Special Edition
Using

FrontPage 2000
Themes

FRONTPAGE 2000 THEMES

Themes are an integral part of FrontPage—they can help set the tone for your entire Web. Good use of themes can keep your site fresh and exciting because of the ability to update the look of your Web site with a few clicks of a mouse. Keep in mind that as you progress you might seek out new themes as well as create your own.

Arcs

Artsy

Automotive

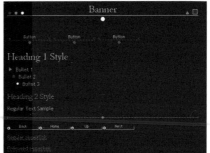

Balance

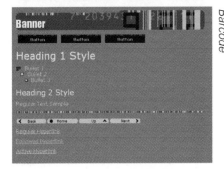

Barcode

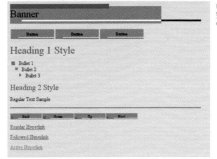

Bars

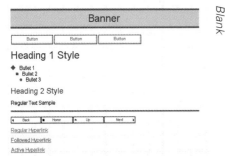

Blank

Blends

Blocks

Banner

Button   Button   Button

Heading 1 Style
- Bullet 1
  - Bullet 2
    - Bullet 3

Heading 2 Style
Regular Text Sample

Back   Home   Up   Next

Regular Hyperlink
Followed Hyperlink
Active Hyperlink

Blueprint

Banner

Button   Button   Button

Heading 1 Style
- Bullet 1
  - Bullet 2
    - Bullet 3

Heading 2 Style
Regular Text Sample

Back   Home   Up   Next

Regular Hyperlink
Followed Hyperlink
Active Hyperlink

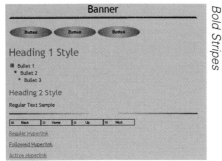

Bold Stripes

Banner

Button   Button   Button

Heading 1 Style
- Bullet 1
  - Bullet 2
    - Bullet 3

Heading 2 Style
Regular Text Sample

Back   Home   Up   Next

Regular Hyperlink
Followed Hyperlink
Active Hyperlink

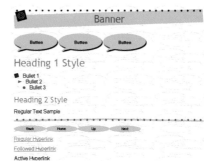

Bubbles

Banner

Button   Button   Button

Heading 1 Style
- Bullet 1
  - Bullet 2
    - Bullet 3

Heading 2 Style
Regular Text Sample

Back   Home   Up   Next

Regular Hyperlink
Followed Hyperlink
Active Hyperlink

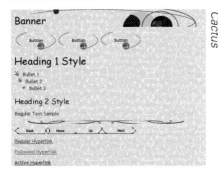

Cactus

Banner

Button   Button   Button

Heading 1 Style
- Bullet 1
  - Bullet 2
    - Bullet 3

Heading 2 Style
Regular Text Sample

Back   Home   Up   Next

Regular Hyperlink
Followed Hyperlink
Active Hyperlink

Canvas

Banner

Button   Button   Button

Heading 1 Style
- Bullet 1
  - Bullet 2
    - Bullet 3

Heading 2 Style
Regular Text Sample

Back   Home   Up   Next

Regular Hyperlink
Followed Hyperlink
Active Hyperlink

Capsules

Banner

Button   Button   Button

Heading 1 Style
- Bullet 1
  - Bullet 2
    - Bullet 3

Heading 2 Style
Regular Text Sample

Back   Home   Up   Next

Regular Hyperlink
Followed Hyperlink
Active Hyperlink

Chalkboard

Banner

Button   Button   Button

Heading 1 Style
- Bullet 1
  - Bullet 2
    - Bullet 3

Heading 2 Style
Regular Text Sample

Back   Home   Up   Next

Regular Hyperlink
Followed Hyperlink
Active Hyperlink

Checkers

Banner

Button   Button   Button

Heading 1 Style
- Bullet 1
  - Bullet 2
    - Bullet 3

Heading 2 Style
Regular Text Sample

Back   Home   Up   Next

Regular Hyperlink
Followed Hyperlink
Active Hyperlink

Citrus Punch

Banner

Button   Button   Button

Heading 1 Style
- Bullet 1
  - Bullet 2
    - Bullet 3

Heading 2 Style
Regular Text Sample

Back   Home   Up   Next

Regular Hyperlink
Followed Hyperlink
Active Hyperlink

Classic

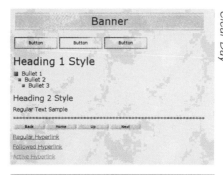

Clear Day

Construction Zone

Corporate

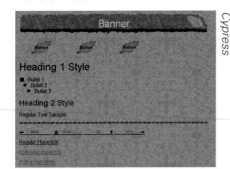

Cypress

Downtown

Expedition

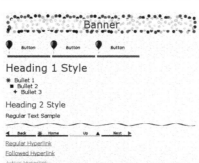

Fiesta

Folio

Geared Up Factory

Glacier

Banner

Button   Button   Button

Heading 1 Style
- Bullet 1
- Bullet 2
- Bullet 3

Heading 2 Style
Regular Text Sample

Back   Home   Up   Next

Regular Hyperlink
Followed Hyperlink
Active Hyperlink

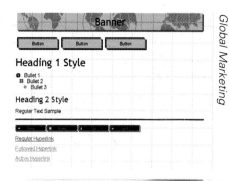

Global Marketing

Banner

Button   Button   Button

Heading 1 Style
- Bullet 1
- Bullet 2
- Bullet 3

Heading 2 Style
Regular Text Sample

Back   Home   Up   Next

Regular Hyperlink
Followed Hyperlink
Active Hyperlink

Highway

Banner

Button   Button   Button

Heading 1 Style
- Bullet 1
- Bullet 2
- Bullet 3

Heading 2 Style
Regular Text Sample

Back   Home   Up   Next

Regular Hyperlink
Followed Hyperlink
Active Hyperlink

In Motion

Banner

Button   Button   Button

Heading 1 Style
- Bullet 1
- Bullet 2
- Bullet 3

Heading 2 Style
Regular Text Sample

Back   Home   Up   Next

Regular Hyperlink
Followed Hyperlink
Active Hyperlink

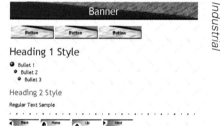

Industrial

Banner

Button   Button   Button

Heading 1 Style
- Bullet 1
- Bullet 2
- Bullet 3

Heading 2 Style
Regular Text Sample

Back   Home   Up   Next

Regular Hyperlink
Followed Hyperlink
Active Hyperlink

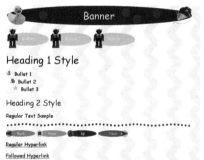

Kids

Banner

Heading 1 Style
- Bullet 1
- Bullet 2
- Bullet 3

Heading 2 Style
Regular Text Sample

Back   Home   Up   Next

Regular Hyperlink
Followed Hyperlink

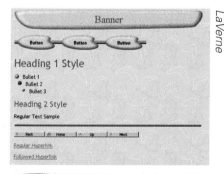

LaVerne

Banner

Button   Button   Button

Heading 1 Style
- Bullet 1
- Bullet 2
- Bullet 3

Heading 2 Style
Regular Text Sample

Back   Home   Up   Next

Regular Hyperlink
Followed Hyperlink

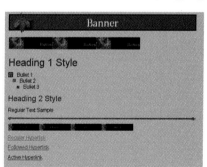

Leaves

Banner

Button   Button   Button

Heading 1 Style
- Bullet 1
- Bullet 2
- Bullet 3

Heading 2 Style
Regular Text Sample

Regular Hyperlink
Followed Hyperlink
Active Hyperlink

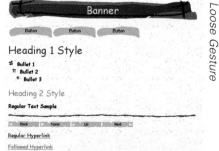

Loose Gesture

Banner

Button   Button   Button

Heading 1 Style
- Bullet 1
- Bullet 2
- Bullet 3

Heading 2 Style
Regular Text Sample

Back   Home   Up   Next

Regular Hyperlink
Followed Hyperlink

Maize

Banner

Button   Button   Button

Heading 1 Style
- Bullet 1
- Bullet 2
- Bullet 3

Heading 2 Style
Regular Text Sample

Back   Home   Up   Next

Regular Hyperlink
Followed Hyperlink
Active Hyperlink

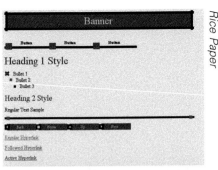

Rice Paper

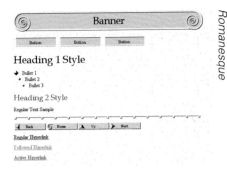

Romanesque

Safari

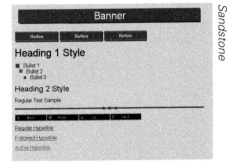

Sandstone

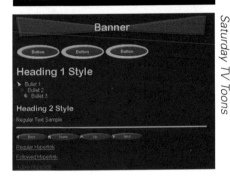

Saturday TV Toons

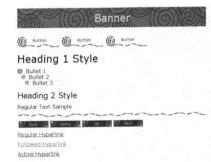

Spiral

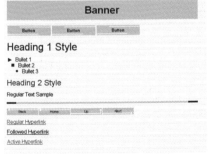

Straight Edge

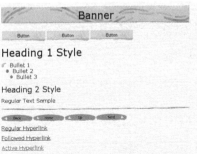

Sumi Painting

Sunflower

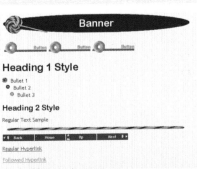

Sweets

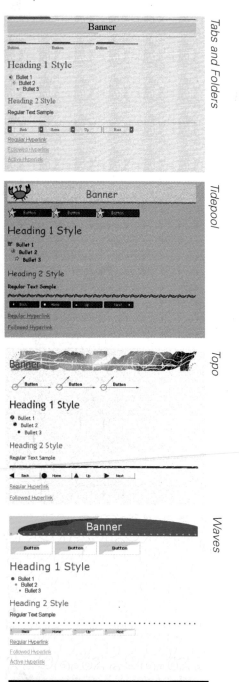

Tabs and Folders

Tidepool

Topo

Waves

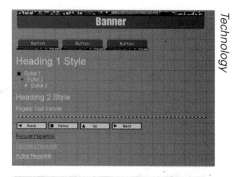

Technology

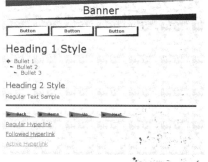

Tilt

Travel

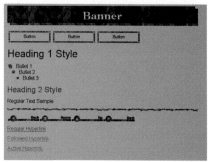

Willow

Zero

Special Edition Using Microsoft® FrontPage® 2000

Dennis Jones

Neil Randall

que®

A Division of Macmillan Computer Publishing, USA

201 W. 103rd Street

Indianapolis, Indiana 46290

G

MICROSOFT™ FRONTPAGE® 2000

Copyright© 1999 by Que

International Standard Book Number: 0-7897-1910-x

Library of Congress Catalog Card Number: 98-87798

Printed in the United States of America

First Printing: May 1999

01   00   99   4   3   2   1

TRADEMARKS

WARNING AND DISCLAIMER

Executive Editor
Mark Taber

Acquisitions Editor
Randi Roger

Development Editor
Scott D. Meyers

Managing Editor
Lisa Wilson

Copy Editors
Heather Urschel

Indexer
Eric Schroeder
Heather Goens
Christine Nelsen
Greg Pearson

Proofreaders
Gene Redding
Kaylene Reiman
Betsy Smith

Technical Editors
Bill Bruns
Robert Crouch
Sunil Hazari

Software Development Specialist
Adam Swetnam

Interior Design
Ruth Harvey

Cover Design
Dan Armstrong
Ruth Harvey

Layout Technicians
Brandon Allen
Stacey DeRome
Timothy Osborn
Staci Somers

CONTENTS

X Extending FrontPage 2000 with VBA

43 Introduction to Programming with Visual Basic for Applications 931

44 Managing Webs with VBA 961

About the Authors

Lead Authors

Dennis Jones is a freelance technical writer and fantasy novelist. He lives near Ottawa, Canada.

Neil Randall (nrandall@watarts.uwaterloo.ca) is the author or coauthor of several books on Internet topics. He has published regularly in computer magazines for 15 years and is currently a technical columnist for *PC Magazine*. He teaches multimedia design and critique, as well as the analysis of computer interfaces, as a professor of English at the University of Waterloo in Canada. You can reach him at http://www.nrandall.com/frontpage.

Contributing Authors

Paul Colligan (colligan@email.com) has been a fan of the Internet since he first logged on with his Mac Plus to something called Gopher. He speaks on Internet-related topics around the country and enjoys an audience that laughs with him, not at him. In his spare time, Paul is a part-time faculty member at both the Leadership Institute in Washington, D.C., and, more locally, Portland Community College. He currently lives with his wife, Heidi, in Portland, Oregon, and would like to thank her for being a constant source of inspiration and support and for putting up with him through this project. When he isn't working on something Internet related, he's a big fan of theater, music, fine dining, and travel. Visit his latest site at http://www.frontpageworld.com.

Mark Fitzpatrick (markfitz@fitzme.com) is a Microsoft Most Valuable Professional (MVP) who specializes in Microsoft Internet technologies and products such as FrontPage, Visual Interdev, and Internet Information Server. He has been designing Web sites for businesses and organizations for five years. When he isn't writing, Mark can be found in the role of Director of Technology for the Inner Reach Corporation (http://www.innerreach.com), Webmaster for the Fibre Channel Community (http://www.fccommunity.org), or working on his own site at http://www.fitzme.com.

John Jay Kottler (jkottler@erols.com) has been programming for 15 years and has spent the past seven years developing applications for the Windows platform. He has also been programming multimedia applications and developing for the Web for the past three years. His knowledge includes C/C++, Visual Basic, multimedia, digital video production, and Internet development. Jay has published several computer articles and has written or contributed to numerous Sams books, including *DHTML Unleashed*, *Visual InterDev Unleashed*, *Web Page Wizardry*, *Web Publishing Unleashed*, *Netscape Unleashed*, *Presenting ActiveX*, and *Programming Windows 95 Unleashed*. A graduate of Rutgers University with a degree in computer science, he enjoys inline skating, cycling, and playing digital music in his spare time.

Kelly Murdock (murdocks@itsnet.com) works as a professional Web developer in the education arena. On the side, he writes Web books and has been involved with too many projects to number, including *3D Graphics and VRML 2*, *Dynamic Web Publishing*, and *HTML 4 Unleashed*. In his spare time he pours his creative energies into the kids education site, which is located at http://www.animabets.com.

Bob Samer provides quality assurance for the FrontPage 2000 extensibility interfaces at Microsoft, working on everything from the Page and Web objects models to building FrontPage 2000 add-ins. He also spent a year working in Microsoft Excel/Visual Basic technical support, providing end-user and developer support for the Excel macro language and cross-application programming. Bob has worked as a Web site designer for netTastic Internet Solutions, a Web development business he co-owns, building sites ranging from simple home sites to complex ASP-driven, e-commerce–enabled sites.

DEDICATION

To the founders of Vermeer Technologies, for their far-reaching vision. —Neil Randall

ACKNOWLEDGMENTS

The first people to acknowledge and thank are the authors who pitched in to contribute specific chapters to this book. In a work of this size and depth, outside expertise is crucial and welcome. Next come those involved in the project from the publisher's perspective, particularly Randi Roger, who skillfully kept all the authors on track and on target, a job both difficult and demanding. Of course, there are all the personal thank yous, the people whose encouragement kept me going through some yucky times. But this time around, my major acknowledgment goes to Dennis Jones, my coauthor, for producing his usual excellent work, reliably and responsibly, in the face of even yuckier times. If I wore a hat, it would be off to him. *—Neil Randall*

TELL US WHAT YOU THINK!

As the reader of this book, *you* are our most important critic and commentator. We value your opinion and want to know what we're doing right, what we could do better, what areas you'd like to see us publish in, and any other words of wisdom you're willing to pass our way.

You can fax, email, or write me directly to let me know what you did or didn't like about this book—as well as what we can do to make our books stronger.

Please note that I cannot help you with technical problems related to the topic of this book, and that due to the high volume of mail I receive, I might not be able to reply to every message.

When you write, please be sure to include this book's title and author as well as your name and phone or fax number. I will carefully review your comments and share them with the author and editors who worked on the book.

Fax: 317-581-4666
Email: office_que@mcp.com
Mail: John Pierce
         Publisher
         Que
         201 West 103rd Street
         Indianapolis, IN 46290 USA

Thanks for Joining Us

In this chapter

We'll cut this introduction short, not because we couldn't write dozens of pages about our own book, but because you're eager to get to the point of it all: the FrontPage 2000 software itself. More particularly, we want to get to creating, updating, and maintaining Web sites.

Special Edition Using Microsoft FrontPage 2000 is devoted to the FrontPage 2000 software package. That might seem incredibly obvious, but it's an important point to keep in mind as you work your way through the book (or, indeed, if you're browsing this book on the shelves and wondering whether you should buy it). This is not a general book about building Web sites; it's about building Web sites with FrontPage 2000 and with any extra software that ships with FrontPage 2000. In your case, that extra software might very well include all of Microsoft Office 2000; if so, you should know that this book covers how FrontPage 2000 works in conjunction with Office 2000. In other words, *Special Edition Using Microsoft FrontPage 2000* focuses squarely on the rich and powerful product you have purchased, with all discussions oriented around that product.

Why are we telling you this? Because this book runs well over a thousand pages, and you deserve to know not only what those thousand pages consist of, but what you'll get out of them. You also deserve to know what the book does not do. It's easy when examining a book of this type to be a bit overwhelmed by the size and elaborate table of contents, which in turn makes it easy to assume that the book will do something it was never designed to do. It's also easy to assume that the book does not do something that in fact it does. We want you to know precisely what you'll get in this book, so that you can make an informed purchase decision.

If you've already bought the book, thank you very much; we will do everything we can to help you get the most out of it. That's why this book has several authors, not just one—we wanted to make sure you got your information from the best source. It's also why we've put up a Web site as an ongoing reference. To access that site, go to the Macmillan Computer Books site at `http://www.mcp.com` and look for the link to *Special Edition Using Microsoft FrontPage 2000*. You'll find a number of resources, including frequently asked questions and links to third-party software. Visit often and enjoy much.

FrontPage 2000 is a powerful but surprisingly easy-to-use package. We hope you find the same to be true of this book. Thanks for joining us.

HOW TO USE THIS BOOK

This book has four purposes:

- Make it easy for you to use FrontPage Explorer to create, maintain, and develop your Web site with the maximum of efficiency and the minimum of difficulty.
- Show you how to use FrontPage Editor to design, create, and maintain Web pages that people will both enjoy and find useful.

- Give you the technical elements of Web design beyond FrontPage 2000, including the coding and details necessary for HTML, Java, scripting, and database integration.
- Help you understand the technicalities of the World Wide Web and the Internet, as well as how you can best design your site to take advantage of the technology as it is now, and as it will become.

Given this, what's the best way for you to approach the book?

You may already be knowledgeable about Web site design and construction. If so, you may want to skim the first chapters and concentrate on the sections that deal with FrontPage's Page view, since that's the tool you'll likely spend most of your time using. Later, when you're using FrontPage in earnest, you'll find that the other views (covered in detail in Part III, "Web Creation and Management") have many features that will make your life as a Webmaster a lot easier. If you're new to site setup but know a lot about HTML, reverse the preceding process and work on site creation and management issues first. Knowing how FrontPage handles web construction will help you when you turn to creating pages with FrontPage Editor.

If you're an experienced Webmaster, browse Parts I, II, and V to learn how to use FrontPage 2000 and how it can make your job easier. Use the Table of Contents to identify areas of immediate interest to you. Be sure to check out FrontPage 2000's advanced features, as well as the chapters devoted to technical coding and the appendixes, which you can keep beside you as you design your site.

Eventually, you'll want to delve into all of the material on FrontPage Editor, FrontPage Explorer, and the Personal Web Server. Together they provide a seamless, powerful environment that can handle all but the most exotic of your site construction needs.

HOW THIS BOOK IS ORGANIZED

Special Edition Using Microsoft FrontPage 2000 covers all the features and functions of the integrated environment. It has 11 major parts, each of which is summarized briefly here.

The organizing principle is to introduce you to the FrontPage suite and then to demonstrate the features of the WYSIWYG Page view. After that, chapters cover Web elements specific to the two major browsers: Microsoft Internet Explorer and Netscape Navigator. You are then introduced to the powerful new Image Composer software included with the FrontPage 2000 Bonus Pack. An entire section is given over to the details of providing active content in your sites, such as Java, ActiveX, scripting, database integration, and VRML.

With all the Web coding issues taken care of, the book shifts to Web site management and creation. Included here is a major section on all the FrontPage Explorer features, the powerful heart of the FrontPage 2000 package, including wizards and templates, Web management and security, and FrontPage's capabilities for building and maintaining intranets.

The next two parts cover FrontPage 2000's integration with Microsoft Office 2000. The book details methods of integration with databases, an increasingly important component of advanced Web design.

PART I: INTRODUCING FRONTPAGE 2000

Chapter 1, "Welcome to FrontPage 2000," introduces the software, explains what's new in version 2000, and offers a history of the product.

Chapter 2, "The FrontPage Environment," outlines each part of the FrontPage 2000 package in greater detail and orients you to its basic and advanced capabilities.

PART II: DESIGNING DOCUMENTS: WORKING FROM THE PAGE VIEW

Chapter 3, "The Page View: Windows, Icons, and Menus," details FrontPage 2000's authoring interface and work space.

Chapter 4, "Developing the Basic Page: Text, Lists, and Hyperlinks," gives you the basics of good page design, the fundamentals of HTML structure, and three fundamental elements of a Web page—text, lists, and hyperlinks.

Chapter 5, "Enhancing Pages with Graphics and Multimedia," offers detailed instruction on images and image layout, colors and backgrounds, graphical hyperlinks, and imagemaps.

Chapter 6, "Working with Themes," outlines FrontPage's themes feature, an important unifying system when developing individual pages and full Web sites.

Chapter 7, "Using Active Elements, Shared Borders, and Navigation Bars," explains the ins and outs of some of FrontPage's authoring elements that can make the most difference in the appearance and functioning of your site.

Chapter 8, "Creating Tables," explores FrontPage 2000's easy-to-use but sophisticated system for creating and editing one of the Webmaster's most important tools—HTML tables.

Chapter 9, "Enhancing Web Sites with FrontPage Frames," teaches you about designing for a framed site, about using frames with links and images, and how to create framed environments with FrontPage's frame templates.

Chapter 10, "Creating Pages with FrontPage Templates," steps you through FrontPage's supplied templates, which speed the creation of pages such as bibliographies, glossaries, directories, and publicity instruments (press releases, for instance).

Chapter 11, "Using Components, Forms, and Interactive Page Templates," covers the numerous automating components in FrontPage, as well as creating and implementing forms. It also details how to work with the FrontPage templates that help you make your pages interactive.

Chapter 12, "Using Style Sheets with Individual Pages and Full Sites," helps you work with the increasingly important design feature called cascading style sheets and FrontPage 2000's sophisticated means of handling them.

Part III: Web Creation and Management

Part III examines the features of FrontPage that let you create, maintain, and manage entire sites.

Chapter 13, "Creating a Web," covers Web creation in detail and introduces the FrontPage wizards that help you set up specialized types of webs.

Chapter 14, "FrontPage's Web Templates and Wizards," steps you through using wizards and templates to set up normal and empty webs and to create the more complex discussion webs, customer support webs, project webs, and personal webs.

Chapter 15, "Working with an Existing Web," deals with FrontPage Explorer's different views of a web, along with the features offered by its menus. This chapter demonstrates how to import existing directories into FrontPage to create a web.

Chapter 16, "Publishing a Web," takes you through the steps required to move a web from your hard drive to a remote Web server.

Chapter 17, "Configuring Webs," shows you how to administer a web by setting web parameters, permissions, passwords, and proxy servers and by configuring editors.

Chapter 18, "Managing a Web," covers managing hardware, software, and people and using the to-do list to keep your site maintenance up to date. This chapter demonstrates how to use FrontPage 2000's advanced maintenance features such as global spell, global search and replace, and hyperlink updating.

Part IV: Collaboration, Workflow, Task Management

Chapter 19, "Establishing a Collaborative Authoring Environment," looks at the managerial and technical side of setting up an environment in which people can effectively collaborate on FrontPage webs and documents.

Chapter 20, "Collaborating on Pages and Webs," shows FrontPage 2000's specific collaboration features.

Chapter 21, "Collaboration and Office 2000," brings Microsoft Office 2000 into the collaboration picture, demonstrating how it integrates with a FrontPage collaborative environment.

Chapter 22, "Managing Workflow and Tasks," outlines the features in FrontPage 2000 and Office 2000 that let a team collaborate effectively and efficiently.

Chapter 23, "Developing Team-Based Internet, Intranet, and Extranet Sites," details how to use FrontPage 2000 as a team-based development tool for creating internal and external sites.

Part V: Scripting, Dynamic HTML, and Dynamic Content

Part V introduces you to FrontPage 2000's expanded capabilities for including a variety of active content in your web designs.

Chapter 24, "Using FrontPage's Dynamic Styles and Effects," explores FrontPage's advanced capabilities for layout and design.

Chapter 25, "Making Your Pages and Webs More Dynamic," shows you how to take existing content—or create new content—and make it change with the users' actions and your own demands.

Chapter 26, "Using Scripts in Your Web Page," looks at some basic applications in which you might want to include scripts.

Chapter 27, "JavaScript and Client-Side Computing," is a more in-depth look at scripting and covers many of the specifics of the JavaScript language.

Chapter 28, "Using Java Applets, Browser Plug-Ins, and ActiveX Controls," looks at the integration between FrontPage and these important web add-ons and controls.

PART VI: CREATING AND ADAPTING GRAPHICS FOR THE WEB

Chapter 29, "Color Concepts," explores the world of computer color, explaining what you need to know to produce top-notch Web graphics.

Chapter 30, "About the Computer Screen," details what you need to know about the workings of the screen itself in order to maximize your graphics' appearance.

Chapter 31, "Web Graphic Formats," differentiates between the variety of graphic formats available for use on the Web.

Chapter 32, "Creating Professional Web Graphics," lets you discover how to produce the great graphics you see on so many other sites.

Chapter 33, "Designing Specialty Graphics," looks at graphics that go beyond the norm and attract even greater attention to your site.

Chapter 34, "Web Graphic Tools," looks at tools for creating and editing graphics in the FrontPage environment.

PART VII: WEB SERVERS AND WEB HOSTING

Chapter 35, "Introduction to Web Hosting and Web Servers," examines the details of serving webs from your own computer, from a remote, and from a rented server.

Chapter 36, "Using a Web Hosting Service," introduces you to commercial web hosting services and explains what to look for when considering subscribing.

Chapter 37, "FrontPage 2000 and the Microsoft Personal Web Server," looks at the details of working with FrontPage 2000 and Microsoft's downloadable server for Windows 95 and 98 machines.

Chapter 38, "FrontPage 2000 and Microsoft's Internet Information Server (IIS)," examines how to make your FrontPage webs work with IIS's advanced features.

Part VIII: Accessing Database Data with FrontPage

Part VIII gives you the details behind building database connectivity into your Web sites, beyond the capabilities of FrontPage 2000 itself.

Chapter 39, "Using Databases with FrontPage 2000," examines the basic but powerful features of database connectivity in FrontPage.

Chapter 40, "Advanced Database Techniques," offers an extensive array of solutions for incorporating databases into your FrontPage webs.

Chapter 41, "Database Development with ASP," shows you how to develop advanced databases using Microsoft's Advanced Server Pages technology.

Part IX: Integrating FrontPage 2000 and Microsoft Office

Part IX provides an examination of the increasing degree of integration between FrontPage 2000 and Microsoft Office 2000.

Chapter 42, "FrontPage 2000 and Office 2000," shows how these two packages work together in a number of important ways and why FrontPage is now fully a part of the Office environment.

Part X: Extending FrontPage 2000 with VBA

Chapter 43, "Introduction to Programming with Visual Basic for Applications," demonstrates the ins and outs of Microsoft's Visual Basic for Applications.

Chapter 44, "Managing Webs with VBA," takes VBA directly into the FrontPage environment from the standpoint of the full array of web management.

Chapter 45, "Accessing Documents," explores the role of VBA in bringing external documents into your FrontPage webs.

Chapter 46, "Using Events in FrontPage 2000," takes you into events programming through VBA and incorporating these events into FrontPage.

Chapter 47, "Cross-Application Programming," demonstrates how to work with VBA in developing routines across multiple applications.

Appendixes

The appendixes offer references for coding HTML documents and their components.

Appendix A, "FrontPage 2000 Resources on the Web"

Appendix B, "FrontPage 2000 and Office 97"

SPECIAL FEATURES IN THE BOOK

Que has a long track record of providing the most comprehensive resource books for users and developers of computer hardware and software. This volume includes many features to make your learning faster, easier, and more efficient.

TIP

These help you use the software more effectively or maneuver around problems or limitations.

Tip #1001	To avoid typing a long URL, you can use Edit, Copy. Copy the URL from your browser's Location box and then paste it where you need it by pressing Ctrl+V.

NOTE

Notes provide information that is generally useful but not specifically needed for what you're doing at the moment. Some are like extended tips.

Note	FrontPage Editor makes it convenient to move among pages. It keeps a history list of the pages you've displayed, and you can choose Tools, Forward or Tools, Back to get around.

CAUTION

These tell you to beware of a dangerous act or situation. In some cases, ignoring a Caution could cause you very significant problems, so pay attention to them!

Caution	You can't change the Quality setting after you've changed it and then saved the image—even if you delete the image and reinsert it from the saved page. Keep a backup if you're experimenting!

TROUBLESHOOTING

Even the best-designed software has dark corners you'd rather not find yourself in. Troubleshooting information gives you a flashlight to dispel the darkness, in the form of advice about how to solve a problem or avoid it in the first place.

CROSS REFERENCES

In a package as tightly integrated as FrontPage, many operations are related to features that appear elsewhere in the book. Book cross references, such as the one accompanying this paragraph, direct you to the related material.

→ **See** "Wizards, What They Are and How They Work," for more information about using wizards, **p. xxx**.

SHORTCUT KEY COMBINATIONS

Shortcut key combinations in this book are shown as the key names joined with plus signs (+). For example, Ctrl+N indicates that you should press the N key while holding down the Ctrl key. This combination opens a new page in FrontPage Editor.

MENU COMMANDS

You'll see instructions such as this everywhere in this book:

Choose Edit, Bookmark.

This means that you should open the Edit menu and select Bookmark. This particular example opens the Bookmark dialog box.

Instructions such as "Mark the Set Color check box" mean that you can either click in the check box to select it or press the C key, which does the same thing.

DESIGNERS CORNER

Most of the chapters throughout the book end with a special section that provides information about the chapter's topic. This includes expert solutions to popular problems, insightful advice on effective uses of features, and general information that will help you get the most out of FrontPage.

INTRODUCING FRONTPAGE 2000

WELCOME TO FRONTPAGE 2000

In this chapter

by Neil Randall

INTRODUCING MICROSOFT FRONTPAGE

Microsoft FrontPage 2000 is the most recent version of the popular all-in-one Web design toolkit. It's the fourth major release of the product, the third since Microsoft acquired it from Vermeer Technologies in 1995 (for a full history, see "Where FrontPage Came From"). This is obviously good news: The last thing you want when you shell out hard-earned money for a software package is to discover that the company who publishes it doesn't intend to support or upgrade it. Microsoft's program of upgrades to FrontPage 97, FrontPage 98, and now FrontPage 2000, in fairly rapid succession, clearly demonstrates that they intend to stick by it. So does the fact that Microsoft is including FrontPage 2000 with one version of the Microsoft Office 2000 package. Knowing that the software you work extensively with will be around for the foreseeable future is an extremely important thing.

> **Note**
>
> If you've never used FrontPage before, the rest of this introduction section explains what FrontPage is and what it does. If you've used past versions of FrontPage, head straight for the section below entitled "What's New in FrontPage 2000".

Microsoft FrontPage 2000 lets you create, maintain, and administer Web sites. The "create" part is hardly unique; many packages, both commercial and shareware, let you create Web pages and build a site consisting of linked pages. FrontPage is a very strong package at creating sites, but it was by no means the first to let you do so, and many have sprung up since its initial launch. Nevertheless, its Web authoring features are definitely up there with the best of any package, especially since it incorporates a rich WYSIWYG (what you see is what you get) display with a very useful HTML (Hypertext Markup Language) display, and you can change between the two simply by clicking a tab at the bottom of the FrontPage screen. In other words, you can work with good old HTML tags and containers, or with a fully graphical environment, or indeed with both. Flexibility, therefore, is one of the package's strengths.

FrontPage's design features are rich. In fact, most of the book is about these features. You can develop basic HTML documents, you can add tables, frames, and multimedia, you can work with style sheets, you can incorporate databases, you can develop JavaScript and Active Server Pages components, and you can add Dynamic HTML and much, much more. Wizards can help you with specific features, while templates and themes give you an excellent start if you don't want to design from scratch. FrontPage 2000 provides power to users of every level, and in fact it has become an important component of the Microsoft Office 2000 suite of applications (it ships with one version of Office 2000). You can design pages in FrontPage, or in Word or PowerPoint or Publisher, and with components drawn from Excel and Access. Office 2000 and FrontPage 2000 work together to give you an even richer design environment.

For many users, however, where FrontPage truly shines is in its Web maintenance and administration features. At first, when you're trying to build your first few Web pages, these features might not seem so important. But before long, you'll find yourself depending on them. These features let you directly work with your Webs once they're on the Web server, eliminating the need to upload new and changed pages from your local machine to the server machine. The features also check your entire Web for hyperlinks that no longer work, a major issue in successful Web maintenance. Non-functional links annoy users and can even destroy your credibility with them.

Another important FrontPage feature is the ability to control access to users and authors. Even if you want part of your Web to be fully public, you can create subwebs that are accessible only to those with assigned usernames and passwords. You can also set your Web as public for viewing purposes, but control access among the authors and administrators of your Web. If you wish, you can even restrict access to the entire site. Access permissions are extremely important for proper Web administration.

FrontPage 2000 offers several features for collaborative Web design as well. If you've involved others in developing your site, you can assign specific tasks to specific authors or administrators, and you can generate a task list to help you track these tasks through completion. You can ensure, with the feature known as Check-in/Check-out, that only one user is editing any given page or file at any given time. You can establish Web discussions for the collaborators as well.

Throughout this book, you will find these features explored in depth. You'll also find countless related features. We wanted do to let you know the overall power of the package you've bought, and to get you even more interested in using it to its fullest extent.

What's New in FrontPage 2000

FrontPage 2000 is a substantial upgrade, offering an essentially new interface, several important new features, and significant enhancements to existing features. Furthermore, with the release of this new version, FrontPage has been tied directly into Microsoft Office 2000, resulting in not only a consistent interface, but also several new collaborative applications.

Designing and Authoring Web Documents

The interface for creating web documents remains largely the same in FrontPage 2000, except for one major alteration: FrontPage Editor, the design staple of past editions, no longer exists as a separate program. Instead, FrontPage Editor has become the Page view in the single program now called *FrontPage*. Users of previous versions, however, will recognize the merged FrontPage as the former FrontPage Explorer with a new view.

Several new or improved authoring features appear as part of the new Page view. Cascading style sheet support has been improved, as has support for Dynamic HTML. You can now easily create special effects using a DHTML toolbar, including DHTML events for mouse clicking or double-clicking, mouse-overs, and page loads. As a further example, for page loads you can assign fly-ins, wipes, zooms, and five other effects, all by highlighting the text and choosing from the DHTML Effects toolbar.

The FrontPage 2000 package includes sixty themes, and you can assign them to individual pages or to the entire web. Furthermore, you can edit the components in all themes to your heart's content, or create new ones. In previous FrontPage versions, you could edit and create themes through a special program available with the Software Development Kit (SDK), but this feature has now been incorporated into the Themes dialog of the main program.

The positioning of specific elements of a document is much more precise in FrontPage 2000. You can place elements exactly where you want on the page, using a new feature called pixel-precise positioning and layering. You can give elements an absolute position, so that it remains at precisely the same location in the browser no matter how you alter the page, or relative positioning, which keeps elements at the same relative proximity to one another. Floating positioning lets you position elements so that text and other elements can flow around it, while Z-positioning lets you layer elements on top of each other. This feature comes from the CSS 2.0 (Cascading Style Sheets version 2.0) specifications, and will be effective only for users who have a CSS 2.0-capable browser, but it can be especially effective in corporate intranets, where the browser version can be mandated. But as more and more people upgrade to version 4.0 browsers, it will be effective for them as well.

If you're accustomed to authoring in raw HTML, FrontPage 2000 offers considerably better support than did earlier versions. First, FrontPage no longer modifies the HTML code you import into the program—a huge improvement for code-based authors. Second, you no longer have to go through the earlier complications of adding raw HTML to your documents: FrontPage 2000 offers an HTML view, available with a simple click, that gives you an easily readable and entirely editable look at the code itself. You can edit HTML, ASP, DHTML, and even XML code in this view. You can also specify in this view how you want the code to appear. That way you can always find the code you want and FrontPage will make imported code look the way you prefer. In addition, a new Reveal HTML Tags feature in FrontPage shows you precisely where the tags exist in the normal (WYSIWYG) Page view. When you select Reveal HTML Tags, the HTML tags and containers will appear in Page view, helping you determine precisely how FrontPage translated your WYSIWYG design into raw HTML code. It is also a useful feature for troubleshooting.

In other words, FrontPage 2000 allows you to be much closer to the raw HTML than ever before. Related to this idea is the inclusion of the Microsoft Script Editor, a powerful tool that lets you edit JavaScript and VBScript for inclusion in your documents. Script Editor also gives you the ability to add controls created with Microsoft's Visual InterDev development package. In fact, integration with other Microsoft development tools has been built in to FrontPage 2000, specifically with Visual Basic for Applications (VBA), which you may now consider a fully functional part of the extended FrontPage environment (although you certainly don't need it to produce strong sites).

Database integration has also been improved in FrontPage 2000, with some new features making their first appearance. The Database Results Wizard is easier to use than database wizards of previous FrontPage versions. It is now a five-step dialog box with several sub-dialog boxes available for advanced features. The dialog box lets you select the database to incorporate, gives you options for how to manipulate that data when loaded into your Web, helps you design the appearance of the data, and provides advanced options such as specialized queries. FrontPage 2000 works extremely well with Microsoft Access databases, even allowing you to automatically create an Access 2000 document from within FrontPage itself, and then using a form to manipulate this data from the Web.

FrontPage 2000's Web components are a crucial element for designers. You can insert an Office spreadsheet directly into a Web page, as well as an Office pivot table or chart. Each has its own Properties dialog box to let you configure the component precisely. The Microsoft Office Chart Wizard appears in the case of inserting a chart component, and it guides you through the selection of data to include in the chart. The Categories component lets you sort information (and even create a Table of Contents) according to the categories into which you've assigned the data. Categories are a new feature in FrontPage 2000, and they help you manage site information.

For advanced FrontPage users, FrontPage 2000 improves the ways it works with Microsoft Visual InterDEV and with Microsoft's Design Time Controls. It adds support for the programming features offered by Document Object Models (DOM), as well as support for Visual Basic for Applications (VBA).

Managing Web Sites

Site management remains the package's central focus. Every part of the interface, including page authoring, is now simply one of several web views accessible via the main FrontPage screen. Most of the older views remain, although some have migrated to a new place.

The most important of these new places is the Reports view, which combines a great many possible reports, including slow pages, non-working hyperlinks, component errors, and much more. In fact, there are so many reports available that FrontPage 2000 offers a new Reports toolbar to let you switch from one to another. You can customize some of these reports to suit your needs, and you can interact with FrontPage through the Reports view. The Folders view has been improved to show all available pages and subwebs, and double-clicking a sub-web opens it in a complete new FrontPage window, letting you keep all webs open simultaneously. As mentioned earlier, the Page view takes the place of the FrontPage Editor, and it's accessed by a single click on the Views bar, just like any other FrontPage view.

Other features abound. You can create Web sites specific to browsers; you can automatically (and more quickly) fix broken hyperlinks. The process of publishing existing webs gives you page-by-page control over what gets published and what doesn't, and FrontPage 2000 works better with disk-based webs than FrontPage 98 did. In fact, you're encouraged to create your webs on disk and then publish them through the program's Publish Web command, rather than spending all your design time online. The program's FTP (File

Transfer Protocol) feature has been improved so that it is faster and less risky publishing directly to a server that does not have FrontPage Server Extensions installed. The one negative change in all of this is that the standalone version of FrontPage 2000 no longer includes the Microsoft Personal Web Server, so you have to download it in order to use it as a practice or staging server. If you buy FrontPage 2000 with Office 2000, however, the PWS is included. The problem here is that features such as database integration don't work properly without the server extensions installed, which means that you never get to see your database queries in action until you publish the Web to the server.

One important addition to the FrontPage 2000 package is a set of collaboration features that allow multiple users to work effectively on the same site. FrontPage 2000 is designed as a multiauthor environment, in fact, and enables multiple users to work on the site at the same time. To keep too many cooks from spoiling the broth, pages can be prevented from being checked out by more than one author and permissions can be set on nested subwebs. *Nested subwebs (page 514)* were not possible with earlier versions of FrontPage (you could create webs one level below the root Web, but no further), and this feature will certainly be welcome to anyone who has attempted to use FrontPage to create large Web sites. Another collaboration features is the workflow report, allowing you to assign individual pages in the Web to specific members of the design team. You can work with the workflow reports, as one example, to establish policies for approving of completed work at various stages in the site design process.

MICROSOFT OFFICE 2000 TIE-IN

FrontPage 2000 is part of Office 2000 and it shares many of the larger suite's features. In FrontPage you can use background spellchecking, and your FrontPage and Office documents can share themes. As with Office 2000, FrontPage's menus tailor themselves to the features each user accesses most frequently, and toolbars can be hidden or rearranged to your content. Like Office 2000, FrontPage now installs specific features only when you need them, keeping your disk clear of unnecessary components. You can customize the toolbars as well, and you can save screen space by placing them all in a single line.

The program also self repairs; it monitors itself on launch and while running, and if it determines that something is wrong (such as a corrupted file that loads with the program itself, it asks you to put in your installation CD so that it can reinstall the parts that no longer function. This is an extremely important function and would be perfect except for the fact that repairing an Office 2000 application takes a long time, sometimes over an hour. Still, it's much better than a simple error message.

Office 2000 documents can be saved directly in HTML format, and HTML is in fact considered a native Office format. You can open Office 2000 documents directly in FrontPage, and you can save Office 2000 documents directly to a web. Office 2000 also includes its own server extensions, allowing collaboration among the various applications, including FrontPage. All in all, Office 2000 has become webcentric, and it uses FrontPage as a basis for its webcentrism.

WHERE FRONTPAGE CAME FROM

Over the years since late 1995, FrontPage has evolved into one of the most significant pieces of software in the Web's brief history. The reason for this is, quite simply, that it was the first package that allowed users not only to design Web pages (lots of packages handle that task), but also to create, publish, and manage entire sites. From the time FrontPage first appeared, anyone buying it needed only an Internet connection to host a Web site—a high-speed 24-hour connection was best, but not required—and that site could include such features as forms, which formerly required a knowledge of programming. That was almost unheard of in 1995. FrontPage, in effect, let anyone create sophisticated Web sites—or glitzy, bouncy, tacky ones if that's what one preferred.

This evolution has been remarkable, especially when you consider that the Internet was almost exclusively the territory of scholars and researchers a very few years ago, and that the World Wide Web did not even exist as late as 1990. It still might not, except that Tim Berners-Lee and his team at the European Organization for Nuclear Research (CERN), based in Geneva, decided to design and release a hypertext system that allowed easier communication among researchers in high-energy physics. The software was written specifically for the Internet and was released in 1991. Berners-Lee called it the World Wide Web.

Not long after that, Marc Andreessen and his programming cohorts at the University of Illinois' National Center for Supercomputing Applications (NCSA) developed a piece of software called Mosaic. Although technically categorized as an HTTP client, Mosaic was referred to as a Web browser almost from its inception. In 1994, Andreessen and many of the same cohorts joined with Silicon Graphics founder Jim Clark to form Mosaic Communications Corporation; in late 1994 they released a browser called Netscape. The name Mosaic, however, is property of the University of Illinois, where NCSA is located, so Andreesen's company changed its name from Mosaic Communications to Netscape Communications. The browser, at the same time, became Netscape Navigator. Suddenly, it seemed, everybody with a Net connection wanted to explore the Web.

That, of course, meant money. Money for software producers, to be sure, but more importantly, money for Internet service itself. A new kind of company formed—Internet service providers—which for a modest fee connected individuals and corporations to the Internet and its World Wide Web. These companies did one more thing as well: They provided disk space on their computers for customers who wanted to post HTML documents, better known as Web pages. Suddenly, many thousands of people became Web designers, working with very basic software to develop sets of hypertextually linked documents accessible to everyone on the Internet. As corporations discovered the value of the Web, and as popular service providers such as America Online provided space for a Web presence as well, designing and developing Web sites became arguably the most popular creative activity on computers.

Putting together a site hasn't been as easy as it might be, though. Until very recently, setting one up required not only an Internet connection, but some pretty specialized knowledge about how Webs are built and maintained, as well as the ability to create the Web site pages using a coding system called Hypertext Markup Language (HTML). Not everyone who wanted a Web site had that knowledge and ability, or the time and desire to acquire them. This isn't to suggest that HTML on its own is difficult—indeed, you can learn the basics in about an hour—but as more and more features were added to HTML, constructing pages by typing all the codes became increasingly difficult and quite tedious. And, of course, in an era of graphical computing, not having a WYSIWYG (what you see is what you get) environment seemed almost entirely inappropriate. Even more important, though, getting a site onto the World Wide Web and then maintaining it was, in many people's minds, simply a matter of mystery, and the tools to help do this were far from advanced.

This is where FrontPage comes in. FrontPage is an integrated site development environment, including a Web creation and maintenance package called FrontPage Explorer, a near-WYSIWYG (what-you-see-is-what-you-get) Web page editor called FrontPage Editor, and a fully functioning Personal Web Server that turns a PC into a Web host machine. With FrontPage, you can create a complete Web site on your PC and link your PC to the World Wide Web and the Internet. Better yet, you don't have to know HTML because FrontPage Editor works like a word processor. You make your page look the way you want it and the software puts the HTML code together for you. It also gives you the ability to put together Web pages that include elements that formerly demanded programming knowledge.

From the moment it was first released by its original producers, Vermeer Technologies, FrontPage 1.0 garnered an unusual degree of critical interest. Everyone who wrote about it had good things to say, and as it made its way into circulation its users quickly agreed with the strong assessments. The package was so well received that software giant Microsoft, realizing that its Internet efforts lacked a Web design package, bought out the program, the technology, and indeed the company; $130 million later, Vermeer Technologies was on its way to Redmond, Washington, to join Bill Gates and company and develop the package from there.

Microsoft revised the FrontPage interface for version 1.1, but touched up the program itself in only minor ways. What the company did do, however, was make the beta versions of the package available as free downloads from its Web site. Users were able to work with the full product for a limited period of time, and over 400,000 took the company up on its offer. The package sold well upon release, and work had already begun on a pumped-up version 2.0.

At the same time, Microsoft placed FrontPage within the Microsoft Office family of applications, thereby announcing to the world that it was intended for anyone in business who wanted to build a Web site. Even though it was not planned as part of the Microsoft Office suite itself (Word, Excel, PowerPoint, and Access), FrontPage was no longer a specialty product, but part of the Office mainstream. As a member of the Office family, FrontPage had to adopt Office's numbering system. When the upcoming main product was named Office 97, FrontPage 2.0 became FrontPage 97. While FrontPage 98 did not adhere to this system, FrontPage 2000 picks up on that system once again.

The challenge for the FrontPage 97 design team was to keep up with the explosive growth of technologies that has come to the World Wide Web over the past year. Version 1.1 let you produce reasonably advanced pages, but the advancements went only as far as the inclusion of frames, tables, and programmable forms. What the package didn't include were those features that professional designers began demanding not long after: Java, JavaScript, VBScript, ActiveX, Netscape plug-ins, and perhaps most importantly, database integration. You could include these things in your FrontPage documents, but you had to put them there manually by writing the code elsewhere and copying it into FrontPage. That was sufficient, but not very helpful.

FrontPage 97 went a long way toward filling those holes. With it you could design JavaScripts and VBScripts directly inside special FrontPage dialog boxes. You couldn't do any actual Java applets or Netscape plug-ins design, but you could import them with their own specialized dialog boxes. Linking to databases began with a newly designed wizard. Support for ActiveX was exemplary, with the imported ActiveX controls displayed in the FrontPage documents as they would appear on the Web. The result? A much more complete package—one that gave you nearly everything you can do with Web pages. A few things remain unsupported—style sheets and the newest Netscape extensions stood out here—but these were browser specific (rather than standard) at that point.

Microsoft FrontPage 97 showed very well the package's power at letting users create all but the most technologically advanced Web sites. It also showed Microsoft's commitment to both the product and the Web design area itself. A wide range of computer magazines rated it at or very near the top of the growing category of Web design software, and almost universally at the top of the smaller but related category of software for Web design and management. Importantly, it also became a favorite among professional and amateur Web site designers alike.

As good as it was, FrontPage 97 wasn't perfect. Important tasks, such as the creation of navigation buttons, the alteration of the dimensions of table cells, and the manipulation of graphic images, either took too long to perform—or worse—weren't included in the product at all. There was no support for the new W3C (World Wide Web Consortium) organization standard known as cascading style sheets (CSS), for example, and frames—another extremely popular feature—were difficult to work with and unintuitive to create. It wouldn't have been so bad if these things were obscure Web design add-ons, but they weren't. They were growing in popularity and, therefore, in importance.

Microsoft FrontPage 98 was designed to address these and many other issues, including some of the difficulties with usability encountered by the product's growing number of users. The result was a product that managed the difficult task of providing both a more complete set of features and an easier learning curve. Sophisticated Web sites were now within the grasp of an increasing number of users.

Once again, the challenge for the FrontPage design team was to make an already strong product stronger, and to keep up with the Web's newest innovations. To that end, FrontPage 98 contained many enhancements to FrontPage Editor, and a few important ones to FrontPage Explorer. FrontPage Editor now contained an extremely rich tables manipulation toolkit, allowing you to customize tables (a highly important layout tool) according to your needs. In addition, frames were now WYSIWYG based, and cascading style sheets were built throughout the product. New and better templates helped produce your site faster, and image manipulation tools let you work directly with graphics. Dynamic HTML made its appearance with FrontPage 98 and made many special effects suddenly possible.

FrontPage Explorer contained an entirely new Navigation view, in which you could easily create new pages and restructure your entire site with simple drag-and-drop actions. All the views were now contained in an interface resembling Microsoft Outlook (part of Office 97), and switching among views was simpler. Also available through Explorer was the Channel Definition Wizard, which let you publish your Web site according to the channel definition format standard for push systems. Push channels never did catch on as a widespread Web technology, but at the time they were considered the future of the Internet. They're still in use, but not nearly as widely as before.

Microsoft FrontPage 98 was, in many respects, the first truly mature version of this acclaimed package. Novice users could get started more quickly, intermediate users could develop and maintain sophisticated sites more easily, and advanced users needed fewer external tools to produce the sites required of them. Room for enhancements remained, but at that stage there was every reason to believe that FrontPage would continue to draw its share of accolades, awards, and editor's choice assignations.

CHAPTER **2**

THE FRONTPAGE ENVIRONMENT

In this chapter *by Dennis Jones*

UNDERSTANDING THE FRONTPAGE 2000 DEVELOPMENT ENVIRONMENT

The Web page editor, where you'll spend much of your FrontPage development time, lets you create World Wide Web pages, otherwise known as HTML documents. It's a near-WYSIWYG (what you see is what you get) system, which means that what you see in its Page view (the workspace in which the page is created) is for the most part what you'll see in your Web browser when you retrieve that page. Not all HTML code displays precisely as it will look on the Web, however, which is why this book refers to it as *near*-WYSIWYG. The point is that authoring Web pages in FrontPage Editor is relatively easy and extremely pleasing because as you create the page, you see almost exactly what it's going to look like to the people who visit your Web sites.

> **Note**
>
> Users of earlier FrontPage versions may be taken aback to find that the Explorer and Editor are no longer two separate applications. This change has made for a much more seamless environment.

Despite the importance of the editor, however, the true core of Microsoft FrontPage is its Web management system. With the management tools, you can create webs, delete webs, import files into webs, and manage your Web sites at all levels. You also have various graphical views of your webs, which let you see how the various pages are linked, as well as tools that update the structure of a changed web.

FrontPage also spares you the difficulty and drudgery of programming your World Wide Web pages by providing code modules called FrontPage *components*. Some components help you create forms that produce usable data, while others track the number of visitors to your site, update information fields whenever the page is loaded, or perform other such useful functions.

A Web server is an optional part of the FrontPage 2000 development environment. This means you have to decide whether to use a Web server to host the webs you are working on or opt for the simpler approach of working with what FrontPage refers to as "disk-based Webs." The information in the next section may help you make up your mind.

DECIDING THE SERVER QUESTION

You can assemble your pages into what is called a *disk-based Web*, which is a collection of linked HTML pages and images stored in one or more folders on your hard drive. In this case, you view a page by first using the browser to open it as a file and then typing a path name (such as C:\My Webs\A_Web\anypage.htm) into the browser's address bar.

However, some of FrontPage 2000's advanced features—forms, for example—require a server-based Web to function; they will not work if the page containing them is opened as a file. You can still create a disk-based Web and insert such server-based elements into your pages, of course. The trouble is that you won't know if these elements work properly until the pages containing them are published to an actual Web server and opened through the server. If you want to take full advantage of FrontPage 2000's resources, you'll likely need to install and use some form of Web server. Furthermore, complete FrontPage 2000 functionality is available only when the server has the FrontPage 2000 Server Extensions installed. Microsoft does not provide a Web server with the FrontPage 2000 package; you'll have to obtain a server of your own if you don't already have one. A very suitable server for FrontPage 2000 development work is the Microsoft Personal Web Server Version 4 (PWS 4).

PWS 4 is not difficult to obtain. You already own it if you own Windows 98—it's on the CD-ROM, in the \Add-Ons\PWS folder. If that's not the case, you can download PWS4 from Microsoft's Web site. The PWS is actually contained in the NT Server 4 Option Pack, despite the name; just be sure you download the correct version for the machine where it is to be installed. There is a version for Windows 9x, for Windows NT Workstation, and Windows NT Server. You will find the download details at
http://www.microsoft.com/windows/downloads/contents/Updates/PersonalWebSvr/.

Install the server once you have it. For detailed instructions on the installation and use of the PWS, see Chapter 37, "FrontPage 2000 and the Microsoft Personal Web Server." To find out how to install the FrontPage 2000 Server Extensions, refer to Chapter 35, "Introduction to Web Hosting and Web Servers."

PART

I

CH

2

DEALING WITH ADAPTIVE MENUS

One particular FrontPage 2000 feature should be mentioned before you go on: the new Adaptive Menus feature. It detects which menu items you used most recently and displays only those when the menu entry is clicked. The less-often used menu choices remain invisible; if you want them, you look at the bottom of the menu, where there is a down arrow. The rest of the menu items appear when you click that arrow.

This feature may not be to everyone's taste; open the Customize dialog box (choose Tools, Customize) if you want to turn it off. Choose the Options sheet and deselect the Menus Show Recently Used Commands First check box. Choose Close; from now on the menus will behave in the traditional manner.

CREATING A DISK-BASED WEB

If you haven't already created a web, you're probably itching to find out what it's actually like to do so—let's begin. This is just a quick run-through to get you used to FrontPage's behavior. You'll learn about web creation in detail later in the book. The web you create here will be disk-based; in other words, it will consist of a collection of folders containing linked pages and page elements, and will not be hosted by a Web server.

See Part III, "Web Creation and Management," for an exhaustive treatment of setting up, configuring, and maintaining Webs. Select the Windows Start button, go to Programs, and select Microsoft FrontPage. FrontPage 2000 opens after a short pause (see Figure 2.1). Choose File, New, Web from the menu bar. You immediately see a dialog box with a list of web templates and wizards.

Figure 2.1
You have a selection of wizards and web templates when creating a new web.

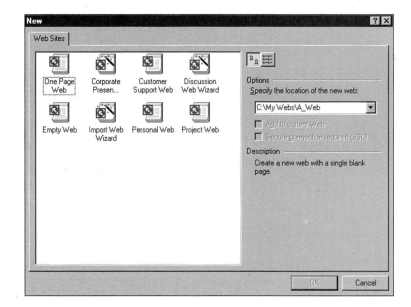

- The One Page Web creates a web with a single blank page, which will be the Web site's home page.

- The Corporate Presence Wizard walks you through the process of creating a web for an organization.

- The Customer Support Web provides you with a framework for developing customer support services.

- The Discussion Web Wizard is excellent for setting up a discussion site; creating one from scratch is a time-consuming business.

- The Empty Web is just that; it creates a web structure without even one page in it. You use this if you've already prepared a home page and need an empty web in which to install it.

- The Import Web Wizard assists you in creating a new web from existing files or folders.

- The Personal Web sets up a single home page for you. It has a selection of hyperlink destinations you can customize.

- The Project Web establishes a web you can use to manage and track a project.

See Chapter 14, "FrontPage's Web Templates and Wizards," for a detailed examination of these webs.

Select One Page Web for your test run. Type the name of the folder that is to contain the web in the Specify the Location of the New Web text box. At default, FrontPage creates disk-based webs in new folders within the *My Webs folder (page 342)*, which was created by FrontPage at installation time. If you want the web to be stored elsewhere, type the desired pathname in the text box. If the folders in the pathname you specify don't exist, FrontPage will create them. The web name is not case sensitive.

Choose OK when you have the path name as you want it; a message box informs you that FrontPage is creating the web. The box disappears and the new web's structure appears in the Folder List (see Figure 2.2). The workspace in the right pane, which is actually the page editing workspace, may already have a new page in it called something like NEW_PAGE_1.HTM. (The page name is visible in the gray bar at the top of this workspace.) This blank page isn't the home page, but a second page that FrontPage has thoughtfully created for you for the web. If you don't want this page, simply click the X button at the right end of the gray bar. Doing so closes the page without saving it.

PART

1

CH

2

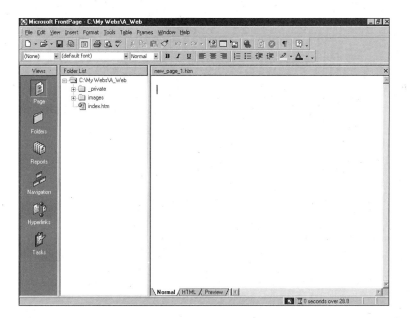

Figure 2.2
A new One Page Web has two folders and a home page already stored in it. Here, the home page has the filename INDEX.HTM.

UNDERSTANDING FRONTPAGE'S WORKSPACE LAYOUT

The FrontPage 2000 workspace has three major sections in it at default: the Views bar, the Folder List, and the right window where the various FrontPage views appear. You can see all these in Figure 2.2. If you find the workspace cramped, you can turn off the Views bar and the Folder List.

Choose View, Views Bar to toggle the Views bar off. To hide the folder list, choose Views, Folder List. Hiding both makes the Views area fill the FrontPage window, thus giving you maximum real estate in which to work.

Tip #1	A fast way to hide the Views bar is to right-click within it and click Hide Views Bar from the shortcut menu. A fast way to hide the folder list is to click the Folder List button, which is on the standard toolbar immediately left of the Print button; use the ToolTips to identify it if need be.

USING FRONTPAGE 2000'S VIEWS

FrontPage provides several views, one of which is Page view, the page editing environment. You can select it by clicking the page icon on the Views bar. There are other available views:

- Folders view, which is much like Windows Explorer; it gives full details about each folder, page, and file of the currently open web.
- Reports view, which shows the status of various components of the current web.
- Navigation view, which provides a point-and-drag method of arranging a navigational structure for the current web.
- Hyperlinks view, which is a schematic not only of all the links within the current web, but also of the links to resources outside it.
- Tasks view, which helps you keep track of complete and incomplete tasks associated with constructing the current web.

These various views are examined in detail in Chapter 15, "Working with an Existing Web." You can leave the workspace set at Page view during this chapter.

DELETING A WEB

You'll notice that there is no Delete Web menu entry. The Delete entry on the Edit menu is good only for deleting pages. That's a safety feature; it prevents you from accidentally deleting a web you've spent a lot of effort on. Deleting a web is a permanent action; there is no Undo for it.

However, sometimes a web must be deleted. To do so, first open it. Right-click the topmost web folder and choose Delete. This opens a dialog box where you choose to either delete the entire web or remove its FrontPage 2000 attributes. Essentially, the latter means that the web is converted into a set of ordinary files and folders.

Assuming you want to delete the web fully, choose Delete This Web Entirely and then choose OK. The web will be removed.

Incidentally, don't remove a web simply by deleting its files and folders in Windows Explorer. If you do this, FrontPage isn't aware of the deletion and can't properly maintain its web records.

CREATING A SERVER-BASED WEB

To do this you must, of course, have a server running on the host computer. Assuming this is the case, choose File, New, Web to open the New Web dialog box. For now, choose the One Page Web, as you did to create a disk-based Web.

In order to create a server-based web, however, you need to use the URL of the server's root web. This is clarified through the following example.

Suppose you have installed PWS4 on a Windows 95 or 98 computer. Upon installation, the server reported that Your Home Page is available at http://MyPC (for example). This actually tells you that the server's root web server is named http://MyPC. All further webs created on this server are contained in the root web, and their names will therefore begin with http://MyPC. If you wanted to create a new web named Another_Web, you'd type **http://MyPC/Another_Web** into the Specify the Location of the New Web text box. The web is created on the server when you then choose OK.

CLOSING AND OPENING WEBS

To close a web, choose File, Close Web. To open a Web, choose File, Open Web. This brings up the Open Web dialog box (see Figure 2.3).

PART

I

CH

2

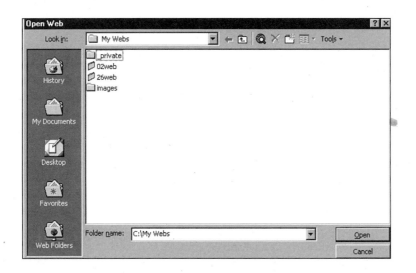

Figure 2.3
You open both disk- and server-based webs by using the Open Web dialog box.

If you are opening a disk-based web, you can type its folder path name into the Folder Name text box and choose OK. Alternatively, use the Look In box to locate the desired folder. When the proper folder appears in the Folder Name box, choose OK.

If you are opening a disk-based web, type its URL into the Folder Name text box and choose OK. Note that the Open Web dialog box's Web Folders button displays only server-based webs when it is clicked. It can't be used to display the folders of disk-based webs.

Note You may notice that the home page filename in a disk-based web is INDEX.HTM, while in a server-based web using the PWS it is DEFAULT.HTM. This has to do with the default page names of FrontPage–extended Web servers; it is not a bug.

UNDERSTANDING THE PAGE VIEW EDITING ENVIRONMENT

While the web management tools are crucial, the Page view editing environment is likely where you'll expend most of your creative energies. The FrontPage 2000 Web page editor is a very robust, full-featured Web page editor, supporting all the HTML standards up to and including 4.0, plus both the cascading style sheets specifications CSS1 and CSS2.

The Page view environment resembles a word processor in many ways. You can open several pages at the same time and switch between them; cut, copy, and paste page elements; perform spell checks; and format character appearance and size. You also have WYSIWYG frames, plus a tool for drawing tables directly on the page. You can follow links from one page to another even while editing them, which in effect turns FrontPage Editor into a mini-browser. Furthermore, you can load World Wide Web pages into FrontPage Editor to study the HTML code that makes such pages work. Most up-to-date of all, the editor provides tools for adding DHTML effects to your pages, without programming or scripting.

For a brief first look into Page view, begin by opening or creating a disk-based One Page Web. Click the page icon in the Views bar. The Open File dialog box appears when you choose File, Open. The only Web page showing in the current web has the filename INDEX.HTM. This is the current web's home page. Click it to select it and then choose Open. The page opens, ready for editing, in the Page view workspace.

Tip #2 You can also drag a page icon from the folder list to the Page View window, where the page will open automatically for editing.

The page has no content yet, but you know you have the right page because the gray title bar of the Page View window says INDEX.HTM. From here you begin the development of your page, adding images, text, hyperlinks, tables, imagemaps, forms, tables of contents—the list goes on and on and by the end of this book you'll be knowledgeable about them all.

You'll go on with this example shortly, but now is a good time to address the question of browser compatibility and how FrontPage helps you develop pages that will behave properly in a given browser.

ALLOWING FOR BROWSER COMPATIBILITY

As you are likely aware, the "Big Two" browsers, Netscape Navigator and Internet Explorer, do not always agree on how a Web page should appear to the user. Furthermore, there are differences in behavior among the various versions of each company's browser; IE 3 and 4 (and soon 5) and Navigator 3, 4, and eventually 5.

PART
I

CH
2

Note

The elegant Opera browser adds another set of display characteristics to the mix, but it is not likely to make a large penetration into the browser market in the near future.

If you are developing pages for one of these browsers specifically, you might accidentally include on a page some elements that the browser either does not recognize at all or displays poorly. You can set up your editing environment to safeguard against this.

Choose Tools, Page Options to open the Page Options dialog box; click the Compatibility tab (see Figure 2.4).

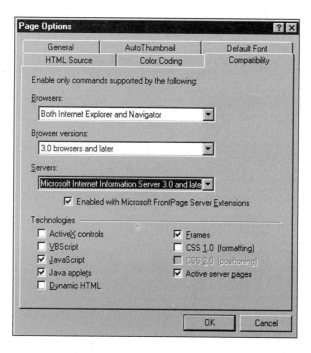

Figure 2.4
The Compatibility tab lets you specify which browser capabilities your pages can use.

On this sheet you can specify which browsers and server type your pages must be compatible with. In the example in Figure 2.4, the pages must behave properly in both Navigator and Internet Explorer 3 and later, as well as with Microsoft Internet Information Server 3 or later. You can see that certain technologies are unchecked. If you leave them this way and choose OK, their associated commands and menu items in Page view will be dimmed, so that the technology can't be used. You can override this by checking the boxes anyway, but doing so defeats the purpose of the exercise.

You can customize the compatibility by choosing Custom in each of the three list boxes, and checking or clearing the technologies as desired.

ADDING TEXT OR IMAGES TO A PAGE

With that out of the way, you might like to experiment with a few of the editor's tools. Try the following:

1. Click the down arrow beside the Style box on the far left of the toolbar. Select Heading 1 and type a title for the page.

2. Center this heading by clicking the Center button on the toolbar. Press Enter to move to the next line. Click Align Left to move the insertion point to the left margin.

3. Now add a graphic below the heading. The Clip Art Gallery dialog opens when you select Insert, Picture, Clip Art. Click the Miscellaneous icon and click the buff-colored cloud (see Figure 2.5). Click the insert clip icon (the top one) on the pop-up menu. The image is inserted onto the page.

4. Click the Preview tab at the bottom of the Page View window to see what the end results of your work will be. (Preview's display is essentially that of the Microsoft Internet Explorer 4 or later browser.)

5. Save the edited page to the web by choosing File, Save. When the Save Embedded Files dialog box appears, simply choose OK; this copies the image from the Clip Art Gallery to the current web.

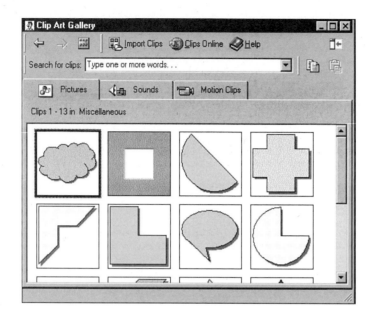

Figure 2.5
FrontPage 2000 ships with a good collection of clip art and other media inserts.

SAMPLING ADVANCED FEATURES

In the previous section you looked at the rudiments of inserting text and images onto pages. FrontPage is capable of far more than this, of course, and in the next three sections you examine some of its advanced features.

USING THE FRONTPAGE FRAME LAYOUT TOOLS

FrontPage 2000's tools for creating and linking framesets and framed pages allow you to see exactly what you're doing while you're doing it. To demonstrate this, you create a frameset with two frames and then populate it. Before beginning, ensure that the open web has at least two pages in it; you need these to best illustrate WYSIWYG frameset behavior. You might also want to make sure the pages have some identifiable material in them, so you'll be able to identify them on sight.

Switch to Page view if you're not already there. (You might want to turn off the Views bar and Folder List to gain more workspace.) Follow these steps:

1. Choose File, New, Page to open the New dialog box; click the Frame Pages tab to display the available frame templates. For this example, select the Header template, which gives you an upper frame whose links will change the page displayed in the lower frame. Choose OK. Now you have the screen shown in Figure 2.6. Note that the page name in the Page view's gray title bar is the name of the frameset page. This page holds the HTML code that controls frame layout and behavior.

Figure 2.6
FrontPage gives you a choice of several different frame layouts, such as this Header and Main Frame arrangement.

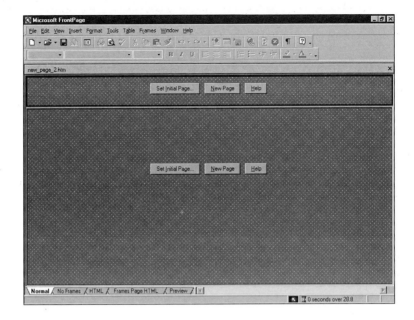

2. You can insert an existing page into any frame, but for purposes of illustration you create a new one for the upper frame. A new, blank page appears in the upper frame when you click the New Page button there. You use this page for the hyperlinks that control the display in the lower frame.

3. In the lower frame, click the Set Initial Page button. This opens the Create Hyperlink dialog box. From the list box, select an existing page of the current FrontPage web; click OK. The selected page opens in the lower window.

4. Click in the upper frame. Type some text there to serve as a hyperlink. Select it and choose Insert, Hyperlink to open the Create Hyperlink dialog box. In the list box, select the page you chose in step 3. (In other words, link to the Initial Page, the page that currently appears in the lower frame.)

5. Repeat step 4, but instead of linking to the page that is currently appearing in the lower frame, link to a different page in the FrontPage web. Your screen should now resemble that shown in Figure 2.7.

6. Use File, Save to save the frameset page and the new or changed pages. You are asked to supply names for the new pages, including the frameset page itself.

7. Use the Preview mode to test the frameset. Clicking the links in the upper frame should switch the page appearing in the lower frame.

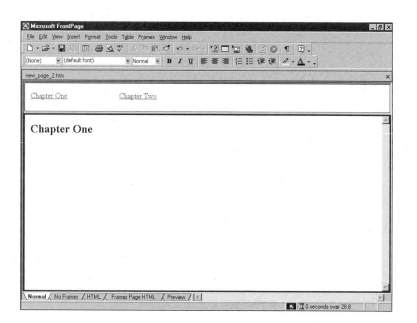

Figure 2.7
The frameset is being set up with two links in the upper frame.

To edit the frameset later, simply open the frameset page in FrontPage Editor. It will appear with its assigned initial pages displayed.

If you want to save the frameset without saving the pages displayed in it, click the Frames Page HTML tab at the bottom of the Editor workspace while you're working on the frameset. When the HTML page appears, choose File, Save As and provide page title and filename.

If you want to establish your web as a framed web as soon as people access it, rename the frameset page DEFAULT.HTM (for a server-based Web) or INDEX.HTM (for a disk-based Web).

DRAWING A TABLE ON A PAGE

Many Web page authors make heavy use of tables to control layout, and FrontPage 2000 provides a drawing tool that makes table setup very easy. To draw a simple table, perform these steps:

1. Choose Table, Draw Table. The Table toolbar appears, and turns into the table drawing tool when you move the mouse pointer into the workspace it. The Table toolbar also appears; if it doesn't, choose View, Toolbars, Table.

2. Drag the table drawing tool through the Editor workspace until you have a rectangle that's about the size of the table you want, then release the mouse button. (It's the same technique as drawing rectangles in a simple paint program.)

3. Drag within the cells to create new cells, columns, or rows. Figure 2.8 shows a partially completed table, with a row boundary being drawn in (indicated by the dotted line).

Figure 2.8
Adding cells, rows, and columns is as easy as drawing with a pencil.

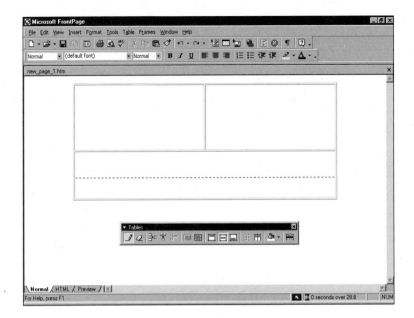

4. To resize a cell, place the drawing tool on top of any cell border until the pointer becomes a double-headed arrow. Drag this to adjust the size of the cell or table.

5. To remove a border, click the Eraser button on the Table toolbar. The mouse pointer turns into an eraser. Hold the left mouse button down while dragging the eraser over the cell border you want to erase. When the border has been selected, it will be highlighted. The cell border vanishes when you release the mouse button. (In some configurations of cells, certain borders cannot be erased.)

You can adjust the table's properties further with the Table Properties dialog box; for example, you likely won't want the borders to be visible if you're using the table as a layout aid. Right-click anywhere on the table and choose Table Properties from the shortcut menu to make the dialog box appear (see Figure 2.9). Modify any properties and choose OK.

To add text to the table, simply place the insertion point in a cell and type. Cells can contain anything a page can, including other tables.

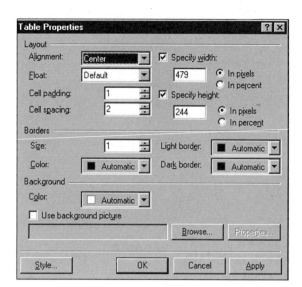

Figure 2.9
Use the Table Properties dialog box to fine-tune the table's appearance.

ADDING A DHTML PAGE TRANSITION EFFECT

On the Web you may have seen fancy page transitions such as fade or wipe and have wondered how they're done. With FrontPage, they are as easy as a few mouse clicks.

Begin by opening the page where you want to apply the transition and choose Format, Page Transition to open the Page Transitions dialog box (see Figure 2.10).

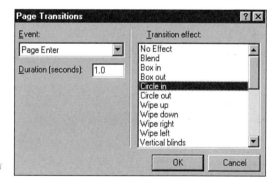

Figure 2.10
You have more than 20 possible transitions (plus No Effect, which turns transitions off) to apply to a page entry or exit, or to a site entry or exit.

In the Event drop-down list box, specify whether you want the effect to take place on page entry or exit. Select the particular transition you want from the Transition Effect list box. Then, in the Duration text box, type the number of seconds over which the effect is to take place. You can apply two different effects to the same page, one for entry and one for exit—the entry effect takes place as the page appears; exit, as the page vanishes from the user's browser.

When finished, choose OK. Create another page and type some text in it to be the hyperlink. Select the text and choose Insert, Hyperlink to open the Create Hyperlink dialog box. Select the name of the page with the effect from the list box and choose OK.

Save the pages and open the link page in Preview. When you click its link, the page with the transition effect appears, complete with the transition.

USING CHECK IN AND CHECK OUT FOR SOURCE CONTROL

More than one person in a collaborative environment may be working on the same Web page. This raises problems of source control: What happens if two authors simultaneously try to modify the same page?

To deal with this problem, FrontPage 2000 has built-in source control, provided you enable it. To do this, open the web that you want controlled. If it is already open, close all open pages. Choose Tools, Web Settings, and then click the General tab. Select the Use Document Check-In and Check-Out check box and choose OK. A dialog box appears, determining whether you do in fact want to modify source control. Assuming you do, choose Yes.

In order to check out a page so that only you can modify it, select it in the folder list or Folders view. Choose Edit, Check Out. A red check mark appears next to the entry. This indicates that you have checked out the file. Other web authors will still be able to open and view the page, but they can't modify it. If someone else has checked the file out, a padlock icon appears next to the entry.

When you're ready to allow other people access to the page again, save and close it; select its entry in Folder view or the Folder List. The red check mark disappears and the page is available after you choose Edit, Check In.

If you want to discard any changes you made to the page since you checked it out, select the file and choose Edit, Undo Check Out. The original state of the page, before you checked it out, is restored.

CUSTOMIZING THE ENVIRONMENT

The FrontPage 2000 environment can be customized several ways. The next sections cover the ways in which you can do this.

USING TOOLBARS AND MENUS

FrontPage 2000 has eight built-in toolbars: Standard, Formatting, DHTML Effects, Navigation, Picture, Positioning, Reports, and Style. Each of these can be displayed or hidden by choosing View, Toolbars, and selecting the desired toolbar. All the toolbars can float; they can be dragged to any convenient place in the workspace.

Similarly, some menus are tear-off menus; they can be "torn off" the drop-down menu and dragged to any desired place in the workspace. You can tell which are tear-off menus by the dark gray line at the top of the menu; an example is the Insert menu's Component sub-menu. Simply place the mouse pointer on the dark gray line and drag the menu—it will turn into a floating toolbar. The main menu bar itself can also be dragged to any position in the workspace.

You can customize existing toolbars, too. To copy a command from one toolbar to another, display both toolbars, press Ctrl, and drag the command onto the destination toolbar.

In addition, you can place menu commands on toolbars. Begin by displaying the desired toolbar; choose Tools, Customize, and then click the Commands tab. Click the group that contains the command you want from the Categories list. In the resulting commands list, click the desired command and drag it to the toolbar.

In a similar manner, you can drag a command to a menu, rather than to a toolbar.

Finally, you can create a brand new toolbar:

1. Choose Tools, Customize, and then click the Toolbars tab. Choose New to open the New Toolbar dialog box.

2. Type a name for the new toolbar in the Toolbar Name box and choose OK. FrontPage adds the new toolbar to the list in the Toolbars box and also displays the new toolbar in your workspace.

3. Click the Commands tab. Then, in the Categories list, click the group that contains the command you want to put on the new toolbar.

4. In the Commands list, click the command that you want to put on the new toolbar; then drag the command onto the new toolbar displayed in your workspace.

5. Repeat steps 3 and 4 until you've added all the commands you want on the new toolbar. Close the Customize dialog box. The toolbar will be available from now on—under the name you gave it—on the View, Toolbars menu.

TROUBLESHOOTING

When you create the first web of a new FrontPage installation, the program defaults to creating a disk-based web in the C:\My Documents\My Webs folder. This occurs even when the host machine has a Web server installed on it. If you have installed a server and want a server-based Web, you must give FrontPage the full URL of this web at creation time: http://MyPC/NewWeb, for example. You'll get a disk-based Web if you don't specify and the Web name can be construed by FrontPage as a path name on the host computer.

There is a further possibility for trouble. If you have a Web server installed, there will be what is called a root Web on your machine. This Web will likely use the name of the host machine (which was given to the machine when the operating system was installed). An example of such a root Web name is http://MyPc, where MyPc is the machine's name. If you try to create a server-based Web on this machine and supply an URL such as `http://test`, you'll get an error message saying you can't create a root Web at that location. To troubleshoot this and to create the Web named `test`, you must use the URL `http://MyPc/test`.

If you attempt to create or open a server-based Web on a machine where there is no server (or the server is stopped; verify that it's running if applicable), you get an error message saying that FrontPage could not find a Web server on port 80.

This chapter mentions that some FrontPage 2000 features require a disk-based web: run-time components (including the form handler component, discussion component, full-text search component, and hit counter component), the database integration features, and Administrative, Authoring, and Browse permissions. To troubleshoot difficulties with these elements, you are advised to install a Web server on the development machine.

DESIGNERS CORNER

At this stage—FrontPage 2000 is installed and you've experimented with a couple of its page editing tools—the temptation is to leap in and start creating that Web site you've set your heart on. That's not a good idea. The best advice you can give yourself at this point is to slow down and think.

Quality Web sites are not produced in a rush. Before you launch FrontPage 2000 for serious work, you should have a good intuitive understanding of your as-yet created Web site. This is the conceptual stage. You must ask yourself questions such as "Who is this Web site for, what audience do I want to attract?"; "What do I want to communicate, what is the site's content?"; "What are the best ways of communicating that information?"; "How do I make the content easily accessible and attractive to my audience?"

Primitive as they are compared to the power of computers, a sheet of paper and a sharp pencil (or a whiteboard and colored markers) are usually the best tools at this stage. Sketch your site's overall structure before committing a single keystroke to it. Elements in this sketch can be individual pages and their linking patterns; for complex sites, elements can be major areas that are then divided into individual pages. Once you can see the your site's structure, it will be far easier to identify redundancies, dead ends, inconsistencies, and omissions. It may also be useful at this stage to start a list of the kinds of non-textual elements—images, animations, sound files, buttons, and bars—that you will need for page design and navigation tools.

If you do it before touching a keyboard, this kind of preparation and thought will save you vast amounts of time once you get to actual construction. Even more importantly, it will help you produce a site that is well designed and a pleasure for people to visit.

PART II

Designing Documents: Working from the Page View

CHAPTER 3

The Page View: Windows, Icons, and Menus

In this chapter *by Neil Randall and Dennis Jones*

Page View's Screen Areas

When you launch FrontPage for the first time, a dialog box explains that the program is trying to determine your machine's network address or local machine name. Once that process is completed and you press OK, you find yourself faced with FrontPage's default multipart interface. This is your workspace; you can do everything from here, by switching among the various FrontPage views.

Figure 3.1 shows the default interface. As with essentially all Windows software, the title bar runs across the top of the screen, with the menu bar immediately below it. Below that comes the standard toolbar and then the formatting toolbar.

FrontPage's three largest screen areas are below these typical components. At the far left is the views bar, and on the right is the largest screen area, the main viewing window. In Page view, in which FrontPage starts by default, only these two areas appear. When you switch to any other view, the Folder List appears between the Views bar and the main viewing window. This chapter deals exclusively with the Page view.

What you actually see, in fact, depends on other things as well. See "Customizing and Creating Toolbars," below, for some ways of changing the interface features. Page view itself offers three tabs at the bottom of the screen: Normal, HTML, and Preview. Each changes the look of the main viewing window (although not the layout of the screen areas), and each alters the menu commands and the right-click menu for specificity.

The Page view is your document editor. In essence, it is the word processor portion of the FrontPage package. You create, format, and edit documents in a word processor, and that's precisely what you do in Page view. From there, in other words, you build the contents of your Web site. In that sense, Page view is FrontPage's workhorse, the area in which you'll spend most of your time.

In earlier versions of FrontPage, document editing and formatting were separated from site creation and management. FrontPage Editor handled the former, FrontPage Explorer the latter. While the distinction offered some useful functionality, including hiding the gory details of site management from those who were assigned solely to authoring tasks, it also caused confusion. For instance those launching FrontPage saw Explorer first and found themselves staring at a screen that had no obvious means of creating their Web pages, which is usually what they bought FrontPage for in the first place. Even for more experienced users there was some confusion: Explorer let you create individual documents—as did Editor—and it wasn't always clear how the two fit together or how working with one affected the other.

FrontPage 2000 brings Page view to the forefront, making it obvious that document editing and creation is fully a part of site management.

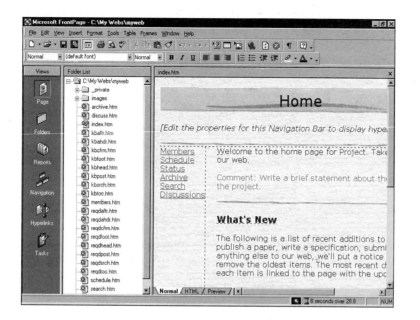

Figure 3.1
The Folder List
appears automatically
when you enter
Folders, Navigation, or
Hyperlinks view.

PART

I

CH

3

TITLE BAR, MENU BAR, AND TOOLBARS

The title bar runs along the top of the FrontPage screen. This bar always displays the name of the product itself, Microsoft FrontPage, and, if you have a web open, the directory path of that web.

When you save a document to a web, the name of the web appears in the title bar. If you save a document to a non-web location such as a data folder on your hard drive, that location's pathname appears in the title bar. The name of the document itself appears only on the grayed bar above the main window.

The menu bar contains the headings for each of the program's menus. As with all Windows software, you can click a menu to reveal the items beneath it, or you can access it by pressing the Alt key and simultaneously pressing the underlined character in the heading. To access the Table menu, for example, hold Alt and press the A key.

The menus are covered in detail in this chapter's "Page View's Menu Bar" section.

The standard toolbar contains a series of icons, each of which corresponds to a FrontPage command or option. Most of them can be accessed with a simple click, although some display a down arrow next to them. In these cases, clicking the icon performs the default task associated with that icon, while clicking the down arrow reveals a submenu. In one case, the help icon at far right, the down arrow leads to another down arrow.

The formatting toolbar also contains a series of icons corresponding to FrontPage commands or options. In addition, it also contains the Style, Font, and Font Size drop-down lists, which are active only when you start a new web document or open an existing one. To access the drop-down lists, click the down arrow to the right of the default entry in the lists: (None) for Style, (default font) for Fonts, and (Normal) for Font Size.

Tip #3

You can modify one or both of these toolbars to suit your needs. You can also move them by clicking and dragging them, as well as reordering and resizing them.

All toolbar details, as well as details about other FrontPage toolbars, are covered in this chapter's "FrontPage's Toolbars" section.

VIEWS BAR

The Views bar appears by default down the left side of the screen. From here you can access the various FrontPage views; you can do the same from the View menu on the menu bar. This chapter discusses only the Page view, accessible by clicking the topmost icon. All other views are detailed in Part III, "Web Creation and Management."

You can't move the Views bar, but you can hide it. To do so, right-click anywhere on the Views bar (even on an icon; it makes no difference where) and select Hide Views Bar. Alternatively, deselect Views Bar from the View menu.

Caution

Whether you hide the Views bar by right-clicking it and selecting Hide Views Bar, or unselecting it from under the View menu, the only way to bring the Views bar back is by selecting it from under the View menu.

FOLDER LIST

When you open a document file in Page view, the contents of the web or non-web folder in which that document resides appear in the Folder List. These contents are presented as a list of folders and documents; the folders are collapsible. The Folder List lets you easily access any file within the folder for editing, without having to switch from the Page view to the Folders view.

Right-clicking in the Folders view brings up a context menu. If you right-click in the white-space (away from the folder and document names), you can add a new page or a new folder, you can paste a page from the clipboard, or you can display the directory above the current directory (through the menu item called Up One Level). You have the following options when you right-click a document name:

- Open—Open the file either into FrontPage Editor or into the editor associated with that file type.
- Open With—Open the file into an editor of your choosing. This option is useful if you have an editor besides FrontPage that you like to use, or if you have a file associated with a program that you want to open with a different graphics package.
- Cut—Cut the file from the list.

- Copy—Copy the file into the Clipboard.
- Paste—Paste the file that's currently in the Clipboard to the web. It will appear in the Folder List. The Paste option appears only if there is something to paste.
- Rename—Rename the document.
- Delete—Delete the document from the web.
- Add Task—Add a task for the currently selected document to the Tasks list. See Chapter 18 for coverage of the Tasks features.
- Properties—Call up the Properties dialog box for that document. The contents of this dialog box are covered in Chapter 4.

The same Context menu appears when you right-click a folder name instead of a document name, except that the Add Task option is grayed out and cannot be used. You can associate tasks only with documents, not with folders.

Main Window

The main window in Page view shows the contents and the format of the currently selected document. You can load a document into the main window the following ways:

- Double-clicking the document's name in the Folders list
- Selecting File, Open and choosing the document from the Open File dialog box (covered in "Page View's Menu Bar," in this chapter)
- Clicking the open icon from the standard toolbar and selecting the document from the Open File dialog box (covered in "Page View's Menu Bar")

Once the file is loaded, you can work with the document through the commands and options on the menus and toolbars. (See "Page View's Menu Bar" and "FrontPage's Toolbars" in this chapter, as well as the remainder of Part II for detailed discussions of these options.) You also have access to context menus by right-clicking in the document. Right-clicking text reveals one set of options, right-clicking a hyperlink another set, right-clicking a graphic another set, and so on. Options common to most of these menus are as follows:

- Cut, Copy, Paste, Paste Special—These are the common editing features. They correspond to the same commands on the Edit menu.
- Theme—Brings up the Theme dialog box, which is covered in Chapter 6.
- Shared Borders—Brings up the Shared Borders dialog box, covered in Chapter 7.
- Properties menus—You can access the Page, Paragraph, Font, Hyperlink, Bookmark, and other properties menus through this Context menu. They are covered throughout Part II.

PAGE VIEW'S MENU BAR

When you are working in Page view, the FrontPage menus contain the commands and options relevant to document creation and editing. Some of these commands are also available as context menus by right-clicking in various screen areas, as covered earlier in this chapter and throughout Part II. The contents of the menus are covered here, but only with commands and options not covered in chapters related specifically to those items are dealt with in detail here.

THE FILE MENU

The File menu covers a range of possible activities, and not all of them have to do specifically with files. As with the majority of Windows software, the File menu collects commands that deal with files, documents, printing, and related activities. FrontPage is no different in this regard.

The items in the File menu are as follows:

- New—Start a new page, a new task, or a new web from the submenu.
- Open—Bring up the Open File dialog box (see Figure 3.2).

  This dialog box's main area is the file window, which shows icons representing the subfolders and files within the folder that is specified in the Look In field at the top of the dialog box. To the left is the list of frequently accessed folders; clicking in one of these folders reveals the contents of that folder (files and subfolders) in the file window. You can browse your computer (or networked computers) using the Look In field and the file window, or you can type the full path of the requested file in the File Name field. You can specify the type of file you want to load in the Files of Type field. By default, this field displays FrontPage document types such as HTML or ASP, but you can select from a wide variety of additional types by clicking the down arrow. The File Name field also offers a down arrow, and clicking it reveals recently loaded files for you to choose from.

  You don't need to specify a local computer location for a file. You can select files from computers on your network, for instance, and you can also type in a Web location (URL). If your site is on a remote server, you'll want to access that server, not your local drive, in which case type the URL for your site. You are prompted for a username and password if the site is password protected; you then have access to the remote folders and files.

  The Open button in the bottom-right corner becomes available when a document is selected. There is a down arrow beside that, which lets you choose between opening the document in the current FrontPage window or in a new FrontPage window. If the latter, a new instance of FrontPage loads with that document in the main window.

  To the right of the Look In field, along the top of the Open File dialog box, is a series of navigation icons. The left arrow changes the location displayed in the Look In field to the location that was displayed before you selected the current location. The left up arrow takes you up one level in the folder hierarchy. The Internet Explorer icon (no, you can't change it) takes you to IE's search engine, which lets you search using other search engines on the Web. With these search engines you can search for files on the Web; once you have located the one you want, FrontPage lets you load that file and work with it. The X lets you delete a file or folder, while the file folder icon lets you add a folder.

The final two icons offer several choices, and thus provide down arrows. The first, Views, lets you choose how to display the files in the file window. List view, which gives you a simple list of folder and filenames, is selected by default. Selecting details gives you a columnar view of the folder and filenames, complete with the files size, type, and last date and time of modification.

If you choose Properties, the file window splits into two panes, with folder and filenames on the left and the properties for the selected folder or file on the right. If you choose Preview, the file window also splits in half, this time with the right side offering a preview of the page (how it will appear in a browser, for example).

The last icon is called Tools. From here you can search for Files (Find), delete or rename a file, print a document, or get the file's or folder's properties. You can also map your local network's drives (yielding Windows' standard dialog box for doing so) or add the chosen folder or file to the Favorites folder. Doing so adds a shortcut in the Favorites folder to the specific folder or file location. You can access Favorites from the Open File dialog box or a host of other Microsoft programs, including Internet Explorer and the Office suite.

- Close—Closes the current document.

- Open Web—Brings up the Open Web dialog box. This is a slightly simplified version of the Open File dialog box described earlier. The differences are as follows: The File Name field has been replaced by a Folder Name field, the Files of Type field has disappeared, the Open button has no down arrow (which means no options), and the Tools button offers only five options—Delete, Rename, Add to Favorites, Map Network Drive, and Properties.

  To open a web on a remote server, type the URL in the Folder Name field.

- Delete Web—Yields the Confirm Delete dialog box. Here you can choose between removing the web entirely by deleting all files and folders, or simply deleting FrontPage information within the web. If you choose the latter, all files and folders remain in place, so you can work on the web as a non-FrontPage web.

  Note that you can remove webs from local drives, network drives, or remote servers. You can't bring a deleted web back.

- Save—Saves the document currently open in the main window to the folder in which it currently resides. If the document has never been saved, this command operates as the Save As command (immediately following).

PART

I

CH

3

- Save As—Brings up the Save As dialog box. This is very similar to the Open File dialog box shown in Figure 3.2, with the following changes: The Open button has been replaced by a Save button with no options arrow; the Files of Type field is now called Save as Type; and the possible file types are much more limited. The title of the current document (the HTML title, not the filename) is shown above the File Name field. A Change button beside this title opens the Set Page Title dialog box in which you can simply type in a new title for the page, click OK, and thus make that change.

- Publish Web—Yields the Publish FrontPage Web dialog box for the purpose of uploading the files and folders of the currently opened web to a remote server. This feature is covered in Chapter 16.

- Import—Brings up the Import File to FrontPage Web dialog box, with which you can bring existing files (such as word processor documents) into the currently loaded web.

- Preview in Browser—Displays the Preview in Browser dialog box, letting you display the currently loaded page in a Web browser. This dialog box is covered in Chapter 4.

- Page Setup—Selecting this option gives you the Windows Print Setup dialog box, from which you select the printer you want to use for the currently loaded document, plus features specific to that printer. This is a Windows function, not a FrontPage-specific function.

- Print Preview—When selected, FrontPage's main window changes to show what the currently loaded document will look like when printed. From this window you can zoom in to see the page in more detail, print the document, and close the window and return to the regular main window. For documents that take up more than one printed page, you can choose Next Page, Prev Page, or Two Pages to see two pages at the same time.

- Print—Yields the standard Windows Print dialog box. This is a Windows function, not a FrontPage-specific function.

- Send—As with other Windows software, Send allows you to email the document. The command automatically opens a new message window in your default Windows email program. The currently selected document automatically appears in this message as an attachment.

- Properties—Brings up the Page Properties dialog box. This box is covered in Chapter 4.

- Recent Files—This selection cascades to reveal the names of the files you have worked on most recently. Up to eight filenames are included. Simply select the desired file; it loads into the main FrontPage window.

- Recent Webs—This selection cascades to reveal the names of the webs you have most recently loaded into FrontPage. Up to four webs are included. Selecting a web name opens that web into a separate FrontPage instance.

- Exit—Exits the program, prompting you for save information.

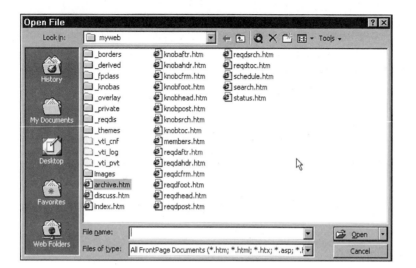

Figure 3.2
The Open File dialog box is common to the Office 2000 suite. The easily accessible typical folders are to the left.

THE EDIT MENU

The Edit menu contains commands that let you (not surprisingly) edit documents. Most of the commands mimic those of the Edit menu in other Windows programs.

- Undo—This command resets the text of the document to what it was before your last action (typing, deleting, inserting, and the like). Each Undo action removes one action, and the number of possible undos depends on your system's memory. The actual command reads Undo X, where X represents the most recent action.

- Redo—The Redo command reverses the most recent Undo action. In other words, it returns things. The actual command reads Redo X, where X represents the last action.

- Cut, Copy, Paste—These commands are standard Windows commands. Cut removes the selected item from the document and places it in the Clipboard. Copy places the item in the Clipboard but also leaves it in place in the document. Paste transfers the item from the Clipboard to the document.

- Paste Special—Brings up the Convert Text dialog box. You choices are to paste the text into the currently active document as one formatted paragraph (it will concatenate separate paragraphs), as the same number of formatted paragraphs as in the original, as normal paragraphs (normal style), as normal paragraphs with line breaks, or as raw HTML.

- Clear—Cuts the selected text from the document without putting it into the Clipboard.

- Select All—Highlights everything in the document. This command is useful for copying, deleting, or reformatting the entire contents of the document.

- Find—Yields the Find dialog box, with which you can search for text strings in the currently loaded document or across the entire active web.

■ Replace—Brings up the Replace dialog box shown in Figure 3.3. Type, in the Find What field, the text string you want to locate; type, in the Replace With field, the text string that will take the place of the located string. Two columns of radio buttons and a column of check boxes guide you through the options. In Find Where, you can choose to find the string in the selected page(s) or across the entire web, while in Direction you can tell FrontPage to search from the cursor position to the beginning of the document (Up) or from the cursor position to the end of the document (Down).

The Options area lets you select any combination of the three options. You can match the entire word (not portions of words) and you can match upper- or lowercase characters. You can also locate the string in the HTML codes themselves. The buttons at the right of the dialog box enable you to find the next (or the first) instance of the string or simply cancel the entire process at any point. The Replace button works in conjunction with the Find Next button: Once a string is found, click Replace to change that selection only, after which the next instance of the string will be searched for. If you're certain at any time that you want to replace all the specified strings in the text without stopping at each one to confirm, you can press the Replace All button.

■ Check Out, Check In, Undo Check Out—These three commands handle the check out and check in features of FrontPage, designed to let only one author work on a document at one time. A web author cannot load a checked-out page. This command is covered in greater detail in Chapter 18.

Figure 3.3
The Find dialog box is identical to the Replace dialog box, except that the Find dialog box does not contain the Replace With field.

THE VIEW MENU

The View menu lets you change what the FrontPage screen displays:

■ Page, Folders, Reports, Navigation, Hyperlinks, Tasks—These first five menu items work identically to the icons on the Views bar that runs down the left side of the FrontPage screen.

■ Views Bar, Folder List—These commands toggle the Views bar and the Folder List respectively. When checked, those features show on the FrontPage screen.

■ Reveal Tags—This command reveals the HTML tags in the currently loaded document. Figure 3.4 shows a document with tags revealed.

■ Toolbars—This menu item cascades into a list of available toolbars. These options are covered in the "FrontPage's Toolbars" section of this chapter.

■ Refresh—Reloads the current document into the main window. This is useful if the display becomes mangled, or for seeing the document with all the changes made. You are asked to save any changes to the file before Refresh takes place.

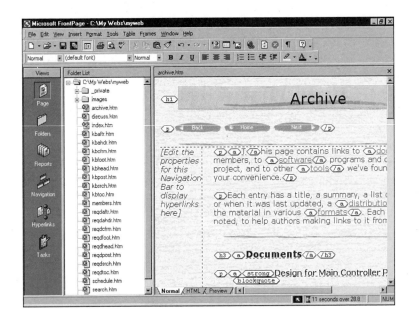

Figure 3.4
You can see the HTML tags when you select the Reveal Tags option. You can edit the document with these tags in place.

THE INSERT, FORMAT, TOOLS, AND TABLE MENUS

These menus are covered in detail throughout Part II, in the chapters devoted to their respective tasks.

THE WINDOW MENU

From the Window menu, you can open a new FrontPage window (another instance of FrontPage) or select from one of the currently open documents. Up to nine open documents will appear in the list; if more are open you can access them by selecting Windows. Each currently running instance of FrontPage has its own separate Window list (although all maintain the same Recent Files and Recent Webs list in the File menu).

THE HELP MENU

From here you can access FrontPage's Help system. The Office Assistant can also do this for you.

FRONTPAGE'S TOOLBARS

By default, FrontPage 2000 loads with two toolbars immediately below the menu bar. Several other toolbars are included with the package, and they can be called up at any time via the View, Toolbar command. Furthermore, you can customize the toolbars to your specific needs. Here you briefly examine the toolbars and look at the customization process.

Figure 3.5 shows FrontPage 2000 with all the toolbars visible. Several are inactive, with grayed-out features. The features become active only if you're performing a task to which they apply. For instance, the third toolbar down from the menu bar in Figure 3.4, DHTML Effects, is active because a *Dynamic HTML (page 506)* event is being added to the highlighted component in the main window. If that component were a graphic, the Picture toolbar (the fifth one down) would be active.

You can change the positions of any of the toolbars. To do so, move the cursor to the far left, where a small vertical line marks the start of the toolbar. The cursor will turn into a four-point arrow; in Figure 3.5 you can see it at the far edge of the second toolbar from the bottom. You can drag the toolbar left, right, up, or down. If the toolbar is *docked* with other toolbars (flush against them so that it does not have its own title bar and exit (X) button), as are all the toolbars in Figure 3.5, you can drag the toolbar along the other docked bars and drop it where you want it. If you drag it away from the docked toolbars, the toolbar becomes a floating toolbar, which you can move anywhere on the screen. By default, only the Standard and Formatting toolbars are docked; the rest, when summoned with the View, Toolbars command, appear as floating toolbars. You move a floating toolbar as you'd move any other window, by clicking and holding its title bar.

Figure 3.5
In this figure, the toolbars are all docked along the top of the FrontPage screen. You can dock them to the left, right, or bottom, or you can leave them floating.

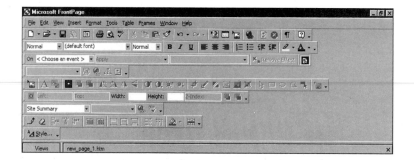

THE STANDARD TOOLBAR

The Standard toolbar contains many icons common to Windows programs. Only a few are specific to FrontPage itself. Follow these from left to right (assuming the default toolbar configuration). Depending on the view you are working in, as well as whether or not a web or page is actually loaded into FrontPage, some of the icons will be grayed out.

- New Page—Click to open a new page in the main FrontPage window. Click the down arrow beside the icon to start a new page, task, folder, or web. Corresponds to File, New.

- Open—Click to yield the Open File dialog box. Click the down arrow to choose between the Open File and the Open Web dialog box. Corresponds to File, Open.

- Save—Saves the current document to your hard drive (or networked drive). Brings up the Save As dialog box if the document is unsaved. Corresponds to File, Save.

- Publish Web—Begins the Web publishing process, covered in Chapter 16. Corresponds to File, Publish Web.

- Folder List—Shows or hides the Folder List. Corresponds to View, Folder List.

- Print—Brings up the Print dialog box. Corresponds to File, Print.

- Preview in Browser—Opens a browser window with the currently active document loaded. Corresponds to File, Preview in Browser.

- Spelling—Initiates the spell-check process, covered in Chapter 18.

- Cut, Copy, Paste—Next three icons. Correspond to Edit, Cut; Edit, Copy; and Edit, Paste, respectively.

- Format Painter—Activates the Format Painter procedure, covered in Chapter 5, "Enhancing Pages with Graphics and Multimedia."

- Undo—Click to undo the most recent action. Click the down arrow to reveal a list of actions ordered from most to least recent and select the action you want undone. Corresponds to Edit, Undo.

- Redo—Click to redo the most recent action. Click the down arrow to reveal a list of actions ordered from most to least recent and select the action you want redone. Active only if a valid Redo action is possible. (Not all Undo actions can be redone.) Corresponds to Edit, Redo.

- Insert Component, Table, Picture, Hyperlink—Next four icons. These commands open the dialog boxes for adding a FrontPage component, a table, a graphic, and a hyperlink, respectively. Click to undo the most recent action. Click the down arrow to reveal a list of actions ordered from most to least recent and select the action you want undone. Correspond to the same commands on the Insert menu.

- Back, Forward, Refresh, Stop—Next four icons. These commands are similar to those in any Web browser. Back takes you to the previous document, Forward to the next one. The down arrows beside let you choose a specific document to return to or to go ahead to. Refresh reloads the current document. Stop halts the loading of a page from the Web. Click to undo the most recent action. Click the down arrow to reveal a list of actions ordered from most to least recent and select the action you want undone. Only Refresh has a corresponding menu command: View, Refresh.

- Show All—Reveals formatting marks, principally carriage returns. This is not the same as Reveal Tags, which displays all HTML tags.

- Help Tool—Click to activate and then click the item for which you'd like help. This activates the Help system.

- More Buttons—The down arrow at the far right of each toolbar lets you customize FrontPage's interface by adding or removing buttons, changing keyboard shortcuts, and so forth. This is covered in "Customizing the FrontPage Interface" in this chapter. Corresponds to Tools, Customize.

PART

I

CH

3

THE OTHER TOOLBARS

The remaining toolbars are covered throughout this book, in chapters devoted to the features that employ them. Here is an introductory overview:

These tables do not appear in FrontPage until you select them from the cascading menu under Views, Toolbars. Once you display a toolbar, it will remain displayed, even after exiting and restarting FrontPage. You must deselect it if you wish to hide it. Toolbars can be placed anywhere on the screen, either as floating toolbars or docked along the sides, top, or bottom of the FrontPage display.

- Formatting toolbar—There's very little difference between the Formatting toolbar in FrontPage and the Formatting toolbar of most other Windows application (especially Microsoft's). With it you can format characters with font styles and sizes by boldfacing, italicizing, and underlining, and by left- or right-justifying and centering. You can produce bulleted and numbered lists, and you can increase and decrease the indentation in outlines. You can also change character colors.

  The only significant difference is the Styles drop-down list (at far left of the toolbar). Here you find HTML styles corresponding to the HTML standards, rather than to the kinds of styles found in a word processor. These styles are covered in Chapter 12, "Using Style Sheets with Individual Pages and Full Sites."

- DHTML effects toolbar—The DHTML Effects toolbar lets you add dynamic HTML effects to your document. The toolbar operates syntactically; the fields create a kind of grammatical sentence to explain the effect. For example, when filled in the fields might read—in order—On Page load, Apply Fly in, from bottom, and that's precisely the effect that is generated. This toolbar is covered in Chapter 25, "Making Your Pages and Webs More Dynamic."

- Navigation toolbar—Operational only when the Navigation view is selected (not in Page view at all). This toolbar is covered in Chapter 15, "Working with an Existing Web."

- Picture toolbar—The Picture toolbar activates whenever a graphic is selected in the main FrontPage window. Covered in Chapter 5.

- Positioning toolbar—Lets you position page elements precisely.

- Reports toolbar—Active only when the Reports view is active in the main FrontPage window; this toolbar lets you select from a variety of reports. Covered in Chapter 18.

- Table toolbar—Active when a table is selected; this toolbar lets you format and position tables in documents. Covered in Chapter 8, "Creating Tables."

CUSTOMIZING THE FRONTPAGE INTERFACE

The menus and toolbars in FrontPage are designed with the majority of users in mind, but all users utilize software differently and most want a customized interface. The FrontPage 2000 interface is somewhat customizable for this reason. It's not as customizable as other Office applications, but it's not bad.

You've already seen two major customization methods in this chapter. The first is changing the major screen components: The View bar and Folder List can be shown or hidden at will. The second is the displaying and positioning of toolbars. You can display whatever toolbars you want (including getting rid of the default toolbars), and you can move them wherever you want on the screen. The trick is to make these basic interface issues as useful to you as possible, and to experiment until you get it the way you want it.

FrontPage 2000 offers formal customization methods as well. Those are covered in detail here.

ADDING TOOLBAR BUTTONS WITH THE MORE BUTTONS ARROW

At the far right of every toolbar is a down arrow called More Buttons. Clicking this arrow yields a button named Add or Remove Buttons; moving the pointer over this button yields a list of the buttons currently on the toolbar. You can click whichever of these you want in order to remove it from the toolbar and then return to this button to re-add the buttons later (if you prefer).

The Reset Toolbar and Customize commands are at the bottom of the list of available buttons. Reset Toolbar restores the toolbar to its default configuration—the way it was when you installed FrontPage 2000. Customize yields the Customize dialog box, which is covered here.

WORKING WITH THE CUSTOMIZE DIALOG BOX

The Customize dialog box is available either via the Add or Remove Buttons option in More Buttons, or via Tools, Customize on the menu bar. The dialog box, shown in Figure 3.6, contains three tabs: Toolbars, Commands, and Options. Each offers different customization options.

CUSTOMIZING AND CREATING TOOLBARS

The Toolbars tab lets you select the toolbars you want displayed on the screen. The toolbar immediately appears when you click the check box. This corresponds exactly to the View, Toolbars command on the menu bar. The Reset button returns the buttons on the selected toolbar to the defaults.

Figure 3.6
The three tabs on the
Customize dialog box
reveal different means
of tailoring the
interface.

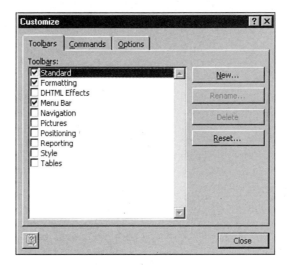

The New button lets you create a new toolbar. You can name it whatever you like in the resulting New Toolbar dialog box, and once the toolbar is created you can rename it by selecting it and clicking the Rename button.

When you click OK in the New Toolbar dialog box, the toolbar name is added to the list of available toolbars. The actual toolbar appears as an empty toolbar beside the Customize dialog box.

Click the Commands tab to add buttons to this new toolbar. The Categories pane shows the menu bar titles, and the Commands pane shows the commands assigned to any particular menu when you click it. You can drag any command from the Commands pane to the new toolbar, where it will appear as a button. A vertical bar helps you position the new button on the toolbar.

The Commands tab's Description button helps you understand what the command actually does. When you select a category or command and click Description, a short description of that item appears from FrontPage's Help system.

The Modify Selection button yields a menu of options that you can apply to the buttons on your new toolbar. The Reset command abandons all changes you've made to the currently selected button, while Delete gets rid of the button. The Name command consists of a field in which you can edit the button name. Place an ampersand (&) to the left of the character you chose as the keyboard shortcut character.

With the next two commands, you can copy the button image to the Clipboard or paste the current image from the Clipboard to the toolbar. (Note that you can work with identical images in different toolbars this way.) Edit Button Image yields the Button Editor and a simplified graphics applet that lets you redraw and recolor the button. Change Button Image yields a palette of button images for you to choose from.

The next four commands let you establish how the button will appear. The Default Style is an image, while Text Only (Always) eliminates the image and replaces it with the name of the button. Text and Image shows both the name and the icon. You can select different styles for each icon on the toolbar.

TROUBLESHOOTING

Once in a long while FrontPage 2000 gets a bit forgetful and throws you into a Page view sub-view you don't actually want. If you open a file in Page view and find yourself looking at an uneditable file as if it's in a browser, or even worse, a file filled with HTML coding, don't panic. Nothing evil has entered your machine. Simply check the three tabs at the bottom of the main window of the Page view and make sure that FrontPage is displaying the sub-view you want: Normal view is the WYSIWYG editing view most people work in; HTML view shows you raw HTML code; Preview lets you see what your document will look like in a browser window. Click the view you want.

Sometimes you'll find yourself having difficulty reading complex HTML code. To make it easier to read, use the HTML Source section on the Page Options dialog. Select Page Options from the Tools menu, then click the HTML Source tab. From here you can choose to Preserve existing HTML code exactly as it is, or you can Reformat it using the rules you define in the bottom half of the dialog. Several options are available, including the spacing before and after each HTML tag or container. You can also specify that HTML tags or attributes be all in lowercase, to help you distinguish among them. From the Color Coding tab of the Page Options dialog, you can carry the HTML Source display further by selecting different colors for normal text, HTML tags, the names of attributes, the values of attributes, comments within the code, and scripts. Using all of these features together, you can customize the HTML Source display precisely to help you read the code most efficiently.

DESIGNERS CORNER

FrontPage 2000's Page view is extremely useful for a number of reasons but, like most Microsoft products today (and for that matter, most products by any software publisher), it significantly fails to take into account that good old 14-inch monitors are still very much in use. For that matter, so are many 15-inch monitors with 800×600 resolution. FrontPage offers most productivity when used with a larger monitor—17 inches or more—at resolutions between 1024×768 and 1600×1200, and with a color depth of 256 colors and up. But not everybody has that, and even those who do often have a second computer with lesser capabilities.

If you have a smaller display, a few options are open to you. First, a significant portion of the FrontPage display is taken up by items other than the main view. When in Page view, specifically, the Folder List and the Views bar occupy the left 25% (by default) of the display. To increase your working area—that is, the main viewing pane—you can hide or shrink both of them. To hide the Folder List, uncheck the Folder List item from the View menu. To hide the Views bar, uncheck Views Bar from the View menu. Presto! Both are gone, and your work area is enlarged.

Doing without the Views bar isn't difficult, because all the views are available from the View menu anyway. You'll want the Folder List quite often, though, so you'll have to toggle it on and off (by checking and unchecking from the View menu). But you don't actually have to get rid of either. Instead, you can simply shrink them. To do so, move the pointer over the vertical border that runs along the right side of the item you want to shrink until the arrow changes to a double arrow. Now drag the border to the left until it is the size you want.

In the case of the Views bar, the icons will keep moving closer and closer to the left border, and the icon titles will abbreviate themselves. You can shrink this bar by two-thirds and still have it remain readable. Shrinking the Folder List, by contrast, simply hides an increasing amount of the folder and file information. Even so, you rarely need the full folder or file-name to work with, and when you do you can always enlarge the list again.

Although it's much smaller than the others, you can also get rid of the status bar (at the bottom of the display). To do so, select Options from the Tools menu, then uncheck the Show status bar option. To get it back, reverse the process.

Unfortunately, FrontPage does not offer the kind of Zoom feature offered in other Office 2000 products (why it doesn't we have absolutely no idea—it would be extremely useful). There are, however, a few other ways to save screen real estate. First, you can minimize the number of toolbars. Select Customize from the Tools menu, and in the Toolbars tab uncheck the toolbars you don't need. In fact, start by unchecking them all and seeing if you can get along without them permanently. The same dialog box lets you switch from small to large icons in the toolbars, useful if you want to minimize but not hide the toolbars. Click on the Options tab and uncheck the Large icons option. Also from the Options tab, you can tell FrontPage to save you a line of screen space by having the standard and Formatting menus (the two default menus) share only one line.

CHAPTER 4

DEVELOPING THE BASIC PAGE: TEXT, LISTS, AND HYPERLINKS

In this chapter   *by Dennis Jones*

THINKING THROUGH YOUR PAGE DESIGN

Compared to writing HTML code with a text editor, making a page in FrontPage's Page view is easy. You can drop in a few headers, some paragraphs of text, three or four images (and maybe an imagemap), a list, a form, a table, some Dynamic HTML effects, some sound, and as many hyperlinks as you please, all in a very short time. Now you've got a home page. Then you do another page, and another, and soon you've got a wonderful Web site ready for the world to visit. Don't you?

Well, maybe, but bad design is the nemesis of many, many Web pages, and you risk producing an unattractive page if you don't know and follow a few common sense guidelines. Most importantly, you have to think about your visitors and how they're likely to experience your site.

PLANNING FOR YOUR VISITORS

If you've spent any time browsing the Web, you've already encountered plenty of sites you won't revisit because the first page you went to had one or more of the following problems:

- Took too long to load
- Had no clear purpose
- Was poorly laid out or badly written
- Had obscure navigational tools
- Didn't link to other sites as it said it would
- Had no useful information

Obviously, you don't want people to have that experience with your site, but how do you make sure they don't? The short answer is to put yourself in your visitor's shoes and think like the audience you want to have. Any author, in print, multimedia, or the Web, has to do this or risk failure.

For illustration, consider your own experience. When you open a new book or magazine or see an unknown Web page appearing in your browser, what's in the back of your mind? You might be barely aware of it, but it's always there, "What's in this for me?" You want something from this page: information, entertainment, aesthetic pleasure, or intellectual stimulation, depending on your tastes and the needs of the moment. If you sense in the first minute or two that you're not going to get it, you very quickly go elsewhere—and so will your viewers if they get that feeling from the first Web page they see on your site.

KEEPING YOUR VISITORS AROUND FOR MORE

This danger of losing the audience on the first page is something all professional authors worry about. The tool they use to prevent it is called *the hook*, and they try very hard to find the best hook for whatever it is they're producing. The idea of the hook is simple: it goes at the very beginning of a work, and it's carefully designed to seize the reader's attention.

More than that, it's designed to make the reader want to go on paying attention, to read the rest of this page, and the next, and the next. As an author of Web pages, you're going to want to keep your audience's attention; otherwise, why are you bothering to make the pages at all? So, put yourself in the mind of the person who's seeing your site for the first time and ask, "What's here for me?" If the honest answer is, "Not much," you need to rethink your approach. You need a better hook, one that makes your viewer want to look around the rest of your site; but, how do you make one?

AVOIDING THE EXTREMES

The first temptation is to pull out all the stops on the technology. That's a considerable temptation because it's gotten a lot simpler to produce decorative or animated marvels on a Web page, and it's fun. The trouble is that it's likely more fun for the page designer to do than it is for the audience to experience. It's true that a visually spectacular page keeps a viewer's interest for a while (assuming the viewer waits for it to download), but if there's nothing to it but spectacle, it's a failure as a page (see Figure 4.1).

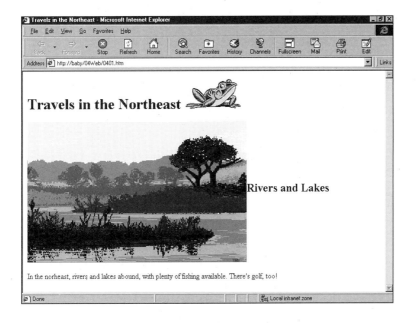

Figure 4.1
Avoid the errors here: a large image that downloads slowly, clumsy layout, no obvious navigation tools, and a distracting and pointless GIF animation (the frog). There's a misspelling, too!

PART

II

CH

4

At the other extreme, a page crammed with solid text, scrolling on and on without whitespace or other elements to relieve the eye, is almost as bad. You, as the author, might feel that the important information you give is enough of a hook. But even if the information the reader wants is there, will she stick around to find it? Her browser controls are in easy reach, and she might decide to go elsewhere for what she's after (see Figure 4.2).

Figure 4.2
Filling screen after screen with solid print is hard on your reader's eyes.

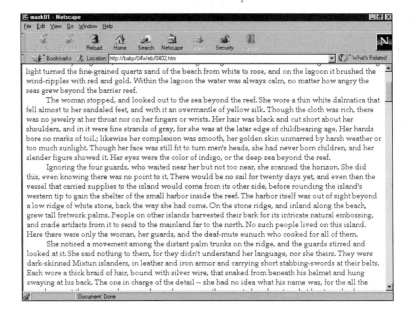

FINDING A BALANCE

When you try to identify the best hook for your site, ask yourself, "What does my viewer want, and how do I show the viewer, in a hurry, that it's there?" Reversing the earlier list of reasons for not staying on a Web site, you get the following:

- The first page appears quickly.
- Its purpose is immediately and clearly identified.
- It's well laid out and well written.
- Its links accurately suggest what the viewer will find.
- Its links behave as advertised when the viewer does use them.
- It supplies the content the viewer expects or a quick path to that content.

Following these suggestions will produce a successful hook for a Web site. Using these guidelines will take you a long, long way toward making all your pages, and therefore your entire site, both pleasing and useful. In short, your key to success is really a balance of presentation and content. An example of such balance appears in Figure 4.3.

You can also produce a very efficient and useful page without using many images and graphical controls. This is a good approach if your intended audience uses a wide range of browsers, including text-only ones such as Lynx. The example in Figure 4.4 is almost entirely text, but its content is balanced by a presentation that directs the user quickly and efficiently to the resources.

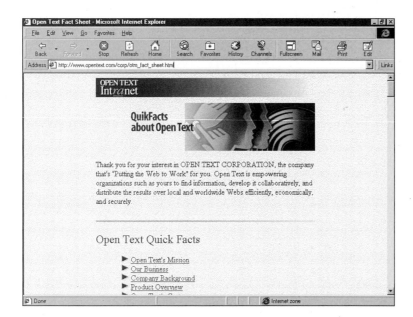

Figure 4.3
This page integrates images, text, and navigation links to make an attractive and functional whole.

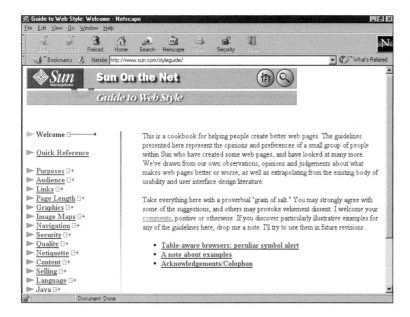

Figure 4.4
This text-based page is laid out clearly and economically.

LETTING VISITORS IN BY THE SIDE DOOR

You need to keep in mind another important fact about Web authoring. With other media, the author has some control over where the audience is going to start. People read novels from page one; movie goers try to reach the theater before the opening credits roll; magazine readers might flip through the magazine, but they usually start reading an article at its beginning. With a Web site, though, your readers can enter at any page depending on which link sent them there. This means that you should design every page with the same care that you lavish on your home page. Because people usually like to have a look at the home page (it helps them get oriented), it's a good idea to include a go-to-home-page control on all your pages. This is especially true if you have a large or complex site or one in which the organization isn't obvious when a person enters it at some point other than the home page.

TIPS FOR QUALITY PAGES

Web authoring is still a young art, but already there is some agreement about its basic principles. The following guidelines list the fundamentals of text layout and hyperlink design.

- Use lots of whitespace on a text-heavy page.
- Avoid very long pages that require endless scrolling.
- Give your page a title that helps the user figure out where she is and what she's looking at.
- Write clearly and pay close attention to spelling and grammar. Nothing undermines a page's authority as much as confused language and bad spelling. Even typos suggest that the author couldn't be bothered to check the work, and what does that say about the other information that's offered?
- If you modify the colors of unvisited and visited links, test the results very carefully to make sure the two states can be distinguished in any display the viewers are likely to use. When in doubt, keep the link colors at their defaults.
- Keep your navigation controls uniform in appearance; for example, a go-to-home-page button should look the same everywhere on your site.

Tip #4

http://www.sun.com/styleguide, Sun MicroSystems' Web site, offers useful general advice on page layout and writing style.

http://info.med.yale.edu/caim, the Yale Center for Advanced Instructional Media, gives extensive information about page design that leans toward the production of scholarly documents.

TESTING

The importance of testing your site can't be emphasized too much. Your pages might look flawless in your favorite browser, but how do they look in another kind of browser? Different browsers, even different versions of the same browser, modify the general appearance of a page, and all recent versions can be user-configured to make drastic changes to the display. Although you can't allow for every possible variation, comprehensive testing ensures that most people can use your site. Just as important, it tells you that your pages are behaving properly before anybody else sees them. Here are some ways of getting things right the first time:

- Test each page with the default settings of Netscape Communicator 4.0 and Microsoft Internet Explorer 4.0. These are now the dominant browsers, and version 5 of each is on the way; when these latest versions appear, test using them as well. In addition, test on a 14-inch monitor that is set to display either the minimal 640×480 resolution in 16 colors, or the middle-of-the-road setting of 600×800 in 256 colors. To test exhaustively, also check your pages out on various other operating system platforms such as the Mac OS and UNIX variants. Finally, it is also helpful to test your page in a text only environment so that your pages can be viewed in the new breed of web-enabled handheld devices.

- Vary the browsers' configurations to see if this drastically changes the appearance of your pages.

- Put in alternate text for images and graphical navigation controls. Remember that many people run their browsers with images turned off to download pages faster.

- Speaking of speed, test your page's downloading time with a phone line connection through your ISP. Simply opening the page in your browser as a local file, using the Preview in Browser command, or retrieving it via an ISDN line is much faster than most real-world situations. Furthermore, even though most new personal and desktop computers have been sold with 56Kb modems for the past year or so, many telephone lines both inside and outside North America do not support this speed. Accordingly, assume that your viewers are using a 28.8Kbps line speed at best and plan your page accordingly. To be really on the safe side, test at 14.4Kbps.

- Get user feedback during testing. Like any author, you're too close to your material to catch every flaw.

- Print your pages and inspect them. Hard copy often reveals problems with the writing in a way that a screen image (for some mysterious reason) doesn't.

- Remember that long, complicated pages are harder to maintain than short, simple ones.

- After making even a minor change to your page, test it thoroughly.

- When everything is working perfectly, test it again.

Tip #5

If you open a page in Page view, the right-hand end of the status bar will show a message such as "9 seconds over 28.8." This tells you that the page (theoretically) will take nine seconds to download from its server to the user's machine. Use this as a guideline, though, not as a certainty.

CREATING A NEW ONE-PAGE WEB AND ITS HOME PAGE

Now that you've had a look at some basic design principles, the rest of this chapter explores how to place text and hyperlinks on a clean page. The page to start with is the home page of a single page Web. To create such a Web, use the following steps:

1. Start FrontPage. Choose File, New, Web, and when the New dialog box appears, select One Page Web. The page created will automatically be the Web's home page.

2. Find the text box labeled Specify the Location of the New Web. Here you must type either the pathname of the new Web (if it is to be a disk-based Web) or the URL of the new Web (if it is to be a server-based Web). Do so, and choose OK. If this is the first time you are running FrontPage, it may ask you if you want to create the directory MyWeb. Accept this default if you wish.

> **Note**
>
> As you might recollect from reading Chapter 2, "The FrontPage Environment," you must append the name of the new server-based web to the machine name: for example, you'd type http://mypc/NewWeb, where *mypc* is the name of the machine and *NewWeb* is the web's name. If you don't append the name of the new web this way, you get an error message saying that you can't create a root Web at this location.

3. A dialog box appears telling you that the new web is being created.

4. When the dialog vanishes, FrontPage arranges a three-pane display showing the Views bar, Folder List, and an empty Page view workspace.

> **Tip #6**
>
> If you've been experimenting with the various views available, your FrontPage window might not look like the one shown in the figures. To make it do so, ensure that the Views bar is visible (choose View, Views Bar). Then, in the Views bar, click the Page icon. Finally, if necessary, choose View, Folder List to display the Folder List.

5. Click the plus sign next to the top folder in the Folder List pane. Now you see the folders and pages in the new web (see Figure 4.5). If you created a server-based web, the new web's home page will be named DEFAULT.HTM; if you created a disk-based Web, it will be called INDEX.HTM.

6. To open the page in the Page view workspace, double-click the home page icon in the Folder List view. The page appears and looks like a blank sheet of paper. Now you're ready to start!

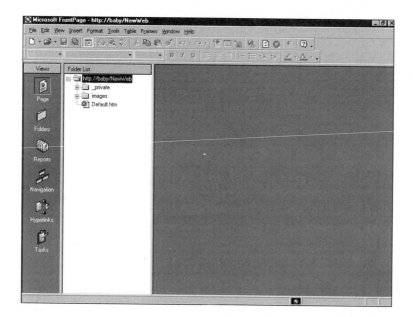

Figure 4.5
After the web is created, FrontPage displays the Views bar, the Folder List, and an empty Page view workspace.

As you work through the rest of this chapter, remember that although Web pages can be very elaborate, most are made up of combinations of the following three basic elements:

- Text
- Hyperlinks
- Images

There's also active content, of course, such as JavaScript, ActiveX, GIF animations, DHTML, and so on. These aren't basic in the sense that they're required for a pleasing, functional page, so they will be discussed in later chapters.

Note

To get the largest Page view workspace, you can use the View menu to turn off the Views bar and the Folder List. In the figures for the rest of this chapter and for later chapters, this has been done.

GIVING YOUR PAGE A TITLE THAT WORKS

Before you start adding content to any page, you should give it a meaningful title. You can always modify the title later. You ought to put some thought into this because a person new to your page usually reads the title for hints about where he is and what he's looking at, and the default titles (as supplied by FrontPage) just won't help much. In fact, there are two more reasons for taking pains with your title. First, it's what your visitor's browser records in its Bookmark list (Netscape) or Favorites folder (Internet Explorer) if he marks the page, so an informative title will jog his memory later about the nature of your site. Second, Internet search programs read the title for indexing and retrieval purposes, and presumably you want your site to show up in their lists. If you don't add a title to your page, it shows up in a search engine with the URL of the page listed instead of a descriptive title.

To change the page title from the default to a more useful one, use the following steps:

1. Open the page in Page view, if it isn't already open. If it is open, click anywhere in the Page view workspace to ensure that Page view is the active view (this applies only if you have other views open as well as Page view).

2. Choose File, Properties or right-click in the workspace and choose Page Properties from the shortcut menu. The Page Properties dialog box appears (see Figure 4.6).

Note

Note that if the Folder List is the active view, then choosing File, Properties will open the New Web Properties dialog.

Figure 4.6
You can change your page title in the Page Properties dialog box.

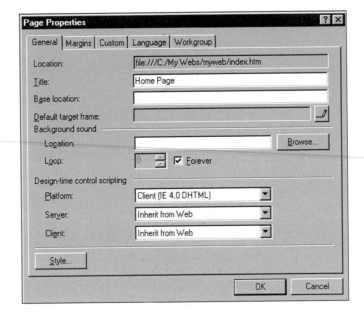

3. Type the new page title in the Title text box. You can use any characters you want. The title can also be any length, but remember that your visitors might be using a lower screen resolution than you are. A width of 60 characters is about the practical maximum.

4. Choose OK.

Your new page title appears in the FrontPage title bar.

Tip #7

Remember that your home page isn't the only one in your site that needs a functional title. Every page should have such a guidepost for its viewers. A title such as "Page 31" or "Section 17" isn't much use in keeping a viewer oriented.

PREVIEWING YOUR EDITED PAGE

Now that you've made a change to the page, you might want to see what it's going to look like in a browser. Here you have two choices.

You can simply click the Preview tab to see how a Microsoft browser displays the page; FrontPage 2000 uses the Internet Explorer 4.0 or 5.0 browser engine. This won't help much for other browsers, though, so you'll certainly also want to use the Preview in Browser command. As you might remember from the discussion in Chapter 2, FrontPage automatically sets up preview browsers when you install it. To use them, follow these steps:

1. Choose File, Preview in Browser. The Preview in Browser dialog box appears (see Figure 4.7).
2. Click the name of the browser you want to use in the Browser list box.
3. Mark the option button for the resolution you want. The Default button uses the current resolution of your display.
4. Choose Preview. The selected browser loads and displays the page that is currently active in FrontPage.
5. Close the browser to return to FrontPage after you check your work.

PART

II

CH

4

Tip #8

A convenient feature of this Preview command is that you can set the browser to save the page before loading it. Mark the Automatically Save Page check box in the Preview in Browser dialog box to enable this feature.

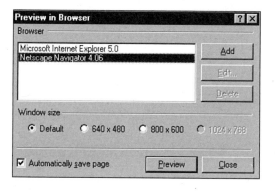

Figure 4.7
You use the Preview in Browser dialog box for fast and easy previewing of a page you're working on.

Note

FrontPage makes it convenient to move among pages you've opened. Choose Window, and the lower section of the menu shows the currently open documents. Click the one that you want to display it.

FORMATTING HEADINGS AND PARAGRAPHS WITH THE STYLE BOX

You use headings—essentially bold type of various sizes—to mark off major divisions and subdivisions of meaning within a page. FrontPage offers the six levels of headings that are standard with HTML, and they are applied to text using the Style box.

Similarly, various HTML paragraph formats are also applied to text using the Style box. If you've used styles in Microsoft Word or other Office products, the technique will be immediately familiar to you.

APPLYING HEADING LEVELS TO TEXT

Applying heading levels to text is quite a simple procedure. Do the following:

1. Type the heading text at the place you want it. Do not press Enter when you're done.
2. Click the arrow button at the right of the Change Style drop-down list box. The list of styles appears (see Figure 4.8).

Figure 4.8
You can apply heading level and paragraph styles easily by selecting from the list in the Style box.

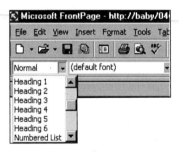

3. Click the heading level style you want. All the text of the heading takes on the new appearance.

You can see all six heading levels in Figure 4.9.

Tip #9

If you make a mistake, you can choose Edit, Undo to undo your last action.

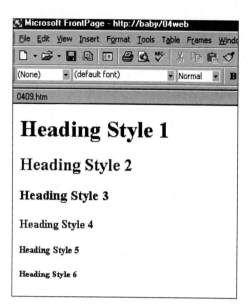

Figure 4.9
FrontPage supplies
very large (1) to very
small headings (6).

Deleting a heading completely can be a little tricky because the heading style can sometimes still be present in the line even though all the text is gone. To delete a heading and its style, use the following steps:

1. Select the heading you want to delete.
2. Press the Delete key or choose Edit, Clear to make the heading text disappear.
3. If the line containing the insertion point still retains the heading style (you can look at the Style box to verify that it does), use the Style box to select Normal. The style of the line returns to Normal (default) style.

Notice that the heading style, unlike some of the other styles in FrontPage, is not retained after you press the Enter key. When you press Enter at the end of a heading-style line, the style of the next line returns to Normal.

Part

II

Ch

4

Tip #10

> Don't overuse the larger heading styles on a single screen. If you do, a visitor to your site might feel shouted at. Think of headings as signaling divisions and subdivisions of content, rather than as a method of emphasis.

CHANGING PARAGRAPH STYLES

As stated earlier, you use the Style box to apply styles to any text, not just to the special case of headings. In some cases, you might want to compose most of the text of your page in the Normal style (the default) and then use the Change Style drop-down list box to modify certain sections.

To use this method to change a paragraph style, use the following steps:

1. Select the paragraph you want to modify by placing the insertion point anywhere inside it.
2. Click the arrow button at the right of the Change Style drop-down list box. The list of styles appears.
3. Click the style you want. All the text of the paragraph takes on the new appearance.

ADDING PARAGRAPHS OF NORMAL TEXT

In FrontPage, you produce most text with the Normal style, which by default is set to the Times New Roman font. In other words, if you see the entry (default font) in the Font box in the Formatting toolbar, any typing you do will display in Times New Roman. Because FrontPage supports the <font face = > and </font> tags, however, you aren't limited to Times New Roman for Normal text; you can change fonts with the Format, Font command. The available fonts are whatever TrueType fonts you have installed on your system.

Before using different fonts, though, be aware that only browsers (MS Internet Explorer 3.0 and later and Netscape 3.0 and later) that support these <font face = > and </font> tags will display the font you choose. In older browsers, or in browsers on machines that don't have that particular font installed, the text shows up in whatever proportional font the browser's user has selected as default. Still, the font-capable browsers are very widely used now, and in most circumstances you can comfortably use a range of fonts.

FrontPage's Normal style produces text in the HTML paragraph style, as defined by the <P></P> tag pair. Unfortunately, there is an ongoing debate over exactly what *paragraph* means in Web authoring, and in fact, FrontPage's Paragraph Format dialog box distinguishes four styles (or *formats*) of paragraphs: Normal, Formatted, Address, and Heading. You'll look at the behavior of the Normal style paragraph first, leaving its font at the default of Times New Roman.

To write your text, use the following steps:

1. Place the cursor where you want the text to begin.
2. If the Style box says (none), simply start typing, and the style defaults to Normal. If the box says something other than (none) or Normal, you must select the Normal style. Click the arrow button at the right of the box and select Normal from the drop-down list.
3. Type your text. When you reach the end of a paragraph, press Enter. This starts a new paragraph, still in the Normal style. Simply go on typing until you're done.

You can see an example of Normal text in Figure 4.10. FrontPage and all other browsers automatically insert whitespace after the end of each paragraph. You can't change this behavior, but a method for closing up the whitespace between paragraphs is discussed later in the section, "Using Line Breaks to Control Text Formatting."

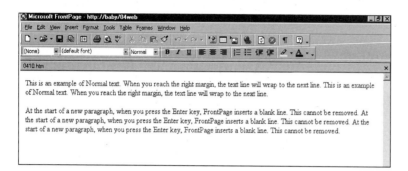

Figure 4.10
You use the Normal style to generate paragraphs of ordinary text.

What if you want extra lines between paragraphs, in addition to the automatically inserted whitespace? It's simple: Just press the Enter key for each extra line you want.

Note

It's not actually that simple under the surface. You might imagine that pressing Enter just adds an empty `<P></P>` container where you want the blank line, but it doesn't. This is because all browsers ignore any such empty paragraph containers (even if you insert a space between the tags) and insist on giving you only the single blank line. FrontPage gets around this by inserting a ` ` (a non-breaking space) whenever you press the Enter key. Browsers that recognize this type of space (including Netscape 2.0 and later, NCSA Mosaic 2.1 and later, and Microsoft Internet Explorer 2.0 and later) give you a blank line for each such space. What you are actually inserting onto the page is a single paragraph composed of a single space.

Tip #11

Sometimes you need a nonbreaking space to force two words or a word and a number to stay together on one line (January 17, for example). Use Ctrl+Shift+Spacebar to insert such a space.

USING LINE BREAKS TO CONTROL TEXT FORMATTING

It's convenient that FrontPage simplifies using whitespace between paragraphs, but what about the opposite problem? You might need short lines of text to remain close together (as in quoting poetry, for example). How do you keep FrontPage from putting blank lines between these one line paragraphs? If you try pressing Enter where you want the text to break, you'll always get a blank line.

The solution is to insert line breaks. The line break orders a browser to jump to the very next line of its window.

The procedure is simple: To keep short lines of text together, press Shift+Enter when you reach the end of each line. This inserts an HTML line break tag into the text stream. The line break tag orders a browser not to leave a blank line before the start of the next line of text. To see where these breaks occur, click the Show All button on the Standard toolbar to display their symbols (see Figure 4.11). These symbols, of course, don't show up in a browser.

Figure 4.11
You use line breaks to arrange text in short lines.

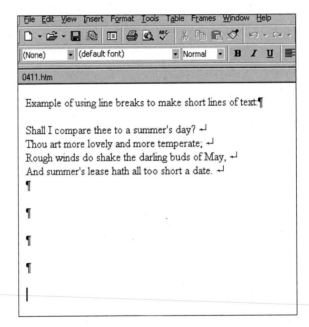

These line breaks don't define the end of a paragraph. Changing the paragraph style affects all the text between the end of the previous paragraph and the start of the next, and treats any line breaks as part of the paragraph content rather than as paragraph end markers.

Note

Choosing Insert, Break provides specialized line breaks as well as the basic one you get by pressing Shift+Enter. These special breaks are discussed in the section "Using Line Breaks with Images" in Chapter 5, "Enhancing Pages with Graphics and Multimedia."

ENLARGING AND SHRINKING NORMAL TEXT

Sometimes you need to increase or decrease the size of text within a paragraph for emphasis or design purposes. You can't do this with a heading because headings are styles, which means they affect the entire paragraph, not just part of it. The way around this problem is to use the Font Size box on the Formatting toolbar. Select the desired text and click the button at the right of this box; the drop-down menu appears listing the seven standard HTML text sizes. Click the size you want, and the selected text is resized (see Figure 4.12).

Notice that it can only approximate the desired size, because the point size of the type isn't fully adjustable as it is in a word processor. The sizes available, in terms of points, are 8, 10, 12, 14, 18, 24, and 36.

The size of Normal text defaults to 12 points in the Netscape Navigator and the Internet Explorer browsers.

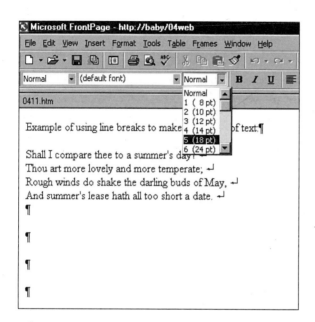

Figure 4.12
Enlarging or shrinking text is simple with the preset sizes in the Font Size box.

ADDING CHARACTER FORMATTING

The physical appearance of words on a page gives your readers clues about how those words are used and how important they are relative to everything else. (All your words are important, but some are more important than others, right?) Italics are for emphasis, but also for book titles and certain kinds of citations. Headings signal blocks of related information. Bold is another emphasis, but is subtly different from italic. Typewriter font gives another effect. In Web publishing (as in paper publishing) you won't go wrong if you stick to normal typographical conventions, especially the one that says "don't overdo it." If half your page displays in italic and half in bold, your reader can't tell the difference between what's important and what's really important.

With FrontPage, you can apply all these character formats simply by selecting and clicking the Bold, Italic, and Underline buttons on the Formatting toolbar. You can also change the text color by clicking the down arrow at the right of the Font Color button and choosing the color you want (to revert to the black default text color, choose Automatic).

Select the text you want to modify and click the appropriate button to apply the effect. If you're starting new text, click the button or choose the color, type the new text, and click the button again (or choose Automatic for color) when you want to turn the effect off. The effects can be *layered*, that is, you can have text that is bold, italic, underlined, and in color.

Usage of bold, underline, and italic in page design is pretty conventional and easy to grasp. Color usage, however, is a more complex matter, and you'll consider it at more length later in this chapter in the section "Using Text Colors and Background Colors on Your Page."

CHOOSING FONTS WITH THE CHANGE FONT BOX

Using different fonts can add enormously to the impact of a page. Fonts do have what you might call (no pun intended) *character*, that is, they suggest a certain mood to the reader. Ornate fonts suggest a different atmosphere from the formal air that surrounds a traditional-looking font such as Times New Roman. Combinations of fonts lend both variety and pacing to the flow of the text on your page.

A common mistake of fledgling typographers, however, is to become overexcited at the vast range of fonts available and change them at the least opportunity. This usually leads to a visual mess. Instead of doing this, start by figuring out the *mood* of the page or of your site as a whole. Is it to be traditionally businesslike? High-technology? Whimsical? Highly personal? Artistic? Counterculture? Of course, the nature of the audience you hope to attract will help define the mood you want to create.

When you've got that worked out, look for fonts that reflect this mood. Experiment with them on the page to see if they work together or cause visual chaos. You'll likely end up with a small selection of fonts: a couple for titles and/or main headings, one for body text, and one or two others for specialized purposes, which will depend on the nature of your site. Properly selected, this range of fonts contributes to giving your page (and site) a feeling of unity and focus. This, in turn, adds conviction to what you want to say. When in doubt, go for fewer fonts, not more.

The simplest way to change fonts is with the Font list box (see Figure 4.13).

To switch to a new font for new text, click the arrow button at the right end of the Font box and select the font you want from the drop-down list. Whatever you type from that point on is in the new font until you either change it or place the insertion point within text of a different font.

To change the font of existing text, select the text to be modified and choose the new font from the Font box. The selected text changes accordingly.

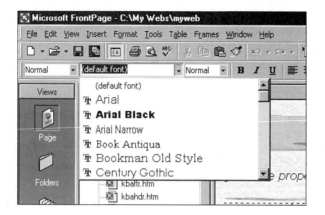

Figure 4.13
Use the Font box to select different fonts.

USING THE FONT DIALOG BOX

These methods are useful shortcuts. However, you can also control your fonts and add additional effects with the Font dialog box. Choose Format, Font to open it. Figure 4.14 shows what it looks like.

PART

II

CH

4

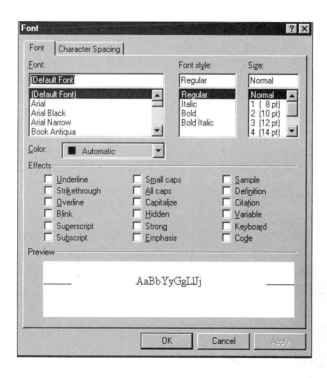

Figure 4.14
With the Font dialog box, you can not only change fonts and their sizes, but also add effects such as strikethrough.

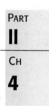

This dialog box has two sheets: Font and Character Spacing. With the former, you can do the following:

- Select the font name from the Font list box.
- Use the Font Style list box to apply regular, bold, italic, and bold italic character styles.
- Choose the font size from the Size list box.
- Use the check boxes in the Effects section to apply effects such as Underline, and for the various HTML-specific effects such as Strong.
- Use the Color drop-down list to apply color to a font or to generate a custom color for the font.
- See what the font will look like in the Sample box.

To make the font look as you want it, select from among the various options and choose OK. Selected text takes on these characteristics, or you can start typing new text that has them. Generating custom colors is discussed later in this chapter in the section "Using Text Colors and Background colors on Your Page."

Tip #12	To quickly format one or more characters, select them, right-click the selection to open the shortcut menu, and click Font Properties to make the Font dialog box appear.

UNDERSTANDING HTML-SPECIFIC EFFECTS

The Font dialog enables you to apply HTML-specific effects to text (by using the check boxes in the Effects section) and these effects need some explanation to clarify their proper use. They represent the HTML approach to character formatting, which distinguishes between logical and physical styles.

The distinction can initially be confusing, but what it boils down to is this. If a browser sees the HTML tags for italic or bold characters (physical styles), it puts italic or bold on the screen, and this display can't be modified. The display characteristics of logical styles, on the other hand, can be redefined by software, for example by a browser. Early browsers allowed users to specify, for example, how the logical style <STRONG> would appear on their screens—they could make it show up in a user-selected font. However, this flexibility is not present in IE 3 and later or in Navigator 3 and later.

Tables 4.1 and 4.2 give more detail about how Web browsers display these styles.

TABLE 4.1   PHYSICAL HTML CHARACTER STYLES IN FRONTPAGE

Style	Effect
Bold	Forces browser to display bold
Italic	Forces browser to display italic
Underline	Forces underlining

TABLE 4.2   LOGICAL HTML CHARACTER STYLES IN FRONTPAGE

Style	Effect
Strikethrough	Strikethrough characters
Blink	Blinks text
Superscript	Applies superscript
Subscript	Applies subscript
Strong	Bold unless redefined by software
Emphasis	Italic unless redefined by software
Sample	Output sample (resembles typewriter font)
Definition	Italic for definitions
Citation	Italic for citing references
Variable	Usually italic for defining a variable
Keyboard	Indicates user-supplied text (resembles typewriter font)
Code	HTML code (resembles typewriter font)

Note

The other effects in the Font dialog box are Overline, Capitalize, Small Caps, All Caps, and Hidden. These are generated by Cascading Style Sheet technology and are not logical or physical HTML styles.

USING THE CHARACTER SPACING SHEET

The second sheet of the Font dialog box is the Character Spacing sheet. You use this to specify horizontal spacing between characters and/or vertical positioning with respect to the text baseline. To select which type of spacing you want, use the Spacing list box to specify Normal, Expanded, or Condensed. Then set the spacing units using the upper By text box. The unit abbreviations are as follows:

- em: width of an "m" relative to the size of the paragraph font
- ex: relative to the height of the paragraph font
- px: pixels, relative to the viewing device
- in: inches
- cm: centimeters
- mm: millimeters
- pt: points; the points used by CSS2 are equal to 1/72 inch
- pc: picas; one pica is equal to 12 points

To set vertical positioning with respect to the text baseline, use the Position list box to select Raised, Lowered, or Normal, and use the lower By text box to set the amount by which the affected text will be raised or lowered.

> **Note**
>
> Character spacing is not the same as kerning. *Kerning* adjusts the space between two specified letters (such as A and T) to improve the appearance of the text.

THE FUTURE OF FONTS ON THE WEB

What happens if you designate a font with the FONT FACE parameter and design your page layout to depend on its look or proportioning, and the person viewing the page doesn't have that font installed on his machine? He'll see either the default of Times New Roman or whatever fonts he's set for his browser preferences. This can ruin your careful work.

A long-range solution (which might or might not come soon) is the OpenType extension to the TrueType font format, which was announced by Microsoft and Adobe Systems in 1997. When fully implemented, this technology will enable Open Type fonts to be embedded into a Web page so that the font is downloaded, along with the page, to the user's browser, assuming the browser supports the technology.

OpenType isn't here yet, so both Netscape and Microsoft have recently come up with interim solutions to the font problem. These solutions are incompatible, needless to say. Netscape Communicator 4 enables downloadable fonts; you can get more information on how it's done from the chapter on the subject at http://developer.netscape.com/docs/manuals/communicator/dynhtml/.

In the same vein, Microsoft offers its WEFT (Microsoft Web Embedding Fonts Tool) software to enable you to add embedded fonts to your site. You can download the preview version of the tool free, and get help on using it, from http://www.microsoft.com/typography/web/embedding/weft/. For more information about how Microsoft is approaching the subject of Web typography, refer to http://www.microsoft.com/typography. The site offers utilities, information, and fonts that you might find useful.

GETTING RID OF CHARACTER FORMATTING

If you've been experimenting with character formatting on a large section of Normal text and have messed it up and want to start all over again, you can easily do so. Select the offending text and choose Format, Remove Formatting. Character size, font, color, and attributes (such as bold) all revert to the default of Times New Roman, size 3 (12 point), regular typeface, color black. Note that this removes character formatting only, and does not affect text that has had a style other than Normal applied to it.

USING FRONTPAGE'S OTHER PARAGRAPH STYLES

So far in this chapter, you've looked at FrontPage's Heading and Normal styles, which produce the page elements that formal HTML calls the heading and the paragraph. On top of that, FrontPage's Style box gives you two other styles: *Formatted* and *Address*.

Note	Because Web publishing is a relatively recent phenomenon, some of its terminology hasn't yet settled down to a standard. FrontPage uses its own vocabulary for certain elements of HTML to make the interface software function more like a word processor. This shows especially in FrontPage's use of *styles* of text, and you might find it easier to think in terms of styles rather than the HTML references such as *preformatted text* or *blockquote*. For consistency with the software, I'll stick with FrontPage's word processor model and refer most of the time to styles.

USING TABS AND EMBEDDED SPACES WITH NORMAL TEXT

The formal HTML definition of Normal text does not allow such text to have tabs or strings of spaces placed within the <P and </P> tags that define it. In FrontPage 2000 this limitation does not apply; you can go ahead and use tabs and embedded strings of spaces when you are typing Normal text.

To see how this works, create a text paragraph, including some tabs or spaces within it, and go to HTML view. You'll see that FrontPage is inserting the nonbreaking space code   within the text, and each   forces a space. Pressing the Tab key inserts a string of three of these spaces. Netscape 3.0 and higher and Internet Explorer 3.0 and higher display these extra spaces and tabs correctly.

This actually does away with much of the need for the Formatted style, which originally was the only simple way to get tabs and spaces into text. However, the Formatted style is still available, so you'll examine it in the next two sections.

USING THE FORMATTED STYLE WITH NEW TEXT

Why would you need the Formatted style? It enables the embedding of tabs or strings of spaces within in it as well as character attributes, such as bold or italic, and most other HTML elements, such as links.

However, when it comes to breaking a line, the Formatted style behaves just as the Normal style does. That is, if you use the Enter key to break a line while you're typing text, you'll get whitespace after the paragraph. To break a line without having this happen, you must use a line break (press Shift+Enter).

A typical use of the Formatted style is for text that needs several levels of indent or that needs various short lines indented (see Figure 4.15). Notice, however, that a paragraph formatted in the Formatted style does not word wrap. Long paragraphs will be rendered as a single line of text disappearing off the right side of the screen. This is true in both the FrontPage workspace and in browser displays.

PART

II

CH

4

Figure 4.15
The Formatted style preserves your program code indenting and lets you indent the first lines of paragraphs.

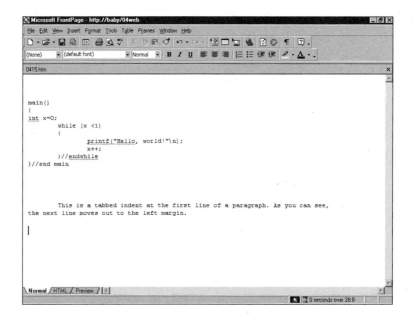

To write new text that is the Formatted style, use the following steps:

1. Place the cursor where you want the new text to begin.
2. Choose Format, Paragraph and choose Formatted from the drop-down list in the Paragraph dialog box (or simply use the Style box to select the Formatted style). The Style box shows you're in Formatted style.
3. Type the text you want, using tabs or strings of spaces as you need them. Remember to use Shift+Enter to keep lines together.

As you can see from Figure 4.15, the default Formatted style does have another drawback, although it's an aesthetic rather than a functional one. Until recently, most browsers displayed Formatted text in a monospaced font such as Courier, which is rather ugly, and that's the default font FrontPage uses. With FrontPage's support of font face tags, however, you're no longer limited to Courier. Choose the Formatted style and select the font you want to use. You'll find that the Formatted style's convenience of tabs and strings of spaces is still available, even though you're not using Courier. Browsers that don't support the font face tags, of course, still show the text in Courier.

INSERTING EXISTING TEXT BY USING THE FORMATTED STYLE

Another use for the Formatted style is to make sure that imported ASCII text retains its indenting and any padding with spaces. (Of course, if the text starts out in another format, you'll have to convert it to an ASCII text file first. If you do this, be sure to save it as text with line breaks, so that any necessary line breaks within the text are preserved.)

To insert an existing text file into your page, position the cursor where you want the text to start and use the following steps:

1. Choose Insert, File. The Select a File dialog box appears.

2. Use the dialog box to find and select the file you want to insert and then choose Open. The Convert Text dialog box appears, giving you five options (see Figure 4.16).

3. Mark the option button that corresponds to the Formatted result you want. (Depending on the format of the source file, you might want to experiment with the various choices.) Choose OK.

FrontPage inserts the file into the page and preserves space padding, line breaks, and tabs. Format marks have been turned off for clarity.

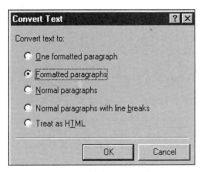

Figure 4.16
You can insert a file as Formatted or Normal text, with options for paragraphing, or choose HTML format.

PART

II

CH

4

Tip #13	If you've made a complicated edit that didn't work out and you want to discard the changes before you go on, you can use FrontPage's Refresh button (note that this button is only active if the page is in an open, server-based web). Click the Refresh button—it's on the Standard toolbar—and FrontPage reloads the page as it was before the edit. You'll be asked if you want to save the changes you did make; assuming you don't, answer No.

USING THE ADDRESS STYLE

This is a simple style used to put the author's address on the page. Browsers usually display it in italics. To insert it, choose Format, Paragraph and choose Address from the list box. Alternatively, type your address, make sure the cursor is within the text, and select Address from the Style box.

Tip #14	It's considered good Web manners to include your name and email address, along with the last revision date of the page, at the end of each page.

LAYING OUT TEXT EFFECTIVELY

Just getting words onto the page isn't enough. Good text layout affects a page's attractiveness and readability. FrontPage has several paragraph formatting tools to help you enhance the appearance of your pages, plus horizontal lines for adding visual interest and organization.

ALIGNING TEXT HORIZONTALLY

You'll often want headings or other text to be somewhere other than at the left margin. To do this, use the following steps:

1. Click anywhere in the text you want to align.
2. Choose Format, Paragraph. The Paragraph dialog box appears.
3. Click the arrow button at the right of the Alignment drop-down list box. The Alignment Options list appears (see Figure 4.17).
4. Select the alignment you want and choose OK.

Figure 4.17
Use the list of alignment options to left align, right align, justify, or center text.

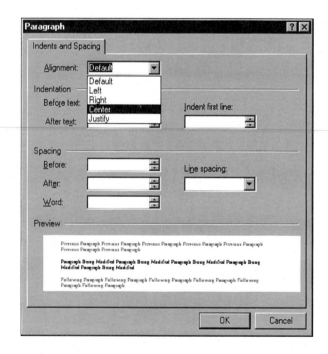

The Left alignment and the Default alignment both put text against the left margin. There is no functional difference between them unless the user has set his browser so that (for example) the default alignment is right aligned.

Tip #15	A quick way to align text is to use the Align Left, Center, and Align Right buttons on the Formatting toolbar.

INDENTING BLOCKS OF TEXT FROM THE MARGINS

In print documents, a chunk of text is sometimes set off from its surroundings by indenting its left and right margins. You often see this in long quotations. The indentations can be set in various units, as follows:

- auto: places text at whatever left margin is defined for the page (for paragraph spacing, it sets the style sheet property "margin-top" to "auto")
- em: width of an "m" relative to the size of the paragraph font
- ex: relative to the height of the paragraph font
- px: pixels, relative to the viewing device
- in: inches
- cm: centimeters
- mm: millimeters
- pt: points; the points used by CSS2 are equal to 1/72 inch
- pc: picas; one pica is equal to 12 points

You set up indents by using the following procedure:

1. Place the insertion point anywhere in the desired paragraph.
2. Choose Format, Paragraph to open the Paragraph dialog box (alternatively, right-click in the paragraph and choose Paragraph Properties from the shortcut menu), shown in Figure 4.18.
3. Set the left indent. In the Indentation section, click the arrow at the right of the Before Text box and select a pre-set paragraph indentation. Alternatively, type a value into the box, remembering to specify the units. To remove all indentation, clear the box.
4. Set the right indent, if desired, by using the After Text box. Note that your changes appear in the Preview section.
5. If desired, set an indent for the first line of each paragraph by using the Indent First Line box. This will automatically indent the first line of each paragraph that you type until it is turned off.
6. Choose OK to apply the setting to the selected paragraph.

PART

II

CH

4

Figure 4.18
Use the Paragraph dialog box to set paragraph indentation and spacing.

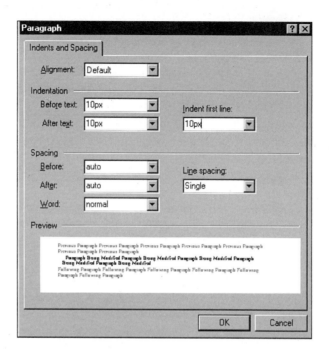

Tip #16

To quickly indent both margins at once, click the Increase Indent button on the Formatting toolbar. The indents increase each time you click the button. To decrease them, click the Decrease Indent button on the toolbar. Notice that this applies a `<blockquote>` tag to the paragraph, rather than the style sheet coding applied by the preceding procedure.

SETTING VERTICAL SPACING BETWEEN PARAGRAPHS

You can adjust the amount of whitespace between paragraphs to help adjust the text density of a page. You can, of course, do this by adding blank lines between the paragraphs, but this technique doesn't give you the fine control that the following procedure does:

1. Place the insertion point anywhere in the desired paragraph.

2. Choose Format, Paragraph to open the Paragraph dialog box (alternatively, right-click in the paragraph and choose Paragraph Properties from the shortcut menu).

3. To set the space above the paragraph, select a value from the Before box or type one in.

4. To set the space below the paragraph, select a value from the After box or type one in.

5. To set the spacing between words, select a value from the Word box or type one in.

6. To set line spacing within the paragraph, select a value from the Line Spacing box or type one in.

7. Choose OK to apply the settings to the selected paragraph.

USING HORIZONTAL LINES

Paragraphs are units of meaning, and a new paragraph signals to the reader that a new unit has begun. However, the horizontal line is effective if you want to announce a more significant shift of emphasis or subject. It's often used with headings, especially to set off the headline of a page or to begin a major section within the page. It is also a design element because it adds visual interest or relief from long blocks of text.

You place a line on a page by choosing Insert, Horizontal Line. The resulting default line, which all graphics-capable browsers display, is a shadowed line that stretches the width of the browser window. Incidentally, it forces whitespace above and below it, so you can't get text to snuggle up close to it.

Note

If you want to position text right next to a line, you have to use a graphic line, which you insert as an image.

You can vary the line's appearance somewhat by adjusting its properties. To do this, right-click on the line and choose Horizontal Line Properties from the shortcut menu. Alternatively, click the line to select it and choose Format, Properties. You can change the line's width; align it; adjust its weight by changing its height in pixels; change it to a solid, unshaded line; or give it a color (see Figure 4.19). You can see various line styles in Figure 4.20.

PART

II

CH

4

Figure 4.19
You use the Horizontal Line Properties dialog box to modify the appearance of a line.

Tip #17

A well-designed page isn't littered with lines. Use them only when they serve a purpose (organizational or decorative). Also, it's better to determine the line width in percent, not in pixels. That way its width will appear to a visitor as you designed it, independent of the screen resolution she's using.

Figure 4.20
Shaded, colored or black lines of varying weight and width can add visual impact to sections of your page.

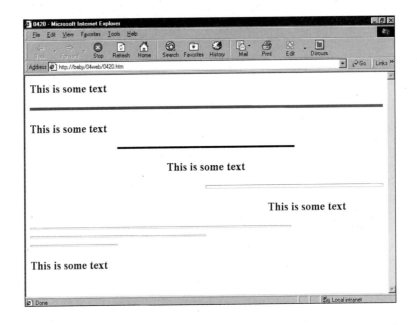

USING SYMBOLS

From time to time, you need characters that don't appear on the keyboard, for example, the copyright or trademark symbols. To insert such a character, place the cursor where you want the symbol to appear and choose Insert, Symbol. The Symbol dialog box appears (see Figure 4.21). Click the character you want (a larger representation of it appears beside the Insert button), choose Insert, and then choose Close. Clicking the Insert button twice inserts the character twice, and so on.

Figure 4.21
When you need specialized symbols, you find them in the Symbol dialog box.

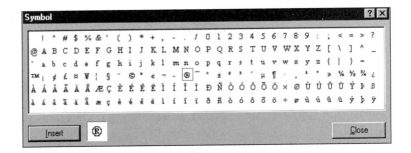

SETTING PAGE MARGINS WITH PAGE PROPERTIES

Setting margins with Page Properties is somewhat unsatisfactory because the results are visible only in Internet Explorer 3.0 and later. A preferable method is to set margins with *style sheets (page 272)* so that all browsers that support style sheets, which includes both IE 3 and later and Netscape 4 and later, display them as desired.

→ For more information about style sheets, **see** Chapter 12, "Using Style Sheets with Individual Pages and Full Sites," **p. 271**.

If you do want to set margins using Page Properties, however, begin by making the desired page active. Then choose File, Properties and go to the Margins sheet in the Page Properties dialog box. Mark the check box for the margin you want (Left or Top) and type a value into the Size box. The units are in pixels.

Tip #18	To open the Page Properties dialog box quickly, right-click anywhere on the page and choose Page Properties from the shortcut menu.

USING LISTS TO PRESENT YOUR CONTENT

As discussed earlier, the content and presentation of your pages should be in balance. That is, all the elements in a well-designed page support and reinforce each other so that the whole is greater than the sum of its parts. (This goes for a well-designed Web site, too.)

Lists are excellent for helping you achieve this synergy in your pages because they are good at integrating presentation and content. They're very adaptable, too, because you can combine different kinds of lists to organize different kinds of information. It's because of this flexibility that lists are everywhere in everyday life, from the humble loaf-of-bread-and-quart-of-milk version to the fantastically complicated checklists that govern the missions of interplanetary probes. In fact, lists are probably the oldest written documents of civilization. Scribes 45 centuries ago were already recording how many bushels of barley the local farmers owed to the king in taxes.

We don't use clay tablets as tax forms today, but our electronic pages do contain lists by the dozens. They not only organize things for our visitors, they also help us organize our thinking as we put them together. What makes lists even more useful is that you can put hyperlinks, styles, and character formatting into them. You're not limited to a fixed font and type size, for instance, and you can nest lists of one kind inside lists of another.

The trouble with coding lists in HTML is that the work is so exact: one tag out of place in a nested list and terrible things happen to your page. Fortunately, FrontPage relieves you of this picky stuff so that you can concentrate on what the list says, rather than how it's put together. You also have a full range of listing tools at your disposal, from bulleted to definition.

MAKING A BULLETED LIST

You use a bulleted list for items that need no particular order, although there's sometimes an implied grading of importance within it. (Formally, these are called *unordered lists*.) Bulleted lists can summarize important points in an argument or emphasize key items of information. They're the most common list type on the World Wide Web, partly because they're visually attractive and partly because they're good for so many different things.

Note that if you use a *themes (page 454)*, the bullets are images attached to that theme. To make the simplest kind of bulleted list—that is, using generic bullets rather than theme bullets—use the following steps:

1. If you are using a theme on the current page, remove it. (You can skip this step if you're not using a theme.) To do so, choose Format, Theme to open the Themes dialog box. Select the item This Page Does Not Use Themes in the list box of theme titles. Choose OK.

2. When the Themes dialog box closes and you're back at the page, put the insertion point where you want the list to start.

3. Choose Format, Bullets and Numbering. The Bullets and Numbering dialog box appears with three tabbed sheets, two of which offer varied bullet styles (see Figure 4.22).

Figure 4.22
With the Bullets and Numbering dialog box, you can choose between numbered lists and bulleted lists.

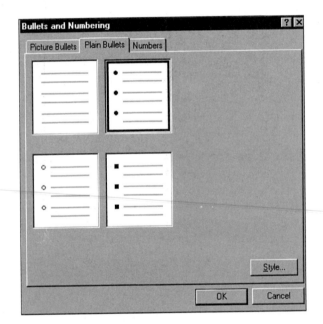

4. Click the Plain Bullets tab and choose the page icon with the bullet style you want (you choose the non-bulleted page icon to turn off bullets).

5. Choose OK. The dialog box vanishes and a bullet appears on the page.

6. Start typing your list and press Enter at the end of each item.

7. Press Enter twice to stop inserting bulleted items when you're finished.

8. To insert a new item into a list, position the insertion point immediately to the right of the preceding item. Then press Enter, and type in the new item (see Figure 4.23).

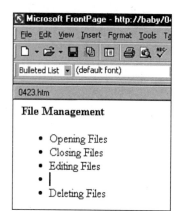

Figure 4.23
A bulleted list that is about to have a new item inserted after the third entry.

Tip #19

A fast way to start a list (of any kind) is to use the Change Style drop-down list box. It contains all the types of lists that FrontPage supports. Alternatively, click the Bulleted List button or the Numbered List button to start a list of that type.

DELETING A LIST OR A LIST ITEM

To delete the whole list, select it and press the Delete key, or choose Edit, Clear.

To delete an item in a list, select the item and press the Delete key or choose Edit, Clear.

MAKING A BULLETED SUBLIST UNDER A TOP-LEVEL BULLETED LIST

You use a sublist (called a *nested list*) to arrange less important points or headings under more important ones. If you've used the outlining tools in applications such as WordPerfect, Word, or PowerPoint, this principle is familiar to you. It's a powerful method of organizing information. To start a nested list under a top-level list, use the following steps:

1. Place the cursor at the end of the line beneath which the nested list will appear. This can be within an existing list or at the end of the last item of an existing list.

2. Press the Enter key to make a new bullet, but don't type anything.

3. Click the Increase Indent button twice. The first bullet of the nested list appears; this bullet will have a different style from those in the superior list.

4. Type the items of the nested list.

5. To end the nested list, press Enter to get a bullet without any text. Press the Delete key and the insertion point returns to the top-level list.

6. To go on with the top-level list, place the insertion point at the end of the appropriate item, press the Enter key, and continue typing items. If you are finished with the top-level list, click anywhere outside the list to relocate the insertion point.

PART

II

CH

4

Lists with more than two levels are a bit trickier. If you are typing items in a third-level list, for example, how do you continue the second-level list after you've ended the third-level one? You can't use the step 5 procedure because this returns you to the top-level list. To get a new second-level bullet to follow the last item of the third-level list, follow these steps:

1. Press Enter to get a third-level bullet without any text.
2. Press the Backspace key twice (or click the Decrease Indent button twice). A second-level list bullet appears beneath the third-level list item.
3. Continue adding items to the second list.
4. Use any of the steps in this procedure or the previous procedure to complete the list.

You can see a nested list with three levels in Figure 4.24. Incidentally, you can create more levels for a list than you're ever likely to need.

Figure 4.24
You use nested lists to arrange less important points or headings under more important ones. Here, an item is about to be added at the end of the third-level list.

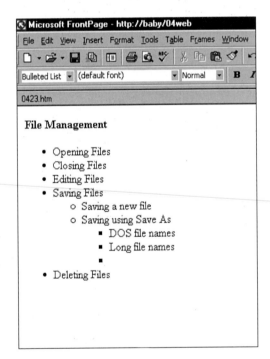

Tip #20

It's easy to *promote* a list item to the superior list above it. Place the insertion point inside the item and click the Decrease Indent button twice. Similarly, to *demote* an item to the list below it, place the insertion point inside the item and click the Increase Indent button twice.

CHANGING BULLET STYLES IN NESTED LISTS

Nested lists by default change their bullet appearance. This might not be what you want, though. For example, you might want all the bullets in the lists of Figure 4.24 to be round, solid ones. To make such changes, do the following:

Note

> The next procedure only works with pages that do not use themes. On a page with a theme, the bullet images are fixed and can't be modified unless you edit the theme itself.

1. Place the insertion point inside the nested list whose bullets you want to change.
2. Choose Format, Bullets and Numbering. The List Properties dialog box appears.
3. Click the Plain Bullets tab and click the type of bullet you want.
4. Choose OK. The nested list immediately acquires the new bullets. Repeat this procedure as desired for any further nested lists.

This also works for the top-most list, not only for the nested lists below it.

Note

> You might have noticed the Enable Collapsible Outlines check box in the List Properties dialog box. Selecting this check box lets you make collapsible lists for Dynamic HTML-enabled browsers (specifically Internet Explorer 4.0 and later).

PART

II

CH

4

USING IMAGE-BASED BULLETS

The trouble with the bullets used thus far is that they're boring. Themes, of course, supply much more interesting bullets, but you might not like any of those, either. The answer is to select your own bullet images.

Follow these steps:

1. Choose Format, Bullets and Numbering to open the Bullets and Numbering dialog box and click the Picture Bullets tab (see Figure 4.25).
2. Mark the Specify Picture option button. If you know the filename of the image you want, type it into the text box under the option button. Alternatively, choose Browse to open the Select Picture dialog box (see Figure 4.26).
3. Assuming the bullet image is stored on your machine somewhere, click the right-most icon on the right end of the URL text box (the folder and magnifying glass icon). This opens a standard Windows 95/98/NT file open dialog box called Select File.
4. Use this dialog box to locate and select the bullet image, and then choose Open. When you return to the Bullets and Numbering dialog box, choose OK. The selected image is the first bullet of the list.

Figure 4.25
Specify your own
bullet image by using
the Picture Bullets
sheet.

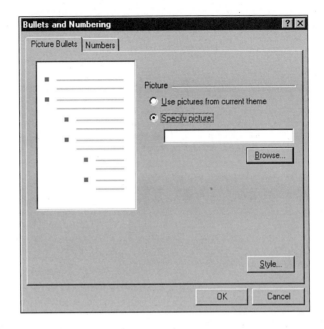

Figure 4.26
Use the Select Picture
dialog box to locate
the bullet image you
want.

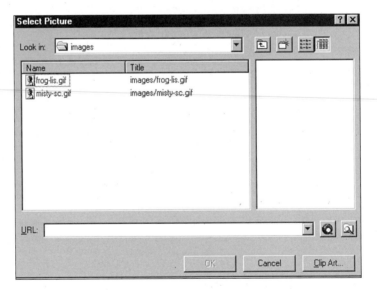

The bullet is applied only to the current level of the current list. If you want a bullet image (even the same one) to apply to a nested list, the image needs to be selected by using the previous procedure.

When you save the page, you are asked if you also want to save the image as an embedded file. If you want to copy the image file to the current FrontPage web so that the page can access it from there, answer OK. You'll be examining image handling in much more detail in the next chapter.

> **Note**
> Changing a page's theme automatically changes all the bullets on that page. However, selecting a bullet image as you just did does not affect existing bulleted lists.

ADDING PARAGRAPH STYLES AND CHARACTER FORMATTING TO LISTS

You can vary a list's paragraph style and character format. In Figure 4.27, some text is in bold and line breaks separate the items of the top-most list. Additionally, the third-level nested list contains a hyperlink. Again, avoid assuming that the Normal mode displays an accurate representation of the real appearance of the page; in the example shown in Figure 4.27, two blank lines are between the top list items, but in Preview mode, only one appears. Notice also that you need two line breaks to force a single blank line in a browser view of the page.

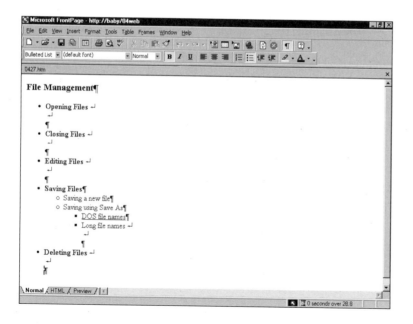

Figure 4.27
You can use character formatting, line breaks, and hyperlinks inside lists. Format marks have been turned on to show the paragraph and line break symbols.

PART

II

CH

4

MAKING A NUMBERED LIST

Numbered lists are somewhat less common on the Web than bulleted lists. They're used for tables of contents, for establishing a rank order from highest to lowest, for a set of instructions, or for any data where relative importance needs to be shown. Because of the numbering, they're formally called *ordered lists*.

You make a numbered list just as you make a bulleted list. Choose Format, Bullets and Numbering and click the Numbers sheet tab. Here you have several different numbering styles that you can arrange into a hierarchy (see Figure 4.28). Themes have no effect on the appearance of numbered lists.

Figure 4.28
The Numbers sheet gives you five numbering styles and the Unnumbered option.

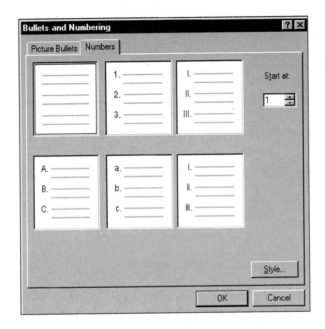

Usually your list starts with 1, or a, and so on. However, if it must start at a higher number, adjust the number in the Start At box accordingly. If you put 2 in the box, for example, and choose the a,b,c type list, the list starts at b.

When you've selected the numbering type, choose OK and the first item of the numbered list appears. FrontPage inserts a new number every time you press Enter. To end the list, press Enter twice. You can use paragraph styles, character formatting, and hyperlinks within numbered lists.

You start a numbered nested list the same way you start a bulleted nested list. Place the cursor at the end of the item before the nested list and press Enter to get a new number. Click the Increase Indent button twice and the nested list starts. Complete it and press Enter once to get a blank entry and click the Decrease Indent button twice. The insertion point returns to the superior list. FrontPage adjusts all numbering to match the additions or deletions.

When you try this, you'll notice that FrontPage doesn't automatically supply a hierarchy of numbering formats. If your superior list uses Arabic numerals, so will your nested list unless you specify otherwise.

You change the style of the nested list numbering by using the following steps:

1. Place the insertion point inside the nested list and choose Format, Bullets and Numbering.

2. Click the Numbers sheet tab.

3. Click the page icon that shows the style you want.

4. Choose OK. The nested list takes up the new style.

You can see an example of an ordered, nested list in Figure 4.29.

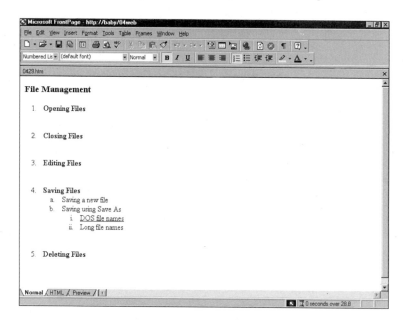

Figure 4.29
You can nest numbered lists inside other numbered lists.

To delete the list or parts of it, or to promote or demote list items, use the methods applied earlier to bulleted lists. (See "Deleting a List or a List Item" and "Making a Bulleted Sublist Under a Top-Level Bulleted List.")

Changing the Style of an Existing List

You might put a bulleted list together and then decide it would be more useful as a numbered list. To make this change, do the following:

1. Place the insertion point somewhere inside the list and choose Format, Bullets and Numbering. The List Properties dialog box appears.

2. Click the Numbers sheet tab. On the Numbers sheet, click the page icon that shows the desired numbering style.

3. Choose OK. The list immediately takes on the new style. You use this procedure going the other way, too, to change a numbered list to a bulleted list.

COMBINING LIST TYPES WITHIN A LIST

You can mix types of lists to fine-tune your presentation of content. For example, you can include a nested list of numbered instructions inside a bulleted list, as shown in Figure 4.30, by following these steps:

1. Place the insertion point at the end of the line before the new nested list. Press Enter but don't type anything.

2. Click the Increase Indent button twice.

3. Choose Format, Bullets and Numbering to open the List Properties dialog box.

4. Select the type of list you want (numbered, in this example) from the available sheets. Select the format you want and choose OK. The new list format appears.

5. Type the list. When finished, press the Enter key to make a blank item but don't type anything.

6. Click the Decrease Indent button twice. The list symbol for the superior list appears.

Figure 4.30
You can use mixed lists to put different types of information together.

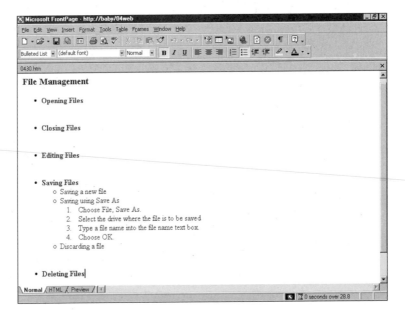

USING THE LIST BUTTONS OR STYLE BOX TO MODIFY EXISTING LISTS

You can use either the Numbered List or the Bulleted List button to manipulate existing lists. To change a list or nested list from one type to another, place the insertion point anywhere in the list and click the appropriate button. Only that list changes; lists subordinate or superior to it aren't affected. If you want to change the formatting of the bullets or numbers, choose Format, Bullets and Numbering to display the List Properties dialog box and make your changes from there.

Alternatively, place the insertion point inside the list and choose the new list type from the drop-down list in the Style box. Finally, you can go to the "Other" sheet in the List Properties dialog and change the list type using the List Style box.

MODIFYING THE PROPERTIES OF ONE ITEM IN A LIST

You won't want to do this often, but here's what you do if you want to mix numbers and letters inside a numbered list:

1. Right-click the item whose list property you want to change. The shortcut menu appears.

2. Click List Item Properties. The List Properties dialog box appears.

3. Click the page icon of the new format you want and choose OK. The item gets its new property, but the other items in the list are unaffected. Notice that you can't mix bullets and numbers.

Tip #21	To get to the List Properties dialog box in a hurry, right-click inside the list and click List Properties to make the dialog box appear.

REMOVING A LIST FORMAT

If you decide your list should be ordinary text, you can get rid of the list style by selecting the entire list and clicking the Decrease Indent button. If you want to remove list styles from nested lists you must select each level individually and click on the Decrease Indent button for each level.

MAKING DIRECTORY OR MENU LISTS

Directory and menu lists are rarely used anymore because they are usually rendered by browsers as bulleted lists. Their exact appearance depends on the tags the browser supports. If you make either list in FrontPage, they will look exactly like bulleted lists. Netscape 2.0 and later and Internet Explorer 3.0 and later also show them as bulleted lists. Internet Explorer 2.0, however, displays them as indented lists without bullets.

A browser that does support directory lists shows the entries evenly spaced across the screen. Neither the Netscape nor the Microsoft browser supports the directory tag, so if you want the effect, use a table. The menu list, in browsers that support this option, shows a list without bullets, and nested lists are simply indented.

→ **See** Chapter 8, "Creating Tables," **p. 193**, for information on using tables for page layout.

DEFINITION LISTS

Also called glossary lists, definition lists are a useful reference format. You can see a typical example of a definition list in Figure 4.31.

Figure 4.31
Definition lists provide structured lists made up of terms and their definitions.

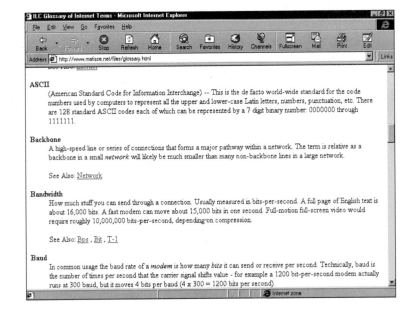

A definition list is a collection of entries, and each entry is made up of a term and its definition. Naturally, this structure isn't only for formal definitions; you can use it for anything that needs a short heading term and one or more indented paragraphs of information beneath it. For the sake of appearance, the term should be short enough to fit on one line of a browser display, but the definition text can be as long as you like. To start a new definition list, use the following steps:

1. Select Defined Term from the Style box.

2. Type the term to be defined and press Enter. The insertion point automatically indents.

3. Type the definition and press Enter.

4. Notice that the Style box says Defined Term again. Repeat steps 2 and 3 until you're finished. Press Enter twice to end the list.

Definition lists are that simple. You can embed other lists inside definition lists, and vice versa. Definition lists can contain hyperlinks and whatever character formatting you want.

Note

Converting lists to and from definition lists causes more problems than it solves. When you convert a list to a definition list, what you get is a list made completely of definitions, so you have to add the terms by hand. If you go from a definition list to a bulleted or numbered list, both terms and definitions convert to first-level bullets or numbers.

Caution

Don't use heading styles inside lists. This style forces line breaks and can leave your list looking very fragmented. If you want to emphasize parts of a list, use character formatting.

USING TEXT COLORS AND BACKGROUND COLORS ON YOUR PAGE

Both content and presentation are important in Web pages, just as they are in any form of communication. However, content is what most people are after, and you should remember this when you add color to a page. If most of the content of the page is in the text (and often it is), don't allow that text to be obscured by even the most stunning visual effects. White text in normal size on a black background, for example, is excruciatingly hard to read; if you want this combination, be prepared to allocate space to a large font or heading style. Some color combinations, such as orange and green or purple and yellow, seem to vibrate, and instantly detract from whatever your words are trying to say. So be careful when selecting background colors and text colors.

Don't bother using color depths over 8-bit (256 colors) either. Most people's systems are still set up for 256 colors, and their browsers may interpret the greater color depth as a pattern instead of a solid color. If such a pattern is behind the text, the text may be difficult or impossible to read.

Finally, always remember to test with different browsers, resolutions, and platforms.

Note

Pages with *themes (page 454)* have their background color and background image fixed. You can't modify these by using the procedures that follow; to do that you must edit the themes themselves, as described in Chapter 6, "Working with Themes." As for text color, you can't modify that globally to the page, although you can change the color of selected text.

PART

II

CH

4

CHANGING THE BACKGROUND AND TEXT COLORS ON NON-THEME PAGES

Both these changes can be made at once from the same dialog box, so I'll consider them together. To change text or background color, use the following steps:

1. Make the desired page active. Choose File, Properties. When the Page Properties dialog box appears, click the Background tab to bring that sheet to the front.

2. Mark the Specify Background and Colors option button.

3. Click the button at the right of the Background drop-down list box. A drop-down list of 16 basic colors appears (see Figure 4.32).

Figure 4.32
Use the Background sheet of the Page Properties dialog box to modify the background color or text color of your pages.

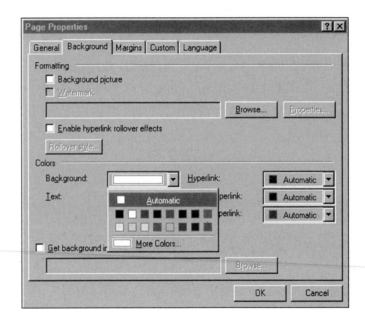

4. Click the color you want. Click OK and the dialog box vanishes. Your page background immediately assumes that color.

5. Click the button at the right of the Text drop-down list box to set the text color. The same color list appears. Select the color you want and click OK.

All new text, and existing text not already colored with character formatting or the Text Color button, takes on the color you selected in step 4.

To restore the default color (white), choose Automatic from the Background list box.

USING MORE COLORS AND MIXING CUSTOM COLORS

If the range of colors available from the drop-down list isn't enough, click the More Colors choice at the bottom of the list box. The Colors dialog appears, with 256 available hues (see Figure 4.33). Click the one you want and choose OK, and then choose OK again to apply the color to text or background.

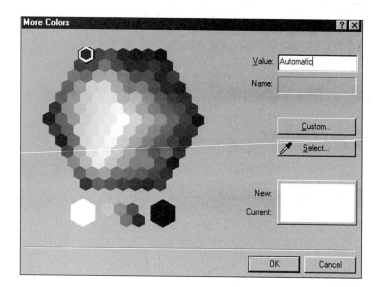

Figure 4.33
The More Colors dialog box expands your range of available colors.

Finally, you can mix your own hue. In the Colors dialog, click the Custom button. The Color dialog box appears (see Figure 4.34).

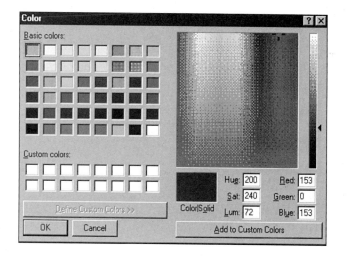

Figure 4.34
The Color dialog box lets you either pick from predefined colors or define your own.

You create a new color in one of the following three ways:

1. Drag the mouse pointer over the large colored rectangle on the right of the dialog box. This changes the color in the Color/Solid box. When you see the color you want, stop dragging. You can change the color's luminance by dragging the black triangle that's next to the vertical bar beside the color box.

2. Adjust the numbers in the boxes for Red, Green, and Blue.

3. Adjust the numbers in the boxes for Hue, Saturation, and Luminance.

After you adjust the color, close the dialog boxes by choosing OK in each box until they all disappear. The page background now has the color you mixed.

This doesn't save your custom color, however. If you want to save it to a custom palette, click the Add to Custom Colors button in the Color dialog box before you leave this box.

Caution

Custom colors might look great in your 256-color or higher display, but they won't appear to the same effect (or at all) on a 16-color system. Using them is more likely a waste of time than an enhancement, unless you are sure that most of your audience will be able to see them.

CHANGING THE COLOR OF PART OF YOUR TEXT

You can make non-global changes of text color even if the page has a theme. Select the text to be changed and do the following:

1. Choose Format, Font to open the Font dialog box.
2. Click the arrow button on the Font sheet at the right of the Color box. A drop-down list of colors appears. (It's the same list as the one you saw in the previous procedures.)
3. Click the color you want. The dialog box closes and the selected text takes on the new color.

Naturally, you can create new text in the new color by following the steps just listed and typing the text. You can also use the color dialogs you saw earlier to specify a text hue.

The best way to understand the effects of these changes is to experiment and see the results through the eyes of your visitors. What will the person using a 16-color, 640×480 display make of your ingeniously coordinated color scheme? Or, if she's got a 256-color display, does she really want to read three screens of yellow text on a black background? Or worse, red on purple?

Caution

The Background sheet of the Page Properties dialog box is also where you change the default link colors to custom colors (for non-theme pages only). If you do this, be sure a visited link remains clearly distinct from an unvisited link.

Note

Many applications, including browsers, have a built-in set of colors, called a color table, that they use for screen display. If a downloaded page contains a color that isn't in the browser's table, the browser either substitutes a similar color or dithers multiple colors from its table to get as close as it can. If you make up a custom color, it might not appear in a browser as it does in FrontPage. As always, test your work.

MAKING COLORS CONSISTENT ACROSS PAGES

Even if (and perhaps *especially* if) you don't use themes, you might want to get a consistent *look* across your site or part of it, and it's a little inconvenient to define the background color and text color for each page as you create it. To get around this, first set up a model page with the color combination you want. Then, for each new or existing page that is to have that combination, open the Page Properties dialog box and go to the Background sheet. Mark the option button called Get Background and Colors from Page and type the filename of the model page in the text box (or use the Browse button to locate the page). Choose OK and the color combination is applied to the current page.

USING THE TEXT EDITING TOOLS

Just as word processors do, FrontPage provides commands for spell-checking, finding and replacing words or strings of words, and a thesaurus. None of these tools is a substitute for careful proofreading and competent writing, but they help.

SPELL CHECKING YOUR WORK

The basic and usually the most convenient method of spell checking is to turn on automatic checking. It is active by default when FrontPage 2000 installs, and misspellings are flagged by a wavy red underline. If you want to turn it off or on, choose Tools, Page Options, and in the resulting Options dialog click the Spelling tab. This displays the Spelling sheet, which has two check boxes. The box labeled Check Spelling as You Type, if checked, turns on automatic checking. Hide Spelling Errors in All Documents conceals or reveals the wavy red line, depending on its checked or unchecked state. If you want to keep checking turned on, but you don't want to be distracted by wavy red lines, check both check boxes. Then, when you're finished writing and want to see how many spelling mistakes you made, go back to the Spelling sheet and uncheck the lower box. Then choose OK. The wavy lines indicating spelling errors now appear.

PART

II

CH

4

Alternatively, you can turn off automatic spell checking and check the document when it's finished. Choose Tools, Spelling (or click the Check Spelling button on the toolbar) and the Spelling dialog box appears. The first possible error is already showing in the Not in Dictionary box (see Figure 4.35).

You can accept the suggested change that appears in the Change To box, select a different change from the Suggestions list box, or type your own correction into the Change To box. Whichever you do, choose the Change button when you're ready to make the change. You can also do one of the following:

- Choose Ignore to bypass the word, or Ignore All to bypass this and all later occurrences of it (you do this if the word is correct, but you don't want to add it to the spell-checker's custom dictionary).
- Choose Change All to change this and all other occurrences of the word.

- Choose Add to add the new word to the custom dictionary. If you do this, it won't get flagged as an error in this or any other document.

- Choose Suggest to get other spelling suggestions from the dictionary. This choice isn't available unless you select a word from the Suggestions list box.

Figure 4.35
Using the spell checker to find suspected errors.

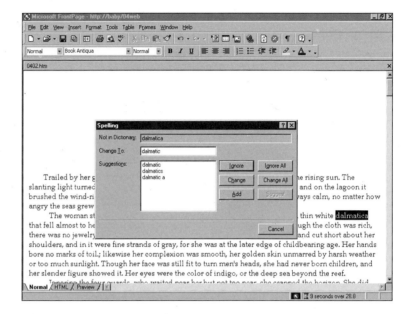

Choosing the Change, Change All, Ignore, or Ignore All buttons immediately takes you to the next possible error, until the page has been checked completely.

USING FIND AND REPLACE

These related commands work just as they do in a word processor. To find occurrences of a string of text, choose Edit, Find. The Find dialog box appears (see Figure 4.36).

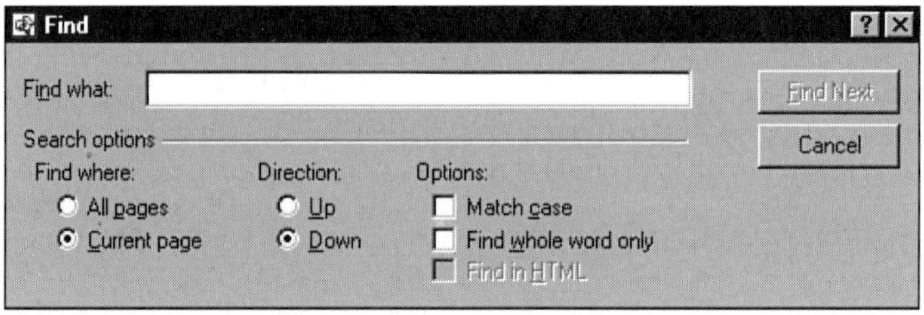

Figure 4.36
You can search for occurrences of a word with the Find dialog box.

You can search the currently active page or all pages of the currently open web. The search direction is specified by marking the option buttons, and you can make the search case sensitive by marking the Match case check box. Depending on what you're looking for, you might want to mark the Match Whole Word Only check box, as well; if you don't, the command finds all occurrences of the text pattern even if it's embedded inside a word. Finally, checking the Find in HTML check box lets you search for text within the HTML code of the page, such as tags or text that is not visible in the Normal mode of Page view.

To search and replace a word or text string, choose Edit, Replace to open the Replace dialog box (see Figure 4.37).

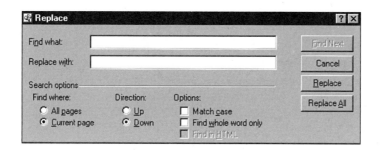

Figure 4.37
The Replace command is handy for selective or global replacement of a text string.

Type the search string into the Find What box and the replacement text into the Replace With box. The various options are the same as in the Find dialog. However, you should consider carefully whether you need to mark the Match Whole Word Only check box. If it's unchecked, and you replace "led" with "brought" (for example), you'll discover that "filed" becomes "fibrought" after the replacement. This might be amusing, but it is counterproductive. If it happens, choose Edit, Undo immediately to cancel the changes.

You can automatically replace all occurrences of the search string by choosing Replace All. To replace selectively, choose Find Next, and if you want to replace, choose the Replace button. If you don't want the replacement, choose Find Next again to go on to the next occurrence of the search string until you finish the document.

USING THE THESAURUS

Mark Twain said that "the difference between the right word and the almost-right word is the difference between a lightning bolt and a lightning bug." If you're staring at the almost-right word and can't think of the right one, try using FrontPage's thesaurus to find it.

> **Note**
>
> The thesaurus might not have been installed yet. If it hasn't been, and you choose Tools, Thesaurus, you will see an alert message saying "This feature is not currently installed. Would you like to install it now?". Assuming you do, place the FrontPage 2000 CD in the CD-ROM drive, close it, and choose Yes. Then follow the onscreen instructions. When installation is finished, the Thesaurus dialog will appear.

Select the word that's giving you trouble (to do so easily, just double-click it) and do the following:

1. Choose Tools, Thesaurus to open the Thesaurus dialog box (see Figure 4.38).

Figure 4.38
Use the Thesaurus when you're having trouble finding the exact word for what you want to say.

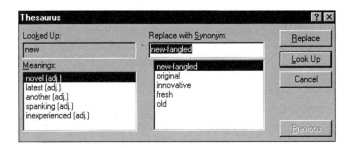

2. Choose Replace if you like the suggested word in the Replace with Synonym box. The dialog box closes, and the original word is automatically replaced with the new one.

3. Select a better one, if the suggested word isn't right, from the right-hand list box and choose Replace.

4. Select a similar meaning from the Meanings list box if that list box doesn't show you what you want. More words appear in the right-hand list box. Select one of these and choose Replace.

5. Select any word from either list box and choose Look Up if you are still not satisfied. More words will appear in the list boxes. (To go back to the previous list, choose Previous.)

6. Keep doing this until you find the word you're after and choose Replace.

You can also use the thesaurus to find antonyms, the opposite of synonyms. The word "antonym" sometimes appears at the bottom of the list in the Meanings list box; select this to get a list of opposites.

There are two problems with using the thesaurus. A minor one is that it's easy to become so fascinated with words that you just keep wandering among them—harmless, though, and perhaps good for your vocabulary. The other, more serious problem, has to do with style. You don't want to become infected with the disorder known as *thesaurusitis*. You know you've contracted the disease when you start replacing words such as "image" with "simulacrum" and "help" with "succor." The effect is often pretentious and can also obscure your meaning. When it comes to style, simple is usually best.

PREVIEWING AND PRINTING YOUR PAGES

Printing your pages is a good idea because language errors seem to stand out better on paper than they do on a screen. Hard copy also gives you another perspective on your page design. You can preview a page before sending it to your printer by choosing File, Print Preview. You print by choosing File, Print or by clicking the Print button on the toolbar.

UNDERSTANDING HYPERLINKS

Without hyperlinks there would be no World Wide Web, just a multitude of isolated pages like unknown islands in an uncharted sea. It's not for nothing that people speak of *navigating* the Web; it really is like a vast and ever-expanding collection of islands, and the hyperlinks are like the trade and communications routes that bind them together across the electronic deeps.

Less poetically, *hyperlink* generally refers to the highlighted words (or specially defined images) that you click on a Web page to access a different resource on the Web or the Internet. Tucked away behind this highlight or image is a string of HTML code that gives your browser the URL for the new location and directs the browser to jump to that location. FrontPage generates this code automatically when you tell it to set up a hyperlink.

USING HYPERLINKS EFFECTIVELY

Most of your hyperlinks will be made up of words rather than images. When you're choosing which words to use for the link, think about them from your readers' point of view. It helps if the link itself suggests what happens if you follow it. An ambiguous link, which a reader must follow to discover whether he really wants to go there, is a potential waste of time. An ambiguous link says "Click here for HTML 4;" a clear one says "HTML 4 Tag Reference." You can make the purpose of a link even clearer by wording the surrounding text to give it context.

→ For detailed information on using images as links, **see** Chapter 5, "Enhancing Pages with Graphics and Multimedia," **p. 121**.

Also, hyperlinks by their very nature stand out from their background. They drag the reader's eye toward them, and if they're not well chosen or there are too many of them, their presence can overpower the meaning of the surrounding text. You should also avoid links that are so short that they're meaningless (such as "Back") or are very long, such as a full sentence. Additionally, you should be careful about using custom link colors. When looking at a page, people want to be able to identify the links they've already visited. So make sure visited and unvisited links are clearly distinguishable. Finally, do not underline text that you do not intend to be a link.

If your page is longer than a couple of screens, you should consider repeating the navigation links at suitable points. This is so that the reader doesn't have to scroll all the way back to the top of the document to get at any links there. You will often find textual navigation controls repeated at the bottom of a page, along with corresponding graphical controls.

PART
II

CH
4

Tip #22

Avoid using the "back" and "forward" labels for navigation links because how they behave depends on how a person reached your site.

SETTING UP A HYPERLINK

The simplest use of a hyperlink is to take your visitor to the top of another page in your Web site. To set this up, make sure you have at least two pages in your current FrontPage web, one to be the hyperlink page and the other to be the destination page, and do the following:

1. Open the hyperlink page in FrontPage. In the hyperlink page, select some text to be the hyperlink.

2. Choose Insert, Hyperlink or click the Hyperlink button on the Standard toolbar. The Create Hyperlink dialog box appears, as shown in Figure 4.39.

Figure 4.39
You use the Create Hyperlink dialog box to select the destination for a hyperlink.

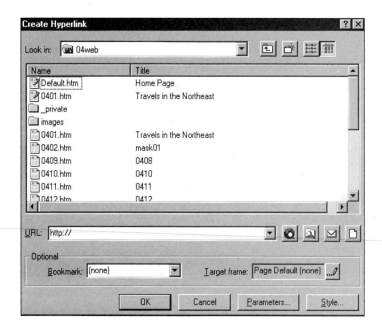

The list box displays all the pages in the web. Some pages might appear twice, once with a standard page icon and once with a pen and page icon. The latter icon simply means the page is currently open in FrontPage.

3. Select the desired destination page by clicking its name and choosing OK.

The dialog box closes, and you've now set up the hyperlink. The text you used as the hyperlink is now highlighted and underlined with the default link color. To test it, hold the Ctrl key down and click the link. The destination page should appear in the FrontPage workspace.

Another way of checking the link is to switch to Preview mode and click the link. The destination page appears. Finally, you can also test the link by using the File, Preview in Browser command; remember to make the hyperlink page the active one, and make sure it's saved before you do this.

Tip #23	If you put the cursor over a hyperlink but don't click it, the URL of the destination appears in the FrontPage status bar. This is handy for identifying the link destination without actually having to go there.

DELETING HYPERLINKS

There are two possibilities here. First, you might want to retain the text of the link, but remove its linking property. To do this, click anywhere in the link and choose Insert, Hyperlink. The Edit Hyperlink dialog appears; except for its title, this dialog is exactly the same as the Insert Hyperlink dialog in Figure 4.39. Now clear the URL text box so that it is blank, and choose OK. The dialog vanishes, and the text remains but is no longer a hyperlink.

If you decide the link isn't worthwhile or if its destination has vanished, you might want to delete it along with its text. To do this, select the entire text of the hyperlink and press the Delete key (or choose Edit, Clear). The link and its text are deleted.

Note	Note that Hyperlink view does not update its link representations until the page is saved.

PART

II

CH

4

EXTENDING THE REACH OF YOUR HYPERLINKS

As stated earlier, hyperlinks are the key element of the Web and its most powerful tool. From any location in your currently open web, you can link to one of the following:

- The top of any page in the open web (as you did earlier)
- A specified location in any page in the open web (*bookmarking*)
- A page in another web on the same host machine
- A resource anywhere in the web or the Internet (pages at other Web sites, FTP sites, Gopher sites, and so on)

Hyperlinks and bookmarks give you tremendous flexibility in structuring your web. For instance, you could keep a table of contents on a single page and set up links to other pages that hold the information itself. In general, hyperlinks make it unnecessary to produce monster pages. This has at least two advantages: shorter pages are easier to maintain, and it's easier to keep navigational aids handy for the reader. Also, most readers start to lose their orientation if they have to keep scrolling through screen after screen of information.

LINKING TO BOOKMARKS

As with all links, you need the hyperlink itself and its destination in order to create a link to a bookmark. In this case, your destination can be either a specific place on the current page or a specific place on a different page. Because it models itself on a word processor, FrontPage refers to this destination as a *bookmark*, which is a common tool in major Windows word processors. This makes sense because you're working with pages, anyway.

You can link to a bookmark from any page in your web, and you can establish bookmarks in any page that you have permission to modify. The formal term for a bookmark is *named anchor*.

> **Note**
>
> The term *bookmark* is also used in Netscape to mean an entry in a quick-access list of Web or Internet sites. FrontPage uses the term bookmark differently, to mean a page location rather than a site address.

To set up the bookmark, which is the destination of the link, use the following steps:

1. Open the destination page in FrontPage and make it the active page. Select an appropriate word or phrase anywhere in the destination page to be the bookmark. An image cannot be used as a bookmark.

2. Choose Insert, Bookmark. The Bookmark dialog box appears (see Figure 4.40).

Figure 4.40
Use the Bookmark dialog box to define the destination of a hyperlink.

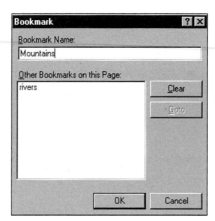

3. Choose the selected text that shows up in the Bookmark Name text box or type something else.

4. Choose OK. A dashed underline appears under the bookmarked text (this underlining does not appear in a browser).

With the bookmark defined, set up the hyperlink itself as follows:

1. Make the origin page active and select the text you want to make into the hyperlink.

2. Choose Insert, Hyperlink or click the Hyperlink button on the toolbar. The Create Hyperlink dialog box appears.

3. In the list box of Web pages, select the page that has the bookmark. This page has two icons, one with a pen and one without, because it's open in FrontPage. You can select either entry.

4. In the Optional section of the dialog, use the Bookmark list box to display the Bookmark list for the page you selected in step 3 (see Figure 4.41).

5. Select the bookmark you assigned as the destination point of the link. When you do, its URL appears in the URL text box.

6. Choose OK.

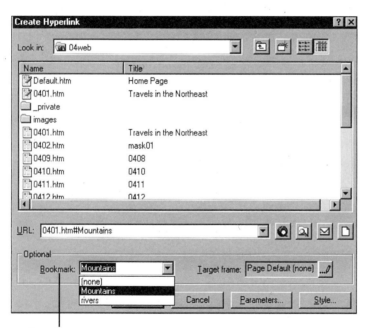

Bookmark List

Figure 4.41
You can choose among a page's bookmarks by using the Bookmark list box in the Optional section of the dialog.

PART

II

CH

4

The hyperlink text is now highlighted and underlined with the default link color. Now switch to the origin page and test the link by using one of the methods described earlier. The destination page should appear with the bookmark at the top of the browser window. If you use Preview in Browser, save the bookmarked page manually before doing so—the automatic saving as provided by Preview in Browser only saves the active page.

Tip #24

> When you put the cursor on top of a link, FrontPage's status bar displays the name of the bookmark that is the link destination (if the destination is a bookmark, of course). In the status bar, the bookmark name is preceded by a pound sign (#), which is the HTML code that indicates a named anchor.

DELETING BOOKMARKS

As with hyperlinks, there are two ways to delete bookmarks. First, you might want to retain the text of the bookmark, but remove its bookmark property. To do this, click anywhere in the bookmark and choose Insert, Bookmark. The Bookmark dialog appears. Select the bookmark you want to remove so that its name appears in the Bookmark Name text box. Choose Clear. The dialog vanishes, and the text remains but is no longer a bookmark.

Alternatively, you might want to delete the bookmark along with its text. To do this, select the entire text of the bookmark and press the Delete key (or choose Edit, Clear). The bookmark and its text are deleted.

LINKING TO A NEW PAGE

FrontPage enables you to create a new page and make a hyperlink to it at the same time. It's a timesaver. To use the feature, carry out the following steps:

1. Open the origin page in FrontPage and select some text or an image for the hyperlink. Choose Insert, Hyperlink.

2. Look at the row of icons to the right of the URL text box (refer to Figure 4.39). The fourth one is a white sheet of paper, which the ToolTip labels as *Create a Page and Link to the New Page*. Click this icon.

3. Select a page type in the New dialog box. Choose OK and the new page opens in the FrontPage workspace.

4. Edit and save it with whatever filename and Page Title you need. Now, when you switch back to the origin page and inspect the link, you'll see that the link points to your new page.

LINKING TO THE WORLD WIDE WEB

It's now that you'll get a real sense of the power of hyperlinks. Local hyperlinks are useful things, but connecting your pages to the Web puts vast resources at your disposal. Remember, though, that it's your visitors who count. They'll use the resources you've selected, so you've got a lot of responsibility to them.

Like the links you just explored, links to the Web are set up through the Create Hyperlink dialog box. If you know the URL of the Web site and/or the specific page within it, you can simply type that into the URL text box and choose OK. If, however, you want to actually access the Web site to make the link, you can do that as well. This a much surer way of making a valid link, especially if the site URL is long and complicated.

Here's how to do this:

1. Log onto your ISP and set up your connection to the Internet and open the origination page (the one that will host the link) in FrontPage. Select some text or an image to be the link.

2. Choose Insert, Hyperlink to open the Create Hyperlink dialog box. The first button to the right of the URL text box has a globe and magnifying glass on it (refer to Figure 4.39). The ToolTip identifies it as *Use Your Web Browser to Select a Page or File*. Click the button. Your system's default browser opens with an instructional message to `Browse to the page of file you want to use, then return to Microsoft FrontPage to continue.`

3. Access the page you want. *Without* closing the browser, switch back to FrontPage.

4. Choose OK when you see the URL of the remote Web site in the URL text box and save the page.

5. Close the browser. Leave your Internet connection active and use either Ctrl+click, Preview mode, or the Preview In Browser command to test the link.

Your links to the World Wide Web work in the same way as the links within your own Web. Clicking a link that references a page somewhere else in the Web will take the visitor there. Likewise, clicking a link to an image file that resides on another server will display that image in a window all by itself.

Tip #25	A fast way to make a link is to choose Insert, Hyperlink from the FrontPage menu bar, but without selecting any text for the link. In the Create Hyperlink dialog box, choose the page you want to link to and choose OK. FrontPage automatically inserts a new text hyperlink onto the current page; this text is the Page Title of the page being linked to.

CREATING A MAILTO LINK

A very common element of a Web page is an email link, which the page visitor can use to send email to the site's management. To add a mailto link to your page, do this:

1. Open the origin page in FrontPage. Select some text or an image to be the link.

2. Look at the four buttons to the right of the URL text box. The third one has an envelope on it. Click this button. The Create E-mail Hyperlink dialog box opens (see Figure 4.42).

3. Type the appropriate email address into the text box.

4. Choose OK and you return to the Create Hyperlink dialog box. You'll now see the email address in the URL text box. Choose OK again and the link is established.

Figure 4.42
Add a mailto link to
your page by using
the Create E-mail
Hyperlink dialog box.

Now, when a visitor to the page clicks the mailto link to open his default mail program,
your address is already inserted as the recipient address. The visitor types the message and
sends it to the mailbox you specified.

EDITING LINKS

To Edit a link, click anywhere in the link text and choose Insert, Hyperlink. The Edit
Hyperlink dialog box appears. Except for the dialog box title, it's exactly the same as the
Create Hyperlink dialog box. Make any changes you want and choose OK.

ADDING LINK PARAMETERS

You might want to edit parameters for the link. You could do this directly in HTML view,
but there's a simpler method. In the Create Link dialog (or the Edit Link dialog, for an
existing link) choose the Parameters button. The Hyperlink Parameters dialog opens (see
Figure 4.43).

Figure 4.43
The Hyperlink
Parameters dialog
enables you to specify
complex properties for
your link.

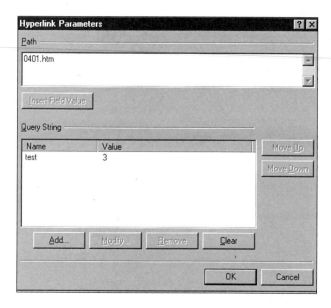

Edit the link path if and as desired. To add a query string to the link, choose the Add button, and an Add Parameter dialog box opens. You use this to insert the parameter name and value. When you close the Add Parameter dialog, the data appears in the Query String list box of the Hyperlink Parameters dialog. Choose OK to insert the parameters and path into the link.

KEEPING YOUR VISITORS OUT OF DEAD ENDS

The Web is a place people like to move around in. Well chosen navigational links laid out in a useful way give your Web pages a professional gleam. But trying to keep visitors at your site by making it hard for them to leave is counterproductive.

A major error to avoid is leaving your visitor at a dead end, which is a page he can't leave without using his browser's Back button. As an example, suppose a visitor turns up at your site, but the link he used to get there brings him to a page that isn't your home page. Suppose also that you didn't bother to establish a link from this page back to your home page or to any other location in your site. So, when he's finished viewing this page, he's stuck. He can only go back to the site he came from, and it's not your site. He won't get a chance to see what else you have to offer him. For this reason alone, you should have a link at least to your home page in every page on your site.

TROUBLESHOOTING

You may edit a page, preview it in a browser, and decide that everything is fine. Then, to save time, you don't close the previewing browser. Then you do another edit and switch back to the browser, but it doesn't show the new edit even when you click the Refresh or Reload buttons.

To troubleshoot this, you have to know that the previewing browser retrieves the page from the file it's stored in, not from the FrontPage workspace. If you don't mark the Automatically Save Page check box in the Preview in Browser dialog box, you will have to save the page each time you want to preview it and then use the browser's Reload or Refresh buttons to display the new version of the page.

Another source of confusion is the distinction between paragraph and character styles. For example, suppose you decide to change from Normal to Formatted style when part way through a paragraph. When you use the Paragraph dialog box to do this, the whole paragraph changes to Formatted style. The same thing happens when you try using the Style box.

This occurs because changing a paragraph style isn't the same as changing character style (for example, selecting Bold or a font). Character style changes affect only selected text or whatever characters you type after the change. However, when you select a paragraph style (the selection method makes no difference) the style is always applied to the entire paragraph. You can't break the paragraph into chunks, each chunk having a different style.

Another thing you may want to do is use an image as a bookmark. Unfortunately, there is no way to do this. This is because an HTML page doesn't actually contain the image data, but rather a *pointer* to the file where the image is stored. HTML doesn't let you define such a pointer as a named anchor, which is what a bookmark actually is. To get around this, you have to use some text near the image (the caption, if there is one) as the bookmark.

DESIGNERS CORNER

As you know from your own experience, most of the time you spend at a Web site is taken up with reading. Graphic elements are indeed a key (and essential) part of a Web page's design, but the bulk of the information is presented in good old-fashioned text. This implies, quite accurately, the importance of good writing to a quality Web site. However, "good writing" doesn't mean just good grammar, spelling, and style, though these are absolutely necessary. A quality Web page also needs a sense of purpose.

What does this mean? Simply this: when you ask yourself what this page is about, you can give a clear, simple answer. If you can't do this, it means that you're not sure why the page exists. Your visitors won't be sure when they see it, either. This is certain to send them away quickly, and they will not come back. Another possibility may be that the page is about too many different things; this is another way of losing focus, frustrating your visitors, and turning them away for good.

In asking yourself the question, you are trying to identify the purpose of the page. Every page in your Web should have a reason for its existence, a purpose related to the overall reason for the Web's existence. If the page has no purpose, or if that purpose has nothing to do with the Web's reason for being, get rid of it.

CHAPTER 5

ENHANCING PAGES WITH GRAPHICS AND MULTIMEDIA

In this chapter   *by Dennis Jones*

GETTING THE MOST OUT OF IMAGES

Images add visual interest, provide information, amplify the meaning of text, break text into manageable chunks, and (very important) give your site character. They're a resource no Web page author should willingly do without.

However, getting the best results from images takes some thought. If you have an artist's eye, you're already ahead of the game. If you're not trained in design, though, all is not lost. However, before you start throwing pictures at a page, ask yourself the following questions:

- What purpose should the image or images serve?
- What content best suits this purpose?
- How big are the images (that is, how long to download)?
- How many should there be?
- How well do they relate to any text and to each other?
- Where do they look best on the page?

Working out these answers helps you avoid building pages that are a hodgepodge of unrelated elements. After you decide what images to use, keep the following guidelines in mind as you choose or create them:

- Don't use a background image that makes your text and graphics hard to see.
- Don't use huge graphics that take forever to download. If you want to make such an image available, put in a thumbnail with a link to the larger image. The largest single image you should consider is 25KB, unless there's a very good reason to go bigger. Keep the total size of all graphics on a page to 30KB or less.
- Speaking of size, be careful about using really wide graphics. If your visitors are running their browsers at less than full screen, or their hardware supports only VGA (640×480) resolution, the image might be lopped off at the side. Keep the image width to less than five or six inches, and test your results.
- When designing imagemaps, be sure the clickable areas are easily identified.
- Pick a browser-safe color palette and stay with it as much as possible.
- Don't overuse special effects such as blinking text, fades, dissolves, and crawls. After the novelty wears off, many people are irritated by a page that flashes, squirms, and slithers. In particular, if you want somebody to concentrate on the meaning of a section of text, don't distract them with something bouncing around right next to it.

UNDERSTANDING IMAGE BASICS

Graphics inserted into a Web page are called inline images. The two most common graphic file formats for Web publications are GIF (Graphics Interchange Format) and JPEG (Joint Photographic Experts Group). All graphics-capable browsers support these two formats and display them without fuss. However, several other formats exist, examples being TIFF, PCX, BMP, and PNG. More recent versions of the Netscape and Mosaic browsers handle these as well by calling up helper applications, which are programs designed to display images stored in these formats. Mostly you should stick with GIF and JPG, and possibly PNG.

Note

> PNG (Portable Network Graphics format) is a relatively new graphics format that might eventually be the standard for Web images. It supports True Color, which makes it better for photographic images than GIF; also, unlike JPEG, its compression is lossless (that is, its quality is not degraded when the image is compressed). It is making inroads only slowly, however.

Which format, GIF or JPEG, should you use in your pages? Each has its own strengths. The advantage of GIF is that it's the bread-and-butter format for the Web, at least for the time being. Browsers decompress it quickly, so it's reasonably brisk about showing up on your visitor's screen. It's the format of choice for line art, that is, art without continuous shading of tones, photographs, for instance. It provides up to 256 colors and can simulate more by dithering. You can also go in the other direction because a useful characteristic of GIFs is that you can use image editors to reduce the number of different colors in them, which reduces the file size. Then again, you can simply reduce the size of the image with a graphics editor. This is a possibility with JPEGs, too.

GIF image files do tend to be larger than equivalent JPEG ones, so what you gain in fast GIF decompression you lose (somewhat) in having to store bigger files on your site. On the other hand, JPEG files, although they can be smaller than GIFs, decompress slower than GIF files. Their advantage over GIFs is that they support up to 16.7 million colors, so that continuous-tone images reproduce better on the screen. However, there's as yet no point in using actual High Color or True Color images on a Web page. It's true that this display technology is more widely used than it was a year ago, but most people are still looking at 256 colors, so the extra quality is probably wasted.

With JPEG images you can also adjust the compression level (in FrontPage this is referred to as the quality) to reduce the size of a graphic. If you choose to do this, inspect the results because the higher the compression, the more the image is degraded. You have to find the right balance of size and quality.

Note

> For best results, you should scale the compression of a JPEG graphic by using a native graphics program (such as Lview or Image Composer) rather than FrontPage's Quality command. You can get an evaluation version of Lview at http://www.lview.com/.

FrontPage 2000 ships with its own Clip Art Gallery of over 1,000 images, and if Microsoft Office is installed on your machine, you will also have access to the Office clip art. Some images, especially of icons and buttons, are also available on the Internet for free use.

However, to individualize your own Web site, you'll likely want unique graphics. Original artwork can be produced either with graphics packages, such as the software included with FrontPage 2000, or by more traditional means such as paint or photography. (If you're not an artist or a photographer, you might want to enlist the skills of someone who is.) Photographs and artwork must be scanned to make the required graphics files, which you can then insert into your pages.

Tip #26 Microsoft itself supplies ready-made images you can use, at `http://www.microsoft.com/gallery/default.asp`.

→ **See** Part VI, "Creating and Adapting Graphics for the Web," **p. 605** for more information about using the FrontPage graphics tools.

PUTTING AN IMAGE ONTO A PAGE

If you installed the Microsoft Personal Web Server 4, FrontPage by default stores server-based webs in an appropriately named folder inside the `C:\Inetpub\Wwwroot` folder. If you create a *disk-based web (page 24)*, the default storage location of the web is in an appropriately named folder at `C:\My Webs`.

No matter which place the Web folder is stored, it has within it several more folders, and one of these is the `images` folder. This is the most convenient place to keep the graphics for your web because storing all your images in one place makes it easier to stay organized.

Note When you reference a graphic that is stored on the local drive or a network drive, and you then save the page that displays the graphic, FrontPage asks if you want to copy that graphic to the current web. If you say yes, the graphic ends up in the web's root directory, not in the `images` folder. To copy the graphic to the `images` folder, or to some other folder, you must supply the relative pathname for that folder.

After you add a graphic to the `images` folder, use the following steps to insert it onto your page:

1. Place the cursor where you want the image to appear.
2. Choose Insert, Picture, From File. The Picture dialog box appears. In the list box, double-click the `images` folder icon to make the list of image files appear (see Figure 5.1).
3. Select the image file you want by clicking its name in the list. Notice that you get a preview of the image in the small window at the right of the dialog box.
4. Choose OK. FrontPage inserts the image into the page (see Figure 5.2).

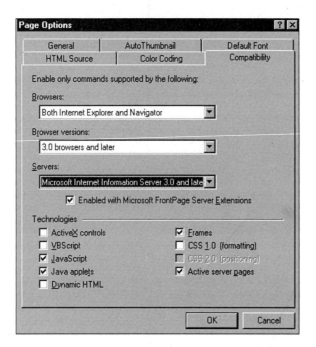

Figure 5.1
Use the Picture dialog box to select an image from the `images` folder.

Figure 5.2
The image you select appears at the cursor position.

PART

II

CH

5

Tip #27	If you want to edit an image that's already on a page, double-click the image. This opens the FrontPage graphics program (if you have installed it) and loads the image file.

DELETING AN IMAGE

Oops! You didn't want that image there. To get rid of it, first click it to select it (you know it's selected when the sizing handles appear on its borders). Press the Delete key and the image vanishes. Alternatively, you can right-click the image and choose Cut.

USING IMAGES NOT IN THE CURRENT WEB

Sometimes, the image file you want isn't in the `images` folder of the web you're working on. FrontPage gives you a quick way to import images from somewhere else on your host machine. Place the cursor where you want the image and use the following steps:

1. Choose Insert, Picture, From File so that the Picture dialog box appears. Look at the URL text box and you'll see two buttons at its right end. The second button, with the folder and magnifying glass on it, is the one you want (its ToolTip is Make a Hyperlink to a File on Your Computer). Click the button.

   The Select File dialog box appears. This is the standard dialog box in Windows 95/98/NT to open a file.

2. Find and select the name of the image file you want and choose Open. All dialog boxes close and the image appears on your page at the cursor position.

3. Continue editing the page until you're finished. Choose File, Save. Because you inserted an image that is not (yet) in the current web, the Save Embedded Files dialog box appears (see Figure 5.3).

Figure 5.3
Use the Save Embedded Files dialog box to add a graphic to your Web.

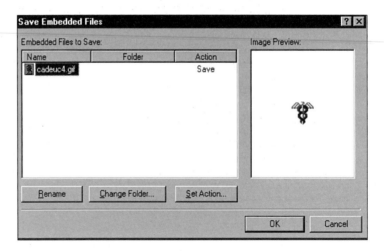

4. To save the new image to the root folder of the current web, select the file and choose OK.

5. To save the file to the current web's `images` folder, select the file and choose the Change Folder Button. This opens the Change Folder dialog box (see Figure 5.4).

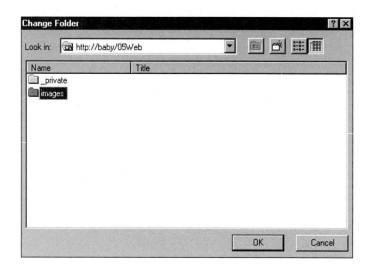

6. Double-click the images folder to select it in the Change Folder dialog box (the folder name should appear in the Look In text box). Choose OK. When you return to the Save Embedded Files dialog box, images/ appears in its list box in the Folder column.

7. Choose OK to save the file to the images folder. You can, of course, use this procedure to save the file to any folder in the current web.

If you now check Explorer's Folder View and click the images folder (or the root folder, depending on the pathname you saved with), you'll see that the graphic has been added to your web. Note that this is a copy of the original; you only copy the graphic, not move it.

Sometimes you don't want the image to be saved to the current web and instead you want to leave it where it is. In this case, begin by following steps 1 through 4 of the previous procedure and then do the following:

1. Click the file in the Save Embedded Files dialog box to select it and choose the Set Action button to open the Set Action dialog box.

2. Mark the option button labeled Don't Save.

3. Choose OK. When you return to the Save Embedded Files dialog box, choose OK again. The image file is now the destination of a hyperlink and is not stored in the current web.

Tip #28

If you have added several graphics to a page before saving it, the Saved Embedded Files list box will list all the unsaved files. You can select and work with these files on an individual basis. Notice that you can rename them, as well: just select the target file and click the Rename button (or select the target file and press F2 to rename the file).

INSERTING IMAGES FROM A REMOTE SITE

You can also access images at other sites, both in webs on your local host and on the World Wide Web. To do this, open the Picture dialog box and type the URL of the remote image into the URL text box. When you choose OK, FrontPage establishes a link to the image and preserves the link when you save the page. If you look at Hyperlinks view with the Hyperlinks to Images option turned on, you'll see an icon for that remote image. (You might need to choose FrontPage's View, Refresh command to update the display.)

However, many URLs are long and complicated, and typing them is prone to errors. To use a more cumbersome, but much more reliable, linking method, first connect to the Internet. Click the first button to the right of the URL text box, the button with the globe and magnifying glass. This starts an Internet Explorer-type browser, which opens with a message: `Browse to the page or file you want to use, then return to FrontPage to continue.`

Use the browser to find the image you want. Without closing the browser, switch back to FrontPage and the Picture dialog box. The URL of the image now appears in the URL text box. Choose OK to create the link. You can now close the browser. You might want to test the link with Preview in Browser before disconnecting from the Internet.

Tip #29	The danger in referencing another site is that it might become inaccessible, vanish entirely, or its Webmaster might delete the image. If it's at all possible, make your images safe by downloading them to your host machine.

Caution	Remember that copyright law applies to the Internet and the Web; many images are for free use, but not all. Don't use the latter without permission from the owner.

ADDING A CLIP ART IMAGE

Shipping with FrontPage 2000 is a Clip Art Gallery. (If you have Microsoft Office installed on your host machine, you will also have access to the Office clip art). These galleries include videos, photographic images, and sound, as well as traditional clip art and Web-related clip art such as icons and buttons.

To use clip art, do the following:

1. Choose Insert, Picture, Clip Art. The Clip Art Gallery dialog box opens (see Figure 5.5).
2. Click one of the tabs (Pictures, Sounds, or Motion Clips) and select the category from the icons box. The dialog box shows you previews of the items in that category in the preview box. Videos and sounds will play.
3. Scroll through the previews until you find the one you want. Click to select it. A shortcut menu appears giving you icons for Insert Clip, Preview Clip, Add Clip to Favorites or Other Category, and Find Similar Clips.
4. Click the Insert Clip icon. FrontPage inserts the clip onto your page.

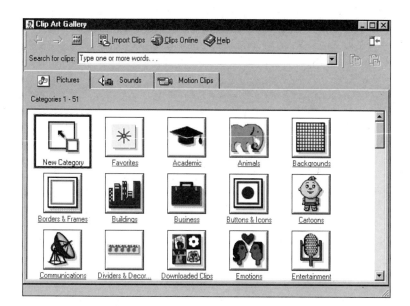

Figure 5.5
Choose from a
selection of clip art to
enliven a page.

You're not limited to the supplied clip art. You can customize the collection by importing items into the clip art categories. Click the Import Clips button and use the dialog boxes to select an item and add it to a category of your choice.

When you save a page into which you have inserted a piece of clip art, you automatically see the Save Embedded Files dialog box. The default name of the clip is useful only to a computer; use the Rename button to give it a better name. Don't use the Set Action button to set up a link to the clip, either. If you do, the clip gets stored in FrontPage's TEMP folder, which is a very poor place to store files.

INSERTING A SCANNED IMAGE

This capability is dependent on your hardware, but assuming you have a TWAIN-compatible device attached to your host machine, open the Picture dialog box and choose Scan. In the Camera/Scanner dialog box, click the Source button to select the device. When it's selected, choose Acquire and the scanned image is inserted onto the active page.

USING FRONTPAGE 2000'S IMAGE PROCESSING TOOLS

You've likely noticed by now that when you select an image, the Picture toolbar immediately appears. You can also force it to appear even when no image is selected by choosing View, Toolbars, Picture.

This toolbar has several very useful image manipulation tools on it, and you'll look at these in the next few pages. To get started, place an image on a page and select it. You see the Picture toolbar with its tool buttons (see Figure 5.6).

PART

II

CH

5

Figure 5.6
The Picture toolbar has buttons for 26 image manipulation tools.

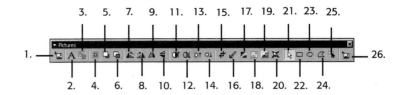

1. Insert Picture
2. Text
3. Auto Thumbnail
4. Position Absolutely
5. Bring Forward
6. Send Backward
7. Rotate Left
8. Rotate Right
9. Flip Horizontal
10. Flip Vertical
11. More Contrast
12. Less Contrast
13. More Brightness

14. Less Brightness
15. Crop
16. Set Transparent Color
17. Black and White
18. Washout
19. Bevel
20. Resample
21. Select
22. Rectangular Hotspot
23. Circular Hotspot
24. Polygonal Hotspot
25. Highlight Hotspots
26. Restore

Some of these tools fall into classes, so you'll examine them in groups when suitable. The very first one, Insert Picture, is of course the same as using the Insert menu to insert an image.

ADDING TEXT TO A GIF

This is an easy way to custom label buttons, but you can also use it in any situation when placing text over an image is necessary (it doesn't work with JPEGs, however).

To add the text, first insert the GIF onto the page. Select it and choose the Text button. A text box appears on the image. You can resize this box with the sizing handles or drag it to any position on the GIF.

With the text box in place, you can type your label text into it and format the text with any of the text tools such as font, sizing, color, and so on. Note, however, that you can't mix fonts or font characteristics in one text box; if you change the font or the font color while the insertion point is in the box, for example, the effect is applied to all text in the box.

Note

Text over GIFs is programmed by a WebBot included in the page. Because of this, text over GIFs will work only if the server hosting the web has the FrontPage 2000 server extensions installed. It works with both IE4 and later and Navigator 4 and later.

You can also apply more than one text box to the same image. This is especially useful for creating text labels that are also hyperlinks; in other words, you can set up an imagemap by using text boxes and their contained text as hotspots. Hyperlinked hotpots are discussed later in this chapter when you do a full treatment of imagemap creation.

UNDERSTANDING AUTO THUMBNAILS

Thumbnails are used when you want to give the user a chance to see a large graphic, but you don't want to force him to wait while it downloads. The thumbnail itself is a small version of the larger graphic; you put the thumbnail on the page and make a link from it to the larger version. If the user wants to see the larger version, he clicks the link to download it to his browser. Thumbnails are image-based links, so they'll be covered later in the chapter.

USING ABSOLUTE POSITIONING

This button forces the selected image to have the style attribute position: absolute. Absolute positioning, which is part of the Cascading Style Sheets 1 (CSS1) specification, places elements at specific points on the page according to the x-y coordinate system, with the 0,0 position at the top left corner of the browser window. The location of absolutely positioned elements does not vary, even if they overlap other elements or if the browser window is resized. Absolute positioning is required for z-indexing (see next section). This will be treated in more detail later in the book.

→ **See** Chapter 25, "Making Your Pages and Webs More Dynamic," **p. 513** for information on layout using style sheets.

SENDING FORWARD OR BACK (Z-INDEXING)

The Send Forward and Send Back buttons are also for CSS positioning. They modify the z-index property of the style assigned to the page element. Z-index positioning is covered at length in Chapter 25, "Making Your Pages and Webs More Dynamic."

IMAGE FLIP AND ROTATE

The Rotate buttons rotate the image clockwise or counterclockwise, 90 degrees at a time. The Flip Vertical and Horizontal buttons reverse left and right or up and down.

ADJUSTING BRIGHTNESS AND CONTRAST

The four Increase and Decrease Contrast and Brightness buttons incrementally adjust these values with each click.

CROPPING AN IMAGE

Select the image and click the Crop button. A gray rectangle with outlined sizing handles appears on the image. Drag and size the rectangle to select the area of the image that you want to crop to. Then click the Crop button again. The image is now cropped.

Note that if the original image had transparent areas, you'll have to restore them with the Make Transparent tool. Also, when you save the page, you see the Save Embedded Files dialog box. In this dialog box, give the cropped image a new name to distinguish it from the original. At the time of writing, FrontPage did not warn you if you were inadvertently about to replace the uncropped image with the cropped one.

PART
II

CH
5

MAKING TRANSPARENT IMAGES

You want to give your pages a unified and harmonious appearance, and you can achieve this through your choice of images, text, and layout. You can add to this sense of unity by using transparent GIF images (only GIFs support this option; it doesn't work with JPEGs). A transparent image lets the page background appear through parts of the graphic, as though the picture were painted on acetate instead of paper. This embeds the image into its surroundings and gives it a sense of integration. You can see the difference in effect in Figure 5.7.

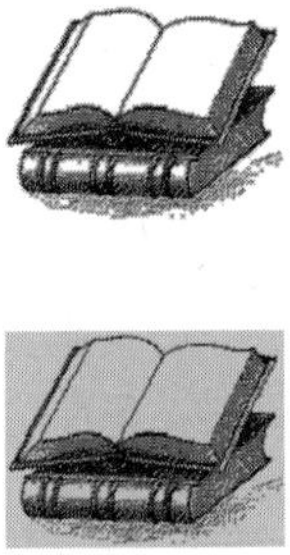

Figure 5.7
The transparent GIF on top is better harmonized with its surroundings than the one below it, which is opaque.

If you feel that a graphic looks better if a particular color is transparent, you can get this effect with the Set Transparent Color tool from the Picture toolbar. To make a particular color invisible, use the following steps:

1. Select the graphic and click the Set Transparent Color button.
2. Put the cursor (it looks like the eraser end of a pencil) on the color you want to render invisible and click. All instances of that color in the graphic become transparent.

Tip #30	When you first look at the image properties for some graphics, the Transparent check box is grayed out because the graphic contains no transparent colors. To establish a transparent color, use the Set Transparent Color tool from the Picture toolbar.

Conversely, you might want to make a transparent graphic into an opaque one. To achieve this effect, select the image and go to the General sheet of the Picture Properties dialog box. Clear the Transparent check box in the Type section. Choose OK and the graphic becomes opaque. You can't check the box again, though, to bring back the transparency. To do that, you have to use the Make Transparent tool as described in the preceding procedure.

BLACK AND WHITE AND WASH OUT

The Black and White button, as you would expect, makes the image black and white. It preserves grayscale quite well. The Wash Out button washes out the image by 50 percent. If you click the button more than once, it has no effect.

BEVELING IMAGE BORDERS

Bevel creates a beveled outline around the image. Because the beveling is white and gray, it shows up better on a background color or image than on a gray or a white page.

USING RESAMPLE

This is an extremely useful tool. It enables you to resize an image to make it larger or smaller. In addition, making a smaller image also reduces the size of the graphic file.

Select the image and resize it by using the sizing handles, and then click the Resample button. When you save the page, you'll see the Save Embedded Files dialog box. Give the modified file a new name or save it in a different folder, unless you want it to replace the original. When you choose OK, the resized file is saved to your web.

ABOUT THE SELECT AND HOTSPOT BUTTONS

The next five buttons on the toolbar, from Select to Highlight Hotspots, are actually for making imagemaps. They'll be discussed after image-based hyperlinks and navigational controls are covered later in this chapter.

USING THE RESTORE BUTTON

This last button is quick to explain, but it's so important that it deserves a section to itself. If you use one or more of the tools to change an image and you don't like the results, click the Restore button. This isn't an undo; it actually re-inserts the original of the image—provided you haven't saved the image yet.

COORDINATING IMAGES AND TEXT

If you've experimented with simple pages where you put blocks of text with an image, you've noticed that the text lines up with the image's bottom edge. Sometimes, this is what you want, but it's typographically limiting; you need more space than that to lay out a good looking page. What about centering images, putting them at the right margin, and getting multiple lines of text to flow down an image's side? FrontPage lets you do all these things.

POSITIONING TEXT AROUND AN IMAGE

As you just observed, if you add Normal text beside an image or insert an image into an existing line of Normal text, the text lines up with the image's bottom edge. If you don't want this effect, you can change it by following these steps:

1. Click the image to select it.
2. Choose Format, Properties. The Picture Properties dialog box appears.
3. Choose the Appearance tab. In the Layout area, click the arrow button at the right of the Alignment box (see Figure 5.8).

PART

II

CH

5

Figure 5.8
You change text position relative to an image by choosing from the Alignment options.

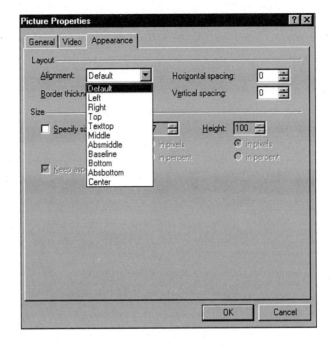

4. Click bottom, middle, or top depending on which alignment you want.

5. Choose OK. The text moves to the appropriate position beside the image (see Figure 5.9).

Figure 5.9
FrontPage lets you align text with the bottom, middle, or top of an image.

Text lined up with the image bottom

Text lined up with the image middle

Text lined up with the image top

Tip #31

You can get to the Picture Properties dialog box quickly by right-clicking the image and choosing Picture Properties from the shortcut menu. Or click on the image and press Alt+Enter.

ALIGNING AND FLOATING IMAGES

Centering or right-aligning an image is easy. Simply select the image and choose Format, Paragraph. When you reach the Paragraph dialog box, open the Alignment drop-down list box and pick the alignment you want. After you choose OK, the image is repositioned. An even faster method is to click the Align Left, Center, or Align Right buttons on the toolbar.

Often you'll want to wrap text around an image. FrontPage lets you float an image to achieve this effect. To make an image float against the left or right margin so that existing or future text wraps around it, use the following steps:

1. Select the image.
2. Choose Format, Properties to open the Picture Properties dialog box. Choose the Appearance sheet tab.
3. Click the arrow button beside the Alignment drop-down list box to open the list of alignment options (refer to Figure 5.8).
4. Select the Left or Right option.
5. Choose OK. The image moves to the appropriate margin and any text present flows around it (see Figure 5.10).

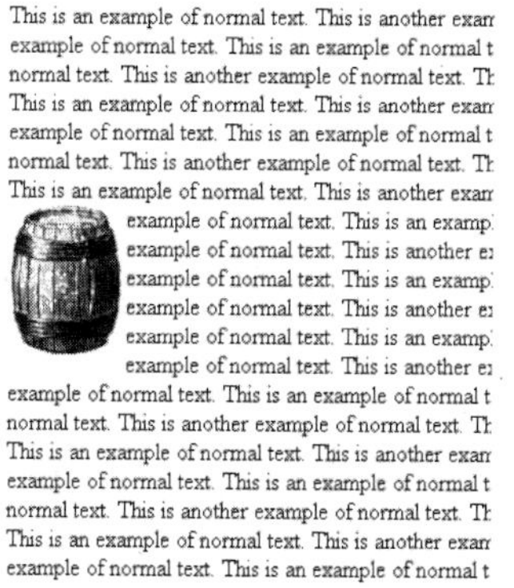

This is an example of normal text. This is another example of normal text. This is an example of normal text. This is another example of normal text. This is an example of normal text. This is another example of normal text. This is an example of normal text. This is another example of normal text. This is an example of normal text. This is another example of normal text. This is an example of normal text. This is another example of normal text. This is an example of normal text. This is another example of normal text. This is an example of normal text. This is another example of normal text. This is an example of normal text. This is another example of normal text. This is an example of normal text. This is another example of normal text. This is an example of normal text. This is another example of normal text. This is an example of normal text. This is another example of normal text. This is an example of normal text. This is an example of normal text. This is another example of normal text. This is an example of normal text. This is another example of normal text. This is an example of normal text.

Figure 5.10
Text wraps around a floating image for better layout.

Tip #32

The Picture Properties dialog box has an Edit button. Click this button to start the FrontPage graphics program (if it is installed) and automatically load the selected image.

USING OTHER ALIGNMENTS

You have four further alignments for lining up text and images. All are accessible from the Alignment drop-down list box in the Picture Properties dialog box. Table 5.1 describes what they do.

Option	Effect
Texttop	Aligns tallest text with image top
Absmiddle	Aligns image with middle of current line
Absbottom	Aligns image with bottom of current line
Baseline	Aligns image with baseline of current line

TABLE 5.1   NETSCAPE ALIGNMENT EXTENSIONS

These extensions actually make little discernible difference in the display of either IE or Navigator.

USING LINE BREAKS WITH IMAGES

So far, you've learned how to align a single line of text at the top, middle, or bottom of an image. You also know how to make text flow around an image that floats against the right or left margin. But how do you put just a few lines next to an image, for instance, if you want a two-line caption beside a graphic that's several lines high?

→ You can also do this sort of thing with style sheet layouts. **See** Chapter 12, "Using Style Sheets with Individual Pages and Full Sites," **p. 271**.

This effect is an important typographical tool, and fortunately it's supported by FrontPage. You adjust the text layout by inserting special types of line breaks.

Let's say you start out with a page that looks like the one shown in Figure 5.11. The image captioning looks very awkward; you want both lines of text beside the image, not broken up as they are.

Figure 5.11
An image sits against the left margin with a caption positioned using the Default image alignment (at the bottom).

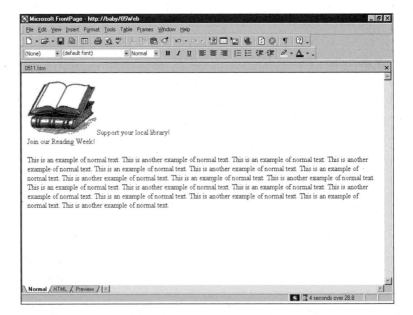

To achieve the desired layout, first change the image properties of the graphic to a left or right floating alignment and then do the following:

1. Place the cursor where you want the special line break to occur. In the example in the figures, it was put right after the "Join our Reading Week" line.

2. Choose Insert, Break. The Break Properties dialog box appears (see Figure 5.12).

Figure 5.12
Specialized line breaks give you more control of the relationship between images and text.

3. Choose Clear Left Margin or Clear Right Margin, depending on where your image is. If you're using a left-floating image and a right-floating image opposite each other, choose Clear Both Margins. (In the example, the text wraps around a left-floating image. As just stated, the break goes after "Join our Reading Week.")

4. Choose OK.

The text following the special line break moves down until it's past the bottom of the image, and then slides over to the appropriate margin (see Figure 5.13). If you have images of unequal size opposite each other, the Clear Both Margins option moves the text down to clear the bottom edges of both images.

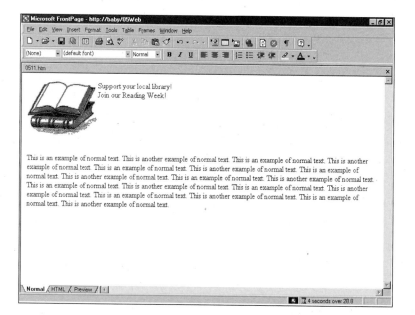

Figure 5.13
A specialized line break forces the text after it to drop below a floating image.

PART

II

CH

5

Spacing Between Text and Image

You know that whitespace is an important component of any page, and you might dislike the way text gets crowded close to your images. Fortunately, you can adjust the text-to-image spacing with the Horizontal Spacing and Vertical Spacing boxes in the Appearance sheet of the Picture Properties dialog box. The values you fill in here determine the spacing; a value of 20 in each gives the result shown in Figure 5.14.

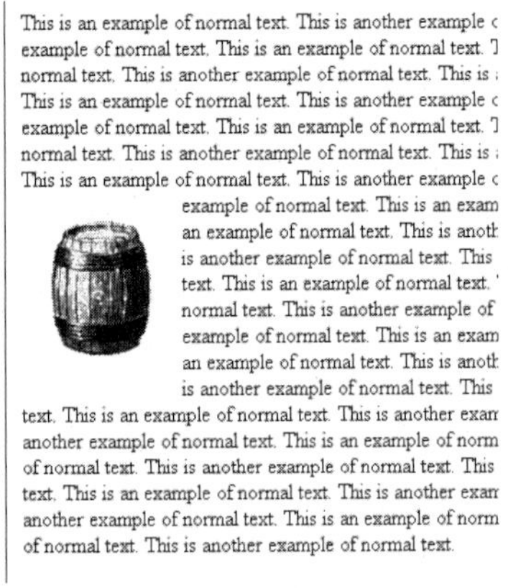

Figure 5.14
Adding whitespace around an image keeps it from seeming crowded by surrounding text. Here the image is also a floating one, so the text wraps around it.

This is an example of normal text. This is another example of example of normal text. This is an example of normal text. Thus normal text. This is another example of normal text. This is a This is an example of normal text. This is another example of example of normal text. This is an example of normal text. Thus normal text. This is another example of normal text. This is a This is an example of normal text. This is another example of example of normal text. This is an exam an example of normal text. This is anoth is another example of normal text. This text. This is an example of normal text. normal text. This is another example of example of normal text. This is an exam an example of normal text. This is anoth is another example of normal text. This text. This is an example of normal text. This is another exam another example of normal text. This is an example of norm of normal text. This is another example of normal text. This text. This is an example of normal text. This is another exam another example of normal text. This is an example of norm of normal text. This is another example of normal text.

Adjusting Image Size

Also on the Appearance sheet, you can mark the Specify Size check box to set the width and height of the graphic in pixels or percent. Fiddling with this can produce weird results, especially if the image is a floating image. The adjustments don't affect the size of the image file, however, so don't try to use this feature to reduce image download times. It's most useful for making minor adjustments to balance the relationship of image and text.

Adding Borders to an Image

You might want a visible boundary around a graphic, although such boundaries aren't used much. When they are, they're often understood to indicate a clickable image. If you want one, there's not much variety; you're stuck with a simple solid line rectangle. You can only vary its line thickness. To add a border, go to the Appearance sheet of the Picture Properties dialog box and type a nonzero value into the Border Thickness box.

Providing Alternative Text

This is important because you must tell people who are running their browsers with images turned off or who are using a text-only browser that there's an image on the page. Even if they have images turned off, they might like to see your graphic, but they have to know it's there.

You add alternative text by using the General sheet of the Picture Properties dialog box. In the Alternative Representations section, use the Text box to type the word or phrase that stands in for the graphic and then choose OK. Remember to test the results! Don't try to give an elaborate description of the picture because a few, well chosen words are plenty. Figure 5.15 shows what alternative text looks like.

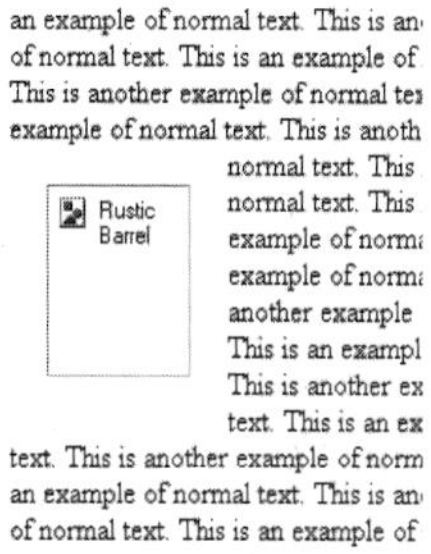

Figure 5.15
Tell your readers about the presence and nature of a graphic by including alternative text.

ADDING A BACKGROUND IMAGE BY USING A FILE

Background images, distinct from background colors, are actual graphics that sit behind your text and your foreground images. You use them to add texture, color, site identification, or other visual effects to your pages. Aesthetics and legibility are important, but remember that it is only a background and should not distract from your content or diffuse the impact of your foreground images.

FrontPage lets you use any graphics file as a background (it doesn't have to be a GIF). A few banks of appropriate images are available on the Web, and you can download them for your own use. Clip art also ships with FrontPage 2000, and if you have MS Office installed on your system, you can use its clip art as well.

Tip #33

Two such image resources are The IconBazaar at `http://www.iconbazaar.com/` and the Microsoft library at `http://www.microsoft.com/workshop/c-frame.htm#/gallery/images/default.asp`.

Caution

If you use a Web or Internet resource find out whether the site wants an acknowledgment that it supplied the resource. Copyright laws apply on the Internet, just as they do elsewhere. Besides, acknowledging someone else's contribution to your work is good manners. Incidentally, be very wary of using obviously copyrighted images, such as cartoon figures. If you put a Disney character on your page, for example, you're asking for trouble.

After you obtain the image, you can make it into your background. FrontPage does this by treating the image like a tile and laying enough identical tiles to cover everything in sight. To put in the image, use the following steps:

1. Choose File, Properties to open the Page Properties dialog box. Click the Background sheet tab and mark the Background Image check box.

2. Click the Browse button. The Select Background Picture dialog box appears. Because the dialog box is identical to the Picture dialog box (except for its title) you already know how to use it.

3. Select the name of the background file and return to the Background sheet by choosing OK or Open, depending on context. Choose OK again and the image tiles across the page to produce your background (see figure 5.16).

Figure 5.16
You can tile an image to produce a background for the main elements of your page. This background is only for illustration purposes; it would be very distracting on a real page.

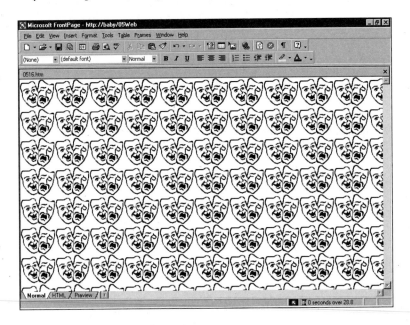

Tip #34

A real time saver is using the Get Background and Colors from Page check box in the Background sheet of the Page Properties dialog box. This copies all the color choices and the background image from another page into the current one. It's very handy for keeping your pages' appearance consistent.

Remember that using a background image from another site puts your page's appearance at someone else's mercy. If the site's URL changes or its Webmaster deletes the image file, you'll lose your background. You're better off downloading the image and storing it locally. (But remember copyright!)

Tip #35

When you use a background image, also set the page's background color so that it's close to the predominant hue of the image. Why? So that a browser running with images turned off (which includes background images) displays your page similar to its intended appearance.

USING WATERMARKED BACKGROUND IMAGES

In a browser, your background images scroll along with the foreground objects and text. Marking the Watermark check box on the Background sheet keeps the background image still, while the foreground material moves across it.

Tip #36	If your page has a background image, you can edit it quickly by choosing View, Toolbars, Picture without selecting a foreground image. When the toolbar appears, you can use it to edit the background image. Not all of the tools are available, but the essential ones are.

USING IMAGES WITH HYPERLINKS

With FrontPage, image-based hyperlinks are just as easy to make as text-based ones. Such images are frequently used as navigational controls within a site, as well as serving as links to remote locations.

CREATING IMAGE-BASED HYPERLINKS

If you know how to make a text hyperlink, you already know how to construct one from an image. Do the following:

1. Insert the image onto the page using any of the methods you learned earlier.
2. Click the image to select it and choose Insert, Hyperlink to open the Create Hyperlink dialog box.
3. Set up the link with any of the procedures you learned in Chapter 4, "Developing the Basic Page: Text, Lists, and Hyperlinks."

That's all there is to it! To edit the link, select the image and choose Insert, Hyperlink.

→ For details on creating and editing hyperlinks, **see** Chapter 4, "Developing the Basic Page: Text, Lists, and Hyperlinks," **p. 61**.

MAKING NAVIGATIONAL CONTROLS

The Web is a place in which people like to move around. Well-chosen navigational tools laid out in a useful way give your Web pages a professional gleam. (And, as stated before, trying to keep visitors at your site by making it hard for them to leave is counterproductive.) Buttons are the most common navigational symbols, and dozens of places on the Web offer these simple images for free-use downloading. Put them onto your page in an organized way, link them to their destinations, and they'll tie your site together so that it'll be a pleasure to visit.

Be consistent with button usage, though; a button that has function X on one page shouldn't have function Y on another. Always provide alternative text for them in case your visitor has images turned off or is using a text browser. Also consider putting a visible text label with each button. It makes life easier for your visitors, and they'll like you for it.

PART

II

CH

5

USING IMAGEMAPS TO MAKE GRAPHICAL HYPERLINKS

Creating an imagemap by hand-coding it in HTML can be a real headache. FrontPage's capability to help you make imagemaps and link them easily is among its most powerful features. The imagemaps it creates, by the way, are client-side. That is, the information about the map structure is embedded in the Web page that's downloaded to the browser client; the information does not reside on the server.

What is an imagemap? Functionally, it's a graphic that has hotspots in it; when a viewer clicks a hotspot, he is automatically sent to another location on the Web or in the current site. To put it another way, imagemaps are graphics with embedded hyperlinks. A good example is Yahoo's Yahooligans page at `http://www.yahooligans.com/` (see Figure 5.17).

Figure 5.17
An image with clearly defined clickable regions (such as the "Cool," "New," Club," and "Help" hotspots down the left side of the page) is a good way to approach imagemap design.

Clickable Regions ——

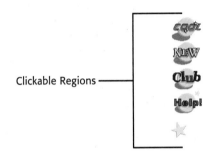

Because you're creating a Web site with its own character and needs, you probably will create or assemble the major imagemap graphics yourself. Before you start, though, think about what the graphic should look like, and especially remember that hotspots don't stand out as much in a browser window. This means you have to let people know where the hotspots are and what will happen if they click them.

The first thing to do is design the graphic so that it has obvious clickable areas. Often the best way to do this is to make those hotspot regions look like buttons, as in the example shown in Figure 5.17. Another thing to consider is whether the destination of the link is made clear by the hotspot. If it isn't, you should consider adding text to describe what will happen if someone follows the link. Alternatively, modify the image itself to make its destination clearer. Try hard to see the imagemap as if you were coming across it for the first time, and try even harder to imagine how it can be misunderstood. (A corollary to Murphy's Law says that if something can be misunderstood, it will be.)

Another thing: Don't jam too many hotspot links into one image. Small hotspots that are only a few pixels across are hard for users to point to, and an image with a dozen clickable regions can be confusing.

Finally, set up text links that duplicate the imagemap's hotspot destinations. This is for people who are running their browsers with images turned off.

Caution

> If your Internet Service Provider (ISP) doesn't have the FrontPage *server extensions (page 301)* installed on the server, your imagemaps probably will not work properly when you copy your web from your PC to the server. If that happens, go to FrontPage's Web Settings dialog box in the Tools menu. The Advanced tab gives some alternate imagemap styles; try Netscape. If this also gives problems or you're concerned about browsers that don't support Netscape-like behavior, contact your ISP administrator to discuss using the CERN or NCSA styles. Better yet, persuade your ISP to install the FrontPage server extensions!

CREATING AN IMAGEMAP

To make an imagemap, you need an image. It can be in any file format, although you should remember that GIF or JPEG are the formats recognized by all browsers without the need for plug-ins or helpers. Begin by inserting the image into the page. Select the image and use the following steps:

1. Decide whether you want the hotspot to be a rectangle, a circle, or a polygon. From the Picture toolbar, select the appropriate drawing tool button (refer to Figure 5.6 for button identification).

Note

> If you can't see the Picture toolbar, toggle it on by choosing View, Toolbars, Picture. When it appears in the toolbar area, drag it to the place you want it.

2. Put the cursor on the image. The cursor changes to a crayon.
3. Hold down the left mouse button and drag to get the outline you want. Then release the mouse button (the black rectangles on the outline are sizing handles). The Create Hyperlink dialog box appears.
4. Establish the link by using the techniques you learned in Chapter 4.

That's all you need to do. If you want to edit the link, select the image, click the hotspot, and choose Format, Properties.

Tip #37

> A quick way to edit an imagemap link is to right-click the hotspot and select Image Hotspot Properties from the shortcut menu.

The nature of imagemaps is to have more than one hotspot in the graphic. To get them to fit neatly, resize each hotspot by dragging its sizing handles or move it around by putting the mouse pointer on its border and dragging it.

DELETING A HOTSPOT

Click the image so that the hotspot borders appear. Click the hotspot you want to delete and either press the Delete key or choose Edit, Clear.

PART

II

CH

5

LINKING TO IMAGES

You now know how to link to pages, bookmarks, and remote locations. Linking to an image is pretty straightforward. Select the text, image, or hotspot you want for the link, and choose Insert, Hyperlink.

Now use the Create or Edit Hyperlink dialog boxes to find the name of the image to which you want to link. Complete the link and choose OK. When the link is clicked in a browser, the browser window clears and the image downloads and displays in that window. That is, the image isn't fitted into or overlaid on the page from which it was called.

USING THUMBNAILS

By now you might be somewhat paranoid about keeping your visitors waiting around for graphics to download, but attractive images are much of the appeal of a good Web site. How do you resolve this conflict between art and efficiency?

In two words: Use thumbnails. This is easy because of the Auto Thumbnail tool. To use it

1. Insert the full-sized graphic into the page and select it.
2. If the Picture toolbar is not visible, open it by choosing View, Toolbars, Picture. Click the Auto Thumbnail button (the third button from the left). FrontPage automatically reduces the size of the image and links it to the original in the original's current location.
3. Save the page. You'll see the Save Embedded Files dialog box with a default name for the thumbnail image. Use the techniques you learned earlier to save the thumbnail to your satisfaction. When you test the page, clicking the thumbnail should display the full size graphic in its own browser window.

Note that if the image width (in pixels) is already smaller than the pixel width pre-set for the thumbnail, nothing will happen. The default width is 100 pixels, but you can change this.

To do so, choose Tools, Page Options, and select the Auto Thumbnail sheet. Here you can customize the size and appearance of the thumbnail image. For example, if you don't want a border around the thumbnail, you can specify this.

The results of using thumbnails can be significant: At the default settings, a GIF that is 340×500 pixels in 256 colors reduces from a file size of 168KB to 31KB. It downloads (all other things being equal) in less than a fifth of the time the original took.

Thumbnails are also good audience psychology; your visitors can judge from the smaller image whether they want to look at the big one, and they won't feel that you've inflicted a finger-drumming wait on them if they choose to download the original. If you have a lot of images to present, you can put a whole gallery of thumbnails on a page and let your visitors wander among them.

The thumbnails should be kept in the images folder. Where you keep the full size pictures is up to you, but remember that if the images are not on your own site, they can disappear without warning.

MAKING THE MOST OF IMAGE FILE FORMATS

Web images are almost all JPEG or GIF files, with the balance at the moment leaning heavily toward the GIF format. You can manipulate these formats to a limited degree with the tools FrontPage gives you (see Figure 5.18). You do this to control image quality and influence download speed.

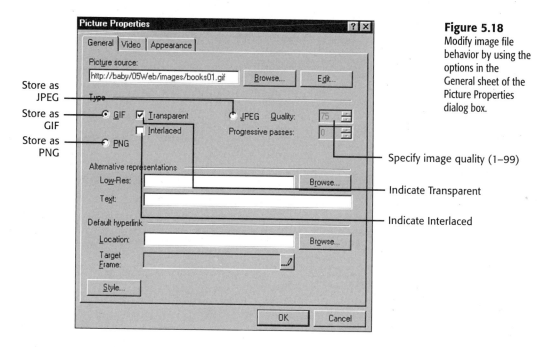

Store as JPEG

Store as GIF

Store as PNG

Figure 5.18
Modify image file behavior by using the options in the General sheet of the Picture Properties dialog box.

Specify image quality (1–99)

Indicate Transparent

Indicate Interlaced

CONVERTING IMAGE FILE FORMATS

When you insert an image, FrontPage checks to see whether it's GIF or JPEG. If it is neither GIF nor JPEG and it is 256 colors or less, FrontPage automatically converts it to GIF; if it is more than 256 colors, it is converted to JPEG.

If you want to store a file in the other formats, mark the appropriate check box for GIF, PNG or JPEG. Then, when you save the page the image converts. If you go from GIF to JPEG, you also get a chance to adjust the quality of the stored JPEG image by typing a number from 1 to 99 in the Quality box (75 is the default). With the best quality (99), you get the lowest file compression and slowest downloading; with the lowest quality (1), you get the highest file compression and the fastest downloading. There's no free lunch, is there?

PART

II

CH

5

Caution

> After you set the Quality setting and save the image, you can't change that setting again, even if you delete the image and reinsert it from the saved page. So if you're experimenting, keep a backup!

Tip #38

> People sometimes link to images on other servers so that they won't have to store many large images on their own Web host. If your Internet Service Provider limits the disk space you can use for your web, this might be the only thing you can do to get the image resources you want.

USING INTERLACED OR PROGRESSIVE IMAGES FOR SPEED

A browser that supports interlaced GIF images or progressive JPEG images builds such an image in multiple passes, with the picture becoming clearer with each pass. On the first pass, the text and links of the page are also displayed so that the viewer can start reading (or clicking a link) without waiting for the image to complete. Again, it's all in the interest of speed.

You can create an interlaced GIF from a non-interlaced one by marking the Interlaced check box in the Picture Properties dialog box. When the page is saved, the image stores as an interlaced GIF. If you want to produce your own interlaced GIFs, Image Composer saves its GIF files in this format.

The analogous JPEG file treatment is to make it a progressive JPEG. This also downloads the image in a series of passes, and you can specify the number of passes in the Progressive Passes text box. Interlaced GIFs download in four passes.

USING LOW RES FOR SPEED

Another tool in your speed-up kit is the Low Res (low resolution) option. To employ this, first use a graphics program to make a lower-resolution version of the original image, and then save that graphic to your images folder. This version should be smaller than the original; a common trick to achieve this is to change it to black and white.

When you want to use the Low Res option, follow these steps:

1. Select the original, full-resolution image and go to the General sheet of the Picture Properties dialog box.
2. Insert the name of the low-resolution image in the Low-Res box in the Alternative Representations section (the Browse button is handy here).
3. Choose OK.

Now when someone goes to the page, her browser loads the low-resolution image and the page text first; only after that does the browser go back and display the high-resolution version of the image. This speeds things up. Notice that you don't have to do any linking here, as you do with the thumbnail technique. The HTML generated by FrontPage takes care of everything for you.

MULTIMEDIA

Multimedia has become much more common on the Web during the past two years, for example the effects offered by use of Macromedia Shockwave files. These effects certainly can increase page appeal, but they're time consuming to download and active content such as JavaScript, and ActiveX present security questions. Keep these factors in mind when you're deciding which (if any) special effects to add to a page.

UNDERSTANDING AND USING SOUND

Sound does have its drawbacks. If you're going to use it, keep it under control and remember that not everyone has the same audio tastes that you do. Actually, many people still think sound is a gimmick, and a fairly useless one at that. This will change when the Web becomes a fully powered information delivery system with short downloads and solid, informative audio content, but that time isn't here yet.

A bit of well chosen and unobtrusive sound can indeed enhance your page, at least for people who have recent browsers that handle audio. (Not everybody has a sound card installed, either, although that's changing fast.) Probably the best design advice is this: Don't make the sound clip too loud and don't loop it and loop it and loop it unless it is a very soft, unobtrusive background noise.

From the technical point of view, the worst problem with sound is that even a few seconds' worth of audio takes a significant time to download; a minute or two of it, depending on the file format and quality, produces downloads in the multi-megabyte range. As a rule of thumb, keep audio clips short enough to make files sizes of 20KB or less. Some audio file types do allow compression, which helps, although there's always the no-free-lunch factor—the higher the compression, the smaller the file, but the worse the quality. These compression formats are as follows:

- AIFF-C (6:1 compression)   The acronym stands for Apple Audio Interchange File Format, and the C indicates the extended version that supports compression (plain AIFF doesn't). The format produces stereo sound at high fidelity and is usually found on Macintosh platforms. The DOS/Windows file extension is AIF, which doesn't actually distinguish these files from the uncompressed version of the format, AIFF.

- MPEG (up to 20:1 compression)   This format, which is the international standard for both video and audio compression, was designed by the Moving Pictures Expert Group, hence MPEG. It provides stereo sound at high quality, and the files can be quite a lot smaller than equivalent ones in uncompressed formats. The DOS/Windows file extensions are usually MPG or MP2.

The uncompressed formats are

- AIFF   It's essentially the same as AIFF-C (just mentioned) except without the compression. For DOS/Windows, the extension is also AIF.
- AU   This is from Sun Microsystems and is very common on the Web. It's as good as telephone quality, which makes it a reasonable choice for sound bites that are mostly speech. The DOS/Windows extension is AU.
- SND   This is a plain vanilla sound format that supports both stereo and mono. The DOS/Windows extension is SND.
- WAV   This is a Microsoft format and another common one. It's useful for both stereo and mono, and the quality is good. The DOS/Windows file extension is WAV.
- MIDI   This Musical Instruments Digital Interface isn't actually a file format; instead, it's a file of instructions that are sent to an electronic sound synthesizer to tell it what to play and how to play it. The computer receiving the file must have a MIDI player for the sound to be heard. MIDI files do, however, enable complex sounds to be stored in relatively small files. The DOS/Windows file extension is MID.

UNDERSTANDING STREAMING AUDIO (AND VIDEO)

Streaming audio technology is an attempt to reduce the problem of long download times of audio files (streaming video uses the same techniques, so what is said here applies to it as well).

The basic principle is simple. In non-streamed audio and video, the original file must be entirely downloaded to a temporary file on the user's machine. Only when the download is complete can he start the appropriate player and see or hear the file. In streamed media, however, a special media player associated with the browser takes the data stream as it reaches the user's machine and starts playing the file before the complete file is delivered. If the user's connection to his ISP is reasonably fast, he might notice no interruptions at all in the playback, although a slow connection will cause the playback to proceed in bursts.

The most common streaming audio/video software is available from RealAudio (at http://www.real.com). The company provides inexpensive conversion software for changing standard video or audio files to streaming format. Once converted, the files can be placed on your Web site and can be heard or viewed by any user whose machine has a compatible player installed. RealAudio makes a free, downloadable version of its streaming player available on its site. The Microsoft Windows Media Player, available from Microsoft's free download site, will also play back most streaming media formats.

ADDING BACKGROUND AUDIO TO YOUR PAGE

Background audio is a sound file that plays automatically when someone downloads a page, assuming the person's browser supports the feature. Adding background sound is fairly simple in HTML, but FrontPage makes the task even easier. Do the following:

1. Go to the page that is to have the sound with it. Choose File, Properties. The Page Properties dialog box appears.

2. Choose the General tab and click the Browse button to open the Background Sound dialog box. Except for the dialog box title, this is the standard file location and opening dialog box used by FrontPage.

3. Locate and open the file; its URL appears in the Location dialog box of the Background Sound section of the Page Properties dialog box.

4. Type the number of repetitions into the Loop box to make the sound repeat; to keep it going, mark the Forever check box (and remember that forever is a long time).

5. Choose OK. The background audio is now inserted into the page. An inconvenience in the way FrontPage handles this is that there's no indication in the editor workspace that a background sound is embedded in the page.

Note

The <LOOPDELAY> attribute, which sets a delay between repeats of the sound file, is not directly implemented in FrontPage. What you must do, if you want the delay, is to use HTML mode to manually add the attribute. For example:

```
<BGSOUND SRC = "SOUND.WAV" LOOP = 10 LOOPDELAY=30>
```

Internet Explorer does not support the LOOPDELAY tag, so there won't be a pause between repeats.

Now test the page in Internet Explorer 3.0 or above, which support the HTML BGSOUND tag (that's what FrontPage uses to insert this type of audio). Netscape 3.0 and later require Java applets to play background sound.

REMOVING BACKGROUND AUDIO

To get rid of audio in the background, open the General sheet of the Page Properties dialog box and delete the filename from the Location box in the Background Sound section. Choose OK and the audio is gone.

LINKING TO A SOUND FILE

Set this up as you would any other link, with the target of the link being the desired sound file. When visitors click the link, assuming their browser has the plug-in or helper application that plays the file format, they'll hear the playback of the file (see Figure 5.19). Internet Explorer 3 and higher, as previously noted, support the BGSOUND tag, so they don't need plug-ins or helpers.

Figure 5.19
Netscape's WAV player plays back a sound file when the link is clicked.

Music

UNDERSTANDING AND USING VIDEO

The basic principle of adding video clips to a page is the same as adding audio clips. Video comes in files of various formats, but they all have one thing in common: they're big. Even with heavy compression and in a small playback window, a minute of video requires megabytes of data. When linking to such a file, you should be sure to indicate how big it is so that people can decide for themselves whether they want to wait for it to download.

The major video formats on the Web now are MPEG Levels 1 and 2, Apple's Quicktime, and Microsoft's AVI. All these offer video compression, the highest ratio being that of the two MPEG formats, which offer good results at ratios even of 20:1.

Whatever scheme is used, though, all video must play back at 30 images (or frames) per second for full motion effects. The larger the images, the more processing power is required of the playback machine, the more storage space the file requires, and the longer the download time. Because of this, full screen video is uncommon on the Web. If you're selecting videos or making your own, remember that smaller is faster in every respect, even when you're working with streaming video. It's a matter of the inverse-square law: An image at 320×240 pixels (which is still pretty big) is one-fourth the size of an image at 640×480.

USING INLINE VIDEO

We owe this development to Microsoft, and so far only Internet Explorer 3.0 and higher support this method of displaying AVI video clips. It's an alternative to the Netscape method of having visitors play back a clip by using the plug-in application installed in their browsers. All the factors of file size and playback image size apply, however; inline video doesn't gain you anything in these respects. Of course, the viewer must be using a browser that supports the method.

The engaging part of inline images is that, once downloaded, they can remain on a page until they are needed. They perform only when called on, which makes them less distracting than infinite-loop GIF animations.

To install an AVI clip into a page, do the following:

1. Choose Insert, Picture, Video. The Video dialog box appears with the familiar file location and selection dialog box.

2. Use the dialog box to find the video file you want and choose Open to return to the page. FrontPage inserts a placeholder to show where the clip will appear.

3. Save the page and use Preview mode or the Preview in Browser command to test the clip in Internet Explorer. (If it's a new file, you'll get the Save Embedded File dialog box).

   As soon as the browser opens, the playback begins and runs until it ends.

4. Click anywhere in the picture to restart; to stop or restart part way through, click in the picture.

You can control the behavior of the clip by using the Picture Properties dialog box. To do this, select the still image by clicking it and choose Format, Properties. When the Picture Properties dialog box opens, choose the Video tab (see Figure 5.20).

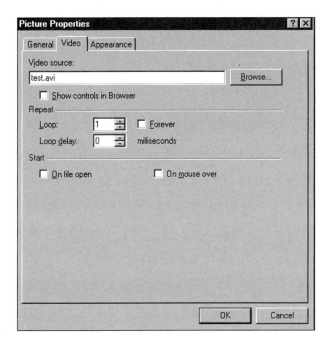

Figure 5.20
You can adjust characteristics of the video playback such as looping and display of controls.

The dialog enables you to browse for another video file and provides more viewer control of the clip, as follows:

- Show Controls in Browser puts a set of simple stop-go playback controls onscreen with the clip.
- Loop and Forever determine how many times the playback of the clip repeats.
- Loop Delay determines the time interval between repeated playbacks.
- On File Open tells the browser to start playing as soon as the clip file loads.
- On Mouse Over, if checked when On File Open is unchecked, halts playback except when the mouse pointer is on top of the image.
- On Mouse Over and On File Open, if both checked, cause the playback to run to completion as soon as the file loads, and then wait until the mouse pointer is on top of it before it runs again.

INLINE VIDEO WITH BROWSERS THAT DON'T SUPPORT IT

Inline videos work for people who are using Internet Explorer, but if you previewed the video-equipped page in Netscape, you see an ugly, blank rectangle where the clip resides.

In this case, you need to put a plain graphic in to provide for browsers that don't handle inline images. To do this, return to the Picture Properties dialog box and select the General sheet (see Figure 5.21).

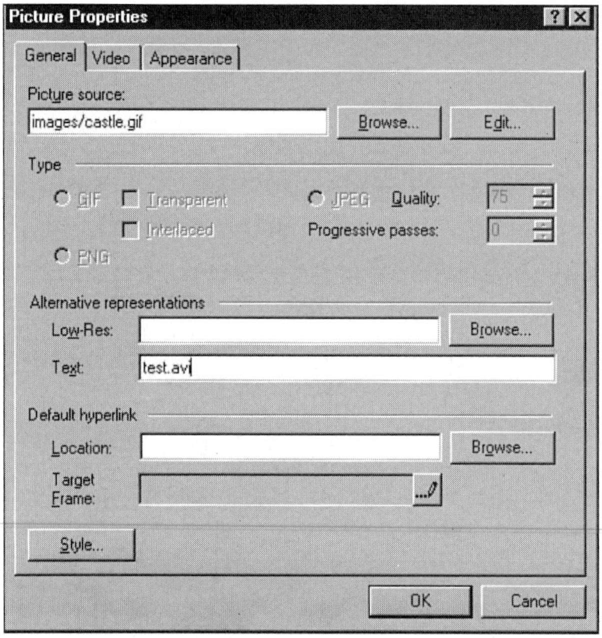

Figure 5.21
Use the Picture
Properties dialog box
to insert a substitute
for a video clip.

Use the Browse button (the one next to the Image Source box) to locate a GIF or JPEG file to use as the substitute and choose OK. From now on, non-Internet Explorer browsers will display the graphic instead of the empty box, while IE browsers automatically play the clip.

LINKING TO A VIDEO CLIP

That's one problem solved, but what about people who don't use Internet Explorer but who do want to see the clip? The answer is to give them a link so that their browser's plug-ins can play it for them. This assumes they know about the clip; your substitute graphic should tell them that it's available.

You might think it is efficient to make the substitute image itself into the link. This seems like a good idea at first, but it has a major pitfall: IE-equipped users who click the clip to stop or start it will not only do that, they'll also activate the link! This gives them a second playback of the clip in an AVI player window. Good as the clip might be, this is probably too much of a good thing.

So, make the link from some nearby text or a clearly labeled graphic. Any file you use for inline video should be reasonably fast to load, but it's polite to indicate the file size with the link, anyway.

Finally, you can include non-inline clips in your pages by setting up a link to them so that they can be played back in a browser. As just mentioned, non-AVI clips must be displayed that way because only AVI can be used for inline video.

DESIGNING FOR ANIMATED GIFs

Animated GIFs have proliferated on the Web for the past year or two. Although they can add vivacity to a page—some are attractively whimsical—they can also distract from the content. There's been some heated debate over their use, and a few basic principles are emerging, as follows:

- Don't overuse them. One per screen is enough, if not more than enough.
- Text is almost always where information is located. Keep a balance between moving images and static words, and remember that motion always draws the attention.
- Because of the preceding point, don't place animations too close to highly important text.
- Consider running the animation sequence once or twice and then stopping it.
- Don't flash; change the animation slowly.
- When a design decision is in doubt, go for simplicity rather than complication.

MAKING AN ANIMATED GIF

An animated GIF works on the essential principle of any animation: a series of slightly differing images that, when viewed in quick succession, give the impression of movement. There is no GIF animator included with FrontPage itself. However, at the time of writing Microsoft had indicated that Image Composer 1.5 would ship with the standalone version of FrontPage 2000, and Image Composer includes the Microsoft GIF animator in its Tools menu. If FrontPage 2000 is purchased as part of the Office 2000 suite, the graphic package will be PhotoDraw 2000, which has no GIF animator. There are other sources for GIF animation packages on the Web; one you might try is GIF Construction Set at http://www.mindworkshop.com/alchemy/gifcon.html.

Making these little creatures is more complex than their appearance suggests, and producing good ones is a lot of work. Still they're fun, and a clever one properly used can catch a new visitor's attention in a way that little else can.

TROUBLESHOOTING

Problems with text wrapping around images will occur if you use the Right alignment option from the Paragraph dialog box to position an image at the right margin, and then try to get text to wrap around it.

Why is this? Well, you might understandably think that the Left and Right alignment options in the Paragraph Properties dialog box are the same as the Left and Right alignment options in the Picture Properties dialog box. However they aren't, although they use exactly the same wording. The difference is that the paragraph alignments don't allow text wrapping; they merely position the image. For text wrapping you must use the floating alignments available in the Picture Properties dialog.

Incidentally, don't apply mixed Picture Properties alignments and Paragraph Format alignments to the same image. A graphic with a Right paragraph alignment and a Right Picture Properties alignment might behave unpredictably. There's no practical reason to mix the alignment types, anyway.

DESIGNERS CORNER

Whole libraries are dedicated to graphic design, and many of these principles are applicable to the design of Web pages as well. The most important principle is likely this one: Think about what you want to do before you do it.

For example, does a particular page absolutely depend on graphics to achieve its purpose? For example, if the page examines a particular work of a particular painter, the answer is almost certainly yes, and the work must be made accessible to the visitor. But does that mean you have to reproduce a large graphic of the work on that page? No, it doesn't, and likely you should not do so—the download time for the page might be very long. Instead, plan to put a thumbnail of the work on the page and link it to a file containing the larger image.

More commonly, graphics are enhancements to a page, helping it to achieve its goals rather than actually being that goal. In this context, remember that you should be able to identify a purpose for every page on your site. Graphic elements should strengthen this purpose and help focus it. If they distract the visitor from the real goals of the page, they are diffusing the page's meaning and lessening its worth. Consequently, just as you can identify the reason for a page to exist, you should be able to identify a reason for the inclusion of each graphic element on that page.

CHAPTER 6

WORKING WITH THEMES

In this chapter

by Neil Randall

ADDING THEMES TO A SITE, TO A PAGE, OR TO PAGES

You have three options for choosing which of your Web pages you want to apply themes to. The first and most obvious choice is to select a uniform theme for your entire site, so that all pages in the site have an identical graphic appearance. You needn't necessarily go that far; you can also add a theme to an individual page inside the site, or to a selection of individual pages. It all depends how totally consistent you want to be.

The procedure is essentially the same no matter how many pages you choose. In all cases, you need to call up the Themes dialog box by selecting Theme from the Format menu. Depending on what you want to do, the process is slightly different:

- To add a theme to an individual page, click the document title in any of FrontPage's views and select Format, Theme. This opens the Theme dialog box, with the Selected Page(s) radio button automatically chosen. You can opt to add the theme to the entire web by clicking the All Pages dialog box instead.

- To add a theme to a selection of pages, go into the Folders view (no other view lets you do this), select the pages as you would any other multiple document selection in Windows, and then select Format, Theme. This opens the Theme dialog box, with the Selected Page(s) radio button automatically chosen. You can opt to add the theme to the entire web by clicking the All Pages dialog box instead.

- There are two possibilities to add a theme to an entire site. The first is to click the Reports, Navigation, or Tasks view and select Format, Theme. The second is to click the Page, Folders, or Hyperlinks view and select the site name at the top of the folder list; then select Format, Theme. In either case, the Theme dialog box opens, with the All Pages radio button automatically selected and the Selected Pages dialog box unavailable.

In other words, you can begin adding a theme to a page (or selection of pages) and decide at that time to add the theme to the entire site; the reverse, however, is not the case.

No matter which of the three themes methods you use, selecting Format, Theme brings up the Themes dialog box. As seen in Figure 6.1, this large dialog box consists of three main sections. The options area runs down the left side, while the modifications area is along the bottom, with buttons for modification and for accepting changes. The largest area, composing the right three-quarters of the screen, is the theme sample area. It's actually called Sample of Theme, but since that's a clumsy name to put into decent sentences, it's given this less clumsy new one.

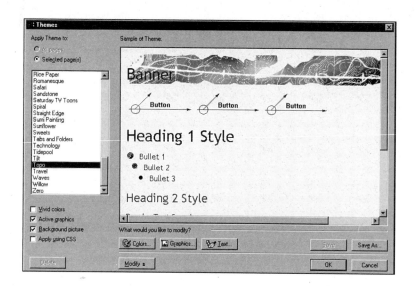

Figure 6.1
Clicking the Modify button in the Themes dialog box brings up the three button choices in the What Would You Like to Modify? area.

THEME SAMPLE AREA

The theme sample area does nothing more than show you what the theme looks like. Here you can see which FrontPage document elements the theme determines. These include banners, navigation buttons, heading styles, bulleted lists, and the three types of hyperlink: regular, followed, and active. (These elements are covered in detail in their relevant chapters in this book.) As you make selections in the options or the actions area, the appearance of all these elements changes accordingly.

The theme sample area functions simply as a noninteractive viewing area no matter which Themes dialog box features you are working with. For example, when you choose any of the three modification choices (see "Modifications Area" in this chapter), the theme sample area reappears, changing as you make any changes to the theme itself.

OPTIONS AREA

The options area, down the left side of the screen, lets you select a theme and alter it to a degree. The changes you make are reflected in the theme sample area.

The topmost options contain the radio buttons for applying a theme to individual pages or the entire site. The themes list is below this. One of these choices is No Theme, which is the one to select if you don't want a theme at all. For the rest, you need only click a theme name; the graphical elements of that elements appear in the theme sample area.

The topmost theme shows as being the default theme. Each of the FrontPage web templates contains a default theme (some contain no theme), and the name of this theme shows as the default in the Themes dialog box. In other words, the default theme depends on the web template chosen when the web is created. To change the theme for that particular web, simply click another and apply it to all pages. This won't change the default for the template itself, which can't be changed.

Tip #39

When you first launch FrontPage, not all themes are installed. You will see an item in the themes list called Install Additional Themes. To give yourself more choices, put your FrontPage 2000 or Office 2000 CD-ROM in the drive and click this item. FrontPage walks you through the installation process.

There are four check boxes below the themes list. The Vivid Colors option provides a richer and brighter set of theme colors, while the Active Graphics option converts the current buttons and bullets into Dynamic HTML elements that supports *DHTML formatting (page 74)*. Background Image uses a graphic for the background if selected, a solid color if selected. Each theme has a default for these, which can be altered through the Modify procedure.

Caution

Once you have chosen a theme for a document, whether as an individual page or by assigning a theme to the entire web, the only two ways to change the background image for that document are by modifying the entire theme, or by opening the Themes dialog box for that page only, selecting No Theme, returning to the page, and then selecting Format, Background.

The final option, Apply Theme Using CSS, lets you establish the theme on your site or individual page as a style using the cascading style sheet standard. The advantage of this is a standardization of code; the disadvantage is that older browsers cannot handle CSS, and older versions of those that do handle CSS often handle them differently.

MODIFICATIONS AREA

There are three buttons along the bottom of the Themes dialog box: Cancel, OK, and Modify. The Cancel button takes you out of the dialog box at any time, without implementing any changes you might have made. The OK button also closes the dialog box, but implements all the changes.

Caution

Once you've clicked OK, you can't use the Edit, Undo command to reverse the action. You must reopen the Themes dialog box and make the changes manually.

The third button, Modify, is the most complex choice of the three. Clicking this yields five additional buttons. Colors lets you change the theme's colors, Graphics lets you alter the graphical components for the theme, and Styles lets you modify the font styles for the theme. Save lets you save changes to the theme, while Save As, a much safer alternative, lets you save your modified theme under a different name, preserving the original theme.

MODIFYING THEME COLORS

Clicking the Colors button yields the Modify Theme dialog box shown in Figure 6.2.

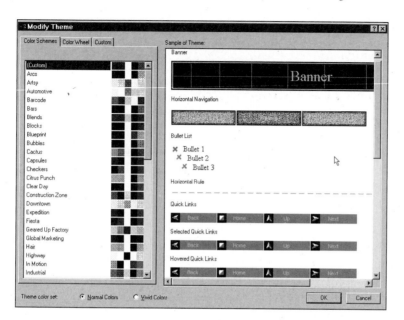

Figure 6.2
The three tabs at the top left of the Modify Theme dialog box give you extensive control over the theme's colors.

From here you can control the colors for each of the current theme's elements. The colors will change in the theme sample area to the right when you click any of the color schemes shown in the list of color sets along the left hand side of the dialog box. Click Vivid Colors at the bottom of the pages to reveal richer colors. Once you've chosen the color scheme, you can click OK to return to the main Themes dialog box, or you can click one of the two remaining tabs at the top left of the dialog box.

The Color Wheel tab contains a color wheel from which you can precisely choose colors. Note, however, that selecting from the wheel changes all colors in the scheme, not specific colors. The scheme's colors are reflected in the five-color bar opposite Colors in This Scheme. You can adjust the brightness of the colors with the Brightness slide. Again, the changes are reflected in the theme sample area.

The final tab, Custom, lets you change the colors of the theme's individual elements. Everything from hyperlink colors to banner colors can be altered via this tab, which gives you a pull-down item list from which to choose the element to alter and a pull-down color palette to select the color for that component.

If you don't like any of the available colors, click More Colors from the Color list; you'll see the Colors dialog box shown in Figure 6.3. Click the Select button and move the resulting eyedropper icon to a specific hexagon on the color palette. Customize the color by clicking the Custom button and choosing your desired color.

PART

II

CH

6

Tip #40

The Value and Name fields of the Colors dialog box show the hexadecimal value and the name (if applicable) assigned to that value. You can use these values directly in HTML code to specify colors.

Figure 6.3
The Colors dialog box lets you establish precise colors for specific theme elements.

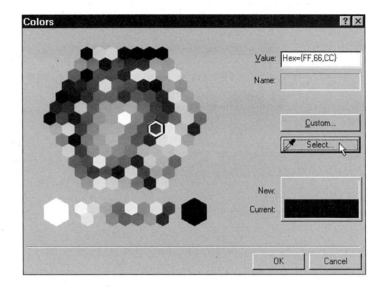

MODIFYING THEME GRAPHICS

Clicking the Graphics button on the main Themes dialog box yields the Modify Themes dialog box. Here, you can adjust the graphics and fonts for the current theme. Although this dialog box seems simplistic at first, with the Image tab offering only a drop-down list for the item to be modified and a Name field for the file to be applied to that item—but clicking the drop-down list lets you choose precisely which theme element you want to change, and the Browse button lets you choose exactly which graphic you want associated with that element. It's quite powerful.

Each of the theme elements in the item drop-down list corresponds to the same element named in the theme sample area. Select the item and choose a new graphic for that item (from your hard disk or from a remote page on the Web). If you have that theme spread across the entire site, all instances of that element will become associated with the new image file.

This dialog box's Font tab, shown in Figure 6.4, works similarly, although it's more complex. Select the item for which you want to modify the associated font from the Item field. The current font shows in the Font field above the Font list, while the current attributes of that font—style, size, horizontal alignment, and vertical alignment—appear in their respective fields to the right of the Font list. Click whatever font you prefer, as well as the attributes you want to give it, to alter the choice for that screen item.

When you've finished the graphics alterations, click OK to implement the changes. You are returned to the main Themes dialog box.

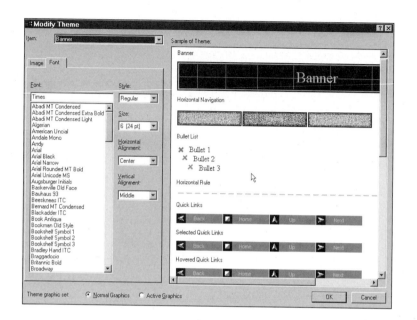

Figure 6.4
You can change the size and alignment of the font associated with each screen element from this dialog box.

MODIFYING HTML STYLES

Clicking the Styles button from the main Themes dialog box brings up a third Modify Theme dialog box, this one pertaining to HTML styles. The Item field displays the major HTML style choices: Body and Heading 1 through Heading 6. These correspond to the `<body></body>` HTML container as well as the six heading containers, `<h1></h1>` through `<h6></h6>`. Select the item you want to change and then click the font you want to use for that item.

For full power with this dialog box as well as to change the style for additional HTML tags and containers, click the More Styles button at the bottom left. This yields the Style menu, also available through FrontPage's Format menu. Once you have finished altering HTML styles, click OK to return to the main Themes dialog box.

SAVING MODIFIED THEMES

You can continue modifying a theme until you are ready. At that point, you must click OK on the main Themes dialog box to have them take effect in the selected document(s) or the current web. If you have made any changes at all, clicking OK displays a dialog box that asks if you want to save the current theme. If you click OK, the defaults for that theme will be overwritten. You can avoid this by first clicking Save on the main Themes dialog box and then clicking OK.

PART
II

CH
6

If you don't want to alter the existing theme, however, click the Save As button instead of the Save button. This yields the Save Theme dialog box, in which you can give the theme a new name and save it to your hard disk. The theme now appears in the themes list in the main Themes dialog box.

TROUBLESHOOTING

If you set up a theme you feel is perfect, but some visitors comment on your site in a way that tells you they don't see the theme, remember this point. All users can change features such as background images and hyperlink colors through the preferences or options menus of their browsers. You have no control over this, although most users are unlikely to change these options at all. Still, it's worth remembering.

You can change hyperlink colors through the Themes dialog box. If you do so, test your web on as many different resolutions and color settings as you can. If a user has a system that works in 800×600 with 16 colors, subtle difference in hyperlink colors simply won't show up—and what if they do? Many people are colorblind.

DESIGNERS CORNER

The first thing to realize about themes is their strengths and their weaknesses. They can be an enormous help in getting a design started, but they can also establish limits in your mind about how the design can proceed. Once you have a theme in place, it's very difficult to think of your web any other way. What can happen so easily is that you let the theme dictate the way you design the information and the interfaces for the web. While that can work fine for a personal web, you don't want it to happen with a web that's for your organization. Those webs need designs tailored to the organization's image and offerings.

For these reasons, you should become familiar with what themes do by building a few sample Corporate Presence and Discussion webs. These webs provide a wizard that, among many other things, lets you decide on a theme for that web. As soon as you know how they work, use one of these samples as a basis for modifying themes using the modification features on the Themes dialog box. Then, create a web with no theme and add individual themes to the individual pages, modifying all of them to achieve some design effect (navigation bar, background image, and so on).

The idea behind all of this is to keep yourself thinking of themes as a starting point, not as a finished design element. In other words, treat them as a helpful tool, but not as a restriction to your own sense of design. The problem with them is that they're so helpful that they can easily become relied upon, and that's not the idea behind them.

Another point to understand themes is that the Themes dialog box lets you decide whether to have the style applied according to the cascading style sheets (CSS) specification maintained by the W3C. If you do not select this option, you might have a problem with visitors who do not use the latest versions of Internet Explorer or Netscape Navigator. To ensure compatibility with older browsers, check the Apply Using CSS box in the bottom-left corner of the dialog box. Doing so creates a CSS file for your web; every time you modify the theme for that web, FrontPage automatically writes the changes into the CSS file.

Furthermore, you can control how much CSS compatibility you want to preserve. On the Page Options menu (available on the Tools menu) you can click the Compatibility tab and select the CSS 1.0 (formatting) and CSS 2.0 (positioning) options. By default, both are checked. As their labels suggest, CSS 1.0 mostly provides formatting instructions for the style, while CSS 2.0 handles positioning on the page. By deselecting one of them, you give control for the specific features to FrontPage. Hence, you depend to a certain extent on what browser your visitors are using. The choice is yours.

CHAPTER 7

USING ACTIVE ELEMENTS, SHARED BORDERS, AND NAVIGATION BARS

In this chapter

by Dennis Jones

UNDERSTANDING FRONTPAGE COMPONENTS

FrontPage components (Microsoft used to call them WebBots, but has settled on the new label) are a key part of FrontPage because they automate certain procedures that other web authoring tools require you to hand code in HTML or in a scripting language. FrontPage puts several different kinds of components at your disposal.

Note

> The term *WebBot* is still around, but if you insert a component into the page and inspect the HTML for that component, you'll see the word webbot within that HTML.

What exactly is a *component*? Briefly, it represents a chunk of programming that gets embedded into a page's HTML code when you insert the component. Depending on the component, the program it represents executes when one of the following occurs:

- The author saves the page.
- A visitor to the site accesses the page.
- The visitor clicks an interactive portion of the page, such as the Submit button, for a form.

You use the Insert, Component menu to put FrontPage components into a page (with two exceptions: the comment and the timestamp, which you look at a little later in this chapter). This chapter examines them in order of appearance on the menu.

Caution

> FrontPage components require a server-based Web to function. They will not work in a disk-based Web (page 24). Furthermore, the server must have the FrontPage 2000 extensions installed for the components to function. In addition to this, there are certain features that are only visible to users of Internet Explorer 4.0 and later.

USING THE BANNER AD MANAGER

This component uses a list of images and displays each for a preset number of seconds. It then switches to the next image and the next, until it is finished with the list. It then starts again from the beginning. As its name suggests, the *Banner Ad Manager* is designed for advertising, but your imagination can no doubt come up with other uses. Because it's a Java applet, the Ad Manager works properly in Netscape 3 and later, as well as in IE 3 and later.

Before placing the banner on the page, prepare the images it will use and store them in a suitable folder. Make a note of the pixel height of the tallest ad and the pixel width of the widest ad in order to determine the largest dimension required for the banner. For best results, all the images should be close to the same size.

Choose Insert, Component, Banner Ad Manager to open the Banner Ad Manager Properties dialog box (see Figure 7.1).

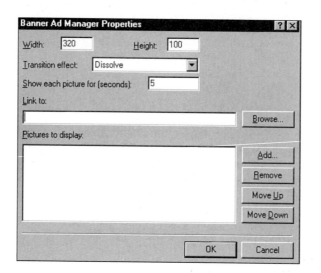

Figure 7.1
The Banner Ad Manager Properties dialog box gives you extensive control over the appearance and behavior of advertisements.

Follow these steps to set up the rotating ads:

1. Type the width of the widest image and the height of the tallest image into the appropriate text boxes. Images that are narrower or shorter than these values display on a neutral background in a window sized with these values. An image bigger than the maximums is cut off.

2. Use the transition effect drop-down list box to select the kind of effect you want for the transition between the images. You have a choice of Dissolve, Horizontal, or Vertical blinds, Box In or Out, and None.

3. Use the Show Each Image For text box to specify how long, in seconds, the ad should display.

4. Use the Link To text box to set up the URL to which the ad will point. If users click the ad, they are taken to that URL.

5. Click the Add button to specify the images that are to rotate through the banner. This opens the standard FrontPage file location and selection dialog box. Use it to select images from the Clip Art Gallery, your local system, or the World Wide Web. After you've selected the images, the URLs or path names appear in the Images to Display dialog box.

6. Select the image you want to move and click the Move Up or Move Down buttons to rearrange the order in which the images cycle. Click the Remove button to delete an image from the display.

7. Choose OK when you're finished. Assuming you are in Normal mode, the first image of the image list appears on the page. If you click it, sizing handles will appear at the boundaries of the banner area. In Preview, a gray placeholder will appear around the image to show where the banner is.

When you preview the banner in a browser, you'll see the images appear and vanish according to the specified effects and duration. The banner works in IE 4 and later and in Netscape 4 and later.

Caution

The Banner Ad applet will not work unless its images are stored in the current web. If you reference an image for the applet and that image is not in the current web, you will get the Save Embedded Files dialog box when you save the page. Make sure you save the image file to a folder in the current web; in other words, don't use the Set Action button to force the image reference to remain external to the web.

USING THE HIT COUNTER

Hit counters in various formats are in almost every Web site—at least those that want a public display of how many times visitors have dropped by. To deploy FrontPage's counter, choose Insert, Components, Hit Counter to open the Hit Counter Properties dialog box (see Figure 7.2).

Figure 7.2
The hit counter is an easily placed module for tracking visits.

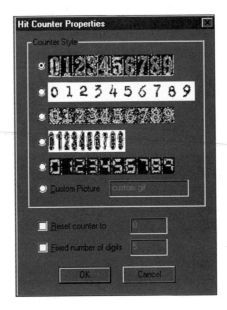

You can choose from five different display formats or choose a custom GIF of your own design. Such a custom GIF must include a full set of the digits 0–9. Make sure the digits are evenly spaced; some adjustment may be necessary for best results.

You can also use the Reset Counter To check box and text box to reset the counter to whatever number you prefer; you can use the Fixed Number of Digits check box and text box to specify how high the counter will count before it starts over.

The hit counter functions properly in Netscape 3 and later as well as in IE 3 and later.

USING HOVER BUTTONS

Hover buttons are animated buttons whose colors and outlines change when the mouse pointer hovers over them. They are intended specifically as navigation buttons. Because they are Java applets, they work fine in Internet Explorer 3 and later and Netscape 3 and later.

To use one, place the insertion point where you want the button to be and choose Insert, Component, Hover Button to open the Hover Button Properties dialog box (see Figure 7.3).

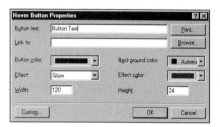

Figure 7.3
With the Hover Button Properties dialog box, you can choose from seven different effects and change colors and button text.

The dialog box allows you to do the following:

- Use the Button Text text box to change the wording. The Font button lets you change the font size, face, and color.

- Use the Link To text box to set up a hyperlink to the button's destination page.

- Use the Button Color and the Effect Color drop-down list boxes to choose the colors for these two attributes.

- Use the Effect Color drop-down list to select among color fill, color average, glow, reverse glow, light glow, bevel out, and bevel in.

- Specify the button's background color. This allows you to match its background color to the page background color.

- Specify the button's width and height.

In this same dialog box, you can choose Custom to set up the hover button with sound or a custom image (see Figure 7.4).

Figure 7.4
You can customize the hover button with sound and images.

This dialog box's Play Sound section enables you to specify a sound file to play when the button is clicked or when the mouse pointer hovers over it. Similarly, you use the Custom Image section to specify your own button images. The Button text box allows you to specify your own image for the button. The On Hover text box lets you select a hover image for the button; if you supply this, that image appears when the mouse pointer hovers on the button. In both instances, the effects applied to the button in the Hover Button dialog box are overridden.

If you use two custom images of different sizes (one for the button and one for the hover effect), you may need to adjust the background color to match the page background color so that the smaller graphic doesn't have colored edges.

USING MARQUEES

Marquees are those boxes that have text moving through them. Opinions vary on their best use; some people keep the text moving, others prefer to slide it into view and then leave it static. Your own design sense is your best guide.

Caution

The <MARQUEE> tag is specific to Internet Explorer browsers and does not work in Netscape browsers; the marquee text appears in Netscape, but does not scroll. Netscape implements marquees through Java applets.

To insert a marquee, choose Insert, Marquee to open the Marquee Properties dialog box (see Figure 7.5).

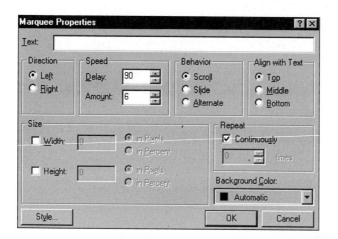

Figure 7.5
Customize the scrolling text with the Marquee Properties dialog box options.

Type the text you want to scroll in the Text box and adjust the marquee properties as follows:

- The Left and Right option buttons determine the scroll direction.
- Amount sets the speed of the scroll. Delay is an adjustment that essentially makes the scroll move smoothly or in increments.
- Slide moves the text onto the screen and stops it.
- Alternate scrolls the text onto the screen and then bounces it back and forth.
- If there's text beside the marquee, the Align with Text option buttons place it at the middle, the top, or the bottom of the marquee height.
- The width and height of the marquee can be set as a percentage of the page or as pixels.
- The repetitions of the marquee movement are set with the Repeat section.
- The background color determines the color of the marquee box where the text appears. Default keeps the box the same color as the page, so that the text appears to float across the page surface.

You can align the marquee on the page by using the alignment buttons on the toolbar. You can also use the Format, Font command to change the marquee font—click the marquee text to select the marquee field and change the font via the usual procedures. Note that you don't make the change with the Marquee Properties dialog box.

To make changes that don't have to do with font, right-click the marquee and select Marquee Properties from the shortcut menu.

PART

II

CH

7

USING THE CONFIRMATION FIELD COMPONENT

This component is associated with forms and is examined in Chapter 11, "Using Components, Forms, and Interactive Page Templates."

USING THE INCLUDE PAGE COMPONENT

The Include Page component inserts the contents of a file into an existing page. You use this if you have several pages in a web that need formatting identical for one or more elements, such as a standard heading at the top of each page. By using the Include Page Component, you can include this heading on as many pages as you like. Furthermore, if you need to change it (inserting a new logo, for example), you can make the change in only one file instead of editing every page on which the element appears. Each page that uses the Include Page component is updated automatically when the included file changes.

To use the Include Page, choose Insert, Component, Include Page. The Include Page Properties dialog box appears (see Figure 7.6).

Figure 7.6
Specify the included file with the Include Page Properties dialog box.

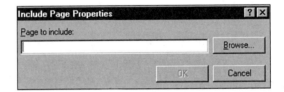

Enter the URL of the file to be included, either by typing it or by selecting Browse to search the current web. Notice that you can only enter page URLs, not image URLs.

USING THE SCHEDULED PICTURE COMPONENT

The Scheduled Picture component inserts a graphic file from the web and displays it for a specified period of time. One of the following things happens if the time period has not arrived or has elapsed:

- A message such as Expired Scheduled Picture appears in Page view. When the page is viewed from a browser, nothing appears.
- A specified alternate image appears in both Page view and in Web browsers.

The scheduled image is particularly useful for advertising or displays that run for a certain period of time. With a scheduled image, you can, for example, insert a client's advertisement for a day or week and, after the time expires, replace it with a specified alternative.

To put a scheduled image into your page, select it by selecting Insert, Component. The Scheduled Picture Properties dialog box appears (see Figure 7.7).

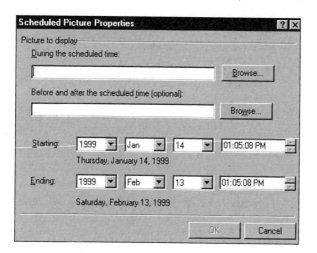

Figure 7.7
Use the Scheduled Picture Properties dialog box to specify how long an image will be included on your page.

Follow these steps:

1. Use the Browse button to select an image from the Web, or type in the image's URL.

2. Specify the starting and ending date and time for the image to appear. The defaults are today's date for the starting date and one month later for the ending date.

3. Optionally specify an alternate image to be displayed before or after the dates given in step 2. If this field is left empty and the system date is outside the specified range, nothing shows up when a user views the page in her browser.

4. Choose OK. If the current system date is within the date range specified in step 3, the image appears on the page in the Page view workspace. If the date falls outside the range, a text message appears in the workspace to state that it is expired.

A Scheduled Picture has the following behaviors:

- Although the image looks like a normal one, you can't select it and edit the image properties, such as borders, image type, or alignment. Attempting to open the Picture Properties dialog box leads you to the Scheduled Picture Properties box instead. In other words, the object on the page is really a component, not an image. (You can manipulate its appearance with the tools on the Picture toolbar, however.)

- The message Expired Scheduled Picture appears in *FrontPage Editor* in place of the image if the computer's system date falls outside the range given by the start and end dates you specified and if there is no optional image specified. Of course, the image and this message do not appear in a browser.

- You can link or unlink the scheduled image or the optional image by using Edit, Hyperlink (or Unlink), and the usual linking methods.

PART

II

CH

7

USING THE SCHEDULED INCLUDE PAGE COMPONENT

You insert a Scheduled Include Page just as you do a scheduled image. (The dialog boxes are identical in function, so the box isn't shown.) The difference here is that an HTML page file is inserted into the document.

Because you're inserting a page, you have some options for making it appear as you want it. Although you can't edit the inserted material directly (trying this just displays the Scheduled Include Page Properties dialog box), you can edit the component's source page. Because of this, the Scheduled Include Page component is more versatile and configurable than the scheduled image. You can create notices, newsletters, limited time offers, holiday pages, and in-depth advertisements, and include them as pages. You can also specify an optional page to display outside the date range specified.

> **Caution**
>
> Sometimes it's better to use the Scheduled Include Page method for inserting an image than the Scheduled Image method. Even though it takes slightly more work (you have to create an HTML page and insert the image into it), inserting an image with the Scheduled Include Page component allows you to create *hotspots (page 224)* on the image as well as modify its properties.

USING THE SUBSTITUTION COMPONENT

The Substitution component inserts the value of a page configuration variable, such as the original author, the person who modified the page, the page URL, or the page description (which can be free-form text). Any page configuration variables you added in FrontPage Explorer are also listed.

To use the component, choose Insert, Component, Substitution. This opens the Substitution Component Properties dialog box. Click the button at the right of the Substitute With list box, select the name of the variable you want, and choose OK. Its value as defined for the current FrontPage web appears on the page.

USING THE SEARCH FORM COMPONENT

When you insert a Search Form component, a simple form appears and allows a reader to search all pages in the current web or in a discussion group for a string of words.

To insert a Search Form component, choose Insert, Component, Search Form. This opens the Search Form Properties dialog box (see Figure 7.8).

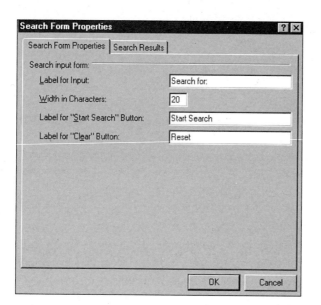

Figure 7.8
Use the Search Form Properties dialog box to establish search parameters.

Note

The Search Form component searches only the current web. It isn't intended as a search engine for locations beyond that web.

The dialog box has two sheets. On the Search Form Properties sheet, you can modify the form's properties in the following ways:

- Put your own text (such as "Search My Web For:") in the Label for Input text box.
- Set the maximum width in characters for the search string.
- Customize the Clear and Start Search button labels.

When you have these to your liking, click the Search Results tab to move to the Search Results sheet. Here you specify the Word List to search to set the search range. All (the default) searches all the pages of the current web. If you've set up a discussion group, you can enter its directory name here, and the Search component searches all entries in that discussion group directory. If you want to exclude some pages from a search, you must store them in a hidden directory.

 See "Using Hidden Directories with FrontPage Components" in this chapter to find out how to exclude pages from a search by storing them in such a directory.

You can also use the check boxes to display the closeness of the match, the last update of a matched page, and the matched page's size in kilobytes (see Figure 7.9).

PART

II

CH

7

Figure 7.9
You determine the search range and other basic information in the Search Results sheet.

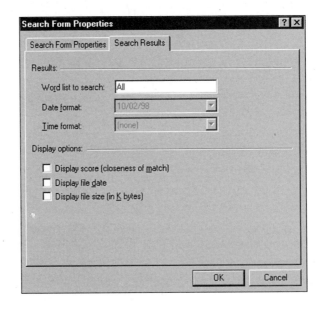

When your site visitor submits words to search for, the Search component returns a list of pages on which the words appear. Whether your web is complex or large, your visitors will appreciate an easily accessible search form.

USING THE TABLE OF CONTENTS COMPONENT

This component creates a table of contents (TOC) for your Web site. Choose Insert, Component, Table of Contents to use it. The Table of Contents Properties dialog box appears when you do so (see Figure 7.10).

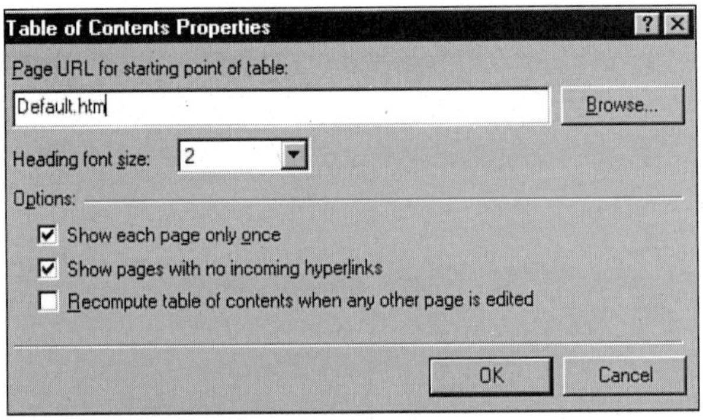

Figure 7.10
The Table of Contents component helps you set up this essential part of a web.

You can do the following with this component:

- Select the page that is the TOC's starting point. Upon execution, the component follows all links from this page. If you want a list of all pages on your web, assign the home page as the starting point.

- Choose the heading size for the table of contents. The TOC heading is taken from the starting page's page title.

- Select the Show Each Page Only Once check box to keep the same page from appearing over and over in the TOC. With the check box deselected, you'll get a TOC entry for the page for each link to it.

- Select the Show Pages with No Incoming Hyperlinks check box to include all pages on the site, even orphan pages with no links to them.

- Select the Recompute Table of Contents When Any Other Page Is Edited check box to update the TOC every time you edit a page in the web. Large Web sites can take a long time to update, so mark this box only if you can wait. To manually update a table of contents, open the page that contains the Table of Contents component and resave it.

Note that you don't see the actual TOC in either Normal or Preview mode—you see only three dummy entries, which you can't edit.

This is because the actual TOC is visible only in a browser that is accessing the page through a server; in other words, to see the TOC properly, it must be on a page in a server-based web. If that is the case, the Preview in Browser command shows you the TOC as it will appear to users. However, if you use the Preview in Browser command to view a TOC that is in a disk-based web (for instance, it's not being accessed through a server) you'll see the words `FrontPage Table of Contents Component` appear where the TOC component is placed. You won't see the actual TOC.

Admittedly, having to use Preview in Browser to view the TOC does make page layout a little more difficult—you can't see directly what the page is going to look like. Remember, however, that this TOC page is inevitably fluid because it changes as your site gains and loses pages.

USING HIDDEN DIRECTORIES WITH FRONTPAGE COMPONENTS

Hidden directories are important to web security and component behavior. Hidden-directory names are indicated by a leading underscore character.

FrontPage puts the special directory _PRIVATE into a newly created web. Browsers can't directly read files in this or in any other hidden directory. For example, if a site visitor tries to access the location `http://www.mysite/_private/header.htm`, he is prompted for a user-name and password.

PART

II

CH

7

By default, FrontPage views do not show files stored in hidden directories. Search Form components do not search hidden directories, and the Table of Contents component does not add links to pages in hidden directories. However, you can configure FrontPage to show the content of hidden directories. Choose Tools, Web Settings from the FrontPage menu bar. (Note that this choice is only available with a server-based web.) When the Web Settings dialog box appears, select the Advanced sheet and mark the Show Documents in Hidden Directories check box.

The _PRIVATE directory is often used with the two include components. For instance, you may want a standard header file for each page in the web but don't want people to be able to directly access that header file. Put it into the _PRIVATE directory and call it from there with the appropriate component.

Tip #41	If you want to create a link to a file in a hidden directory, select the Show Documents in Hidden Directories check box so that you can use Browse buttons to locate the file.

USING COMMENTS

Although the comment isn't part of the Component menu, it behaves like a component; that's why it's examined here. Essentially, the comment lets you insert text that appears only in FrontPage's Page view. It works much like a comment or an annotation in a word processor in that it's invisible to end users. In this context, that means that when someone views the page in her Web browser, she doesn't see the comment text.

The comment component is extremely useful, especially if different people are editing the same Web page and need to leave explanations for each other. In fact, FrontPage itself sometimes writes little notes for your benefit—several of its wizards and templates have embedded comment components that prompt you how to use that page's features.

To insert a comment, position the cursor where you want the comment to appear; then choose Insert, Comment. The Comment dialog box appears (see Figure 7.11). Enter the text you want for the comment and choose OK. The Comment dialog box closes and the comment appears in the FrontPage Editor workspace in purple text.

Figure 7.11
Use the text box to enter the comment text.

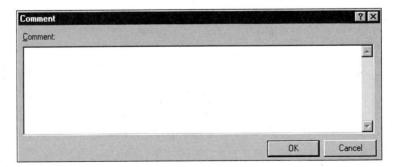

If you want to change the comment text, double-click it. Make your changes in the Comment dialog box and choose OK.

Tip #42	You can also right-click the purple text and choose Comment Properties from the shortcut menu.

DATE STAMPING A PAGE

One other component that has a menu entry to itself is the Date and Time component. To place a date stamp on a page, choose Insert, Date and Time; this brings up the Date and Time Properties dialog box. Here you specify whether the date stamp shows either the last edit date of the page or the date of its last update, which can be the last edit date or the date the page's URL was regenerated owing to a change in the web structure. Finally, you can specify the date and time format, if any.

USING SHARED BORDERS AND NAVIGATION BARS

Shared borders provide a quick and convenient way to give your web a consistent appearance. *Navigation bars*, which reside within these borders, greatly simplify creating and maintaining the links within a web. You can apply shared borders and navigation bars to an entire site at once and then (if you need to) individualize the borders of single pages within the web.

A handy thing about shared borders is that you can modify a border in Page view and apply that modification to all pages in the current web. Pages whose borders you have modified on an individual basis, however, do not change.

Shared borders and navigation bars, incidentally, work in Navigator 3 and later as well as in IE 3 and later.

CREATING SHARED BORDERS FOR THE CURRENT WEB

To create a shared border for the current web, open it and choose Format, Shared Borders. The Shared Borders dialog box appears (see Figure 7.12). Select the All Pages option button, select the check boxes for all or some of the borders you want to apply, and then choose OK. (For the moment, ignore the Include Navigation Buttons check boxes; they are covered later in the chapter in "Adding Navigation Buttons and Bars to Shared Borders").

Note	If none of the pages in the web is open in Page view, then the All Pages option of the Shared Borders dialog box is automatically marked. If you have already opened a page in Page view, the Current Page option is automatically marked.

Figure 7.12
If you select the All Pages option, you can add top, bottom, left, or right borders to an entire web at once.

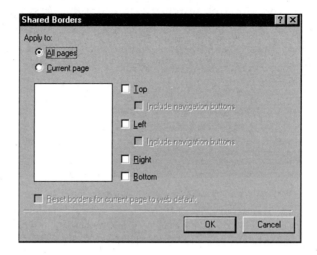

Tip #43

The borders are stored as HTML files in the hidden _borders folder. To see the hidden folders, choose Tools, Web Settings. Go to the Advanced sheet and select the Show Documents in Hidden Directories check box.

Now when you open an existing page or create a new page, these borders are automatically applied. Each one contains a comment component, which you can replace with your own material. Anything you place in the border will automatically appear in the corresponding border of every closed or open page in the current web, and if you create a new page, the borders and their contents will also appear on that page.

ADDING NAVIGATION BUTTONS AND BARS TO SHARED BORDERS

Navigation bars, which contain navigation buttons, are useful tools for establishing your web's links. To see a very basic example of how buttons can be installed in a navigation bar, first apply shared borders to your web as you did in the previous section. As you recollect, the borders show no navigational tools.

Now right-click any open page and choose Shared Borders; alternatively, choose Format, Shared Borders. Ensure that the All Pages option is marked and then mark both the Include Navigation Buttons check boxes. (Note that these check boxes are grayed out unless All Pages is selected.) The page appears, as shown in Figure 7.13, when you choose OK.

The buttons are shown as [Button] and are actually contained within a navigation bar. To see this, click once on any [Button] label; the navigation bar element will be highlighted in reverse video. (A page banner has also been added to the top border; this element is examined later, beginning in "Working with Navigation Bars and Shared Borders.")

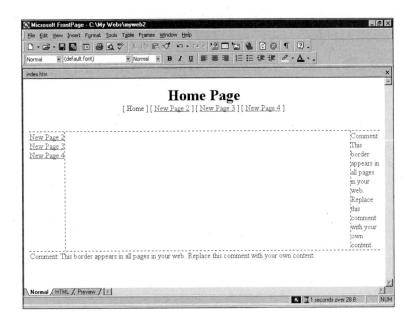

Figure 7.13
You can add basic navigation tools to every page in a web with a few clicks of the mouse.

The appearance of the navigation bars depends on the theme chosen for the web. If there is no *theme (page 454)*, the navigation bars appear entirely as text, as shown in this example. The links established through the navigation bars are determined by the web's structure as set up in Navigation view. However, if you haven't set up a Web structure in Navigation view, the navigation bars will be too generic to be of much use. What it boils down to is this: The most useful combination of tools is the Navigation view (to set up the web's linkage structure) and shared borders (applying them to that structure).

A detailed explanation of how to use Navigation view appears later in this book (see Chapter 15, "Working with an Existing Web"). You might find it useful to glance over the topic before proceeding with this chapter. To get you started, though, the next section briefly covers the basics of Navigation view.

Tip #44

Clearing the check boxes in the Shared Borders dialog box does not actually remove the HTML border files from the _borders folder. If you really mess up the border edit and want to begin over, you should deselect the appropriate check box or boxes in the Shared Borders dialog box and go to the _borders folder and delete the appropriate border file; then reapply that particular border with FrontPage Explorer's Tools, Shared Borders command.

WORKING WITH NAVIGATION BARS AND SHARED BORDERS

To create a navigational structure for a Web, make the views bar visible and click the navigation icon. This opens Navigation view; if the navigation toolbar is also visible, close it—it is not required for the following examples.

Make the folder list visible and drag page icons from it into the Navigation view, placing each page in the correct relation to the home page and other pages. An existing page's page title supplies the title of the Navigation view icons. When shared borders are in effect, these icon titles are used as the page banners in the top borders of the pages.

Assume for the moment that the current web's Navigation view looks like the one in Figure 7.14, that the web does not use themes, and that no shared borders have so far been applied to the web or to any individual page in it.

Figure 7.14
A web's Navigation view determines how the navigation bars in the borders are set up.

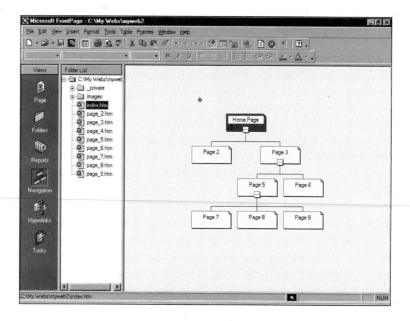

Now choose Format, Shared Borders and apply all four borders to the pages in the entire web, as you did earlier. Also select both the Include Navigation Buttons check boxes. (Note that it doesn't actually matter whether you apply borders before or after creating the navigational structure; the example works this way for clarity.) When you're done, choose OK.

Now open one of the pages in Page view. The example uses the home page, DEFAULT.HTM, as shown in Figure 7.15.

Figure 7.15
The top and left borders automatically supply navigation links and a banner, both as defined in Navigation view.

WORKING WITH THE TOP SHARED BORDER

The top border has two default elements, one of which is the page banner—in the example, Home Page. The banner text is supplied from the page icon title in Navigation view.

This banner is actually a page element, as you'll see if you click it once—the area of the page occupied by the element is displayed in reverse video. If you delete this banner, you also delete the banners for all the other pages in the web—be careful.

> **Note**
>
> Although the Navigation view icon title is initially obtained from the page title, editing the icon title will not change the page title. In addition, using the Page Properties dialog box to change a page title does not change an existing icon title in Navigation view.

If you want to change the text of the banner, right-click it and choose Page Banner Properties from the shortcut menu. In the resulting dialog box, type the new text into the Page Banner Text box and choose OK.

You can also modify the banner's alignment or font. Right-click it and choose the Paragraph Properties dialog box or the Font Properties dialog box to make the changes.

> **Tip #45**
>
> You can also change the banner text in Navigation view. To do so, go to Navigation view. Right-click the desired page icon, choose Rename from the shortcut menu, and edit the name on the icon itself.

By now you'll have noticed that the bracketed word [Button] appears three times under the banner. This second default element is a navigation bar and is actually a set of hyperlinks. You take a closer look at it shortly.

Caution

When you use FrontPage to view a page at the top of the Navigation view hierarchy (the home page in this example), you'll see that the top border's navigation bar has [Button] placeholders for navigation buttons. You can simply leave these placeholders; they do not show up in a browser, although they do in Preview mode. Don't try to delete them. If you do, you will delete the top border's navigation bar not only in this page, but in every page of the current web!

WORKING WITH THE LEFT SHARED BORDER

If you look at the left border of the example in Figure 7.15, you see that it has two preset text links: Page One and Page Two. FrontPage obtained the link text from the page icon titles in Navigation view, and this link text can be changed by editing the icon titles in that view.

You can also change the hyperlinks themselves by going to Navigation view and dragging the page icons to different orientations and connections. It's a good idea to close all pages in Page view before you do this so that their links are properly updated when you reopen them.

Caution

When you want an accurate assessment of shared border and navigation bar behavior, use the Preview in Browser command, not Preview mode. The latter can be misleading—for instance, it shows [Button] placeholders, which don't actually show up in a browser.

WORKING WITH BORDERS WITH COMPLEX LINKAGES

Now consider a page with more complicated linkages, such as Page Four from the navigational structure example in Figure 7.14. When you open such a page in FrontPage Editor, it resembles the example shown in Figure 7.16.

You see that the top border possesses multiple, automatically generated links instead of the [Button] placeholders that appeared in the home page. These links are as follows:

- A Home link that takes the viewer to (where else?) the home page
- An Up link that takes the viewer to page two, the page immediately above page four in the Navigation view hierarchy
- Links to pages three and five, which are at the same level as page four in the Navigation view hierarchy

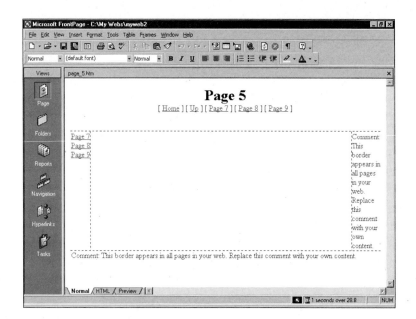

Figure 7.16
A page from the middle of a web has more complex navigation bars than does the home page.

To let the user go downward in the Navigation view hierarchy, the left border provides automatically generated links to pages six, seven, and eight, which (as you can see from Figure 7.14) are below page four in the hierarchy.

EDITING NAVIGATION BARS

You can add your own links—and any other page element—to the navigation bars. Click in the bar to place the insertion point and use the normal FrontPage editing tools. Do not accidentally delete the navigation bar page element; doing this deletes the corresponding navigation bar from every page in the web!

You can adjust the links included in the navigation bar with the Navigation Bar Properties dialog box. To use it, right-click in the navigation bar and choose Navigation Bar Properties from the shortcut menu (see Figure 7.17).

From this dialog box, you can specify which position in the hierarchy the link will lead to:

- Parent Level inserts links to all the pages in the hierarchy level immediately above the current page.

- Same Level inserts links to all the pages at the same level as the current page. This is the default for the top border navigation bar.

- Back and Next inserts links that allow the user to move across the pages in a level and back again. These links don't let you move outside that level.

- Child Level inserts links to all pages in the level below the current page. This is the default for the left border navigation bar.

- Top Level inserts a link to any page other than the home page. It is linked at the hierarchical level of the home page.

- You can also add a link to the home page or to the parent page. The latter is not quite the same as using Parent Level because it links only to the parent page, not to all pages at the parent level (assuming there is more than one page at that level). It supplies a link named Up.

Figure 7.17
You can change the linkages of a navigation bar with the Navigation Bar Properties dialog box.

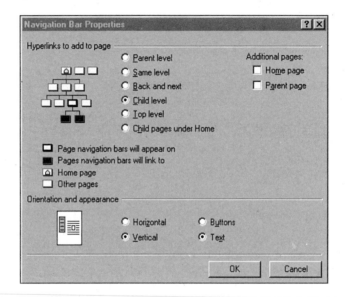

Note that the schematic display in the dialog box changes as you select among these options, to show how each set of linkages will operate.

You can use the Orientation and Appearance section to specify whether the navigation links are buttons or text, and whether they run vertically or horizontally. If the web uses no themes, though, you only get text—even if you select the Buttons option.

Caution

When you use FrontPage to view a page at the bottom level of the Navigation view hierarchy, you'll see that the left border's navigation bar has [Button] placeholders for navigation buttons. You should leave this border and its navigation bar as they are—the placeholders do not show up in a browser, although they do appear in Preview mode. Don't try to delete them—if you do, you delete the left border and its navigation bar not only in this page, but in every page of the current web!

WORKING WITH THE RIGHT AND BOTTOM BORDERS

These are simpler entities than the other two borders, since they don't have navigation controls. They default to comment components with purple comment text. Click inside either border, which selects the purple comment text, to add your own page elements. Insert any elements you like; the first element you insert replaces the comment text. Remember that the changes you make will appear in the borders of all pages on the Web site. The exception to this is if you individualize a page's borders. You examine this procedure later in this chapter in "Individualizing a Page's Borders."

USING BORDERS AND NAVIGATION BARS WITH THEMES

So far, adding a theme to the borders and navigation bars has been avoided. You can do this now.

Assuming you want the theme to appear in all the pages in the web, open the web in FrontPage Explorer and use the method you learned in Chapter 6, "Working with Themes," to apply the theme. The one chosen for the following examples is the Global Marketing theme, with the background image turned off for clarity. In Figure 7.18 you can see the results as they appear in Internet Explorer 4.0.

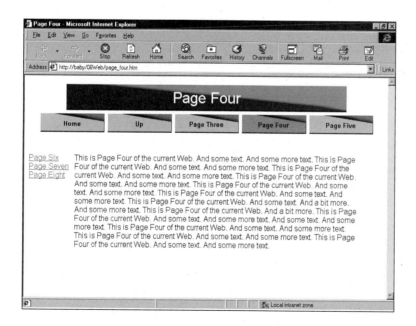

Figure 7.18
This browser display uses both shared borders and navigation bars.

As you can see, the *navigation buttons (page 682)* are supplied by the theme. You cannot customize navigation bar buttons with your own button images.

Sometimes you may want to change the banner so that it's plain text and doesn't use the theme image. To do this, right-click the banner and choose Page Banner Properties from the shortcut menu. This opens the Page Banner Properties dialog box where you can select either Image or Text option buttons. The Text option button will replace the banner image with plain black text.

At default, the navigation bar in the left border uses text links. To change them to buttons, right-click the bar and select Navigation Bar Properties from the shortcut menu. In the resulting dialog box, select the Buttons option. This replaces the textual links with buttons. Conversely, you can change the buttons in the top border's navigation bar to text links. Right-click the bar, go to the Navigation Bar Properties dialog box, and select Text (instead of Buttons).

Marking the Horizontal or Vertical option button in the Navigation Bar Properties dialog box changes the orientation of the button strip on the page—but only the orientation of the buttons in the top border. The buttons in the left border are not affected by this option.

Note that the changes affect all the pages in the web except for those that have individualized borders.

INDIVIDUALIZING A PAGE'S BORDERS

From time to time, you may want a page treatment different from that applied by the web's shared borders. You get this result by individually customizing each page's borders.

To do so, open the desired page and choose Format, Shared Borders. The Page Borders dialog box appears, as shown in Figure 7.12. Select the Current Page option and then select or deselect the check boxes that correspond to the borders you want to remove or keep. The unwanted borders disappear from that page only when you choose OK. If you don't like the changes, you can reset all borders to the current web default by returning to the Shared Borders dialog box and selecting the Reset Borders check box.

Caution

The Current Page option is somewhat misleading. With this option you can only remove or add a particular page's borders; you can't edit that page's borders on a border-by-border basis. Even if you select the Current Page option button, any changes you make to the content of any page's border will be repeated in the corresponding border of all the other pages of the web.

If the web has a theme, the borders that remain will reflect that theme. Follow these steps to make the borders on a page use a different theme:

1. Open the desired page. Use the Borders dialog box to remove or add the desired borders. Choose OK.

2. Choose Format, Theme to open the Themes dialog box. Make sure the Selected Pages option is marked.

3. Select the theme you want from the list box and choose OK. The theme is applied to the borders of the selected page, and to no others.

If you want no theme at all in the borders of the selected page, select No Theme in the list box of the Themes dialog box and choose OK. The theme buttons and images are replaced by the default shared borders with their text banner and links. The drawback is that you're forced to use the supplied text links for navigation—as mentioned earlier, you can't edit the content of a border, even when you've specified that the borders are to affect this page only.

CREATING NEW PAGES IN A SHARED BORDERS ENVIRONMENT

Inevitably, you need to create more pages to go into a web that already has shared borders. To do so, choose File, New, Page, and then select the kind of page you want. When the new page appears, it has [Button] placeholders in the top and left borders, although the content of the right and bottom borders is the correct content.

To set up the top and left borders properly, save the page with a suitable page title and file-name. Close it and go to Navigation view. Open the Folder List and drag the new page to its correct position in the Navigation view hierarchy. The banner and links appear as they should when you open the page.

INSERTING A NAVIGATION BAR WITHOUT SHARED BORDERS

You can place a navigation bar on a page without using shared borders. To do this, choose Insert, Navigation Bar. This opens the Navigation Bar Properties dialog box you saw in Figure 7.16. Specify the navigation bar properties you want and choose OK to make the bar appear on the page. The bar's appearance is determined by the theme of the page; it will be a textual navigation bar if no theme is present. Adding a navigation bar to one page does not add a navigation bar to any other page.

INSERTING A BANNER WITHOUT SHARED BORDERS

Similarly, you can place a banner on a page without using shared borders. Choose Insert, Page Banner; the Page Banner Properties dialog box appears (see Figure 7.19).

If the page uses a theme, selecting the Image option makes the banner use that theme; selecting the Text option forces a text banner. Either use the Page Banner Text box to type in the banner wording or accept the default.

PART

II

CH

7

Figure 7.19
You can add a page
banner to a page
without using shared
borders.

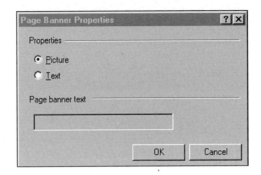

USING THE FRONTPAGE SPREADSHEET COMPONENTS

FrontPage includes three specialized components for managing spreadsheet data on a Web page. These components are the Office spreadsheet, the Office pivot table, and the Office chart. They are all versions of various Microsoft Excel tools.

ADDING A SPREADSHEET COMPONENT TO A WEB PAGE

Choose Insert, Component, Office Spreadsheet when you want to add a spreadsheet component to a Web page. An Excel worksheet appears on the page, including a comprehensive Help system, which is available through the Help button on the spreadsheet toolbar. You can restrict what your users are allowed to do with the spreadsheet, but the user can both change spreadsheet data and use the tools on the spreadsheet toolbar when all permissions are set to Available.

ADDING A PIVOT TABLE COMPONENT TO A WEB PAGE

Insert a pivot table by choosing Insert, Component, Office Pivot Table. It requires source data, which is retrieved from an Excel worksheet or a database accessible through your web. Extensive help is available from the Help button.

A *pivot table* is an interactive tool that can analyze data and present it in different views that you specify; in the case of the FrontPage pivot table, these views are specified and presented in a browser by using the Pivot Table toolbar. Data in a pivot table cannot be edited in the browser.

ADDING A CHART COMPONENT TO A WEB PAGE

Insert a chart by choosing Insert, Component, Office Chart. Right-click the chart and choose Help if you need assistance. Charts are used with data sources such as databases, FrontPage's Office spreadsheet component and its Office pivot table component.

DELETING AN OFFICE COMPONENT

To do this, click the component to select it and then choose Edit, Delete.

TROUBLESHOOTING

You may run into difficulty if you create a new page. If so, click Insert, Navigation Bar to insert the navigation bar. The page may be blank when you preview the page in the browser—the navigation bar might not appear.

It's likely that you have not defined the site's navigational structure by dragging your pages, including this newly created page, into FrontPage's Navigation view. You must create such a structure and place the new page in it before the navigation bars will function.

DESIGNERS CORNER

One way of telling a professional-quality Web site is the consistency of its navigational tools. Using FrontPage's navigation bars, especially in combination with the graphical enhancements of themes, allows you to achieve a uniform appearance. Even if you elect not to use navigation bars, you should study their layout and design for useful tips on constructing your own navigational tools.

Similarly, shared borders easily give your site a consistent look. Remember that once you design the borders for a page, those borders are available to all the pages in the current web. If you want a custom look repeated across all the web's pages, you need only design the borders once; they are automatically applied to each new page you create, as well as to all existing pages.

PART

II

CH

7

CHAPTER 8

CREATING TABLES

In this chapter

by Dennis Jones

USING TABLES FOR BETTER CONTENT ORGANIZATION

Like lists, tables are common—especially in business and science. Web pages can contain text and images, just as printed tables do, and you can use them to arrange text in parallel columns or to set an explanatory block of text beside the image that resides in the adjacent cell. You can insert lists into cells and even insert tables into other tables. All this gives you tremendous flexibility in arranging data and images (see Figure 8.1).

Figure 8.1
In this Preview mode Page view, an image is in the left cell of the table's top row and a bulleted list is in the right. Table borders are shown for clarity; they're optional.

Tables can also contain hyperlinks to other resources, which gives them a whole new dimension. For example, you can make a table containing *thumbnails (page 131)* of images and link these to the larger versions.

→ **See** "Using Thumbnails," to discover how to easily create thumbnail versions of existing graphics, **p. 144**.

In another example, each entry in a periodic table of elements can be linked to a resource that gives detailed information about that element. You can also insert forms or FrontPage components into a cell, which can turn a table into an interactive tool.

You can see this in Figure 8.2, where the bulleted hyperlinks are actually contained inside the cells of a two-column table. (In this example, the cell and table boundaries don't show.)

Figure 8.2
The two-column bulleted list in the lower half of the screen is contained in the cells of a two-column table. The cell contents are hyperlinks.

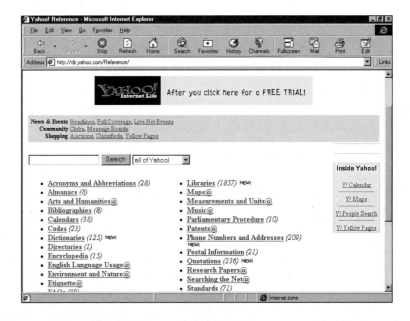

Tip #46	To understand better how tables work in FrontPage, you can save a World Wide Web page to a file, import that file into a FrontPage web, and manipulate the table properties to see what happens.

Tables have been supported by the major browsers ever since Netscape 2.0 and Internet Explorer 2.0 were released. Different browsers treat visible cell borders differently, though, so you should check to see what the borders look like in each browser before you settle on a design. Equally important is remembering that many people cruise the Web at 640×480 resolution; if you create tables that take advantage of the width of a 1024×768 display, visitors using a lower resolution may not see what you envisioned.

Setting Up A Table

FrontPage gives you many options for table appearance, but don't begin a complicated table by plunging right in. Begin by planning it, if only by roughing it out on paper, to organize the data and its presentation. You'll save yourself a lot of time and revision.

Once you've worked out the table's content and structure, follow these steps:

1. Open the desired page in Page view. The Tables toolbar appears when you choose Table, Draw Table. When you move the mouse pointer into the Page view workspace, the pointer turns into the table drawing tool.

2. Drag the table drawing tool diagonally through the workspace until you have a rectangle that's about the size of the table you want. When you release the mouse button, the table border appears with a default thickness of 1 pixel.

3. Drag the drawing tool within the cells to create new cells, columns, or rows. A dotted line snaps into position as you drag the drawing tool and indicates where the new cell border is going to be (see Figure 8.3).

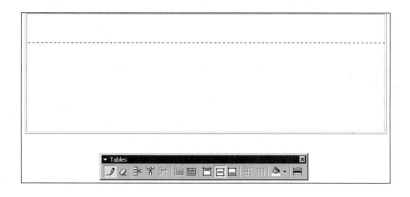

Figure 8.3
You get a pilot line, which shows where the cell boundary is going to be, while dragging the drawing tool.

4. Place the drawing tool on top of any cell border until the pointer becomes a double-headed arrow. Drag this to adjust the size of the cell or the table.

5. Select the eraser tool from the Tables toolbar if you've made a mistake. Hold the left mouse button down while dragging the eraser perpendicularly across the cell border you want to erase. The border is highlighted when selected. Release the mouse button and the cell border vanishes. (Certain borders cannot be erased in some configurations of cells.)

Tip #47

If the Tables toolbar isn't visible and you need it, choose View, Toolbars, Table to make it appear.

If you prefer not to use the drawing tool, you can create a table by using the Table, Insert, Table command. You must also use this command to insert a table into an existing table; you can't use the drawing tool to insert tables inside tables.

The Insert Table dialog box appears when you use this command (see Figure 8.4). Here you can establish the essential characteristics of the table:

Figure 8.4
The Insert Table dialog box is an alternative way of creating a table.

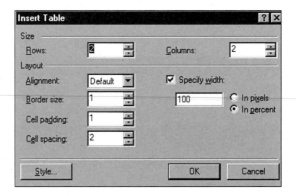

1. Specify the number of rows and columns in the Rows and Columns text boxes.

2. Specify whether you want the table against the left margin, centered, or against the right margin in the Alignment drop-down list box.

3. Specify how many pixels thick the cell and table borders are to be in the Border Size text box. A value of 0 specifies no borders.

4. Specify how many pixels of space you want between the cell contents and the inside edge of the cell boundary in the Cell Padding text box.

5. Specify how many pixels of space you want between cells in the Cell Spacing text box.

6. Specify how wide you want the table to be, either in pixels or as a percentage of the browser window, in the Specify Width text box.

7. Choose OK when you are done; the table appears. If you chose a Border Size of 0, the cells are outlined in dotted lines in the workspace and are in Normal mode. These dotted cell boundaries don't appear in a browser or in Preview mode.

To place content into a cell, click in the cell. If it's text you want, just start typing. The text wraps when it reaches the cell margin, pushing the bottom of the whole row down so that you can keep going. To insert images, other tables, lists, or any other page element, click in the cell and use the appropriate menus to insert the component. The cells resize to suit the content.

Note

The appearance of the table in Page view's Normal mode is not exactly WYSIWYG. To see an accurate picture of the table, use Preview mode.

USING THE TABLE MENU

Now that you have a table, you can get a better look at the Table menu. (Except for Draw Table and Insert Table, the entries for the Table menu were grayed out when you last saw them.) Click anywhere in the table and choose Table to make the menu appear (see Figure 8.5).

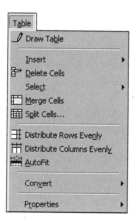

Figure 8.5
Use the Table menu to manipulate and select parts of a table.

Many of the operations you perform on table elements require you to select those elements. You can use the menu to select cells, rows, columns, or the entire table. You can also drag across table elements to select them.

Tip #48

You can also select a row or a column by placing the cursor on the table border to the left of that row or above that column. When the cursor changes to a small black arrow, click once to select the row or column.

MODIFYING THE PROPERTIES OF AN EXISTING TABLE

As you work on a table, you may discover that you need to change some of its characteristics. To do so, click anywhere in the table and choose Table, Properties, Table. The Table Properties dialog box appears, as shown in Figure 8.6.

Figure 8.6
Change the settings for an existing table with the Table Properties dialog box.

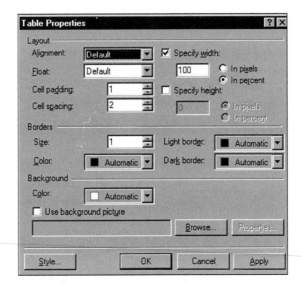

The Table Properties dialog box duplicates part of the Insert Table dialog box. You can modify the table layout and the width of the table by using the same procedures. (The use of the Minimum Size section is discussed later in this chapter.) When selected, the Float option under the Alignment text box allows text to wrap around the table, just as floating images allow the same effect.

You can also apply colors to the table; you see this procedure a little later, in this chapter's "Adding Colors and Backgrounds to Tables and Cells" section.

Tip #49

To get to the Table Properties dialog box quickly, right-click anywhere in the table and select Table Properties from the shortcut menu.

DELETING A TABLE OR PARTS OF A TABLE

When you're experimenting, you need to know how to delete an experiment gone wrong. To get rid of a table entirely, click anywhere in it and choose Table, Select, Table and press the Delete key. Another way is to double-click in the left margin to select the entire table and press the Delete key or choose Edit, Clear.

PART

II

CH

8

You remove columns, rows, and cells via a somewhat different method:

1. Click in the column, row, or cell you want to delete.
2. Choose Table, Select. Then choose either Column, Row, or Cell.
3. With the table element selected (it is in reverse video) choose Table, Delete Cells.
4. The table element is deleted.

Tip #50	You can also select the desired cells, right-click in any one of them, and choose Delete Cells from the shortcut menu.

There is one thing to watch out for when doing cell deletion. If you delete a cell (distinct from deleting its content), all the cells to its right slide over to fill the empty space, and a gap is left at the right side of the table (see Figure 8.7).

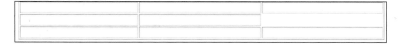

Space caused by deleted cell in center of middle row

Figure 8.7
Deleting a cell leaves a blank area in the table because the cells to its right moves into the space left by the deleted cell.

Tip #51	Yet another way to delete a cell, row, or column is to select it and click the Delete Cell button on the Tables toolbar.

ADDING ROWS OR COLUMNS

Even with the best planning, you sometimes discover a class of information you didn't allow for, and need a new row or column for it. To add either one, select the existing row or column that is to be adjacent to the new one. Choose Table, Insert, and either Rows or Columns. The Insert Rows or Columns dialog box appears, as shown in Figure 8.8. Fill in the data for the number of rows or columns to insert and where they should go relative to the selection you made; choose OK.

Figure 8.8
Use the Insert Rows or Columns dialog box to add data space to your tables.

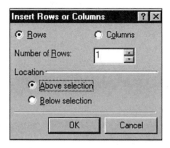

Tip #52

You can use the Tables toolbar as a shortcut to column and row insertion. A blank row appears above the selected row when you select a row and click the Insert Row button. Use the Insert Column button similarly to insert a column left of the selected column. If you select two rows or two columns, two new rows or columns are added, and so on.

INSERTING A CELL

If you delete a cell and decide you want its real estate back, you can insert a new cell by using Table, Insert Cell. The new cell's location is governed by the following:

- If the cursor is in an empty cell, the new cell is added immediately to the left of the current cell.

- If the cursor is at the left end of any data in a cell, the new cell is added to the left of the current cell.

- If the cursor is at the right end of any data in a cell, the new cell is added to the right of the current cell.

ADDING AND FORMATTING A CAPTION

To add a caption, click inside the table and choose Table, Insert, Caption. The insertion point moves to the line immediately above the table's first row. The caption you type automatically centers itself.

You have some flexibility with its placement and appearance. To make adjustments, click anywhere in the caption and choose Table, Caption Properties to open the Caption Properties dialog box (see Figure 8.9). Mark the appropriate option button to place the caption above or below the table. For lateral placement, click the Left Align, Center, or Right Align buttons on the toolbar.

To change the caption font, select the text and choose Format, Font; make the changes within the Font dialog box. You can also use the character formatting buttons on the toolbar for bold, italic, underline, or color.

To delete a caption, select it and press the Delete key twice.

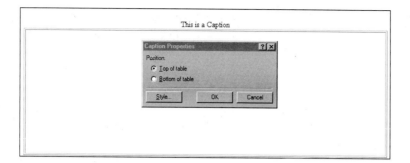

Figure 8.9
Captions can go above or below a table, according to the selections in the Caption Properties dialog box.

INSERTING A TABLE INTO AN EXISTING TABLE

You can get an interesting and powerful effect by putting a table inside another table's cell. To do this, click the cell where you want the subtable to appear and choose Table, Insert Table. Set up the subtable properties as you like and choose OK. You can see an example of a table in another table's cell in Figure 8.10.

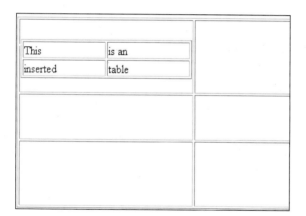

Figure 8.10
Placing a table within the cell of another table gives a subdivided effect.

SPLITTING AND MERGING CELLS

A perfectly regular grid of cells may not exactly match the way your data needs to be laid out. To change the cell patterns so that they serve your purposes better, you can split or merge them. To split a cell, click in it and choose Table, Split Cells. The Split Cells dialog box appears, as shown in Figure 8.11.

Now you have a choice of dividing the cell into columns or rows. Set up whichever you want and choose OK. Splitting the cells leaves the data intact in the left cell (row split) or the upper cell (column split). You can see a table with both row-split and column-split cells in Figure 8.12.

Figure 8.11
You can change a table's cell subdivisions by splitting cells.

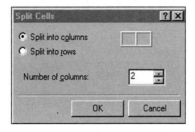

Figure 8.12
The top-right cell has been split into two rows and the bottom-left cell into three columns.

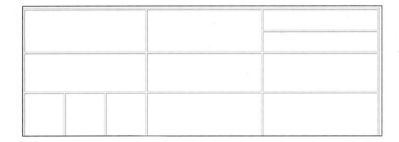

To put cells together, select them and choose Table, Merge Cells. The data is intact in the resulting cell, although you may have to do some reformatting.

Tip #53

Use the Split Cells or Merge Cells buttons on the Tables toolbar as shortcuts for joining and dividing cells.

MODIFYING THE TABLE'S APPEARANCE

A plain-vanilla table is good for organizing content, but you also need to think about presentation. Using column and row headers, captions, color, and suitable alignment of cell content can make your tables pleasing to the eye.

ADDING HEADERS

Most tables have column headers to denote the kind of data in each column; many tables also have row headers. An example is a sales report with product names as row headers and sales for each quarter as column headers. You often want to emphasize such headers, and one way is to select the text and use character formatting. Another method is to change the cell properties. To do this, select the cell or cells you want as header cells and choose Table, Properties, Cell; this displays the Cell Properties dialog box (see Figure 8.13). Select the Header Cell check box and choose OK.

Tip #54

To reach the Cell Properties dialog box quickly, select the cell and press Alt+Enter.

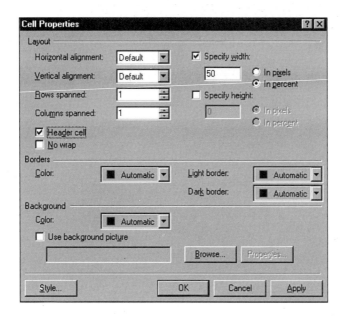

Figure 8.13
The Cell Properties dialog box lets you turn a cell into a header cell.

The text in the selected cell is rendered in bold. If you want to remove the header formatting, reopen the Cell Properties dialog box and deselect the Header Cell check box.

ALIGNING THE CONTENT OF A CELL

Depending on your cell content, you may want it positioned in different places. An image, for example, usually looks better if it's centered within the cell borders. You can also get these effects by using the Cell Properties dialog box. You can specify horizontal and vertical text alignment with the drop-down list boxes in the Layout section. Figure 8.14 shows an image with the horizontal alignment set to Center and vertical alignment set to Middle.

Figure 8.14
Centering images and text in cells may improve their appearance.

Tip #55

The Align Top, Center Vertically, and Align Bottom buttons on the Tables toolbar are shortcuts to locating cell content vertically within the cell.

Using No Wrap

The No Wrap check box, if marked, prevents word wrap from being applied to the contents of a cell. This can have profound effects on a table's layout when a browser gets it, so be sure to check your work in a browser if you use the No Wrap option.

Specifying Minimum Cell Width

The Cell Properties dialog box gives yet another way to proportion cells, or in this case, full columns. As usual, you should keep the minimum width units set to percent, not pixels, to allow for different resolutions your viewers may be using.

Tip #56

Sometimes the pixel measurement is a better choice than percentage—if you are basing the cell width on the absolute width of an image, for example.

A three-column table has the default minimum cell widths set at 33%. The cells take up at least 33% of the total table width each (to be precise, 33%, 33%, and 34%, from left to right). Changing these percentages lets you adjust the width of a whole column, independent of other columns, as shown in Figure 8.15. Getting the cell width percentages coordinated with the table width percentage can be tricky and will take some experimentation and browser previewing.

Figure 8.15
You create columns of differing widths by using Minimum Width cell settings.

35% min. width	10% min. width	40% min. width	15% min. width

Evening Out Row and Column Proportions

If you've done a lot of dragging and fitting of row and column boundaries, they may not be as evenly proportioned as you'd like. To make an even distribution of rows and columns, select those you want affected and click either the Distribute Rows Evenly button or the Distribute Columns Evenly button on the toolbar. There are also menu commands for these operations on the Table menu.

Making Cells Span Rows and Columns

Another way of modifying your table's grid is to make a cell bigger or smaller. This is called *spanning*, and you change a cell's span by selecting a cell and using the Cell Properties dialog box. In the Cell Span section, enter the number of rows or columns you want the cell to stretch across and choose OK. The ultimate effect can be very similar to merging or splitting cells. The difference is that when you span a cell, the cells it spans across are pushed down or sideways, as if you had inserted cells. You can delete these extra cells, of course. In Figure 8.16's example the large center cell was produced by setting its span at 2 rows and 2 columns. The cells that were pushed to the right and downward by this were then deleted.

Figure 8.16
Using cell spanning lets you customize your table's appearance.

ADDING COLORS AND BACKGROUNDS TO TABLES AND CELLS

Both the Table Properties dialog box and the Cell Properties dialog box have sections in which you specify background colors, images, and border colors (unless the page has a theme). Because these sections are identical, they are considered together.

Figure 8.17 shows the Table Properties dialog box with the More Colors dialog box for the background color displayed. This dialog box is identical to those used elsewhere in FrontPage, including the capability to mix a custom color.

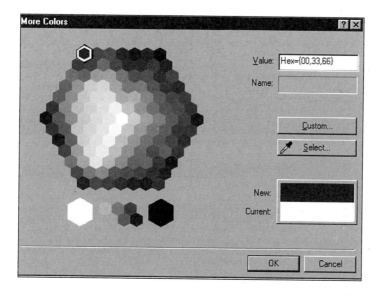

Figure 8.17
The More Colors dialog box lets you pick colors for table or cell backgrounds as well as for table or cell borders.

The major difference between using Table Properties and Cell Properties is that using the former sets the colors for the entire selected table, while using the latter sets the colors for the selected cell.

Entire tables or selected cells can have a background image, which you choose by selecting the Use Background Image check box and inserting the filename of the desired image in the text box. The procedure is identical to the one you learned in Chapter 5, "Enhancing Pages with Graphics and Multimedia."

Finally, a word about design: Don't make the backgrounds of your tables too busy or their colors garish and distracting. The table is a means to an end, not an end in itself—the information it organizes is the most important thing.

Note

Background colors or images for tables will cover any background color or image for the page that normally would appear behind the table.

INSERTING PAGE ELEMENTS INTO A TABLE

To add text to a table, click in the cell and start typing. All of FrontPage Editor's text formatting tools are at your disposal.

As for images, links, and multimedia components, you add these to a table cell by clicking in the cell and continuing as if the new element were standing by itself on the page. The fact that it's in a table makes no difference at all. Again, don't make your table too busy.

In Figure 8.18, you can see a page that puts a series of elaborately equipped tables to good use.

Figure 8.18
The tables on this page put a lot of information into well-organized spaces.

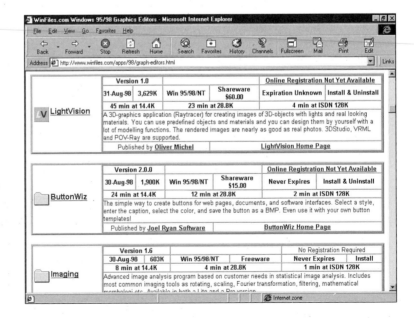

Graphics, graphical hyperlinks, text hyperlinks, and variously sized cells and columns are included in each table. The author has also used different fonts to suggest different types of information, but hasn't gone overboard with them. There's a lot of information here, and adding decorative elements such as cell colors and backgrounds would have been too much.

USING AUTOFIT

Sometimes you find that you are putting small amounts of content into cells that are too big for them. In this case, try using AutoFit. It shrinks the cells to make a neat fit around their content. It works best if the content of all the cells are close to the same size.

USING CONVERT

The Table menu provides a useful utility named Convert. This changes a text selection into a one-column table, and a table into normal text with the content of one cell per line.

To convert text to a table, select the desired text and then choose Table, Convert, Text to Table. This opens the Convert Text To Table dialog box (see Figure 8.19).

Figure 8.19
You select the text delimiter as needed in the dialog box.

Depending on how your text elements were delimited, choose the appropriate delimiter to separate the text elements. These can be Paragraphs, Tabs, Commas, Other (type the delimiting character into the box), and None (if you want all the text to end in a single cell). Choose OK after selecting. The text will convert to a table of one column, with as many rows as there were delimited items.

To convert in the other direction, click anywhere in the desired table and then choose Table, Convert, Table to Text. Each cell's content becomes a paragraph of normal text. You cannot specify a delimiter for this conversion.

Although Convert's menu suggests that it can only be used for text, this is not precisely so. For example, an image in a table is placed on a line by itself when the table is converted, and hyperlinks are preserved. Similarly, hyperlinks, images, and other page elements are moved into the table when they are selected for conversion.

TROUBLESHOOTING

Creating tables with FrontPage is a fairly problem-free activity. The major problems are likely to be associated with fitting the desired HTML elements into the cells. For example, a graphic may look cramped by the cell borders if they're visible or by the content of surrounding cells if the borders are invisible. To "loosen" the layout's look, increase the cell padding.

DESIGNERS CORNER

As mentioned earlier in this chapter, tables are a very useful and effective tool for many page layout tasks. Conceptually, this can be a good aid for visualizing a page before you begin; better yet, sketch the table on paper to help work out the spatial relationships and sizes of the main page elements. For example, if you're placing text inside certain table cells, it's a good idea to know how much room is available for that text. Then, when you come to actually write the copy, you'll know you have space for 500 words but not for 1,500. That may also force you to make your writing more concise, which is much better than being wordy. Similarly, you'll get a better idea about how graphics will appear when sized properly for their table cells. If they won't fit, or look bad when resized or cropped to fit, you can make changes at this design stage rather than when you're actually creating the page.

Be aware that you can use graphical table captions instead of the text captions that are the default when you choose Table, Insert, Caption. To do so, first design the graphical caption, remembering to set its width and height values to suit the dimensions of the proposed table. Create the table, click in it, and choose Table, Insert, Caption, to create the caption line with its insertion point. Then choose Insert, Picture, From File, and then select the prepared graphic. Choose OK as necessary to complete the insertion.

ENHANCING WEB SITES WITH FRONTPAGE FRAMES

In this chapter   *by Dennis Jones*

Frames were originally developed by Netscape, and their use in Web sites has been expanding ever since. Simply put, *framing* is a method of placing two or more windows on the screen and giving the viewer individual control of none, some, or all of them. Frames can even contain other frames, and the page within a frame can reference other pages independently of the rest of the display. This gives a web designer great flexibility in choosing how to organize and present information, whether it's text, graphics, or other varieties of content.

To see what this means, look at the example in Figure 9.1. The narrow, dark fixed frame at the top of the screen contains navigation controls. The leftmost frame contains a scrollable menu. The pages referenced by the menu items appear in the large frame at the right.

Figure 9.1
Frames allow different pages to appear and behave independently in the browser screen.

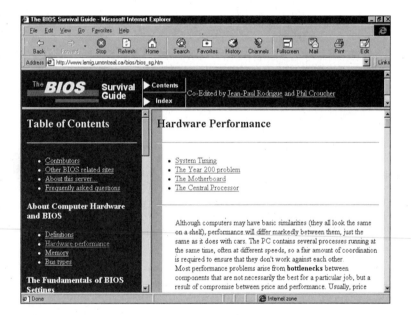

WHY USE FRAMES?

You should use frames if you want your user's browser window to display both static and dynamic elements. A *static element* remains visible no matter what your user does; the *dynamic element* changes according to his input. The menu frame in Figure 9.1 is static (you can scroll it but cannot change its content) and the large frame is dynamic (its content changes according to the menu selection).

One great advantage of the frame environment is the way it can keep your visitors oriented. The static part keeps a map of the site (or part of it) in front of them, and the dynamic elements show different parts of the site on command. The user doesn't have to scroll up or down, for example, to find the hyperlink that returns her to the home page or to another major section of the site. The links are always there, right in front of her.

You can also present an image within one frame and give your visitor several screens' worth of information about it in an adjacent frame. While the information scrolls within its frame, the image remains visible at all times. The only way to do this without frames is to repeat the image for each screen of data, which is a waste of space, time, and energy.

Back in 1995, when many people used nonframe browsers, it was important to provide non-framed pages to meet their needs. The use of frame-supporting browsers is now so wide-spread that this is less of a consideration. Still, many people do not like frames—especially if their viewing area is limited to a 14-inch display. This may eventually change, but until it does you should be aware of these differences of opinion when creating a framed environment. At the very least, don't cram a lot of frames into the same screen.

DESIGNING FOR THE FRAMED ENVIRONMENT

As with tables, handmade frame creation with HTML coding is a picky business. The presence of a WYSIWYG frameset creation environment in FrontPage 2000 makes setting up and managing frames immeasurably easier. This environment works with *framesets*, which is what FrontPage calls several frames that appear together in a browser display. You don't actually insert framesets into a page; a frameset acts like a scaffolding in that it relates pages to each other.

Before you start creating a frameset, though, you need to think about how—or if—you're going to use the frame environment. Keep the following in mind:

- Use frames only if you need them, not just because they're decorative.
- Don't crowd a page with frames. This obviously reduces their sizes. In particular, a viewer shouldn't have to scroll to see all of an image; the practical maximum is three frames.
- Use static frames sparingly. Use them for navigational tools, table of contents information, or for site identification such as a logo. Static frames are like the instrument panel of a car, which drivers indeed need to refer to—but drivers spend most of their time looking through windshields.
- Commit most of the screen area to dynamic frames where information can be retrieved and displayed.
- Don't develop your frame layout for monitors with screens bigger than 15 inches. Many people—and many businesses—don't use the larger screens yet. Even a 15-inch monitor has about 20% more viewing area than a 14 inch. In fact, you'd be wise to assume your visitor has a 14-inch monitor running at 800×600 resolution in 256 colors at best, and plan accordingly.

USING THE WYSIWYG FRAME ENVIRONMENT

In the next sequence you create a frameset with two frames and populate it. To best illustrate WYSIWYG frameset behavior with this frameset, you need two or more pages, so create any you require, give them titles and filenames, and save them.

After the pages are created (you can close them after you've done this), continue by choosing File, New, Page to open the New dialog box. Click the Frames Pages tab to display the available types of frame (see Figure 9.2). You get a concrete example of how the procedure works by setting up a specific frameset.

Figure 9.2
FrontPage 2000 gives you a selection of predefined framesets.

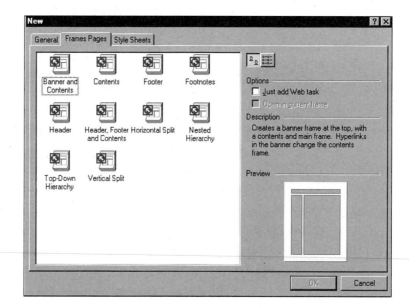

Now follow these steps:

1. Select the Header frameset. This layout produces an upper frame whose links change the page displayed in the lower frame. After selecting, choose OK. The WYSIWYG frame environment appears (see Figure 9.3).

2. You can insert an existing page into any frame, but for purposes of illustration, you'll create a new one for the upper frame. In the upper frame, click the New Page button; a new, blank page appears there. You'll use this page for the hyperlinks that control the display in the lower frame.

3. In the lower frame, click the Set Initial Page button. This opens the Create Hyperlink dialog box. Select an existing page and click OK from the dialog box's list box. This existing page opens in the lower window. (You see a new page filename if you now look in the gray page title bar of Page view. This new filename is the name of the frameset file itself.)

4. Click in the upper frame. Insert a hyperlink to the page that currently appears in the lower window. Insert a second hyperlink to a different page while you are still in the upper frame.

5. Use File, Save (or Save As) to save the frameset file and the new page you created for the upper frame. In the dialog box, you are asked to supply page titles and filenames for these new files—don't use the defaults. You know when you're saving the frameset page because a schematic representation of it appears in the right side of the Save As dialog box.

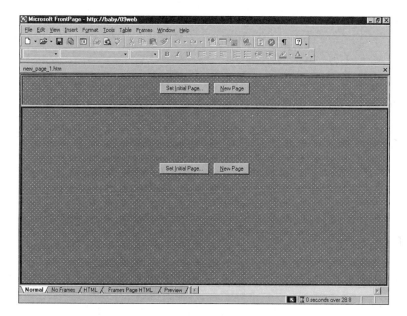

Figure 9.3
The WYSIWYG frame environment lets you lay out your frames so you can see how the design and proportions look.

Test the frameset by using Preview mode or the Preview In Browser command. The display should resemble the one in Figure 9.4. Clicking the links in the upper frame should change the pages in the lower frame.

Figure 9.4
The results of creating a two-frame frameset with a navigation pane in the upper frame.

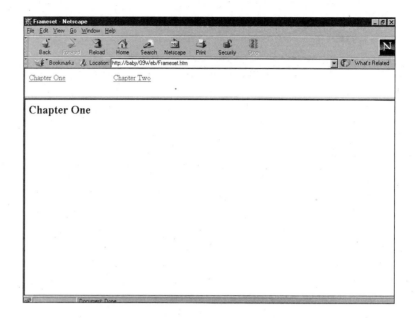

Editing a Frameset

You can adjust the appearance of the frameset during the previous procedure or in a later editing session. To edit the frameset later, open the frameset file in Page view. It appears with its initial pages displayed.

Here is a listing of the other frame-handling tools available directly from the WYSIWYG frame environment:

- To work on a page that appears in a frame, click that page. The active page is indicated by the thick dark line around its frame.

- To adjust the proportions of the frames, drag their boundaries.

- To view the HTML of the frameset file itself, click the Frames Page HTML tab at the bottom of the editor workspace while you're working on the frameset.

- To view a page's HTML within a frame, click it and then click the HTML tab.

- To edit the message that appears in a non-frame–supporting browser, click the No Frames tab. Edit the default warning message normally. This message gets saved with the frameset file, so you don't have to take any further action.

- To add frames to an existing frameset, you can split a frame into further rows or columns. Choose Frames, Split Frame, and use the resulting Split Frame dialog box to specify the number of rows or columns you want the frame split into.

- To delete a frame, select it and choose Frames, Delete Frame. Note that deleting the frame does not delete the page, if any, contained in it.
- To establish your web as a framed web as soon as people access it, rename the frameset page with the filename **DEFAULT.HTM**.

MODIFYING A FRAMESET'S FRAME

There are two sets of framesets properties that you might need to modify from time to time: those for the individual frames within a frameset and those for the frameset itself.

To modify an individual frame's properties, first click in the frame to select it; then choose Frames, Frame Properties to open the Frame Properties dialog box (see Figure 9.5).

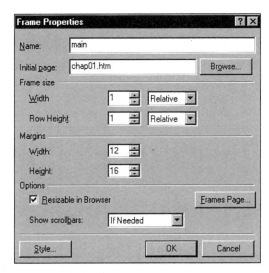

Figure 9.5
You set specifications for features such as scrolling, margins, and frame size within the Frame Properties dialog box.

You can do the following in this dialog box:

- Specify the frame name. This is not the name of the page that is contained in the frame, but the label of the frame itself; it is used to identify the individual frame of the frameset. You use this name in various FrontPage dialog boxes (such as Create Hyperlink) to specify the *target frame*, which is simply the frame in which a page should appear when the user clicks a link to that page. Specifying target frames can be a confusing process, and is treated at length later in this chapter.
- Specify the initial page appearing in the frame. To do this, type the page URL into the Initial Page text box (or use the Browse button to locate and identify the page).

- Specify frame width or height (if the selected frame belongs to a column or row of frames), as relative to that of other frames, either as a percentage of the size of the window or as a set number of pixels. Click the drop-down list boxes in the Frame Size section to choose among Relative, Percent, or Pixels. Given that you won't know what screen resolution your visitors are using, Percent may be the safest choice.

- Specify the frame size as *fixed* (which means the user can't resize it by dragging the frame border) by deselecting the Resizable in Browser check box.

- Adjust the margin width and margin height, which control the separation of the frames in a browser.

- Specify scrollbar behavior by choosing Never, If Needed, or Always from the Show Scrollbars drop-down listframesets.

MODIFYING FRAMESET PROPERTIES

To do this, choose Frames, Frame Properties, and click the Frames Page button in the Frame Properties dialog box. Because this is a frameset page, you get the Page Properties dialog box with one extra sheet (see Figure 9.6).

Figure 9.6
The Frames sheet lets you change just two values: spacing and borders.

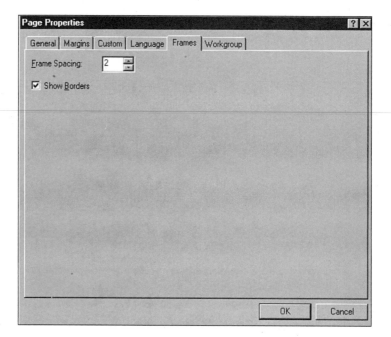

Here you can specify whether the frames have borders (deselect the Show Borders check box to remove them) and set the frame spacing in pixels. Frame spacing determines the amount of padding to display between frames when they are viewed in a browser.

CREATING CUSTOM FRAMESET LAYOUTS

The basics of this are quite simple, but can get confusing when you start customizing the target frames for the pages that show up in the frameset. Because of this, a concrete example will be used to illustrate (among other things) the use of *static frames*, those that don't get written over by other frames. These, you may recall, are often used to contain navigation aids.

There will be one frameset—which you'll eventually call FRAMESET.HTM—and five pages, one of which will be a navigation page containing links and will reside in the static frame; the others will be content pages. The example assumes that you have created the required pages before constructing the frameset; in the example, the page filenames and their titles are as follows:

- NAVIG.HTM   Navigation
- CHAP01.HTM   Chapter One
- CHAP02.HTM   Chapter Two
- NOTES.HTM   Notes
- BIBLIO.HTM   Bibliography

Begin by choosing File, New, Page and switching to the Frames sheet. Select the Contents template and choose OK. You now have a page that looks like the one in Figure 9.7.

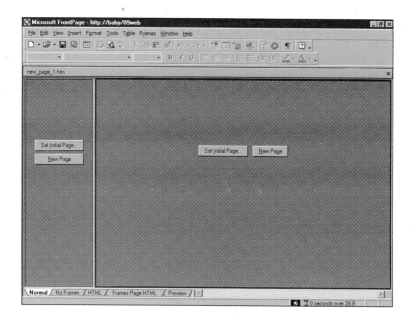

Figure 9.7
The best way to create a custom frameset is to start with a template similar to the one you want.

This frameset is going to be modified so that the links in the content frame (on the left) will change the page in an upper-right frame, and the links in the upper-right frame will change the page in a lower-right frame.

Before going on, right-click in the left frame and choose Frame Properties from the shortcut menu. You see in the Frame Properties dialog box that this frame's name is CONTENTS. Close the dialog box and do the same in the right frame. Observe that its frame name is MAIN. You didn't assign these names, so where did they come from? They were supplied by the template.

To go on, close the Frame Properties dialog box. In order to split the right frame in two, click inside it and then choose Frames, Split Frame. The Split Frame dialog box appears (see Figure 9.8).

Figure 9.8
You can change the frameset layout with the Split Frame dialog box.

Note You can also delete a frame. Click in the frame to select it and choose Frame, Delete Frame.

You want a horizontal split, so select the Split into Rows option button and choose OK. You now have two right frames that are stacked one above the other. If you check the frame names of your new right frames (right-click and choose Frame Properties, as you did earlier), you see that the upper is still MAIN, but that the lower is MAIN1. You can, of course, change these names. For convenience, leave them at their default values.

The Create Hyperlink dialog box appears when you click Set Initial Page in the left frame. Select NAVIG.HTM and choose OK.

Similarly, click Set Initial Page in the top-right frame and make the initial page **CHAP01.HTM**. Use the same method in the lower-right frame to make the initial page **NOTES.HTM**.

In the left window, create a link to CHAP01.HTM. While the Create Hyperlink dialog box is open, look at the text box labeled Target Frame. The value in this box is Page Default (main). Main is the important piece of information—it tells you that the page is going to appear in the MAIN frame, which is in the top right. This target frame is also labeled a default because MAIN is the default target frame property for this page (see following note).

It's necessary to distinguish between a *target frame*, which is a link attribute and is specified in the hyperlink dialog box, and a *default target frame*, which is a page property and specifies the frame where the links in that page display their destinations. In effect, setting a page's default target frame also sets the target frame of any hyperlink created on that page.

If you wanted `CHAP01.HTM` to appear in the lower-right frame, you'd change this target frame value to `MAIN1`. You examine how to do this in a minute, but leave the value as it is for the moment. Complete the Chapter One link and create a hyperlink to `CHAP02.HTM` still using the left frame.

Now click in the top-right frame. Create some text there as a hyperlink to `BIBLIO.HTM`, select the text, and choose Insert, Hyperlink. Select `BIBLIO.HTM` in the list box. Notice the Target Frame text box. It reads Page Default (none). None means the link's destination page will appear in the same frame as the page that owns the link—in other words, `BIBLIO.HTM` replaces `CHAP01.HTM` in the upper-right frame.

Assume that you don't want this to happen—you want to be able to see both `CHAP01.HTM` and `BIBLIO.HTM` at the same time. In other words, you want the upper-right frame to be a static frame with respect to the lower-right frame, so that the pages opened by links on the upper-right frame don't overwrite what's already there. To achieve this, click the pencil icon button at the right of the Target Frame text box. The Target Frame dialog box appears (see Figure 9.9).

Of course, the upper-right frame is not static with respect to the contents (left) frame because the contents frame's links do change the pages that appear in the upper-right frame. The contents frame, though, is a true static frame—nothing alters it. To make a fully static frame, be sure that it is not any hyperlink's target frame in the current web.

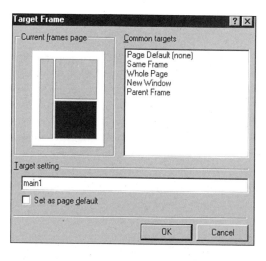

Figure 9.9
The Target Frame dialog box makes selecting a target frame as easy as clicking in it.

To specify where the link's destination page should appear, click the desired frame in the small preview display; Figure 9.9 shows this. Choose OK twice (do not double-click) to complete the specification for the destination page.

Tip #57	Selecting the Make Default for Hyperlinks on the Page check box specifies that any destination pages linked from the active page appear in the selected frame.

Place a link to the NOTES.HTM page in the upper-right frame, and change the target frame of NOTES.HTM to MAIN1 as well. To complete the example, open CHAP02.HTM and add to it the same links you added to CHAP01.HTM.

Choose Save or Save As; you are asked for a filename and page title for the frameset file. In the example, it was christened (not very originally) FRAMES.HTM and Frameset, respectively. Again, you can tell when you're saving a frameset page because a schematic representation of it appears in the right side of the Save As dialog box.

The completed frame layout resembles that shown in Figure 9.10. The contents frame's hyperlinks will change the page in the upper-right frame, and the links in the upper-right frame will change the page in the lower-right frame.

Figure 9.10
A three-frame display
with navigation links
in two of the frames.

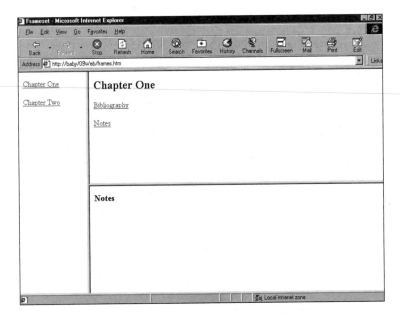

CREATING A CUSTOM FRAMESET TEMPLATE

If the frame layout is one you use often, you may want to save the frameset file as a template. The procedure is the same for both page templates and frameset templates. Note that only the frameset file is saved as the template, even if you have inserted initial pages into it.

→ For the template-creation procedures, **see** "Creating Custom Templates," **p. 241**.

SPECIAL TARGET FRAMES

There are also four special target types you can use. Typing one of these into the Target Frame box of the Create or Edit Hyperlink dialog boxes produces links with the following behaviors:

- New Window—The page the link points to loads into a new browser window. HTML for this target is _blank.

- Same Frame—The page the link points to overwrites the page where the calling link resides, but the frame layout in the browser window is not disturbed. HTML for this target is _self. This is the default.

- Parent Frame—The page the link points to overwrites the page where the calling link resides. The browser window is reset. HTML for this target is _parent.

- Whole Window—The page the link points to loads into the whole window of the browser, replacing the frameset. HTML for this target is _top.

Caution

If your link loads the destination page into the same frame as the origin page, it's extremely important to avoid a dead end at the destination. If users can't find a way out of a frame, its contents will sit there until they move to another site entirely. This tells them that you designed your site carelessly. Make sure you add a link to such a page in order to keep it from becoming a dead end.

INCORPORATING NEW AND EXISTING PAGES INTO A FRAMESET

This is where the default target frame specification—which you can find in the Page Properties dialog box's General sheet—becomes especially important.

There are two likely situations for using this specification. One is where you have a frameset and you want to create new pages for it. The best way to do this is to open the frameset file where the page is going to appear and then follow these steps:

1. Select any frame—it doesn't matter which one—and choose File, New, Page. In the New dialog box, make sure you select the Open in Current Frame check box. Select the page template you want and choose OK. The new page opens in the selected frame.

2. Right-click the page to get the shortcut menu and choose Page Properties. The Page Properties dialog box appears.

3. Click the button at the right of the Default Target Frame text box to open the Target Frame dialog box (refer to Figure 9.9). Just as you did when creating custom frameset layouts, select the frame you want for the page's default target frame and choose OK. When you return to the Page Properties dialog box, the frame name appears in the Default Target Frame text box.

4. Choose OK again. Links created on this page now have the specified frame as their default target.

Are you wondering why you went to the trouble of opening the frameset and creating the page there? If you don't do it that way, you don't get the handy Target Frame dialog box, which shows the small graphic of the frame layout. You get the dialog box without the graphic and have to type the frame name into the Target Setting text box, which is prone to errors.

The other situation in which you need to set a page's default target frame is when you have some pages that never were part of the framed environment and you want to include them in it, with their own default target frames.

To achieve this, open the frameset, select any frame, and choose File, Open. The Open dialog box has the Open in Current Frame check box, just as the New dialog box did. Select the box and choose OK; the page opens in the frame. Now follow steps 2 through 4.

Caution

FrontPage doesn't warn you if you get the default target frame name wrong in the Page Properties dialog box. You'll learn about your mistake when testing. When you click such a faulty link in the source page, you get the destination page showing up in a new browser window. There's no harm done, however, except to your pride. Go back and edit the page properties to fix the problem.

MORE ABOUT STATIC FRAMES

Now that you've had a look at default target frames, you can elaborate a little further on static frames. These are important entities because you often have frames on a page (navigation areas are a good example) that must not be changed.

To create a static frame (one whose content is not changed by the content of any other frame), specify a default target frame for the page that displays in the static frame. Once you've done this, the content of the static frame is fixed (see the accompanying Caution). Only the display in the target frame changes as links are clicked.

Note

This can be worded as a general principle: If a default target frame is specified for a page, every link on that page displays its destination in that target frame only.

Caution

> You can overwrite a static frame's content two ways. If another page's default target frame specifies the static frame, that will do it; so will specifying the static frame as a hyperlink's target frame. Of course, you may encounter situations where you actually do want to overwrite the content of the static frame.

USING TARGET FRAMES AND HYPERLINKS IN THE CURRENT WEB

You've so far concentrated on using a page's default target frame to determine where its linked pages show up, but you can also specify a page's display frame by creating or editing the link that calls it. To do this, open the page in the frameset and select some text or an image for the link; then choose Insert, Hyperlink (or set up to edit an existing link; the procedure is identical for both new and existing links).

Assuming you're working with the current web, select the destination page. Click the button at the right of the Target Frame text box to open the Target Frame dialog box (see Figure 9.9). Select the target frame for the link, choose OK twice (do not double-click) to return to the Page view workspace. The hyperlink now displays the destination page in the specified frame, overriding the default target frame of the page where the hyperlink resides.

Note

> You may be wondering why you have two ways of deciding in what frame a destination page displays. After all, if you can specify the target frame for each link, why do you need the Default Target Frame option in the Page Properties dialog box? Convenience is the answer. The default target frame enables you to specify the target frames for all links on that page so you don't have to set them individually. Because it's merely a default, you override it when you specify the target frame for a particular link.

USING TARGET FRAMES AND TEXT LINKS WITH WORLD WIDE WEB URLs

This task is the same as setting up a target frame for the current web, except that now you use the techniques from Chapter 4, "Developing the Basic Page: Text, Lists, and Hyperlinks," to set up the link to the remote site. The Web site's page shows up in the frame you specify. Remember, however, that it has less room for display and it may look cramped.

USING TARGET FRAMES AND BOOKMARKS

Bookmarks (page 114) and frames don't really have much to do with each other, although you can specify both when creating or editing a link. The destination page simply scrolls to the bookmark when it displays in the named frame.

COPING WITH BROWSERS THAT DON'T SUPPORT FRAMES

This situation is rapidly becoming less common, but you may still need to consider it—if for no other reason than a lot of people haven't gotten used to frames and therefore don't like them. The best thing to do (apart from not using frames) is to supply an alternative area of your web that works properly without frames. When your visitor links to the framed part of your web, he should be notified that there is a nonframe alternative so that he has a choice.

SHOULD I SET UP MY HOME PAGE AS A FRAMESET?

You should not set up your home page as a frameset unless you're determined to force people with frame-capable browsers to view frames from the moment they reach your home page. If this is what you really want, you can set up a framed home page by creating an empty web and then creating a frameset for it. Give this frameset the filename DEFAULT.HTM;—that's your framed home page.

USING TARGET FRAMES WITH IMAGES AND IMAGEMAPS

Setting up image-based links to use target frames is very similar to the procedure for establishing text links. Choose Insert, Hyperlink and use the Hyperlink dialog box to select the frame name for the Target Frame text box.

See Chapter 4 and Chapter 5, "Enhancing Pages with Graphics and Multimedia," for information about creating and editing various hyperlinks.

Likewise, drawing a *hotspot* (the portion of an image that acts as the link) on an image brings up the Create Hyperlink dialog box, and you use it to enter the target frame name in the Target Frame text box.

USING IMAGE PROPERTIES WITH FRAMES

If you open the Picture Properties dialog box for an image, you find a Default Hyperlink section at the bottom. Use its Location box (with the Browse button, if appropriate) to set a default destination for the image's hyperlink. Use the Target Frame box to specify the frame where the destination page will appear (see Figure 9.11).

Note

Are you wondering why you'd use Image Properties to set a default destination and target frame for an image's hyperlink, when you can get the same result by specifying both when you establish a link? You'd do this when the image has hotspots in order to set a default if the user clicks an area not covered by the hotspot.

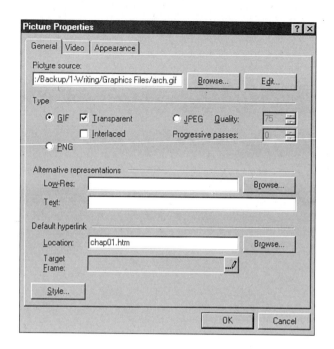

Figure 9.11
The Default
Hyperlink area is
where you specify
the location and tar-
get frame of an
image's link.

PUTTING FORMS INTO FRAMES

You can instruct a form to send its results to a frame. You do this with the Form
Properties dialog box, where you type the name of the target frame into the Target
Frame box; click OK.

FLOATING FRAMES

Although FrontPage doesn't support it, there is an alternate way to create compound documents: You can place frames in your HTML document by using the IFRAME element. Called
floating frames, this design technique allows you to insert HTML documents into your document the same way you insert images by using the IMG element. This means you can use
the ALIGN= attribute just as you do with IMG to align the frame with the surrounding text.
The following example aligns a frame at the left margin and wraps subsequent text around
the right side of the frame:

```
<IFRAME SRC="xx.htm" ALIGN=LEFT>
<p>Your browser does not support floating frames, so you can't see the page that
➥ would display in this space.</p>
</IFRAME> Here's some text to the right of a frame.
```

The IFRAME syntax is Microsoft–specific and is incompatible with all non-Microsoft
browsers, including the Netscape browsers. You can add a message for users who can't see
the floating frame, as in this rewritten code:

```
<IFRAME SRC="xx.htm" ALIGN=LEFT>
<p>Your browser does not support floating frames, so you can't see the page that
➥ would display in this space.</p>
</IFRAME> Here's some text to the right of a frame.
```

DELETING A FRAMESET

You can delete a frameset with FrontPage. The frameset file, with its normal HTM extension, appears in the Folder List or in Folders view just as a page would; you simply select it and press the Delete key. However, if you delete a frameset, you must also remove all frame target entries in any page properties or links that referenced the deleted frameset. If you don't, browsers become confused about where they're supposed to look and may give undesirable results.

USING FRONTPAGE'S FRAME TEMPLATES

FrontPage supplies 10 templates to help you create different framesets:

- A bannered, two-column document in which the links in the banner change the left (contents) frame
- A table of contents with a left frame that changes the frame on the right
- A footer document; links in the footer change the main frame
- A document with footnotes; links in the main frame change the footnotes
- A header document where links in the header change the main frame
- A header, footer, and contents document where header and footer links change the main frame
- A horizontal split with independent top and bottom frames
- A nested, three-level hierarchy
- A top-down, three-level hierarchy
- A vertical split with independent left and right frames

Creating your own custom framesets is so easy that you may prefer that approach if you use frames to any extent. However, because they can be very useful, do take a look at the templates.

USING THE BANNER AND CONTENTS TEMPLATE

Choose File, New, Page, and then select the Frames Pages sheet to create a frameset from this template. Assuming you create and save a page for each frame, you end up with four new files: the frameset file itself and three ordinary pages—one to populate the banner frame, one for the contents frame, and one that will appear in the main (lower-right) frame and change according to the links in the contents frame.

In a real site, naturally, there would be many different pages appearing in the main frame. To put the frameset into service, use Page view to add page elements to the banner and contents pages and create as many main pages you need. Figure 9.12 shows an example of how the results might look in a browser.

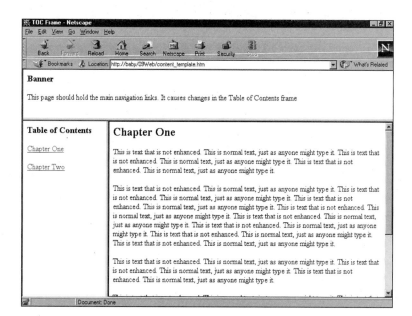

Figure 9.12
Your visitors can use the left table of contents frame to see other pages without losing the table of contents itself.

USING THE CONTENTS TEMPLATE

This is actually a simpler version of the template discussed earlier. The banner frame has been removed, but the links in the left frame still change the pages that appear in the right frame.

USING THE FOOTER TEMPLATE

The display produced by this template looks like the one in Figure 9.13. The links in the footer frame change the content of large main frame.

Figure 9.13
Use the Footer template to put navigational controls at the bottom of the browser display.

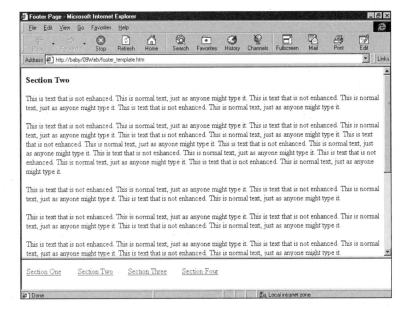

USING THE FOOTNOTES TEMPLATE

This is the same as the Footer template, but the links go in the opposite direction. Clicking the footnoted text in the upper frame makes the footnote appear in the scrolling lower frame. The virtue of this is that it's much more convenient for your visitor than flipping back and forth through a single page—or linking to another full screen page—every time he wants to read a footnote. The viewer just clicks a footnote entry in the main document and the note appears at the bottom of the screen. To implement this application, put all the footnotes on one page, bookmark each one, and link to the bookmarks from the appropriate places in the main document.

Note

As you know, the traditional footnote indicator is a superscript number. You can get these by going to the Font dialog box and selecting them in the Effects section. However, a footnote superscript in a printed document is really just a link to the bottom of the page. Because the reader can already see a web link, do you really need superscripts in a Web page to indicate a footnote? Probably not. Moreover, using superscripts in FrontPage makes line spacing slightly uneven.

USING THE HEADER TEMPLATE

This was discussed earlier in this chapter.

USING THE HEADER, FOOTER, AND TABLE OF CONTENTS TEMPLATE

This is the most elaborate in appearance of the templates, but is merely built on the simpler ones. It gives you *static frames (page 217)* at the top and bottom of the page and is a good starting point for a complex, framed environment that requires extensive navigational tools. For example, one static frame could be a site identification area and the other could be the navigation control panel. Your imagination can certainly fill in other possibilities.

Two more frames lie between these two static areas: The left might be a table of contents and the right would usually be the main data display area. Again, you can use your imagination to work out other uses for the arrangement.

This is a frameset more complex than you've looked at so far. The links in the upper static frame make their destination pages appear in the left frame (the TOC frame) and the links in the TOC frame and in the bottom frame make their destination pages appear in the right frame (the main frame). Links in the main frame—unless you set them otherwise—make their targets replace the current page in that frame.

You can change all this, as you know. For example, you can reset the page properties of the page in the top static frame to make its target document appear in the bottom frame (but then the bottom frame won't be static) and so on. With a frameset as potentially complicated as this one, you'd need to do some careful page and data organization. You would also need even more careful testing if you decided to modify the targets of the various frames.

PART
II
CH
9

USING THE TOP-DOWN HIERARCHY TEMPLATE

Use the top-down hierarchy template for all or part of a site whose page and data organization is, as the name suggests, hierarchical in nature.

The frameset establishes the hierarchy as follows:

- The default target of the top frame is the middle frame.
- The default target of the middle frame is the bottom frame.
- The bottom frame's default target is itself.

You'd use this scheme to go from broad categories to more precisely distinguished ones to finely detailed ones. Depending on how much information you had for each entry, you would use either full pages or bookmark entries within pages. An example of a hierarchical information structure is shown in Figure 9.14.

Figure 9.14
A hierarchical frame structure gives a cascade effect—in this case, from general to more specific to quite detailed information.

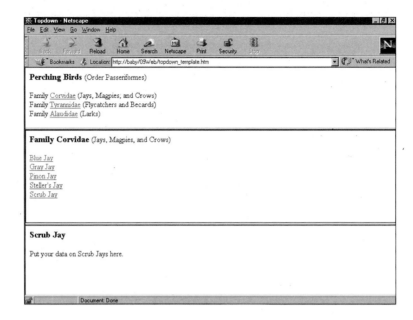

USING THE NESTED HIERARCHY TEMPLATE

The nested hierarchy template is similar in approach to the previous frameset, but the hierarchy works from left to top right and then down.

In practice, the links in the left frame display their destination pages in the top-right frame; those in the top-right frame display their destination pages in the bottom-right frame. You can see in Figure 9.15 a nested version of the pages that appeared earlier in the top-down hierarchy. The visual characteristics of your page content (such as large or small images, number of images, quantity of text) influence which frame layout you choose.

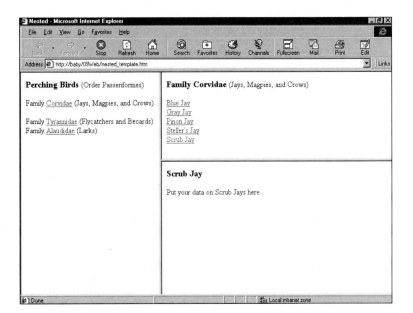

Figure 9.15
A nested hierarchy gives a different effect from a vertically organized one.

USING THE HORIZONTAL AND VERTICAL SPLIT TEMPLATES

These are identical except in their orientation. The two frames are independent of each other—the links in each frame simply overwrite the current contents of that frame.

TROUBLESHOOTING

A common source of misbehavior in FrontPage-generated frames is setting an incorrect default target frame. Remember that the *default target frame* is a page property that specifies the frame where the links in that page display their destination pages. If this property refers to a nonexistent target frame, the link's destination page shows up in a new browser window. If it refers to an existing but incorrect frame, the page appears where you don't want it.

Similarly, setting a hyperlink's target frame (using the Edit Hyperlink dialog box) so that it references a nonexistent frame also forces the link's destination page to open in a new browser window. In general, if your frames are behaving badly, begin troubleshooting by checking for errors in the target frame name (in the Hyperlink dialog box) or the default target frame name (in the Page Properties dialog box).

DESIGNERS CORNER

Before you decide to use frames on any part of your site, you should be aware that framed pages inspire loathing in many Web users. This isn't new—dislike of the technique was evident in 1996, when frames began popping up here and there on the Web. However, it was believed then (mostly by those Web designers who liked frames) that this irritation would go away as people got used to the technique. However, the dislike is still very much with us in 1999.

The chief advantage of frames, allowing one part of the screen to change its content in response to links in another part, seems to be outweighed by their drawbacks. A major problem is that the URL of a framed page (the URL appearing in the browser's address or location bar) is that of the highest level of the frameset. The URLs of the contained pages are not readily accessible to the user, if at all. This makes bookmarking a contained page extremely awkward. Furthermore, the frames make the Back button's behavior counterintuitive, and they plunge search engines into utter confusion. Even worse, saving a framed page is difficult and confusing for an unsophisticated user; simply clicking File, Save As in his browser saves the top-level frame, which is probably not the item he wants.

Smaller monitors (14" and 15") also don't really give enough room for frames, especially when navigation bars are added. The screen ends up being elaborate in form and meager in content, which is not at all how you want your Web site to be perceived.

All this is not to say that you should never use frames. They may serve a purpose you can achieve no other way. However, you should think of them as a specialized tool for reaching specialized goals, rather than as a general-purpose approach to Web site design. Unless you are very adept, don't base your entire site around a framed structure.

CHAPTER 10

CREATING PAGES WITH FRONTPAGE TEMPLATES

In this chapter

by Dennis Jones

USING THE CONTENT-ORIENTED TEMPLATES

FrontPage offers three basic, commonly used templates that are oriented toward particular forms of information: bibliographies, frequently asked questions, and guest books.

Note

The New dialog box lists more templates than are covered in this chapter. These other templates are oriented toward the production and use of forms, and are discussed in Chapter 11, "Using Components, Forms, and Interactive Page Templates."

USING THE BIBLIOGRAPHY TEMPLATE

Bibliographies are taken very seriously in the world of research. They not only give credit to your sources, but allow other people to refer easily to those sources. Bibliographies on the World Wide Web are fairly *static documents (page 448)* and usually imitate their paper-based counterparts. A bibliography has a strict format (format depends on the discipline), so FrontPage provides a template that conforms to a widely accepted style.

Tip #58

FrontPage's bibliographic format represents only one of many permissible styles. You may need to refer to a reference manual such as the MLA (Modern Language Association) Handbook for more complex formats. You can also go to the Association's Web site at http://www.mla.org.

You start any template-based page in the same way. Because of this, it's examined here just once and is not mentioned again. Choose File, New, Page and then select the template you want from the list; in this case, Bibliography. Choose OK; the template immediately opens in the Page view workspace (see Figure 10.1). To help you further, the template includes instructions for use in the form of a *comment*, which is the purple text. Comments don't show up in browsers, so you don't have to remove this one unless you want to.

Tip #59

To create a new, default blank page without going through the template-choosing procedure, click the New button on the FrontPage toolbar.

If you've ever struggled with bibliographic formatting, you'll appreciate the help the template gives you. The A, B, and C before LastName indicate that all entries must appear in alphabetic format from A to Z down the page. From this point, replace the LastName, Initial, Title, City, State, and Publisher with those that correspond to your particular references. Remember to retain the punctuation and italicization the template has set up for you.

You also get bookmarks with the formatting: ALastName, BLastName, and CLastName have the dotted underlines that signal these link targets. Once you link to them from the original document page, your reader can inspect your reference materials with little effort.

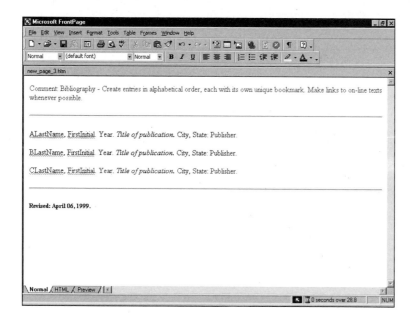

Figure 10.1
This Bibliography template can be customized according to your particular needs.

When the page is complete, save it. Remember with all templates to use the Page Properties dialog box to give the page a meaningful title and change its filename to something other than the default.

You can see a real-world example of a bibliography in Figure 10.2.

Note

Although not all of the real-world examples in this chapter have been prepared with FrontPage, they show you design approaches that can easily be reproduced with FrontPage's editing tools.

The author compiling this bibliography did not use hyperlinks to other documents because these were exclusively print references. However, *hyperlinking (page 111)* in bibliographies will become more common as more and more resources are put online. Notice that the citation style closely follows that of the FrontPage template.

Figure 10.2
This formal bibliography refers you to the documents cited in the Web site (http://www. newciv.org/ISSS_ Primer/biblio. html).

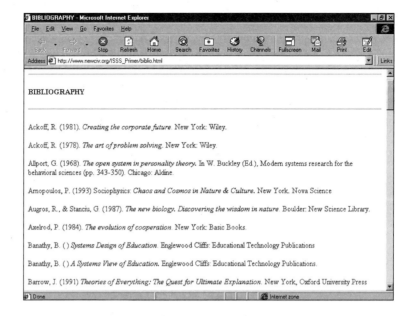

CREATING A FREQUENTLY ASKED QUESTIONS (FAQ) PAGE

With so many people browsing through the tangles of the World Wide Web, the number of questions posed to Webmasters increases by the minute. FAQ lists try to target the most frequently repeated questions and provide a single, thorough answer. So many answers are needed that FAQ lists now accompany almost every newsgroup and mailing list on the Net and the Web. To help you set up one of your own, FrontPage offers you a template. Open it to get the screen shown in Figure 10.3.

The FAQ template provides users with an introductory area from which they can access all major sections of the FAQ page. The Table of Contents hyperlinks work like the This Month, Last Month, and Previous Month divisions in the Press Release Directory, giving readers suitable points of entry to the site's information areas.

The FrontPage template is adequate if you plan on only a few questions and responses. However, if your FAQ page is extensive, you should consider setting up separate pages for each class of question and linking to bookmarks in them. As usual, this is to enhance response speed.

You can see an example of a large FAQ site in Figure 10.4. It offers a header area from which you can access mirror sites in several languages and from which you can download the FAQ answers in several file formats. The Contents entries are links to bookmarks farther down the page. These bookmarked areas, in turn, each have tables of contents, and each entry in these subtables is a link to a page where you find the answers to the question. These pages have further hyperlinks to places that give you even more information on the subject.

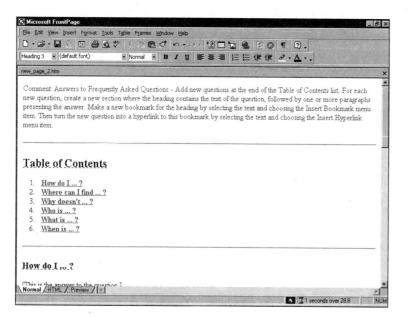

Figure 10.3
The FAQ template provides a Table of Contents menu ready for customization.

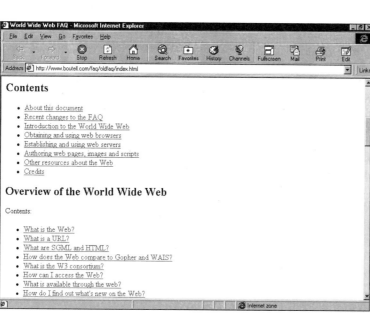

Figure 10.4
This site classifies questions into specialized areas for more efficient access to information (http://www. boutell.com/faq/ oldfaq/index. html).

Tip #60

When wording the responses to your FAQs, remember that you may be addressing an Internet newcomer, or at least a newcomer to your site. Avoid highly technical answers that could confuse such people.

USING FRONTPAGE'S LAYOUT TEMPLATES

Over a dozen layout templates are available and can be grouped as follows:

- Layouts with single or multiple text columns
- Layouts with single or multiple text columns with menus or sidebars
- Layouts with multiple staggered columns

The secret is that all these layouts are specified by tables. As you saw in Chapter 8, "Creating Tables," tables are a very efficient way of controlling a page's arrangement. One principle to remember when using table layouts is that just because a table column, row, or cell exists doesn't mean it needs to have something in it. With cell borders turned off, as they are in all these layouts, such a cell looks like blank space.

In the next few sections you'll look at some representative samples of each group. As you select different templates, you can get an idea of what the page will look like by examining the Preview pane in the New dialog box.

SIMPLE LAYOUTS WITH SINGLE OR MULTIPLE TEXT COLUMNS

The layouts in this category are as follows:

- One-column body—This is a three-column table with one row; you can adjust the width of the center column to whatever you like and type your text there.
- Wide body with headings—This is a more complex table. If you inspect it in FrontPage, you'll see that the heading text's hanging indent is created by making the heading text's cell occupy the table's entire width, whereas the text under the heading is pushed to the right by an empty cell on the table's left margin. Notice how an empty, full-width cell is inserted to establish the spacing between the main title and the first section title.
- Two-column body—Here you have a reorganization of the one centered column layout. In the two-column arrangement, the table's main text area has three columns, but the center column is squashed thin to provide the whitespace between the two text columns. Empty cells again are used to create spacing between the page title and the text area.
- Three-column body—This layout actually has five columns in the main text area; three are for text and two are spacers. Empty rows again are used to control vertical spacing between page elements.

LAYOUTS WITH SINGLE OR MULTIPLE TEXT COLUMNS WITH MENUS OR SIDEBARS

This group consists of the following:

- Narrow, right-aligned body—This template has no title area; it simply presents three columns of varying widths. The left is the sidebar area, the middle is for text, and the right is whitespace.

- Narrow, left-aligned body—This merely reverses the layout just described and adjusts the column widths by dragging the cell boundaries.

- One-column body with contents on left—There is a title area at the top. The leftmost column in the main informational area is essentially a navigation section, suitable (for example) for a site map. The middle column is extremely narrow and serves as a spacer. The right column is for text, and anything else you want to put there, as the template graphic suggests.

- One-column body with contents on right—Essentially a mirror image of the previous layout, but this has four main columns. The leftmost column serves to provide a margin of whitespace, the next is the main information column, the third is a spacer, and the fourth and rightmost column is the navigation section.

- Two-column body with contents on left—This layout has five columns. The left-most column is the navigation section, followed by a spacer column and two main information columns again separated by a spacer column.

- One-column body with contents and sidebar—Another five-column table, this one reserves the leftmost column for the navigation section, puts the text into the wide center column, and reserves the rightmost column for a sidebar (populated by graphics in the template). There are narrow spacer columns between the three main columns.

- One-column body with two-column sidebar—This is five columns, but takes a different organizational approach. The main text area (leftmost) is under a title area. A spacer column follows, then a column populated by (suggested) graphical hyperlinks. Then there's another spacer and a column for a text sidebar.

- Two-column body with contents and sidebar—This actually sets up four columns but reserves the center two for the main text area and gives the outside columns over to other purposes. In the basic template, the leftmost column could be a menu area with hyperlinks to other sections of the page, while the rightmost functioned as a text or image sidebar.

LAYOUTS WITH MULTIPLE STAGGERED COLUMNS

These provide visual variety by avoiding a strictly linear arrangement. The layouts in this group are:

- Two-column staggered body—The table has four columns (the outside two providing whitespace margins) and multiple rows. Alternating blank cells with filed ones in each column give the staggered effect.
- One-column body with staggered sidebar—The table again has four columns, but does away with the margin columns. The leftmost two columns alternate page elements with whitespace by breaking the columns into rows. A spacer column separates these columns from the main text area, which has one row and thus isn't staggered.
- One-column body with two sidebars—This might equally belong in the section on sidebar layouts, but it's here because it staggers the sidebar content. Here you have five columns, two of which are spacers. The two leftmost columns are broken into rows to provide a staggered-entry navigational section. The main central column is for text and a suggested graphical sidebar occupies the rightmost column.
- Two-column staggered body with contents and sidebar—This is about as elaborate as you should get: six columns, two of which are spacers. The leftmost column has one row and is the navigational area. The rightmost column is a sidebar column. The two large center columns are broken into rows, allowing page elements to be inserted in a staggered arrangement.

WHAT A REAL-WORLD EXAMPLE LOOKS LIKE

Figure 10.5 shows how the two-column body with contents on left template might be applied as the basis of a layout in a real Web site. This page is from the Yale/CAIM Style Manual, an excellent guide to the principles of Web page design, which you can find at `http://info.med.yale.edu/caim/manual/contents.html`.

The page is shown in the FrontPage workspace, so that the table boundaries are visible as dotted lines. This page's arrangement differs from the FrontPage template only in the addition of two narrow spacer columns on the left of the table, and one spacer at its right. The leftmost spacer is margin whitespace, and the one next to it provides a hanging indent for the section title (Page Design). Next come the main navigation area in the third column, a spacer, the main text area, and the right margin spacer. You can see from this how using tables is a very efficient way of organizing information on a page.

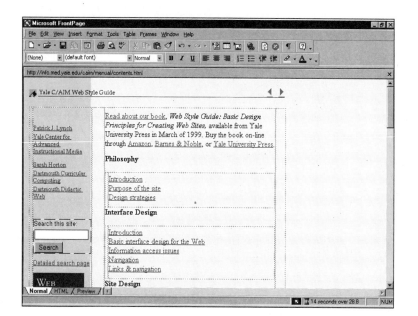

Figure 10.5
The Yale/CAIM Style Manual uses tables to control the arrangement of page elements.

CREATING CUSTOM TEMPLATES

This is basically a page-editing task, although it may be a long and complicated one, depending on how elaborate your template is. Begin by loading the template that will serve as the basis for your own, or by creating an entirely customized page. Once the template page is completed to your satisfaction, take the following steps:

1. Use the Page Properties dialog box to give the template page an appropriate title.

2. The Save As dialog box appears when you choose File, Save As.

3. In the Save As Type list box, use the arrow button to select the FrontPage Template entry. This specifies a TEM extension.

4. Choose Save. The Save As Template dialog box appears (see Figure 10.6).

5. Edit the template's Page Title in the Title box if you prefer and then type a filename into the Name box. You don't need to add an extension; FrontPage adds a TEM extension by default.

6. Type a description of the template into the Description box. This appears in the New Page dialog box when you choose the template to create a page. The Description is required, so if it isn't there, the OK button is grayed out.

7. Choose OK.

Figure 10.6
You can save a page layout and design as a custom template.

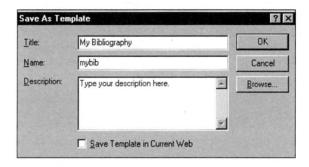

Because a template is merely an HTML file, any page can be a template. That means you can open any page from the Web, save it, and use it as such.

Assuming a default installation, the custom template will be saved in the
C:\Windows\Application Data\Microsoft\FrontPage\Pages folder, within a subfolder bearing the name you assigned to the template. This name has a TEM extension. From now on, the custom template's name appears in the list box whenever you choose FrontPage's File, New command. If you want to remove the template both from the system and from the New Page list box, use Windows Explorer to go to the Pages folder and delete the folder bearing that name.

Using the templates described in this chapter, you can also create hybrid templates. Open the templates you want to use and cut and paste the appropriate parts of them into the new template. Save the new template as a custom one, using the previous procedure. It's no more complex than cutting and pasting with a word processor.

Of course, you can add themes and shared borders to pages created with the FrontPage templates, and you can also add such elements to custom templates.

UNDERSTANDING TEMPLATES FOLDERS

As indicated, FrontPage stores your custom templates in their own folders in the
C:\Windows\Application Data\Microsoft\ FrontPage\Pages folder. When you save an HTML page as a template, its unique folder is created with the name you assigned to the template. Unlike most folder names, this one has an extension, TEM (for template, obviously). It's this extension that makes the template accessible through the New command, and if it isn't there, the template won't appear in the New Page list box.

The template file, which is simply an HTML file, is within the folder. The template folder name must match this file's name. An INF file is also in the folder. This is a text file storing the name and description of the template, as well as the path names of any separate files (such as image files) required by the template file. There's no official limit on the number of templates you can have; the unofficial limit is probably as large as your hard drive has room for.

PART
II
CH
10

Note

> There are four other folders under the `C:\Windows\Application Data\Microsoft\ FrontPage` folder: `Css`, `Frames`, `State`, and `Webs`. These store your templates for custom cascading style sheets, frames, content advisor rules for rating site content, and entire FrontPage webs.

The templates supplied with FrontPage 2000 are stored in the `C:\Program Files\Microsoft Office\Templates\1033` folder. This is the case even if you don't have the rest of Office installed on your machine.

Finally, a custom template can be stored in the current web itself. You set this up in the Save As Template dialog box by selecting the Save Template in Current Web check box. When you save the template this way, it's stored both in the `C:\Windows\Application Data\Microsoft\FrontPage\Pages` folder, as it normally is, as well as in the current web in the `_sharedtemplates\pages` folder. (This set of subfolders within the current web is automatically created if it does not already exist.) You do this if you want the template to remain accessible in the Web if the Web is moved to other machines.

Tip #61

> If you can't see the `_sharedtemplates\pages` folder, choose Tools, Web Settings, to open the Web Settings dialog. Select the Advanced tab, and select the check box labeled Show Documents in Hidden Directories.

TROUBLESHOOTING

Because templates are essentially tables, the main difficulty in using them is likely to be fitting the page elements into the table cells, so that the overall look is balanced. For example: A template with scattered whitespaces all over it, the result of having cells whose contained elements vary widely in size, may look disorganized and fragmented. If possible, bring the element sizes closer together so that the unity of the page, as visible on the screen, is preserved.

DESIGNERS CORNER

Some of the templates supplied with FrontPage may meet your needs on an as-is basis. It's equally likely, though, that they'll be almost, but not exactly, what you need. In these cases, feel free to modify and experiment. Design elements from one template may be mixed with those of another, to produce a hybrid that better suits the intent of the page.

You may want to consider making a collection of custom templates based on the various page layouts that your site will need. This comes back to planning—rather than reinvent the wheel for every new page you create, can you perceive the pages as falling into various types of layout? If so, so much the better. You can then make up a template for each type, and use those templates as needed. This will have the side benefit of helping your site's pages have a consistent design.

For instance, suppose you have a main Web with half a dozen nested subwebs. Each subweb, and the pages of the main Web, may need a characteristic look and layout. Rather than repeat the layout work for each page you create, consider creating a template for the main Web and every subweb, including elements such as logos, FrontPage components, and navigation tools. You can then adjust the looks of the various templates so that they are coordinated with each other, before you start creating the actual pages. This will give a cohesive design to the whole Web and its subwebs and save you work in the bargain.

CHAPTER **11**

USING COMPONENTS, FORMS, AND INTERACTIVE PAGE TEMPLATES

In this chapter   *by Dennis Jones*

FORMS: WHY BOTHER?

Nobody knows who invented the first form (he or she must have been a bureaucrat), but forms have been proliferating like weeds ever since. There's a good reason for this—they're useful. In a society like ours, which depends so heavily on the processing of information, they're essential for organizing both the way the information is gathered and how it's presented. If a census-taker merely asks a person to "tell me all about your household," she'll probably get some of the data she's after, but she'll miss some and receive other, unwanted information. In this disorganized state, the information is almost useless. Give the same census-taker a form with which to guide the data collection, and life suddenly becomes much easier.

DESIGNING EFFECTIVE FORMS

Because you intend for your forms to gather information, you have to persuade people to fill them out. People dislike forms almost on principle, and if the form is badly organized, too long, and filled with irrelevant questions, nobody will touch it. Here are a few things you can do to create user-friendly forms:

- If you can, create an enticement to complete the form. Remember how people ask, "What's in this for me?" when they first enter your site? This inclination is multiplied when they run into a form.

- Keep the form brief. List the form's objectives and ask only for data that applies to those objectives. Don't get sidetracked by nice-to-know items—stick to the need-to-know items, in other words information you intend to use. If a form takes more than a minute or two to fill out, most people won't bother.

- Briefly tell the reader why you want the data and how it is to be used. If she understands the form in this context, she'll be more likely to fill it out correctly. Don't overburden her with explanations, however; a couple of sentences should summarize your intentions adequately.

- Ask general questions first, starting with a couple of easy ones, and then go for the detail. Ask demographic questions (age, income, sex, education, occupation, and so on) lastly. Don't ask anything unless it is necessary. Too many personal questions make the reader apprehensive about submitting the form.

- Nobody reads forms carefully, so ask your questions as briefly and as clearly as you can. If the question takes multiple sentences to ask, find a way to shorten it and don't ask two questions at the same time. Remember that if something can be misunderstood, it will be.

- Avoid ambiguous questions, such as "Do you find our service good?" That's brief, but it's a badly designed query. Is the "service" your delivery speed or your customer response line? What is "good"? Fast but expensive? Slow but cheap?

■ Avoid leading questions, where the wording influences the answer. They're unethical, for one thing, and they can give you results you don't want or intend. If you ask "Is our aggressive Web advertising campaign offensive?" you're almost asking for a Yes answer because many people detest the idea of advertising on the Web—especially aggressive advertising.

■ Before putting the form into service, test it on some real people and use the feedback to modify it. Even professional form and survey designers don't get it right on the first try.

UNDERSTANDING WORLD WIDE WEB FORMS

When a visitor fills out a form and clicks the Submit button, this action sends the information to a program on the Web server. The server program must exist—without it, nothing happens and the data doesn't get saved anywhere.

When the data comes in, the server program processes it. This process can be as simple as saving the data to a file, or as complex as sorting the data and calculating results from it before the information is sent to the intended recipient. The program also sends the respondent a confirmation that the information was received.

The software standard that controls how your visitors interact with your site is called the *Common Gateway Interface* (CGI). The server programs that deal with such incoming information are called *CGI scripts* and are written to conform to the CGI specifications. When your visitor clicks that Submit button on your form, the data goes to the script and it processes the data according to the way the script was written.

Without FrontPage, you have to write a CGI script to handle your forms and install that script on the Web server. Writing these scripts is a headache for anyone who doesn't have some programming experience; worse, poorly written ones can cause severe misbehavior at the server end, and many ISPs won't let you put your own scripts in their servers. Fortunately, FrontPage enormously simplifies the whole messy business. You don't have to write any CGI scripts because certain FrontPage components take their place. FrontPage calls these components *form handlers*.

PART

II

CH

11

> **Caution**
>
> To use forms generated by FrontPage, your Web pages must reside on a server that runs the proper FrontPage extensions. If the Web server doesn't have these extensions, it won't have the software that evaluates the submitted information and your forms won't work. Contact your ISP administrator if this happens.

If you're already familiar with programming and compiling CGI scripts, though, you'll be happy to know that FrontPage fully supports them. However, you need them only when adding specialized features or when a page dependent on a CGI script is imported from another Web server.

Caution

Just as writing CGI scripts is, CGI security is far beyond the scope of this book. However, you should be aware that because CGI opens the door to end-user interaction (in fact, that's its purpose), there's always the possibility that an aggressive and unethical user could submit statements and codes that, in effect, control your Web server's behavior if it is not configured properly. For more on CGI security issues, see `http://hoohoo.ncsa.uiuc. edu/cgi/security.html` and `http://www.go2net.com/people/paulp/cgi- security/`.

Note

For an exhaustive treatment of CGI scripting, refer to Que's *Special Edition Using CGI.*

UNDERSTANDING FRONTPAGE FORMS

You can get just about any information you want from your visitors with FrontPage forms (assuming they're willing to give it). You can also instruct FrontPage to save the data in various HTML or text formats, allowing viewing and manipulation by various external soft-ware applications and macros.

Every FrontPage form has the same basic structure: at least one question, one or more fields for the reader to enter information, a Submit button to send the information to the server, and a Clear (or Reset) button to remove existing entries from the fields. Also associated with the form, at the server end, is some component-generated software to process the submitted data.

You can create a FrontPage form in any of three ways: with the Forms Wizard, by designing a custom form of your own, or via a template. You'll explore each of these in the next sections.

Tip #62

Do a draft on paper before starting the form in FrontPage. This enables you to organize and visualize the form and you'll create the software version with less backtracking and revision.

CREATING A FORM WITH THE FORM PAGE WIZARD

The Form Page Wizard lets you easily and quickly create many of the forms you need. The wizard takes a lot of the drudgery out of the work, supplies you with suitable formatting, and inserts the required form handler components for you.

To start the wizard by opening the New dialog box, choose File, New, Page. Select Form Page Wizard from the New sheet and choose OK. The first dialog box of the Form Page Wizard appears.

No input from you is required for the first dialog box, so choose Next to move to the second one to start creating your form's content.

You might not want the form to stand on a page by itself. To insert it into an existing page, first complete the form on its own page; then copy just the form to the Windows Clipboard and paste it at the appropriate place in the desired page.

ADDING QUESTIONS TO YOUR FORM

The second dialog box is where you get down to business and start asking questions of your respondents (see Figure 11.1).

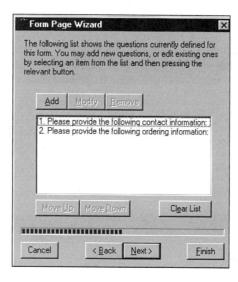

Figure 11.1
Use the Form Page Wizard dialog box to specify the questions for your form. This one shows contact and ordering information.

PART

II

CH

11

When you choose Add, the wizard opens a list box from which you can pick the type of input this question collects. The list is pretty comprehensive. You can see what it does by reading the Description section of the dialog box. If the Description section lists several items (form fields), don't worry. You can customize the form later as much as you like.

The Edit Prompt for This Question text box shows the question's default wording. The prompt differs depending on which input type you select. You can edit it if you need to. When you have the prompt right, choose Next.

SPECIFYING FIELDS FOR THE INPUT TYPE

Now decide which data items to collect from users (see Figure 11.2). These chunks of data are assigned to fields. From the user's viewpoint, fields are simply the text boxes on the form to type input. The wizard uses terms such as *value*, *field name*, and *variable*. For your purposes, think of the variable name as being the same as the field name, and the variable value as being the data itself. Better yet, think of the variable as a bucket with the field name painted on it, and the value as whatever someone pours into the bucket.

Figure 11.2
You can choose several data items and two subtypes in this section of the Form Page Wizard.

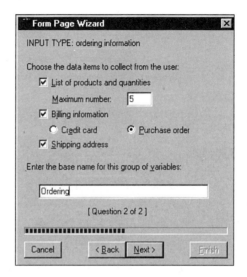

Although this dialog box is slightly different for each input type (ordering, account, and so on), it's always divided into three parts: a section that reminds you of the input type, a section that lets you choose data items, and a section that lets you specify the base name for this particular group of form variables.

No matter what the input type, the second section is always set up the same way. A check box adds a field and the option buttons and text boxes modify what the field looks like. For example, marking the Billing Information check box shown in Figure 11.2 tells the wizard to insert fields for billing information. The Credit Card and Purchase Order option buttons further define what type of fields appear. If you don't want a particular data item to be asked for, clear the check box.

Usually you needn't worry about changing the contents of the Enter the Base Name for This Group of Variables text box. This is what the wizard uses to help organize the field structures of the form. Changing it merely changes the standard prefix of the field names.

When the data in the input type dialog box is the way you want it, you can choose either Next or Finish. If you choose Finish, FrontPage immediately generates the form page. If you choose Next, you return to the previous dialog box (the second dialog box of the wizard) where you select further questions to add to the form. (Be careful with the Clear List button—it removes all the questions from the list box.)

Go through this cycle until you have all the input types you want and you have returned to the dialog box shown in Figure 11.1. If you have several input types, you can change the order of presentation via the Move Up and Move Down buttons.

If you choose Finish at this point, FrontPage immediately generates the form. However, there are some refinements you can make. To do so, choose Next.

FINISHING THE FORM WITH PRESENTATION OPTIONS

When you use the Next button to leave the dialog box, you find yourself looking at another of the Form Page Wizard's dialog boxes (see Figure 11.3).

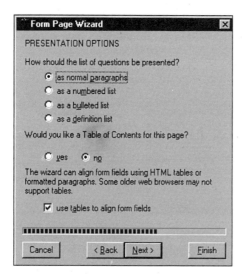

Figure 11.3
This dialog box gives you control of how some of your form elements appear.

You can format your questions as one of the following:

- Paragraphs
- Numbered lists
- Bulleted lists
- HTML definition lists

You can also create a table of contents for the form. Do this if your form has many sections; otherwise, don't bother. Remember that if you have a form that long, you may have difficulty getting anybody to use it!

You can automatically create tables to keep the form fields aligned. If you don't want this to happen (because browsers' handling of forms differ somewhat), deselect the Use Tables to Align Form Fields check box.

When you are finished with this dialog box, you can choose Finish to generate the form immediately. However, you'll likely want to choose Next—that's how you get to decide a very important part of the whole information-gathering process: how to save the data so that you can look at it.

> **Note**
>
> Are you wondering whether you can edit a template-based form? You can. Form customization is discussed a little later in this chapter in the section "Getting Started on Customized Forms."

SPECIFYING FORM OUTPUT OPTIONS

The dialog box shown in Figure 11.4 allows you to choose how the data will be saved. You have the following options:

- Save Results to a Web Page—This creates an HTML file in the web. Whenever a user clicks the Submit button on the form, each field's name/value pair is added to that file. *name* is the field name (such as ORDER_QTY) and *value* is whatever data the user typed into that field on the form.

- Save Results to a Text File—This creates the same results that choosing Save Results to a Web Page creates, except that the output is in ASCII text. Use this if you want to import the data into another application, such as a database or spreadsheet.

- Use Custom CGI Script—This tells FrontPage that a CGI script, which you have to write, accepts the data and produces a results file.

Figure 11.4
In this dialog box you determine the format of the results file.

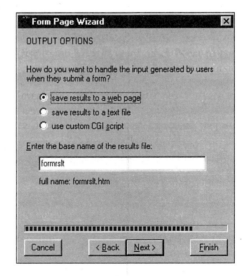

The Enter the Base Name of the Results File text box is where you type the name of the file that stores the output (avoid using the default). *Base name* simply means that this is the name to which the appropriate extension is added: HTM, TXT, or CGI, depending on the kind of output you asked for.

At last you can choose Next, then Finish, and let FrontPage create the form. You're not quite done, though. You need to edit the This Is an Explanation section at the top of the form to suit your needs. You will also want to modify the form title and the copyright information at the bottom of the form. (Notice that there's a date stamp component included with the copyright data—it's with the word Revised.) When you've finished, save the form page.

GETTING AT THE INFORMATION PEOPLE SEND YOU

If you told the wizard to save the results as a Web page, take a look at FrontPage's Folder List. You'll see that you now have a results page whose filename is formsrslt.htm. Its default page title is pretty cumbersome, so you should change it via the Page Properties dialog box.

This results page stores the data sent when a user fills out the form and clicks the Submit button. To see the information that somebody sends you, open the results page in an application compatible with the data storage format and look at it.

If you told the wizard to save the results as a text file, the file shows up in the Folder List. However, if you open it from there, it is retrieved into whatever application handles TXT files on your system. (The default is Windows Notepad.) If you chose Use Custom CGI Script, that script processes the information and stores it as the script instructs. Whatever you did to save the data, you now have it and can use it as needed.

GETTING STARTED ON CUSTOMIZED FORMS

The forms FrontPage generates for you are generic; they're good, but they're not great. You can customize them extensively by editing the text, inserting images, adding or removing text boxes, and modifying the form's properties. Alternatively, you can begin from scratch and build a form from the ground up.

Before you begin, there's an important point to be made about form pages. If you inspect any form, you see a dashed line surrounding it. This identifies the form boundary. If you insert a form field onto the page outside this boundary, you're actually starting a new form—be careful.

Note

You can customize a form created by the Form Page Wizard. Everything about customization, as described in the following paragraphs, also applies to modifying forms you've created with the wizard.

Rough out your form design on paper to get an idea of how it should look; then open the page where you want the form and place the insertion point at the desired place. Follow these steps to create a brand new form on the page:

1. Choose Insert, Form. The Form submenu opens.

2. Choose the top entry: Form.

3. A new form is inserted onto the page, complete with Submit and Reset buttons. Note that the form boundaries are displayed as a dashed line.

4. To make room for your fields above these buttons, press the Home key to put the insertion point to the left of the Submit button. Press Return as much as you like in order to get some blank lines.

You insert and edit text and images with the standard editing and insertion tools. At this stage, creating the form is just like creating any kind of page. When you start adding the form fields, though, life becomes a little more complicated.

Before adding the form fields, you need to look more closely at how the software actually handles the data returned from these fields. With the wizard, you only needed to decide whether the saved information should be passed to a custom CGI script, and if not what the information's format should be. For custom forms, you need to understand how the Save Results component works.

UNDERSTANDING THE SAVE RESULTS COMPONENT

The Save Results component is the most common form handler used in FrontPage. This component takes the information submitted by a form and saves it to a file in a format you select. These are various flavors of HTML, text, and database formats.

To specify the behavior of the Save Results component for a particular form, right-click any field in the form and select Form Properties from the shortcut menu. The Form Properties dialog box opens (see Figure 11.5).

If needed, you can change the form results destination file by changing the entry in the File Name text box. More importantly, you can set up many other options, including the capability to direct form results to an email address.

SENDING FORM RESULTS TO EMAIL

Many Web site managers prefer to get user feedback via email rather than results files, which can be cumbersome to handle and maintain. Setting this up is as simple as filling in the target email address in the E-mail Address text box of the Form Properties dialog box. This email is handled on the server and is transparent to the user. The server-side processing takes the form results, encodes them for email, and transmits them on to an email server. You'll look at options for configuring email submission of form results a little later in this chapter, in the section "Using the E-Mail Results Sheet."

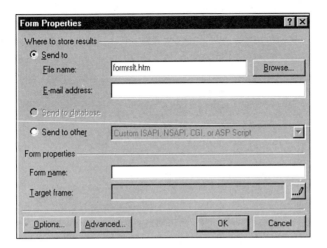

Figure 11.5
The Form Properties dialog box is the starting place for extensive customization of the way form results are recorded and acknowledged.

USING THE FORM PROPERTIES OPTIONS

Click the Options button, which is on the Form Properties dialog box. This opens a tabbed, four-sheet Options for Saving Results of Form dialog box. This dialog box opens to the File Results sheet by default.

USING THE FILE RESULTS SHEET

You use the sheet shown in Figure 11.6 as follows:

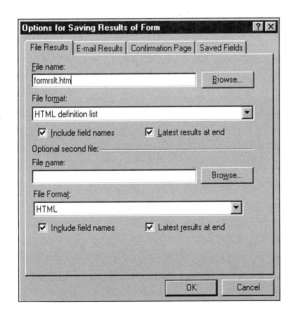

Figure 11.6
You specify the destination file and format of the user-submitted information with the File Results sheet.

- Enter the name of the file where the form data will be stored in the File Name text box. Supply an absolute pathname if you want to save the file outside the web but in the server (for example, `C:\TEMP\RESULTS.HTM`).

- Use the File Format drop-down list box to select the format for the result file. Select the Include Field Names check box to also save the variable name and value of each field in the results file.

- Selecting the Latest Results at End check box puts the latest submitted information at the end of the results file rather than at the beginning, but only if it is an HTML file. Text file results are always appended at the end; this can't be changed.

- The Optional Second File section allows you to specify another file in which the user-submitted information will be stored. This is useful if you need to store submitted data in one format to suit a database and in another format for human readability.

USING THE E-MAIL RESULTS SHEET

This sheet lets you specify the email results address, which actually duplicates the E-mail text box in the Form Properties dialog box (see Figure 11.7).

Figure 11.7
The E-mail Results sheet provides options for mail formatting and message headers.

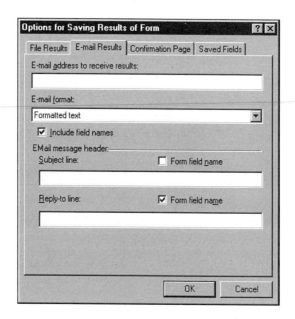

You can do many additional things on this sheet:

- Specify the email format. Formatted text is the default, which is the preferred format for most email programs.

- Include field names with the data by selecting the Include Field Names check box.

- In the Subject Line text box, specify the subject line that should appear in the email message header. This is, of course, to help you figure out from what form the information came and why you were collecting it. If you want the subject line to contain the results of a form field, select the Form Field Name check box and type the name of the field into the Subject Line text box.

- Use the Reply-To Line text box to specify the form field whose value should appear in the email's reply-to line. If you don't want this result, deselect the Form Field Name check box (it's marked On by default) and type the desired text into the text box.

USING THE CONFIRMATION PAGE SHEET

You can enter an optional confirmation page in the URL of Confirmation Page text box. A standard HTML confirmation page is automatically sent to the reader's browser if this text box is left blank. Use the URL of Validation Failure box to send a page telling the submitter that the information submitted is invalid; this is optional. Note that this field is grayed out until at least one validation is created for a form field.

USING THE SAVED FIELDS SHEET

You can use the Saved Fields sheet to specify which form fields to include in the results file. When this sheet is first opened, the Form Fields to Save list box displays the names of all the fields on the form (see Figure 11.8). You can delete or rearrange these fields. Whatever fields you make appear in the list box are written to the results file in the order of their appearance.

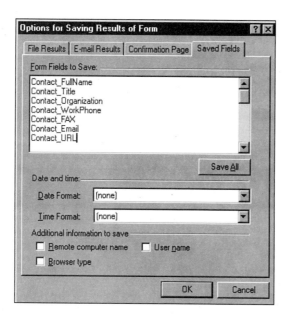

Figure 11.8
Use the Saved Fields sheet to specify the fields to be saved and the order of their appearance in the results file.

You can save the date and time the respondent submitted the form by specifying a date or time format in the appropriate text boxes. The Additional Information to Save section includes three check boxes that can provide additional information to the results file about the respondent.

USING HIDDEN FIELDS

There is a provision for hidden fields in the Form Properties dialog box. To access it, click the Advanced button. These fields don't show up in a browser but are sent to the form handler as a field name plus the value in that field. This is called a *name-value pair*. You create name-value pairs by choosing Add and filling in a field name and a value for the field in the Name/Value Pair dialog box. You can modify or remove the entry once it's created.

Now that you've sorted all that out, you can continue to put more form fields onto your page.

Note

The Target Frame text box deals with a framed environment. For details, see Chapter 9, "Enhancing Web Sites with FrontPage Frames."

SELECTING FIELDS TO ADD TO YOUR FORM

To insert a field, choose Insert, Form and select the desired field from the submenu that appears. The field gets inserted at the cursor position. You have eight field types, ranging from one-line text boxes to labels.

ADDING A ONE-LINE TEXT BOX

The one-line text box gives you a field one line high and up to 999 characters long. You use it for short answers, such as name, phone number, or email address. When you select it, a text box appears on the screen inside the dotted form boundary. Type the label text of the box next to it (or wherever you like) to identify the box for its users.

Tip #63

You can use the Increase Indent and Decrease Indent buttons to line up blocks of fields. Remember also that you can use tables inside forms to arrange your form fields.

What about configuring the form field content? You do this by clicking the field to select it and choosing Format, Properties. The Text Box Properties dialog box appears (see Figure 11.9).

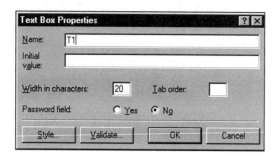

Figure 11.9
Use the Text Box
Properties dialog box
to set up the
parameters for the
form field.

You set up a text box via the following steps:

1. Assign a name to the Text Box field by entering an appropriate name in the Name text box. This is the *name* part of the name/value pair associated with the field. (It has nothing to do with the prompt or question text that appears on the form itself.)

2. If you want the box to start off with some specific wording, type that text into the Initial Value text box. If you don't want such an initial value, leave the text box blank.

3. Type a number into the Width in Characters text box to set the width of the box when it appears on the form.

4. Choose the Yes option button in the Password Field section if you want the text box to be a password field, so that characters typed into it are masked.

If you are targeting Internet Explorer 4 or later as the main browser, you can specify a tab order in this or in any other Form Field dialog box; do so by entering a number in the Tab Order box.

Tab Order works like this: Assume you have five fields in a form column and have given the top field the tab order 2 and the third field the tab order 1. The insertion point starts in the third field in this case. Pressing the Tab key moves the insertion point to the top field (because you designated it as tab order 2). Remember that this only works with IE 4 and later. To remove the field from the tab order, enter -1.

Now comes a very important step: data validation. This allows you to reject spurious data at the browser or client side of the information transaction. The server isn't burdened with validation if you do this, thereby relieving it of much of its data-processing load. Choose the Validate button to open the Text Box Validation dialog box (see Figure 11.10). Or you can right-click the field and select Form Field Validation from the shortcut menu.

The Display Name dialog box specifies a name the user sees in error dialog boxes if the internal field name is different from the text beside the field as it appears on the form. Make this name the same as the text that the form shows for the field; the user will know which field to correct.

PART

II

CH

11

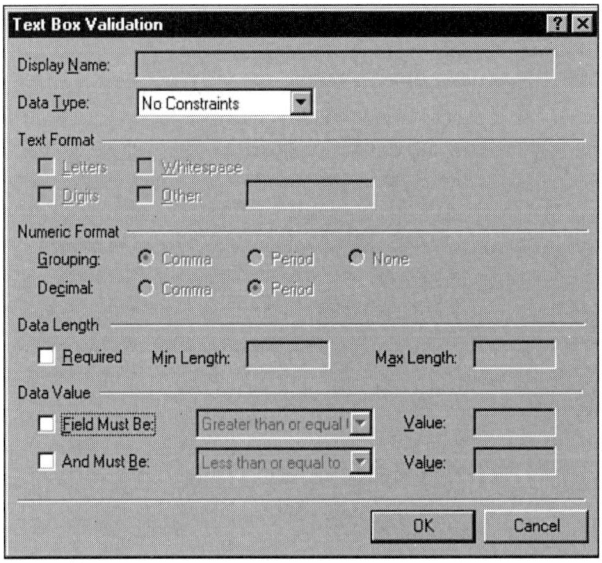

Figure 11.10
Validate your users' input before it's sent to the server.

The other fields here are self explanatory. You can specify the data type (no constraints, text, numeric, integer), kinds of text allowed, numeric format, minimum, maximum, and required data length, and data value ranges. To get this right, you must have a thorough understanding of the information formats you want. Plan ahead and test, test, test.

Once you've specified the validation parameters, choose OK to return to the Text Box Properties dialog box; choose OK again to place the completed field on the form. When a user types the wrong kind of data into a field (numbers instead of text, for example) and presses the Submit button, a message requests a specified correction.

Caution

Several sheets are displayed if you open the Form Properties dialog box and choose Options. (You saw the sheets earlier.) Confirmation Page is one such sheet. On this sheet you can specify a page that indicates whether there has been a validation failure of a particular field. If you do so, users don't see error messages if they try to submit an incorrect form. Instead, the validation failure page appears.

Tip #64

Sizing handles appear when you click a text box. You can change the size of the box, within limits, by dragging the handles.

ADDING A SCROLLING TEXT BOX

This field lets the user type in multiple lines of text. The Scrolling Text Box Properties dialog box resembles that of the one-line text box, except that here you can specify the number of lines allowed for a scrolling text box. Setting the properties for a scrolling text box is similar to setting them for a one-line text box, except that you can specify the number of lines, but no password. The validation procedure is identical.

Tip #65	To quickly open a field's Properties dialog box, double-click the field in the FrontPage workspace.

ADDING A CHECK BOX

You use check boxes for a list of fields that can be selected or deselected (see Figure 11.11). For example, if you want to know which books on a supplied list a reader owns, the reader can check several fields, one, or none. You can specify the field's initial state as marked or unmarked. The default value is ON; this means that if the check box's initial state is unmarked, ON is the value returned to the form handler if someone does mark it. A null value is returned if the box remains unmarked. You use these values to figure out which fields are true or false for a given respondent.

Because a check box returns only ON or null, no validation is required.

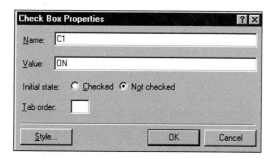

Figure 11.11
Use the Check Box Properties dialog box to set the returned data values.

ADDING RADIO BUTTONS

You use radio buttons instead of check boxes when the reader must provide one—and only one—answer from a list. One button in a group of buttons is always selected; clicking another deselects the initially chosen button. You must have more than one button in order for the tool to be useful; a single button will always be ON, which doesn't tell you much.

You use the Radio Button Properties dialog box to set up the group (see Figure 11.12). All the buttons that work together must have the same group name, which you enter in the Group Name text box. In the Value text box, type the value that the field returns when clicked. The initial state can be Selected or Not Selected.

Figure 11.12
Option buttons must be grouped into sets with the Radio Button Properties dialog box.

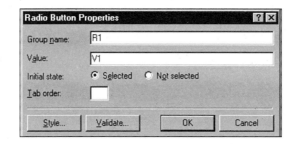

There is also a validation procedure for option buttons; if the Data Required check box is selected, the user must check one of the radio buttons. The Display Name box serves the same purpose the one-line text box serves.

USING A DROP-DOWN MENU

A drop-down menu is another way to give a user choices. The Drop-Down Menu Properties dialog box is a little more complicated than the others (see Figure 11.13).

Figure 11.13
You can give the user a menu by using the Drop-Down Menu Properties dialog box.

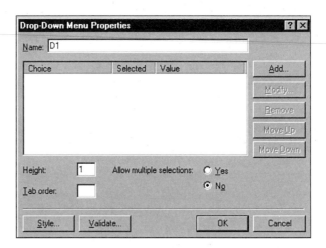

Set up a drop-down menu via the following steps:

1. Choose Insert, Form, Drop-Down Menu to insert a menu, then double-click it to open the Drop-Down Menu Properties dialog box. Type a name for the menu in the Name text box.

2. The Add Choice dialog box appears when you choose Add. In the Choice text box, type the menu entry as it appears to the user.

3. Leave the Specify Value check box unselected if you want the form to return the value specified in the Choice text box. If you select the check box, a new, untitled box automatically opens in which you can type the value that is returned instead. The user's menu entry remains the same, however, as in the Choice text box.

4. Click Selected or Not Selected to specify whether the menu entry is highlighted in the user's browser. Selected returns the value in the Choice text box; Not Selected returns a null value.

5. Choose OK to return to the Drop-Down Menu Properties dialog box. Repeat steps 2 through 4 until the menu is complete.

6. Select Yes or No in the Drop-Down Menu Properties dialog box to enable or disable multiple selections.

7. Specify the menu box's height. The menu behavior varies depending on the browser, so experiment.

8. Modify or rearrange the entries, if necessary, with the Modify, Move Up, and Move Down buttons.

9. Use the Validation button to go to the Validation dialog box and set the required conditions, if any, for the data.

10. Choose OK to insert the menu field into the form.

ADDING A PUSH BUTTON

Finally, life gets a little simpler with the Push Button Properties dialog box (see Figure 11.14). Assign the button a name and type the label you want into the Value/Label box. Mark the appropriate option button to choose whether it's a Normal, Submit, or Reset button. (Submit you know about; Reset clears all the form's fields.) Submit and Reset buttons were automatically added when you created the form, of course, but you might want to relabel them (or you might accidentally delete one and have to replace it). A Normal button is a generic one that does nothing until you assign a script to it. The button appears on the form when you choose OK.

> **Note**
>
> You can also use style sheets with the button text. For more information, see Chapter 12, "Using Style Sheets with Individual Pages and Full Sites."

ADDING A PICTURE FIELD

You might think that inserting a picture field has the same purpose as inserting an image, but it doesn't. A picture field does the same thing a Submit button does. When you insert a picture field, you give it a name in its Field Properties dialog box, edit its properties if

PART
II

CH
11

needed, and choose OK. You can't edit its link, though, because a picture field cannot have a link. It's really just a fancy Submit button.

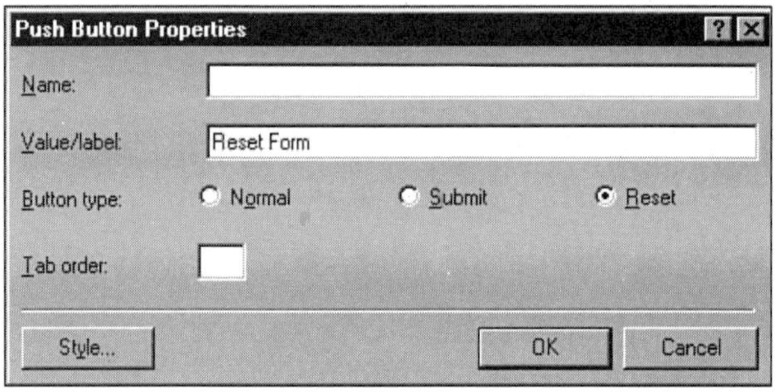

Figure 11.14
The Push Button Properties dialog box gives you a bit of control over the look of the Reset and Submit buttons.

ADDING A FORM LABEL

This command assigns the label text to the `<LABEL>` tag's `VALUE` attribute. To use it, insert the form field and type some text next to it to be the field label. Select both the form field and the label text and choose Insert, Form, Label to carry out the command. If you inspect the page's HTML, you'll see that the `<LABEL> </LABEL>` container is applied to the field label's text.

CHANGING THE FORM PROPERTIES

Changing the form's properties is the final way of customizing a form. Right-click anywhere inside the form boundaries and then select Form Properties from the shortcut menu. This opens the Form Properties dialog box that you looked at in detail earlier.

CREATING A CUSTOM CONFIRMATION FOR YOUR VISITORS

When a visitor submits a form, FrontPage automatically returns a confirmation of what he entered. This is a bare-bones confirmation; you might like something a little more decorative. You achieve that decoration with the confirmation field component, which you use in a confirmation page you create.

To do this, open the form and double-click any field you want to confirm. Write down the field name that appears in the Name text box and click Cancel. Do this until you have a list of all the field names you're going to confirm.

You can then create a new Normal page and edit it to be the Confirmation page. Use the following steps at each place you want a confirmation to appear:

1. Choose Insert, Component, Confirmation Field. The Confirmation Field Properties dialog box appears.
2. The dialog box has one text box—Name of Form Field to Confirm. Type the name of a field from your written list into this text box and choose OK. The field name appears in your page.

3. Repeat steps 1 and 2 until you've entered all the confirmations. Save the Confirmation page.

4. Go to the form you want to confirm. Right-click it and select Form Properties. The Form Properties dialog box appears.

5. Choose the Options button. When the Options for Saving Results dialog box appears, click the Confirmation Page tab.

6. Insert the URL of the Confirmation page you just created into the URL of Confirmation Page text box. Choose OK twice (do not double-click) to close the Form Properties dialog box.

7. Save the page and test it. When you submit the form, you should see your custom Confirmation page in your browser.

UNDERSTANDING THE DISCUSSION FORM HANDLER

You've likely noticed that the Form Properties dialog box offers a grayed-out text box next to a Send To Other option button. Select this option button to make the text box active and then click the arrow button to the right of the text box. This option lets you send results to a script or to two specialized form handlers, one of which is the Discussion handler.

This *Discussion handler* is specifically designed to handle inputs from a discussion web, which you create by using the Discussion Web Wizard. This is certainly the best way to set up a discussion group. However, you might want to modify some of the pages' properties.

Use the normal editing tools to change the look of the page; a discussion group page is like any other except in its form handler and some of its properties. To modify the properties, right-click within any form boundary and choose Form Properties. When the Form Properties dialog box appears, choose the Options button. This opens the Options for Discussion Form Handler dialog box, which has three tabbed sheets. The dialog box defaults to the Discussion sheet.

UNDERSTANDING THE DISCUSSION SHEET

The Options for Discussion Form Handler sheet specifies how the Discussion web behaves in normal operation (see Figure 11.15):

- Use the Title text box to edit the name of the discussion group. This name appears on all articles.

- Use the Directory text box to specify in which directory FrontPage should store all the articles. This directory must be hidden. The text box has an initial underscore (the sign of a hidden directory) to remind you of this.

- Use the Table of Contents Layout section to customize the TOC's look, which automatically regenerates every time someone submits an article. You can modify what appears in the TOC's subject descriptions by typing field names into the Form Fields text box. You can have more than one field; just separate them with spaces. Selecting the Time and Date check boxes displays the date and time of submission for each article. Selecting the Remote Computer Name and User Name check boxes displays remote computer names and the usernames of the authors, respectively. Finally, you can decide whether the articles appear from oldest to newest or the reverse.

Figure 11.15
The Discussion sheet lets you customize the group title, TOC appearance, and Confirmation page.

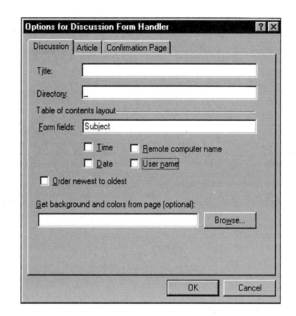

UNDERSTANDING THE ARTICLE AND CONFIRMATION PAGE SHEETS

The Article tab establishes additional information that shows up in each article. You can specify the URLs of your standard header and footer, time and date of the article's submission, and remote computer and author names. If you want a custom confirmation or validation failure page, insert their URLs into the appropriate boxes on the Confirmation Page sheet.

UNDERSTANDING REGISTRATION FORMS AND WEB SECURITY

A Registration form gives you some control over who gets into a particular web on your host. The basic procedure is this: A new user accesses a Registration form stored in your site's root Web and registers with a username and password for a particular root Web child web. This is done through the user's Web browser, and isn't very tight security. However, it does make it unnecessary for registered users to keep entering their name into some types of form fields; the server finds out who they are when they log on. In addition, there's some assurance to others that it's really you communicating with them, not an impostor.

Note that setting up a registered-access web requires the web to be server based, not disk based. This is because the registration information is saved in the server's root Web. *Root Web* may sound mysterious, but it isn't. If you're running the Microsoft Internet

Information Server, for example, and if your machine's name is MyPC, then the root Web's URL is simply http://MyPC. Accordingly, you would open the root Web in FrontPage by using this URL in the Open Web dialog box.

> If you have created some server-based webs in PWS 4 by now, you'll notice that they appear as subfolders of C:\Inetpub\wwwroot. These webs under the root Web are called *subwebs* or *child webs*. The root Web is thus the parent web of all child webs.

However, there are some significant limitations to using registration forms. To begin, Web security in FrontPage 2000 depends on the type of server that is being used to host the webs. Some servers provide excellent security tools, others none at all. If you're using PWS 4, for example, you won't be able to test your registration forms because PWS 4 does not let you set permissions for your webs.

Furthermore, FrontPage security for Microsoft servers is based on ACLs (Access Control Lists). If you are using Microsoft Internet Information Server (IIS), this means that your webs must be hosted on a Windows NT NTFS disk partition, rather than on a Windows 95/98 FAT disk partition. UNIX and non-Microsoft servers also use access lists, but of course do not require webs to be on an NTFS partition; refer to their documentation to determine how you should handle security issues.

Finally, Windows NT security and Microsoft Internet Information Server (IIS) do not allow registration through a Web browser.

CREATING A REGISTRATION FORM

As noted previously, using a registration form successfully depends on setting up an appropriate Web server in the correct manner. Assuming this has been done, follow these steps to create the registration form:

1. Open the server's root Web. (All registration forms must reside in the root Web to work properly, even though users are registering for a child web.)

2. Choose File, New, Page and then select the User Registration template from the list box.

3. Use the instructions included with the template as a guide to modifying it. After that, change the title and heading of the page to suit the web it's for. If you want more information from the registrant, add form fields to collect it.

4. Once you are satisfied with the form, right-click any form field and select Form Properties to open the Form Properties dialog box. Notice that the form handler is automatically set to be the Registration Form Handler.

5. Click the Options button in the Form Properties dialog box. This opens the Options for Registration Form Handler dialog box, which has four tabbed sheets. The Registration sheet is the default.

6. Type the name of the protected web for which the users are registering in the Registration sheet's Web Name box.

7. In the User Name Field text box, provide the name of the field where the user types his username.

8. In the Password Field text box, provide the name of the form field into which the user will type a password.

9. In the Password Confirmation Field text box, provide the name of the form field where the user confirms his password.

10. Select the Require Secure Password check box to force the user to specify a password with at least six characters. For better security, choose a password that does not resemble the user name.

11. Give the URL of the page the user sees if his registration fails in the URL of Registration Failure Page box. A default failure page is used if you leave this box blank.

12. Choose OK. The File Results, Confirmation Page, and Saved Fields sheets are identical to those you saw earlier. Use them to set other parameters for the form. By default, the results file is stored in the root web's _private folder.

13. Choose OK again to close the Form Properties dialog box and save the page. The web is now set up to accept only registered users.

Note

Step 4 refers to the Registration Form Handler's appearance in the Form Properties dialog box's Send to Other text box. This handler is specifically written to handle registration forms. Don't change this setting. The forms won't work if you do.

USING THE REGISTRATION FORM

To register for the protected web, users have to access the root Web and complete the form page for that particular web. This includes choosing a username and password, so if you have more than one protected web, you need a Registration form for each one. Remember that the registrants must have access to these forms.

The security check is actually made at the browser level. When a user's browser contacts the page's URL, a username and password box appear in the browser window. The user can't get into the web unless he knows both of these items. Once he's in, however, all pages in that web are accessible to him—even if he leaves the web and returns. The security isn't enforced again until the browser is shut down and restarted.

USING TEMPLATES TO CREATE INTERACTIVE PAGES

FrontPage supplies five templates that have components or similar interactive elements. The way the templates use these components and form fields gives you useful examples to follow when you're setting up the interactive parts of your site. Now that you know a lot more about how your visitors can communicate with you through forms, it's time to have a look at these types of pages.

Caution

When you use the templates, remember to use their form properties to rename the files where they store their results (if applicable). Leaving the result files at their default names may cause data to be overwritten or jumbled.

- The Guest Book template uses a scrolling text box to gather comments about a site. It sends the data with the commentator's username to a file named GUESTLOG.HTM. This file is displayed in the lower part of the page via an include page component; the visitor can see what other people have said about the site. This page also has a comment component at the top to give instructions for use, and a Date and Time component at the bottom to show when the page was last updated or edited. All the templates have these two components, so they aren't mentioned again. See Chapter 7, "Using Active Elements, Shared Borders, and Navigation Bars," for more information on using them.

- The Search Page template uses the search component to find instances of a text string in the current web's public pages. The page includes two bookmarks for navigation and a section that describes how to use the query language. See Chapter 7 for more information.

- The Table of Contents template is nothing more than a page with a Table of Contents component in it. Remember that you don't see the real TOC unless you view the page in a browser.

- The Feedback Form template is really an elaborated example of the Guest Book template. An interesting addition is the set of four radio buttons that help classify the kind of feedback being given. Inspect these buttons' properties to see how default button values are used.

- The Confirmation Form template is a general-purpose tool for letting users know that you've recorded the information they sent you. The template uses several Confirmation field components. To use it, type its name into the URL of Confirmation Page text box for the page you want confirmed. See "Creating a Custom Confirmation for Your Visitors," in this chapter.

TROUBLESHOOTING

Forms can be error-prone creatures. One way to minimize problems in debugging them is to use uniquely named and easily identified labels for the various fields of the form. Another is to make sure that the parameters you specify for field verification are suitable to the information that people will type into that field; also make sure that the parameter ranges (if applicable) are correctly set. Finally, ensure that the proper form handler is active for the kind of form you're using. For example, if you create a Registration Form and accidentally set the form handler to Custom or to Discussion, the form will not work.

DESIGNERS CORNER

Form design is something of an art, but the basic principles are easily understood. They were examined earlier in this chapter, but a checklist for forms design is always a good thing to have. Here is one you can use:

- Be up front with your visitors. Tell them exactly why you need the information they submit via the form, and how you will use it. If they might have privacy concerns, address these suitably and honestly.

- Do not clutter the form. Keep it simple.

- Keep the questions brief, and proceed from the general to the specific.

- If you would like an item of information, but don't absolutely require it, indicate to the user that filling in that particular field is optional. Better yet, if it really isn't necessary, don't ask for it.

- Do not ask leading questions.

- Do not ask ambiguous questions.

- Test the form before putting it into service. You want accurate information, and if there is a way to misinterpret a question and give you incorrect data, people will find it.

CHAPTER **12**

USING STYLE SHEETS WITH INDIVIDUAL PAGES AND FULL SITES

In this chapter

by Dennis Jones

WHAT ARE STYLE SHEETS?

A style sheet is a page styling template you create yourself; it embeds special commands within HTML formatting tags to specify the appearance of a Web page or pages. Style sheets provide

- More complex formatting capabilities, especially greater control over text appearance and placement. These formatting effects can be achieved without complex and awkward HTML workarounds.

- More flexible and simpler control of the formatting across multiple pages. You don't need to turn tags on and off to change the look of individual page elements, and the reduced number of tags makes your HTML code much easier to read and follow.

- Fast changes to the formatting of a page or pages, by changing a few parameters in a linked style sheet. This lets you make major changes to the appearance of a whole site, without the drudgery of modifying every page the site contains.

- Greater potential for sophisticated page design, based on a style sheet standard that all browsers will (eventually) be able to recognize.

The implementation of style sheets in FrontPage 2000 is based on that of the World Wide Web Consortium's CSS1 specification. You can access this at `http://www.w3.org/TR/ REC-CSS1`.

If you want information about CSS2, refer to the W3C site at `http://www.w3.org/TR/ REC-CSS2/`.

The term *cascading style sheets* refers to the fact that you can use multiple styles to determine how your page looks. A style sheet-supporting browser follows a set hierarchy to determine which formatting elements get displayed and which don't.

With Internet Explorer 3 and 4 and later and Netscape Navigator 4 and later, you have several different approaches to employing style sheets: linked styles, imported styles, embedded styles, and inline styles. All four styling methods work with these browsers and behave as follows:

- *Embedded style sheets*—You actually insert a style sheet specification into a particular page. Changing a parameter modifies the look of the complete page.

- *Inline styles*—These modify the behavior of a single tag, a group of tags, or a block of information on a single page.

- *Linked style sheets*—Your regular Web pages link to such a sheet (this is actually just a text file with a CSS extension) that determines how they'll look. With linking, you can change the look of many pages by changing only the style sheet file.

- *Imported style sheets*—These style sheets, which also have the CSS extension, are imported by the browser rather than simply linked to the Web page. The difference between linking and importing is that styles specified in imported style sheets can be combined with other style declarations in a `<STYLE>` block on the Web page—in fact, imported style sheets *must* be referenced in a `<STYLE>` block, not with the `<LINK>` tag. This lets you combine external style sheets with local styles within the `<STYLE>` block for flexibility in setting up page appearance. Styles specified by linked style sheets can't be used this way.

You can mix these approaches on a single page, too—using one doesn't preclude the use of others. The rules of precedence for the different style sheets are described later in this chapter in the "Understanding Cascading" section.

No doubt you're eager to explore the tools provided by FrontPage 2000 for the creation of style sheets. You'll get to this, but the way FrontPage handles style sheets will make much more sense if you examine the underlying syntax of style sheet HTML. The next few sections will cover this, and then you'll go on to using FrontPage.

BUT WHAT ABOUT BROWSER COMPATIBILITY?

If you have already used style sheets, you will be aware that the Internet Explorer 4 and Netscape 4 browsers are not fully compatible when it comes to rendering styled pages. The upcoming version 5 of each browser may alleviate this situation, but you'll have to wait and see. Until then, or until Microsoft and Netscape browsers achieve reasonable compatibility in handling CSS, the safest course is to test all aspects of a style in each browser.

However, to avoid reinventing the wheel and doing all the testing yourself, you can use the Web to find out what style elements are compatible—or not—with the major browsers. One such resource is at `http://webreview.com/wr/pub/guides/style/mastergrid.html`.

More resources regarding style sheets can also be found at `http://webreview.com/wr/pub/guides/style/`, the parent of the previous page.

This page has links to a "danger list" of style elements, as well as to a "safe list," and also provides tutorials on style sheet usage.

PART

II

CH

12

UNDERSTANDING STYLE SHEET SYNTAX

With linked and embedded style sheets, you include at least one definition of the style in the HEAD section of the page. The style definition format is as follows:

```
<ANY HTML TAG>{ property1 name: property1 value; property2 name: property 2
value }</ANY HTML TAG>
```

Note that curly braces were used to set off the definition itself. (The extra spaces between the curly braces and the contained code are for readability; you can leave them out if you wish.) There can be as many properties as you like within these braces. The style definitions are enclosed in the `<STYLE>` `</STYLE>` tags. Where these are placed within the HTML file depends on the kind of style sheet you're using.

USING EMBEDDED STYLES

Embedding a style sheet is straightforward. Insert a <STYLE> </STYLE> tag pair into the document between the <HEAD> tags. This styling block controls the appearance of the entire Web page in which it's embedded. Internet Explorer 3 and later automatically registers the MIME media type for style sheets, so you can include the TYPE="text/css" parameter within the style tags to direct non-supporting browsers to disregard the style sheet.

In addition, to make sure non-supporting browsers don't display the text of the style definitions, you can comment out the style block with <!-- and -->.

Here's an example of what it looks like:

```
<HTML>
<HEAD><title>Some Styles</title>
<STYLE TYPE="text/css">
<!--
BODY { font: 10pt "Arial"; color: maroon }
H1 { font: 24pt "Courier New"; color: blue }
P { font: 10pt "Arial"; color: red }
-->
</STYLE>
</HEAD>
<BODY>
<H1>A HEADING </H1>
<P>Some Text</P>
</BODY>
</HTML>
```

If you edit this directly into a page and then use Preview or the Preview in Browser command, you'll see a 24-point blue heading in Courier New font, and the words "Some Text" in 10-point Arial in red. Note that the <BODY> tag specifies that text is to be maroon unless some other style specification changes it. The <P> tag's style definition of color: red did exactly that, which is why "Some Text" appears in red rather than maroon.

Tip #66	You would assign styles to the <BODY> tag to set the overall appearance of your page, as in the previous example. These effects take place globally. Then, to set individual styles for particular elements, you define these in the rest of the <STYLE> block, as is done with the <P> and <H1> tags.

The values inside the curly braces next to the H1 define the style for all Heading 1 headings in the page; the values inside the curly braces next to the P do the same for all paragraph (normal) text in the page. You can change the global look of the page by changing the values within the curly braces.

USING INLINE STYLES

You use inline styles to set the properties of a single tag and its contents. To do this, you place the style attributes within the tag itself. To set the color and attributes of a normal paragraph of text, you'd use this syntax:

```
<P STYLE ="color:green;font-style:italic">
This text is green and in italics.
</P>
```

As you can figure out for yourself, the result is green, italicized text. Note that quotation marks, not curly braces, are used to define the attributes list.

Note also that if an inline style differs from the embedded style block of the page, or from a linked or imported style, the inline style takes precedence. In the previous example, no matter how the <P> tag is defined in the page's <STYLE> block, the inline style will make the text of this paragraph into green italics.

Sometimes you want to change the look of a large block of a page, and inserting the same inline attributes for each tag within that block would be tedious and error-prone. For this, you use the <DIV> tag. For example:

```
<DIV STYLE = "font-size: 14pt; color: red">
. . . block of HTML code . . .
</DIV>
```

This makes a global color and font size change to all the text contained within the <DIV> tags. In other words, if you have several <P> sections and a <UL> section or two, you don't have to set inline styles for each tag. However, if you do add an inline style to one tag of that larger block, the style will override the <DIV>-defined style and apply the different appearance to the part enclosed only in that tag.

Another handy inline style tag is the <SPAN> tag. This is used to affect text within a block element, such as the <P> element. You can use it as an inline attribute, as follows:

```
<P>This is black text. This is <SPAN STYLE="color:red">RED TEXT</SPAN> and now
this is black text. </P>
```

The result of this HTML will be the phrase RED TEXT appearing in red within a line of black text.

SPAN can also be used within the STYLE block. Within the block, write "SPAN {color:lime}" and then use the <SPAN> </SPAN> tag pair to wrap some text within some text. The wrapped text will be a lime color (pale green). These principles can also be applied to the <DIV> tag.

PART

II

CH

12

Note

The <DIV> and <SPAN> tags are similar enough in function to cause a bit of confusion. Briefly, DIV provides a way to group style properties for elements that may not have them in common. The properties can be applied to the elements as a group rather than individually, which reduces the amount of HTML code you have to write. SPAN is more limited, and is intended as a text-level tag to surround small quantities of text that are to be rendered inline.

GROUPING TAGS

Sometimes you want several different tags styled the same way. You can define the styles individually for each tag in the embedded style section, but there's a shortcut. If you wanted formatted and normal text to have the same look, for example, you'd write

```
H1,H2,H3 { font-style: italic; color: blue }
```

and this would affect all three heading styles. You *must* use the commas to separate the tags or the grouping won't work.

USING LINKED STYLE SHEETS

To set this up, create a file with the desired style definitions, using exactly the same techniques you use for embedded styles. Save the file with a CSS extension and link to it from the page that is to have that style. In practice, if you wanted all the pages in your Web to have the same style, you'd link each one to the style sheet. The syntax is as follows:

```
<HEAD>
<TITLE> Title of Page </TITLE>
<LINK REL=STYLESHEET HREF= "mystyles.css" TYPE="text/css">
</HEAD>
```

The forward link type REL=STYLESHEET indicates that LINK specifies a link to a style sheet, and that this style sheet is to be applied to the page where the forward link resides (for example, the page where the LINK statement appears).

SPECIFYING A STYLE CLASS OR ID

Creating a class lets you make up variations on a base tag (like <P>) and use these variations either globally on a page (if the class definition is in an embedded style) or globally in the Web (if the style definition is in a linked or imported style sheet).

Let's say you want three types of <P> text: one bold, one italic, and one bold and green. The code for this would be:

```
<STYLE>
<!--
P.bold { font-weight:bold }
P.italic { font-style:italic }
P.boldgreen { font-weight:bold; color:green }
-->
</STYLE>
```

Here, for example, P.bold is the name of a style class. You would place the code above either in the STYLE block at the head of the page (for embedded styles) or in the linked style sheet (for linked styles). Then, when you wanted to use the tag classes on the page, you would write:

```
<P CLASS=bold>Bold is easy using the class attribute.</P>
<P CLASS=italic>Italic is easy using the class attribute.</P>
<P CLASS=boldgreen>Bold and green are easy using the class attribute.</P>
<P> This text is unaffected by any styles.</P>
```

The bold, italic, and boldgreen are arbitrarily chosen names for the three classes. You could have a class style called P.aardvark if you wanted to. These are of course trivial examples meant as illustration of the method; depending on your needs, you might prefer to use the <I> tag to italicize the text, rather than go to the trouble of creating a style class.

Note

> Netscape 4 doesn't work with classes defined in the header style declaration if you use a number in the class declaration. An example that doesn't work would be p.3 {font-weight: bold}. Netscape 4 does work if the class is a letter (p.b {font-weight: bold}, for example).

IDs are assigned on an individual basis to define the style of an element. An ID is specified by using the indicator # to precede a label for the identifier. ID syntax looks like this:

```
#xyz { color:red }
```

This would be referenced in HTML by the ID attribute:

```
<P ID=xyz >Red Text</P>
```

IDs are most useful in scripts because they can be used to reference specific page elements so that the script can change them.

SPECIFYING LEADING

Leading (pronounced "ledding") is the adjustment of the space between lines of text, measured from text baseline to text baseline. Typographers use leading to make subtle changes to the text density on a page. To set leading in your page, use the line-height style attribute. For example, to set the <P> tag to produce Normal text with 24 points between text baselines, you'd use the attribute as follows:

```
P { line-height:24pt }
```

If you were doing a lot of variable line spacing, using the CLASS attribute would be useful. You'd insert some modified <P> tags into a STYLE block, like this:

```
<STYLE>
<!--
P.12 { line-height:12pt }
p.18 { line-height:18pt }
p.24 { line-height:24pt }
-->
</STYLE>
```

Then you'd use them in your text, like this:

```
<P CLASS=18>This line is 18 points from its baseline to the baseline of the
line above it.</P>
```

PART

II

CH

12

UNDERSTANDING CASCADING

If you use several style sheets whose definitions conflict, the results are settled by cascading. Cascading is simply a set of rules for determining which style takes precedence if there are conflicting style declarations: for example, if an embedded style says that <P> elements are to be blue, but an inline style down the page says that <P> elements in that part of the page are to be green, the green takes precedence over the blue. Overall, the W3C specification states that inline styles will override embedded styles, which will in turn override imported styles, which will then override linked styles.

CREATING STYLE SHEETS WITH FRONTPAGE

Style sheet use in FrontPage is not exactly WYSIWYG, but it is certainly easier than coding the HTML by hand. Essentially, you insert styling code into a STYLE block using preset choices from a dialog box. Alternatively, you can add inline styles to a page element by using the Class sheet of the Style dialog box. Finally, you can create an external style sheet and reference it as an imported or linked style sheet.

CREATING AN EMBEDDED STYLE

As you'll remember from the discussion earlier in this chapter, embedded styles are those you define with the STYLE block inside the HEAD section of the page. An example of creating such a style block is given in the following procedures. The example sets up a page that uses the Courier New font as default with maroon as the default text color (in other words, the <BODY> tag is to have these style attributes). Furthermore, the STYLE block will set all H1 level headings to appear in black Arial, bold italic, with a solid-line border, and all paragraphs will have a left margin of 16 pixels.

SETTING FONTS AND COLORS

FrontPage's method of creating a style sheet requires that you select the page element tag from a list box; the software will then fill in the attributes you want for the page element by using a set of styling dialog boxes. To get started, do the following:

1. Open the page that is to have the style applied to it; it's assumed in the example that the page already has H1 headings and paragraph text on it. Then choose Format, Style. The Style dialog box appears (see Figure 12.1).

2. The Style list box shows all the HTML tags that FrontPage supports and that can have styles applied to them. Begin by selecting the one to which you want to apply a style. (In the example, it's BODY, since you want to define the BODY style as Courier New, colored maroon; this will set the default text of the whole page to this font and color).

Note

The tags in the dialog box are in lower case. Following convention, however, in this book they'll be rendered in upper case. HTML tags aren't case sensitive, of course.

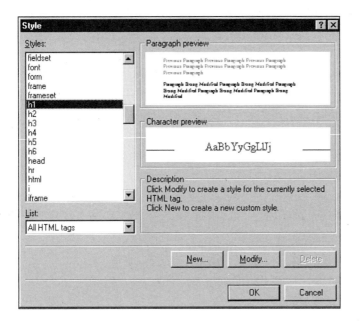

3. Choose Modify. The Modify Style dialog box opens. Choose Format to reveal the drop-down menu of styling choices (see Figure 12.2).

Figure 12.2
You can choose styles of font, paragraph, border, or numbering.

PART

II

CH

12

4. Choose Font. This opens the standard FrontPage Font dialog box. In the Font list box, choose Courier New. In the Color drop-down list, choose the maroon swatch, which is fourth from the left in the top row. If you were inclined, you could also specify font style, size, and effects for the new BODY style.

5. Choose OK to return to the Modify Style dialog box. You'll see a representation of the style in the Preview box, and the actual CSS style code under the Description section. In the example, this reads font-family:Courier New; color: #800000. Note that colors are specified by the hexadecimal RGB code rather than by name (although you can use color names if you are hand-editing the HTML for the style later).

6. Choose OK again to return to the Style dialog box. Note that the Styles list box has only one entry in it—BODY. This is because it's now a user-defined style. This is shown in the drop-down List box beneath it, which now says User-Defined Styles. To return to the full list of HTML tags, you would use the arrow button at the right of this drop-down list box and select All HTML Tags.

7. Choose OK again to close the Style dialog box. The H1 headings and the paragraph text in the page immediately assume the values specified for them by the new BODY style. If you inspect the HTML for the page, you'll see that a <STYLE> block is now present in the HEAD section, with the style code you specified present in it.

You've now established the font and the font color of the BODY element, thus establishing the default font and font color of the page as a whole.

Changing Existing Style Attributes

Suppose you made a mistake in the previous examples and wanted the BODY foreground color to be something other than maroon. Or perhaps you decided that the <BODY> tag should revert to standard HTML values—in other words, that the styles applied to it should be deleted.

Corrections and deletions are quite simple. Do the following:

1. Open the Style dialog box with Format, Style. Select User-Defined Styles from the List box.

2. Select the desired tag from the Styles list box.

3. To remove all user-defined styles from the page element, choose Delete and then OK. However, if you need to modify the styles, choose Modify and use the menu to go to the needed dialog box. (In this example, it would be the Font dialog box, where you can make changes to text colors and fonts.) Make the required changes, and exit from the dialog boxes.

4. Your corrections or deletions will take effect immediately.

SETTING UP TEXT, PARAGRAPH, AND BORDER STYLES

You remember from the introduction to this section that the H1 headings of this page are to be in bold italic, and in Arial font rather than Courier New; they are to have a left margin (an indent, actually) of 16 pixels and be surrounded by a solid border. To set this up, choose Format, Style to open the Style dialog box again. You'll notice again that the Style list box displays only the tag <BODY>, and that the List box under it shows User-Defined Styles. This is because you, the user, have already defined a style for BODY.

However, at the moment you want to define a font style for H1 elements. Click the button at the end of the List box, and select All HTML Tags to display the full list. Now do the following:

1. Scroll to H1, select it, and choose Modify.

2. Choose Format, Font. Use the Font sheet, as you did earlier, to specify Arial, Bold Italic.

3. Choose OK to return to the Modify Style dialog box. Choose Format again, and this time select Paragraph to open the Paragraph dialog box (see Figure 12.3).

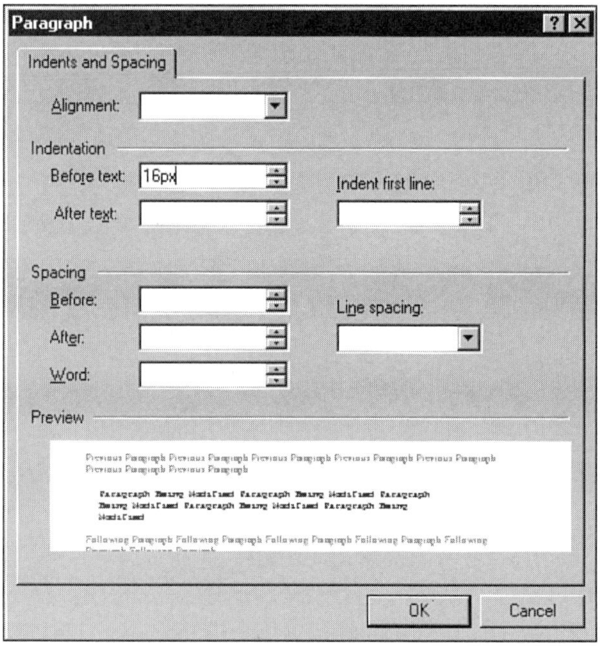

Figure 12.3
You specify paragraph alignment styles with the Paragraph dialog box.

PART

II

CH

12

4. You saw this dialog box back in Chapter 4, "Developing the Basic Page: Text, Lists, and Hyperlinks," in the sections on paragraph layout. Type a value of **16px** into the Before text box and choose OK to return to the Modify Style dialog box.

5. Choose Format again, and then choose Border. This opens the Borders and Shading dialog box (see Figure 12.4).

Figure 12.4
Set borders and bor-der styles with the Borders sheet.

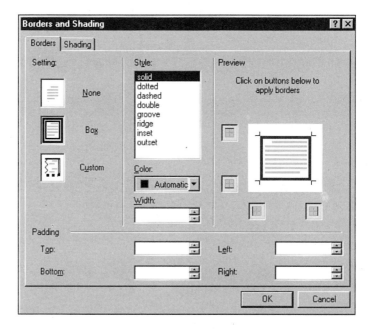

6. To put a simple box around the heading text, click the Box icon to select it. In the Style box, select Solid. In the Color box, select Automatic if it is not already selected.

7. Choose OK to return to the Modify Style box. Since you're finished, choose OK and OK again to close the Style dialog box.

8. The heading will now be in Arial, bold italic, inside a border.

As you probably noticed, the Borders sheet has several other features. With it you can do the following:

- Specify the four borders of the element, with eight different line styles. To apply or remove each border, click the buttons around the preview icon in the Preview section. If you can't see the borders, make sure the Color box shows a color swatch.

- Apply customized borders by specifying the border styles individually for each of the four borders. To do this, select the Custom icon. Then use the Style box to select a border style, and then click a button in the Preview section to apply that style to that particular border.

- Set the color and width for each of these borders.

- Set the padding (spacing) between the insides of the borders and the content within them.

USING THE SHADING SHEET OF THE BORDERS AND SHADING DIALOG BOX

Styles can also be used to apply background and foreground colors for specific page elements, and background images for them as well. Note that this differs from setting page backgrounds and images with the Page Properties dialog box—here, the effect is applied only to the specified page element. For example, setting the background color of the H1 element makes that color appear only behind Heading 1 text. It does not appear on the entire page.

To set these style attributes, do the following:

1. Choose Format, Style to open the Style sheet. Choose Modify, Format, Border to open the Borders and Shading dialog box (see Figure 12.5).

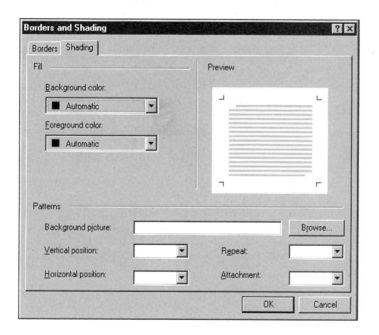

Figure 12.5
The Borders and Shading dialog box is used to apply background effects to page elements.

2. Click the Shading tab to open the Shading sheet.
3. You can now do any or all of the following:
   - Set the Background Color, which will be applied behind the element. This will display on top of any background color specified in the Background sheet of the Page Properties dialog box.
   - Set the Foreground Color, which applies to foreground elements—text, normally.
   - Specify a background image, by using the Browse button or typing the image URL into the Background Picture text box.

- Set the Attachment of the background image. The list box gives you Scroll or Fixed, which determine whether the background image moves along with scrolling text or stays put (if the latter, it's also called a *watermark*).

- Set Repeat value for the background image of the element; the drop-down list gives you repeat, repeat-x, repeat-y, and no-repeat. Repeat tiles the image behind the entire element. Repeat-x tiles the image horizontally in one row across the top of the element, while repeat-y tiles it vertically in one column at the left of the element. No-repeat places one instance of the image at a position defined by the Horizontal and Vertical settings (see the next item).

- Set the Vertical and Horizontal positions of the background image with respect to the top-left corner of the element.

4. When you've finished, use OK to back out of the dialog boxes until you're back in Page view. The effects are applied to the element immediately.

USING STYLES WITH BULLETS AND NUMBERING

The next option on the Format menu of the Styles dialog box is the Numbering selection, which actually controls the styling of both numbered and bulleted lists. When you open it, you get the Bullets and Numbering dialog box you used in Chapter 4. The dialog box here is used in the same way as you learned earlier.

Note that you would use this option to style only <OL>, <UL>, and <LI> tags. Applying bullet or numbering styles to other page elements has no effect.

USING POSITIONING

The last option on the Format menu of the Styles dialog box is Position. This is used to control the relationship of text and images and is treated fully in Chapter 25, "Making Your Pages and Webs More Dynamic."

USING STYLE CLASSES WITH FRONTPAGE

The basic principles of embedded style sheet usage are pretty simple. Using the previous procedures, you specify the styles you want for various page elements, and when you insert the elements into the page, the styles are automatically applied. So, using your example style sheet from the previous sections, you'd get maroon Courier New text whenever you put Normal text on the page. That's the basic use of embedded styles—you get one style per element.

But suppose you need several different styles for paragraphs, or for any other element for that matter. That's where classes come in—you create them with FrontPage and then apply them.

The class creation procedure is exactly the same as you used earlier to create styles for tags—it just involves a bit more typing to add the class name to the tag name. For example, to create an H1 class called H1.indent5, you'd do this:

1. Open the Styles dialog box. From the list box of All HTML Tags, select H1.

2. Choose Modify to open the Modify Style dialog box. You'll see H1 in the text box labeled Name (Selector). "Selector" in our context simply refers to the label—H1 in this case—that selects an HTML tag.

3. Place the insertion point right after H1. Type a period. Then type **indent5**. The whole class name should read H1.indent5, without spaces.

4. Choose Format, and apply the formatting for the style as before. In the example, it's simply to change the H1 heading so that it has an indentation of 5cm.

5. Choose OK to back out of the dialog boxes until you've reached the Style dialog box. Change the Styles list box to show User-Defined Styles, and you'll see the style class H1.indent5 there.

6. Choose OK to exit from the dialog box. If you inspect the style block in the HTML for the page, you'll see the line

   ```
   H1.indent5 { margin-left: 5cm }
   ```

   This is the definition statement for the class H1.indent5.

This is all very well, but how do you apply it? Actually, it's very simple.

Type the text that is to have the style. Click in it. Now open the Style drop-down list box on the Format bar and scroll down to the bottom, past the standard style choices. There you will find the style Heading1.indent5. Click it. The style is immediately applied to the text. You can also select the style before you start typing, and the style will be applied to the new text as you create it.

As you can see, creating a style class is like adding a new style to FrontPage's formatting capabilities. However, the style is an embedded style and therefore is available only while the page where you created it is active—if you close the page or switch to another page, the style is no longer in the Style box.

PART
II

CH
12

Tip #67

> However, if you place a style class in a linked or imported style sheet, the class will be available to all pages in the current web—it will appear in the Style box no matter which page is active.

CREATING A NEW STYLE DEFINITION

You've examined the use of classes to create what amount to custom HTML tags; it's very simple, for example, to create a tag like P.quote that indents a paragraph of text from both margins and leaves half an inch above and below it. As you learned, though, such style classes are bound to their tags and can't be applied in a general way.

However, there is a method of creating a style class so that the style can be applied to any tag. Do the following:

1. Choose Format, Style to open the Style dialog box.
2. Choose New. The New Style dialog box opens. Except for the dialog box title, it is identical to the Modify Style dialog box.
3. Type a name for the style into the Name text box.
4. Choose Format to open the Format menu, and choose the type of formatting you want. Specify the style as you learned earlier.
5. Choose OK until you have returned to the Style dialog box. Note that the name of the style now has a period in front of it. Choose OK again to close the dialog box.

Now go to the HTML sheet of Page view and inspect the style block for the page. Suppose you had specified a style called "narrow" that indented text 75px from each margin and allowed half an inch of whitespace above and below it. You would see this in the style block:

```
.narrow { margin-left: 75px; margin-right: 75px; margin-top: .5in; margin-
bottom: .5in }
```

The style name is .narrow; it differs from the style classes you created earlier only in that it does not have a selector (the name of a tag) prepended to it—in other words it doesn't say, for example, p.narrow or h2.narrow.

You can now apply this style to any text by using the Style box, just as you did with the tag-based classes you created earlier.

USING CLASS AND ID LISTS TO APPLY STYLES

There is another way to apply custom style classes to page elements. This is to use the Class or ID list available in certain dialog boxes.

As an example, suppose you need different appearances for different bulleted lists that appear on the page. You'd begin by creating the required style classes for the various lists, using the procedures described earlier. You might, for instance, use the Style dialog box's New dialog box to create a class called UL.one and another called UL.two (UL, remember, is the tag for an unordered list—that is, a bulleted list). The style definitions, which you can see by inspecting the HTML in the page's STYLE block, might look like this:

```
ul.one { font-family: Arial Black; color: #008000; margin-left: 2cm; margin-
right: 2cm }ul.two { font-family: Courier New; color: #FF0000; margin-left: 3cm }
```

Suppose now that you have created the various bulleted lists and want to apply the UL.two style class to one of them. Do the following:

1. Click anywhere in the list.
2. Choose Format, Bullets and Numbering to open the List Properties dialog box.
3. Choose the Style button. The Modify Style dialog box opens.

4. Click the arrow button at the right end of the Class drop-down list box. This opens a list of all style classes (see Figure 12.6). Note that the tag names are not present, only the style class names.

5. Click the entry that says two. Choose OK twice to back out of the dialog boxes. The style is immediately applied to the entire list.

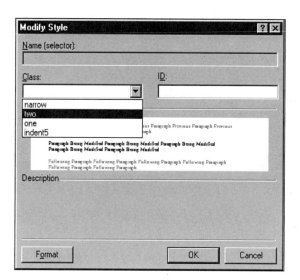

Figure 12.6
Use the Class list box to select an existing style class to apply to an element.

PART

II

CH

12

Note

If you want to apply a class to an element, the class must have been defined for that element. That is, if you have a class P.xyz and try to use the Class dialog box to apply the xyz style to anything but Normal paragraph text, it will have no effect. It would be convenient if the list of classes included the tag (if any) associated with each class; unfortunately, it does not.

If you defined an ID for the style, you can alternatively type its name into the ID text box. Use of the ID attribute for style sheets is discouraged by the W3C, however, as it leads away from the structural approach to style sheets. IDs are recommended for scripting and other uses on the page; for style sheets, you should stick to using classes.

You may have noticed that some dialog boxes have the Style button and others don't; the Paragraph Properties and Font dialog boxes, for example, do not, while the List Properties dialog box does. This is a design decision by Microsoft—it was felt that some types of styling, such as font formatting, are better done with straight HTML rather than with styles.

USING INLINE STYLES

Inline styles are those applied to an HTML tag directly, without using a style definition or a class definition in the STYLE block. You recall that a style block looks like the following:

```
<STYLE>
H2  { margin-left: 5cm }
</STYLE>
```

This indents all H2 headings on the page by 5 centimeters.

However, you might not want to indent some H2 headings. To achieve this, you could create a style class called, for example, H2.indent5, and apply that when you wanted H2 headings indented.

On the other hand, you might want to use the indentation just once, and creating a style class might be overkill. This is where you'd use an inline style. It would be in the page body itself, not in a style block, and it would look like the following:

```
<H2 style = "margin-left: 5cm"> Heading2 Text <H2>
```

But how do you create such code, given that using the Style dialog box creates an embedded style with the style definition placed in the STYLE block?

The answer is that certain options in certain other dialog boxes actually do create inline code for you. For example, when you use the Paragraph Properties dialog box to indent a heading by 5 centimeters, the inline code (previous example) is generated by FrontPage.

Inline code can also be generated through dialog boxes that have Style buttons, for example the Bullets and Numbering dialog box. (Not all dialog boxes have one—as mentioned earlier, the Paragraph Properties and Font dialog boxes do not.)

Suppose you have a bulleted list and want to apply an inline style to it. You'd do the following:

1. Click inside the list. Then choose Format, Bullets and Numbering (or right-click and select List Properties). The List Properties dialog box appears.

2. Choose the Style button, and the Modify Style dialog box appears. You used this in the previous section to style page elements with the Class dialog box. This time, however, you can't use an existing class, because none has been created for the style you want (and that's why you're resorting to an embedded style, of course).

3. To set up the new style for the list, choose the Format button and go on to specify the desired style, just as you've done before.

4. When finished, click OK to back out of the dialog boxes until you're in Page view. The style has now been applied to the list.

5. Inspect the HTML for the list. You'll see the inline style code right after the initial <UL> tag of the list.

CREATING A STYLE SHEET FOR LINKING OR IMPORTING

A linked or imported (external) style sheet is essentially a page with nothing on it but a style definition like the following:

```
P { margin-left: 5cm }
H1 { color: blue }
```

That's all there is on the page—no STYLE tags, no HEAD, no BODY, nothing but CSS styling code. The page's filename must simply have a .CSS extension to indicate that it's a style sheet.

FrontPage 2000 provides several style sheet templates that you can use either as-is or with modifications. To create a style sheet, choose File, New, Page and select the Style Sheets tab. You're provided with a template for a blank style sheet (Normal Style Sheet) and about a dozen prepared examples. Select the one you want and click OK.

Assuming you've chosen the normal, blank sheet, you next choose Format, Style, and apply what you've learned so far to create the styles you want. When you're done, click OK to back out of the dialog boxes. Back in the workspace, you'll see the CSS code on the new style sheet page. Save it with a meaningful name; the .CSS extension will be applied automatically by FrontPage.

LINKING A STYLE SHEET OR SHEETS TO WEB PAGES

You can link more than one style sheet to a single Web page. This provides flexibility because you can apply different styles to different pages, depending on which selections of style sheets you link to them. Be aware, however, that if styles conflict between style sheets, the last style sheet in the link list will take precedence.

To link the sheet (or sheets) to the desired Web page or pages, do the following:

1. If all the pages in the current Web are to use the style sheet(s), go straight to step 2. Otherwise, you must select the particular Web pages that will use the style sheet(s). Do so by opening Folders view and selecting the desired pages.

2. Choose Format, Style Sheet Links. The Link Stylesheet dialog box opens (see Figure 12.7).

3. If all the pages are to use the style sheet(s), mark the All Pages option button; if only selected pages, mark the Selected Page(s) button.

4. Choose Add to open the Select Hyperlink dialog box. Use this dialog box to locate the desired style sheet and select it. Then click OK to return to the Link Stylesheet dialog box. The name of the style sheet appears in the list box.

PART

II

CH

12

5. If there are other style sheets to be linked, repeat step 4. To remove a style sheet, select it and choose Remove. To change the order of loading for the style sheets, use the Up and Down buttons.

6. When you're finished, click OK. If you now open the page or pages (assuming they have some appropriate content) you should see the styles applied there. If you inspect the HTML of a page, you'll see the <LINK> tag(s), one for each linked sheet.

REMOVING STYLE SHEET LINKS

This is essentially the reverse of installing the links. Select the page(s) whose links you want to remove and open the Link Stylesheet dialog box. In the list box, select the style sheet to be unlinked, and choose Remove. Click OK, and the linkage is removed from the Web page(s). Repeat the procedure if more than one sheet is to be unlinked.

Figure 12.7
Use the Link
Stylesheet dialog box
to set up the link
between your Web
page and the external
style sheet or sheets.

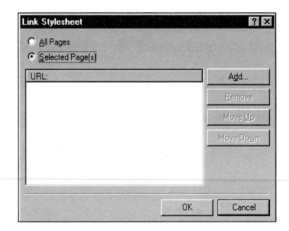

IMPORTING STYLE SHEETS

FrontPage does not provide a method for importing style sheets. Imported sheets, as you may recollect, are inserted into the STYLE block and can be used in conjunction with embedded styles to achieve the desired effects.

If you want to use them, you'll have to edit the STYLE block HTML by hand. On completion it should resemble the following example, which uses two imported style sheets and a P style definition:

```
<STYLE>
@import URL ("one_style.css")
@import URL ("another_style.css")
P { color: blue }
</STYLE>
```

CSS PROPERTIES SUPPORTED BY INTERNET EXPLORER BROWSERS

The following section provides lists of the CSS properties that can be safely used with Internet Explorer 3, 4, and later (the three properties that only work with Internet Explorer 5 are in a separate section). If you propose to use any of these properties in Netscape 4 or later, test their behavior in those browsers.

PROPERTIES SUPPORTED BY INTERNET EXPLORER 3

The style sheet properties supported by Internet Explorer 3 are shown in Table 12.1.

TABLE 12.1   INTERNET EXPLORER 3–SUPPORTED PROPERTIES

Attribute	Description	Values	Example
font-size	Sets text size	points (pt) inches (in) centimeters (cm) pixels (px)	{ font-size:12pt }
font-family	Sets typeface	typeface name	{ font-family: courier }
font-weight	Sets type thickness	extra-light light demi-light medium demi-bold bold extra-bold	{ font-weight: bold }
font-style	Italicizes text	normal italic	{ font-style:italic }
line-height	Sets the distance between baselines	points (pt) inches (in) centimeters (cm) pixels (px) percentage (%)	{ line-height: 24pt }
color	Sets color of text	color name RGB triplet	{ color: blue }
text-decoration	Underlines or highlights text	underline italic line-through none	{ text-decoration: underline}

PART

II

CH

12

continues

TABLE 12.1 CONTINUED

Attribute	Description	Values	Example
margin-left	Sets distance from left edge of page	points (pt) inches (in) centimeters (cm) pixels (px)	{ margin-left: 1in }
margin-right	Sets distance from right edge of page	points (pt) inches (in) centimeters (cm) pixels (px)	{ margin-right: 1in }
margin-top	Sets distance from top edge of page	points (pt) inches (in) centimeters (cm) pixels (px)	{ margin-top:-20px }
text-align	Sets justification	left center right	{ text-align: right }
text-indent	Sets distance from left margin	points (pt) inches (in) centimeters (cm) pixels (px)	{ text-indent: 0.5in }
background	Sets background images or colors	URL color name RGB triplet	{ background: #33CC00 }

The named colors you can use are:

black	silver	gray	white
maroon	red	purple	fuschia
green	lime	olive	yellow
navy	blue	teal	aqua

Tip #68

To place a background image in a style sheet, specify the URL in parentheses with the <BODY> tag:

```
BODY { background: URL(books.gif) }
```

Internet Explorer 4–Supported Style Properties

Internet Explorer 4 supports the following style sheet attributes, in addition to those in Table 12.1.

- `background-attachment`   If a background image is specified, the value of `background-attachment` determines if it is fixed with regard to the canvas or if it scrolls along with the content.

  Syntax: { background-attachment: scroll¦ fixed}

- `background-color`   Sets the background color of an element.

  Syntax:{ background-color: <color> ¦ transparent}

- `background-image`   Sets the background image of an element.

  Syntax:{ background-image: <url> ¦ none}

- `background-position`   If a background image has been specified, the value of `background-position` specifies its initial position.

  Syntax:{ background-position: [<position> ¦ <length>]{1,2} ¦ [top ¦ center ¦ bottom] ¦¦ [left ¦ center ¦ right]}

- `background-repeat`   If a background image is specified, the value of `background-repeat` determines how/if the image is repeated.

  Syntax: { background-repeat: repeat¦ repeat-x ¦ repeat-y ¦ no-repeat}

- `border`   Specifies the border to display around the element. The `border` property sets the border for all four sides while the other border properties only set their respective sides.

  Syntax: { border: <border-width> ¦¦ <border-style> ¦¦ <color>}

- `border-bottom`   Specifies the bottom border.

  Syntax: { border-bottom: <border-bottom-width> ¦¦ <border-style> ¦¦ <color>}

- `border-bottom-width`   Sets the width of an element's bottom border.

  Syntax: { border-bottom-width: thin ¦ medium¦ thick ¦ <length>}

- `border-color`   Sets the color of the four borders.

  Syntax: { border-color: <color> Syntax: {1,4}}

- `border-left`   Sets the left border.

  Syntax: { border-left: <border-left-width> ¦¦ <border-style> ¦¦ <color>}

- `border-left-width`   Sets the width of an element's left border.

  Syntax: { border-left-width: thin ¦ medium¦ thick ¦ <length>}

- `border-right`   Sets the right border.

  Syntax: { border-right: <border-right-width> ¦¦ <border-style> ¦¦ <color>}

- `border-right-width`   Sets the width of an element's right border.

  Syntax: { border-right-width: thin ¦ medium¦ thick ¦ <length>}

- `border-style` Sets the style of the four borders.

  Syntax: { `border-style: none ¦ solid`}

- `border-top` Describes the top border.

  Syntax: { `border-top: <border-top-width> ¦¦ <border-style> ¦¦ <color>`}

- `border-top-width` Sets the width of an element's top border.

  Syntax: { `border-top-width: thin ¦ medium¦ thick ¦ <length>`}

- `border-width` This is a shorthand property for setting `border-width-top`, `border-width-right`, `border-width-bottom`, and `border-width-left` at the same place in the style sheet.

  Syntax: { `border-width: [thin ¦ medium ¦ thick ¦ <length>] {1,4}`}

- `font-variant` Sets the variant of the font to normal or small caps.

  Syntax: { `font-variant: normal¦ small-caps`}

- `height` This property can be applied to text, but it is most useful with inline images and similar insertions. The height is to be enforced by scaling the image if necessary. When scaling, the aspect ratio of the image should be preserved if the `width` property is `auto`.

  Syntax: { `height: <length> ¦ auto`}

- `left` Sets the left position when in a 2D canvas.

  Syntax: { `left: <length> ¦ <percentage> ¦ auto`}

- `letter-spacing` The length unit indicates an addition to the default space between characters. Units are in ems.

  Syntax: { `letter-spacing: normal¦ <length>`}

- `margin-top` Specifies the top-margin for the text.

  Syntax: { `margin-top: [ <length> ¦ <percentage> ¦ auto ]`}

- `margin-bottom` Specifies the bottom-margin for the text block.

  Syntax: { `margin-bottom: [ <length> ¦ <percentage> ¦ auto ]`}

- `position` Specifies whether the element can be positioned.

  Syntax: { `position: absolute ¦ relative ¦ static`}

- `text-transform` Transforms the text.

  Syntax: { `text-transform: capitalize ¦ uppercase ¦ lowercase ¦ none`}

- `top` Sets or returns the top position for elements that are positioned absolutely or relatively.

  Syntax: { `top: <length> ¦ <percentage> ¦ auto`}

- `vertical-align` Affects the vertical positioning of the element.

  Syntax: { `vertical-align: baseline¦ sub ¦ super ¦ top ¦ text-top ¦ middle ¦ bottom ¦ text-bottom ¦ <percentage>`}

- width   This property can be applied to text elements, but it is most useful with inline images and similar insertions. The width is to be enforced by scaling the image if necessary. When scaling, the aspect ratio of the image should be preserved if the height property is auto.

  Syntax: { width: <length> ¦ <percentage> ¦ auto}

- z-index   Specifies the z-index for the element. Positive z-index is above the text, negative z-index is rendered below the text.

  Syntax: { z-index: number}

CSS PROPERTIES SUPPORTED ONLY IN INTERNET EXPLORER 5

The following properties are usable only in Internet Explorer 5.0.

- table-layout   Sets or retrieves whether the table layout is fixed

  Syntax: { table-layout : auto ¦ fixed }

- border-collapse   Sets or retrieves whether the row and cell borders of a table are joined into a single border or detached as in standard HTML

  Syntax: { border-collapse : separate ¦ collapse }

- direction   Sets or retrieves the reading order of the specified object

  Syntax: { direction: [ltr ¦ rtl ¦ inherit] }

UNSUPPORTED CSS ATTRIBUTES

The following CSS attributes are not supported in any Microsoft browser:

- word-spacing
- !important
- first-letter pseudo
- first-line pseudo
- white-space

Note

For the most recent list of CSS attributes supported by Internet Explorer 4 and later, go to http://www.microsoft.com/workshop/c-frame.htm#/workshop/author/ default.asp and go to the CSS section of the menu.

PART
II

CH

12

TROUBLESHOOTING

Using CSS with the tools by FrontPage 2000 is pretty well trouble free. If you write the CSS code directly into a page, however, you may run into problems. Most of these are caused by syntax errors in the code. Check for missing or extraneous colons, semicolons, curly braces, parameter or value errors, and so on.

DESIGNERS CORNER

As you've seen in this chapter, style sheets are an extremely powerful tool for the design, layout, and modification of Web pages. The ability to change the entire look of a Web site with a relatively small number of style specifications has been a great boon to page designers.

When you're analyzing the best ways to apply CSS to your Web pages, try to mentally separate the content of the pages from their presentation. Where possible, place the presentation specifications (such as margins, colors, methods of text emphasis, paragraph formatting, and so on) in style sheets. Reserve the HTML pages for content as much as you can, while minimizing the amount of presentation information you incorporate into these pages. This isolation of form and content makes it easier to modify either the form or the content independently. This in turn makes Web site and document maintenance less of a headache.

As an example, you might create a style class called "Emphasize Paragraph" and place it in a linked style sheet. This would allow the way that the paragraphs are emphasized to be changed with a simple modification to the style's definition in that style sheet. Consequently you don't need to edit the HTML pages to which this style sheet is linked—the change is applied globally as soon as the style sheet is put into use.

WEB CREATION AND MANAGEMENT

CREATING A WEB

by Neil Randall

Requirements for Creating a Web

You can create a FrontPage web directly on a Web server, or you can develop it on your local hard disk and transfer it to a Web server later. Here's the difference:

In order to make a web available for external access, either on the Internet or in a company intranet, you must work with a computer running HTTP (Hypertext Transfer Protocol) server software. More simply, it has to be on a Web server. The server software can reside either on a remote computer accessible over the Internet or on your local computer. FrontPage 2000 lets you create webs directly on your server and edit documents across the Internet in order to eliminate the steps of downloading, then editing, then uploading. In fact, this has always been one of FrontPage's most significant features, and the concept of remote editing has made its way into Office 2000 as well.

> **Note**
>
> Earlier versions of FrontPage shipped with a Web server (two, in fact), but FrontPage 2000 does not. If you have Windows 98, however, you can install the Microsoft Personal Web Server from the installation CDs and use it to serve your webs. (See Chapter 37, "FrontPage 2000 and the Microsoft Personal Web Server," for details on installing and using the Microsoft PWS.) You can also get it from the Microsoft site, but it's a huge download. If you prefer, you can find HTTP (web) servers on download sites across the Web (see `http://www.winfiles.com/` for an example), and if you're using Windows NT 4 or Windows 2000, servers install with the operating system.

You don't need a server to create a FrontPage 2000 web. You can create the web on your local hard disk (or a network drive) and publish the web later using File, Publish Web. (See Chapter 16, "Publishing a Web," for details on publishing webs this way.) However, if you create a web without a server, there are some important features you can't test. You can design fill-in forms, for example, but they won't actually work; when you load them into a browser, fill in the fields, and click Submit, the information won't go anywhere. In fact, you'll receive a message that tells you that you need a server to do this. Still, *disk-based webs* *(page 24)* are a very good way to get started, and most of the design work for most types of webs can be handled without the server in place.

You'll eventually need a server, and eventually that server must be connected to the Internet or your company's network. Server details are covered in Chapter 16 and in all of Part VI of this book.

When you create a web, you must specify where you want the files for that web to be saved. You can save them onto a local hard disk, a network drive, or onto a Web server. You determine this location when you access the File, New, Web command, as you see in this chapter's "Starting a New Web Site" section. If you are saving to a Web server, you are in essence telling FrontPage where you want your web served from. Usually this is a remote machine; a fully accessible web must be served from a machine that is connected to the Internet on a 24-hour basis and (ideally) at high speed.

If you want to build a local web, which you do primarily for the sake of testing it, and if you have Web server software such as the Microsoft PWS running on your computer, you can specify the server address as `http://localhost` or `http://127.0.0.1`. (The two addresses are the same thing.) Addressing is covered later in this chapter. When you begin the web creation, it will be immediately functional.

Of course, you might have a server in place already. Several server packages are popularly available, including O'Reilly & Associates' WebSite and Netscape's FastTrack. To use all of FrontPage 2000's features with these servers, you must install the *server extensions* for them. These installations are handled during the initial FrontPage installation process, but if you add a server later you must install the extensions for it manually. The server extensions let the server handle FrontPage 2000's advanced features, such as forms programming and advanced server pages; server extensions are covered in Chapter 35, "Introduction to Web Hosting and Web Servers." As shipped, FrontPage supports several popular Web servers for Windows, including the Netscape Commerce and Communications servers and O'Reilly's WebSite server. Additional extensions—including those for the most popular Web server software of all, Apache (for UNIX)—are available on Microsoft's FrontPage Web site (`http://www.microsoft.com/frontpage/`).

If you're running a Web server that isn't supported by a FrontPage extension, you can still make use of FrontPage. Once your web is completed locally, you can export it to the Web server machine using FrontPage's File, Publish feature (see Chapter 16).

Tip #69

> Even if you have a machine with a server supported by FrontPage extensions, you should seriously consider designing, developing, and testing your webs on a non-public machine, using either disk-based webs or, better still, server software such as the Microsoft Personal web Server that ships with Windows 98. This is a much better idea than developing on a live Web server because you can guarantee that nobody will be able to visit it while it's in progress. That way, data is secure, errors and difficulties don't become public, and the final public web is exactly the one you want people to see.

STARTING A NEW WEB SITE

To create a web site, load FrontPage and select File, New, Web. This brings up a dialog box named New, shown in Figure 13.1.

The left third of the dialog box consists of icons for the new various FrontPage web wizards and templates. To the right are three elements: icon viewing options, web options, and a description. The icon viewing options let you choose between seeing the web wizard and template icons as large or small icons. The description gives you a one-sentence overview of what the currently selected wizard or template will do for you.

Figure 13.1
The New dialog box contains the FrontPage templates and wizards available for automatic web creation.

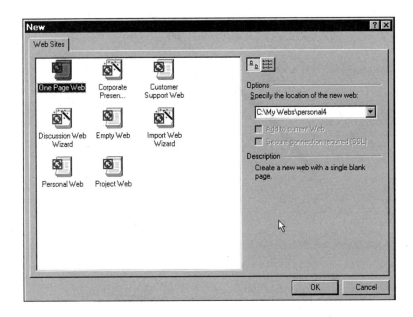

The Options area lets you specify the location where the new web is to reside—the machine and directory where the files will be stored. FrontPage creates this directory and a file named default.htm as that web's home page. By default, FrontPage offers the storage directory created on installation, typically c:\mywebs in Windows 95/98, or the user's profile directory in Windows NT 4 or Windows 2000. Also by default, FrontPage offers a name for the web, although this is anything but creative. FrontPage simply takes the most recently created web and increments the number of that web by 1 (so that personal3 becomes personal4, for example). If only to keep track of your webs, it's a good idea to type in a different name. At any time, however, you can change the name of the web by choosing Tools, Web Settings.

If you want to create your web on a remote server, type the URL of that server in the location field of the New dialog box. Typically, this takes the form http:// www.*yourserver*.com/*webname*, with *yourserver* and *webname* being replaced with the actual server name and web name. Note that you cannot create a *root Web* (the default Web site at that URL) with this method. You must specify a subdirectory for the URL, and indeed you can specify a subdirectory of a subdirectory, should you want to create webs inside other webs.

Tip #70

If you are creating a web on a remote server, it is always a good idea to open the root Web, or a web inside the root Web, before proceeding. This way, you can easily decide to create a new web in a separate directory, or add it to the current web.

One important option here is Add to Current Web. As mentioned earlier, when you create a new web, FrontPage creates a new directory for the site and adds a home page called default.htm. For instance, using www.mysite.com as an example, if you create a web called works, FrontPage will create the directory www.mysite.com/works and transfer its files to that directory along with any relevant subdirectories. If you choose to add the new web to the current web, however, FrontPage transfers the files into the current directory, creating the needed subdirectories within the current directory. Using the same example, if you create a web called works and add it to the currently loaded www.mysite.com site, FrontPage does not create a works subdirectory. Instead, it transfers the default.htm file into www.mysite.com and creates subdirectories from there.

Obviously, this procedure is fraught with potential problems. Since the current site already has a default.htm file and the new site has one as well (all new sites automatically have one), one of them has to go. No operating system allows more than one file of the same name in a single directory or folder. FrontPage will ask you if you want to replace the existing default.htm, and you may do so. However, either your existing or your current default.htm file gets the nod in either case, and you might not want to lose either. In such a case, simply cancel the new web creation process and next time leave the Add to Current Web check box unselected.

Tip #71

> The Add to Current Web option is extremely useful if you've developed a new home page that will incorporate the navigation links from the existing home page in the web, or if you originally opted for a one-page or empty web and now have a more detailed home page.

Another option is a check box called Secure Connection Required (SSL). If your server supports Secure Sockets Layer (SSL) connections, you can establish your new web as requiring these connections.

The web wizards and templates range from Empty Web through Corporate Presence Wizard. The difference among the selections lies in the relative simplicity or complexity of the possibilities. An empty web is exactly what its name suggests; you get a web, but there's nothing in it. Selecting the Corporate Presence Web, on the other hand, launches a wizard that takes you step by step through the initiation of a web site fully populated by page templates designed specifically for establishing a corporate presence. The choice is yours: start with nothing or start with a sophisticated template.

Why would anybody forego the templates and start with an empty web? The answer lies very much in your confidence and creativity, as well as your experience in Web page design. If you've put together a number of webs and you know exactly how you want to start and what you want to include, a template might very well be a detriment rather than a benefit. If you're about to begin your first site or know very well that you could use a good assistant, by all means start with a template.

PART

III

CH

13

The real problem with templates is that they tend to produce webs that are very similar to other webs out there. In fact, as FrontPage becomes more and more popular, there's a very real danger that you'll see all kinds of FrontPage–assisted web designs that offer nothing distinctive. Still, the templates in FrontPage are strong enough that even a moderate amount of tinkering produces something at least worth looking at, which is far better than nothing.

If you select Empty Web, you'll have to create all Web pages from scratch. This process is covered throughout the entirety of Part II, "Designing Documents: Working from the Page View." For now, adding to an empty web means editing the home page (the default.htm file) via FrontPage 2000's Page view, then adding pages to the web choosing Tools, Show FrontPage Editor in Explorer. Once Editor loads, choose File, New Page and proceed from there.

USING THE WIZARDS FOR CREATING NEW FRONTPAGE WEBS

FrontPage Explorer offers two wizards for creating new webs: the Corporate Presence Wizard and the Discussion Web Wizard. Both offer an extremely usable system of dialog boxes, and once you've completed them all, you'll have a web filled with easy-to-alter Web page templates.

Note

Microsoft has done a great deal to develop and improve on FrontPage over the past few versions, but it has added almost nothing to the wizards and templates area. The authors of this book would love to run through something besides the Corporate Presence Wizard, but it remains the most comprehensive wizard in the package. It's also essentially unchanged from its original version. Let's hope Microsoft releases a few more wizards before these expire under the statute of computing limitations.

To see how these wizards work, you'll step through the Corporate Presence Wizard, creating a site for a company you just created called FrontPagers Corporation. In this hypothetical example, you've applied to the InterNIC registry service (http://rs.internic.net/rs-internic.html) for the domain name frontpagers.com, but you haven't yet received confirmation of ownership. As a result, you establish the web first on a local hard disk, understanding that you'll publish it to a Web server later by using FrontPage 2000's Publish feature.

Note

As of this writing, the domain name **frontpagers.com** was still unclaimed, as revealed by a WHOIS search at the InterNIC site. This book's authors didn't actually buy the name, so it might very well be unavailable by the time this book is published. Then again, Microsoft might object if someone actually did take it.

STEP 1: LOAD FRONTPAGE 2000

Load FrontPage 2000.

STEP 2: START THE CORPORATE PRESENCE WIZARD

Select New, Web from the File menu. From the resulting New dialog box (refer to Figure 13.1), highlight Corporate Presence Wizard in the left pane. Don't yet click OK.

STEP 3: SPECIFY WHERE YOU WANT YOUR NEW WEB TO RESIDE

In the Options area on the right side of the dialog you'll see a field for the web's location. Here you can specify a hard disk location or a Web server location. By default, FrontPage displays a hard disk location within the c:\My webs\ folder and gives your new web a default name.

You can change the folder and the web name. If you've decided to store your webs in d:\fpwebs\ (and in order to call your new web smithproject), type d:\fpwebs\smithproject in the location field. Use c:\My webs\frontpagers for this example.

If you're running a Web server on your local machine in Windows 95/98 or Windows NT, you can locate the new web within the server's control. To do so, type http://localhost/webname in the location field. In this example, you would type http://localhost/frontpagers.

Finally, if you're creating the web directly on a remote Web server, you would replace the localhost portion of the location with the Web server's URL. In this example, you would type http://www.companyname/frontpagers (replacing companyname with your actual domain name, of course).

Note

> When publishing to a server, you can use the server's numerical IP address rather than the domain name or the **localhost** designation. If your company's IP number is **207.148.35.7**, for example, you could type **http://207.148.35.7/webname** to place the new web on the server. In the case of **localhost**, the IP address is always **127.0.0.1**—it's the standard address reserved for the local machine. IP addresses are the real addresses on the Internet; domain names are associated with them because human beings aren't great at remembering numbers.

Once you have the Corporate Presence Web selected and the location of your web specified in the location field, click OK to begin the process of creating the web. FrontPage 2000 launches the Corporate Presence Web Wizard, which consists of a series of interactive dialog boxes.

STEP 4: SELECT THE TYPES OF PAGES YOU WANT IN YOUR WEB

The Corporate Presence Web Wizard walks you through this procedure of creating your web, beginning with an opening screen that tells you what you're about to do. From this screen, click the Next button to go to the second stage.

Figure 13.2 shows your first array of choices. You have to create a home page (it's required; thus, the option is grayed out), but you can also include the types of pages shown in the following list. At this point, you're concerned only with the type of pages you want in your web. FrontPage creates the pages you decide you need, and they are all template pages. After the web is created, you use FrontPage's Page view to change the details on each page; you use other FrontPage views or menus to delete unwanted pages or add new ones.

The page types that you can create from this dialog box are as follows:

- What's New—The What's New page, a standard offering on almost all corporate web sites, gives readers who revisit your site a quick means of determining whether you've added information that might be to their benefit. This page is linked from your home page.

- Products/Services—The Products/Services page, also very common in business sites, allows you to supply information to your readers about what you're actually selling. This page is linked from your home page.

- Table of Contents—Since the Corporate Presence Web is quite extensive, a Table Of Contents page helps your readers find their way around. This page looks like (obviously) a table of contents from a book, with each item linking to the appropriate page.

- Feedback Form—The wizard can create a form for users to fill in and comment on the site. You can revise this form in any way you like after it's created. Note, however, that the form will be created, but will not actually work (it won't collect user data) unless you store it on a Web server that has FrontPage extensions operating.

- Search Form—If you have an extensive site, you should provide a search form for users to locate specific information. Note that this isn't a search form for the entire web (that is, it's not HotBot or InfoSeek), but rather to all the pages within your own Web site.

For this example, you create all possible pages from this wizard. To do so, click the check boxes for all page types that aren't already checked by default. Click Next to continue.

Caution

Although this example suggests creating all available pages, in practice you might want to be more selective. Remember that the more pages you create, the more pages you'll need to edit and customize after the web is in place.

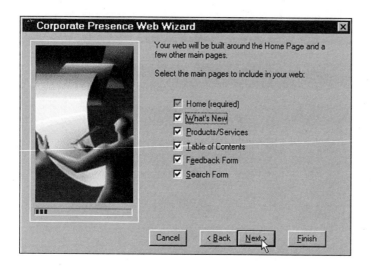

Figure 13.2
The more page types
you select, the larger
your Web site will be
and the more pruning
you might have to do.

STEP 5: SELECT THE TYPES OF INFORMATION YOU WANT ON YOUR HOME PAGE

The wizard creates areas on the home page itself for specific kinds of information. The Introduction offers you a place to tell your users what your home page is about. You can also include a mission statement about the company and a full company profile. Finally, the wizard creates contact information for users to get in touch with you.

Again, you'll create all possible template areas. Click the check boxes for all types; click Next to continue.

STEP 6: SELECT ELEMENTS FOR THE WHAT'S NEW PAGE

In the "Step 4: Select the Types of Pages You Want in Your Web" section, you told the wizard to create a What's New page. Now you're asked to select the various elements that appear on that page (see Figure 13.3). Web Changes offers an area in which to tell users what new pages have been added to the web since their last visit. If your company issues press releases, mark the appropriate check box. If your company is well served by articles and reviews about your products and services or about further research into your product type, include these as well. In this example, mark all of them for the fullest possible What's New page. Click Next to continue.

STEP 7: TELL THE WIZARD HOW MANY PRODUCTS AND SERVICES YOU WANT TO LIST

Since you decided in the "Step 4: Select the Types of Pages You Want in Your Web" section to create a Products/Services page, the dialog box lets you determine how many products and services you want to list. The default is three products and three services, but change it to four products and one service. To do so, enter **5** in the Products text box and enter **1** in the Services text box. Click Next to continue.

PART

III

CH

13

Figure 13.3
This dialog box lets you tell your reader exactly what's been going on with your company.

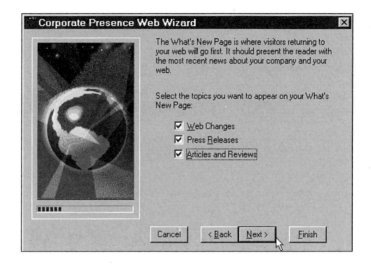

STEP 8: ENTER INFORMATION TO BE DISPLAYED ABOUT THE PRODUCTS AND SERVICES

The dialog box shown in Figure 13.4 lets you set the information you want to offer about the products and services included in step 7. Select Product Image if you have a graphics file with a picture of the product. Pricing Information gives you a place to tell users how much the product costs, while Information Request Form produces a form that potential customers can use to get additional information about the products. For your services, you can offer a list of capabilities, and you can point to satisfied customers with the Reference Accounts option (but make sure you check with those customers first). A separate Information Request Form lets readers ask for more details about your services.

For this example, check all the items. Click Next to continue.

Figure 13.4
Determine in advance how much information you need to provide about each product and service in order to satisfy your visitors.

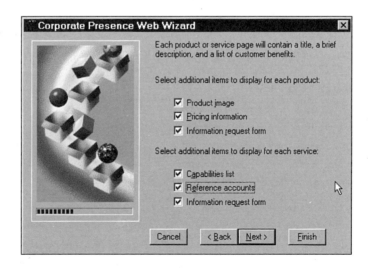

STEP 9: TELL THE WIZARD HOW TO CONSTRUCT THE FEEDBACK FORM

In this step, you specify the fields you want to appear on the feedback form you chose in the "Step 4: Select the Types of Pages You Want in Your Web" section (see Figure 13.5). The choices are straightforward, and they include Full Name, Job Title, Company Affiliation, Mailing Address, Telephone Number, FAX Number, and E-mail Address. Keep in mind that the more information you ask users to produce, the less likely it is they'll fill out the form. Because you're after the most complete site possible, mark all of them. Click Next to continue.

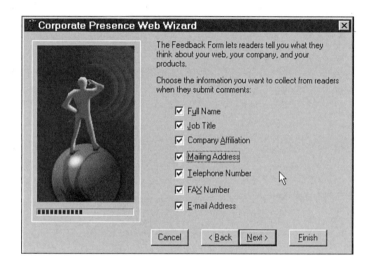

Figure 13.5
FrontPage creates a feedback form page with all the options you select.

STEP 10: DETERMINE WHICH FORMAT YOU WANT FOR FORMS INFORMATION

When users fill in the feedback form, the information is stored in one of two ways. You can have it in *web-page format (page 74)*, which is good if you're going to take all the information directly from that page. If you want the information to be fed into a spreadsheet or database, however, you can choose *tab-delimited format (page 74)*. This format is especially useful if you construct a script to place it directly into such a package. Choosing the tab-delimited method becomes important as your data needs become more extensive, so leave the default radio button selected. You can change this information once you're inside FrontPage's Page view, where you can add multiple methods for receiving the information. Click Next.

STEP 11: SET THE OPTIONS FOR THE TABLE OF CONTENTS PAGE

Keep Page List Up-To-Date Automatically does just what its name implies; FrontPage monitors your web, adding pages and links to those pages as you create them. Show Pages Not Linked into Web tells Explorer to display, in its viewing area, pages you've created that you haven't actually linked to the main web (experimental pages or abandoned pages, for example). Use Bullets for Top-Level Pages puts bullets in the Table of Contents beside the

PART

III

CH

13

main pages, helping your users navigate through your web. Select all three and click Next to continue.

STEP 12: TELL THE WIZARD THE INFORMATION THAT SHOULD BE SHOWN ON EACH PAGE

Essentially, this dialog box provides a means of adding headers and footers to all the pages in your site (see Figure 13.6). This dialog box lets you specify what elements you want to see on every page in the site, although you can use Editor to alter or delete these elements on individual pages once the web is created. If you have a company logo, you might want it to appear on every page, in which case mark Your Company's Logo. The page title appears on each page if you prefer (that is, the HTML title you specify in the document preferences in Editor), and you can include a navigation bar with Links to Your Main Web Pages. You can also offer links to your main Web pages at the bottom of the page; you probably don't want this navigation bar both on top and bottom, though, so mark only one. You can also include your webmaster's email address (in other words, you), a copyright notice that handles the legal thing, and the date the page was last modified.

Figure 13.6
Several options for presentation style are available for global inclusion across your web.

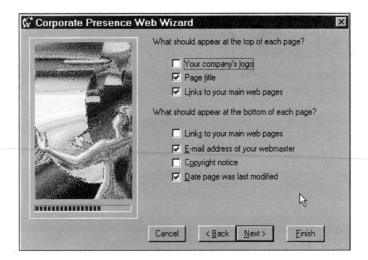

Once again, mark all the boxes, except for the Links to Your Main Web Pages box in the top section of the dialog box. Place the navigation bar at the bottom instead. Click Next to continue.

STEP 13: SPECIFY WHETHER YOU WANT UNDER CONSTRUCTION SIGNS ON YOUR UNFINISHED PAGES

One of the most common symbols on the Web is the Under Construction sign. It tells you that the page has not yet been completed, but at this stage in the Web's history the sign is so overused that it's practically meaningless. This dialog box lets you decide whether you want these signs on your pages. Explorer automatically creates a to-do list of uncompleted pages in your web, which you can update as you complete them (see Chapter 18, "Managing a Web"). As you do so, the Under Construction sign disappears from these pages. Some people find the Under Construction sign objectionable, so you should take a few seconds to decide whether you want to include it. If so, choose Yes; if not, choose No. Click Next to continue.

STEP 14: ENTER THE NAME AND ADDRESS OF YOUR COMPANY

The next step is to type your company's full name, abbreviation, and address. This information appears on your Web pages throughout. Your company's full name goes in the top text box, and the street address in the bottom text box. Type `FrontPagers Corporation` in the first and any address you want in the bottom. In the middle field there goes a one-word version of this name, and the obvious choice is `FrontPagers`. When you've completed these entries, click the Next button.

STEP 15: COMPLETE YOUR COMPANY INFORMATION

In the dialog box following the name and address dialog box, you can enter the company's telephone number and fax number, along with your webmaster's email address and the email address for general information about the company. Typically, the webmaster's address is `webmaster@yourcompany.com`, and the information address is `info@yourcompany.com`, so for this example type in `webmaster@frontpagers.com` and `info@frontpagers.com`, respectively. Keep in mind, however, that the domain name is still not fully registered. You therefore can't assign email addresses to it. As a result, you might want to enter your own email address instead. Click Next when you're done.

STEP 16: SELECT A WEB THEME FOR YOUR SITE

The next step is to select an optional theme for your Web site. A theme (covered in Chapter 6, "Working with Themes") establishes common fonts, bullet types, background patterns, and other graphical styles for all the pages in your web. Every page is created based on the theme you choose, and if you want some pages to appear differently you can alter them by using the document options in Editor. For this tutorial, click Choose Web Theme. Select the theme you want from the choices in the left pane when the Choose Theme dialog box loads (see Figure 13.7). Click through the themes to see the differences. Select the Vivid Colors and Active Graphics options at the bottom left of the dialog and then click OK. This places you back in the Corporate Presence Web Wizard; click Next to continue to the next stage.

STEP 17: DECIDE WHETHER TO VIEW THE TO-DO LIST

The last step in the creation of the Corporate Presence Web is to choose whether you want the to-do list to appear whenever the web is loaded into Explorer. It's always a good idea, so select the check box. Click Finish this time; it has replaced the Next button because the wizard has taken you as far as it can go.

Now that you've created the web, your to-do list appears in the FrontPage Explorer main window. This is the Tasks view, which you can access any time by clicking the Tasks icon in the Views toolbar at the left side of the screen. Here, you are shown the pages you have yet to complete, along with a number of other important details. As explained in detail in Chapter 18, you explore how to work with this list, but for now take note of it as an important step in the building of your web. FrontPage continues to revise this list as you finish some pages and add others. For now, click the Navigation icon in the Views toolbar and bring this important view to the main window.

Figure 13.7
Cycle through the theme choices on the left side. Several will do nicely for your corporate site.

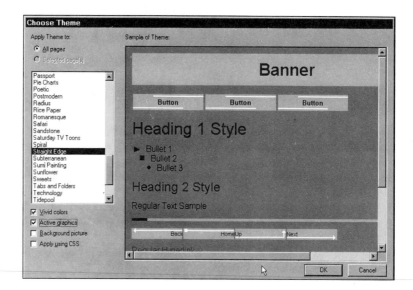

→ **See** "Managing a Web," **p. 385**, for information about the Tasks feature.

The Navigation view (see Figure 13.8) shows what you've been aiming for: a web in place and ready for action. If you were connected to the Internet and had assigned this web to a real IP number, your site would be accessible from any computer in the world connected to the Internet. From this point on, all you need to do is modify and alter your new web. Once it's finished, you can transfer it to a fully-operational, 24-hour Web server machine.

TROUBLESHOOTING

If you mount your new web directly onto the server of an ISP or a Web Presence Provider (a.k.a, Web Hosting Service), you might occasionally find that you can't access your web, or that you can access it but you can't create new webs or save documents to existing ones. In such a case, a warning box will tell you that your FrontPage client can't see the FrontPage *server extensions (page 301)* on the remote server. It will also tell you to contact your Web server administrator. Certainly this does not happen all the time, and not with all ISPs or WPPs, but it does happen.

The warning box is correct: You must contact your Web server administrator (a technical support person at your ISP or Hosting Service). Typically, he or she can correct the problem by reinstalling the FrontPage server extensions on your account. In some extreme cases, however, you will have to reinstall FrontPage itself. Whatever the case, be firm with the ISP/WPP; don't let them tell you that this is not their problem. You paid for a FrontPage-compatible server, and you deserve to have it work properly.

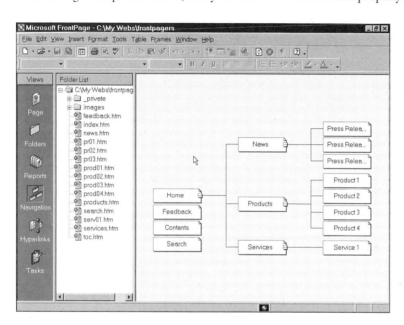

Figure 13.8
Presto! Your new web is ready for your loving care. (Note that your screen might not look like this, since Navigation view defaults to a vertical display, not the horizontal one shown here.)

DESIGNERS CORNER

This chapter looked briefly at the issues concerned with mounting a web site, and here we'll delve a bit more deeply into it. While you can design all the webs you want using either disk-based webs or on a "localhost" server on your own machine, you'll want even at this point to know a bit more about actually mounting your web.

Chapter 35 of this book looks at the role of Web servers in mounting webs, while Chapter 36, "Using a Web Hosting Service," examines the benefits and drawbacks of mounting your web on a Web Hosting Service. But before continuing towards those chapters, let's deal with an issue shared by many of you who access the Internet through a modem and a dial-up account. This issue impacts directly on the idea of building a web, which is why it's included here.

The fact is that you can, technically, mount a web on a machine with a modem and a dial-up account. The problems, as covered in greater detail in Chapter 35, are speed and ease of access to your web. The speed issue is very simple: With a standard modem running at anywhere between 28.8Kbps to 56Kbps, your visitors will receive information very slowly, and your server will be hard pressed to serve more than one or two concurrent visitors. But the access problem is even worse. You won't be able to have your own domain name for your web, because InterNIC requires that a domain be operative on two full-time servers. Even your IP number won't be consistent if, as is the case with most dial-in customers, your ISP assigns a new IP number every time you log on. Furthermore, unless you're willing to leave your computer on 24 hours a day, your site won't always be available. Even if you are willing to do so, your ISP might object. Even ISPs that give you unlimited access time often have a policy that lets them deny you access time if you severely overuse it.

Now for the interesting part. High-speed access options are now coming into the picture. ISDN lines are probably on their way to a well-deserved death (well-deserved because the phone companies never seemed to get the ISDN idea right), but ADSL modems and cable modems are on their way in. ADSL modems make use of the fact that telephone conversations use only about 10% of the available bandwidth on the phone line, and they use the rest of it for simultaneous and high-speed Internet access. Cable modems make use of the existing cable lines strung throughout cities, including Net services along with regular cable television service. Although rates vary, about $30-$40 per month for either seems to be where the industry is moving.

Of the two, only cable services seem willing to give you a fixed IP number, because ADSL service requires that you dial in to your ISP (albeit much more quickly than with current modems). With a cable service, your computer is on the Net at all times, and the IP number doesn't change (your particular cable company might have a different way of handling this), even if you turn your computer off.

So yes, it's possible that you *could* mount a web on a cable modem service. But here too, there are problems. A major one is that, while cable access is certainly fast (up to 30 times as fast as a 33.6Kbps modem), it's fast in only one direction: downloading. It's no faster than current 56Kbps modems when it comes to uploading. And uploading is precisely what you do when someone visits your web. Your server *uploads* information to the Net, and that information finds its way to the visitor's computer. Professional Web servers are connected to the Internet through high-speed lines such as T1 or T3, which means they upload information faster than you can download through a modem. They work with cable modems because cable modems reach closer to the server's speed; essentially, the cable modem (like the ADSL modem) lets download speed more closely match upload speed. But if you're serving information at 56Kbps, which a cable modem does, you're no better off at serving a web than if you had a standard 56Kbps modem. ADSL does not have the uploading limitations, but it has the dial-up limitations of inconstant connection and non-fixed IP numbers. Rest assured, finally, that phone companies and cable companies will be watching very closely to ensure that you're not using your connection to serve a web. They don't want that, because you'll tie up too much bandwidth.

The answer? Unless your web is designed for your twenty close friends, to whom you can give times of operation and changes in IP numbers, don't host a web from your modem-connected computer.

CHAPTER **14**

FRONTPAGE'S WEB TEMPLATES AND WIZARDS

In this chapter

by Neil Randall

THE DISCUSSION WEB WIZARD

The procedure for creating webs based on one particular FrontPage wizard, the Corporate Presence Wizard, is covered in Chapter 26, "Using Scripts in Your Web Page." Explorer offers a second wizard, the Discussion Web Wizard, and it deserves a close look as well. Its purpose and requirements are considerably different from and, in some ways, more advanced than the Corporate Presence Wizard. The discussion web creates an area where readers can participate in a forum on a topic of their choice and, as such, demands some special considerations at the time of creation.

Creating a discussion web from scratch requires an intimate knowledge of FrontPage forms. These are covered in Chapter 11, "Using Components, Forms, and Interactive Page Templates." Creating one from the Discussion Web Wizard, however, requires none of this knowledge—at least not in the initial creation stage. FrontPage's forms features let documents created with FrontPage cooperate with the Web server in a fully interactive way, and the Discussion Web Wizard directs these forms into a specific and organized use.

> **Caution**
>
> It's important to keep in mind as you build webs with FrontPage that its interactive capabilities, although immensely useful and time-saving, are limited. If you want to develop a full Web site with extensive links to databases and other information sources, you need to understand scripting and programming. What makes FrontPage so welcome in this regard is that it takes care of the most common interactive elements, and thus lets the majority of web designers accomplish their interactive tasks quite easily.

The first step in creating a discussion web is to choose File, New, Web. Choose Discussion Web Wizard from the resulting New dialog box, assign the new web a location (see Chapter 13, "Creating a Web," for a discussion of possible locations), and indicate whether you want to add this to the current web and if you require SSL security; click OK. You'll see the introductory page of the Discussion Web Wizard; click Next to continue.

> **Tip #72**
>
> To keep easy control over access to your webs and to help you keep track of HTML files you've added, create new webs rather than adding them to your existing web. This places your web files in a new directory and helps compartmentalize your web designs.

TYPES OF PAGES TO INCLUDE

The first choices you have to make come from the second screen in the wizard. Here you can choose to include the following pages of information:

- Submission Form—The submission form is necessary for readers to compose and post articles. You don't have a choice about including this one, but it's the only required element.

- Table of Contents—This page offers readers an easy-to-navigate area from which to choose whether they want to search or read the discussions, or post a message of their own. If you want, the discussion web (on a later dialog box), will replace the web's current home page with this Table of Contents, a recommended procedure if the discussion forum will be a primary focus of your web. You can just as easily offer a link to the contents page from your existing home page (or any other document for that matter), so at this stage it's probably better to say no to that replacement.

- Search Form—The wizard will create a Search Form with which your readers can find articles in the web that have the specified text strings or patterns. If you're planning a site with numerous postings, especially on a variety of topics, be sure to include this form. Without it, the forum will be less useful than it might otherwise be.

- Threaded Replies—Threaded replies are practically a necessity in any kind of discussion forum, especially those with numerous postings. *Threads* let readers reply to specific articles within a topic, rather than posting only the topic itself. Again, this is a good choice to make, although you might find that articles tend to be disordered if your readers don't use threading effectively. A well-run discussion forum can make extremely good use of threaded replies, so unless you know why you wouldn't want them, they're always a good idea.

- Confirmation Page—The Confirmation Page lets readers know whether they've successfully sent their postings to the web. Without this page, readers' articles are posted without them having any way of knowing it. Like the other possible elements, the Confirmation Page is a good idea, so there's every reason to include it.

After you've made your selection, click Next to call up the next dialog box.

TITLE AND INPUT FIELDS

After selecting the pages you want to include, give your discussion forum a descriptive title by typing that title in the Enter a Descriptive Title for This Discussion field. Don't just call it Discussion—instead, give it a name that makes its purpose clear to all your readers. This title appears on the top of all pages in the discussion web, so giving it a bit of thought is worthwhile.

The second fill-in field on this dialog box asks you to enter the name of the discussion folder. FrontPage fills in this field automatically, and there's no real reason to change it. The folder name isn't very descriptive—it doesn't have to be; you won't likely be searching for it on your hard drive because it will appear automatically when you open the web to which it belongs. If you decide to change it, however, keep the opening underscore (_) intact. The underscore indicates a hidden folder, and because this folder holds the actual discussion entries, you don't want other authors of your web to have easy access to it. You can reveal hidden folders in FrontPage in the Web Setting dialog box, as described in Chapter 17, "Configuring Webs."

PART

III

CH

14

After completing these fields, click Next. In the subsequent dialog box, you must decide which input fields you want on the submission form for the web. At the very least, this form will include a Subject field and a Comments field. The user will enter the topic the posting is about in the Subject field; the user will type the actual message in the Comments field. You can determine the possible topics of discussion by including all possibilities in a pull-down menu; with that you can ensure that all messages are assigned a meaningful topic.

You can add either a Category field or Product field to this list. If you have a discussion about a large topic (types of Internet software, for example), you might want to offer categories in addition to subjects. As with subjects, you can specify the available categories through a pull-down menu on the Submission Form. The Product field replaces the Category field on the final grouping of input fields, and if you offer several different products to your customers, or if your subjects are product-based rather than category-based, choose the Product field instead. As always, click Next to move to the next dialog box in the wizard.

REGISTRATION

The most difficult (and perhaps significant) decision you make when creating a discussion web is whether to insist that your readers register in order to read or post articles. You will build a *protected* web if you choose to have them register, and all who register will have their usernames and passwords built into your web's permissions area. Your other choice is to leave the web unprotected, meaning that anyone can post messages.

On the surface, an unprotected web might seem the more desirable choice. After all, the World Wide Web is known as a place of freedom and openness, and offering a discussion group in which users must register might seem inappropriate or even offensive. But there are a few things to keep in mind about this issue: First, on a purely nice-to-have basis, articles posted within a registered web will automatically include the user's registered names.

More importantly, though, you should consider the purpose of the discussion forum. If you want to offer your readers a place all their own in which to post messages, questions, and suggestions, why not give them a protected area in which to do so. Of course, there's nothing stopping anyone on the Web from registering, so even here the discussion can be considered open. To prevent this, you can build in further password protection to your web, based on product serial numbers, passwords based on the words in a document, or anything else you can devise.

ORDER OF ARTICLES AND HOME PAGE

After deciding on registration and clicking Next, you can elect to sort the posted articles from oldest to newest or newest to oldest. They then appear on the Web's Table of Contents in the chosen order. The former gives a chronological feel to the discussions, and as readers scroll the messages they can see how the discussion has developed. On the other hand, this means that extended discussions require scrolling at virtually all times, and that could become a bit annoying. Sorting from newest to oldest places the most recent articles at the top of the page, and frequent readers will know what has come before. Newest to oldest is generally the preferred order.

After making this decision, you're given the option of having the Table of Contents page become the home page for the discussion web. If you take the option, the Table of Contents page replaces the current home page. This option actually takes effect only if you have not chosen to add the discussion web to the current web when first creating the web—if you've not made that decision, the Table of Contents page automatically becomes the home page for a discussion web on its own. Nevertheless, you're given the choice.

SEARCH DETAILS

The next dialog box lets you select the criteria by which the Search Form will report that a search has located documents. There are four choices: Subject; Subject and Size; Subject, Size, and Date; or Subject, Size, Date, and Score. All searches will reveal the subject of the located article; adding size gives information about the size of the article in kilobytes. Date adds information about when the article was posted. Score shows the reader a measure of how relevant the article is to the search string entered. A score of 1000 is a direct hit, while lower scores denote lesser relevance.

The choice here has to do with how much information you want your server to compute, as well as how much your feel your readers need. For a large discussion forum, the more information you provide, the more useful the searches will be. Smaller discussion forums, on the other hand, might not need this much information about the search.

WEB THEME AND FRAMES

The wizard for the discussion web lets you select the global Web theme for text and link colors, button styles, and the background graphics or color. After selecting the theme, the Discussion Web Wizard carries the design choice one step further by offering a selection of frame options. This dialog box is shown in Figure 14.1.

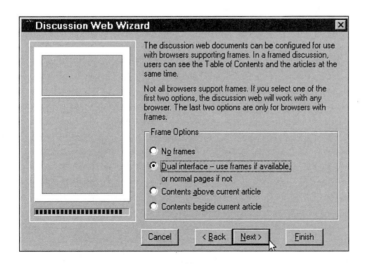

Figure 14.1
The Discussion Web Wizard's Frames dialog box offers four choices.

The purpose of this dialog box is to let you display your articles on a Web page that contains frames. *Frames*, windows inside a main window, were first offered with Netscape Navigator 2.0 but have since become an important design component on the Web in general. All current Web browsers support frames without difficulty, so the hesitation behind designing pages with frames—a hesitation present when they first became possible—should no longer influence your design decisions.

The Discussion Web Wizard offers to divide the discussion articles page into zero, two, or three frames. If you want to guarantee that all Web users will be able to access your articles, choose No Frames. If you want to use frames to their fullest extent, choose either Contents Above Current Article or Contents Beside Current Article. Both choices create three frames, one showing the page's contents, one the actual articles, and the third a banner displaying whatever you choose. If you want the best of both worlds—an articles page that offers frames to those with frames-capable browsers and an articles page with no frames for those without—choose Dual Interface. (This option is pictured in Figure 14.1.) The frames in this last case include one showing the contents and another showing the actual articles' text; the banner frame is not included.

THE SELF-REGISTRATION FORM

You've completed the wizard after making your decision about frames. Clicking Finish starts the actual creation of the web with all your pages in place. You're finished.

However, if you chose earlier to restrict access to the web to registered users, the wizard loads a file called webreg.htm into the Page view (see Figure 14.2).

Figure 14.2
The self-registration form allows your users to register themselves.

Installing the self-registration form into your Web is a bit complex, and even a bit confusing. Nevertheless, the instructions provided on the template page itself are complete enough to guide you through.

To get the self-registration system working properly, you must first access Tools, Security, Permissions and choose the Use Unique Permissions for This Web option. Click Apply from that dialog box to set these permissions and then click the Users tab to make another change. Select Only Registered Users Have Browse Access and then click Apply once more. (You can add users at this stage.) Finally, click OK to close the dialog box. You have set the permissions in your discussion web to accommodate registered users.

You probably noticed that you can manually set users in the Users dialog box. What makes the self-registration form particularly useful is that you don't have to do so. The information from the self-registration form is passed to Explorer in order to create the users automatically. This saves you both time and trouble.

Note

> Chapter 17 contains information about Web security. Included there are the differences in adding users in systems running Windows 95/98, Windows NT, and UNIX servers. Adding users differs depending on which system you're running.

The next step makes the self-registration page available for your readers to add the information necessary to update the Users configuration area. With the web self-registration form still loaded in FrontPage Editor, return to Explorer and select File, Open FrontPage Web; click More Webs and then click List Webs (for the current server). Open the server's *root Web (page 266)*. Switch back to Editor and use the File menu to save the self-registration page into the root web. Leave the title and filename as suggested by the Save As dialog box.

To assure yourself that the self-registration form is being properly applied to the discussion web, click in any of the form fields (Username will do) to select it. Right-click in the field and select Form Properties. Click Options in the resulting Form Properties dialog box; you'll see the Options for Registration Form Handler dialog box that's shown in Figure 14.3. The form should show the same name in the Web Name field that you entered when you began building the web. This ensures that the registrations are applied to that web alone.

Figure 14.3
Make sure the correct Web name appears in the Forms Settings dialog box.

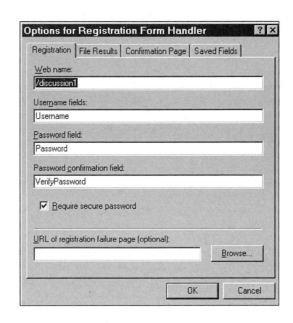

At this point you should test the self-registration form. With your Web server running, launch a Web browser such as Microsoft Internet Explorer or Netscape Navigator and enter the URL for the file WEBREG.HTM (the file containing the self-registration form). If you're running the Personal Web Server from the localhost address, for example, enter **http://localhost/webreg.htm** or **http://127.0.0.1/webreg.htm** in your browser's Location box. (If you changed the name of the file from WEBSELF.HTM, enter it instead.) If you've saved the file to a remote Web server, enter the appropriate IP number or domain name in place of **localhost** or **127.0.0.1**. Because the self-registration form was saved to the root web, you need not enter a path for the file, merely the filename itself. Later, you'll want to link the self-registration file from your home page, so users can access it without typing the filename. The self-registration form is shown in Figure 14.4.

Fill in the username and password fields with whatever names and passwords you want; then click the Register Me button. You receive a confirmation page showing that the registration has been successful, unless the username is already in the FrontPage database (which happens if you choose your administrator username as a name here), if your password is shorter than six characters, or if the password doesn't verify because of mistyping.

To see if the user has been registered, open the discussion web in Explorer, select the Permissions dialog box from the Tools menu, and click the End Users tab. You should see that the registered username now appears in the user area. As more and more users register themselves, this listing increases. You may close this dialog box.

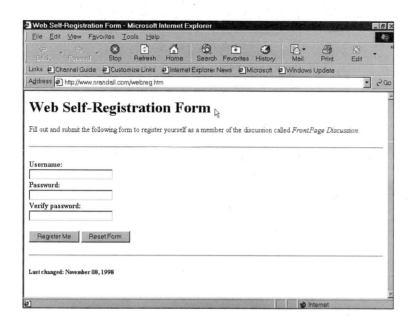

Figure 14.4
The self-registration form in Internet Explorer 4, ready to accept its first registrant.

Returning to the confirmation page, you'll see that it contains a link to the discussion web itself. When you click that hyperlink, you get a dialog box requiring you to enter a username and password. You are allowed into the web when you type the newly registered name and password. At this stage, you can begin posting messages to the discussion forum. If you establish more than one username, you can experiment by sending and replying to messages, then searching them and checking the contents page for results.

FINISHING THE DISCUSSION WEB

With the discussion web in place, very little remains to put it into place. You'll probably want to edit the registration form and give it a title that clarifies what web it belongs to, and you'll definitely want to provide a hyperlink from your main home page to both the registration page (to allow users to register) and to the discussion web's home page (to let them sign in and participate). Assuming you allowed the wizard to establish the Table of Contents page as the discussion web's home page, the name of that file will be *WebName*/INDEX.HTM (replacing *WebName* with the web's actual name). The registration file will be in the root web directory and will be named whatever you called it when you saved it to that directory after the wizard's completion.

Inside the web, you might want to edit the contents page and the Welcome page to add some spice to them. Open other pages in Editor and see which you want to edit in addition to these. The last change you might want to make is setting password protection for the posting page itself. This must be done from your Web server's administrator, however, not from within FrontPage.

PART

III

CH

14

POSTING TO A DISCUSSION WEB

Once the discussion web is in place, users can post articles to it. To do so, they need only enter the URL in the Location or Address field of their Web browser (or you can provide a direct link from your home page). Once there, and depending which frames option you used, they'll see a page that includes existing articles plus hyperlinks to Post a New Article or conduct a Search through the existing articles. If they click an existing article in the Contents frame, they can read that article and then reply to it or post a new one. Replies are hierarchically organized (visually threaded) in the Contents frame so that it's clear which reply belongs to which thread.

DELETING ARTICLES FROM A DISCUSSION WEB

Given the ease with which FrontPage's designers let you create a discussion web, it's surprising that they apparently gave no thought to an easy means of managing it. Nobody wants articles to accumulate on these things indefinitely (as many discussions currently on the Web attest), and the Webmaster needs to clean it out once in a while. Posted articles in a FrontPage discussion web stay there forever, however, accumulating until the page becomes a scrolling nightmare. As it stands, there's only one way to deal with unwanted postings in a discussion web. First, load the web into FrontPage Explorer. Choose Tools, Web Settings to bring up the FrontPage Web Settings dialog box. Click the Advanced tab and then click the Show Documents in Hidden Directories option. Click Apply.

Now enter the Folders view for your discussion web. Click the _discx subdirectory (x may be any number). Inside, you'll see eight-digit filenames preceding the .htm extension. These are the postings. The first posting, for example, will be 00000001.htm, the hundredth posting 00000100.htm, and so on. Deleting the file deletes the posting from the web.

How do you know which file belongs to which posting? Using your Web browser, enter the discussion web in your browser and click the posting you want to delete; this brings it up for reading. Call up the properties for that posting (the manner differs for each Web browser); the resulting box tells you the name of the associated .htm file.

Go back to the Folders view in FrontPage Explorer and highlight the file again. From here you have two choices. First, you can retain the file, but if you do, you should open the file in Page view and change the text to say something like, "This posting deleted." This means, of course, that this message will appear in the discussion web's table of contents, but the filename itself is preserved. Unfortunately, there's no way around this.

The second way is to delete the file from the web, then select the Recalculate Hyperlinks command from the Tools menu. This will clear the file and, in the discussion web itself, the heading (the subject line, for instance) for the message.

EMPTY WEB AND ONE-PAGE WEB

Two of FrontPage's web templates are designed to offer minimal help to you as web designer. The Empty Web template creates, as its name suggests, a web with nothing in it.

Its only purpose is to create the directory (which it take from your web's name) into which all documents will be stored, after which it's your task to develop the web as you want. The One-Page Web template, available at the top of the New FrontPage Web dialog box as a radio button, adds only one element to this: a home page that gives you a place to start. This home page, however, doesn't actually include any text or graphics; it's simply an empty HTML page, waiting for your design decisions.

CUSTOMER SUPPORT WEB

Creating the Customer Support Web does not require working through a wizard; in fact, there is no corresponding wizard. To create this web, select Customer Support Web from the New Web dialog box. FrontPage creates a Web that looks like that shown in Figure 14.5.

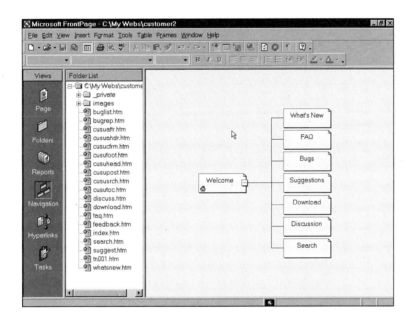

Figure 14.5
The Customer Support Web features all you need to offer top-notch service.

This web is designed to let you provide a full range of services for your clients. Its design, however, replicates the many computer company sites on the Web. If you have a different kind of product or service, not all the pages will be of use to you. They can be modified, and certainly two or more of the pages will be useful, but expect to do a significant amount of redesign on this web. If you plan to offer software or hardware products, on the other hand, the Customer Support Web will get you halfway to your goal.

To make the suggested changes to this web, you need to load each individual page into Page view, which is usually done by double-clicking the page's icon from Folder or Navigator view. To get an idea of what the page looks like, load it into your Web browser by using the appropriate URL with the /Support Web Name/INDEX.HTM path.

PART

III

CH

14

PAGE 1: WELCOME

The first page in the Customer Support Web welcomes your users to your site and provides a set of links to all the other pages on the site. This page provides a general welcome, along with parenthesized "fields," which you are expected to alter to customize the page for your own company. Begin at the top of the file, giving a clear company name and adding a logo if you have one, and be sure to use the Page and Web Properties features to give your site a color and graphical thematic unity. Be sure to change the copyright information at the bottom of the page as well.

The important thing to realize is that this page provides the entry to the entire Web site. As such, it gives your readers an all-important first impression, and you don't want to let that get away. Work hard on this Welcome page—perhaps even harder than on all the rest.

PAGE 2: WHAT'S NEW

The purpose of the What's New page is to show your readers what has been added to the site recently. Again, the page needs a great deal of work to make it consistent with your company's image. More importantly, you must decide precisely how to display the links to the new information, as well as—and this is crucial—how often to update. In a true customer service site, the What's New page is perhaps the single most important component of the site. If you don't intend to keep the page up to date regularly, get rid of it and erase all links to it. If you do keep it, make sure that the links point correctly to their corresponding documents. One link is already provided, and this is to a template for a technical document, complete with *inline graphic (page 122)*. Use this document as a basis, but if you have your own, use it instead.

PAGE 3: FREQUENTLY ASKED QUESTIONS

One of the main reasons for offering customer support over the Web is to minimize the need for support over the telephone. The most effective way of doing so is to provide answers on the Web site to questions the telephone support staff receive regularly. The FAQ (Frequently Asked Questions) page is designed as a template to help you put these together. This page offers a set of questions early in the page that contain internal links to answers farther down the page. This is a good structure by which to get started, but if questions demand a response longer than a paragraph or two, it is better to instead link to other, longer documents.

PAGE 4: BUGS

If your business sells software, you'll inevitably run into the problem known as *bugs*. The purpose of the Bug Report page in the Customer Support Web is to allow your users to report bugs they find in your product. It's unacceptable for software companies to insist their product does not contain bugs—all computer users know differently and generally accept the fact that bugs exist. This page shows that you're up front about trying to fix them, rather than suggesting that they're not there in the first place. One very good reason for a page like this is for testers of your company's beta products. Even Microsoft has an area for this purpose in its beta support sites.

The Bug Report page offers a form for readers to fill in and submit. This form is shown in Figure 14.6, and it contains two drop-down selection menus and several fill-in fields. Your primary task, aside from introducing the bug report according to your company policies and redesigning the page according to a consistent color and graphic scheme, is to customize the form and invite the information you need. Spend some time considering exactly that question because an effective Bug Report Form can optimize the usefulness, and thus the salability, of your product.

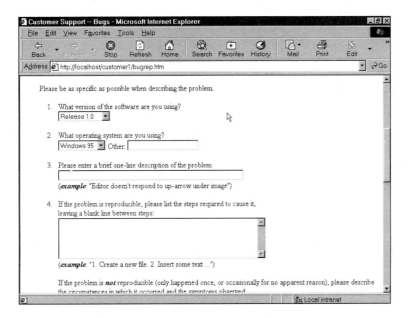

Figure 14.6
The Bug Report Form offers several fields for readers to select.

PAGE 5: SUGGESTIONS

If you're genuinely uninterested in what your site's visitors think of your Web site or your products, get rid of this page immediately. There's nothing worse than offering a suggestion page that you never pay attention to. Visitors who make suggestions want to feel that they're making a difference. If you are interested in your visitors' suggestions, however (and any good service-oriented company should be), customize this page to invite the feedback you need in order to make your products or services more successful. Customizing the Category portion of the form is of particular importance because through this drop-down menu you encourage readers to speak up about specific topics.

Page 6: Download

It's become a given on the Internet that if you want to sell software, you have to let users download at least a demo version so they can try it out. When people purchase your software, you must provide downloadable upgrades from your Web site as well. The Download page lets you provide these services, although to make it work properly you have to customize it significantly. The template page provides a simple suggestion for how to deal with different file formats and multiple download items, but visiting any software or hardware company on the Web will give you some much better ideas about how to offer your product.

Caution

Failing to test the Download page will cause a negative impression from your readers. If a click does not produce the software, your users will be angry or at least disappointed. Be sure to test—and not just from one machine. Log in to your site through a modem and make sure everything works right.

Page 7: Discussion

The Discussion page on the Customer Support Web offers a place for your readers to discuss your products and services with other users and with company representatives. Note that while there's no requirement in the web itself for a company representative to take part, it's extremely important that one be present. It helps avoid the embarrassing possibility of customers saying incorrect or demeaning things about your products. The discussion area resembles the one created with the full discussion web examined earlier in this chapter, and you can customize it to provide as full a discussion forum as you want, including offering user registration.

Note

As with the Download page, be absolutely certain the discussion area works well before making it public. Also be sure that you intend to pay attention to the discussion.

Page 8: Search

Figure 14.7 shows a portion of the Search page created by the Customer Support Web template. It's simple, but as the description of the query language at the bottom of the page demonstrates, it's not simplistic. You can't possibly know how or even if your readers will make use of this page, but it's a good idea to have one, and it's a good idea also to construct pages that anticipate reader searches, building in common keywords and text strings.

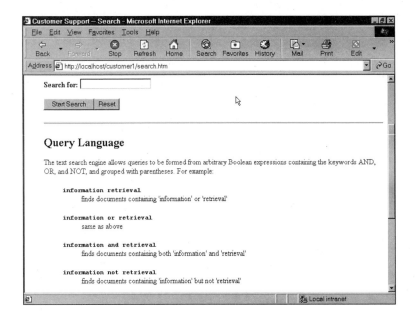

Figure 14.7
The Search page contains a description of the query language used by FrontPage.

PROJECT WEB

The Project Web offers a means for members of a team project to keep in touch with each other, and perhaps more importantly, a place for you to put all information about the project that everyone involved should be able to retrieve. Its primary use will be in an intranet. For some organizations, the Project Web will be sufficient to replace more complex software packages such as Lotus Notes, but even within these organizations, a Project Web might suffice for a small working group collaborating on a specific project or portion of a project.

PAGE 1: HOME

The template home page for the Project Web offers a brief description and a What's New area, as well as a series of links to the other pages in the web. Because a Project Web is meant primarily as an internal site, there's not as much need for extensive editing to appeal to customers. The design decisions made here should reflect your management goals of professionalism and efficiency, and should be less marketing-driven than the customer support site. Members of the Project Web are usually your co-workers, who can expect a certain amount of "cutting through the hype." The efficiency is displayed in providing ease of access to information, and by constantly updating the What's New information.

PAGE 2: MEMBERS

The Project Web's Members page offers an alphabetical listing of those involved in the project, and the links from that list lead to the type of generic profile shown in Figure 14.8. By

PART

III

CH

14

replacing all the names with real names, the pictures with real pictures, and the email addresses with valid ones, you can create a useful, dynamic page of information that members can share. From this page, members can email one another and visit one another's home page, and the page can therefore act as a team bond. Be absolutely certain, however, that all information is correct, or risk anything from embarrassment to downright anger.

Figure 14.8
Team members can interact with one another from the Members page.

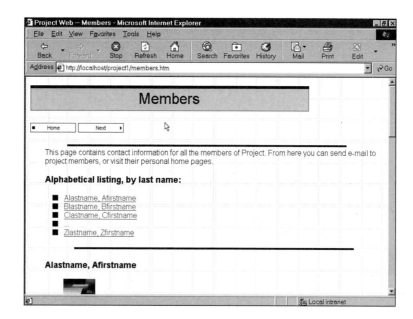

PAGE 3: SCHEDULE

What's a project without a schedule? Nothing, obviously, so the template creates a schedule page for you. On this page are three main sections: a list of goals and activities in the current and following weeks, a showcase of upcoming events pertaining to the project, and a listing of milestones and deliverables.

The function of the schedule, of course, is to keep all project members aware of progress to date and necessary progress to come. To that end, it's imperative that this page be kept updated constantly. Slip here, and you risk losing the Web site's credibility. The best bet is to alter this page as soon as you can to fit the project you're running rather than the one the template suggests. Continue returning to it to keep the project team focused.

PAGE 4: STATUS

Assuming the project is large and long enough, you'll probably be required to file status reports as the work continues. The Status page offers a place to collect those reports and make them available to members of the project team. The titles of the hyperlinks on the template page assume monthly and quarterly reports for the current year, quarterly and annual reports for last year, and annual reports for previous years of the project. The links on the page don't lead anywhere; it's your job to supply the actual documents. Clearly, this page is only as useful as your status reports allow, and you might not want it as part of your web if you have no reports to include. It can be easily modified to allow weekly reports, subteam reports, and so forth.

PAGE 5: ARCHIVE

If your project team has developed a significant number of documents, prototypes, programs, tools, and other demonstrable items, you will want to offer them as a project archive. The Archive page (see Figure 14.9) is designed as a kind of catch-all for this kind of material. Each internal link leads to a description of the item and further links to the documents in a variety of formats. Obviously, it's up to you to provide the materials, and in all likelihood you'll want to completely revamp the presentation of this page—but it's an excellent suggestion for a page within the web.

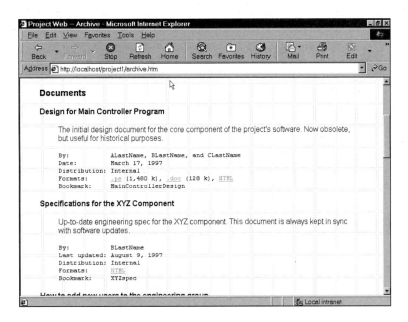

Figure 14.9
The Archive page offers links to documents in various formats.

PAGE 6: SEARCH

The Search page is identical to the one offered in the Customer Support Web discussed earlier, and requires only a minor degree of tinkering. Otherwise, leave it as it stands.

PAGE 7: DISCUSSIONS

Page 7 of the Customer Support Web was also a discussion area, but the difference here is that the Project Web's Discussions page contains two discussion groups already built in.

PART

III

CH

14

The principle is to provide a separate discussion forum for as many topics as your project members require, and the page describes each forum and invites participation from the appropriate parties. You can add as many discussion groups as you want, but starting with two or three (to keep things under control) seems the best idea.

PERSONAL WEB

The Personal Web is essentially a combination résumé and special interest web. Figure 14.10 shows the generic home page information offered by this page, all of which is in obvious need of customization before this web becomes public.

Figure 14.10
The Personal web is little more than a résumé, but a complete one.

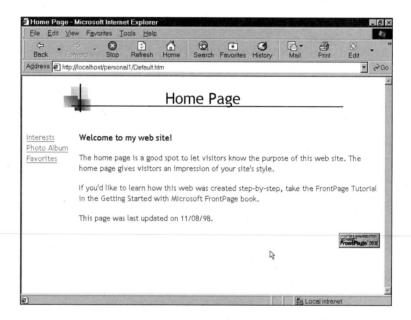

Lower on the page, the template offers a place to insert links to external sites, as well as contact information and even a form for comments from outsiders. There's also an area on this page for links to reports from associates and employees, and obviously you want to make sure these are flattering. In fact, this entire web template is of questionable value—a personal site should be handled with very great care depending on its purpose. If you want employers to look at it, be sure to keep that audience in mind. "If I want friends or random Web visitors to see it, why include job information?" and so on. Consider carefully and change the site dramatically.

FILES CREATED BY FRONTPAGE'S NEW WEBS

When you build a web with the FrontPage New Web feature, several directories and files are created on the machine running the Web server software. Note that these are in addition to the directories and files created by installing the FrontPage server extensions in the first place.

Each web produces the same directory structure, although individual files differ according to the type of web (Corporate Presence, Project, and so on) being built. This structure is as follows and is shown in Figure 14.11 in a Windows 98 Explorer window.

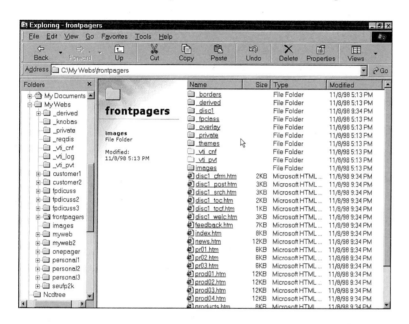

Figure 14.11
All FrontPage–created webs share this rather elaborate directory structure.

WebName/

The files and directories for the individual Webs you create are stored within a directory that bears the name you gave the web in the New Web dialog box.

private/

In general, all directories that begin with the underscore character (_) are hidden from Web visitors. They're also hidden from the view in FrontPage Explorer, unless the option Show Documents in Hidden Directories is toggled on within the Advanced portion of the Web Settings dialog box.

The _private/ directory works somewhat differently. It contains files that you want to keep invisible to your Web's visitors, and these files will not show up in a search produced by the Search Bot. The directory is visible within FrontPage Explorer because it's one to which you'll want frequent access.

fp-class/

The fp-class/ directory holds the Java classes for the hover buttons and navigation buttons, both of which are Java applets created through the process of designing your Web.

You can use it to store other Java applets you develop as well. This directory doesn't exist by default; it is created when FrontPage automatically creates Java items.

images/

The images/ directory offers a place to store image files (GIF and JPG, for example). This directory makes it easy for FrontPage Editor to locate your images when you use the Insert Image dialog box.

themes/

The _themes/ directory stores the files necessary to display the theme chosen for your web. Whenever you select a theme, FrontPage automatically uploads the GIF (graphics) and CSS (cascading style sheet) files necessary to ensure that the theme is displayed correctly. These files are stored in a subdirectory that bears that theme's name. Each time you select a different theme for a particular Web, FrontPage replaces that specific theme's subdirectory with one bearing the new theme name and stores the new theme information. Each web can therefore have only one theme at a time.

vti_cnf/

Every Web page you create—every .htm file within the Web—has a corresponding file of the same name within the Web's _vti_cnf/ directory. This private directory holds files that contain name values for the public page, with information such as the last author to edit the page, when the page was edited, and so forth.

vti_bin/

The private _vti_bin/ directory contains three executable programs to be used in conjunction with FrontPage's WebBots and administrative functions. _vti_bin/ itself contains the file SHTML.EXE, which handles all HTML documents in your Web that control some aspect of the browser's behavior (such as WebBot forms). Within _vti_bin/ are two subdirectories, _vti_adm and _vti_aut. The first of these contains the ADMIN.EXE file, which handles administrator procedures such as permissions and Web creation. The second contains AUTHOR.EXE, which handles author procedures, including permissions.

vti_txt/

To make searches possible, each Web contains a _vti_txt/ directory that contains a text index file. Within each _vti_txt/ directory is a default.wti/ directory, which contains one set of files for discussion groups created with the Discussion Group Web Wizard (if you've done so for that Web) and another set for all other HTML documents.

| Tip #73 | If you don't plan to allow searches against your site, consider deleting the _vti_txt/ directory completely. This reduces the memory needed for the Recalculate Links command. |

`vti_pvt/`

The `_vti_pvt/` directory contains several private files, including the Web's parameters, the list of subwebs (in the root directory only), the to-do list, and the to-do list history.

Some Web types created by FrontPage have a subdirectory unique to the functions of that web. The Project Web, for example, stores information for its Knowledge Base in a directory called `knobas`, necessary for user searches against the Knowledge Base. Also in the Project Web is `reqdis`, which contains the files for the discussion of requirements among team members. Discussion webs contain a directory called `_discx` (where *x* represents a single digit), in which posted articles are stored. Customer Support Webs contain the `_cusudi` directory for the Customer Support discussion.

TROUBLESHOOTING

One of FrontPage 2000's more important web creation and management features is its use of *nested subwebs (page 514)*. These are webs that are created inside other webs. The value of such webs is that you can assign overall permissions to an overall web, and different positions inside each of the subwebs. By doing so, you gain greater control over the subwebs.

For nested subwebs to function properly, though, you must mount them on a server with the most current server extensions, those that ship with FrontPage 2000 or that can be downloaded specifically for FrontPage 2000. Earlier versions of the extensions allowed for only one level of subwebs, those immediately below the *root web (page 266)* on the hierarchy. For example, you could have a web at `http://www.mycompany.com`, and any number of subwebs a level below that, such as `http://www.mycompany.com/products`. But you couldn't have `http://www.mycompany.com/products/peripherals`, because that's two subwebs deep.

Make sure, therefore, that your ISP or *Web Hosting Service (WPP) (page 764)* is using the FrontPage 2000 extensions. If they're not, make a demand. If you can't make use of everything FrontPage 2000 has to offer, your purchase isn't a very useful one. But if you have to wait a few weeks for the ISP or WPP to install and test the extensions, patience is probably a good idea.

DESIGNERS CORNER

Don't feel hamstrung by the documents created by the wizards or templates. These are simply a starting point, ideas to consider, and you should plan extensive changes to what FrontPage initially creates. You'll want to completely rethink the Customer Support web, for example, because every business has unique service needs. You'll want to add pages and even full sections, and you'll find that some you simply don't need. But when you make changes, remember to ensure that the navigation pages work after each change.

You'll also want to customize the way the web works. For example, as shown above, the Customer Support web includes a bug report page. If you decide to keep this area, make sure that you modify the form fields to ask for specific bug information, and also to direct the customers' reports to the appropriate personnel. You might also want to ensure that only registered customers have access to the bug reports (if everyone on the web has access to it, you're liable to get lots of prank reports). One way to protect a single page or two such as this is to create a subweb called, say, /bugreports, move these two pages into that web, and restrict browsing permissions to registered users only. If you do something like this, however, be sure to provide a link from a relevant page.

CHAPTER 15

Working with an Existing Web

In this chapter

by Neil Randall

LOADING A FRONTPAGE WEB

Once you have one or more webs created with FrontPage 2000, you can load them by choosing File, Open Web or by clicking the down arrow beside the Open icon on the FrontPage toolbar, then selecting the Open Web icon from the drop-down menu. A third way is to select Recent Webs from the File menu and then select the web you want to load (but only four will be listed here).

Finally, you can specify that when you launch FrontPage, you want the most recently modified web automatically loaded as well; you specify this in the Startup area of the Options dialog box (available through Tools, Options). Obviously, this is even more limiting than the Recent Webs menu item, but it's a useful feature if you're working primarily on one web.

Either of the first two options yields the Open Web dialog box. Studying this dialog box is important because some of its elements are somewhat hidden. First, there are two main areas to look for your webs: the first is in Web Folders, the second in the My Webs folder. Web Folders is found in the lower-left corner of the Open File dialog box, inside the Action bar. It can also be found in your computer's My Computer folder, accessible by clicking the down arrow beside the Look In field, and then on My Computer at the top of the list. My Webs is found in the c:\ directory and is accessible by clicking the down arrow beside the Look In field, selecting (C:), and then double-clicking My Webs in the body of the dialog box. My Webs is the default folder in the Look In box.

The bottom of the dialog box offers a more comprehensive means of retrieving recently open webs than the Recent Webs menu command. A drop-down menu reveals a list of webs you've worked on recently when you click the down arrow beside the Folder Name field. You can select your web from here instead of from the Look In field.

If you open a *root web* (the web associated at the root of the folder or the URL—http://localhost, for example) all *subwebs* (webs within a subfolder of that web) are displayed as web icons in the Folder List. Figure 15.1 shows an open localhost web, with several subwebs displayed as icons near the top of the list.

Note that this command is useful only for loading webs created with FrontPage itself. If you have a web created outside FrontPage, use the Import Web feature described later in this chapter to load that web into FrontPage.

The remainder of this chapter assumes you'll be working with the Web created in Chapter 13, "Creating a Web," called FrontPagers, which was built with the help of the Corporate Presence Web Wizard. A dialog box might appear when you click OK (depending on the server you're using); the dialog box will require a username and password for author permissions, which you established earlier. Once the FrontPagers Web is loaded and you click the icon for Folders view, you see the window shown in Figure 15.2.

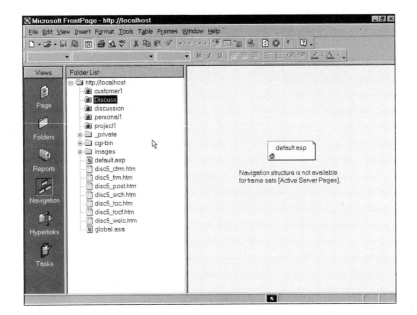

PART

III

CH

15

Figure 15.1
To see the webs associated with a root web, open the root web and examine the Folder List. All sub-webs are displayed beside web icons toward the top of this list.

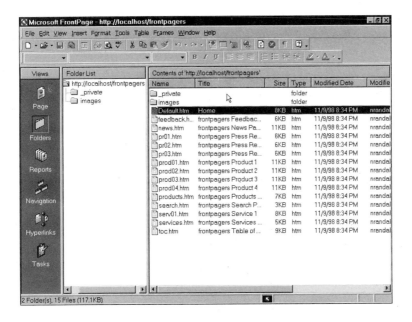

Figure 15.2
The FrontPagers web is now loaded and ready to edit in any of the various views.

USING THE FOLDER LIST

The Folder List is primarily a navigation aid. When you click a folder, the subfolders and files contained within that folder appear in the Contents pane. You move from folder to folder by clicking in the Folder List (the Contents pane has no navigation tools to move up a level or go back), although you can open a subfolder of the currently displayed folder by double-clicking it in the Contents pane.

As a navigation aid, however, the Folder List has one important quirk. While you can use the Contents pane to view subfolders of the currently selected folder, you cannot use it to view subwebs of the currently open web. The web icons in Figure 15.3 (folders with tiny globes in the middle) in the Folder List and Contents pane represent subwebs. If you click one, the Contents pane displays "Files in a subweb cannot be viewed here. Double-click on the Web folder to view its contents."

When you follow these instructions, FrontPage will open the subweb in its own FrontPage *instance* (you'll have two FrontPages running). The new instance then lets you display the subweb's folders, subfolders, and files in the Contents pane, but if that subweb has subwebs of its own, they must be opened in a new instance as well.

You can select specific FrontPage instances from the Windows taskbar, or through the time-honored tradition of cycling through the open programs and windows by using the Alt+Tab key combination.

> **Caution**
>
> It's entirely possible to have several instances of FrontPage 2000 open at the same time. However, each takes its own share of system resources, so it's a good idea to close the ones you aren't actually using. This applies to all programs, of course, not just FrontPage. Multitasking is nice, but it has its limitations.

If you right-click a folder or a subweb in the Folders view, several options appear on the context menu. The same context menus appear if you right-click a folder or subweb in the Contents pane. The options are as follows:

Relevance	Command	Explanation
Common	Copy	Copies the item into the Clipboard; Paste appears as an option on the context menu.
	Delete	Deletes the item; FrontPage asks for confirmation.
	Properties	Yields the Properties dialog box for the item. No options are available for subwebs. For the main web and for subfolders, options allow programs or scripts from this directory, and allow files to be browsed (a directory listing, for instance). The more you select, the more access users have to your site and its features, but security becomes an issue.
Folders only	New Page	Adds a new FrontPage document to the folder.
	New Folder	Adds a subfolder to the current folder.
	Cut	Cuts the folder into the Clipboard; Paste appears as an option on the context menu.

Relevance	Command	Explanation
	Rename	Allows you to rename the folder. You can also do this by clicking the folder name, waiting a few seconds (don't double-click), clicking it again, and then typing in the new name. All references to this folder in the web will be changed to reflect the new name.
	Convert to Web	Converts the folder from a folder into a web. FrontPage issues a dialog box with two warnings. First, documents that include files (such as Office documents) might no longer be updated if you change the files themselves (an obvious inconvenience). Second, the hyperlinks on the navigation bars might become external instead of internal. In other words, the conversion might not work exactly as you expected it to; you might need to do additional work for the new web, and the old one as well, to have them work completely correctly.
Subweb only	Open	Opens the subweb in a new FrontPage instance.
	Convert to Folder	Converts the web into a folder. FrontPage issues a dialog box with four warnings. First, pages with themes might change to match the theme of the parent web. Second, users without access to the parent web will not have access to the newly created folder (which makes sense). Third, hyperlinks that pointed to the web will no longer work, and must be manually changed or deleted. Fourth, any tasks related to the converted web are lost.

Be careful when cutting, deleting, or renaming folders (cutting puts them on the Clipboard; deleting gets rid of them permanently). Remember that internal links within your web use the folder name as part of the hyperlink reference; changing the folder means invalidating those links. Fortunately, FrontPage keeps track of renamed folders and automatically changes the links when you choose Tools/Recalculate Links. Cut or deleted folders appear as broken links in your FrontPage Web.

WORKING WITH FRONTPAGE'S VIEWS

Each web you work on will later open in the most recent view you've used. As you use FrontPage, you'll find yourself gaining a favorite view, one that you use most frequently, and quite likely even a different favorite view for each type of web you create. You examine the various views here, and they will reappear throughout this section of the book.

FOLDERS VIEW

FrontPage's Folders view isn't nearly as graphically pleasing as Navigation view or Hyperlinks view (both of which are covered later), but it provides a perspective on your site that is well suited to those of you who are used to dealing with files and folders. Folders view exists for web designers and maintainers who want to see the web as a series of individual files in various folders and work with them on that level. For many users, this is the most efficient way to work.

You can access the Folders view either by clicking the Folders View icon on FrontPage's Views bar or by selecting Folders from FrontPage's View menu.

As Figure 15.3 shows, Folders view offers both the Folder List and the Contents pane. The Folder List shows, in a collapsible list, the folders for that Web, and consists of both the folders that FrontPage created when it built the Web you're working with, and those you create yourself. The Contents pane shows the files and subfolders within the folder currently selected in the Folder List. In other words, Folders view is very much like the Windows Explorer file viewer found in Windows 95 and Windows NT 4.0.

Figure 15.3
The Folders view for the FrontPagers web shows the folders on the left and the contents of the folder, including subwebs and subfolders, on the right.

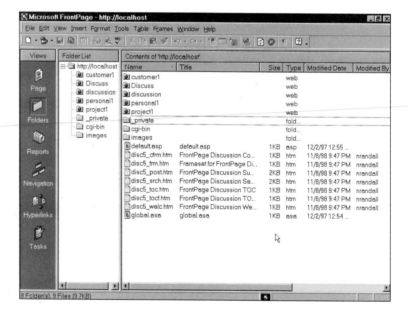

As with all Windows file viewers, FrontPage gives you the choice of seeing hidden files in addition to normal files. If you want to see all hidden folders in the Folders view, open the Web Setting dialog box from FrontPage's Tools menu and select Show Documents in Hidden Directories from the Advanced tab. Incidentally, it's clear from the name of this command that Microsoft hasn't quite completed the shift in terminology from *directories* to *folders* either—but let's give them a few more years.

Across the top of the Folders view's Contents pane is a series of seven columns offering details about the subwebs, subfolders, and files. You can shrink or expand the width of each column by moving the mouse pointer to the border between two columns (it turns into a cross) and dragging the border left or right. The columns are as follows:

- Name

  Displays the computer name of the web folder (in the case of subwebs), the folder, or the filename (in the case of FrontPage documents).

- Title

  The title of the FrontPage document. You assign titles when you create the document, and you can change the title by opening the Properties dialog box for an individual page. This title appears on the title bar of the Web browser when it displays that document.

- Size

  The size of the file, in kilobytes (KB) or, in the case of large files, megabytes (MB).

- Type

  The folder or document type. Web folders display web, regular folders display folder. Files display the filename extension, such as .htm for HTML files, .asp for Active Server Pages files, and so on.

- Modified Date

  Displays the date and time, in mm/dd/yy hh/ss format, of the last modification made to the file. Does not appear with folders or web folders.

- Modified By

  Displays the username of the person who did the last file modification. Does not appear with folders or web folders.

- Comments

  Displays the comments added through the Properties dialog box's Summary tab for the document. Not available for folders or web folders.

WORKING WITH INDIVIDUAL PAGES

Once you reach a page you want to work with in Folders view, you can work with it by clicking it. At this point, you have several choices. Double-clicking opens that page in the Page view, where you can edit and save it directly back to the web. Right-clicking the icon reveals a pop-up menu with the following options:

- Move to Center (Hyperlinks view only)—Centers the selected document in the graphical representation in the Hyperlinks pane.

- Check Out *or* Check In (Folders, Reports, Hyperlinks views)—If you have the check-in/check-out feature enabled through the Web Preferences dialog box, one of these commands will be on the right-click menu. Check Out lets you open the file in Page view and prevent any other user with authoring permissions open on the same page. Check In returns the page to the state of being editable by users with authoring permissions. The Check In option appears only when the file is checked out.

- Open (all views except Tasks)—Loads the page either into the Page view or into an editor you have specified for that file. (See Chapter 17, "Configuring Webs," for details on how to configure FrontPage to work with a different editor.)

- Open With (all views except Tasks)—Loads the page into an editor you select from the resulting Open With dialog box (again, see Chapter 17).

- Cut (Folders, Reports, Navigation views)—Removes the page or folder from the display and places it in the Clipboard, making it available for pasting elsewhere. Simultaneously erases links to other pages and restores them when you paste. Use Cut to move files or folders.

- Copy (Folders, Reports, Navigation views)—Copies the page or folder to the Clipboard and makes it available for pasting to other locations.

- Rename (Folders, Reports, Navigation views)—Lets you change the name of the file or folder and simultaneously changes names in links to that item.

- Delete (all views except Tasks)—Permanently erases the page from the web and simultaneously erases links to other pages.

- Add Task (all views called New Task in Tasks view)—Opens the Add Task dialog box for that specific file. (See Chapter 18, "Managing a Web," for a full discussion on FrontPage tasks.)

- Properties (all views except Tasks)—Opens the Properties dialog box. (See the "FrontPage Menus" section later in this chapter for more details.)

Beyond that, any work you do on individual pages occurs through the Page view. The point of the other views is to let you see your web, keep track of it, and add or remove folders and pages—not to edit individual pages.

REPORTS VIEW

The Reports view collects a number of extremely useful views of the web. Its primary purpose is as a means of maintaining your web, offering several tools for doing so. The reports included with this view range from the site summary, which offers a set of one-line summaries of the contents of your web, through lists of recently added and recently changed files, a list of pages that load slowly in users' browsers, a status of publishing for the pages, and lists of broken hyperlinks and other errors.

These reports are covered in Chapter 18.

NAVIGATION VIEW

The Navigation view offers a visual display of your web, one that makes it easy to add to and reorganize your web. Its purpose is to help you organize your web's navigation bars. It is accessible by clicking the Navigation icon on FrontPage's Views toolbar, or by selecting Navigation from the View menu. When you do, you see a screen resembling Figure 15.4. Note that for the sake of the screen looking good in this book, I've rotated the default view (by right-clicking in the main viewing window and selecting Rotate).

PART

III

CH

15

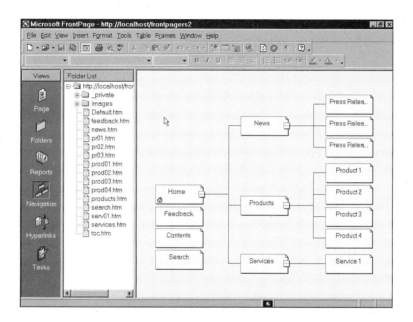

Figure 15.4
The Navigation view displays your web's structure in clear and unambiguous detail.

As Figure 15.4 shows, Navigation view has the Folder List and the main window (which is unnamed). Each box in the main window represents a page in the web and displays the page's title. Each box also has a corresponding filename in the Folder List. To see which filename corresponds to which title, right-click in the main window on a page and select Properties. The Properties dialog box displays the full path and filename in its (unchangeable) Location field.

The Navigation view lets you structure your web quickly and easily, simply by dragging and dropping files from the Folder List, or by adding pages directly in the main window and dragging them among the boxes to create your web's hierarchy. Here you can easily rename your pages, giving them a new title.

Let's see how this view works. Start by opening the FrontPagers Web you created in Chapter 13; select the Navigation view. Doing this gives you a Navigation view showing several boxes in the Presentation pane and several folders and files in the Contents pane. Your screen should look much like Figure 15.5.

Figure 15.5
You must scroll hori-
zontally to see all of a
large web in
Navigation view.

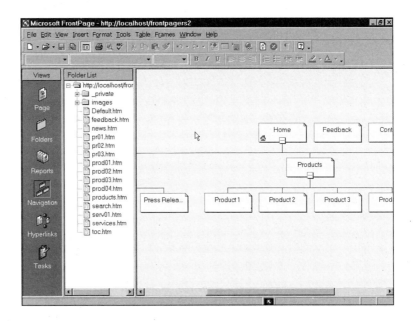

Notice the lines running between the boxes. These demonstrate the web's hierarchy, showing which pages are subordinate to other pages. Several pages lead directly from the home
page—News, Products, and Services—and several more lead from that second row into the
third. Note also that pages with subordinate pages also have an expansion toggle (the plus
or minus sign). Click the expansion toggle to expand or collapse the structure.

First rename a few pages. Find the box Product 1 in the third row and click it. After a
pause, click it again to highlight the text. The pause is necessary because clicking twice
quickly is read as a double-click, which loads the page into Page view. With the text highlighted, type **Books** and press Enter.

Tip #74

> You can also rename a box by right-clicking it and selecting Rename. Furthermore, if
> you've just finished renaming a box, you can tab to the next one and Rename will still be
> active. This way, you can rename several of the web's pages easily in succession.

Now add a second product page to the web. To do so, select the Products page again by
single-clicking it, then clicking the New Page icon in the toolbar. You can do the same
thing by right-clicking the Products page and selecting New Page. You'll see a new box
with the title New Page *x*, where *x* is a number that varies according to what's already in the
web. This new page is connected to the Products page. Rename this new page **Magazines**.
Finally, create two pages leading from the Magazines page, one called **Computer** and the
other called **Fashion**. Your Navigation view should look like Figure 15.6 (which is rotated).

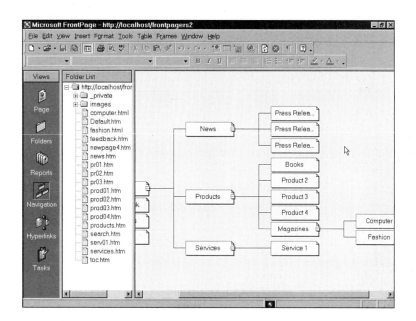

Figure 15.6
This web now has three hierarchical levels, but it still needs a lot of work before publishing.

What you've done is add three pages to the web and, more importantly, added three links to the web's navigation bars. FrontPage formats the navigation bars according to the positioning of pages in the Navigation view, so this view is your primary assistant in designing your web's user interface. If users can't find what you make available to them, your site is worthless.

You can also easily delete a page from your web. Select the page and either press the Delete key, right-click and choose Delete, or select Delete from the Edit menu. When you do, you are presented with the Delete Page dialog box, which allows you to remove the page (and all its child pages) from only the web's navigation bars or from the entire web itself. In other words, you can keep the pages but simply not have them show up in the navigation bars, in which case it is still available in the other FrontPage views, or you can delete the page entirely.

To show the complete power of Navigation view, you'll move a child page from one parent to another. Assume you don't need all three Press Release pages, only one. You also need one more Product page and a subordinate page to the Feedback page. Instead of creating new pages, you can drag the two unneeded Service pages to their new locations.

To do so, first click the page, called Press Release 2. (If you can't see the whole name, right-click the box and choose Rename—but don't rename it.) Drag it toward the main Products page until the line from the Press Release 2 box detaches itself from the News page and attaches itself to the Products page. The page will be in its new location when you release the mouse button. Rename it **Software** to account for the third product in your line. Now drag the Press Release 3 box to the Feedback box, rename it **Archives**, and apply your changes. You've successfully restructured your web.

If your web is too wide for your display, you can rotate it 90 degrees. To do so, right-click in the Presentation pane and select Rotate. Scroll down until the home page, Feedback page, and Products pages are visible. Your screen should look like Figure 15.7.

Figure 15.7
The Navigation view lets you rotate the appearance of the Web to give you a different perspective on your Web's structure.

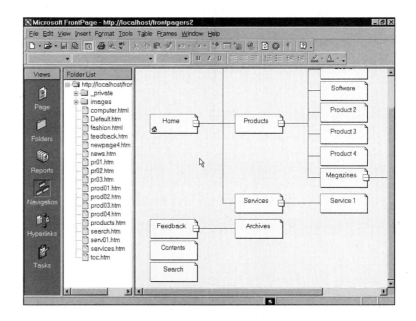

Tip #75

You can also create new pages in Navigation view by dragging files from the Content pane into the Presentation pane until the line attaches to the parent page you want.

Several options are available through the Navigation view's context menus. The following commands appear depending on whether you right-click on a box or outside a box:

Right-Click Area	Command	Explanation
on box	Open	Opens the page in the default editor (usually Page view).
on box	Open With	Lets you select which editor to load the page into.
on box	New Page	Inserts a new page into the web as a child page to the currently selected page.
on box	External Hyperlink	Lets you add an external hyperlink to the hierarchical structure of your web (and thus to your navigation bars).

Right-Click Area	Command	Explanation
on box	Cut	Cuts the page into the Clipboard. Paste appears as an option on the context menu.
on box	Copy	Copies the item into the Clipboard. Paste appears as an option on the context menu.
on box	Paste	Allows you to paste the page you have copied (or cut) into the web at the location of the cursor. Since you perform this action while the cursor in on an existing page, Paste will create a copy of the copied (or cut) page and link it to the page on which it is pasted. *(Grayed out unless Copy or Cut already performed.)*
on box	Rename	Allows you to rename the page. You can also do this by clicking the box name, waiting a few seconds (don't double-click), clicking it again, and then typing in the new name. All references to this page in the web will be changed to reflect the new name.
on box	Delete	Deletes the item; FrontPage gives you a choice of removing the page from the navigation bars only or from the entire web.
on box	View Subtree Only	Displays only the selected box and its child boxes; select this option again to view the entire web.
on box	Included in Navigation Bars	When toggled on, the box is included in the web's navigation bars; when toggled off, the box is grayed out on the display, and it does not appear in the navigation bars.
on box	Add Task	Adds the selected page to the Task List. See Chapter 18 for details on working with FrontPage tasks.
on box	Properties	Yields the Properties dialog box for the page. No options are available for subwebs.
outside box	Zoom	Lets you zoom the web to make it more visible on the display.

Right-Click Area	Command	Explanation
outside box	Rotate	Rotates the web 90 degrees for easier viewing.
outside box	Expand All	Expands all the collapsed subtrees in the web. You can expand individual subtrees by clicking the expansion toggle (the plus sign) on any applicable box.
outside box	View Subtree Only	Lets you exclude all boxes from view except the currently selected box and its children. (*Grayed out unless you select a box to which children are attached.*)
outside box	New Top Page	Adds a box to the Navigation view, on the same level as the top box in the hierarchy (which is usually the `default.htm` document).
outside box	Apply Changes	If you have made any changes to the Navigation view, this command makes them permanent. (*Grayed out when no changes have been made.*)
outside box	Web Settings	Opens the Web Setting dialog box described in Chapter 17.

HYPERLINKS VIEW

The Hyperlinks view is shown in Figure 15.8. This view explicitly shows the links among the individual documents in the web. In other words, the view shows the web as a web, relating each page to one another. You can display the web with any selected page at the center, thereby altering your perspective on the web's structure. To center the hyperlink display on a different document, either click the document in the folder list or right-click the document in the Hyperlinks pane and select Move to Center.

The Hyperlinks pane is more helpful than the Folders List at showing you the web's structure. Documents are linked to other documents in a series of loops (a document is linked to other documents and eventually back to itself), and only the Hyperlinks view shows this. Click the plus sign on the top left of the document icon to see all related links; this expands the icon to show the pages linked to it.

The Hyperlinks Context menu is displayed when you right-click in the main viewing window, away from the documents themselves. The available commands are as follow:

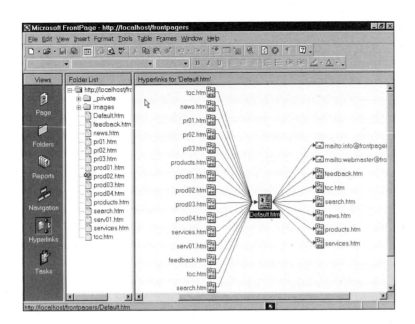

Figure 15.8
The Hyperlinks view
portrays the links
from page to page
across the web.

Command	Explanation
Show Page Titles	By default, the documents in Hyperlinks view are labeled with their filenames. If you want to label them with their page titles instead (which are often more explanatory), select this command. This toggles the command on, and you can return to filename labels by selecting it again to toggle it off.
Hyperlinks to Pictures	To keep your web from looking cluttered, by default FrontPage doesn't show links to images (images in your Web pages). If you want a more complete view of your web, toggle this command on. Images are then displayed with the image icon.
Repeated Hyperlinks	Often your pages contain multiple links from one page to another page. There's usually no reason to see these links more than once in the Individual Pages pane, but for a complete picture you can toggle Repeated Hyperlinks on.
Hyperlinks Inside Page	When you create pages, you can include a link to another place within that same page. This gives your readers strong navigational assistance. By default, however, FrontPage doesn't show these links because they clutter the display. If you want to see how many of these links you've created, toggle Hyperlinks Inside Page on to get a more complete view.
Web Settings	This command brings up the Web Settings dialog box, also available through the Tools menu. This dialog box is covered thoroughly in Chapter 17.

FRONTPAGE MENUS

FrontPage offers several main menus through which to complete its tasks. Chapter 3, "Page View: Windows, Icons, and Menus," covers those available for Page view, and the rest are covered here.

FILE, NEW, PAGE

This command lets you create a new document file in the web.

FILE, NEW, WEB

With the New Web command, which is available in all views, you begin the process of creating brand new webs. Choosing this command opens the New Web dialog box. Here you can select a wizard or a template to help automate the creation of a web.

One option is to add the new web to the current web. If you have a web currently loaded, you can create a new web and insert it directly into the loaded web. In this case, you are asked if you want to replace or retain files with duplicate names.

FILE, NEW, FOLDER

This command lets you create a new folder in the web, and thus a new directory on the Web server.

FILE, NEW, TASK

Lets you create a new task for inclusion in the Tasks view.

FILE, OPEN AND FILE, CLOSE

If you have already created documents (Web pages), you can load them into FrontPage via the Open command. The File menu's Close command unloads the current web.

FILE, OPEN WEB AND FILE, CLOSE WEB

If you have already created webs, you can load them into FrontPage via the Open Web command. The File menu's Close FrontPage Web command unloads the current web.

FILE, SAVE AND FILE, SAVE AS

Save lets you save the file currently loaded in Page view; it updates the file of that name already stored on your hard drive or server. Save As lets you save the current document under a new filename.

FILE, PUBLISH FRONTPAGE WEB

When you complete a web and want to store it on another Web server, use the File menu's Publish Web command. This is covered in detail in Chapter 16, "Publishing a Web."

FILE, IMPORT

If there are files or folders you want to bring into the current web from your hard drive, choose Import from the File menu. You'll see the Import dialog box shown in Figure 15.9. Clicking Add File displays the Add File to Import List dialog box, while clicking Add Folder yields the Browse for Folder dialog box. You can add multiple files and folders into the Import File box before clicking OK, and you can change the hyperlink reference by clicking Modify.

You select the appropriate file in the Add File to Import dialog box and click Open; the Add File to Import dialog box disappears and the filename appears in the Import dialog box. When you import a folder, FrontPage adds all the files within that folder (including those within subfolders) to the Import dialog box. You can add additional files by clicking the Add File button again, and if you change your mind about importing them, you can remove files from the list box by clicking Remove. You can highlight any file in the list box and click Modify URL to change the location within the web of the selected page. When you've made your decisions, click OK to add the file to your web. You can click the Stop button as the file is importing if you change your mind.

You can also import files and folders to a web through drag and drop. A web should be open in a FrontPage view. Simply drag files or folders from Windows Explorer into either the Folder List or the main viewing window and then drop them. FrontPage immediately uploads the file to the Web server, even if the server is on a remote machine. Once the files are in place, you can provide links to them or manipulate them as you manipulate other files in your webs.

If you import files created in Microsoft Office, FrontPage 2000 creates icons for these files that reflect the program of origin. When you double-click these files, the file loads into the appropriate Office application. There is one very important point to keep in mind: Unless your visitors are using Microsoft Internet Explorer, they won't be able to view these Office documents (at least not without a special add-on or plug-in for the non-IE browser). For this reason, directly importing Office files is best reserved for private intranets, in which the choice of browser can be guaranteed.

If no web is currently loaded, the Import command acts as a New Web command.

FILE, PREVIEW IN BROWSER

Instead of loading pages into your browser to examine or test them, you can use the Preview in Browser command instead. You will see the Preview in Browser dialog box, from which you can select your desired browser and screen *resolution (page 634)*.

FILE, PAGE SETUP

This command lets you set up the current page for printing. It brings up the standard Print Setup dialog box for your printer.

FILE, PRINT PREVIEW

As with most application programs, FrontPage lets you preview how the pages will look when you print them. This command lets you see the pages, and you can print directly from it.

FILE, PRINT

This command brings up the standard Print dialog box for your printer.

FILE, SEND

The Send command opens your default email program with the current file attached to a new message. You can fill in the message with recipient and any other text and send it via your network or the Internet.

FILE, PROPERTIES

This command opens the Properties dialog for the currently selected item. In Page view, it will yield the Page Properties dialog for that page. In other views, it will yield the Filename.htm Properties dialog.

FILE, RECENT FILES

This command offers a cascaded menu of the eight most recently opened pages. Selecting one loads that page into Page view.

FILE, RECENT WEBS

This command gives you a cascaded menu of the four most recently opened pages. Selecting one opens that web in a separate FrontPage window.

FILE, EXIT

This command exits the FrontPage program, shutting down all FrontPage windows. You will be asked if you want to save any changed documents.

EDIT, CUT

The Cut command removes the selected file or folder from the web and places it in the Clipboard. It is now available for pasting elsewhere on that web or another web. Links to that item are destroyed and then reestablished where the document is eventually pasted.

EDIT, COPY

Copy lets you duplicate the selected file or folder elsewhere—in that web or on another. Highlight the item, copy it, and then paste it wherever you prefer.

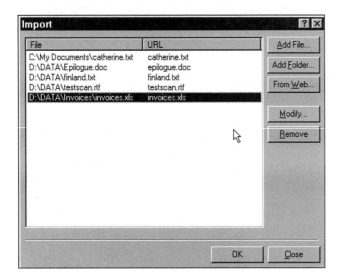

Figure 15.9
If you have documents on your hard disk, this procedure lets you import them into your web.

EDIT, PASTE

The Paste command will be available if you have used the Cut or Copy command. Move to the web and location where you want the item to be placed and select Paste.

EDIT, DELETE

Delete permanently removes the currently selected page or graphics file from the current web. The Confirm Delete dialog box appears when you choose this command.

EDIT, RENAME

Use the Rename command if you want to change the name of a file or folder. Links are changed to reflect the name change.

EDIT, SELECT ALL

This command selects all the files and folders in the current web. You may then cut, copy, or delete them. You should obviously use this command with caution.

EDIT, TASK

As you work on building your web, you will often decide to add elements that you don't currently have time to complete. The Task command lets you add these elements to your to-do list.

VIEW, FOLDERS; VIEW, ALL FILES; VIEW, NAVIGATION; VIEW, HYPERLINKS; VIEW, HYPERLINK STATUS; VIEW, THEMES; VIEW, TASKS

These commands let you switch among the various FrontPage views and are identical to clicking the corresponding button in the Views toolbar.

VIEW, REFRESH

Because several people can be working a web at the same time, it's entirely possible for new pages and links to be added without your knowledge. Choose View, Refresh to ensure that you have the most complete web showing in FrontPage. The entire Web, complete with all current changes, is then visible.

TOOLS, SPELLING; EDIT, FIND; EDIT, REPLACE

These three separate commands are tasks for web managers. As such, they are covered in full in Chapter 18.

TOOLS, RECALCULATE HYPERLINKS

The Recalculate Hyperlinks command performs several important maintenance functions. The command is covered in Chapter 22, "Managing Workflow and Tasks."

TOOLS, SECURITY

This command yields the Security dialog box, which is covered in Chapter 17.

TOOLS, WEB SETTINGS

This command is covered in Chapter 17.

TOOLS, OPTIONS

The Options dialog box is covered in Chapter 18.

DESIGNERS CORNER

When using FrontPage 2000 for the first few times, you might find it difficult to keep track of the number of FrontPage *instances* that are open. An instance is a separate running of the program. If you used earlier versions of FrontPage, you'll remember that you had only one FrontPage instance open. Now each instance appears as a separate document on the Start bar at the bottom of the screen, and also through the Alt+Tab method of switching from program to program.

Actually, this isn't new only to FrontPage; Microsoft has made it a standard for all of Office 2000. Each Word document, for example, opens as a separate Word instance, and each appears in the Start bar. One obvious problem is that if you have three Word documents, a couple of Excel documents, three Outlook messages, and four FrontPage documents open, your Start bar suddenly looks very, very busy.

Two points here: First, increase the space on the Start bar by dragging the top of the bar upwards (or down if you have it docked on the top). That will let you read the icons for the open documents and programs. More importantly, though, you should understand when FrontPage 2000 opens a new instance. It's quite simple, but perhaps not immediately apparent.

Here are the guidelines:

When you first launch FrontPage, you will begin, by default, with no web loaded. However, if you specify in the Options dialog box (Tools, Options) that you want to open the last web automatically when FrontPage starts, the most recently opened web will be open whenever you launch FrontPage from scratch. In the latter case, if you open a web, it will appear in the default FrontPage window. In either case, you have a single FrontPage instance running at this point.

With one web already open, every other web you open or create will appear in its own FrontPage instance. You can accomplish this by double-clicking on a subweb (not a page) in the Folder List, or you can create a copy of the currently opened web by selecting Window, New Window. In both cases, a new FrontPage instance begins.

Within a given web, you can open any number of individual pages. But they all open as separate windows in the Page view of the current web and are available via the Window menu of that web. They do not create new instances.

All you have to do, then, is pay attention when you're opening or creating a web. Those are the ones that produce all those extra items on the Start bar and the Alt+Tab selection list.

PUBLISHING A WEB

by Neil Randall

THE BASICS OF WEB PUBLISHING

There's nothing magical about publishing a web, although FrontPage 2000 does its best to make it seem so. A web can be made available to the public if its files are placed in a publicly accessible directory on a computer that is connected to the Internet and running Web server (HTTP server) software. Your web will be available even if you don't have a home page available. In server-speak, the *home page* is simply the page that loads by default when a user types in the root directory's URL. Your users need only know the filenames of the documents you want them to see. If your server software is set to allow directory listings, your users can select whichever file they prefer.

The complexities of web publishing come into play with issues such as scripting, proprietary features, and hyperlinking. First of all, the server must be able to handle scripts and proprietary features: Internet Information Server 4.0, for example, handles Active Server Pages—but earlier versions did not and many existing server packages still do not. If you're running early versions of Netscape, Apache, or Microsoft servers, you won't be able to use Java applets or JavaScript scripts, and you won't be able to serve Dynamic HTML or cascading style sheets unless you're using the most recent server packages. The first thing to be aware of when publishing your webs is what your server is capable of doing.

For most users, of course, the server's capabilities will be entirely out of your control. Either your hosting service or your organization will determine which server and which version of that server is running. In the case of hosting services to which you can subscribe, you can be well assured that server updates will occur reasonably quickly; these services need to remain competitive. It's often a very different thing with companies not only because of the need for coordination with corporate policy but because of the need to maintain strict security and reliability. This isn't to suggest that hosting services don't care about those things; they do, of course, but the situation is much different since hosting is their business.

The other major publishing issue, *hyperlinking (page 111)*, reveals its difficulties in the need to keep track of the hyperlinks references in the web. Anyone who's put together a Web site from scratch knows how trying it can be to ensure that the links on each page point to the correct document locations. Of course, there's not much you can do about links to external Web sites beyond checking them periodically and perhaps contacting the Webmaster of the external site when there are problems, and you can always put a disclaimer on the page telling visitors that you have no control over what goes on with other companies' Web sites. If a link to a file within your own site doesn't work, however, your credibility takes an instant beating.

There's actually one other important issue when it comes to web publishing: when to make your web public. While the Under Construction notice was once the signal to all users that your web was still in progress, it has become taboo to include such an indication. Everybody realizes that all webs are under construction at all times, so telling people you're not finished is redundant. Secondly, it's unprofessional to show your unfinished work and to leave the impression that you don't have much to offer. Asking people to come back soon only works if they absolutely need what you have to offer.

FrontPage's web publishing features are designed to overcome the problems typically associated with putting up your web on time and technically strong. Specifically, FrontPage gives you the following:

- The ability to develop a web on your local hard disk or a *staging* server (a non-public Web server) and then to transfer the web to a public Web server when you are ready
- The choice of publishing all web documents as a whole, or of selectively publishing by keeping some documents for later addition to the web
- Automatic changing of internal hyperlinks to reflect new document locations on the public server
- Full compatibility with the FrontPage extensions if installed on the public server, but will also retain as many of your web's advanced features as possible if the FrontPage extensions are not present
- Compatibility with HTTP and FTP upload protocols

PART

III

CH

16

Tip #76

> FrontPage can alter hyperlinks to ensure that they are compatible with the new file paths once they are on the server, but it can't do anything about links that are incorrect before you publish your web. In other words, double- and triple-check your web to ensure that links work locally before starting the publishing process.

HTTP AND FTP

FrontPage 2000's publishing features offer compatibility with the two primary protocols for uploading information on the Internet: HTTP and FTP. HTTP stands for Hypertext Transport Protocol, while FTP is short for File Transfer Protocol. Depending on the type of web you're creating, as well as the capabilities of the server on which your web will be published, you'll use one or the other of these protocols.

HTTP is best known as the protocol that makes the World Wide Web possible. It allows the interaction between the user's Web client software (the browser, for instance) and the Web server software on which the files reside. In a typical web interaction session, HTTP translates the user's mouse clicks into requests, sends them to the server machine, and arranges for the requested data to be sent back to the user. While most HTTP requests are for data to be sent from the *server* to the client, HTTP can also handle data that flows the other way—from the *clients* to the server. In other words, users will use HTTP primarily to download data, but they can use HTTP to upload it as well.

FTP is one of the oldest protocols on the Internet, older than HTTP in fact by nearly 20 years. It has been the primary protocol for the transfer of files from one Internet machine to another since its implementation, and until the advent of HTTP it remained so. Even now, FTP lives on for the purpose of uploading to and downloading from all over the Internet and is still a prominent download protocol for large files from Web sites. Even when it's possible to download files via HTTP, many Web sites also offer a download through FTP. The reason is simple: FTP is significantly faster than HTTP. For some reason, dedicated FTP client software (widely available as freeware or shareware) almost always performs FTP transfers faster than Web browsers do, again to a significant degree.

If you download a file via HTTP across a 56Kbps modem connection, you'll be lucky to maintain a consistent speed of 56Kbps. If you download the same file via FTP through your Web browser, you should triple or even quadruple that speed. If you perform the same FTP transfer through a dedicated FTP program, you'll reach speeds of 30Kbps or higher, sometimes well into the 40s and 50s.

FrontPage supports protocols for publishing webs. The difference is essentially this:

1. Use HTTP if your server has the FrontPage server extensions installed.

2. Use FTP if your server does not have the FrontPage server extensions installed.

Because of the server extensions, HTTP uploads offer a greater ease of use and the possibility of publishing using the security of an SSL connection (the HTTPS protocol). Still, you don't have to use HTTP to publish to a server with FrontPage extensions; you can use FTP if you like. You cannot, however, publish via HTTP to a server that does not have the extensions installed.

THE PUBLISH WEB DIALOG BOX

When you have a web you want published to a server, select Publish Web from the File menu. This brings up the Publish Web dialog box, which you can extend by clicking the Options button. Doing so yields the complete version of the dialog box, as shown in Figure 16.1.

Figure 16.1
The Publish Web dialog box contains a button called WPP's, which takes you to the list of FrontPage-specific hosting providers linked to Microsoft's Web site.

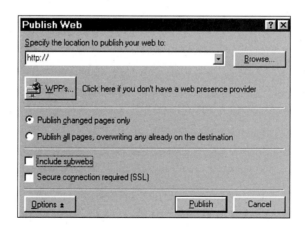

The most important area of this dialog box is the location field, formally called Specify the Location to Publish Your Web To. Here you can specify either an HTTP address, an FTP address, or a local or networked hard disk location.

Publishing via HTTP

When this dialog box opens, the location field shows only `http://`. If you want to publish to an HTTP location, you need only fill in the rest of the address and click the Publish button. FrontPage will start the transfer process.

Caution

FrontPage publishes to the web directory you specify; if you specify the domain name only, such as `http://www.mycompany.com/`, you will essentially overwrite the root Web on that server. FrontPage's warning dialog boxes will help you out here, but you're better to specify the exact web directory in the first place.

If you attempt to publish to an existing web directory, FrontPage will warn you if you're about to overwrite a file with the same filename as the file currently uploading. Do You Want to Overwrite This File? appears in such a case, telling you the filename, the web directory in which the overwrite is taking place, and the date of the last modification of the original file as well as the username of the person who modified it. The publishing process stops if you click No, with no files having been transferred. If you click Yes (or Yes to All), the file is replaced.

FrontPage also warns you if you are about to replace the existing web's navigation structure. If you click Yes, you're presented with the Publishing Web Structure dialog box, which gives you three choices. The first, Do Not Replace the Navigation Structure of the Destination Web, publishes your files but leaves the existing navigation structure in place. The second, Replace the Navigational Structure of the Destination Web, does exactly what it indicates. The third, Let FrontPage Merge the Changes, replaces the navigation structure but replaces the changes made by another author only if the file you're uploading is newer than the existing file.

Rather than overwrite an existing web, you'll usually want to publish your web in a new folder. To do so, type the folder name as you want it to appear in the new location. For example, if you want to publish your Sales department's web as your root Web's subweb, you might want it in a subdirectory called sales. To do this, you would type `http://www.mycompany.com/sales`. In such a case, FrontPage would create the new directory and place the web in it.

Publishing via FTP

To publish a web to a server on which the FrontPage server extensions are not installed, you need to publish via FTP. To do so, change the address in the location field from `http://www.mycompany.com/directory` to `ftp://mycompany.com/directory` or whatever your

FTP site is called. You can also access FTP sites from the FTP locations in FrontPage's standard Windows Save/Load dialog box.

You are presented with the Publishing FrontPage Components dialog box if you're publishing via FTP and any files contain content that requires the FrontPage server extensions. This box lists the files that contain such content and asks you to click either Continue or Cancel. If you choose Continue, the web keeps uploading.

PUBLISH WEB OPTIONS

Several important options are available from the Publish Web dialog box:

- Publish Changed Pages Only (HTTP and FTP)

  This option instructs FrontPage to upload only files that have changed since the last upload—files with newer modification dates and times. There is never any reason not to use this option, since uploading an unchanged page simply takes unnecessary time. Indeed, things might be worse, since (for example) uploading a new form results page will erase all the data saved from an existing form results page. Always use this option. Among other benefits, it lets you keep your site up to date quite easily.

- Publish All Pages, Overwriting Any Already on the Destination (HTTP and FTP)

  This is the reverse of the Publish Changed Pages Only option, instructing FrontPage to upload all pages to the destination site, automatically overwriting any identically named files on the site. Use only if you're absolutely sure you want to do this. It might be useful for fixing an existing page, just as an example.

- Include Subwebs (HTTP and FTP)

  By default, FrontPage uploads only the currently selected web. Select this option if you want to upload that web's subwebs as well. Use with caution, however, since your chance of damaging existing data increases if you have subwebs going several layers deep. FrontPage will warn you subweb by subweb of overwrites it's about to perform. Of course, if you select both the Publish All Pages and the Include Subwebs options, you're essentially letting FrontPage have its way with a significant portion of your Web site.

- Secure Connection Required (HTTP only)

  If your Web server supports Secure Sockets Layer (SSL) connections—a much more secure connection system than the simple username/password system of typical servers—you can specify that an SSL connection is needed. FrontPage will ensure that your computer and the remote computer perform the procedures necessary to make the connection; it will refuse the connection if necessary.

TROUBLESHOOTING

The Publish Web process is, in the large majority of cases, problem free. However, if you don't watch one particular feature of the dialog box, you can cause lots of trouble for yourself. That feature is the field labeled Specify the Location to Publish Your Web To. Be careful that you don't select the root web, or any other existing web on your server, unless you really want to put it there. Once you start the publishing process, and even with FrontPage's dialog boxes during that process, it's far too easy either to overwrite your existing work or to render it non-functional by replacing important support files. Be sure, quite simply, that you publish your web to a location that you know to be the correct site. Do not, for instance, type a subweb location in the box without checking to make sure you don't already have a subweb of that name.

Sometimes, for no apparent reasons, a FrontPage web on a server becomes partially non-functional after several publishing instances, particularly in cases where only the changed pages were uploaded. In such a case, it can be a good idea to ensure that the entire web is correct on your local drive, then publish it, overwriting existing pages. This was certainly the case in earlier versions of FrontPage, including FrontPage 98, and it seems mostly fixed in FrontPage 2000. But in the late beta version, the problem resurfaced a bit, albeit rarely.

DESIGNERS CORNER

You can use an independent FTP client to publish your webs, instead of using FrontPage's Publish Web process. In fact, if you run one of the many, many FTP clients available for Windows 95/98/NT users (see www.winfiles.com or www.shareware.com to find some), you will notice that FTP is a richer and even faster experience than with FrontPage. And besides, you can use the client to do all your FTP work, not just FrontPage FTPing.

But if your web depends on FrontPage server extensions, use the FrontPage publishing features instead. Often, FrontPage uploads additional files to allow the extensions to do their work, and the FrontPage publishing system is designed to ensure that everything gets uploaded properly. If you have a subweb, however, that you know does not rely on the server extensions, you can certainly adopt a separate FTP client.

CHAPTER 17

CONFIGURING WEBS

In this chapter   *by Neil Randall*

ESTABLISHING PARAMETERS, CONFIGURATIONS, ADVANCED SETTINGS, AND LANGUAGE OPTIONS

The major settings for the currently loaded web can be set via the Web Settings command in FrontPage's Tools menu. For the most part, only the web administrator can change these settings, but since you're probably that person (having established that during program setup), you'll continue as if that's a given. If that's not the case, you need to contact your Web administrator if you want to alter any settings.

Selecting Tools, Web Settings opens the Web Settings dialog box (see Figure 17.1).

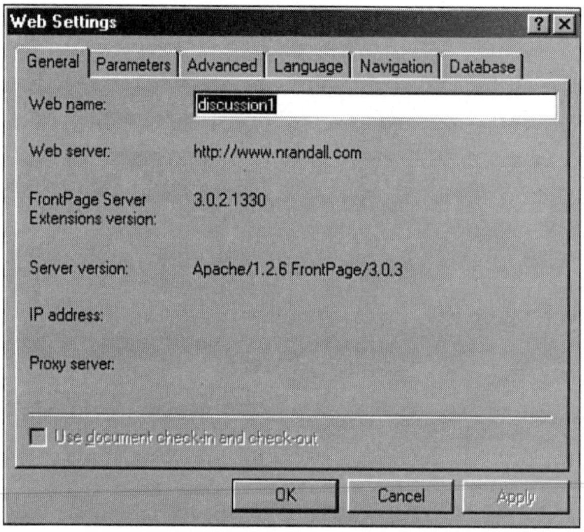

Figure 17.1
The General, Parameters, Advanced, Language, Navigation, and Database tabs compose the Web Settings dialog box.

GENERAL

The following information is in the General tab:

- Web Name—The name of the web as it appears in the Open Web dialog box and as it appears as a directory in your Web server software. You can change that name if you are the root web's authorized administrator and if your server (Personal Web Server for instance) supports the changing of web names. The name of the web is the same as the name of the directory on the server in which that web is stored. The web name must therefore be permissible as a directory name on the server's file system (usually UNIX or NT). And keep in mind that, while Windows 95/98/NT/2000 will take spaces in the name, these show up unattractively (as a percentage number) in the location area of your browser if they are served from a UNIX server. Including spaces is considered bad form.

- Web Server—This is the Web server's URL. If your server does not have a domain name, this URL is the same as the IP address information shown in this tab. You can't change the Web server information; this was set when you created the web.

- Server Version—This gives you information about the version of your Web server. This cannot be altered unless you upgrade your server, in which case the change is automatic.

- IP Address—Your server's IP address, always expressed in numerical format (for example, `129.97.48.53`). This is the actual number Web browsers look for; the domain name is simply a more easily remembered alias for the IP address and is subject to the Internet's Domain Name System and the capability of DNS servers to locate it. This field need not show information.

- FrontPage Server Extensions Version—FrontPage installs software in your server software that allows the two to work together. These are known as *server extensions*. This link shows you the version of those extensions and cannot be altered except automatically through software upgrades.

- Proxy Server—This line shows the URL of the *proxy server*, the server that's connected to your internal network and acts as a firewall or buffer between the internal network and the external Internet. You set this information with Explorer's Tools, Proxies. If you are not working through a proxy server, this field will be blank.

- Use Document Check-in and Check-out—If you wish to prevent two web authors from working on the same file at the same time, you can activate the Check-in/Check-out feature. This feature notifies an author who requests a document if that document has already been "checked out" by another author. The feature is off by default.

PARAMETERS

Initially, the Parameters tab is probably the most confusing of the three tabs available from the Web Settings dialog box, mainly because it's not obvious what this tab is supposed to accomplish. Clicking the Help button is somewhat helpful, but even here the purpose is a bit obscure. Once you go through the procedure of establishing even one parameter on your own, however, it's all crystal clear.

To fully understand what these parameters are all about, you have to know what *Substitution components* do. (These components (automated procedures) are covered in Chapter 11, "Using Components, Forms, and Interactive Page Templates.") When you create a Web page in Page view, you can create a component that tells the Web browser to substitute the text in the component for text stored in the web's parameters. You establish the parameters for each web through the Parameters dialog box for that web.

In other words, it's like entering a variable time and date stamp in a word processing document; when the file loads into the word processor, the time and date are automatically changed by the software itself, without any action on your part. You might want to show your web visitors the name of the author who developed a certain page in your web, but the information might change; you might want to have the exact current URL for the page, instead of a fixed URL; you might want your company's phone and fax numbers to appear throughout the web. To do any of these things, create a Substitution component to take care of the substitution, thereby letting FrontPage—instead of you—make the changes.

This is especially useful if you want that information to appear on multiple pages in your web. Instead of having to type the information on individual pages, you need only include the Substitution component on each applicable page, and whenever that page is loaded in a visitor's browser, the component locates the information on the server and performs the substitution. The major benefit is that, if the information changes, only the Value item in Web Settings' Parameters area need be altered.

You insert a Substitution component into a document by loading the document into Page view and then selecting Insert, Component, Substitution. The dialog box contains a pull-down menu that lets you select from the variables for that web. Four variables are available by default; Author, Description, Modified By, and Page URL are taken from the Properties information for that particular page.

To add new variables, open the Web Settings dialog box, click the Parameters tab, and click Add. Give the variable a name by typing whatever you prefer in the Name field (a new variable might be Location, for example). Type the text you want associated with that name in the Value field (for Location, this might be Our corporate offices are located in San Jose, California). When you return to Page view for that page, you can select Location from the Substitution component drop-down list, and the phrase Designed at the head office... will appear when the page is loaded into a browser.

The magic is this. Say you put this Substitution component on every page in the web, and after six months the company moves to Phoenix, Arizona. Instead of changing every single page in the web to reflect where the head office has relocated, you simply open the Web Settings dialog box and change the value for the variable Location. The Substitution component for each page, when it loads, checks for the value of that variable and displays the new text.

Tip #77

> To see your new configuration variables in action, load a page from your web into Editor; choose Insert, FrontPage Component; choose Substitution Component from the resulting dialog box, and click the arrow to the right of the Substitute With drop-down list box.

Click OK when you've finished specifying the name and its value. The new configuration variable (which is a combination of the Name and Value fields) appears in the Parameters tab. From here you can click OK or Apply to place it into the web and thus make it available as a Substitution component item. You can also modify or remove it, but remember to click OK or Apply to actually place it in the web when you do so.

ADVANCED

The Advanced tab (see Figure 17.2) gives you access to four items: default scripting language, hidden directories, and temporary files.

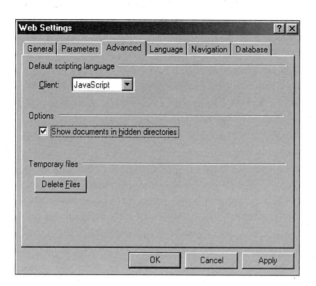

Figure 17.2
The Advanced tab lets you see what's inside FrontPage's hidden directories.

The dialog box's Default Scripting Language area) lets you specify the scripting language you will be using as a default in this web. (It can be different for each web.) The two choices are JavaScript and VBScript.

FrontPage defaults to JavaScript because JavaScript is the scripting standard on the Web, while VBScript is used much less (there was once an actual battle between the two languages, but JavaScript dominated quite easily). VBScript is easier for some programmers and scripters, and the Internet Explorer browser supports it fully (Netscape browsers to a lesser extent). If you're more comfortable with VBScript, use it, but only if you're certain that your users will all be using Internet Explorer or a compatible version of Netscape Navigator. If you're unsure, use JavaScript instead. In company intranets, however, you might very well find that VBScript is the standard—using it allows companies to standardize their development staff entirely on Visual Basic—so again, make sure before you start.

If you decide to use one as the default, you can still add elements of the other. You can code in straight HTML within Page view, or you can use the Microsoft Script Editor (found in Tools, Macro) to create JavaScripts or VBScripts. The Advanced tab simply determines the default for scripts in your web.

The Advanced tab's Options section also contains the Show Documents in Hidden Directories option. As explained in Chapter 14, "FrontPage's Web Templates and Wizards," FrontPage 2000 installs some directories as hidden directories. If you want to display these in FrontPage's Folders and Reports views, thereby giving yourself the opportunity to work with all the files, you must specify this option in the Web Settings dialog box. Visitors can't access the folders and files because they will not be visible in the web itself, but any user given administrator permissions for the web will be able to see them. Unless you have a specific reason for working with these directories, it's best to leave them hidden. If you want full control over all directories, however, or if you want to see every single file that FrontPage generates, by all means display them.

FrontPage 2000 will refresh the page when you select to show the hidden directories, which can take a bit of time if the web is on a remote server. If you subsequently uncheck this option in order to remove the hidden directories from view, FrontPage will take a minute or two to refresh the web again.

The final option in Web Settings' Advanced tab is to delete the temporary files on your web. Like many other applications, FrontPage creates several temporary files as it does its work; these can collect and eat up hard disk space. To see how many have been created by various applications on your own machine, select Start, Search, Files and Folders and then search your hard drives for *.tmp files. You'll find lots—most not from FrontPage itself. By clicking the Delete Files button in the Web Settings dialog box, you erase the temporary files from the web and free the space.

LANGUAGE

You can change the server message language and HTML coding via the Language tab of the FrontPage Web Settings dialog box.

The Default Web Language refers to the human language in which error messages are displayed in your visitors' browsers. If your audience is primarily English speaking, leave this setting as the default. You can also return error messages in French, German, Italian, Japanese, or Spanish, and you should keep this in mind if developing pages for audiences whose primary language is one of those.

Tip #78	If you want to offer your web in multiple languages, you should design completely separate webs. If you wish, you can use the Copy Web command to copy the finished web and then translate the copy, but remember that icons and symbols might mean very different things to different cultures. In fact, that's another reason to maintain different webs for different languages.

Default Page Encoding refers to the character set that will be used across your web. By default, the character set is U.S./Western European, but many others are available, including Korean, Greek, Baltic, Cyrillic, Thai, and several flavors of Japanese. All pages you create will be saved with the chosen default encoding, and your visitors must set this encoding in their browsers in order to view your pages the way you designed them. You can alter this for individual pages through the Properties dialog box. Finally, to stop FrontPage from remapping your keyboard to reflect the current encoding selection, until you are finished making the selection, you can click the field called Ignore the Keyboard When Deciding the Encoding of New Pages.

NAVIGATION

Figure 17.3 shows the contents of the Navigation tab in the Web Settings dialog box. From here, you can change the text that appears on the labels of the default elements in your web's *navigation bar (page 179)*. By default, for example, the label for the navigation button for moving to the previous page is Back, while the label for the navigation button that leads to the home page (default.htm, default.asp, index.html—whatever your server requires) is Home. These make obvious sense, but for the sake of having a unique web, or because you like different terms for these activities (or perhaps company standards dictate), you might want to change them.

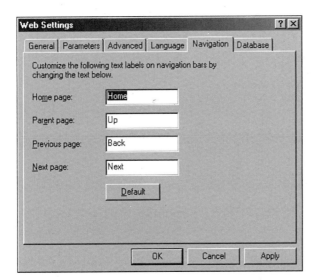

Figure 17.3
From the Navigation tab, you can change your web's navigation button labels.

PART

III

CH

17

You can change these defaults for these navigation elements in the Navigation tab. Home Page lets you change the label for the web's default document from Home to anything you choose. Similarly, Previous Page lets you change the label for the return option from Back to something else (Previous, for example); Next Page allows you to change the label for the "go to the next document" option from Next to something you like better.

Parent Page allows you to alter the label for the button that moves the user to the page above the current page. For example, assume your web leads visitors from the home page to a child page called Products. Products has several child pages, one of which is Cameras. If a visitor is on the Cameras page, the Up button (or whatever you choose to label it) takes him to the Products page. The Home button, by contrast, would take him all the way up the hierarchy, past the Products page to the web's default document.

GIVING PERMISSION TO ADMINISTER, AUTHOR, AND BROWSE YOUR WEBS

Your webs are important primarily because they show off your company documents or your personal preferences to the world, as well as offer important information to members of your company or organization. Because of this, you don't want just anybody putting information on your site. In fact, you need strict control over who can make changes. If FrontPage didn't offer a system for setting permissions, anyone on the Internet could make changes to your web; you'd wake up every morning wondering exactly how your public image had been modified. Who needs that kind of excitement?

FrontPage lets you set permissions for users to administer, author, and browse your webs. Each of these is explored in detail in this section.

The differences are as follows:

- *Browse this web* permissions are given to users who are permitted to visit your web via a Web browser such as Netscape Navigator. They can read your pages, but they cannot alter them in any way, nor can they add, delete, or otherwise manage your webs. Their only access to your Web site is through a browser, not through FrontPage. By default, all visitors have browse permissions—it's a fully public web—but you can set FrontPage so that only specific users can browse.

- *Author and browse this web* permissions are given to users who are permitted to create and edit content in the web. They cannot add or delete webs, nor can they manage them in any other way. In other words, they can use FrontPage in conjunction with a particular web (and only that web), and they're restricted to authoring and editing. Users with author permissions have browse permissions as well.

- *Administer, author, and browse this web* permissions are given to users whom you want to have full access to web administration. They can add and delete webs and they can set web permissions and configurations. Note, however, that only the overall web administrator—established at installation time—has the ability to restrict administrators to individual webs, with only one administrator having full access to the root web. Those with administer permissions automatically have author and browse permissions as well.

In other words, people with administer permissions on a web have unlimited access to that particular web, while those with author permissions have less access, and those with browse permissions have the least complete access of all.

You can set the permissions for the root web using the Server Administration dialog boxes. The root web is the one that FrontPage creates as the primary web for your server. All your webs can contain the same permissions. Using the Permissions dialog box, however, you can set unique permissions for each web on your server. This allows you maximum flexibility for determining who will work on your webs. This might be your most important administrative task as Webmaster.

ESTABLISHING THE MAIN SETTINGS

To access the Permissions dialog box, select Tools, Security, Permissions.

Figure 17.4 shows the Settings tab of the Web Permissions dialog box. You have two choices in this area. You can have the currently loaded web use the same permissions as the root web, or you can establish unique permissions for this web. If you mark the Use Same Permissions as Parent Web option button, you can set no other permissions in this dialog box; the options in the remaining tabs will be grayed out. By marking the Use Unique Permissions for This Web option button, you can establish specific permissions for the current web, although by default this web automatically inherits the root web settings until you change them.

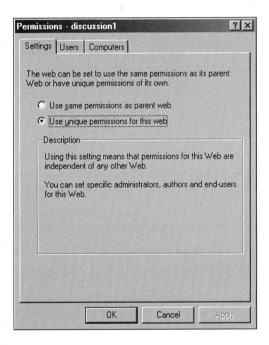

Figure 17.4
For maximum security, establish unique permissions for each web and each child web. This can, however, be inconvenient if you're dealing with a large number of webs.

PART

III

CH

17

SETTING PERMISSIONS: PEOPLE VERSUS COMPUTERS

FrontPage offers two ways of setting browse, author, and administer permissions. You can give these permissions to people via the Users tab, giving each user a name and a password; this is the most common way (see Figure 17.5). Through the Computers tab, you can also restrict access via the IP (Internet Protocol) address of computers themselves. You can restrict access to individual computers or to computers that share portions of an IP address.

Figure 17.5
Adding users requires that you specify a name and a password for the person, as well as the level of permissions you're granting.

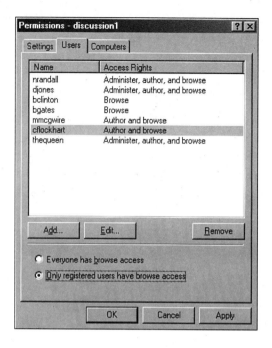

Why would you choose the Computers option? The most obvious choice is to restrict browse permissions to groups of computers in a single organization. For example, you might be creating a web that contains important company information and is designed to be seen only by that company's employees (an intranet, in other words). Each machine in that company will have an IP address such as 139.205.104.72 (for example), and all machines on the company network will likely have IP addresses that are identical for the first 3–6 numbers (139.205). In this case, you can tell FrontPage 2000 to restrict browse access to computers with an IP address of 139.205.*.* (the asterisks are *wildcards*); this prevents outsiders from seeing the information. The server checks the IP address when anyone tries to access the web, and if the address is not within that restricted range, the server won't serve any information. This process is called setting an *IP mask*.

By default, all webs give administer, author, and browse permissions to all computers on the Internet (IP *.*.*.*), but to no user other than the root web administrator. This means that only the users you set up can get into your web (with whatever level of permissions you grant them), but that they can do so from any computer on the Net. By carefully combining user and computer restrictions, you can specify exactly who gets to do what on your web.

SETTING ADMINISTER PERMISSIONS

Administrators play an important role in creating webs. They have permission to create webs and individual web documents, to delete pages and webs, and to establish permissions for authors and users. In other words, administrators control exactly who gets to work on the web and, in fact, who gets to see it. Administrators are automatically registered as end users and authors.

The root web administrator can give administer permissions on individual webs to users or computers via the Users and Computers tabs. The process is simple, but it's extremely important.

Caution	When you create a web—especially if you're not a large company—your first inclination might be to give administer positions to just about anyone. However, you should give careful thought to this decision; administrators have a lot of power over the web.

The Add User dialog box appears when you click the Add button in the Users tab. The username and password are entirely up to you, but be sure to remember the password so that the new administrator can access the site. Then select the option Administer, Author, and Browse This Web (under Allow Users To) and click OK. The new name appears in the Permissions dialog box. When you have finished adding users, click Apply.

PART

III

CH

17

Tip #79	Don't let users with administrator permissions set their own passwords. Only one person should be the chief administrator of the web, and that person should establish all access. That should be policy as soon as you install FrontPage.

To further ensure controlled permissions in your webs, you can click the Computers tab and restrict administer permissions to specific IP addresses or address masks. IP address masks are ranges of IP addresses. You can specify a full IP address or you can use the wildcard asterisk character to specify IP addresses within a certain range.

For example, if you want to restrict access so that administrators can access the web only from one specific machine, you can enter that machine's full IP address. Click Add and then fill in the machine's IP number in the resulting New IP Address dialog box. The IP address looks something like 135.201.123.91. It's always a four-part number.

More likely, you'll want to restrict access to an IP address range. Because users with dial-up connections are usually given a *dynamic* IP address (one that changes with each new logon), specifying a full IP restriction means that dial-up administration is next to impossible. Instead, you can use the wildcard asterisk character in place of some of the IP numbers. In the previous example, the first two numbers (135.201) specify the high level of the domain, so a restriction to that portion of the address means that users have to be logged on to that overall domain—which means a specific organization, such as your company—to perform administrative tasks. For this example, you click the Add button and type 135.201.*.* in the New IP Mask dialog box.

When you've set your administrator's and IP address masks, click Apply to save them to the web. Remember that they apply to the current web only; you must set individual restrictions for each web you administer.

SETTING AUTHOR PERMISSIONS

In addition to establishing administrative authority for each web, you can also set authoring authority. Authors can create and delete individual web pages from the specific web for which they're authorized. They cannot create or delete the webs themselves, nor can they establish authorial permission for other authors.

Setting author permissions is identical to the process described in the previous "Setting Administer Permissions" section. Click Add on the Users tab, provide a name and password, and select User Can Author and Browse This Web; click Apply. From the Computers tab, you then restrict Author permissions according to IP number or IP mask for added security.

Establishing author permissions is one area in which web management becomes just that—web management. As chief administrator, you have the sole authority to authorize administrators for each web. Each of those administrators, in turn, can establish as many new authors as she wants. It's extremely important to set firm guidelines about who has permission to author, and this has to be done through frequent communication with your administrators.

SETTING BROWSE PERMISSIONS

One of a web administrator's most important security tasks is to establish who is allowed to visit your web. Doing so restricts who gets to look at your web, and this can be useful for any number of reasons. When you're first constructing a web, for example, you don't want the world to see it. Once it's established, you might want it to be accessible only to users you choose to register.

Establishing browse permissions with the Users or Computers tab is identical to establishing administer and author permissions except that, after providing a name and password, you select Browse This Web from the Allow Users To section. If you've set your web so that everyone has browse access (in the Permissions dialog box), restricting by IP number or IP mask comes into play if you want to control access. Setting user browse permissions effectively does nothing at all if you've established that everyone has browse access and that all computers have access.

Restricting user access by name can be valuable if you want to set up a web on which purchasers of your service or product are given a common username and password that allow them to access a special web just for them. The only way they can learn the username and password is to buy the service or product (perhaps you include it in the packaging), so you can establish all customers as registered users with one username and one password.

As a matter of fact, this is what happens when you access the "Chapter Upgrades" section of this book's Web site, at http://www.nrandall.com/frontpagers/.

CREATING USER REGISTRATION FORMS

This process is obviously tedious if you're attempting to establish a web where all individual users have their own unique usernames and passwords. Use FrontPage's Registration component to allow users to register themselves and to provide you with valuable information for your database. You can initiate this component either while authoring a page or from the Discussion Web Wizard.

Caution

If you establish a web on Microsoft's Internet Information Server on a Windows NT machine, don't bother creating registration forms. Users cannot register through a browser onto a Windows NT machine. They must be added via Windows NT user administration.

→ **See** Chapter 11 and Chapter 14.

Using Page view, you can create a registration form that you can specify as belonging to the precise web you want. When users fill in this form and submit it to your server, their usernames and passwords (which they supply) are automatically added to the end user permissions of that web. The following steps describe this process:

1. Specify the current web as being accessible to Registered Users Only; this is accomplished through the General tab of the Web Permissions dialog box.

2. Open your server's root web.

3. Choose File, New. Select User Registration from the resulting list of page types.

4. Find the form itself in the new page. Right-click inside the form and choose Form Properties. The Form Properties dialog box appears, showing that the results will be sent to the registration form handler.

5. Click the Options button. This yields the Options for Registration Form Handler dialog box, shown in Figure 17.6.

6. In the Registration tab, type the name of the subweb for which you want to register users (the web that you've just established unique user permissions for). Type the label for the Username field, the Password field, and the Password Confirmation field. Except for the subweb name, FrontPage's defaults are perfectly fine. Leave the rest of the fields as they are.

7. In the File Results tab, you'll see the name of the file in which the usernames are kept. It is stored in the (hidden) folder private/ in your root web. You may change this, but there's no reason to do so unless you plan to have several registration pages, in which case you should give this file a more meaningful name. You can also select the format of the results file; again, it's best to leave it at the default of text database using tab as a separator. You can create a second results file if you prefer, using the same—or an entirely different—file format. Click OK twice to return to the Page view.

8. Change the page however you like. Replace information in the square brackets to reflect actual content. Save the page into the root web (where it already is). Now your visitors can start registering themselves; the results appear in the Users tab of the Web Permissions dialog box, as well as in the results files. As you'll discover, this is an extremely powerful system.

Tip #80

Registration forms grant browse permission only to each added user. If you want to grant author or administration permission, you must access the Permissions dialog box.

Figure 17.6
These two dialog boxes let you create the elements necessary for users to register on your site.

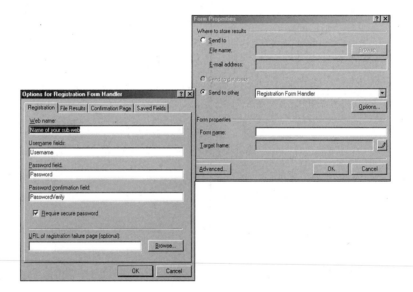

CHANGING PASSWORDS

As with most network-based programs, you can change your password to prevent unwanted access. In fact, as long as the root web administrator agrees, you should change it frequently. To do so, choose Tools, Security, Change Password. You are presented with the Change Password for Username dialog box, in which you type the current password, the new password, and the new password a second time (to make sure you don't accidentally type something you'll never remember).

Any users with administer or author permissions can change their own passwords. You should set policy on password changes if you're the main administrator for your organization's webs, instructing those with administer or author permissions when they can make such changes—and whether you're even permitting them to do so. This is a significant issue in managing your Web site because you'll want full control over who gets to access it for the sake of adding, editing, and deleting webs and files, and you should clarify password procedures immediately.

SETTING OPTIONS FOR THE WEB

Several options are available for each web through the Options dialog box, accessible through the Tools menu. Click whichever of these you want to activate or deactivate.

- Open Last Web Automatically When FrontPage Starts

  This option activates whenever you load FrontPage. Instead of beginning with no webs loaded (the default), FrontPage loads the last web you worked on. This is obviously useful if you're working with one web over a period of time.

- Check if Office Is the Default Editor for Pages Created in Office

  When you create a Web page in an Office application, you'll want to edit it in the same application to make use of that application's particular features. This option tells FrontPage to check that the Office application will load when you double-click an Office document in FrontPage.

- Check if FrontPage Is the Default Editor for Pages

  When you double-click a document in FrontPage, you normally want to display that page in Page view. This option sets Page view as the default editor for Web pages. It also specifies that FrontPage is to be the default editor when you double-click any web document from the desktop or a Windows file viewer. This option is turned off automatically if you toggle the Office default option.

- Show Status Bar

  The status bar runs along the bottom of the FrontPage screen, offering various information. This option lets you hide it or redisplay it.

- Warn When Included Components Are Out of Date

  When creating pages, you can specify a date for certain FrontPage components. This option displays a message telling you that the date for that component has passed.

- Warn When Text Index Is Out of Date

  FrontPage automatically creates a text index for your web, allowing you to keep track of text references inside your documents. If you change something in the web that makes this index incorrect, FrontPage warns you. For instance, if a navigation button refers to a specific page and you delete that page or rename the file, the index will be out of date and FrontPage will warn you. It will also ask if you want to recalculate the text index at the same time.

- Warn Before Permanently Applying Themes

  When you apply a theme, FrontPage must upload a number of files, including graphics files, to the server. This option lets you choose whether or not to display a message warning that it is about to apply the theme (and letting you cancel the operation).

PART

III

CH

17

CONFIGURING EDITORS

As you work in FrontPage 2000, you will realize that the package does a great deal—but not everything. The package includes a graphics package, for example (Image Composer or PhotoDraw), but you might have a favorite image editor you'd like to use as well. Nor does FrontPage have a tool for editing sound or video files. To compensate, FrontPage lets you configure editors to handle specific types of documents.

To establish the editors, choose Tools, Options and click the Configure Editors tab. The Configure Editors dialog box appears. The file extension is shown in the Type column, while the editor you want to use for viewing that kind of file is displayed in the Editor column.

The Add Editor Association dialog box appears when you click the Add button. This dialog box allows you to specify a file type, the editor name, and the location of that program on your hard disk. For example, if you want to use a specific graphics editor when modifying GIF files, you open the Add Editor Association dialog box, type GIF in the File Type field, type the program's name in the Editor Name field, and then click Browse to find the program file for the application itself.

Once the editors are established, you can invoke them by double-clicking that file type anywhere in a FrontPage view. The appropriate editor automatically opens with the specified file loaded into it and ready for viewing or editing.

Also in the Configure Editors area, you can choose whether to open Office documents in the applications in which they were originally created.

SETTING OPTIONS FOR REPORTS VIEW

Figure 17.7 shows the default for the Reports View tab. This tab lets you tell FrontPage what to display in the Reports view. (See Chapter 18, "Managing a Web," for a detailed look at this view.) The Reports view informs you which pages are recent, which ones are older, and which are slow to load at a specific connection speed. In this dialog box, you can set precisely what you mean by these terms. You can also specify whether you want to display the *gridlines* (the lines between the columns and the rows) when examining the Reports view.

TROUBLESHOOTING

I restricted access to a domain mask, but my administrators can still get in from anywhere they like. What happened?

All administrators listed in the Administrators tab share the same restrictions. You can't restrict one administrator to access from one IP range and a second from a different IP range. Because of this, be sure to remove the default *IP address mask (page 376)* (*.*.*.*) if you're going to restrict ranges at all. This mask allows access from anywhere, which is exactly what you don't want.

It tells me my name already exists with administrator permissions when I try to add myself as an author. Does this mean I can't author pages in my own web?

Not at all. All administrators automatically have authoring permissions for that web, even though their names do not appear in the Authors tab.

Figure 17.7
You can use the Reports View tab to let FrontPage know what you mean by that view's settings.

PART

III

CH

17

ADMINISTRATOR'S CORNER

USING HIDDEN DIRECTORIES WITH DISCUSSION GROUPS

As described in this chapter, one of the options under the Advanced tab of the Web Settings dialog box is to show the web's hidden directories. Discussion webs offer one especially good reason to toggle this feature on.

The problem with discussion webs is that the messages just keep piling up. And the more they pile up, the more unwieldy the web becomes. FrontPage offers no interface specifically designed to help administrators delete messages, and the only way to do so is by displaying the hidden directories and deleting the specific messages from inside them.

To delete a message, first open the discussion web, find the message you wish to delete, right-click on it and select Properties, and note its filename. Then toggle the hidden directories feature on, then refresh the web and view the messages directory for that particular web (it bears the web's name, preceded by an underscore). Click on the filename of the message you wish to get rid of, then delete it. Return to the open discussion web (in FrontPage), and choose the Recalculate Links feature in the Tools menu. Your discussion list will no longer include the deleted file.

It would be nice if FrontPage had an archiving feature for discussion webs, but it doesn't.

ASSIGNING USER PERMISSIONS ON WINDOWS NT–BASED SERVERS

A Caution earlier in this chapter suggested that there's no point creating registration forms if you're using Internet Information Server on a Windows NT machine. The reason is that the only way to add users to WinNT is through that operating system's user administration features; if you want to restrict access to users, you must do so by first creating the users in your NT Server domain. You can restrict the permissions of each user as well, although typically you'll want to use the default user accounts that IIS sets at installation time as the accounts for your web's visitors. This group is restricted to IIS's web directories, and you can further restrict access to files within those directories.

If you want to password-restrict visitors to your IIS/NT-based web, you must establish this access through the Security dialog boxes accessible through FrontPage's Tools menu. From this dialog box you can include any users who already have accounts on the NT domain on which IIS resides.

One way to work extremely effectively with NT is to establish the web server on a separate domain from the rest of your organization's domains. The server domain should be *trusted* by the main domain (NT domains can contain *trust* relationships with one another to determine the degree to which the domains can access one another). Establishing the appropriate trust relationships between the two domains will keep your visitors from outside the organization restricted to the web server domain only, and you will be able to keep them out of portions of the web, while internal users, who already have their own accounts on the main web, will have accounts to the web server domain through their accounts on the main domain. The trust, in other words, goes from the main domain to the web server domain, but not the other way.

CHAPTER 18

MANAGING A WEB

In this chapter *by Neil Randall*

WEB SITE MANAGEMENT

FrontPage makes designing Web sites and creating individual web documents easier than ever before. Creating webs, however, isn't the greater part of a Webmaster's work. Instead, that dubious honor falls to maintaining and updating webs. In fact, from start to finish, managing a Web site is every bit as important as creating one, even though the glory clearly goes to the people who make it look like something. Once a web is in place, however, it remains of interest to users only if it is frequently updated, with new information and new reasons for visiting constantly being built in. Your job as Webmaster is to make sure that everything gets done, and that the new and replacement elements are placed in the web so that they work right from the start.

MANAGING PEOPLE

You might be in the position of using FrontPage 2000 to create and manage a web alone. In this case, the only person you need to manage is yourself. Assuming that you can be relied on to listen to yourself, FrontPage offers all you need to do the job. If you're creating and developing a Web site in conjunction with others, like a growing number of Webmasters, the management of people becomes quite probably the most difficult task of any you'll face. It's one thing to force a computer to do what you want it to do; it's quite another to get a group of people, no matter how small, to work together on a top-notch creative effort like a Web site. Workgroup dynamics, thankfully, are far beyond the scope of this book.

One of FrontPage 2000's greatest strengths is its ease of use. What this means, from a manager's perspective, is that you have a far greater choice when hiring potential web authors. In the past, you needed to find someone who knew HTML and probably CGI if you wanted to get anything done with reasonable speed—and those skills were hard to find. With a graphical package such as FrontPage 2000, you can begin focusing your recruitment on people with an eye for design rather than those who can code or program. This isn't to suggest that you no longer need people with programming experience, but FrontPage makes it much easier to share tasks among contributors with differing talents.

Here you take a look at the tools within FrontPage that will at least partly ease the assignment of tasks to authors and coadministrators. These tools—the Permissions dialog boxes of the FrontPage Configuration menus and the Tasks view with its limited but effective tracking mechanism—are by no means extensive, but they're better than nothing by a long shot.

MANAGING INFORMATION

After managing people, the hardest thing about creating a Web site is managing all the information. Information itself changes constantly, but more importantly, so do the needs and the expectations of its users. If you want your Web site to be effective—which translates into many users visiting many times and finding many rewards for doing so—you have to change the information and its presentation regularly. You also need to change the ways your readers interact with that information and, as a result, you'll frequently have to reconsider the interface your Web offers to its users.

With the advent of intranets, a new kind of information has appeared in Webs. This information—which consists of everything from procedures documents, meeting and event schedules, project milestones, and financial details—is restricted to viewing by members of the organization to which it belongs. As the manager of an intranet site as opposed to an Internet site, your attention to information will be different but at least as important. The organization's information must be complete, readily accessible, and secure. Changes to some intranet information might be less frequent than for an Internet site, but that doesn't make it less demanding.

While information management is an organizational issue and hardly something one person can be responsible for, FrontPage offers a few tools that make such management a bit easier. First, the integration of Page view and the other FrontPage views makes on-the-fly editing and adding of Web pages easier than ever before. Second, FrontPage's built-in links management system helps you keep your pages properly connected to one another, solving the problem of hyperlinks that lead nowhere or to the wrong page entirely. Finally, FrontPage's multiple views let you see the way the information is presented, thereby negating the need for flow diagrams or such niceties as index cards. Your information is easier to manage because you can visualize it easily.

MANAGING COMPUTERS

At this point in the Web's history, there's still nothing easy about setting up a Web server and making all connected computers work with it happily and without incident. Simply put, managing a web is still very much about managing computers.

This is one area in which FrontPage does as good a job as anything out there. The fact is that most Web servers exist on UNIX or Windows NT machines. The other fact is that most would-be web designers work with computers running Windows 95, Windows 98, Windows NT, Mac OS, or Linux. Through its server extensions, and hence its capability to let you work directly with the Webs on your server, FrontPage makes setting up a Web site relatively transparent. Similarly, by incorporating into the authoring software many of the tasks normally given over to the *Common Gateway Interface (CGI) (page 247)*, FrontPage lets you take command of the server in a way that most nonprogrammers could barely even dream of.

None of this is to suggest that using FrontPage replaces an intimate knowledge of UNIX, networking, CGI, Java, or the workings of an HTTP server. What FrontPage does, however, is render computer management something apart from those highly technical concerns. As long as the server's administrator cooperates, FrontPage gives you a considerable amount of power when it comes to managing computers. In this sense, real cooperation means having the most recent FrontPage server extensions installed on their servers, and you should make sure that your ISP or web hosting service *fully* supports those extensions, including database and forms programming (which they can selectively leave out if they wish). If not, then you won't get everything you can out of your FrontPage purchase.

FRONTPAGE'S TASKS VIEW

The single most useful piece of direct Web management available through FrontPage is the Tasks view. Although it's certainly no replacement for sophisticated project management software, it is nevertheless a surprisingly powerful assistant. From the Tasks view you can launch and work on every one of the outstanding projects, and you can get an entire history of who did what and when during the building of your site.

FrontPage automatically creates a Tasks view for each Web you create, although depending on the web you've created there is not necessarily a set of tasks in that view. The principle behind the Tasks view is this: All pages are incomplete (under construction) on a newly created Web. They will show in the Web as being under construction and will bear the Under Construction icon (unless you've specified in the wizard not to include that icon). As you work on individual pages, you can load them into FrontPage from the Tasks view. If you change anything on that page and then save it to the web, FrontPage will, if you want, automatically mark the task as completed within the Tasks view. You can add new tasks in the Tasks view from within the Tasks view itself, or you can add them from within the other views. You must have the Web currently open in FrontPage to use the Tasks view.

TASKS VIEW COLUMNS

Figure 18.1 shows the Tasks view. Along the top of the list are the following column headings: Status, Task, Assigned To, Priority, Associated With, Modified Date, and Description. Most of these are created through the Task Details or Add To Task dialog boxes, which are discussed later. The exceptions are Modified Date and Linked To, and their appearance is also discussed later.

Figure 18.1
The Tasks view contains enough information to keep track of a web's planned progress.

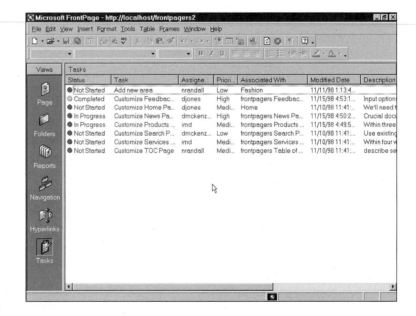

STATUS

The Status column shows the status of each task in your web. Three statuses are possible: Not Started, In Progress, and Completed. A task is in Not Started status until the page is loaded into Page view. At that point, it enters In Progress status. A task is marked Completed either by choosing Mark as Completed from the Tasks views Context menuTasks view, or as a dialog box option within Page view. Tasks in Not Started or In Progress status display with a red circular icon; those in Completed status display with a green circle (but only as described next.

You tell FrontPage that you finished a task by right-clicking that task in Tasks view and choosing Mark as Completed. This changes the icon in the Status bar for that task to a green light and the status to Completed. You don't usually see this change because completed tasks disappear from the Tasks view unless you right-click in the Tasks view and select Show Task History.

TASK

The Task column simply lists the names of the tasks themselves. FrontPage automatically adds a name when you use a wizard to create a web, but when you add a task manually you can give it whatever name you prefer (up to 256 characters). You can edit the name of manually created tasks at any time by double-clicking the task; by right-clicking the task and selecting Edit Task; or by selecting File, Properties. In all three cases, the Task Details dialog box appears, as shown in Figure 18.2.

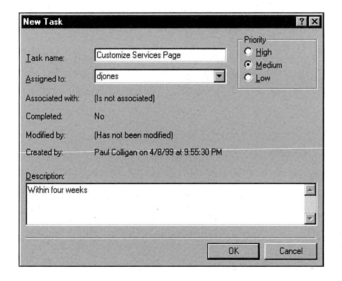

Figure 18.2
The Task Details dialog box lets you change the name of the task, the person it is assigned to, its priority, and its description. You can also start the task from here.

ASSIGNED TO

All tasks contain an Assigned To field. You can type whatever you like in this field, but the idea is to assign each web task to a member of your authoring team. FrontPage does no internal checking for names or user IDs; this field is entirely freeform. The names already entered in the Task Details dialog box appear in a drop-down list, from which you can select any of them. The web administrator's name appears in this field by default, but you can edit the field by right-clicking the task and selecting Edit Task (or File, Properties). When you create a task manually, you can assign the task at the same time you give it a name.

PRIORITY

Whenever you create or edit a task, you assign it a priority. There are three priority levels: High, Medium, and Low. You can change priority on the Task Details dialog box by right-clicking the task and selecting Edit Task (or File, Properties). Assigning a priority in FrontPage doesn't actually do anything to the task in that FrontPage doesn't check due dates or alert you to unfinished tasks (as a Personal Information Manager such as Microsoft Outlook or Lotus Organizer does). You can, however, sort by priority as a means of helping you organize your team's work.

ASSOCIATED WITH

The Associated With field shows the title of the page (in the FrontPage web) that the task actually belongs to. This field appears only when you create a link through Page view, at which point the task takes the title of the page you're working on as its association. The link performs the central function of telling FrontPage what to do when you select Start from the Edit menu (or Start Task from the right-click menu). Start Task simply indicates that this page should be loaded into the editor associated with that file type. For Web pages, this means load into Page view; for graphics and other files, it means load into whatever editor is assigned to files of that type. Start Task is unavailable if a task does not have an association.

You cannot add a link to a manually created task.

MODIFIED DATE

The Modified Date column shows the date and time the task was last modified. In other words, it shows when the linked page was last changed and saved, or when the task was marked as Completed. This field cannot be manually modified.

Tip #81	You can change the Not Started status and a task's modified date by simply starting the task, thereby loading it into Page view, changing the page in any way, and then resaving. As far as Tasks view is concerned, the task is in progress as of the current date and time.

DESCRIPTION

As its name suggests, this column is simply a description of that task. FrontPage offers its own generic descriptions of tasks it creates through wizards, but you can (and should for clarity's sake) change the description at any time through the Task Details command. The Edit Task dialog box's Description field is completely free-form, so feel free to be as explanatory as you like. In fact, you can use it for simple checklists for the task, milestones, due dates, and so forth.

SORTING TASKS

You can sort the tasks in Tasks view according to any of the columns, by clicking the column heading itself. While there might seem little need for this kind of sorting in the pictured Tasks view, it can be of obvious usefulness on a much longer list sorting by priority, by page linked to, or by person assigned to. You can toggle the elements in a column between ascending and descending order simply by clicking the column heading twice.

TASKS VIEW COMMANDS

You get a shortcut menu showing four commands when you select a task and right-click it: Edit Task, Start Task, Mark as Complete, and Delete. Start Task and Mark as Complete are also available through the Edit, Task cascading menu. Edit Task is available, when a task is selected, by choosing File, Properties.

You get a menu of three choices when you right-click in the Tasks view away from the task list. New Task lets you add a task to the list (as does Task, Add Task in the Edit menu). Show Task History displays the tasks in Completed status as well as those in Not Started and In Progress status (also available in Edit, Task). Web Settings opens the Web Setting dialog box, which is covered in Chapter 17, "Configuring Webs."

PART

III

CH

18

START TASK

Although simple in concept, this is an extremely powerful tool. When you select a task in the Tasks view and click Do Task, the file associated with the task opens into its appropriate editor. HTML files open by default inside the Page view, while graphics files load inside the associated graphics editor. You establish these editors and their associations in the Configure Editors dialog box, which is available with Tools, Option.

→ **See** "Configuring Editors" for details on how to establish editors and associations, **p. 382**.

EDIT TASK

The Task Details dialog box appears when you select a task and Edit Task from the shortcut menu (or Properties from the Edit menu). As Figure 18.2 shows, this dialog box contains several fields; some are alterable but four of them are not.

The first item in the dialog box is the Task Name. This name is created either by the FrontPage wizard that created the web or by the person who added the task to the Tasks view. You can change this name as you like.

The Assigned To text box lets you specify who should complete the task. This box is wide open, meaning that its contents aren't checked against the list of authors or administrators for the web. (An option to do so would in fact be helpful.) However, a drop-down list provides a list of people whose names you've already entered into the Assigned To column for that web.

To the top right of the dialog box are the Priority option buttons. You can set the selected task as High, Medium, or Low priority, and the choice appears in the Tasks view's Priority column. While it's tempting to set everything at high priority, as a Web manager you'll want to set only the most truly important tasks as such.

The Description list box is another free-form field. Type in anything that might be helpful here, including specific suggestions to the person to whom the task has been assigned. The first few characters of this description appear in the Tasks view's Description column. The other four fields are determined by FrontPage itself, and cannot be altered except by working on the task.

MARK AS COMPLETE

When a task in the Tasks view has been finished to your satisfaction, select Mark as Complete from the shortcut menu (or Edit, Task, Mark as Complete). The task is shown on the Tasks view with a green icon and with the status of Completed.

DELETE

Not surprisingly, the Delete command erases the task from the Tasks view. The document to which it refers is unaffected; it's still on your web. Notice that there's a difference between deleting a task and marking it Completed. If you want to keep track of what's been done, use Mark Completed; if you have no interest in the history of your web's tasks, use Delete.

ADDING TASKS

The Add command, available through New Task on the shortcut menu when you right-click in the Tasks view, lets you enter an entirely new task into the Tasks view. The dialog box is identical to the Task Details dialog box shown in Figure 18.2, except that the Task Name and Description text boxes are not filled in, and the Associated With field shows Is not Associated. Because the task hasn't been created through a FrontPage view in which you create new documents (Page view, Navigation view, or the like), the task is not associated with a file in your web. Thus, you cannot open it automatically into an editor. In fact, selecting a task added this way results in the Do Task button being grayed out.

As a manager, you can use this button to add to the list tasks that aren't actually web creation tasks. For example, you might need several graphics created for a page or series of pages, or you might need pictures or documents scanned for presentation in a document. For that matter, you can use the Add button to schedule meetings if it helps get your assistant's attention. This method of adding tasks, however, is less effective than adding them from FrontPage's main programs; they can't be completed as part of FrontPage activity itself.

ADDING A TASK FROM PAGE VIEW

Often, when working on a page in Page view, you'll realize that something needs to be completed that you don't have time or resources for at that particular time. Instead of jotting down a note to yourself in a text file or a word processor, you can add a task to the Tasks view directly from within Page view itself.

When editing a page in Page view, select Edit, Task, Add Task (it's the only item of that submenu available) or File, New, Task. This yields the Task Details dialog box, which you complete. Click OK. The task appears immediately in the Tasks view.

The Associated With field is an important element of this dialog box. The document's filename appears in that field. This means that selecting the Start Task command in Tasks view (or selecting Edit, Tasks) loads the file into Page view.

ADDING TO THE TASKS VIEW

Adding a task to the Tasks view—if you're working in the Folders, Navigation, Hyperlinks, or Reports view—is almost identical to the procedure for adding from Page view. With the View visible, click the page to which you want to associate the task. With the page highlighted, right-click and choose Add Task .

The New Task dialog box appears, with the selected page appearing in the Linked To field. The task, ready for action, appears in the Tasks view after you fill in the appropriate information.

MANAGING THROUGH FRONTPAGE VIEWS

Throughout Part III, "Web Creation and Management," you've seen examples of the graphical Hyperlinks view or Navigation view in FrontPage. So far, the suggestion has been that these views help you create a Web site and develop all the associated pages. That's true—but if your role is that of site manager rather than (or in addition to) page creator, these views will help you here as well. In fact, two other views, Folder and Reports, are also useful in this regard.

HYPERLINKS VIEW

Figure 18.3 shows a Customer Support Web as created by FrontPage. The view here, which you've seen throughout these chapters, is the Hyperlinks view. There's a textual hierarchy of hyperlinks in the left pane and a graphical view of these links in the right.

PART

III

CH

18

Figure 18.3
The Hyperlinks view for a Customer Support Web.

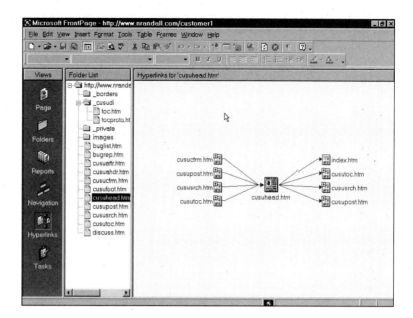

TheFolder List offers one possible assistant for Web management. Using this pane, you can quickly get a top-level hierarchical look at your web by keeping all the headings compressed, or you can look in detail at any particular heading and its components by selectively expanding them. As you expand headings by clicking the plus signs to the left of the items, you get a sense of the size and scope of your web and can move quickly to an individual component for editing or assigning.

The Hyperlinks view's main viewing window shows you the web in a graphical format. With this view you can tell exactly which pages link to which pages and how the links fit together to form the overall web. The strength of the Hyperlinks view lies in its capability to show you exactly what needs to be added or completed, rather than simply presenting it (as does the Tasks view) as yet another item in a list. The weakness of the Hyperlinks view, however, is that it can show you only a portion of the web at any one time. A 21-inch monitor set to ultra-high resolution can obviously display a larger portion than a 14-inch monitor and low resolution, but the Hyperlinks view can become unwieldy on such a display. From a management perspective, the graphical Hyperlinks view is best as a means of assessing and detailing specific portions of the web.

FOLDERS VIEW

In Figure 18.4 you see the same web that's shown in Figure 18.3, but this time the Hyperlinks view has been replaced by the Folders view. The Folders view is similar to the file view of Windows Explorer: folders in the left pane, subfolders and files in the right. Obviously, the Folders view is text-based rather than graphical and as such doesn't provide the same kind of information the Hyperlinks view offers. What it does provide, however, is a summary of all the details pertaining to the files in your Web site.

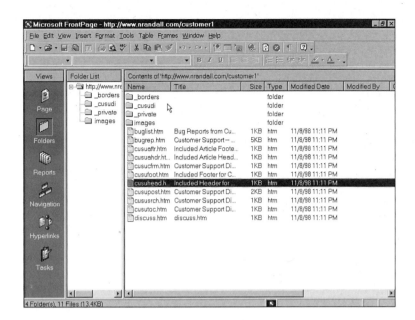

Figure 18.4
The Folders view shows you exactly which files make up your web.

PART

III

CH

18

The columns in the Folders view display the following data:

- Name—This is the actual filename of the folder or file. Web documents will almost always end in .HTM or .HTML. (Note that Windows 95/98 and Windows NT accept extensions of more than three characters.) Graphics will usually end in .JPG or .GIF. You can use the filename information, for example, if you want to edit the file directly by using a different editor or a text editor such as Windows Notepad.

- Title—The title of the Web file as set during the creation of the page. You can change the title using the Page view's Page Properties dialog box. In the case of images, the Title column shows the path and filename instead of a title.

- Size—The Size column shows the size of the file in bytes. Files smaller than 1Kb (1,024 bytes) are shown with their actual byte count, while files greater than 1Kb are displayed in kilobytes and rounded to the nearest kilobyte. Files larger than 1M (1,024Kb) are displayed in megabytes, rounded to the nearest megabyte.

Tip #82

> It's entirely possible that files greater than one gigabyte (1,024Mb) appear in number of gigabytes, but like most people, this book's authors didn't have a large enough system to test this properly. If you have a file that large in your web, you should get rid of it immediately; otherwise, you might find yourself with hordes of angry modem users storming your house.

- Type—The file type simply repeats the extension shown in the filename—except for directories and subdirectories (which show the type as Folder) and subwebs (which display the type as Web).

- Modified Date—This column shows the last date and time the file was modified.
- Modified By—This column shows who did the modifications for that page or file.
- Comments—The Comments column shows the comments about the document as entered through the Properties dialog box.

Together, these columns can provide a wealth of information. You can sort the Folders view according to any of these columns by clicking the column heading. This shows you precise details ordered as you need them. For example, sorting by Modified Date lets you instantly see which pages haven't been updated recently enough to suit the site's needs as established during planning. With large webs, it's extremely easy to overlook one or two pages that need updating (especially pages that are less frequently accessed); this column can help keep your attention focused on that strategy.

NAVIGATION VIEW

FrontPage's Navigation view gives you a rich graphical look at your web. From a web creation standpoint, Navigation view is indispensable. From a management standpoint—working with a web once it's in place, for example—it offers an extremely convenient means of reorganizing and adding to a web. The Navigation view is covered primarily in Chapter 15, "Working with an Existing Web."

REPORTS VIEW

The Reports view collects a number of extremely useful web views. Its primary purpose is maintaining your web, offering several tools for doing so. The reports included with this view range from the Site Summary, which offers a set of one-line summaries of the contents of your web, through lists of recently added and recently changed files; a list of pages that load slowly in users' browsers; a status of publishing for the pages; and lists of broken hyperlinks and other errors.

Tip #83

> If you're managing a large site, you'll practically want to live in the Reports view. From there you can determine everything that's working and not working in the web, and you can separate work items into a variety of categories to help you plan.

The best way to work with the Reports view is to show the Reports toolbar. It lets you select exactly which reports you want to see. Selecting View, Toolbars, Reports displays it. It appears as a floating toolbar inside the Reports view's main viewing window.

Tip #84

> In order to make full use of the Reports view, ensure that hidden files are showing. Otherwise, FrontPage will not display them in the individual reports.

SITE SUMMARY

The Site Summary is shown in Figure 18.5. It offers a top-level overview of the currently loaded web. From here, you can access other reports in the Reports view. The Site Summary shows you the number of files in the web and their total size, the number of image files and their total size, and so forth.

The Site Summary has three major purposes. First, you can see at a glance if your site favors of one type of file (multimedia, for example) or another. Second, you can get a quick sense of the number of problems that have to be fixed. Third, you can use the Site Summary as a launching pad to individual reports. By hovering the cursor over the rows, you can see which rows will respond to a double-click by opening a different report (Older Files is an example). You're instantly into that report when you double-click.

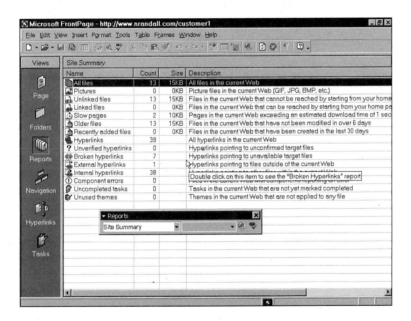

Figure 18.5
The Reports toolbar is open and cursor is hovered over a specific row.

ALL FILES REPORT

The All Files report provides a look at all the files in your web, plus their location and their status. You can see the All Files report by selecting All Files from the Reports toolbar's drop-down menu.

As Figure 18.6 shows, the All Files report displays the filename in the leftmost column (Name) and all associated information about that file in the remaining seven columns. These columns include the folder in which the file can be found, the file's title within the web, its size and type, when it was last modified, who performed the modifications, and any comments that have been recorded about that file. This information is merely taken from the File Properties box (right-click a filename anywhere in FrontPage and select Properties), but having it all in one place is extremely useful.

Figure 18.6
This is the complete
All Files report, with
all hidden files and
directories showing.

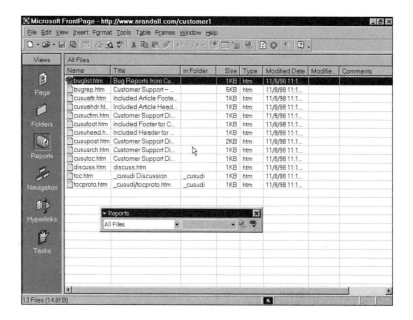

The power of the All Files report comes into play when your web takes on multiple files across multiple folders. It's extremely easy to lose track of where all your web's files are located and what their current status is. The All Files report gives you this information at a glance and also lets you access any of those files for renaming, cutting, deleting, copying, or loading into Page view.

RECENTLY ADDED FILES REPORT

This report shows you the files recently added to the web. You access the report by selecting Recently Added Files from the Reports toolbar, and at the same time you can determine what you mean by *recent*. The second drop-down menu of the Reports toolbar lets you set *recent* to anything from 0 days (today), through 365 days. You can set the default number of days by selecting Tools, Options, clicking the Reports View tab, and changing the number in the Recent Files line.

The benefit of this report is to let you see at a glance what your team has added to the web in the past *x* number of days. In other words, it's a managerial tool. The report itself shows the name and title of each recently added file, along with who created it, who last modified it, its size and type, and the folder in which it is stored.

RECENTLY CHANGED FILES REPORT

This report shows the files modified on your web within the number of days selected in the Reports toolbar's drop-down list. The display is identical to the Recently Added Files report, except of course that the files are those that have been modified recently rather than added from scratch.

OLDER FILES REPORT

As you keep developing your web, the information and links on many files get outdated; of course, you'll keep track of these. Other files, however, sit out there and get no attention from the standpoint of modification because the information hasn't changed in any way. Despite this, you should check them; they might be showing inconsistencies or other kinds of signs of age. This report displays (in columns identical to the Recently Added Files report) the files that are older than a number of days specified in the Reports toolbar's drop-down menu. Use it to weed out old, unneeded documents and to make sure all documents sport recently determined designs.

You can set the default number of days by selecting Tools, Options, clicking the Reports View tab, and changing the number in the Older Files line.

UNLINKED FILES REPORT

This report shows the files that are not linked from the web's home page, either directly or indirectly—files that you can't reach without typing the precise name of the file into your browser's address field, in other words. Sometimes you want files to be unlinked—it's a good way of keeping them relatively hidden—but for the most part unlinked files are useless to you. This report shows you the unlinked files and lets you work with them to change (or confirm) their status.

SLOW PAGES REPORT

There's nothing worse for your visitors than pages that take ages to download. The WWW has been nicknamed the World Wide Wait for a reason, and you don't want your site to add to the joke. To help you keep tab on lengthy download times, Page view's status bar shows the approximate download time of the currently loaded document, and the Slow Pages report gives you a list of offenders. All the usual report information is here, with headings for name, title, folder, modification times, and so on, but also here are the page's size and approximate download time.

You can set a download time on the Reports view toolbar of up to 600 seconds; pages taking longer than that to load are shown in the report. You can change the number of seconds you want to use as the default download time by selecting Tools, Options and clicking the Reports View tab. Here you can select not only the number of seconds to use as a default (you can go way beyond 600 seconds in the Slow Pages line), but also the connection speed this calculation will assume.

The connection speed ranges from that supplied by 14.4Kbps (kilobytes per second) modem to a dedicated T3 line, which hits 45 million bytes per second. If you're designing for the public World Wide Web, you can probably assume 28.8Kbps, although certainly many users still log in at 14.4. If you're designing purely for internal use, your systems administrators can tell you what speed to expect.

> **Note**
>
> The download time displayed in the Slow Pages report is simply an estimate. Many factors contribute to the speed of a download, including bottlenecks across the Internet and the degree to which the viewer's Internet provider's network is busy while the download is taking place. If anything, you should consider FrontPage's estimates too fast, not too slow.

BROKEN HYPERLINKS REPORT

The Broken Hyperlinks report gives you a quick glance at the documents in your web that contain invalid hyperlinks: the documents to which the hyperlink points cannot be reached. When you select this report, FrontPage shows you links with broken pages according to the last time it verified the hyperlinks; if you want to check again, click the Verify Hyperlinks icon on the far right of the Reports toolbar. FrontPage will go onto the web and attempt contact with each hyperlink in your web and then return the results of uncompleted contact here.

The Broken Hyperlinks report shows the status of the link in the first column, the hyperlink that doesn't work in the second column, and the page on which that hyperlink occurs in the third column. You can edit the hyperlinks for each page by selecting the row and clicking either the Edit Hyperlink icon on the Reports toolbar or Edit Hyperlink from the right-click context menu.

COMPONENT ERRORS REPORT

This report displays the pages in your web that contain errors in their included FrontPage components, whatever those errors might be. This report shows the name and title of the page and a description of the error, along with the folder in which the document resides. To correct the error, open the document for editing in Page view by double-clicking the appropriate row.

REVIEW STATUS REPORT

The Review Status report is an important part of managing your web's authors and administrators. It is described in detail in Chapter 22, "Managing Workflow and Tasks."

ASSIGNED TO REPORT

The Assigned To report is an important part of managing your web's authors and administrators. It is described in detail in Chapter 22.

CATEGORIES REPORT

The Categories report is an important part of managing your web's authors and administrators. It is described in detail in Chapter 22.

PUBLISH STATUS REPORT

Obviously, an important part of web design is the publishing of documents to that web. You can, however, create documents that you have no intention of publishing, at least at this point in the web's development. Documents should be withheld from publishing if they are to appear on the web at a specified future date, if they are created in case of a specific event, or if they are created against the possibility of something that might require them.

The Publish Status report (see Figure 18.7) shows you which pages are marked for publication and which are marked *not* to be published. The usual Name, Title, and Modification columns are here, as well as the folder in which the file resides and that file's review status (which is the basis for the Review Status report). In addition, the report has a Publish column, which you can click to change the document's Publish status. The drop-down menu appears when you click the column twice (which, again, is not a double-click). You can also change this value by right-clicking the file, selecting Properties, clicking the Workgroup tab, and then checking the box labeled Exclude This File When Publishing the Rest of the Web.

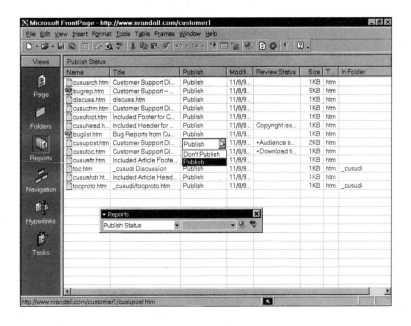

Figure 18.7
The drop-down menu shown here is completely hidden from view until you click once, pause, and then click again on the Publish column.

PART

III

CH

18

MANAGEMENT TOOLS: SPELLING, FIND, VERIFY HYPERLINKS, AND RECALCULATE HYPERLINKS

FrontPage 2000 offers four important tools specifically designed to help Webmasters manage their webs. These tools tackle four simple but crucial tasks: Global Spell-Checking, Global Find and Replace, and two means of checking a web's links—Verify Hyperlinks and Recalculate Hyperlinks.

GLOBAL SPELL-CHECKING

One of the problems every Webmaster encounters is the difficulty of ensuring accurate spelling across the entire site. Authors can check their work on individual documents in Page view, but it's essential that spelling be checked for errors and for lack of standardization when all the documents in a web are linked. Almost nothing can reduce the professional appearance of a site more quickly than a measly little spelling mistake. It simply looks bad.

To invoke global spell-checking, choose Spelling from FrontPage's Tools menu. This can be done from any of FrontPage's views. You are asked if you want to check all pages or only the pages you've selected, as well as whether you want to add a new task to the Tasks view for any pages that contain misspellings. (In Page view, only the current page is checked for spelling.)

If you double-click the file from the Spelling dialog box, you open that document in Page view, along with the Spelling dialog box. The Spelling dialog box is essentially the same as that found in a word processor, with options to select a word from the Suggestions field, to ignore the current misspelling, or to add the located word to the dictionary (so it's not marked as incorrect next time).

GLOBAL FIND AND REPLACE

Sometimes, several documents in a web contain a piece of information that needs to be located or changed. The names of products or corporate contacts, the prices of services, or any other type of repeated information might need to be found and altered. Changing repeated data in a large web is extremely tedious, requiring the Webmaster to load each page individually and edit the material. FrontPage 2000 makes this considerably more convenient by providing a global Find feature and a separate global Replace feature.

To perform a global Find, select Find from the Edit menu. Type the text string you want to find, and whether you want to match the whole word or the upper- or lowercasing of the word as typed. You can also decide to find the text string in the HTML code itself, which is extremely useful for locating specific formatting codes. Finally, you are asked if you want to find the string in all pages in the web, or only in the selected pages.

The results of your search appear in the Find dialog box's occurrence window. This box shows the pages on which the search string has been found. By double-clicking a page, you load the document into Page view, where the text string is highlighted and you can do what you intended. You can place the page in the Tasks view by clicking Add Task.

Performing a global Replace is almost identical. Select Replace from the Edit menu and then type the text strings in the respective Find What and Replace With fields on the Replace dialog box (shown in Figure 18.8). Here you are asked, as with Find, to specify case and whole word matches, whether to replace the string across the Web or in selected pages, and whether you want to search for the string in HTML code.

The results of the Replace command appear in the occurrences box shown in Figure 18.8. Here you see the titles of the pages on which the string is found, as well as the number of times it occurs on each page.

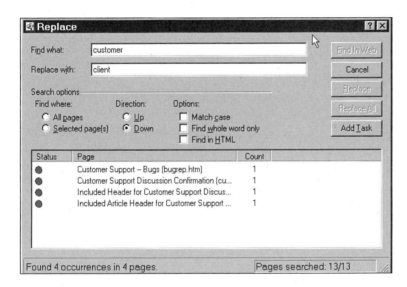

Figure 18.8
You can add each document to the Tasks view to edit later or you can edit directly from here.

Double-clicking an occurrence loads the document into Page view, where you are immediately presented with the Replace dialog box, complete with the Find and Replace fields filled in. In other words, you haven't actually replaced anything yet; you have to perform the replacement operations from there.

If you add the document to the Tasks view by clicking Add Task instead, you are presented with the same Replace dialog box when you load the page from within the Tasks view.

VERIFY AND RECALCULATE HYPERLINKS

Another of a Webmaster's crucial but tedious tasks is to check the hyperlinks within and without your site. This task is crucial because broken links frustrate the web's users. It is also tedious because a heavily linked site (as most webs are) contains any number of potential erroneous hyperlinks.

FrontPage 2000 offers two ways of checking hyperlinks across the web. The first, Verify Hyperlinks, is available only as an icon on the Reports toolbar. Verify Hyperlinks determines whether hyperlinks to pages external to your site are valid. The second, Recalculate Hyperlinks (available from the Tools menu), updates the views of your webs as well as various components of your webs. Both ways require that you first be online.

Selecting Verify Hyperlinks causes FrontPage to ensure the validity of hyperlinks external to your web. Clicking the Verify Hyperlinks icon on the Reports toolbar yields the Verify Hyperlinks dialog box, in which you can verify all links or just those from the currently selected page on the report. The result is to display the status of the links in the Broken Hyperlinks report's Status column. The statuses are Unknown, Broken, or OK.

Recalculate Hyperlinks performs several important updating functions. First, it updates the views of the web in FrontPage, which is extremely important if you've edited hyperlinks or added or deleted pages. Next, it updates the text indexes that are produced by any Search component you have in your web. Search components create indexes of all searchable pages, and these indexes become incomplete as you add or delete pages. Finally, Recalculate Hyperlinks regenerates all the Include components in your web. These components are, in a sense, empty containers with pointers to fields in your webs that contain specific information; the components retrieve the most current version of that information when a visitor calls the page. Recalculate Hyperlinks updates all the Web content that depends on these components.

You should run the Recalculate and Verify Hyperlinks commands frequently—certainly after any significant changes to your web.

DESIGNERS CORNER

In the Designers Corner for this chapter, we'll look at two items. The first will cover the automatic creation of tasks, while the second will revisit the Categories feature.

AUTOMATIC GENERATION OF TASKS

For the most part, tasks are created for a web either automatically through a web wizard or manually as you create them yourself. In some instances, however, FrontPage will create a task for a web document as a result of a specific action. For example, if you perform a spell check and FrontPage notes a spelling error, a task will be created for that error automatically.

It makes sense, therefore, to check your tasks regularly. In fact, you might want to switch to Tasks view before closing your web; when you reopen it, Tasks view will be showing. If you're working primarily on only one web, you can have FrontPage automatically reopen that web in the last-used view by checking the Open Last Web Automatically When FrontPage Starts option in the Options dialog (available through Tools/Options).

MORE ON CATEGORIES

It's nearly impossible to overstate the potential usefulness of setting categories. For one thing, categories help you manage the tasks and workflow of the web team, and that's a huge value in and of itself. But they can also be used in another useful way, as a basis for generating a table of contents for a web.

To create a table of contents based on categories, open the home page for the web in the Page view. Then click where you want the list to appear, in order to set the cursor position. Next, select the Categories component from the Insert/Components cascading menu. In the resulting Categories Properties dialog box, you can choose the category or categories to show on the page, and you can sort the entries by document title or date last modified. You can also choose to include the comments associated with each listed page.

If you choose multiple categories, they will be sorted as you chose in the dialog box, but not actually by category. To get a multi-category listing, you must create a category listing individually for each category. You can do this in a table if you want.

PART

III

CH

18

COLLABORATION, WORKFLOW, TASK MANAGEMENT

CHAPTER 19

ESTABLISHING A COLLABORATIVE AUTHORING ENVIRONMENT

In this chapter

by Paul Colligan

As the requirements of Web design become more and more elaborate, the concept of the lone Webmaster or Webmistress quickly becomes as antiquated as the Gopher server or version 1.0 of anything. Today the complexities and requirements of Web development require a team effort.

The individualistic nature and tendencies of programmers and authors makes the process of team development a difficult one. In the instant reply and always on world of the Internet, developers seem to always want to go their own way and work under their own terms using the programs and techniques that they know best. Controlling a group of authors, programmers and developers has understandably been likened to herding cats but must be done none the less. This chapter will cover the process of developing the workflow process for developing a Web collaboratively using the technology provided by FrontPage 2000 to do just that.

While people have been working on the Web in teams for years now, the software has finally caught up to this trend. There are a number of tools provided by FrontPage 2000 that, when implemented properly, can make the process possible and successful. This chapter examines them and then shows you how to use them.

Also in this chapter you look at the process of setting up a web project utilizing the collaborative tools provided by FrontPage 2000. The human bandwidth (personnel and time) issues that go into such a project and how to deal with those issues are examined as well.

A COLLABORATIVE AUTHORING ENVIRONMENT

Developing a collaborative authoring environment is a blend of the technology and workflow process. FrontPage 2000 provides the technology. The developing of the workflow process is the project manager's job.

When working with a team, someone or something must take on the complex task of tracking who is doing what and who is allowed to do what. FrontPage 2000 provides a means to track these issues simply and quickly. Without a proper understanding and communication of the project at hand, a team can waste countless hours trying to achieve a goal that isn't possible because it doesn't exist or wasn't communicated well.

| Tip #85 | An effective collaborative development environment will never be accomplished without a single individual in charge of the process with whom the "buck stops." There needs to be one person whose job is to watch the entire project from overhead and make sure that the task at hand is being met. While it is the nature of Web designers to want to work in a communal type of atmosphere, there still needs to be someone in charge. Choosing the right project manager is at least as important as choosing the technology with which you will implement the project. |

TECHNOLOGY

Technology is a key part of the successful collaborative development environment. There is no longer any need to communicate task requirements by email or spend a great deal of time tracking anything that the computer could do a much better job of. FrontPage 2000 provides a set of tools that help make a collaborative environment much easier and effective while letting the computer track the elements as required.

Previously the only option for task management in FrontPage was a limited tasks file—seldom used by anyone and with no direct impact on the Web site. In FrontPage 2000, the tasks tracking capabilities have been greatly increased in scope and a number of new collaborative features that benefit the collaboration process directly have been added. The new Office server extensions (part of Office 2000, not of FrontPage) also provide a number of collaboration features that you examine here as well.

FRONTPAGE SERVER EXTENSIONS

The FrontPage *server extensions* are a series of programs and executables that work in collaboration with FrontPage and a Web server to provide a lot of its server-side capabilities (often found in the FrontPage components). FrontPage server extensions have been part of the program since the beginning and each version of FrontPage brings a new version of the server extensions with new capabilities and functionality. With FrontPage 2000 comes version 4 of the FrontPage extensions.

Unlike typical Microsoft programs that require the Windows platform to run, there are versions of the FrontPage extensions for most of the Web server programs available today. Chances are very good that there will be server extensions for whatever Web server you choose to place your site on.

If you install FrontPage 2000 on a machine that has a Microsoft Web server running on it, the program automatically installs the latest version of the FrontPage extensions during the installation process. If there is no server located on the machine that you install FrontPage on, you'll want to make sure that the server you'll be working on has the extensions installed. Also ensure that the latest version of the FrontPage server extensions are installed on the machine to make use of the all the features discussed in this chapter.

The role of FrontPage server extensions and Web servers are discussed in great detail in Chapter 35, "Introduction to Web Hosting and Web Servers." If you feel uncomfortable with the concept of server extensions or need more information, feel free to read the chapter now and return to this after.

While the use of FrontPage server extensions is encouraged and their use is described in great detail, it is important to note that if for some reason you do not want to use them, the program still provides a high degree of functionality.

PART

IV

CH

19

Note

If you have used previous versions of FrontPage and have been frustrated by the program's inability to perform much more than simple page design without the use of server extensions and a Web server, note that the program has changed considerably. FrontPage 2000 now provides much of the previous functionality of server extensions without requiring their use. It is even possible to develop an entire site without server extensions using the disk-based web feature described later in this chapter.

OFFICE SERVER EXTENSIONS

As mentioned previously, one of the more interesting aspects of FrontPage 2000 is that it is now an official part of the Microsoft Office Suite and is provided with the Premium Version of the product. New to Office 2000 is the introduction of Office server extensions, which provide a high degree of functionality and collaborative assistance to the web (and document) development process. Similar to the Web server extensions, the Office server extensions provide an additional level of functionality to the web experience in the areas of *web discussions, web subscriptions (page 453)*, and a web-based administration page. Unlike FrontPage server extensions available for most commercially available Web-server programs, Office server extensions can only be installed on a server running Microsoft Internet Information Server on NT 4 or later. They cannot be installed on Microsoft personal Web server or the FrontPage server.

Tip #86

If the final home for your Web site is going to be a third-party ISP or hosting firm, you might want to consider the support of Office server extensions in both the platform and ISP decision process.

Web discussions, as shown in Figure 19.1, provided by Office server extensions, allow threaded discussions on specific Office documents. These discussions are supplemental to the document and are viewable only by participants in the online discussion process.

Web discussions are useful because they provide an additional communication channel for participants in the development process: Instead of making comments to documents in the Task view or by email, comments can be made directly to the document.

Web subscriptions (see Figure 19.2) provide an email notification whenever a specific document is changed. They can help keep members of a team up to date on any changes made to the Web site if they are subscribed accordingly. They act almost as a third-party monitoring service that alerts you to changes as they happen.

One of the most powerful Web Subscription option applications is its requiring that each person responsible for a page or document in a Web site subscribe to that page. As a result, any time a change or comment is made to the document, the person responsible for the document is notified and can, if needed, act accordingly. Previously, a user was unaware if someone else changed her work and the effective use of Web subscriptions eliminates this problem.

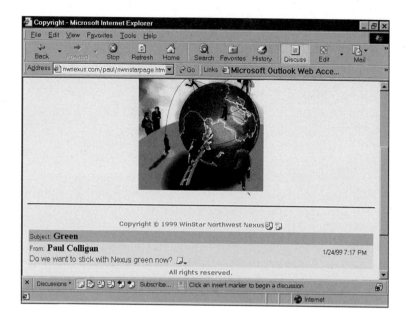

Figure 19.1
The Web Discussion option provides a means to comment on a Web document, line by line if necessary.

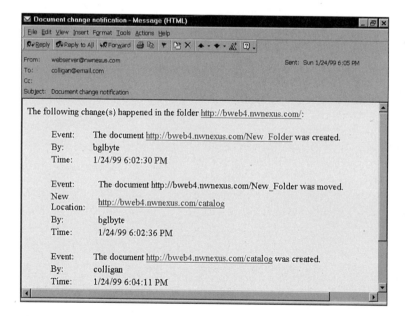

Figure 19.2
The Web Subscription notification provides a very specific reporting of changes made to a Web site.

The web-based administration page shown in Figure 19.3 provides a means of simple site administration through the Web browser. Provided on the page are means to manage and configure web discussion and subscriptions, configure database settings, and search the entire site.

The most useful aspect of the administration page is the capability to manage all user subscription and discussion information from a single point. A user could be subscribed to dozens of pages and be involved in multiple discussions during a collaborative effort. A single source reference point for this potential information overload is desirable.

Figure 19.3
The Office Server Extensions Start page makes Office server extensions available to any Web browser that supports frames.

Browser type determines the ease of functionality for the Office Server Extensions. Internet Explorer 5 has the discussion option built into the main toolbar (see Figure 19.4) but earlier versions of Internet Explorer and all versions Netscape Navigator can support the feature; they just require starting at the Office Server Extension Start page to begin a discussion.

Figure 19.4
The Discuss button is an option on the Internet Explorer 5 toolbar.

WORKING WITHOUT SERVER EXTENSIONS

Much to the frustration of many previous FrontPage users, FrontPage server extensions were required for any sort of Web-based development. This is no longer the case. FrontPage 2000 provides the new option for a *disk-based web (page 965)* that provides much of the functionality provided by a Web server with the server extensions installed. If desired, a disk-based web could be placed on a shared directory and edited by anyone with access to the directory.

Although this is possible, it is not a recommended development platform—especially when working with the collaborative features provided by the program.

TASKS TRACKING

From the Tasks view (see Figure 19.5), FrontPage 2000 provides the capability to assign and track tasks during the development process. Users assigned to the tasks during the development process can go directly to their jobs and complete them as required by double-clicking the task. FrontPage opens the document immediately and when a document is closed, FrontPage asks the user whether to mark the task as completed or in process.

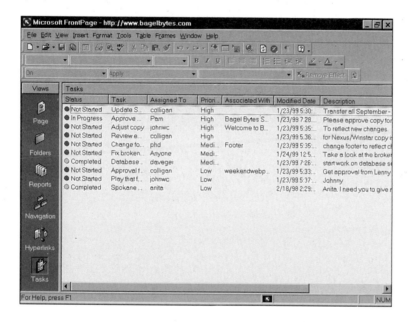

Figure 19.5
The Tasks view in FrontPage 2000 shows the status for each task, who it is assigned to, its priority, what document it is associated with, the last date it was modified, and any comments.

The tasks tracking feature provides two services: It allows an overview of the entire project status as needed and it provides a jumping off point for team members. The project manager can easily see what remains to be done from a simple view and team members can quickly get to work without bothering the manager with a typical "What should I do now?"

Pushing any of the field buttons in the Tasks view sorts the list by the field. This is powerful when assessing priority, status, modification dates (to see which task has been around the longest), or the amount of tasks assigned to an individual.

ESTABLISHING WORKFLOW

A Web site is an entirely different entity than a traditional document (or any other traditionally linear work). Multiple items within a single document are linked at different locations and the final product might be the result of many people including a graphic designer, copy editor, page layout director, and programmer. Because a change in any of the elements can have an immediate effect on the complete document, the need to establish a set of rules and project etiquette is necessary.

Blending the provided technology with a firm understanding of the project is the key to successful collaborative efforts. It might seem that because FrontPage 2000 provides such powerful collaboration tools, developing workflow would be easy as well. This is not the case. The workflow for any project may be many times more complicated than the development of the project itself.

Establishing workflow is a three-step process of developing a site goal, designing the project flow, and assigning duties to the team in charge of the project. Once these three things are complete, workflow has been established and the site development process is both well under way and on a path to success.

There are a number of computer programs available on the market today that can help with the design and establishment of a project workflow. If you are looking for one, make sure that the program assumes multiple participants in the project, not a single user. Microsoft Project 98 is one such powerful tool and can help in the workflow process. More information about Microsoft Project can be found online at
`http://www.microsoft.com/project`.

THE SITE GOAL

All too often technology gets in the way of the task at hand. The desire to jump right into a project, embracing the forgiving nature of web design, is a powerful draw. It may seem obvious, but a very clear site goal should be developed and communicated to all team members before the site's first page is designed.

If the purpose of a Web site is not clearly understood, creating it will be very hard to accomplish. The larger the project team, the more important the clear communication of the site's goal and purpose. This obviously requires that the manager know what she wants from the site. Sadly, many Web sites and projects have been taken on without the slightest clue as to what the project purpose is. In the rush to get online, people often forget the reason they're headed there in the first place. Don't let this happen to you.

An effective Web site goal takes into account the user and platform base, aesthetic requirements, team assignments and responsibilities, and a growth and maintenance schedule. An understanding of these four issues and how they are related to each other is an understanding of the project ahead. Some of the questions that should be asked to achieve such an understanding follow.

The Web site is still a very new medium that might be viewed by many different users on many different platforms (different browser versions on different operating systems) on many different devices (handheld devices, WebTV-type machines, computers, and so on). This new presentation paradigm requires a level of attention that simple print projects have never required. The user and platform base is very important when working with a team. A technology restriction must be put into place if the site is to be viewed by users without the latest technology. Programmers and Web site designers tend to love to put the latest and greatest at the site (and FrontPage 2000 provides enough flash to accomplish this goal). It must be well understood by everyone what to do with technology that might not be supported or understood by the user base. Questions to ask include:

- Should it be utilized at all?

- Should there be alternative pages for users without the technology?

- Should the site provide information for users on how to download and install the latest technology?

- Do you want to provide technical support to users who try to use the technology but are unable to do so on their own?

- Do potential viewing platforms such as handheld devices or television set top browsers have an effect on the technology that will be utilized?

Tip #87

Although not a perfect answer to all of these questions, the Compatibility tab in the Page Options dialog box can be utilized to quickly prevent you from using technology that might not be supported universally. Selecting Microsoft WebTV in the Browsers drop-down menu will at least ensure that the product will work on that specific device and prevent you from using some technologies that are not universally available.

Aesthetic requirements are especially important when working with a team because all members must understand, and be able to reproduce, a specific look and feel for the entire site. Questions to be asked:

- Will this be done with the use of themes?

- Does your team understand how to design sites so that they can be effectively managed and updated with themes?

- Will you use Web page templates?

- Will you require that everyone use them?

- Who will design them?

- What will the color scheme for the site be?

- Where will the graphic library come from?

- Do your graphic designers understand the graphic and color palette issues specific to web design?

Team assignments and responsibilities must be carefully understood and communicated from the very beginning. Everyone needs to know what is expected of him or her in the site development (and maintenance) process:

- Who is in charge of proofreading and editing?
- What sections of the site should be legally approved before publication?
- Who has the authority to change look and feel, colors, or themes?
- Who is responsible for providing links to newly added pages?

What happens once the site is up is always very important. Unlike a printed document that once printed is complete, a Web site is traditionally a constantly changing entity that requires an upkeep schedule. The Tasks view mentioned earlier only works when team members go to FrontPage to view their tasks. It does not have the capability to send them reminders or even assure that their task has been completed. Everyone in the team needs to not only understand what is expected of him in terms of site maintenance and upkeep, but should also know what type of update schedule he is required to follow.

It cannot be stressed enough how important a clear site goal is. The tendency to take it as it comes with a technology that is so forgiving is understandable, but hardly an effective means of developing an online project.

Tip #88	Communication of the goals and purpose of a Web site is as important as both the technology used to develop it and the people who make use of the technology. If it is not made perfectly clear what is expected from all of the players, chaos will always result.

DESIGNING WORKFLOW

Once these questions have been answered, the workflow design has to be created. *Workflow* is best described as the specified order in which projects are completed, reported, and verified. In what order are the elements of site design going to come into play and who is going to be responsible for what? If one element takes too long (or is completed early), how does that affect the project? How much has to be done before the first page is designed and how much effect on the site does any one page or user have?

The elements of workflow that need to be established and placed into order include content development, structure development, establishment of site look and feel, publication, alpha testing, beta testing, and maintenance. Obviously, not all sites will contain all of the elements listed, but the workflow elements that will be utilized need to be put into place.

The workflow design should be simple enough to fit on a single page that can be distributed (electronically if possible) and communicated to the entire team so that it knows what is expected.

Tip #89	Consider adding a special section that is only accessible by the team that clearly states the site goal and workflow requirements. Ask your team to refer to this section on a regular basis so that they are reminded of the project requirements. You can also update the area as things change and your teams can automatically be updated when such changes occur via the use of subscriptions.

Content development is one of the more important issues in web design. A popular catch phrase in the world of Web design is "content is king." If the project you are working on has a team of writers attached to it, the source for your content is clear. If (as is often the case) your team does not contain professional writers, the source of your content won't always be so. Don't automatically assume everyone on your team has the skills required to write for the Web.

Once the content is completed (or at least started), the content presentation and linkage structures must be determined. Common issues include how many links away do you want any document to be from another and how many hyperlink choices you want to offer on any one given page. Documents that are hard to find and documents offering too many choices on them can create unnecessary confusion at the site. Use of the Navigation view is a powerful tool for determining structure development.

The site's look and feel is extremely important because it dictates how content is to be imported into the Web site. If the site is going to make use of themes, it is especially important that the team use similar style tags so that all pages look the same. If style tags aren't used and the site theme is changed, the result could be quite awkward. If templates are used, the templates' source, the template number, and the final templates' approval need to be determined as well. A further discussion of the use of themes in Web design can be found in Chapter 6, "Working with Themes."

Issues of site publication include

- How often the site is going to be published
- Who has the authority to publish the site
- What elements of the site are going to be prevented from being published

A publishing schedule and rule set must be established in the workflow design.

Alpha testing is the process of bringing in external users to examine the site's basic flow before it is completed. A shell needs to be put into place before alpha testing can take place, but site usability can be examined once this has been done. If the initial alpha testing team determines that the initial flow or feel of the alpha site is ineffective, a restructuring plan can be put into place without requiring a remake of the entire site.

Beta testing is the process of bringing users to the final site before it is open to the public (or specified audience) in order to catch bugs and problems that are seen much easier by someone who has not spent hours on the project. The results of the beta test can range dramatically from simple bug fixes and content edit to large overhauls of issues missed during the design process.

Maintenance is key and sometimes more complicated than the rest of the issues mentioned earlier because it determines the life of the site after it has been published to the initial audience. Understanding and communicating who is in charge of each level of maintenance ensures that the site is updated as required.

ASSIGNMENT OF DUTIES

Once the purpose of the site has been determined and the workflow process has been established, the next step is to assign duties to the team.

Tip #90	The Tasks view (see Figure 19.6) is the most important view when working on a collaborative project. It provides a snapshot of all the work that remains to be done on the project as well as an assessment of the current work in progress. You can sort the tasks by selecting the appropriate column in the view with the mouse.

Figure 19.6
The Tasks view not only shows the status and task of each project but also shows who each task is assigned to and what priority it has been given.

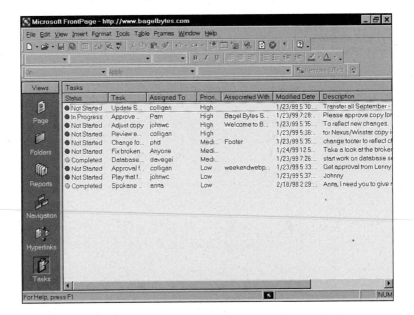

Choose File, New, Task to assign a generic task to a web. Enter the task name, who it is assigned to, the priority for the task, and a short description. To associate a task to a specific document, have the document selected before you create the new task. You can assign a task to any document list in the Pages view by right-clicking the document and selecting Properties.

Specific directions for assigning and completing tasks are given in Chapter 20, "Collaborating on Pages and Webs."

THE DEVELOPMENT ENVIRONMENT

Collaborative development is typically done on what is called a *development server*. The development server holds the collaborative project until it is ready to be published to a live server for the intended audience to see and interact with.

Traditionally, the development server is built on the same hardware and software platform that the final project will be launched on, which provides a means of testing all aspects of the final project. This practice is encouraged because it not only gives the developers a chance to work on the same system they expect the audience to work with, but it also helps identify unforeseen problems with the chosen platform. Interestingly, development servers have also historically been used to provide back systems when the deployment server goes down.

Budgets and other issues sometimes prevent a separate development server. It is possible, although not recommended, to develop the site on a disk-based web or in a section of the site rendered unavailable to anyone but the development team.

DISK-BASED WEBS

Disk-based webs are new to FrontPage 2000. They are a means to develop a site without the need for a separate Web server. All that is required is sufficient hard disk space. Although it is limited in some areas of functionality, a disk-based web provides a simple web development platform not previously available by FrontPage.

By default, FrontPage 2000 assumes that all Web sites are going to be disk based. You must indicate otherwise, when the Web site is created, if you would like to create a server-based web (see Figure 19.7).

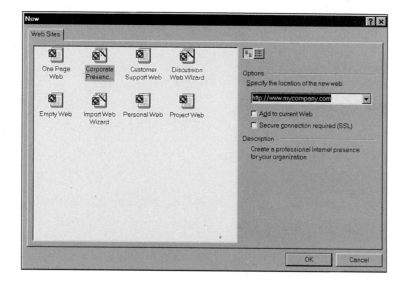

Figure 19.7
You must indicate that a web is going to be server based in the New dialog box by specifying a server for the new web's location.

PART

IV

CH

19

Tip #91

If you have already created a disk-based web with which you would like to make full use of the FrontPage server extensions, publish the disk-based web to a server and then edit the web on the server accordingly.

Obviously, webs must be server-based in order to make use of the capabilities provided by FrontPage server extensions.

SERVER-BASED WEBS

The development site is ideally server-based. Obviously, if FrontPage or Office extensions are going to be used in the final product, it would be ideal to have them installed on the development server as well.

In many cases, Microsoft personal Web servers (which comes with Microsoft Windows 98 or can be downloaded from Microsoft for Windows 95) is a fine development server. The server type is usually not important unless a large team of people is working on it. It is important to note that FrontPage server extensions must be installed on personal Web servers (despite the logical assumptions, they don't come preinstalled). As mentioned earlier, Office server extensions must be installed in Microsoft's Internet Information Server, which requires (and is bundled with) Microsoft Windows NT Server 4.

PUBLISHING ISSUES

One of FrontPage 2000's new features is the capability of marking a page or document to prevent it from being published during the normal publication process. All documents are marked for publishing by default, but you can quickly change the status of anything on the site.

This is powerful because it keeps the development web from becoming an all-or-nothing situation. You can publish your development server on a regular basis without fear of half-completed documents or other such problems that can come from the use of multiple participants in the web design process.

To exclude a specific file from being published with the rest of the web, select the Exclude option from the Properties dialog box's Workgroup tab, shown in Figure 19.8; do so by right-clicking the document and selecting Properties from the menu.

CHECKING DOCUMENTS IN AND OUT

Another new FrontPage 2000 feature is the capability to check documents in and out from a Web site. During the time that a document is checked out, the individual who checked it out is the only person allowed to edit it. This option can be used to both prevent users from making multiple edits to a single file and prevent users from editing a file they shouldn't (see Figure 19.9). This option was not available in previous versions of FrontPage and was the source of a number of problems.

This option was originally only available on Web sites hosted on a Windows NT server running an additional program called Microsoft Visual SourceSafe. Now the feature comes built into the program.

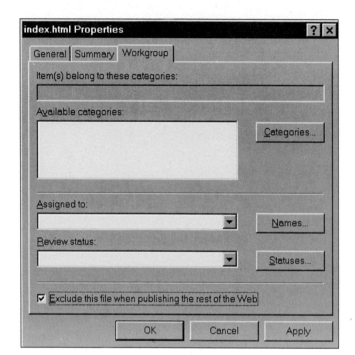

Figure 19.8
You can exclude a file from being published to the web until you are assured that the file is ready to be published.

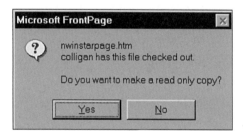

Figure 19.9
FrontPage makes it clear when the document is not yours to check out. It also lets you know who you have to contact to get the document.

Tip #92	Be sure to stress to your team the importance of checking a document back in after it has been edited. It is very frustrating to find that someone who has gone home for the day, weekend, or year has checked out the document and not checked it back in.

WITHIN FRONTPAGE WEBS

To turn on the feature (it works in all webs, including disk-based ones), simply click the Use Document Check In and Check Out option in the general tab of the Web Settings dialog box. This can be reached by selecting Tools, Web Settings. The option can be turned on and off as needed. The results can be seen in Figure 19.10.

Figure 19.10
The periods next to each document indicate that the web is using the document check-in and check-out feature. The documents you have checked out are indicated with the check icon. Documents checked out by somebody else are indicated with the small lock icon.

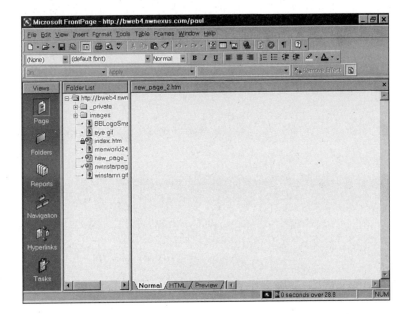

Once the feature has been turned on, every document opened by a user will result in the user being asked if they want to check out the document just requested. If he says no, he is given a read-only version of the document that can be saved under a different filename. If the user wants to simply check out a document without opening it, they can right-click the document in the folder list and select Check Out from the menu. This option is useful for preventing unauthorized edits to important pages.

Tip #93	Consider using the feature on any collaborative Web site that you work on. It provides an extra level of protection that, although not always necessary, might prove to be very useful when you least expect it.

INTEGRATION WITH VISUAL SOURCESAFE

Although FrontPage 2000 allows for checking documents in and out, it does not contain all of the functionality of Microsoft Visual SourceSafe. Visual SourceSafe also provides extensive version control capabilities that can be very powerful during a collaborative effort.

Version control is a tool that keeps copies of previous document and program versions. This is powerful because it makes it possible to return to a specific date and time's version. Mistakes made aren't often realized until later in the project and the capability to go back and undo a mistake at its point of origin is powerful.

Visual SourceSafe also provides more features to the documentation check-out process: cross-project tracking and separate access level control. The degree of power offered to the administrator is considerably more than is given with FrontPage 2000.

Visual SourceSafe only runs on Microsoft Internet Information Server on Windows NT. At this time there are no plans to port it to any other server platform.

Although the cost of Visual SourceSafe might make it appear a bit out of reach, it is often recovered in simple man hours when one problem is promptly fixed because of a revision history.

More information about Microsoft Visual SourceSafe can be found online at `http://msdn.microsoft.com/ssafe/`.

PERMISSIONS

Permissions are key when multiple users are going to access and edit different areas of a Web site. Chaos would reign if all users had all levels of access and permission to a Web site. Imagine what would happen if anyone viewing the site had permission to change it or if the graphic designer were suddenly placed in charge of which programs the server can and cannot execute. Levels of permission on all projects include no access at all, browsing authority only, authoring authority, and the ability to administer the site. Permissions can be set on the level of the user, group, or computer.

Permissions can also be utilized to give a small audience browsing access to a site that you don't yet want open to the general audience. This is very useful when performing alpha or beta tests on your site.

Although the server administrator always has the final word on site permissions, FrontPage offers an interface for granting permission that can do much of the server administration work without requiring other server administration knowledge.

If your Web site is located on a third-party server that you have limited access to the controls for, the capability to set and change permissions from FrontPage may be the only permission control you have on your project.

It is important to note that the level of permission control you get from FrontPage 2000 on a web is based on decisions made by the server administrator. Some of the capabilities described later might not be available to you if your server administrator has decided to prevent you from using them.

PART

IV

CH

19

Tip #94	If you are going to place your site at a third-party ISP or web hosting company, you'll want to check what level of permission control you will be given and what type of response time is promised to permission change requests. Some companies charge fees for changing permissions and others take a long time to make such changes.

ADDING USERS

Permission for individual users is given through the Users tab in the Permissions dialog box; this is reached by selecting Tools, Security, Permissions. You can add, edit, or remove a user from the list via the Users tab. You can also select what access level the user has.

ADDING GROUPS

If provided by your server, permissions can be set on a group level through the Groups tab in the Permissions dialog box; this can be reached by selecting Tools, Security, Permissions. The Groups tab enables you to add, edit, or remove a group from the list and select what access level the user has. Note that you cannot create new groups through FrontPage.

ADDING COMPUTERS

If provided by your server, permissions can be set on a computer level (identified by IP addresses) via the Computers tab in the Permissions dialog box, which is reached by selecting Tools, Security, Permissions. From this tab you can add, edit, or remove computers from the list and select what access level the computer has.

ASSIGNING DOCUMENTS

FrontPage 2000 gives you the ability to mark documents with a specific user assignment or review status. Although the markings have no direct effect on the file, the marking can be used to help the project team better understand the site's needs and requirements. By viewing either the Review Status or Assigned To report, participants in the development process have an additional view of the project status.

To assign a specific file to a specific user, click the Assigned To cell in the column of the Assigned To report; select or type in the name of the person you want to assign the document to. You can also assign Review Status to any document using the same procedure in the Review Status report. You can also assign a document or Review Status through the Page Properties dialog box's Workgroup tab (see Figure 19.11).

Remember that assignment of documents to users or the assignment of Review Status is little more than a label that has no control over who has authority to edit or delete the document. Assignment status should be used for reference purposes only.

PUBLISHING THE SITE

Publishing your site to a live server is a simple task and is explained in great detail in Chapter 16, "Publishing a Web." When multiple users are in control of different areas of content on the site, the timing and requirements of publication duties become even more important.

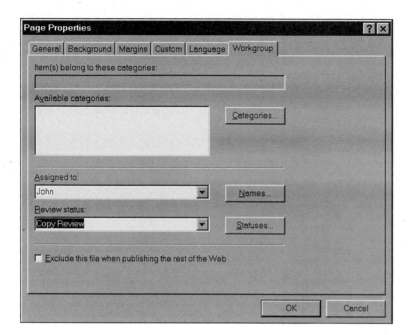

Figure 19.11
The Workgroup tab shows who the document has been assigned to and what Review Status has been assigned to the document.

TROUBLESHOOTING

The collaborative process adds a new element of problems. The more users involved in the process, the more likely the chances for them to make mistakes.

An effective collaborative endeavor requires that the person in charge of the project be able to both understand where the mistakes come from and assist in preventing them from happening again. The later chapters in this section help explain how to do just that.

DESIGNERS CORNER

Collaborative authoring adds an interesting element to the design process because it adds many people to a procedure that was at one time only completed by one. Having a team decide on (or even develop) design elements may be an invitation to disaster and should be approached carefully.

Whiteboarding a site and providing initial planning screenshots to an approval team is an effective way to handle many in the design process if such is deemed necessary. Making sure that everyone understands exactly what the site is going to look like and requiring that everyone follow the directions is a mandatory step.

The best way to get around the problems associated with group design is to divide the team in such a way that the actual design process is limited to as few participants as possible. Make a decision on who is in charge of the design and aesthetic aspects of the project and trust them to bring the project to completion.

PART
IV

CH
19

CHAPTER 20

COLLABORATING ON PAGES AND WEBS

In this chapter   *by Paul Colligan*

THE MANAGER

The Manager position has been called by other names that include, but are not limited to web master, web mistress, web architect, web facilitator, project lead, program lead, and "boss." What's important in collaborative design is that a single individual has a final say in the development process—the name for that individual is unimportant. For the rest of this text, we will refer to the position as "the Manager."

The job of the Manager is a difficult and complex one. The first role is responsibility for the growth of the site. Equally important is the role of assessing the site during the development process to bring the project back on course should it sway. This requires a firm understanding of the development process, the tools provided by FrontPage 2000, and how those tools interact with FrontPage 2000.

Typically the duties of the Manager are best performed by a single individual. While a large project may have many people in a leadership position, a single leader who heads the project still best suits a collaborative effort.

ASSIGNMENT

The first duty of the Manager is that of assignment. This includes the assignment of documents to specific categories, documents to specific individuals, specific tasks to groups, and specific tasks to individuals.

FrontPage 2000 has the ability to assign variables to specific documents and users. This helps the collaborative environment by providing a clear online presentation of who is responsible for what and what is expected from each person in the project. Variable assignment is new to FrontPage and helps the Manager distribute the project requirements as needed in an effective and manageable format.

Assignment is accomplished through the Properties dialog box for each document. To reach the Properties dialog box, either right-click the document in FrontPage and select Properties or select File, Properties in an already open document.

Figure 20.1 shows the information made available in the Workgroup tab.

Note

The Document Properties dialog box, reached by right-clicking the document in FrontPage, has fewer options than the one reached through selecting File, Properties, but both options offer the Workgroup tab, discussed here.

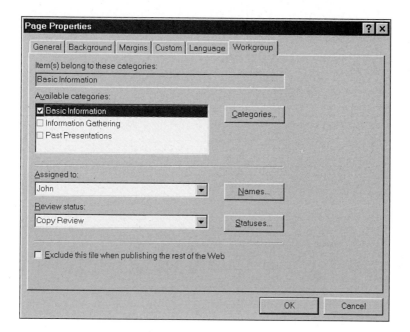

Figure 20.1
The Workgroup tab of the Page Properties dialog box lets you assign categories, users, review status, and publishing status to any document in your web.

CATEGORIES

A document can be assigned to one or more *categories (page 431)*. By assigning documents to categories, the Manager can assess and modify the workload distribution and the Developer can quickly determine which documents have been placed under their responsibility.

Category variables can be added, edited, or deleted at any time. A site-wide Master Category List is reached by selecting Categories in the Page Properties dialog box. In the Master Category List dialog box, categories can be added and deleted as necessary. There is no limit to the number of categories that can be assigned to a web site. Feel free to get as specific as you like. See Figure 20.2 for a look at the Master Category List.

The ability to assign categories to a specific document helps distribute the workload of the total project. It also helps make maintenance of the site a bit more approachable. Instead of being an unwieldy mass of hundreds (or thousands) of documents, a web can be divided into manageable categories. The site reports (discussed later in this chapter) help assess how documents are assigned, and the effectiveness of such a distribution.

DOCUMENTS

As well as being assigned to categories, a document can also be assigned to a single individual. As with category assignment, this is done in the Workgroup tab of the Page Properties dialog box. Unlike category assignment, it is not possible to assign a document to more than one individual.

PART

IV

CH

20

Figure 20.2
The Master Category List lets you assign category possibilities for the entire web site.

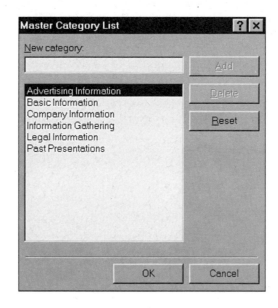

Document assignment is a powerful tool because it provides a working environment and site profile where a Developer can go directly to the site, see what documents are assigned to him, and work on the documents as necessary. It also helps the Manager see the load balance for the site.

Through this assignment, there is no constant need for direct interaction between the Manager and Developer. Often members of a project team are in different physical locations and communication is scarce at best. A pattern of document assignment enables a clear workflow process.

A Manager can choose to assign documents on a category or user level or, for a higher level of specificity, assign to both with users being viewed as a sub-category. For example, a Manager might assign document A to Mary in Marketing and document B to Mark, also in Marketing. Documents can share categorization but have different Developers assigned to them.

Like the Master Category List, a Usernames Master List is also available. This is reached by selecting Names in the Page Properties dialog box. See Figure 20.3 for an example Usernames Master List.

Note

The Usernames Master List is independent of the Users list assigned to the site reached through Tools, Security, Permissions. Assignment of a name to the Usernames Master List does not automatically grant that name access to the site.

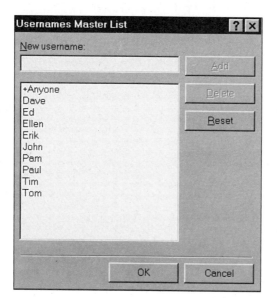

Figure 20.3
The Usernames Master List lets you assign username assignment possibilities for the entire web site.

REVIEW STATUS

The third element on the Workgroup tab in the Page Properties dialog box is Review Status. Review Status is an optional indicator for documents that require review before publication. Possible statuses include, but are obviously not limited to, Legal, Marketing, and Sales. Review Status could also include technical requirements, such as code review or proper use of color palettes (see Figure 20.4).

Like the previously mentioned master lists, a Review Status Master List is available. This is reached by selecting Statuses in the Page Properties dialog box.

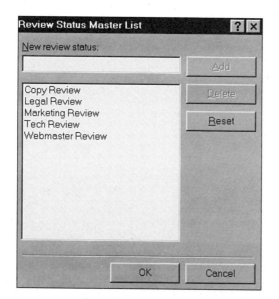

Figure 20.4
The Review Status Master List lets you review status possibilities for the entire web site.

PART

IV

CH

20

PUBLISHING EXCLUDE

The previously mentioned Category, User, and Review assignments have no direct effect on the document. They are for reference only and have no control over any specific aspect of the site. For example, James could easily edit a document assigned to Linda or Marketing might not ever read a document that was assigned to them for review. Make sure that everyone in the project understands this fact.

The check box at the bottom of the Workgroup tab of the Page Properties dialog box is the one tool that has a direct impact on the web site. When the check box is selected, the document is excluded when the web is published and can't be published until the box is unchecked. See Figure 20.5 for an example.

Figure 20.5
When selected, the Exclude check box prevents a document from being published.

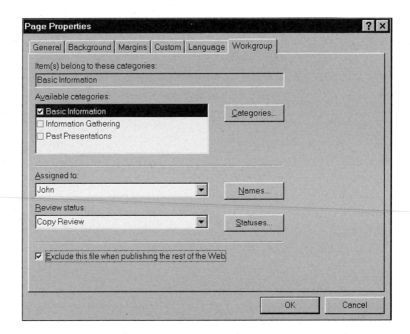

Use the Publishing Exclude option when a document needs review or an edit before it should be published. This is an important issue when holding content for legal or code review. Upon completion of the review, the reviewer can deselect the option. Make a note to the person in charge of the document to be sure to deselect the option when the task is completed.

Tip #95

It might be difficult to get a team to remember to deselect the Publishing Exclude option. This could result in a complete site that isn't allowed to be published. Before publishing the site, run the Publish Status report to determine if there are any pages that require additional work.

DOCUMENT SUMMARY

The Summary tab is available only in the Page Properties dialog box, reached by right-clicking the document and selecting Properties. You can place text in the Comments box that can be viewed (and edited) by anyone with access to the FrontPage web. Figure 20.6 shows the Summary tab.

Note

Text placed in the Page Summary tab is not placed in the HTML—unlike the Comments Component, which places the comment text directly into the HTML (although not viewable through the browser). Be careful to put sensitive information about a page in the Page Summary tab, where it can only be seen by members of the collaborative team.

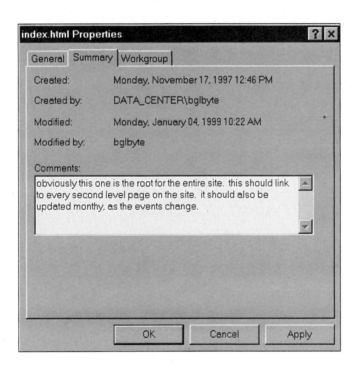

Figure 20.6
You can make comments about a specific document in the Summary tab of the Page Properties dialog box.

The Comments box for each document is a great place to present information about the document that you don't want made available in the HTML of the final document. Typical information found in the Comments box includes, but is not limited to, workflow commands, document purpose statements, editing requirements, and documentation-specific requests.

TASKS

The assignment abilities of the Manager are not limited to categories, users, and review status. A Manager can also assign *tasks (page 435)* to a web that are either assigned to a specific document or are independent in nature. By providing tasks as a common reference point,

PART

IV

CH

20

Developers can quickly determine what jobs are expected of them by examining and reacting to the Tasks view. See Figure 20.7 for an example of the Tasks view.

Figure 20.7
The Tasks view shows each task, to whom it is assigned, the priority given to the task, the document the task is associated with (if there is one), the date the task was last modified, and any comments about the task.

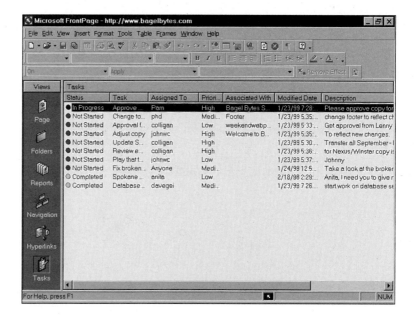

The Manager can assign a task at any time by selecting File, New, Task. The New Task dialog box will open, enabling the Manager to enter the task name, who it is assigned to, the priority of the task, and a description for it. The rest of the variables are completed automatically by FrontPage.

To associate a task with a specific document, the document needs to be open when the New Task dialog box is selected. Another option is to right-click the document either in the Folder List or Contents view and select Add Task.

Tip #96

During the site development and maintenance process, you'll find that there are a number of tasks that can be accomplished by anyone in the group. Consider creating an Assigned To variable of "Anyone" or "Volunteer" so you can place the tasks in the Tasks view with an open call to anyone who will take it on.

ASSESSMENT

The second job of the Manager is assessment of the project. One person needs to understand how the overall project is doing so that workflow can be adjusted accordingly if needed. With a team of Developers that are each focused on a specific page, file, or program, it is extremely important to have someone who concentrates on the overall project. Without such focus, a web can quickly degrade into little more than a collection of individual documents.

FrontPage 2000 provides the tools to make an assessment of a document and the review process. The program also provides a number of reports, new to FrontPage 2000, that can help the Manager understand how different aspects of the project are doing.

THE REPORTS

FrontPage 2000 provides 13 reports that can be used to assess the status of the site. Each report provides a different picture of the project's overall health. These reports are new to FrontPage 2000, providing a powerful assessment tool that wasn't previously available.

Tip #97	If you have hidden folders in your web site (and you will by default) the hidden folders will not be reported on in any of the reports. If you want to view (and report on) hidden folders, select the Show Documents in Hidden Directories option in the Advanced tab of the Web Settings dialog box, reached by selecting Tools, Web Settings.

The first report, Site Summary, acts as an overview or inventory of all of the reports and lists the total number of files, pictures, unlinked files, linked files, slow pages, older files, recently added files, total hyperlinks, unverified hyperlinks, internal hyperlinks, component errors, uncompleted tasks, broken hyperlinks, external hyperlinks, and unused themes. Double-clicking any of the lines of the report takes you directly to that specific report.

Tip #98	In all reports with elements that can be defined variably (how long does a slow page take anyway?), the definitions of each report can be changed by selecting the Report Setting drop-down menu to the right of the Report drop-down menu in the Reports toolbar. Although the default variables for each report often provide a valuable view of the site, consider manipulating the variables for a more specific reading of you site. The default values for some of the reports can be changed in the Reports View tab of the Options dialog box, reached by selecting Tools, Options.

All Files shows all the files in the web site in one long list. As is true with all of the reports, selecting any of the column headers in the report will allow you to sort by that variable.

Use this report to assess just how big your site has become. A quick glance through all of the files at once can give you a powerful overview of the project and can quickly point you in the direction of immediate site needs and requirements.

Recently Added Files shows you what elements have recently been added to the site. This is an especially powerful option for the Manager who wants to make sure that nothing has been added to the project that shouldn't be there.

If you aren't sure of the purpose or the validity of a document, open or view it to get a better idea of what it is. The *Modified By* column lets you know who placed the item into the web in the first place, should you need to take action.

PART
IV

CH
20

Recently Changed Files reports on changes made to any document in the site over a certain period of time. If necessary, the Manager can use the report to verify every change made to the site.

If the Manager's team includes an overzealous member who tends to makes unnecessary or problematic changes, the report can be used to track the individual's work. One of the biggest problems in collaborative web design is that a single user can edit key areas of the site, resulting in a snowballing effect on the rest of the web.

The *Older Files* report shows you the oldest files in the site. A Manager might choose to remove older files as a result of the report or use the information to identify which documents need updating or archiving.

Unlinked Files are files without a link to or from the file. They tend to signify either a forgotten or incorrect link or a document that should have been deleted from the site. The Manager should take time to verify the purpose of any Unlinked File and act as necessary.

Tip #99	Instead of deleting files from a site, consider creating a Deleted folder in which all documents marked for deletion could be placed.

The *Slow Pages* report can help the Manager identify potential problem files that should either be reduced in size or split into two or more files.

Remember that the default for the Slow Pages report is meant to rate the site in relation to a typical modem connection. If your project is an intranet with typical LAN connectivity, this is hardly an issue.

Broken Hyperlinks cause user frustration and inhibit site success. They are often the result of a simple typographical error but are hard to trace because the link path doesn't appear in the WYSIWYG FrontPage interface. This report quickly lists all broken hyperlinks and provides a quick repair option through the Edit Hyperlink dialog box, reached by double-clicking the specific broken link.

The *Component Errors* report lists problems with any FrontPage *components (page 24)* in the site. This report prevents the Manager from having to double-check every component in the site to make sure that they work. Just because a component has been placed in a web does not mean that it will automatically work. Most components call for additional files and variables that, if not listed, will result in the component not working.

The *Review Status* report lists every file in the site, providing a column for Review Status, if any. The Reviewed By column is marked with the person who assigned the review. Use this report to determine which files still need to be reviewed before project completion.

The *Assigned To* report, like the Review Status report, lists every file in the web, with a column for whom the document was assigned to and who assigned it.

Use the report to determine the distribution of work in the project. Sometimes a Manager might not realize that he or she has placed a large amount of work on a single individual, and the report can help identify such trends.

Categories lists all files in the web, with a column provided for category assignment. You can use the report to make sure the right pages were assigned to the right categories and review the category distribution.

Publish lists all files, their review status (if any), and their publish status. Documents that were excluded from publication are marked as Don't Publish in the report.

It's always a good idea to review the Publish report right before you think a project is completed. There might be a file remaining that needs to be reviewed (or has already been reviewed and needs to be marked accordingly).

HYPERLINKS VIEW

Another tool made available to the Manager is the Hyperlinks view. The view provides site information in terms of how every document relates to other documents in the site.

When the Hyperlinks view is opened, the home page for the site is shown in the center of the screen, with links to the left showing all documents that link to the page and links to the right showing all documents to which the page links. Selecting any document in the view provides a similar report that continues as long as the user is interested.

Use the Hyperlinks view to examine and assess the flow of the site. If a page has only one link attached to it, you might want to consider providing additional paths to the document. If a document seems to have too many pointers to it, you might want to consider taking a few away. See Figure 20.8 for an example of the Hyperlinks view.

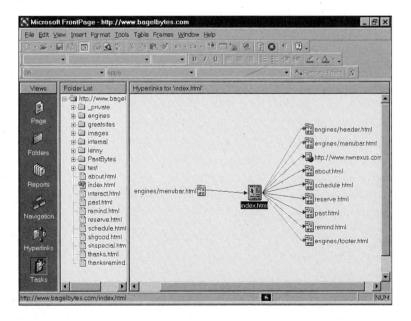

Figure 20.8
The Hyperlinks view can be used to assess how every document relates to every other document in the web.

PART

IV

CH

20

THE DEVELOPER

As the world of web design moves from simple text and graphics to interactive multimedia, not only does the need for a team-based approach to web design become obvious, it also become necessary. Very few people can provide all of the skills needed to produce an effective web site. Those who think that they can tend to have a higher opinion of themselves than they should.

The Developer in a collaborative project could be a Mac user accessing the site with the Macintosh version of FrontPage, a programmer accessing the site with a version of Microsoft Visual InterDev, or a technical writer that only feels safe using Word. Sure, the Developer might have the same system you do (it sure makes communication and training easier) but it's not always so. Sometimes the Developer might be using a third party development tool instead.

The Developer can use the same tools provided to the Manager to make his daily job a little more productive. Use of the Tasks view and reporting features is as useful to the Developer as it is to the Manager.

Tip #100	Although Microsoft Visual InterDev (version 6.0 and earlier) and previous versions of FrontPage (including the Macintosh version) can access a FrontPage web, they will not be able to make full use of all the features provided by this release of the program. Make sure to be aware of exactly which options are available to team members who aren't using FrontPage 2000.

THE TASKS VIEW

The most powerful tool for the Developer is the Tasks view. It lets the Developer quickly check the site for a list of any tasks that might be assigned to him and react accordingly. Instead of task meetings or waiting for an email note with the work for the day, a Developer can go directly to the web to see what is required/expected of him in the project.

Assigned tasks can also be generic in nature, not necessarily assigned to particular individual. The smaller the team, the more likely for a Developer to wear multiple hats. This is provided for in the program.

When the Developer double-clicks the task, the Task Details dialog box opens, giving all the specifics for the task. From there the Developer can select Start Task to open the document so the work can be done. When the Developer closes the document, FrontPage automatically asks if the user wants the task to be marked as completed. If the user says yes, the Tasks view will list it as such. If the user says no, the Tasks view will list the task as *In Progress*. See Figure 20.9 for an example of the Task Details dialog box.

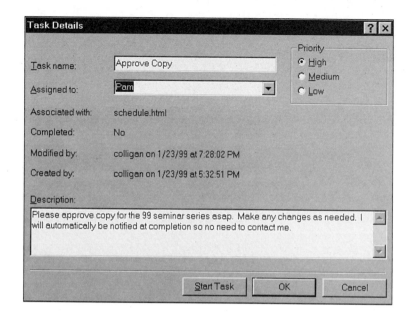

Figure 20.9
The Task Details dialog box shows the Developer exactly what is expected of him in the collaborative process.

REPORTING

The Developer can also use a number of the reports in the Reports view to determine what tasks are expected from him.

If the Developer is in charge of elements of the site specific to a report, he can run the report to determine site requirements and individual action. For example, a developer in charge of making sure that the site loads quickly can run the Slow Pages report to determine which pages require action.

Developers should understand which of the reports apply to their specific tasks and should be trained in how to run the reports and react appropriately.

Tip #101	Site reports are a very new concept in web design. Experienced Developers might not immediately recognize their purpose in the development process. It is the job of the Manager to communicate the benefits of site reporting to everyone involved in the project.

DEVELOPERS NOT USING FRONTPAGE

You might be faced with Developers on the team who aren't using FrontPage. Although this provides an additional level of complexity, for the first time in FrontPage's history it is not an impossible task to accomplish.

The key to Developers working in a FrontPage web without FrontPage is the program's commitment to 100% HTML preservation. What this means is that if a document is edited by a third-party program, FrontPage will not re-edit the HTML to make it work inside the system. A Developer could edit a page inside a web with any program (including Notepad) and expect it to remain as edited.

If development work in a FrontPage web is going to be done without FrontPage as the proprietary editor, you should use the Recalculate Hyperlinks option on a regular basis. Recalculating hyperlinks makes FrontPage aware of all the files in the web so it can act and report accordingly.

Tip #102	You do not want to recalculate hyperlinks when any part of the site is being edited by any of the Developers, as it might not provide a complete view of the site.

COMMUNICATION AND DISCUSSION OPTIONS

Obviously telephone calls and email notes are legitimate discussion options between team members. Their effectiveness is not questioned and we won't try to sway you from using them.

There are other communication and discussion options provided by FrontPage 2000 that are even more effective to communication in the collaboration process. The two main features are the Discussion and Subscription options provided by Microsoft Office Server Extensions. In this section, we'll also examine a few additional communication and discussion options that don't require the Office Server Extensions but still make use of the tools provided by FrontPage.

Tip #103	If you haven't yet picked the development platform for your collaborative project, consider the extra features offered with Microsoft Office Server Extensions. They offer a set of communication and discussion tools that are well worth the installation and maintenance effort.

OFFICE SERVER EXTENSION DISCUSSIONS

Office 2000 Server Extensions provides a means to carry on threaded discussion about any document in the server. If the user is using Internet Explorer 5.0 or higher, pushing the Discuss button on the Internet Explorer toolbar activates discussions with *threads* that are placed and identified directly onto the document. If the user is using an earlier browser version, he can start a discussion through the Browse Web Folders option on the Office Server Extensions Start Page. Through this option, discussion will take place through a frames interface.

Discussions are valuable because they provide document-based discussions that are attached to the document for the rest of the team to see. Instead of taking the form of email notes between the Developer and Manager, a document-based discussion is open for the entire team to read and make note of. Additionally, document-based discussions don't require any additional software, making the process that much easier. Figure 20.10 shows an example of the discussions tool.

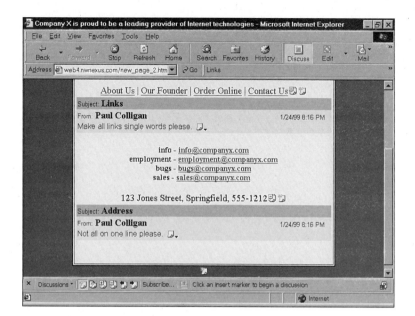

Figure 20.10
Discussions about a document can be used as a communication tool between developers on a web site.

Additional use of web discussions with Office 2000 is discussed in Chapter 21, "Collaboration and Office 2000."

OFFICE SERVER EXTENSION SUBSCRIPTIONS

Office Server Extensions also enables users to subscribe to a document in the Web site that they are discussing. When a user is subscribed to the Web page, he will be notified by email every time a change is made to it.

Subscriptions can be used as a notification service for the development team. Possible implementation options include requiring that every Developer subscribe to pages assigned to him. Whenever a change is made to the page, the owner will be notified and can double-check the page to make sure the changes were acceptable.

When combined with the document discussion options, a user can subscribe to a document he is discussing and be notified when changes have been made to the discussion. If a developer has a specific question about a document that he is waiting for an answer on, he can work on other tasks in the project, knowing that when the question is answered he will be notified.

Users subscribe to a page by selecting the Subscribe button in the web discussion interface described earlier.

PART

IV

CH

20

Tip #104

It is easy for a user to be subscribed to hundreds of pages. This would make management near impossible were it required on a page-by-page basis. Chapter 21 explains how to use the Office Server Extension Administration Page to manage subscriptions effectively.

Additional uses for web subscriptions are discussed in Chapter 21.

ALTERNATE COMMUNICATION AND DISCUSSION OPTIONS

There are a number of other ways to communicate with the development team using the tools provided by FrontPage 2000.

One option is to make extensive use of the Insert Comment feature during the web design process. Leave comments wherever you feel they're necessary in any file in the web site so that Developers will know exactly what you expect and where. Be careful to ensure that the comments are removed after they are used because, although they don't show up in the web page, they are viewable in the HTML code. See Figure 20.11 for an example of how comments can be used.

Figure 20.11
Comments can be used in pages to direct the Developers in the right direction.

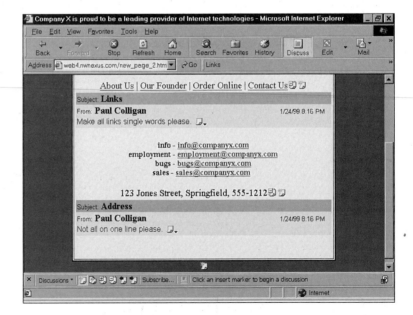

Another option is to create an Inbox directory in your web that contains short notes to different team members. Save the short notes as text files so they can be viewed by anyone with access to the development site. This enables users to communicate without requiring them to run their email program. Making the Inbox directory part of your regular communication process will encourage your Developers to open the site regularly, possibly checking the Tasks view to see if a new job is waiting for them.

You can also create a Tasks HTML file. Set the permission for the file so you are the only one able to modify it. List the requirements for the site in the page and require your team to view it on a regular basis. You might even want them to set the Tasks file as the default page in their browser.

Some people develop a single Master Tasks HTML document if they have specific requirements in assigning tasks that can't be met with FrontPage's capabilities. Place whatever requirements you have in tables in the document and require your team to treat the document as a living status report that they check in and out of daily, almost as if it were a virtual dry erase board. You'll want to use the Document Check In and Out feature to make sure that the master plan document is only edited by one person at a time.

FrontPage 2000 is considerably more than a WYSIWYG editor. The program tools provide a number of communication opportunities between the Developers and the Manager.

TROUBLESHOOTING

The reporting features of FrontPage provide one of the best troubleshooting tools available. An understanding of your site from the macro view will both provide you direction in correcting problems and prevent them from happening in the first place. Start all troubleshooting efforts from the Reports view.

It is also important to note that use of the collaboration features provided by FrontPage requires that people actually use FrontPage in the design process. There are no safeguards that will make sure that this important rule is followed outside of the program. Care should be taken to make sure that the development team understands this issue.

A document opened in any program other than FrontPage won't be affected by the Check In and Out features. For example, nothing will prevent them from editing or deleting the file from within the Windows Explorer. If you have users who plan on editing files within the Web using programs other than FrontPage, the feature becomes pointless.

The use of subscriptions and discussions also requires that users check their email on a regular basis and view sites in the discussion mode. If users don't use the supplemental tools, your collaboration endeavors are in vain. Make sure that your users know exactly what is expected of them outside of the FrontPage interface.

DESIGNERS CORNER

The Web Discussion options discussed earlier provide a very valuable tool in the design process. They provide, essentially, a virtual post-it note environment that will enable a level of commentary on the project previously unavailable.

Use the Web Discussion to make comments on the project as they arise. Have the rest of the team subscribed to their pages so that they are alert when comments are made and can react accordingly.

PART

IV

CH

20

CHAPTER 21

COLLABORATION AND OFFICE 2000

In this chapter   *by Paul Colligan*

OFFICE 2000 AND THE INTERNET

Office 2000 is Microsoft's attempt at integrating its Office applications with the Internet. Office 2000 Internet protocols and file formats are actually native to all of their applications. Every program in the Office suite is able to write its content to a Web page as easily as it could the computer screen or printer. This integration makes Office 2000 a viable Internet content creation option.

Also included in Office 2000 is the introduction of HTML as a native file format and Web folders as a file storage option. These two features help bring users unfamiliar with traditional Internet tools into the world of content creation.

Note

> Understand that the HTML generated by Office 2000 is a very advanced/hybrid/altered (pick your term) version of HTML specific to the performance issues required by each of the applications. For example, it is obviously impossible to program a spreadsheet in standard HTML and Office 2000 makes no attempt to do so. Office 2000 will often create many lines of HTML that is simply unfamiliar to people familiar with traditional HTML.

Also new to Office 2000 is the fact that FrontPage 2000 is now offered as part of the Premium version of the development suite. FrontPage was previously only made available as a standalone program, although it was always Office-friendly. This means, among other things, that thousands of desktops and users are going to find themselves with a copy of FrontPage 2000 and wonder exactly what to do with it in relation to, and independently of, Office 2000.

Office 2000 has an excellent toolbox for anyone creating Web sites with FrontPage 2000. The toolbox provides a number of tools for content creation and editing that aren't available in FrontPage. Where FrontPage is a great tool for creating *static HTML pages (page 448)*, the Office 2000 suite provides the tools for creating Web-based spreadsheets, databases, and presentations. The format is understood by the general Office suite user, enabling him or her to use tools that have been around much longer than the Internet has been popular.

Most importantly (at least in terms of this chapter), the other programs provided by Office 2000 provide an additional batch of tools for an entirely new workforce than is mentioned in other chapters of this section. It is no longer necessary to put Internet-savvy members on your content creation team.

HTML AS NATIVE FILE FORMAT

The concept of HTML as a native file format for all Office 2000 applications is an interesting one. While it is probably not as altruistic in purpose as it may sound at first, it certainly brings a new level of publishing options that weren't previously available.

In short, almost every Office application has the option to save the file as an HTML file in addition to the file format native to the application. This means that the Web browser has the capability to become the universal viewer and interface for all Office documentation. The implications of this are discussed later in this chapter.

Note

Obviously, you cannot save an entire Access database to HTML—but you can save sections and reports (discussed elsewhere).

Note

Again, a document saved in HTML by any of the Office applications might in fact be saved as a number of different files. Don't assume a single file will be saved as a single HTML file.

In the past, if someone wanted to read a Microsoft Word document or view a PowerPoint presentation and didn't have the application, she had to use a free viewer program for Microsoft that usually took some time to find (or download) and install. Often it was never worth the effort and people simply wouldn't go through the hassle. Excel and Access never had a free viewer program and there was no way to view their data short of using the original creation application.

The only other option was to have the author turn the document into a Web page and let the world view the content accordingly.

Publishing content to the Web quickly changed the face of document distribution. Instead of requiring that everyone in the office have copies of every program that might be used to generate content, all content was generated for the Web and required only one application for viewing—the browser. This very fact may help you gain insight as to why Microsoft's dedication to Internet Explorer is so strong.

Because Office 2000 provides the user the opportunity to publish directly to HTML from any of the Office applications, any Office application user suddenly has the ability to provide Web content.

Note

There are some problems that come with publishing documents into HTML. In some cases, HTML simply doesn't have the capability to present things exactly as the user prefers. In some cases this requires something as simple as changing footnotes to end notes. In other cases, the translation is simply impossible (you can't publish an entire database into HTML) and requires creativity.

The use of HTML as a native file format is a two-way street. Documents saved as HTML in any Office application can be reopened in HTML by the same application and allow the user to edit the file exactly as it was saved in the native file format. Obviously, there are

PART
IV

CH
21

components of every Office program that have no equal translation into HTML. Elements not made available to the browser are still stored in special HTML tags added to the file when opened by the proper application.

DOCUMENT PUBLISHING

The concept of *document publishing* is another feature new to Office 2000. You can save to any machine hooked up to the Internet using this feature instead of saving to a hard drive or somewhere on the corporate network (providing they have the appropriate extensions installed). All that is required? A connection to the Internet, an address, a login, and a password. There is no need for complicated files transfer options such as FTP, email attachments, or even FrontPage webs. All that is required is that you publish to the right Web folder. Figure 21.1 shows an example of Web folders in action.

Figure 21.1
In addition to printing and saving locally, most Office 2000 documents can be published to a Web folder located anywhere on the Internet.

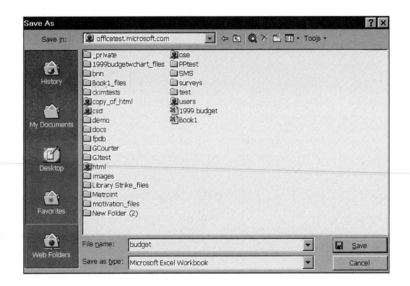

This means that in the long run training people to participate in the collaborative process is even easier than it was before. If people are only required to perform certain simple steps, you can train them in a short amount of time. Saving to a Web folder is an extremely simple step that can be taught quickly.

For example, an administrative assistant whose job it is to print a weekly report can be taught to not only print the document to the printer for the office but publish the document to the intranet via Web folders. You just made that administrative assistant a web documentation specialist and added a new member to your team.

Note

> Just because someone can publish a document online doesn't mean that he is going to do
> so correctly, or at least the way you want him to. Users who use Office 2000's publishing
> features aren't guaranteed to put things in the right places online. Carefully guide them
> through the process the first couple of times; you'll find that they'll do well after that.

OFFICE 2000 WEB COMPONENTS

Because not everything translates well directly into HTML, the Office 2000 web components (two programs) have also been added into the mix. These programs let you manipulate Access and Excel data through the Web browser, almost as if you were using the
applications themselves.

These programs are simply ActiveX versions of the very same viewer programs discussed
earlier (with a few modifications). However, unlike their earlier counterpoints, the programs
don't require an installation process. They are automatically part of the Web site.

The Office 2000 web components are not without their faults. They only work on Internet
Explorer 4.0 or later and do not port to any of the other browsers. Most importantly, they
require that the user have a copy of Office 2000 installed on the machine she intends to
view the content on. As a result, these components have little use for any application other
than an intranet application, where all viewers have the application installed on their
machine.

Figure 21.2 shows an example of the Office 2000 web components in action.

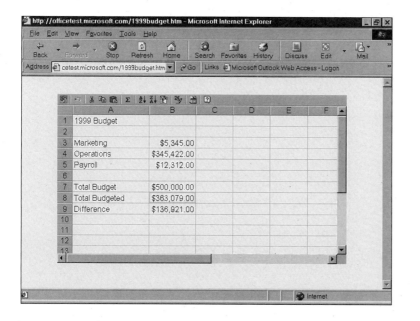

Figure 21.2
The Office 2000 web
components make
data examination
and manipulation
possible through the
Web browser.

THE OFFICE EXTENDED SERVER

Office 2000 also provides the option for an Office extended server (OSE). Office server extensions are in addition to FrontPage extensions and, unlike FrontPage extensions, can only be installed on a server running Windows NT. An Office extended server allows for Web discussions and subscriptions, two tools that assist greatly in the online collaborative process.

WEB DISCUSSIONS

One of the most powerful products of the Office extended server is the option for Web discussions. Through Web discussions (and subscriptions, discussed next), the collaborative process is made much easier. The Office server provides an additional communication vehicle for participants in a collaborative endeavor.

Any document in a Web site can be discussed through the Web discussion option. By using this tool, anyone in the group can make comments on or discuss any element of a Web site. The comments are stored in such a way that anyone viewing the site with the same discussion server can see all of the comments, as well as who made them and when they were made. A manager or editor can use the tool to help direct the author as to what should come next in the process. Other participants in the collaborative process can also use it to make comments when appropriate. Figure 21.3 shows an example of the concept.

Figure 21.3
Web discussions provide a means to comment online about any document in a Web site.

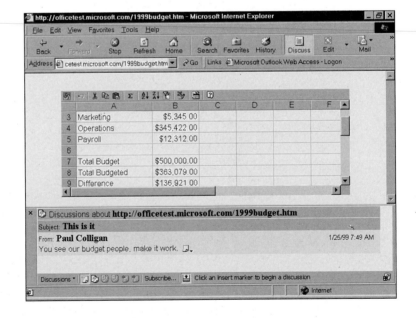

For example, a site manager could use the Web discussion option to provide edits to his project team. Each member could then edit the documents per the discussion comments. Following this type of editing process would keep everything online and accessible by any connection to the Web. Obviously this opens additional project opportunities for telecommuters and contract workers.

Consider Web discussions as a virtual sticky-note option that has the additional value of being seen only by the appropriate team members.

WEB SUBSCRIPTIONS

Web subscriptions enable a user to subscribe to a Web document so that she is notified any time an edit was made to the document (or a comment was made on the document. This automated change notification system is a valuable tool in the online collaborative process.

Although this tool will most often be used by people interested in knowing when key sites have been updated, it can also be a very effective tool for collaborative efforts on two levels.

A team member who wants to monitor whenever a suggestion has been made about her document can utilize web subscriptions as an alert system. By subscribing to the document, she can be notified by email whenever a change is made and not be required to check back in to the site on a daily basis.

At the same time, a manager can use web subscriptions to monitor key documents on the Web site. By subscribing to them, the manager can be notified via email whenever a change has been made and then act accordingly.

Web subscriptions enable a site monitoring aspect that once required the constant attention of a paid employee.

Note

It is unwise to assume that everyone on your team checks his email on a regular basis. If you decide to use subscriptions as a primary change notification system, make sure your team checks email on a suitable schedule.

COLLABORATION AND THE OFFICE PROGRAMS

The specifics of Office 2000's Web-based capabilities are discussed in great detail in Chapter 42, "FrontPage 2000 and Office 2000." This section gives specific examples of how the tools can be used in the online collaborative process.

Tip #105

Sometimes the quickest and most effective translation of Office 2000 (or any other version) content to a web is done by copying the content in the Office application and pasting it into FrontPage. FrontPage also allows you to drag Word and Excel files directly into a Web page and will translate the copy on that action. If these simple steps provide the help that you need, feel free to use them.

In short, the greatest collaboration options provided by Office 2000 come from the fact that the programs provide an entirely new batch of people who can help in the design process. Although many people would be scared to pick up a new program such as FrontPage, the same people might be more than willing to assist in a project if they can use the programs they are most familiar with. Many more people are familiar with the Office environment than with any other Internet development application.

THE EDIT BUTTON

Internet Explorer version 5.0 and later includes a more expanded version of the Edit button in the toolbar. It not only enables you to edit Web pages but edit them in the application that they were originally developed in. For example, pushing the Edit button on a Web page created in Word will open the file for editing in Word, instead of FrontPage. When browsing documents through a Web browser, a simple push of the button opens the appropriate editing program and allows the user to edit from there. The implications of this tool are obvious.

Figure 21.4
The Edit button allows a simple jump from document viewing to editing.

When a document is edited via this feature, all that is required to save the document to the Web location is closing the program. Internet Explorer saves the file and reopens it in the browser.

The Edit button makes the collaborative process even easier. There is no need for everyone in a team to run things from the FrontPage interface. Although it is easier that it has ever been, it is still an interface that the general public is unfamiliar with. For example, a copy editor can walk through a Web site page by page and upon need for edit make the appropriate action with the simple click of a button. There is no need to require that the editor use FrontPage.

THEMES

With FrontPage 98 came the introduction of *themes*—a common pattern of fonts and graphics that enable an entire Web site to have a common look and feel. Themes are not utilized (or appreciated) by every FrontPage user, but their reach has been expanded in Office 2000.

All elements in Office 2000 that publish to HTML enable the use of themes in their publication. Documents published to the Web from Office can be published with themes, enabling them to have the same look and feel as the rest of the site (if themes are being used throughout the site).

If implemented properly (and if desired), themes can assist greatly in the collaborative process because they enable team members the chance to make their content look like it belongs with the rest of the site. By subjecting an Office document to themes, it can quickly look like it belongs with the rest of the site.

Tip #106	Be careful when subjecting Office content to the use of themes. They were designed to make Web pages look great but don't always translate well to Office documents. It is always a good idea to preview documents subjected to themes before they are published.

The use of themes is discussed in great deal in Chapter 6, "Working with Themes."

WORD 2000

Microsoft Word is one of the most popular and recognized applications on the desktop today. If anyone knows anything about computers, chances are good that they understand word processing. If they use a word processor, chances are good that they use Microsoft Word.

All of the people mentioned earlier are viable candidates for online content creation with Word 2000. They can complete their tasks in that program without having to spell FrontPage. They may not have the skill required to link everything or to understand the key issues of Web design, but they can be used to create site content.

Tip #107	Even today the concept of making Web pages carries a certain mystique that can be used to your advantage. You might be surprised how many people in your company might want to help with your Web project when you tell them all they have to know how to use is Microsoft Word.

Team members who create content for a Web project in Microsoft Word (or any other Office application) have two options for content publication. The first option is to teach them how to publish the document to the Web site and the second option is to skip that process and have them deliver the content to another team member who does the publishing work. The majority of the work in Web design is content creation and if the issue is covered, publication is often easy and best handled by as few team members as possible.

Tip #108	You don't have to translate the documents into HTML if you are developing an intranet where all of the users are going to use Microsoft Internet Explorer. Internet Explorer can read Word documents in the native .doc file format.

PART

IV

CH

21

Word 2000 also provides a number of Web page creation templates that can be used by content developers who need additional creation assistance. You can create *Web templates* from Word the same way you create a normal Word template. Two of the more powerful templates include the **Feedback Form** template that helps a user with the questions that are asked on a typical feedback form and the **Frequently Asked Questions** template, which helps a user put together a FAQ.

EXCEL 2000

Number crunchers love to show off their handiwork. Before Office 2000, porting Excel content to the Internet was a tedious task that was not often deemed worth the effort. Now that it is easy to save content to the Web, adding said number crunchers to an online collaborative team is always a good idea. Their charts and columns might be a welcome addition to your project.

The first means of porting Excel data to the Web comes by using the Save as Web Page option from the File menu. When the Add Interactivity box is not selected, it creates a static page of data (or a multicolored chart) that can either be published directly to a Web site or sent to someone else for later publication.

Note

Be careful not to think that Excel's Save As feature produces a single HTML file. It also often produces an additional folder of content and graphics that needs to be ported to the Web site.

The second option for Web publication, and by far the more exciting of the two, is the capability to publish Excel content to the Web with an additional interactivity element. It comes in the form of the *web components* (discussed earlier in this chapter) and adds a level of complexity to your site that you simply can't get from FrontPage 2000.

Selecting the Add Interactivity button in the Save As dialog box causes the data from the Excel spreadsheet to be published in such a way that the user can manipulate and examine the data from the Web browser. Uses for this option are many and include the capability to play with "what if" situations and to provide a means of performing online calculations. Figure 21.5 shows a simple example of the power provided through this feature.

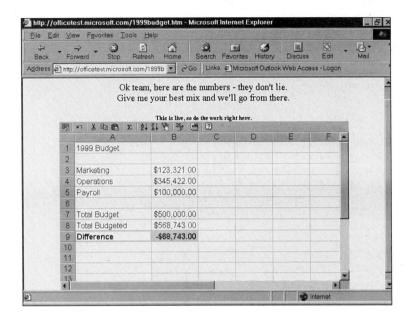

Figure 21.5
The Excel web component can be used to provide interactive "what if" scenarios to a Web site.

POWERPOINT 2000

The Publish to HTML features available to PowerPoint 2000 open an entirely new source for content to the collaborative effort. As there are many people familiar with Word who aren't with FrontPage, the same is true for PowerPoint.

Unlike Word, PowerPoint documents published to the Web translate exactly the way they originally looked. There is no need to worry about translation issues.

PowerPoint 2000 even makes considerations for the different browser versions that are used by the viewing audience. Obviously, the best possible viewing options are in Internet Explorer 4.0 or later, but PowerPoint also offers solutions for Netscape Navigator.

Figure 21.6 shows how easy it is to publish a PowerPoint slideshow to the Web.

Many companies have untold fortunes of material stored away in the form of PowerPoint presentations. From sales presentations to slideshows about the company's status, a great deal of content is sometimes available and can quickly be ported to the Web. Consider such treasures when putting together a Web project.

Tip #109

A PowerPoint slideshow integrated into a Web site can help break up the monotony typically associated with such. The Web interface provided by PowerPoint 2000 is an impressive one that is sometimes fun for users to navigate.

PART

IV

Ch

21

Figure 21.6
PowerPoint 2000 takes the different Web browsers into account when publishing to the Web.

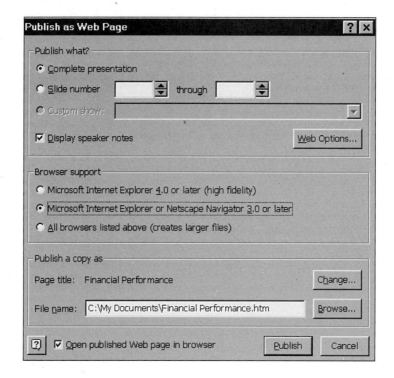

Many companies also have a number of employees who feel comfortable and are quite talented PowerPoint users. Consider bringing them into your collaborative process.

Tip #110	The HTML content generated by PowerPoint 2000 is very impressive but creates files and download times considerably larger than a standard HTML file. If download time or file size is an important issue, this must be taken into consideration.

ACCESS 2000

Access 2000 is a major advance in the Access product line. Advances include, among other things, the capability to pull and manipulate data from external database systems. The product also integrates seamlessly with Excel for reporting options and with SQL for integration with legacy systems. In short, Access 2000 is a considerably more powerful application than previous versions.

The Access web component described earlier provides a means by which to bring Access 2000 data management options to a Web browser. Through the Access web component, a user could access and manipulate all aspects of any internal database system (legacy or otherwise) through a Web browser. It also enables the use of Excel's graphing capabilities to further make a point. This reality can place information in the hands of people who either never had the opportunity to see that data or never had the tools. Access 2000 brings the opportunity for data access that simply wasn't there before.

Tip #111

> Although Access 2000 makes it possible to make incredible amounts of data available to a large audience, you still must determine whether doing as much is a good idea. User data access is often limited because not everyone needs to see the data. Other times it is limited because not everyone should see the data. Either way, make sure that the tools provided by Access 2000 don't make data accessible to people who simply shouldn't see it.

Bringing database integrators into your collaborative team enables an entirely new level of power and interactivity to your project. The limits of FrontPage and static HTML prevent any sort of realistic large-scale database integration to a system. Access 2000 is a viable option for such needs. Consider adding an Access programmer to your collaborative team and making use of the content he could bring to your final project.

BROWSER ISSUES

The introduction of Office 2000 as a viable HTML generation tool means the problem of browser compatibility issues needs to be re-examined. Issues include which browsers will run the Office 2000 web components, in addition to broader issues of the multiple platforms that might be viewing the site.

In short, every browser views things a little bit differently. Where some issues might be small, other issues can make a significant difference. Browser compatibility issues are discussed at great length throughout this book.

The most important Office 2000 content creation and browser compatibility issues center around the fact that users who create content on Office applications will be far less likely to take compatibility issues into account. It is realistic to assume that users who only create content from Office will never consider the important issues.

The solution to the problem is simple. Make sure that all content created by Office is screened for the applicable browser compatibility issues. This point is obviously moot if the site is going to be created for a specific browser (common to an intranet or extranet application).

CHOOSING THE RIGHT EDITOR

The introduction of Office 2000 as a suite of content creation tools brings a new issue to surface. Now there are multiple options of content creation; there are different programs to accomplish the same task. A decision now needs to be made—which one to use. The decision depends on what type of content is to be created.

PART
IV

CH
21

Microsoft Word is one of the most used content creation applications (Notepad and WordPad come first). The ability to create HTML content in Word is an attractive option because it is a familiar one. It is important to point out that FrontPage contains most of the design tools available in Word, but deciding which tool to use is personal. Most people tasked with choosing between the two will decide upon FrontPage because of its Internet capabilities.

On the other hand, using Excel as a development tool makes a lot of sense when working with charts and tables. The IntelliSense options are not available in FrontPage and make creation in Excel a very viable option. There are also many more classes and tutorials available for Excel than for FrontPage and it might be easier to train people in Excel.

Remember that FrontPage provides the option to import Word and Excel options directly into a FrontPage web. If that is all that is required, don't make things harder than you need to.

Using PowerPoint for content creation makes a lot of sense when trying to put together an online presentation. The automatic layout and spacing functionality provide a presentation development application much easier to use than FrontPage at this point.

In many ways, Access' Internet capabilities are simply unavailable in FrontPage. Using Access to develop the online database integration options provided by the program simply makes great design sense.

EDITING OUTSIDE OF THE CREATION APPLICATION

It is possible to edit documents in programs other than the original creation application. Assume a user tries to edit a file (either through the Edit button on Explorer or by double-clicking the document from within FrontPage). By default, Windows opens the file in the original creation application (if the program is installed on the machine). If the original creation application is unavailable, the program will open FrontPage for editing.

Be careful when editing HTML documents in programs other than the original creation application. Because the HTML created by the Office applications has code specific to each of the applications, the possibility that file edit will affect the file integrity is there.

TROUBLESHOOTING

Working with documents created by applications that don't think first in terms of the Internet will always create certain problems. Trying to translate some documents into HTML is like trying to translate a television show into a radio program. Most of the elements work, but some things sometimes just don't.

The best way to get around this problem is by making sure that everyone on your team understands what does and does not translate well to the Internet. Take a few minutes to walk them through the realities of the Internet and teach them how to make the right decisions.

If a document doesn't look right, it is often best to open the document in FrontPage and do the editing there. It simply isn't worth trying to get Office to do something that you will eventually need to do by hand.

DESIGNERS CORNER

Many of the applications discussed here do the best possible job that a machine could do for an automated translation of document data to the Internet. The transition in many cases is smooth, but there are times when someone needs to come in and clean things up. Right now there is no way to program a computer to have the formatting look the same between programs in a way that will work right every time. There are just too many places were a document that looks good in one format does not translate well to the Web. There will always be the need for the designer in the final process.

If your site makes use of occasional documents translated from Office programs, it might be wise to take a look at each of these documents individually to make sure that the desired result was achieved. If the site makes frequent use of translated documentation, it might be worth your time to examine the process by which the document is translated to ensure that things are done the way you want them to every time.

Although it is possible to use themes in Office documents published to a Web, be careful when doing so. All of the applications merely subject the HTML to the theme rules without any concern for what that may look like. Whereas a site created from a wizard or template might look fine with themes, a report generated via Access or a Word document published to the Web might not have the same success.

As mentioned previously, it is possible to cut and paste Office content directly into FrontPage and edit accordingly. Many times this approach will result in the best possible look and feel because the developer is in control of the final product instead of the corresponding application.

CHAPTER 22

MANAGING WORKFLOW AND TASKS

In this chapter

by Paul Colligan

ASSESSING

From file assignment to reporting, many of the tools and features new to FrontPage 2000 help the user better understand the status of the project she is working on. The focus on site assessment is new to FrontPage 2000 and assists greatly in the collaboration process.

As sites grow larger and larger, it is extremely important to have an accurate understanding of the entire project. When building a bridge, construction quality means little if the foundation is sinking. In site design, the quality of the graphics means little if the site has ineffective flow or the task load on any one member of the team prevents that member from performing his assigned job. Proper use of the tools provided by FrontPage 2000 gives the user an understanding of the project, which enables him or her to make proactive decisions in terms of continued site development.

SITE FLOW

There is no doubt that the Internet contains millions of pages of great content. The problem has always been finding an effective way to direct people to that content. Greater than the problem of bandwidth, technology, or crashing operating systems is the problem of site flow. Very few sites provide a clear path to the content it works so hard to present.

How many pages does someone need to click to get to the information he is looking for? Much the same way people get disgusted when they have to push 10 numbers before they can speak to a real human in a phone tree, clicking through 10 pages to get to the content they are looking for is equally as discouraging.

Site flow is defined as the means by which a user goes from one page to another. Are the possible paths well defined? Do they make sense? Is there more than one option for getting to the information he is seeking? Once the user has gone down one path, does he need to return to the beginning to go down another one?

Effective site flow comes from an effective navigation scheme and manageable and navigational depth level.

NAVIGATION

One option in assessing site navigation is the Hyperlinks view (shown in Figure 22.1). This view enables you to see each file and how it relates to each other file in terms of links from and to the document.

Hyperlinks view lists each document and folder in the Web on the left side of the screen. To assess how any document relates to the rest of the Web, select the document from the folder list. The view shows the document in the middle of the screen with documents that link to the item on the left and items the document links to on the right. Selecting the plus symbol on any of the documents in the screen results in the same presentation for that document. You can follow this view as many times as you'd like, placing as many hyperlinks on the screen as desired. This is shown in Figure 22.2.

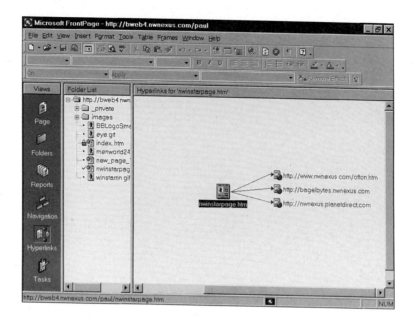

Figure 22.1
The Hyperlinks view lets you examine your site in terms of links to and from each document.

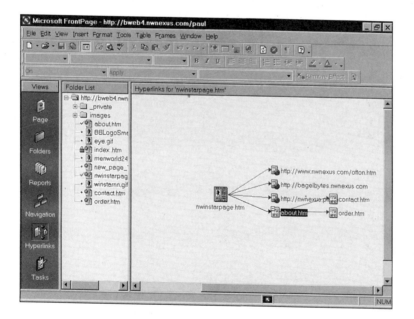

Figure 22.2
Hyperlinks view lets you examine the link relationships to multiple documents on the same screen if desired.

It is important to examine the possible paths to each document in the site when assessing the navigation options on your site. If a document has only one path to it, the chances for a user finding that document are greatly diminished. The power of hyperlinked text is in the fact that is nonlinear, allowing the user to approach the text however he wants to.

Tip #112

It is a good idea to have at least two paths to every document in your site. People aren't guaranteed to follow any specific direction so providing multiple roads will help increase chances that a user will find what they are looking for.

If a document only has one possible path, track back through the path and see if there are any other path options that can be offered. For example, a document could also be listed in a general page of important site documents or in a New Links section that directs users directly to documents recently added to the site.

Tip #113

Another popular site navigation tool is a Site Guide page, which provides a map or overview of the entire site for the first-time visitor.

Navigation can also be assessed through a simple examination of the Web site. Take a look at your site through a browser and consider how the first-time user might approach navigation. You can also bring in an outsider to view the site for the first time. Ask her what she thinks of the site and documents links.

Tip #114

Shared borders and the Include component are tools that can be used effectively in promoting a simpler site navigational scheme. More information about these tools can be found in Chapter 7, "Using Active Elements, Shared Borders, and Navigation Bars."

DEPTH

The depth of your site is also very important. If it takes too many clicks for a user to get to a certain document, the chances are good that she either won't take the time to do so or will get extremely frustrated in the process. Most users come to a Web site looking for a specific item and if that item is too hard to find they'll often leave quickly and disappointed.

If your site was developed using the *Navigation view (page 44)*, shown in Figure 22.3, you already have a great overview of the site depth; use the view to see just how deep the site goes. There is no way to view a site in Navigation view unless it was created under that view.

If you didn't build your site in Navigation view, you'll have to assess the site depth on your own. You can use the Hyperlinks view mentioned previously to some success, but effective assessment requires an understanding of the site that, at this point, can only be reached by clicking your way through the site.

Tip #115

One good way to manage site depth is to put each level in a new folder on the site. You'll quickly be able to determine how deep a site is if you follow this design process from the beginning.

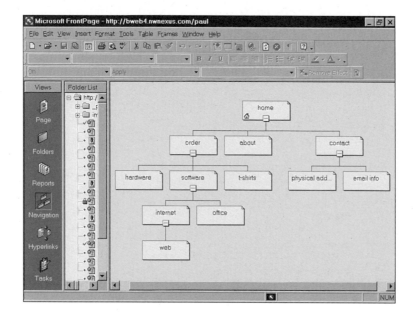

Figure 22.3
Navigation view quickly lets you see how many documents are required to get to any particular item on your site.

There is no need for a site to become too deep. FrontPage's capability to rewrite paths on the file makes site reorganization a simple and worthwhile task. If the site has become too deep, it is time to reorganize the site navigation.

TASK LOAD

A domino effect of inefficiency can take place if too much responsibility lies on the shoulders of a single individual or team. If team members are waiting on someone else to complete his part of the project, you can have a cyber traffic jam in your design process.

Cross training individuals in your team is always a good idea. Not only does it provide a certain protection from the repetition factor, but it also provides an additional workforce should one group's workload become too heavy.

REPORTING

There are 13 site reports new to FrontPage 2000. They provide an incredible overview of the site workflow and task status. Understanding how to utilize and respond to each of the reports is key to managing the development and maintenance process.

Remember that the variables assigned to each of these reports are defaults and might not necessarily represent a realistic view of your site. Make sure you adapt the variables in each of the reports to your requirements.

Tip #116	Sometimes moving a printed presentation from the electronic form of the report by individuals in the project is effective. You can use the printed form on which to edit. The change of view that comes from working with a printed report helps team members see the project differently, facilitating the understanding of the need for change and action.

SITE SUMMARY

The Site Summary report provides a basic snapshot of the site, which can be used to make a number of important decisions and assessments. It lists the basic elements of all of the reports listed above allowing you to quickly determine your next step.

Use this report as a jumping-off point for your site maintenance duties; refer to it on a regular basis as it provides a view of your *entire* site—not just a single aspect of it. You can click any of the items in order to jump to the corresponding report.

ALL FILES

The All Files report, shown in Figure 22.4, provides a way to quickly view and sort through a list of every document in the entire site. You can sort by any aspect in the report by clicking it. For example, you can click on the Type column header to sort all of the files by type, enabling you to quickly identify all non-HTML files. You can also use the feature to sort by Name or Title if you aren't sure exactly what file you are looking for.

Figure 22.4
The All Files report can be quite long. It gives a powerful, exhaustive overview of everything contained in the site.

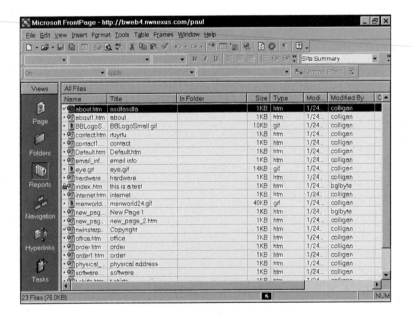

Use this view to assess a number of things, including how many types of a specific file are in the site, an overview of the site's history in the modified date field, and a list of people who have been modifying documents in the site. You can also use the report to tell just how many files there are, where they are located, and who is modifying them.

It is important to have a good understanding of just how big your site is. Depending on the site's purpose, it might be a good idea to institute a practice of archiving or deleting files after they have met their purpose. A site can sometimes become simply too big to handle.

RECENTLY ADDED FILES

The Recently Added Files report gives you the chance to see what was recently added to the site. Double-clicking any item in the report opens the document for your inspection or approval. You can sort by any of the fields in the report by clicking the field header.

If you are working with a team, chances are good you will run into an overzealous participant who is adding things that simply shouldn't be there. This can get you into trouble from a content, flow, or legal standpoint. Use this report to prevent that from happening by double checking that all recently added files are there for the right reason.

On a more serious note, a hacker might have placed an item into the web that shouldn't be there.

Tip #117	Don't assume that HTML files can't contain viruses or other forms of malicious code. They can call viruses from an outside source; scripts in the file can contain malicious code as well. If a suspicious file has been added to your Web site and you are not sure what it does, consider bringing an expert in scripting or programming in to examine the file to make sure it is acceptable.

RECENTLY CHANGED FILES

Like the Recently Added report, Recently Changed Files can help you understand what changes have been made to the site and when. Someone needs to keep track of what changes have been made to the site and this powerful tool accomplishes that task.

OLDER FILES

Older Files does just what its name implies: lists the oldest files in your site. The report is useless if your site performs the role of archive and you need to keep a copy of everything. If, however, you want to maintain a site of specific size or need help weeding out older documents and files, this report is for you.

It is a common practice for many to keep a copy of everything the site has ever presented online. While this may have a certain nostalgic effect, it can create a site that is simply too large to manage. A site can quickly become tens of thousands of pages and at the same time become a large management headache. Use this report to identify older files and to determine a plan for them.

PART

IV

CH

22

Tip #118	If you need to keep an online copy of every file ever posted to your Web site, consider storing documents of a certain age in an archive file. It makes them more easily identifiable.

UNLINKED FILES

An unlinked file is an interesting problem. It identifies either a file no longer needed or a file that can't be reached because it is missing an important link to it. The first problem requires either deletion or archiving, while the second problem requires further investigation and action. All files should have at least one link or they will not be able to be found.

Tip #119	If you know that there should have been a link to an unlinked file, chances are good that the link to the file was misspelled. If this is the case, you can use the Broken Hyperlinks report to determine potential sources for the link.

An unlisted file that shouldn't have been deleted obviously requires some sort of link to it. If it is unclear where the document should be linked from, create a task that requires the right team member to find and implement the link.

SLOW PAGES

A common problem in Web development is the developer or team who forgets that the average user will be connecting to the site over a modem (often at speeds less than optimal), instead of over the high speed network the site was developed on. A lot of FrontPage developers don't even have a network to deal with; most have likely developed their sites on the Web server that came with the program.

As some developers might have the tendency to forget the reality of the world they are designing for, the Slow Pages report is a powerful tool because it enables a quick view of all potential download speed problems in the entire site without requiring a look at each individual page.

The Slow Pages report provides a look at pages that might have speed problems when being downloaded by modem. You can choose what speed you consider a slow download to have and examine your site from that perspective.

How slow is a slow page? How long should you expect your audience to wait for a page to be viewed? These are some of the great questions of Web design that can't be answered here. You need to determine who your audience is, what it is they are looking for, and how long they are willing to wait for it. If you want a hint at what works best, look at the world's most popular Web sites (Yahoo!, MSN, Amazon, and Excite) with a stopwatch and see what they do.

Tip #120

> It is always a good idea to design your pages to load as quickly as possible, despite your audience's probable connection speed. Although you may be designing your site for a high-speed network such as an intranet, the chances are solid that users will want to access the site from a traditional dial-up line (either through the Internet or via a direct-dial connection into the network).
>
> Telecommuters and remote staff are becoming more and more common in today's workspace. You should do what you can to be ready for them. It is always easier to design with them in mind than it is to later modify a site for their use.

There are three things to do with slow loading pages: split them into pieces, decrease graphic sizes in the document, or leave the document as is.

Splitting a document into pieces is by far one of the easiest ways to solve the slow page problem. You can do the entire process in a few minutes with FrontPage's cut-and-paste capabilities. Make sure to identify and hyperlink the files accordingly.

Tip #121

> If you split a document into pieces, you want to take note of what might happen if a person enters the site from one of the middle pages. Spider-based search engines make a note of a site's every page and might, for example, send one of your users to page 4 of 7. In a multiple page document, hyperlinked notations (such as page 4 of 7) are a great navigation tool and help prevent potential confusion.

Decreasing graphic size on a page is another means of decreasing page download time. A simple tweak to a color palette or a change in file type can result in a significant decrease in image file size. Another option is to shrink the physical size of the image, which always results in a smaller file size (as shown in Figure 22.5).

Sometimes you just need to leave the file as it is. There are some pages that need every item to remain just the way it was designed. Although this is rare, it is still an option that needs to be considered. If the document is valuable enough and people know the wait is coming, it can be worth the slow load time.

Tip #122

> If you have a page on your site that takes a long time to download, it is always a good idea to make a note of that fact on all hyperlinks to that document.

Broken Hyperlinks

Broken hyperlinks are always a problem in a site of any size. A broken hyperlink can be a frustrating experience to anyone who is looking for specific information and can result in the perception that the site is sloppy.

Figure 22.5
Decreasing the size
of an image on a
page can quickly
decrease its down-
load time.

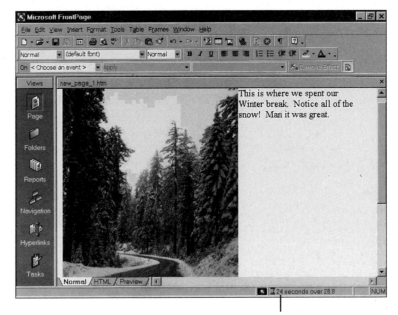

note download time

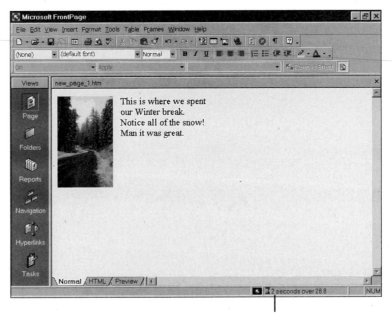

note download time

Webmasters sometimes receive an email note that says little more than "Your link to that page is down." In the past, they had no choice other than to check each hyperlink individually. In the past, third-party programs (some costing more than the retail price of FrontPage 2000) helped track down such hyperlinks. The program is now included with the program.

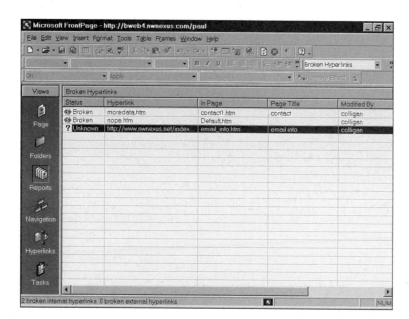

Figure 22.6
The Broken Hyperlinks report provides a quick listing of all such links—internal and external—in your site.

A broken hyperlink's source is usually either a typographical error or a file or external Web site that has been deleted. You can use the broken hyperlink path in conjunction with the All Files report to make a solid guess at what the hyperlink might be. If the problem is a deleted file, you are on your own as to how to resurrect the file.

Tip #123

> It takes a great deal of time (especially when using a modem), but be sure to run the Broken Hyperlinks report when you are connected to the Internet. If generated while online, the report also tells you what links are down outside your Web site.

COMPONENT ERRORS

As discussed previously, FrontPage *components (page 24)* provide the site design process high level of power and interactivity. They enable you to provide interactive elements to your site traditionally assigned to complicated (and expensive) programming or programmers.

FrontPage components require a number of elements that aren't as obvious as other elements in a Web site. The chances for problems are obvious and care should be taken to prevent them. Problems could be as simple as a missing file or could result from something as complicated as the server permissions not being properly set.

The Component Errors report is a valuable time saver because it identifies problems in site components without requiring that you test every element individually. It is a good idea to run the Component Errors report on a regular basis in order to identify any potential problems early.

If you find a component error on a page in your site and aren't certain what is required to fix it, consider eliminating the component from the page altogether and then reinserting it.

REVIEW STATUS

The Review Status report gives a complete overview of every file in the site and any review status (or reviewer) that is assigned to the document. Clicking any of the fields sorts the list by the variable, allowing you to quickly identify any files that still need to be reviewed.

As mentioned previously, it is important to identify potential problems in the workflow process as early as possible. One large potential problem is too much work being assigned to an individual or group. An astute manager will make frequent use of the Review Status report to identify any potential bottlenecks.

ASSIGNED TO

Like the Review Status report, the Assigned To report gives an overview of every file in the site and who it has been assigned to.

Use the report to determine if too large of a workload has been placed on an individual or group or if the same individual or group has not been performing as expected. If a single person has been placed in charge of hundreds of files while others have only a few, it might be a good idea to shift some of the workflow around.

CATEGORIES

The Categories report shows the category (if any) that every file in the site was assigned to. The report enables both an assessment of workload as well as an overview of the ratio of site content. For example, if a site seems to be more marketing content than anything else, it might be wise to encourage other departments to include their share.

The Report Settings drop-down menu in the Reports toolbar lets you view only files assigned to a specific category. Use this option to verify that documents have been assigned to a proper category.

If you make use of category assignment in your site, it is a good idea to run this report on a regular basis. That way you can make sure documents have been assigned to their proper categories. If users go directly to the category list to determine what is expected of them, it is important to make sure that categories are assigned properly.

PUBLISH STATUS

The Publish Status report shows every file in the site, whether it is flagged for *publishing* *(page 791)*, and what the review status is, if any. The report can be used to determine which work remains on the site and quickly direct you as to the review responsibility.

Tip #124	A document flagged as not to be published does not automatically mean that the required task is incomplete. A team member might have completed the required task but might have simply forgotten to switch the flag.

RESPONDING

Once the site has been assessed and the reports have been run, it is important to know how to respond to the gathered information. While the natural instinct is to immediately issue a new set of tasks and assignments, this might not be the best first step.

Responding to site status requires identifying site problems and then implementing the proper corresponding solution. Establishing a means to prevent further such problems is a good idea as well.

PROBLEMS

Problems in project workflow come from either ineffective assignments or an unequal workload. In short, problems arise when your team members are unable to accomplish the tasks at hand in the amount of time given them. It is the manager's job to keep track of the project workload as well as make sure that the assignments are effective.

You can usually identify a problem via a quick assessment of the tasks list or from the Assigned To or Publish Status reports. An individual or a group often rises to the top as having much more to do than anyone else. This unequal distribution results in others waiting for elements from the slowest team and, because of a domino effect, being unable to accomplish their tasks as a result.

A group or individual that can't keep pace with the rest of the team needs discipline, training, or additional help. Discipline is an individual matter, but FrontPage can assist with training or help.

Tip #125	Make sure your entire team understands the tools made available to them. Take a few minutes to point out to everyone on the team the tools that will have the biggest impact on their project and make sure that they know how to use them.

SOLUTIONS

Solutions to workflow and task assignment problems are found either in better training or by the task reassignment. Solutions can also be reached by creating wizards and templates that guide a team member through a process not previously understood or handled well.

Sometimes team members are hard workers with the potential to complete their requirement and are simply unaware of how to use FrontPage's tools. Web design requires a special way of thinking and understanding that is sometimes forgotten in the world of the WYSIWYG interface.

Training can take many forms. Possibilities include direct training by the manager, letting users work their way through this book (or others), and sending team members to third-party training.

Sometimes the manager must walk the team member through the fundamentals of design with FrontPage—especially in terms of the project being worked on. While there are some aspects of FrontPage a team will never use, there are an equal number of tools that, although not obvious, will greatly assist in the development process. Don't assume that the team knows and understands what has been made available to them. A few examples of using the tools often provide the team member with all of the required information and allow them to make great production advances that they wouldn't have made with a simple understanding of the program. The tutorial that comes with FrontPage, although basic, walks the user through the fundamentals of the program as well and might be a great place to start.

If you are looking for a book about FrontPage that isn't the 1200+ page tome this is, consider either *Using FrontPage* (not the *Special Edition* version) or *Sams Teach Yourself Microsoft FrontPage 2000 in 24 Hours*.

Tip #126	The quality (as well as the price) of professional training varies greatly. Take great care when choosing a vendor. The best way to choose an effective training vendor is to talk to past program participants and see what they learned.

Task reassignments, shown in Figure 22.7, can be based on a logical shifting of responsibilities to one group or another. Another option is to create virtual users and groups and that can be claimed by anyone who has the time to accomplish the task. Assigning a document to *Anyone* or to a group called *Extra* is a viable option that gives team members with time on their hands additional direction towards project completion. This practice, used in conjunction with the ability to check documents in and out, provides a smooth workflow.

Use of this tactic requires a team capable of completing each other's work. Whereas it is fine to let anyone transfer a preexisting memo to a Web site, it is not a good idea to let a temp undertake the legal review tasks on his first day.

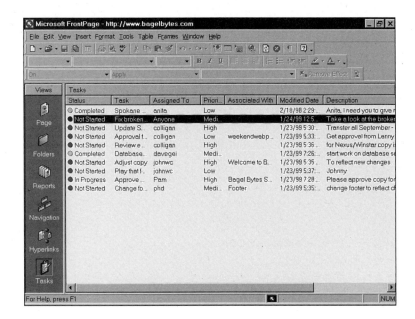

Figure 22.7
Assigning tasks to virtual users can be a subtle means of offering the task to anyone with the time to complete the project.

Wizards and templates are another possible solution to problems that may arise during the collaborative process. The team might not have the skills or time to create pages and sections from scratch. Not everyone has the eye for layout that another team member might have.

If desired, you can make page templates in FrontPage as you would any other page and simply save the file as a FrontPage template (as shown in Figure 22.8). Make sure to select the Save Template in Current Web check box (in the Save As Template dialog box). This ensures that the template is saved to the entire Web and not to your local machine.

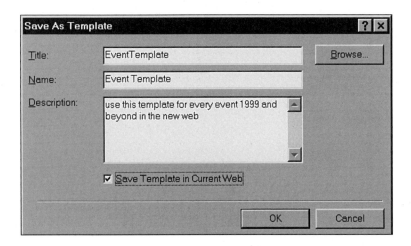

Figure 22.8
Selecting the Save Template in Current Web check box saves the template to the entire Web so that it can be used by everyone on the team.

Remember in template design to use the Insert Comment option; this further directs users regarding what is expected of them on the page. Comments are viewable only in FrontPage and are not seen when the page is viewed through a Web browser.

Tip #127

> When assigning a task that requires a template, make sure to note that fact specifically on the task assignment. There is no way to force anyone to use a template, so good training is the best way to assure that one is used.

PREVENTION

Good preventative measures for protecting against potential problems are a necessity in the collaborative process. Use of the assessment tools described earlier in this chapter is most effective if they are used to spot trends and problems that the manager can help protect against in the future.

Problems and corresponding preventative measures vary greatly from project to project. It is useless to mention all of them here. It is important to stress that FrontPage 2000's assessment tools can be used in combination with the rest of the program to provide a number of powerful preventative measures.

Some preventative measures are quite clear. An overzealous team member who tends to edit or create more than she should can quickly be identified and dealt with accordingly. Likewise, older files can be archived and broken hyperlinks can be fixed. A quick note to the team about the problem and its probable cause is often all that is needed to prevent it from happening again.

In issues of greater importance—bottlenecking, for instance—prevention comes from identifying problems before they become too big and acting accordingly. Reassigning tasks to another individual or group as needed is the typical response.

Tip #128

> Sometimes users view the task list once and don't return until they complete what they were originally assigned. It is not the practice of everyone to view the task list on a regular basis. If you tend to edit a user's task list (especially in terms of task reassignment) on a regular basis, you might want to notify the user via an additional means of communication.

NEW TASK LOAD

When assigning a new task load, assure that the recipient(s) understands the tasks and why they were reassigned. Help the team understand that they are working for the sake of the project and everything is assigned accordingly based on that need. You don't want to foster low team morale by not giving team members a reason to work hard. You don't want to encourage slow workers to continue to be so by taking their tasks away from them. Everyone should be encouraged to work their hardest and a new task load should be implemented in a way that does so.

Because of the way Web sites are so closely interwoven and the kinds of action required by developers, it is hard to balance the requirements of new task loads with the personal implications of assigning them. Good management requires effective communication skills as much as it does effective design talents.

Often the best method is to assign a few tasks at a time so that users are gently guided to the task ahead of them; it helps avoid their being too overwhelmed with the scope of the project. This obviously requires that the manager have an excellent understanding of the site needs and requirements.

Tip #129	If you choose to assign tasks a few at a time, make sure to foster a practice within your teams of looking to the tasks list on a regular basis for the latest updates. It is also a good idea to put future tasks on the list without specific user/group assignments so that the team can become aware of what is coming ahead on the project.

PUBLISHING

Excluding a file from publishing with the rest of the web is another possible solution to workflow and task problems. If it is possible to separate some of the problem issues from the rest of the general site, it is possible to publish a good chunk of the site while waiting for the problem areas to be fixed.

If possible—if, that is, it doesn't affect the site flow too much—tag the problem files as shown in Figure 22.9 and continue to publish the completed areas of the site on a regular basis.

Choosing not to publish certain areas of a Web site is always a risky undertaking. It requires that you break the site into different sections. Much the same way it is difficult to separate part of a spider web, it is hard to take away part of a Web site without deeply affecting the remainder of the project.

Tip #130	You want to be careful when marking files not to be published. Make sure that there are no hyperlinks to the file that are otherwise published. This results in broken hyperlinks.

Figure 22.9
Selecting the Exclude
This File When
Publishing the Rest of
the Web option in
the Workgroup tab
keeps you from pub-
lishing a page that
isn't ready.

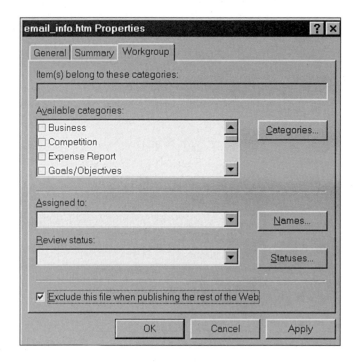

TROUBLESHOOTING

It is important to understand that proper management of workflow and tasks is one of the most powerful preventative elements you can add to a collaborative online effort. Placing someone in the position of viewing and maintaining the site on a macro level helps ensure a cohesive project. As Web projects become bigger and bigger, it is more important than ever to make sure that the site stays true to its original purpose.

It is also important to point out that a lot of things can go wrong in the management process. If team members are only given snapshots of an entire project, they simply cannot be expected to understand where their work fits into everything else and the project "big picture." As a result, a page or section can conflict with another if care is not taken to prevent this from happening. This is the job of the manager.

Take great care to make sure that your team members understand how their part of the site fits into everything else. Expect and require your team to create the sight to this understanding. If the site shares a common look and feel or lexicon, make sure that everyone on your team understands and creates to it.

If something goes "wrong" in the process of site design, the most common sources are either an ineffective communication of the big picture to team members or an ineffective big picture in the first place. You either didn't explain what you needed or didn't have something worth explaining.

If your site woes are determined to be a result of poor communication, find a means to better present the issues at hand. Sometimes this requires the much dreaded physical meeting but sometimes it can take the form of a note to the group or a one on one conversation with everyone on the team to better walk people through what is expected of them. When communicating to your team what is expected of them, or more importantly, what they have been doing wrong, remember the KISS principle: Keep It Simple, Stupid (or Silly).

If your problems are in fact a poor site design or purpose, you should first stop the team from going any further. There is no reason for them to continue going in the wrong direction, even if you have to pay them for a full day's work. As quickly as possible, reform the site to do what you now realize it needs to do and get back to work.

If you do have to redesign the purpose, flow, or mission statement for the site, consider getting help from your team. As they participated in the process of getting you to the point of realizing that you were heading in the wrong direction, they might be able to help point you in the right one as well.

DESIGNERS CORNER

If you previously found yourself in a position of Web designer and have now found yourself in a position managing a team of developers, there are two courses of action you can take. Your first choice is to humbly take on your new position and pat yourself on the back for advancing in the world. If, on the other hand, you need to continue being the designer that you were in the midst of your new role as manager, there is a way to do both.

There is no rule that prevents a manager from designing the templates to be used by the team. There is also nothing preventing the same manager from designing a site theme or even Web shells and bringing the team in to "fill in the blanks." Not everyone might have the eye for design that you do and designing the basic building blocks for the project that your team must take on is not always the worst idea.

It is important to point out that some designers have a messiah complex and feel that they need to do everything on a project, despite team size. This can often cause all sorts of problems and is something you want to be careful not to do. If you have been given a team of people to work with, make sure to make use of this valuable resource. You'll find that your team is more valuable to the project than FrontPage will ever be.

CHAPTER 23

DEVELOPING TEAM-BASED INTERNET, INTRANET, AND EXTRANET SITES

In this chapter

by Paul Colligan

DEVELOPING THE TEAM

Putting together the right team is key to any collaborative effort. The right team is made up of willing participants with the talents that enable them to get the job done.

More than anything else, developing the team requires a solid understanding of the project at hand. Participants should be chosen in light of their abilities in relation to the project requirements. All too often a Web site has been designed with far too many artists or programmers, without the needed qualified writers and content editors. Choose your team based on what is needed, not based on a preconceived notion of how many people should be on the team.

PARTICIPANTS

It might seem like a good idea to bring a lot of people into a Web-based project. Many decide that everyone can be a part of the project if the only thing required is access to the Web site (or even corporate network).

This reasoning is never a good idea. The same way too many cooks spoil a soup, an over-sized team can work a project into the ground. The meetings and planning sessions that exponentially multiply with the size of a group seldom do more than get in the way.

Like any other project, a collaborative Web-based effort needs to have a clear beginning and end. Effective leadership is required to move the project from concept to completion. Including everyone in the process will most likely keep both from occurring.

At the same time, beware of thinking that you need fewer people than you do. There is a common misunderstanding that just because you can, you should. Sometimes subtlety and brevity work better than any fancy graphic or layout ever can.

No matter how wonderful the tool, an understanding of what to do with the tool is always more important than having the tool. Be careful with participants who think that because they have a graphic program they are suddenly an artist; be careful also of those who believe they can suddenly program now that they have wizards at their disposal.

As mentioned in the previous chapter, FrontPage 2000's reporting features provide a number of valuable options for tracking the movement and progress of the teams. Use these reports on a regular basis to understand and react to what you participants are doing. It is a very powerful toolbox for understanding your project's status in its entirety.

TALENTS

There are seven talents required for a successful collaborative Web-based project:

- Ability to create content
- Effective layout skills
- Graphics capabilities
- Programming capabilities

- Knowledge of the data that's to be presented (and how to present it)
- Understanding of the project flow
- Management skills

A single person can obviously provide more than one talent. It also goes without saying that some talents are important enough to require multiple participants. The best collaborative team blends these talents.

Tip #131

> The ability to work with a team is an obvious but often disregarded requirement for anyone participating in a collaborative online effort. Don't assume that just because someone spends his time in front of a computer means he lacks people skills. Nothing slows a team project faster than someone who doesn't work well with others.

CONTENT

The ability to create clear and concise content is one of the most overlooked talents in a collaborative project. All too often people assume that anyone who has a keyboard in front of him can create good content for the site. This is simply not the case. Understanding what to present does not come naturally to everyone. Team members will sometimes use a Web site as a dumping ground for every piece of information available. Key elements will at other times be missing because it is assumed that "everyone knows that." Nothing frustrates a user faster than a Web site that lacks the information she is looking for.

Get someone who has an understanding of content presentation. English majors, copywriters, and communication specialists are always a good place to start. Many times it is the same people who write your marketing or training material that should be brought into the project.

The kind of content required for intranet projects can be very different from traditional copy sources. This content often contains phrasing and slang understood by the company but is Greek to the outside world. This is understandable but needs to be carefully monitored; the documents may one day be ported to a traditional Internet or extranet, which might be viewed by individuals unfamiliar with the corporate lingo. The audience for any project needs to be clearly understood before the first line of copy is written.

"Content is king" is a popular Internet catch phrase. Without good content, the rest of the site isn't worth much at all.

LAYOUT

A firm understanding of Web design layout requirements is mandatory whenever a site is being created. This is especially important in a collaborative effort; as you divide the project into manageable pieces, it will become even more important to trust that the other participants are completing their ends of the project. Someone who writes good copy or codes database searches well should not be expected to understand how their work will look on different platforms. As can be seen in the following figure, lousy layout can have the effect of overshadowing fabulous content.

Figure 23.1
Although the content might be great, lousy layout prevents the reader from ever getting to that content.

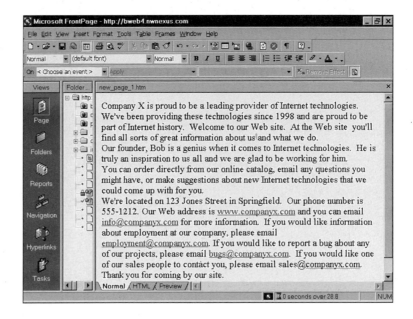

To put things simply, someone with skills for layout simply has an "eye" for it. She must understand the maximum amount of words that should be on the screen at any one time and has the ability to place them together in a way that is pleasing to the eye. She knows how to create a look and feel that flows through the entire site. It is obviously best if she has worked on a Web site before. The following figure shows how good layout can help direct the user in whatever direction you want them to go.

Often the person with the layout talent should be one of the first involved in the development process. FrontPage 2000's template capabilities can help prevent some layout mistakes made by the uninformed or the overly zealous, but those capabilities should never take the place of team talent on a large project.

The required layout skills vary based on the type of project. A project that will only be viewed by employees can be a bit more forgiving than projects presented to the entire world.

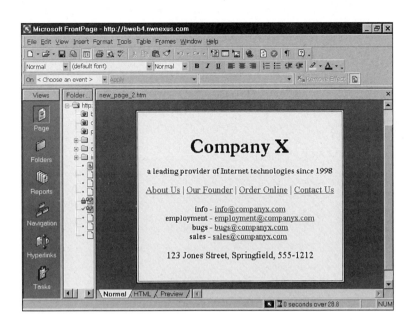

Figure 23.2
Good layout directs the eye to the content and leads the reader along. Compare this to Figure 23.1.

GRAPHIC SKILLS

Graphic skills require more than the ability to use the graphics programs available to the group. An eye for aesthetics and an understanding of the requirements and limitations of a screen-based presentation are required for anyone who is going to be put in charge of the graphics and images for the site.

It may seem that everything is different on the Internet, this is seldom the case. Many of the same skills taught to and understood by traditional graphic designers can be utilized in a Web environment. The effect of certain colors on mood or the impact gained from a certain font can help make a powerful Web project.

Go for the "eye" first if you have to decide who to assign to layout. Someone in charge of layout or content can always manipulate the users' work so that it can be presented online. The graphics chapters in this book can help walk you through that process. Some help for the art of using graphics with Web design can be found in Section VI, "Creating and Adapting Graphics for the Web," Chapters 29-34.

PROGRAMMING CAPABILITIES

There will be times in the life of a Web-based project when programming skills are required. It might not be required in the beginning, but the chances of programming becoming necessary at some point are too strong to ignore.

There is also the reality that many Web project requirements can be better performed via a program rather than via traditional HTML. If you understand the options, you can make the best decision. In short, FrontPage is not always the right tool for Web design.

It is a good idea to have someone available from the project's beginning who can help you determine whether (and when) programming will ever be needed. Even if you think that you don't need a programmer immediately, it is a good idea to have one available for both project consulting and possible later use. No one knows better than a programmer when a programmer is needed.

Scripting is the first type of programming you'll see in a Web project. In this approach, the programmer writes scripts (on either the server or client side) that interact directly with the data or the user. Typical examples of this programming type include reactions to mouseovers or direct responses to entered data. Scripting is typically accomplished in DHTML, JavaScript, or VBScript. JavaScript and VBScript should never be confused with their executable-based Visual Basic or Java counterparts.

There is also an option for *server-side scripts* (scripts that are stored and executed on the server). Such scripts result in HTML being written based on user input or other external data sources. This is typically utilized when the user is searching information in a database and HTML code has to be written on-the-fly to respond to their search. ASP is one of the most popular implementations of server-side scripting.

Because it doesn't require program execution, scripting is one of the most popular practices for Web-based programs. If your programming requirements can be accomplished via scripting, it is best to do so.

The second type of programming is more traditional. It results in individual programs that run in conjunction with the Web browser or server. These can be found in the form of traditional .exe executables, Java programs, and ActiveX controls.

When looking for a programmer, bring someone to the team who can program in Visual Basic and VBScript for Microsoft-specific projects or C++, Java, and Perl for more universal applications. Make sure you hire someone who understands both programming approaches and understands when to utilize each. If you don't know enough about programming to make a good decision, bring on board someone who does.

It is also a good idea to utilize programmers who make use of additional software tools. While programmers will at some point have to code something by hand, the assistance given by such tools almost always speeds the development process. Beware of programmers who say they don't need additional development tools—they sometimes separate themselves from the tools because they fear being replaced.

Tip #132

> Programming must be approached carefully in Web-based projects when the browser version used by the viewer is unknown. There is less need to worry when implemented on an intranet or extranet level, where you might be able to control the browser version. If you can't control your audience's browser type use, use programming that can be deployed on as broad a level as possible. You will never be able to make everyone happy all of the time, but you should do what you can to include as many as possible.

DATA MANAGEMENT

Web sites often contain tremendous amounts of data. Whether it is in the form of a database or hundreds of pages of copy, the amount can sometimes be overwhelming. Making sense of all of the data is an important skill set for successful Web design. Sometimes site data management requires more than effective layout skills and an understanding of flow.

Someone on the team needs to understand and be able to manipulate the amount of data presented at the site. The requirements are minimal if the amount is relatively small. Having a person skilled in data management is always a good idea, however, if the amount of data is as large as is typical to intranet and extranet applications.

Tip #133	Sometimes it appears as if the requirements of a Web site can be met through traditional HTML. If the amount of data contained on the site is expected to grow on a regular basis, it is a good idea to examine whether the site could best be designed and implemented via a database-driven interface. Obviously FrontPage is not the only tool utilized in such a situation.

INFORMATIONAL FLOW

Understanding (and controlling) how the information flows from one page of the site to the next is mandatory for an effective site design. This concept is discussed in greater detail in the first three chapters of this section and should be reviewed if necessary.

There should be either an individual or a tightly knit team responsible for how the project's information flows. The larger the number of people working on the project, the better chance that the content will be haphazardly thrown together. This needs to be prevented.

Someone often meets this talent need with previous site design and Web building experience. Chances are good that they will have made mistakes in the past and can bring their current knowledge to the project. The larger the site they have worked with in the past, the more experience they have with issues of informational flow.

The type of person required is someone who understands the site as an entity as well as understands how everything relates to everything else. These are certainly "big picture" people who see things in terms of the site instead of the Web page.

MANAGEMENT SKILLS

Someone must manage the project. Introducing a new leader to the perils of command when working on a collaborative Web project is never a good idea. The person in charge of the project should have some past management experience and should enjoy working with people; he or she will work with others more often than anything else. All of the clichès in this case are true—you'll want a people person with good communication skills.

Someone with previous online or computer-based management experience is especially desirable. Someone with the experience of communicating with a team via email (or other forms of electronic communication) will have an advantage. Anyone who has used a computer system to track his or her progress is in the right location as well.

DIVISION OF LABOR

Dividing the work among your team members is always easier said than done. Expecting everyone to complete his or her work in such a way that no one else in the group is adversely affected is nothing short of wishful thinking. Because the relationships between different elements in every Web are so interconnected with each other, great care must be taken in dividing the tasks between the team members.

The best way to approach the division of labor problem is to divide the project into smaller tasks—as many as you can. If at all possible, design the project so that everything comes together as late in the process as possible. Follow each of the teams as they complete their tasks and make sure that they follow some kind of schedule.

It is often wise to have content developed independently of the rest of the site. Upon completion, the content can be added to the final product without requiring constant revisions.

Putting placeholders in a Web project is no problem. Filling pages with dummy text or a database with multiple copies of the same entry is fine in the initial stages. Placing "graphic goes here" placeholders on the pages is also completely acceptable.

PLATFORM DECISIONS

Deciding what platform the final product will be created in and reside on is not an easy task. You should consider several things: an understanding of the desired Web type; the server type; the best possible physical location of the server; the type(s) of browsers expected to be used by the project audience; and any additional tools that might be part of the development process.

Platform decisions vary greatly based on the type of project being developed. Whereas Microsoft Personal Web Server is a fine platform for an intranet of a company of fewer than 100 employees, an extranet designed for a worldwide client base certainly requires something a bit more robust. The tools used in the Web and design process also help dictate the project's final shape.

WEB TYPE

The web type is the first decision that needs to be made. *Web type* is defined as the technical means by which the information is presented. This dictates the requirements for the development and deployment platform.

If your site will only use HTML, your options are unlimited and you are free to use any Web server available. If you expect to use additional features such as database integration, streaming media serving, or other server-side applications, the web type requirements become much more clear.

Tip #134

> Don't be surprised that the complexity of your site grows over a short amount of time. Many sites that start as a few short pages about a subject become multimedia presentations in a short amount of time. Consider what might happen in the future when considering web type.

SERVER TYPE

The first question you'll ask in the server type is whether FrontPage extensions will be required. If so, make sure that the final placement of the project is on a server with the extensions installed.

Obviously, installation of the server extensions makes the development and update process easier. As discussed earlier, it allows people to log into the site and make changes from their own machines. It is still one of the most powerful aspects of the program and should not be underestimated. The power provided by Office server extensions is also very attractive in light of the collaborative process.

Note

> While FrontPage extensions are available for most professional Web servers today, it is important to note that Office server extensions must be run on Microsoft's Internet Information Server, which only runs on Microsoft NT.

If you want to run other server-side applications such as *database integration (page 491)*, make sure that the server supports the tools you are looking for. If you want to use Microsoft applications on the server side, you probably need to run your site on Microsoft Internet Information Server on Windows NT.

Different server-side applications such as electronic commerce, database parsing, and media streaming work best on different server platforms. Spend some time researching your options (they change all the time) so that you can make the right decision.

Tip #135

> It is no secret that computer costs decrease on a regular basis. A platform priced in one month could be considerably less in 60 to 90 days. If you are going to host the site internally or will buy your server (and software), consider developing the project on a simple server and have it published to a robust platform upon completion.

It is important to point out that not all Web servers provide the same degree of reliability. When investigating Web servers, make sure that you either have a reliable one or a response plan for when things go wrong. On the Internet it is never a question of if you'll go down, it is a question of when you'll go down and what you plan to do about it.

SERVER LOCATION

The server's physical location isn't as obvious a decision as you might think. While many companies locate their servers at their physical location, this might not be a good idea.

If the project is an intranet and only serves people in one physical location, the server's typical location is the local network. There is often little need to place the information outside.

If the project is a traditional Internet Web site, it is a good idea to place the server where as many potential customers as possible can easily reach it with as few hops as possible. If your company is located far away from some of the Internet Network Access Points (called *NAPs*), it is a good idea to place the server in a location that takes fewer hops to a NAP. Where it might seem strange to locate your Web server hundreds (even thousands) of miles away, the speed at which your customers can connect to your server is well worth the effort.

An extranet is also best served in a location where it is as few network jumps as possible away from as many customers as possible.

In all circumstances—including the corporate intranet—it is a good idea to examine possibilities for outsourcing the server to an Internet service provider or Web hosting firm. Their connectivity most often rivals what any company can bring and the pressures of keeping hundreds of sites running can result in an uptime guarantee that the average IS staff simply can't provide. For more information, see Chapter 35, "Introduction to Web Hosting and Web Servers," and Chapter 36, "Using a Web Hosting Service."

There are also obviously security issues associated with placing your server in a location anywhere other than your own property. Spend some time considering these issues as well.

BROWSER TYPE

The audience browser question is an important one. Browser type dictates which technology can be used at the site and the addition of every type and version increases the scope of the project.

| Tip #136 | Remember that when viewing a Web site, browser version is not the only variable that dictates the way the Web is viewed. The viewer's screen size and resolution can also dictate certain elements. Don't assume that any site will be viewed in the same screen dimensions that it was designed in. FrontPage lets you view your site on a number of screen resolutions. Make constant use of this option. |

Many times an intranet can be developed for a single browser version. A corporate decision or mandate can require that anyone wishing to view the site must do so on a certain browser type and version. If this is the case, development in terms of browser type is an easier task.

Tip #137

The choice of browser is by far the most personal of software decisions. Feelings about Microsoft (pro and con) sometimes cause individuals to insist on a certain browser type at their desktop. Performance issues also often dictate browser choice. Different browser types simply work better on different systems. Just because a corporate decision has been made about a browser type doesn't mean that it is always going to be followed.

Extranet results are also subject to specific browser versions, but introduce probabilities that the site might be viewed on another platform. Users might not think that using a specific browser is as necessary as the developers think it is and approach the site accordingly. A traveling sales force might be forced to use handheld devices or someone else's platform during their travels. It is also important to note that it might not be a good idea politically to dictate what browser any customers or re-sellers use if your extranet is being positioned as a service.

Tip #138

If you are developing an extranet for a single browser version, consider making copies of that browser available to everyone who will make use of the Web. Choices include a simple Download option on the site's home page and distribution of CDs to all participants. Programs such a *Microsoft Internet Explorer Administration Kit (IEAK) (page 493)* make customization of browsers an interesting option as well.

A traditional Web site opens the possibilities of dozens of browser versions and types viewing your site. Interestingly enough, there are surfers running version 1 or 2 of their program and who simply refuse to upgrade. In addition to that reality, remember that nontraditional Web devices such as Windows CE machines, Palm Pilots, and television set top devices (such as Microsoft WebTV and the Sega Web Browser) are surfing the Internet as well. Also remember that some browser versions are available on multiple platforms including the PC, Macintosh, Linux, and more.

FrontPage 2000 does offer some help. It is not nearly enough to not require additional attention, but is a start in the right direction and offers more than the program ever did.

The Page Options dialog box's Compatibility tab lets you choose a number of variables for a specific page. These variables can affect the browser in use. You can choose to include or exclude specific features and browser versions. The browser versions are limited to Internet Explorer, Netscape Navigator, and Microsoft WebTV and should not be mistaken as a list of all possible options.

Figure 23.3
The Compatibility tab lets you define exactly which commands that page will support.

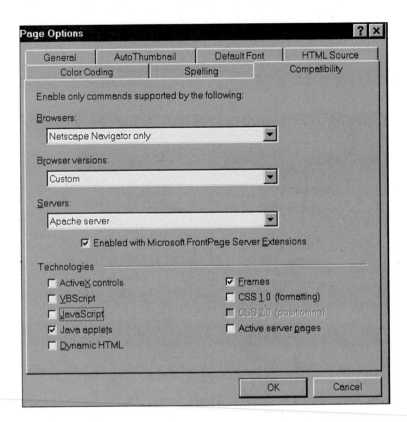

Tip #139

If you are not going to use the Compatibility option on a sitewide basis, consider designing a series of template pages with the desired options for the site and designing all pages in the site from that initial template.

Tip #140

If for some reason browser version is an absolute requirement for your Web site, code your site home page such that it permits only that specific browser version. Talk to your project programmer if you are unfamiliar with how to implement such a requirement.

ADDITIONAL DEVELOPMENT TOOLS

FrontPage 2000 is obviously not the only development tool available for Web site design. Not only are there previous versions of FrontPage to consider, but other products such as Microsoft Visual InterDev and non-Microsoft products such as Dreamweaver, Net Objects Fusion, HomeSite, and others.

You can't assume that everyone in the group will use FrontPage 2000. Some users might have previous versions of the program and others might be using the Macintosh implementation of the program. It is important to understand the implications of this and react accordingly.

What FrontPage does, it does well. What it doesn't do well requires the use of additional software.

OTHER FRONTPAGE VERSIONS

Because FrontPage allows collaboration in the FrontPage web, other versions can be used in the development process. They may not be capable of using the latest technologies provided by the new program, but will always be capable of accessing and editing site content.

The same is true for the Macintosh version of FrontPage. Although the two programs are on a different development schedule, the Macintosh version will always be able to open and edit text on any FrontPage web.

Tip #141	If you or your team members are using a previous version of FrontPage, look into the upgrade costs. They might be smaller than you expect.

MICROSOFT VISUAL INTERDEV

Microsoft Visual InterDev is an additional Internet development tool from Microsoft. The program provides for a higher degree of programming than is provided by traditional HTML. Typical uses for InterDev include database integration and Active Server Page (ASP) development. It is a powerful tool that adds a degree of programming capability that FrontPage is simply unable to deliver.

FrontPage 2000 does provide a tiny amount of database support, but you'll want to use an additional tool if you intend on doing any significant work with databases in your site. InterDev's purposeful integration with the FrontPage environment makes it the ideal tool for such integration.

Tip #142	FrontPage 2000 is designed to be as simple to use as possible. The program purposely looks and acts like other programs in the Microsoft Office suite. Microsoft Visual InterDev is meant to be a powerful application development tool that requires and understanding of programming and database integration. Don't feel that you can pick the program off the shelf and learn it much the same way you can FrontPage.

More information about Microsoft Visual InterDev can be found online at http://msdn.microsoft.com/vinterdev/, and in *Special Edition Using Visual InterDev*, 0-7897-1549-x.

MICROSOFT VISUAL STUDIO

In addition to Visual InterDev, Microsoft also has an entire line of development products that fall under their Visual Studio line. The programs include Visual Basic, Visual C++, Visual FoxPro (a database development program), and Visual J++ (a Java development program). Like InterDev, these products require a high degree of programming proficiency, but are all excellent tools and are designed to work within the FrontPage development environment.

More information about Visual Studio can be found online at `http://msdn.microsoft.com/vstudio/`, and in *Special Edition Using Microsoft Visual Studio*, 0-7897-1260-1.

OTHER WEB DEVELOPMENT PROGRAMS

If in the past you used a third-party Web development program to edit content for a FrontPage web, you know that FrontPage would often rewrite certain elements of the code and sometimes undo edits. This was a frustrating problem and generated more complaints than any other issue. Microsoft claims to have fixed the problem in this revision.

Microsoft claims that FrontPage 2000 supports 100% HTML preservation and, unlike previous versions, promises not to edit any HTML placed within the site. As a result, it is possible to use additional HTML editing programs (or any other additional Internet development applications) within the FrontPage environment. This can either by done by editing the files externally and importing them into the Web site or by opening the files directly on the server and editing them with the specific application.

While Microsoft's commitment to 100% HTML preservation is admirable, it is not yet proven. While it is possible to use other development programs during the development process, you'll always want to take great care when doing so. Regularly backing up a project is a good idea. This is especially smart if you work with third-party applications.

TASK ASSIGNMENT AND DISTRIBUTION

As discussed previously in this section, electronic task assignment and distribution is made possible via the FrontPage 2000 environment. There is no need to run a separate jobs board or to provide the team members any other kind of distribution system.

Although using a piece of Web design software to manage your task assignment and distribution system may seem a bit awkward at first, it is ideal. Placing the requirements directly into the system (and having FrontPage provide automatic linking) lets your team go to one place to gather and accomplish its tasks. Doing so also provides a level of supervision and guidance that you won't be able to find elsewhere. Once the team members are used to it, they will find themselves wondering how they ever got along without it.

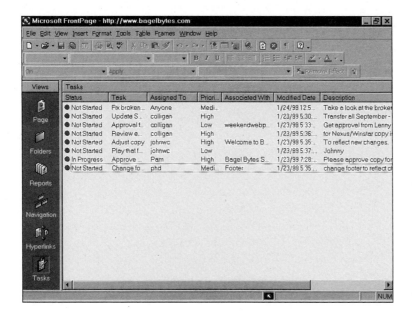

Figure 23.4
The Tasks view lets any team member get an overview of what is expected from him or her.

SERVERS

Traditionally team-based development is done in a two-phase process. The site is first built and approved on a production server in which the entire team has access. Once completed or ready for viewing by the entire world, the content from the production server is published to a launch server, to which the intended audience is given general access.

Whereas everyone in the team has access to the development server, traditionally only a few have access to the launch server. This helps prevent all sorts of potential problems. The benefits of this two-tiered approach are obvious: It prevents the audience from viewing content not yet ready for its consumption and it provides an experimental platform for the development team to preview its ideas and concepts before letting the world at them.

Use this two-tiered approach if at all possible. The benefits are plentiful and the potential problems from not implementing such an approach are obvious.

Tip #143	One benefit to the two-tiered approach is the fact the two servers act as an additional backup system. If one server goes down completely, the other one can be used to bring it back to a certain level of functionality.

PRODUCTION SERVER

The production server does not have to be a costly endeavor. The number of people accessing the site will traditionally be small and can almost always be handled on an individual user's machine. The past exception to this rule is a highly complex Web site on the server side that would require a production server capable of testing the implementation.

LAUNCH SERVER

Choosing the launch server for your final product is one of the most important decisions you can make. Who has access to the launch server is another important issue that must be decided.

It is almost always a good idea to store the launch server in a location other than the production server. This is in case there are any problems with the physical location of either.

DAMAGE CONTROL

Mistakes will be made. The more people involved in the development process, the more mistakes will be made. As mentioned earlier, it is never a question of if you'll have problems, it is a question of what you will do when you have problems.

Effective damage control comes from a gentle balance of preventing mistakes, undoing mistakes, backing up the project on a regular basis, and if possible, using some form of version control.

PREVENTING MISTAKES

There are many ways you can help prevent mistakes in a collaborative environment. They can be summed up as making effective use of the tools provided, making use of whatever tools are made available, and working with intelligent people during the process.

The most common mistake made in collaborative Web design is a user editing or deleting a file he shouldn't have. This stems from a variety of problems, which include an improper understanding of what files and tasks are assigned to him and making simple mistakes. The remedy is preventing the user from being able to edit or delete the wrong file in the first place.

The document check out process described in Chapter 19, "Establishing a Collaborative Authoring Environment," is a very effective tool in preventing this kind of mistakes. If users specifically assigned to a file check out the file, they prevent other users from altering them. They also provide a clear message as to who to contact for more information.

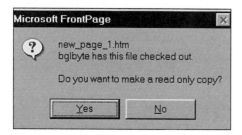

Figure 23.5
A document that has been checked out will quickly prevent an unauthorized user from modifying or deleting the file.

Another way to help prevent mistakes is to assign every document in the Web to a specific user. The second step is making sure that users pay attention to the assignments and react accordingly.

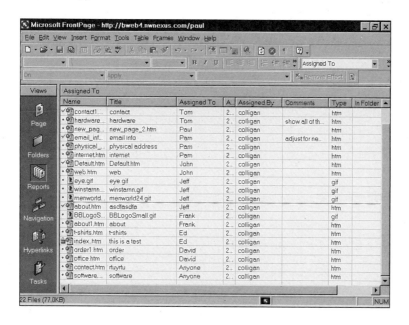

Figure 23.6
Getting a team member to check which documents are assigned to him can help prevent him from editing the wrong file.

You can also use the FrontPage 2000 security options. By making certain directories available to certain groups or users, unauthorized access is not permitted and mistakes are less likely to be made.

There is nothing preventing you from creating as many directories and webs on your site as you'd like. Consider placing everyone's work in his or her own folder so that he or she only deals with (and has the potential to damage) a small area of the Web site.

Figure 23.7
Setting access limitations to certain areas of the Web site is a sure-fire way of preventing some mistakes.

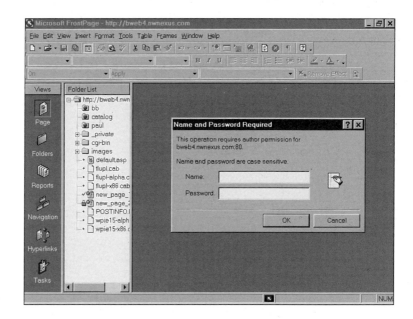

BACKING UP THE WEB

Backing up anything on a regular basis is always a good idea. Disk drives are prone to failure and the constant accessing of files typical to a Web server puts a lot of strain on any drive.

Back up both your production and launch server on a regular basis. Removable media that can be stored somewhere else—CD-ROM or tape drives, for example—provide additional archiving capabilities.

Tip #144

Consider maintaining an archive of backups for your Web site. If you make your backups on the same media, you will only have the most recent backup to return to. Many times a mistake made on a site isn't realized until a significant amount of time has passed. Without a series of different backups, you will be unable to get a backup as close to the mistake as possible.

INTEGRATING WITH SOURCESAFE

Microsoft Visual SourceSafe is one way to provide version control and change management for your site. *Version control* is the practice of making an actual copy of every change made to a project; that way any problems noticed in the future can be fixed. SourceSafe automates the entire process on any server it is running on.

If you perform collaborative work in Visual SourceSafe, all changes made at any time to the site are recorded in an exhaustive database. If a mistake is realized anywhere in the process, the exact change can be tracked and the correct modifications made.

Microsoft Visual SourceSafe requires that the site be developed on the Windows NT environment using Microsoft Internet Information Server. If this is an unacceptable platform for your project, you will be unable to use the program. It also requires proficient Windows NT knowledge. If you do not have such a member on your team, approach the program cautiously.

More information about Visual SourceSafe can be found online at
`http://msdn.microsoft.com/ssafe/`.

WORKING WITH SHARP PEOPLE

The ease with which anyone can approach Web design is often confused with the idea that anyone should be able to do it. The skill set required to make a Web page is small.

It is also sometimes difficult for people to begin working as a virtual team. Put those people in a room together and they can accomplish almost any task. Place that same group in front of computers and they are unable to perform. They're part of a group they can't see and this isn't a task for everyone.

Collaborative teams are special groups of people. They must understand the need to be self starters, realize their position in a larger picture, and know how to work in a team environment in which they might never see the face of anyone they are working with.

Hiring a good team to produce your product is as important as any technology or platform decision you will ever make. People who are unable to take on the challenge will often make mistakes that can have a disastrous effect on the entire group.

TROUBLESHOOTING

Troubleshooting on a team-based site is much more difficult than on one you developed yourself. Not only are there mistakes that might have been made, but you might not be aware of them because you weren't part of their creation. It is just hard to fix something you didn't create, or know nothing about.

In short, before you can effectively troubleshoot a team-based site, you must first view the thing before you can identify the problems to fix. This means every single page, like it or not. The role of the manager is to know the entire site so that troubleshooting site-wide is possible.

If you are unable to view every page in the site, there are a few tools that can help you with some of the biggest potential problems.

Viewing the site-wide reports discussed in the last chapter can provide a great heads-up of potential problems. This suite of reports will point in the direction of many of the biggest problems with a site. If you are unable to review a site completely, at least run all of the reports to identify the biggest problems.

The other feature of FrontPage 2000 that can help with troubleshooting on a site-wide basis is the ability to spell check an entire site. You can perform a Web spell check by selecting Tools, Spelling and choosing the entire site. If you find that a certain page has an unusually high number of spelling errors, you might want to go back and make sure that it was otherwise written to your specifics.

DESIGNERS CORNER

A team-based Web site is one of the more exciting opportunities for the *true* designer. Whereas the old paradigm of a single Webmaster required that he/she learn all aspects of the development process (including Web security and database programming), a true team environment can allow people to perform the duties they are the most skilled at.

The biggest challenge for a designer in a team environment is often in convincing others in the team to follow your design—not develop their own. Because the design process (as opposed to the skill) is so easy with FrontPage 2000, many will fancy themselves developers, regardless of their talent. Effective project management obviously also requires an appreciation (and understanding) of the role of the design in the development process.

This is why the role of the project manager is so important. This individual is tasked with making sure that everyone on the team complete the tasks assigned to them while letting others do what they do well. On any project where the design process seems to get out of control, a good manager can help bring everything back into focus.

Scripting, Dynamic HTML, and Dynamic Content

CHAPTER 24

USING FRONTPAGE'S DYNAMIC STYLES AND EFFECTS

In this chapter

You saw in the previous chapter how scripting can be used to provide on-the-fly changes to text styles and page appearance. This is, of course, an example of Dynamic HTML (DHTML), an important software technology—or collection of technologies—that helps you create pages whose structure, content, or appearance can be changed in response to user input.

Until DHTML, most such changes had to be made with custom programming at the server side of the web connection, so that any change in a page required that an entire new version of the page be downloaded to the user's machine (the client). If there were many such changes, the load on the server became very high and response times suffered. However, all the changes are made on the client machine with DHTML (assuming a DHTML-capable browser is receiving the pages). Because there is no server round-trip time for page modification, the user gets faster results and the server breathes a sigh of relief. The end result, from the user's point of view, is that the page changes its appearance and its behavior in response to his use of the mouse or keyboard. This enhanced capability to respond to users' input is the reason for characterizing this development of HTML as *dynamic*.

The specification for this extension of HTML has been laid down by the Word Wide Web Consortium (W3C), the organization responsible for standardizing the HTML language. This specification is referred to formally as the *Document Object Model* (DOM). This originated with Netscape in the first version of JavaScript used in Navigator 2.0; in 1997 it was extended by Microsoft and SoftQuad in anticipation of W3C's recommendation of a DOM standard. This recommendation is now in force; you can examine it at
http://www.w3.org/TR/REC-DOM-Level-1/.

Netscape and Microsoft have both tended to take their own approaches to DHTML, which has unfortunately led to browser compatibility problems. The behavior of Microsoft's IE4 and IE5 browsers is fairly compliant with the DOM specification, while Navigator 4 tends to use more proprietary methods of doing things. These methods, such as JavaScript style sheets, layering, and font technology, are not supported by IE 4 and IE5. It would be much preferable if both browsers rendered Web page content in exactly the same way, but so far it hasn't happened.

Note

The reference page for Netscape's version of DHTML is found at
http://developer.netscape.com/library/documentation/communicator/dynhtml/.

The reference page for Microsoft's version of DHTML is found at Netscape's
http://www.microsoft.com/workshop/author/default.asp.

FrontPage 2000 also uses Microsoft's DHTML approach. That being the case, you will notice that the DHTML effects produced by FrontPage 2000 work best (or only) in IE 4 and later. If you use these effects in a public-access Web site, where you can't control what browser is in use (as you often can with an intranet) you should create alternate Web pages for people who are not using IE4/5, and direct such people to those pages. Creating such pages is obviously more work, so you may want to think hard before liberally salting your Web site with FrontPage's DHTML effects.

The W3C Document Object Model

The W3C has this to say about the model and about DHTML:

"The Document Object Model is a platform- and language-neutral interface that will allow programs and scripts to dynamically access and update the content, structure and style of documents. The document can be further processed and the results of that processing can be incorporated back into the presented page. [The term] 'Dynamic HTML' is a term used by some vendors to describe the combination of HTML, style sheets and scripts that allows documents to be animated. W3C has received several submissions from members companies on the way in which the object model of HTML documents should be exposed to scripts. These submissions do not propose any new HTML tags or style sheet technology. The W3C DOM WG is working hard to make sure interoperable and scripting-language neutral solutions are agreed upon."

As mentioned earlier, you can get up-to-date information on the DOM spec at `http://www.w3.org/TR/REC-DOM-Level-1/`. The general W3C site for DOM is at `http://www.w3.org/DOM/`.

PART

V

CH

24

The best way to understand FrontPage 2000's implementation of DHTML is to actually use it. The remainder of this chapter examines the tools that FrontPage 2000 offers to create interesting DHTML effects. Keep in mind, however, that overuse of dynamic elements on a page can be irritating and distracting. DHTML effects are a means to an end, not an end in themselves. There should be a constructive purpose for every piece of DHTML included in your web.

Tip #145	Remember that FrontPage gives you control over browser compatibility settings so that you can disable FrontPage components that won't work with a particular browser version. These adjustments for browser types are examined in Chapter 2, "The FrontPage Environment."

USING THE DHTML EFFECTS TOOLS

FrontPage 2000 gives you a broad range of DHTML effects that are oriented to the appearance and behavior of text and images—including basic font and color changes for text, and animating the arrival of text and images on a page. The majority are created using the DHTML Effects toolbar, which is organized around mouse behavior and page loading.

UNDERSTANDING CLICK, DOUBLE-CLICK, MOUSE OVER, AND PAGE LOAD

FrontPage applies DHTML effects by tying them to three mouse events and one page event. With respect to the mouse, the effect occurs when the mouse is either clicked or double-clicked on some defined text or on a defined image, or when the mouse pointer is on top of some defined text or a defined image. In the fourth case, page load, the effect occurs when the page is loaded into the browser.

Associating these events with text or images is very straightforward—simply use the DHTML Effects toolbar.

CREATING DYNAMIC FONTS AND COLORS

These are perhaps the simplest of the effects. To create them, follow this procedure:

1. In the Page view workspace, create the text as you want it to appear in its "original" state; that is, before it is clicked, double-clicked, or the mouse pointer is over it. The text can be of any style listed in the Style box—normal, heading, and so on. It can also be hyperlink text.

2. Click anywhere in the text.

3. Choose Format, DHTML Effects. The DHTML Effects toolbar appears.

4. Click the arrow button at the right end of the On box (the box shows <Choose an Event>). A drop-down list appears, giving the four available events (see Figure 24.1).

Figure 24.1
You choose an event
from the On list box
in preparation for
linking an effect to it.

5. Select Click, Double Click, or Mouse Over, depending on the event that will trigger the font change. (Page Load is for another type of effect, which is examined later.) The event label appears in the On list box, and <Choose an Effect> appears in the Apply box.

6. Click the arrow button at the right of the Apply box. Select Formatting from the drop-down list that appears.

7. Select Choose Font from the third box of the toolbar. (It has no label, but shows <Choose Settings>.) This opens the Font dialog box.

8. Select the font face, style, color, and size you want. You can also apply font effects such as Small Caps, Strikethrough, and Hidden by selecting the appropriate check boxes.

Note

If you choose Hide as a font effect, the text vanishes when the mouse event occurs. However, if the event is Click or Double Click, it stays hidden even when you click or double-click the region containing the text. In effect, it's gone until the page is reloaded. With the mouse over event, however, the text reappears when the mouse pointer leaves its region.

9. When you have the font you need, choose OK to close the Font dialog box.

10. The affected text will be highlighted in Page view, to indicate the existence of a DHTML effect. If you don't want the highlight, click the Highlight Dynamic Effects button at the extreme right of the DHTML Effects toolbar.

11. Test the effect in Preview mode or Preview in Browser. The effect appears when the specified mouse event occurs—the original text will take on the new appearance in response to the event.

REMOVING A DHTML EFFECT

If you decide you don't want the effect, click the text in the Page view's Normal mode. Choose Format, DHTML Effects to display the toolbar. The effect and any highlighting vanish when you click the Remove Effect button.

APPLYING DYNAMIC BORDERS

You can make text borders appear and disappear just as you make fonts change. Follow steps 1 through 6 in the procedure for dynamic fonts, but select the Choose Border entry in step 7. This opens the Borders dialog box, which you learned about in an earlier chapter. Set up the borders the way you want them and choose OK. The effects appear in response to the specified mouse event. See Chapter 12, "Using Style Sheets with Individual Pages and Full Sites," for more information on using borders.

FLYING TEXT OFF THE PAGE

To create this effect, begin by clicking in the text that is to be flown. Display the DHTML toolbar; choose Click or Double Click for the event and then select Fly Out in the Apply box. You can choose the fly-out effect itself from the third list box: the direction the text flies in and whether it leaves all at once or word by word.

SWAPPING IMAGES

This method switches between two images with a click, a double-click, or a mouse over event. Follow these steps:

1. Insert the starting image into the page.

2. Click the image to select it.

3. Display the DHTML toolbar. Select Click or Mouse Over in the On box. (Note that Double Click will not apply swapping.)

4. Select Swap Picture in the Apply box.

5. Select Choose Picture in the final box. The Picture dialog box opens. Locate and select the image you want and then choose OK.

6. Test the effect in Preview or Preview in Browser. The two images will swap back and forth as the mouse event occurs.

FLYING OUT IMAGES

If you want the image to fly off the page, as was done earlier with text, you can follow the previously described steps to step 4. At that point, select Fly Out from the On box. Note that you have to choose one of the two click events for this to work; Mouse Over does not let you fly either images or text.

This causes the image to leave the page on the mouse event, just as the text did.

You can also place multiple images on one line and apply the Fly Out effect to all of them. Simply select one image and apply the effect to it; this applies it to all the other images on the line as well. If you then use the third box to select a Fly Out setting that is not By Word, all the images on the line will fly out together. However, select one of the By Word settings if you want a more exotic effect—the images will fly out one by one, starting with the leftmost.

FLYING IN TEXT ON PAGE LOAD

The Page Load effects occur, as you might expect, when the page is loaded into the browser. To use them with text, follow these steps:

1. Create the text and click in it. Display the DHTML toolbar.
2. Select Page Load in the On box.
3. There are several choices in the Apply box: Drop In by Word, Elastic, Fly In, Hop, Spiral, Wave, Wipe, and Zoom. Select one.
4. Select the effect's attributes from the third box. Some effects, such as Drop In by Word, have no attributes; the box is therefore grayed out.

The best way to get an understanding of the Page Load effects is to put some text on a page and actually use them. The Hop, for example, is more impressive when there are several words on the line rather than one.

FLYING IN IMAGES ON PAGE LOAD

This works just the same way as flying in text. Zoom, however, has no effect on the image—it simply appears. Hop, Wave, and Drop In by Word are most impressive if there are multiple images on the line. Again, experiment.

APPLYING EFFECTS SIMULTANEOUSLY TO IMAGES AND TEXT

With images and text on the same line, Click and Double Click events can be used to apply borders around both types of page element, and font changes can be applied to the text. Fly Out can also be used. The image(s) and text will be treated as a unit, unless you use the By Word attributes. In this case, each image is treated as a word.

Note that Page Load doesn't allow the effect to apply to images and text on the same line. The image will have the effect applied, but the text does not appear at all.

USING THE HYPERLINK ROLLOVER EFFECT

Text hyperlinks usually sit on a page, fulfilling a vital function but otherwise keeping a pretty low profile. With Hyperlink Rollover, though, you can make them stand out from the crowd.

The effect isn't actually applied to individual hyperlinks; it's found in the Page Property dialog box, and when turned on it affects all the text hyperlinks on the page. This is good for consistency, but it does mean that you can't have different hyperlink effects on the page.

Tip #146	If you do want different text hyperlink effects on the same page, simply apply different DHTML font effects to them.

Assuming you want consistency, right-click the page and choose Page Properties. Select the Background sheet and mark the Enable Hyperlink Rollover Effects check box. Choose the Rollover Style button, which opens the Font dialog box. Select the attributes you want for the link (Hidden is probably a bad choice) and choose OK. Choose OK again to close the Page Properties dialog box. Test the page in Preview or Preview in Browser; the selected effects appear when the mouse pointer passes over a link.

PART

V

CH

24

TROUBLESHOOTING

The most frustrating part of using the FrontPage DHTML styles and effects is that they are tailored to the capabilities of IE4 and IE5. As long as you view them in either of these browsers, they are trouble free. In Navigator, however, the results are not likely what you're looking for.

However, an effective page should behave itself in either Netscape or Internet Explorer. If the desired behavior is highly browser dependent, be prepared to create browser-specific versions of the pages and allow visitors to link from the home page (which should not be browser dependent) to the appropriate set of pages. This admittedly is a very labor-intensive and cumbersome way of troubleshooting the browser incompatibility problem; unfortunately, it is at the moment the only way to deal with it.

DESIGNERS CORNER

Dynamic HTML and the effects it makes possible have already changed the look and behavior of the Web to a considerable degree, and the rate of change will no doubt accelerate. Most creators of Web sites are vividly aware of the speed of this change, and this awareness can lead one into temptations that may be better resisted.

Such temptations come from the very natural desire not to be left behind, especially in such a competitive field as Web design. The consciousness of rapidly advancing software technology exerts considerable pressure on a Web designer to "keep up with it"—in other words, to grab whatever is newest and most eye-catching and use it on the next page she creates. The pressure increases when one reads authoritative-sounding pronouncements along the lines of "if other Web designers use dynamic fonts, DHTML animations, and special effects, and you don't, pretty soon nobody will visit your site because it won't be up-to-date and splashy enough. Everybody will be at the sites with the most bells and whistles."

Such pronouncements are simply not true. It *is* true that many people surf the Web for enjoyment and to look for "neat" sites, but vast numbers use it to look for and obtain hard, useful information. If your site has the data they are looking for, and you provide that data efficiently and quickly, you do not necessarily need an animated mailbox, pop-up windows, pages that use dissolve transitions, or fonts that change size and color. Such add-ons may actually be more of an annoying distraction than a positive attraction to your visitors.

This doesn't mean you should never use DHTML effects, of course. Simply make sure that the ones you do use agree with the context of the page, and don't use them just because they are available. Remember that you are *designing* sites and pages, not tossing them together from the most flashy elements at hand.

CHAPTER **25**

MAKING YOUR PAGES AND WEBS MORE DYNAMIC

In this chapter

by Dennis Jones

USING COLLAPSIBLE OUTLINES

Anyone familiar with the outlining tools of any high-end word processor or document-processing application recognizes *collapsible outlines*. The *DHTML (page 506)* version allows you to create an interactive outline so that clicking a topic heading displays the information under that heading, and clicking it again makes the information vanish. Headings can be nested so that a large amount of information can reside on one screen—it's invisible when it's not needed; it's visible, at the user's command, when it is needed.

Caution

> Collapsible outlines do not function in Netscape Navigator 4.0. The full text of all the lists is visible, but sublists cannot be made to vanish and reappear.

The collapsible outline in FrontPage 2000 is built around lists, either bulleted or numbered. You may remember (from your examination of lists in Chapter 4, "Developing the Basic Page: Text, Lists, and Hyperlinks") that there was an Enable Collapsible Outlines check box in the List Properties dialog box. This is the option you use.

Begin by setting up a list with at least one sublevel list (a *nested* list). Figure 25.1 shows a list with two levels of *nesting (page 514)*; when fully collapsed, it shows only the top-level headings.

Figure 25.1
This set of nested lists collapses and expands in a DHTML-enabled browser such as Microsoft Internet Explorer 4 or 5.

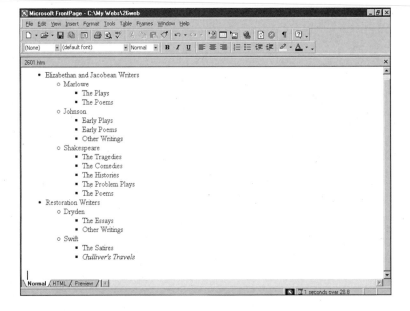

Place the insertion point in any list item in the topmost list and choose Format, Bullets and Numbering. When the List Properties dialog box appears, select the Enable Collapsible Outlines check box. Now the list(s) subordinate to any element in this list will vanish or appear as the element is clicked.

In the example, if Marlowe is selected and marked as collapsible, this attribute also applies to Johnson, Shakespeare, and the list elements under these entries. However, marking Marlowe does not make the superior list, the one containing Elizabethan and Jacobean Writers, a collapsible one. In other words, the collapsible attribute is applied only downward in a list, not upward.

Furthermore, each sublist is treated as a separate list. In the example in Figure 25.1, the sublist containing Marlowe, Johnson, and Shakespeare is independent of the sublist containing Dryden and Swift. If you wanted both of these sublists to be collapsible, you would have to enable collapsible outlines for each one. Alternatively, to make the entire collection of lists collapsible, you would simply mark the entry Elizabethan and Jacobean Writers as collapsible. Marking Restoration Writers would have the same effect because you don't have to mark the first item of a list to get the effect.

Assume that you've created the bulleted list shown in Figure 25.1 and that you've enabled collapsible outlines for the headings of the top level as well as for each top level's sublist. When you open the page in IE 4 or 5, the entire list is visible (which allows for non-DHTML browsers). All the second-level headings below a top-level heading vanish if you click that heading. Click it again and they reappear. Click one of these, and their subordinate levels vanish, and so on.

If you want the list to be collapsed when the page loads, select the Initially Collapsed check box. This check box is only available with an item in the topmost list.

USING PAGE TRANSITIONS

As you move away from bare-bones Web page presentations, the creative itch grows stronger in web authors. Why, for example, should pages just appear? Why shouldn't an author be able to do neat things with *transitions*, the way she can with slide transitions in PowerPoint?

Caution

Page transitions do not function in Netscape Navigator 4.0 or 4.5. The page changes with no errors, but no transition effect appears.

Now it can be done. Begin by opening the page where you want to apply the transition and choose Format, Page Transition to open the Page Transitions dialog box (see Figure 25.2).

Figure 25.2
You have more than 20 possible transitions (plus No Effect, which turns transitions off) to apply to a page entry or exit.

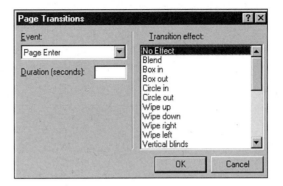

Now you're in the Event drop-down list box. It's here you can specify if you want the effect to take place on Page Entry or Exit; alternatively, you can choose Site Entry or Exit. Select the particular transition you want from the Transition Effect list box; in the Duration text box, type the number of seconds over which the effect is to take place. You can apply two different effects to the same page, one for entry and one for exit—the Entry effect takes place as the page appears; Exit, as the page vanishes from the user's browser. The Site Entry and Site Exit options create the effect when the user enters or exits the Web site via the page to which the effects have been applied.

USING DHTML LAYOUT AND POSITIONING

Until recently, web authors had to rely on some rather crude layout tools: floating alignments, paragraph alignment, and tables. These are not precise enough to satisfy graphics professionals, and it was only a matter of time until something better was introduced.

The "something better" is *CSS (page 272)* layout and positioning. These tools are actually part of the CSS specification, but they are so often considered part of the DHTML toolkit that they're examined in this chapter. This is all the more suitable because the layout and positioning tools lend themselves to creating dynamic effects through scripting.

First, however, you should be aware that the positioning code as generated by FrontPage 2000 works consistently only with the IE4 and IE5 browsers. Netscape browsers 4.0 and later understand positioning, but they are not fully compatible with FrontPage's way of implementing it. The examples in the following sections, therefore, are guaranteed to display properly only in IE4 or IE5.

Caution

Don't use DHTML effects with positioned elements—even with the Microsoft browsers. Doing so may lead to unpredictable results.

USING ABSOLUTE POSITIONING FOR LAYOUT

Absolute positioning places an element on a page at an exact position relative to the page's top left corner, using x,y coordinates. It is called *absolute* because the position of the element cannot vary. In other words, if it is at 133,345 (133 pixels right of the top-left corner and 345 pixels down) it will stay there, no matter how the browser is displaying it or what else is happening on the page.

This can be useful in several ways. One is to control the captioning of images, so that the caption does not wander off by itself owing to the settings of a user's browser. It's a good example, so this chapter goes through the procedure to see how it works.

First, you need the image and the caption that is to go with it. Insert the image into a page and type the caption as well. It doesn't matter if these two elements are in their proper places—they'll end up there.

Now follow these steps:

1. Click the image to select it. The Position dialog box opens when you choose Format, Position (see Figure 25.3).

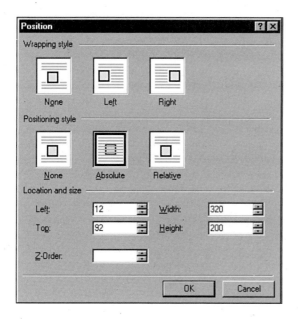

Figure 25.3
You specify absolute positioning values in the Position dialog box.

PART

V

CH

25

2. Click the icon labeled Absolute. Use the Left and Top text boxes to set the coordinates of the picture's top-left corner. The Width and Height boxes will already contain the image's dimensions, so you can leave them as they are. (Decreasing or increasing them will squash or stretch the image, respectively.)

3. Choose OK. The image appears on the page. It may cover up the caption, but don't worry—that will be fixed.

You don't actually need to specify the pixel coordinates, unless they have to be very precise. This is because you can drag an absolutely positioned element around the page to place it where you want it. To do this, move the mouse pointer over the image until it becomes a four-headed arrow; drag. Note that you can drag the image over top of other page elements, including the caption.

Now make the caption text an absolutely positioned element. Click in the text; choose Format, Position and click the Absolute icon. You can set the pixel coordinates in the Top and Left boxes now or you can leave them as they are, so as to position the caption by dragging it. Finally, choose OK.

Now there will be a position box around the text (which you don't get with images). You can detect its outlines by the eight black sizing handles that define it. If you drag these handles to squeeze the box laterally, you can force the caption to wrap. You can also enlarge the box vertically to allow room for more text. With the caption the way you want it, drag it to its position with the four-headed arrow pointer. (The pointer may be a bit difficult to find at first; it should appear when you move the mouse pointer between any two sizing handles on the invisible box boundary.)

The results might appear as in Figure 25.4. No matter how the browser is set up now, the position and layout of the caption and the image will not change.

Figure 25.4
The caption and image here are absolutely positioned. Their relationship will not change in a browser, regardless of browser settings.

Absolute positioning enables you to stack page elements on top of one another. This is called *layering* or *z-indexing*. However, you still need control of which element appears in the top layer, next layer down, and so on. You learn how to do this later, in the section "Using Z-Ordering for Layering."

Tip #147

> If you want to use a toolbar for absolute positioning, choose View, Toolbars, Positioning. This puts the Absolute Positioning toolbar in the workspace. You can use it to set top, left, width, and height values, as well as the z-order.

USING RELATIVE POSITIONING FOR LAYOUT

Relative positioning shares a basic characteristic with the ordinary positioning that occurs when you place an element on a page. This ordinary positioning is sometimes called *static positioning*. However, relative positioning also has points in common with absolute positioning in that its location can be set with Top and Left values, and that it can use z-indexing.

How, then, is relative positioning different from absolute positioning or static positioning? One difference is that relatively positioned elements are part of the text stream, as are statically positioned elements. This means that relatively positioned elements flow onto the page in the order they appear in the HTML file and that their location doesn't need to be explicitly set, as is necessary with absolute positioning.

As with absolute positioning, the element's location is controlled by the Position dialog box. Relatively positioned text elements also show a location box with sizing handles if you click the text.

The *relative* also means that relatively positioned elements are located relative to where they would be if they flowed normally onto the page. That is, the origin for relative positioning is the default location of the element—the origin it would have if it were a statically located element.

As an example, consider the image in Figure 25.5. When it was initially set to be a relatively positioned image, its Top value (its default top, if it were statically positioned) was 61. The Top value was then changed to 200 and the image moved down the page as shown, so that the top margin was then 200 pixels below the default—261 pixels below the very top of the page. This is, of course, different from absolute positioning; a Top value of 200, in absolute positioning, sets the top of the image at just 200 pixels below the very top of the page, not 261.

Note

If the results of relative positioning don't appear properly in Normal mode, switch to Preview mode.

Figure 25.5
The image here is relatively positioned, which means that it is placed with respect to its static position.

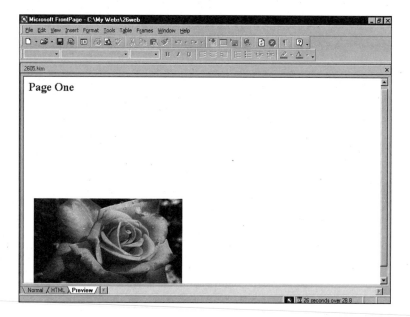

This characteristic has a side effect. If you place a relatively positioned image in text that flows around it and then change the Top or Left values away from the default values, the image will show up in the newly specified location in a browser. The problem is that the text will not fill in the image's default space; a blank white area will remain. This isn't a bug, it's just the way relative positioning works.

A corollary to this is that when you move a relatively positioned element, any elements positioned relative to it will also be moved.

Note

You can't drag relatively positioned elements around the workspace the way you can drag absolutely positioned ones.

USING Z-ORDERING FOR LAYERING

This is a simple but powerful concept. z-ordering (or z-indexing or layering as it is often called) lets you stack images in a specified order. For example, you might want three images to overlap: a street background, a car, and a person. You want the street to be farthest away (the lowest layer), the car next (the middle layer), and the person to be standing in front of the car (the top layer).

The essential thing to remember about layer arrangement is that layers are specified relative to each other, with layer zero as the foreground of the page. The layers' z-orders can be positive or negative.

Another important consideration is this: Since you presumably want your layered elements to maintain their exact relationships, it's best to use absolute positioning with layers. Trying to use relative positioning, since it repositions elements with respect to their original place in the text flow, can be very confusing.

You set the z-order via the Position dialog box (see Figure 25.3) by typing the layer value into the Z-Order text box. In the streetscape example, you would first select the streetscape image, give it absolute positioning, and then set its z-order value to 0. Choose OK and then drag the image where you want it. Repeat the procedure with the car, whose z-order is 1, and then with the person, whose z-order is 3. When they are all dragged to their desired positions, they will overlap in the order specified.

You could use negative layers, too. The person could be set at 0, the car at -1, and the streetscape at -2. You could also leave blank layers to be occupied later, by setting the z-orders to 0, 3, and 5 for streetscape, car, and person, respectively.

Text layering and mixed text and image layering is handled in the same way as the image layering example. A heading and two paragraphs, for example, can be layered to overlap in a specified order, with each paragraph and the heading being treated as a separate element. Similarly, the caption that was set beside the rose image in the absolute positioning previous example could be layered and moved to lie partly or entirely on top of the image.

Collecting Multiple Elements in One Position Box

It's already clear that positioned elements are actually contained inside a position box; with text elements, the outlines of the box are visible as sizing handles and a positioned image's sizing handles similarly define its position box.

It can be useful to place multiple elements in one box so they can be manipulated as a group. For example, you could place some graphic and text elements inside an absolutely positioned position box in order to drag them around the page together.

This is possible because a positioning specification is applied to all currently selected elements. As an example, type some text on a line and insert an image next to it. Select both text and image, choose Format, Position, and use the Position dialog box to specify absolute positioning; choose OK. Both the image and the text will move when you drag the position box. If you set z-ordering, all the elements in the box will take up the specified z-order.

DYNAMIC POSITIONING

These layout tools also lend themselves to dynamic positioning. This is because the positioning attributes can be manipulated by scripts, so that the layout of the affected elements is changed when the script runs. FrontPage 2000 does not provide methods of scripting dynamic layout, but you can insert the required code yourself. The following example gives a script that moves an image from one place to another when the image is clicked; the picture of the arch begins at pixel position 10,25 and when clicked moves to 250,125.

```
<HTML>
<HEAD>
<TITLE>Dynamic Layout Example</TITLE>
<SCRIPT LANGUAGE="JScript">
function MovePic() {
    {
    arch.style.top = 250;
    arch.style.left = 125;
    }
}
</SCRIPT>
</HEAD>
<BODY>
<DIV ID="arch" style="position: absolute; top:10; left:25px;"
onclick="MovePic();">
<img src="arch.gif">
</DIV>
</BODY>
</HTML>
```

SETTING WRAPPING STYLE

Wrapping specifies how text will flow around a relatively-positioned page element. It is similar in concept to the left or right alignments used with floating images, and makes use of the CSS property called *float*. You apply wrapping by first specifying relative positioning for the element, and then using the Position dialog box's Wrapping Style section to set Left or Right float. To remove the float attribute, choose None.

TROUBLESHOOTING

Relative positioning (page 519) may present you with some difficulties when you try using it at first. Unlike absolute positioning, it places an element at a fixed point in the text flow. Unlike static positioning, however, relatively positioned elements are located relative to where they would be if they flowed normally onto the page.

When you are editing a page in Page View, the effects of setting relative positioning do not show up in the Normal mode, only in Preview mode. This isn't a bug. In most cases, relative positioning is used for animation purposes. In cases where the initial setting might place some text off the page, and then a script is used to "warp" it onto the page, making relative positioning appear as WYSIWYG would cause this text to be uneditable.

DESIGNERS CORNER

The collapsible outline tool available with FrontPage is very useful for hiding text in sublists until the user wants to see this text. However, collapsible outlines will hide images in a sublist as well. Simply insert an image into the sublist, perhaps with its superior list item as a caption if this is appropriate. The only glitch is that the bullet for the image item (assuming you've used a bulleted list) is visible. To get around this, create a very small GIF that is the same color as the page background, specify a picture bullet in the List Properties dialog, and use this small GIF for the bullet.

On a broader scale, DHTML/CSS layout gives you much finer control over page element positioning than was possible with straight HTML. For an effective page, use the positioning tools to create a clear, consistent visual hierarchy that will be the first thing the visitor sees when the page appears. His first impression, that of text masses and color blocks as the page loads, will be succeeded by perception of individual graphics, animated elements if any, and then the words themselves along with the text hyperlinks. The positioning of all these elements should draw the eye with good contrast, good proportion, and a sense of balance among them. A page without proportion or balance will give the impression of a disorganized, messy hodgepodge of unrelated text, graphics, and links. Even if the information the visitor wants is there, she may leave in frustration before she finds it.

PART

V

CH

25

CHAPTER 26

USING SCRIPTS IN YOUR WEB PAGE

In this chapter

by John J. Kottler

SCRIPT WRITING

As the Web has evolved into a more robust environment, there is an increased need for Web site designers to control more and more the presentation of the site. In the past, interactive sites were accomplished by using simple forms and passing data from those forms to applications that ran on the Web server. The results could then be generated by an application developed in a programming language such as C, Perl, or even Visual Basic. With more current Web sites however, it is not uncommon to find yourself truly interacting with the Web page because of advancements such as Java applets, plug-ins, or ActiveX controls such as Flash, as well as the onslaught of Dynamic HTML.

Even though the use of simple forms is still appropriate today for accessing databases or other large or diverse information sources on a server, it is not effective for more simple actions such as verifying that the user input data into a field. This is not the optimal platform for simple field validation because each time the user submits data from a form, the information must be passed up to a Web server. There an application reads the data passed from the browser, performs actions such as checking that the fields are filled, and returns an appropriate message. In a world where connectivity to the Internet is not that quick, this can be a painful experience for the end user. Also, it is not quite intuitive to the user for another Web page to appear and state the errors on a previous page. In the world of Windows, the user would expect and prefer a warning message that does not interfere with their data input.

To make Web pages within a site more responsive to the end user, the Web browser developers began to incorporate client-side capabilities for performing basic logical operations and programming. The idea was that the page would react more quickly if some of the logic used to build responses on the Web server via an application were available locally within the user's Web browser. In order to create custom logical commands and programs, a language is required to instruct the computer what to do with a Web page.

BRIEF HISTORY OF SCRIPTING

When scripting was first introduced to a Web browser, it was with Netscape 2.0. Because of an increasing demand for Java in the programming community at the time, the scripting language developed for controlling actions within a Web page of the browser was derived from Java's syntax. This scripting language was quickly referred to as JavaScript because its syntax was nearly identical to Java. The key differences between Java and JavaScript were the objects that are available for access via the language. Java has the capability to create full-blown applications similar to those that you would find available for the Windows operating system. JavaScript, on the other hand, is not as feature-rich as Java; it does contain the same basic syntax for creating programmatic instructions. For example, you cannot create a graphical game using JavaScript because it does not have inherent exposure to graphics commands. Instead, you can think of JavaScript more as a macro language, or the glue that binds information on a Web page to some form of logic.

With the continuing advancement of Web browsers, Microsoft quickly acknowledged and began including client-side scripting capabilities as well. For their Internet Explorer implementation, they decided to include a more generic method for embedding scripting. If you have used any of Microsoft's other development tools, you probably know that Visual Basic and its associated language is a powerful and simple language that Microsoft embeds in many of its products. Even if the product they develop is not a programming tool, Microsoft's strategy is that all macro commands should be written using the same language. As a developer, this is a good strategy if you use predominantly Microsoft tools. This means that you only need to learn Visual Basic's language once and can instantly program almost any other Microsoft application. Therefore, Microsoft decided that this language should be made available within the Web browser as well so that these same developers can easily create Web page macros or scripts.

Fortunately, Microsoft also realized that they would need to include JavaScript in their browser in order to be compatible with many sites on the Internet that were beginning to use the language. JavaScript was not a standardized language at the time and was not open for any company to include in their products. To maintain compatibility, Microsoft developed a JavaScript-like language known as JScript. This version of JavaScript is nearly 100 percent compatible with JavaScript; veteran programmers know, however, that there are a few things that Netscape's version of JavaScript can do that older versions of JScript could not handle. This small battle has disappeared with the formation of a standard JavaScript language that has been defined as ECMA-262. If both Netscape and Microsoft browsers follow this standard for JavaScript, developers can be assured that their code will execute properly on either platform.

ADVANTAGES AND DISADVANTAGES OF SCRIPTING

You are probably thinking that JavaScript is a very powerful solution for aiding in the development of Web pages and that there are no reasons you should not be using it. It is true that JavaScript offers a variety of features, but it is also important to note that there are some things you need to consider when using any scripting language within a Web browser. Let's quickly review these advantages and disadvantages.

THE POSITIVES

There are many good reasons to implement client-side JavaScript on a Web page. One of the foremost reasons is that it is fast. Consider an example where you want to create an online order form for a Web-based store. As the user begins specifying quantities for items he wants to order, the form should update at the bottom of the screen to show subtotals, shipping charges, and a grand total for the merchandise to be ordered. In the older world of Web-based development, the user would have to enter the number of items to purchase and click a Submit button. A script on the server would then make the appropriate calculations and send the results back to the Web browser. Unfortunately, many users access the Internet through dial-up modems and a procedure such as this could take quite a long time. This would likely discourage the user and prevent him from returning to your site.

With the capability of client-side scripting, it is possible for the same user to enter information about the products that he wants to order. In this case, however, the mathematical computations for determining shipping costs and a grand total could be calculated instantaneously. With the capability for the browser to provide immediate feedback to the user without another hit to the Web server, you can quickly see how client-side scripting can be used to orchestrate more than just mathematical calculations on a Web page. It could easily update information in a Java applet, for an example, to change the color of an item to be purchased. The applet could then render a graphical preview of the item based on the information provided by the script. With script running on the client, it is possible for the browser to have more direct control over the user's experience and his computer than a remote server on the Internet.

THE NEGATIVES

Client-side scripting within a Web browser has become fairly commonplace and is certainly only going to increase as Web developers create more complex Web sites. What are the negatives of such a technology? In general, the biggest concern with client-side scripts revolves around security. Since the script is designed to run on the Web site visitor's computer, it must be downloaded to her machine when she visits the page. The easiest method for implementing this was to include the script within the actual HTML file that is downloaded to the browser. With special HTML tags that identified blocks of script, the browser could then extract the information that was programming logic and use it when necessary.

As a Web site developer, you are keenly aware that it is possible for any visitor to view your Web pages' HTML source code. Practically every browser on the market provides the capability to view the source for an HTML document or even save it locally on your computer. It is therefore equally possible for that same visitor to view the logic for the client-side scripts, since they are contained within that same HTML file. If your scripts contain proprietary logic that you want to keep secret, this is obviously a security concern. Even less obvious is the fact that a user could actually change the way these scripts act.

If a savvy site visitor decides to download a Web page and save it locally, there is no reason she cannot open that file locally within her Web browser. She can therefore take the liberty of changing the HTML page's content, which in itself is no threat. If she decides to change the operation of the scripts within that page, you could begin experiencing problems. Assume that you perform calculations in your script to determine the totals for the items to be ordered on an order form. There is no reason someone cannot examine the script logic and change it so that she is charged a fraction of the price she should be billed. When she loads her modified page into the browser and enters the appropriate information, the grand total could be significantly less than what it should be. She could then submit this content to the server, which happily places the order, none the wiser.

Tip #148

> Although you cannot hide JavaScript source code within an HTML page or scramble it, you can put more sensitive information within a hidden frame of the Web page. Although this is not foolproof, it helps hide information or scripts from the viewer. One limitation to this approach is that the Web browser supports frames, but most browsers that support JavaScript should support frames as well. To make a frame invisible, you can, for instance, split a window into a top and bottom frame. When defining these frame sets, you simply expose the top frame by utilizing 100 percent of the browser's height. This way the bottom frame is essentially hidden as there is no room left in the browser to render contents from that frame. The following sample HTML illustrates how to set up this frameset:
>
> ```
> <frameset rows="100%,*">
>   <frame name="top" src="main.html">
>   <frame name="bottom" src="hidden.html">
> </frameset>
> ```

The good news is that most of these security issues can be avoided by carefully programming safeguards. In the example just outlined, for instance, it is highly recommended that the server-side application not rely on the results of the JavaScript code on the client computer to determine final prices. JavaScript could still be used on the client's computer to speed calculations and provide immediate response on the forms, but the final values should be calculated and checked again on the server when the form is ultimately submitted.

Tip #149

> You could even be more tricky and make the server-side application that receives the form data check the origin of the data submitted. To do this, the server programmer could merely check the referrer information that is passed to the server as an environment variable. If it does not match the valid URL for the Web site, information from the form was submitted from another location than the form on the Web server. In this case, it would likely indicate that the form was modified and invoked from either the client's computer or another server.

One final note on security involves the access that scripts have on the client machine. For most users, JavaScript is limited and cannot directly interact with the operating system on a client machine's hard disk. However, some languages do allow such access, or at least limited forms of this access. In this case, it is quite easy for a malicious program to be executed via a client script that adversely affects the clients computer. As a developer, you should make certain not to affect your site visitor's machine negatively. As a user, you should always be careful about what programs you download and allow to execute on your machine. Even the best-looking programs may be mere Trojan horses.

A second negative is that JavaScript is a slightly limited language. With the capability of adding programming logic to the Web page the client retrieves, you may be inclined to think that it extremely powerful and that you can do anything with JavaScript. You can add

PART

V

CH

26

quite a bit of functionality to your Web site with client-side languages such as JavaScript, but it is important to remember that these types of scripting languages are simply the glue that binds data within a Web page together. Languages such as JavaScript lack many of the capabilities that you would find with Java applets, browser plug-ins, or ActiveX controls. For instance, a JavaScript application does not have the capability to draw graphics such as circles, lines, or boxes on the page. It does not have by itself the capability to play back music or sounds. You could easily use JavaScript, however, to interact with a Java applet that does draw graphics or a plug-in that plays media.

HOW TO USE JAVASCRIPT

Before continuing, it is imperative to clarify that although this chapter concentrates on JavaScript, many of the rules about using scripts apply no matter what language is used. Even though the language is syntactically different, many of the same principles hold if you are using VBScript. This book concentrates more on JavaScript's use because in its standardized form, it is the language that is most likely supported on the widest variety of Web browsers. Although you can use additional languages such as VBScript at your discretion, many are not supported in every version of Web browsers.

Another important point to make is that since JavaScript is embedded within the HTML for a Web page, you can edit it with a variety of tools. This chapter concentrates on the use of FrontPage 2000 as an editing tool for JavaScript logic. In this section you see how Microsoft's tools can help you create scripts quickly and easily, even if you are not an advanced programmer.

As already stated, JavaScript is identified as a block of programming statements embedded within an HTML page. These script blocks are uniquely distinguished by opening and closing <SCRIPT> tags. Any content that falls between the <SCRIPT> and </SCRIPT> tags is treated as scripting commands and must abide by the rules and syntax of the language used. An important feature to note is that some software vendors support JavaScript on the server side of the process as well. For instance, Microsoft's Active Server Pages technology, which is included with their Internet Information Server, supports the capability to write JavaScript or VBScript applications that execute on the server. Learning JavaScript as a development language may not limit you to creating client-side applications.

Note

Sometimes you can use scripting languages for creating either client- or server-based applications, depending on the software solutions you have installed. If you can develop applications on a Web server such as Microsoft's Internet Information Server using scripting languages, it is important to remember that you do not necessarily need to be consistent in the choice of languages for your overall Web site. You can easily mix and match JavaScript on the client-side of the process with VBScript on the server. As long as the software can interpret the specified language, you can use either interchangeably. In fact, it is possible to use both JavaScript and VBScript on the same page.

The <SCRIPT> tag accepts additional parameters: language, src, and the Microsoft server-script parameter runat. Let's quickly review each parameter:

- language—As you are well aware, you can use a variety of languages for writing script commands. The languages available depend on the software that is interpreting the language. In the case of client-side scripts, the browser must support the language in order for the programming statements to take affect. As you see later, scripting languages can be used on the server as well. In this case, languages used for server-side scripts depend on what the server software supports. To specify what language you want to write your script commands in, you can set this parameter to the name of the language. Examples you could use here include LANGUAGE=VBScript and LANGUAGE=JavaScript.

- src—As you begin programming routines in JavaScript, you will find that you would like to reuse many of the commands that you write. By using the src parameter, you can specify a URL from which the common script can be retrieved. Note that the URL should point to a file that contains only JavaScript commands, it should not contain any HTML references.

- runat—This parameter is reserved for server-side scripts, particularly those written to execute within the context of Active Server Pages found in Microsoft Internet Information Server. With this parameter, script code that exists between script tags can be forced to either run on the client machine or on the server. This parameter can contain the value server if it is to execute on the Web server; otherwise, the default is to execute the script on the client.

HELLO WORLD

Once you have identified the section of the Web page that is to be treated as script, you are probably wondering how this script is started. If the script exists within the standard body section of the HTML page, it will be executed when the body of the page is displayed within the browser. The page is rendered in the Web browser as the file is parsed from the top to the bottom. Once the browser reaches the section that contains script, that script executes and its results are displayed.

Another method for invoking script is to attach script commands to *events* that other objects on the Web page invoke. Object-oriented technology is reviewed a little later; the review more fully explains the concept of events. For now, simply consider that script can also be invoked when some action (such as a user clicking on a button) occurs on the page.

You can create a basic example of JavaScript on a Web page with what you know so far. For this simple test, you write the classic "Hello World!" example that has been used countless times when introducing other computer languages. In this example, you create a Web page that displays a message box that floats on top of the Web browser window. JavaScript features an alert command, which can accomplish this task. Listing 26.1 demonstrates using a simple JavaScript command within a Web page, while Figure 26.1 illustrates the results of the page up until the "Hello World!" line is displayed.

PART

V

CH

26

LISTING 26.1   JAVASCRIPT COMMANDS CAN BE EASILY EMBEDDED WITHIN A WEB PAGE

```
<HTML>
<BODY>
<H1>Hello World Example</H1>

<SCRIPT LANGUAGE="JavaScript">
    alert("Hello World!");
</SCRIPT>

This is a sample JavaScript page.
</BODY>
</HTML>
```

Figure 26.1
This "Hello World!" message appears halfway through the rendering process of the Web page.

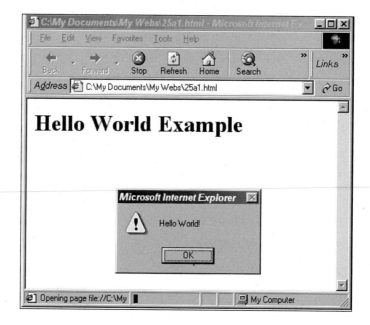

If you open the Web page created in Listing 26.1 within your Web browser, you will notice that the JavaScript executes in the order in which it exists in the page. The Web browser in your example will first display the line `"Hello World Example"` in a large header font. You are then greeted with a message box that pops up on top of the Web browser with the text "Hello World!" and an OK button. Nothing else will appear within the browser until you dismiss this pop-up window by clicking the OK button. After doing this, the browser continues and displays the text `"This is a sample JavaScript page."`

SAME OLD ROUTINE

You can quickly see how you can use JavaScript to control the output displayed within the Web browser—place logic within the body section of an HTML page. There will be occasions when you want to have JavaScript routines available, yet not want to necessarily display them immediately within the browser's output window. If this is the case, it is possible to create JavaScript functions or subroutines, just as a developer would create these functions in another language such as Visual Basic, C, Java, or even BASIC.

A *function* or *subroutine* is simply a collection of scripting commands that are identified with a name. When grouped, your application can call the routine at any time and as many times as necessary. This often helps the programmer share common functionality for the entire application or help logically group actions of the application. For instance, it wouldn't be uncommon for a developer to write an application and group functionality for opening or closing files into separate subroutines.

Once the block of logical statements has been added to a subroutine or function, the program can invoke those routines by *calling* that routine by name at any time. When you define a function, you define the block of code with a name that is unique in the application. You can always invoke the functionality of that block of code by simply calling the name of the function anywhere within your application. Any script or commands that are to be included within a program block in JavaScript must be surrounded by curly braces ({ }). Just like HTML tags, you need a closing brace for every opening brace; otherwise, your JavaScript will not function properly.

So far you've been using the words *function* and *subroutine* interchangeably. There is one substantial difference between the two terms. *Functions* are blocks of programming code that return some form of result, whereas *subroutines* do not return results. A square root function is an example of a function. When you call this function, you would expect a number to be returned that represents the square root of another number. A subroutine may be something more direct, such as opening a document in an editor.

Consider one final note on routines and functions within a programming language. When you create a reusable section of code and define it as either a function or subroutine, there is the option to specify parameters of information that can be sent into that routine. You can add as many parameters as you need to a function or subroutine definition, provided they exist within parentheses and are separated by commas. This parameter list often sits directly after the name of the function or subroutine when it is defined.

Subroutines in JavaScript are simply functions that do not return values. Therefore, the function command is all that is required to define a block of reusable code within an application or Web page. Example functions defined in JavaScript could be as follows:

```
Function SquareRoot(number as int){
    // Code to determine square-root of a number
    Return result;
}

Function OpenDocument(file as string){
    // Code to open filename passed to function
}
```

OBJECT-ORIENTED TECHNOLOGY

Computers improved with the advent of operating systems that use a Graphical User Interface such as those found on the Macintosh and Windows machines; with that improvement there developed a need for a better programming model. In the past, developers could simply write a series of computer program statements that would be executed sequentially. Even with functions and subroutines defined, the program executed from a beginning and ended at some point.

These starting and ending points became less obvious in the world of Windows-based operating systems because the user interface opened the possibility for programs to react based on user input. For example, in the past you could run a DOS-based application that performed one function based on a series of parameters provided to it, such as copying a file from one drive to another. This copy program had a start and finish and no user interaction between those two points. However, even a somewhat simple application (such as Notepad in Windows) suddenly opens a large amount of user interactivity. The user can click menus to open files, close files, exit the program, search within documents, and perform other tasks. She can type on the keyboard and those actions must be translated to characters that appear within the text editor. Even though an application such as Notepad had a definite start and eventual end point, the user controlled when that end point occurred (exiting the application) as well as all actions between those points.

Object-oriented technology helps provide a programming model that among other things eases the ability to interact with the user. It also provides numerous other features such reusing an object's capabilities across applications or hide information so that developers do not need to know the intricacies of how a particular object works. It is a powerful model in which each object can be either an entire application or separate components within that application.

Objects have many features and characteristics, but concentrate here on the primary capabilities most every object utilizes. These capabilities include *properties* for the object, *methods* that can be invoked for the object, and *events* that can be raised by the object. Often in scripting languages such as JavaScript or VBScript, methods and properties for an object are identified after the object's name itself. In the case of JavaScript or VBScript, a single period (.) delimits the object and the method or property for that object. To invoke a method for an object in script, you would therefore use the `object.method()` syntax.

PROPERTIES

To explain the concepts of object-oriented programming a little more clearly, think of an everyday object such as a door as an object. Take a look at any door and you'll quickly notice that there are a wide variety of types. What makes each door different from another? Most often it is obvious characteristics such as the color or size, whether it has windows, and what it is made of. You could consider each of these characteristics a *property* of the object we call a *door*.

Once a set of properties is available for an object, the developer can choose which should be made available for change and which should only be viewed. For example, the color of a door can be changed with a new coat of paint. A color property for the door is editable. Some other door properties could be its state, such as whether it is opened or closed. This type of property is more of a read-only property, where you could query the door's state. In this case you can open or close the door object, but that is more of an action *performed on* the door, not a property *describing* the state of the door.

One final word on properties: They can be set or read. The action performed on the property depends on the direction of the assignment statement in a programming language. In JavaScript, you can assign information to *variables (page 535)* or objects by using the equal sign (=). For instance, you use x = 1 to set the variable X to 1. Likewise, you can set properties for an object using this same syntax, such as `object.property` = 1. Conversely, you may also retrieve the values from a property and store them in other variables, x = `object.property`, for example.

METHODS

Properties are used to define or retrieve the state of an object's characteristics. If you want to invoke an action on an object, use a method defined for the object. *Methods* are similar to function calls except that they are directly related to the object itself. They are also *public*; they are exposed so that other programs can use them. They are a secure mechanism by which only the functions that an object wants to have exposed are shown to the world. They also ease development because the programmer does not necessarily need to know how the method works on an object, rather trusts that the action will get done.

Using a door as an example again, there can be two methods for that object: open and close. The action of opening a door can be called for the door object and you don't care exactly how this occurs. Some doors may be double and one must open before another. Another door may slide instead of swing open. As a developer, you may not care for the details about how a door is opened—you just want to open it.

EVENTS

The third area of object-oriented technology lies in the use of *events*. As you can see, objects can be used by setting or retrieving their properties, or invoking actions via there methods. However, there will be occasions when you design an application and want to know when something happens with another event. Events are the inverse of methods. You call methods on other objects to force those objects to do something. Certain objects can do something and then force your program to do an action as a result if you choose to allow them. An event is basically a way in which your program is notified that some action has occurred elsewhere.

Back to the doors example: If someone knocked on the door, knocking could be an event. If your program cares about someone knocking on a door, you could write a function that performs an action when the knocking occurs. Functions written in your application that execute when an action occurs are often referred to as *event handlers*, since they handle what happens in your program when an external event happens.

OBJECT MODELS

Now that you are somewhat familiar with the core components behind object-oriented technology, this chapter can discuss the concept of object models. As you can quickly see, each object has its own set of properties, methods, and events, based on how the developer who wrote the object decided to implement functionality for that object. Since each object can be drastically different in functionality, you cannot assume what a particular property or method for an object will be. Therefore, the properties, methods, and events for objects are usually well documented. This collection of properties, methods, and events is sometimes referred to as the object's *model*.

It is important to remember that an object model can be available for any object, including the Web browser. With the advent of fourth-generation browsers that support Dynamic HTML, it has become increasingly necessary for the Web page developer who incorporates script on the page to know how the browser object works and what properties, methods, or events it exposes. Because a Web page is known as a *document*, the object model for an HTML file is often referred to as the *Document Object Model* or *DOM*. More often than not, your JavaScript components within a Web page are going to interact in one way or another with other components on the Web page. You will therefore see that it is common for JavaScript to constantly rely upon the DOM's capabilities. In a moment you see how Microsoft FrontPage 2000 helps with the use of JavaScript and its interaction with other objects, including the document object.

CREATING SCRIPTS WITH FRONTPAGE

As already stated, keeping track of the objects available for Web page development and their possible properties, methods, and events can be a daunting task. Fortunately, Microsoft has made the process of writing scripts for Web pages easier with FrontPage 2000. There is a macro script-writing tool included with FrontPage 2000. Additional features include the capability to browse the objects available within the page of the Web browser and invoke methods on those objects, set properties for those objects, and create JavaScript routines to handle events fired by those objects.

A QUICK SCRIPT EDITOR TOUR

To invoke the script editor within FrontPage, you can choose the editor from the FrontPage menus. It exists under the Tools, Macro submenu and is labeled Microsoft Script Editor. Once you have invoked it, you should see a screen similar to the one in Figure 26.2. Quickly review the primary windows used within the Script Editor.

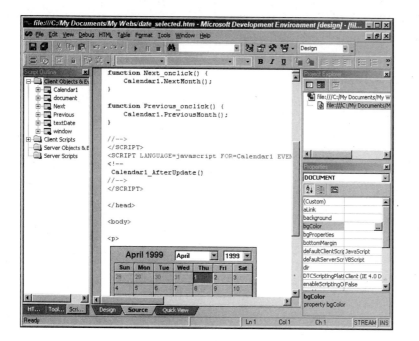

Figure 26.2
The Microsoft Script Editor is a powerful tool included with FrontPage 2000; it aids in the process of generating JavaScript routines.

DOCUMENT WINDOW

If you are familiar with other Microsoft Web development tools such as Visual InterDev, you will quickly realize that this is the same script editor used to edit scripts within that environment. The center window contains the HTML page, displayed as either a graphical preview or as HTML source code. The appearance of this window is set by choosing the appropriate tab directly underneath the window: Design, Source, and Quick View.

- Design—This mode is not usually available within the Microsoft Script Editor for FrontPage 2000. It often allows the developer to design a Web page in a WYSIWYG fashion. FrontPage 2000 was designed just for this and includes more advanced features for creating your Web page. You may therefore find that this tab is disabled when you try to activate it.

- Source—The Source mode is probably the one you will use most when editing Web pages within the Script Editor. This tab forces the document window to display all of the HTML source for the page, including any script within that page as well as any objects such as ActiveX objects or design time controls. Fortunately, this source mode still hides extraneous information such as the Class IDs for ActiveX objects or the source for design time controls. It instead displays a graphical object representing that object, but allows the user to change properties for that control.

PART

V

CH

26

- Quick View—Sometimes you will want to see how the page you are working on will appear within the Web browser without necessarily invoking Internet Explorer. A representation of the page is rendered inside the document window when you click this tab. This is only possible, however, if Internet Explorer is installed on your computer; this option makes use of Internet Explorer's Web browser object.

PAGE EXPLORER WINDOW

To the left of this Web page document window exists another window that can be toggled between one of three modes: HTML Outline, Toolbox, and Script Outline. Depending on the mode chosen, this window will update with information about the Web page being edited. In a sense, this window allows you to explore components for the Web page.

- HTML Outline—When you pick this tab, the window updates with all information about the Web page that is loaded. In particular, it shows a hierarchy of HTML tags that are used within the Web page and how they are nested within each other. This is sometimes useful when you are writing script that affects other objects in the page. In such cases, you may need to see how objects are related to each other.

- Toolbox—If you are familiar with other development environments (such as Visual Basic), then you know that you can place objects onto the application's window. The objects that are available to be dragged and dropped onto the application window can be found in the toolbox window. In the case of the Script Editor, you can find many objects that you would usually use in HTML pages (such as buttons, forms, or entry boxes). You can also expand this toolbox's capabilities and add new ActiveX objects as necessary.

  You may also have noticed that there are General and HTML indexes within the Toolbox view. These buttons allow you to navigate through sets of controls within the toolbox. Clicking the General button, for instance, brings up general editing tools such as the selection pointer. Selecting the HTML button brings up a list of intrinsic HTML controls for the Web browser. You can think of each button as opening a particular drawer of your toolbox. You can easily right-click inside the toolbox and choose to add new drawers as well as move objects within the toolbox into these different categories. With this type of interface, you can place all ActiveX controls into its own group of the toolbox or place all objects related to a project within another category. The object organization is up to you.

- Script Outline—Besides the toolbox, this is probably the most used tab within this page Explorer window. When you select this tab, a list of all of the components on the Web page is displayed within this Explorer window. Four main folders are presented: Client Objects & Events, Client Scripts, Server Objects & Events, and Server Scripts. Additional objects that logically fall into that category are in these folders. If you have placed several pushbuttons on a Web page, for instance, each of those buttons will be listed by the name given to them via their ID or Name attribute in HTML. If you have other objects on the page (such as ActiveX controls or other HTML form objects), those are listed within the Client Objects & Events folder. As you investigate the objects on the page, you can expand each object to see the events that each supports. In the case of a button for instance, Microsoft Internet Explorer 4.0's DOM supports events for when a user clicks the button (onClick). This event would be displayed as a member of the button object within this Explorer window.

PROJECT EXPLORER

The Project Explorer window that exists near the top-right corner of the editor contains a hierarchical list of all objects for a given Web project. This information is usually imported from the FrontPage Web project that you were working on. In most cases, you will see objects that were retrieved from the FrontPage web on the Web server. These objects certainly include HTML files, but may also include Active Server Page script files or other objects that exist within the Web site. To open another file from the web project into the editor, simply double-click the item you are interested in examining.

ADDING SCRIPT

As discussed earlier, you can directly embed script within the context of an HTML document that executes when those lines are parsed by the Web browser. It is more common and accurate, however, to place JavaScript commands within the appropriate context of an event for the Web page. For instance, modify your example in Listing 26.1 so that a button is placed on the page instead where the original JavaScript resided. In this case you add the capability to the page so that the message "Hello World!" appears when the site visitor clicks this button.

To complete this task, keep in mind what is occurring in the browser. The page is painted and all of the JavaScript is read and prepared for execution when necessary. When the user clicks the Show Message button, a click event is generated by the Web browser for that button. The script on the Web page must therefore provide an event handler for catching the occurrence of a button click. After creating the event handler linkage, the script must then create the message box with the appropriate text. Listing 26.2 demonstrates the complete source code; the script can be easily tweaked by Microsoft Script Editor so that a button invokes the message box.

PART

V

CH

26

LISTING 26.2 THE "HELLO WORLD!" SAMPLE SCRIPT

```
<HTML>
<HEAD>
<SCRIPT ID = "ClientEventHandlersJS" LANGUAGE = "JavaScript">
<!--

function button1_onclick() {
    alert("Hello World!");
}

//-->
</SCRIPT>
```

continues

LISTING 26.2   CONTINUED

```
</HEAD>

<BODY>
<H1>Hello World Example</H1>

<INPUT type = "button"
       value = "Show Message"
       id = "button1"
       name = "button1"
       language = "JavaScript"
       onclick = "return button1_onclick">
</BODY>
</HTML>
```

ADDING EVENT HANDLERS IN SCRIPT EDITOR

Adding *event handlers (page 1025)* within the Script Editor is incredibly simple. First you need to locate the object that you want to write an event handler for in the leftmost Script Outline view. You're looking for the button you placed on the HTML page named button1. After finding it in the list, double-click or click the + expand symbol to see all of the events for this button. The DOM within Internet Explorer 4.0 and later is quite extensive, so you will see many events that can be invoked for a button. In this example you want to simply allow the user to click the button; you are looking for the onClick event. Double-clicking that event leads the Script Editor to automatically add a JavaScript function named button1_onclick and set up a script block for all of your page's event handlers.

You will also notice that the Script Editor automatically updates the HTML information for the button1 HTML object on the page. It adds appropriate attribute information for handling events such as onclick = "return button1_onclick". This is the way scripting language applications handle events. Where the object is defined on the HTML page, there can be an additional attribute that specifies the action to perform on a particular event. This attribute consists of the name of the event to trap (onClick) in this instance, and the JavaScript commands to perform when the event occurs (in this case the JavaScript function to call). Of course, you can add as many attributes for as many events as you need to take care of within the HTML tags for the object. If you begin adding many events or large amounts of programming logic to perform for each of these events, the definition of the object can become unwieldy in the HTML source. It is therefore highly recommended that you invoke script functions instead of embedding the logic directly into the definition statement for the object in HTML. This makes your HMTL code much more legible and helps you when you are creating your applications.

With all of the tedious setup actions automated for you by the Script Editor, you can simply add the logic to perform on the click event of the button within the button1_onclick function. In this case, you simply need to add a single line of JavaScript that creates an alert message with the text Hello World!. Although this seems like a simple example, remember that this technology also applies to other objects such as *ActiveX controls (page 541)*. This makes the process of binding ActiveX control actions to JavaScript commands easier.

Note

Make sure that you have the correct language selected for your client- or server-side applications when editing scripts with the Script Editor. You can control what languages are used for client- or server-side applications on a per-page basis. If you are in doubt, make sure to check the current settings under the Page Properties tab within the Script Editor. If you write JavaScript code while the VBScript language preference is selected, you will most likely create pages that produce errors; the automated portions embedded by the Script Editor will be written in the language chosen in the preferences.

MAKING INTELLISENSE OF IT ALL

Another nice feature that is supported by Microsoft's Script Editor is a capability referred to as Intellisense. This technology, which was introduced in Visual Basic 5.0, allows the developer to quickly and easily invoke methods or properties for objects. With Intellisense enabled within the Script Editor, you can quickly see a reference of all properties and methods supported by an object as you are writing JavaScript code.

For instance, say that you are writing JavaScript code that changes the name of a button on the Web page. As you are aware, a button's name is set by its value attribute in HTML. If you have a button named button1 on the Web page, you can begin typing the name button1 in your script. As you will recall earlier in the discussion of object-oriented technologies, JavaScript separates the object from its methods or properties in code by using the period. With Intellisense, you see a small pop-up window as soon as you press the . key after the button1 object text; it's next to the object name with a list of properties and methods. Properties are identified by an icon that resembles a finger pointing at a sheet of information, while methods are denoted by an icon resembling a flying block.

Note

JavaScript is a case-sensitive language, therefore you must type the ActiveX control name exactly as it appears in the ID property where it is defined in order to use Intellisense. Therefore in this example when you write the JavaScript and want to see the methods and properties available for an object, you must use the capital "C" in "Calendar1" since that is how it was named. JavaScript wouldn't recognize the control if a lower-case "C" was used, and so the Script Editor won't allow you to make that mistake.

If you are expecting for a list of methods and controls for an object in JavaScript but do not see them after you type the ".", make sure to double-check that the name of the control is spelled properly and that the proper letters are upper- or lowercase.

While this separate window is displayed, you can begin typing the first few characters of the property or method you want to use or you can simply scroll through the list and pick the component you need. In this simple example, you are looking for the value property and select that appropriately.

The benefit of Intellisense clearly is that you do not need to memorize the properties and methods for each object you may use; neither do you depend upon written or electronic documentation for reference. It simply makes getting to the information you need quicker. Another added benefit is that Intellisense works equally as well with other objects such as ActiveX controls on the Web page or the actual DOM for Dynamic HTML.

COMPLETE JAVASCRIPT EXAMPLE

Without knowing much about the actual syntax of the JavaScript language, it is difficult to construct an example at this point that clearly outlines its usefulness. Do not be dismayed; JavaScript is covered in more detail in Chapter 27. Consider a quick calendar page to get a better sample of properties, methods, and events in action. This example Web page features a calendar ActiveX control that is available from Microsoft. With such an object on a Web page, you don't need to worry about users entering illegal dates such as February 31 on an entry form. It also makes your life easier as a Web page developer because you don't need to write convoluted logic to test that the user's input was accurate; you can trust that the ActiveX control will do that work for you. Figure 26.3 shows the final Web page with the calendar ActiveX control, as well as a standard HTML text area that shows a textual equivalent of the date whenever a new date is picked in the control. There are two additional HTML buttons that allow the user to move backward and forward through the calendar by month; they're at the bottom of the screen. Listing 26.3 contains the source code necessary to implement the JavaScript on this sample page. This event is handled by JavaScript on the Web page that updates the HTML for a textual equivalent of the date.

Figure 26.3
JavaScript can act as the glue on a Web page to bind ActiveX controls to other HTML objects on the page.

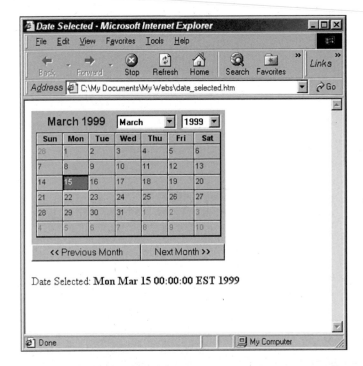

LISTING 26.3 THE CALENDAR CONTROL RAISES AN EVENT WHENEVER ITS DATE CHANGES

```html
<html>

<head>
<META name=VI60_defaultClientScript content=JavaScript>
<meta http-equiv="Content-Language" content="en-us">
<meta http-equiv="Content-Type" content="text/html; charset=windows-1252">
<meta name="GENERATOR" content="Microsoft FrontPage 4.0">
<meta name="ProgId" content="FrontPage.Editor.Document">
<title>Date Selected</title>

<SCRIPT ID=clientEventHandlersJS LANGUAGE=javascript>
<!--

function Calendar1_AfterUpdate() {
    textDate.innerText = Calendar1.Value;
}

function Next_onclick() {
    Calendar1.NextMonth();
}

function Previous_onclick() {
    Calendar1.PreviousMonth();
}

//-->
</SCRIPT>
<SCRIPT LANGUAGE=javascript FOR=Calendar1 EVENT=AfterUpdate>
<!--
    Calendar1_AfterUpdate()
//-->
</SCRIPT>

</head>

<body>

<p>
<object classid="clsid:8E27C92B-1264-101C-8A2F-040226009C02"
        id="Calendar1" width="288" height="192">
  <param name="_Version" value="526288">
  <param name="_ExtentX" value="7620">
  <param name="_ExtentY" value="5080">
  <param name="_StockProps" value="1">
  <param name="BackColor" value="-2147483633">
  <param name="Year" value="1999">
  <param name="Month" value="4">
  <param name="Day" value="1">
  <param name="DayLength" value="1">
  <param name="MonthLength" value="2">
  <param name="DayFontColor" value="0">
  <param name="FirstDay" value="1">
  <param name="GridCellEffect" value="1">
  <param name="GridFontColor" value="10485760">
```

continues

PART

V

CH

26

LISTING 26.3 CONTINUED

```
    <param name="GridLinesColor" value="-2147483632">
    <param name="ShowDateSelectors" value="-1">
    <param name="ShowDays" value="-1">
    <param name="ShowHorizontalGrid" value="-1">
    <param name="ShowTitle" value="-1">
    <param name="ShowVerticalGrid" value="-1">
    <param name="TitleFontColor" value="10485760">
    <param name="ValueIsNull" value="0">
</object>
<br>
<input type="button"
      value="&lt;&lt; Previous Month"
      name="Previous"
      LANGUAGE=javascript
      onclick="return Previous_onclick()">
<input type="button" value="Next Month >>"
      name="Next"
      LANGUAGE=javascript
      onclick="return Next_onclick()">
</p>
<p>Date Selected: <b><span id="textDate">Today</span></b></p>

</body>

</html>
```

By examining the JavaScript in Listing 26.3, you'll see that there is one event for the calendar object. Whenever someone changes the date displayed within the calendar object, it raises an event named AfterUpdate. By adding a JavaScript function Calendar1_AfterUpdate, the Web page can perform some form of logic whenever the date is changed on the calendar control.

In this example, you want to update the HTML for the Web page so that a textual representation of the date picked in the calendar control is displayed. Use Dynamic HTML and the Internet Explorer Document Object Model to do this. With Dynamic HTML, you can define a region of HTML using the <SPAN> and </SPAN> tags. If you name this region textDate by setting the <SPAN> tag's ID attribute, you can then reference it in JavaScript code. Within the Calendar1_AfterUpdate function, set the text property of the textDate HTML region to the actual date value picked in the calendar control. To do this, use the innerText property found in Dynamic HTML to set the HTML inside the <SPAN> region and reflect the new date chosen. In this case, the calendar control stores the currently selected date in its value property. The line of code necessary for setting the text on the Web page to the current date is textDate.innerText = calendar1.value. As you use this example, you'll also notice that the textDate area also updates whenever you click on the Next and Previous buttons. This is the correct action since these buttons update the calendar and therefore raise the AfterUpdate event.

To finish exploring this example, notice that there are two additional JavaScript functions for two buttons underneath the Calendar control. These buttons allow the Web page viewer to change the calendar displayed by moving forward or backward through the year by month. By clicking the Next Month button, the calendar is updated to display the next month past the one currently active. Likewise, the Previous Month displays the month before the currently displayed month. To accomplish this in JavaScript, two buttons—buttonNext and buttonPrevious—were created and their respective functions for handling their onClick events were added. To actually change the month displayed within the calendar control, the ActiveX object exposes two methods: NextMonth and PreviousMonth. By calling these methods within their respective JavaScript button events, the Calendar control is updated to reflect the new month as the user navigates through the year.

Although this example uses very limited amounts of JavaScript, you can quickly see how powerful JavaScript can be when gluing components together on a Web page. With some more advanced logic added to the page, there is virtually no limit on the amount of creativity that can be applied when creating Web sites with JavaScript.

TROUBLESHOOTING

When I add scripts using the Script Editor, the functions built for me are in the wrong language and don't match the settings I made in FrontPage 2000. Why is this and how can I fix it?

The Microsoft Script Editor is actually a separate application that can create scripts for your Web pages, but can also be used to create VBScript applications for other Microsoft products such as Microsoft Word. Therefore some settings that you make in the current version of FrontPage 2000, such as the default scripting language, are not automatically brought over to the Script Editor. To change the default scripting language for the Web page you are editing in the Script Editor, look at the Properties toolbar that is normally docked in the lower-right hand corner of the editor. Within this properties sheet, you should find two properties: defaultClientScript and defaultServerScript. You can change either of these to be VBScript or JavaScript. Once set, future functions that you attempt to define via the editor's interface will be built in that language. Remember that this default setting is based on each page and can be different for every new page you create.

Some applications such as the Calendar example in this chapter does not seem to work within my browser. Why is that?

The Calendar example in this chapter makes use of Microsoft ActiveX technology. If you are using a Web browser that does not support ActiveX, then the calendar control cannot be created and therefore the JavaScript will fail.

But if you are using an ActiveX capable browser such as Internet Explorer and are still encountering problems, make certain that you have client-side scripting enabled for the browser and that ActiveX controls can be executed. These options are available within the Browser's Internet Options menu. While verifying that scripting and ActiveX controls are available, you must also make certain that the security settings for the Web browser enable the execution of ActiveX controls.

DESIGNERS CORNER

Scripting with JavaScript is a very exciting prospect, but don't overdo it. Use the scripts where they seem appropriate and don't add unnecessary script. Unnecessary script can add up quickly and burden the Web browser with longer download times. It can also make the Web page more complex than it needs to be from a usability perspective.

Avoid using JavaScript to build the Web page. In Chapter 27 you will see how you can use the Document Object Model within the Web browser and the methods for writing text to the Web browser window. However you probably don't want to use this technique for writing static HTML to the Web browser window. In the long run it will make your Web page much more difficult to support and change.

Finally don't write JavaScript applications that contain information that you wouldn't mind being made available to the public. Scripts are not secure and anyone that can view the Web page can examine the JavaScript determine what the code is doing. Make sure that you don't have anything confidential in these scripts at any time.

CHAPTER 27

JAVASCRIPT AND CLIENT-SIDE COMPUTING

In this chapter

by John J. Kottler

SIMPLE JAVASCRIPT PROGRAM: HELLO WORLD!

A popular example used for introducing a new language is the "Hello World!" program. This is perhaps the easiest program you could ever write. It simply displays the words "Hello World!" onscreen. Although terribly simple, it illustrates some introductory points of JavaScript. Listing 27.1 shows a sample "Hello World!" application.

LISTING 27.1   THE HELLO WORLD! PROGRAM IN JAVASCRIPT

```
<HTML>
<HEAD>
<SCRIPT LANGUAGE="JAVASCRIPT">
        document.write("Hello World!")
</SCRIPT>
</HEAD>
<BODY>
...
</BODY>
</HTML>
```

As you can see, the JavaScript application code is embedded in the HEAD section of the HTML document. You can place the JavaScript code anywhere in the document, however. Notice the single line of code between the <SCRIPT> and </SCRIPT> tags. This line is the command that writes output to the screen.

Tip #150

> Put scripts that are *functions* into the HEAD section of the HTML document, and put the main program that calls these functions in the BODY section. Placing scripts in the HEAD section of the page reserves them for future access. If scripts are added to the BODY area, they will be executed as soon as the page is displayed.

The write statement is considered to be a *method* of the document *object*. Functions and methods are blocks of script code that may be invoked from another place in the code. Typically, functions and methods provide access to commonly used routines. In this case, writing resulting data is a very common function. The following sections review objects, methods, and properties in greater detail. For the moment, understand that the output "Hello World!" is being written to the currently viewed Web page (document) through the write command.

WHAT'S YOUR FUNCTION?

In the code shown in Listing 27.1, the write method is a common action. One of the purposes of a function is to simplify the code you write by making a common feature a single block of code that can be referenced numerous times. In this way, functions are similar to the SRC attribute for the <SCRIPT> tag discussed earlier. If there were no functions, you would have to key in that block of code at each point you wanted to use it, which would be a maintenance nightmare in the future if a particular piece of that common code were changed. Instead of updating it in one spot, you would have to manually find each occurrence of that code and update it.

Suppose you wanted to write an application that determined the number of notebook computers available for sale at an online computer store. If this number needed to be determined multiple times in a JavaScript application, it could be placed inside a function and invoked as needed. In this example, determining the number of computers available may require several lines of code behind the scenes: attaching to a database, retrieving information from a database, reformatting that information and returning it if no errors were encountered, and disconnecting from the database. As a Web page developer, you may want to be shielded from these actions. You especially do not want to include all these actions independently in your source code each time you want to determine the number of available laptops. It's more efficient to issue a single command such as `GetNumberOfPCs`.

A function enables you to group multiple actions together to be invoked by a single command. To extend the Hello World! application a bit further, you can add a function that does some math. Add a function called `FigureTip` that calculates a 15% tip based on an initial amount (see Listing 27.2).

LISTING 27.2   A SIMPLE FUNCTION (`FigureTip`) THAT DETERMINES A 15% GRATUITY

```
<HTML>
<HEAD>
<SCRIPT LANGUAGE="JavaScript">
        function FigureTip(amount){
                var TipAmount

                TipAmount=amount*.15
                document.write("A 15% tip for $",amount," would be: $",TipAmount)
                return TipAmount;
        }
</SCRIPT>
</HEAD>

<BODY>
<SCRIPT LANGUAGE="JAVASCRIPT">
        FigureTip(20)
</SCRIPT>
</BODY>
```

As you can see, functions are declared in JavaScript through the `function` command. Immediately following the `function` command is the name by which you will identify this function's block of code in other areas of the script.

Immediately following the name of the function is the list of arguments, enclosed by parentheses. *Arguments* are variables that allow communication between the function and other portions of the script that called the function. Arguments often determine the actions and results of a function by providing information to the function. In Listing 27.2, `FigureTip` is a function that accepts one argument (amount). It then uses the value passed into the function through the amount argument as part of the equation to determine a tip. Although this example shows only one argument being used, you can have multiple arguments, which are separated by commas.

After the function has been named and the arguments that are necessary for the function have been established, you can declare the body of the function, which is the lines of code that will be used many times. You must write these lines of code in the same language that's specified in the <SCRIPT LANGUAGE> attribute.

You must then mark the lines of script code that implement the function. You can specify this block of code by enclosing the lines of code in the script with curly braces ({ at the beginning and } at the end). In Listing 27.2, TipAmount=amount*.15, document.write("A 15% tip for $",amount," would be: $",TipAmount) and return TipAmount are commands for the function because of the position of the braces.

The first line of code in the function in Listing 27.2, var TipAmount, declares a variable that will be used elsewhere in the function. This type of line is one place where JavaScript shows some of its C roots. You should declare each variable you plan to use in your JavaScript code. In C and other languages, you have to declare a variable as either a number (such as an integer or floating value), as a type of character string, or as another object. In JavaScript, you simply declare the variable; you don't need to specify what type of variable it is.

You also can set a default value for a particular variable when declaring it. In the preceding example, you could initialize the variable TipAmount to be zero when the function is first called by modifying the first line to read: var TipAmount=0.

Note

> The JavaScript language doesn't require you to declare variables before using them. JavaScript declares them automatically the first time you use them in your code. However, it's recommended that you explicitly declare *variables (page 535)* because it helps to make your code easier to understand and maintain.

The second line of the function does some multiplication to determine the appropriate tip, based on the amount of money passed into the function. Because the average for tips is 15 percent, the program function takes the amount of money passed into it and multiplies it by .15. The result is then stored into the variable declared in the line above, TipAmount.

The next line of code displays the results of the equation for the viewer to read. Recall that you can use the write method to display text on a Web page using JavaScript. Document.write indicates that the results should be printed to the current Web page. On the inside of the parentheses, notice that text you want printed onscreen is enclosed by quotation marks. Also notice that the variables used to store the total amount of money, as well as the tip amount on that total, are located within the write method. If you want to display the results of a variable, insert that variable into the write statement without quotation marks. JavaScript prints the text to type within quotation marks literally and prints the values of the variables that aren't surrounded by quotation marks. The line in the example code in Listing 27.2 displays the following onscreen:

```
A 15% tip for $20 would be: $3
```

Variables and literal text must be separated within the `write` statement. The example in Listing 27.2 uses a comma for that separation. You don't have to use commas, however. You may be more comfortable with the use of a plus sign (+) instead of a comma, which also concatenates these text strings and variables together.

Finally, the function returns a variable that holds the results of the function. You don't necessarily need to return a result, depending on the nature of the function you're writing. If you're writing a function that does some mathematical calculations, chances are you would want to return the result to the place in the program where the call to the function was made. For instance, if you wrote a function `FindSquareRoot` that determined the square root of a number, you would want that function to return the result. That way, a section of the main program could write the results using a single line of code:

```
document.write("The square root of 4 is: ",FindSquareRoot(4))
```

Because the function you wrote (`FindSquareRoot`) returns a result, you could use that result in the `write` statement immediately. You could also assign the result of `FindSquareRoot` to a variable and then write out that variable, but the preceding example compacts the code.

THE OBJECT FAMILY TREE

Of course JavaScript does not allow you only to invoke functions within the Web page. A key option that JavaScript offers is the ability to access information within a Web browser via specific objects inherent to the browser. These objects allow the scripts to monitor information about the Web page and browser or change these characteristics.

No object in the Web browser's Document Object Model (DOM) stands alone. Each object is related in one way to another object and can be referenced by a scripting language such as JavaScript. This relationship has been determined from a top-down approach to the browser window. Everything you view inside the window is part of the window. Therefore, the `window` object is the topmost object in the hierarchy for the Web browser objects. Figure 27.1 illustrates how these objects are related to each other.

Immediately beneath the `window` object are the `document`, `location`, `history`, and additional `window` objects. If you think of a typical Web page, you realize that these attributes describe the overall window. The browser window has information regarding the URL or location of the page you are viewing, historical information tracked by the browser for going back and forward through pages, a document that has the actual page data, and additional windows such as *frames (page 210)*.

PART
V

CH

27

Figure 27.1
The JavaScript language can access a hierarchy of objects exposed by the Web browser.

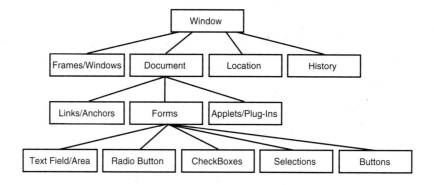

The Web page document you view in the browser is typically the most complex object in this hierarchy because it is where all information is presented to the viewer and where data is retrieved through forms. Therefore it shouldn't be surprising to find numerous objects that are related strictly to the document object. Figure 27.1 shows that there are three basic types of information that describe a document: links and anchors, applets and plug-ins, and forms. forms consist of many objects themselves. Forms can contain any number of buttons, radio buttons, check boxes, or text entry fields. All these objects fall beneath the form object in the hierarchy.

> **Note**
>
> With the advent of *Dynamic HTML (page 506)*, the object model for the Web browser has expanded tremendously. With the current version of Dynamic HTML, it is now possible to address all objects on the Web page, not just specific ones. Dynamic HTML offers a more robust Document Object Model (DOM) for programming the Web browser using JavaScript. However, keep in mind that the DOMs for different browsers may not be identical.

NAMING OBJECTS

Now that you know the relationships between the numerous family members of the JavaScript language, it's important to understand how to reference each object individually. If you have experience designing Web page forms, you're probably familiar with the concept of naming form controls. Naming was necessary to pass information from the form to a CGI script on the server. This naming concept is even more important in JavaScript and other object-oriented languages.

Each object in JavaScript must be given a name in order to be uniquely identified in the language. The objects you cannot create in JavaScript have their own unique default names. For instance, you cannot create new documents or location information objects dynamically through JavaScript, so each of these objects uses its default name: document and location, respectively. You can update some of these objects or read information from them, but you cannot create new *instances*, or additional copies, of any of these objects.

You must appropriately name objects that you create. To name an object, use the NAME attribute when creating the object. For instance, if you were creating a new text field for entering a name on a form, you would use the following syntax:

```
<INPUT TYPE="text" NAME="yourname">
```

REFERENCING OBJECTS

After all custom objects have been named appropriately, you can reference any object within the browser window. You can use the top-level objects by themselves in your JavaScript applications. However, if you want to reference any of the objects that are descendants of the window object, you need to explicitly state the hierarchical path. Simply put, this statement means you must include all objects in your code between the root object (window) and the object you want to reference. Fortunately, you don't need to include the root object (window) each time you reference an object because everything must come from this starting point anyway. Use the . character to separate elements in the hierarchy path that you specify in a JavaScript application.

For example, to check an attribute on an entry field called yourname in a form on your Web page document, use the following syntax to identify that field:

```
document.myform.yourname
```

or

```
document.forms[0].yourname
```

The first example shows how to traverse the path if you have assigned a name to the form in your Web page. The second example depicts how you can use the forms default object to reference a form on the Web page. Notice the [0] syntax. This syntax indicates to JavaScript that you want to read the first form on the page. Additional forms on a page are identified by using [1], [2], [3], and so forth.

ARRAYS OF OBJECTS

As you can see in the previous example showing how to reference an item in a form, JavaScript can distinguish between multiple forms on a Web page, even if they're not all properly named, because each object is stored in an array. An *array* is a series of similar objects that are grouped together logically and uniquely identified by a number, or index. Indexes in JavaScript range from zero to one less than the number of objects on the page. This rule has been inherited from the JavaScript ancestor, the C language.

You can think of an array as a row of houses on a street. Each house may be different, but they are all houses. In addition, each house has a street number associated with it. If you wanted to reference a particular house, you would use that house's street number. The same goes for arrays. In the example with forms, each form on a Web page may be different (different entry fields and buttons), but they are all still forms. They can each be referenced by a unique form number. Forms aren't the only object that may be considered an array. You also can use arrays to identify a series of frames, hyperlinks, and anchors on a Web page.

OBJECT PROPERTIES

So now that you can uniquely identify an object on a Web page, what can you do with it? Depending on the object, you can set and read properties (attributes) of the object. Each object in JavaScript has properties. Some properties are unique to a particular object, and others are shared across all or multiple objects.

You can change an object's attributes by setting a property of an object equal to the value you want. For example, suppose you want to change the value entered in the yourname field in the form on a page. In that case, you would be modifying the value property for the yourname object. You could use the following syntax:

```
document.forms[0].yourname.value="John Doe"
```

Likewise, you could read property values to use elsewhere in your JavaScript application. For instance, you could read the value from the yourname field to print a welcome message:

```
Document.writeln("Hello " + document.forms[0].yourname.value + ", good to see you
again!")
```

OBJECT METHODS

Properties alter the attributes of an object, and methods invoke a particular action that's unique to a specific object. To execute a method in JavaScript, you specify an object with its hierarchical path and then reference its method by name and a set of parentheses. Several common methods in JavaScript simply invoke events, which the next section discusses. Table 27.1 shows some common JavaScript methods.

TABLE 27.1 JAVASCRIPT METHODS

Method	Description	Applies To
focus()	Sets the input cursor to a particular entry field or object on a form.	Text fields Text areas Selections
blur()	Deselects an entry field or object on the form. Opposite of focus().	Text fields Text areas Selections
select()	Highlights text in an entry field.	Text fields Text areas
click()	Simulates a mouse click on either a link or other object.	Buttons Radio buttons Check boxes Submit buttons Reset buttons
enable()	Allows an entry field to be typed into or an object to be clicked on.	All input objects
disable()	Does not allow entry fields to be typed into or objects to be clicked on. These objects are grayed out to show disabled status.	All input objects

Therefore, if you wanted to select all the text in the yourname field on a Web page form, you would use the following JavaScript code:

```
document.forms[0].yourname.select()
```

OBJECT EVENTS

Events are similar to methods for an object, except that you can explicitly determine what actions are to be taken when an event is triggered. Most events are caused when a user interacts with an object, such as clicking on a button, selecting text, or moving between entry fields and objects. Each of these actions may trigger an event that you may want to act upon in your JavaScript application.

Events are coded in the attribute section of a new object created on a form. The name of the event to be coded for is used as the attribute name, and the actual JavaScript code to be performed is enclosed in quotation marks afterwards. For instance, to create a new button labeled My button that performs a function called myfunction, use the following line of code:

```
<INPUT TYPE="button" VALUE="My button" NAME="mybutton"
onClick="writeln('Result='+myfunction())">
```

Note

Some functions of JavaScript require you to use quotation marks within an event. This requirement complicates matters because the attribute that holds the event code is surrounded by quotation marks of its own, as in the following example:

```
<INPUT TYPE="button" VALUE="My button" onClick="writeln('CLICK!')">
```

Typically, the writeln method requires double quotation marks around the text you want to write to the window. However, JavaScript is flexible enough to interchange single and double quotation marks as necessary to accommodate these situations.

Tip #151

As you begin to add more attributes to an object on one line of code, you can see how easy it is to get confused. Consider spanning attributes across multiple lines and indenting code instead of stretching a single line as wide as it can go. Take the following line for example:

```
<INPUT TYPE="button" VALUE="My button" NAME="mybutton"

onClick="result=myfunction();writeln('Result='+result)">
```

This line would be more legible if it were broken and stored in your HTML document as the following:

```
<INPUT TYPE="button"
        VALUE="My Button"
        NAME="mybutton"
        onClick="result=myfunction();
          writeln('Result='+result)"
```

Several events may be triggered in JavaScript. Table 27.2 shows some valid events in JavaScript and with which objects you can use them. In the following sections, you will see many more events that are available for specific objects.

TABLE 27.2   AVAILABLE EVENTS IN JAVASCRIPT

Events	Description	Applies To
onBlur	The opposite of onFocus, onBlur code is executed when you click an object other than the current object or tab off of the current object.	Text fields Text areas Selections
onChange	Code for onChange events is executed when the value of a field has been changed.	Text fields Text areas
onClick	When you click an object, the JavaScript code for that object's onClick event is executed.	Buttons Radio buttons Check boxes Submit buttons Reset buttons
onFocus	This code executes when an object is activated. Typically, activation is either through clicking or tabbing to an object.	Text fields Text areas Selections
onLoad	When a Web page is loaded, this event is triggered once the page has finished being loaded.	Web page body frame sets
onUnload	This event is triggered when a Web page is exited as a result of the user navigating to a different page.	Web page body frame sets
onMouseOver	You can control what happens when you pass the mouse cursor over a link on a Web page using the onMouseOver event.	Links
onSelect	When you highlight text in an entry field, the onSelect code is executed for that object.	Text fields Text areas
onSubmit	If you want to execute JavaScript code when the Submit button has been pressed, you can use the onSubmit event.	Form submission

EVENT DETAILS

Events captured by JavaScript functions can also be further interrogated for more useful information. For example, it's important to invoke a JavaScript function when a key on the keyboard is pressed, but it may become necessary to determine exactly which key was pressed. To accomplish this, Web browsers such as Netscape Navigator and Microsoft Internet Explorer provide an `event` object. The `event` object contains various properties that are set when an event is triggered within the Web browser:

`data`—This property contains an array of information that represents the URLs of objects that were dropped during a `DragDrop` event.

`height`—The height of the source window or frame can be determined via this property for the `event` object.

`layerX/layerY`—When using Dynamic HTML and layers, the `layerX/layerY` properties represent the X and Y coordinates of the mouse cursor. When resizing a layer, these properties represent the new width and height of the object. Otherwise they represent the X and Y position of the mouse cursor, relative to the top-left corner of the layer in which the mouse cursor was when the event was triggered.

`modifiers`—In situations such as mouse or keyboard events, there could be additional special keys used in conjunction with the original event. For example, the user could hold down the Alt key while clicking an object. Valid modifiers include `ALT_MASK`, `CONTROL_MASK`, `META_MASK`, and `SHIFT_MASK`.

`pageX/pageY`—These properties are very similar to the `layerX/layerY` properties. The primary difference is that the `pageX/pageY` properties represent the mouse cursor's position relative to the *entire* Web page, not just the object in which the event was triggered.

`screenX/screenY`—Not unlike the `pageX/pageY` properties, the `screenX/screenY` properties represent the mouse cursor's position relative to the entire computer screen. This includes the area outside the browser window.

`target`—This property contains a string value that indicates the object to which the event was sent.

`type`—In your JavaScript application you can determine the type of event that was raised by interrogating the textual value represented in this property. This is useful if you wish to create generic event handlers.

`which`—As discussed earlier, the `which` property specifies detail information for an event, such as the key pressed during keyboard events or the mouse button used during mouse events.

`width`—Logically, just as the `height` property holds the height of the current window or frame, this property contains the corresponding width.

`x/y`—Instead of using the `layerX/layerY` properties, you could use these equivalent properties.

In the case of determining which key was pressed, the `which` property holds an ASCII value representing the key on the keyboard. By checking this property in the JavaScript function that handles the `onKeyPress` event, you can perform actions based on particular keystrokes.

UNDERSTANDING OBJECT DETAILS

The previous sections acquainted you with the fundamentals of properties, methods, and events for JavaScript. This section investigates some specific attributes of the standard Web browser objects. Certain objects contain their own properties and methods. In the sections that follow, each object is presented, followed by specific properties, methods, and events, with appropriate descriptions of each.

There is a large number of properties, methods, and events associated with each object, and covering each would clearly extend beyond the focus of this chapter. The object model becomes increasingly more complex when you begin considering the entire Dynamic HTML model. This chapter is an introduction to JavaScript and the basic Document Object Model. For more information on JavaScript and document object components, visit the Netscape developer Web site at
http://developer.netscape.com/docs/manuals/js/client/jsref.

window

The `window` object, as you should recall from Figure 27.1, is the highest level object in the hierarchy of objects. It is the root and because of its status, it doesn't have to be included in the hierarchy path when objects are identified. Because all objects are descendants of this object, the `window` object is inferred by JavaScript.

OBJECT PROPERTIES

`frames[index]`—To uniquely identify frames within a window, use the `frames` property. The index refers to each frame on the Web page in the order the frames were defined in the HTML document. The indexes begin at zero and end at one less than the total number of frames per page.

`frames.length`—If the number of frames used on a page is uncertain, you can use this property to determine the total number.

`innerHeight/innerWidth`—These two properties return the dimensions of the browser's content area of the window. The two properties describe the window's height and width, respectively, in pixels.

`outerHeight/outerWidth`—Like `innerHeight` and `innerWidth`, `outerHeight` and `outerWidth` properties identify the size of the overall browser window in pixels.

`parent`—This property identifies the parent window of the current window. Often the parent window is the frameset.

`self`—This property refers to the current window. It is especially useful when a Web page has multiple frames.

`top`—This property identifies the topmost window, the one in which all other windows are embedded.

OBJECT METHODS

`alert("text")`—Sometimes you need to post a warning message. You can use the `alert` method to accomplish this task and use your own custom message. For example, the following code produces the dialog box depicted in Figure 27.2.

`alert("Your order has been canceled.")`

Figure 27.2
The `alert` method can post a warning message.

`close`—If you have multiple browser windows open, you can choose to close one by invoking this method on the `window` object you want to close.

`confirm("text")`—This method is similar to the `alert` method. The `confirm` method, however, enables the user to choose to either continue (OK) or cancel. Again, you can pass a custom message as a parameter to this method. The method returns TRUE if OK is selected and FALSE if Cancel is selected. The following line of code produces the message box displayed in Figure 27.3.

`confirm("You are about to make a purchase. Is it OK to continue?")`

Figure 27.3
The `confirm` method enables the user to make a choice of whether to continue.

`find(string, caseSensitive, backward)`—You can search for information within the currently loaded Web page by calling this method, followed by the string you want to search for within the Web page. Optionally, you can choose whether the results of the search rely on the case of the text or if the search should look backward through the data in the document to find a string within the page.

`home`—Invoking this method causes the Web browser to redirect to the home page as defined in the options for the browser.

`open("URL", "window name")`—The `open` method enables you to jump from the current Web page to another Web page, opening an additional browsing window to display the new page. This method accepts a URL to jump to as well as the name you want to see in the caption bar of the newly created browser window.

`print`—Prints the currently loaded Web page to the default printer for the computer.

prompt("Message", "defaultValue")—A new dialog box has been added to more recent versions of JavaScript. This window displays particular text with OK and Cancel buttons. One major difference is that this window also provides a single line for entering data. The return value of this method contains the data that the end user enters into the dialog box.

close()—The opposite of the open method, the close method closes the currently selected window.

OBJECT EVENTS

onBlur—Whenever the user clicks outside the browser window and deselects it, this event is triggered for the window.

onFocus—The opposite of onBlur, the onFocus event triggers when the user clicks the browser window to select it and make it the active window.

onDragDrop—When the drag and drop operation is used, this event is fired.

onError—If an error occurs during the execution of a JavaScript statement, you can choose how to handle this occurrence.

onLoad—When the Web page is first loaded within the Web browser, the onLoad event is invoked.

onUnload—This event is the opposite of the onLoad event and therefore occurs whenever the Web browser is about to leave a page.

onResize—As its name implies, this event is registered whenever the user resizes the dimensions of the Web browser window or a frame within that window.

location

The location object holds information regarding the current URL for a Web page. Because this object is a descendant of the window object, preface any location properties or methods with location.the *name of the object*. This object is equivalent to the line that contains the URL in the browser.

OBJECT PROPERTIES

hash—For use with CGI scripts, the hash property contains any information that follows the # (number) symbol in a URL after submission.

host—After the protocol portion of a URL, there is a host name that typically includes domain names and ports, if any are used. The host property returns the entire host name and port.

hostname—If you want to retrieve only the host name without port information, use this property.

href—This property contains the entire URL as it appears in the browser's location line.

pathname—This property is the entire string that appears after the third / (slash) in a URL. This string is typically the directory structure and file that uniquely identify the document you are viewing in the browser.

port—To return to only the port for the current document, examine this property.

protocol—This property is the type of protocol used for the Internet that precedes URLs. This property returns either HTTP:, FTP:, GOPHER:, or any other protocol for the page currently viewed in the browser.

search—For use with CGI scripts, this property returns information after the ? (question mark) symbol in an URL after a form has been submitted.

post—This property holds any post headers that may exist.

OBJECT METHODS

reload—Forces the current Web page to be reloaded within the Web browser.

replace(URL)—Renames the URL found within the Web browser address line for the current page to the value set in the URL parameter.

history

The history object holds information about pages that were recently visited. It contains the URLs for pages that the client has visited that are typically found in the drop-down list of the location line of the browser. It also allows you to traverse backward or forward through the history, which is similar to using the Back and Forward buttons on the browser.

OBJECT PROPERTIES

previous—Access this property to find the URL of the last page visited.

next—If there is a URL for the next entry in the history file, this property returns it.

current—This property retrieves the URL of the current page.

length—This property provides the total number of items in the History list.

OBJECT METHODS

back—Forces the browser to load the last visited page into the browser window.

forward—Causes the Web browser to load the next page as defined in the history queue.

go(# of pages)—You may jump forward or backward any number of entries that are in the History list. Each entry in the History list contains information on the page last visited, including the document's URL. If you specify a positive number for the go method, you jump forward that many entries. Negative numbers cause the browser to jump back a specified number of entries.

go("title or URL")—Because entries in the History list change often, you may need to jump to an entry in the list by using the title of the document or its URL. You can specify either the document title or URL in the go method. JavaScript finds the first entry that exists with all or part of the information you specify in the entry's URL or title.

document

The `document` object contains and enables you to set information regarding the overall appearance of the document presented in the browser. Again, remember to preface properties and methods in your JavaScript application with the `document.` notation.

OBJECT PROPERTIES

`alinkColor`—While you hold down the mouse button on a link (without letting go of the button), the link changes to a color that is neither the default `linkColor` or the visited `vlinkColor`. You may read or set this highlight color using the RGB hexadecimal codes and the `alinkColor` property.

`anchors[index]`—Multiple anchors are treated as an array, just like forms and links. The index indicates a specific anchor based on the order in which the anchors were created in an HTML document.

`anchors.length`—As with links and forms, you can determine the total number of anchors on a page with this property.

`applets[index]`—Similar to the forms array, the `applets` property is an array of values that point to the specific Java applets that may exist on the Web page. The index identifies which applet on the page is to be used in JavaScript.

`applets.length`—To help determine the number of applets that exist on the Web page, you can use this property.

`bgColor`—This property identifies the color used as a background for the Web page. It consists of a string of three hexadecimal codes. Each code identifies the amount of red, green, or blue color to be mixed. Code values may range from `00` to `FF` hexadecimal (0–255 decimal).

`cookie`—The `cookie` property enables you to specify cookie information as well as retrieve cookie information related to a particular Web page.

`domain`—Retrieves the domain name of the current Web server on which the Web page can be found.

`embeds[index]`/`plugins[index]`—Just as you can have multiple Java applets within a single Web page, you can also place multiple plug-ins within a Web browser window. To act upon each one, you can use the `embeds` array where the index specifies which embedded plug-in you want to reference.

`embeds/plugins.length`—You can easily determine the number of plug-ins available on a page by interrogating this property.

`fgColor`—Similar to `bgColor`, this property controls the color to use for the standard foreground text color.

`forms[index]`—As mentioned earlier, multiple forms on a page are stored in an array. You may then reference each form uniquely by using the appropriate index. Indexes range from zero to one less than the total number of forms on a page. The order of the indexes is based on the order in which the forms are generated in the HTML document. You may also use the form name you identify with a new form to access a specific form.

`forms.length`—A single Web page can have multiple forms. The `forms.length` property returns the total number of forms on the currently viewed page.

`images[index]`—With all of the arrays currently available to the `document` object, you should not be surprised to find an array that uniquely identifies all images that exist within the Web page.

`images.length`—The number of images embedded on the Web page or the length of the `images` array can be determined via this property.

`lastmodified`—This property holds the last date on which the document was modified and returns the result as a string.

`linkColor`—Because the default colors for links may blend into the background, it's necessary to change the color of the links as well. The `linkColor` property specifies the color of links on the page that have not been visited yet. It uses the technique of combining hexadecimal codes to specify a color.

`links[index]`—Just like forms, links on a web page are stored in an array. Each link may be referenced by its appropriate index. Indexes range from zero to one less than the total number of links on a form and are determined by the order in which they appear in an HTML document.

`links.length`—From experience, you know that a web page contains multiple links to other places. To determine the total number of links on a page in your JavaScript program, use the `links.length` property.

`referrer`—The `referrer` property is the URL of the page that was loaded just prior to the current page.

`title`—Use this property to modify or use the current title of the document, which appears in the caption bar of the browser window.

`url`—You can obtain the URL of the current document from this property of the `document` object instead of the `location` object.

`vlinkColor`—This property specifies the red-green-blue (RGB) combination that indicates a color to use for links that have already been visited.

OBJECT METHODS

`write(data or "text")`—The `write` method displays additional text on the currently viewed window in the browser. It does not affect paragraphs or other structures, but it appears in sequence with the HTML document. This method can display text or data. Enclose explicit, static text with single or double quotation marks. Do not enclose dynamic text, such as the results of variables, with quotes. You may also concatenate text using the comma (,) or the plus sign (+). The `write` method displays text without placing a carriage return at the end of the line. Therefore, when using multiple `write` statements, the data appears to be concatenated. For example, the following code would display the sentence `This is a test` on one line:

```
document.write("This ")
document.write("is ")
```

```
document.write("a ")
document.write("test")
```

> writeln(data or "text")—This method works identically to the previously mentioned write method, except that it appends a carriage return at the end of the line each time the method is called. However, this only applies to text that you are writing using the preformatted tags such as <PRE> or <XMP>. For example, the following code

```
document.writeln("Hi ")
document.writeln("there!")
```

> would display

```
Hi
there!
```

Note

You can use several special characters, such as new line characters, within write statements, writeln statements, and strings within JavaScript. The following list shows each of these special characters and how to identify them in JavaScript. These characters are the same as those you would find in the C programming language.

\"   Specifies that an actual quotation mark is to be written between the quotation marks that otherwise surround a string.

\\   Specifies that an actual backslash character is to be written within a string. This is essential, since the backslash usually indicates a special character and is otherwise ignored.

\n   Specifies a new line character, which forces text onto the next line when output.

\r   Specifies the carriage return character.

\t   Specifies the tab character, which is useful for indenting text.

Each special character is preceded by the \ (slash) character. The slash instructs JavaScript to use the following character as a special character (if it is one of the letters in the preceding list) or the literal character after the \. For instance, if you wanted to use a quotation mark within a write statement, you could use the following syntax:

write("\"This is great!,\" she said.")

> clear()—This method clears the contents of the current window.

> open("*MIME Type*")—This method opens a specific MIME-supported file type, launching the appropriate plug-in or helper application as necessary.

> close()—This method closes the document windowwrite method displays.

OBJECT EVENTS

> onClick—When the user clicks anywhere within the document window, this event is triggered.

> onDblClick—Similar to onClick, the onDbdClick event is raised when a user double-clicks anywhere within the Web page.

onKeyDown—When the user presses and holds down a key on the keyboard, the onKeyDown event is triggered and can be captured by JavaScript.

onKeyUp—The opposite of onKeyDown, this event is raised whenever a key on the keyboard is released after being previously held down.

onKeyPress—Not to be confused by the onKeyDown or onKeyUp event, this event represents the entire process of pressing down *and* releasing a key on the keyboard. The onKeyDown and onKeyUp events can be thought of as subsets of this overall event.

onMouseDown—When a mouse button is depressed and held down, JavaScript within the Web page can be notified via this event.

onMouseUp—Similar to onKeyUp, when the user releases a mouse button, this event is fired.

FORMS

JavaScript still uses forms and objects on the form, such as buttons or text entry fields, extensively. Each form is an object in itself and may be referenced either by the forms[] property or by the name you associate with the form in the HTML document when you create it. If you use the forms[] property, each form on the Web page is stored in the order in which it appears on the page. Also, the first form may be identified with an index of zero (forms[0]), the second with an index of one (forms[1]), and so forth. The last form on a page may be referenced with an index that is equal to one less than the total number of forms on the page.

OBJECT PROPERTIES

action—The action attribute of a form may be returned as a string through this property. The action attribute typically contains information on what CGI script or additional program is to be run.

elements[*index*]—This array categorizes all elements within the form and stores them so that each element within a form can be identified by an index.

elements.length—This property indicates the number of elements that may exist within a form.

method—Not to be confused with object-oriented methods, this property specifies what method the form uses for information. It returns either a 0 for the GET method or 1 for the POST method.

name—This property holds the name that identifies a form. This name comes from the HTML source code that creates the form. This property is an optional method for referencing forms instead of using forms arrays.

target—Newer Web browsers enable you to create multiple windows for formatting information. Each window that's created either by links or forms may be identified by a name, which is stored in the window's target property. The unique window name allows for window maintenance capabilities from your JavaScript application. Figure 27.4 shows an instance where the whole story in a new window link in the window on the left displays the new window on the right when clicked.

Figure 27.4
The `whole story` `in a new window` link creates a new browser window when clicked.

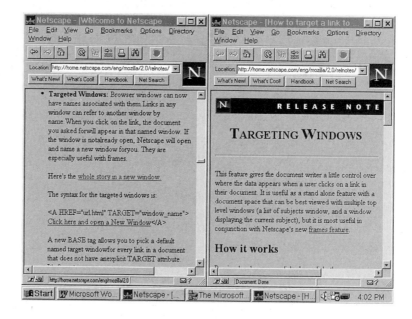

OBJECT METHODS

`reset()`—The `reset` method causes the form information to be cleared, similarly to clicking a Reset button on the Web page.

`submit()`—This method forces the form to be submitted. This action is the same as if you clicked a Submit button.

OBJECT EVENTS

`onReset`—Once the user clicks a Reset button and the `reset()` method is invoked, this `onReset` event is fired. JavaScript routines can then process the actions that must occur when a Web page's form data is reset.

`onSubmit`—When a Submit button is clicked or the `submit()` method is invoked, the `onSubmit` event is triggered. At this point, you can write JavaScript code that does some work before sending the data.

TEXT FIELDS AND AREAS

Because single-line text fields and multiple-line text areas are very similar in nature, they share the same properties, methods, and events. The "Object Methods" and "Object Events" sections in this chapter reviewed the common events and methods for text fields.

Note

Because text, buttons, radio buttons, check boxes, and selections are part of a form, you must include the form name when identifying these objects. For example, if a text field named `yourname` exists in a form, you need to use the full qualifier `document.forms[0].yourname` to correctly access that object.

PROPERTIES

defaultValue—This property contains the default value, if any exists, for a text object. The value returned is the value of the text object before any changes were made to it.

name—This property is the name of the text object, which uniquely identifies it on the form. It is set with the NAME attribute when defining the text object in the HTML document.

type—This property corresponds to the type of text object as identified by the TYPE attribute within the text field's HTML syntax.

value—The purpose of text objects is to accept information. The value property of a text object holds typed information and enables you to change that information through JavaScript programming.

METHODS

blur()—This method forces the blur event to be triggered for the text field.

focus()—You can set the current focus, or the text input cursor, to a particular text entry field using this method.

select()—To highlight all of the text within an entry field, you can use this method with the entry field you wish to highlight.

EVENTS

onBlur—This event is triggered on an entry field if it originally had focus and lost it because you pressed the Tab key or clicked another form object.

onChange— If data is changed within an entry field, this event is triggered.

onFocus—When a user tabs into this field or selects it with the mouse, the entry field receives focus and this event is triggered.

onKeyDown/onKeyPress/onKeyDown— These events are available to text areas only. In addition to standard text field events, text areas can also use the keyboard-specific events.

onSelect—Whenever the text within an entry field is highlighted by the user, the onSelect method is triggered for that field.

CHECK BOXES

Forms on a page may include check boxes or switches that you can turn on and off to make selections on the form.

PROPERTIES

checked—The checked property of a particular check box contains the value TRUE if the box is checked and FALSE if it is unchecked.

defaultChecked— This property returns TRUE if the specified check box was initially checked. FALSE is returned otherwise. The default status of a check box is determined by the CHECKED attribute when the check box is created by the HTML document.

name— This property uniquely identifies each object on a Web page, including check boxes. For instance, if you created three check boxes on the form, they might be named option1, option2, and option3.

type/value—The type or value property of a check box contains the information for the check box as defined by its TYPE attribute in its HTML declaration.

METHODS

click()—You can simulate a check box being set or cleared by invoking the click() method for an object.

EVENTS

onBlur—As with most objects, the onBlur event is triggered whenever a user deselects a currently selected check box.

onClick—The onClick event is triggered whenever a user clicks a check box to set or clear its status.

onFocus—The opposite of onBlur, onFocus is invoked whenever a check box receives the focus without necessarily being clicked. For example, if a user presses the Tab key to navigate through a form, the check box will become highlighted or receive focus. The user can then press the Spacebar to toggle the state of the check box.

RADIO BUTTONS

Radio buttons are similar to toggle switches. They enable only one option to be selected at a time from a group of options. In HTML, radio buttons in the same group share the same name but return different values. To access a radio button called gender on a form named myform in a JavaScript application, you would use document.myform.gender to qualify that object.

Once you have access to the object, you will find that there may be several radio buttons related to that radio button group's name. To make it possible for you to choose a specific radio button within the group, JavaScript assigns a numeric property to each radio button within that group, starting at zero. You can then access an individual radio button by its number. For example, to access the first radio button in the gender group, you would use document.forms[0].gender[0] in your JavaScript code.

PROPERTIES

checked—If the current radio button is selected, the Boolean value TRUE is returned for this property; otherwise, FALSE is returned.

defaultChecked—This property indicates if the default setting for the current radio button is selected (TRUE) or not selected (FALSE).

name—This property is the name of the radio button group, as defined in the HTML document when the group is created.

type—The type property is a reflection of the TYPE attribute specified in the HTML source code for the radio button.

value—This property reveals the value a radio button returns when selected. The value is specified in the HTML source code as an attribute when you create the radio button.

METHODS

blur()—By invoking this method, you can remove the focus or highlight for a given radio button object.

click()—You can simulate a radio button being selected by invoking the click() method for a particular radio button option.

focus()—The result of this method is the exact opposite of the blur() method. It sets the focus or highlights a given radio button.

EVENTS

onBlur—Once the user deselects a currently selected radio button, the onBlur event is raised for that radio button.

onClick— Whenever a user clicks a radio button option, the onClick event is triggered for that option.

onFocus— Similarly, the onFocus event is invoked when the user highlights a radio button without necessarily clicking it. Again, this could occur when the user presses the Tab key to navigate to that radio button.

SELECTIONS AND LISTS

Another popular control for selecting information on a form is the selection object. This object enables you to create lists of answers where one or more elements in the list may be selected at once. Options within selection objects are grouped within <SELECT> and </SELECT> tags. Each option is stored in an array. This array is identified as an *option* parameter for the selection list object.

For instance, assume that there is a choice on a form for a person's eye color. This choice would be implemented nicely using a selection object named eyecolor. The JavaScript code would then access the first item in the list using the following statement:

```
document.forms[0].eyecolor.options[0]
```

Each option for a selection object is maintained in an array. As you can see from the preceding statement, the first option is identified with an index value of 0. Subsequent options are identified by increasing this index. The index range is the same as for other arrays in JavaScript, between zero and one less than the total number of items.

PROPERTIES

defaultSelected—You can determine which items are selected by default within a selection list. The defaults are determined through the SELECTED attribute for each <OPTION> tag. This property returns TRUE if the currently indexed option was a default; FALSE is returned otherwise.

length— This property contains the total number of elements that exist in the selection list.

options —This property holds an array of options specified in the HTML page. This array can be indexed either by name or by number.

selected —This property returns the Boolean value TRUE if the currently indexed option item is selected or highlighted. FALSE is returned otherwise.

selectedIndex —This number identifies the position of a list item in the selection. Zero indicates the first row, and one less than the total number of items in the selection object represents the last row.

text—The text property hold the string that appears at the current index in the selection element. This text follows the <OPTION> tag in the HTML document for a selection element.

value—As with most other objects, the value sent to the server doesn't need to be the same text included in the selection list. This property holds the value to be sent to the server during submission, as defined in the VALUE attribute for an <OPTION> tag in the HTML document.

METHODS

blur()—Opposite of the focus() method, the blur() method removes the focus of a specific selection list.

focus()—To force a specific selection to receive the focus, you can invoke this method.

EVENTS

onBlur—Once the selection or list object has lost focus because the user pressed the Tab key or clicked another form object, the onBlur event is triggered.

onChange—If the highlighted choice in a selection or list has changed, this event is triggered.

onFocus—When a selection list receives the focus because of the user pressing the Tab key or clicking the list with the mouse, the onFocus event is triggered.

BUTTONS

Web page developers have wanted greater control over buttons for the longest time and now they have it. Custom button capability has been added to the newer Web browsers and JavaScript. You can add buttons for submitting forms, clearing forms, or performing any custom functions.

PROPERTIES

name—The name used to uniquely identify a button within a form may be referenced by the name property.

value—In the case of buttons, the value property is the caption that appears on the face of the button.

METHODS

click()—To simulate the action of clicking a button object, you can use the click() method for that particular button.

EVENTS

onBlur — Once the button object has lost focus because the user pressed the Tab key or clicked another form object, the onBlur event is triggered.

onClick—You can create JavaScript code to handle what happens when a user clicks a button with this event.

onFocus—When a button receives the focus because of the user pressing the Tab key to select the button, the onFocus event is triggered.

onMouseUp/onMouseDown—The onMouseUp/onMouseDown pair of events is available whenever the user presses down or releases the mouse button on a form or button object.

ANCHORS AND LINKS

No hypertext Web page would be complete without hypertext links. This isn't a new feature to Web browsers, but there are a few properties and events that may be associated with links that allow you greater control.

EVENTS

onClick—This event is triggered when a user clicks a link.

onDblClick—When the user double-clicks a link, this event is triggered.

onKeyDown/onKeyUp/onKeyPress—These three related events are raised when the user presses a key and holds it, releases a held key, or presses and immediately releases a key, respectively.

onMouseDown/onMouseUp—Like the keyboard events, the onMouseDown/onMouseUp events are fired when the user presses and holds a mouse button or releases a held mouse button.

onMouseOut—Whenever the user moves the mouse cursor outside of an area, link, or layer object, this event is invoked.

onMouseOver—It's possible to perform a specific JavaScript action when a user passes the mouse cursor over a link. A practical example is to create more meaningful descriptive text that appears in the bottom-left corner of the browser window. For example:

```
<A HREF="http://www.netscape.com/"
   onMouseOver="window.status='Clicking here will jump
                          to Netscape's Web site.'>
```

USING JAVASCRIPT STATEMENTS

In addition to objects, JavaScript has commands that do things such as control program flow. This section examines multiple statements that control how your JavaScript application runs. This section is where JavaScript really shows its C roots—the statements and operators covered in the following pages are nearly identical to those found in the C programming language.

USING LOOPS

There are several different ways to perform loops (or iterations) in JavaScript: the `for` loop, the `for-in` loop, and the `while` loop. There are significant differences between these loops and, depending on your application, one may be more appropriate than another. For instance, suppose you want to perform an action for a predetermined number of times. You could use a `for` loop to accomplish this task.

Tip #152	Avoid infinite loops. These special loops can continue forever because the user has no way to interrupt them. Under such circumstances, the only way to terminate the loop is to terminate the browser. Often this action requires pressing Ctrl+Alt+Del on the keyboard to invoke the Windows 95 Close Program dialog box and then choosing Netscape or Internet Explorer and clicking the End Task button. Infinite loops are caused by conditions that are never met in the loop. Make sure that all your JavaScript programs have legitimate endpoints and that your conditions are valid.

for LOOP

The `for` loop performs a line of code or a series of lines of code a predetermined number of times. The number of times a loop occurs is maintained by the loop index. In a `for` loop, you specify the starting and ending values for this index, as well as how much the index should change after each iteration. The `for` loop appears as a function and accepts three parameters:

```
for (starting point; ending condition; increment)
```

> *starting point*—This parameter is either a variable initialization or a statement that determines the starting index value.

> *ending condition*—This parameter checks the index for the specified condition. If that index meets the condition in the `for` loop, the statements that occur in the block of code are executed. Once this condition stops being met, the `for` loop is terminated and program execution continues after the block of code. For more information on conditions, see the section on `if` statements.

> *increment*—Each time the condition for a `for` loop is met, the index is increased or decreased by the amount specified by this parameter. Typically indexes for `for` loops end at a greater value then they begin with; therefore, it's common to increase an index by one. Use the ++ syntax to accomplish this task.

Any line of code that exists immediately after the for loop is iterated for the number of times the loop occurs. If you want to include more than a single line of code to be looped, you must enclose that block of code with beginning and ending braces ({ }). It's also recommended that you indent your code inside of the for loop to make it easier to determine which code is executed multiple times. The following loop prints the words *Hello World!* 10 times onscreen:

```
for (i=1; i<=10; i++){
        document.writeln("Hello World!")
}
```

for-in LOOP

A close relative to the for loop is the for-in loop. This kind of loop is similar to a typical for loop in that it executes a block of code a predetermined number of times. However, the number of times this loop is executed depends on the object. This function is primarily used for traversing all properties of an object. It requires two parameters, the index for the loop and the object you want to traverse:

```
for (index in object)
```

For example, the JavaScript function in Listing 27.3 displays all the properties for an object name that is passed into the function.

LISTING 27.3   AN EXAMPLE for-in LOOP

```
function DisplayProps(obj){
        result = "";

        for (i in obj)
                result += "{object}." + i + " = " + obj[i] + "\n";

        alert(result)
}
```

while LOOP

Another loop that's very similar to the for and for-in loops is the while loop. The while loop executes a block of code multiple times until a condition is reached. Unlike the for loop, it doesn't require an index, and JavaScript code within the loop may be executed until any condition occurs. This function accepts one parameter, which is the condition that must be met in order for the loop to occur.

```
while (condition)
```

Suppose you wanted to create a text string of 10 stars (*). Listing 27.4 demonstrates how to accomplish this task using a while loop. As you can see from the example, the condition tests the length of the string built so far. If the string is less than 10 characters long, the function continues to add to it.

LISTING 27.4   THE while LOOP IS USED TO CONSTRUCT A STRING OF STARS

```
s="";

while (s.length<10)
        s += "*";

alert(s)
```

break AND continue STATEMENTS

At times you may find it necessary to prevent a loop from continuing or to skip an iteration of the loop. The break and continue statements enable you to do each of these actions. To understand each statement, examine the code in Listing 27.5. This example displays a dialog box with the word Looped! each time a loop occurs.

LISTING 27.5   AN EXAMPLE OF A LOOP WITH A break STATEMENT

```
for (i=1;i<=5;i++){
        if (i==3)
                break;
        alert("Looped!");
}
```

The loop is supposed to execute five times; however, this example only shows the resulting message twice because of the check to see whether the loop index reached three. When the loop index reaches three, the break statement aborts the loop completely. Program execution continues at the first statement after the loop.

If you changed the break statement in Listing 27.5 to be a continue statement instead, the resulting message would appear four times. The continue statement causes the program execution to continue with the next loop iteration, skipping any remaining code for the current iteration. From the example, the loop would execute twice and then the condition to see whether the loop index is equal to three would be executed. When this condition is true, the continue statement causes the loop to skip to the end of the block of code (skipping over the alert method). The loop then continues to execute the last two times.

USING OPERATORS

There are several operators that may be applied to values to perform mathematical or other arithmetic functions. Although JavaScript employs the standard operators such as addition (+), subtraction (-), multiplication (*) and division (/), it also employs many more powerful operators common to C programmers. Table 27.3 demonstrates some of these more commonly used operators.

TABLE 27.3 OPERATORS TO USE IN CONDITIONAL STATEMENTS

Operator	Function	Description
++	Increment	Increments a value by 1. In a sense, adds one to a value.
- -	Decrement	Decrements a value by 1 or subtracts one from a value.
+=	Addition Assignment	Example: x += 5 is equivalent to x = x+5, which simply adds five to the current value of x.
-=	Subtraction Assignment	Example: x -= 5 is equivalent to x= x-5, which subtracts five from the current value of x.
*=	Multiplication Assignment	Example: x *= 5 is equivalent to x = x*5, which multiplies the current value of x by five and assigns that result to x.
/=	Division Assignment	Example: x /= 5 is equivalent to x = x/5, which divides the current value of x by five and assigns that result to x.
-	Negation	The negation operator negates a value. Example: If x=5 then -x would yield -5. If x=-5 then -x would yield 5.
%	Modulus	This operator returns the remainder when two values are divided integrally. Example: 16 % 5 returns 1.
<<	Bitwise Shift Left	Converts a value to its binary equivalent and shifts the bits one place to the left. The result is converted back to a value.
<<<	Bitwise Double-Shift Left	Converts a value to its binary equivalent and shifts the bits two places to the left. The result is converted back to a value.
>>	Bitwise Shift Right	Converts a value to its binary equivalent and shifts the bits one place to the right. The result is converted back to a value.
>>>	Bitwise Double-Shift Right	Converts a value to its binary equivalent and shifts the bits two places to the right. The result is converted back to a value.
&	Bitwise AND	Converts both values to their binary equivalents and compares each bit by ANDing their values. The result is converted back to a value. Example: 10001000 & 11001010 would yield 10001000.
¦	Bitwise OR	Converts both values to their binary equivalents and compares each bit by ORing their values. The result is converted back to a value. Example: 10001000 ¦ 11001010 would yield 11001010.
^	Bitwise Exclusive OR	Converts both values to their binary equivalents and compares each bit by XORing their values. The result is converted back to a value. Example: 10001000 ^ 11001010 would yield 01000010.

USING CONDITIONS

Conditions were briefly discussed in relation to the use of loops. You also can test for conditions and have JavaScript code act appropriately in other sections of your program. Before looking at additional statements, review some of the common forms of comparisons that may be performed. To compare information in JavaScript, use the operators in Table 27.4.

TABLE 27.4   OPERATORS TO USE IN CONDITIONAL STATEMENTS

Operator	Function	Description
==	Equal	TRUE is returned if the two operands in a condition are equal.
!=	Not equal	If the two operands aren't equivalent, then TRUE is returned.
>	Greater than	TRUE is returned if the first operand is greater in value than the second.
>=	Greater than or equal to	When the first operand's value is greater than or equal to the second's value, TRUE is returned.
<	Less than	The result is TRUE if the first operand is lesser in value than the second.
<=	Less than or equal to	If the first operand's value is less than or equal to the second operand's value, TRUE is returned.
&&	Logical AND	When comparing multiple conditions, && returns TRUE when the first condition's result is TRUE and the second condition's result evaluates to TRUE.
||	Logical OR	When multiple conditions are compared, || returns TRUE if either the first condition or the second condition evaluates to TRUE. If one condition is TRUE, the other condition is basically ignored.
!	Logical NOT	The NOT operator inverts an operator's value. For instance, if an operator is TRUE, the NOT operator causes it to evaluate to FALSE.

if AND if else STATEMENTS

The if condition is a fundamental statement in any programming language. It is a function that evaluates multiple operands using the comparisons listed in Table 27.4 and allows the program to execute code based on the result. If the result is TRUE, the block of code that follows the if statement is executed. If the result is FALSE, that block of code is ignored and program execution continues with the first line of code after that block. Use the following syntax for an if statement:

```
if (condition)  {
        TRUE condition JavaScript code
}
```

You also can execute specific code when an if condition is FALSE. When you use an else statement in conjunction with an if statement, the block of code that follows the else statement is executed when a condition is FALSE. This is different from just allowing the code to resume after an if statement. Use this syntax for an if else statement:

```
if (condition)  {
        TRUE condition JavaScript code
}
else  {
        FALSE condition JavaScript code
}
```

Listing 27.6 depicts an example of an if else statement in use. This example checks whether a user wants a free catalog and prompts for appropriate information based on his or her choice.

LISTING 27.6 A SAMPLE if else STATEMENT

```
result = document.forms[0].sendcatalog.value;

if (result = "y" |¦ result = "yes"){
        alert("Please fill out the form so we can send you a free catalog.");
        FreeCatalog();
}
else {
        alert("You have chosen not to receive a free catalog. Please tell us
why.");
        NoCatalog();
  }
```

SHORTCUT STATEMENTS

As you code more JavaScript applications, you will find yourself constantly coding long lines that identify the hierarchical path to an object. For example, to access the value of the field yourname, you typically need to use the following syntax:

```
document.forms[0].yourname.value
```

This syntax is fine if you're only infrequently accessing one property at a time. However, if you want to access multiple properties at once, this syntax can become frustrating.

with

JavaScript includes a with statement that replaces the need to constantly retype the full qualifying path to an object. The statement simply accepts one parameter, which is the object you want to use.

```
with object name  {
        properties or methods to use with object
}
```

As you can see by the definition, the with statement applies only to attributes and methods that are enclosed within braces ({ }). Listing 27.7 shows a code fragment that uses the with statement.

LISTING 27.7 AN EXAMPLE OF THE with STATEMENT

```
with document.forms[0].yourname {
        alert("Name = " + name);
        alert("Value = " + value);
}
```

Tip #153

Instead of using the with statement, you can also assign a variable to an object and use that variable to invoke methods or access properties for that object:

```
obj = document.forms[0].yourname
alert("Name = " + obj.name);
alert("Value = " + obj.value);
```

this

Sometimes you want JavaScript code to work on the currently active item on a Web page. But how do you determine the currently selected object? JavaScript provides the this statement to indicate that you want to use methods or properties associated with the currently selected object. The following example shows how to display the value of the current object:

```
alert(this.value)
```

COMMENTING YOUR JAVASCRIPT CODE

An old saying states, "It was hard to code, it *should* be hard to understand." But this situation isn't very effective or productive. It's recommended that you comment your JavaScript code. If anyone ever has to maintain your application, he or she will have no idea what you were thinking at the time you wrote the application. In fact, if you were to maintain the code after not looking at it for a year, *you* probably wouldn't remember what you were thinking.

It's important to make textual comments that briefly describe what the JavaScript code is doing in your application. Comments don't have to be verbose, but they should clearly outline key points. Likewise, you don't need to comment every line you write. Try keeping comments to those routines or lines of code that were tricky to write and are confusing to understand without some type of description.

Comments are supported in JavaScript code with the // characters in front of a line in the script. The double slashes indicate to the browser that any text afterwards is a comment and shouldn't be interpreted as JavaScript code. If you want to be more eloquent with your comments and need more than a line to make your point, use the /* and */ symbols to surround your text. Listing 27.8 gives a quick example of the proper use of comments.

LISTING 27.8   ADDING COMMENTS TO JAVASCRIPT CODE

```
/*
Form Calculation Program
Written on: November 23

This program updates subtotals and totals on a form based on values
entered by a user.
*/

// The following line calculates a 25% discount.
discount = amount*.25
newAmount = amount - discount
```

TROUBLESHOOTING

I am experiencing problems with my scripts and can't figure out what is wrong. How can I troubleshoot my applications?

As with any programming language, troubleshooting problems with your application in JavaScript can be a complicated process. The world of debugging is what takes a great amount of time when developers write software solutions. Typically the Web browser will return some form of error when the JavaScript it encounters cannot be handled correctly. When this occurs, typically only a line number is returned.

To begin troubleshooting script errors, you must first be able to access the script. If a page is downloaded from a Web server, you must change the page on the server. But for temporary work, you can always choose Save As from the File menu to save the current HTML file to your local hard disk. In any case, you'll want to look at the actual Web page HTML and code that is loaded locally within the browser. In certain cases, the Web page file on the server may contain additional information such as Active Server Pages code or server-side Include statements that are translated to actual HTML tags. When the Web browser reports an error on a particular line number, it's the line number that it sees in the fully assembled and downloaded Web page. Therefore if the Web page contains a server-side Include statement at the top that contains an additional 100 lines of code, the line number reported back by the Web browser includes the lines that were generated by this server-side Include statement or other commands. In such cases, it is quite possible for the Web browser to report an error on line 400 when there are only 350 lines total in the HTML file as you see it on the server because other HTML was generated dynamically by embedded commands.

The next thing you need to do is open the offending HTML page in a text editor. It is also recommended that you use a text editor other than Notepad, which comes with Windows. You may want to consider using an editor that includes line numbers or at least indicates the position of the cursor. This is important especially when debugging large HTML files with complex JavaScript routines. In these cases, there could be hundreds or thousands of lines of code intermixed with the HTML, and it is nearly impossible to count the lines manually to find the offending line of JavaScript.

Once you have found the exact line that is in question, the error reported by the browser should give you a hint as to what is wrong with the syntax of the line. In some cases, it may be as simple as missing a ; at the end of the line. In other cases, you may not know exactly what is going wrong because the line in question is dependent on variables. If this is the case, consider using the alert command in JavaScript. By using the alert statement, you can display a message box that contains the value of a variable. This can help you track down what is going awry in the script.

Another use for the alert command is to use this statement throughout a section of code that seems to be misbehaving. For example, if you suspect that a for loop is not ending correctly, you can place an alert statement just before the loop and another after the loop. When you execute the script and don't see the second alert statement, chances are you have a problem within the loop itself.

DESIGNERS CORNER

Good programming practices are always good to follow when writing applications or scripts for the Web. There are several things you'll want to consider doing within your code, such as commenting and indenting appropriately.

Commenting is important because it helps future developers who may maintain your Web pages to understand the logic you used when writing a particular script. You should always comment confusing sections thoroughly. Don't feel that you need to write a novel; you should keep your comments succinct and clear.

Indenting is incredibly important as well. As a basic guideline, you should indent all commands that fall between the opening { and the closing }. This will help identify the blocks of code when you are looking at a complete listing. You should also indent deeper as you encounter additional opening { symbols.

```
Function testResult() {
    for (i=0;i<5;i++) {
        if (result[i] == 0) {
            Alert("Result met.");
        }
    }
}
```

With proper indenting, it is much easier to see that the conditional statement occurs within the loop, within the function testResult.

Finally, when designing your scripts, remember to test that they function correctly within several browsers and with several versions of each browser. If you're creating an Internet Web site, you do not want visitors being frustrated because they cannot see your JavaScript application.

CHAPTER 28

USING JAVA APPLETS, BROWSER PLUG-INS, AND ACTIVEX CONTROLS

In this chapter   *by Dennis Jones*

UNDERSTANDING NETSCAPE PLUG-INS

High-end browsers, such as the Netscape browsers and Microsoft Internet Explorer, handle many different media types, but no browser handles everything. Both Netscape and Microsoft put *hooks* into their products to allow programmers to write code that extends the media types supported by the browser. Netscape browsers depend on *helpers* and *plug-ins*. Internet Explorer browsers use ActiveX technology rather than plug-ins to achieve similar effects.

Starting with version 1 of Navigator, Netscape provided ways to enhance its browser with *helper applications (page 582)*, which support data formats beyond the built-in graphics and HTML. With Netscape Navigator version 2, Navigator began supporting plug-ins, another way to extend the range of data types that can be presented on or with a Web page. This continued with Navigator 3 and has been carried into Navigator 4 (which Netscape refers to as Communicator 4). No doubt it will persist in the upcoming Communicator 5.

To see why plug-ins are useful, go to the desktop of a Windows 95/98/NT computer and double-click a few documents. If you choose a document that your system associates with a particular application, that application launches; but, if you double-click a document whose type and creator are unknown, you'll get a dialog box like the one shown in Figure 28.1.

Figure 28.1
A Windows 98 user is invited to *associate* a file extension with an application.

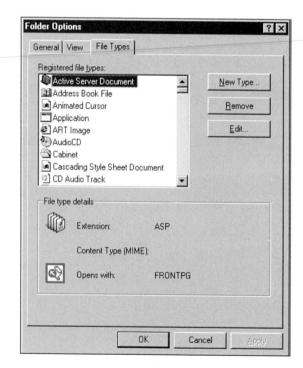

On the whole, operating systems designers have developed workable schemes for mapping documents to applications.

But today, the user's world goes far beyond their local hard drive. The user may have files on a file server on the local area network and may access files on a coworker's machine on the other side of the room or, through a company intranet or the Internet, the other side of the world.

When a Netscape 4 user attempts to open a document that the browser does not recognize, the user gets the dialog box shown in Figure 28.2. This dialog box allows the user to select an external viewer application with the Pick App button or to save the file.

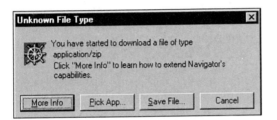

Figure 28.2
A Navigator 4 user attempts to open an unrecognized file type.

Note

Netscape Communicator is quite adaptable; before showing the Unknown File Type dialog box, it looks for an installed application that can handle the file. For example, if you have WinZip on your machine and try to open a ZIP file in Communicator, Communicator automatically calls WinZip instead of opening the Unknown File Type dialog box. (In the example for Figure 28.2, the host machine did not have WinZip installed, so the Unknown File Type dialog box appeared.)

External viewers, also known as *helper applications*, allow the Web user to see a variety of data types that are not built into browser. The downside of helper applications is that they are, indeed, applications. This means that they are fully separate programs launched outside the browser, whereas plug-ins work more or less seamlessly within the browser environment. Therefore, to view a file with a helper application, the user's machine must start a whole new program. This fact means the following:

- The user has to wait while the new program loads.
- The user may run out of memory and not be able to launch the new program.
- If the helper application launches, the document will appear in its own window, out of context from the Web document.
- There's no interaction between the Web document and the external file—for example, if the external file is a movie, there's no provision to allow the user to use buttons on the Web page to control the movie viewer.

PART

V

CH

28

UNDERSTANDING MIME MEDIA TYPES

To understand helper applications and plug-ins, you must first understand MIME media types, formerly known as MIME types. Multimedia Internet Message Extensions, or MIME, were developed to allow users to exchange files by email. Although the Web does not use the full MIME standard, it is convenient to use media types to tell a Web browser how the file is formatted.

MIME is described in detail in Request for Comments (RFC) 1521 and updated in RFCs 2045-2049 (draft standards). Although MIME was originally intended for use in email systems, and RFC 1521 was written with that application in mind, today's user encounters MIME in a variety of multimedia settings.

Note

> RFCs are supervised by the Internet Engineering Task Force (IETF), which is the protocol engineering and development arm of the Internet. The IETF is a large open international community of network designers, operators, vendors, and researchers concerned with the evolution of the Internet architecture. For more information on the IETF and RFCs, go to `http://www.ietf.org/`.

MIME is designed to have a limited number of top-level types, such as `application`, `text`, and `video`, which can be extended by subtypes. Table 28.1 shows some typical MIME-compliant media types.

TABLE 28.1   MIME TYPES CONSIST OF A TYPE AND A SUBTYPE

Type	Subtype	Meaning
application	msword	Format of Microsoft Word documents
application	rtf	The Rich Text Format for word processors
application	octet-stream	A catchall type for a collection of bytes
application	zip	The compressed-file format of PKZIP and its kin
application>	pdf	Adobe's Portable Document Format
audio	aiff	An audio interchange format developed by Apple Computer
audio	midi	A music format based on instruments
audio	wav	The RIFF WAVE sound format developed by Microsoft and IBM
image	cgm	Computer Graphics Metafile image format
image	gif	Graphics Interchange Format image format
image	jpeg	File interchange format of the Joint Photographic Experts Group

Type	Subtype	Meaning
text	plain	ASCII text
text	html	The Hypertext Markup Language
video	mpeg	Video format of the Motion Picture Experts Group
video	quicktime	Format developed by Apple Computer

When a Web browser requests a document from a server, the server sends several header lines before it sends the document itself. One of the headers is `Content-type`. This header line contains the MIME type and subtype, separated by a slash. Thus, most Web pages are preceded by the following line:

```
Content-type: text/html
```

Note

MIME media types are assigned by the Internet Assigned Numbers Authority (IANA) in response to a formal request process. If you plan to develop your own plug-in, check out the list of IANA-approved MIME types at `ftp://ftp.isi.edu/in-notes/ iana/assignments/media-types/media-types`.

If you need a private MIME media type for use on an intranet or in a limited distribution application, use the most appropriate type and select a subtype that begins with the characters `x-`. For example, `application/x-myType` is an acceptable name for a private type.

HOW NETSCAPE BROWSERS PROCESS PLUG-INS

When the Microsoft Windows versions of Navigator 3 or Communicator 4 start, they look in the directory that holds the browser executable for a directory called Program. Inside that directory, they look for a directory named Plug-ins. They next examine the files in the Plug-ins folder and read out the MIME type. You can see which plug-ins either browser found by choosing Help, About Plug-ins.

Tip #154

On a Windows machine, the names of the plug-in files must begin with the characters `np` or Netscape browsers will not recognize them as plug-ins.

Later, when the Netscape browser encounters a `Content-type` header with a type it does not recognize, it looks through the list of MIME types registered by the plug-ins. If it finds a match, it loads that plug-in Dynamic Link Library (DLL) into memory and passes the contents to the plug-in.

If none of the plug-ins on the list match, the browser looks at the list of helper applications. If none of those match, the browser starts the plug-in assisted installation process by displaying the Unknown File Type dialog box shown earlier in Figure 28.2.

USING FRONTPAGE TO INVOKE A NETSCAPE PLUG-IN

FrontPage's plug-in insertion command generates the <EMBED> tag, which is recognized by both Netscape browsers and Internet Explorer. Essentially, the <EMBED> tag is a type of link; objects specified by it automatically download and display when the document is displayed. To insert a plug-in, do the following:

1. Choose Insert, Advanced, Plug-in. The Plug-In Properties dialog box appears (see Figure 28.3).

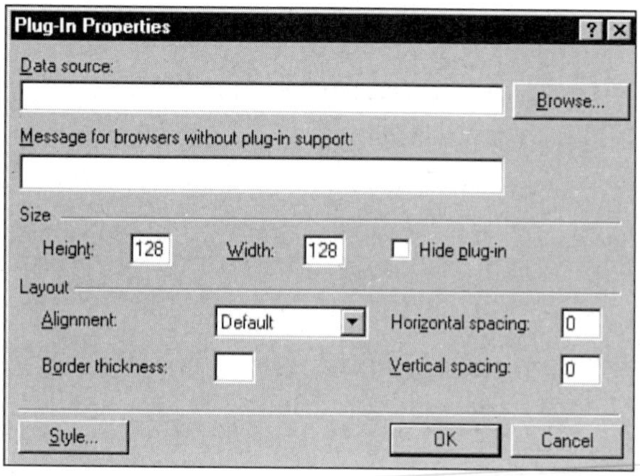

Figure 28.3
The Plug-In Properties dialog box lets you specify the behavior of the plug-in.

2. Type the path name of the data file to be loaded in the Data Source box, or use the Browse button to locate the file. (The Data Source is the file the browser tries to read with its plug-in.)

3. Using the Message box, type a message that browsers that don't use plug-ins can display.

4. Specify the size and height of the plug-in region (in pixels) that you want in the browser window. If you don't want any visible evidence of the plug-in region in the browser, mark the Hide Plug-in check box.

5. Use the Layout section to specify where the plug-in will sit in relation to text, its border thickness, and its spacing away from text.

6. Click OK. A generic plug-in placeholder appears in the FrontPage workspace.

The workings of such an embedded object can be a little confusing. (For this example, you'll assume a default Netscape Navigator 4 installation without any third-party plug-ins). If you plug in an object whose MIME type is supported directly by either browser (such as a WAV file) and view it in Navigator 4, a WAV audio player automatically loads with the page and is embedded in the page from which it was called. The user can now play the file with the controls (see Figure 28.4).

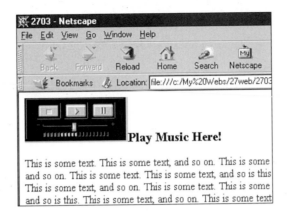

Figure 28.4
You can embed a WAV player in a Netscape-displayed page by using the <EMBED> tag.

This result of using the <EMBED> tag is quite different from using a link to access the data source file: in the latter case, the WAV player appears only when the viewer clicks the link, and it is not integrated with the page on which the link resides.

An interesting side effect of making the WAV plug-in hidden is that the sound file automatically plays when the page loads in a Netscape browser. This is a workaround for getting background sound into these browsers without using an applet, although they don't enable you to loop the sound for continuous playback.

As was noted in Chapter 5, "Enhancing Pages with Graphics and Multimedia," Navigator 4 doesn't support inline video with AVI files, as Internet Explorer 3 and 4 do. If you simply use the Insert, Video command to put the animation file into the page, Netscape browsers won't display it. However, if you use a plug-in and make the data source the AVI file, Navigator displays the animation without the user needing to click a link to go to it. Don't hide the plug-in, though, or you'll get an error message that the window could not be created.

With Netscape browsers, if you use a MIME type for which the user's browser has no plug-in, an icon appears in the browser window at the plug-in location. When the user clicks the icon, the message shown in Figure 28.5 appears. In this case, the MIME type was X-PN-REALAUDIO, and the Navigator 4 installation being used didn't have this plug-in. After clicking the Get the Plug-in button, a user is linked directly to Netscape's plug-in resource site.

Browser responses to embedded data sources vary considerably with the MIME types used and the capabilities and configurations of the browsers, so you'll have to do some experimenting to get things just right.

Figure 28.5
Netscape asks if the user wants to download a plug-in for an unsupported MIME type.

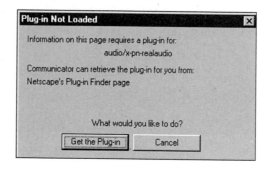

JAVA AND JAVA APPLETS: AN OVERVIEW

The Java programming language was originally designed and implemented as a language for programming consumer electronics. However, under the auspices of Sun Microsystems, it has been developed to be a general-purpose, high-level programming language, like C++. Java is not specifically oriented to Web programming, and stand-alone Java programs do not need to be run from inside a Web page.

The language was designed to be platform-independent and to have a high level of inherent runtime safety. Because of this, standalone Java language programs may eventually enjoy success in areas such as major applications programming, although that day is not yet here.

Java has been applied to Web programming mostly in the form of Java applets. These are specialized Java programs designed for executing within Web pages. To run a Java applet, you need a Java-enabled Web browser; both Navigator 3 and later and Internet Explorer 3 and later fulfill this requirement. These browsers can download Java programs as specified in the page, and then execute these programs on the user's computer by using the Java virtual machine that is integrated into the browser software.

Java applets are therefore a specialized subset of the overall Java development environment. Although you won't write code for Java applets in this chapter, you will work through the procedure for including Java applets in your pages.

You can get more background on Java from `http://java.sun.com/aboutJava/index.html`.

If you want to experiment with actually programming in Java, many tools for creating Java applications now exist. Symantec's Café, Visual Café, and Microsoft Visual J++ come immediately to mind as excellent, GUI-based development tools. If you want to start with the basics, the original Java tools are freely available from the creators of Java, Sun Microsystems. These tools are as follows:

- *javac*—The Java compiler
- *appletviewer*—A Java virtual machine for testing and debugging your applet
- *javadoc*—Automatically generates an online manual documenting your program's classes

You can download a free copy of the Java Developer Kit at `http://www.javasoft.com/`.

Java requires a 32-bit operating system and support for long, case-sensitive filenames. In the PC arena, Java supports only Windows 95, 98, or Windows NT.

WHY USE JAVA APPLETS?

In the context of the Web, Java applets offer the following advantages:

- Because they run on the client, not on the server, Java applets can make better use of computing resources.

- Java is designed to be *architecture-neutral*. This is the software equivalent of "one size fits all." For vendors, it means larger potential markets, fewer inventory headaches, and the elimination of costly software porting efforts. For consumers, it means lower costs, increased choices, and greater interoperability between components.

- Although other languages can be considered architecture-neutral, Java programs can typically execute much faster and more efficiently. The Java virtual machines built into recent Web browsers can make Java programs run almost as fast as native executables.

USING FRONTPAGE AND JAVA APPLETS

In the following sections, it's assumed that you've either created some applets yourself or have obtained some from the Web. When you want to add an applet to one of your pages, use the following procedure:

1. Copy the applet file into the same folder as the page that will include the applet. (The applet file likely has the extension CLASS or CLA; but see the next Caution.) Also, copy into this folder any other files the applet needs to work properly.

2. Choose Insert, Advanced, Java Applet. The Java Applet Properties dialog box appears (see Figure 28.6).

3. Type the name of the source file into the Applet Source box and the Applet Base URL if the applet isn't stored in the Web site's root folder. Note that the source file name is case sensitive.

4. Type an appropriate message in the Message for Browsers without Java Support box.

5. Use the Applets Parameters section to add any required parameter values needed by the applet. Because Java does not provide a mechanism for displaying what the parameters and values are for a given applet, you'll have to consult the documentation that comes with the applet (if you didn't write it yourself) to learn the correct parameter names and the legal values for each parameter.

6. Type values for the applet's size and layout into the appropriate boxes and click OK. A placeholder for the applet appears.

7. Use the Preview in Browser command to test the applet.

PART

V

CH

28

Figure 28.6
The Java Applet Properties dialog box lets you install and fine tune Java applets and their parameters.

Java Applet Properties `? X`

Applet source:

Applet base URL:

Message for browsers without Java support:

Applet parameters:

Name	Value

Add...
Modify...
Remove

Layout

Horizontal spacing: `0`   Alignment: `Default ▼`

Vertical spacing: `0`

Size

Width: `128`   Height: `128`

Style...   OK   Cancel

A calculator applet is shown in Figure 28.7. This is a simple applet in the sense that it doesn't use any parameters to modify its appearance or behavior. The HTML code that FrontPage uses to insert the applet into the page is

```
<applet code="PocketCalc.class" width="395" height="179"></applet>
```

Figure 28.7
A simple calculator applet running in a page.

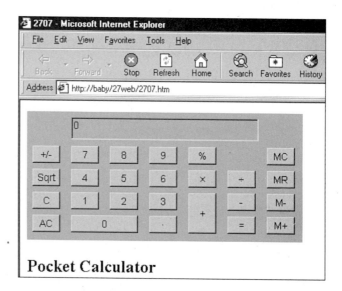

2707 - Microsoft Internet Explorer

File   Edit   View   Favorites   Tools   Help

Back   Forward   Stop   Refresh   Home   Search   Favorites   History

Address http://baby/27web/2707.htm

0					
+/-	7	8	9	%	MC
Sqrt	4	5	6	×	÷	MR
C	1	2	3	-	M-
AC	0	.	+	=	M+

Pocket Calculator

Note that the values for the width and height of the applet, in pixels, must be specified using the Applet Properties dialog box. This is because the screen area needed by an applet isn't detected automatically by FrontPage and you have to get this information from the applet documentation and add it by hand.

Caution

When typing the name into the Applet Properties dialog box, you have to preserve the spelling and case exactly as it is given in the applet documentation. Renaming the applet file in FrontPage and using that name in the page will cause errors. This is especially important to remember if you unzipped a downloaded applet with an unzip utility that doesn't preserve long filenames. If this happens, you must restore the correct filename before using the applet. In the previous example, the correct applet name is `PocketCalc.class`. Calling the applet with `PocketCalc.cla` will not work, even if that's the way the applet's name appears in the Web folder.

Two instances of a digital clock applet are shown running in Figure 28.8. This is a somewhat more interesting example because the applet display parameters can be changed.

Figure 28.8
Two instances of the same applet showing the differences obtainable by changing the applet parameters.

The upper applet uses white *LEDs* on a dark gray background; the lower is 24-hour time with red LEDs on a white background. The HTML coding for the upper applet is as follows:

```
<applet code="Timer" width=120 height=36 align=absmiddle>
<param name=ledcolor value=white>
<param name=backcolor value=gray>
<param name=mode value=24>
Clock
</applet>
```

Clock in the code is the text that is displayed by browsers that don't support Java. The HTML for the lower applet is as follows:

```
<applet code="Timer" width=120 height=36 align=absmiddle>
<param name=ledcolor value=black>
<param name=backcolor value=white>
<param name=mode value=12>
Clock
</applet>
```

Remember that the names of the parameters are defined by the applet code; you have no control over these names. There may be required or out-of-bounds values for some parameters, so check the applet documentation. As is clear from the preceding examples, you don't have to write your own applets to begin experimenting with them. There is a growing number of applets, which you can use in your own pages, available for download from the Web. The following are two of those applet sites:

Gamelan: http://www.gamelan.com

Java Applet Rating Service (JARS): http://www.jars.com/

UNDERSTANDING ACTIVEX CONTROLS

Microsoft introduced ActiveX Technologies in 1996, at the time it released Internet Explorer 3. By building on its highly successful Object Linking and Embedding (OLE) technology, Microsoft was attempting to set a standard for adding active content to Web pages. This standard was to allow the capabilities of the Web browser to evolve continually and also allow data and information from existing applications to be easily accessed.

ActiveX controls have not become the standard for dynamic content and Web page data access that Microsoft hoped—it appears that scripting and DHTML will provide that set of capabilities. Microsoft, in fact, appears to be reducing its commitment to ActiveX in favor of DHTML-related tools. They are no longer developing controls for customer use or giving much support to the ones they did generate, and the creation of new controls has been delegated—or relegated—to third-party developers. Nevertheless, ActiveX controls may still have a place in your Web pages—especially if you have programming skills—so in the following sections you will examine their use with FrontPage.

WHAT ARE ACTIVEX CONTROLS?

Like Java applets, ActiveX controls can be automatically downloaded to your system if they are not currently installed or if the installed version is not the most recent. Like plug-ins, ActiveX controls remain available to your Web browser continuously once they are installed. However, ActiveX controls are more than simple Web Browser plug-ins or add-ins. Because of their nature, not only can they be used to extend the functionality of Microsoft's Web browser, but they also can be used by any programming language or application that supports the OLE standard. For example, an ActiveX control could be written to enable Internet Explorer 4 to automatically search Usenet newsgroups for specific information and, at the same time, perform a similar function through integration into Microsoft Office products such as Excel or Access. Netscape Navigator plug-ins, on the other hand, can be used only in Web browsers and often work only with those that are Netscape-based; although, to be fair, ActiveX controls that use specific features of the container sometimes don't work properly outside a Microsoft browser environment. In this case the control should detect its container and issue an error message.

As with Netscape Navigator's plug-ins, ActiveX controls are dynamic code modules that exist as part of Microsoft's *Application Programming Interface* (API) for extending and integrating third-party software into any OLE-compliant environment. For Internet Explorer users, ActiveX controls support allows you to customize Internet Explorer's interaction with third-party products and industry media standards. Microsoft's ActiveX control API also attempts to address the concerns of programmers, providing a high degree of flexibility and cross-platform support.

WHAT ACTIVEX CONTROLS MEAN FOR END USERS

For most users, the presence of ActiveX controls is transparent because they open up and become active whenever an ActiveX-enabled browser is opened. Furthermore, you will often not even see ActiveX controls at work because most ActiveX controls are not activated unless you open up a Web page that initiates them. For example, after you install the Shockwave for Macromedia Director ActiveX control, you will notice no difference in the way Internet Explorer functions until you come across a Web page that features Shockwave.

Once an ActiveX control is installed on your machine and initiated by a Web page, it manifests itself in one of the following three potential forms:

- Embedded
- Full-screen
- Hidden

EMBEDDED CONTROLS

An embedded ActiveX control appears as a visible, rectangular window integrated into a Web page. This window may not appear any different from a window created by a graphic, such as an embedded GIF or JPEG picture. The main difference between the previous windows supported by Internet Explorer 3 and 4 and those created by ActiveX controls is that ActiveX control windows support a much wider range of interactivity and movement, and thereby remain live instead of static.

In addition to mouse clicks, embedded ActiveX controls also can read and take note of mouse location, mouse movement, keyboard input, and input from virtually any other input device. In this way, an ActiveX control can support the full range of user events required to produce sophisticated applications.

FULL-SCREEN CONTROLS

A full-screen ActiveX control takes over the entire current Internet Explorer window to display its own content. This is necessary when a Web page is designed to display data that is not supported by HTML. An example of this type of ActiveX control is the VRML ActiveX control available from Microsoft. If you view a VRML world using Internet Explorer 3 with the VRML ActiveX control, it loads into your Web browser like any other Web page, but it retains the look and functionality of a VRML world, with 3D objects that you can navigate through and around.

HIDDEN CONTROLS

A hidden ActiveX control doesn't have any visible elements, but works strictly behind the scenes to add some features to Internet Explorer 3 that are not otherwise available. An example of a hidden control would be the Preloader control, discussed later in this chapter. This ActiveX control is used to preload a graphic, sound, or other element that is subsequently viewed by the Internet Explorer user. Because the element is downloaded while the user is browsing through the current Web page, the response time of the element appears to be much shorter.

Regardless of which ActiveX controls you are using and whether they are embedded, full-screen, or hidden, the rest of Internet Explorer's user interface should remain relatively constant and available. So even if you have a VRML world displayed in Internet Explorer's main window, you'll still be able to access the browser's menus and navigational controls.

WHAT ACTIVEX CONTROLS MEAN FOR PROGRAMMERS

For programmers, ActiveX controls offer the possibility of creating Internet Explorer add-on products by using existing ActiveX controls to assemble Internet-based applications. Creating a custom ActiveX control requires much more intensive background, experience, and testing than actually using one. If you are a developer or are interested in creating an ActiveX control, the following discussion will be useful.

The current version of the ActiveX control Application Programming Interface (API) supports four broad areas of functionality.

ActiveX controls can do the following:

- Draw into, receive events from, and interact with objects that are a part of the Internet Explorer 3 and 4 object hierarchy
- Obtain MIME data from the network via URLs
- Generate data for consumption by Internet Explorer 3, by other ActiveX controls, or by Java applets
- Override and implement protocol handlers

ActiveX controls are ideally suited to take advantage of platform-independent protocols, architectures, languages, and media types such as Java, VRML, and MPEG. ActiveX controls should be functionally equivalent across platforms as well as complementary to platform-specific protocols and architectures.

When the Internet Explorer 3 or 4 client launches, it knows of any ActiveX controls available through the Windows Registry, but does not load any of them into RAM. Because of this, an ActiveX control resides in memory only when needed, but many ActiveX controls may be in use at one time, so you still need to be aware of memory allocation. By having many ActiveX controls readily available, without taking up any RAM until just before the time they are needed, the user is able to view seamlessly a tremendous amount of varied data. An ActiveX control is deleted from RAM as soon as the user moves to another HTML page that does not require it.

Integration of ActiveX controls with the Internet Explorer client is quite elegant and flexible, allowing the programmer to make the most of asynchronous processes and multi-threaded data. ActiveX controls can be associated with one or more MIME types, and Internet Explorer 3 or 4 can, in turn, create multiple instances of the same ActiveX control.

At its most fundamental level, an ActiveX control can access an URL and retrieve MIME data just as a standard Internet Explorer client does. This data is streamed to the ActiveX control as it arrives from the network, making it possible to implement viewers and other interfaces that can progressively display information. For instance, an ActiveX control can draw a simple frame and introductory graphic or text for the user to look at while the bulk of the data is streaming off the network into Internet Explorer's existing cache. All the same bandwidth considerations adhered to by good HTML authors need to be accounted for in ActiveX controls.

Of course, ActiveX controls can also be file-based, requiring a complete amount of data to be downloaded first before the ActiveX control can proceed. This type of architecture is not encouraged due to its potential user delays, but it may prove necessary for some data-intensive ActiveX controls. If an ActiveX control needs more data than can be supplied through a single data stream, multiple simultaneous data streams can be requested by the ActiveX control, so long as the user's system supports this.

If data is needed by another ActiveX control or by Internet Explorer while an ActiveX control is active, the ActiveX control can generate data itself for these purposes. Thus, ActiveX controls not only process data, they also generate it. For example, an ActiveX control can be a data translator or filter.

ActiveX controls are generally embedded within HTML code and accessed through the <OBJECT> tag.

Note

Whereas creating an ActiveX Control is much easier to do than, say, writing a spreadsheet application, it still requires the talents of a professional programmer. Third-party developers offer visual programming tools or BASIC environments that provide ActiveX control templates, making the actual coding of ActiveX controls much less tedious. However, most sophisticated ActiveX controls are, and will be, developed in sophisticated C++ environments, requiring thousands of lines of code.

Tip #155

The main source for ActiveX information is on Microsoft's Web site under the Component Development menu at `http://www.microsoft.com/workshop/default.asp`.

ACTIVEX CONTROL SECURITY

ActiveX controls are pieces of software; therefore, all of the dangers of running unknown software apply to them as anything you download from the Internet. ActiveX controls are unlike Java applets, which run in an environment designed to ensure the safety of the client and can usually cause trouble only by exploiting bugs or flaws in the Java runtime security systems. ActiveX controls, on the other hand, can do anything on the client computer. Although this increases their potential to perform functions within your Web browser and other compatible applications, it also poses an added security risk. How do you know that a downloaded ActiveX control won't erase your hard drive?

To address this concern, Microsoft's Internet Explorer Web browsers (version 3.02 and later) support *Authenticode code-signing technology*. This enables vendors of ActiveX controls and other software components to digitally *sign* these components. When they are downloaded and the digital signature is recognized, a code signature certificate is displayed onscreen. This certificate ensures that the software component is coming from the named source and that it hasn't been tampered with. At this point, you can choose to install the software component.

Internet Explorer 4 and 5 provide graduated, customizable levels of security in dealing with downloadable components like ActiveX (see Figure 28.9). Internet Explorer 4 and 5 automatically install at the Medium security level, which warns you before you download and run potentially dangerous content. Knowledgeable users can select Custom and click the Settings button, which opens a dialog box where you can specify precisely how much security is to be applied to signed controls, unsigned controls, and so on. You can also set up "zones" of sites, each of which has a different security level.

Caution

You should almost never select the Low security level, because this leaves your system completely unprotected from malevolent or poorly written software. Only select this level if you are certain that all the sites you are visiting are safe.

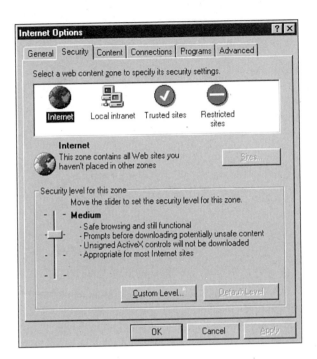

Figure 28.9
In Internet Explorer
5, Medium security
level puts the burden
on the user—you will
be warned of poten-
tial security risks, but
you are given the
option to continue.

HTML IMPLEMENTATION OF ACTIVEX CONTROLS

Implementing ActiveX controls in HTML Web pages requires the use of the HTML <OBJECT> and <PARAM> tags to include and configure each desired control. Although not too difficult, the syntax for using these controls and determining the correct configuration parameters for each can be an intimidating task. This is all the more so because Internet Explorer 4 implements plug-ins, applets, and ActiveX with the <OBJECT> tag.

FrontPage makes the process easier through its point-and-click method of control installation. Before you work with this, however, a brief discussion of how ActiveX works in a page will be helpful.

As just stated, including ActiveX controls in HTML documents requires use of the <OBJECT> tag to embed the control within the page. Controls are configured through the attributes of the <OBJECT> tag, and configuration parameters are set by using the <PARAM> tag within the <OBJECT>...</OBJECT> container.

Using FrontPage, any locally installed ActiveX control can be placed within a Web page. Individual Label controls can be displayed as they would appear, as will images and other elements. FrontPage also allows you to configure the many options of each embedded ActiveX control—set the <OBJECT> and <PARAM> configuration values—using a simple dialog box customized for each control. When control configuration is complete, the HTML code needed to implement the control in your Web page is written into the HTML document.

PART

V

CH

28

THE <OBJECT> TAG

ActiveX controls are embedded in HTML documents through the use of the HTML <OBJECT> tag and are configured through use of the <PARAM> tag. Listing 28.1 is an example of using an ActiveX control embedded within an HTML Web page. The attributes of the <OBJECT> tag itself determine the ActiveX control (or other Web object) used, as well as its size and alignment on the Web page. The <OBJECT>...</OBJECT> container tags also enclose the <PARAM> tags that are used to set the control-specific parameters.

On their own, neither Netscape Navigator nor Communicator supports ActiveX controls and will ignore any controls embedded in a Web page through the use of the <OBJECT> tag. However, with one of the Ncompass Labs plug-ins installed, Netscape browsers do support ActiveX controls and will interpret embedded objects correctly.

Note

> http://www.ncompasslabs.com/ provides examples of using Microsoft's ActiveX Technologies in Netscape Navigator through NCompass Labs' ScriptActive plug-in.

The next sections discuss each of the important attributes of the <OBJECT> tag and some of the possibilities for using the <PARAM> tags.

LISTING 28.1   Marquee.htm—EXAMPLE USING THE ACTIVEX MARQUEE CONTROL OBJECT

```
<HTML>
<HEAD>
<TITLE>Marquee Example</TITLE>
</HEAD>
<BODY BGCOLOR=#FFFFFF>
<CENTER>
<HR>
<OBJECT
    ID="Marquee1"
    CLASSID="CLSID:1A4DA620-6217-11CF-BE62-0080C72EDD2D"
    CODEBASE="http://www.somesite.com/some.ocx"


    TYPE="application/x-oleobject"
    WIDTH=100%
    HEIGHT=100
>
<PARAM NAME="szURL" VALUE="image.gif">
<PARAM NAME="ScrollPixelsX" VALUE="2">
<PARAM NAME="ScrollPixelsY" VALUE="2">
<PARAM NAME="ScrollStyleX" VALUE="Bounce">
<PARAM NAME="ScrollStyleY" VALUE="Bounce">
</OBJECT>
<HR>
</CENTER>
</BODY>
</HTML>
```

ID

The `ID` attribute of the `<OBJECT>` tag is used to give the ActiveX Control a name that can be used within the Web browser (or other application) environment. This is the easiest way for the parameters of the ActiveX Control to be accessed and manipulated by other elements running within the Web browser (usually VBScript or JavaScript applications). For example, in Listing 28.1, a VBScript to change the background color of the Marquee control to red, if clicked, would look like the following:

```
Sub Marquee1_OnClick()
    Marquee1.BackColor = 16711680
End Sub
```

CLASSID

The `CLASSID` attribute is perhaps the most intimidating looking piece of the `<OBJECT>` tag of an ActiveX Control. However, it is simply the identification code for the ActiveX Control being used. It is what Internet Explorer uses to load the correct ActiveX Control code module from your computer, and its value is set for each control by the control's author. The code for the ActiveX Marquee Control, displayed in Listing 28.1, is `CLSID:1A4DA620-6217-11CF-BE62-0080C72EDD2D`.

CODEBASE

Unlike Netscape Navigator plug-ins, ActiveX controls can be automatically downloaded and installed when Internet Explorer 3 (or another compatible application) encounters a document that makes use of them. The key to this feature is the `CODEBASE` attribute. The `CODEBASE` attribute defines the URL from which the ActiveX Control can be downloaded and defines the version of the control used. Then, when Internet Explorer attempts to render the Web page on a client machine, the `CODEBASE` attribute checks if each ActiveX Control embedded in the HTML document exists on that machine and checks if it is the latest version. If a more recent version exists at the URL defined by the `CODEBASE` attribute, it is automatically downloaded and installed, subject to the security settings in place in the local copy of Internet Explorer being used.

Tip #156	Whenever possible, only use ActiveX controls that have been digitally signed by their vendors in your Web pages. This helps to ensure that these controls can be downloaded and installed on your users' machines without a problem.

TYPE

The `TYPE` attribute defines the MIME type of the ActiveX Control. In general, this will be `application/x-oleobject`. For other object types embedded in an HTML document using the `<OBJECT>` tag, the value of this attribute will be different.

WIDTH AND HEIGHT

The WIDTH and HEIGHT attributes of the <OBJECT> tag define the size of the ActiveX Control within the Web page. For hidden Controls, such as the Timer or Preloader controls, these attributes can be kept at their default values of 0. For controls such as the Marquee or Label controls, these attributes need to be sized correctly for their desired appearance.

THE <PARAM> TAGS

The <PARAM> tags are used to configure the appropriate parameters of each ActiveX Control. In general, the syntax of the <PARAM> tag is as follows:

```
<PARAM NAME="ParameterName" VALUE="ParameterValue">
```

For instance, in the Marquee control example shown in Listing 28.1, the URL of the document being placed in the marquee is given by:

```
<PARAM NAME="szURL" VALUE="image.gif">
```

To make use of an ActiveX Control effectively, you need to know the names and possible values of all of its parameters that can be set with the <PARAM> tag. The trick is that you have to know the parameters and their possible range of values. This information is normally provided by the vendor of the control at the time of purchase.

ADDING AN ACTIVEX CONTROL IN FRONTPAGE

Microsoft provides a set of ActiveX controls with FrontPage. Unfortunately, it no longer hosts its ActiveX Gallery, which used to give parameter details for its proprietary ActiveX controls, and the parameter specifications for the included controls were not available at the time of writing. Microsoft has lately shown less interest in encouraging ActiveX development, apparently preferring to direct most of its energies toward developing DHTML tools. However, ActiveX has capabilities that are very useful in a controlled environment such as an intranet, so the technology will continue to be used.

If you want to experiment with a control or two, start by choosing Insert, Advanced, ActiveX Control. The Insert ActiveX Control dialog box appears (see Figure 28.10). Then do the following:

1. Select the control you want and click OK. An ActiveX icon (with some controls it's an image of the control) appears on the page.

2. Double-click the icon to open the ActiveX Control Properties dialog box. This will vary according to the control, but it will always have at least two sheets: the Object Tag sheet and the Parameters sheet (see Figure 28.11).

Figure 28.10
The Insert ActiveX Control dialog box allows you to select from the controls available on your host system.

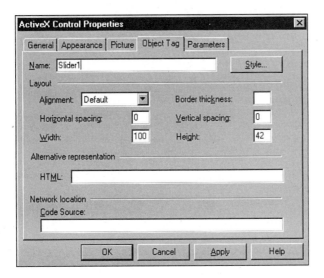

Figure 28.11
You configure an ActiveX control's general appearance with the Object Tag sheet.

3. You use the Object Tag sheet to set the attributes of the control's `<OBJECT>` tag. To begin, type a name for the component in the Name box. This label makes it easier to figure out what each control is doing when you look at the HTML code later.

4. Specify the control's alignment, spacing (to separate the control from surrounding page elements), height, and width in the appropriate text boxes.

5. In the HTML box, type the code for an alternative representation of the control, for browsers not supporting ActiveX. For instance, `<img src="inkwell.jpg" width="116" height="103">` in this box produces a JPEG image in Netscape in place of the control.

PART
V

CH
28

6. Use the Code Source text box to specify the URL from which the ActiveX control can be downloaded. This is actually an alternate method of specifying the CODEBASE parameter for the control. (See "The <OBJECT> Tag" section earlier in this chapter for more on CODEBASE.)

7. Click the Parameters tab to go to that sheet. Here you'll see the control's parameters and the default values for them (see Figure 28.12).

Figure 28.12
The Parameters sheet gives you the opportunity to add, modify, and remove parameters.

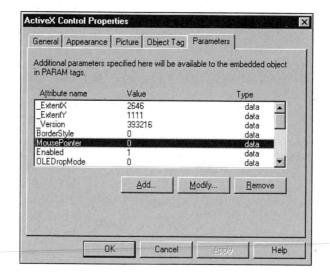

8. To modify a parameter's values, choose Modify to open the Edit Object Parameter dialog box. Here you can change the values assigned to that parameter. Choosing Add opens the same dialog box, but allows you to create a new parameter. Choosing Remove deletes the parameter.

8. Click OK. The dialog box closes and the component attributes and parameters have been updated. To see the control, you may have to go to Preview mode.

TROUBLESHOOTING

The most likely source of trouble with applets or ActiveX controls is incorrect parameter specification. If the component isn't behaving properly, check these parameters and their values carefully. Plug-ins cause less trouble; if one isn't working right, check to see if the path to the data source is correct.

DESIGNERS CORNER

If you're looking for plug-ins for experimentation, one place to start is the Netscape site, specifically at `http://home.netscape.com/plugins`. Here you'll find plug-ins for 3D and animation, audio and video, image viewing, and business utilities, along with links to other plug-in vendors and suppliers like Macromedia. Another list, even more comprehensive, is available at `http://browserwatch.internet.com/plug-in.html`.

Although there is an ActiveX plug-in for the Netscape browsers, you might be well advised to avoid extensive use of ActiveX components unless your target audience is guaranteed to be using Internet Explorer on Windows machines. This is unlikely to be the case unless the Web site is on an intranet. If it is the case, however, ActiveX may be a good choice because the controls are very fast and efficient. They run natively on Windows machines, and are usually smaller than plug-ins.

Java applets may provide useful effects and tools if your target audience uses a wide range of browsers. Note however that applets are slower than ActiveX components because their code must be interpreted by the browser's Java machine before it can run.

CREATING AND ADAPTING GRAPHICS FOR THE WEB

COLOR CONCEPTS

by Kelly Murdock

COLOR THEORY

If you have a window nearby, look out. In the natural world, you have quite a wide range of colors. There's everything from the bright green of a new leaf to the shocking orange of an Arizona sunset. Between these bold extremes, nature shows her subtle hand—a soft blue sky, a slate gray rock, the light tan patches on a cat's fur.

The computer environment is more limited than nature, and when you take a closer look at the Web environment, these limitations become even more stringent. Yet, an understanding of the colors that exist and how they work gives you an undeniable edge when it comes to using color that leaves a lasting impression.

SUBTRACTIVE COLOR

Colors in the natural world are made up of pigments. Pigment is a substance that reacts to light. You might have heard it said that without light, there is no color. This is true, and without pigment, there is no variation in color.

Subtractive color is the theoretical premise on which color in the natural world is based. It's called *subtractive* because it absorbs light before transmitting or reflecting the results that your eyes perceive as color.

Subtractive color theory exists to help both industrialists and artists understand and try to recreate nature's own design. With this premise as a guide, pigments are recreated chemically in paints, dyes, and inks.

Remember the color wheel? A color wheel is the circular representation of subtractive color, with different colors making up pie slices within the wheel. The color wheel begins with what are known as the *primary* colors: red, green, and yellow.

Each of these colors can be mixed together to come up with an entire spectrum of colors.

Digital information, however, is dealt with quite differently. Computers and computer hardware are quite limited in their ability to deliver color to a screen. You can't compete with Mother Nature!

You do try. And the way you do this is by using a different color method. Since it's impossible for a computer to first absorb light, it must *generate* light. Therefore, the type of color you see on your computers is backed by a theory referred to as *additive synthesis*.

ADDITIVE SYNTHESIS

In additive synthesis, color is created by the addition of colors. Computers use three colors to do this: red, blue, and green. It's almost like three individual paint guns are being fired at your screen, combining color and light to create variations.

Red, blue, and green color is referred simply as "RGB." As you look into how to work with digital color, this will be the technical foundation for the decisions you make. However, it's the subtractive world from which you gain your inspiration. It's important to keep this distinction in mind.

How come the natural world can make all colors from red, blue, and yellow, but computers cannot? It goes back to the difference between the ability to absorb versus the ability to transmit light, and how light then interacts with what is absorbed or transmitted. If you mix red and green by using paint, you'd get brown. But guess what happens when a computer mixes those same colors? The resulting color is yellow.

COMPUTER DELIVERY OF COLOR

Computers rely on three primary pieces of hardware to deliver color information to you:

- The CPU (Central Processing Unit)
- A video graphics card
- The computer monitor

It stands to reason, then, that the quality of color you see on your computer depends on the quality and capability of these components. If any one of these components is incompatible or unequal in its properties, the end results will not be as true and refined as possible.

Furthermore, computer platforms and operating systems (OSs) have differing capabilities when it comes to color. In terms of the computers and OSs you might be using: the Macintosh is known for its higher-end color, Windows 3.1 is usually limited, Windows 95 and later has very good color control, and, if you're using a standard UNIX machine, you're at a disadvantage, with lower color capabilities.

The reason this is important to you is so that you have an understanding of how, and why, you must learn to work with the color limitations and standards that exist. Knowing your own machine, and the capabilities of your viewing audience, will help you do just that.

Add to this the fact that any graphical interface, such as a browser, will affect the management of color, and you've got an important issue in color technology: In Web design, it is the browser that limits color significantly.

This is the bane of the Web designer's existence when it comes to color, but it's not insurmountable. FrontPage is replete with color controls that will help you manage color effectively.

> **Note**
>
> Does the fact that hardware and software are limited mean that computer color is considered substandard? Not at all. This is especially true of very high-end, specialty machines such as *SGI (Silicon Graphics Incorporated)* machines. SGI is used in film and video because the colors it's capable of are truest to those found in the natural world.

If you come from a graphics background or have worked with Photoshop or other professional graphics programs, you're probably familiar with other color management methods. One of the most familiar is CMYK (Cyan, Magenta, Yellow, Black). *CMYK* is a method used for print output. Other management systems include grayscale (contains black, white, and gradations of gray) and indexed color (a limited palette of specific colors defined by the designer). In Web design, indexed color is extremely important, and you'll have a chance to work with it in Chapter 31, "Web Graphic Formats."

COLOR DEPTH

If you've been shopping for video cards, the measurements of 8-bit, 16-bit, and 24-bit color might sound familiar. These values refer to the number of bits of computer memory required to represent the different levels of color depth.

These values mentioned aren't the only possible color depths, only the most popular. The simplest level is 2-bit color. This requires only two memory places—one for the color white and another for the color black.

For every additional bit of memory, the number of possible colors increases. 3-bit color has 8 unique colors, and 4-bit color has 16. The next major color depth worth mentioning is 8-bit color. 8-bit color can display 256 colors. This is what Photoshop refers to as indexed color and the GIF format still uses this color depth.

16-bit and 24-bit color includes colors that your eyes cannot even detect with 65,536 colors and 16,777,216 colors, respectively. Somewhere among these colors are the hues of that Arizona sunset and the patches of a cat's fur. 24-bit color is often called photographic quality color.

Web designers use all these color depths, and FrontPage deals with each of these separately.

Note

If you've shopped around for scanners while looking for video cards, you've no doubt seen ads mentioning 30- and 36-bit color depths. These are 24-bit color scanners with an additional 6- or 12-bits added to measure the opacity of an image. These extra bits are called the alpha channel and define how much of the underlying image shows through.

ELEMENTS OF COLOR

As mentioned earlier, there is no color without light. Of course, that could be said for all of life. Plants and animals (including the human variety) require light for their very existence.

While light is necessary, color is not. In fact, many people cannot perceive color, or they perceive color improperly such as in the common condition known as color blindness. However, for those with normal color perception, color is a significant aspect of your emotional and artistic life. In fact, it's so much a part of you that you might not necessarily even know what motivates you to pick out certain colors for your wardrobe—yet you do it.

Artists and designers have been trained to understand and use the elements of color as a method of communication. Web designers, however, often do not come from design backgrounds and don't have a full understanding of what color can do, what it means, and how to harness its power and use it to create sites with maximum communicative potential.

This section will help those of you who do not have a strong background in design look at a variety of color elements that impact design, including color types, properties, relationships, and special effects. For those of you with an artistic background, revisiting these elements will help you put them into the perspective of the Web.

CATEGORIES OF COLOR

Color is defined by how colors are combined. While the method of combination is going to differ when you compare the subtractive, natural world to the digital, additive one, the end results are the same in terms of your perception of color.

Colors categories are defined as follows:

- *Primaries*—All colors are the results of some combination of three colors: red, yellow, and blue. These colors are referred to as primary because they are the first colors to technically exist. Without them, no other color is possible.

- *Secondaries*—The next step is to mix pairs of the primaries together. If you mix red and yellow, you come up with orange. Blue and yellow create green, and violet is created by mixing red with blue. Orange, green, and violet are the secondary colors found on the color wheel.

- *Intermediates*—When two or more primaries, or secondaries are mixed together, the results are referred to as intermediate color. These colors are gradations that lie between the primary and secondary colors.

Along with these categories, you can achieve additional categories by adding white or black. When you add white to a given color, you achieve *tint*. Black added to a color darkens it. This is referred to as *shade*.

> **Note**
>
> Colors that are next to one another on the wheel, such as blue and violet, have a distinct relationship and are considered to be *similar*. Opposing colors, such as orange and blue, are *complementary*. Red and green, which are three colors removed from each other on the wheel, are *contrasting* colors.

PROPERTIES OF COLOR

The past several years have been very exciting in the fashion design world. There's a lot of texture, plenty of style, and a wide host of colorful names for color.

Bordeaux. Banana. Spice. Where do these colors fit into the spectrum? What determines the difference between cobalt and peacock, even if they are both blue?

The way in which differentiation of this nature is made is by defining the *properties* of color. Color properties are determined by the type and amount of color as well as how much light is used in that color, as follows:

- *Hue*—This term is used to differentiate one color from another. For example, red is different than green, and purple is different than brown. Whether a color is primary, secondary, intermediate, or tertiary (third level) isn't important with regard to hue, that they are different in terms of actual color is.

- *Value*—Chocolate brown is darker than tan, and sky blue is lighter than navy. A color's value is defined by the amount of light or dark in that color.

- *Saturation*—Also referred to as intensity, you can think of saturation as being the brightness of a color. Peacock blue is very bright, whereas navy is rather dull. Similarly, those popular neon lime greens reminiscent of the 1960s are much more intense than a forest green.

- *Warmth*—Hues found in the yellow-to-red range are considered to be warm. They emit a sense of heat.

- *Coolness*—Cool colors are those ranging from green to blue. Think of ice blue or the cool sense of a forest a deep green can inspire.

If you look at these definitions, you can see that a given hue can contain a value and saturation. When you think of all the variations that are potentially held within each of these properties, you can begin to see that color is much more than meets the eye.

Of course, you might notice that black and white are missing from this list. Black can be described as absence of light, and white as being light. A more technical way to think about black and white is to refer to the properties of hue and saturation. The fact? Neither black nor white possess hue *or* saturation.

Note

Why then are there "shades" of gray? The reason is found in value. The amount of light or dark in white or black determines the resulting value of gray.

COLOR RELATIONSHIPS

Colors are emotional, and they have emotional relationships with one another. In a compatible relationship, harmony reigns. In a discordant relationship, clashing occurs.

In design, relationships are very important, because both harmonious as well as *discordant* color schemes can be effective, depending on the circumstances.

If I'm trying to convey a peaceful environment, I'm going to want to use *harmonious* colors. An example of this would be creating a palette from soft, subtle pastels. The end result is going to be calm and even feminine.

However, if you want to wake people up and jangle them up a bit, you might try a discordant relationship. Bright yellow and red with black is going to create discord, but the visual impact is intense. Depending on the audience and the communication issues at hand, the discordant relationship might be a more appropriate choice than the harmonious one.

SPECIAL COLOR EFFECTS

Light, and how it interacts with color, creates special color effects. As a designer, you can learn to use these effects to enhance your designs.

Color effects include the following:

- *Luster*—Luster is the term used to describe a shining quality usually seen in fabrics such as satin or silk. Luster results from the way light is absorbed by certain areas of a texture contrasting with black areas of the background color.

- *Iridescence*—The inside of seashells, pearls, and opals are iridescent. Instead of the light splotches contrasting with black, the background color is usually some shade of gray.

- *Luminosity*—Similar to luster and iridescence, the difference here is the quantity of contrast. When there is very delicate contrast between the lighter areas and background areas, luminosity is created.

- *Transparency*—Think of a piece of tape or colored glass. Light passes through, creating a clear or transparent effect.

You can create all of these effects by mimicking what happens in nature.

To demonstrate what these effects look like, play around with FrontPage's hover buttons. You can follow these steps to make examples of special color effect buttons. Follow these steps and take a close look at the results.

1. In FrontPage, select View, Page.
2. Create a new hover button by selecting Insert, Component, Hover Button. The Hover Button Properties dialog will open as shown in Figure 29.1.
3. Set the dimensions of the button large so that the color effect is easy to see. Set the button Width to 400 and the Height to 320.
4. Click the Button Color drop-down list and choose Black.
5. Next, click the Effect Color drop-down list and choose a gray color.
6. Finally, click the Effect drop-down list and select Light Glow. Click the OK button to close the dialog.
7. Select File, Save, and save the page as HoverTest1.htm.
8. Click the Preview tab at the lower right of the Page View window.
9. Move the mouse over the button to see the results, as shown in Figure 29.2.

The results show the lustrous effect.

Figure 29.1
The Hover Button
Properties dialog box.

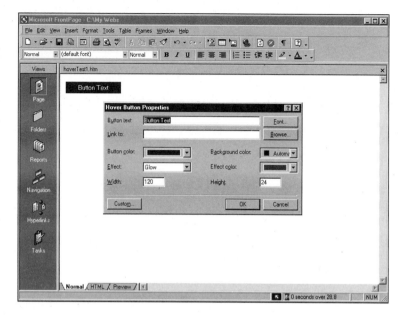

Figure 29.2
Luster is achieved by
contrasting color with
black.

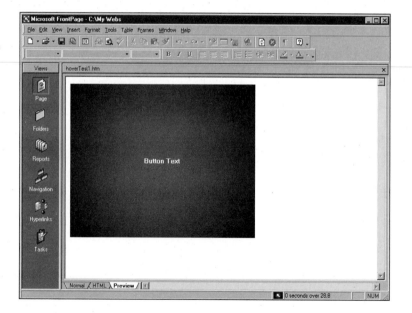

To create an iridescent button, follow these steps:

1. Return to HoverTest1.htm in Page view.

2. Right click the hover button and select Hover Button Properties from the pop-up
menu.

3. Change the Button Color from Black to White.

4. Save the file once again and click the Preview tab.

5. Mouse over the button to see the iridescence example. Figure 29.3 shows the results.

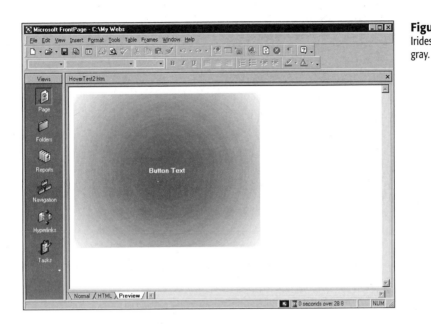

Figure 29.3
Iridescence: light and gray.

Since luminosity is a more delicate approach, use a lighter gray for the Effect Color, and then change the background in the previous example to a dark gray color. Figure 29.4 shows the result.

Transparent effects are different from the Set Transparency Color control found on the Picture toolbar. The transparent effects referred to here deal with the opacity of an image. PhotoDraw and Image Composer can create this effect easily.

1. In PhotoDraw, create a new workspace by clicking New and selecting Default Picture.

2. Switch PhotoDraw into Draw Shapes mode by clicking the Draw Paint icon and then clicking the Shapes icon.

3. Drag the mouse across the workspace to create a simple blue rectangle.

4. Repeat steps 2 and 3 to create an additional overlapping rectangle.

5. Click the small red box in the right pane to change the color of the new rectangle to red.

6. With the second rectangle selected, click Effects, Transparency.

7. Drag the Transparency slider in the right pane over about half way. This will increase the transparency of the rectangle. Figure 29.5 shows the semi-transparent rectangle.

Figure 29.4
Luminescence: delicate, subtle contrast is the name of the luster game.

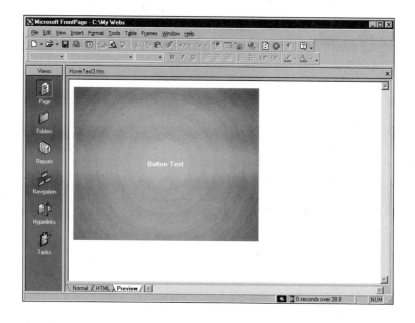

Figure 29.5
Rectangle with increased transparency. You can save this file for later reference.

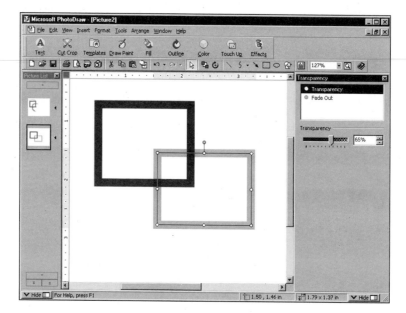

COLOR SIGNIFICANCE

To those of you who are familiar with it, the "Wired" look is memorable. Using neon and discordant colors, the magazine as well as the HotWired Web site (http://www.hotwired.com/) communicate energy.

My mother hates me in black. She says it makes my skin look lackluster and yellowish. She's right, but I still like to wear black. Why? It soothes me. It neutralizes my sense of my body and calms me.

Ever notice how all-night restaurants are usually very brightly lit? This is thought to help keep people awake.

The more you look for examples of the significance of color, the more of them you'll find. Colors are even associated with specific professions, ages, and sexes: white and green for doctors and nurses; darker or more neutral colors for older people, pink for girls, and blue for boys.

None of this is accidental. In fact, it's very specific. Color has very strong impact on the human psyche. This has been shown to be true in countless studies.

However, the intriguing issue is that color alone doesn't create this impact. Culture has a profound influence in how you perceive color, too.

Recently, there was a trend in some Western countries to marry in black—the bride and her bridesmaids as well as the men used black material in their formal bridal wear. This upset a lot of people, as Westerners tend to associate black with death and mourning.

But in some cultures, the color that you normally associate with purity and brides—white— is the color of death. In East India, for example, white is the color of the death shroud and mourning costumes.

It's important for you—a Web designer working in a global medium—to have some sense of what colors signify. While it's not possible to give you a run-down of cultural color significance in one chapter, giving some general meanings of color is. Be advised that if you're doing work for a client from a different culture, it will be well worth your while to ask a bit about color perception in that individual's culture. This can help you avoid uncomfortable, time-consuming situations.

Here's a bit about color significance in the Western world. Remember, these are generalizations, and other interpretations do exist.

Color	Significance
Black	Death, darkness, elegance, sophistication
White	Purity, cleanliness, refinement
Red	Passion, intense energy, anger
Green	Healing, nature, earth
Blue	Dignity, power, stability
Yellow	Happiness, vibrancy, youth
Purple	Royalty, riches, sumptuousness

Color designer and researcher J.L. Morton offers up fascinating information on color at her Web site, Colorcom, at http://www.colorcom.com/. Electronic "Color Voodoo" books can help inspire and guide you when working with color. You can download these (for a fee) from http://www.jiffyart.com/cvoodoo.html.

Now that you are familiar with the types and meanings of color and have a good foundation in color theory, it's time to apply these ideas to the Web.

WEB COLOR TECHNOLOGY

You've already become familiar with color management methods for the computer screen. The one emphasized as a starting point for Web-based color is RGB, or red, green, blue color management.

To effectively work with color on the Web, however, you have to take RGB a step further and convert it into a system of values that HTML will recognize. This system is known as *hexadecimal*.

Hexadecimal, referred to simply as "hex," is the base 16 number system. Base 16 is an *alphanumeric* system, consisting of both numbers and letters in combinations that translate into a color. Hexadecimal uses the numbers 0–9 and the letters A–F. All hexadecimal values should contain a total of six characters for HTML to understand it. The first pair in the series of six will equal the amount of red in the color; the second pair will equal the amount of green; and the third pair, blue.

Tip #157

> If at any time you get a single character in hex conversion, such as a single 0 or letter D, simply enter a 0 before the hex character so that the resulting binary information will be accurate.

Remember your computer science? A single byte is made up of 8 bits of information. Every two characters within a hex value makes up one byte, or 8 bits. This means that each hex value contains 24 bits of color information.

It's no accident that RGB color is also known as *24-bit color*.

How do you find the hex value of RGB colors? You're in luck. FrontPage automatically does the conversion and shows you these values when you select a color.

USING HEX COLOR VALUES

If you examine HTML code, you'll find places where colors are specified in hex values. These are easy to identify because they begin with the # sign followed by six characters.

Although FrontPage uses the standard Windows color selector dialog box, there is an additional dialog box that shows a range of colors useful on the Web. This is the More Colors dialog box, and it also shows the hex values for all the colors.

You can use these hex values to replace the hex values in the HTML code to change colors manually. To find the hex value for a color, follow these steps:

1. Find one of the many color selection drop-down lists through FrontPage, such as the ones in the Page Properties dialog box on the Background tab. You can access this directly by clicking Format, Background.

2. Clicking the color drop-down list opens a small pop-up menu showing the Standard Colors, Document Colors, and a link to the More Colors dialog box. Figure 29.6 shows these options. Click the More Colors option.

3. The More Colors dialog box (see Figure 29.7) presents a hexagonal array of colors. Select a new color by clicking it.

4. The hex value for this color is shown in the Value field at the upper right. Remember to drop the commas when using the hex value in code.

Note

A select few colors have familiar names associated with them. When a color in the More Colors dialog box shows a value in the Name field, then that color can be specified within HTML code by that name. These names include: blue, cyan, lime, fuchsia, yellow, red, maroon, white, silver, gray, and black.

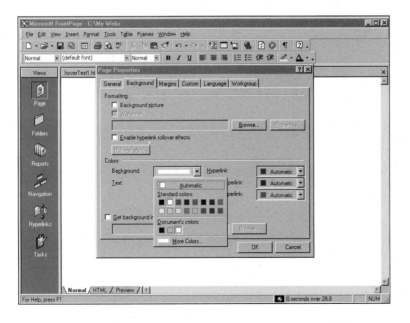

Figure 29.6
Color Selection drop-down list in the Page Properties dialog box.

Figure 29.7
The More Colors dialog box shows the hex value for each color.

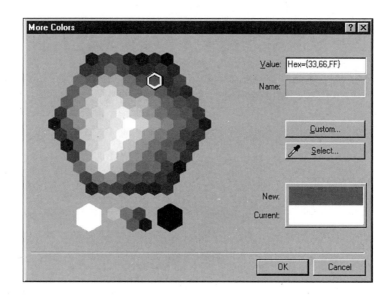

Many imaging programs also provide hex support.

BROWSER-BASED COLOR

Think of it this way—if you never had to download a graphic, your pages would load really fast. But would you sacrifice speed for visual attraction?

The answer is: probably. But that doesn't mean that you can't use color to create a rich base for the graphics you will use. What this does is offer the opportunity to have faster loading pages because you're using less graphics to achieve visual appeal.

Smoke and mirrors? Hardly! But if you understand how to tap into the colors that are native to your browser, you'll have stable, attractive splashes of color before a graphic is ever downloaded.

To make this happen, you have to understand the *safe palette*. This is a palette of 216 colors that are reserved by browsers on the Macintosh and Windows platforms for immediate access. Instead of having to download information from a remote server, the browser will parse the hexadecimal color codes from the page right away.

Does this sound great? The FrontPage creators are one step ahead of you. The colors in the hexagonal array within the More Colors dialog box just happen to be these 216 colors.

THE SAFE PALETTE

A safe palette is the palette made up of 216 colors that are going to remain as stable from one browser to another, between platforms, and at different monitor color capacities and resolutions as possible.

It's important to use the safe palette in most instances, because it ensures cross-browser, cross-platform stability. If you use colors outside of the safe palette, you can run into serious problems.

Picture this: you choose a soft, pale blue color for your background, and a very dark blue for your text. There's enough contrast to be readable, and you're happy with the look—proud of your hard design work done on an upper-end machine capable of full 24-bit color.

You put your page up on the Internet, and along comes a pal to check out your work. He gets to the page and sees you've chosen a bright peacock blue for your background, and a very similar color for your text. He can't read the content on your page, and he's confused.

How did this happen? Well, you didn't use safe color. Your friend came along with a more limited set of hardware and software, and his color management system chose to *dither* the colors. This means that his computer grabbed the first blues available because it couldn't identify your unsafe color.

To avoid this, you'll need to choose from the safe palette. It may seem that 216 colors is a very limited number, and it's true. My only words of solace are to encourage you to be creative. There are enough colors within the safe palette to create beautiful designs—it's done every day on the Web, and I have no doubt that you can do it, too.

Note

> If most color systems can display at least 256 colors, how did the safe palette end up with only 216? It's a complicated story that involves Windows 3.1 having reserved colors for the operating system. Browsers then went on to use just the available colors to avoid the problem, and the end result was a limited palette. The good news is that the 216 color palette is very stable and addresses many problems that occur across platforms—something over which Web designers can breathe a sigh of relief.

If you're using an external drawing package, try to find and use a palette made of Web-safe colors. You can also look in the following places on the Web.

Safe palette information and tools can be found by visiting the following Web sites:

Victor Engel's Color Cube: `http://the-light.com/netcol.html`

Lynda Weinman: `http://www.lynda.com/hex.html`

WORKING WITH THE SAFE PALETTE To work effectively with the safe palette, you have to draw from all of the information we've covered in this chapter. Beginning with what you know of color, you can think about the look-and-feel, special effects, and emotional expression you wish to express on your site.

Let's say you want to create a warm and welcoming personal presence that expresses your personal energy. Begin by selecting colors that are warm as well as vibrant: orange, red, yellow. Then find an appropriate combination of hues—you want the site to be harmonious, not discordant. The harmony of colors will help express the welcoming and personal presence, offering comfort while still conveying energy.

Turn to your understanding of RGB and hexadecimal values. Add to that the fact that you know you want to choose your colors from a safe palette, and you've narrowed down your choices to a very specific set of colors.

What you can do at this point is create what I call an *individual* palette. This is a selection of five to seven colors that you choose from the safe palette.

FrontPage offers an easy way to keep track of the colors you've selected. In the drop-down menu on any color selector is a section of Document Colors; these are the unique colors that you've chosen for this document. By examining these colors and checking the harmony between them, you should be able to tell which colors need to be changed.

So where do you go from here? By using the hexadecimal values in combination with HTML and cascading style sheets, you can employ your colors to create a design. Be creative, combining your colors for backgrounds, links, text, and table cells.

SPECIAL CONCERNS

There are two issues to bring to your attention regarding color. The first is contrast and readability, the second is the use of unsafe color.

CONTRAST AND READABILITY

Contrast is a necessary element when designing with color. Simply defined, *contrast* is two colors that are different enough from one another to provide an obvious separation to the eye. Contrast is necessary to produce readable sites.

Many of you have undoubtedly visited sites where the background and body text have been very difficult to read. In most cases, the problem is due to poor contrast. A light blue on a slightly darker blue isn't going to have enough contrast to be readable, as you can *try* to see in Figure 29.8. However, black on white is going to be very readable (see Figure 29.9).

Tip #158	Accessibility experts have found that for visually impaired individuals, severe contrasts such as black and white are the best for readability in low vision circumstances. If you know that your audience has a lot of older individuals or visually impaired persons, it's wise to plan ahead and ensure that your contrast colors are as solid as possible: black on white for body text is a sure-fire way to go.

Another approach is to *reverse* this concept, placing light colors on dark colors. This is known as *reverse type* and, if the contrast is good enough, it can be quite effective. Bottom line? Be sure that your content is readable on your background, so people are sure to be able to get to the information you're delivering.

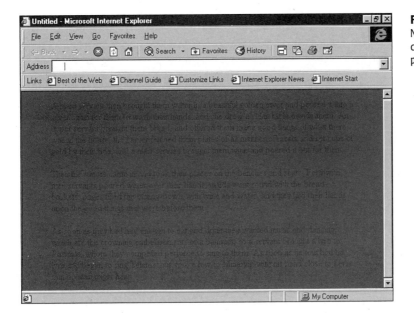

Figure 29.8
Not enough contrast creates readability problems.

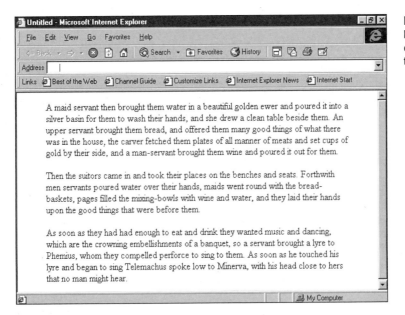

Figure 29.9
Black on white is high contrast, so it's easy to read.

Usually, body text should be darker than the background—dark enough so that significant contrast is created, allowing for maximum readability.

UNSAFE COLOR

Using unsafe color is risky, and it's not recommended. However, there are times when unsafe color can be used. Here's a helpful set of guidelines:

- You know your audience. And I *mean* know them! One situation where you might know them well would be a corporate intranet.
- If you're less certain about your audience, but still interested in using unsafe color, test the colors for dithering at lower resolutions.

To test colors, drop your monitor down to 256 colors when viewing your page. If the color appears differently from what you originally determined, it's probably a good idea to revert to a safe color. You'll also want to be very thorough, testing your pages on a variety of browsers, platforms, and computer systems.

COLORS IN FRONTPAGE

Colors are all around and in everything. Mother Nature didn't provide a magic rainbow that is the source of all colors. You need to search and find the colors for yourselves. You need to visit the forests to find greens, a flower shop to find the red of roses, or lay back lazily to breathe in sky blue.

In a similar manner, FrontPage doesn't have a single control for managing color, but rather, several entry points to the color controls. Whether it's text color, a background, or a complete color theme, the controls always seem to be there when you need them.

SELECTING COLORS

If you look at the Web, you see a lot of color. It seems to fill every corner of every page and it isn't just found in graphics. Most of the color selection tools are part of the various format dialog boxes. Table 29.1 is a list of which elements can be colored and where the color selector is found.

TABLE 29.1 COLOR SELECTOR LOCATIONS IN FRONTPAGE

Element	Location
Text	Font dialog or Formatting toolbar
Borders and Shading	Borders and Shading dialog box
Normal Hyperlinks	Page Properties dialog box, Background tab
Active Hyperlinks	Page Properties dialog box, Background tab
Visited Hyperlinks	Page Properties dialog box, Background tab
Page Text	Page Properties dialog box, Background tab
Page Background	Page Properties dialog box, Background tab

Element	Location
Table Background	Table Properties dialog box
Table Borders	Table Properties dialog box
Cell Background	Cell Properties dialog box
Cell Borders	Cell Properties dialog box
Horizontal Lines	Horizontal Line Properties dialog box
Hover Buttons	Hover Button Properties dialog box
Marquees	Marquee Properties dialog box

All of the color selection drop-down menus are initially set to Automatic. This setting allows FrontPage to manage the color by using Themes or predefined Style Sheets. Selecting a color overrides this automatic setting, but the first option in the color pop-up menu will allow you to re-enable the automatic setting.

STANDARD AND DOCUMENT COLORS

The next section in the color pop-up menu contains the Standard Colors. These 16 colors are standard across a broad range of operating systems and browsers. They also make it quick to choose and apply a basic color to an element.

Any new colors selected and applied to your current Web page are added to the Document Color section. This provides a quick look at the range of colors that your page is using. This is a good reference for piecing together a pleasing color scheme. If the Document Color section shows a mess of unharmonious colors, you should rethink your color selections.

BROWSER-SAFE COLOR PALETTE

The More Colors option opens a dialog box with the browser-safe colors presented in a pleasant hexagon shape. You can safely select any of these colors and rest assured that the same peacock blue you designed your site with will show up the same no matter the system or browser.

If the safe colors still don't have what you need, you can select a color by using the eye dropper tool or select a custom color.

USING THE COLOR DROPPER

Have you ever painted a room? Choosing the perfect color can be the trickiest part of the process. To find the matching color requires several trips to paint store. Each time you return with several small strips of colors. When you finally find the right one, you are usually holding it in your hot little hand. If you lose the color strip, it's back to the drawing board to start the process over again.

Sometimes this happens when designing a site. If you have an image that holds the exact tones you need, you might struggle to match the same tones from a palette. The eye dropper tool, found in the More Colors dialog box, lets you grab any color you can see. Suppose you wish to grab a color for your page background, this is how it works:

1. Open the Page Properties dialog box, Background tab by selecting Format, Background.

2. Click the Color drop-down list for the background color.

3. Select More Colors.

4. Choose the eye dropper tool by clicking the Select button shown in Figure 29.10. The cursor will change to an eye dropper tool.

5. Click the color you wish to select. This color becomes the new color.

Figure 29.10
Selecting existing colors with the eye dropper tool.

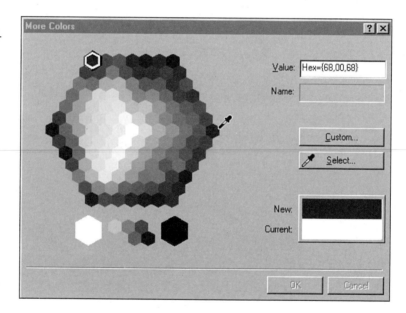

CUSTOM COLORS

The Custom button is the final option for colors. This opens the Color dialog box. This dialog box is the default Windows color selector shown in Figure 29.11. By using the controls on the right, any color within the 16.7 million colors in the 24-bit spectrum are possible. This should be more than enough colors for even the most demanding designer.

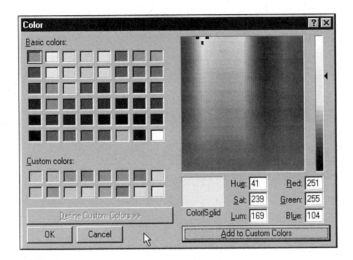

Figure 29.11
The default Windows
color picker is used
for custom colors.

Any custom colors that are selected will become instantly available in the color pop-up
menu thereafter.

THEME COLORS

A surefire way to make your colors match is to use themes. Chapter 6, "Working with
Themes," covered the details about themes, but theme colors are unique enough to be
mentioned here.

The Themes dialog box has a toggle button for turning vivid colors on or off, but the really
interesting color options show up when you click the Modify button. This makes three buttons appear, as shown in Figure 29.12. One of these buttons is Colors.

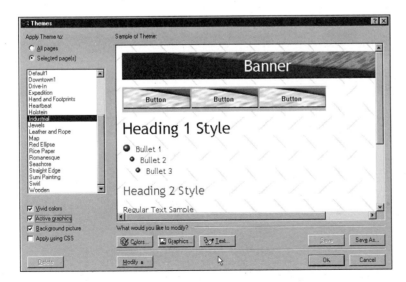

Figure 29.12
Themes can be modi-
fied in three different
ways.

Clicking the Colors button opens the Modify Theme dialog box for colors. There are three tabs in this dialog box: Color Schemes, Color Wheel, and Custom. The Color Schemes tab (see Figure 29.13) shows the color schemes for each of the loaded themes. You can choose any of these schemes for your current theme by clicking it. The Sample of Theme pane shows the current theme with the new color scheme.

Figure 29.13
Choosing a color scheme.

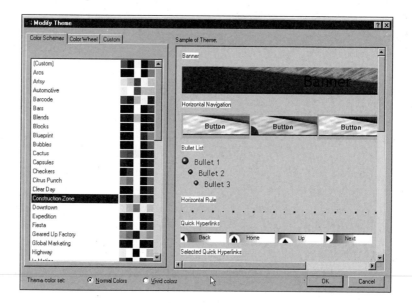

If none of the current color schemes fit the bill, click the Color Wheel tab. This opens a color wheel where you can select a new custom color scheme. The five colors that make up the color scheme are interrelated, so when a new default text color is selected in the color wheel, complementary colors are automatically updated. Figure 29.14 shows the color wheel at work.

The Custom tab allows you to hand pick the colors for a variety of Web page elements including hyperlinks, background, and all heading levels.

Once you've applied a theme, the theme colors will show up in the color pop-up menu for easy selection.

STYLE SHEET COLORS

Chapter 12, "Using Style Sheets with Individual Pages and Full Sites," covered the basics of style sheets, part of which is color. Style sheet colors are selected in the same manner as other colors in FrontPage. Notice in Figure 29.15 how the colors are specified by using hex values. The Preview pane provides a visual feedback that helps identify the colors.

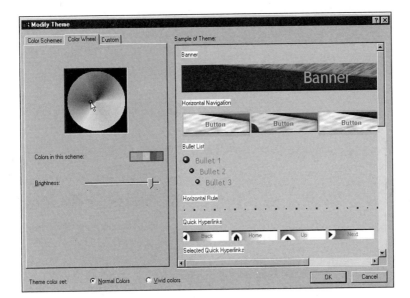

Figure 29.14
Selecting a custom color scheme by using the color wheel.

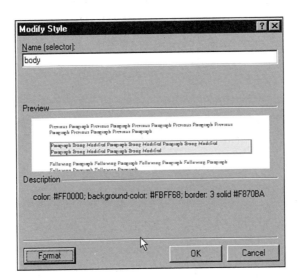

Figure 29.15
Style sheet colors are specified by using hex values.

TROUBLESHOOTING

I'm having trouble choosing colors. Can you give me some tips?

Colors are everywhere. Take a look at the purpose of the site. What type of images do you expect on the site? If it's a company site, start with the colors in the company logo. Look for brochures, signs or business cards that have colors. If you don't have some basic colors to start from, then select some colors from magazines or ads that look good together and use them.

I'm working on some pages for events taking place on around the holidays. How do I use the holiday colors and not mess up my color scheme?

If you have a color scheme established, then don't be afraid to deviate on one or two pages. The holiday colors provide a great chance to add some variety to your pages. Try using small splashes of the holiday colors, or you can abandon your basic scheme for hot pink during Valentine's Day. Visitors will be understanding since they know it's only temporary, and they'll know you have a festive attitude.

DESIGNERS CORNER: CREATING A COLOR-SAVVY TEMPLATE

Creating a template with positive, correlating colors can be tricky. It is also one of the most important aspects of Web design. The colors you choose will define the mood of the site to your visitors. If incorrectly defined, the site can alienate visitors.

The first step is to understand the theme and mood that you wish to convey. For this example, I'll be working on a site for a waterpark. The imagery that I want to portray will include water, waves, oceans, beaches, and sun. I hope to present a cool, calm and relaxing mood. Given these definitions, my colors will be light blues and tans.

Next, consider the graphic formats that you intend to use. I plan on using mainly GIF images, so my colors should be selected from the 216 browser-safe colors in the More Colors dialog box. Visit the dialog box and look at the possible colors, then think of the places in your pages that you'll need these colors.

To create a template of site colors, follow these steps:

1. Open a new Web page by selecting File, New, Page. From the New dialog, select Normal Page and click OK.

2. The first colors to select can be found on the Page Properties dialog box. Open this dialog box by right-clicking your new page and selecting Page Properties from the menu.

3. Choose a color for the background by clicking on the arrow to the right of the Background drop-down list. Then, select the More Colors option and pick light blue (#CCFFFF) and click OK.

4. Repeat the above step for selecting a text color. Make sure that the text color has a good contrast to the background color (#000066).

5. With the Page Properties dialog still open, select Hyperlink (#0000FF), Visited Hyperlink (#0000CC) and Active Hyperlink (#000099) colors.

6. With the Page Properties colors defined, add some text to the page to check the results.

7. Next add a table and open the Table Properties dialog. Set the Background color to be the same as the page background and choose some colors for the border (#FFCC99), light border (#FFFFCC) and the dark border (#FFCC66).

8. Add a Horizontal Line by selecting Insert, Horizontal Line and open its properties dialog. Select its color to be the same as the dark border color on the table (#FFFFCC).

9. Next, add a Hover Button component using Insert, Component, Hover Button and select a Button Color (#0000FF), Background Color (#FFFFFF), and an Effect Color (#66CCFF).

10. Finally, save the page as a template by selecting File, Save As. Select FrontPage Template in the Save As Type drop-down list. In the Save As Template dialog, include the colors used in the Description box.

CHAPTER 30

ABOUT THE COMPUTER SCREEN

In this chapter   *by Kelly Murdock*

SCREEN RESOLUTION

What many web designers are surely familiar with, but many of their site visitors don't know, is how to manage their computer monitors' resolution.

Resolution refers to how many pixels appear on the horizontal and vertical axes of your computer screen. If the resolution is set to the lowest common denominator of 640×480 pixels, that means 640 pixels are available in width and 480 pixels are available in height for the whole screen.

Most computers ship with 640×480 as a default resolution, and many older computers are capable only of that resolution. For this reason, many Web site visitors are seeing the web at 640×480—and they either cannot or do not know how to change the resolution.

Similarly, many notebook computers ship at a default of 800×600 resolution. This is a very popular resolution. The disadvantage of 640×480 resolution is that there is less space to work within (see Figure 30.1). The advantage is that everything appears larger.

Figure 30.1
640×480 screen resolution: the lowest common denominator.

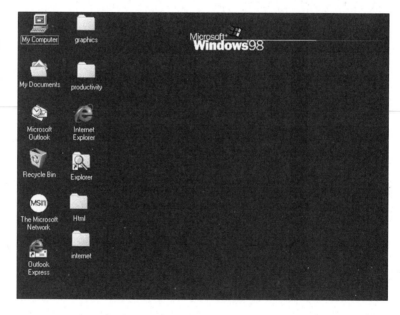

Now look at Figure 30.2; you can see what 800×600 looks like. Much more space to maneuver in, but smaller-looking objects. Of course, you can adjust the size of the objects to make things visible while maintaining the extra workspace on many platforms.

Figure 30.2
800×600: more
workspace on my
Windows 98
machine.

There are higher resolutions, too—1024×768 alters the look of a desktop considerably (see Figure 30.3). You can go even higher on that particular computer—to 1280×1024 (see Figure 30.4).

Figure 30.3
At 1024×768, this
desktop is
dramatically altered
visually.

Figure 30.4
A screen resolution of 1280×1024 is reserved for special situations.

Higher resolutions have their advantage when an individual has a very large screen for specialty reasons—computer-generated design (where detail matters), large data management, or low vision problems.

The bottom line when it comes to screen resolution is this: Web site visitors are seeing your site at a variety of screen resolutions. This directly affects the way your Web sites will be experienced, and it's up to you to design sites that look good no matter the resolution.

Tip #159

Professional web developers should have monitors that support a range of resolutions, so they can test their sites at those various resolutions. Several Windows machines are a good idea. You can also use the Macintosh and PowerPC, which allow you to test the look of pages from the Macintosh OS point of view, too.

MANAGING RESOLUTION

Consider this, from the *Yale C/AIM Web Style Guide:* "It's bad enough to have to scroll in one [vertical] direction; having to scroll in two directions is intolerable."

When it comes to Web site design, one of the worst—yet easiest—mistakes to make is not designing for the audience. If you're a computer buff, you might enjoy working at higher resolutions and won't immediately think of your audience's limitations.

Knowing how serious some of the mishaps that occur when ignoring audience needs are, you're certain to not only know why it's so important to manage screen resolution, but also how to do it.

One of the first issues you need to address is making sure that your pages fit into any screen resolution. This ensures that you'll avoid what the Yale style guide refers to: a horizontal scrollbar. This is a bar that appears along the bottom of a page when too much information is contained along the horizontal axis (see Figure 30.5). To demonstrate the problem, the table in Listing 30.1 fits a higher rather than a lower resolution. The screen shot is shown at a lower resolution—and the horizontal scrollbar appeared.

LISTING 30.1 DEMONSTRATING A HORIZONTAL SCROLL

```
<HTML>
<HEAD>
<TITLE>Horizontal Scroll Bar</TITLE>
</HEAD>
<BODY>
<TABLE border="0" width="750">
<TR>
<TD valign="top" width="400">
A maid servant then brought them water in a beautiful golden ewer
and poured it into a silver basin for them to wash their hands, and
she drew a clean table beside them. An upper servant brought them
bread, and offered them many good things of what there was in the
house, the carver fetched them plates of all manner of meats and set
cups of gold by their side, and a man-servant brought them wine and
poured it out for them.
</TD>
<TD valign="top" width="350">
Then the suitors came in and took their places on the benches and
seats. Forthwith men servants poured water over their hands, maids
went round with the bread-baskets, pages filled the mixing-bowls
with wine and water, and they laid their hands upon the good things
that were before them.
</TD>
</TR>
</TABLE>
<P>
As soon as they had had enough to eat and drink they wanted music and
dancing, which are the crowning embellishments of a banquet, so a
servant brought a lyre to Phemius, whom they compelled perforce to
sing to them. As soon as he touched his lyre and began to sing
Telemachus spoke low to Minerva, with his head close to hers that no
man might hear.
<P>
</BODY>
</HTML
```

Figure 30.5
A horizontal scrollbar equals unhappy site visitors.

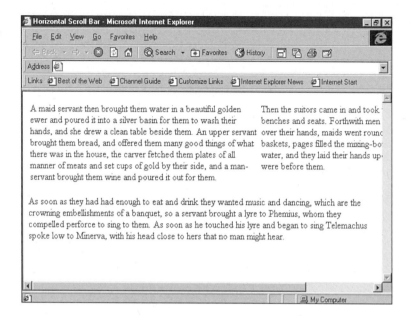

This bar will disappear at higher resolutions. At this time most people are viewing the Web at 640×480 resolution, with 800×600 getting close in popularity.

Theoretically, this means that anything you create must be 640 pixels wide or less to avoid the horizontal scroll. Anything longer than 480 pixels will go off the screen along the vertical axis as well.

The following is a sobering exercise that shows you why you don't even have 640×480 pixels per screen:

- Open your Web browser. In this case Netscape is opened in a portion of the desktop.
- Make sure all of the toolbars (the browser appears before you make custom modifications) are on (see Figure 30.6).
- Notice that there's a title bar at the top. Beneath that, a navigation toolbar. Beneath that, a location bar, and below that, a personal toolbar. All of this takes a significant amount of space away from the viewing section of the browser.
- You'll notice there are pixels taken up around the browser edge.
- If you move your eyes to the right side of the computer screen you'll see a vertical scroll bar. This takes up additional space.
- A status bar (along the bottom) is also responsible for reducing the browser viewing area.

Note

Different browser brands and versions take up different pixel amounts. The 595×295 recommendation addresses these differences.

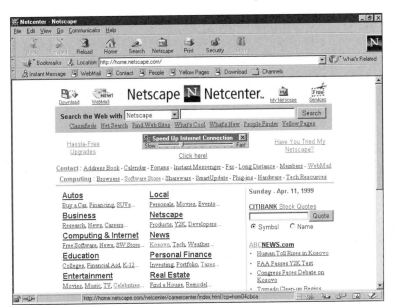

PART

VI

CH

30

Figure 30.6
The Netscape interface: Note all the real estate it eats up.

All told, the viewing area is so significantly reduced by the browser's interface that professional Web designers use a new total screen dimension to avoid problems: the dimension—595 pixels×295 pixels.

But wait. Be reassured that there are ways to work with this small space to ensure compatibility for higher resolutions, as well as give the illusion that more space exists. The following are some guidelines:

- Design to the lowest available resolution. Always design with the 640×480 screen resolution in mind—meaning that you'll need to employ the 595×295 rule.

- Don't forget that there are people using higher resolutions. Background graphics always tile, so you need to control the way those graphics work (see Chapter 32, "Creating Professional Web Graphics"). When working with tables and frames, you need to be aware that fixed-width tables and frames cause extra space to appear around the fixed design (see Figure 30.7) at higher resolutions (see Figure 30.8).

- Test, test, test! This rule should be firm no matter what the circumstances. Test your pages on different systems, different browsers, and at different resolutions. Now—before your site goes live—is the time to troubleshoot horizontal scrolls or any other troublesome areas.

- Work within the allotted space. In other words, don't pretend you have more space than you really do. You'll need to focus on proportion, dimension, and whitespace, which this chapter discusses later.

Figure 30.7
Fixed frame design at 640×480.

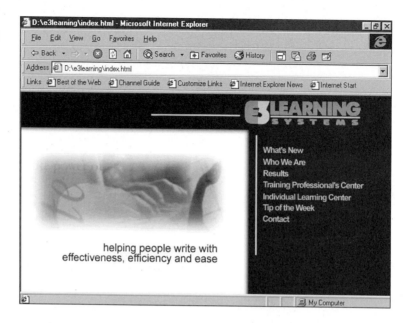

Figure 30.8
The same design at 800×600—more whitespace to the right and bottom.

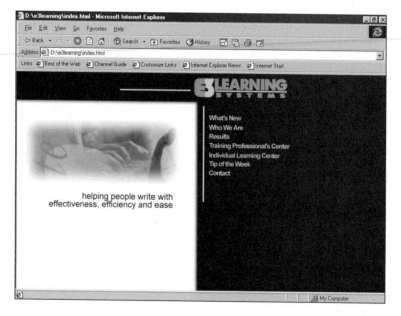

These simple guidelines save you from more trouble than you might imagine. You have greater control over your pages and better manage your sites, providing your audience a much more stable and effective product.

Testing your pages can't be stressed enough—even if you are employing maximum control over your page dimensions.

Tip #160

> If you're just getting started working with resolution issues, set your screen resolution to 640×480 and do all of your graphic design and HTML work at that resolution. You'll become familiar with the way things look at that resolution.

Some designers actually work only in 640×480 resolution and test at higher resolutions. Whether you choose to do this, or to work at higher resolutions but test those pages doesn't really matter. The bottom line is that you must check and re-check your work in a variety of circumstances to fully troubleshoot problems.

You can download a helpful ruler for measuring your Web page from `http://www.wpdfd.com/wpdtame.htm`.

SCREEN COLOR AND GAMMA

Another concern is screen color. Older hardware used on the Web is limited to 256 colors, which asks the Web designer to do some pretty fancy tricks.

The test-everything rule also applies with color. If a visitor is limited to 256 colors and you've been doing your design work in full 24-bit color, what you see and what your audience sees are going to be very different. More information on working with color can be found in Chapter 29, "Color Concepts."

Another important color issue often overlooked by Web designers: Gamma.

Gamma is complex to describe because it involves a lot of math. Put into its most simple terms, *Gamma* is a system that significantly influences the way data appears on a computer screen.

Gamma must often be manipulated, or *corrected*, to provide your monitor the most accurate information.

Your hardware is what determines how Gamma is corrected. One of the reasons Macintoshes have been so popular in the graphic design industry? A fair amount of Gamma correction is available on the Macintosh. This is especially true with Silicon Graphic machines. It's no wonder SGIs are the computers of choice for film, animation, and video production.

Because of this correction, Macintoshes and SGIs can display color with greater accuracy. Windows machines, prevalent on most desktops, are problematic.

There was little, if any, Gamma correction available to the Windows platform prior to Windows 95 and 98. Since the release of these more sophisticated GUIs, however, a bit more gamma correction is available, particularly if you've bought top-of-the line hardware. The better and newer your computer, video card, and video monitor are, the better your chances are of having some inherent Gamma correction.

The video displays problematic images when Gamma is improperly corrected. The dominant problem is that very dark images are displayed—so dark that much of the image is obscured. This is especially true in environments such as the World Wide Web.

What a problem for the Web designer who has worked so hard to get very high- color for his or her site visitors!

To learn more about Gamma, check out the following resources:

- "An Explanation of Monitor Gamma," by Robert W. Berger. This excellent article explains monitor problems across platforms, and even provides a visual method of determining your computer's Gamma (`http://www.vtiscan.com/~rwb/gamma.html`).

- "Frequently Questioned Answers About Gamma," by Charles Poynton. Facts and fallacies about Gamma are examined in great detail at `http://www.inforamp.net/~poynton/notes/color/GammaFQA.html`.

- The Gamma Correction Home Page is a comprehensive article and has related Gamma resources (`http://www.cgsd.com/papers/gamma.html`).

Experts claim that working in high contrast colors is a way around Gamma problems. Of course, this translates into the loss of subtlety in design. Your best defense against Gamma problems is to learn what it is and how it affects your design. As ever, be sure to test your sites with a variety of equipment, gaining a feel for what variations of your design might appear.

WORKING WITH SCREEN SPACE

Now that you understand screen color and Gamma, here are a few more helpful methods for gaining maximum control over screen space when designing for the limitations of the Web.

The first step in finding control over screen space is to understand that the screen space within a browser is a very small space that allows little or no opportunity to vary its borders.

Let's refer to this problem as *constraint*. Web space is *constrained space*.

Learning how to manage your sites effectively in constrained space will immediately affect the comfort of your site visitors, making them feel relaxed, at ease, and prepared to enjoy your Web site.

Look at your computer monitor. It is itself a constrained space with distinctive borders. The borders physically separate the unit from its environment. More borders create a visual frame around the desktop.

If you revisit the earlier browser discussion, you'll remember that the browser adds its own borders around the viewing window.

As if these constraints weren't enough, many designers add constraints to their designs. Table borders around tables (see Figure 30.9), borders around images (see Figure 30.10), and large, chunky headers or graphics (see Figure 30.11) all add to the sense that browser space is very limited.

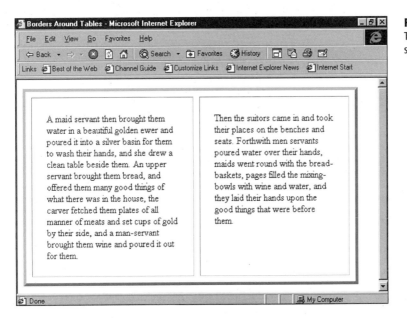

Figure 30.9
Table borders add spatial constraints.

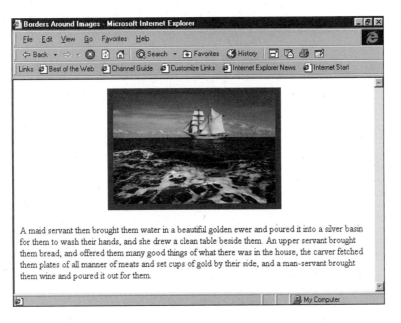

Figure 30.10
Image borders also add to a sense of containment.

Figure 30.11
Chunky headers and graphics crowd the available space.

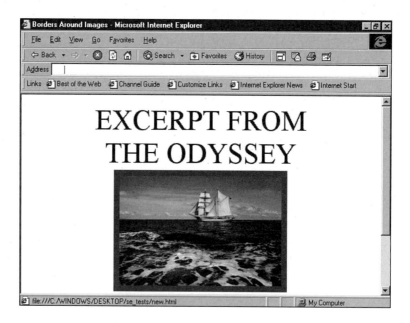

To make your site visitors more comfortable, you need to divert their attention away from the spatial limitations of the Web.

Tip #161

> Why does it seem natural to put borders around tables and images? Many designers do it and they like the results. Matting, or *framing*, space is a familiar method of handling artwork or design. For example, if you look at the art in your office, it's probably matted and framed. The frames can be thought of as similar to your computer monitor's external boundaries, and the matte similar to a browser's interface.

The first thing to do is manage your visual space.

MANAGING SPACE

Several design techniques help you create pages that are visually freed from the constraints of the computer and Web environments. They include the following:

- Use margins—Add margins wherever you are working with long blocks of text.
- Think about whitespace—This is the use of background space (not always white) as a cushion and guide for the eye.
- Eliminate clutter—Everything on a page should be there for a reason.
- Control dimension and proportion—Keep the size of your graphic and media elements in balance with not only the size of available space, but with other elements on the page.

Now take a closer look at how to put these methods work.

ADDING MARGINS

Margins are simply the addition of space, sometimes referred to as *gutters*, along the right and left edge of text. Figure 30.12 shows a page with no margins, and Figure 30.13 is the same page with margins. You can easily see that margins make sections of text easier to read—and the page looks better, too.

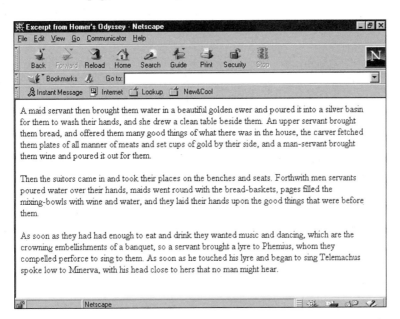

Figure 30.12
An HTML page of text without margins.

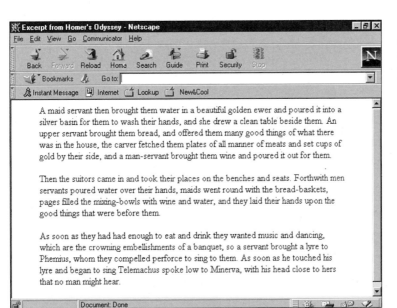

Figure 30.13
Add margins and achieve greater readability as well as aesthetic appeal.

Margins can be achieved several ways via FrontPage. The most visible is setting margins for the entire page using the Page Properties dialog box, which is found on the Margins tab. Margins can only be set for the top and left of the page. Follow these steps to set margins for the entire page:

1. Open a Web page in Page view by selecting View, Page.
2. Right-click anywhere on the page and select Page Properties from the pop-up menu. This opens the Page Properties dialog box.
3. Select the Margins tab (see Figure 30.14).
4. You can specify only the top and left margins. Select which to include by checking the appropriate box.
5. Enter the number of pixels for the margin and click OK.

Figure 30.14
Setting the page margins.

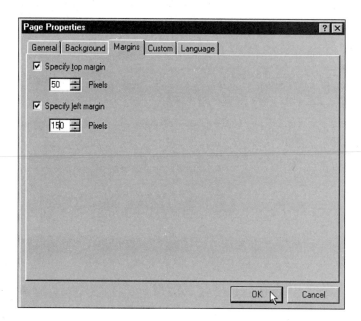

Global margins aren't the only margins available. FrontPage can also set the margins for individual paragraphs using the Paragraph dialog box (see Figure 30.15):

1. Place the cursor within the paragraph you want to format.
2. Select Format, Paragraph.
3. Under the Indentation section, type the number of pixels in the Before Text and After Text fields.
4. You can also indent the first line by placing a value in the Indent First Line field.
5. Click OK when finished.

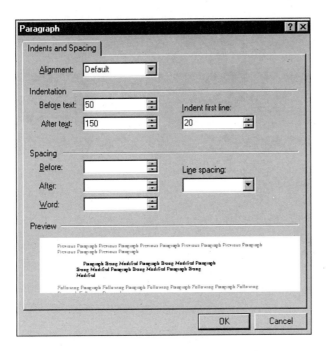

Figure 30.15
Setting individual paragraph margins.

Setting paragraph margins with the Paragraph dialog box uses the `leftmargin` and `right-margin` style sheet attributes within the opening <P> tag :

```
<P style="leftmargin:100; rightmargin:300">
```

You can see this code by clicking the HTML tab at the bottom of the Page View window.

You can control the margins of almost any Web page element with style sheets. Check out Chapter 12, "Using Style Sheets with Individual Pages and Full Sites," for more information on using these.

Tables are another way to gain margin control. More about this technique can be found in Chapter 8, "Creating Tables."

ADDING WHITESPACE TO GRAPHICS

Whitespace is the absence of design, but it is wholly design. While you might think of design as being the elements and objects that go into creating a Web page, design is also what is not there.

Some areas in Figure 30.16's layout are blacked out. Focus only on the white. If you look carefully, you'll notice that the white area is a shape in and of itself. Different shapes, like those in Figure 30.17, change the whitespace.

Figure 30.16
Notice the space in between the blacked-out elements.

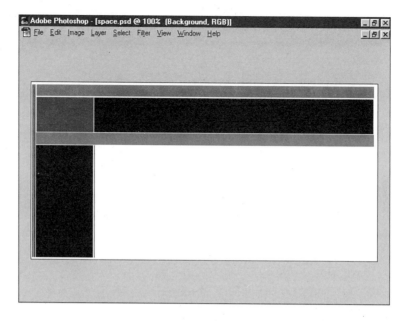

Figure 30.17
Different shapes are used for these elements; the shape of the whitespace changes.

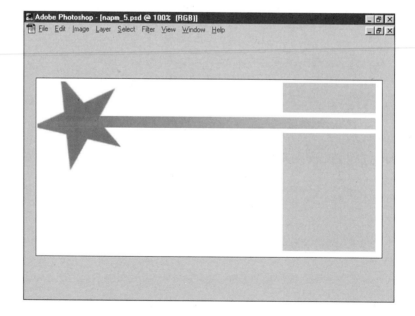

Whitespace adds to design by providing texture and cushioning for page elements. It also can help serve your design by leading and resting the eye.

To work with whitespace, you have to gain a feel not only for what you put on to a page, but what shapes are created between those elements.

One of the most essential places to use whitespace is around graphical images. FrontPage allows you to set the space surrounding an image:

1. Select a picture on the current Web page.

2. Right-click the picture and select Picture Properties from the pop-up menu. This opens the Picture Properties dialog.

3. Select the Appearance tab (see Figure 30.18).

4. You can specify only the top and left margins. Select which to include by selecting the appropriate box.

5. Enter the number of pixels for the margin and click OK.

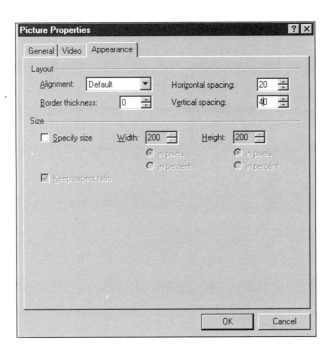

Figure 30.18
Add whitespace
around a picture.

ELIMINATING CLUTTER

As designers, eliminating clutter is one of our biggest jobs. How would you decorate a small, dark room without windows in order to make it look larger? Here are several recommendations.

- Paint the room a light color.
- Furnish it simply, even sparsely.
- Make sure the furnishings in the room are not too heavy or ornate.

You can use these suggestions to directly apply some sensible ideas to a heavy Web page (see Figure 30.19). In most cases, you'll want to keep your pages light. Of course, there will be exceptions to this guideline, but it's a good one to keep in mind. Next, you'll want to ensure that your graphics are carefully chosen and—most importantly—that each one serves a purpose. Finally, your graphics should not be too heavy or complicated for the page.

Figure 30.19
A heavy, cluttered page.

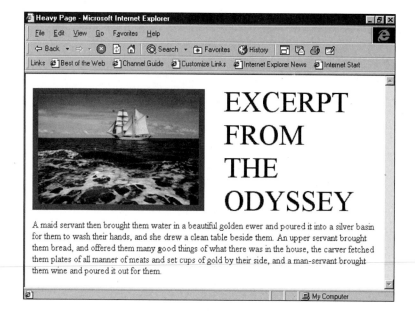

To sum it up, less is more when it comes to Web design. While this is not always practical—especially when dealing with large amounts of data—working toward a simpler goal improves your chances of having a more spacious, relaxed page (see Figure 30.20).

DIMENSION AND PROPORTION

Dimension is the size of a given element. *Proportion* is the relationship of elements to each another.

Dimension is particularly important on a Web page. If a graphic is too large, it causes not only a visual imbalance but potential problems with scrolling.

There's an odd tendency for some designers to create objects that are far too big for a page, as shown in the block layout in Figure 30.21. The page's impact is lost when this occurs. When sizing images, always keep the 595×295 per screen guidelines in mind. This is sure to help you size your graphics and media elements more appropriately.

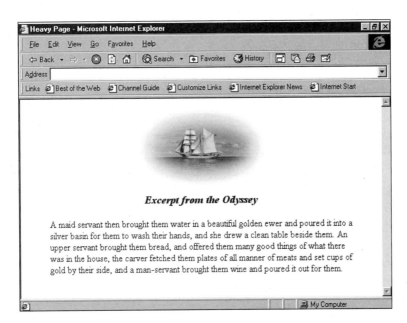

Figure 30.20
A lighter, happier page.

Figure 30.21
An element that is too large for a page will weigh it down.

The relationship between elements is important. To create visual harmony, you want elements to be the right distance from one another, as well as proportional to one another. The header area, graphic image, and text in Figure 30.22 are all balanced within the page's layout.

Figure 30.22
A more harmonious layout—visually interesting whitespace, balanced elements.

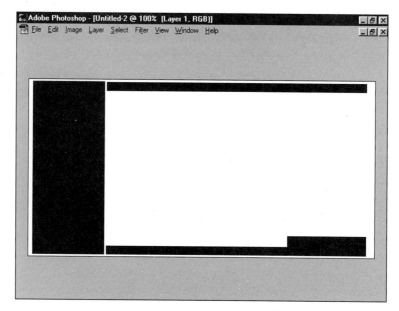

If any one of these elements were too much larger or smaller, the balance of the page would be the size of your graphic and media lost.

TROUBLESHOOTING: USING FRAMES

I want to use frames in my site, but I've read that many people don't like the use of frames.

The major problem with frames is that they constrain screen space even more. Frames typically have additional scroll bars and borders that take up additional browser space. You should consider carefully your design before using frames. Another alternative is to give visitors a choice—to view the site with frames or without.

I keep my computer resolution set to 1024×768. Is there a way to view my pages at different resolutions without changing my computer's resolution?

Yes, you can always resize the browser window to any size you want, but FrontPage has an easier method. "Designers Corner" shows you how to set the browser and resolution to preview your pages. This makes it easy to view your pages at many different resolutions.

DESIGNERS CORNER: REVIEWING SCREEN SPACE IN FRONTPAGE

If there were one point worth stressing in this chapter concerning screen size, it is test, test, test. FrontPage makes this easy with the capability to preview the current page in any number of browsers and resolutions.

For a quick look at the current page, use the Preview tab at the bottom of the Page View window. This is useful for giving you a quick once-over, but shouldn't be relied on for the final test. To really test your pages, you need to use the Preview in Browser function.

SETTING THE PREVIEW WINDOW SIZE

Clicking the Preview in Browser button opens the current page in the default browser. The page must be saved before it can be viewed. The default preview browser and resolution can be set using the Preview in Browser dialog box. Change the default preview browser by following these steps:

1. Open the Preview in Browser dialog box by selecting File, Preview in Browser.
2. Select the browser that you want to use to preview your pages.
3. Browsers can be added to the list with the Add button.
4. Select the window size by clicking the desired resolution. Your current computer resolution is the default option.
5. Click on the Automatically Save Page check box to save the page every time you click the Preview in Browser button.

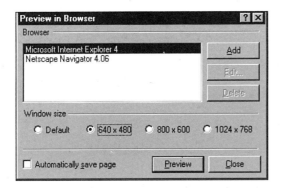

Figure 30.23
Changing the default preview browser and resolution.

CHAPTER 31

WEB GRAPHIC FORMATS

In this chapter

by Kelly Murdock

GRAPHIC INTERCHANGE FORMAT (GIF)

GIF is a file format that uses a type of compression known as *lossless*, which means that none of the image quality is lost during the compression process. Compression, as a general rule, is based on complicated mathematical algorithms that are best saved for those developers interested in working with compression.

For all individuals developing Web pages, you are best served by learning that GIF compression works by figuring out how much of the image uses the same color information. At that point, the compression algorithm saves those sections by using a numeric pattern.

GIF compression is limited to a total of 256 colors, so that numeric pattern is very specific. This is one of the main reasons it's so important to understand more about color theory and restrictions on the Web. If you have 15 shades of blue within your graphic, that translates to 15 individual patterns. With more than 256 patterns, the algorithm has to decide what to leave out. It does this by limiting those blues to a few or even one blue color.

Because of this process, your neon blue might end up a sky blue. This is where experience and a skilled hand come to play—knowing when and how to deal with color and file types will enable you to gain control over colors within your graphics.

> **Note**
>
> There's a bit of confusion over the pronunciation of GIF. Many people say it with a hard G, because logically, if the *G* stands for *graphic*, it would follow that *GIF* (as in GIFt) would be the proper pronunciation.
>
> However, many people, including myself, pronounce the G like a J, or JIF as in JIFFY. Interestingly, when on the phone with Unisys, the owners of the GIF algorithm, pronounced it just that way.

GIFs have been the longest supported graphic file type on the Web, and they are extremely useful for a number of graphic file applications.

WHEN TO USE GIFs

There are several important guidelines that help determine if you should choose the GIF compression method for a specific graphic:

- Line-drawn images—Any graphic that uses few lines, such as a cartoon, is a good choice for GIF compression.
- Images with few, flat colors—With only a few colors and no light sources or gradations in that color, there's not going to be a lot of competition for those 256 colors in the compression method.

Figure 31.1 shows a line-drawn cartoon image, which is an excellent choice for GIF compression. Figure 31.2 uses four solid colors, with no light sources or gradations, which also makes the image perfect for GIF compression.

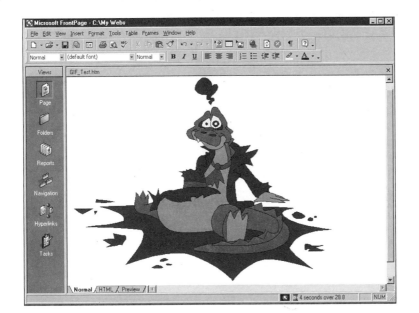

Figure 31.1
A line-drawn cartoon image from the Animabets.com site is a perfect choice for GIF format. .

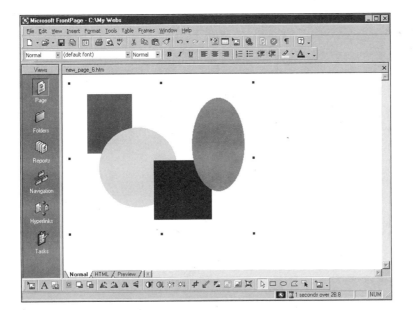

Figure 31.2
This image, using only solid colors, is also a good choice for the GIF format.

JOINT PHOTOGRAPHIC EXPERTS GROUP (JPEG)

Frustrated with the limitations of GIFs, a group of photographic experts went to work on compression methods that would allow high-quality compression while retaining millions of colors. The results are what is known today as Joint Photographic Experts Group (JPEG or JPG).

> **Note**
>
> The appropriate file extension for JPEG files is .jpg. There's a lot of confusion around this issue, because of JPEG. Always follow standard filenaming conventions and use the .jpg suffix for all JPEG images.

The algorithm that makes up the JPEG is by nature more complicated than that using the GIF. JPEGs use a *lossy* compression method, which means that some image quality is sacrificed during the compression process. The algorithm focuses on removing data that is considered unimportant, instead of first mapping out areas of information that should be saved.

The JPEG method does this by dividing the image data into rectangular sections before applying the algorithm. On one hand, this method gives you a lot of control in terms of how much information you're going to toss away; at high compression ratios, however, you can end up with a blocky, blurry result.

These blocky sections are known as *artifacts*. Artifacts occur when you've overcompressed an image. You'll look at this a bit later, when you step through the optimization process. Working with JPEGs, just as with GIFs, requires a bit of skill and a fine hand to achieve the best results.

WHEN TO USE JPEGS

Because the JPEG format was specifically designed to manage files with a lot of color, there are certain types of images that best lend themselves to JPEG compression. The following list is a helpful guide to use when determining if JPEG is the best format for your image:

- A lot of colors, such as with color photographs
- Graphics using gradient fills (see Figure 31.3)
- Graphics using light sources
- Photographs with much gradation, such as skies, sunsets, and oceans (see Figure 31.4)

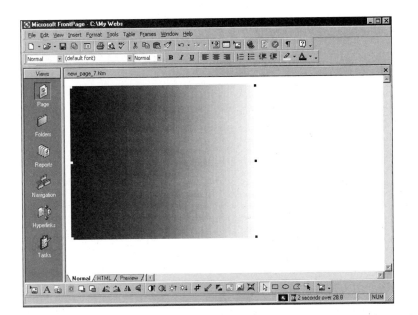

Figure 31.3
Gradient fills are appropriate for JPEG format.

Figure 31.4
Sunset pictures, particularly when in full color, contain a lot of gradation and will normally be processed via the JPEG format.

Portable Network Graphics (PNG)

Another file format supported by some Web browsers, including Internet Explorer 4.0b1 and later and Netscape Navigator 4.04 and later is the Portable Network Graphics format, PNG for short. While it's still not widely supported by many graphic tools, it is felt that PNG offers even better compression than a GIF.

Caution

> Despite the fact that 4.0-generation browsers have chosen to support the PNG format, that support is sometimes buggy. The biggest perpetrator of this is Netscape Navigator. As a result, using PNG for Internet-based Web sites is, at this time, risky at best.

Using the lossless method, the difference between PNG and GIF compression is that PNG isn't limited to a 256-color palette. It can also be interlaced, making it a very attractive option for the future.

FrontPage, as well as many other Web graphic imaging programs, has PNG support for file development and optimization. For more information on the PNG format, visit the World Wide Web Consortium's specification for PNG at `http://www.w3.org/TR/REC-png-multi.html`.

When to Use PNGs

PNG format is best when you find yourself in middle ground, in need of a lot of colors, and still desiring lossless compression. Interlacing images with lots of colors is another reason to use PNG. This isn't an option with standard JPEG images.

Keep in mind that it is still a risk to use PNG on the Internet. This format is better used on a intranet with a homogenous browser base:

- Line-drawn images with more than 256 colors (see Figure 31.5)
- Interlaced graphics with lots of colors
- GIF images in need of better compression rates

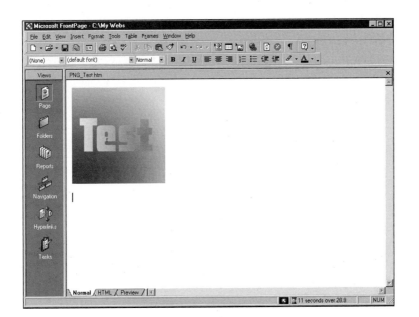

Figure 31.5
An image with straight lines but lots of colors is ideal for PNG.

VECTOR FORMATS

In addition to the standard bitmap formats, new vector formats are becoming available. These formats, such as Macromedia Flash, require plug-ins to work. Why would anyone want to use a graphics format that requires a plug-in? The biggest advantage on the Web is that vector graphics are represented by mathematical formulas and numbers. This makes their file size much smaller when compared to bitmap images.

Animations are another area in which vector formats are a huge advantage. GIF animations require the space of several images shown one after another, but vector animations only need to know how the mathematically defined lines, curves, and colors change over time. This yields a dramatic size savings and can really open your Web presentations to some elaborate full-screen effects. The cost to users is a plug-in.

MACROMEDIA FLASH

The most popular vector format by far is Macromedia's Flash. The 3.0 version offers advanced features such as music and interactivity. Figure 31.6 shows a snapshot of an 81KB introduction piece done for the International Olympic Committee's Web site. The introduction includes background music, flying text, and fading images.

By comparison, a single frame of this animation weighs in at 39KB for a GIF image and 19KB for a JPEG image. The vector animation has over 150 frames of animation and much more. For some reason, installing a plug-in doesn't seem like such a big deal now.

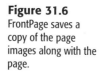

Figure 31.6
FrontPage saves a
copy of the page
images along with the
page.

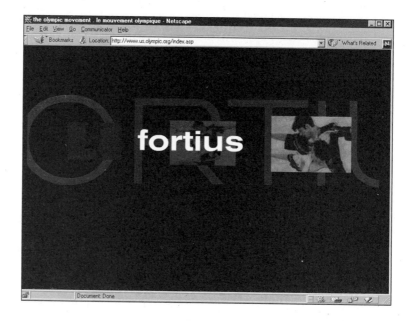

Unfortunately, FrontPage doesn't support any vector formats. You can import vector images such as WMF or EPS, but these get converted to bitmap images when the Web page is saved.

GRAPHIC OPTIMIZATION

Optimizing graphics is the technique by which a Web graphic designer reduces a graphic's file size for acceptable download times, but maintains the highest quality image he or she can produce.

Optimization is all about reducing an image's file size. The file size can be reduced by getting rid of graphical information, preferably the unneeded information, such as extra white space that surrounds an image. One way to reduce file sizes is to reduce image size—with fewer pixels, there's less information and the file is smaller.

Another way to optimize an image is to throw away colors that aren't being used. If a GIF image holds the information for 256 colors and an image only uses 56 colors, the extra 200 colors is unnecessary information that can be deleted.

Another method for reducing file sizes is built into the GIF format. Suppose you have an image of a flag. Reading the information for this image is something like pixel number 1, blue; pixel number 2, blue; pixel number 3, blue, and so on. The long stretch of redundant colors could be more efficiently represented with this: The next 31 pixels are blue. This method of compression is built into the GIF format.

Understanding how this compression works gives you another method for optimizing images. If you can replace large sections of multiple colors (such as dithered areas) with a single color, the resulting image saved as a GIF will be much smaller.

Before applying any of these techniques, determine which file format is appropriate for the file. GIF, JPEG, and PNG formats will help you to achieve this step if you use the general guidelines given earlier.

To recap: The general rule of thumb is to use the GIF file format for line art and images with few areas of flat color. JPEGs are more appropriate for full-color, gradient images; PNG is useful if you have a line art image with more than 256 colors and you're certain that the people accessing the image are using a browser that supports PNG graphics.

Interestingly, the guidelines discussed within this chapter for these formats are not always accurate. A black and white photograph (or even a color photograph) with very little color information, light source, and gradients is an example. With this example, it's going to take a little experimentation to determine which file type will help you achieve the smallest file size while retaining the most important information.

PART

VI

CH

31

No cut-and-dry answer can be found any other way than through trial-and-error or by using one of the many graphic optimization tools available (see "Optimization Tools" later in this chapter).

The optimization tools in FrontPage are limited, so you may need to rely on additional tools to complete your optimizations. First you see an example of optimizing a GIF image by reducing the number of colors. Since this requires that you change the image's bit depth, Photoshop 4.0 is used.

Note

> You can optimize graphics with a wide range of tools. Photoshop is used here because its palette control is superior to many of the less professional programs on the market.

Before you begin the step-by-step, here's a list of helpful terms that are used throughout the remainder of the chapter:

- Color palette—There are several types of color palettes. They are numerically determined sets of colors within the graphic program that enable the designer to make specific choices over how an image is processed.

- Adaptive palette—This palette allows you to make adaptations to a given image, including controlling color, depth, and dithering.

- Indexed color—A software program such as Photoshop will take an image file and count its colors. If there are more than 256 colors in an image, indexing will reduce the image's palette to 256 colors, making it ready for GIF production. At that point, you can use the adaptive palette to further control aspects of the palette.

- Exact palette—You'll see this appear when an image already has less than 256 colors because the colors fit within the indexing limits, the specific number of colors used will appear. You can then determine whether to keep this number or to reduce with the adaptive palette.

- Bit depth—Also known as *color depth*, this is the amount of total bit data that will be saved with your image. The optimization of images into the GIF format depends upon your ability to control bit depth.

- Number of colors—In GIF optimization, there can be as few as 8 colors or as many as 256 colors. Limiting the number of colors is how you reduce the size of a GIF file during the optimization process.

- Dithering—This is the process by which the computer and imaging software determine which color to use when reducing a palette. Remember the discussion of the GIF algorithm earlier in this chapter? It was mentioned that a neon blue could conceivably show up as a sky blue during reduction. That is *dithering*. Ideally, you don't want your images to dither at all, which speaks to the issue of proper file format selection.

- Maximum, High, Medium, Low—These settings are specific to JPEG optimization and refer to how much information is removed during the lossy compression process.

With the terminology down, you can begin optimizing a graphic.

OPTIMIZING A GIF

With an appropriate file for GIF optimization in hand, let's step through the optimization process. Here's a checklist to be sure you're ready:

1. Your file is obviously ready for GIF optimization. It has flat color, few colors, and is line-drawn.

2. You've scanned and sized your file to appropriate Web dimensions (see Chapter 32, "Creating Professional Web Graphics").

3. The file is in RGB format—either a native Photoshop file, an EPS, or a JPG set to Maximum.

In Photoshop:

1. Select Image, Mode.

2. Choose Indexed Color.

3. When the Indexed Color dialog box pops up, select the Adaptive palette, No Dither (see Figure 31.7).

4. Reduce the bit depth to 7.

5. Save the file using the File, Export, GIF89 feature (see Figure 31.8).

6. Name the file `gif_test_7.gif`. (Be sure to save your original file; you'll be going back to it.)

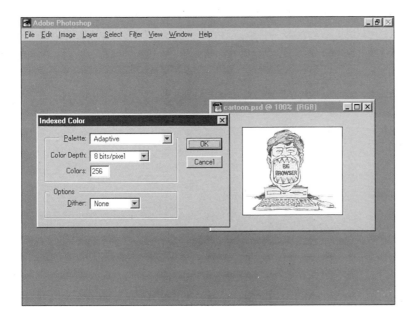

Figure 31.7
The Adaptive palette
in Photoshop.

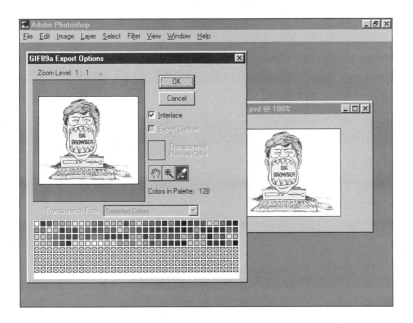

Figure 31.8
Exporting the image
with the GIF89
export feature.

View your results. Figure 31.9 shows mine.

Figure 31.9
The GIF, optimized at
7 bits.

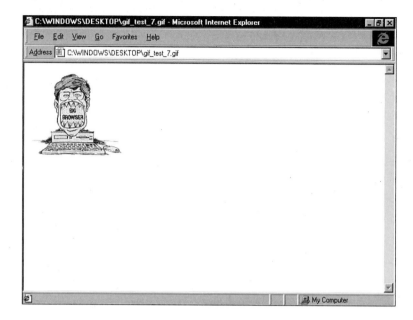

Now try reducing the bit depth even more:

1. Open the original file. In this case, it's `gif_optimize.psd`.
2. Select Image, Mode.
3. Once again, select Indexed Color.
4. Choose the Adaptive palette, set to No Dither.
5. Reduce the bit depth to 3.
6. Export the file (File, Export, GIF89).
7. Name the file `gif_test_3.gif`.

View your results. Are they acceptable, or did they reduce the colors or line integrity too much? If you liked the first example but weren't happy with the second at 3 bits, try optimizing at a variety of bit depths until you find the right one for your file.

Figure 31.10 shows the results. Note that there's not much difference between the two images visually, but the first file, `gif_test_7.gif`, is a total of 9KB, and the second, only 4KB.

Figure 31.10
The GIF example, this time at a bit depth of 3.

OPTIMIZING A JPEG

JPEG optimization is easier to control. The ability to optimize an image is one of the key benefits of the JPEG format. Since the JPEG format is a lossy format, it automatically throws away image information based on the user-specified settings. It first throws away the information that no one will miss, but eventually, if you squeeze hard enough, it will discard some noticeable information.

You can use FrontPage to control the level of JPEG compression. Begin with a file appropriate for JPEG optimization. Here's a list of helpful guidelines:

- Images appropriate to optimize as JPEG files should have many colors, light sources, or color gradients.
- Your initial file should be in RGB format, preferably a maximum set JPEG.
- The file to be optimized should be appropriately sized for Web use.

Start by opening a Web page containing a JPEG image. Now you're ready to optimize the file:

1. First, view the JPEG at its current settings by clicking the Preview tab at the bottom of the window. Figure 31.11 shows the image at its maximum quality setting.
2. Right-click the JPEG image and select Picture Properties from the pop-up menu.
3. Under the General tab, the Quality setting determines the amount of compression applied to the image.
4. Change the Quality value to 25 and click OK.
5. Save the file and click again on the Preview tab (see Figure 31.12).

Notice the difference between the two images. The maximum quality JPEG is very clear and crisp, with no degradation or appearance of artifacts, but it also weighs in at a hefty 23KB.

For this example, the quality value of 25 is pretty severe. It's there so that you notice the obvious difference caused by too much reduction. You should be able to see the blocky artifacts through the sky of Figure 31.12, even in the black and white picture in this book. The file size was reduced to a paltry 4KB. In reality, the optimum setting is somewhere in the middle.

Figure 31.11
The JPEG at a High quality setting.

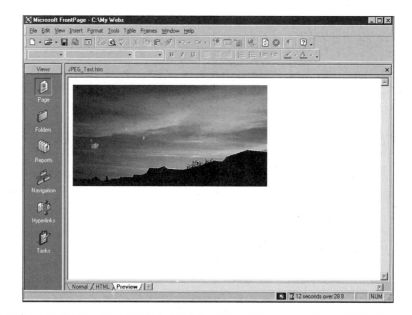

Figure 31.12
At a quality setting of 25, the JPEG becomes blocky, blotchy, and blurry-filled with artifacts.

> **Note**
>
> Quality settings of 75 and 50 are often similar in visual quality, but not always similar in terms of weight. Most of your JPEGs are going to be saved at a setting of 50, with some at 75, and—if you truly are looking to keep image integrity—very few will be saved at 25 or lower. A setting of 100 is a good setting should you have a reason to want full color with absolutely no degradation. This is helpful when using larger files for specialty viewing.

Your JPEG mileage may vary. The more you practice optimization techniques, the more skilled you will become at knowing what type of file format to use, how much or how little to optimize a graphic, and when your specific circumstances allow you leeway for variation in file weight.

ADDITIONAL GRAPHIC TECHNIQUES

There are several graphic techniques involving the GIF and JPEG file formats critical to your Web graphic production work. They include progressive rendering, transparency, and animation. FrontPage can be used for progressive rendering and transparency, but you'll need an addition tool to create animations. See Chapter 34, "Web Graphic Tools," for information on animation tools.

PROGRESSIVE RENDERING

This technique keeps a site visitor's visual attention while graphics are downloading from a server to a Web page. The concept is that the individual will see portions of the graphic until all of its binary data is loaded into the browser.

It's an effective method. If you prefer to having your images "pop" into a page, there's a sense that the downloading process is smoother when progressive rendering is in place. You should learn progressive rendering techniques and make your own decisions based on personal and professional preferences.

Progressive rendering can be achieved in both the GIF and JPEG format.

INTERLACED GIFS

Interlacing is the term used for GIFs that progressively render.

Photoshop supports interlacing, as do all the popular Web graphic applications.

To create an interlaced GIF in FrontPage, simply be sure that the Interlaced box is checked in the Picture Properties dialog box. You need to save the graphic as well as the page before you can see this effect.

An interlaced GIF will first appear fuzzy, and then slowly clarify as the GIF data downloads to the Web browser.

Note

If you view these images in the Preview window or in a browser on your local machine, you might not see the interlacing effect. Even large images will take almost no time to load from your local hard drive, so the interlacing effect isn't noticeable. To see the effect, load the image from a Web server.

PROGRESSIVE JPEGS

It's important to note that you cannot interlace a JPEG. However, a technology has been developed to allow JPEGs to progressively render. This is the *progressive* JPEG format. FrontPage, as well as many contemporary Web imaging programs, allow you to create JPEGS that render progressively.

As mentioned earlier in the chapter, the JPEG algorithm works by reducing rectangular sections of color data within an image. If you conceptually reverse this process and imagine data flowing into the rectangular blocks, you'll be visualizing the way a progressive JPEG renders. There's an integrated series of blocks that create the image and first appear with little graphic data. With each new delivery of information from the server, the JPEG blocks receive more data until the download is complete.

While interlaced GIFs first appear fuzzy and then get clearer, progressive JPEGs first appear blocky and blurry.

Note

When serving progressive JPEGs at high speeds, the blurry effect is reduced or eliminated, improving the visual experience.

Another consideration when working with progressive JPEGs is that they are not supported by most browsers prior to the 3.0 generation. Therefore, visitors using older browsers will not see your graphic.

The Picture Properties dialog box holds the key to progressive JPEGs. You can set the number of passes that are required before the entire image loads. These passes are divided by the total time to load the image. If you have a fairly small JPEG image that takes five seconds to load with a setting of five passes, each pass will take roughly one second. This will create a rippling effect as the graphic comes into view.

To create a progressive JPEG, follow these steps:

1. Open a page with an embedded image.
2. Right-click the image and select Picture Properties from the pop-up menu.
3. Select the General tab (see Figure 31.13).
4. Select the JPEG option and set the quality value.
5. Select the number of progressive passes and click OK.
6. Save the Web page and the image.

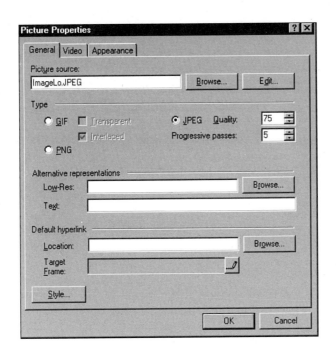

Figure 31.13
Create a progressive
rendering JPEG by
setting the number of
passes.

Part

VI

Ch

31

Tip #162

> Standard GIFs and JPEGS scroll into place rather than render progressively. Some people prefer this look. Still, most usability studies and anecdotal information suggest that progressive rendering helps keep individuals on a page. Therefore, in many cases it's usually wise to progressively render your graphics.

TRANSPARENCY

Transparency can be described as an effect that places your graphic on a clear piece of tape. This means you can place that tape on a background and the background will show through the tape.

This is particularly effective when you're creating graphics that sit on a background—especially graphics that aren't a standard rectangular shape.

The technique takes a little bit of time, patience, and an excellent hand and eye to learn.

Again, FrontPage can create transparent images, but your favorite Web graphics program is likely to have a helpful method by which to make an image transparent.

Note

> Only GIFs can be transparent. JPEG technology does not include a transparency option.

Assume you want to place a text header image over a background texture. The text selection is ornate, with a lot of circular shapes. Follow these steps to create a transparency:

1. Open a new page in Page view.

2. Add a background image by clicking Format, Background. This opens the Page Properties dialog box with the Background tab selected.

3. Check the Background Picture box and then use the Browse button to locate the background image.

4. Click OK to accept the background image. The Page view should tile the background image.

5. Load the header image by selecting Insert, Picture, From File. If the file doesn't include transparency information, it will look like Figure 31.14.

6. Click the image to access the picture toolbar at the bottom of the window; click the Set Transparent Color tool.

7. The cursor will change to look like an eraser. Click the color in the image that you want to make transparent.

8. The color you clicked becomes transparent (see Figure 31.15).

Figure 31.14
Adding a non-transparent image to a page with a background image.

Figure 31.15
A transparent GIF appears seamless over textured backgrounds.

Tip #163

Creating transparent GIF images can leave ragged edges around your image. To reduce the visibility of this edge, try to match the background color in the image to the background color on the Web page.

GIF ANIMATION

Another inherent aspect of file formats is the GIF animation. This very handy effect is actually an exploitation of GIF technology. This chapter briefly mentions animation because the GIF animation is directly tied to the file format that parents it.

GIF animations are essentially several GIF images stitched together into one file. You can create an animation effect by crafting your images carefully. FrontPage cannot be used to create GIF animations, but it can place any such animations on a page. You'll need to save the Web page to view GIF animations.

For more information on how to create animated GIFs, see Chapter 33, "Designing Specialty Graphics."

SPECIAL CONCERNS

Several considerations regarding graphic file formats should be discussed before moving on to other aspects of Web page creation. These include using lo-res images, splitting large images into several smaller ones, using the Web palette, and working with optimization tools.

USING LO-RES IMAGES

As an alternate to progressive rendering, consider this approach. FrontPage supports, in the Picture Properties dialog box, a lo-res alternate to any image. This lo-res alternate loads before the actual image loads. If you can create a compressed or black and white version of the actual image, it will give visitors something akin to the image to look at while the actual image is downloaded.

FrontPage can help create a low resolution (Lo-Res) alternate. With the image selected, click the black and white tool in the Picture toolbar. This creates a black and white version of the image. Save this version with a name that is unique and include this name in the Lo-Res Alternatives field of the Picture Properties dialog box.

SPLITTING LARGE IMAGES

Another trick for managing large images that are slow to download is to cut a large image into several smaller ones. As the page loads, these pieces will download and become visible before the entire image does.

This technique gives visitors a quick look at portions of the image without the blurry blotches that are common with progressive rendered images.

When using this technique, it is best to place the cut up images within a table so that they won't wrap if the browser window is reduced. Be sure to set the borders, cell padding and cell spacing properties in the Table Properties dialog box to 0.

ADAPTIVE VERSUS WEB PALETTE

Editions 4.0 and 5.0 of Photoshop, as well as in other graphic programs, the inclusion of the Web-safe palette has offered designers a way to save their GIFs specifically to that palette.

There's some dissention over this concept. Doesn't it make perfect sense to just use the *Web-safe palette (page 620)* when saving GIFs? There are at least two reasons you might consider not using this method of saving a file:

1. The 216 color palette is just that—it contains 216 colors that are common between Macintosh and Windows computers. Using the Adaptive palette, you can reduce that number of colors significantly for greater control over your file weight.

2. Limiting colors by hand gives you much greater control over the palette. The 216 color palette will always dither colors to match that palette, sometimes giving you unacceptable results (see Figure 31.16). The same file is optimized in Figure 31.17, with profoundly better visual results and only a 4KB increase in file weight.

Figure 31.16
The 216 Web-safe palette can sometimes dither graphics unacceptably. The weight is low: 4KB.

Figure 31.17
The same file, optimized with the Adaptive palette. The weight is slightly higher: 9KB.

How, then, can Web graphic designers ensure that their graphics don't dither when viewed in unsafe circumstances? You can certainly decide to use the Web-safe palette if you prefer. Here are a few other tips:

- If you're creating graphics from scratch, begin with colors selected from the safe palette.

- If you must use unsafe color and are concerned about support, try to be sure that the graphics are enhancements rather than necessary to your site. An example of a necessary GIF is anything that contains text pertinent to the page. If this dithers, it could seriously affect readability.

Note

Remember, unless you create a JPEG yourself or replace every color in that JPEG by hand with a Web-safe color, JPEGs will always be unsafe. The JPEG algorithm doesn't limit the palette and, in fact, supports up to 24 bits of color information—that's a lot of color! Users with browser or monitor limitations will see a poorer quality of graphic in these cases.

OPTIMIZATION TOOLS

Several good tools to assist you with the comparison of Web graphic formats exist, including the following:

- Debabelizer Pro (http://www.debabelizer.com/)   This is the professional-level graphic production tool. It can very successfully manage the optimization process and it includes a batch processing utility that lets you optimize many graphics at once. This is a particularly good choice for Web graphic designers. It's an expensive program!

- Ulead Systems SmartSaver (http://www.ulead.com/)   For the Windows platform only, this helpful utility allows you to import and then compare graphic optimization types and weights before saving.

- Web Vise Totality (http://www.autofx.com/html/webvise totality.htm)   A complete optimization package for both the Windows and PowerPC platforms.

- GIF Optimizer (http://www.gifoptimizer.com/)   You can optimize your GIF online using this tool, free of charge.

TROUBLESHOOTING

PNG and GIF are comparable. I have a graphic tool that can output to PNG, should I use it instead of GIF?

Although the PNG format has better properties, there are still many people on the Web that are using older browsers that cannot display PNG images. If you are worried about this group of surfers, then I'd stick with GIF images. If the advantages of using PNG are of more concern than visitors with older browsers, then use PNG.

Is there a difference between interlaced GIF images and progressively rendered JPEG images?

The difference is in the formats. GIF images use only 256 colors and JPEG images can have millions of colors, but they both accomplish roughly the same result of displaying the image is several passes. In some graphic tools, you can set the number of passes that a progressively rendered JPEG requires.

DESIGNERS CORNER: GRAPHIC FORMATS AND FRONTPAGE

FrontPage makes it easy to work between different graphic formats. Although you would expect FrontPage to support only GIF, JPEG, and PNG formats, FrontPage actually can place images in any of the following formats:

- Internet formats (GIF, JPEG, PNG)
- Windows bitmap (BMP)
- Tagged image format (TIF)
- Windows metafile (WMF)
- Sun raster format (RAS)
- Encapsulated Postscript (EPS)
- Zsoft Paintbrush (PCX)
- Kodak PhotoCD (PCD)
- Targa (TGA)

CONVERTING BETWEEN FORMATS

Although FrontPage can import any of these graphic formats, FrontPage automatically converts the image to either GIF, JPEG, or PNG when the page is saved. The format depends on the setting in the Picture Properties dialog box. When the page is saved, you are given a chance to rename the image before it is saved along with the HTML file for this page. Follow these steps to convert between formats:

1. Open FrontPage in Page View mode by selecting View, Page.
2. Add an image to the page by selecting Insert, Picture, From File.
3. Click the Explorer icon in the lower right of the Picture dialog box.
4. Click the File Types drop-down list in the Select Files dialog box to see the formats that FrontPage can import (see Figure 31.18). Select the file to import.

Figure 31.18
FrontPage supports many industry-standard graphic formats.

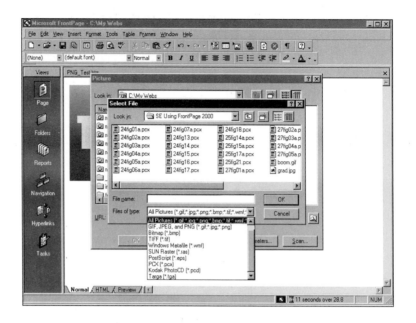

5. Right-click the image and select Picture Properties from the pop-up menu.

6. In the Picture Properties dialog box, select the file type that you want to use; click OK. Figure 31.19 shows a JPEG image being changed to PNG.

7. Save the page by selecting File, Save. The Save Embedded Files dialog box lets you rename or save the image to a different folder (see Figure 31.20).

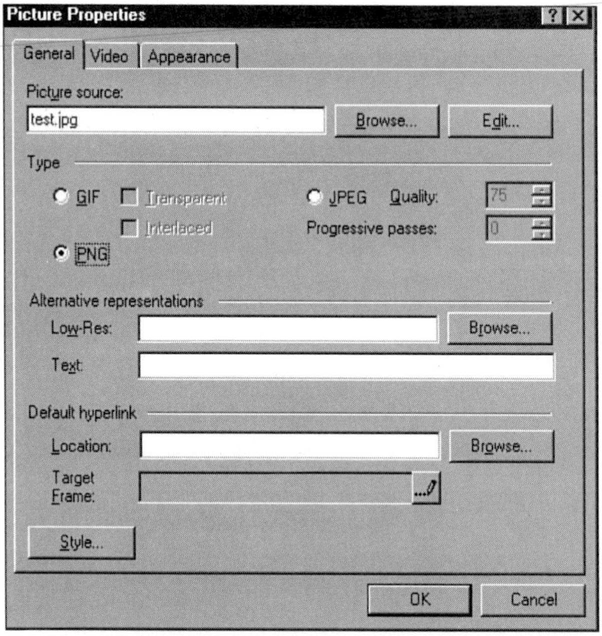

Figure 31.19
Converting between JPEG and PNG formats.

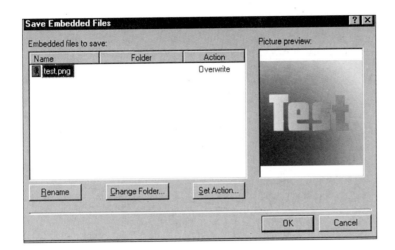

Figure 31.20
FrontPage saves a copy of the page images along with the page.

CHAPTER 32

CREATING PROFESSIONAL WEB GRAPHICS

In this chapter

by Kelly Murdock

IMAGES FOR YOUR PAGES

A Web site typically uses graphics to design, identify, and navigate.

Some of the images you'll want to consider for your pages include the following:

- *Background images*—These are images that load into the background of the page. Sometimes referred to as wallpaper, background images set the tone of a page.

- *Headers*—Headers give an individual page its identity They can also include the parent site's identity, too, as in Molly's Site: What's New.

- *Navigation buttons*—One click of a navigation button and you're on your way to another page within a site.

- *Bars and rules*—Used to separate text or elements on a page, graphic bars and rules can customize a site's look.

- *Spot art*—This is the term used to describe clip art or photography that will accentuate the textual content on a page.

FrontPage has some unique dialog boxes to create some of these types of images, but you'll want to use a graphics tool like PhotoDraw or Image Composer to create others.

Within these types of images are a variety of techniques to employ to ensure professional quality.

SCANNING TECHNIQUES, CLIP ART, AND STOCK ART

How do you get images? Essentially, three ways exist:

- Scanning and manipulating photographic and organic (real items) materials
- Working with clip and stock art and photography
- Designing your own graphics from scratch

Sometimes you'll employ all three methods to create a single image. It all depends on the look and feel you've planned for your site.

I like to refer to a famous acronym, GIGO. This means "Garbage In, Garbage Out" and is most appropriate in terms of Web graphics. If you begin with poor images, whether from scan or stock, you'll end up with poor images.

To avoid that, you'll learn some basic scanning tricks and then take a look at how to choose quality clip art, stock art, and photos. To design your own graphics, there's an entire section of this chapter to walk you step-by-step through Web graphic creation.

SCANNING IN FRONTPAGE

Scanning is in and of itself an art. The good news is that for the Web, you don't need high resolution scans. This translates into less money spent on hardware, as well as a shorter learning curve for those individuals wishing to get right to the business at hand.

For hardware, a flatbed color scanner is highly recommended. You can buy very inexpensive scanners that will work well for the Web. The guideline is in resolution—because your final image will be 72dpi (dots per inch), you need a scanner capable of scanning only at this resolution. Just be sure it supports millions of colors and will work with your computer and imaging software (see Chapter 34, "Web Graphic Tools").

After your scanner is in place, you'll want to choose the item to be scanned. Typically, this will be a photo, hand drawings, prints, or an organic object, such as a pen or bottle. (Yes, you can scan "stuff"!)

Here are some guidelines to follow as you prepare to scan your work:

- Be sure photos are crisp, clean, and free of dust.
- Drawings and prints should be free of smudges and speckles.
- Organic objects should be wiped down and cleaned before they are placed on the scanner screen.
- The scanner screen itself should be clean and free of dust. Follow your manufacturer's guidelines when cleaning your scanner.

The next step is to place the item to be scanned on the scanner. On the software side, FrontPage is all you need. Notice the Scan button in the Picture dialog box (see Figure 32.1). This button holds the key to importing images by using a scanner or a digital camera. The Scan button opens another dialog box with a Source button for selecting the scanning device and an Acquire button for beginning the scanning process. The actual software that does the scan depends on scanner type.

PART
VI

CH
32

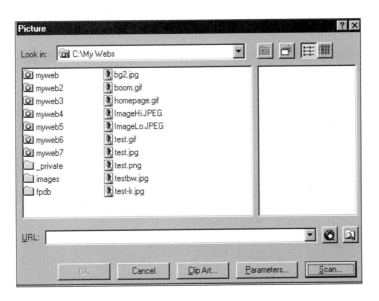

Figure 32.1
Scanning a photo into FrontPage.

After your item is scanned, you'll want to crop it. At this point, you're probably working larger than any recommended Web graphic—both in terms of dpi and dimension. For now, your crop is a preliminary one to remove any whitespace or extra information that you don't want (see Figure 32.2).

The Crop tool can be found on the Picture toolbar. Click it once to enable the cropping boundaries. Move the boundaries by dragging the edges or corners. Once you are comfortable with the crop marks, click the Crop tool again to complete the action.

Figure 32.2
Cropping the scan.

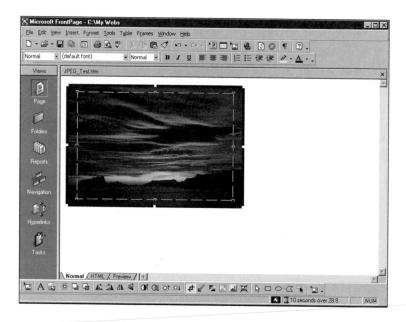

Now you'll want to look for any problems with the scan. Is everything smooth and crisp, or are there smudges and speckles? If the scan isn't acceptable, go back and do it right. It can be time consuming, but it's well worth it.

If you're happy with the scanned results, you'll want to set your dpi to 72. If you scanned in at a higher resolution (check your scanning hardware and software for adjusting this), you will see an automatic reduction in the image's dimension.

If you're at 72dpi, you're ready to make any adjustments to the scan. Crop any areas that you won't want in your final product, make alterations to the color, blur or sharpen, and generally sweep, dust, and clean the image to your tastes. FrontPage has a number of tools to help modify your scanned images, including Brightness and Contrast. See Chapter 34 for more information on FrontPage's image editing tools.

When you're satisfied, resize the image to the size you want. Bear in mind that you might be adding a photographic edge effect, such as a drop shadow or a bevel. For this reason, *save your work* at this point—this is your resource file.

It is best to save photographs in the JPEG format to maintain the entire range of colors. Be sure to save a copy of the original in case you need to start over.

A discussion of dimensions for each kind of graphic in the individual work exercises is found in the "Building Web Graphics" section of this chapter. At this point, it's most important to remember that you're designing for the screen (see Chapter 30, "About the Computer Screen").

If you're looking to create a page that is accessible across platforms and browsers, you're working at 640×480 screen resolution. No graphic should exceed the 640 width in this case, with the exception of backgrounds, which will be explained in just a bit. As for height, some occasions exist where you'll be designing longer graphics; but typically, you want to stick to sizes that fit within the screen.

> **Note**
>
> In some instances, you will want to design for higher resolutions. One example is a corporate intranet where hardware and software specifications are highly controlled.

You're now ready to make additions or changes to your scanned image or to put it aside for later use.

USING CLIP ART LIBRARY IMAGES

Another valuable resource for graphics is the Clip Art Library that ships with FrontPage. Not only is this a good place to find new images, but it is a great resource for managing all your graphic files.

Looking again at Figure 32.1, you'll notice a Clip Art button. This button opens the Clip Art Gallery (see Figure 32.3). The Gallery lets you search for clips by keywords, browse through numerous categories, and even import your favorite clips. There is also a Clips Online feature that lets you find and download clip art from the Web.

PART

VI

CH

32

Figure 32.3
Finding an image in
the Clip Art Gallery.

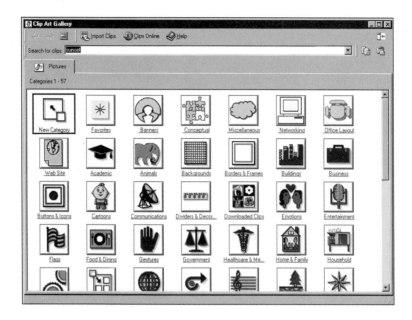

To add clips to the Gallery, follow these steps:

1. Click the Import Clips button at the top of the Clip Art Gallery.

2. A File dialog box will open. Locate the clip to add and click Import. You can specify whether to copy the image to the gallery, move it into the gallery, or let the gallery link to the image.

3. Next the Clip Properties dialog box opens. This dialog box is where you define the image, select a category, and specify any searchable keywords (see Figure 32.4).

Figure 32.4
Defining an image
imported into the
Clip Art Gallery.

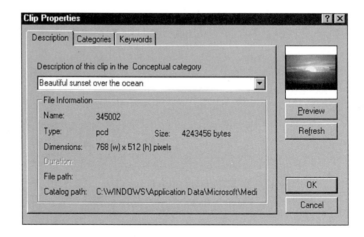

SELECTING STOCK ART

Chapter 34 provides you with several important resources for stock images. Use the resources in that chapter to get started with the selection and use of stock art.

The following are some guidelines for choosing stock art:

- Photographic images should be crisp and clear, not blurry.

- Line drawings should have no marks or speckles on them.

- You should be able to choose from the file type. Typically, a JPEG file is acceptable, particularly if it's been saved to maximum capacity. What you want to avoid are optimized GIFs, unless you're going to use that file as is or make very minimal changes to it.

- Read the licensing agreements *very carefully*. You want to be absolutely certain that you can use the image you're downloading.

Figure 32.5 shows Photodisc (`http://www.photodisc.com/`). You'll notice that you are allowed to choose the kind of file you want to purchase—options are available for file type as well as resolution.

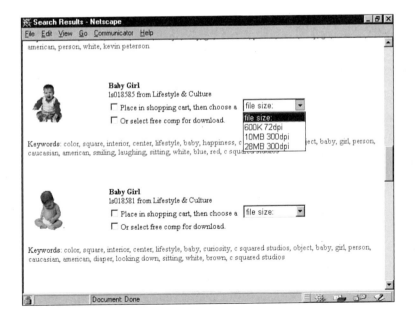

Figure 32.5
Browsing through the stock photos at Photodisc.

PART

VI

CH

32

ArtToday (http://www.arttoday.com/) is a great resource, too. Be a little more selective when choosing images from this site (see Figure 32.6). Many high-quality images are available, but quality consistency is less than that of the more expensive vendors such as Photodisc.

Figure 32.6
Selecting images from ArtToday.

Free art sites are variable. You can find great stuff, but you need to use the guidelines stated earlier to make good decisions when selecting from free clip art and photos.

BUILDING WEB GRAPHICS

With a good foundation beneath you, you're ready to create some graphics. I'll step you through a variety of tasks and demonstrate and describe features, pitfalls, and helpful hints that will make your graphics creations as professional as they get.

BACKGROUNDS

Three kinds of background images exist:

- *Wallpaper patterns*—These are small squares that tile in to create a smooth, seamless texture that looks like well-installed wallpaper (no burps, seams, or bungles!).

- *Margin tiles*—Also referred to as *strips* because they are wide and short, margin tiles can be functional or decorative in nature.

- *Watermark style*—This is one large background graphic, usually square, that adds an image, logographic material, or color to the background of a page.

One important issue to remember is that *all backgrounds are tiles*. They may not look like tiles, but they will always, always act like tiles whenever the resolution of a screen changes. Wallpaper patterns, which are squares, will tile into the browser one-by-one until the available space is filled.

Margin tiles fill the browser in the same way—except it might seem as though they don't because of their size and shape. One way to understand this process is to create a strip that isn't as long as it should be and then view it in your browser. You'll see that it does, in fact, tile along both the horizontal and vertical axes (see Figure 32.7). Finally, watermark tiles, which are very large squares, tile in the same way that wallpaper and margin tiles do (see Figure 32.19 later in this chapter). Therefore, you have to be careful when creating watermarks.

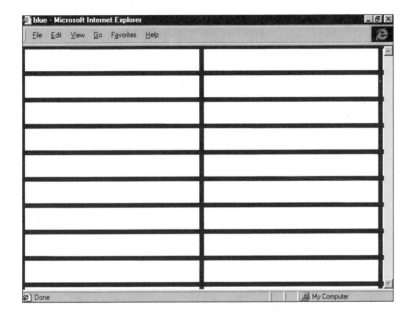

Figure 32.7
I outlined this longer, thin tile so you can see how it flows into the page.

PART

VI

CH

32

Take a closer look at individual types of backgrounds.

WALLPAPER PATTERNS

Wallpaper patterns were the first wave of background graphics. You've probably seen lots of them, in all kinds of styles. They're problematic for a number of reasons, including the fact that if they're too dark or busy, they'll interfere with readability. They're also demanding on the designer—it takes a bit of skill if you're making them completely by hand.

However, if you design them properly, they can create an extremely attractive look for your site.

The following are some general guidelines to use when creating tiles:

- Individual tiles should be at least 50×50.

- Work hard to ensure that tiles appear seamless.

- Avoid repeating the same image (imagine one egg in a single square, tiled repeatedly into the browser) over and over unless you have a darned good design that supports this repetition.

- Always ensure that you do *not* interlace background graphics (see Chapter 31, "Web Graphic Formats").

Now create a simple background tile. For this exercise, you're going to use PhotoDraw, but you can follow along with almost any imaging program (see Chapter 34).

1. Open the program and select Blank Picture from the Start-up dialog box, or select File, New. The Design Templates are very handy and you'll use them later.

2. From the New dialog box, choose Default Picture and click OK.

3. Resize the current workspace by selecting File, Picture Setup.

4. In the Picture Setup dialog box, change the Units to Pixels and the Width and Height to 50 and click OK.

5. Zoom in on the workspace by selecting View, Pan and Zoom. In the Pan and Zoom window, drag the slider up until the workspace is large enough.

6. The image is now ready for painting. Click the Draw Paint icon and select Paint. A Paint sidebar will open.

7. In the Paint sidebar, select Artistic Brushes and choose the Chalk-Even brush. Then pick a nice light color. Click the arrow next to the colors for more options. Finally, set the width of the brush by dragging the slider. For this project, set it for 12.0 pt.

8. To create the background tile, draw a circle in the center of the workspace and a quarter circle in each corner (see Figure 32.8).

9. Save the file as a GIF image by using File, Save As.

Now you can load the image as a background graphic in FrontPage. Figure 32.9 shows my flowery results!

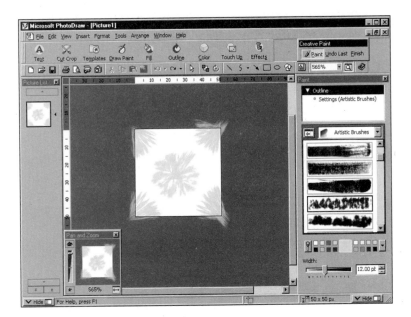

Figure 32.8
A background tile
created in
PhotoDraw.

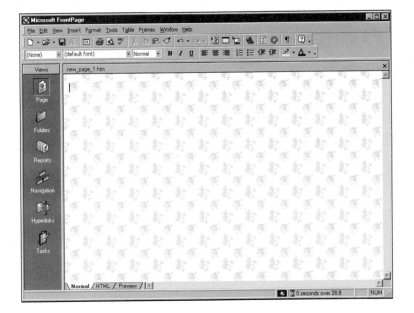

Figure 32.9
Flowered, seamless
wallpaper.

MARGIN TILES

Margin tiles are quite prevalent on the Web. Essentially, two types of margin tiles exist:

- *Functional*—This is a background margin tile that uses the margin space for navigation or other graphic and text information. Because it will be a significant part of your color and design scheme, functional margin design means making sure text, links, and other functional items can be seen and integrated into the margin's space and design (see Figure 32.10).

- *Decorative*—Decorative margins serve to enhance a design aesthetically. They have no function other than to provide visual interest to a page (see Figure 32.11).

Figure 32.10
This site makes use of a functional margin background.

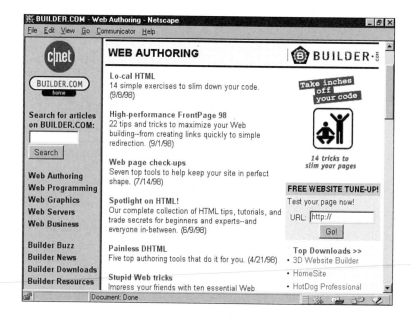

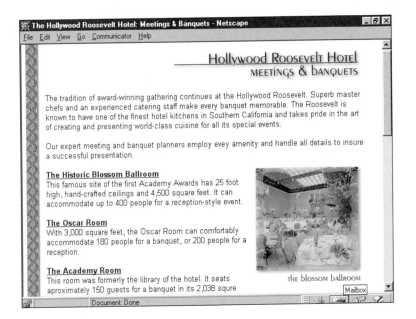

Figure 32.11
This Web site uses a decorative margin background.

The design within the margin portion of the tile can be decorative, as can the body portion. You can use flat areas of color or texture—whatever your imagination and creative influences suggest. However, always lean toward readability.

For effective margin tile design

- Create long tiles, anticipating various screen resolutions (see Chapter 30, "About the Computer Screen"). You'll want your background margin tiles to be at least 1024 pixels wide. You might even consider making them 320 pixels wide, but it's up to you and your awareness of your audience. Choose longer if many of them are using very high resolution monitors; 1024 is a typical choice for standard Internet sites. Height will range from around 50 pixels to 250 pixels or so, depending on your design.

Note Although it would seem that a graphic with these dimensions would be huge, the actual file size isn't that great at all. The reason is that most of the graphic is a single color (like white) and the GIF format can compress long sections of solid color very efficiently.

- Design using few colors, but be sure to add interest by employing shadow, shape, or texture. Flat margin tiles are very common on the Web. Although they're not unattractive, challenge yourself a bit and create something with a bit more verve.
- Because you have to anticipate a wide range of resolutions, design your image to size. If you're creating a right margin, this means making sure that the design begins within the allotted visual space of 595 pixels. Your image should look good no matter the viewing resolution.

PART

VI

CH

32

To create a functional left-margin image with color and texture, do the following by using PhotoDraw.

1. Open the program and select Blank Picture from the Start-up dialog box, or select File, New.

2. From the New dialog box, choose Default Picture and click OK.

3. Resize the current workspace by selecting File, Picture Setup, set the Units to Pixels, the Width to 1024, Height to 50, and click OK.

4. Zoom in on the right edge of the workspace by selecting View, Pan and Zoom. In the Pan and Zoom window, drag the slider up and resize the red box to show just the right end.

5. Click the Draw Paint icon and then select Shapes.

6. In the Outline sidebar, select a normal line, the color white, and move the Width slider to 1.0 pt.

7. Drag the cursor over most of the right end to create a rectangle.

8. With the rectangle selected, click the Fill icon and select Texture. Choose a texture from the sidebar.

9. Keep in mind that margin graphics will tile vertically, so try to match up the top and bottom edges. Also, PhotoDraw will flatten the image when you save it, so don't worry about lining up the texture with the workspace.

10. With the rectangle still selected, click the Effects icon and select Shadow. Choose a shadow type to apply to the image (see Figure 32.12).

Save the file as a GIF image by using File, Save As.

Figure 32.12
Selecting a Shadow effect for the margin background image.

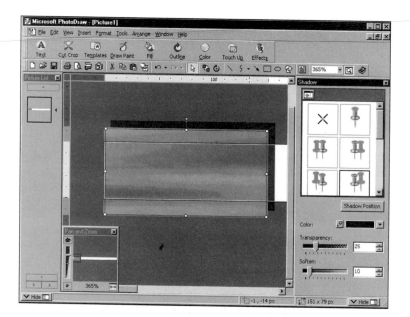

You can see the result in Figure 32.13.

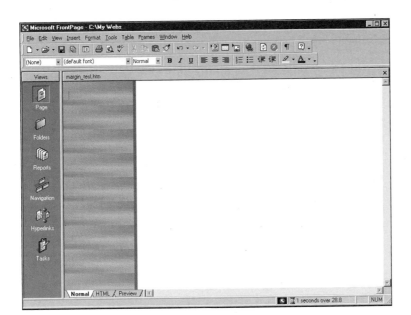

Figure 32.13
A textured, functional margin background.

WATERMARKS

Watermarks are especially difficult to create because of the repetitive issue. The idea with watermarks is to keep them simple, with very few colors, because this is the only way you can make larger graphics look good.

I created a watermark using PhotoDraw. First, I created a very large tile, 1024×1200 pixels. This way I know that no matter the resolution, the effect will generally be the same.

I then drew a stylized wave shape onto the tile. I used two colors: white and light blue. To save the file this time, I'll use PhotoDraw's Save for Use In Wizard.

1. With the image ready to save, select File, Save for Use In.

2. Select On the Web and click Next.

3. PhotoDraw will show you the various options for saving, including GIF and JPEG at four different image quality settings. It will also compute the file sizes and download times for different connection speeds (see Figure 32.14).

4. For this graphic, I selected GIF with a file size of only 4KB, not bad for an image of this size. Click Next to continue.

5. Finally, click Save to access a File dialog box.

Figure 32.14
Creating a watermark-style background.

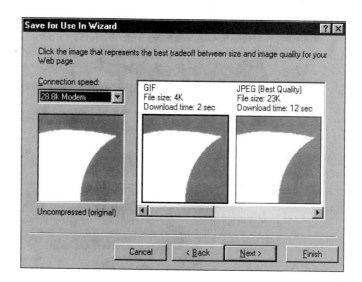

To see the result, create a new page in FrontPage and load the watermark graphic as the background image (Figure 32.15). One of the options in the Background tab of the Page Properties dialog box in FrontPage is a Watermark check box. This check box causes the background graphic to not move as the page is scrolled. This is only supported in browsers that support this feature.

Figure 32.15
A watermark-style background in FrontPage.

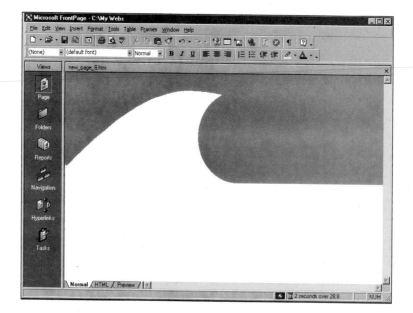

HEADER GRAPHICS

Headers are used to identify a site and a page within a site. One type of header is the *splash header*. This typically fills a larger piece of real estate on the opening page only. It identifies the site with the company logo or brand and sets the visual tone for the rest of the site.

A *page header* is smaller, but still boldly visible along the top and left, middle, or right of an internal page.

FrontPage can automatically create Page Banners, but there are times when you'll want to use individually created headers.

BUILDING A SPLASH DESIGN

Creating a splash design is a perfect opportunity to use the Design Templates that are part of PhotoDraw.

1. In PhotoDraw, select File, New Template.
2. The Templates sidebar opens with the Web Graphics category selected.
3. Choose Banners from the types and select the Banner style to use (see Figure 32.16), and then click Next.

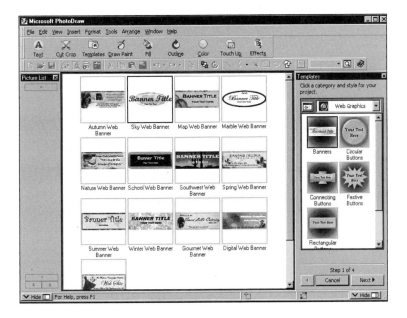

Figure 32.16
Selecting a Banner style.

4. In the second step, you can load a new background image for the banner. I used the default.

5. Next I changed the text for the banner (see Figure 32.17).

6. After the Template Wizard finishes, save the file as a JPEG image by selecting File, Save As.

Figure 32.17
Changing the banner text.

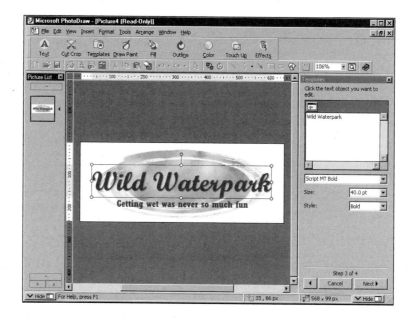

To create a page using the banner image you just made, use FrontPage's Insert, Picture, From File. The resulting splash page will look like Figure 32.18.

From the original splash header, creating internal page headers is just a matter of resizing the original. In FrontPage, just grab on to one of the corners and drag it to the desired size. To resize the actual graphics file, click the Resample button on the Picture toolbar. This page header can then be used on additional pages as needed or loaded into the Navigation Bar.

Figure 32.18
The splash graphic in place.

BUTTONS IN FRONTPAGE

Button, button, who's got the button?

You will, of course, in just a few minutes.

Navigational buttons can be made up of text, images, or a combination of both.

You're going to learn about two kinds of buttons: a beveled button, and FrontPage's simple method of doing mouseover text buttons, called Hover buttons.

Tip #164	Another good source of buttons is in PhotoDraw's Design Templates.

CREATING A BEVELED BUTTON

For this exercise, start with a simple graphic image that you want to make into a beveled button.

1. In FrontPage, load the button graphic by selecting Insert, Picture, From File. I like to use textured graphics to create buttons.

2. Select the graphic and click the Bevel button on the Picture toolbar.

3. Using the text tool, I added some text to the button.

PART
VI

CH

32

The beveled button was added to the page with the watermark graphic. The results are shown in Figure 32.19.

Figure 32.19
A beveled button on a watermarked background.

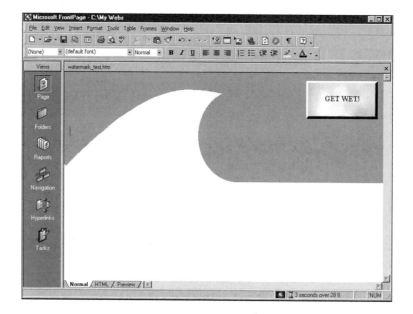

USING HOVER BUTTONS

Hover buttons were used in several of the examples for Chapter 29, "Color Concepts." In those example, you saw the basic functionality of Hover buttons. But there is more you can do with them, including using custom button images and sounds. To create a hover button with a custom graphic, follow these steps:

1. Create a new file to the appropriate size and dimension of your button(s). I'm creating a 150×50 pixel file.
2. Fill the background layer with the color or texture appropriate to your design.
3. Now create another version of the graphic to display when the mouse is over the button. An easy way to do this is to create a negative version of the same graphic.
4. Insert a new Hover Button by selecting Insert, Component, Hover Button.
5. In the Hover Button Properties dialog box, enter the button text, colors, and link.
6. Click the Custom button.
7. Browse to load the custom button images you created and some sounds and click OK.
8. You can resize the button once it is completed.

You now have the makings of an attractive mouseover. The nice thing about hover buttons is that the text remains in the exact position. One of the most common problems seen with mouseover images is that they move slightly due to inexact creation.

BARS AND RULES

I'm not a big fan of separating portions of text, but at times you might like an effective, decorative bar or rule to demarcate visual sections of a document.

If you're going to create your own bar, I'd recommend the following:

- Don't stretch the bar from margin to margin. Instead, make a bar that is either centered with some whitespace to either side or aligned to the right or left. Cutting off the margins separates space dramatically and could cause disruption in cohesiveness of both the design and the experience of the content.

- Use a treatment such as a drop shadow, curved or angled lines, something that's hand drawn, or broken lines—anything to give the rule a fresh look.

FrontPage can create a variety of horizontal rules for you, or you can make your own and import them as a normal graphic.

STANDARD HORIZONTAL RULES

To use FrontPage's horizontal rules (or lines as FrontPage calls them), select Insert, Horizontal Line. Within the Horizontal Line Properties dialog box, you can specify width, height, alignment, and color (see Figure 32.20).

Figure 32.20
Setting the Horizontal Line properties.

SPOT ART

Spot art serves to enhance and accentuate text. It can be clip art or photographs.

To make spot art stand out from the norm, it's fun to add edges, shadows, or bevels for effect. However, you do have to be careful with the use of effects because of the additional weight they can add to a page.

Hand-drawn art, cartoons, and clip art can add variety and personality to your sites, too.

Whichever you choose, you should be consistent and creative—not conflicting and cliche—throughout a site. It always surprises me to find that people have created slick graphics only to mix them with a piece of overused, worn clip art.

Another concern is dimension. Spot art is akin to italic or bold on a page—it's about emphasis, not dominance. You want your spot art to blend well into the overall scheme of your design. Pay close attention not only to the dimension in relation to the screen size (see Chapter 30), but from one photo to another.

Backgrounds, headers, rules, and spot art—you're wrapped up and ready to go!

TROUBLESHOOTING

I've seen images used on the Web that don't fall into any of the categories mentioned here. How would you categorize them?

Web page design is a creative process. There are no hard, fast rules on using images. The categories in this chapter represent some of the more common uses, but it isn't a complete list. Don't be afraid of trying different ideas of your own.

If I use a background image, how can I insure that visitors to the page will be able to read the text?

If you use a background image with lots of details and colors, you could be in danger of making the text on your page illegible. One good method to try is to use the Wash Out tool on the Picture toolbar in FrontPage. This will reduce the brightness of the image and make the text easier to read.

DESIGNERS CORNER: CREATING SPOT ART

For the final example of this chapter, I'll create a spot art image using an advanced image editing style made possible by PhotoDraw. This example will give you an idea of the possibilities available for Web graphics.

I like to add edge effects to my photos, and to do this, I'm once again going to use PhotoDraw's Design Templates. In this example I'm going to take a photo and add an edge to it.

1. In PhotoDraw, select File, New Template.
2. In the Templates sidebar, select the Designer Edges category.
3. Choose Artist from the types, select the Mesh Edge style, and then click Next.
4. In the second step, you can load a new background image for the banner. I will use the default.
5. I load the photo I want to use by clicking the Browse button and then repositioning the photo with the Picture Position button.
6. After the Template Wizard finishes, save the file as a JPEG image by selecting File, Save As. Since this is a photo, it is best to save it as a JPEG.

Figure 32.21 shows the edge results in FrontPage.

Figure 32.21
A treated photo on a
Web page.

CHAPTER 33

DESIGNING SPECIALTY GRAPHICS

In this chapter

by Kelly Murdock

IMAGEMAPS

Imagemaps allow a designer to take a single image and break it down into multiple sections of varying shapes. Each of those sections can then be linked to a different web page.

While this sounds convenient, and while imagemaps have certainly been a significant part of web design for some time, the reality is that they are becoming less present on professional sites. Whether this has to do with the fact that more sophisticated and attractive technologies, such as JavaScript mouseovers, are taking precedence over imagemapping, or that mapping is too fixed for today's regularly updated web sites, is difficult to determine.

Despite these changes, the technology and tools related to mapping have remained current, and you will certainly want to add the technique to your repertoire of graphic skills.

METHODS

There are two methods for imagemapping. The old-fashioned method is *server-sided mapping*, which requires the browser to work with the server to interpret your imagemap.

The newer, more popular, method is *client-side mapping*. This means that the browser can interpret the map data without relying on the server to do so. This is the method that FrontPage supports.

The client-side mapping technique is preferred, but because some older browsers don't support it, many individuals combine the two techniques, ensuring that no matter the browser, the visitor will be able to use the imagemap.

CLIENT-SIDE MAPPING IN FRONTPAGE

Client-side maps are fast and stable because they rely on the browser to do the interpretation for them.

The process is to select an image, then to choose sections within that image called hotspots and assign a link to them. A *hotspot* is an area within an image map that is hyperlinked. These hotspots can be circular, rectangular, or polygonal. FrontPage allows you to create these hotspots by simply drawing on an image.

Once an image is loaded into a page, you can create an image map. Rectangular hotspots are perhaps the most common way to define regions. Create a rectangular hotspot by following these steps:

1. Make the image active by clicking it.
2. Click the Rectangular Hotspot button at the right end of the Picture toolbar.
3. Click and drag the mouse within the image to create a rectangular shaped hotspot. The Create Hyperlink dialog box appears.
4. Within the Create Hyperlink dialog box, enter the URL or bookmark for the link.
5. Click the OK button to complete the link.

Once the hotspots are created, they can be moved, resized, or deleted. The Highlight Hotspots button on the Picture toolbar is useful if you want to see just the hotspots with no image underneath. Figure 33.1 shows the image with rectangular, circular, and polygonal shaped hotspots.

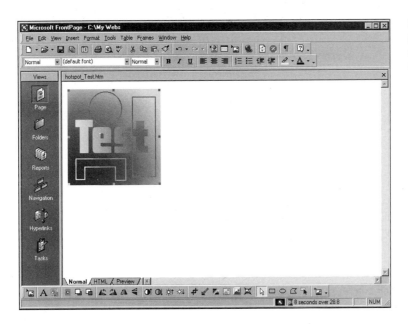

Figure 33.1
An image with three defined hotspot regions.

PART

VI

CH

33

Note

If you overlap two hotspots, the overlapped area will link to the hotspot that was created last.

SERVER-SIDE MAPPING

To accommodate older browsers, many coders like to use server-side mapping. This requires the creation of a map file with the coordinate locations within it. The file must be saved with a `.map` extension.

This type of imagemapping becomes more complicated because of several factors:

1. The `.map` file will have to reside on the server. Depending on your ISP, this may be a designated spot. Either way, you'll have to find out where your ISP would like you to store this map—it will affect the way you write the HTML output.

2. There are two kinds of map files. One is NCSA style, the other is CERN style. Typically, you'll want to use NCSA, but some servers, such as Microsoft's Information Server, require the CERN style. Once again, you'll have to check with your provider before mapping your image to a server.

3. Because server-side mapping relies on CGI, you'll be required to find out from your ISP where the mapping utility is and what its name is.

Here's an example of NCSA map code:

```
#contact info for phoenix office
rect phoenix.html 86,173, 245,224
#click for tucson contact information
rect tucson.html 152,245, 259,331
```

Here's the same map in CERN format:

```
rect (86,173) (245,224) phoenix.html
rect (152,245) (259,331) tucson.html
```

Notice that the information is not only ordered differently, but the CERN map leaves out alternate text information shown in the NCSA code.

If you have the information necessary from your ISP, you are now ready to add the map data to your HTML. Server-side imagemaps require an attribute added to the IMG tag, known as ismap.

```
<IMG src="images/arizona_map.gif" width="278" height="328" border="0"
alt="imagemap of arizona" ismap>
```

The ismap attribute lets the server know that this is a mapped image.

To invoke the script that will interpret the imagemap, you'll need to link your image. Listing 33.1 shows the code for an HTML page with an NCSA-style server side imagemap.

LISTING 33.1 SERVER-SIDE IMAGEMAP SYNTAX

```
<HTML>
<HEAD>
<TITLE>Contact Our Company</TITLE>
</HEAD>
<BODY>

<H2>Contact Our Company</H2>

For contact information, please select a city from the map below.
<P>


<A href="/cgi-bin/contact.map"><IMG src="images/arizona_map.gif" width="278"
height="328" border="0" alt="Imagemap of Arizona" ismap></A>

</BODY>
</HTML>
```

If you've uploaded the appropriate .map file to the correct area on your server, and you've linked to the correct area and file on that server within your HTML, this map will now be active.

ANIMATED GIFs

Another popular specialty graphic is the Animated GIF. GIF animations exploit a looping process in the GIF89a technology. Compact in size and easy to make, Animated GIFs are a great way to give a page some verve.

There are many tools available for making Animated GIFs. Chapter 34, "Web Graphic Tools," provides excellent resources for GIF animation software.

Caution

> It's important to keep in mind that animations should enhance, but never detract from, a page's design. Many enthusiastic individuals will place more than one animation on a page. Combine this with mouseovers, audio, and other multimedia, and you will lose your message—and your audience—very quickly. Always use a light hand when adding active media to a page.

CREATING AN ANIMATED GIF

Since FrontPage cannot be used to create animated GIFs, I'm going to show you how to make an animated GIF using GIF Construction Set and PhotoShop. No matter your preferred imaging and animation tools, the methods are very similar, and my example will serve to get you started making GIF animations right away.

You will first need to create the individual images used within the animation. Known as *cells*, imagine each individual image as being a unique action within the animation.

You can use this concept to create as simple or complex an animated gif as you wish. However, I recommend starting out with something quite simple. You should always think about what you're going to need—any specific graphic images or text—in advance. It's also good to know the dimensions of the animation, so you can create or modify your cells to that size.

PART

VI

CH

33

Tip #165

> Try to select images that are going to be lightweight, because you always want to keep your individual file weight down. This will help when you combine all the images into the final format. The smaller the input, the less heavy the output.

My plan is to create an animation that reads "I love my cat." However, the words "love" and "cat" will be replaced with a heart and the image of a cat, respectively.

I first need to collect or create my images. To get the heart and cat, I visited ArtToday at `http://www.arttoday.com/` where I'm a member (see Chapter 34). I went to the clip art section and did a search for a heart and then a cat.

I found the files I wanted and downloaded them.

Now I'll take you through the steps I followed to create the animation:

1. Open an imaging program (in my case, PhotoShop).
2. Create the first image in the series. Because the image is 100×100 pixels, select File, New and then input the file dimensions and type (RGB).
3. Because the first word is "I," select the typeface and set the type by using the Type tool.
4. Position the type to the center.
5. Flatten the image.
6. Optimize the image as a GIF.
7. Save the file as `image_1.gif`.

To create the next image

1. Open the existing image in your imaging program.
2. Size and crop your image to the appropriate dimensions.
3. Index the image.
4. Export as a GIF.
5. Save the file as `image_2.gif`.

Now repeat the steps in the first or second sample, depending on whether you are adding text or a graphic. Name each image with its appropriate numeric value in the sequence.

When I was finished, I had the following:

> `image_1.gif`—A 100×100–pixel GIF of the word "I"
>
> `image_2.gif`—A 100×100–pixel GIF with the image of a heart
>
> `image_3.gif`—A 100×100–pixel GIF of the word "my"
>
> `image_4.gif`—A 100×100 pixel–GIF with the image of a cat

All of these files are now resident on my hard drive (see Figure 33.2).

Follow these steps to animate the graphic with GIF Construction Set:

1. Open the GIF Construction Set.
2. From File, select Animation Wizard.
3. Click Next when asked if you are ready to proceed.
4. Select Yes, for Use with a Web Page.
5. Click Next.
6. Select your looping preference. I recommend only once!

Figure 33.2
Viewing my four animation cells.

7. The next dialog box offers preferences for types of graphic. Choose the description that best suits your graphic—mine is Drawn (see Figure 33.3).

8. Now you'll set the delay. For demonstration purposes, stick with the default of 100 hundredths, although you can select any delay you prefer in the future—and you can change this setting later.

9. Click Next.

10. Choose Select.

11. Go to the area where your GIFs are stored.

12. To animate each image, select them in the order of their appearance.

13. Click Next, Done.

14. When GIF Construction Set is done animating the image, select Save As and save your file. Mine is saved as `animation_1.gif`.

15. Now view your animation by using the View selection.

To add your animated image to a FrontPage web page, simply insert the image in the same way that you'd insert a normal GIF image. Compliant browsers will understand that this is an animated GIF and play it properly.

PART

VI

Cн

33

Caution

You'll notice that I've recommended looping your animation only once. Animations that keep looping tend to be annoying. There are some instances in which you'll want to loop continuously, such as if you have a slow moving animation or an advertisement. For accent animations, however, be subtle!

Figure 33.3
Selecting the image
type in GIF
Construction Set.

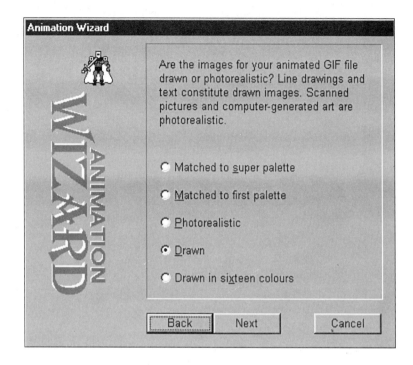

For more on GIF animation techniques and technologies, I recommend a visit to Royal E. Frazier's famous GIF Animation site at `http://members.aol.com/royalef/gifanim.htm`.

ADVERTISING BANNERS

One of the most popular methods of advertising web sites is getting involved in an advertising banner campaign. *Banners* improve visibility of a product or web site and, in some cases, have proven a helpful method for gaining product recognition and boosting sales on the Web.

Typically, advertising groups require specific, standardized sizes and guidelines for banner creation. You do have to check with the methods employed by the group you decide to work with, as their guidelines will differ.

The following are some general specifications:

- An average banner size is 468×60 pixels.
- GIF or JPG files.
- Small file sizes—8KB is the recommended maximum.
- Use bright colors—This enhances appearance on the page.
- Animated GIFs are considered very effective. Looping is often acceptable with ad banners, but be sure to check with your ad banner partner for more specific guidelines.

For more information on ad banners, check the popular ad site Doubleclick at `http://www.doubleclick.net/`.

BUILDING AN ADVERTISING BANNER

Following the specifications listed earlier, I'm going to walk you through the creation of a static banner.

You'll need

- Your ad material, such as a logo and byline
- An image editing program such as PhotoDraw

With your materials on hand, do the following:

1. Open PhotoDraw.
2. Select Blank Picture, Default Picture from the opening dialog boxes.
3. Select File, Picture Setup and adjust the Width to 468 pixels and the Height to 60 pixels.
4. Add your graphic logo.
5. Add your text.
6. Select File, Save For Use In and compare the size versus quality and save the image.

Weigh your image. My GIF image (see Figure 33.4) came out to 3KB, well within the guidelines.

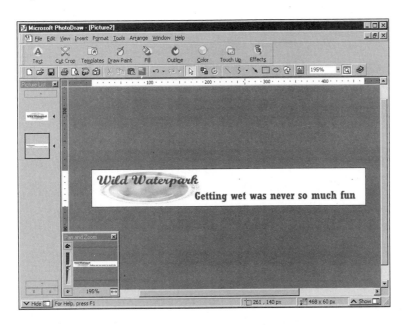

Figure 33.4
An ad banner image.

Note

Your advertising banner company will tell you how to properly add banners to a page. Very often, they have the banners on a rotation. You'll send your banner to them, and they'll send the syntax necessary for your page.

MISCELLANEOUS FRONTPAGE GRAPHICS

In the last two chapters I've presented a lot of different graphic types and styles, but there are still some graphic techniques yet to be explored.

USING GRAPHICAL BULLETS

Most of the FrontPage themes include graphical bullets, but you don't need to use a theme to add graphical bullets to your pages. To add graphical bullets to any bulleted list, do the following:

1. First, create the bullets in an image editing program like PhotoDraw.
2. Add a bulleted list to your page.
3. Open the List Properties dialog box (Figure 33.5) by right clicking the bulleted list.
4. Click Specify Picture, locate the graphical bullet, and click OK.

The results are shown in Figure 33.6.

Figure 33.5
Locating a graphical bullet to use.

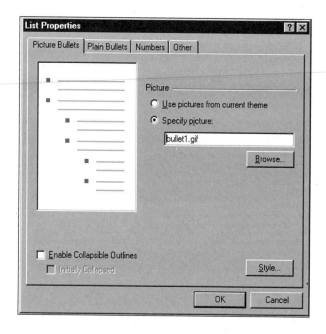

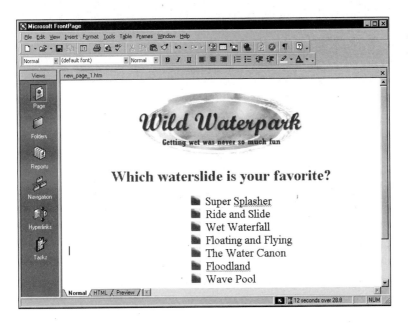

Figure 33.6
Graphical bullets add a nice touch to this list.

USING SCHEDULED PICTURES

Creating pages that are regularly updated is a must in today's web world. FrontPage has a wonderful component that makes updating images automatic. Using the Scheduled Picture component, you can specify when new graphics will appear.

To add a Scheduled Picture, follow these steps:

1. Select Insert, Component, Scheduled Picture. The Scheduled Picture dialog box opens, as shown in Figure 33.7.

2. Browse to the images to load during and after the scheduled time.

3. Specify the Starting and Ending times by selecting a date and time and click OK.

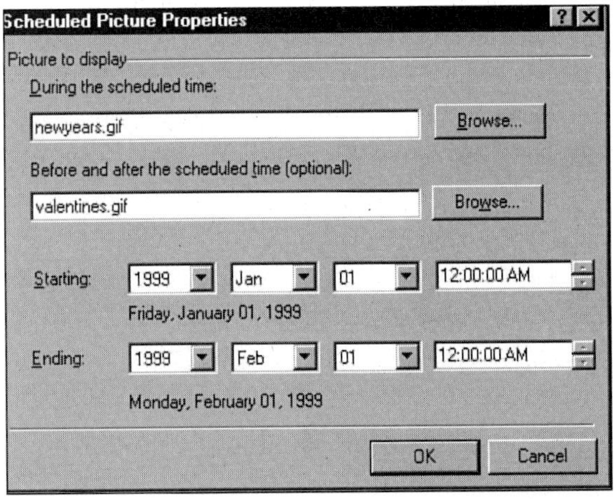

Figure 33.7
Scheduled Pictures are shown only during the specified dates and times.

TROUBLESHOOTING

Can I create Animated JPEGs or Animated PNGs?

The GIF format is the only format currently that supports animation. You can however convert the JPEG and PNG images to GIF format and animate them that way.

How do some sites flip the advertising banners between several different ads?

There are a couple of ways to do this. One is to create an Animated GIF that cycles through the various banners. Be sure to modify the frame rate settings so that each frame shows up for a long enough time. Another way to do this is with JavaScript. JavaScript will let you randomly select an image from a list and display it. It could even be used to randomly select from several Animated GIFs.

DESIGNERS CORNER: TILING GRAPHICS BETWEEN TABLES AND FRAMES

Tables are very useful for positioning graphics and in Chapter 32, "Creating Professional Web Graphics," I suggested splitting large images into several smaller ones for quicker loading. This can pose a problem if the graphics get pushed to opposite sides of the browser window.

The solution as I mentioned before is to use tables to keep the graphics together. This same technique can be used to tile a single image across two different frames. To tile graphics between table cells and frames, follow these steps:

1. Open the graphic in an image editing program like PhotoDraw and split the original into several pieces. I split my car3.jpg image into four equal pieces.

2. Save and name each piece. I've named mine s-car1.jpg, s-car2.jpg, s-car3.jpg, and s-car4.jpg.

3. In FrontPage, create a 2×2 table by selecting Table, Insert, Table and entering the values in the Table Properties dialog box.

4. Load an image into each cell of the table.

5. Open the Table Properties dialog box again by right-clicking the table and selecting Table Properties from the pop-up menu.

6. Uncheck the Specify Width check box, set the Border, Cell Padding, and Cell Spacing values to 0, and click OK.

Without borders, padding, or spacing, the table collapses the pieces close together like I wanted (see Figure 33.8).

Figure 33.8
After the split graphics are collapsed together.

CHAPTER 34

WEB GRAPHIC TOOLS

In this chapter   *by Kelly Murdock*

MYTH: TOOLS DON'T MATTER

For die-hard supporters of tools that are not industry standards, you'll be happy to hear that many of your favorite programs are making a concerted effort to bring you the highest quality output possible. Another exciting issue in the area of Web graphic software is new-and-improved image editing suites from a variety of industry standard vendors.

But the idea that tools don't matter is a *very* disturbing untruth. While it's not meant to imply here that shareware or a variety of professional tools are useless for the Web designer, there is a major concern for those of you who are seeking to be employed in the Web design field.

If you're pursuing professional Web design, you *must* be willing to purchase and learn the sometimes expensive, higher-end tools to compete.

Furthermore, knowing the skills associated with those tools puts you in the driver's seat when it comes to being able to find employment with design firms. They're going to be using industry standards, and you're not going to be as marketable if you don't have the skills.

You are infinitely more attractive as a Web graphic designer with Adobe Photoshop and Illustrator or Freehand skills than you will be with, say, CorelDRAW skills, PHOTO-PAINT skills, or Paint Shop Pro know-how.

On the other hand, if your design needs are more personal, any one of these and other tools will be helpful to you. It's finding the right fit that counts, particularly if you're not interested in pursuing professional level jobs where the pro standards are typically Adobe products.

That said, take a look at some of the Web graphic design tools out there.

EDITING IMAGES IN FRONTPAGE

One of the best places to start is with FrontPage. Although you probably won't be using FrontPage to create your images, you can use it to perform some simple image editing. These editing features appear on the Picture toolbar, which is accessible anytime an image is selected.

Before examining the external image editing tools, take a look at what FrontPage can do. In many cases, it can save time and enable you to make minor adjustments without using an external tool.

You can make the Picture toolbar appear at any time by selecting View, Toolbars, Picture. But, if an image isn't selected, most of the buttons on the Picture toolbar are disabled. If an image is selected, the toolbar magically appears at the bottom of the window with all the buttons enabled.

The buttons on the Picture toolbar include the following:

- Insert Picture From File: This button is the same as the one on the Formatting toolbar. It opens the Select File dialog to load an image.
- Text: This button adds text to the current image.
- Auto Thumbnail: This button reduces the size of the current image and links it to the actual full-size image.
- Position Absolutely: This button sets the position property to absolute causing the image to be positioned relative to the browser's upper-left corner.
- Bring to Front: This button sets the image on top of the stacking order.
- Send to Back: This button sets the image at the bottom of the stacking order.
- Rotate Left: This button rotates the image 90 degrees to the left.
- Rotate Right: This button rotates the image 90 degrees to the right.
- Flip Vertical: This button replaces the image with a vertical mirror image.
- Flip Horizontal: This button replaces the image with a horizontal mirror image.
- More Contrast: This button increases the image contrast.
- Less Contrast: This button decreases the image contrast.
- More Brightness: This button increases the image brightness.
- Less Brightness: This button decreases the image brightness.
- Crop: This button places crop guides on the image. After positioning these, click again on the Crop button to cut the image to the size of the guides.
- Set Transparent Color: This button lets you select a single color in the current image to make transparent.
- Black and White: This button reduces the colors in the image to grayscale.
- Wash Out: This button reduces the overall brightness and contrast making the image much lighter.
- Bevel: This button adds beveled edges to the image.
- Resample: This button resizes the actual image file after dragging the image's handles.
- Select: This button enables the default setting that allows the image handles to be moved.
- Rectangular Hotspot: This button adds a rectangular image map hotspot to the image.
- Circular Hotspot: This button adds a circular image map hotspot to the image.
- Polygonal Hotspot: This button adds a polygonal image map hotspot to the image.
- Highlight Hotspots: This button shows the hotspots on the current image.
- Restore: This button replaces the current modified image with the original image.

PART

VI

CH

34

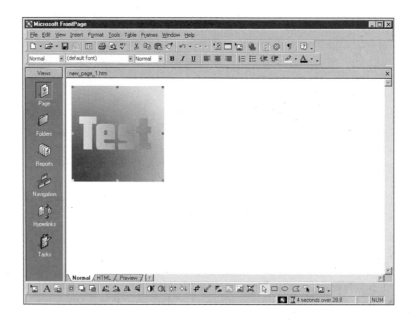

ADDING TEXT TO AN IMAGE

If you want to add some text to your image, you can do so without having to return to your image editing package. FrontPage makes it easy with the Text tool on the Picture toolbar.

These text labels can be edited at any time by selecting the image and clicking the text label. The text font, size, color, and style can be changed with the standard text features on the Formatting toolbar. Any formatting applied to the text label is applied to all the text. FrontPage will not allow you to change the formatting on only a portion of a text label.

To add text to an image, follow these steps:

1. Click the image to make it active. The Picture toolbar appears.
2. Select the Text button. A box with a cursor in it appears in the image.
3. If the image is not a GIF image, an alert box will ask if you wish to change it to a GIF image. Click OK.

Caution

Converting to a *GIF image* will reduce the number of colors in the image. This may degrade the visual quality of your image. Also, JPEG images saved at low quality may degrade the text to an illegible level.

4. Type the text for the label.
5. Move the text label to its position by deactivating the text label. This is done by clicking somewhere in the image away from the text hotspot and then dragging it to the desired location.

6. Resize the text hotspot by dragging its handles.

7. Change the text style by selecting the style from the Formatting toolbar.

8. Edit the text by clicking the text after it is selected and typing the changes.

9. Double-click the hotspot to open the Create Hyperlink dialog box. Within the dialog box, you can specify a hyperlink for the label.

Figure 34.2 shows a text label.

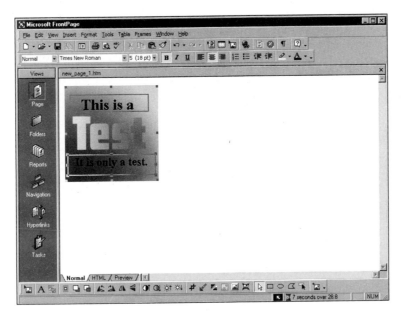

Figure 34.2
An image with two text labels.

Tip #166	One way to use this text feature is to create multiple instances of the same image, each with a different text label. These multiple images can be used throughout the site without requiring the *background image (page 682)* to be downloaded several times.

CREATING AUTO THUMBNAIL

The Auto Thumbnail feature lets you quickly create a gallery of images complete with links. *Thumbnail images* are smaller representations of the larger image. These smaller images download much more quickly and give the user an idea of what the image looks like. By clicking the thumbnail image, the complete image is loaded into the browser.

To create Auto Thumbnail images, follow these steps:

1. Click the image to make it active. The Picture toolbar appears at the bottom of the window.

2. Click the Auto Thumbnail button.

3. The image is reduced in size (Figure 34.3) and linked to the original larger image.

Figure 34.3
An auto thumbnail image.

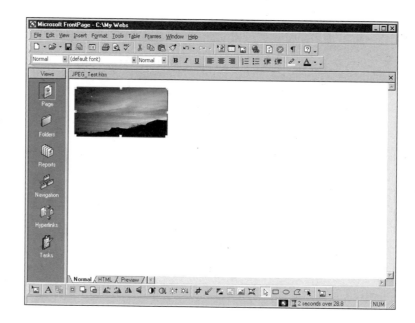

The Page Options dialog box includes some controls for Auto Thumbnail images. You can set the thumbnail dimensions, border thickness, and whether the edges are beveled (see Figure 34.4).

CONTROLLING IMAGE POSITIONING

Standard HTML lays out Web page elements sequentially. You can control whether elements are aligned to the left, center, or right, but the page layout changes depending on the size of the browser. Dynamic HTML allows you to position Web page elements, including images, absolutely. By using this feature, images will stay in the same position regardless of the browser size.

To position an image absolutely, follow these steps.

1. Click the image to make it active.

2. Click the Position Absolutely button.

    Handles are positioned around the image and its surrounding area.

3. Click and drag on the handles to resize the absolutely positioned area.

4. Click and drag when the cursor shows four arrows to move the image. Figure 34.5 shows the image after being moved.

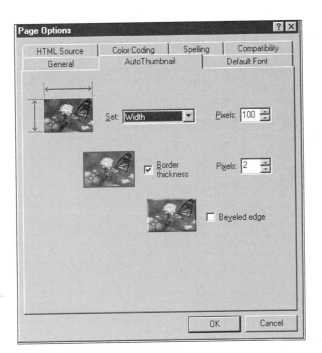

Figure 34.4
Auto Thumbnail options.

Figure 34.5
An absolutely positioned image.

PART

VI

CH

34

Absolutely positioned images make it possible to place images on top of another. If two pictures overlap, the stacking order can be controlled with the Bring Forward and Send Backwards buttons. To alter the stacking order, follow these steps.

1. Load several images onto a page. I chose the car, sunset, and test images.

2. Select each image and click the Position Absolutely button on the Picture toolbar.

3. Move each image until it overlaps the other images.

4. Click the Bring Forward button to restack the image on top of the other elements (Figure 34.6).

5. Click the Send Backwards button to restack the image below the other elements.

Caution

Not all browsers support absolute positioning or image stacking. Check with your target browser before using these tools.

Figure 34.6
Two images stacked on one another.

Absolutely Positioning Text

The Absolutely Position tool can also be used on text. Just select the text and click the button and the same absolutely positioned area encloses the text. You can then move and position the text as desired. This only applies to paragraphs of text and not individual characters.

CHANGING IMAGE ORIENTATION

FrontPage has four buttons that can change the image *orientation*. They are: Rotate Right, Rotate Left, Flip Horizontal, and Flip Vertical.

To rotate or mirror an image, follow these steps:

1. Click the image to make it active. The Picture toolbar appears at the bottom of the window.

2. Click the Rotate Right button to rotate the image 90 degrees to the right. Alternatively, click the Rotate Left button to rotate the image 90 degrees to the left.

3. Click the Flip Horizontal button to flip the image about its horizontal axis (Figure 34.7), or click on the Flip Vertical button to flip the image about its vertical axis.

Figure 34.7
Rotated and mirrored images.

ADJUSTING BRIGHTNESS AND CONTRAST

The controls for adjusting brightness and contrast are especially helpful for scanned images. Scanners are notoriously bad at getting these two image properties correct. Since FrontPage has the ability to scan images, it is common sense that they would have brightness and contrast adjustment.

FrontPage is lacking a histogram feature to help analyze how much contract increase is necessary, so you are left to your eyes. Use More Contrast, Less Contrast, More Brightness, Less Brightness until the image looks right. Chapter 29, "Color Concepts," speaks more about contrast.

PART
VI
CH
34

CROPPING IMAGES

Another tool that comes in handy when working with scanned images is the Crop tool. ping is the process of cutting a portion of an image and deleting the rest. Scanned images usually have sections that you don't want to include. Cropping can help remove unwanted sections. It can also be used to quickly reduce file sizes.

Suppose that your car image is too big and you decide that you don't need the mountains in the background. To crop to just the car, follow these steps:

1. Click the image to make it active.
2. Click the Crop button.
3. A dashed line outline appears with handles around it.
4. Move the handles by dragging them about the image, or you can create a new outline by clicking and dragging a rectangle around the area you wish to keep.
5. Click the Crop button again to complete the crop.

Figure 34.8 shows the car image after the crop.

Figure 34.8
An image after a crop.

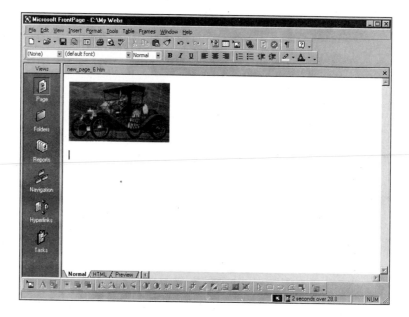

SETTING THE TRANSPARENCY COLOR

One of the features of the GIF image format is the ability to specify a single color to be *transparent*. This makes the background color or texture show through the GIF image wherever the transparent color is located.

Chapter 31, "Web Graphic Formats," has an example showing how to select a transparent color within FrontPage.

CREATING BLACK AND WHITE AND WASHED-OUT IMAGES

A common trick to make images appear to load faster is to load them first in black and white with smaller file sizes and then to load in full-color. Chapter 31 explained the details on this trick.

Similar to the Black and White tool is the Wash Out tool. Detailed images can make text placed on top of it illegible. One solution is to increase the brightness and decrease the contrast of the image, but an easier way is to use the Wash Out tool.

To wash out an image to make text on top of it legible, follow these steps:

1. Click the image to make it active.
2. Click the Wash Out button.
3. The image's brightness is decreased.
4. To add text to the image, click the Text tool and type the text in the box.

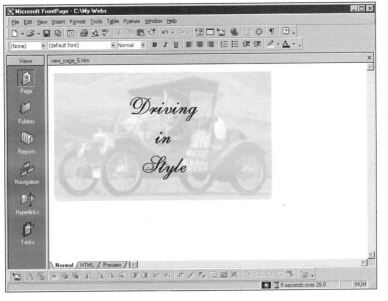

Figure 34.9
A washed-out image with text added.

PART

VI

CH

34

RESAMPLING IMAGES

A selected image has handles that can be used to resize the image, but resizing an image by dragging its handles doesn't resize the actual graphic file that is saved with the Web page. To modify the actual file, click the Resample button. Then, when you save the page, a file dialog box will enable you to rename and save the file.

Adding Beveled Edges

A quick way to turn any image into a button is to add beveled edges. Chapter 32, "Creating Professional Web Graphics," explains how to create beveled buttons.

Restoring an Image to Its Original Look

The final button on the Picture toolbar is the Restore button. If you've tried several tricks and you are dissatisfied with the results, you can use the Undo feature to return the image to its original look when you first loaded it, or you can restore it instantly with the Restore button.

Tools of the Web Graphic Trade

Now that you've seen what FrontPage can do, move on to additional tools that complement FrontPage graphics. You'll be looking at a variety of tools here, including imaging and illustration programs, optimization tools, multimedia development tools, plug-in and enhancement programs, and stock art and photography resources.

Imaging and Illustration Programs

These are programs that allow you to work with photographs, actually create images with color and type, scan images, add enhancements, and optimize graphics.

Microsoft PhotoDraw

If you've purchased a version of Microsoft Office that includes PhotoDraw, you already have a great tool for creating graphics. PhotoDraw is targeted at the business professional, so its interface and tools are designed to be powerful and user-friendly.

PhotoDraw includes both illustration and image editing tools in one package. This opens a wide range of possibilities and allows you to work with different, comfortable tools on a single project.

If you feel that your design skills are lacking, look into PhotoDraw's design templates. These templates include pre-built elements like banners and buttons that are easy to modify to fit your specific project.

PhotoDraw's features include:

- Familiar interface similar to other Office products
- Save for use on the Web Wizard for comparing size versus quality
- Multiple effects galleries
- Automatic photo editing and touch-up tools
- Visual menus that show a sample of results

Figure 34.10 shows an image created easily from a design template.

Figure 34.10
Part of Office,
Microsoft's
PhotoDraw.

MICROSOFT IMAGE COMPOSER

A very nice, compact imaging application (see Figure 34.11), Microsoft Image Composer works in tandem with Microsoft GIF Animator, which gives it maximum impact as a Web imaging program. Image Composer is shipped with FrontPage 98 (Windows versions only). More information on how it works, how to use it, and new and improved enhancements can be found at http://www.microsoft.com/imagecomposer/.

The following are some of Image Composer's features:

- Sprites are similar to layers, allowing you control over your images.
- Text and text styles help you create headers, buttons, and typographic images.
- Patterns, fills, and effects give you a lot of power over your images.

ADOBE PHOTOSHOP

This is the "Big Daddy" of all professional Web graphic production tools (see Figure 34.12). Its features include the following:

- As a design industry standard application, Adobe Photoshop features, support, and third-party solutions are vast.
- Photoshop creates raster graphics, which are the suitable type for Web image optimization.
- Photoshop layers are a powerful way to work with images.
- The GIF89 Export feature allows the creation of transparency and interlaced GIFs.

PART

VI

CH

34

- Versions 4.0 and later contain a Web-safe palette that is useful when optimizing graphics for the Web.

- Full-feature photographic manipulation and filters allow you to improve the quality of photos, as well as alter and arrange them as you please.

- Photoshop 5.0 offers powerful type setting options and other filter features such as bevel, drop shadow, and light sources.

Figure 34.11
Working in Microsoft's Image Composer.

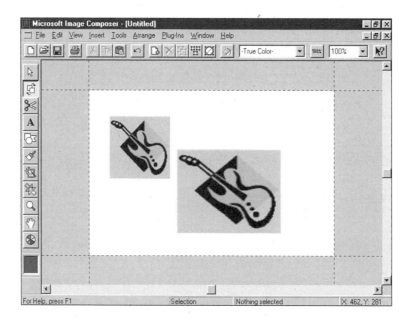

Figure 34.12
The Adobe Photoshop interface.

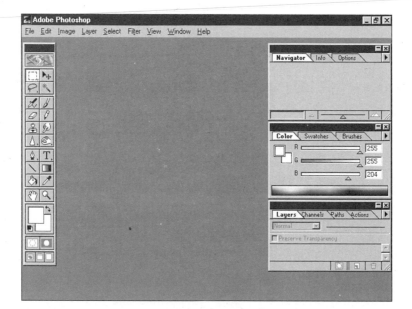

For product information, costs, and support, visit Adobe at n.

ADOBE ILLUSTRATOR

An excellent tool for creating *vector-based graphics*, Illustrator also offers advanced typesetting options (see Figure 34.13).

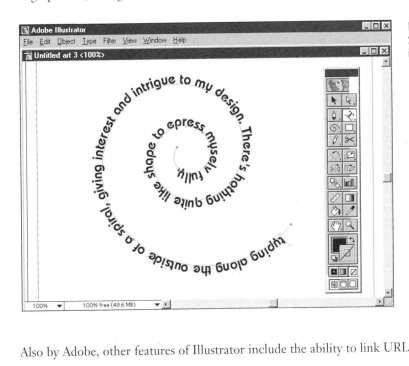

Figure 34.13
Setting shapely type in Illustrator.

Also by Adobe, other features of Illustrator include the ability to link URLs to images.

ADOBE IMAGEREADY

This exciting new product is designed specifically to optimize graphics for Web use. One of its most powerful features is that its interface is similar to Photoshop's (see Figure 34.14), so there's easy adaptability for Photoshop users.

ImageReady offers real-time compression and batch processing, as well as tools for animating images.

As with Photoshop and Illustrator, more information on ImageReady is available at http://www.adobe.com/.

Figure 34.14
The ImageReady interface and an optimized image tab view.

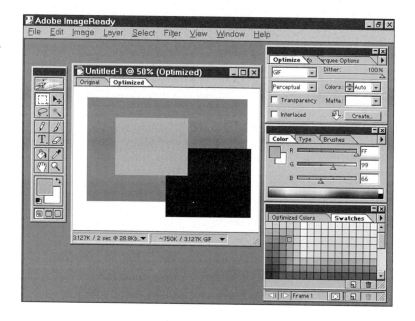

CorelDRAW

CorelDRAW holds an esteemed level as a drawing program among certain computer users—usually those involved in business and industry. However, it's not considered the standard when it comes to professional graphic design. Still, the recent edition of CorelDRAW, version 8.0, includes a number of attractive new features:

- Customizable interface for power users
- Kerning and leading for type
- More sophisticated palette control than in previous versions
- Guidelines for image rotation, nudging, and multiple select

Corel PHOTO-PAINT

Corel's photographic program allows users to scan and manipulate images. Its features include the following:

- Ability to assign hyperlinks to objects for imagemap creation
- Support for animated GIFs
- Ability to preview JPEGs for optimization determination
- Web-safe palette support

Visit the Corel Web site at http://www.corel.com/ (see Figure 34.15) for more information on CorelDRAW and PHOTO-PAINT.

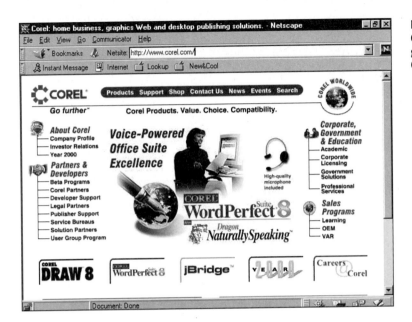

Figure 34.15
Corel's Web site uses
graphics created by
Corel software.

JASC PAINT SHOP PRO

A favorite among many Web designers, Paint Shop Pro is gaining features as we speak. Unfortunately, it's only available for the PC platform, making it a tough sell to professional graphic companies.

In version 5.0, Paint Shop Pro allows users to

- Work in layers, as you can in Photoshop
- Create transparencies
- Interlace GIFs
- Make GIF animations with the built-in Animation Shop

Download a demo of Paint Shop Pro from its parent company, Jasc, at `http://www_jasc.com/`. You'll also find support information, extended information about Jasc products, and links to related resources (see Figure 34.16).

MACROMEDIA FIREWORKS

This exciting program is brand-new from Macromedia. Geared specifically to the creation and management of Web graphics, Fireworks includes the following features:

- Advanced support for imagemapping.
- Slicing graphics for table positioning.
- HTML generation for graphic positioning.

PART

VI

CH

34

- JavaScript rollovers—Fireworks generates the code for you.
- Special effects such as bevels and drop shadows.
- Live redraw: no need to undo, simply reset the parameters of an effect and it will automatically redraw.

Figure 34.17 demonstrates working on a graphic with Macromedia Fireworks.

Figure 34.16
Jasc's home page.

Figure 34.17
Designing graphics with Macromedia Fireworks.

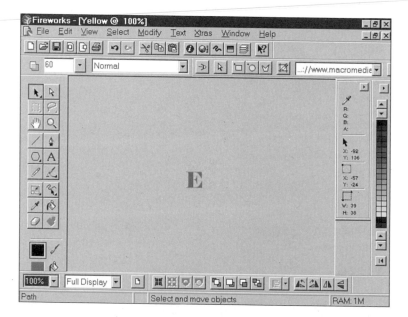

MACROMEDIA FREEHAND

A competitor to Adobe Illustrator, Freehand is a vector graphics design tool with new features added in version 8.0 that make it easier to produce Web-ready image files.

Like Adobe ImageReady, Freehand includes animation capabilities and handy batch processing of graphics.

Macromedia products are available at `http://www.macromedia.com/` (see Figure 34.18). You can download demos, read and join in discussions about Macromedia software, and see Macromedia results in action on their colorful, active Web site.

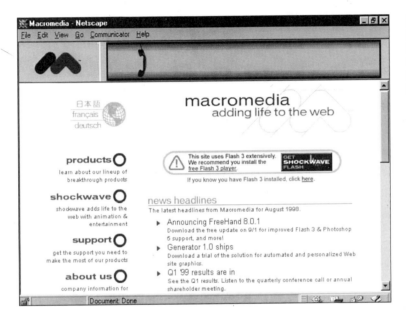

Figure 34.18
Macromedia's exciting Web site makes use of a wide range of Macromedia software.

MACROMEDIA FLASH

For vector graphics with their tiny file sizes, check out the industry-standard Flash from Macromedia. The current shipping version (3.0) includes support for interactivity and streaming sound. For the same file space as two large images, you can create a complete presentation complete with sound.

Flash requires users to download a plug-in that is freely available at Macromedia's site.

ULEAD PHOTOIMPACT AND WEB RAZOR

A very impressive product for a low price: Ulead PhotoImpact and Web Razor are suites designed with the Web in mind. I'm especially impressed with their combined ability to make great specialty graphics, such as *backgrounds (page 682)*. Note that Web Razor is the effects package that not only works in tangent with PhotoImpact but can be plugged into both Adobe Photoshop *and* Paint Shop Pro. Other features include the following:

- Imagemap support
- Button maker
- SmartSaver (a very handy optimization tool)
- Specialty filters

Visit Ulead at `http:www.ulead.com` for a variety of Web and image-related software applications, clip art, and resources.

ANIMATED GIF PROGRAMS

One of the easiest ways to add a bit of life to your Web pages is through the use of animated GIF images. The animation is encoded within the image file, meaning that all browsers can read it. Other animation options may cost more money and not be as cross-platform, cross-browser compatible.

The following are some helpful GIF animation programs. As you've already found out—animation is fast becoming part of the new wave of image production tools, including Photoshop.

MICROSOFT GIF ANIMATOR

GIF Animator works with Microsoft's Image Composer. Its features include the following:

- Drag-and-drop images directly from Microsoft Image Composer.
- Special effects such as loop, spin, and fade.
- Customize palettes, or let the application optimize the animation for you.

You can find out more about Microsoft GIF Animator at `http://www.microsoft.com/image-composer/gifanimator/gifanin.htm`.

GIF CONSTRUCTION SET

A popular shareware tool for constructing animated GIFs on the PC, GIF Construction Set contains a Windows 95-based wizard that walks the creator through the simplified process of creating an animated image. For users more comfortable with the animation process, GIF Construction Set also offers the ability to bypass the wizard and build the images yourself. GIF Construction Set is available at `http://www.mindworkshop.com/`.

GIF MOVIE GEAR

The power of this animation tool lies primarily in its palette control and its ability to optimize each individual graphic, removing unnecessary data. GIF Movie Gear is available from Gamani at `http://www.gamani.com/` (see Figure 34.19). Alas, it's only for the PC.

Figure 34.19
Gamani's home page.

ULEAD GIF ANIMATOR

I personally love the way you can add special effects to your graphics by using Ulead GIF Animator, another great PC utility. Sweeps, fades, fills, and general fun can be had, all with the click of a mouse.

Ulead products are long on productivity and short on expense. A perfect combination for lower budget projects, they can be found at http://www.ulead.com/.

OPTIMIZATION TOOLS

Optimization tools help get your graphics down to Web-ready size (see Chapter 31, "Web Graphic Formats"). Here's a look at some of the particularly helpful applications.

DEBABELIZER PRO

You can take tedious guesswork out of optimization with this powerful program that processes and optimizes graphics. While you can do everything that Debabelizer does to a graphic by hand in Photoshop, Debabelizer has the added advantage of batch processing files as well as offering up file type and size comparisons. Debabelizer Pro can be found at http://www.debabelizer.com/.

Be wary, however. Debabelizer Pro is a considerable expense. I've only used it when working for design companies requiring large quantities of graphic production. For smaller clients and specific applications, I prefer to use Photoshop (and do my optimization by hand) or one of the other tools listed in this section. You'll need to evaluate your circumstances to come up with the most sensible approach.

PART
VI

CH
34

ULEAD SMARTSAVER

For the PC user, SmartSaver cannot be beat for a simple interface and great output. What's more, it's a *whole* lot less expensive than Debabelizer—perfect for smaller Web graphic production facilities and personal use. Ulead SmartSaver can be found at `http:www.ulead.com/`.

GRAPHIC ENHANCEMENT PROGRAMS AND PLUG-INS

The way you present a graphic is as important as the graphic's quality itself. A well-processed image, while strong on its own, is rendered even more classy when enhanced with drop shadows, feathered edges, and geometric edge designs, just to name a few.

These effects, as well as innumerable others, can be achieved through the use of plug-ins to Photoshop or Photoshop-style imaging programs.

ALIEN SKIN SOFTWARE

With 21 filters, Alien Skin's premier plug-in package is Eye Candy. It offers a wide range of powerful standards as well as fun creations such as drop shadows, glows, motion trails, jiggle, weave, and water drop (see Figure 34.20). Find out all about Eye Candy and other Alien Skin products at `http://www.alienskin.com/`.

Figure 34.20
Weird and wacky filters from Alien Skin.

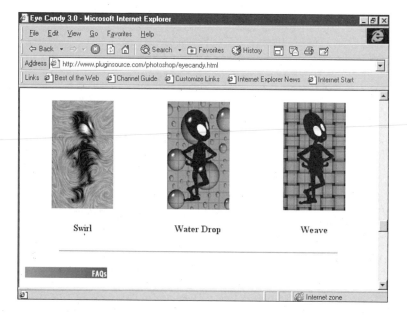

AUTO F/X

With such enhancements as photo edges from Photographic Edges (see Figure 34.21), type edging with Typographic Edges, and a powerful image optimizer and color palette controller known as WebVise Totality, Auto F/X makes some mighty plug-ins available for the Macintosh and PC platforms. Visit Auto F/X at `http://www.autofx.com/`.

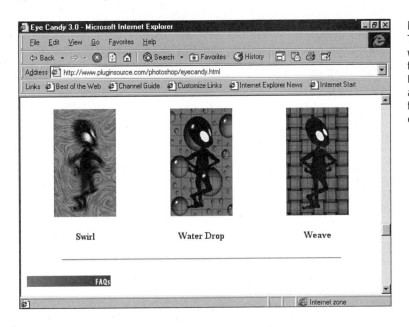

Figure 34.21
This graphic uses a wavy edge effect from Auto F/X Photographic Edges and a drop shadow for a professional edge.

KAI'S POWER TOOLS

The king of enhancements, Kai's Power Tools can help you create background tiles, Web buttons, and complex color blends. Kai's Power Tools is available for both the Macintosh and Windows platforms from MetaCreations at `http://www.metacreations.com/kpt/` (Figure 34.22).

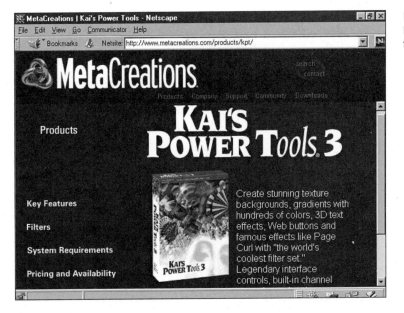

Figure 34.22
Kai's Power Tools from MetaCreations.

GRAPHIC SOURCE MATERIAL

You'll also want to have sources for icons, patterns, stock photos, and fonts. There are numerous sources of freeware or shareware material on the Internet. Higher-quality material can be acquired on CD-ROM and must be used according to the associated license.

For professional projects, it's definitely worth your while to accumulate a solid library of stock photography, clip art, and fonts.

CLIP ART GALLERY

It's quick, it's easy and it's at your fingertips. FrontPage gives you immediate access to the extensive Clip Art Gallery that ships with Office. The gallery is expandable and can be used as a management tool for all your graphics.

It allows you to index and search for images by keyword. It can also connect to Internet resources for even more clip art.

ADOBE STUDIOS

Adobe Studios offers an excellent line of quality stock materials. You can get a regular paper catalog delivered via snail mail, or you can browse and purchase stock materials online at http://www.adobestudios.com/.

PHOTODISC

A visit to the Photodisc site will provide you with a shopping source for plenty of stock photos, backgrounds, and links to other sites of interest. Free membership entitles you to downloads of comp art and photos at http://www.photodisc.com/. You can also order a standard mail catalog.

ART TODAY

An inexpensive alternative to high-end stock materials such as Adobe Studios and Photodisc, a membership to Art Today (http://www.arttoday.com/) gives you unlimited downloads for a very reasonable yearly fee. The quality varies, but you can find a variety of useful images and art. I've found this resource to be well worth the price tag of only $29.95 per year.

FUN AND FREE SITES

The Web is *filled* with sites that offer downloadable clip art, photos, backgrounds, and animations galore. It would be impossible to list them all here, but here are a few favorites.

- The Internet Baglady (see Figure 34.23)—She's a personal friend (well, when she remembers to clean up after her dumpster-diving forays), and her site is simply all-too-fun! The Baglady has searched for and found a wide number of inexpensive and free ways to get art for and information about building a Web site. The Internet Baglady can be found at http://www.dumpsterdive.com/.

- Caboodles of Clip Art—A great site for the home page enthusiast or design novice, Caboodles of Clip Art can be found at `http://www.caboodles.com/`.

- Microsoft Images Gallery—High-end selection of images from Microsoft at `http://www.microsoft.com/gallery/images/default.asp`.

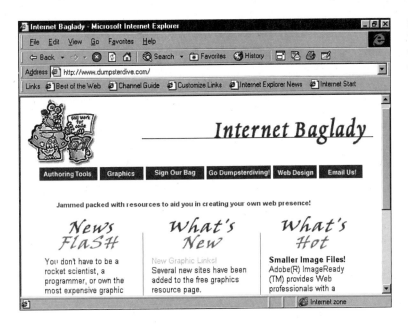

Figure 34.23
The Internet Baglady can help you find free and cheap gems.

TROUBLESHOOTING

I want a full powered graphics tool, but I don't have a lot of money. Which tool should I pick?

There are several shareware graphic tools available on the Web, but many of them lack the powerful features of the more expensive tools. If your budget is tight, try checking out Paint Shop Pro. It can be purchased for about 1/5 the cost of Photoshop and has many powerful features.

Another alternative for students is to look for academic versions of these products which are usually available at discounted prices.

There are so many different tools, I don't know which one to pick. Is there a way to try some before I buy?

Almost every tool mentioned in this chapter has a demo or an evaluation version available online. Try downloading the ones you are interested in and playing with them for a while. This way you can choose a tool that you are comfortable with.

PART

VI

CH

34

DESIGNERS CORNER: CREATING A BACKGROUND GRAPHIC—COMPARE AND CONTRAST

To give you a feel for graphic design tools and how they work, this section discusses the evolution of a Web background graphic using a compare/contrast process with different tools. The times will give you an idea of how long it takes with each tool.

To be as fair as possible with this test, I chose three software programs to run the test with which I feel confident: Photoshop, PhotoImpact, and Paint Shop Pro.

USING PHOTOSHOP

Start time: 6:53 PM

End time: 6:55 PM

The first thing I did was create a new file. Then, I filled the file with a color and added noise to give it a speckled look. I then optimized the image.

Now I'm going to write some HTML code and load the image into the browser so you can see it (see Figure 34.24).

Figure 34.24
My background image as created with Photoshop.

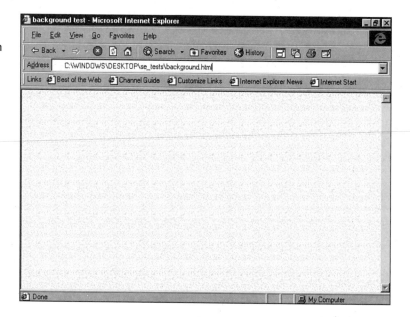

USING PHOTOIMPACT

Start time: 7:00 PM

End time: 7:03 PM

In PhotoImpact, I went first to the Web and then to the Background Designer (see Figure 34.25). I chose a background effect I liked, colorized it, and then lightened it enough for Web use. After that, I loaded the image into SmartSaver to help me optimize it. This is what took the extra minute. Adept Photoshop users will typically be able to optimize by hand slightly more quickly than having to go through the extra step of using a specialty application.

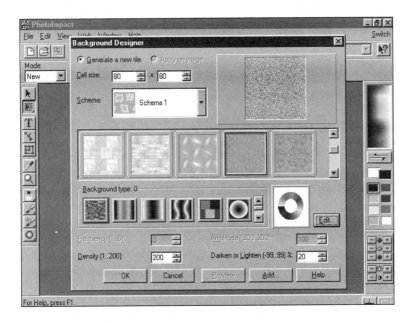

Figure 34.25
PhotoImpact's
Background Designer.

USING PAINT SHOP PRO

Start Time: 7:05 PM

End Time: 7:11 PM

Using Paint Shop Pro, I first started a new file. Then, I filled the file with color and added noise, just as I did with Photoshop. However, Paint Shop Pro didn't have a monochrome option (see Figure 34.26), which is my preference when creating speckled backgrounds. I saved the file as a GIF, and Paint Shop Pro defined the palette for me. It did a good job of keeping the file size low, but I had little control over the resulting image. I also wasn't able to quickly adjust the contrast or brightness.

Here's my analysis of the comparative exercise:

PHOTOSHOP

Advantages: I liked the control I had with Photoshop. From being able to choose directly from a color-safe palette to controlling exactly how I would optimize the image, I felt that all decisions were left to me. This enabled me to work quickly and meet my goal with quality results.

PART

VI

CH

34

Disadvantages: To manage Photoshop quickly, users will need to have some experience working with it. It has so many features that it can be confusing to those who aren't comfortable with it.

Figure 34.26
Monochromatic options were not available when adding noise in Paint Shop Pro.

PHOTOIMPACT

Advantages: While the control wasn't the same as with Photoshop, what PhotoImpact offers are *options*. The Background Designer is so much FUN that I could spend a lot of time playing around with it. It is a very creative tool. The interface is also quite easy to maneuver, and SmartSaver helped me to see up front what file formats would work best for optimization. While I already knew what would be the best option in terms of optimization, those designers with less experience are sure to appreciate the features of SmartSaver.

Disadvantages. As with Photoshop, there's a lot of stuff here. Opening up the different applications, which are truly like smaller programs within the parent program, is more time consuming than the pop-up windows in Photoshop and Paint Shop Pro.

PAINT SHOP PRO

Advantages: The easy-to-use interface makes this program especially powerful. There's not a lot you have to think about; you can pretty much jump right in and do what you want to do. And Paint Shop Pro makes the process very simple and straight-forward.

Disadvantages: Paint Shop Pro's simplicity is both its power and its problem. I wanted a lot more control over my image production than the program allowed me, and I had to search for workarounds to accommodate my needs.

Web Servers and Web Hosting

CHAPTER 35

INTRODUCTION TO WEB HOSTING AND WEB SERVERS

In this chapter

by Neil Randall

No matter how well designed and full featured your web might be, it is of no use whatsoever if nobody can see it. You have to place your web on a server in order to make it a part of the World Wide Web or of your organization's intranet. A *server* is a computer that contains web server software and (ideally) a full-time, high-speed connection to the Internet. This computer can be on a machine running any flavor of Microsoft Windows (3.*x*, 95, 98, NT 3.5, 4.0, or the upcoming Win2000), an Apple Macintosh, a UNIX workstation such as a Sun or Hewlett-Packard (and many others), a PC running Linux, FreeBSD, or OS/2, or any other computer for which Web server software is available.

The standalone version of FrontPage 2000 does not ship with Web server software. By contrast, if you've acquired FrontPage 2000 as part of the Microsoft Office 2000 suite, the Microsoft Personal Web Server (for Windows 95/98 only) is included as part of the package. If you want the Microsoft PWS—and it's an excellent server, especially for testing purposes—you can download it from the Microsoft Web site. Be aware, however, that the download is huge (about 24MB). Chapter 37, "FrontPage 2000 and the Microsoft Personal Web Server," covers the Microsoft PWS in detail.

Other servers covered in Part VII, "Web Servers and Web Hosting," of this book include Microsoft's Internet Information Server (Chapter 38, "FrontPage 2000 and Microsoft's Internet Information Server (IIS)") and Netscape's line of servers. Any server must be running the FrontPage *server extensions (page 301)* in order for it to work with all of FrontPage's features, including Microsoft's servers.

This chapter offers an introduction to the workings of Web servers, as well as to the FrontPage Server Administrator software.

HOW A WEB GETS "SERVED"

To serve your information to the World Wide Web, you almost certainly need a computer with Web server software and a full-time, high-speed connection to the Internet. The hardware and software combination together is called a *Web server*. You can run a server entirely on your own or you may be assigned to it as part of your organization's local area network (LAN).

Web servers are increasingly owned by companies that exist precisely to provide such services. They're often called *Web presence providers*, or WPPs, but they go by Web Hosting Services and Web Service Providers as well. It's likely that your Internet service provider (ISP) offers some free Web space for its subscribers. Check the Web page for your ISP and see if it offers this service. If not, and if you need a web, switch to another provider. Some providers offer users as much as 20–30MB for this purpose.

If you get an account with a WPP or an ISP that provides web hosting services, you won't need Web server software, nor will you need a full-time connection to the Internet. Anyone with an account with the provider, a modem, and a copy of a web creation tool such as FrontPage can develop sophisticated webs and then transfer them to the server or develop them directly on the provider's server with FrontPage. In such a case, however, be sure that your provider is willing to allow the FrontPage extensions for its server; if not, you will be restricted to using certain FrontPage package features. Later in this chapter you see what server extensions allow you to do.

It's not necessary to have a full-time, high-speed connection to the Internet to serve a web. You can create a web and run it whenever you log on to your ISP if you use FrontPage's Personal Web Server or any other Web server software on your machine. The problems with doing so are threefold: First, your readers can access your Web only when you're online; second, the connection is slow; third, most ISPs give you a different Internet Protocol (IP) address every time you log on, so you won't be able to provide permanent hyperlinks to your site from anywhere else on the Web. This only works if you have a web designed for private use, and you can supply those included with the IP number every time you're up and running.

Caution

At this point you might be thinking that you've paid for an Internet account with unlimited access—why don't you just get a separate phone line, dial in, and leave your machine connected 24 hours a day, seven days a week? Forget it. Your ISP knows all about these tricks and probably has an automatic disconnection ready to go. In fact, if you read the terms and conditions that are part of your account, you might very well find that your access isn't truly unlimited, and that you can be kicked off your ISP if you stay online for too long.

On the other hand, your ISP might be willing to provide you (at significant cost) with a 24-hour modem connection and a fixed IP address. This, however, requires a second phone line in your house, and the scheme is usually more expensive than renting server space from the same ISP. Several megabytes of server space are typically available for anywhere from $50 to $250 per month.

There is one other possibility currently available in some regions. Hooking up to the Net through your cable company (you need a cable modem and an account to do this) usually means that you have a 24-hour connection and a fixed IP address. If you have such an account, you can install Web server software and serve all the webs you want. The only problem with this approach, apart from the fact that you have to leave your machine running most of the time, is that cable access is excellent for data transfers *to* your machine (most cable users claim about 1.5 megabytes per second), but no faster than 300-400 *kilo*bytes per hour for transfers *from* your machine. In other words, downloads are fast, but uploads aren't. This means that visitors would receive their pages relatively slowly.

Web server software is available for practically all types of computers, but the most common serving platforms are UNIX (by far the most prevalent), Windows NT, Macintosh, and more recently, Windows 95 and Windows 3.*x*. This software exists solely to serve files; it waits for incoming requests from the Internet and then sends the requested file to the requesting machine. This is primarily handled through the protocol known as *Hypertext Transport Protocol* (*HTTP*). All requests from Web browser software begin with a protocol statement. This is usually `http://`, but it can also be one of several others. The other most common protocols follow:

- `mailto://`—Sends an email message to the specified address.
- `ftp://`—Requests a document via FTP.
- `https://`—Requests a document using SSL security technology.
- `gopher://`—Requests a document from a Gopher server (uncommon today, but still exists).

> **Caution**
>
> It's no longer necessary for users to type the protocol itself in the Location or Go To field in browsers such as Netscape Navigator and Microsoft Internet Explorer. To reach the Microsoft site, for example, users need only type `www.microsoft.com` (or just plain `microsoft`), not `http://www.microsoft.com`; to download from the Netscape FTP site, they need only type `ftp.netscape.com`, not `ftp://ftp.netscape.com`. Be sure to include the full address—complete with protocol—in the links you create in your Web documents. Otherwise they won't work.

In effect, the server acts as a communications assistant between the user's machine and the machine on which the web is stored. When the browser registers a click from the user, the server software initiates the transfer of the HTML file and all its subfiles, such as graphics, imagemaps, and Java scripts.

SERVER ADMINISTRATION AND SERVER EXTENSIONS

Even though FrontPage ships with fully functional Web server software, FrontPage's Server Administration tools do not actually control the Personal Web Server; instead, they provide an interface to whatever Web server software you happen to be running. You can still use Server Administration if you're running O'Reilly's WebSite, the Netscape FastTrack or Enterprise Servers, or the NCSA UNIX server, although you will do so in conjunction with the Server Administration tools provided by that server.

What does FrontPage Server Administration do? It primarily exists as a means of installing FrontPage's server extensions so that FrontPage's features work smoothly with your existing server. All Web servers ship with server administration tools, but in all cases these tools let you configure only that particular server. FrontPage Server Administrator, on the other hand, works hand in hand with a wide number of popular servers, with more to be added by Microsoft as the product matures. FrontPage accomplishes this task through the use of *server extensions*, which (as their name suggests) extend FrontPage's capabilities to other Web server software.

The Web servers supported by FrontPage are listed in Table 35.1. Note that these are current as of the end of January 1999. They can be found at
`http://officeupdate.microsoft.com/frontpage/wpp/platforms.htm`.

TABLE 35.1 WEB SERVERS SUPPORTED BY FRONTPAGE EXTENSIONS

Computer Platform	Web Server Software
Microsoft Windows 95, 98, NT Workstation 3.5x and 4.0, NT Server 3.5x and 4.0, Windows 2000	Microsoft Personal Web Server 4.0
	FrontPage Personal Web Server (included with past versions of FrontPage)
	Microsoft Internet Information Server 2.0 or later, including IIS 4.0
	Microsoft Peer Web Services (Windows NT Workstation 4.0)
	O'Reilly WebSite (and Pro) 1.0 and 2.0
	Netscape Communications Server 1.12
	Netscape Enterprise Server 2.0 and 3.0
	Netscape FastTrack Server 2.0
UNIX (includes Intel, HP, IBM, Silicon Graphics, and SPARC hardware); includes operating systems BSD 2.1 and 3.0, Linux 3.0.3; SCO OpenServer Release 5, SCO UnixWare 7, HP/UX 9.03, 10.01, AIX 3.2.5, 4.x; IRIX 5.3 and 6.2; Solaris 2.4 and 2.5; SunOS 4.1.3, 4.1.4	Apache 1.1.3, 1.2.4, 1.2.5
	CERN 3.0
	Netscape Commerce Server 1.12
	Netscape Communications Server 1.12
	Netscape Enterprise Server 2.0 and 3.0
	Netscape FastTrack Server 2.0

HOW SERVER EXTENSIONS WORK

FrontPage's server extensions are designed to work in conjunction with existing Web servers, such as those available from O'Reilly & Associates, Netscape Communications, the National Center for Supercomputing Applications, and Microsoft. You will want to know the principles under which the server extensions operate, especially if you have a server for which a FrontPage extension does not currently exist. With this information, you can use FrontPage to develop your Web pages despite having an unsupported server.

The server extensions provide support for the administration, authoring, and programming/special functions features of FrontPage 2000. Basically, the server extensions communicate with the Web server through either the *Common Gateway Interface* (*CGI*) or the Internet

Server Application Programming Interface (ISAPI). These are the interface mechanisms by which servers themselves communicate with databases and other non-Web functions (CGI controls many fill-in forms, for instance); the server extensions are designed to use CGI exactly as each specific server demands. CGI passes user-configured variables and environment specifics to the server, and CGI returns the requested information in one file format or another—typically HTML. The FrontPage server extensions use this generalized process to communicate with the different servers.

It's often necessary for the server extensions to communicate directly with the server. This happens in the instance of setting server configuration and establishing permissions for administrators, users, and authors. Most Web servers have their own idiosyncratic way of managing this information, and the server extension's task is to interact appropriately with the type of server being run. In addition, newer servers have their own rich interfaces for setting these details (O'Reilly, OpenMarket, and Netscape servers are examples) and the configurations must often be set using the server's software before FrontPage's Server Administrator can deal with them.

In practical terms, the server extensions allow FrontPage to do the following:

- Authoring—The extensions handle some of FrontPage 2000's advanced authoring features, such as including navigation bars across the entire web, page formatting across the web, and the automatic hyperlinks maintenance. In addition, the extensions allow you to use FrontPage's discussion groups, search forms, hit counters, and forms that specify where the data is to be sent. Certain page templates, such as Discussion Form, rely on the server extensions for functionality. The extensions also make possible multiuser authoring and remote authoring (saving pages directly to remote servers). More specifically, the server extensions provide the following author-level features:

  Display the webs already on a server and open a web for editing in FrontPage

  Create and rename directories and files

  Apply and edit themes and shared borders

  Implement FrontPage components

  Use the check-in and check-out features for documents

  Produce a searchable text index for the web

  Create the navigation structure for the web

- Administering—The FrontPage server extensions allow you to set security permissions for your webs. You can set security without the server extensions, but not through FrontPage's Tools/Security dialog boxes. Instead, you need to contact your WPP for instructions on how to restrict access to your site for browsing, authoring, and administrative purposes. Often the WPP has documents on its Web site outlining these features. Related to security, the server extensions also let you control whether scripts and programs (executable files) can be run from your pages.

More specifically, the server extensions provide the following administrator-level features:

Set permission levels for each web (Browse, Author, and Administer permissions); use Windows NT user features to set these levels when run on a Windows NT-based server

Create, rename, and delete webs

Work remotely with site administration

FRONTPAGE SERVER ADMINISTRATOR

While the majority of the administration for your individual webs is handled through FrontPage Explorer configuration dialog boxes (see Chapter 17, "Configuring Webs"), administration of the Web server itself is performed through the FrontPage Server Administrator.

FrontPage 2000 has no separate icon for running the Server Administrator. In fact, to get to the Server Administrator you have to locate—via My Computer, Windows Explorer, or the Run dialog box from the Start menu—a file named `fpsrvadm.exe`. By default, this program can be found in the following location on your hard drive: `c:\Program Files\Common Files\Microsoft Shared\Web Server Extensions\version 4.0\bin`.

When you launch the program, you get an MS-DOS box with the following menu:

0. Quit
1. Install
2. Upgrade
3. Uninstall
4. Check and Fix
5. Enable Authoring
6. Disable Authoring
7. Change Security Settings
8. Recalculate Links
9. Delete
10. Rename
11. Set Directory Executable
12. Set Directory no Executable
13. Putfile
14. Recalcfile
15. Create a Subweb
16. Merge a Subweb into Its Parent Web
17. Full Uninstall of All FrontPage Information

PART
VII

CH
35

The `fpsrvadm.exe` interface allows you to issue these commands interactively, asking you for information at each step of the process. If you want, however, you can forgo this interface by issuing the commands on the command line of a normal DOS box (Win95/98), Command box (NT), or system prompt (UNIX). The general syntax for a command is as follows:

`fpsrvadm.exe -o command -p portnumber -x option`

-o is the operation or command, -p is the port number, and -x represents addition commands or arguments. The command line operator is shown beside each menu name in the following description. You can get a listing of all commands and arguments by issuing the command `fpsrvadm.exe -h` at a command prompt.

Note

In order to work with `fpsrv.adm`, you must run it on the computer where the Web server software is installed.

The Quit command closes the DOS box, while Install (-o `install`) places the server extensions on the specified port (80 is the typical port, 8080 a frequently used secondary port).

Uninstall (-o `uninstall`) deletes the server extensions from the web. Upgrade does what its title implies: upgrade the existing server extensions.

Check and Fix (-o `check`) determines whether the server extensions are in full working order and repairs those that are not. You can check or fix a specific web by entering the web name at the name prompt; you can alternatively leave this blank and have all webs checked, beginning with the root Web. Check and Fix ensures that the DLL and EXE files are in place and uncorrupted, and that the necessary FrontPage *directories(page 342)*, such as _vti_bin, _vti_private, are in place and uncorrupted.

Enable Authoring (-o `enable`) allows you to use FrontPage's authoring and administering features (which are enabled by default). Disable Authoring (-o `disable`) reverses this process. Enable Security (-o `security`) is related to the authoring-enabling command in that it lets you establish or delete the username and password of a specific author or administrator.

Recalculate Links (-o `recalc`) ascertains that all links within the web are functional. You must specify a web name for this operation, just as you must with the Delete (-o `delete`) command, which lets you delete a web or subweb, and the Rename (-o `rename`) command, with which you can change the name of an existing web or subweb.

Set Directory Executable (-o `setdirexec`) establishes the web you name as capable of containing programs (executable files). Set Directory No Executable (-o `setdirnoexec`) establishes the web you name as *not* capable of containing executable files. You can set these options from within FrontPage itself, but not with UNIX Web servers (only with Win95/98 or Windows NT servers).

Putfile (-o putfile) lets you transfer (publish) a file from the local machine to the specifically named web on the server. Recalcfile (-o recalcfile) checks and repairs the links that exist on a specific file in the named web.

Create a Subweb (-o create), as its name suggests, lets you create a new subweb to the named web. Merge a Subweb into Its Parent Web (-o merge) converts the named web to a folder within its parent web (by deleting the server extension information within the subweb).

Full Uninstall (-o fulluninstall) uninstalls the server extensions from the server, but it goes beyond the simple Uninstall command by removing all FrontPage information, thereby rendering it impossible to easily recreate the webs on that server by simply reinstalling the extensions (which Uninstall allows you to do).

Table 35.2 shows the arguments that can follow the commands.

TABLE 35.2   ARGUMENTS FOR THE SERVER ADMINISTRATOR COMMANDS

Abbr.	Full Name	Stands For	Values
-p	-port	Port number	The number of the port through which webs will be served. Usually this number is 80. If you use a different port number, you must ensure that links to your site include the number at the end of the domain name, as in the following example: `http://www.mycompany.com:8080/`
-w	-web	The name of a FrontPage web	The web's URL, relative to the root Web. For example: `http://www.mycompany.com/services/`
-t	-type	The Web server type	`apache, ncsa, netscape-enterprise, netscape-fasttrack, stronghold, website, frontpage, msiis, mspws, website. frontpage` refers to the no-longer–supported FrontPage Personal Web Server; `msiis` is the Microsoft Internet Information Server, `mspws` is the Microsoft Personal Web Server.
-s	-servconfig	A Web server configuration file	Required if your server (usually non-Microsoft servers) require a configuration file (usually `httpd.conf`).
-m	-multihost	The server's name or IP address, or, in the case of IIS 4.0 or later, a server instance number	Domain address or IP number.

continues

PART

VII

CH

35

TABLE 35.2 CONTINUED

Abbr.	Full Name	Stands For	Values
-u	-username	The user's username	Either an existing username or a new one. With IIS servers, only existing names can be applied; they must be taken from NT's user profiles.
-pw	-password	The user's password	The user's password. It's not needed on IIS servers, since the password is part of the user profile.
-i	-ipaddress	IP address	The four-part IP number of the user's computer, such as 129.97.185.21.
-a	-access	The level of access you want to grant a user or group	Administer, Author, or User (browse-only permission). Instead of one of these, you can use Remove, which remove access privileges for that user or group.
-d	-destination	The URL for the file or folder you want to work with	In the case of Putfile and Recalcfile, specify the exact path and filename. For Setdirexec and Setdirnoexec, specify the folder only.
-f	-filename	The name of the file	The full path and filename for the specific file.

USING FRONTPAGE WITHOUT SERVER EXTENSIONS

Server extensions do not exist for all Web server software, but that doesn't mean you can't make use of FrontPage's Web creation and page creation features. You won't be able to use all of them, but it will be an extremely useful program for building webs. The following sections discuss items to keep in mind when dealing with a server without FrontPage extensions.

COPYING WEBS

Copying webs from your computer to a server without FrontPage extensions requires the following considerations:

- Don't use the Publish Web feature found in FrontPage Explorer. Instead, transfer files via FTP from your machine to the appropriate directory on the server. Alternatively, use the Web Publishing Wizard that comes with the FrontPage Bonus Pack, and which when installed appears in Start, Programs, Accessories, Internet Tools.

- Don't transfer directories beginning with _vti_. These directories are proprietary to FrontPage's extensions system.

- Don't transfer files that contain access control information, such as Author and Administer permissions. These access controls will not work on a server that does not support FrontPage extensions.

SERVER DIFFERENCES

Web server software packages differ in the way they treat files and documents. The following points must be considered when building Webs for a server without FrontPage extensions:

- Web servers vary in what file types they recognize. UNIX servers, for example, typically recognize as Web documents only files with an .HTML extension, while FrontPage for Windows generates these files with an .HTM extension. You might need to change the extension on all files either before or after FTPing them to the destination server. Other file incompatibilities might occur as well, depending on the operating system and the server software on the destination machine.

- Access control differs from server to server. Even FrontPage's server extensions don't solve all the possible access control problems. In general, try to avoid extensive access restrictions on your web.

- Find out what the destination server needs as the name for its default document, that is, the document that appears when users enter your domain name but don't specify an actual document name. Some servers recognize INDEX.HTML as this name, but others use other names (such as WELCOME.HTML). You need to know this before transferring your web to the server.

FRONTPAGE COMPONENT INTERACTIONS

FrontPage's Bots are extremely powerful, but they won't work with a Web server for which FrontPage server extensions do not exist. The following are points that must be considered if building webs for such a server:

- Don't use FrontPage imagemaps. Instead, set them as appropriate for your server when you create them.

- Some of FrontPage's components depend on the existence of server extensions for correct operations. These include the Search Bot, Registration Bot, Discussion Bot, Save Results Bot, and Confirmation Bot. Avoid building these into your documents.

FRONTPAGE TCP/IP TEST

A surprisingly useful FrontPage 2000 package utility is the TCP/IP Test. TCP/IP Test is found in the FrontPage Explorer's Help menu. Choose Help, About Microsoft FrontPage Explorer, and then click the Network Test button. This yields the FrontPage TCP/IP Test box, where you see a Start Test button. Clicking this button gives you useful information about the behavior of your TCP/IP network connection.

The TCP/IP protocol is the protocol under which the Internet operates. To be on the Internet, in fact, a computer must be running the TCP/IP protocol. You can be on other networks without it, but not on the Internet. Computers connected to LANs sometimes share the TCP/IP stacks necessary to connect to the Internet, but the protocol is there even if the individual machine doesn't know it.

> **Note**
>
> If you are connecting to the Internet through a dynamic IP address system, as is usually the case with modem connections to an Internet service provider, you and your readers can access your site only by typing the actual IP number (for example, `http://129.97.38.164/`). This is because your IP address does not have a publicly available domain name associated with it.

TROUBLESHOOTING

Windows NT with IIS 4.0 can be difficult when it comes to working with the FrontPage server extensions. If you have the NT Options Pack installed (Microsoft not only recommends it, they practically assume it), you use the Microsoft Management Console (MMC) to install and upgrade the server extensions. But sometimes you can install the newest extensions and FrontPage still won't work the way you think it will, because you must remember to upgrade them through the MMC after installing. The problem is that the MMC doesn't make it particularly easy to do anything at all, despite Microsoft's proclamations to the contrary.

The point is this: If you're using NT and IIS, be sure to learn the MMC thoroughly. You should anyway if you're running NT Server, and for some of you that's part of your job, but if you're an NT do-it-yourselfer, this is an absolutely essential component to learn.

DESIGNERS CORNER

By the time this book hits the shelves, two high-speed connections, cable and ADSL, will be available in several areas. This could influence your decision to host your own web. Before you buy an account with a cable or ADSL provider, however, ask questions. For the first while, they won't likely let you serve webs from your own machine; instead, you'll have to buy hosting accounts on their servers. Usually a small amount of server space comes with a connection account, but sometimes you can't serve this space with an individual domain name.

The ability to host a web through a dial-in account *might* be possible with the release of Windows 2000. If your ISP adopts Windows 2000 Server, you should be able to reroute your domain name using Dynamic DNS. Dynamic DNS, in effect, tells the Internet whenever your domain name is associated with a new IP number, letting you host a web even if your IP address changes, as it does when you dial in to most ISPs. However, Win2000's features are far from final at the time of this writing, and ISPs might choose not to allow this, so don't count on it. Besides, you'd have to stay connected at high speed, and if your site had any significant traffic at all, even ADSL wouldn't be fast enough to serve it properly.

CHAPTER 36

USING A WEB HOSTING SERVICE

In this chapter

by Neil Randall

Running your own server isn't nearly as easy as the producers of Microsoft, Netscape, IBM, or other server software and hardware would have you believe. In fact, it's a demanding, often grueling chore that can cast you into the murky world of high-tech problems faster than you'd ever thought possible. Thankfully, tons of companies want to take these problems away from you, and all they ask is some money for their trouble. These companies are called *web hosting services* or *web presence providers*, and this chapter examines the ins and outs of working with them. The terms *web hosting service* and *web presence provider* will be used interchangeably throughout the chapter because when you begin searching for one, you'll find they're referred to as both.

Tip #167

> You can find a long list of web hosting services tailored for Microsoft FrontPage users (they have the FrontPage server extensions installed) on Microsoft's FrontPage Web site at `http://microsoft.saltmine.com/frontpage/wpp/list/`. Another excellent site, and one that rates hosting services, can be found at `http://webhostlist.internetlist.com/`.

THE PROBLEMS WITH SERVING YOUR OWN WEBS

Web server software is widely available, and if you look around the download sites you'll even find some excellent packages that are free. You can download the Microsoft Personal Web Server for free if you use Win95/98, and if you buy Windows NT 4.0 or the upcoming Windows 2000 (NT 5.0), you'll get Web server software with it. If you want to get away from Microsoft's platforms completely, you can get Linux (the UNIX clone that runs on PCs) either through free downloads or at minimal cost from companies such as RedHat or Caldera. The Apache server comes with the packages and can be downloaded free.

Why not set up your own server? Lots of reasons, actually. Here are a number of them, and you can decide which ones apply to you.

You need a computer with Web server software and a full-time, high-speed connection to the Internet in order to serve your information to the World Wide Web. The hardware and software combination together is called a *Web server*. You can either run a server entirely on your own or you can be assigned it as part of your organization's local area network (LAN).

Right away, you can see a few potential problems. First, you need a 24-hour connection to the Internet. If you're running from a standard modem, even the most liberal ISPs that offer "unlimited access" won't permit that for any length of time. You can get an exclusive modem connection with most ISPs, and for a considerable cost—but even here you won't meet the high-speed criterion. Modems are too slow for serious Web serving. This is true even of cable modems because while cable modems let you bring data into your computer extremely quickly, data gets sent from your computer at the speed of a regular telephone modem. Since serving your webs means primarily sending data to other computers, your server will be slow. New modem types such as ADSL might change this equation, but for common usage those technologies remain in the future.

The only way to realistically have a full-time Internet connection that operates at high speed in both directions is to hook your machine up to a high-speed shared line such as a T-1 or T-3. Unless you're rich, this means hooking up as an employee of an organization (such as a business or university) that already has such a connection. The problem here is that, as you might expect, such organizations almost certainly have policies against your personal use—including a side business—running on their networks. These policies exist for a number of reasons, including security, network overload, and the simple fact that the organization wants you to do some work for them. The other problem with connecting this way is that it's rarely possible for you to set up your own *domain name (page 769)* through such an organization. In order to get a domain name, an existing organization has to be willing to host it—and these organizations usually won't do that. If they don't, then you'll need to maintain a high-speed connection yourself, and that will run you thousands of dollars per year.

Say you can get your own domain name (or you don't care about having one), and that either your organization is willing to let you serve your own webs or you've set up and paid for your own high-speed connection—you still might not want to serve your own webs. You have to administer not only the webs, but the server itself. Security becomes a major issue here, even if your server uses Windows NT Server or UNIX as its operating system. You must be constantly aware of new attempts to crack the security guarding these OSs, and you must learn how to defend against them. The other side of maintenance, of course, is keeping your system running, backing up data, and all the other tasks that go with being an Information Technology professional.

Of course, some readers will be thinking that you've run a server for months, even years, without incident. That's entirely possible—but if your business or organization depends on the server for its livelihood, you'll want to look at possibilities other than doing it all yourself. That could mean a systems contract of some sort, or it could mean not serving your own web at all.

If you decide not to serve your web at all, you can have a company do the entire job for you, including design and information gathering. That costs money. For far less money, you can compromise and design your webs yourself, be in full control over which documents and files get onto your webs, and turn the administration of the server hardware and software (but not the administration of your webs) over to a company that specializes in such services. This might be your ISP or a dedicated web hosting service (WPP).

ISPs VERSUS WPPs

Why choose a WPP over your ISP? There are two reasons. The first is that a dedicated WPP almost always offers a better range of web serving features (not Internet features, just web serving features) for a better price than does the ISP. Second, ISPs are primarily concerned with keeping users connected to the Internet, including corporate connections; it takes precedence over all other activities. For WPPs, on the other hand, serving webs is the only business. For that reason, they have to provide competitive pricing (there are hundreds of WPPs available to users) and they have to make sure their Web servers stay up and running with a strong, fast connection to the Net.

This brings up another advantage to WPPs: If your ISP is having network problems, your web will also have problems. Splitting the two services means you don't have all your eggs in one basket. Of course, the other side of this argument is that you have double the potential difficulty, but the business competition for both types of providers helps with that kind of problem. You can always switch to another service.

WPPs offer more web services, more options, and greater ease of use for posting webs. They're also more likely to keep on top of new technologies for serving webs, again because of competition. Equally important to FrontPage users is the fact that WPPs are more likely than ISPs to mount FrontPage server extensions. To all of these points, of course, you'll find exceptions. In fact, the ISP you have now might very well surpass all WPPs for features, quality, and price. Using a WPP makes sense, however, for the majority of FrontPage users.

In one area, however, many WPPs usually aren't as good as ISPs. That area isn't in web services, but in email. The problem is this: WPPs typically offer POP (Post Office Protocol) servers but several do not offer SMTP (Simple Network Mail Protocol) servers. You receive your Internet mail through a POP server, but you need an SMTP server to send it. WPPs assume that you already have an ISP who provides SMTP services, and this assumption allows them not to configure and maintain SMTP services.

> **Note**
>
> The lack of SMTP services isn't by any means universal. Some WPPs offer SMTP and many other mail services. One feature WPPs tend to be good at, for instance, is email aliases and mailing lists.

The reason is that SMTP servers can be configured so that they do not *relay* mail. This means that they will send Internet email only if it originates from an account on that server, not from accounts on other servers. This is primarily important if you use the WPP to set up and host your domain name, and you want to send and receive mail using that domain name.

Assume that you use an ISP called goodnet.net. You use a WPP to serve your webs, and with that WPP you establish the domain name mycompany.com. Your userid is ceo@mycompany.com. You set the POP servers as mail.mycompany.com in your email program, and say your WPP doesn't provide an SMTP server. As a result, you set your outgoing mail to the SMTP server mail.goodnet.com. When you try to send a message under the username ceo@mycompany.com, your SMTP server might very well reject it, saying it cannot relay.

The solution to this isn't difficult, but it's inconvenient. You have to set your reply address different from your email address in your email program. In the preceding example, you set your email address as joe@goodnet.net, the server as goodnet.net, and your reply address as ceo@mycompany.com. That way you send a message as a goodnet.net subscriber, but when people reply to it using their own emailers, the message will go to ceo@mycompany.com and can be received using the WPP's POP server. This is far from perfect, but it works.

FEATURES OF A WEB HOSTING SERVICE

You'll see almost as many different features in hosting services as there are hosting services themselves. Competition in the hosting service game is fierce, and as a result it pays you to shop around to get the best combination of features and price. Here are the most important features and issues you should look for, and a general range of what you'll find out there. Figure 36.1 shows the features of one sample hosting service.

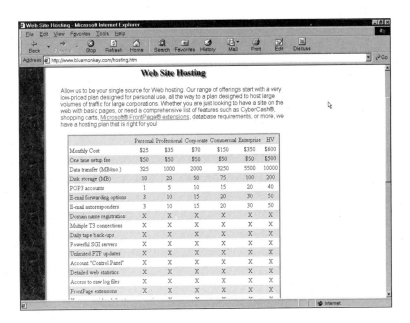

Figure 36.1
This hosting service, Blue Monkey Enterprises, outlines its hosting prices and services in a single, easy-to-read table.

PRICE

Price matters. Web hosting can cost you anywhere from a few dollars to hundreds of dollars per month. At first, of course, you'll look for a way to pay the least amount possible, which only makes sense. Be sure to budget for what you can afford and—just as importantly—what you need. If you're beginning a Web-based business that will depend on Internet financial transactions, your needs are much greater than those of a FrontPage user who just wants to put a small site up for the experience and the enjoyment. You need to consider what you'll be doing with your site and also what your visitors will be doing.

You'll find hosting services ranging from less than $10 per month to greater than $100 per month, plus corporate plans that go far above that. If you pay more than $100 per month, however, ensure that you're getting a wide range of extra services. Some plans include site design, high-speed office connections, and more.

Generally speaking, you should be able to get a hosting service account with lots of bells and whistles for under $50 per month. The bells and whistles are as follows.

DISK SPACE

This is a huge differentiator among hosting services. Typically, you'll get between 10MB and 50MB of space for your $10–$25 per month account, with additional space available for additional rates. In some cases, however, you'll find up to 300MB of disk space for not much more. You should try to determine fairly early how much space you'll need, keeping in mind that multimedia files can take up loads of space. To get a sense of this, design some disk-based webs with FrontPage and determine how much disk space they occupy, then go from there.

CONNECTION SPEED

As with your modem or LAN connection, the connection between your web hosting service and the Internet can vary considerably in speed. Essentially, though, only two speeds are worth looking for: T-1 and T-3.

T-1 lines run at 1.544Mbps (millions of bits) per second. T-1 lines consist of 24 channels, each at 64Kbps, and each of which can be configured and sold separately. If your provider boasts *fractional T-1*, only part of the connection is available for web services.

T-3 lines are much faster than T-1s, running at 43Mbps. The T-3 consists of 672 separate channels of 64Kbps, each of which, again, can be configured separately. Most Web presence providers offer T-3 speeds.

TRAFFIC ALLOWED

Because you're sharing your provider's connection to the Internet with all of their other account users, you have to be careful about how much traffic your site receives. *Traffic* is the amount of data sent between your site and your visitors. You'll be billed extra charges by most web hosting services if you exceed a specific amount of traffic over a specific period of time (usually a month). Sometimes, this figure is 1000–2000MB per month, but many providers offer amounts in excess of a gigabyte. Figure 36.2 shows one hosting service offering unlimited traffic (hits and transfers).

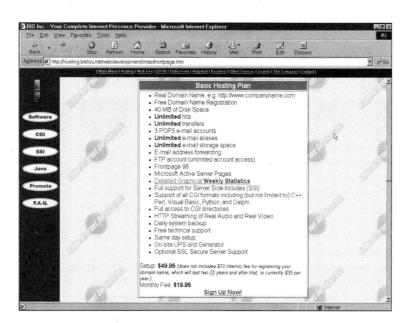

Figure 36.2
Ballou Internet Services highlights several features that offer unlimited use.

As you're selecting a hosting service, this point should be primary in your mind, which means you should try to determine in advance how much data will actually be transferred from your site to your visitors' machines. If you have a full multimedia site with large downloads and many visitors, you'll create much more traffic than a text information site accessed less often.

FRONTPAGE SERVER EXTENSIONS

This is an obvious point, but be sure to look for it. You don't need the FrontPage extensions to mount a perfectly fine Web site, but you can't do without them if you want to make full use of FrontPage's features. Check your hosting service's Web site to ensure that your account will include the *server extensions (page 301)*, as well as to ensure that you don't get charged extra for them.

DOMAIN NAME HOSTING

One of the benefits of signing on with a web hosting provider is that they frequently offer a good deal on registering domain names. A *domain name* is a text-based address (such as mycompany.com) that is associated with an IP number (such as 138.211.67.113). If you want to establish a domain name, you have to apply to the InterNIC registration services, fill in some jargon-laden forms, and ensure that you have at least two servers on which the domain name is already set up at the time of registration.

Your hosting service can cut through all the technical details and provide a quick and easy way to do all this. They fill out all the necessary forms and put the domain name on their servers. Furthermore, they do so for not a great deal of money; some, in fact, offer a free domain name registration as part of your new account purchase. No matter which hosting service you use to host your domain name, you won't be able to avoid the annual fees charged by the InterNIC itself. As of this writing, those fees are $35 per year, with a two-year payment of $70 right off the bat; typically you are responsible for paying them directly to the InterNIC.

A large number of hosting providers offer both virtual and non-virtual hosting packages. The difference is quite simple. *Virtual* plans are those in which your site's URL takes your domain name; for example, `www.mycompany.com`. *Non-virtual* plans are those in which you do not buy a domain name; the URL for your site will display the hosting service's name with your username as a separate folder (*subweb* in FrontPage terminology). In this case, your URL would be, for example, `www.hostingservice.com/~jsmith`. Figure 36.3 shows the difference between the two offerings at one hosting service.

Figure 36.3
The features of both the virtual and non-virtual plans at CyberVision Network, including a very large disk space offering for either.

EMAIL ACCOUNTS AND MAILING LISTS

Your hosting service will probably include at least one email account for your new domain name. Some services offer more. Some offer email aliases that aren't the same as POP accounts—aliases aren't really individual accounts—but which work well enough to sustain email for a small business. In many cases, you can also establish mailing lists to serve your employees or customers. Compare a variety of services to see what they offer.

FTP ACCESS

FrontPage uses the Internet's FTP to upload files with its Publish feature, and you should ensure that your hosting service provides you with at least one FTP account. FTP accounts are also useful as a place to store non-Web documents, if you have enough disk space.

TELNET ACCESS

If your hosting service runs on UNIX machines, you should be offered a Telnet access account. This allows you to access the account for a number of UNIX-specific purposes, including changing permissions and reading mail.

SECURE SERVER AVAILABILITY

Your hosting service will likely offer the ability to place a portion of your web on a secure server for the purpose of offering greater security to your visitors when transmitting forms data. You'll want this even if you plan to simply ask your visitors to fill in their name and address; fears of hackers stealing data from the Net are strong.

E-COMMERCE AVAILABILITY

If you plan to develop a Web-based storefront, check to see if your provider offers e-commerce solutions. These often cost more than the basic package, but it's far better to let the provider worry about credit card transactions (as an example) than doing it yourself.

CGI CAPABILITY

The Common Gateway Interface (CGI) has been the central technology behind Web programming for several years. All important Web server software handles CGI without the need for special extensions (such as the FrontPage Server Extensions), and many CGI scripts and solutions are available on the Net and on CD-ROMs. FrontPage itself supports CGI scripting, first for users who do not have access to a server running the FrontPage extensions, and second because if it didn't the product would be worthless to many experienced Web developers (for instance, an important potential user base for FrontPage). Check to see if your hosting service gives you your own directory for CGI scripts (the directory is called `cgi-bin`). If your service uses UNIX servers, it almost certainly will provide you with your own `cgi-bin`, but if it uses NT servers it might not.

TROUBLESHOOTING

You can delay the usefulness of your account by neglecting to request that the hosting service set up the FrontPage extensions. With some services, this is a special checkbox, or even a special email request, and if you don't request it immediately you might have to wait an extra week or so. Not only can this wipe out your initial enthusiasm, it can also be disastrous if you need to start your site immediately.

As soon as your account is operational, test it to make sure everything works. Create new webs directly on the server. Publish webs you have stored on your hard disk. Add new items to existing webs on the hosting service, and make full use of FrontPage components to ensure that the server extensions function properly. If anything negative occurs, contact your WPP immediately and insist on the help you need.

If you buy FrontPage 2000 when it first hits the shelves, it will probably take some time for your WPP to upgrade to the new server extensions. They have to test them first, and they're also reluctant to upgrade software if the existing software works fine. The last thing they want is to install the new extensions and then discover that some of their clients' sites don't function properly anymore. But by all means remind them fairly frequently (weekly, for instance) that you need the new extensions. If your site isn't crucial, you might even offer to be a guinea pig willing to test the new extensions on your account.

DESIGNERS CORNER

Selecting a WPP can be an exercise in frustration, simply because there are so many of them to choose from. A site such as InternetList.com (`http://webhostlist.internetlist.com/`) offers ratings of WPPs and provides useful browsing. Look also to Yahoo's section on Web Hosting (`http://dir.yahoo.com/Business_and_Economy/Companies/Internet_Services/Web_Services/Hosting/`), remembering that the list here is for services with or without FrontPage server extensions. Also look at Microsoft's listing of FrontPage-compatible services at `http://microsoft.saltmine.com/frontpage/wpp/list/`, but Microsoft offers no ratings. You can find ads for WPPs on Web pages (look for banner ads in particular) and in computer magazines as well as some business and hobby magazines (such as computer games mags).

Before making a decision, go to the WPP's site and read everything about what you might be getting, and what you might be paying for it. Test out the customer service by emailing a couple questions to the contact address and seeing how long it takes to get a response. Check for extra charges for such features as additional email accounts, RealMedia service, Internet Chat services, shopping carts, and so forth. And make sure that the price you're quoted on the site or through email has special conditions attached to it. For example, the monthly price showing for the selected hosting plan is frequently based on your paying an entire year up front. If you want to try the service out for three months, you'll usually be paying more per month to do so.

Be sure that your service offers FTP uploads. No matter how much you rely on FrontPage to upload your documents to your web site, there will be times when either FrontPage isn't working (programs break), or when you're at a computer on which FrontPage isn't installed. But also be sure to inquire if uploading via FTP will cause any problems with your account; some WPPs advise against any FTP uploading of pages because doing so can (in some cases) cripple the FrontPage extensions for your account. Ask about the policy for this.

FTP services have another benefit. Since you're buying disk space, you can use space that your webs don't use for storage of other types of files. For instance, you can use your server space as a backup for your data files. You can never have enough backups, and a good place to put your backups is on a completely separate machine.

CHAPTER 37

FRONTPAGE 2000 AND THE MICROSOFT PERSONAL WEB SERVER

In this chapter   *by Dennis Jones*

WHY USE THE MICROSOFT PERSONAL WEB SERVER?

Some of the most powerful features of FrontPage 2000 (such as several Dynamic HTML features, interactive forms, and various FrontPage components) will only work or display properly when the page containing them is accessed through a World Wide Web server. That is, you must open the page in your browser by using the Web server address of that page (such as `http://MyWeb/anypage.htm`).

Nevertheless, you don't actually need to use a Web server with FrontPage 2000 to create a Web. You can assemble your pages into what is called a disk-based Web, which is essentially a collection of linked HTML pages and images stored in one or more folders on your hard drive. In this case, you view a page by using the browser to open it as a file by typing a pathname such as `C:\webs\anypage.htm` into the browser's address bar.

If you do create a disk-based Web using FrontPage 2000, you can still insert FrontPage's advanced server-based elements into your pages. The trouble is, you won't know if these elements work properly until the pages containing them are published to an actual Web server and opened through the server, rather than opened as files. So, if you want to set up a full development environment using FrontPage 2000, it's pretty essential to install and use some form of Web server (and one, moreover, that supports the FrontPage 2000 server extensions). For development purposes, version 4 of the Microsoft Personal Web Server (PWS) will fill most if not all of your needs. This server is available either by free download from Microsoft; or, if you own Windows 98, it is on the Windows 98 CD-ROM.

The components and capabilities of the PWS somewhat overlap those of FrontPage 2000 (such as provision of a Personal Home Page Wizard), but you may find them to be useful supplements to the tools provided by FrontPage itself. For this reason, this chapter will be devoted to a full examination of the Personal Web Server, version 4.

UNDERSTANDING THE PERSONAL WEB SERVER AND THE PERSONAL WEB MANAGER

The PWS is a light-duty World Wide Web server, and is not intended for supporting large Webs that are accessed by many people (it can sustain only 10 simultaneous connections). It is designed to install easily on machines running Windows 95, Windows 98, and Windows NT Workstation. It does not run on Windows NT Server, which requires the PWS's big brother, Internet Information Server.

Associated closely with the PWS is the Personal Web Manager. As its name suggests, this is for managing Webs that are hosted by the PWS. The Manager also furnishes Web publishing facilities, a Home Page Wizard, and configuration tools.

The PWS is well suited to a FrontPage 2000 Web development environment. In addition, you could use it as the working server for a small intranet on a modestly-sized network. The tools provided by the Personal Web Manager component, along with the server itself, can give you a very effective way to share resources within your organization.

If you do this, however, keep in mind that the PWS has no built-in user authentication, so it isn't a good choice for information environments where high security is a concern. In addition, the PWS does not provide an FTP service, so you will need to install an FTP server from another software source if you wanted to provide this option on your intranet. The PWS does, however, support *Active Server Pages (ASPs) (page 878)*, so if you need to host or develop ASPs, the PWS can do the job.

PART

VII

CH

37

> **Note**
>
> The earlier versions of the Microsoft PWS (1.0 and 1.0a) did include an FTP service, but this was dropped in version 4. There was no version 2 or 3 of the PWS, by the way.

INSTALLING THE MICROSOFT PERSONAL WEB SERVER

As previously mentioned, the PWS does not ship with FrontPage 2000. You can install it either from a downloaded version available from the Microsoft Web site, or from the Windows 98 CD-ROM, if you own that. The next two sections cover each of these types of installation.

INSTALLING THE PWS FROM THE WINDOWS 98 CD-ROM

To carry out a basic installation, excluding any networking or TCP/IP configuration, use the following procedure.

> **Caution**
>
> The PWS will not work unless the TCP/IP networking protocol is installed correctly on the host machine. Refer to the documentation and/or Help files for your particular operating system (Windows 95, 98, or NT Workstation) for information about how to set up TCP/IP networking.

1. Save all your work and close all applications. Insert the Windows 98 CD-ROM into the CD-ROM drive. If the Windows 98 splash screen appears, close it.

2. Choose Start, Run, to open the Run dialog box.

3. Assuming your CD-ROM drive letter is D, type **D:\add-ons\pws\setup.exe** into the Open text box. (If the CD-ROM drive is another letter, substitute that for D:.) Choose OK.

4. The Microsoft Personal Web Server Setup splash screen opens. This is merely introductory, so choose Next.

5. The next dialog box offers you a choice of Minimum install, Typical install, and Custom install. Choose Typical.

Note

> The Custom install allows you to set up optional components of the PWS, including additional data access components, the Microsoft Message Queue, additional Transaction Server components, RAD support for Visual Interdev, and various advanced documentation. These components are for advanced Web designs and designers and are well beyond the scope of this chapter.

6. The next dialog box allows you to specify your default Web publishing Home Directory, that is, the folder where your Web's home page is stored. The default folder is C:\Inetpub\wwwroot. If you need to change this, either use the Browse button to locate a new default folder or type the folder's path name directly into the WWW Service text box (see Figure 37.1).

Figure 37.1
You can specify a new default publishing folder in the Setup dialog box.

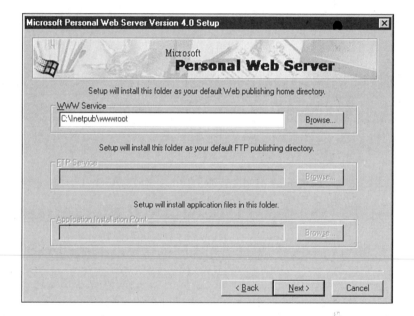

7. Choose Next. Setup completes this stage of the installation and opens a final dialog box when it has finished. Choose Finish or press the Enter key to leave Setup.

8. The Systems Setting Change dialog box appears, asking if you want to restart your computer to put the new settings into effect. You can't use the PWS until you do this, so go ahead and choose Yes to restart and complete the installation.

After the computer has restarted, you will see a new icon in the System Tray of the Status bar. This icon indicates that the PWS is running. Note that the PWS is a system service and, once installed, will always load at startup. Although you can't prevent the service from loading when the computer boots, you can start, stop, and pause the server. This will be covered a little later in this chapter.

DOWNLOADING AND INSTALLING PWS4

Microsoft has made PWS4 available for download on its Web site. The server is actually part of the NT Option Pack, so don't be alarmed when you find yourself navigating the Windows NT Web pages.

To download the files, connect to the Microsoft web site at `http://www.microsoft.com/ntserver/nts/downloads/recommended/NT4OptPk/default.asp`. You can get information here about the Option Pack and how to download its files. The Windows 95/98/NT Workstation pack is about 27MB in size for a minimal install, so expect to spend some time downloading if you have a slow connection.

Follow the instructions on the page to download the Option Pack download wizard (about .5 MB in size) to a folder on your machine; the name of this wizard is download.exe. When you've got it, remain connected to the Internet and launch the wizard. When it runs, it allows you to specify:

- Whether you want to download the actual Option Pack files or install directly from the Internet. You should likely download the files, so you will have them if you need to reinstall the Option Pack at a later time.
- The user's language, and what kind of machine (X86 Intel CPU or Alpha CPU) and operating system (Windows 95/98, NT Workstation, or NT Server) on which you will install the package.
- Whether you want typical, minimal, or full installation.
- The folder where the files are to be stored (you can accept the default supplied by the wizard).
- The Web site from which you want to download the Option Pack files. Choose the one you want to begin the download process.

Select the appropriate options to begin downloading the desired version of the Option Pack. When the download is complete, close all applications, disconnect from the Internet, and run the setup.exe program from the download folder. At this point, the installation procedure is exactly the same as that in the previous section.

TESTING THE PERSONAL WEB SERVER

It's a good idea to test the PWS before going on. The machine on which you installed the PWS will be either a standalone or a networked machine, so we'll cover these two essential cases.

TESTING THE PWS ON A STANDALONE MACHINE

The PWS communicates only through the TCP/IP protocol. Therefore a standalone machine, from the point of view of the PWS, can be either a PC that has no networking connections at all (except possibly a dialup connection to the Internet) or is connected to a network that does not use the TCP/IP protocol.

> **Note**
>
> If you are testing the PWS on an NT Workstation machine that has no network interface card at all, you will need to install the MS Loopback Adapter. This software driver can be installed when Workstation is first installed, or later by choosing Control Panel, Network, Adapters, Add, and choosing MS Loopback Adapter from the adapter list.

Once the server is installed, you should verify that it's working properly. Begin by starting Internet Explorer. In the browser's address bar, type the Web address `http://127.0.0.1`; this is a reserved IP address, valid on all computers for the local machine. The `127.0.0.1` address will always work (assuming the server installation is error-free) even if the machine is not connected to a network or to the Internet.

> **Tip #168**
>
> With Internet Explorer 3 or later, or Navigator 3 or later, you don't have to type the http:// part. In the example, typing `127.0.0.1` and pressing Enter will open the page.

Once you've typed in the address, press Enter. After a brief pause, the default startup page, which was created when you installed the PWS, appears in the browser window (see Figure 37.2).

Figure 37.2
The PWS's default startup page allows you to test the server installation.

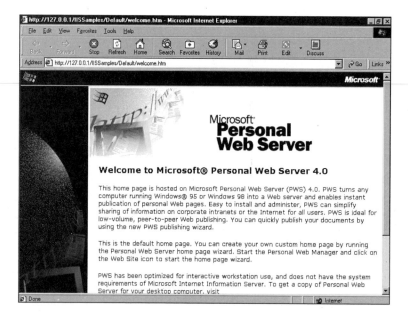

If you look in the address bar, you'll see that the page location (or URL) is `http://127.0.0.1/IISSamples/Default/welcome.htm`. If you want to check this out with Windows Explorer, you will find the file `WELCOME.HTM` (which is what you're looking at in the browser) stored on your hard drive at `C:\Inetpub\iissamples\default\`. As you can tell, this isn't the default publishing folder you specified during installation. Instead, it's a special sample folder to help get you started. The default publishing folder (`C:\Inetpub\wwwroot`) is where you would put the pages of your actual Web, assuming you did not change this default during installation.

A more user-friendly address is to use the actual name of the computer, which you assigned during your original Windows installation. If you've forgotten the name, you can get it from the Personal Web Manager—simply double-click the Publish icon to start the Manager, and you'll see the line Web Publishing Is On. Your Homepage Is Available At is in the Manager's Main window. Under this line, in blue, is a Web address—`http://` followed by a name; an example might be `http://mypc`. To use this name as the Web address, simply type **`http://mypc`** into the browser address bar (or just **`mypc`**, for recent browsers) and press Enter. The default startup page should appear in the browser window.

Once you know the server is working, you can close the browser.

PART

VII

CH

37

> **Note**
>
> You may be familiar with earlier versions of the Microsoft PWS running on a standalone Windows 95 machine. In the Windows 95 environment, you need a HOSTS file to make the computer name into a valid Web address, although the IP address 127.0.0.1 will always work without a HOSTS file. However, the new PWS running on a standalone machine does not need a HOSTS file; the PWS handles the mapping of the computer name to the 127.0.0.1 IP address for you.

TESTING THE PWS ON A TCP/IP NETWORKED MACHINE

This assumes that the machine is connected to a properly configured TCP/IP network, and that the network is properly configured to recognize your machine and its name.

The simplest method of testing the PWS is to do it on the local machine. Start a browser and type **`http://`** followed by the computer name—the name by which the network recognizes the machine—into the address bar. Then press Enter. The PWS welcome page should appear in the browser window.

> **Tip #169**
>
> You can get the machine name from the Personal Web Manager, as described in the previous section. Alternatively, you can obtain it from the Network Neighborhood, Properties, Identification tab.

For a more rigorous test, start a browser on another machine on the same TCP/IP network, and repeat the previous procedure. If the PWS welcome page does not appear, there may be something wrong with the network configuration. This must be corrected before you can proceed further.

REMOVING OR ADDING SERVER COMPONENTS

After the server has been completely installed, you can remove or add PWS components with the PWS setup program. If you need to do this, launch either the PWS Setup program that is on the Windows 98 CD-ROM or the PWS setup program you downloaded.

Tip #170	There is an alternate method, providing you have the Windows 98 CD-ROM. Insert the CD-ROM into the drive. Then choose Start/Programs/Internet Explorer/Personal Web Server/Personal Web Server Setup to start the install procedure.

When the Microsoft Personal Web Server Setup opening screen appears, choose Next. In the next screen, you have two choices (see Figure 37.3).

Figure 37.3
You can remove the PWS completely or add and remove components of it.

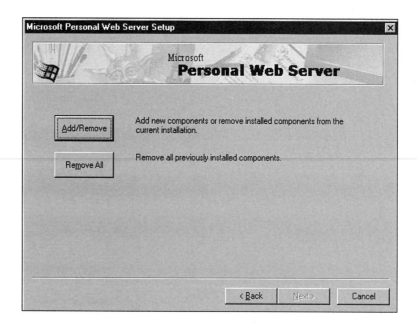

If you want to remove the server completely, choose Remove All and wait until you are instructed to restart the computer. Restarting completes the removal of the PWS.

If you want to remove or add server components, choose Add/Remove. This opens another screen, where you can specify what's to be added or removed (see Figure 37.4).

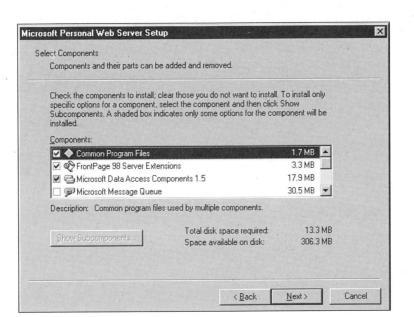

Figure 37.4
The Select Components dialog box gives you a complete picture of the PWS components available for addition or removal.

Note

The Windows 98 CD-ROM version or the downloaded version of the PWS may list "FrontPage 98 Server Extensions" (as shown in Figure 37.4) instead of "FrontPage 2000 Server Extensions". Upgrading the PWS to the FrontPage 2000 Server Extensions is covered later in this chapter.

In the Components list box, clear or check the appropriate check boxes to indicate which components you want added or removed. When you have finished, choose Next, and the setup program will modify the PWS installation. Depending on your selections, you may have to restart the computer to complete the setup.

USING THE PERSONAL WEB SERVER AND PERSONAL WEB MANAGER

The PWS and the Personal Web Manager are tightly integrated. The Manager is the main control point for the PWS and gives you access to the rest of the Personal Web Services. You'll explore these tools and services in the next part of the chapter.

USING THE MAIN WINDOW OF THE PERSONAL WEB MANAGER

The shortcut icon for the Personal Web Manager, which was installed on the desktop during the setup process, is titled Publish. Double-click this to start the Manager. Alternatively, choose Start/Programs/Internet Explorer/Personal Web Server/Personal Web Manager.

The Tip of the Day screen now opens over the main Manager window; if you don't want this to happen every time you start the Manager, clear the Show Tips at Startup check box. To step through all the Tips, choose Next for each new Tip.

When you finish with the Tips window, choose Close. Now you can use the services in the various Manager windows (see Figure 37.5). The Main window of the Manager, which is the default opening window, provides basic start/stop tools and some usage statistics that may be useful if the PWS is used as an intranet server.

Figure 37.5
The Personal Web Manager is your base for using Windows 98's Personal Web Services.

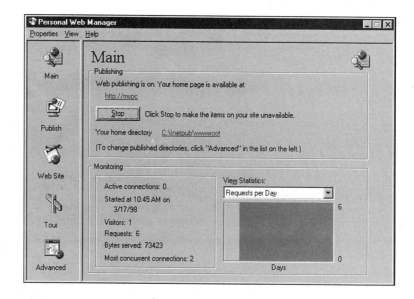

UNDERSTANDING THE HOME PAGE URL (THE WEB ADDRESS)

In the Publishing section of the Main window, you'll see the line Web Publishing Is On. Your Homepage Is Available At. Under this line, in blue, is a Web address—http:// followed by a name. This name is actually the one you assigned to your computer when you installed Windows. It is also a name that you can use to access your Web; you will remember doing this in the earlier section on testing the PWS.

For example, if you originally named your computer mypc, the blue line is http://mypc. To access the Web under this name, type **http://mypc** into the address bar of a browser and press Enter to open the page. Upper or lowercase is not important; either will work.

You'll remember that you can also use the local-machine address 127.0.0.1 to open your Web, provided that the browser is running on the machine that contains the Web. However, if the machine is connected to an intranet, the browsers on the other intranet machines can't access the Web with that address because it is local-machine only. Those other browsers can instead use the computer name—mypc, in the previous example—to open the Web. This assumes that the intranet is properly configured to recognize your machine and its name.

STARTING, STOPPING, AND PAUSING THE SERVER

To stop the server, click the Stop button. This changes the button to a Start button, which you click again to restart the server. You stop the server if you need to make the Web site unavailable to users. Note that the server icon in the system tray remains visible, though there is a red × on it when it's stopped. Stopping the server, as mentioned earlier, does not unload it from memory.

You can also pause the server. You must do this by right-clicking the server icon in the system tray (the Manager does not have to be open). This opens a popup menu with four choices: Start, Stop, Pause, or Continue. Left-click the one you want.

The functional difference between Stop and Pause is this: If someone tries to access the server when it is stopped, the server simply does not respond, and the person will eventually get a browser message that it was not possible to connect to the server. If the service is paused, the person's browser will get a message that says "The System Cannot Find the File Specified." This lets him or her know that at least the Web site exists.

PART
VII

CH
37

Tip #171	If you choose Pause, and if the Personal Web Manager window is open, the Start button changes to a Continue button.

USING VIEW STATISTICS AND MONITORING

You can use the View Statistics list box to show requests per day or hour or visitors per day or hour. The Monitoring box also shows other server performance information:

- The Active Connections entry shows how many connections are transferring data to or from the server at the moment.

- The Started At entry shows when the server was last started, that is, at the boot time of the computer (not when the Start button was last pressed).

- The Visitors entry shows how many unique addresses have connected to the server since it last started.

- The Requests entry shows how many requests were received since the server last started.

- The Bytes Served entry tells how many bytes of information were sent out since the server last started.

- The Most Concurrent Connections entry shows the maximum of simultaneous connections the server handled since it was last started.

TAKING THE PERSONAL WEB SERVICES TOUR

The Manager has a short but useful tour built into it. Click the Tour icon in the left pane of the Manager window to view this introduction to the Personal Web Services that are built around the PWS.

USING THE WEB SITE SERVICE

The first time you choose the Web Site service, the Home Page Wizard opens (see Figure 37.6). You need to run this Wizard before you can use the Publishing Wizard, which is started when you click the Publish icon.

Note

The Home Page Wizard is not connected in any way to the Personal Web that can be created through FrontPage 2000. In other words, if you create a homepage with the PWS Wizard, this page does not automatically end up in the FrontPage 2000 Personal Web (assuming you have already created one).

Figure 37.6
You can use the Home Page Wizard to create a home page on your Personal Web Server.

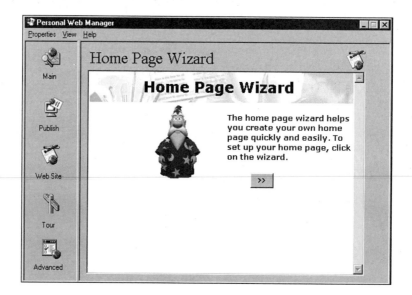

Note

If you're even moderately experienced at Web design and configuration, you may not want to use the homepage produced by the Wizard. This is perfectly possible, but may require some minor Web reconfiguration. You'll learn how to do this later in the chapter.

To create the home page, start the Wizard as described earlier, and do the following:

1. In the Home Page Wizard opening window, click the picture of the Wizard. A Security Alert opens. Assuming you have no security concerns, choose Yes. Now you can choose among three basic templates for the page appearance. Select any of them (the simplest is Looseleaf) and choose the Forward button, which is marked with a >>. To return to the previous step, choose the button marked with a <<.

2. The Security Alert dialog box shows up again. This time, mark the "In the future…" check box to prevent the alert from appearing every time you go to the next step of the Wizard. Then choose Yes to move to the next step.

3. Mark the Yes or No option buttons to specify if you want a guest book. (In the example, all available options are selected.) Choose the >> button.

4. Mark the Yes or No option buttons to specify if you want a drop box. Choose the >> button.

5. At this point, you're told you will next get to personalize your homepage information. Choose the >> button to move on.

6. The PWS Quick Setup page opens in the browser (see Figure 37.7). This is really a form that you fill out with various kinds of information.

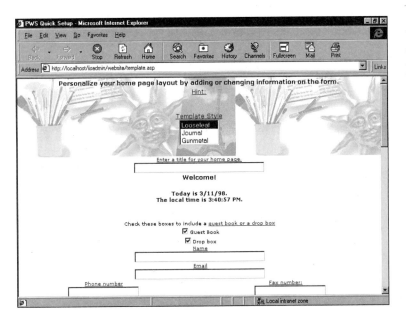

Figure 37.7
The Quick Setup Page allows you to personalize the content of your home page, and provides on-line assistance while you do this.

7. The Hint link at the top of the page leads to a complete help screen for using the setup form. There are various other links on the page that give you help for specific items. Fill in the various heading boxes and text boxes with the appropriate information, referring to the Help links for guidance. You do not have to fill in all the boxes—if you leave a box blank, the wizard will ignore that particular entry when it creates the page.

8. You can also specify what links to other Web sites will appear on the homepage. Locate the URL box and type the Web address of the site into it. Be sure not to delete the `http://` protocol designation.

9. In the Description text box, type the words that are to appear on your page as the link. For example, if the link was to a news site, the URL might read `http://www.world-news.com`, and the Description box might read World News. Then the link on your homepage would appear as World News. (If you leave the Description box blank, the link appears on the page as the full URL.) When you're finished, click the Add Link button to place the link on your homepage.

10. When you are finished creating the page, click the Enter New Changes button. The Wizard will generate the new homepage and show it to you. If you need to make changes, you can do so as described next.

EDITING AN EXISTING HOMEPAGE WITH THE WIZARD

Once the page is created, you can edit it. Open the Manager, if necessary, and click the Web Site icon. The Wizard opens again and allows you to edit your page or view your guest book and drop box (see Figure 37.8).

To edit the page, click the Edit Your Home Page Link. This opens the form you used to create the homepage. Modify the entries as needed and click the Enter New Changes button when you are done.

Figure 37.8
Editing your home-page or viewing guest book and drop box information is done through the Home Page Wizard.

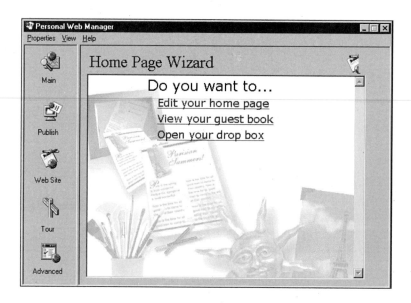

USING THE GUEST BOOK

Including the Guest Book in your homepage, either at the time you create the page or if you add the option later, places a link to the Guest Book on the page. This allows visitors to leave you a record of their visit. Visitors can also read the Guest Book entries of other visitors to the site.

When you want to look at this record, open Personal Web Manager, click the Web Site icon, and choose the link to the Guest Book. This displays a query form where you can sort and select the entries you want to see.

To look at all the entries, set the Message Date to "Less Than" and the date to today's date. (This is the default condition, so you may not have to change it). When you click Submit Query, links to all the entries are displayed (see Figure 37.9).

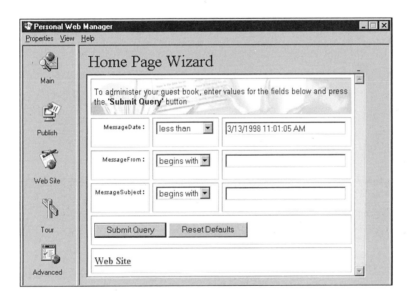

Figure 37.9
Select all or some of the Guest book entries with this Home Page Wizard form.

You can also select entries according to date, sender, and subject. Use the query form to specify the values you want and choose Submit Query. Links to the guest book entries are displayed on a scrollable form. Click the one you want to look at, and it will display. After it's displayed, you can use the >> and << buttons to move among the selected Guest Book entries.

Tip #172 | Clicking on a column header sorts the display by that header.

To delete a Guest Book entry, open the entry by clicking its link. Then, with the Guest Book entry open, click Delete. You can't restore a deleted entry, so be careful.

Once you have finished viewing the entries, you can return to the selection form by clicking the Return to the Guest Book link at the bottom of the page (scroll down if you can't see it). You can also return to the Initial Home Page Wizard screen by clicking the Web Site link at the bottom of the page.

USING THE DROP BOX

If you add the Drop Box option to your homepage at creation time or with a later edit, a visitor can leave you messages by clicking the drop box link and filling in a form. The difference from the Guest Book entries is that other visitors cannot see the message.

To view your messages, open the Personal Web Manager and then click the Web Site icon. Click the Open Your Drop Box link to display the message links. As with the Guest Book, clicking a column header sorts the display by that header. Click the links to display the message texts and use the >> and << buttons to move among the messages.

If you need to delete a message, first display it. Then, with the message open, click Delete. Deleting a message cannot be undone.

You can return to the main Drop Box list by clicking the Return to the Drop Box link at the bottom of the page (scroll down if you can't see it). You can also return to the initial Home Page Wizard screen by clicking the Web Site link at the bottom of the page.

UNDERSTANDING THE HOME DIRECTORY

Once the Home Page Wizard has run and the homepage has been created, open the Home Directory. This, as you remember, is the folder C:\Inetpub\wwwroot. You can look at it by using Windows Explorer, but if you have already opened Personal Web Manager, there's a faster way: in the Main window, simply click on the blue path name next to the words Your Home Directory. This automatically opens Windows Explorer to the Home Directory, whatever you have assigned it to be.

Tip #173

> You can also open your homepage quickly, by clicking the blue URL that sits immediately above the Stop button in the Main window.

In the Explorer window, click the wwwroot folder in the left pane, if it isn't already selected. In the right pane, the files and folders contained in wwwroot appear. If you're moderately familiar with Web files, you may wonder why you don't see DEFAULT.HTM, the default homepage of the Web, in this folder. What you do see, instead, is a file named DEFAULT.ASP.

Nevertheless, DEFAULT.ASP is the homepage you created with the Wizard. ASP stands for Active Server Pages, a Microsoft software technology that (this is very oversimplified) allows the server to combine HTML, scripts, and ActiveX components to do on-the-fly creation of interactive Web pages. However, you need to have some knowledge of programming and scripting, as well as HTML, to create Active Server Pages from scratch. That's why the Personal Web Services include a Home Page Wizard—it's so you can set up an interactive homepage, with a Guest Book and Drop Box, without knowing anything about Active Server Pages.

At some point you may want to replace the Wizard-produced ASP-type homepage with a different page. As mentioned earlier, this may require some minor Web reconfiguration, and will be dealt with later in the chapter.

Note

Some non-Microsoft servers require that the default homepage be named INDEX.HTM. If you're going to publish your site to a non-Microsoft server, check with the server administrator to see if this is the case. As well, most non-Microsoft servers don't support ASP. You should take this into consideration when working out the software design for your Web site.

PUBLISHING DOCUMENTS

Once you've created the homepage with the Home Page Wizard, you can start using the Publishing Wizard. The Publishing Wizard allows you to easily add documents to your Web and automatically adds links to them to your homepage. Other people with access to the Web—through an intranet, for example—can then access these documents. Making documents available in this way is what is meant by *publishing*. Documents do not have to be Web pages; that is, they do not have to be HTML files.

Of course, you can make documents available without using the Publishing Wizard. This will be covered later in the chapter.

UNDERSTANDING THE PUBLISHING DIRECTORY

The Publishing directory is a special folder called webpub, located at C:\Inetpub\webpub, and is created during installation of the PWS. It is a read-only directory, which means that documents placed in it cannot be modified. This protects them from being changed by curious, malicious, or meddling visitors to your site—or by you, accidentally.

When you use the Wizard to publish a document, a copy—not the original—of the document is made in the publishing directory. The wizard also maintains a record of the document's original location, so you can easily update the copy if the original is modified. Deleting a document in the publishing directory does not delete the original document. Finally, the Wizard puts a link to the document on your homepage so that people can get to it once they have your homepage open.

USING THE PUBLISHING WIZARD

To use the Wizard, start the Personal Web Manager and click the Publish icon in the sidebar. The Publishing Wizard introductory dialog box opens. Then carry out the following procedure:

1. Click the >> button to move to the next step of the Wizard. The Publishing Wizard entry form appears (see Figure 37.10).

Figure 37.10
The Publishing Wizard form is where you select the documents that will be copied into your webpub publishing directory.

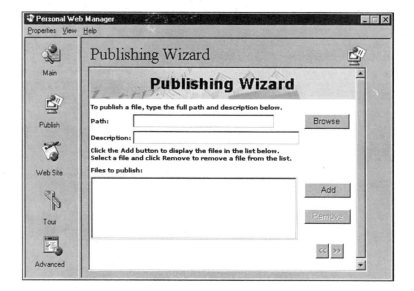

2. Assuming you know the name and full path of the document, type it into the Path text box. (If you don't know it exactly, or you prefer to use Browse, use the procedure described in the next section, "Browsing for Documents with the Publishing Wizard").

3. Type a description of the document into the Description text box. This description will appear on your page to provide information about the link.

4. Choose Add. This places the document name and description in the Files to Publish box.

5. If you have other documents to publish, repeat steps 2 through 4. If you decide not to publish a particular file after all, select its entry in the list box and click the Remove button to delete it from the list. The end result might look like that shown in Figure 37.11.

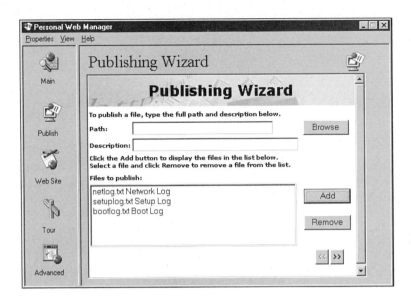

Figure 37.11
Here, three documents have been specified for publication and appear in the Files to Add list box.

6. Once you have selected all the required documents, click the >> button to move to the next step.

7. In the next screen, you are notified that the documents have been added to the webpub folder (also known as the publishing directory). If you're satisfied with what you've done, you can close the Personal Web Manager or use it to do some other task.

8. However, if you need to make changes to your work, click the << button to go back. You now get the What Do You Want to Do dialog box (see Figure 37.12).

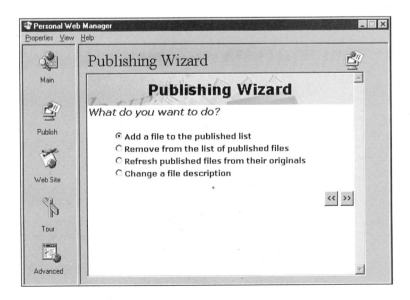

Figure 37.12
The Publishing Wizard also lets you carry out editing and document maintenance of the contents of the webpub folder.

9. To add a file to the published list, mark the top option button and click >>. This takes you to the dialog box where you add documents to the publishing directory, as in steps 2 through 7. Follow these steps and, if necessary, go through step 8 again to return to the What Do You Want to Do dialog box.

10. Assume you're back in the What Do You Want to Do dialog box. To remove a file from the publishing directory, mark the second option button and choose >>. This opens a dialog box showing all the documents in the publishing directory (see Figure 37.13).

Figure 37.13
You use this dialog box to remove documents from publication.

11. To select one document for removal, click its entry in the Published Files list box. To select several documents, hold down the CTRL key while clicking the document entries. The File and Description boxes display the filenames and description of each selected entry.

12. Choose >>. A notification dialog box appears, telling you the document was deleted.

13. If you need to make more changes, choose << to return to the What Do You Want to Do dialog box.

14. Assume you're back in the What Do You Want to Do dialog box. To refresh published files with new versions from modified originals, mark the third option button, and choose >>. As before, a dialog box opens to show all the documents in the publishing directory.

15. Using the Published Files list box, select the files you want refreshed, following the procedure in step 11. Then choose >>. The notification dialog box appears again, with the appropriate message. If you need to make more changes, choose << to return to the What Do You Want to Do dialog box.

16. Assume you're back in the What Do You Want to Do dialog box. To change a file description, mark the bottom option button and choose >>. A dialog box opens to show all the documents in the publishing directory.

17. Using the Published Files list box, select the file whose description you want to change and type the new description in the Description text box. Choose Update. The entry in the Published Files list box is updated. Choose >> to move to the confirmation dialog box. In the confirmation dialog box, you can again choose << if still more changes to the publishing directory are needed.

PART
VII

CH

37

After you run the Publishing Wizard for the first time and have placed at least one document in the publishing directory, the Wizard automatically opens with the What Do You Want to Do dialog box when you run it again. Follow the appropriate steps to add, remove, refresh, or re-describe any documents published.

Caution

If you accidentally specify an incorrect document path name, the Wizard will still add it to the list of documents to be added, removed, or refreshed. You finally get an error message, which asks you to restart the Wizard, when you choose the >> button to carry out the operation. If you've just assembled a lengthy list of documents for processing, this can be an annoyance, so be sure all filenames and pathnames are correct. Using Browse will reduce such errors. Note that this also happens if you try to add a file to the publishing directory and the file is already there. However, duplicated file descriptions, as distinct from duplicated filenames, do not cause an error.

To see the results of the Publishing Wizard, open the home page in your browser. You will see that a link called "View My Published Documents" has been added to the page. Click this link to view the content of the publishing directory. You might see something like the display in Figure 37.14.

As you've already realized, the Publishing Wizard does not care about the file formats it places in the publishing directory. A visitor will be able to view a non-HTML file, however, only if his machine has a program that is capable of displaying that kind of file.

BROWSING FOR DOCUMENTS WITH THE PUBLISHING WIZARD

You can select documents to add by using the Publishing Wizard's Browse button rather than typing the document path names. This is less prone to error, especially when the path names are long and complicated. Do the following:

1. In the Personal Web Manager, click the Publish icon to start the Wizard, and choose >>. If you don't have any documents in the publishing directory, you will be taken straight to the screen where you get to add them. If documents already exist in the publishing directory, you'll be taken to the What Do You Want to Do dialog box. In this case, mark the top option button and choose >> to move to the publishing dialog box.

2. In the publishing dialog box, click the Browse button. This opens a browser window to a special page called Server File System that shows the file structure of the C: hard drive (see Figure 37.15).

Figure 37.14
Four documents are available in this publishing directory. Note that they are not all Web pages (HTML files)—three of the four are text files.

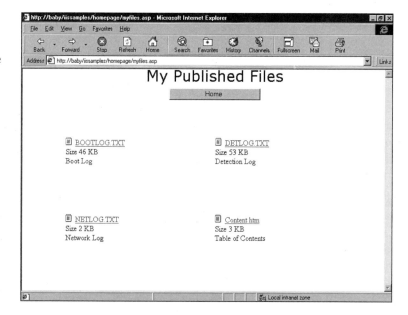

Figure 37.15
The Browse button opens a browser window where you can select files for addition to the publishing directory.

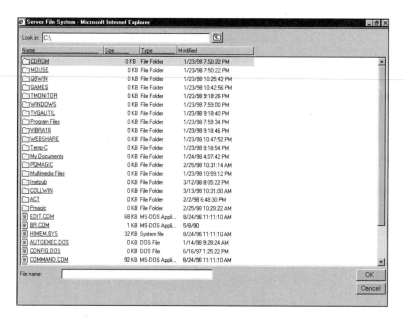

3. Navigation is similar to that used in Windows Explorer. Navigate among the folders until you have located the file you want. Click its entry so that the filename appears in the File Name box at the bottom of the browser window.

4. Choose OK. The browser closes, and the full pathname of the selected file appears in the Path text box of the Wizard. Type a description into the Description box and choose Add to place the file on the list of documents to be added.

5. Repeat steps 2–4 until all desired files have been added to the list.

6. Choose >> to place the listed documents in the publishing directory.

PART

VII

CH

37

USING WINDOWS EXPLORER TO ADD DOCUMENTS TO THE PUBLISHING DIRECTORY

You can also use Windows Explorer to copy or move an existing document from somewhere in your file system into the webpub folder. This removes any need to use the Publishing Wizard, and you also get some of the Wizard's benefits—the very act of placing a file in the webpub folder automatically inserts a link to that file into the homepage. You can then use the Wizard to edit the link description. The drawback is that you can't refresh the document by using the Wizard—if you try to, the Wizard politely informs you that this is not possible.

Note, however, that placing a document into the Home Directory of `C:\Inetpub\wwwroot` does not place a link to this document on the homepage. This automatic linking only works with the webpub publishing directory. Also, if you have a homepage other than the one produced by the Home Page Wizard, this automatic linking does not occur.

ADDING DOCUMENTS AND SUBDIRECTORIES TO THE HOME DIRECTORY

The simplest way to do this is to use Windows Explorer to create folders and subfolders within the Home Directory. Once the Web structure is set up, you can use a Web page editor to create, store, and link HTML pages and other types of documents within that structure.

In some cases, however, you may find that *Virtual Directories (page 802)* are a better method of adding content to a Web. The use of Virtual Directories will be examined later in this chapter.

USING ADVANCED SERVICES TO CONFIGURE YOUR WEB

The Advanced Service of the Personal Web Manager allows you to reconfigure your Web site according to new or changed circumstances. As mentioned earlier in this chapter, you may (for example) need to replace the homepage generated by the Wizard with a homepage of your own design. This is just one possibility of several, all of which will be examined in the next sections.

REPLACING THE DEFAULT HOMEPAGE IN THE PWS HOME DIRECTORY

Before beginning this task, let's briefly examine how homepages and Home Directories behave when accessed by a browser. When a user accesses a site, he or she usually does so by using one of two basic methods. If he or she uses a pathname that ends with a filename (such as `http://mypc/reviews/books.htm`), the named page—`books.htm`, in this example—appears in his or her browser.

However, if he or she leaves out the filename and types only the path, such as `http://mypc/reviews`, the server has to figure out what file to send him or her. Usually there is some sort of default page in the specified directory, and this is the page the server sends to the browser. The default page of the Home Directory (`http://mypc` in the example) is the one usually refereed to as the homepage of the Web. Note, however, that each subdirectory of the Home Directory can also have its default page—it's sort of a homepage for the subdirectory.

As you remember, the default homepage created by the Home Page Wizard is C:\Inetpub\wwwroot\default.asp. If you have a different homepage you want to use, such as `DEFAULT.HTM`, you can simply copy it into the `wwwroot` folder by using Windows Explorer.

Then, however, you may need to make a configuration change. Start the Personal Web Manager and click the Advanced icon. The Advanced Options dialog box opens (see Figure 37.16).

Figure 37.16
You use the Advanced Options dialog boxes to modify the configuration of your Web.

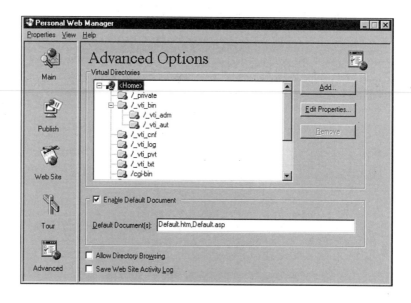

Look at the text box labeled Default Documents(s). As installed, it will have the file names `DEFAULT.HTM` and `DEFAULT.ASP` in it. The entries in this box specify what page the server will send to the browser when the browser first accesses the site.

Let's assume that the name of your PC is mypc, and therefore your Web's name is mypc. When a user types `http://mypc` into her browser, the page she first reaches is specified by the entries in the Default Document text box, and by their order. `DEFAULT.HTM` is the first entry, so the server will try to find that file in the Home Directory, `wwwroot`. Because you put the file there, the server will find it and send it to the browser.

As you likely have figured out, if `DEFAULT.HTM` were not present, the server would search for the next name in the list, and find `DEFAULT.ASP`. Since `DEFAULT.ASP` is still in the directory (unless you deleted it) the server would send that page to the browser.

You can also delete the existing `DEFAULT.ASP` and replace it with one of your own design. If you want the server to search for `DEFAULT.ASP` first and `DEFAULT.HTM` second, edit the list in the Default Documents text box to reverse the search order. You must put a comma between each filename.

If you want the server to search only for only one default filename, edit the list to show only that name.

But what happens if the document is not found? This can result from leaving a comma out of the file list, from naming errors, or because the file is not present. In that case, the server returns an error message saying Directory Listing Denied. This will also happen if you unmark the check box labeled Enable Default Document, unless Directory Browsing is allowed. Directory Browsing is discussed in the section after next.

SPECIFYING DEFAULT DOCUMENTS IN SUBDIRECTORIES OF A WEB

You can extend this principle to subdirectories. Suppose you wanted to use `SUBDEF.HTM` as the name of the default file of each subdirectory of your Web. First, name all the desired subdirectory default pages to `SUBDEF.HTM`. Then, in the Advanced Options dialog box of the Personal Web Manager, edit the list in the Default Documents text box to read `DEFAULT.HTM, SUBDEF.HTM`. When a user visits the Web and navigates to a subdirectory of it, the server will search for these two names when it opens the subdirectory. It can't find `DEFAULT.HTM` in the subdirectory, but it does find `SUBDEF.HTM`. It then sends `SUBDEF.HTM` to the browser.

ALLOWING DIRECTORY BROWSING

This is a plain-vanilla way of displaying the documents on your site; you might consider using it if you frequently add to or delete from your site content, or if you have a lot of documents in non-HTML format in the site.

To enable Directory Browsing, go to the Advanced Options dialog box of the Personal Web Manager. Unmark the Enable Default Document check box and mark the Allow Directory Browsing check box. Now, when a visitor enters the site, he or she will see a display like the one in Figure 37.17.

Figure 37.17
Directory Browsing gives a straightforward list of files and subdirectories within a directory.

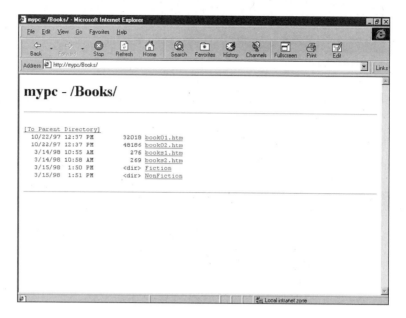

To navigate the site, the visitor clicks the various links.

MIXING DEFAULT DOCUMENTS AND DIRECTORY BROWSING

For some Webs, you may find it convenient to mark both the Enable Default Document and Allow Directory Browsing check boxes. With this arrangement, a visitor who enters a directory containing a default document will see that document. However, if you omit a default document from a particular directory and set up a link to that directory rather than to a page in it, the visitor will see a directory listing when he or she clicks the link. This means you can set up frequently-changed directories to use directory browsing, while relatively static directories can have a normal HTML default page.

CHANGING THE DEFAULT HOME DIRECTORY

Before going into this, it would be a good idea to explain briefly the usage of default documents in the context of a Web's structure. Every Web has a Home Directory that serves as the primary entry point for visitors; this is where the Web's homepage is stored. Using the earlier example of a Web name, when a visitor types the address http://mypc into his or her browser, he or she is automatically taken to the homepage DEFAULT.ASP of the C:\Inetpub\wwwroot folder (assuming a default installation).

Suppose, however, that you already have an existing Web nestled in its own carefully thought-out folder layout, and this is the Web you want people to access when they type http://mypc into their browsers. However, you don't want to endure the complications of moving all the Web's folders and files over into the C:\Inetpub\wwwroot structure.

As an example, imagine that this existing Web has a top-level folder called `C:\Reviews`, and this folder in turn has two subfolders, one called Books, and the other called Movies. You want the homepage that is stored in the Reviews folder to be the page that visitors first see when they access your Web site. Finally, assume that this homepage in the Reviews folder is named `DEFAULT.HTM`.

To change the default Home Directory to from `C:\Inetpub\wwwroot` to `C:\Reviews`, do the following:

1. Start the Personal Web Manager. Click the Advanced icon in the sidebar to open the Advanced Options dialog box.

2. Click the Home icon at the top of the directory tree. Then choose Edit Properties. The Edit Directory dialog box appears (see Figure 37.18).

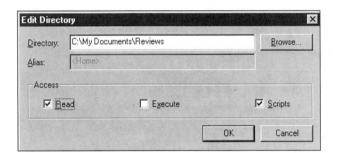

Figure 37.18
The Edit Directory dialog box allows you to change the Home Directory and modify the permissions associated with it.

3. In the Directory text box, type the pathname of the folder that is to be the new Home Directory. Alternatively, use the Browse button to open a Browse dialog box where you can select the desired folder. When you close the Browse dialog box, the pathname of the selected folder appears in the text box.

4. Set the access permissions for the directory by marking or unmarking each check box. You can turn on or off the access for Read, Execute, and Scripts. The details of the access permissions are given in the next section of this chapter.

5. Close the Edit Directory dialog box. The Home Directory has now been changed.

You'll notice that even after the change has taken place, the directory tree shown in the Virtual Directories window shows no visible difference. This is because the window is a display of a virtual directory structure, not a display of a physical directory structure like that of Windows Explorer. All three folders of the Reviews Web, in the example, are "contained" in the <Home> folder at the top of the virtual directory tree.

However, if you now open the Reviews Web in a browser, your changed homepage will appear, and its links will lead to the other pages and files of that Web. You can, by the way, still use the webpub directory, if you need to. You don't have to physically move it to the Home Directory of your new Web. This is because it's also a virtual directory of the Home Directory in this display. You'll learn more about virtual directories later in this chapter.

UNDERSTANDING DIRECTORY ACCESS PERMISSIONS

You encountered the PWS directory access permissions for the first time in the previous section. As you saw, access permissions come in three flavors: read, execute, and scripts. Each has its own characteristics, as follows.

- With Read access turned on, visitors can read or download files stored in your Home Directory and all directories stored in the Home Directory. If a directory's Read access is turned off, the browser displays an error message. If you turn off Read access for your Home Directory, Read access is also turned off for all directories physically contained in the Home Directory. If you need to set directory access permissions on a directory-by-directory basis, you have to use virtual directories, which will be discussed later in the chapter. Directories containing Web content, such as HTML pages, should have Read access. However, you should deny Read access for directories containing *Common Gateway Interface (CGI) (page 753)* applications, Internet Server Application Program Interfaces (ISAPI), and dynamic link libraries (DLLs), to prevent curious or malicious users from downloading the application files. All directories created during setup have Read access set to on by default.

- Execute access allows an application to run in its owner directory. To enhance security, don't allow Execute access for directories where you have placed Web content.

- With Scripts access turned on, a script engine can run in the directory. This occurs even without having Execute permission set. Use Script access for directories that contain ASP scripts, *Internet Database Connector (IDC) scripts (page 878)*, or other scripts. Script access is safer than Execute access because you can limit the applications that can be run in the directory. All directories created during setup have Scripts access set to on by default.

> **Caution**
>
> Even if you don't provide links to certain content in the Home Directory, in its contained folders, this content can still be viewed by visitors, provided they can discover the file and folder names. Keep only public-access material in the Home Directory and its contained folders.

UNDERSTANDING VIRTUAL DIRECTORIES

A virtual directory is a directory that is not physically contained within the Home Directory. With the PWS, this Home Directory (at default) is the folder C:\Inetpub\wwwroot. If you add virtual directories to your Web, browsers see these directories as being contained in the Home Directory, though they are not physically there.

There is a very important security point to be noted about the Home Directory. It and any subdirectories physically within it are effectively *publishing directories (page 791)*, accessible by anyone who visits your site—even if you haven't included any links to those subdirectories or to their content. This is because the access permissions applied to the Home Directory affect both it and the subdirectories physically contained within it; you can't apply permissions on a directory-by-directory basis. So, if you remove Read access from your Home Directory, nobody can view anything in it or in its subdirectories. This rather defeats the purpose of your Web! Virtual directories provide a way around this.

Also, virtual directories make your site more secure because they use an alias. An alias is a name that a browser uses to access a directory, but it is not the real pathname to the directory; hence users can't determine where your files are physically located on your PC.

Finally, virtual directories make it easier to modify or reorganize a Web site. If your Web site uses virtual directories, you can rename and move the real ones as much as you like and simply use the Personal Web Manager to re-map the connection between the virtual directories and the real ones.

PART

VII

CH

37

UNDERSTANDING THE PWS VIRTUAL DIRECTORIES

Earlier, you looked briefly at the virtual directory structure provided by the PWS. Now it's time for a more detailed examination; start the Personal Web Manager, and click the Advanced icon. The Advanced Options dialog box appears with the Virtual Directories Tree displayed (see Figure 37.19)

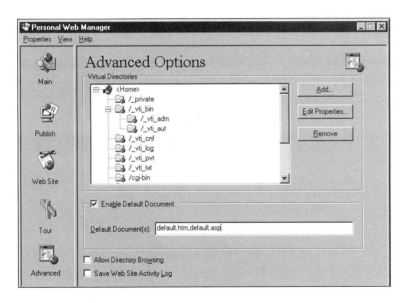

Figure 37.19
The Virtual Directories tree helps you organize the "virtual structure" of your Web.

You've probably wondered what all these virtual directories do, especially since they are present even when you change the Home Directory from the PWS default to a Home Directory of your own choosing. The essentials are as follows:

- <Home> contains all the directories that are physically contained in the physical Home Directory; in other words, the directories as they appear in Windows Explorer.

- IISADMIN, IISHELP, and IISSAMPLES refer to utility directories used by the PWS. Do not remove these virtual directories.

- SCRIPTS is a script directory used by the PWS. If you don't need it, you can remove it; however, leaving it alone will do no harm.

- WEBPUB is the special publishing directory you worked with earlier. You can remove it if you will not be publishing your documents with the PWS-generated Home Page and the Publishing Wizard. Again, leaving it there does no harm.

- msadc references some system files needed by the PWS. Do not remove this virtual directory.

- cgi-bin contains Common Gateway Interface scripts for the forms in your Web. Do not remove this virtual directory.

The list did not include the virtual directory _private, and all the directories beginning with _vti. These directories are associated with the FrontPage server extensions, and are needed if the PWS is to run pages you create with FrontPage's advanced server-dependent features.

INCLUDING WEB CONTENT AS VIRTUAL DIRECTORIES

Using virtual directories can extend the content of your Web without requiring drastic changes to your disk's file structure. However, because virtual directories can be a bit confusing at first, let's work with a concrete example. This will be the Reviews Web examined in an earlier section of this chapter, "Changing a Home Directory." This Web has a top-level folder called C:\Reviews, and this folder in turn has two subfolders, one called Books, and the other called Movies. Within each folder are pages with links to other pages in other folders.

Assume that this Web is now the Home Directory of the PWS. You can verify the identity of a Home Directory with the following procedure.

Open the Personal Web Manager and click the Advanced icon. In the Virtual Directories tree display, select the <Home> icon, and then choose Edit Properties. The Directory text box will tell you that the Home Directory is indeed C:\Reviews. As mentioned earlier, the virtual directory tree does not show physical subdirectories, such as Movies or Books. This is because they are included under the <Home> virtual directory.

Now assume you have another folder, called C:\Writing, whose content you want to include in your Web. You could, of course, physically move or copy this folder into your Web's Home Directory (C:\Reviews in our example). But it's easier to simply make it into a virtual directory. Then, if you later decide to remove the folder's content from the Web, all you need do is remove the virtual directory from the Personal Web Manager's virtual directory tree. Doing this has no effect on the real folder called Writing or on its content.

Here's what you do to create a virtual directory that references a physical directory. This example assumes that the virtual directory will be a subdirectory of the Home Directory.

1. Open the Personal Web Manager and click the Advanced icon to go to the Advanced Options dialog box.

2. Select the <Home> icon at the top of the virtual directory tree. Then choose Add to open the Add Directory dialog box (see Figure 37.20).

Figure 37.20
You use the Add Directory dialog box to add a virtual directory to the tree.

3. Type the full pathname of the physical directory (C:\Writing in our example) into the Directory text box, or use the Browse button to open the Browse dialog box and select the file. When you close the Browse dialog box, the pathname appears in the text box.

4. In the Alias text box, type an alias for the directory. This is the "fake" name browsers will use to access the subdirectory; as a rule you should make the alias different from the name of the real directory. In the example, it's Novel.

5. Mark the Read, Execute, and Scripts check boxes according to the access you want to allow.

6. Close the Add Directory dialog box. After a pause, the alias you specified (Novel, in the example) appears in the Virtual Directories window. This entry is your new virtual directory.

7. To remove a virtual directory, select it and choose Remove in the Advanced Options dialog box.

Note that a virtual directory can be added as a subdirectory of any higher virtual directory. For example, you could have created Novel as a virtual subdirectory of the /SCRIPTS virtual directory. This gives you enormous flexibility in creating Web structures.

Now you can set up links on your other pages to reference the pages in the new virtual directory. Note, however, that the links that reference the pages of a virtual directory must use the directory's alias in the URL of the link, rather than the actual name of the physical directory. For example, if the physical directory is named Writing, and the alias assigned to the virtual directory is Novel, the URLs of such links must reference Novel, not Writing.

Now, when a user goes to your Web and accesses a page in the virtual directory, the address he or she will see (in the example) is http://mypc/novel/. The existence of the Writing folder is hidden from him or her.

MANAGING LINK CHANGES WITH VIRTUAL DIRECTORIES

Using virtual directories has one very, very big advantage over using physical directories, as described next.

Suppose you have a homepage that has a dozen links to pages in a physical (not virtual) directory. The name of this physical directory is Writing. Now suppose you move the physical directory Writing and all its content to somewhere else in your PC's file structure. You then have to manually edit the URL of each link on the homepage to reflect the change in the location of Writing. If you don't, the links won't work. In addition, for each moved page, you need to construct a forwarding Web page that will send the viewer to the new location. This is in case your viewers have those older pages bookmarked; you don't want them getting "Page Not Found" messages.

All this can be a big job if a lot of links and pages are involved. But if the links are to a virtual directory, the change is simple.

> **Note**
>
> Web restructuring is one reason why the subdirectories of the Home Directory are not listed in the virtual directory tree. If you need to move the Home Directory's subdirectories around, you do so only in Windows Explorer, and don't have to repeat the operation in the virtual directory tree.

Now suppose that the physical directory is Writing and your Web uses a virtual directory to access it under the alias Novel. Suppose also that the links on the homepage reference the virtual directory Novel, instead of the physical directory Writing. Then use the following procedure:

1. Move the physical directory to wherever you like. When you've done so, go to the Advanced Options dialog box of the Personal Web Manager and use the virtual directory tree to select the name of the virtual directory (Novel, in the example).

2. Choose Edit Properties to open the Edit Directory dialog box, and use the Browse button to locate and select the new location of the physical directory (Writing, in the example).

3. When you've selected the location, close the Browse dialog box. The new pathname of the moved physical directory appears in the Directory text box. Do not change its alias.

4. Choose OK. The virtual structure of your Web is now updated. You don't need to edit links that point to Novel because they are still correct. That is, the PWS has changed the mapping of Novel to the new physical location of Writing, so the links still work.

MANAGING PERMISSIONS WITH VIRTUAL DIRECTORIES

Assume now that you create another directory called Programs as a physical subdirectory of C:\Reviews. You put some utility programs into Programs that you want visitors to be able to run. However, you don't want your visitors to be able to see the program files themselves—in other words, you don't want this directory to have Read access, just Execute access so the utility programs can run.

However, you soon realize that visitors can indeed see and even download the files containing these utilities. This is because the files are in a physical subdirectory of the Home Directory and are therefore in a readable directory, because all the subdirectories of a Home Directory must inherit the Home Directory's access permissions. What do you do?

The answer: You make the Programs directory a virtual directory and set its access permissions in that directory. Begin by using Windows Explorer to move (not copy) the Programs folder to some other place in your file structure so it's no longer a subfolder of the Reviews folder.

Then, by using the procedure you learned earlier in this chapter, create a virtual directory that references the physical directory; for security, use a different name as the alias. Then unmark the Read and Scripts check boxes and mark the Execute check box. Now the programs can be run by users, but the users will have no other access to them.

USING ACTIVITY LOGS

If you go to the Advanced Options dialog box of the Manager and mark the check box labeled Save Web Site Activity Log. The PWS then will maintain a log of who has visited your site. This can be a useful security check on site activity. The files are stored in the Windows\System folder (in NT Workstation the folder is winnt\system32) in a subfolder named W3svc1. The names begin with NC followed by year, month, and day as numbers. The logs are in NCSA log file format and are viewable in any text editor.

INSTALLING THE FRONTPAGE 2000 SERVER EXTENSIONS

The FrontPage Server 2000 Extensions allow PWS4 to support all the special Web features that FrontPage 2000 provides, such as DHTML effects. If the PWS was already installed on the host machine when FrontPage 2000 was installed, its extensions were upgraded automatically (at the user's option, however).

If the PWS is installed after FrontPage 2000 was installed, you need to manually upgrade the server extensions. Do the following:

1. Choose Start, Programs, Microsoft Office Tools, Server Extensions Administrator. This opens the Microsoft Management Console dialog box.

2. In the left pane of the dialog box, click the plus sign icon next to the entry FrontPage Server Extensions. Doing so displays a subfolder that has the name of the PWS's root Web next to it (see Figure 37.21). In the example shown, the name of the root Web is BABY; this is also the name of the host machine, of course.

Figure 37.21
You upgrade the server extensions of the root Web through the Management Console.

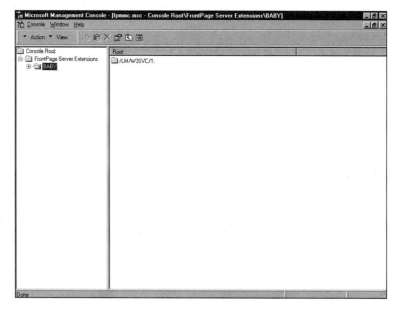

3. Click the root Web entry to select it. Then, in the menu bar, choose Action, Task, Upgrade Extensions.

4. The PWS FrontPage Extensions will be upgraded and a dialog box will be displayed to tell you this.

5. Close the Management Console dialog box. You don't need to save the console settings unless you want to.

TROUBLESHOOTING

The Personal Web Server is reasonably bullet-proof. If you're merely using it as the development server for FrontPage 2000, you'll likely be unaware of its existence most of the time. One essential thing to remember is not to accidentally delete the Root Web, which at default is located at `C:\IntePub\wwwroot`. You cannot delete the Root Web from within FrontPage, but you can do so through Windows Explorer. Deleting it takes all its subwebs with it, and these are precisely the Webs you've worked so hard on!

DESIGNERS CORNER

While you don't absolutely have to install a Web server to develop a FrontPage Web, you can likely see from this chapter that PWS 4 has a lot to recommend it if you are designing and creating webs on a Windows 9x or NT Workstation machine. You'll be able to install and use the FrontPage 2000 extensions if they are available on the target host (that is, where the Web will be when it's in actual use). Alternatively, if the target host does not run the extensions, you can remove them from the PWS and thereby make sure you don't use page elements that require these extensions.

The major drawback to the PWS is that it doesn't provide very good security, so this kind of testing will be difficult. Keep in mind that once the Web is moved to the host machine, you should test the Web's security or arrange for it to be tested if you don't have the required permissions to do so yourself.

PART

VII

CH

37

CHAPTER 38

FRONTPAGE 2000 AND MICROSOFT'S INTERNET INFORMATION SERVER (IIS)

In this chapter

by Mark Fitzpatrick

Internet Information Server (IIS) 4 is Microsoft's latest entry into the commercial Web server market. Even though Microsoft entered the Internet era a little later than most companies, no time has been wasted making Internet-enabled products that are second to none. IIS 4 is without a doubt the fastest Web server for the Windows NT Server market and is one of the most feature-rich Web servers available. If you're interested in comparing IIS 4 to other Web servers, such as Netscape Enterprise or Apache, Microsoft has published a comparison datasheet at `http://www.microsoft.com/ntserver/web/exec/compcompare/` `NSEnterprise.asp`. This comparison was originally written at the time of IIS 4's release and may not reflect the current capabilities of the new versions of Netscape Enterprise or Apache. IIS is now the second most used Web server available according to Netcraft (`http://www.netcraft.com`) reports on the current numbers and types of Web servers being deployed. Although Apache dominates the web server market with an install base of over 53% of the web servers worldwide (according to the January 1999 Netcraft survey), IIS has gained a respectable 23% of the market.

This chapter's goal is to show how FrontPage 2000 integrates with IIS 4. This chapter also helps provide some basic information on IIS 4 features, installing the Windows NT Option Pack, configuring the FrontPage 2000 server extensions, special issues encountered when using FrontPage 2000 with IIS 4, and troubleshooting common problems. In order to get a better understanding of IIS 4 and its features, first look at the evolution of the IIS 4 product line and that of its cousin, the personal Web server (PWS).

IIS 3 AND PWS 3

Because IIS 3 and its cousin the Personal Web Server 3 are the minimal requirements for the FrontPage 2000 Server Extensions we'll review a little about IIS 3. Although this chapter is geared towards IIS 4, much of the material will be applicable to IIS 3 users who haven't upgraded yet.

IIS 3 was released as an upgrade to IIS 2 and was available on the Windows NT Service Pack 3 CD-ROM as well as for download at `http://www.microsoft.com/iis/`. IIS 3 added major functionality to IIS, including *Active Server Pages (page 878)* (ASP) for server-side scripting, Index Server 1.1 for cataloging documents, and Crystal Reports for generating reports from the IIS log files. Even though IIS 3 lacked an advanced user interface and some management features found in Apache and Netscape Enterprise, it was a major step forward for Microsoft's vision of distributed computing.

Like IIS 3, PWS 3 was also an upgrade from the previous version. Unlike the upgrade to IIS 3, the upgrade files were not easily found. As it turned out, PWS 2 used the same file to upgrade to version 3 that IIS 2 used to upgrade to version 3. The upgrade was also made available as part of the FrontPage 98 CD-ROM in a file called `ASP.exe`.

IIS 4

Now that you've looked at the roots of Internet Information Server, you can focus on the newest incarnation—IIS 4. If you aren't running IIS 4, many of the issues involved in IIS 4 are present in earlier versions as well.

Microsoft released the much-awaited Windows NT 4 Option Pack in early 1998. The Windows NT Option Pack was more than just a new Web server—it was more akin to a major upgrade of IIS 4 than to some new applications. The Option Pack introduced the Microsoft Management Console (MMC), which allows for the development of *snap-ins*, which control various services and applications. The MMC offers a uniform feel to managing services such as IIS 4, Microsoft SQL Server 7, Microsoft Exchange Server 5.5, and the FrontPage 2000 server extensions. The MMC is a preview of features that are being fully incorporated into Windows 2000.

In addition to the MMC and IIS 4, the Option Pack also included Microsoft Transaction Server 2.0 for transaction processing, Microsoft Index Server 2.0 for document indexing and searching, and an improved version of Active Server Pages, called ASP 2.0.

INSTALLING IIS 4 AND THE WINDOWS NT 4 OPTION PACK

HARDWARE AND SOFTWARE REQUIREMENTS

Some hardware and software requirements must be met before installing the Option Pack. Microsoft lists the following minimum hardware requirements and their recommendations.

For Intel and compatible systems:

- Pentium 66MHz or higher; Pentium 90MHz recommended
- 32MB of memory (RAM); 64MB recommended
- 200MB of available hard-disk space

For Risc-based systems:

- System with Alpha processor
- 48MB of memory (RAM); 64MB recommended
- 200MB of available hard-disk space

The hardware just listed should be adequate if you are going to install IIS 4 on a development server that will be used only for testing purposes or on a production server that will host a number of static Web sites. However, the following minimum requirements are recommended if you are going to install IIS 4 on a production server that will be hosting a number of sites that use numerous ASP or generate database-driven pages.

For Intel-compatible systems:

- Dual 200MHz or higher Pentium Pro or Pentium II
- 128MB of memory (RAM)

For Risc-based systems:

- System with dual Alpha processor
- 128MB of memory

Dual processor configurations can greatly improve IIS 4 performance when hosting a large number of *static web sites (page 448)* but are especially useful to improve ASP performance by allowing the ASP engine to spawn more threads across additional processors. IIS 4 can also cache Web pages and applications in memory for faster access, but also requires more RAM.

In addition to the hardware requirements already mentioned, there are some software requirements. The Option Pack requires Windows NT Service Pack 3 and Internet Explorer 4.01. If you received a new copy of Windows NT 4.0 server, these should already be installed. If you received the Windows NT 4.0 Option Pack CD-ROM, Service Pack 3 and IE 4.01 are available on the CD-ROM. The Service Pack and Option Pack can be downloaded from http://www.microsoft.com/ntserver/ and IE 4.01 can be downloaded from http://www.microsoft.com/windows/ie/download/.

Since the release of the Windows NT 4.0 Option Pack, Microsoft has released Service Pack 4 for NT and IE 5. Service Pack 4 contains a number of fixes to IIS 4, but should be installed with caution. Applying Service Pack 4 can cause secondary problems to your NT Server installation depending on what additional services or applications are also running on the server. Consult the Service Pack 4 documentation and the Microsoft Knowledge Base carefully before installing to make sure that there aren't any known issues with other hardware or software that is running on your system. It also may not be possible to remove Service Pack 4 and return to your previous configuration without problems so install Service Pack 4 after careful consideration.

CHOOSING FEATURES

Before you begin installing IIS 4, you should consider which features you want to install. The following is a brief description of each of the major components included with Option Pack 4.

CERTIFICATE SERVER

Certificate Server allows for the creation and request of digital certificates. Certificate Server enables Web sites to use the secure https protocol. Secure Socket Layer (SSL) allows browsers to negotiate a secure channel to the Web server. SSL is an ideal solution for protecting items, including a user's personal information or electronic commerce.

MICROSOFT TRANSACTION SERVER 2.0

Transaction Server 2.0 is Microsoft's latest gift to transaction processing. Transaction processing enables you to guarantee that any changes an item made are returned (*rolled back*) to their original state if that item fails to attain a certain result. IIS 4.0 even allows an ASP to be treated as a transaction, enabling you to write complicated database-driven pages; this allows the database to be rolled back to its original state if a problem is encountered.

MICROSOFT INDEX SERVER 2.0

Microsoft Index Server 2.0 allows directories and Web sites to be indexed for searching. Advanced queries can be designed via the Internet Database Connector (used in Index Server 1.1) or ASP (the preferred method). In addition to indexing Web pages, Index Server can also index Microsoft Word documents and Adobe Portable Document Format (PDF) files (which are available through a plug-in from Adobe).

MICROSOFT MESSAGING QUEUE SERVER 1.0

Microsoft Messaging Queue Server (MSMQ) allows for asynchronous communication between servers or applications. For example, if you sent a message such as a sales order to an unavailable server, that message is stored until the server becomes available. This is very helpful when ensuring that information is not lost due to power outages, hardware failure, or a downed network connection.

MICROSOFT INTERNET INFORMATION SERVER 4

In addition to the Web and FTP services available with IIS 4, the Option Pack also includes a news server for running newsgroups and a new SMTP server. The SMTP server can be a critical component if you want to send email messages from your Web server. The SMTP server that comes with the Option Pack is not the same as the SMTP server that ships with older Windows NT 4.0 server CD-ROMs and contains extra functionality for use by IIS 4.

Typical configurations will include the following: IIS 4 (required), the FrontPage 98 *server extensions (page 301)*, the IIS 4 HTML-based administration, Index Server 2.0, and Microsoft Transaction Server. Some optional items include the Software Developer's Kits for the various Option Pack components, additional documentation, and multiple language support for Index Server 2.0. Because the FrontPage 2000 server extensions are not part of IIS 4, they must be installed from the FrontPage 2000 CD-ROM or downloaded and installed from http://www.microsoft.com/frontpage/. The FrontPage 2000 server extensions can then upgrade any FrontPage 98 server extensions-based webs present.

Because no software package is ever complete or bug-free, it is recommended that you check often for software updates. Updates for IIS and the Windows NT Option Pack can be found at the download section of the Microsoft Windows NT Server Web site (http://www.microsoft.com/ntserver/). Service Pack 4 contains a Quick Fix Engineering patch for the Option Pack. If the system IIS is to be installed on is not running Service

Pack 4, it is then recommended that the QFE is installed to maintain performance. Microsoft also distributes hot fixes for service packs that address issues that arise after the release of a full service pack.

ADMINISTRATING IIS 4

IIS 4 allows for both local administration through a Microsoft Management Console snap-in, and remote administration through an administrative Web site that IIS 4 generates.

LOCAL ADMINISTRATION

IIS 4 uses an MMC snap-in to provide its administrative interface. The new MMC architecture can make things much easier for a weary administrator. The new architecture allows for some customization, but also allows for the creation of custom MMC files that tailor the snap-ins you want. This allows users administrative control of IIS 4, Index Server 2.0, Transaction Server 2.0, and the FrontPage 2000 server extensions—all in the same application.

The IIS snap-in also allows for the control of IIS 4 on remote computers. The addition of remote servers is best saved for IIS servers that are located on the same network or domain in order to avoid wrangling with domain permissions. IIS also installs an HTML-based remote administration utility that is discussed in this chapter's following section.

Upon installation, IIS generates a root Web site for your server. This should appear under the computers tree with your server's name. By default this will be installed on the same partition that NT Server is installed on. You might want to change this to an alternate partition where common data is stored. The default Web site that IIS creates is bound to your drive\Inetpub\wwwroot directory, or an alternate directory path that you can assign during the IIS 4 install. The default Web site is not bound to any IP address by default and will answer to any IP address bound to the server that doesn't already have a web bound to an IP address. This means that if you have 3 IP addresses in use but 10 bound to the server, the default Web site will respond to requests for the remaining 7. To keep the default Web site from responding you can either specify an IP address for it to respond to or stop the default web altogether.

You can invoke the new Web site wizard by right-clicking the server name and selecting New, Web. The new web wizard guides you through the process of naming your web, choosing the home directory for the web, and configuring base settings for your web.

In order for the FrontPage server extensions to work properly with your new Web site, you need to configure the web in IIS to use the FrontPage server extensions. This can be done by performing the following steps in the Internet Service Manager:

1. Right-click the web name.
2. Select Properties from the drop-down list.

3. Select the Home Directory tab.

4. Select the FrontPage Web box.

This helps ensure that IIS treats this as a FrontPage web.

HTML-BASED REMOTE ADMINISTRATION

By default, IIS will install a Web site for remote administration. In order to use the HTML-based remote administration, two things must be done:

- The Web site must be set to grant access to non-local IP addresses. The following steps illustrate how to grant access to IP addresses other than those assigned to the server:

  1. In the Internet Service Manager, open the property sheet for the Administration Web site.

  2. Select the Directory Security tab.

  3. Edit the IP address and domain name restrictions.

  4. Set the default to Grant Access to All.

- The port number assigned to the Administration web must be determined. IIS installs the administration web to a random port number instead of to the default port 80. This helps prevent a rogue hacker from running across your remote administration site. The port number for the Administration web can be found by the following steps:

  1. In the Internet Service Manager, open the property sheet for the Administration Web site.

  2. Select the Web Site tab and look at the number listed for TCP port.

The HTML-based remote administration has the same features that the MMC snap-in has. The largest difference between working locally and working remotely is the loss of other features such as adding and removing users or altering file permissions. Microsoft provides the Web Administrator 2.0 for Microsoft Windows NT Server 4.0 for download at http://www.microsoft.com/ntserver/. The Web Administrator encapsulates the most commonly used administrative Windows NT features into an HTML-based system.

SPECIAL FRONTPAGE 2000 FEATURES WITH IIS 4

The FrontPage Server Extensions are very adaptive and will offer different features according to the web server that they are installed on. Some features of the FrontPage 2000 Server Extensions will be unique to an IIS 4 web server, and others will behave similarly to other web servers.

CREATING VIRTUAL SERVERS

FrontPage 2000 Web sites can be created automatically when an IIS 4 virtual server is created. To create a new virtual web in IIS 4, the New Web Wizard must be invoked via the following steps:

1. Open the IIS MMC if it's not already opened.
2. Expand the view for the computer in order to reveal all the virtual Web and FTP servers already created
3. Right-click the computer name and select New, Web.
4. Follow the directions provided by the wizard to choose a name, the basic permissions, and a home directory for the web.
5. Once the virtual Web server is created, right-click the newly created virtual server and select Properties.
6. Select the FrontPage Web check box, which is located on the Home Directory tab.
7. Press the Apply button and OK to close the Property sheet.

Once complete, it is always useful to open the new virtual web with the FrontPage 2000 client to ensure that the setup was completed properly.

SECURITY AND PERMISSIONS

The FrontPage server extensions are very adaptive and offer different capabilities for different Web servers. Knowing some of these differences can save hours of struggling for solutions. The most visible difference between IIS and other Web servers is the way IIS handles security.

Windows NT Server 4.0 thrives on security. Every file has security information saved with it—who can access the file and what can a user or group of users do with it? This is native to the Windows NT file system (NTFS). IIS uses this security information to determine who can access a file. If an IIS hosted web site is located on a partition that uses FAT then security cannot be implemented by IIS and any FrontPage security-related features will be disabled. Other Web servers use a special database of usernames and passwords to determine who can access a secured page instead of relying on NTFS permissions. This method bypasses the secure nature of Windows NT and can open a Web server and network to security problems.

Windows NT security uses the concept of users and groups. A *group* is a collection of users; for instance, the administrator is part of the Administrators group. By default, most users belong to the users group. Windows NT allows for custom groups to be created and the ability to assign a user account to more than one group. This means the Administrator account could be assigned to the Administrators group and to the Users group. IIS uses a special account called IUSR to authenticate a request for a Web page.

The Internet User (IUSR) account is created by IIS upon installation. The account is actually a combination of IUSR and the name of the server that IIS is installed on and will appear as IUSR_machinename. To make the account easier to remember, it is simply referred to as IUSR. When a browser connects to an IIS server to request a Web page, IIS first checks to see whether the IUSR account has read access to the page in question. If the IUSR account isn't listed as having read access the user will be prompted for a valid username and password.

The FrontPage server extensions do a very good job of checking files for the proper permissions. The server extensions compare the settings for a web that were made in FrontPage 2000 to those that are on each file. The server extensions correct any errors they find and also offer the opportunity to constrict the permissions list for each file as tightly as possible. Permissions can be set through the Windows Explorer, but this can cause problems because FrontPage uses certain files that require special permission settings. Altering permissions through Windows Explorer can lead to odd behavior in FrontPage webs or in IIS itself. Microsoft publishes a list of these special security settings as part of the FrontPage Server Extensions Resource Kit (SERK), which is available at http://www.microsoft.com/frontpage/wpp/serk/.

When FrontPage applies restrictions on permissions, it does them for an entire web. Sometimes there is a need to restrict a small number of pages. This can be done via the Windows Explorer, but can lead to previously mentioned problems. The best way to handle these cases is to create a *subweb (page 971)* that holds all pages that have the same security requirements. This prevents the sloppy task of manually editing permissions for each file and the trouble of attempting to maintain the permissions for any period of time.

DATABASE CONNECTIVITY

ASP is an integral part of IIS 4 and allows web developers to write Web pages that contain both static elements and server-side code. This new paradigm allows for greater flexibility and decreases the amount of time needed to develop web applications and dynamic Web pages. FrontPage 2000 leverages the power of ASP to create dynamic, data-driven Web pages.

Because ASP is such an integral part of IIS 4, little needs to be done to ensure the proper functionality of FrontPage's database features. The database connectivity does require ODBC to be installed as well as Microsoft's newest database access technology, ActiveX Data Objects (ADO). Both of these should be installed by IIS 4 if not already available on the server. The latest versions of ADO can be found at http://www.microsoft.com/data/ado.

For more information about integrating FrontPage 2000 with databases, refer to Part VII of this book.

PART

VII

CH

38

USER REGISTRATION FORMS

There is one feature in FrontPage 2000 that does not work with IIS: the User Registration Form (also known as a Registration Web or Bot). The User Registration form was part of the earliest versions of FrontPage when most Web servers were running UNIX and before IIS was widely used.

The User Registration form allows authors to create an area where users enter basic information about themselves in order to gain access to a web or directory. The User Registration form was often incorrectly used as a method of securing access to Web pages. The form simply requires a user to enter information about himself and then grants the user access to the pages. Because there is no way to verify this information, anyone can gain access to pages protected in this manner whether the information is truthful or not. This sort of protection violates the strong Windows NT and IIS security models.

Since IIS does not allow the User Registration form, it is possible to duplicate the effects by creating a simple form that gathers information about a user and designing a custom confirmation form. The Confirmation form can contain links to the file or files that require some form of user registration. While not a solution, this can be used as a simple replacement in lieu of other, more complicated custom solutions such as creating individual Windows NT user accounts for every user.

Creating users for a FrontPage Web site has a major disadvantage in the form of a client license. Things could get costly if you have to create a number of user accounts for FrontPage Web sites. Each username requires a distinct Client Access License (CAL) for Windows NT. Microsoft has moved to a per-seat licensing scheme, which now means that every user must have her own CAL. Previously, licensing was determined by concurrent connections to the server, which meant you could have 100 users and only pay for 10 connected at any given time. CALs can be very expensive. In addition to monetary price, having a large number of users in the Security Accounts Manager (SAM) can create a performance bottleneck.

Other solutions for restricting access to individual Web pages are available. The most common solution involves using IIS 4's Active Server Pages to query a database of usernames and passwords when a page is visited to determine whether a user is allowed access to a page or group of pages. This can work well for simple sites, but the issues become more involved for complex sites.

Another solution is to use a custom component, such as an ActiveX server control, to handle user authentication. While these components are not likely to be free, they can save a lot of time in development. Additional information on both solutions can be found at http://www.activeserverpages.com and http://www.15seconds.com.

For full-fledged membership systems, Microsoft offers Microsoft Site Server, a collection of Internet and intranet applications designed to enhance content and publishing. Site Server has built-in Personalization and Membership (P&M), which integrates directly with IIS 4; it also has Active Server Pages and is usable with FrontPage 2000. The P&M allows for member authentication without using Windows NT CALs and also tracks how a visitor uses a Web site in order to offer personalized content based on his usage patterns and preferences.

TROUBLESHOOTING AND COMMON PROBLEMS

Every software application or service has its own set of issues and IIS 4 is no exception to the rule. Some of these directly effect how FrontPage can operate in conjunction with IIS 4. There are some problems that can occur just because of the way IIS is set to operate, but they can be easily corrected. Understanding some of the common problems before setting up FrontPage webs can be a great boon to any system administrator. When setting up IIS 4 and FrontPage for the first time, it is always advisable to test several configurations before rolling a system into a production environment. If the server will be hosting multiple domains, testing all features under several dummy domains is extremely useful before going live—especially for an ISP who is entering the FrontPage hosting market for the first time.

PART

VII

CH

38

Most issues that occur with IIS fall into two categories: FrontPage server extension configuration issues on IIS and problems with the way IIS operates. There is no clear line between the two, but it helps to categorize problems when truly trying to understand where they are coming from. An application might behave oddly through no fault of its own because it often relies on other resources. The same can be said of using FrontPage on IIS. System administrators can waste valuable resources tracking down what they think is an error in FrontPage, only to find that it is an error with IIS or their security settings. The following problems are common problems seen with IIS 4 since its beta days. Most of the same problems can be found in IIS 3 and may be present in the upcoming IIS 5.

SEARCH PROBLEMS

One of the most common and most visible problems involves the FrontPage search engine. Normally, the FrontPage server extensions use a WAIS-based search utility, which builds a searchable text index of the web. There can be some problems when Microsoft Index Server is installed on the Web server also, which is the default setting for the Option Pack installation. In previous server extensions versions, Index Server took over as the default search mechanism. The FrontPage 2000 server extensions should remain the default search mechanism, but there may be times when an error occurs and Index Server could take control.

The FrontPage 2000 server extensions contain a configuration variable called `NoIndexServer`. This should be set to `0` by default, which allows the FrontPage server extensions to retain control of the search functions. If this variable is set to `1`, Index Server becomes the default search engine. This configuration variable can be set globally and by each virtual server, but cannot be a subweb.

The `NoIndexServer` configuration variable can be set globally in the following Registry key:

`HKLM\Software\Microsoft\Shared Tools\Web Server Extensions\All Ports`

It can also be set by individual virtual server:

`HKLM\Software\Microsoft\Shared Tools\Web Server Extensions\Ports\Port` *hostname:nnn*

hostname is the name given to the virtual server and *nnn* is the port number for the virtual server (the default is 80). In order to set a virtual web to be indexed by Index Server, the Index This Directory check box on the Home Directory tab for the individual Virtual Server must be checked.

There are some items that should be known about using Index Server. Since Index Server works as a background service, it indexes files at regular intervals. This can result in the search index not always reflecting the most current web content. In addition to normal HTML pages, Index Server can also index Office documents and Adobe PDF documents (using a plug-in available from Adobe's Web site at `http://www.adobe.com`).

Other than the capability to use Index Server as a search engine, the FrontPage 2000 server extensions search feature will work the same on IIS as it will on most other systems. If a large number of sites will be set up not to use Index Server, it may be wise to recommend that users not edit their webs directly on the server and that they work locally and then publish to the server. When FrontPage saves a page, it scans the page and adds references to the text search indexes. This can cause an unnecessary performance lag on the server and slow response for other FrontPage clients and Web site visitors.

AUTHENTICATION AND SECURITY

The most common problems that occur with IIS and the FrontPage server extensions are due to the way IIS validates users and NTFS permission settings. As mentioned previously, IIS and FrontPage rely on the Access Control Lists that are stored with each file on an NTFS partition. If the web site is installed on a FAT partition then IIS cannot implement any security so it is very important to host virtual servers on an NTFS partition.

By default, IIS sets each web to use NTLM authentication and to allow anonymous users. NTLM authentication is used by Windows NT and Windows 9x networks to authenticate users on a Windows NT domain. This authentication scheme is supported by Internet Explorer, but not by Netscape Navigator or Communicator. In order to support Netscape users, IIS also offers basic authentication. Basic authentication sends passwords unencrypted, clear text.

In a situation where NTLM authentication is enabled but basic authentication is not, Netscape users are repeatedly asked for a username and password. This continues until the Windows NT Server rejects any further attempts to log on as a security precaution against outside attacks. Follow these steps to enable basic authentication:

1. Open the IIS 4 Internet Service Manager.
2. Right-click the appropriate Web site and select Properties.

3. Select the Directory Security tab.

4. Press the Edit button (under the Anonymous Access and Authentication Control).

This allows Netscape users to authenticate their usernames and passwords properly. Internet Explorer always tries to use the most secure level of authentication possible. This allows both NTLM and basic authentication to be enabled, which in turn allows for the best security possible for both sets of users.

At least one authentication method must be enabled when altering the authentication methods for a Web server. When FrontPage users connect to a server enabled with the FrontPage server extensions, the FrontPage client expects to be prompted for a username and password. When there is no request, FrontPage reports a user to the error, detailing that no authentication header was sent to the server. Enabling NTLM authentication allows FrontPage to connect to the server with little fear of the client password being intercepted and decoded.

NTFS FILE PERMISSIONS

In addition to the various problems that can occur through user authentication, problems can also stem from the permission settings on individual files and directories.

Errors in permissions usually appear as a nonfunctional server component. This most commonly occurs with forms; forms are required to post data to a server extension DLL and then save the information to a file. These errors usually appear as an inability to process the request or an error stating that the user doesn't have the permissions required to access the file.

The FrontPage server extension MMC provides the capability to check the state of the server extensions and correct any problems that it finds. Check server extensions task in the FrontPage MMC will scan for any errors in the configuration of the server extensions. In addition to scanning for configuration errors, the Check server extensions can also constrict the webs' permissions as tightly as possible. Allowing the permissions to be tightened forces FrontPage to verify that the basic permissions requirements are met and that all users and groups have the proper level of access. During this check, FrontPage loosens permissions that are given too little access.

Unfortunately, the server extension check can still miss improperly configured permissions. Microsoft has a published list of the minimum permissions requirements for FrontPage as part of the SERK. The most current version of the SERK is available online at `http://officeupdate.microsoft.com/frontpage/wpp/serk/`. It is best to consult the SERK before manually altering any file permissions. Understanding the minimal permission requirements and keeping track of what files the permissions have manually altered can save hours of trouble verifying permission settings.

The topic of security and permissions leads to one last topic: the Everyone group. The Everyone group is special in that users aren't specifically assigned to it. The Everyone

PART

VII

CH

38

group means just that—every user listed in the domain or Web server is included in this group. Giving the Everyone group permissions to files and directories allows other FrontPage users the ability to edit webs that they wouldn't normally have permissions to. This could also include allowing anonymous IUSR account permission to edit a web.

To prevent this, it is recommended that the Everyone group be deleted from the list of authorized groups immediately upon creating a new virtual web. This can be done through the Tools, Security menu in the FrontPage 2000 client. Since any new subwebs or directories created inherit their permissions from the virtual web parent, this should only need to be done once. New directories and files inherit their permissions from their parent directory. By default, the Everyone group has full access to all directories and files. Unless the Everyone group is removed from a directory, all files and directories that inherit from it will also grant the Everyone group full access—so be careful to remove it from the permissions list as soon as possible.

TROUBLESHOOTING IIS 4 AND THE FRONTPAGE 2000 SERVER EXTENSIONS

Because of the wide range of technologies used in both IIS and FrontPage it can be difficult to narrow down the cause of certain problems. There are a number of common problems that occur with FrontPage 2000 and IIS 4. Many of these problems we have already discussed as they are integrally tied into how IIS 4 works with Windows NT.

SECURITY PROBLEMS

As we've discussed before, IIS and FrontPage 2000 use NTFS permissions to determine who has security rights to a particular file. To even of the most experienced administrators, file permissions and minimum security rights can be scary topics. Attempting to manually adjust permissions should be considered a last resort since even the slightest error could leave your web server vulnerable or non-functional.

When looking at security related problems it often helps to look at where security begins on your network. Some networks have Proxy Servers or Firewalls as their first line of defense. If FrontPage 2000 users outside of a network with a Proxy Server or Firewall are having trouble connecting to the server from a remote site, make sure that the FrontPage 200 clients have the proper proxy settings. Many Proxy Servers will also block NTLM password authentication, which can result in a FrontPage 2000 client or Internet Explorer user from being granted access to a FrontPage web or other restricted area. Disabling NTLM Authentication and enabling Basic Authentication can often solve this type of problem.

Another common problem involves authenticating users against a Domain Controller. IIS 4 offers the ability to specify a base domain to authenticate users against. A simple typo can cause IIS to search for a non-existent domain controller when attempting to authenticate users. If IIS 4 is installed on a Primary Domain Controller then care needs to be taken regarding how the user accounts are set up. A Primary Domain Controller (PDC) is an odd beast because, by design, users don't log on to it directly. Accounts in the Administrator group are usually the exception as they have to be able to log on to the PDC directly. This behavior is usually noticed when administrators can open FrontPage 2000 webs on the server but non-administrators cannot. This problem can usually be overcome by granting a FrontPage 2000 user's account the ability to "log on locally" through the User Rights in the User Manager for Domains.

Lastly, if all the settings with IIS and the FP Server Extensions seem correct, it may be time to adjust the file and directory permissions manually. Before adjusting any permissions, it is always advisable to make a copy of the entire directory tree that you will be working on. This way if something goes wrong a backup is readily available with all the original security information intact.

Once a copy of the directory structure has been made the real work can begin. In most cases, when FrontPage 2000 reports a problem opening a web or a file on an IIS web server this is due to incorrect settings on one or more files used by the FrontPage Server Extensions. Microsoft publishes a set of minimum security requirements for key files as part of the FrontPage 2000 Server Extensions Resource Kit (SERK). The most current version of the SERK is available at `http://officeupdate.microsoft.com/frontpage/wpp/serk/`. Often, by comparing the minimum permissions requirements to those of the troubled web, the problem will become apparent.

There are times, however, where the security problem doesn't expose itself even with the most careful examination. Before using the following steps make sure that the directory tree of the problem virtual server has been completely backed up with all its security information intact. The goal of the following steps is to return the permissions on the web server to it's simplest and broadest form to allow any errors to be removed before the permissions are re-tightened.

1. Uninstall the Server Extensions from the troubled virtual server. The Extensions do not need to be uninstalled or removed from any virtual server other than the one that presents problems. If more than one virtual server is presenting problems it is still best to handle them one at a time.

2. Using Windows Explorer, select the primary directory of the virtual server and bring up its property sheet. Open the permissions dialog by clicking on the permissions button of the security page. Add the Everyone Group with Full Access to the directory and remove all other accounts. When applying this change, make sure that the Replace Permissions on Subdirectories box is checked so that the permissions are inherited by the rest of the web.

   Once the permissions have been set, re-install the FrontPage 2000 Server Extensions to the Virtual Server.

3. With the FrontPage 2000 client, open the root web of the virtual server.

4. Select Tools, Security in the FrontPage 2000 client to bring up the security dialog. Add at least one account with Administrate, Author, and Browse access to the root Web; remove the Everyone Group from the list of authorized groups; apply the changes.

5. In the FrontPage Server Extensions Administrator right click on the virtual server and select Tasks, Check and Fix to have the server verify that all files now have the correct permissions.

6. Once the permission changes are applied, the web site should be limited to registered users only. Select the Everyone has Browse Access radio button and apply the changes.

7. It is advisable to repeat step 6 to guarantee that the changes are made correctly.

Most of the subwebs should inherit these security settings, but some may need to be set manually by repeating steps 5 through 8 on each subweb that has been set not to inherit permissions from the root web. Once the root web and subwebs have the proper minimum permission settings then additional users can be granted author or administrator access. If, at some point, something goes wrong simply copy the backup of the web site over the original to restore the permission settings and try again.

ACTIVE SERVER PAGES ERRORS

ASP often presents some very odd problems to administrators new to IIS and FrontPage. ASP makes use of pre-built components often known as ActiveX Server Controls, that are based on Microsoft's COM component architecture. FrontPage's database features use the Active Data Object (ADO) controls, which are installed with IIS 4 to ODBC-compliant databases. Most FrontPage 2000 users who will receive an ASP error will be using the database features.

Like domain names, COM objects have user-friendly names that mask complicated registration numbers. One of the most common errors from ASP reports of the failure to create an object such as an `ADODB.Connection` or an `ADODB.RecordSet`. Sometimes, the Registry can lose track of the common names for an object. This will lead to errors stating `Server.CreateObject(objectname) failed`. When this happens the `.dll` that contains this object must be tracked down and re-registered using `regsvr32.exe`. In the case of ADO objects such as the `Connection` or `RecordSet` objects, the `.dll` that must be registered is the `msado15.dll`. This is installed on the same partition as NT and is located in the `Program Files\Common Files\System\ado` directory. To re-register any COM object, open an MS-DOS command prompt and run the `regsvr32.exe` program found in the `winnt\system32` directory.

Another common ASP error occurs when insufficient data is provided. A common example of this mistake is having a form that searches a database. If one of the required form fields is left blank this can cause the query to fail and result in an error. If a field is required, use FrontPage Form Validation to guarantee that the form field is filled. If a form field is not filled in an empty string is passed instead which will cause many database queries to fail.

DESIGNERS CORNER

When installing IIS or any web server for the first time it is a good policy to plan your system ahead of time. Determining how your server will be set up can save time further down the road.

PLANNING YOUR USERS

It is good to have a policy laid out as to how you will handle requests for new users or granting users access to a FrontPage Extended web or virtual server. Creating user groups for FrontPage administrators can help keep confusion down when looking through a list of users in a Domain. User Groups help when you need to determine who an account belongs to and as well as helping to avoid security problems.

PLANNING YOUR STORAGE

There are several considerations to make when deciding where to actually store the physical copy of your web site(s). If the server has two or more hard drives, using RAID to mirror or stripe your web site data might be very useful. In a simple two drive configuration, mirroring your web sites on each drive can give a certain peace of mind to a careful administrator. Employers and clients, while they understand that mechanical failures do happen, do not take kindly to any loss of data. Even with a mirrored system, errors can happen as most mirrored systems run off the same SCSI controller. If the SCSI controller begins performing oddly, errors can be written to both drives which will damage the data or render them completely useless. Keeping to a stringent backup policy will help lessen the impact of a massive failure.

In addition to hardware concerns, there are also simpler administrative concerns. Planning a logical structure to your web sites can save many administrative headaches down the road. A logical structure such as `d:\web sites\company1\website1.companyname.com` can help quickly identify a site, and keep the directory tree clean and simple.

ACCESSING DATABASE DATA WITH FRONTPAGE

CHAPTER 39

USING DATABASES WITH FRONTPAGE 2000

In this chapter

by John J. Kottler

WEB DATABASES

Since the inception of the Internet, we have seen the capabilities of this worldwide network grow from basic text pages to elaborate marketing-based Web sites, to online shopping centers. In each case, the technological capabilities behind the Internet have increased vastly to accommodate each new type of Web site. Most recently, many portions of Web sites have been controlled by databases. With databases, site visitors can query the most recent information from a site as well as contribute new information. For instance, the most elaborate shopping sites on the Web require database connections in order to query current stock for products as well as allow the user to order a specific item.

As you probably can guess, databases are everywhere that computers exist. Computer systems need to store vast amounts of information for purchase orders, product inventory, personal contact information, and just about anything else you can imagine. A *database management system (DBMS)* is required in order to store large quantities of data. With a database management system, large quantities of information can be stored on a single computer or even distributed across multiple systems. It is up to the database management system to understand how to best store information and optimize that storage. By optimizing the storage of data, a DBMS can quickly and easily perform searches on information within the database and return accurate results.

Between the high demand for databases and database applications within corporations and the increasing popularity of the Internet, there has been a phenomenal need for Internet-based database systems over the past year. However, being able to easily tie information from a database into a Web site has typically required large amounts of custom programming using a variety of tools. Many complex Web sites on the Internet today require more than one tool to manage. For instance, one tool may be used to edit the HTML content for a site, while another application language is used to write scripts or programs on the Internet Web server, and yet additional software is required to manage data within the database on the system. You can clearly see that managing a Web site with database connectivity can be a daunting task. Fortunately, Microsoft is attempting to make managing database content easier with FrontPage 2000.

WHERE TO USE DATABASES

You can probably guess the appropriate places in which to use databases on a Web site. Databases are typically used in one of the following areas, although these are certainly not the only areas:

- Real-time systems—Every user in the Information Age expects to have the most up-to-date information at her fingertips. With real-time systems, users can connect to databases that house the most current information. Examples include an inventory system that keeps track of products and the stock on-hand and a database of news content to be published on the Web.

- Connecting to legacy systems—Large corporations still use mainframes and other legacy systems that require special connectivity. In some cases, Web sites simply tie into the legacy data stores instead of rewriting all of these older applications as new client/server systems.

- Data processing—As people have used the Internet for more information gathering, users have decided that they want more interactive Web sites. Instead of simply viewing static Web site data, they want to control what information is displayed via accurate searches. In some cases, they are expecting to enter information into the Web-based system to accomplish a particular task, such as purchasing a product on-line.

You can accomplish several things by making these types of systems available online: your site's capabilities; give visitors more control over what they see as well as the timeliness in which they see it; and give them the ability to update pertinent information. However, there are many advantages and disadvantages that must be considered before implementing database information on a site.

Advantages of Databases

As you have already seen, databases are important for holding large volumes of information and for making the data available to visitors of a site. In fact, this is their specialty and database management software handles data better than any other type of application can. If database systems are used for Web sites, there are many advantages that can be exploited immediately:

- Information stores—Without an adequate database management program such as Oracle, SQL Server, or Access, a developer would be required to create his own format for storing data. On systems this typically requires creating text-based files that contain rows of information pertaining to each database record. Databases allow developers to quickly create a structure for database information and invoke simple language commands to populate the database store or retrieve data from it. There is no need to invent a storage system each time a new Web site is developed.

- Large storage support—Database management software is designed to scale in order to handle very large volumes of information, such as thousands—or even millions—of records. To create a system that accommodates this volume of information from scratch would require tremendous resources and skill. It typically requires implementing numerous complex computer algorithms and for efficiency requires low-level support in some cases.

- Quick indexing/searching—Storing information within a database is only part of the problem. The second half is being able to quickly and easily extract data from the system and display it for the viewer. Many databases index the data within them in order to make the searching component faster. Again, this typically utilizes algorithms in computer science that can be duplicated, but not easily or efficiently.

Note

It is important to note the difference between database searching and site searching. With databases, a search is typically an instruction to the database to retrieve data that meets particular criteria. Site searches are usually classified as search engines for the Web site. Though they search against HTML pages, the actual technology is similar to a database. The Search Engine parses through all pages on the site and stores relevant words into a database directory for future searches. This is why search engines on the site are able to be retrieved quickly, no matter how many pages exist on the site.

- Structured Query Language (SQL)—Most, if not all, database management systems on the market today support this English-like syntax for performing commands on the database. This language supports commands for extracting information from a database, grouping those results, deleting information within the database, and inserting new information, in addition to a plethora of additional capabilities. It's a relatively simple language to learn, and more importantly it is a standard in the industry.

- Concurrent user support—Practically every database system on the market supports some form of information locking so that multiple people can use the database and update content within it. Again, this is a feature that comes with the management system and the developer does not need to write specific application code to coordinate multiple users.

DISADVANTAGES OF DATABASES

If you read the preceding section, it appears that databases are the panacea for solving most of the problems that computers face for information storage. In all, databases are very efficient and have proven themselves as a viable computer technology for several decades now. There are, however, some disadvantages that need to be considered, particularly when publishing information on the Web. In particular, there is a notion that database engines are required on Web servers in order to provide instant information updates to a site. The following points help outline why databases are not always the most optimal approach for all Web content:

- Site searching versus database searching—You will have to consider searching options if you create standard HTML pages with content across the site as well as attach a database system. More often than not, you will want your site viewers to be able to search the site for any information they desire. To accurately represent the entire site, you need to search the HTML information as well as the database contents. This usually requires two separate searches that must appear as a single search. In addition, database search capabilities do not typically match Web search engines capabilities.

- Scalability—Although database servers are designed to handle millions of records of information and hundreds of users working on the database at once, they are not very well suited for handling millions of hits per day. In the world of the Web, where this type of access is common, static pages of information can be cached and displayed more efficiently than dynamic content from databases. In addition, each hit to the database management system typically opens its own communication channel. If thousands of these occur at once, the server machine can easily be inundated by requests.

- Security—Security itself is a high concern on the Internet; people want to keep private their individual information, such as credit card numbers. Likewise, corporations that deal on the Internet want to keep their internal information confidential. Therefore, connecting a database to the outside world of the Internet can open a potential security risk in that a hacker could access or modify information in a database. Although many database vendors have security options implemented in some format, the best type of security is creating a separate instance of the database information for the Internet that is not directly connected to a corporation. That way if information is destroyed or viewed illegally, it is a remote subset of the database that has confidential information parsed out of it.

- Expense—Costs are incurred when a database system is acquired and set up. They also require ongoing maintenance and support, which is a hidden expense.

FRONTPAGE AND DATABASES

As you can see, there are many issues to consider before implementing databases as a final solution to all of your Web problems. Now that we have reviewed the topic of database technology and its advantages and disadvantages, we will take a look at how to utilize databases and maintain their information within the realm of FrontPage 2000.

FrontPage 2000 has enhanced database capabilities that were not found in previous versions. Microsoft has truly realized that many people do want to provide real-time information, particularly in an intranet environment as corporate Information Technology departments begin migrating current internal database applications to the internal web. Even if you have limited experience with database technologies, you can still quickly implement a Web page with database results or with forms that post information to a database. FrontPage 2000 supports databases via many methods, including its database results wizard, data form entry, database creation, and Access 2000 data access pages.

In order to illustrate database connectivity more effectively, you examine within this chapter (and the next several) a typical example Web site. You build a computer shopping Web site that allows the viewer to examine which products are in stock as well as their brief description and price. The viewer will also be able to order products by filling out information on an order form, which is then routed to a database.

DATABASE RESULTS WIZARD

One of the more common functions that a Web page developer wants is the ability to include information from a database into the current page. This functionality has been built in to FrontPage 2000 as a wizard, which will certainly increase non-developers' ability to include complex database results. This is a good situation for both developers and basic Web page authors. It gives the power of complex database results to the author, which reduces cycle time in developing Web pages. It also frees the developer to create more complex solutions on the server rather than constantly tweaking database results.

The Database Results Wizard in FrontPage 2000 supports a plethora of database formats including Microsoft Access, Microsoft SQL Server, and Oracle. It also supports additional database software and legacy systems via *ODBC (Open Database Connectivity) (page 836)* drivers that link between common database functions exposed by FrontPage and equivalent system-specific results on the destination system. To begin the Database Results Wizard, you must be working on a page within FrontPage 2000. Because of the context-sensitive menus within FrontPage, the option to insert database results will not appear on the menu until you either create a new page or edit an existing one.

Note

> To embed database results within a page, you must be editing the HTML document within a FrontPage web. If you are editing a Web page and the Database Results Wizard is unavailable, it is probably because the document you are editing is not associated with a FrontPage web. Database results via the wizard require that the FrontPage extensions must be installed on the server for your site.

Once you have an HTML page to work with, you can invoke the Database Results Wizard by selecting Insert, Database, Results from the menus within the FrontPage Editor. Figure 39.1 illustrates the resulting dialog box that appears after making this menu choice.

Figure 39.1
When inserting database information within FrontPage, the Database Results Wizard begins by prompting for a database to use.

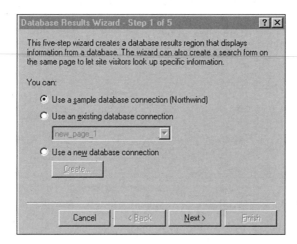

The resulting window prompts for a database connection. There are three choices to select from:

- Use a sample database connection (Northwind)—As the title implies, this choice allows you to connect directly to the Northwind company database. This is a sample database that is included with FrontPage 2000 to help illustrate database connectivity. It is often used as a tutorial database as an example of production data. You should only need this database for testing connectivity or experimenting with FrontPage.

- Use an existing database connection—If you have already added database connections to the current FrontPage web via other pages in the site, you can choose to link to those databases again. If, for instance, in your CompuShop database you use one Web page to display monitors and another page to display notebook computers. When you create the second page you can reuse the database connection information that was established from the first page.

- Use a new database connection—No matter what database is available on the network, you must create a connection to it so that FrontPage can access it. If a database connection is not previously established in your Web site, you must create that new logical connection at this point. It is important to notice, however, that this option allows you to neither create the actual database nor enter data into it.

The first two options of this window allow you to connect to some previously established database connection. These are, by far, this window's simplest options. In either case, you choose a database connection and instruct FrontPage which information to display from that database as well as any additional formatting information. In the event that you choose to create a new database connection, you still get to this same point of the Database Results Wizard—but you are first asked some additional information for actually creating the database. Start the database wizard discussion by creating a new database connection.

MAKING THE CONNECTION

Figure 39.2 depicts the window that appears after you click the Create button in the database wizard's first step. This window is the same window you can access via Tools, Web Settings from the FrontPage Editor. In this case, however, the Database tab is highlighted by default.

Within this window you can either add a new database connection, modify a previous connection's information, remove a connection from the FrontPage web, or simply verify that the connection still functions properly. In this example you add a new connection by clicking the Add button.

Figure 39.2
When creating a new database connection, you are given the chance to configure all the database connections associated with your Web site.

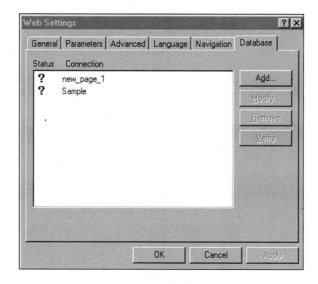

Figure 39.3
After deciding to add a new connection, FrontPage asks for more information about where the database for the connection can be found.

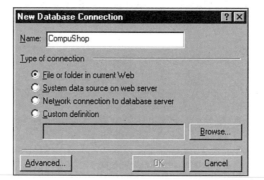

A window similar to the one in Figure 39.3 is displayed when you click the Add button. The example in this figure is the easiest selection to describe: File or Folder in Current Web. This implies that the database connection you want to establish links to an actual database file that is stored in the same location as your Web site. In this example, you use Microsoft Access and therefore point to an Access database file that exists in the same path as your Web site. To actually select the Access compushop.mdb database, you simply click the Browse button and select the database file within your Web site.

Note

A database file must already exist in your Web site's folder list for you to be able to select it. To do this, you must import the standard database into your FrontPage web using the File, Import option. Once the database file has been imported into your FrontPage project, you can create a new database connection that points to that file.

Within this dialog box, you may notice that there are two additional options: Data Source on Web Server and Other Database Server on the Network. There is an important difference between these two choices. Assume you select the Data Source on Web Server radio button. When you then click the Browse button, a window will display valid ODBC connections on the Web server hosting your site. In this case, you are creating a link to another ODBC link that points to the actual database. In order for this ODBC link to be available on the server and point to your database, you must either configure it yourself via the *ODBC Data Source Administrator* on the Web server or ask that server's administrator to do it for you.

If you choose the Other Database Server on the Network option and then click Browse, you are presented with another dialog box. This window asks for information about the database server you are connecting to. This information includes the type of database server you are using, the name of the actual server, and the name of the database on that server.

> **Note**
>
> You must choose the Browse button to make a more detailed selection, no matter what option is highlighted within the New Database Connection window. Only after you click this button can you specify the more detailed information necessary to create the connection and continue with the Database Results Wizard.

You may also notice that there is an Advanced button in the New Database Connection window. This button allows you to define advanced options such as a user ID and password, timeout values, or additional necessary parameters for the database.

You are brought back to the Database Results Wizard's initial screen after you create the new connection. This time, however, the Use an Existing Database Connection option is selected and the drop-down selection box contains the name of the new connection you created. In this example, the name is CompuShop as defined in Figure 39.3.

EXTRACTING THE DATA

After the database connection information has been defined, it is time to move on with the Database Results Wizard. The wizard next prompts for a choice regarding what data should be extracted from the database. A database source typically contains multiple tables of information. A *field* usually represents a type of data to store. For instance, a person's last name can be captured within a field of information. A collection of fields such as name, address, and phone number can be grouped to form a record of data within the database. In this case, each person listed in the database would have his or her own record of information. A *table* is basically a logical collection of these records within the entire database and it is important to note that there may be several tables within a single database. For your simple CompuShop database, you can have one table that holds records of product information and another table that holds incoming orders. These two tables contain entirely different information, but are logically connected by being placed within the same database project.

In Figure 39.4 you'll notice that in this step you must either choose to extract all data from a table within the database or create a more specific query. The easiest choice is to extract all data from the table and select the table from which the database should retrieve information.

Figure 39.4
To extract data to dis-play within a Web page, you must either choose a table in the database or specify a query.

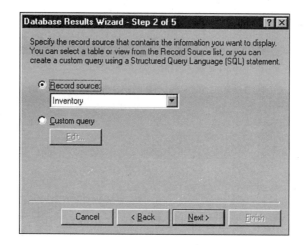

However, in some cases you may want to construct your own query for retrieving informa-tion from the database. There are several reasons you may prefer creating your own query. If, for example, you want to extract multiple pieces of information that range across several tables, you may need to join this information using an appropriate SQL query. If you are conscious of Web site performance, you may want to distribute work evenly—examples include data input validation on the client's Web browser, performing the dynamic page assembly using FrontPage extensions or Active Server Pages on the Web server, and per-forming data-intensive tasks using the database server. If you are processing thousands or millions of information records, you may want the database server to perform the task because it is best optimized for this purpose. This is more efficient than expecting the FrontPage extensions or an Active Server Page task to parse the data. Figure 39.5 shows the basic window in which you define custom queries.

Tip #174

> Sometimes designing the SQL code can get a bit confusing or unruly. To help out, you may want to turn to the aid of some SQL builder software such as the component built into Microsoft Access. With Microsoft Access, you can design your SQL query more easily by reviewing a graphical representation of the database and the relationships between tables. After designing the SQL code graphically, you can copy the resulting SQL text and paste it into FrontPage 2000.

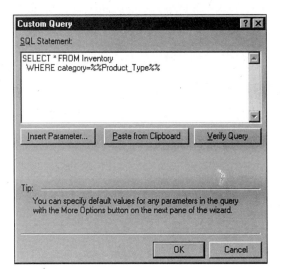

Figure 39.5
If you need to specify
a custom query to
extract database
information, you can
do so within the
Database Results
Wizard.

An important feature to notice within the Custom Query window is the Insert Parameter button. With this button you can type the name of a data entry field from an HTML form for use within the query. With this capability, you can take choices made by a Web form visitor and extract data from the database that meets this user's criteria. For example, the choice to browse monitors within the CompuShop store can be made on a Web form and then fed to this query. This query takes the Web form results and then executes the respective query. This way a user can also choose to view desktop computers on that same form and receive the appropriate results using the same query. The Web pages are the same and the basic query is the same as well. The only thing that changed between these two scenarios is the parameter data passed into the query. Parameter data is identified by the parameter's name, enclosed by two percent symbols (%%) on each side of the parameter name. Figure 39.5 illustrates a parameter used within the query.

Tip #175

> Basic SQL commands are the syntax used within the custom query window. You can perform complex joins, selections, grouping, ordering, or any other database function within this entry window using the proper SQL syntax. But you should always verify the SQL code before continuing. You want to always try to insure that you will not be retrieving too many records of information or tie up the database server.

CHANGING DISPLAY OPTIONS

The Database Results Wizard's next several steps ask for choices to be made about the appearance of data on the Web page. Figure 39.6 shows the step that asks which fields from the database table should be formatted and displayed on the final Web page that is rendered for the site visitor.

Figure 39.6
After making the database connection and specifying necessary criteria for extracting data, FrontPage allows you to select which fields from a database table are actually displayed.

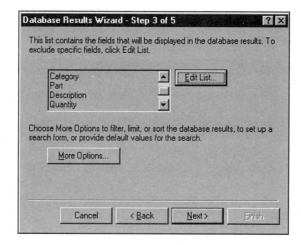

If you specify a custom query for retrieving data from the database, you may not see all of the fields for the table listed in Figure 39.6. If you specify particular fields to retrieve data from within the custom query's SQL command, only those fields are available in the Displayed Fields list box. For example, the SQL statement SELECT description FROM Inventory in the Custom Query Entry field allows only the Description field to be displayed in the Displayed Fields box.

In Figure 39.7, you can see the dialog box that clicking the Edit List button of the wizard presents. This is an interface for selecting or removing fields to be displayed as well as for specifying the order for displaying them.

Figure 39.7
FrontPage 2000 makes it easy to choose which fields to display in the database results for a Web page.

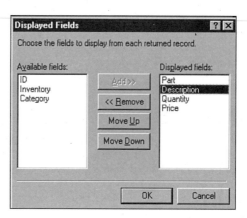

If you examined Figure 39.6 fully, you probably also noticed that there is a More Options button in addition to the Edit List... button. Clicking the button displays another dialog box, which allows you to specify criteria for retrieving data from the database as well as sort orders and other default parameters. Figure 39.8 shows the More Options dialog box, which is brought up by clicking this button.

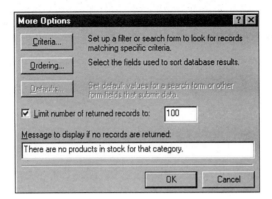

Figure 39.8
Like many FrontPage features, there is a More Options dialog box for tweaking the data returned from a database.

MEETING THE CRITERIA

If a database contains millions of *information records (page 843)*, you will want to allow the user to narrow the search results. To do so, you must indicate specific requirements that the data must meet in order for it to be displayed. In your CompuShop example you store products by the type of product they are, such as monitors, laptop computers, or desktop computers. With theoretically thousands of products supported by the shop, you want the user to choose what type of product he is interested in. By selecting the type of product from a web search form, this criterion can be passed to the FrontPage extension and used to prune the database results. This restriction is associated within the FrontPage web using the More Options dialog box.

For your CompuShop example, you set up the criteria for the database results as shown in Figure 39.9. In this example, you only want to retrieve products within the category that a user chooses, such as monitors. To enhance this example, you also make sure that only products that are in stock are displayed by returning records where the inventory quantity is greater than zero.

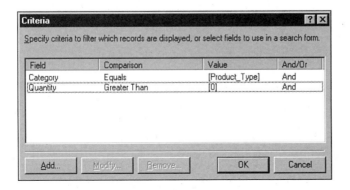

Figure 39.9
Varying logic can be applied to fields within the database to define the set of results returned for display in the Web page.

By examining Figure 39.9, you can see that it is possible to build fairly complex queries by simply adding lines of logical conditions to the overall criteria list. Each line is logically connected to each other by either an AND or an OR condition.

Tip #176

Remember that AND commands take precedence when mixing AND and OR conditions across lines in the criteria builder window. Two criteria lines joined by an AND statement are executed before two lines connected with an OR statement. For example, say CompuShop has a negative quantity (backorder) on a particular type of monitor. If you built the criteria query as follows, you could expect to retrieve from the database all products that are either laptops or monitors and in stock (quantity greater than zero):

```
Category Equals Monitor OR Category Equals Laptop AND Quantity
Greater Than 0
```

Unfortunately, this example does not work as constructed and instead returns all laptops and monitors, whether they are in stock or not. This occurs because the AND condition is determined before the OR. The query therefore finds all laptops that have a stock quantity greater than zero and returns those records in the result set. In addition, the OR condition states to include all products that meet the category Monitor, but there is no check made to see if the quantity of monitors in stock is greater than zero.

You could use parentheses to override the natural precedence of logical commands in computer languages such as SQL, but you cannot do this with the criteria builder. The criteria builder simply adds AND and OR statements between your criteria in the order in which you define your criteria. If you have complex criteria for retrieving data from a table, consider implementing it in the custom query section as a SQL statement. Or use the criteria builder to build the basic conditional checks and then click the Back key in the Database Results Wizard to return to the Custom Query option that contains an Edit button. Clicking on this button will reveal the source SQL code built via the criteria builder. At this point you can tweak the code to include parentheses as necessary.

To add a criterion to the list, you can simply click the Add button to display another entry screen (as shown in Figure 39.10).

Figure 39.10
The criteria builder in FrontPage allows you the flexibility to specify logical conditions and HTML form fields to use.

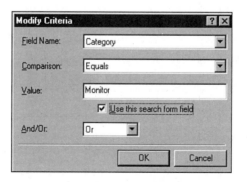

The Modify Criteria dialog box prompts for the name of the field in the database to perform the criteria against, a comparison operation such as equal to or greater than, and the value to compare a database field to. In addition, there is the option to specify whether this value is a constant value or one that is inherited from an HTML form. Finally, the logical command to tie this criteria to additional criteria in the list can also be specified as either an AND or OR condition.

SORTING THE RESULTS

You can sort the result set after including all of the criteria for retrieving results from the database. You can choose to sort on one or more data fields and even specify the direction of the sort, such as ascending or descending. Figure 39.11 shows the Ordering dialog box, which appears after clicking the Ordering button of the More Options dialog box in Figure 39.8.

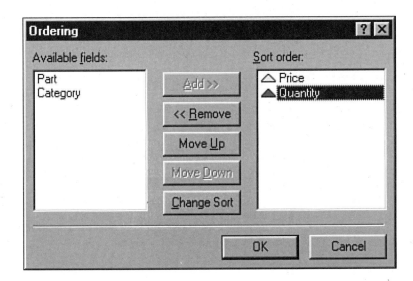

Figure 39.11
After determining what criteria is used to display data, you can choose the order by which the information is displayed.

PART

VIII

Cн

39

When selecting more than one data field to sort on, you are specifying the sequence in which the sort is performed. The results are sorted primarily on the first data field selected. If there are multiple records and the data of each record contains repetitive information in the first field, the second field in the order list is used to sort the subsequent data. For example, if you sort your CompuShop results first by category, there would obviously be many records that meet the Monitor criteria. To further sort the monitors returned, you could add a second sorting order on the monitor's price.

SETTING DEFAULTS

The final button in the Advanced Options dialog box is Defaults. This button displays a list of default values for use in the criteria list for database results. To be more specific, this button allows you to set default values for parameters that are otherwise specified via HTML forms; if a form is not filled out completely and a choice is not made, the default selection is still used. The Defaults button is only available for items in the criteria list that retrieve query parameters from HTML forms. This button is disabled if all criteria is based on constant values.

FORMATTING RESULTS

By far the most complicated portion of the wizard is the criteria selection section. After you have made the necessary data retrieval selections, you can choose exactly how you want the information to physically appear on the Web page. Figure 39.12 shows the next Database Results Wizard step, which features an option for formatting resulting data within a table or as separate sections of information.

Figure 39.12
The Database Results Wizard can automatically create tables or page sections to format data results more logically.

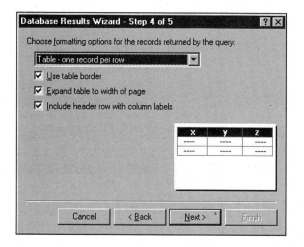

The table option results are fairly obvious—the rows of database results are displayed as rows in the table. Likewise, each column within the table represents the respective field of the database. You can further adjust the table's properties by deciding whether borders should be displayed, whether the top row of the table should include the column field names, or whether to expand the width of the table to accommodate the entire page.

When finished setting the options on this page, the final step of the wizard is displayed. On this fairly simple page, you decide whether you want all database results to be displayed on a single page or you want to add navigational buttons at the bottom of the database region on the Web page. If you decide to add *navigation buttons (page 682)* , you can select how many data records you want to display on a single page. If you enter 5 in the Records per Group field, then only five rows of the database will be displayed within the Web page. If there are more than five rows returned, you could click the Next button when viewing the Web page to retrieve the next five records. This is similar to many search engines on the Web in which there are so many results returned that they must be split into multiple pages of information. This final step is highlighted in Figure 39.13.

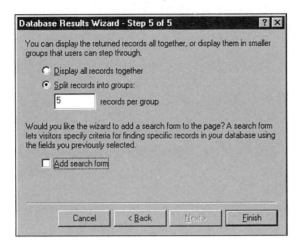

ADJUSTING DATABASE RESULTS

After you have successfully embedded a database results region on your Web page, you may need to edit it or add additional fields to the database. Figure 39.14 illustrates the final addition of the database region to a particular page in the CompuShop site.

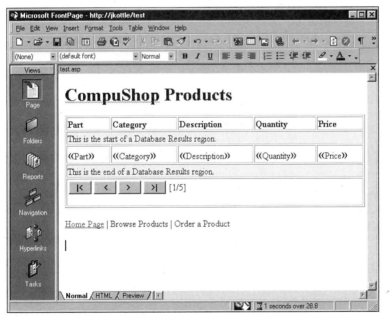

Figure 39.14
The Database Results Wizard embeds itself within the Web page being edited by FrontPage.

Even though this database results region sufficiently displays data, the results should be cleaned up. When viewed within a Web page, the category section repeats for the selected category. For instance, assume a viewer at the site chooses to display all monitor products. Those products are displayed, but the Category column would have the text Monitor repeating down the column at the same time. You should really only display this information once at the top of the screen in the format Product Categories: Monitor.

To do so, you must first remove the Category column from the database within the results region. There are two options for removing the Category column from the database results. The first option is to highlight that column and delete the cells. Another option is to invoke the Database Results Wizard by either double-clicking the database results region or right-clicking the database results region and choosing Database Results Wizard from the pop-up menu. When the Database Results Wizard appears, you can step through to the screen that prompts you to choose which fields to display. You can then choose to remove the Category field from the displayed list.

Don't be alarmed if you accidentally remove the wrong column of data. You can just as easily add columns to the data results region by reinvoking the Database Results Wizard and choosing new fields to add to the results. As an option, you can also place your editing cursor within the database results region and choose Insert, Database, Column Value from FrontPage's menu to insert a particular column from the database connection.

Once you have successfully removed the Category database field from the Web page, you have to add it again as a separate, single result at the top of the page. To start, you can simply move the cursor in FrontPage 2000 to a blank region of the page between the header and the table of results and type **Product Category:**. You can then add the single field from the database. To do this, you must choose to insert a new database results region via the Database Results Wizard. Individual columns on a page cannot be embedded because there is no inherent association with a particular database connection. The only way this connection can be made is by adding a new database results area with the wizard.

To add the Category field, you invoke the Database Results Wizard in a manner very similar to the one already reviewed. This time, however, you want to display the information in a table with borders or other properties disabled. Of course, you will only select the Category field from the database table. An important thing to notice is that all of the rows of information are returned when you choose to embed database results within a FrontPage Web page. In this case—even though you want only each unique category to appear once—the Database Results Wizard will display each row that is returned from the database. Therefore, there are repeating categories in this new database results region.

To repair this problem, you must know a little about SQL syntax. Instead of choosing the category from the Database Results Wizard, you should build a custom query that contains the SQL statement discussed in the following section.

`SELECT Category FROM Inventory GROUP BY Category` The `SELECT` statement instructs SQL-aware databases to retrieve data from a table. In this case, the `SELECT` command is extracting only the Category field from the Inventory database. The `GROUP BY` syntax instructs the database to group the results by a particular field; the Category field in this example. The `GROUP BY` clause effectively groups the categories by category. If there is more than one result for a category, those results are grouped into just one result.

Figure 39.15 demonstrates the fully functional Web page as it would appear within the Web browser. As you can see, the resulting categories no longer repeat in the output results and the navigation buttons are available at the base of the database results region to page through the products.

Figure 39.15
The final Web page as rendered in Internet Explorer shows a complete list of products based on categories picked by the site visitor.

CAPTURING DATA FROM FORMS

Displaying content from databases within a Web page is only half the battle of database maintenance in most cases. There is usually a need associated for updating information in a database or for somehow connecting entry fields on a form to data storage for future retrieval. In the CompuShop example you need not only display the products that are available for purchase, but also provide a form by which people can place orders.

To solve this, you first need to create an HTML form for capturing key criteria for order processing. This form can be created either manually using FrontPage's HTML form editing tools or by using the Form Wizard. No matter which approach you use, a sample order form for the CompuShop will include the part number for the product and the quantity of items the user wants to order. There are usually additional fields on this form in which to enter credit card information and shipping information. The sample order entry form used by CompuShop is shown in Figure 39.16.

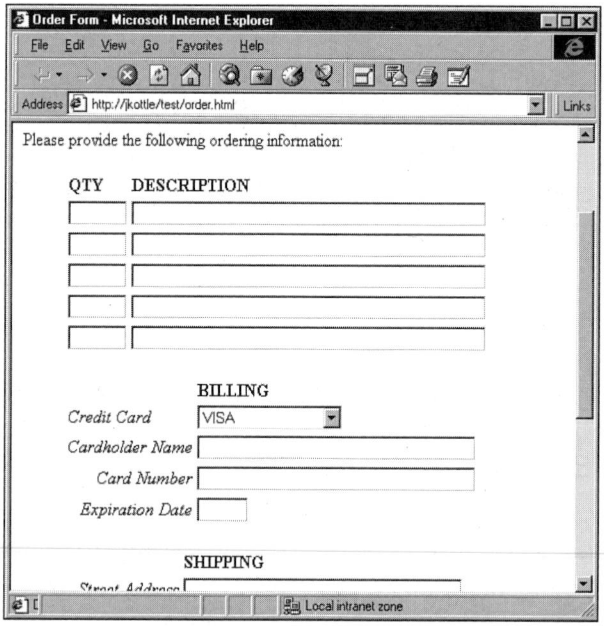

Figure 39.16
HTML forms can be
easily connected to
databases using
FrontPage.

When a user fills out the information for a Web form, that information must go someplace for storage or review. After laying out the form for the Web page, you can attach the fields in the form to respective fields in a database table. This way the database can be interrogated later by a representative at the CompuShop to fulfill the order.

To begin the process of taking results typed by a user and entering them into a database, right-click the HTML form area of the Web page within FrontPage and choose Form

Properties from the pop-up menu. A Form Properties dialog box allows you to choose how you want to store HTML form results. Possible solutions include routing the information to a mailbox, storing it in a text file on the Web server, passing it to another server-side application such as an Active Server Pages, or adding it directly to a database.

To add information directly to a database from an HTML form, you simply choose the Send to Database option in the Form Properties window and click OK. After clicking OK for the first time, you should receive a message from FrontPage asking if you would like to edit the form's settings now because they may be invalid. If you click Yes at this point, the Options for Saving Results to Database dialog box appears as depicted in Figure 39.17. You can also access this window by clicking the Options button. The Options for Saving Results to Database dialog box allows you to configure the database information for saving results entered by a site visitor on the HTML entry page.

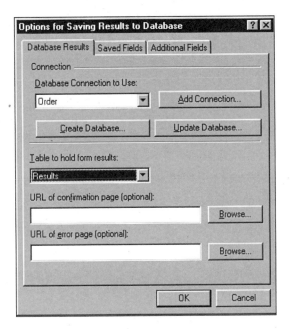

Figure 39.17
FrontPage 2000 offers the option to store user input from HTML forms directly into a database.

PART

VIII

CH

39

The Connection section of the Database Results tab allows you to specify the database connection to use when storing data from the HTML form. Within this section you can choose a previously established database connection or add a new connection (as you did earlier) to display results from a database. The beauty of FrontPage 2000, however, lies in this tool's capability to automatically create a database if one does not already exist. By clicking the Create Database button, FrontPage automatically creates an Access database for you and stores this database file in a folder named fpdb, which is within your FrontPage web.

Note

> FrontPage 2000 creates a new database file using the same name as the HTML filename. For example, if the Web page were named order.html, the resulting database for the form on this page would be order.mdb. In the event that there are multiple HTML forms on a Web page, each subsequent database filename that is created automatically by FrontPage contains the Web page name, followed by a sequential number, and the .mdb extension. In addition, the table that holds the information from the HTML form within the database is named results by default.

You will also notice that within the Saving Results to Database dialog box you can specify the table to store information in if more than one table exists. An additional feature that saves the page editor a lot of work? The capability to quickly specify which Web pages should be displayed after either the database has been successfully updated or if an error has occurred.

There are two additional tabs in this dialog box: The Saved Fields tab must be reviewed before you commit the settings in this dialog box. This tab provides the ability to explicitly choose which fields on an HTML form should be stored in the database as well as to define the respective database field names to use in the database for identifying this information. You must define the form fields that you want to store in the database; otherwise, no information may be stored at all. Similarly, the Additional Fields tab allows you to record optional metadata in the database, such as the Web browser the visitor uses when accessing your site, the visitor's computer name, the visitor's username, and the time at which the form data was submitted.

You are finished after configuring all of the options available in the Save Results to Database window and committing the changes. To verify whether the new settings function properly, you can load the Web page that contains the HTML form into your Web browser and try to submit data. After you have submitted data, you should receive either an error or a success message as determined by the options for Save Results to Database dialog box. If no custom Web pages are configured for result messages, a prebuilt confirmation message is generated by FrontPage's extensions on the Web server. To actually review the data that was sent to the database, you can open the database by double-clicking the appropriate .mdb file in the FrontPage Web Folder List. This opens Microsoft Access and the respective database file (as long as Access is installed on your system).

TROUBLESHOOTING

Can I edit my database information within FrontPage?

FrontPage provides only basic capabilities for connecting to database to retrieve data or create a new database from scratch to mirror form data. Although it has a query wizard that can help you build queries to issue to databases, you may want to consider using Access 2000 in conjunction with FrontPage 2000. Access 2000 is becoming more of a "front-end" tool for connecting to and managing databases such as those found on SQL Server.

I know that you can store form data in an Access database file that FrontPage creates automatically for the form. Can FrontPage automatically create databases tables using other database management software such as SQL Server or Oracle?

Currently when you use FrontPage 2000 to link form fields to a new database, only Access databases can be created by FrontPage to store information. If you wish to store information from a form within other databases, you need to create the appropriate databases and tables using tools provided by the database management software you use. Then you can connect the form fields within FrontPage to their respective data fields in the database.

DESIGNERS CORNER

If you are creating a Web site that contains a lot of changing Web page content, it is natural for you to assume that a database system is required. In some cases this may be necessary, but you should consider the type of project you are creating, especially if you are creating a high-traffic Web site.

Most people turn to database systems to help manage the content of Web sites and to make the publication of static information appear more instantaneous. However in such an environment, it is not efficient for the Web server to be constantly invoking database commands via Active Server Pages, just to present a document on the Web site.

There is no reason why you cannot pull document data from a database, but instead of doing this live for each page that is "hit" by a visitor to the site, consider running a server-side process that assembles the results of a database as a series of HTML files. From a scalability perspective, HTML pages require fewer resources on the Web server than complex database queries and Active Server Pages. You can be sure that you will run into fewer issues with concurrent users on your site if you use more traditional HTML files.

To make the process appear more instantaneous, you can also consider invoking the assembly process for only the pages that changed. Likewise you can invoke this assembly process as many times as necessary. Each time this application executes, it will simply update the HTML files that have changed.

Many Web-based document management systems include the ability to pull document information directly from the database "live" during a site visit, or to create static information in the method described here. Essentially, the server-side assembly process reads a template file that describes the overall appearance of the resulting HTML pages. Within that template are control codes that the assembly program recognizes and substitutes with actual data from a database. The final results are merged and unique HTML files are created as a result.

You should reserve true database interaction for portions of your site that truly require it, such as storing information from Web forms or interacting with real-time product databases for electronic commerce applications.

CHAPTER **40**

ADVANCED DATABASE TECHNIQUES

In this chapter

by John J. Kottler

BEYOND THE BASICS

In Chapter 39, "Using Databases with FrontPage 2000," you were introduced to FrontPage's basic capabilities for incorporating database results and updating information in databases. This chapter expands upon the knowledge you have already gained and begins looking at creating more complex database systems. In this section you examine the differences between smaller database engines, such as Microsoft Access, and larger database management systems, such as Microsoft SQL Server or Oracle. Additionally, you are introduced to more advanced concepts; an example is using Microsoft's Active Server Pages to retrieve customized information within FrontPage as well as the use of server-side objects to enhance the functionality, speed, and security of your Web sites.

The computer industry has recently seen a revolution in the way computer systems are developed. First was the concept of the mainframe, a type of computer that acted as a host to any number of additional terminals that contained minimal computing power.

In this world all application development was concealed on the mainframe system and any database management was handled by the same system. As computer technology evolved and the concept of personal computers was introduced, it was quickly realized that not all of the work needed to be placed on a single host system. Instead it became more logical to break up the work and assign different tasks to the components that best met the environment. In a data entry application for example, the database server contained all of the information and did the hard work of managing that information. In this same application, a simpler application could be designed to run entirely on a personal computer that provided the interface screens necessary for users to interact with the system. The server worked on the parts of the problem for which it was best optimized and the client application did the work that it handled best.

Ironically in the world of the Internet, technology has migrated slightly back to the mainframe-type of mentality. For instance with a Web page that updates data in a database, the client is considered to be a "thin" client and therefore is somewhat limited in its capabilities. A large dependency is again placed on the Web server and the database servers for verifying and managing information.

This previous model, which included a server and a client, quickly became logically labeled as *client/server* technology. This technology was the industry buzzword for the past few years, until the advent of the Internet. The Internet changed everything in the world of computers, and the creation of complex systems is no exception. With the Internet, the prospect of creating elaborate systems that can be used anywhere in the world on virtually any computer system has become highly desirable—yet it has also introduced a new layer of complexity in the overall solution.

A developer in the client/server arena was concerned with two primary levels, or *tiers*: the client tier and the server tier. This server was usually a database server that handled strictly database functions and some logic related to the database. The actual program an end user would work with in order to access and update that data would be written using an application such as Microsoft Visual Basic or Sybase PowerBuilder. The end-client application became the conductor which housed the instructions that the entire application followed.

The introduction of the Internet, however, encouraged the use of a standardized, thin-client application more commonly referred to as a *Web browser*. This Web browser attaches to a server somewhere on the Internet network to retrieve information and format it appropriately. The server it attached to on the network made up the second tier of the overall solution. As the Internet matured from a basic file-sharing network to a complete marketing solution with complex applications, there became an increasing need to share actual updated data. This is even more strongly reinforced as Internet technology has overtaken corporations for use on internal intranet networks. With the onslaught of the Web, a third layer has been introduced for Web application development. As already noted, the client attaches to a Web server to form a two-tier architecture. As soon as a database server is introduced, the third tier is inferred. In a typical Web-based application, the client will communicate with a Web server, which may in turn connect to a database to format results based on real-time data. The middle tiers often accomplish their respective tasks and pass the results onto other dependent servers in the chain.

To finish this discussion of levels used within applications, also consider that additional servers may be used in more complex solutions on the Internet. For example, media servers may be used in addition to database servers on the third tier, or a transaction server may be introduced between the Web and database servers, creating a four-tier architecture. Whatever the case, it is important to notice that there may be any number of tiers in an application. Thus, you may hear within the computer industry constant referral to an *n-tier* architecture, which simply implies that the servers are expandable such that many can be combined to form an overall solution. Figure 40.1 illustrates more clearly the concepts of multiple-tier systems and the communications between these tiers.

PART
VIII

CH
40

2-Tier Client/Server Architecture

Client   Database Server

Figure 40.1
The use of Web technology with database servers has introduced several layers, which an application can utilize.

Sample N-Tier Web Application Architecture

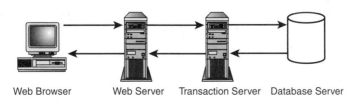

Web Browser   Web Server   Transaction Server   Database Server

With multiple layers or tiers comprising an application, one of the primary problems a Web developer must grapple with is the question of when to use each layer. This is particularly true when creating optimized applications for both security and speed. When considering factors such as these, the choices made about where application code should reside will clearly affect the application's overall performance. As you move along through this chapter, you will hopefully begin to understand where the optimal location for portions of an application belong.

WHEN TO USE LARGER SYSTEMS

By now you are likely wondering why you'd bother using multiple tiers for a Web application. After all, you've already seen how Microsoft Access databases are easy to use and integrate with FrontPage 2000. In reality, there are many reasons you would consider approaches other than just Access for creating Web applications. Among the top reasons are performance, reliability, robustness, and security.

INDUSTRIAL-STRENGTH DATABASES

Microsoft Access is a terrific application that is very easy to use from an end-user's perspective. However, it was originally designed to be a more personal database system—a small workgroup database system at most. In the world of the Internet, where a Web site could receive thousands of visitors within an hour, a small database system is not capable of the stress that a high-volume Web site generates. More advanced database management systems, such as Microsoft SQL Server or Oracle, can be used. These systems have been designed years ago as mission-critical database engines for large volumes of data. They have many of the features that a smaller database system (such as older versions of Access or dBASE files) may not contain.

SECURITY

First of all, you should review the area of security. Security on the Internet has been raised as a priority issue that all sites consider. Security is foremost considered when posting information from a database on the Internet or updating information from the network into a database. If the integrity of that database data is compromised in any way, there can be many adverse affects. To prevent hackers and malicious programs from invading data, database servers such as Microsoft SQL Server have made great efforts to secure database information using the newest schemes.

When creating Web sites—particularly those that offer electronic commerce—it is highly important to ensure that no prying eyes will retrieve secure information. Database servers (again, SQL Server) make high use of permissions and roles with distinct IDs and passwords. Additionally, information in the database can be encrypted to further ensure that information cannot be recovered illegally. Smaller systems often offer forms of encryption as well as some form of user identification protection, but the larger systems are designed to truly integrate security on a more granular level.

Security should be considered for almost any application, but particularly for those that contain confidential or personal information. Electronic commerce applications are particularly good examples of systems that should contain high security implementations. You wouldn't want a hacker to invade a database and obtain your personal credit card information, would you?

In addition to relying on valid identification and database encryption, you may want to consider some additional factors. For example, the further the critical information is away from the Web server or other exposed servers on the Internet, the better the chances that it will not be compromised. In this case, distance obviously is not measured by physical distance, but by the number of barriers that exist between servers in the application. As more blocks (firewalls, for example) are placed in between the Internet and the information, the more likely an intruder is to stumble and eventually retreat.

Another more tacit consideration is the use of replication. Many industrial-strength database servers such as SQL server make use of replication services. *Replication* means that you do not need to have a direct connection between the external Internet and your organization's internal network. At first it seems that you should attach an internal network database directly to an external Web site for instant updates, but this poses a serious security hole. As soon as you open a hole between the outside world and your internal network, there is no way a skilled person cannot find his way through this hole and expose all of your personal organization's information. A more viable approach is to create a copy of the internal database information on the external site on a routine basis. The information stored on the internal database is replicated to the outside world for all to read and any updates made they can be replicated in the opposite direction to the internal network. If for any reason a copy of the database exposed to the Internet is compromised, an internal copy remains intact and the external source can be easily restored.

Besides securing the actual database storage, it is important to secure the actual network over which data is passed. Some time ago a technology was introduced on the Internet that helps ensure that confidential information remains confidential as it is passed around the network. With a disparate network such as the Internet, it is easy for packets of information to pass through several computer systems before reaching their destination. During this journey, the information being passed could be sniffed (picked up through networking monitoring software or hardware) and reviewed rather easily. To prevent this from happening and to keep information from getting into the wrong hands, a *Secure Sockets Layer (SSL) protocol* was introduced. This protocol basically encrypts the data so that if a person did attempt to view the information as it is passed over the network, she would not be able to read it unless she were able to decrypt the data. In the example of an electronic commerce application in which a user buys a jacket at a store, confidential information such as credit card numbers are encrypted by the client Web browser before being sent to the server. The information is decrypted only after it has reached its final, approved destination.

Although SSL effectively prevents information from being retrieved illegally as it passes around the Internet, it should not be used as the sole form of security. Some form of

PART

VIII

CH

40

security measures should be implemented wherever there is potentially secure information. The greater number of security features you add, the lesser the chance of an attack.

There are many facets of security that can make your site as bullet-proof as possible. These are just a few to consider when designing your Web applications. Coverage of security features would clearly extend the scope of this book; to learn more about implementing specific security measures on the Internet, see *Maximum Security, A Hacker's Guide to Protecting Your Internet Site and Network*, Sams Publishing (ISBN 0-672-31341-3).

SCALABILITY

If you are working on a site that can serve thousands of clients at a single moment—and that server must be constantly available—you should look toward using a system with high levels of scalability. *Scalability* is basically the capability for computer systems to easily expand in order to accommodate greater volumes of user access or demand. Large and popular sites such as www.microsoft.com receive millions of hits per day. No single system can handle the entire load placed by users during the period of a day. Instead, the Web site must be scaled to handle an increasing number of users by adding either servers or components to those servers.

Similarly, database systems that your Web site relies upon must be highly scalable. You need a database server that can handle the tremendous amount of access that will be placed upon it by Web browsers. This same system must also be highly reliable—particularly for applications that involve electronic commerce—unless your organization can do without transactions being accomplished for a period of time.

High reliability almost infers scalability. In order to be reliable, there must be contingencies in place for when systems fail. In this case, multiple database servers can be used so that if one fails, the others can be relied upon. This, of course, also implies the use of replication, which keeps the data between database servers synchronized.

It is important to remember that scalability is not only used for reliability, but also for performance enhancement. Instead of using the second database as simply a backup database, there is no reason you cannot split your Web application's workload such that some users use one database while others use the second database. This helps increase the site's performance levels instead of a single database serving all users that attach to the Web site.

Another scalability feature is adding components to systems that are already in place. In addition, those systems automatically recognize and make use of these additions. For example, by adding another processor, more memory, or other physical hardware to a system, that system should recognize that there is additional capability. Realizing this, a scalable application can be adjusted to make optimal use of the resources added to the mix. Many industrial-strength database systems contain scalable solutions for creating complex systems.

LARGE DATABASES

You may think this is a subtle point, but it is important to remember. Smaller databases have a theoretical limit on the number of records that can be stored in a database. File-based databases such as Access are bound by the constraints placed by the operating system for files. Assume you have a 4GB hard drive PC. Even if the database system allows you to use all of the hard disk as a single data file, you cannot store more than 4GB of data.

Larger database systems such as Oracle and SQL Server make use of complex computer algorithms to achieve higher storage capacities. Microsoft's SQL Server, for instance, boasts that it can accommodate a terabyte of data—a thousand gigabytes. If you are looking at creating a system with this level of data storage, you clearly need to choose a database management system that can accommodate your requirements.

REPLICATION

As mentioned before in the security and scalability sections, it is important for Internet Web sites to use databases that are replicas of internally hosted databases. If you are creating a site in which you want to obtain a secure environment and that can function across multiple databases, you should consider a management system that supports replication. With replication, data is automatically updated between two sources as necessary on a routine cycle. If data is updated in one copy of the database and also changed in a second copy, only the respective changes will be synchronized between both databases when those two copies are replicated.

MULTIPLE USER ACCESS

Almost every database system on the market allows multiple users to simultaneously read data from the database. Larger systems provide higher scalability for supporting many more concurrent users than smaller systems; they also allow more granular control of access by users. In the role of updating content in the database, the number of people changing content in the system is an important measurement when selecting a database manager.

To prevent inconsistent information updates, databases lock information so that one person cannot touch information while another person is finished editing it. This is similar to the check-in/check-out capabilities in FrontPage 2000. Think about this: You finish making your changes first and save the file. The second person saves his copy of the file. A problem is introduced. Because the second person opened the file last, but opened it before you saved your changes, he has the original document without your work. When he saves his changes, the file you saved your information to will be overwritten by the file that he is working on, erasing your changes.

Database systems work very similarly. Imagine that two people are attempting to change a piece of information in the database at the same time. Whoever saves his changes last will have the permanent changes in the database. To prevent this from occurring, database manufacturers provide a locking capability in the database management system. When one user decides to work on a piece of data from the database, a lock is placed on that piece of information, which prevents others from working on it until the first person has finished.

Here's where there is a difference: Some database vendors create locks on the entire database or the entire data table. In this case, users cannot update the database at all while a record is being changed. Some other database designs, however, lock a single row of data within the database table. This makes more sense in that only the record being worked on is locked; other activities can still be accomplished on the database.

GUARANTEED TRANSACTIONS

The idea of guaranteed transactions may be important to a developer of a complex Web site. In a nutshell, a transaction occurs each time a database is read from or updated. In some cases these transactions may not be completed; the network going down temporarily is just one reason this may occur. In applications, however, it is particularly essential that each transaction is completed successfully and even more important that related transactions are completed together.

A typical example of complete transactions can be illustrated by a banking Web site. Assume there is a Web site that allows you to examine your checking and savings accounts as well as transfer money between those two accounts. When you decide to move money from savings into checking, you may actually be invoking two database functions: one to withdraw an amount of money from savings and another to deposit that same amount of money into your checking. You want both transactions to complete, your accounts will otherwise be left inaccurate.

Now assume that you transfer $500 from savings into checking and that the actual process of transferring this money involves the two steps mentioned previously. If, for some reason the network connection fails between withdrawing money from your savings account and depositing in your checking account, you will lose the $500; Your savings account is debited before the checking account is credited. Likewise, if the checking account is credited before the savings account is debited and the same connection error occurs, you would gain $500.

The concept of *transaction management* ensures that these conditions don't occur. In the realm of databases, there is the capability to set up a transaction by which all database functions occur within that transaction space. If, at the end, there are any problems during the processing, the entire set of actions that occurred within the transaction can be *rolled back*— the database is returned to its original state. Similarly, only if everything succeeded can the entire transaction be committed. This type of implementation enforces an all-or-nothing approach. Many database management systems support this kind of transaction management; it may be a feature required for your particular Web site.

TRIGGERS AND STORED PROCEDURES

Again, depending on the complexity of the Web application you are attempting to design, you may need to consider another capability that's typically found in more advanced database systems. Triggers and stored procedures are functions that can be designed to execute on the database server. This aids in the n-tier development function; the capabilities that databases handle best can be controlled by scripts on the database server. You should consider using stored procedures or triggers within a database for many reasons, as you see shortly in some demonstrations.

The primary difference between stored procedures and triggers is the method by which they are invoked. *Stored procedures* can be thought of as functions within the database that contain one or many database commands. They are essentially small program files that control database actions within the system and can be customized by accepting parameters specified by external sources. An advantage to using stored procedures is that they are optimized for use on the database server, while your custom script (that accesses the database) may not be as optimized. The database is also local to the stored procedures, instead of being located somewhere across the network. Finally, multiple functions can be batched within a stored procedure script, which means some of the consistency issues addressed earlier are solved.

Triggers are cousins to stored procedures. They also are made up of a series of database commands and execute locally on the database server. The primary difference is in the way that they are started. Stored procedures must be explicitly started by another program or application that calls that stored procedure. Triggers are kicked off by events that occur within the database. For instance, when a user deletes a record from a table in the database, it is possible to create a trigger with logical commands that are executed whenever an item is removed. Other events occurring in the system are the only method by which triggers can be executed.

USING NETWORK DATABASES

Now that you have an understanding of why you should consider using larger-scale database systems, you need to understand how FrontPage 2000 makes use of these databases. As complex as advanced database management systems appear, connecting to them with FrontPage 2000 is not very difficult. This chapter concentrates on using Microsoft SQL Server, although many of the techniques can be used equally on other database systems, such as Oracle, or on legacy systems via ODBC drivers.

PART

VIII

CH

40

MAKING THE CONNECTION

To incorporate results from databases within a Web page, you can use the Database Results Wizard (which is covered in Chapter 39). After you have created your Web site and added a page to the project, choose Insert, Database, Results from the FrontPage 2000 menu to invoke the wizard.

The first window that appears within the wizard prompts for a database connection for the database from which you want to retrieve information. If a connection has not already been created for the Web site, be sure to choose Use a New Database Connection from the dialog box and click the Create button. After you have clicked the Create button, you are brought to the FrontPage Web Settings dialog box which is within the Database tab. You can add a new data connection for your Web site by clicking the Add button.

Adding a new database connection brings up the New Database Connection dialog box. The dialog box is shown in Figure 40.2. This window wants to know where the database that you want to connect to exists; it also prompts for the name of the connection you want to use to identify this database within your FrontPage Web site. Since you are going to connect to a separate database server on the network, choose the Network Connection to Database Server option and then click the Browse button to specify information about that network database.

Figure 40.2
When connecting to database servers, you must create a connection using the Network Connection to Database Server option.

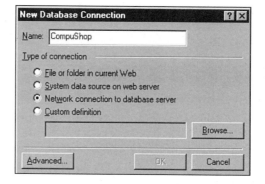

Another Network Database Connection dialog box, as shown in Figure 40.3, is displayed after you click the Browse button. This window asks for three parameters: the type of network database being connected to, the name of the network database server, and the name of the database to be used on that server.

Note

In Figure 40.3, Microsoft SQL Server is listed as the database type for this connection. However, the drop-down list within this dialog box allows you to specify additional database types. The Microsoft ODBC for Oracle driver is included with FrontPage 2000. It is important to note that these are not the only network database types that are supported by FrontPage. In reality, this list is generated by the ODBC Data Source Administrator program found in your system's Control Panel. Within that management application there lies a Drivers tab, which contains both file-system database connections and network database connection drivers. FrontPage 2000 displays any network database drivers that are configured in this ODBC Data Source Administrator. To add support for legacy databases (such as those found on the mainframe), be sure to add the appropriate ODBC drivers on your development system as well as the Web server that contains your FrontPage Web site.

After filling the appropriate information in the Network Database Connection dialog box, you are returned to the New Database Connection dialog box. You should notice that the gray field beneath the Other Database on the Network text is filled with the information you provided in the Network Database Connection dialog box. In this case, this text would include CompuShop@jkottle.

At this point you could commit the changes made in these windows and continue, but for this example you want to specify some additional parameters for the database. Those include a user ID and password for use when accessing the database. To specify this additional data, simply click the Advanced button, which is at the bottom of the New Database Connection dialog box. A window similar to that shown in Figure 40.4 is displayed.

Figure 40.3
To connect to network databases, FrontPage allows you to specify the database type, as well as its server and database names.

As you can see in Figure 40.4, there are provisions for you to specify a user ID and password. Likewise, it is possible to adjust time-out properties for the database, or include parameters that the database may require when starting.

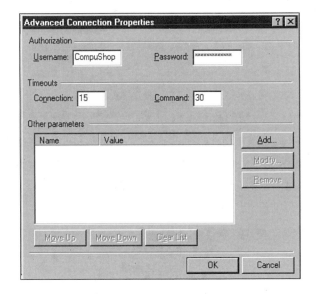

Figure 40.4
Some network database connections require that additional information be specified.

PART

VIII

CH

40

Once you have specified the necessary data and committed the changes via clicking the OK button, you can continue to click OK on all of the parent windows until the original Database Results Wizard dialog box reappears. At this point, you should notice that the selected radio button is now Use an Existing Database Connection and that the name of that connection matches the information you specified earlier in the New Database Connection dialog box—CompuShop in this case. If the connection names do not match, you need to double-check the connections that you already defined or create a new database connection.

If you click the Next button to continue with the wizard, you will notice that it takes a bit longer to proceed in the wizard. At this point the initial connection between your development system and the database server is being made. Depending on the connection speed, this could take several seconds or minutes. When the second step of the wizard appears, it is very similar to the window shown in Figure 40.5. This is indeed similar to the method described in Chapter 39, in which you select the database table from which you want to retrieve results. An important difference, however, is that there may be more tables listed now.

Note

You will see table and database information based on the permissions set by the database administrator. If at first you do not see all of the database tables in the Database Results Wizard that you expect, it may be because the ID and password you used do not contain privileges sufficient to display every table. Make sure to verify your user IDs permissions if you do not see everything that you think you should.

Figure 40.5
Depending on the network database used, your database permissions, and the information available within that database, you may see many unexpected tables.

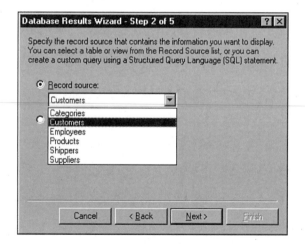

In Figure 40.5, the drop-down list box that contains the list of database tables available clearly illustrates many more tables in the system aside from the Inventory table used to store CompuShop's current inventory. Many of these tables are system specific that are particular to the database system being used. In some cases you may want to connect to these tables to extract additional information from the database, but in most cases you do not need to display this information within a FrontPage Web site.

Tip #177

It can be difficult to distinguish your own tables from system tables when there are many in a database. It is highly recommended that you follow some standard, either your own or one enforced by a database administration group within your organization. If, for instance, each custom table started with the prefix MY_, you could find all of your tables together in the list box instead of searching line by line through the results.

Another consideration: Start your personal tables with a prefix beginning with an A or other character at the beginning of the alphabet. List boxes are typically sorted alphabetically in ascending order. This way all of your database tables will appear at the top of the list instead of lower.

Another option when selecting the table from a list box is to create your own query via SQL. Just as it is demonstrated in Chapter 39, you can add custom or complicated SQL language statements to FrontPage by choosing the Custom Query option within the Database Results Wizard and directly editing the commands.

Tip #178

If you write your own queries for network database systems, be sure you are familiar with the specific database provider's SQL language. Each database vendor typically implements SQL's basic features in a standard manner. However, each vendor also includes different features and capabilities that may be exposed by additions. Never assume that a SQL command that works with one network database system will necessarily work the same with another.

In reality, the only difference between formatting results for local databases such as Access and network databases such as SQL Server lies in the connection to those databases. After you have specified the connection properties and established which table you want to connect to, the Database Results Wizard continues to ask questions about the formatting of this information. For additional information on how to use the rest of the wizard, check Chapter 39.

PART

VIII

CH

40

UPDATING DATABASE INFORMATION

Of course, displaying information from a database source is only half the battle. A truly useful Web site also takes information from a user and populates a database. For example, your CompuShop example site should display all products available at the store as well as allow users to place orders for products thy want to purchase. To do this, you can simply attach the entry forms within FrontPage 2000 to a network database.

To start, you must create a basic form within FrontPage that contains the entry fields necessary for updating the database. In this case, start by creating a Customer Profile form. This form allows the customer to update information about him or herself. It includes information such as the user's name, address, phone number, and credit card number. Figure 40.6 shows a sample form that can be used for this purpose.

Figure 40.6
In addition to providing database results, a Web site can provide an entry form, which can update a database.

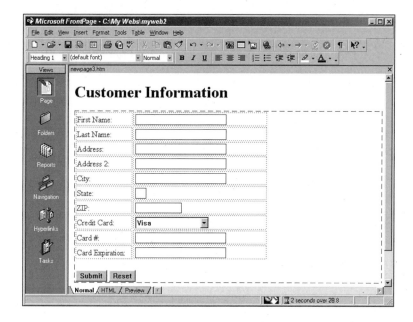

To connect the entries to a database, simply right-click somewhere within the form and choose Form Properties from the pop-up menu. A dialog box prompts you with form results instructions. In Figure 40.7 you see that in this case, you've chosen to redirect results entered on the form to a database. In particular you choose a network database for depositing the results.

Figure 40.7
The Form Properties dialog box allows you to choose where you want form data routed.

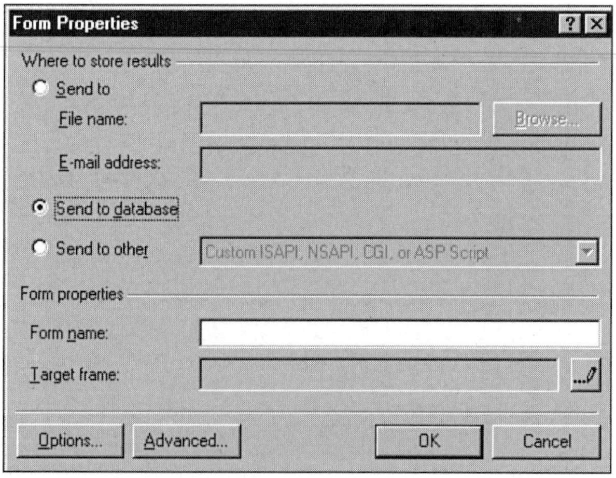

Tip #179

> It may seem confusing, but the Options button that appears within the Form Properties window changes depending on which radio button is selected. For example, the Send to Database selection yields options different than the Send to Other selection.

Clicking the Options button while the Send to Database radio button is selected displays a dialog box similar to that shown in Figure 40.8. This window allows you to specify the database connection that you want to associate form data with or add new database connections to. Selecting which table within that database you would like to store information in is shown in Figure 40.8. In this case, the SQL Server database displays only those tables for which the user defined in the database connection has update privileges. If a table does not appear, verify the permissions set on the table that you are trying to access with your database ID and password.

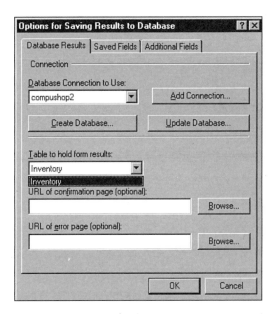

Figure 40.8
You can easily associate form data to a database connection.

PART
VIII

CH
40

Note

> Unfortunately, FrontPage's current version only allows you to create new Microsoft Access databases from the Options for Saving Results to Database dialog box. If you want to create new tables or databases for other ODBC-compliant databases, you must do so through alternative methods such as creating the database and respective tables using tools included with the database server.

As you set up your *entry forms (page 869)* in FrontPage, you will likely have form fields named differently than database fields within your destination database table. To map the form entry fields to their respective database fields in a table, you can choose the Saved

Fields tab and modify each form field that you want to store in the database. When you do choose to modify a form field to save, a secondary dialog box asks you to choose which database field to use. These database fields are displayed within a drop-down list box and are determined directly via FrontPage interrogating the database table.

Choose OK after remapping all of the form fields to database fields. However, you may receive one of two warnings while committing your changes to FrontPage. The first error may alert you that a form field type does not match the database field type. This means that a particular field in the database expects data of a particular type. For instance, a product number should be a series of numbers while the customer's name should be all text. If you receive this warning, it is easiest to change the validation of the form field within FrontPage. This validation criteria in FrontPage basically determines whether an input field on the form is a number, an integer, or text. Choosing one of these data types for each object in the form should resolve any problems.

A second error that you may receive while trying to save the final mappings has to do with mandatory fields. This error that states that you must specify a form field for a database field in order for an update to be successful. A database field in the table cannot be NULL; there must be some sort of information filled in that database field, it cannot be left in empty state. If you receive this warning, you must associate a form element on the HTML form to that database field mentioned in the warning. If you do not want to make this a user-input field, you can consider adding to the form a hidden field with default information that should be placed into this database field.

Once you have successfully set the field mappings and committed all changes, your Web site form is ready. Whenever anyone updates information on this form, the results of the submitted data will be routed directly into a database on the network.

DOING MORE

Reading data from a network database and populating new information into this database are obviously the two strongest Web site developer requirements. There may be times when you want to implement more functionality within your site. This is particularly true as developers begin creating Web sites on the intranet that manage data within databases. In addition to reviewing and adding data, users want to update and delete information within a secure environment. FrontPage 2000 does not provide a large amount of flexibility for more advanced data maintenance, such as deleting information or editing information. This section, however, briefly discusses some solutions and explains more advanced database concepts such as stored procedures and triggers in detail.

In the case of the CompuShop Web site, you need to create a mechanism in which multiple records in several database tables are removed concurrently. The Customer table from the customer profile example contains individual customer information such as name, shipping address, and billing information. One of those fields in that table is a key that uniquely identifies each customer. The customer's phone number was used, because in most cases that should be unique for each individual.

With this unique customer identifier available, you can place multiple orders under the CustomerOrder table and maintain orders for each customer. This is accomplished not only by creating within the CustomerOrder table specific fields related to orders, but also by including the customer's unique identifier (phone number) as a database field for each order record. Using the customer's unique identifier instead of each piece of information related to the customer such as their name provides a couple of advantages: The database size is smaller because redundant information need not be stored multiple times within a database table for each record. In addition, the information is guaranteed to be consistent in all places if it is changed. If a unique key identifies each customer, then that customer's information can change without affecting other database tables. Each order in the CustomerOrder table can look up the respective shipping address by the key and not worry about it being out of date. Each additional copy in the database must be found and changed explicitly if data were scattered multiple times throughout the entire database and one piece of information (such as the shipping address) changes.

Because customer orders are stored in one table and customer information is stored in another, all of a customer's orders should be deleted when that customer is deleted from the system. Like the banking example, the customer information and his respective orders should be deleted simultaneously. You do not want orders in the database for a nonexistent customer.

STORED PROCEDURES

One method for ensuring that a customer is deleted with his respective orders is to encapsulate both deletions into one function on the database server. If this function exists on the database server, there is only one call (not two) to this function from the calling server over the network: one to delete the customer and another to delete that customer's orders.

As discussed earlier in this chapter, *stored procedures (page 863)* allow you to encapsulate several database commands into one function that can be easily invoked. Because they reside on the same physical server as the data, they also provide the utmost in speed and reliability when interacting with database information. Stored procedures can help ensure that work is accomplished; this is done by encapsulating multiple steps into a single function.

Creating stored procedures varies widely depending on the database management system being used. For instance, Oracle implements a different stored procedure language and offers slightly different features than does SQL Server. With Microsoft SQL Server 7.0, stored procedures can be created within Transact SQL via ODBC, or within the Enterprise Manager for SQL Server. Regardless of what method you use to import the stored procedure function, they all follow this format in Microsoft SQL Server 7.0:

```
CREATE PROCEDURE ProcedureName
     @myVariable int
AS

SQL Commands
```

In the case of the CompuShop customer deletion, you could write a single stored procedure, DeleteCustomer, that deletes both customer information and their respective orders:

```
CREATE PROCEDURE DeleteCustomer
    @custid int

AS

DELETE
FROM Customer
    WHERE  Phone = @custid

DELETE
FROM CustomerOrder
    WHERE CustomerID = @custid
```

You'll quickly notice that in addition to standard SQL commands, SQL Server stored procedures make use of a peculiar @ syntax. When this @ symbol immediately precedes a command, it indicates that the word following the symbol should be treated as a variable. The beginning of your procedure makes use of the @ command; it defines a variable named @custid as an integer data type. A key point is that this declaration is made before the AS statement, which indicates that SQL Server should use this variable as a parameter to the function. Therefore, your DeleteCustomer function expects a single integer value to be passed into it whenever it is invoked. This parameter will logically indicate the unique ID number for the customer to delete from the database.

To invoke this stored procedure, you can use the following SQL syntax:

```
EXEC DeleteCustomer 5551234
```

In this example, the DeleteCustomer stored procedure is invoked and the @custid variable will be set to 5551234. The SQL commands in the stored procedure itself will delete records from the customer database where the customer's phone number is equivalent to 5551234. Likewise, the second SQL command will delete orders from the CustomerOrder database where each order's customer ID is equal to 5551234.

TRIGGERS

You are probably convinced that stored procedures are the best way to delete dependant information within a database. Although the method described will clearly meet the needs of related deletions within the database, stored procedures are not the perfect mechanism for doing this. The main problem with using the stored procedure approach is that you must invoke the stored procedure in order for the information to be consistently deleted. This is fine if all database modifications and data deletions are performed strictly by your controlled application. What if someone deletes a record within the Customer table using either another tool or direct SQL statements and does not use your stored procedure? Information can become inconsistent within the database.

Triggers help you avoid this. *Triggers* are a form of stored procedure in that they exist on the database server and contain command syntax similar to stored procedures. A key difference lies in the way they are activated. Stored procedures need to be explicitly called in order to execute. Triggers are associated with particular events that can arise within the database. For instance, it is possible to attach commands for execution within a trigger that is invoked whenever data is deleted from a particular table. This is clearly the best approach for your application. With a trigger executing essentially the same commands as the stored procedure, both the customer information and the respective orders will be deleted whenever a single record of information is deleted.

Like stored procedures, triggers can be defined either in the SQL Server Enterprise manager, Transact SQL, or within ODBC calls. Whatever method is used to create the trigger, an important difference between triggers and stored procedures is that triggers are associated directly with tables within the database, whereas stored procedures are not. As just mentioned, triggers are invoked based on particular events that occur on a table in the database. You must therefore explicitly define which tables a trigger is to work with.

The following syntax is used to define a trigger within SQL Server 7.0:

```
CREATE TRIGGER TriggerName ON TableName
FOR DELETE
AS

SQL Commands
```

Similar to stored procedures, triggers are assigned unique names. One thing you will immediately notice is the use of the ON command. This command indicates the relationship between the trigger and its respective table. The name of the table for the trigger to associate itself with follows the ON command.

In stored procedures, parameter values are defined before the AS command. In the case of triggers, however, the type of event on which the trigger executes is defined. The FOR command indicates that the trigger should be invoked for a particular event within the specified table in the database. The DELETE preference in this brief example follows the FOR command to indicate that this trigger is to be invoked whenever database information is deleted from a table. Other trigger events for SQL Server 7.0 include UPDATE and INSERT.

PART
VIII

CH
40

Tip #180	There is no reason you cannot use both stored procedures and triggers together. If the function you want to accomplish is complex or has already been defined in another stored procedure within the database, you can invoke that stored procedure from within the trigger by using the EXEC SQL command, followed by the stored procedure name and any applicable parameters.

You want to keep the Customer table and the CustomerOrder table synchronized in the CompuShop example. You could define the following trigger on the Customer table:

```
CREATE TRIGGER DeleteOrder ON Customer
FOR DELETE
AS

DELETE CustomerOrder

FROM CustomerOrder INNER JOIN deleted
    ON CustomerOrder.CustomerID = deleted.phone
```

You should define this trigger on the Customer table only, not on the CustomerOrder table. This follows the logic that a customer may have placed several orders and that you may want to cancel one of those orders without removing the customer.

You also make use of the deleted table in the example. This is not a custom table within the database, but rather a system table introduced by SQL Server 7.0. This table contains a copy of the records that are to be deleted from the system. If you delete a single record of information from the Customer table, the deleted table will be populated with a copy of the record you are deleting. That way you can discover the customer ID number from the deleted table of the customer being deleted and perform a search to delete the respective customer's orders.

INVOKING WITHIN FRONTPAGE

Now that you have a firm understanding of stored procedures and triggers as well as the benefits they provide, you are probably wondering how to make use of them within your FrontPage site. Triggers, as pointed out, are invoked automatically by changes in the database. The good news is that there is nothing special you need to perform in FrontPage to invoke them.

Stored procedures, on the other hand, can be invoked by FrontPage via one of two methods. You'll remember that when you are using the Database Results Wizard within FrontPage 2000 that it is possible to not only choose a table to use for the results, but to create custom queries. Within that custom query, you can choose to invoke a stored procedure or to issue other database SQL commands such as DELETE or INSERT. Figure 40.9 depicts a simple query that includes invoking the DeleteCustomer stored procedure with a parameter specified by a form field.

One thing to keep in mind is that FrontPage 2000 currently requires that information be returned in the Database Results Wizard. Because no data results are returned, you cannot create a custom query that only invokes a stored procedure that deletes information. The custom query in FrontPage must contain a SELECT statement as the first item in the query.

If you want to use SQL statements or stored procedures without returning results, there are a few approaches you can consider. You can return data from an empty table or populate that data with HTML that you would like to display within the Web browser after the stored procedure executes. If you are using HTML style sheets, you can hide the region in which database results are returned; as an alternative, you can invoke advanced database functions using Active Server Pages script embedded within the page. Listing 40.1 illustrates a sample ASP script that can be embedded within your Web page by altering the HTML directly for the page within FrontPage.

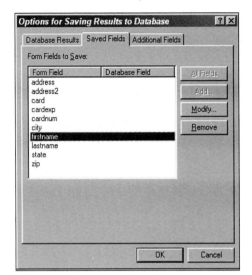

Figure 40.9
You can invoke stored procedures or other complex database functions within the Database Results Wizard.

LISTING 40.1   ACTIVE SERVER PAGE SCRIPT

```
<%
set myConn=Server.CreateObject("adodb.connection")
myConn.Open "CompuShop","compushop","compushop"
set rs=myConn.Execute("EXEC DeleteCustomer 5551234")
%>
```

As you can see, using advanced database features in some cases (such as advanced SQL or stored procedures within FrontPage) is not terribly convenient when using the Database Results Wizard. In these circumstances, it is more effective to use Microsoft's Active Server Pages or server-side objects. Chapter 41, "Database Development with ASP," covers these issues in more detail and explains how to create more robust server applications.

PART
VIII
CH
40

Troubleshooting

I understand that there is the ability to control databases at the client level with Microsoft's Active Data Objects. Should I use that capability?

The beauty of Microsoft's data access technology is that it can be used anywhere using the same syntax. It is easy to develop database connection code and that code can execute locally as well as be reused on a server without any code changes whatsoever. With local database access, information can be controlled more dynamically and more quickly. However you need to carefully consider the visitors that will be frequenting your site. This capability only works if ActiveX is available on the client's workstation. If the visitor does not have the ability to use ActiveX controls because they are not using Internet Explorer or because ActiveX has not yet been made available for their platform, then you will need to consider creating alternate methods. In general, you should not design your Web sites to make use of specific features of a particular browser or operating system unless you know for sure that all of your potential visitors meet those requirements.

Designers Corner

When creating large and complex database systems for the Web, the best approach is to split the work for the application such that the best components are used for the work they were designed to do. If you are creating a site in which the deletion of one record should force other data to be erased, triggers should definitely be considered. For enhancing security and ease of maintenance, database stored procedures can also be used.

CHAPTER 41

DATABASE DEVELOPMENT WITH ASP

In this chapter

by John J. Kottler

Custom Solutions

So far you have seen how FrontPage 2000 can be used to significantly improve the rate at which you develop Web sites. Chapters 38 and 39 exposed you to creating Web sites that even include real-time database connectivity. In most cases, the understanding you have gained to this point will help you create most of your Web sites, even more complex ones. There is always the prospect, however, that you need to control your Web site in more ways than FrontPage 2000 alone offers. Fortunately, there is a fairly straightforward solution; it's offered by Microsoft for solving highly complex application development on the Web. This solution includes their Active Server Pages technology included with Internet Information Server, as well as incorporating server-side objects. If this seems daunting, don't be alarmed—these technologies and more are covered in this chapter.

Evolution of Active Server Pages

You may or may not already be familiar with the term *Active Server Pages* or ASP for short. This technology has evolved over the course of several years and is an feature included within Microsoft's own Web server, Internet Information Server (IIS). As the Web has matured into a more dynamic, database-driven environment, there has become an increased need to easily connect to databases.

Rumor has it that during development of one of the early versions of IIS, a team from that server group decided to put an idea into practice after hours at Microsoft. The idea was to make database information easily accessible through the use of a two simple text files. This technology was quickly dubbed the *Internet Database Connector* and became popular because of its ease of use. This IDC technology used one file to define database connection information such as the database to connect to, a SQL command, and other necessary parameters. The second file acted as a template and consisted of HTML content in addition to special tags that the IIS could translate into actual data retrieved from the database.

The first file that set up the initial connection parameters needed to simply be saved as an .IDC file; it contained information such as the ODBC data source from which to retrieve information, the template with which to process the results, and a SQL statement for use when retrieving data from the database. A simple .IDC file, which could be used to set up database connections to an ODBC data source, would be similar to the one illustrated in Listing 41.1.

Listing 41.1   A Simple .IDC File

```
    Datasource: ODBC_CompuShop
      Template: inventory.htx
 SQLStatement: SELECT * FROM Inventory WHERE Category = '%frmCategory%'
```

As clearly demonstrated by Listing 41.1, there are three parameters that can be included in the .IDC file:

- DataSource—This property identifies the database connection to use when retrieving data. It is the name of the connection as defined in the ODBC Data Source Administrator within the system's Control Panel settings.

- Template—As indicated, once the data has been returned from the database it must be merged with a template file to be output to the browser. This template file contains basic HTML formatting, as well as special tags that indicate where data is to be inserted in the result stream. The Template parameter must be set so that IIS knows which template file to use when formatting results.

- SQLStatement—By now you are probably familiar with the concept of using SQL statements within FrontPage. These statements are standard database commands that can extract data based on particular criteria. Only products of a particular category will be extracted at a time by the code in Listing 41.1.

You'll also notice in Listing 41.1 the use of a variable in the SQLStatement line: %frmCategory%. The developers at Microsoft quickly realized that it was not only to retrieve generic data from a database, but that it would be more useful for users when they specified particular information in order to customize the returned data. They provided the ability in the IDC for parameters such as HTML form field information to be passed in to customize results. In this case, assume that there is a entry field named frmCategory on the HTML submission form. When executing on the Web server, the information typed or selected in this field is then passed into the IDC file and replaces the variable to narrow the database search.

For completeness, take a look at the HTML template file that often wears the extension .HTX. Listing 41.1 defines the template to use when populating data as inventory.htx. The returned data could be formatted using an HTML template file (.HTX). Listing 41.2 illustrates a sample HTML template file that could be used with the IDC.

LISTING 41.2 AFTER SPECIFYING CONNECTION INFORMATION

```
<HTML>
<BODY BGCOLOR=#FFFFFF>
Products Available:<BR>

<% BeginDetail %>
    <% Part %> - <% Description %> - <% Quantity %> - <% Price %> <BR>
<% EndDetail %>
</BODY>
</HTML>
```

The HTML file in Listing 41.2 is hardly pretty, but you get the idea. The object of this template is to strictly list the products available as defined by the .IDC file in Listing 41.1. You'll quickly notice that the file appears just as a normal HTML file, with a few exceptions. You will see several special tags denoted by the `<% tag %>` syntax within that file's listing. Each tag represents one of two things: either a database field to display within the template or a language command that the IDC generator recognizes and translates to its logical equivalent.

In this case, the database results are displayed and include database fields such as the product's part number, its description, the number available in stock, and its price. Around the single line in the template file that indicates these fields are the commands `<% BeginDetail %>` and `<% EndDetail %>`. There are many commands supported by the IDC that control how the IDC behaves. Some of these commands include traditional programming commands such as loops and conditional logic statements. In this case, the `<% BeginDetail %>` and `<% EndDetail %>` pair indicate to the IDC that information between these lines is to be repeated for as many records that are returned by the database query. The database fields for each record and HTML between these commands are to be returned to the Web browser for every record of information returned from the database. The template in Listing 41.2, when combined with the IDC, generates the following results:

```
Products Available:
12619 - 233MMX Laptop/13.3 TFT/3.0GB/64MB/2MB Video - 12 - $1,599.95
12622 - 166MMX Sub-Notebook/32MB/2.0GB - 31 - $1,449.95
12664 - Pentium II 300 Laptop/3.0GB/64MB/4 MB Video/DVD - 27 - $2,495.95
```

As you can see, retrieving database results or in theory updating information in the database can be accomplished rather easily by using the IDC. To invoke the IDC at any time, you simply need to connect your HTML form's ACTION property to the name of the IDC file on the server. If you didn't use a form, you could simply use the IDC filename as part of the URL line to invoke the IDC.

Note

> You have probably noticed that the IDC file makes use of a special syntax to identify variables by enclosing the variable name with % symbols. Make sure that when using the IDC that you do not confuse this syntax with FrontPage's use of double %% symbols to surround variables. They are not interchangeable. Notice, however, that the `<%` and `%>` tags used in the IDC template file are similar in syntax to those used in ASP.

ENTER ASP

Based on what you know now about the IDC, you're probably wondering what was wrong with the technology? Why can't all Web sites today be designed to use strictly the IDC? As discussed earlier, there is a growing need for robustness and scalability in the server marketplace, particularly on Web sites with mission-critical applications such as electronic commerce. Similarly, the IDC was a good advancement, but the Web site developer needed more. As you have seen in the previous section, it is possible to write fairly rich database functionality using the IDC. In addition to the basic capabilities that you have reviewed, there are additional commands and capabilities that this book has not explored, such as the ability to create loops or conditional logic statements. Each of these subsequent commands makes use of additional specialized tags within the IDC. Soon the syntax language of the

IDC became burdened with many specialized tags, where a more advanced programming language would have been more suitable.

Leveraging the experience already gained with the IDC, Microsoft introduced the concept of Active Server Pages. This technology is very similar to the IDC technology in that templates are used to format the end results passed to the Web browser; it is quite different in that it uses a standard programming language such as Visual Basic Script or JavaScript (instead of countless dedicated tags) to control the behavior of Active Server Pages logic. It is also highly extensible, so that you can include additional components within your application to provide capabilities that Active Server Pages does not include inherently.

An Active Server Page is basically identified on the system as an HTML file with the extension .ASP. This extension associates that file with the Active Server Pages engine so that any logical commands that exist within the page can be executed and the final results rendered as output to the Web browser. In a sense, whenever an ASP page is invoked it is read and sent to an ASP parsing engine. That engine analyzes the data file and looks for script commands or variables within the page. As it encounters program script, the commands are compiled and executed and then the results are returned. These results replace the actual script commands in the final HTML file that is generated and sent to the Web browser. Similarly, any variables that are defined within the Web page are replaced with their corresponding data and the results of those variables only are passed back to the browser. Figure 41.1 illustrates this process in a little more detail.

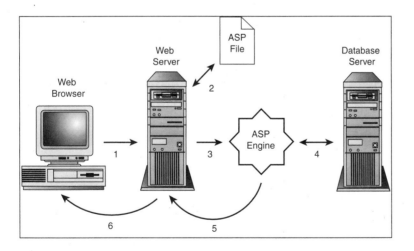

Figure 41.1
Active Server Pages analyzes script in an ASP file and converts it to actual results that are passed back to the browser.

You can follow the process that is used to interrogate an ASP file in Figure 41.1. As you can see from the figure, in step 1 the Web browser asks the Web server for a page—in this case an ASP page that contains HTML and some script that connects to a database. In step 2 the Web server takes the URL request from the Web browser, finds that ASP file on the system (step 2), and sends it over to the ASP engine to be handled (step 3). The ASP engine may then invoke other database servers or other objects on the network to complete its task. This example assumes that the script included in the ASP page instructs the engine to retrieve data from a database; hence, in step 4 a connection is made to the database server to retrieve results.

As the ASP engine plods through the ASP file, it finds scripting commands that needs replacing. If the script is written legally, it will be interpreted and the output results of the script will be included in place of the actual script code itself. Likewise, any variables used within the ASP page will be resolved to their actual value. Like script results, the actual values for a variable will replace the variable syntax within the ASP page. It is important to note that even though this information is being "replaced" within the ASP page, it is only being replaced in the output stream that is ultimately sent to the browser, not the physical ASP file that was first retrieved in step 1.

After all of the relevant information has been parsed in the ASP engine, the results are handed back to the task that called it originally or—in this case—the Web browser (step 5). The results from the ASP engine are ultimately sent to the Web browser from the Web server as a standard output string that can be read by the Web browser and formatted appropriately (step 6).

INTERROGATING THE ASP FILE

Now that you have a familiarity with Active Server Pages and how it works, you should get a taste of the ASP file itself. Listing 41.3 contains a sample ASP file with script embedded within it. If you are familiar at all with Visual Basic, you may recognize the syntax of the commands; this example was written using Visual Basic Script (VBScript). This simple example extracts data from your CompuShop Inventory table and displays the results accordingly. To understand what this sample accomplishes, take a look at Figure 41.2. This figure includes results extracted from the Inventory table and formatted in the cells of a table.

LISTING 41.3 FIGURE 41.2 GENERATED EASILY WITH ASP

```
<html>

<head>
<meta name="GENERATOR" content="Microsoft FrontPage 4.0">
<meta name="ProgId" content="FrontPage.Editor.Document">
<title>New Page 4</title>
</head>

<%
  set myConn=Server.CreateObject("adodb.connection")
  myConn.Open "CompuShop","compushop","compushop"
  set rs=myConn.Execute("SELECT * FROM Inventory")
%>

<body>
<table border="1" width="100%">
  <tr>
    <td width="20%" bgcolor="#000080">
      <font color="#FFFFFF">Category</font>
```

```
        </td>
        <td width="20%" bgcolor="#000080">
          <font color="#FFFFFF">Part # </font>
        </td>
        <td width="20%" bgcolor="#000080">
          <font color="#FFFFFF">Description</font>
        </td>
        <td width="20%" bgcolor="#000080">
          <font color="#FFFFFF">In Stock </font>
        </td>
        <td width="20%" bgcolor="#000080">
          <font color="#FFFFFF">Price</font>
        </td>
      </tr>

    <% while not rs.eof %>
    <tr valign="top">
      <td width="20%"><%= rs("Category") %></td>
      <td width="20%"><%= rs("PartNum") %></td>
      <td width="20%"><%= rs("Description") %></td>
      <td width="20%"><%= rs("Quantity") %></td>
      <td width="20%"><%= rs("Price") %></td>
    </tr>
    <%
        rs.movenext
        wend
        rs.close
        myConn.close
    %>
  </table>
  </body>
  </html>
```

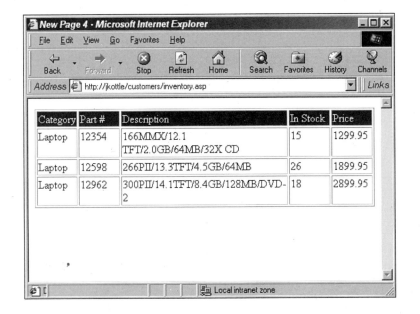

Figure 41.2
With Active Server Page scripts, you can achieve the same database results that you can with the Database Results Wizard in FrontPage.

PART

VIII

Cн

41

You will immediately recognize that the ASP syntax in Listing 41.2 is surrounded by the opening and closing <% %> symbols. Certain commands within the ASP file are contained on their own dedicated lines and others are embedded between HTML table tags. The opening and closing <% %> symbols indicate a *block* of the ASP file that is to be treated as commands or as script. You can therefore extend the script across multiple lines without having to include these symbols for each line in the script.

Tip #181	Incidentally, the HTML in Listing 41.3 was generated using the FrontPage WYSIWYG editor, and the ASP code was injected within the HTML tab view. There is no reason you cannot continue to do this in your environment, even if there are multiple authors. Just be careful about changing the layout drastically; that may affect the ASP code that was injected into the file. For instance, the Web page designer may not want to delete the entire row of the table that contains the ASP script.

As you further interrogate the content within the ASP file, you'll notice that there are actually two different types of symbols used to separate the ASP code from the HTML in the file. The usual <% and %> symbols wrap the ASP code within an ASP file, but there are also the tags <%= and %>, which wrap particular pieces of information between table tags.

The difference between the two is obviously the opening symbol, either a <% or a <%=. The functional difference between these two syntax codes is the way the ASP engine interprets what to do with the results for each. This is executed within those blocks that start with the standard <% syntax, but the results are not necessarily written to the result stream unless explicit ASP commands within those blocks instruct the engine to write data to the output such as response.write.

On the other hand, if the block of ASP code begins with a <%=, the = character indicates to the ASP scripting engine that whatever results may come out of the script should be sent to the standard output for the Web page. Therefore, the ASP scripts within the table tags in Listing 41.3 imply that the data from the database fields should be substituted in the final Web page presented to the browser. Likewise, the database connection and flow control commands (such as while and wend) do not need to be within a block starting with a <%= because you want to execute those commands without writing output results.

Making the Connection in ASP

As usual, one of the first things you need to do in your ASP example is connect to the database in order to retrieve results. This is another area where ASP is significantly different than the IDC. You'll recall that the IDC has the capability to connect to databases built inside itself. ASP, however, is a generic engine that can accomplish much more overall. In the process of making it as such, some things that are not so generic, such as database connectivity, were stripped out. This certainly does not mean that you cannot do database connections in ASP. What this does mean is that database functionality has been encapsulated into a separate server-side object that ASP can invoke and make use of. This approach, in the long run, is more effective; ASP capabilities can be expanded simply by invoking and using additional objects that perform different tasks. For instance, in addition to connecting to databases, there is no reason a server-side component that allows ASP to send email could not also be developed.

When establishing a database connection, the script in Listing 41.3 first creates the database object on the server (since it is the ASP script on the server that will be communicating with the database server). This object creation is accomplished using the CreateObject method on the Server object within ASP. The resulting object that is created can then be further referenced in the ASP script by setting the object to a variable via the set command.

```
set myConn=Server.CreateObject("adodb.connection")
```

You'll notice that the Active Database Object created in the ASP file object creation line in Listing 41.3 is named adodb.connection. This is the standard convention used to identify the advanced database object. Essentially, it is possible that each object can contain many subobjects and therefore the . notation separates the higher-level object name from its more specific class names. In this case, the adodb.connection string indicates that ASP would like to use the connection class of the object in order to connect to a database. For more details about ADO, you can visit Microsoft's Web site at

```
http://www.microsoft.com/data.
```

OPENING THE DATABASE

After the ASP script has created the database object, the next thing you need to do is actually open the database from which you are interested in obtaining information. In this case, open the Inventory table, which exists in your CompuShop database. To do this, invoke the Open method on the ADODB object that was just created. This method accepts three parameters to specify: database name, login ID, and login password. The last two parameters are optional and obviously do not need to be included if the database does not require them. In this case you open your CompuShop database, which is currently in Microsoft SQL Server 7.0. You must therefore specify a valid ID and password for access. The ID and password in this instance is the database-specific login information.

```
myConn.Open "CompuShop","compushop","compushop"
```

Once you have opened the database for access, there is quite a bit you can do with the database depending on the permissions set for the ID and password used. For this example, you simply want to extract data from a table in the database. The easiest method for acting on a database is to use the common SQL language to create a command that performs your desired action. You can simply use the Execute method to invoke a SQL command on the database server. It is available on the same database connection object that you have defined.

```
set rs=myConn.Execute("SELECT * FROM Inventory")
```

As you can see from this snippet of code, the Execute method expects a parameter that contains a string to be used as the actual SQL statement to pass to the database. In this case,

PART

VIII

CH

41

you have chosen to select all data fields from the Inventory database table. There is an important consideration to remember, however. When using the Execute command, the resulting data from the database is stored in a temporary container referred to as a *result set*. This result set is essentially an object that can be referenced by script and contains properties such as the actual data field information returned and methods for navigating through the records such as MoveNext. To make use of this record set within the ASP file, you must remember the record set object by assigning it to a variable you can reference later in the script. Much like defining the database connection initially, the record set can be assigned to a variable via the set command.

TAPPING FIELD INFORMATION

Now that the connection has been established, a SQL command has been issued, and a result set has been generated, you can continue to process the information in the database. For this example, you use the result set returned and stored in the variable rs. As you can see from Listing 41.3, there are several references made to this record set object to retrieve database field information. Basically, the easiest method for retrieving data from the database is to print the results of a record set database field by using the following:

```
<%= rs("Category") %>
```

As you can see from this quick example, the record set that is returned after a SQL Execute statement contains an array of database fields. Each field can then be referred to in your script by using the name of the field within parentheses and double quotation marks. If you examine ASP more deeply, you'll find that this is only one method that is available for retrieving data from the database. It is just as possible to retrieve database fields based on their numeric position in the database. Also notice that the results of the database field Category for the current row of the database in this case will be printed. As you will recall, this is accomplished by preceding the database field information with the ASP delimiter <%=, where the = character implies exporting the results.

An important aspect is that the data returned from the database is stored in a *set* of records. That is, when you use the rs("category") syntax, only a single record's item is returned, not all of the records. If there are three records in the result set with the categories Laptop, Desktop, and Monitor, only the word Laptop is returned. It's returned because it was in the first database record.

To traverse through the entire set of records that is returned, you must add some basic scripting commands to complete the task. Listing 41.3 uses the WHILE command, which is included in the VBScript scripting language for ASP, and its respective wend command. When used together these two commands indicate a block of code that is to be repeated. The number of times that this block is to be repeated depends upon the conditions placed by the WHILE command. When the condition specified after the WHILE command has been met, the looping process stops and execution continues in the script at the statement immediately after the wend command. The following instruction infers that the loop is to continue until the condition rs.eof is met:

```
<% while not rs.eof %>
```

What does rs.eof mean? As mentioned earlier, the set of records returned by the database execution statement is identified as an object. This object, like many other in object-oriented technology, contains numerous properties and methods that can be invoked on the object. In this case, the record set object contains an EOF property. This property is an abbreviation for *end of file*. When you have reached the end of the record set, this property is automatically set to TRUE and therefore causes the WHILE loop to stop repeating. Remember, statements within the WHILE loop only execute when the condition that follows the WHILE statement is true. If you simply used the syntax while rs.eof, the loop would never repeat unless you were already at the end of the record set. The process of displaying record information should repeat while you are not at the end of the record set. Hence, the correct syntax includes the NOT operator, which inverts the result afterward, such as TRUE to FALSE or vice versa.

WHEN TO USE ASP

As you can see, Active Server Pages is an extremely powerful interface that allows Web site developers the flexibility to customize Web sites as much as possible. You can now also appreciate the benefits of FrontPage 2000. For those site designers who are uninterested in creating all advanced functionality on a Web site from scratch, you can see how FrontPage's basic support truly helps the process. You can probably appreciate what FrontPage does for you now that you have seen the long way of implementing database support.

Why would you choose to use Active Server Pages? In a sense, FrontPage 2000 makes use of Active Server Pages already. If you examine the HTML that is generated by FrontPage when you use the Database Results Wizard, you will notice that there are several FrontPage *WebBots (page 166)* that are embedded automatically. These WebBots facilitate the connection and extraction of data from databases. You may also notice that there are FrontPage-generated ASP commands throughout the HTML file.

Active Server Pages is obviously an important technology and will be used even more often in the future. The more you understand this technology, the better choices you will make when creating your own Web sites. Like many computer technologies, ASP is unfortunately not a magic bullet that is a perfect solution for all problems. Sites that require advanced functionality should consider using ASP.

Active Server Pages can be simply thought of as the glue that bonds the pages of a complex Web site. An advanced application contains many *static pages (page 448)* as well as pages that are dynamically generated. Those pages that need to be created dynamically can easily be controlled by logic and data as determined by scripts in ASP.

PART

VIII

CH

41

ASP ADVANTAGES AND DISADVANTAGES

There are many benefits of using ASP, but there are also some drawbacks. The following list illustrates some of the basic advantages to using ASP:

- Simple to develop—ASP uses standard Internet programming languages such as VBScript or JavaScript to control logic within a Web page. If you are familiar with writing browser-side applications within a Web page using either of these languages, you can quickly pick up on programming ASP.

- Highly extensible—As you have seen already, ASP can invoke server-side objects such as database connection objects. There is no reason these objects must be limited to database connectivity. In reality, they can be any type of object, such as a control that works with email or a custom control that contains business logic about your company.

- Included in IIS—If you are running Windows NT as your Web server platform and have decided to use IIS on that platform, Active Server Pages is included with IIS free of charge. To get started using ASP, you simply need to rename your file with an .ASP extension and embed some script within that file.

- State management—The Internet is *stateless* by definition, which means that as a user travels from one page to another on the Internet (or even on the same server), neither the server nor the browser remembers the previously visited page. This was originally designed to prevent the need for continuous connections to an Internet server and therefore relieve the server, which could send more volumes of data to more users at once. In complex database applications such as e-commerce, it is important for the Web server to remember who logged into the system from the browser and keep that information available while that user is logged in. This usually requires a bit of tricky programming, but fortunately ASP provides an easier mechanism by which developers can rely on steady application information.

- Executes on the Web server—This statement does not require much clarification, but it is an important concept to remember. With all of the database access and additional logic being performed on the Web server, there is no need to write varying scripts that depend on the browser's capabilities. The ASP engine does not care what browser is being used and can easily perform complex tasks and send those browser-neutral results to any Web browser.

With all of these points, it is hard to imagine any negative impact when using Active Server Pages. In reality, you must weigh the following considerations before making a decision:

- Requires programming—ASP is basically a platform on which developers can write applications. These applications can be designed in any scripting language (such as VBScript or JavaScript), but software development experience and skills are recommended for larger projects. There are many considerations when developing a larger system and application developers are better trained to handle these situations and write script accordingly. For example, an application developer should know how to best optimize database usage on a heavily used site so that ASP does not bog down a visitors response time.

- Requires Microsoft solutions—If you do not prefer using Microsoft's server technologies, then you probably will not find yourself using Active Server Pages. ASP is definitely a powerful platform, but currently it is only supported on Microsoft's IIS, which is only available on Microsoft Windows NT Server. You cannot write ASP applications on another server platform (such as UNIX with a Netscape Web server) with Microsoft's software. Some third-party vendors are marketing ASP-compatible server extensions for Netscape and other Web servers that do run on varying server platforms. It is important, however, to consider that ASP, like every other Internet technology, is evolving at a dizzying pace. Make sure the solution you implement continues to meet your requirements for using the newest Microsoft ASP features.

- DCOM server-side objects—Whenever ASP invokes a server-side component such as the database connector object, it is invoking an object that adheres to Microsoft's Distributed Common Object Model (DCOM). These objects can be created using a variety of languages, including Microsoft Visual Basic, C++, J++, or even Microsoft COBOL. The key point? These objects must be compiled as 32-bit Windows applications that can execute on a Windows NT server. If you prefer to use a different vendor's server or if you want to use other objects that follow competing object standards such as CORBA (Common Object Request Broker Architecture), you must consider something other than ASP as your application's platform.

Script Support in ASP

The previous source code examples exhibit some basic features of Active Server Pages in use. You may have also noticed that there were very few script commands used in the examples, but that written was accomplished using VBScript. In theory, script within an ASP file can be designed in any language that conforms to Microsoft's Active Scripting model. ASP currently supports two primary languages that are also common for client-side browser scripting: VBScript and JavaScript.

You can determine the scripting language for use within an ASP file by either setting the language attribute globally for the file or by configuring each block of script as code written in a particular language. To set the language of an ASP file for the entire document, you can use the following command at the top of the ASP file itself:

```
<% @Language= "JavaScript" %>
```

In this example, the default scripting language for the scripts that execute within an ASP file is JavaScript. The code designed within the entire file must therefore adhere to JavaScript's conventions in order for it to execute and produce results.

A second method for specifying the language for use within a script is to use the `<SCRIPT>` tag. If you have create client-side scripts that run within the context of the Web browser, you are probably already familiar with this tag. It allows you to specify a block of an HTML file that is to be treated as script. Likewise, the tag allows you to specify blocks of script within the ASP file. A parameter named LANGUAGE lies within the `<SCRIPT>` tag. You can set the language for use for that block of code by following this parameter with a language name such as JavaScript or VBScript.

> **Note**
>
> When using the <SCRIPT> tag within your Active Server Page files, be sure to indicate where you want the script to execute. Any program code that exists between the <SCRIPT> </SCRIPT> tags will, by default, execute on the browser. To indicate script that should execute on the server or be translated by the ASP engine, make sure that you add the RUNAT parameter. This parameter allows you to specify Server as an option, which forces the script to run on the server. To set up a block of code to run within an ASP page using JavaScript, for example, you could use the following:
>
> ```
> <SCRIPT LANGUAGE="JavaScript" RUNAT="Server">
>     JavaScript Commands...
> </SCRIPT>
> ```
>
> Keep in mind that in order to use the RUNAT parameter, ASP requires that you also specify the LANGUAGE parameter.

Tip #182

> There is no reason all code written in an Active Server Page must be in one language. You can use the <SCRIPT> </SCRIPT> tags to indicate some blocks of code that are written in JavaScript and others that are written in VBScript.

KEEPING IT IN SCOPE

If you are a developer, chances are you have heard of the concept of *variables (page 535)* and their scope within an application. You can typically define a variable as well as exactly where that variable can be made available within a program. For instance, a variable could be defined as available throughout the application. This type of variable is often referred to as a *global* variable because any portion of the application can retrieve or set the variable's content. It is also quite possible to define variables that last only within a particular function. These variables are available within a function and any variables that were declared in that function are reset once that function has terminated.

You may be wondering why this is important. You must understand where variables can be defined in ASP and how long each of those variables will persist. Otherwise you may try referencing variables that no longer contain data because you are accessing them outside of the scope in which they were intended. There are three basic scopes in which variables can be defined within ASP:

- Session variables—These variables are defined when a user visits the Web page for the first time and persist until that same user leaves the site. These are truly the most global of Active Server Page variables and can be referenced from any ASP page within an application. Information such as the name of the user logged into a system can usually be maintained in a session variable.

- Page variables—When writing multiple blocks of script within an ASP page, you can define variables that are globally available to that single page, but not to other pages. These variables can be accessed or set from any functions or code blocks within the page. Since the Web is stateless by nature, global variables can not be passed across multiple pages unless you use the "session" object that is available in ASP to set session variables.

- Function variables—Any variables declared and used within a function persist only for the duration of the function. Once the function finishes, any variables that were used are released and cannot be accessed by outside functions or script.

Note

It is important to point out that any variables used within <SCRIPT> tags in an ASP file are also available only within those blocks of code. A variable declared in one block of code declared by the <SCRIPT> tag is unavailable to other blocks of code within the ASP file. Therefore it is important to declare reusable variables such as object pointers within the overall scope of the file, not just within a function or <SCRIPT> block.

SERVER-SIDE COMPONENTS

By now you have a good understanding of what Active Server Pages can do for your Web site and how it can enhance your development abilities. The reality is that as good as ASP is for some applications, it is insufficient for very highly accessed or very complex Web sites. For such sites, Microsoft encourages the use of another technology: server-side objects.

You will recall from your previous database examples that an ASP must make use of the ADODB.Connection object in order to attach to a database connection. Database capabilities are not inherent in ASP and must therefore rely on the use of external objects to create an application your ASP application. This makes Active Server Pages a very extensible environment because there is no reason these external objects must be database connections only. In fact, they can be objects that accomplish any variety of tasks. For instance, your Active Server Page file could invoke an object that routes electronic mail, retrieves additional information, or performs tasks specific to your organization.

The use of server objects in complex applications is recommended for many reasons:

- Separation of logic from presentation—As many people begin maintaining a Web site, it is natural to break responsibilities into several areas such as programming, graphics and layout, and content. With more people involved with the Web site's creation, it becomes exceedingly difficult to prevent content authors or layout artists from accidentally overwriting program code. Separating program logic into individual objects prevents another person from destroying the object's logic itself, although he may accidentally remove a reference within the file to the object.

PART

VIII

CH

41

■ Enhanced security—Many of the objects that are referenced within Active Server Pages are compiled objects that cannot easily expose their internal logic. By being separate compiled objects on the same server (or even remote servers), there is less of a chance that an intruder can determine any sensitive business logic that the object contains.

■ Reusability—By encapsulating core logic as objects that reside on the server, common actions can be easily reused. In order to use a server-side object within an ASP page, an instance of that object simply needs to be created. If other pages within a Web site also want to use the same functionality, such as database connectivity, they can simply create their own instances of the main object. There is no need to copy and paste the actual logic that the object implements into every potential application page. Likewise, any improvement made to an object is inherited to all pages that used the object. If objects were not used and logic is instead embedded into each page, each page that contained a copy of that logic would also need to be maintained or corrected.

■ Enhanced speed—In most cases, Active Server Pages is a fairly quick running environment. If large amounts of data are being parsed and returned, however, the interpreted language commands within an ASP file may slow performance. As alluded to earlier, server-side objects are compiled and optimized for execution on the server. If an object is written in C++, it will therefore be compiled to the machine's native language and executed very quickly. This is much quicker than the execution of an ASP page, particularly when you consider all of the overhead required to execute an ASP file such as the Web server, the actual ASP engine, and more.

■ Less rewrite—If you have been using a development tool such as Visual Basic to write logic for applications within your organization, chances are you do not want to throw away all of that work. With server-side object technology, you can encapsulate the predetermined logic into an object. By compiling that logic into an object, you can reuse the code previously written on new platforms such as the Internet or an intranet. Separating core business logic into a component allows you to easily create multiple front ends to that object. For example, with the core logic in a separate object, either a Web page could make use of that object or another Visual Basic application could use it. It is important to remember that languages other than Visual Basic support this architecture.

As you can see, there are many good reasons to consider writing your main components for a Web site as a server-side object instead of including it all within ASP script. Here's a brief review about how to create a server-side object.

CREATING AN OBJECT WITH VISUAL BASIC

Creating an object can be surprisingly simple. This example creates a basic object that retrieves information over the Internet via the HTTP protocol and returns the result as a string. You basically create an object with a single method, getURL, which accepts a single parameter that specifies the URL to retrieve; the actual method returns a string with the URL results. This object type can be useful when creating ASP scripts that read information from other sources across the Internet or can be used to invoke subsequent ASP files.

To begin, you need to start Visual Basic version 5.0 or 6.0 and choose to create an ActiveX DLL from the New Project dialog box. After doing so, the appropriate window is assembled within the Visual Basic workspace and the project window contains a single class module within the project. Figure 41.3 more clearly illustrates the workspace that will be created by Visual Basic after starting the new project.

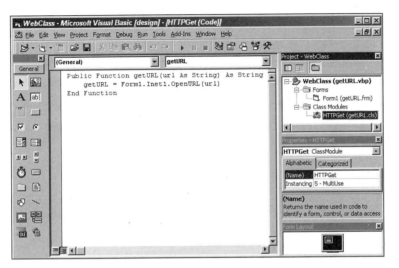

Figure 41.3
Server-side components can be easily created using Visual Basic.

Note

There is a difference between ActiveX DLLs and ActiveX EXEs. The basic difference lies in the fact that one creates applications that run in-process of the Web server context and the other creates applications that run outside the Web server's process.

A server component DLL (in-process) will run in the same process of other applications, which improves its overall performance. It does not need to be continually loaded and unloaded. If it crashes, any other tasks associated with it may crash as well.

An EXE component runs in its own memory space. If it crashes, it will not affect other processes on the system—but each process that executes will require additional memory and processing. These components form are not as optimized as server-side DLLs, but are sometimes more stable.

PART

VIII

CH

41

At this point it is important to mention how this Visual Basic application will be identified via the CreateObject command in an ASP script. The name of the Visual Basic class in Figure 41.3 is HTTPGet. This name is set by interrogating the properties for the selected class module. Also notice that the name of the project is WebClass. This setting can be controlled via the Visual Basic application's Project Properties dialog box, as demonstrated in Figure 41.4.

Figure 41.4
The Visual Basic project's name, `WebClass`, is used when identifying which object to create using the `CreateObject` command.

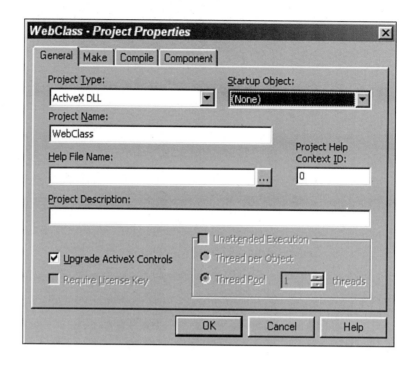

When you want to create this object within an ASP script using the `Server.CreateObject` method, specify the object to create as `WebClass.HTTPGet`. The following is an example:

```
set myURL = Server.CreateObject("WebClass.HTTPGet")
```

It is therefore important to name your project and classes both appropriately and logically. You may want to consolidate similar classes into a single project. For example, if there are a variety of financial functions defined within your organization, it may help to create a `myOrganization` project and then identify classes within that project by function such as `finance`.

ADDING THE LOGIC

After you have started the project, it is important to add some programming logic to carry out when a method is invoked on the object. In this case you want to create a simple method named `getURL`, which accepts a parameter that specifies an URL to retrieve on the Internet. Once the information has been retrieved, send the resulting HTML file or data file back to the ASP script that invoked this method.

In the left side of the screen shot in Figure 41.3 there exists a single function, `getURL`, in the class you are creating. This function, which serves as the main method for our server-side object, is defined as follows:

LISTING 41.4   A SIMPLE FUNCTION IN VISUAL BASIC

```
Public Function getURL(url As String) As String
    getURL = Form1.Inet1.OpenURL(url)
End Function
```

Functions within a Visual Basic class can be exposed as methods for the final rendered objects within ASP script or other programming environments. It is important to remember that you can specify both functions that are exposed to other applications as well as functions that remain visible only internally to the application object. Use the `Public` keyword in Visual Basic to determine which functions are available outside the object. Similarly, you can define functions that are available only internally within the object by using the `Private` keyword in front of the function declaration.

Specifying a parameter within the parentheses of the function declaration line indicates that the function requires an input parameter—or in this case an URL—to open on the Internet. By specifying the function `As String`, you infer that the function will return a result; in this case that result will be a text string. It is equally possible to create methods that do not return results, but these methods would be defined as subroutines (`Sub`) within Visual Basic.

In your one-line function, you invoke the `OpenURL` method on an Internet `Control` object. To make programming this object as simple as possible, include the Microsoft Internet Transfer Control in our Visual Basic project, which allows you to perform some basic Internet functions. Including this control in the Visual Basic project requires that you add the component by choosing Components from the Project menu within Visual Basic. A list of objects such as those in Figure 41.5 appears, including the Microsoft Internet Transfer Control.

Once the object has been included with the Visual Basic project, it is important to actually invoke the object. Adding the ActiveX object to the project does not mean that it is instantly available; you must activate it. The easiest method for activating such a control is to add a basic form to the Visual Basic project and simply drop this control onto the form by itself. Now you can see why Listing 41.4 needs to invoke the `OpenURL` method on the fully-qualified Internet Transfer Control object `form1.inet1`.

Note

By now you are probably wondering why you must bother to wrap the Internet Transfer Control object within a second object. There are a few reasons. First, the Internet Transfer Control cannot currently be invoked by using the `CreateObject` command. The only way that it can be successfully loaded into memory is to include it within the Visual Basic project's application. Therefore, you should not be able to create the object within the context of an ASP page either. The second reason for this wrapper is that you can add more logic to the control as necessary. In this simple example, you are merely returning the results of a requested URL. In reality, you could add business logic to determine information such as security rights before allowing the URL to be opened.

PART
VIII

CH
41

Figure 41.5
The Internet Transfer
Control can be easily
added to a Visual
Basic project to help
create interesting
server-side objects.

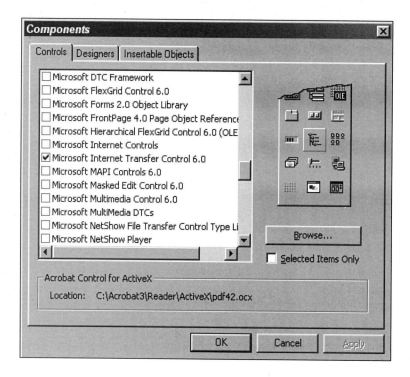

That's the jist of creating a server-side component in Visual Basic. Once you have finished adding the code, you can compile the project as a final .DLL file. After the compiled file has been added to the Web server, you can use ASP script to create an instance of this Visual Basic object and invoke methods such as getURL.

Tip #183

After you have compiled your Visual Basic DLL, you need to install it on the same Web server on which you plan on executing your ASP script. This installation includes both copying the file to the destination server as well as registering the new object in the server's system Registry. You can install this DLL on a Web server with one of two methods.

The first is to create a basic installation program via the Visual Basic Application Setup Wizard and then execute that setup program on the remote server. This automatically copies the files and registers the component within the server's system Registry. Although this seems convoluted, it is a recommended method. Visual Basic objects such as WebClass.HTTPGet requires numerous dependant files such as the Internet Transfer Control and associated Visual Basic runtime files. If you handle this process manually, you might forget to install necessary files.

A second approach is to simply copy the files manually onto the destination server. After the files have been copied, register the new object into the server's Registry. To do this under Windows NT Server, you can run regsvr32, followed by the name of the DLL file to register. This is an example: regsvr32 WebClass.dll.

INVOKING THE OBJECT IN ASP

Recall creating the database connection object and invoked methods associated with that object? To activate your custom object's getURL method, you can create very similar script code for your ASP application. Listing 41.5 illustrates a basic Active Server Page that creates an instance of the new object, invokes the getURL method to retrieve a data file from a Web server, and displays that file's content using the response.write method inherent to Active Server Pages.

LISTING 41.5   ASP-CREATED OBJECT

```
<HTML>
<BODY>

<% set myURL=server.CreateObject("WebClass.HTTPGet")
   myVar = myURL.getURL("http://jkottle/inventory.txt")
   response.write (myVar)
%>

</BODY>
</HTML>
```

DESIGN-TIME CONTROLS

By now your mind is swimming with the potential capabilities that Active Server Pages offer as well as server-side components created with development tools such as Visual Basic. As efficient as these technologies are, there is an additional technology Microsoft has introduced with Visual InterDev that FrontPage 2000 can make use of as well.

Design-Time Controls are objects that can be embedded within the Visual InterDev or FrontPage 2000 environments. These controls are basically objects that you can choose to embed within your Web page or Active Server Page. They are named Design-Time Controls because they contain properties and methods similar to other objects, but are controlled while you design the page. For instance, it is possible to embed a database control that provides navigation through pages of data. You can set up the properties for this control when you add it to your page by determining how many rows you would like to have returned per page, how you would like the navigation buttons to appear, and more. After you have included this Design-Time Control within your Web page, the actual script required to perform the object's actions are embedded within the page. In a sense, Design-Time Controls represent reusable script that can be embedded directly into your site's Web pages. A key advantage to Design-Time Controls is that they can allow the developer to set various properties for the control via a rich user interface. When finished, those changes are translated into simple code that is embedded within the page. These controls provide essentially a wizard for customizing script that is inserted into a page.

To understand Design-Time Controls more fully, add a simple Design-Time Control to your Web pages within the CompuShop Web site. When you install Visual InterDev 6.0, several Design-Time Controls (DTCs) are included with the installation. You add the PageTransitions Design-Time Control for this simple example. This control basically helps the page developer add page transitions, similar to those transition effects that you are accustomed to seeing in PowerPoint. To add a Design-Time Control to a page within FrontPage 2000, choose Insert, Advanced, Design-Time Control from the FrontPage Editor menu. Once you have chosen this option, a window lists all Design-Time Controls currently installed on the system. Figure 41.6 illustrates a sample list of available Design-Time Controls with the PageTransitions control selected for insertion.

Figure 41.6
There are many Design-Time Controls that can be embedded into a Web page through FrontPage.

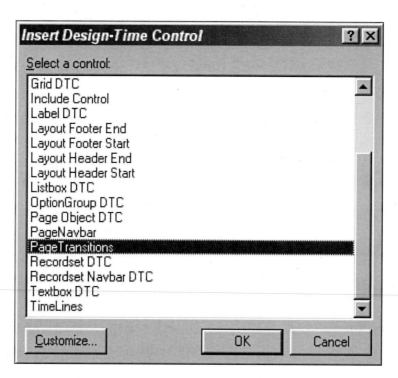

The highlighted control is added to the Web page currently being edited within FrontPage 2000 when you click OK within the Insert Design-Time Control dialog box. In the Normal WYSIWYG mode of the FrontPage editor, the control inserted appears as a long, button-like rectangle within the page. In the HTML mode, you simply see an <OBJECT> tag embedded for the control you are using. To change the behaviors for this control, simply click the control to select it and choose Properties from the Format menu within FrontPage.

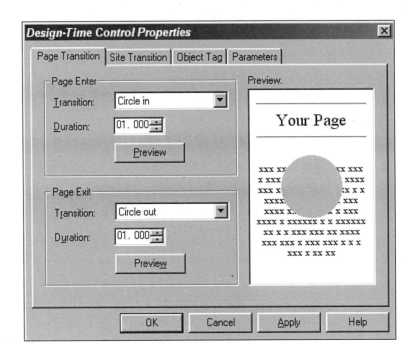

Figure 41.7
Design-Time Controls allow you to customize control properties through exposed interfaces.

With the PageTransitions control, you can select a fade-in or fade-out effect either for the current page you are designing or for the entire site. As you can tell from Figure 41.7, the Design-Time Control provides a simple yet powerful interface in which the page designer can specify properties for the transition. For example, a list box provides choices for the style of transition that can be used, such as Circle In. To see a preview of this transition, click the Preview button and watch the pane on the right side of the window.

Additional tabs across the top of the Design-Time Control interface allow you to specify other properties, including site transition properties, how the object will appear within the FrontPage designer, and using straight parameters versus user-friendly forms for the DTC. These tabs, of course, vary from control to control. Once you have completed the settings for the Design-Time Control, its properties are automatically updated on the Web page and any necessary script is embedded automatically.

The PageTransitions control simply allows the page developer to specify page transitions for use when entering or exiting a Web page, similar to changing slides in a PowerPoint presentation. To understand what exactly is being accomplished to perform these effects, take a look at the final Web page generated by FrontPage 2000 as shown in Listing 41.6.

LISTING 41.6 THE WEB PAGE HAS BEEN REPLACED WITH APPROPRIATE SCRIPT

```html
<html>

<head>
<meta http-equiv="Content-Type" content="text/html; charset=x-undefined">
<meta name="GENERATOR" content="Microsoft FrontPage 4.0">
<meta name="ProgId" content="FrontPage.Editor.Document">
<title>New Page 1</title>
</head>

<body>
<p align="left">

<!--metadata type="DesignerControl" startspan
<object classid="clsid:8EA785B1-4738-11D1-B47C-00A0C959BB15"
              id="PageTransitions1"
           dtcid="1" width="160" height="23">
  <param name="EnterPageDuration" value="1">
  <param name="EnterPageTransition" value="2">
  <param name="EnterPageType" value="0">
  <param name="ExitPageDuration" value="1">
  <param name="ExitPageTransition" value="3">
  <param name="ExitPageType" value="0">
  <param name="EnterSiteDuration" value="1">
  <param name="EnterSiteTransition" value="-1">
  <param name="EnterSiteType" value="0">
  <param name="ExitSiteDuration" value="1">
  <param name="ExitSiteTransition" value="-1">
  <param name="ExitSiteType" value="0">
</object>
-->

<META HTTP-EQUIV="Page-Enter"
        CONTENT="revealTrans(Duration=1.000,Transition=2)">
<META HTTP-EQUIV="Page-Exit"
        CONTENT="revealTrans(Duration=1.000,Transition=3)">

<!--metadata type="DesignerControl" endspan-->
</p>

<table border="1" width="100%" height="100%">
  <tr>
    <td width="100%" height="305" valign="middle" align="center">
      <p align="center">
      <font size="5" face="Abadi MT Condensed">Welcome to</font>
      <font size="7" face="Arial Black"><font color="#FF0000"><br>Comp</font>
      <font color="#000080">u</font>
      <font color="#FF0000">Shop</font></font></td>
  </tr>
</table>

</body>

</html>
```

If you think that the code in Listing 41.6 seems quite long to accomplish a relatively simple task, you're right. Many Design-Time Controls substitute a large amount of information that is required because the logic is fairly complex and the scripts that handle that logic can require many lines of code. If you know about Microsoft's DHTML Document Object Model, which is supported in Internet Explorer 4.0, you'll quickly realize that the only lines in this example necessary to creating the transition effects are those with the `META HTTP-EQUIV="Page-Enter"` or `META HTTP-EQUIV="Page-Exit"` tags. Even if you are not familiar with the transition capabilities of Internet Explorer 4.0, you may have noticed that the entire block of HTML that contains the `<OBJECT>` tag and associated `<PARAM>` tags is embedded within an HTML comment.

FrontPage basically uses two comments to indicate where a Design-Time Control is embedded within a Web page. The `<!--metadata type="DesignerControl" startspan` tag indicates where the DTC begins and the corresponding `<!--metadata type="DesignerControl" endspan-->` tag marks the end. The actual script that represents the end results of the Design-Time Control can be found between those comments.

The actual `<OBJECT>` tag is the actual Design-Time Control and the `<PARAM>` tags are the properties for that control. Since they are within the first comment, they are not displayed within the browser—yet FrontPage 2000 knows to read this information and use it appropriately when editing Design-Time Control information. The Page Transitions Design-Time control in this case is an object made up of the logic that embeds the correct script into the Web page, as well as the property window that allows you to set the attributes for the control and resulting script.

> **Note**
>
> The actual `<OBJECT>` tag within the Web page represents the Design-Time Control. A Design-Time Control is essentially an ActiveX control that can be specifically used within development environments such as FrontPage 2000 or Visual InterDev. If you remove the comments around the `<OBJECT>` tag in an editor such as Notepad and reload that page within Internet Explorer, you see the same button-like rectangle representing the Design-Time Control as that in FrontPage.

SUMMARY

In this chapter you were exposed to some advanced Web site development using technologies such as Active Server Pages, Server-Side Objects and Design-Time Controls. As you can clearly see, there are many options and technologies available to help you design your industrial-strength Web site. As you create heavy-duty Web sites, hopefully the experience you have gained form this chapter will help you to determine when to use the right technologies to accomplish your objectives.

TROUBLESHOOTING

What servers does Active Server Pages work with?

ASP was designed by Microsoft to work properly on Microsoft technologies such as Internet Information Server with Windows NT. If you wish to use Active Server Pages on a machine that uses another Web server package such as Netscape, or another operating system such as UNIX, you may want to consider purchasing an additional piece of software that emulates ASP for other platforms. A good example of this sort of software can be found at http://www.chiliasp.com.

DESIGNERS CORNER

As you already saw in Chapter 40, there can be many components used to create an overall site. Your particular site may require connectivity to databases or other servers to complete a task. It's obvious that you should optimize your site so that work for the site is performed by the right components. For example, that the database-specific commands are controlled by the database management system, validation and business logic is performed on the Web server, and whatever requires the most interactivity with the client is placed on the visitor's browser.

Just as you separate components to execute in their most optimal environments, you should also consider creating reusable Microsoft DCOM (Distributed Component Object Model) objects. By creating DCOM objects that are used on the server, you can gain many benefits such as application reusability, enhanced security, and increased stability. By building DCOM objects that control more of the business logic for your site, you can make use of other technologies to increase the robustness of your site.

For instance after creating DCOM objects, you can place all of related objects within a Microsoft Transaction Server transaction. This way system integrity is maintained since all respective actions are to either perform successfully or all be undone to revert the system to a previous state. You can also make use of message queue systems such as Microsoft Message Queue to guarantee that data is transmitted successfully across a network in which network response could be interrupted. Additionally with DCOM objects handling your business-specific actions, you can make components that are reusable for other sites or internal applications as well as components that execute faster and can be used more securely.

PART X

INTEGRATING FRONTPAGE 2000 AND MICROSOFT OFFICE

FrontPage 2000 and Office 2000

by Paul Colligan

Office 2000 is Microsoft's third attempt to integrate its office applications with the Internet. In this round it makes Internet protocols and file formats native to all of its programs.

Office 95 offered additional Internet assistants (by download) that help translate office content into HTML. They were simple at best and seldom provided attractive results, but they helped start an important trend—making Office content available by Web browser. Office 97 went a step further and offered a number of features built into each of the programs that enabled the user to save content as HTML files.

The Internet is integrated with every aspect of every program in the Office 2000 suite, including the introduction of *Web folders (page 907)* as a viable file storage option. It also introduces the use of HTML as a possible native file format.

The Web is so integrated into Office 2000 that FrontPage is now offered as part of the Premium Version of Office 2000. FrontPage was previously only made available as a stand-alone program.

Office 2000 can be very effective for anyone creating Web sites with FrontPage 2000 because it provides a number of tools for content creation and editing. Where FrontPage is a great tool for creating static HTML pages, the Office suite provides the tools for creating Web-based spreadsheets, databases, and presentations. Because FrontPage is part of the Office suite, integration between the program is much easier than it was before.

CHANGES IN OFFICE 2000

Included in the Internet-specific changes to the Office 2000 suite are the introduction of the Office extensions and web components, Web folders, and themes that spread through all of the suite's programs.

Office 2000 is no longer a set of programs that offer some Internet options. It is a set of programs that rely on Internet technologies (both existing and those developed specifically for Office) for a platform of interoperability.

OFFICE EXTENSIONS

Since the first version of FrontPage, server extensions were required to make full use of the program's functionality. In Office 2000, FrontPage server extensions have been upgraded and renamed *Office server extensions*. Office server extensions provide similar functionality across all of the applications in the suite. Many of the features discussed in this chapter are impossible to implement without the use of Office extensions on the Web server storing your files.

OFFICE WEB COMPONENTS

Excel and Access 2000 provide web components that let you manipulate program data through a simple Web interface. These powerful tools help you combine the publishing flexibility of HTML with the data mining power of Excel and Access via a simple COM object embedded in a Web page.

The power of this option should not be underestimated. Whereas many people feel uncomfortable using a traditional data manipulation tool such as Excel or Access, the simplicity of a Web browser as the interface can win over even the biggest technophobe.

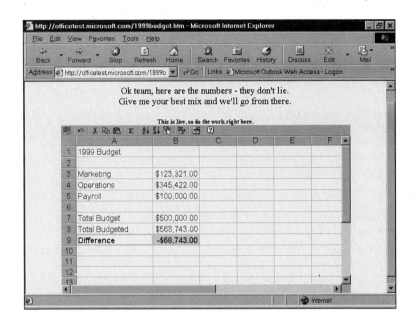

Figure 42.1
The Excel web component embedded in a Web page makes for an easier data manipulation interface.

An intranet that provides real-time sales figures to a company through the browser is one example application for Office web components. Company employees could choose which sales reports they want to view through a familiar interface and receive instant information.

Web components provide new opportunities for web development because they provide a simple way to provide Web-based data manipulation that once required extensive programming work. At this point they are unfortunately limited largely to intranet-type applications; their use requires an Office 2000 license and the files that make such interactivity possible are only made available on machines that have Office 2000 installed.

WEB FOLDERS

One of the new Office 2000 features (it's in all of the individual Office applications as well) is the introduction of Web folders as a file storage option. Simply put, *Web folders* are remote file shares that enable you to save your files to a remote server on the Internet. A corporate Web folder can be located anywhere—on your machine, in your company's LAN, at a local ISP, or on a server farm across the country. Internet access is all that's required. Access to Web folders is controlled through login and password entry—little different than a LAN.

Tip #184

> Placing a Web folder on the Internet, where it can be accessed by the entire world, opens a huge potential security risk that needs to be examined—and done so before such a tool is implemented on a corporate level. Make sure you understand the implications of Web folders before you make use of them.

The power of Web folders is not in what they do, but how they do it. File storage could be achieved remotely through FTP since the Internet's birth, but by making Web folders an option from within the application and making the interface simple, anyone can use them. The metaphor that they are familiar with using and the only knowledge required is a folder name (usually in the form of www.company.com), a login, and a password.

Web folders on servers with Office server extensions provide a number of features and capabilities in terms of collaboration. These things are covered in great detail in Part IV, "Collaboration, Workflow, and Task Management."

Placing your files and content at a remote Web folder location provides access to your files that might not have been previously available. It is no longer required that your desktop remain on for all users to share files from your machine. Even the need for a corporate file server can quickly be replaced by a similar Internet offering.

The introduction of Web folders enables Internet service providers to provide intranet services, either on purpose or by default. ISPs often provide hardware and backup capabilities small business can't afford, and by making use of a Web folder intranet, a small business can have these services at their disposal.

Web folders add a level of functionality to data storage that simply wasn't there before. Having all of the functionality of file shares that's now provided by the Internet—instead of an internal information services staff—lets you put the focus on content, not where and how that content will be stored.

SAVE AS WEB PAGE

Because Microsoft embraced HTML as a native file format, the programs in Office 2000 give you the chance (wherever possible) to save your content in HTML. *Headers (page 682)* saved into the HTML allow you to reopen the files in the programs they were created in for further editing.

What this means, for example, is that a slideshow created in PowerPoint can be saved to the corporate intranet as an HTML file viewable on all browsers by everyone in the company—not just those with PowerPoint (or the now-obsolete PowerPoint Viewer). If at any time the content needs to be edited, PowerPoint can open the HTML file directly and edit as needed. There is no need to utilize the proprietary PowerPoint file format. The same is true of any elements saved as a Web page by the Office suite.

Tip #185

> When using the Save as Web Page option, all of the content is rarely saved as a single HTML file. It is often saved with a number of other files and directories (graphics and the like) that contain all of the content in your original file. If you have saved a document as a Web page to your own machine for later uploading to a Web server or folder, make sure that you also copy all of the accompanying files.

Some items obviously won't translate perfectly into HTML. There are some things in world of publishing that don't have a counterpart on the Web. Elements such as page numbering, header and footer notations, page breaks and the like won't always look right on a browser. Check content saved as HTML in your browser to make sure that it meets your requirements. It is also a good idea to check the HTML files on multiple browser versions.

In any Office program, the Web Options tool found in the Save As dialog box's Tools drop-down menu gives you the ability to specify the type of HTML file you want to save your files as. You can disable features not available to earlier browsers, as well as specify the screen size for each of your files. If you are *publishing (page 791)* Office documents to the Web for a broad audience, make sure that you provide HTML that is viewable on a broad range of browsers. If you are building for an application where you control the browser type, make sure to make full use of the functionality provided by the later browsers.

Tip #186

> With a feature as impressive as being able to save all of your content into HTML, you might consider the option of never using Office's native file formats again. While possible, this creates files that are much larger and with a file structure that's sometimes harder to figure out. Often a single Office file is saved as multiple Web files. As a result, it is wise to use the native file formats wherever possible.

It is important to point out that the Save As Web Page option is merely a shortcut to the Save As dialog box; it saves the content as a Web page. There is no functional difference between the two paths.

WEB PAGE PREVIEW

PowerPoint 2000, Excel 2000, and Access 2000 provide a Web Page Preview in the File menu; the preview gives you the chance to immediately view the content you are creating in a Web browser. If you are curious how your content translates to HTML, you can use this feature for a quick examination. It is unavailable in Word because the Web Layout option provides the same effect directly from within the program. The Web Layout option in Word is discussed later in this chapter.

PART
VIII

CH
42

Tip #187

> It is always a good idea to see how your content appears in a Web browser if you are going to publish it in this manner. The Web Page Preview option is a quick way to accomplish this and no longer requires that you save the document as HTML in order to do so.

PUBLISHING DOCUMENTS

In addition to saving content as a Web page, Access, Excel, PowerPoint, and Outlook provide the option of publishing content to a Web server. Unlike saving static HTML files, publishing is associated with dynamic content.

The publishing dialog boxes provide a number of tools and options that enable you to specify the type of browser, user, and application you are publishing to.

It is important to point out that publishing almost always requires the use of Office extensions while the Save as HTML options can almost always be converted to any Web server.

THEMES

Themes were introduced in FrontPage 98 to mixed reviews. Now they are no longer just part of FrontPage; they are part of every program in the Office suite. Any data saved as HTML can be subjected to a theme, which helps give an entire site of static HTML and database-driven content the same look and feel. You can use FrontPage to change the theme of all content in the Web site, whether or not it was created with FrontPage, at any time.

More information about the use of themes in Web design can be found in Chapter 6, "Working with Themes."

FRONTPAGE 2000—AN OFFICE PROGRAM

Historically, FrontPage was positioned as a program that worked well with Office. Microsoft consistently offered some sort of rebate if you bought both of the programs and spent a lot of marketing money convincing you to do so.

FrontPage 2000 is included in the Office 2000 Premium package. Not only does this say interesting things about the future of publishing and the modern office but it also means that a lot of people are going to get their introduction to FrontPage from the new Office bundling.

Chances are good that a number of people reading this book purchased it because they have no idea of what to make of that FrontPage icon in their programs bar. If you are one of these people, welcome.

WORD 2000'S WEB TOOLS

Since Microsoft realized the importance of the Web and began to reorganize itself as an Internet company, it has explored the opportunity of utilizing Word as a Web page editing tool. It started in Word 95 with an add-on tool called the Internet Assistant. It made Word a rudimentary Web browser and provided limited Web page creation capabilities. It was a crude effort at best.

In Word 97, the option to save the file as an HTML document was built right into the program but still offered, at best, the simplest of options for Web development. Hyperlinking from within a Word document was made easier with the addition of a Web toolbar, but that and a few Web page design wizards was all that the program offered in terms of Web design.

Microsoft is almost there with Word 2000. Word is now a viable Web page design tool and offers a number of features that make it an attractive option. A Web layout view, a Themes option, a better Web toolbar, and a number of Web page wizards make Word 2000 a viable application for Web development.

The Web tools built into Word 2000 also open up the notion of a single document being publishing in a number of ways. For some a document will be printed, for others it will be faxed, and for others it will be placed on a Web site. Because Word now creates documents for both the printed and Web page, its power is increased.

Tip #188	It is important to point out that a number of people uncomfortable with the thought of Web design through a program such as FrontPage might not be opposed to the same task in Word. If your Web design duties require the work of many individuals, consider Word as an alternative design tool.

WEB LAYOUT VIEW

The traditional Normal and Print Layout views are in Word 2000, but a new view—Web Layout—lets you see your document if it were to be saved to the Internet. If you decide to use Word to develop Web pages, use this view during creation.

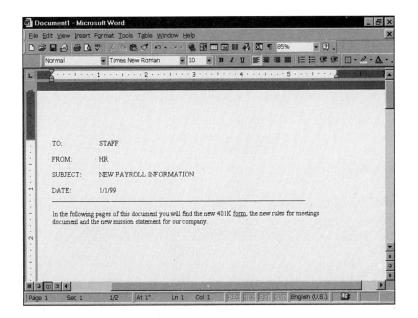

Figure 42.2
A Microsoft Word document seen in the Print Layout view.

Figure 42.3
The same document seen in Web Layout view.

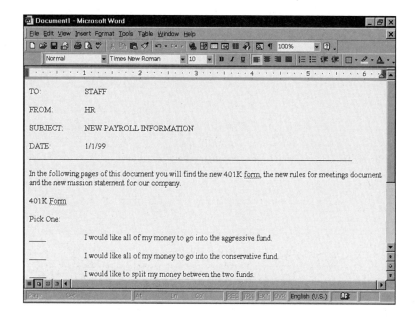

Be careful though—elements common to word processing but complicated in Web design (footnotes, headers, page numbering, and the like) don't always translate well.

THEMES

As discussed earlier in this book, *themes* are a group of color and graphic controls that control the appearance of a Web page or site. A theme can be set for an entire Web site through FrontPage 2000, giving every page in it a specific look and feel. If implemented properly, the theme can be changed, on either a *by-page* or *by-site* basis resulting in a new look and feel—and the content is not affected in any way.

When a theme is chosen for a Word 2000 file, it only affects the Web version (.HTM) of the file; it has no impact on the printed version (.DOC).

Click Format, Theme to choose a theme for a Word document. The Theme dialog box opens and allows you to either select or change a theme. Make sure Word is in Web Layout view.

Tip #189

> Themes don't always translate well into Word documents saved as HTML. If they originally weren't intended for the Web, little to no thought went into formatting the documents to make use of themes. It is a good practice to preview all Word documents saved with themes before making them available to the general public.

Themes give a site a consistent look and feel, which is important when trying to demonstrate that all of the content works together for a specific purpose or reason. Web sites are often the work of large teams, with each person having a different style that can come across in the design process. This is especially true if some are designing pages in FrontPage while others are using Word. By implementing themes as a common element throughout the entire site, the Web can have a cohesive, common look that portrays a particular feeling.

THE WEB AND WEB TOOLS TOOLBARS

Word 2000 contains two toolbars specific to the Internet: Web and Web Tools. You add them to your desktop the way you do any other toolbar; click View, Toolbars and then select the desired toolbar.

The Web toolbar was included with Office 97 and essentially makes the program a simple browser with limited capabilities. The toolbar is also made available in Excel 2000, Access 2000, PowerPoint 2000—even Outlook 2000—but is most often used in Word 2000.

Figure 42.4
The Web toolbar in Word 2000 gives the program simple browser capabilities.

The buttons on the Web toolbar are as follows (from left to right):

	Back	Moves back to the previous page
	Forward	Moves ahead one page
	Stop Current Jump	Stops the command in process
	Refresh Current Page	Reloads the current page
	Start Page	Opens you default search page
	Search the Web	Opens your browser search page
	Favorites	Opens your Favorites folder
	Go	Provides a drop-down menu of a number of navigational options
	Show Only Web Toolbar	Toggles the rest of the toolbars on and off

The Web Tools toolbar is new to Word 2000 and provides a tool set by which to add Web-type functionality to the page.

Figure 42.5
The Web Tools toolbar in Word 2000 enables you to insert Web functionality into your Word documents.

The buttons on the Web Tools toolbar are as follows (from left to right):

	Design Mode	Toggles the Design Mode option
	Properties	Shows (and allows you to edit) the properties of the selected item
	Microsoft Script Editor	Opens the Microsoft development environment
	Check Box	Adds a check box to the document
	Option Button	Adds an Option button
	Drop-down Box	Adds a drop-down box
	List Box	Adds a list box
	Text Box	Adds a text box
	Text Area	Adds a text area
	Submit	Adds a Submit button
	Submit with Image	Adds a graphical Submit button
	Reset	Adds a Reset button

	Hidden	Adds a hidden value to the form
	Password	Adds a Password box
	Movie	Adds a movie to the document
	Sound	Adds a sound to the document
	Scrolling Text	Adds a marquee (*scrolling text*) item to the document

Tip #1001

If you find yourself putting a lot of *interactivity* into a document, it is a good idea to use FrontPage instead of Word to do so. Just as Word specializes in the layout and editing functionality that you expect from a word processor, FrontPage is best at adding interactivity to a Web page. Both programs can do the work of the other but, by default they make it much harder than when the proper program is used.

HYPERLINKS

Long before the Internet was the multimedia extravaganza that FrontPage helps make it, the Web's focus was on the concept of *hypertext*—linking concepts, documents, and ideas in a non-linear format. The ability to breeze through libraries of documentation the way you wanted to—at the click of a mouse—was an intoxicating option and a powerful new reference tool.

You can hyperlink to any item or document (Word, HTML, Excel, and so on) from within Microsoft Word. This has applications both Web based and otherwise. Instead of requiring that content be developed linearly, you can create it in whatever format you want, link it wherever you want, and leave the rest to the viewer.

Hyperlinking is done by selecting the text (or item) to be hyperlinked and choosing Insert, Hyperlink or selecting the Insert Hyperlink button from the standard toolbar. From there the Insert Hyperlink dialog box gives you a number of hyperlinking options.

WEB PAGE WIZARDS

When creating a new document in Word 2000, the New dialog box devotes an entire tab to Web pages. It provides the following options:

- Column with Contents creates a Web page template. A column to the left provides internal links to the page's different sections. Use this template to create a single Web page with multiple sections.

PART

VIII

CH

42

- Frequently Asked Questions creates a Web page template for a Frequently Asked Questions (FAQ) page. This template also makes use of internal linking to make document navigation easier.

- Left Aligned Column creates a Web page template with a photo to the left and content to the right. Use this if you are uncomfortable laying out a Web page in Word and need some basic assistance doing so.

- Personal Web Page creates a Web page template for a basic personal Web page.

- Right Aligned Column creates a Web page template similar to the one created by Left Aligned Column, but with a reversed layout.

- Simple Layout creates a Web page template with a very plain layout that is pleasing to the eye and can be viewed on almost any browser.

- Table of Contents creates a Web page template that can be used as the home page for a larger Web site.

- Web Page Wizard creates a multipaged Web site with themes and a navigational structure that, although impressive, can be developed much quicker in FrontPage. A site developed in the Web Page Wizard could easily be imported into FrontPage for later editing.

Tip #190	You will often find it easier to create a Web page from FrontPage's wizards than it is from Word's.

WORD 2000'S OTHER WEB TOOLS AND FRONTPAGE 2000 FEATURES

Because Word 2000 and FrontPage 2000 share many of the same features, functions, and code, a number of tricks can be utilized to get quick results when using elements from both programs:

- A Word file can be dragged from the desktop into FrontPage, where FrontPage automatically translates the document into a Web page. There is no need to use the Insert, File option commonly used and encouraged for file importing.

- Elements of a Word file can be dragged directly from Word into FrontPage. To do so, select the area you would like to move from Word and drag the selection into FrontPage.

- Copying the entire contents of a Web file to the Clipboard and then copying it directly into an open page in FrontPage 2000 is another way to quickly transfer content between the two programs.

- You can make a quick edit to a Word file saved as HTML in your Web without opening Word. To accomplish this, right-click the item in the FrontPage 2000 folder list, select Open With, and then select FrontPage as your editor.

FrontPage 2000 and Word 2000 can be used hand in hand. You'll quickly find that you can use either program to achieve the result you are looking for.

EXCEL 2000'S WEB TOOLS

Through Office's use of HTML as a native file format, Excel 2000 gives you the capability to save worksheet and workbook content directly to the Web. This content can be used for reporting information and data without the need for the Excel client. Excel 2000 makes the process simple.

With the use of the Excel Web component, Excel 2000 also gives you the ability to publish worksheet information with interactivity elements that bring much of the functionality of Excel to the Web browser. Data analysis can be provided through the Internet Explorer without requiring that Excel be on the desktop (and understood by the user).

It is also important to point out that the use of hyperlinks can be added to Excel files through the use of the Hyperlink function in an Excel formula.

SAVING WORKSHEETS TO THE WEB

To save worksheet content to the Web, select the Save as Web Page option from the File menu. When the Save As dialog box opens, decide whether you want the entire notebook or the selected area to be saved. For simple porting of worksheet data to the Web, make sure that the Add Interactivity option button is deselected.

Figure 42.6
The Excel Save As dialog box gives you the ability to save your files as HTML or publish them with interactivity.

The content produced through this procedure can be viewed on any Web browser and requires no special plug-ins or programs to be viewed. It is a very powerful way to present information online, but is limited by the static nature of the data presented. This function should be used mostly to present informational snapshots, much like the tradition use of Excel data in Word documents.

PUBLISHING EXCEL DATA TO THE WEB

You can also publish Excel content to the Web, providing a level of interactivity previously unavailable through the use of the Excel Web component. To do so, select the Add Interactivity option button in the Publish area of the Save As dialog box when publishing your content.

Figure 42.7
An Excel sheet published with the Add Interactivity check box selected to enable the user to manipulate data in a Web page.

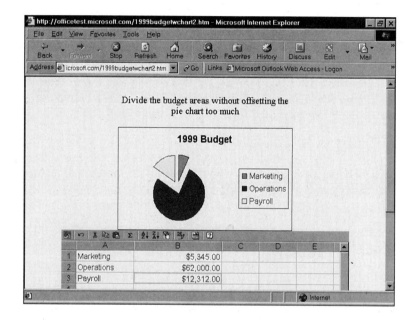

Excel data published with interactivity lets you change information within the Web page and see the results instantly. Formulas and table are updated on-the-fly as the user changes the data. Excel's interactive, analysis, and data manipulation options provided are now ported to the Web browser via this option.

Publishing Excel content with interactivity requires Internet Explorer 4.0 or later and the Excel Web component installed on the machine viewing the content. Microsoft requires an Excel 2000 license on a desktop using the Excel Web component; its application, although powerful, is limited on a larger scale. At this time, the Excel Web component's primary use is on an intranet with users manipulating and analyzing data through the Web browser instead of Excel.

HYPERLINKS IN EXCEL

It is possible to add hyperlinks to Excel worksheets through the use of the HYPERLINK function. Use the following syntax to put a hyperlink in a cell:

```
=HYPERLINK ("link location","friendly name")
```

`link location` is the hyperlink source and `friendly name` is what you want to call the hyperlink. It is that simple.

If you are familiar with Excel formulas it is worth noting that you can use the `HYPERLINK` function within other Excel functions.

POWERPOINT 2000'S WEB TOOLS

Microsoft has provided a means of outputting PowerPoint slides to the Web since PowerPoint 95. The benefits of placing slides online for the entire world to view are obvious. Where a slideshow was normally only viewed by the participants in the program, an online version can be referenced at any time by anyone with access to your Web site. A Web version of a past presentation is a powerful archive of previous work and it enables you to share it with as many people as possible.

The past two attempts at integration accomplished the task of putting the slides online but only resulted in simple HTML versions of the presentation that required a bulky PowerPoint player application for any form of interactivity. The PowerPoint player was eliminated with the introduction of PowerPoint 2000.

The new Internet features in PowerPoint 2000 give you an additional level of functionality. You can now publish an online slideshow specific to browser types (including Netscape) and broadcast the presentation online.

HYPERLINKING WITHIN POWERPOINT SLIDES

If you are going to place slides online, the capability to provide hyperlinks within the slideshow opens a new level of interactivity to your presentation. Instead of just describing a Web site or application, you can directly link to it, allowing the user to interact with it.

The practice is also effective if you are presenting a slideshow that refers to other content. Simply hyperlinking the content from within a slide provides another possible presentation track.

Hyperlinking from within PowerPoint is done by selecting the text (or item) to be hyperlinked and choosing Insert, Hyperlink; you can also select the Insert Hyperlink button in the standard toolbar. The Insert Hyperlink dialog box provides your hyperlinking options from there. Hyperlinking has been an option in PowerPoint since PowerPoint 97.

PUBLISHING A SLIDESHOW

Once a slideshow is complete and you are ready to make it available online, you can either save the content as a Web page or you can publish it to a Web server with Office server extensions installed on it. Where the first option provides an impressive HTML version of the presentation, publishing provides a number of features new to this version of the program.

Figure 42.8
The Publish as Web Page dialog box allows you to specify the browser type you expect to be viewing your presentation.

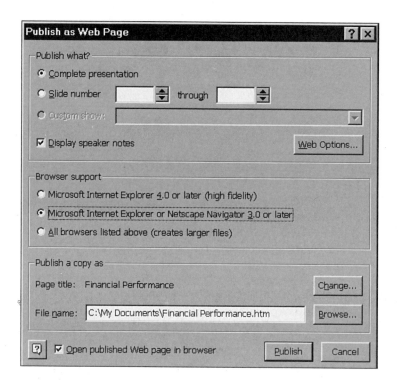

The Publish as Web Page dialog box gives you the option to publish your slides with or without speaker notes and to choose the browser type for the presentation. You can also choose which slides will be published and whether you want to preview the final product after it is published.

Tip #191

When you publish a PowerPoint presentation online, realize that the notes from your presentation will also be made available by default. Individuals who keep little or poorly edited notes might want to consider not making this option available.

THE PUBLISHED PRESENTATION

The published presentation offers a number of capabilities based on the variables that you saved the presentation with, as well as the browser type and version you use when viewing the presentation.

A slideshow saved specifically for the browser and viewed in Internet Explorer 4.0 or later provides a number of interactive options:

■ The frame to the left of the screen contains the program outline. You can jump to any slide in the presentation by clicking the slide title.

- The outline can be collapsed or expanded with the Expand/Collapse button on the lower-left side of the screen.

- The outline can be eliminated completely with the Outline toggle button, which is to the left of the Expand/Collapse button.

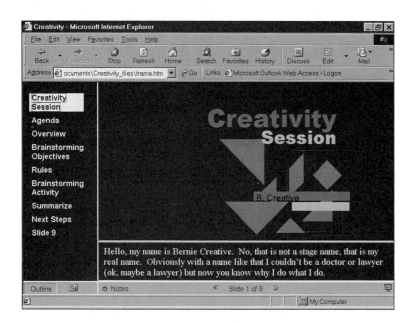

Figure 42.9
A published presentation provides frames for both the presentation outline and the speaker notes in Internet Explorer version 4.0 or later.

Figure 42.10
This slide presentation is viewed in Full Screen mode on Internet Explorer 4.0.

PART

VIII

CH

42

Directly under the slides are a number of buttons that—from left to right—open or close the notes frame, let you navigate through the slides, and provide a full screen option similar to the PowerPoint Slide Show option. Pressing the Esc key returns you to normal viewing mode.

Figure 42.11
This slide presentation is viewed in Netscape Navigator version 3.0.

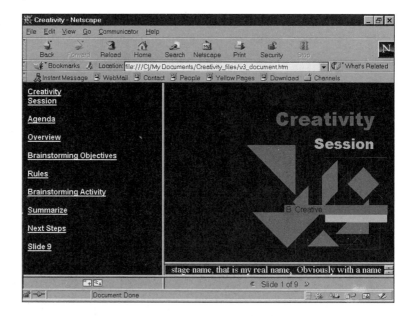

In presentation saved for Netscape version 3.0 and later, the screen also divides into different frames for the outline, slides, and notes. You can still select any slide from the outline, collapse the outline with buttons on the bottom of the screen, and navigate through the slides but have no toggle or full screen options provided by the Internet Explorer versions.

Tip #192

When saving your presentations for viewing by the general public, it is smart to enable the All Browsers Listed Above option. You never will know the type of browser your audience is using and giving the best chance possible to see your content is always a good idea.

PRESENTATION BROADCASTING

Another option new to PowerPoint 2000 is the capability to broadcast a PowerPoint presentation over the Internet to any user with Internet Explorer version 4.0 or later.

Up to 15 users can view the presentation on a normal Web server. If you have more viewers than that or use audio or video, you must use Microsoft's NetShow server.

Options for communication with the presenter include regular email and, if the proper services are installed and made available, chat.

To set up a broadcast, choose Slide Show, Online Broadcast. The dialog box walks you through the process and places the presentation on the server for broadcast. You have the option to schedule your broadcast through Outlook, which will provide linking options for users with Outlook and any other HTML-compliant email program.

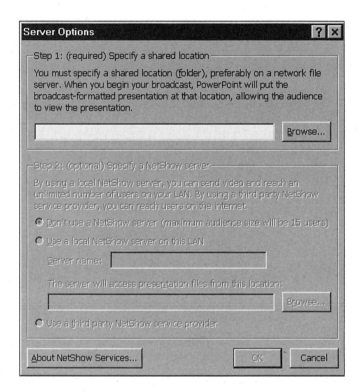

Figure 42.12
The Server Options dialog box lets you specify your broadcast location and walks you through the necessary steps required to go live with your presentation.

Tip #193

During the course of developing your broadcast presentation, PowerPoint 2000 creates a Presentation Broadcast Lobby page, which you can point to from your Web site.

Once you are ready to broadcast, PowerPoint will walk you through the process step by step.

ACCESS 2000'S WEB TOOLS

A complete guide to database integration with FrontPage 2000 can be found in Chapter 39, "Using Databases with FrontPage 2000," and in Chapter 40, "Advanced Database Techniques." This chapter focuses on saving Access 2000 data to the Web and examining the concept and creation of the data access page.

Access 97 provides a Save to the Web Wizard lets you save database elements as HTML. This straight feature was dropped in Office 2000. In Access 2000, any table or query results can be saved as a Web page from Access 2000.

This option provides a quick and easy way to port data from Access to the Web. The results aren't pretty but it beats cutting and pasting each element individually.

Access 2000 really shines in its capability to design data access pages, a concept new to Access 2000.

DATA ACCESS PAGES

A *data access page* is a Web page designed for viewing and working with data stored in a database, typically Microsoft Access or Microsoft SQL. It makes use of the Access Web component and can also contain Excel chart and pivot table information.

Data access pages are powerful tools because they provide a Web interface for data analysis that was previously impossible without extensive programming talent. With data access pages, powerful browser-based analysis tools can quickly be developed.

Figure 42.13
Access 2000 lists data access pages as native objects.

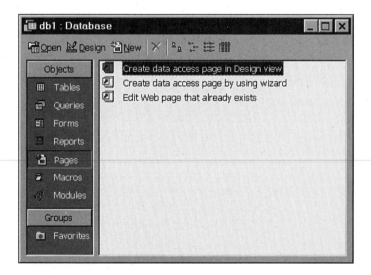

Access 2000 gives you the ability to create data access pages directly within the program. The Objects frame in the Access database interface gives you the option to create a data access page in either Design view or by wizard. It also gives you the option to edit an existing data access page.

When creating a data access page in Design view, Access 2000 opens a data access page design window that lets you control almost every element. It opens up the toolbox, alignment, and sizing toolbars, which are what give you complete control.

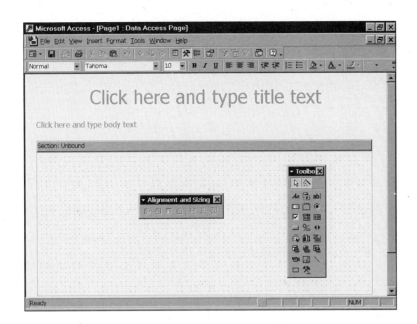

Figure 42.14
Design view gives you control over every element of the data access page design process.

If you desire assistance in the creation of a data access page, use the Create Data Access Page by Using Wizard option. The wizard will ask you to choose the fields desired on your page; it will then ask you for the records' sort order. The shell for the page is completed and you can either modify it to meet your specific needs or view the completed product.

Remember that viewing data access pages requires Internet Explorer 4.0 or later and a licensed copy of Access 2000 on the machine that is running the browser.

Adding Office Charts and Data to the Data Access Page

The most powerful tools in the data access page toolbox is the Office PivotTable, Office Chart, and Office Spreadsheet tools that enable you to add Excel pivot tables, charts and spreadsheets to a data access page. You can develop a data access page that pulls data from multiple sources charted and presents them on a single Web page in a very easy-to-understand format.

Should You Upgrade to Office 2000?

The question of upgrading your version of Office obviously arises if you purchased FrontPage 2000 and have an older version of Office. In determining whether you want to upgrade, ask yourself the following questions:

- Are all of your needs currently being met with the version of Office that you are currently using? What exactly would you get from upgrading?
- Is the project that you are working on ready to make the jump to Office 2000? Does your Web server have the Office server extensions installed?

- If you intend on making use of the Web components discussed in this chapter, will all of the people you expect to make use of the components be able to upgrade as well? Can you afford the cost of upgrading everyone?

- If you are working with a team and want to make use of the collaboration tools enabled with Office 2000?

If you find that FrontPage 2000 and your current version of Office will meet most of your requirements, don't worry about upgrading yet. Appendix B, "FrontPage 2000 and Office 97," covers Office 97 and FrontPage 2000, and the Web options made available to Office 95 are so simple that little explanation is required to use them.

TROUBLESHOOTING

Problems in working with other Office 2000 programs and FrontPage will almost always come from an incomplete understanding of the other program, or how the document is translated to HTML.

A firm understanding of the program is the first step in making a smooth transition to a Web page. If you aren't able to make the program perform as you'd like it to, the transition to a Web page will obviously go poorly as well.

The help files that come with Office 2000 are very good at explaining specific answers to frequently experienced problems. If it seems that your problem "shouldn't be that hard" there is most likely an answer quickly available.

The assistants that come with Office 2000 are a bit cutesy for most but they will search Microsoft.com for additional answers if what you are looking for can't be found in their database. Consider using them as a last resort.

Many problems will come from trying to make another Office program do something that FrontPage 2000 does well. Check this book first if you are looking to do something specific and you might be surprised what you find.

DESIGNERS CORNER

The other Office 2000 programs provide a fleet of additional design tools that can be used to make your Web site more attractive. If you have them, make sure that you make use of them. As mentioned previously, don't use them to do the things FrontPage 2000 does well—use them to do the things the other programs do well.

The HTML options provided by Word are very similar to what you'll find in FrontPage. The biggest boost offered by this program is the ability to save previous Word documents as an HTML file without ever having to port them into FrontPage. This can be a huge timesaver and is something you can train almost anyone to do.

The HTML options provided by Access have little to do with the design process but can assist when developing the result pages for your database queries. Don't spend time developing results pages when you have the tools provided by Access.

Excel's chart making features can help you quickly design charts and graphs that can help make a point that would takes hours with FrontPage. If you need to present data at your site, consider Excel's chart wizard to give you the look you desire.

PowerPoint's design features have been around longer than the Web. There is simply no better way to develop presentation slides. If you are putting slide information online, use PowerPoint to develop it.

EXTENDING FRONTPAGE 2000 WITH VBA

INTRODUCTION TO PROGRAMMING WITH VISUAL BASIC FOR APPLICATIONS

In this chapter   *by Bob Samer*

WHY WOULD WEB DEVELOPERS WANT TO DO THIS?

In other Microsoft Office applications, VBA is used most often to create runtime type of effects. For example, a programmer may create a VBA checkbook manager "application" that is embedded inside of an Excel workbook. When the workbook is opened, the VBA program displays its user interface to the user.

Runtime effects for FrontPage documents (since they are just HTML files) are created by using scripting languages in conjunction with standard HTML elements and Active elements (ActiveX controls, Java Applets, and so on). FrontPage's VBA is designed for a much different purpose: creating programs that function in a design-time environment. Here are a few examples.

VBA can be used to publish a specific Web (or list of Webs) from the development server to the production server at a specified time of day.

VBA might be used to enforce corporate standards by trapping the `OnBeforePageSave` event and scanning the HTML document for inappropriate content or apply the corporate style sheet.

The possibilities that exist for the programmer using the VBA in FrontPage are effectively limitless.

WHAT IS VBA?

Visual Basic for Application is the core language implementation for the Visual Basic programming language. VBA contains all of the elements shared between the Microsoft Visual Basic programming environment and the programming environment used by Microsoft Office applications to create macro languages, the Visual Basic Editor (VBE).

You learned about Visual Basic Scripting Edition (VBScript) earlier in the book. VBScript is a subset of the VBA language. VBA is, itself, a subset of the Visual Basic programming language.

WHAT IS VBE?

VBE stands for the *Visual Basic Editor*. This is the Integrated Development Environment (IDE) that ships with all Microsoft Office applications. VBE allows the user to create and execute VBA code and provides mechanisms to manage your programming projects. Figure 43.1 shows the VBE window.

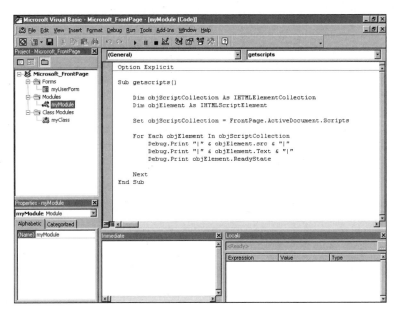

Figure 43.1
The Visual Basic Editor.

THE PROJECT EXPLORER

The VBE Project Explorer displays the current list of modules that are defined for your project. A *module* is an object that contains related sections of code. The modules are arranged in the VBE Project Explorer in much the same fashion as files and folders are arranged in the Windows Explorer. VBA programmers have access to three types of modules in VBE: Code modules, Form modules, and Class modules. Figure 43.2 shows the Project Explorer window.

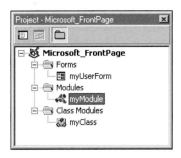

Figure 43.2
The VBE Project Explorer.

The three top-level folders that are displayed in the Project Explorer contain nodes for each of modules that are stored in the current project. Use the Project Explorer to add, delete, and modify the modules in your project.

CODE MODULES

Code modules are the most basic of the modules available in VBE. Code modules contain sections of code that are self-contained. The code may depend functions or variables in other sections of the same module or different modules, but does not depend on any information from the code module itself. To create a new code module, choose module from the Insert menu inside of VBE. This will add a new code module to your project.

USER FORM MODULES

User Form modules are used to provide user interface features for FrontPage macros as well as an area for sections of code. User Form modules are different from code modules in that they provide an area, called a User Form, onto which user interface components called controls can be arranged. Figure 43.3 shows this staging area with a Text Box control centered on it.

Figure 43.3
A User Form module in VBE.

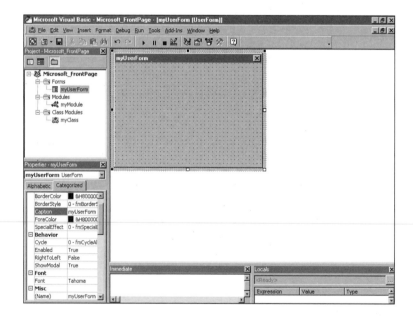

Controls are added at design time to the user form by selecting them from the VBE Control Toolbox. To show the toolbox, choose Toolbox from the View menu. The VBE Control Toolbox is shown in Figure 43.4.

To add a control to a user form, drag it from the VBE Control Toolbox onto your form. Most controls are resizable and they can be arranged anywhere within the boundaries of the form.

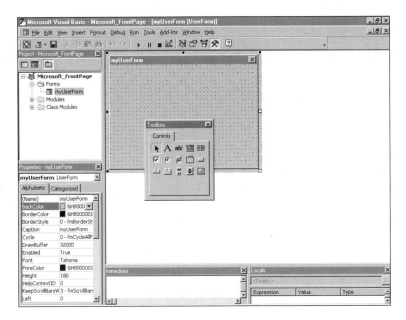

Figure 43.4
The VBE Control Toolbox.

The User Form module, and the controls it contains, expose pre-defined code that enables the programmer to manipulate the contents of the form and controls. The User Form and its controls also expose sections of code in the code area called *event handlers*. These are special procedures that are automatically run when specific events occur. For example, every User Form module defines a `UserForm_Initialize` event handler that runs when the form is first displayed.

Note

Handling events is explained in detail in Chapter 46, "Using Events in FrontPage 2000."

From the Insert menu in VBE, choose User Form to insert a new User Form module.

CLASS MODULES

Class modules enable the VBA programmer to create his or her own objects that define properties, methods, and events. Instances of these objects can then be used within other code sections.

One of the most common uses for Class modules in FrontPage VBA is to trap events. Using Class modules to respond to FrontPage generated events is covered in detail in Chapter 46.

To insert a new class module, choose Class module from the Insert menu in VBE.

THE VBE CODE EDITOR

Once a module is inserted, its content can be manipulated by using the VBE Code Editor. The Code Editor is a window that provides text editor functionality that VBA programmers can use to work with their code on the different types of modules. Double clicking a module node in the Project Explorer will open the module into the VBE Code Editor window for editing. Figure 43.5 shows the VBE Code Editor.

Figure 43.5
The VBE Code Editor.

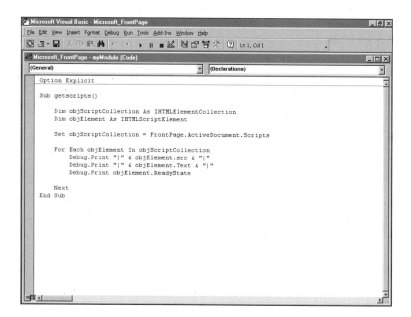

THE OBJECT LIST BOX

The Object List Box that is located at the upper-left of the VBE Code Editor is used to navigate the objects that are defined for a particular module. Depending on what type of module is open in the Code Editor, the Object List Box will contain items pertaining to that type of module.

Since Code modules do not expose any intrinsic objects, their Object List Boxes only contain one item, the general area of the module. This item is defined for all module types and selecting it displays the entire module contents in the VBE Code Editor, beginning at the top of the module.

User Form modules contain the User Form object and any controls that are defined on the User Form. Class modules contain the class object as well as any other objects defined on the Class modules.

> **Note**
>
> Chapter 46 covers objects defined by using the `withevents` keyword to create event handlers. Objects defined with this keyword will show up in the Object List Box of the Class module on which they are defined.

Changing the selection in the Object List Box will affect what procedures appear in the Procedure List Box. If the general item is selected, then all procedures that exist on the module are displayed in the Procedure List Box. If an object is selected, all procedures that are *available* for that object are displayed in the Procedure List Box.

THE PROCEDURE LIST BOX

The Procedure List Box that is located at the top-right of the VBE Code Editor enables the programmer to navigate through the different procedures defined for the object that is selected in the Object List.

If the general item is selected in the Object List, all procedures defined in the form are displayed in the Procedure List Box.

If the item listed in the Procedure List Box exists in the current module, the item is displayed in bold. Selecting a bold item from the List Box will display the procedure in the VBE Code Editor. If the item is not bold, the procedure does not yet exist. Selecting the item will place a procedure handler into the module and navigate the VBE Code Editor to the new procedure.

For example, if the current module is a User Form module, and the User Form object is selected in the Object List Box, the procedures that a User Form can have defined for it will appear in the Procedure List Box, even if none of these procedures is currently defined on the User Form module. Selecting the Initialize item will add the following code to the User Form module and then navigate to the procedure in the VBE Code Editor.

```
Private Sub UserForm_Initialize()

End Sub
```

The programmer can now add programming statements to the area between the `Private Sub` and `End Sub` that will produce the desired effect. Programming statements are covered a bit later in this chapter.

THE PROPERTIES WINDOW

Each of the three types of modules that VBA programmers work with exposes properties accessible via the VBE Properties window. The Properties window is shown in Figure 43.6.

Figure 43.6
The VBE Properties
window.

To show the VBE Properties window, choose Properties Window from the View menu in VBE. The VBE Properties window displays the module's properties. At design time, the programmer can change these properties to affect the module's behavior.

Code modules expose one property, Name. This property is used to identify the module in the Project Explorer and also provide a method for other modules to access the code on the module.

User Form modules expose a host of properties that define the behavior of the form. As it does in the Code module, the Name property identifies the form in the Project Explorer, but also allows other modules to access the code defined for the User Form. For example, the following code uses the User Form's Name property to execute its Show method to display the User Form.

```
frmMyUserForm1.Show
```

Working with User Form modules to create a user interface is discussed in more detail later in the chapter.

Class modules expose the Name property that works just as it does for Code and User Form modules. In addition, class modules expose an Instancing property. This property controls whether or not the class is creatable outside of VBE.

Note

For work within FrontPage and VBE, the Instancing property should be set to private.

THE IMMEDIATE WINDOW

The Immediate window is a very useful tool to the VBA Programmer. As its name hints at, the Immediate window executes whatever code is entered into it immediately after the programmer presses Enter. To show the Immediate window, choose Immediate Window from the View menu in VBE. The Immediate window is shown in Figure 43.7.

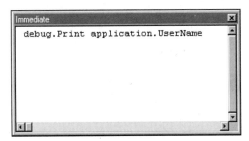

Figure 43.7
The VBE Immediate window.

The Immediate window is useful when debugging or trying out code to see how it works. The `Print` statement can be used to print the value of a variable or function in the Immediate window. For example, typing the following code into the Immediate window and pressing Enter will display the current time below the `Print` statement.

```
Print Today()
```

Tip #194	Substitute the question mark (?) for the `Print` statement to output variables and functions to the Immediate window. The following code is equivalent to code listed before this tip. `? Today()`

The VBA programmer can also print to the Immediate window from code defined in modules by using the `Debug.Print` statement. This is useful when debugging code.

EXECUTING YOUR CODE

Now that you know how to add procedures to modules in VBE, you are probably wondering how to execute the code. There are a few ways to run your code, depending on whether you are executing with VBE as the active window or FrontPage as the active window.

EXECUTING INSIDE VBE

To execute your code within VBE, place the cursor inside of your procedure and press F5, or choose Run Sub/UserForm from the Run menu.

To see a list of procedures that are available to run, move the cursor outside of a procedure and press F5, or choose Run Macro from the Run menu. This will display the Macros dialog box that lists all of the available procedures in the current project.

Note	The Macros dialog box displays all of the procedures available to run in the current *project*—not the current module. Don't be surprised if you see a larger list than you were expecting.

To execute the macro, select it from the macro list and click the Run button.

EXECUTING INSIDE FRONTPAGE

To execute your macro while FrontPage is the active window, press Alt-F8 or choose Macros from the Tools/Macro menu. This will display the Macros dialog box. Choose the macro from the macro list and click the Run button.

Tip #195	You can also assign a macro to a toolbar button or menu item. To do this, choose Customize from the Tools menu to display the Customize dialog box. Switch to the Commands tab and select the Macros item in the Categories list box. Drag the Custom Button item from the Commands list box and drop it onto a toolbar. Next, right click the new button and choose Assign Macro from the context menu. This will display the Macros dialog box. Select the macro you wish to execute when the button is accessed and click OK.

Code can also be fired in response to FrontPage-generated events. Trapping FrontPage-generated events is covered in Chapter 46.

PROGRAMMING WITH VBA

Programs created by using VBA can vary in complexity from one line to a series of many different blocks of code. These blocks of code are stored on one of the three types of modules mentioned earlier and are arranged into discrete sections called procedures. VBA provides three types of procedures: *Sub Procedures*, *Function Procedures*, and *Property Procedures*.

SUB PROCEDURES

Sub Procedures are blocks of code that perform a specific task or set of tasks, but do not return a value to the caller.

Tip #196	*Caller* refers to what code originally called the Sub Procedure. This could be another Sub Procedure or Function in the current program, some code in a COM AddIn (discussed later in the chapter), or FrontPage itself via the Tools, Macros, Macro dialog box.

Sub Procedures can take arguments if necessary and are always enclosed between a Sub and End Sub statement. For example, the following code displays the name of the current user when executed.

```
Sub ShowUserName()
    MsgBox Application.UserName
End Sub
```

To add a new Sub Procedure to your module, choose the Procedure menu item from the Insert menu inside the Visual Basic Editor (VBE). This will display the Add Procedure dialog box. Choose the Sub radio button, type a name for the Sub Procedure, and click OK. This will add the Sub and End Sub statements to the current module.

FUNCTION PROCEDURES

Function procedures are sections of code that perform some task or set of tasks and always return a value to the caller. Function procedures can take arguments and are enclosed with the Function and End Function keywords.

For example, the following function verifies whether the currently logged in user's username is "Administrator" and returns true or false.

```
Function IsUserAdmin() as Boolean
    if Application.UserName = "Administrator" then
        IsUserAdmin = True
    else
        IsUserAdmin = False
    End If
End Function
```

To add a new function procedure to your module, choose the Procedure menu item from the Insert menu inside the Visual Basic Editor (VBE). This will bring up the Add Procedure dialog box. Choose the Function radio button, type a name for the function procedure, and click OK. This will add the Function and End Function statements to the current module.

PROPERTY PROCEDURES

Property procedures are a special kind of *sub procedure (page 940)*. These are only allowed inside Class modules and are used to access data from an instance of a class.

Property procedures are usually defined in pairs that allow the get and set of the data defined inside a class.

The procedure that sets some data contained in the instance of the class is defined with the Property Let keywords and closed by the End Property keywords. For example, the following code defines a property called URL that sets the m_URL string to whatever value is contained in the argument sURLPath.

```
Property Let URL(ByVal sURLPath As String)
    m_URL = sURLPath
End Property
```

The procedure that retrieves some data contained in the instance of the class is defined with the Property Get keywords and closed by the End Property keywords. The following code defines a property "set" called URL that returns the value of m_URL as the value of the URL property.

```
Property Get URL()
    URL = m_URL
End Property
```

The following example demonstrates the use of the URL property defined in the previous two paragraphs as it is used inside of a class called CMyWebPage.

```
Dim m_URL As String

Sub Class_Initialize()
    Set m_URL = ""
End Sub

Property Get URL() As Variant
    URL = m_URL
End Property

Property Let URL(ByVal sURLPath As String)
    m_URL = sURLPath
End Property
```

To add a new *property procedure (page 940)* to your class module, choose the Procedure menu item from the Insert menu inside the Visual Basic Editor (VBE). This will display the Add Procedure dialog box. Choose the Property radio button, type a name for the property procedure, and click OK. This will add the appropriate property procedure keywords to your class modules.

WORKING WITH VARIABLES IN VBA

Variables are used in VBA to store the data values for your program. *Variables* are often defined as a specific data type. The data types provided by VBA are listed in Table 43.1.

TABLE 43.1 SIMPLE TYPES

Variable Type	Description
Byte	Byte value
Integer	Integer
Long	Long integer
Single	Single-precision floating-point number
Double	Double-precision floating-point number
Currency	Currency value
Decimal	Decimal value
Date	Date value
String	String
Boolean	Boolean value
Variant	Can contain any data type

Using the Dim keyword in VBA creates variables. For example, the following line of code defines a variable called iCounter that is of type Integer.

```
Dim iCounter As Integer
```

> **Note**
>
> Variable identifiers must begin with a letter, cannot exceed 255 characters, and must be unique within the procedure.

Variables that are not given a specific type by using the As keyword are stored in the Variant data type by VBA. The Variant data type is large enough to hold any type of data. For example, the following code defines the iCounter variable, but does not assign it to a specific data type. VBA treats iCounter as a Variant and allocates the maximum amount of storage space for it.

```
Dim iCounter
```

> **Note**
>
> It is a good practice to explicitly assign your variable a data type. Using Variants for your variables wastes memory in your procedure and decreases performance because of all the conversion activity that takes place.

> **Tip #197**
>
> Add the Option Explicit declaration to your module to force the VBA compiler to complain about untyped variables. You can enable this as the default for all modules by checking the Require Variable Declaration check box in the Options dialog box.

Understanding Scope in VBA

Scope refers to what level of access is defined for a particular variable or procedure. VBA programmers can define both variables and procedures with either public or private scope.

Procedures declared with the Public keyword are available to all other procedures in the project. Procedures declared with the Private keyword are available only to other procedures on the same module.

Variables defined with the Public keyword must be defined outside of a procedure. This makes them available to all other modules and procedures in the project. Variables defined with the Private keyword that lie outside of a procedure are available to all procedures in the module, but not procedures on other modules.

Variables that lie inside a procedure can also be defined with the keyword Static. This forces the variable to retain its value after the procedure is finished executing.

The following example demonstrates the scoping of procedures and variables in VBA.

```
Public g_sName As String
' g_sName is a global variable, available to all procedures on all modules
' in the project

Private sLocalName As String
' sLocalName is a local variable, available only to procedures on this
' module.
```

```
Public Function CalcSum(iNum As Integer) As Integer
'CalcSum is a global procedure that is available to all modules in the
'project.
Static iRunningTotal As Integer
' iRunningTotal is private to CalcSum
' Also, since it has the static keyword, it
' keeps its value each time CalcSum finishes executing
iRunningTotal = iRunningTotal + iNum
CalcSum = iRunningTotal
End Function

Private Function OutputName() As String
' Output name is only available to procedures on this module
OutputName = sLocalName
End Function
```

DECISION STATEMENTS

Decision statements allow the programmer to choose an execution depending on a decision. VBA defines three different types of decision statements: If Then, If Then Else, and Select Case.

If Then

Use the If Then construct when the program needs to execute one or more statements based on a condition. The following example demonstrates the use of the If Then statement. If the Boolean variable bDocIsInWeb is true, the code displays a message box to the user.

```
If bDocIsInWeb = True Then
    MsgBox "Document Found in Web"
End If
```

The If Then construct can handle more complex conditions. The following example demonstrates the use of a more complex conditional.

```
If bDocIsInWeb = True And sUrl = "Default.htm" Or sUrl = "Index.htm" Then
    MsgBox "Document Found in Web is the Home Page"
End If
```

An End If statement must close IF Then.

If Then Else

Use the If Then Else construct when the program needs to execute one of a number of sections of code depending on a condition. The following example demonstrates the use of the If Then Else statement.

```
If bdocisinweb = True Then
    MsgBox "Document Found in Web is the Home Page"
Else
    MsgBox "Can't find document in web"
End If
```

For each section of code needed, the programmer can define an `ElseIf` statement. The following example demonstrates.

```
If sUrl = "index.htm" Then
    MsgBox "The document is the home page"
    ElseIf sUrl = "index.html" Then
        MsgBox "The document is the home page"
        ElseIf sUrl = "default.htm" Then
            MsgBox "The document is the home page"
            ElseIf sUrl = "default.html" Then
                MsgBox "The document is the home page"
            Else
                MsgBox "The Document is not the home page"
End If
```

Many nested `ElseIf` statements will get very tedious and hard to maintain. Replace them with the `Select Case` statement to improve readability and maintainability of the code.

An `End If` statement must close IF Then Else.

Select Case

Use the `Select Case` statement to select different code sections depending on a specific condition. The following code creates the same effect as the `If Then ElseIf` code sample previously listed.

```
Select Case sUrl
Case "index.htm"
  MsgBox "The document is the home page"
Case "index.html"
  MsgBox "The document is the home page"
Case "default.htm"
  MsgBox "The document is the home page"
Case "default.html"
  MsgBox "The document is the home page"
Case Else
  MsgBox "The Document is not the home page"
End Select
```

The `End Select` statement must follow the `Select Case` statement.

LOOPING STRUCTURES

VBA defines three looping structures: the `Do While` statement, the `For Next` statement and the `For Each Next` statement.

Do While

Use the `Do While` statement to execute a series of statements a number of times depending on a looping condition. There are a few different forms of the `Do While` statement.

Use the Do While Loop form to execute a series of statements zero or more times. For example, depending on the value of bCondition, the following code executes the statement zero or more times:

```
Do While bCondition
    MsgBox "Continuing Loop until bCondtion is false"
Loop
```

Because VBA evaluates the looping condition before executing the loop, no statements in the loop are executed if bCondition is false or nonzero.

Note

> If you are familiar with VBA, you may be wondering why we didn't discuss the While Wend structure. This structure works exactly the same as the Do While Loop structure. The following code works exactly the same as the preceding example:
>
> ```
> While bCondition
>     MsgBox "Continuing Loop until bCondtion is false"
> Wend
> ```

Use the Do Loop While form to execute the statements inside the loop one or more times. For example, the following code will always execute the statement at least once:

```
    Do
            MsgBox "Continuing Loop until bCondtion is false"
Loop While bCondition
```

In this case, VBA doesn't evaluate the looping condition until the loop has executed once, regardless of the value of bCondition.

For Next

Use the For Next *structure* to execute statements a specific number of times. The For Next structure iterates from a lower bound to an upper bound by a certain increment each cycle of the loop. For example, the following loop executes its statements 10 times:

```
Dim x As Integer
For x = 1 To 10
    MsgBox "Loop iteration #" & x
Next x
```

Note

> The ampersand (&) symbol used in the preceding example is an operator VBA uses to concatenate values together. In this instance, the value of x is joined to the string that is passed to the MsgBox function.

In the preceding example, x is the counter variable for the loop. During each iteration of the loop, x is incremented by one. Once the loop is complete, x has the value of 10. The For Loop assumes an increment amount of 1. To increment by a different value, or event decrement, add the `Step` statement to the `For Loop` structure. For example, the following example loops from 1 to 10, but uses an increment value of 2:

```
Dim x As Integer
For x = 1 To 10 Step 2
    MsgBox "Loop iteration #" & x
Next x
```

In the preceding example, the loop executes five times instead of 10. `For Loop` structures can also count down from an upper bound to a lower bound. The following example counts from 10 down to 1 by setting the `Step` value to -1:

```
Dim x As Integer
For x = 10 To 1 Step -1
    MsgBox "Loop iteration #" & x
Next x
```

EXITING LOOPING STRUCTURES

Programs will often need to drop out of a loop before the loop is finished iterating. For example, you may want to drop out of the `For Loop` before hitting the tenth iteration. Use the `Exit For` and `Exit Do` statements to drop out of `For Loop` and `Do Loop` statements. The following example exits the `For Loop` when x is equal to 5, even though the loop is supposed to execute ten times:

```
Dim x As Integer
For x = 1 To 10
    MsgBox "Loop interation #" & x
    If x = 5 Then
        Exit For
    End If
Next x
```

WORKING WITH OBJECTS

One of the key features of VBA is its support for objects and collections. VBA exposes its own objects and collections and also provides facilities to access other applications' objects and collections.

WHAT IS AN OBJECT?

Since Microsoft introduced them back in 1994, objects have gone by a number of different names.

They were available under the umbrella of a technology called Object Linking and Embedding (OLE).

OLE 1.0 was originally introduced as a means to provide document embedding between Microsoft Excel and Microsoft Word. The idea was that a user could create a table in Word that was a representation of an Excel spreadsheet. When the user selected the table, Excel would start up and allow the user to work with the table inside Excel itself and any changes made were saved to both the Excel sheet and the Word document.

Next, OLE 2.0 appeared and allowed Word to provide Excel's commands inside itself (and vise versa) without having to execute Excel. When the user selected the Excel table inside of Word, the menus and toolbars switched themselves to those of Excel.

When OLE 2.0 transformed itself into OLE Automation, the first instances of "objects" as they are known in VBA came on the scene. For example, programmers could create instances of Excel from their own code, instruct Excel to perform some calculations, and then close Excel. Excel was now a programmable object.

Objects can be complete executable programs, like Microsoft Excel, or objects that exist inside a program, like a the Worksheet object that exists in Excel. Objects that exist inside programs usually follow a hierarchy and are part of what is called an Object Model.

An *Object Model* is a structured hierarchy that represents the functionality of a specific program. This hierarchy is usually only available from a top-level object, the `Application` object.

FrontPage 2000 has an extensive Object Model that encapsulates almost all of the features of FrontPage. This Object Model is only available via the FrontPage `Application` object.

> **Note**
>
> If you are working with VBA inside FrontPage's Visual Basic Editor, the `Application` object is automatically created for you. The entire FrontPage Object Model is available from this object.

Objects manage their own data and provide services for other code to access and manipulate that data. These services are called methods and properties.

> **Note**
>
> VBA exposes the methods and properties of objects via the . symbol.

METHODS

Methods are facilities that an object exposes that perform some sort of action. For example, Microsoft FrontPage exposes an object called `Web`. The `Web` object encapsulates the idea of a FrontPage-based Web and provides a number of methods that correspond to actions a user can perform on the Web. For example, the following code calls the `ApplyTheme` method of a `Web` object that corresponds to the active Web in FrontPage:

```
Dim myweb As Web
Set myweb = ActiveWeb
myweb.ApplyTheme ("Blends")
```

Note

VBA requires the use of the `Set` statement to assign objects to variables that are dimensioned as objects. In the proceeding example, we are assigning the `ActiveWeb` object to the `MyWeb` object, so we have to use the `Set` statement.

Methods work somewhat like function procedures. Some take arguments, some return values, and so on. Methods perform actions to modify the data that the object encapsulates. In the preceding example, the `ApplyTheme` method modifies that data of the `Web` object that represents the theme information of the Web.

PROPERTIES

Properties are facilities that an object exposes that provide a `get` and `set` mechanism used to access the data that the object encapsulates. They are different from methods in that they do not necessarily perform an action. Rather, they simply return or set data specific to the object. For example, the following example retrieves the `URL` property of a `Web` object:

```
Dim myweb As Web
MsgBox myweb.url
```

The preceding example got the value of the URL from the `Web` object. `URL` is a read-only property, meaning that FrontPage sets the `URL` to a value automatically and the programmer cannot set it to a new value directly. Some object's properties are settable. For example, the following code sets the `UserName` property of the FrontPage `Application` object to `"Administrator"`:

```
Application.UserName = "Administrator"
```

Some properties return objects instead of the base types that VBA provides. In these cases, VBA requires the use of the `Set` statement when accessing the property. For example, accessing the `RootFolder` property of the `Web` object to retrieve an object of type `WebFolder` requires the `Set` statement. The following example demonstrates:

```
Dim myFolder As WebFolder
Set myFolder = ActiveWeb.RootFolder
```

In addition, objects provide a means to notify the code that is accessing them when certain actions take place. These notifications are called events.

EVENTS

Some objects in an Object Model have specific *events* defined for them. VBA programmers can set up Event Handlers for these events that are essentially Sub Procedures that are set to execute when the event occurs. The FrontPage Application defines a number of events. Working with events in the FrontPage 2000 Object Model is covered in great detail in Chapter 46.

THE VBE OBJECT BROWSER

As you work with objects in VBA you will find that it is difficult to keep track of what properties, methods, and events each object exposes. One of your best resources to solve this problem is the VBE Object Browser. The Object Browser is a window in VBE that lays out the Object Model of the application in a hierarchical form.

To access the Object Browser, choose Object Browser from the View menu. Figure 43.8 shows the object browser and the FrontPage Object Model.

Figure 43.8
The VBE Object Browser for FrontPage 2000.

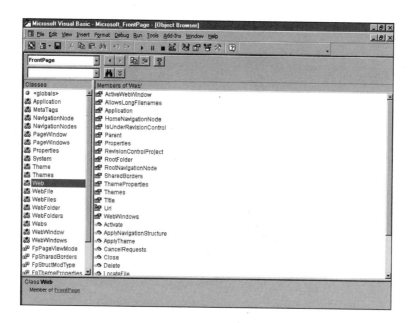

The Object Browser consists of two adjacent list boxes, the Classes list box and the Members list box, an Application drop-down box, and an information pane.

As different libraries are selected in the Application drop-down box, the Classes list box is populated with the objects defined for that application's Object Model.

As objects are selected in the Classes list box, the properties, methods, and events that are exposed on the object are displayed in the Member list box.

Clicking a member in the Members list box displays information about the selected property, method, or event in the information pane at the bottom of the Object Browser.

For example, Figure 43.9 shows the display of the information pane when the ApplyTheme method of the Web object is selected.

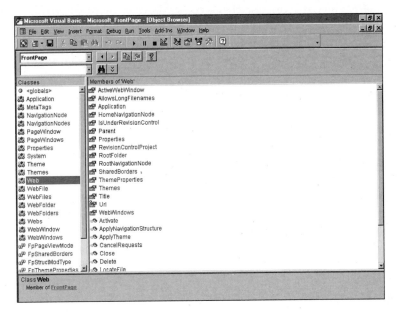

Figure 43.9
Using the Object Browser.

COLLECTIONS

Collections are special types of objects that encapsulate similar objects. In most cases, collections are pre-defined by the Object Model, or the Object Model controls the additions, deletion, and selection of the collection's objects via a series of methods and properties.

ADDING OBJECTS TO THE COLLECTION

All collections provide a means to add new objects to the collection. The Add method will place a reference to the new object into the collection and update the Count property for the collection. For example, the following code uses the Add method to create a new Web site and make it available in the Webs collection:

```
Dim newweb As Web
Set newweb = Webs.Add("http://www.bigcompany.com", "username", "password")
```

The Webs collection now contains an instance of a Web object corresponding to the FrontPage Web site (http://www.bigcompany.com).

Note

The name of the method used to add new objects to a collection will vary depending on the collection and the application. In addition, many collections contain multiple methods to add objects. For example, the Webs collection exposes an Open method as well as the Add method. Use the Open method to open an existing Web and place an instance of its Web object into the Webs collection.

ACCESSING AN OBJECT IN A COLLECTION

Most collections expose the Item method to access individual objects in the collection. For most collections, Item takes one argument. This argument is of type Variant, meaning that it can be of any other type. The two most common types sent to the Item method are integer and string values. This allows the programmer the luxury of indexing into a collection by a string value, such as the Web's URL, or a numerical index, such as zero. For example, the Web collection's implementation of Item takes either the URL of the Web or a numerical index corresponding to the position of the Web object in the Webs collection. For example, the following code accesses a Web with the URL of http://www.bigcompany.com that is currently opened in FrontPage:

```
Dim w As Web
Set w = Webs.Item("http://www.bigcompany.com")
```

The following code will return the same Web by using its numerical index into the Webs collection.

```
Dim w as Web
Set w = Webs.Item(0)
```

> **Note**
>
> Objects and collections that are defined in an Object Model will often set one of their methods or properties as the default action. The default action for most collections is the Item method. This means that it is not necessary to use the actual name of the method or property in your code. For example, the following two code segments are equivalent:
>
> ```
> Dim w as Web
> Set w = Webs(Error! Bookmark not defined.)
> ```
>
> ```
> Dim w As Web
> Set w = Webs.Item("http://www.bigcompany.com")
> ```
>
> To determine the default action for an object, use the Object Browser to view the properties and methods for an object. Default actions are marked with a small dot above the property indicator.

DETERMINING THE NUMBER OF OBJECTS IN A COLLECTION

All collections expose a property used to determine the number of objects in the collections. Normally this is the Count property. As objects are added or removed, the Count property is updated to reflect the current contents of the collections. The following example uses the Count property of the Webs collection to determine how many Webs are currently opened in FrontPage:

```
Dim iCount as Integer
ICount = Webs.Count
MsgBox "There are " & iCount & " webs open!"
```

Note

> The FrontPage Page Object Model (POM), discussed in Chapter 45, "Accessing Documents," does not implement the Count property for its collections. Instead, the POM exposes a Length property to determine the number of objects in a collection.

REMOVING OBJECTS FROM A COLLECTION

Collections expose facilities to remove objects as well as add them. For example, the Webs collection exposes a Delete method. Use the Delete method to remove the Web object from the Webs collection and delete the Web site itself.

Some objects expose methods that remove them from their collections as well. The Web object exposes a method called Close that is used to remove the instance of the Web object from the Webs collection. The following example closes each Web object in the Webs collection.

```
Dim x As Integer
For x = 0 To Webs.Count - 1
    Webs(x).Close
Next x
```

USING THE For Each STATEMENT WITH COLLECTIONS

VBA exposes a special form of the For statement designed to work especially with collections. The For Each statement iterates over each object in the collection and does not require the programmer to know how many objects are in the collection. For example, the following code uses the For Each statement to close each Web object that is opened in FrontPage:

```
Dim w as Web
For Each w In Webs
    w.Close
Next w
```

For each iteration of the For Each loop, the next Web object in the Webs collection is placed into the w variable.

The FrontPage 2000 Object Model exposes a number of collections that represent features of FrontPage. The Webs collection mentioned in the proceeding section is one example of such a collection. Chapter 44, "Managing Webs with VBA," and Chapter 45 cover these collections and their corresponding objects in detail.

DEBUGGING

One of the most valuable tools in VBE, or any programming environment, is the debugger. VBE includes a robust, easy to use debugger that the programmer can use to root out and fix bugs that will inevitably crop up.

VBE DEBUGGER

Access the VBE debugging features via the Debug menu. One of the coolest features of the VBE debugger is the ability to "step" through code a line at a time. Use the Step Into menu item on the Debug menu or press F8 to step to the next line. As you step into your program, a yellow highlight bar will appear on the line that will execute next. Each time you step to the next line, execution of the code pauses, allowing you to check the value of variable, change code later in the program, and so on.

As you step through code, you may come across a line that calls into a procedure somewhere else in the code. When you reach the line that calls into the procedure, you can either step into the procedure by choosing the Step Into or pressing F8, or step over the procedure call by using the Step Over menu item on the Debug menu (or Shift-F8).

Stepping into the procedure call will navigate the VBE code editor to the first line of the procedure and allow you to continue stepping through the procedure. Once the last line of the procedure is executed, control will return to the line *after* the procedure call.

> **Note**
>
> You will often want to stop stepping into a procedure once you have entered it. Use the Step Out menu item (or Ctrl+Shift+F8) to step out of the procedure and return to the line after the procedure call.

Another important feature of the VBE debugger is the ability to set breakpoints at certain points in your code. When the code is run, execution will enter break mode when each breakpoint is hit. Break mode will pause code execution, allowing the programmer to use the other debugging features of VBE. To set a breakpoint in your code, choose the Toggle Breakpoint menu item from the Debug menu. Lines of code in the VBE Code Editor that have breakpoints set are designated with a red ball to the left of the line of code. Figure 43.10 shows a line of code with a breakpoint applied to it.

The true power of the stepping and breakpoint features comes from combining these features with the VBE Locals and Watch windows and the Immediate window.

LOCALS AND WATCH WINDOWS

The Locals and Watch windows are frames in VBE that can contain variable references. These variable references can be to any type of variable or object. References to basic VBA types will show their values in the window and references to object types will display the properties for the object and their corresponding values.

To display the Locals windows, choose the Locals Window menu item from the View menu. While code is in break mode, the Locals window automatically contains references for all of the variables that are local to the procedure. For example, the Locals window shown in Figure 43.11 shows the variable references that are automatically added when the following code is stepped into:

```
Option Explicit

Sub LocalsWindow()
Dim iValue As Integer
Dim sMyString As String
Dim myWeb As Web

iValue = 10
sMyString = "My String"
Set myWeb = ActiveWeb
End Sub
```

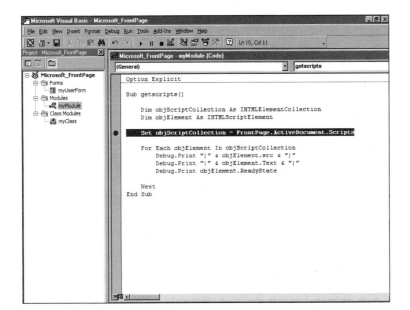

Figure 43.10
A VBE breakpoint.

Note

The properties and their corresponding values for the myWeb object are displayed in the Watch window. If the properties in question are not read-only, the programmer can change them directly in the Locals window by selecting the value and typing a value.

The Watch window works exactly like the Locals window in form and function. The difference is that the programmer can add *any* variable to the Watch window, not just variables local to the procedure. To display the Watch window, choose Watch Window from the View menu. To add a variable to the Watch window, highlight the variable in the code editor and choose Add Watch. From the Debug menu, press Shift+F9, or drag and drop the item onto the Watch window.

Figure 43.11
The Locals window.

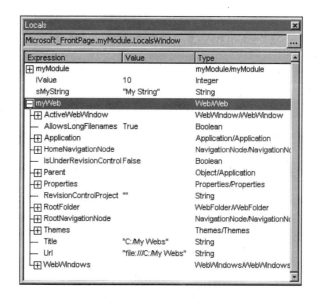

USING THE IMMEDIATE WINDOW

The Immediate window was discussed earlier in the chapter in the section titled "VBE Code Editor." The Immediate window provides a powerful method to execute code while in break mode.

SHARING YOUR WORK WITH OTHERS

Now that you have a solid grasp on developing code VBE in FrontPage 2000, you are probably wondering how you can show off to all of your friends. There are a number of different ways to share code developed in FrontPage VBE.

Most of the other Microsoft Office applications that expose VBA provide a separate VBA project for each document. FrontPage only provides one client project to store all User Form, Code, and Class modules and their corresponding code. This VBA project is stored in the Microsoft FrontPage.fpm file located in the application data area of the user profile on your system.

Note

If you are using Windows 2000, this is stored at c:\winnt\profiles\<username>\ application data\Microsoft\FrontPage\Macros\Microsoft FrontPage.fpm. For Windows 95 and Windows 98, the VBA project file is stored at C:\WINDOWS\Application Data\Microsoft\FrontPage\Macros\ Microsoft FrontPage.fpm.

COPYING THE DEFAULT VBA PROJECT FILE

The quickest method to transport your VBA code to another machine or user is to replace the Microsoft FrontPage.fpm file on the target system with the one from your system. When FrontPage is booted, it automatically loads the Microsoft `FrontPage.fpm` file located in the application data area. All of the modules and code that was available in your original project file will be available on the target machine.

EXPORTING AND IMPORTING MODULES

Another method to transfer code is to export the User Form, Code, or Class modules from your VBA project file to the file system and then import the modules into the VBA project file on the target system. To export a module, open the module into the VBE Code Editor and choose Export File from the File menu. The Export File dialog box shown in Figure 43.12 will appear. Choose the path to which you wish to export the module and click OK.

PART

VIII

Cн

43

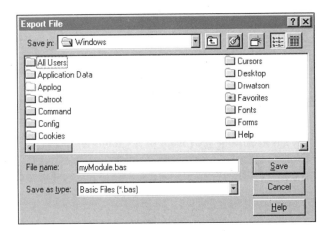

Figure 43.12
The Export File dialog box.

Once the module is exported to a file, switch to the target system and import the module. To import a module, choose Import File from the File menu. This will display the Import File dialog box (see Figure 43.13). Use the dialog box to navigate to the file you exported and click OK. The module is now part of the VBA project file on the target machine.

Note

Exporting User Form modules will generate two files, one with the extension `.frm` and the other with the extension `.frx`. Because User Forms can contain other controls, they must retain some binary information when exported. This information is stored in the `.frx` file. To import a User Form module, its associated `.frx` file must be in the same directory.

Figure 43.13
The Import File
dialog box.

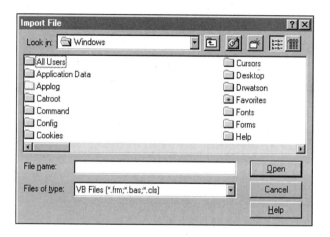

There are a few other methods to share code between users. One method is through the use of COMAddIns. All of the Microsoft Office 2000 applications provide support for the COMAddIn specification. These AddIns are developed by using Microsoft Visual Basic 6.0 or Microsoft Visual C++ and provide an interface to the FrontPage Object Model. Please see FrontPage VBA online help for more information on developing and using COMAddIns.

One other means to shared code is the Microsoft Office Developer Editor (ODE). *ODE* is an add-on for Microsoft Office applications that allows VBE developers to create their own VBA projects and save them to file systems. ODE is especially helpful to FrontPage VBA users because it allows them to have more than just the default Microsoft FrontPage VBA project. ODE is available as a separate project. See FrontPage VBA online help for more information on obtaining and using ODE.

TROUBLESHOOTING

Just like any other programming environment, programming with VBE requires its users to overcome a bit of a learning curve. There are a number of tools to help get you going more quickly.

First, the most powerful tools available to the VBE programmer are VBE's debugging tools: the Immediate window, the Watch window, the Locals windows, and so on. The Watch window is an especially powerful tool in that it allows the programmer to see the values of all the properties for an object at a specific instance of time.

Second, most of the Microsoft Office applications include a Macro Recorder feature that allows the user to start a recording session, switch to the Office application and perform an action, and then stop recording. The VBE Code Editor will then contain the actual Object Model code that will recreate the action that was performed.

Unfortunately, FrontPage 2000 does not expose a macro recorder. However, if you are simply wondering how an Object Model works or how VBA code interacts with the Object Model interfaces, another Office application's macro recorder can be used to generate code for analysis.

In addition to the information available in this chapter, FrontPage 2000 provides an extensive help system that covers all aspects of the FrontPage 2000 Object Model and, more specifically, the VBA language. To access online help for VBA, switch to the VBE editor and choose the Microsoft Visual Basic Help menu item from the Help menu.

Finally, VBE is a common editor used across the Microsoft Office suite of applications since the advent of Microsoft Office 97. Because VBE has been in use for more than two years, Microsoft maintains an extensive database of technical articles dealing with specific problems and solutions. This database is call the Microsoft Knowledge Base and is available at http://www.micorosft.com/kb.

DESIGNERS CORNER

Writing programs in VBA is simpler than in many other programming languages, but VBA programmers should still use good programming practices. Following good programming conventions will help VBA programmers debug their code as well as make it easier to maintain. Here are a few rules of thumb to follow to make sure your code follows good programming practices.

One practice is to make sure that you understand the layout of your code. If your code is basically one big procedure or functions, examine it to see if you are repeating code in any areas. For example, does your code add apply the same effect in the same manner to a number of different elements. If so, you may want to move the code that does the effect out to a new function. This will accomplish two things. First, moving the repeated effect code out of the main procedure will make it easier to understand and maintain. Second, if you wish to change the way the effect is applied, having it centrally located in a separate procedure means it only needs to be changed one time.

Another trick to enforce good programming practice is to name your variables in such a manner that illustrates their type and function will help you avoid type mismatch errors. For example, supposed I have a variable called count. If count is going to hold a value that is of integer type, count should be named icount. Prefacing the variable name with its type will remind you and other programmers who deal with your code what type of value icount should hold.

This naming convention can be extended to objects as well. If the variable is a generic type, preface its name with an o. For example, myobject should be named omyobject. If you know the object type, use a convention that will remind you of that object type. For example, the FrontPage 2000 Object Model exposes an object named WebFile. Variables that contain WebFile objects could be named with a 'wf' prefix, for example.

CHAPTER 44

MANAGING WEBS WITH VBA

In this chapter *by Bob Samer*

INTRODUCTION

COLLECTIONS IN THE CONTEXT OF THE WOM

In Chapter 43, "Introduction to Programming with Visual Basic for Applications," you learned that the Page Object Model grouped related objects into their own type of object, the collection. The WOM exposes collections as well. Groups of web sites, HTML files, and Folders in a web site are all exposed in their own collections.

WOM Collections work the same way as POM collections for the most part. Both are zero based and both use the Item property to get at the elements contained in the collections. For example, the following code accesses a Web object that is contained in the Webs collection and keeps a reference to the web in the variable w.

```
Dim w as Web
Set w = Webs.item("http://www.microsoft.com")
```

Note

Just as with the POM collections, the Item property is the default property for the Webs collection and can be assumed. So the following code works exactly the same as the previous code example.

```
Dim w as Web
        Set w = Webs("http://www.microsoft.com")
```

WOM OBJECTS

Just as the POM exposes a myriad of objects to allow the manipulation of an HTML page, the WOM exposes a number of objects used to manipulate files and folders that make up a web site. Figure 44.1 shows the hierarchy of the objects that make up the WOM. Table 44.1 gives a brief description of each of the objects.

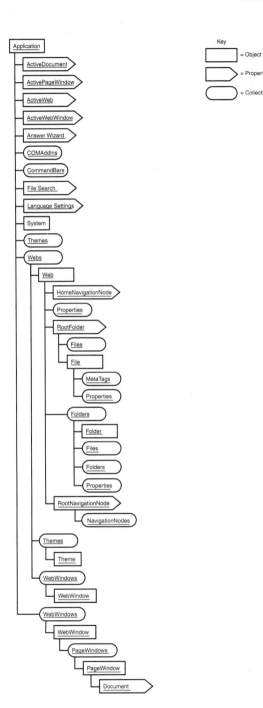

Figure 44.1
The hierarchy of the objects that make up the WOM.

TABLE 44.1 THE WOM OBJECTS

WOM Object	Description
Webs Collection	Encapsulates all the open web sites in FrontPage
Web Object	Corresponds to one FrontPage-based web site
WebFolders Collection	Encapsulates all the folders exposed at a certain level of the web site's hierarchy
WebFolder Object	Corresponds to Directory inside a web site
WebFiles Collection	Encapsulates all the files contained in a particular WebFolder object
WebFile Object	Encapsulates a file contained within a web site's directory
PageWindow	Represents an HTML or CSS file opened into the Pages view of FrontPage
Theme	Represents a FrontPage theme
NavigationNodes Collection	Encapsulates a series of nodes in the Navigation structure of a FrontPage-based web site
NavigationNode Object	Corresponds to one node in the navigation structure of a FrontPage-based web site
Properties	Encapsulates the Meta Info for a web, WebFolder or WebFile
Meta Info	Corresponds to the collection of <meta> tags for a document

ADDING AND REMOVING FRONTPAGE WEBS USING THE Webs COLLECTION

The Webs collection is a top-level collection that enables the programmer to create and manipulate FrontPage-based web sites. The Webs collection contains the web sites that are currently opened into FrontPage. Use the item property to access the Web objects corresponding to a particular web. The item method can take either a numerical index or a string representing the URL of the target web.

The following code sample uses the item property to access a Web object for the web site at c:\my webs\mynewweb.

```
Dim theWeb as Web
Set theWeb = Webs.item("http://www.bigcompany.com")
```

To create a new web, use the Add method of the Webs collection. The Add method takes three arguments: WebURL, UserName, and PassWord. The WebURL argument is required and specifies where to create the web. UserName and PassWord are required if the currently logged in user does not have permission to create webs at the specified URL. For example, the following code creates a new web site at c:\my webs\mynewweb.

```
Dim theWeb as Web
Set theWeb = Webs.Add("c:\my webs\mynewweb","username","password")
If theWeb.URL = "http://www.bigcompany.com/newweb" then
    MsgBox "New Web Create"
End If
```

To open an existing web, use the Open method. Open takes the same arguments as Add:WebURL, UserName, and PassWord. Again, UserName and PassWord are required if the user currently logged in does not have access to the web site. The following example uses the Open method to open the web created in the last example and displays a message box containing the number of files in the root folder of the web.

```
Dim theWeb as Web
Set theWeb = Webs.Open("c:\my webs\mynewweb","username","password")
MsgBox theWeb.RootFolder.Files.Count
```

PART

X

CH

44

> **Note**
>
> The Open and Add methods require the programmer to already have access to the URL that indexes the web site, or to specify the username and password for that URL. For *disk-based webs (DBW) (page 24)*, authentication is not required unless access to the drive where the DBW resides is restricted. Regardless of the location of the web site, if the authentication information has been provided once during a session it is not required again until FrontPage is restarted.
>
> The preceding examples create webs on your local disk drive. They assume that you already have a FrontPage based web created at c:\my webs. The Add and Open methods and the Item property of the Webs collection work with any URL that FrontPage can work with. This includes file based URLs, http based users, UNC paths, and so on.

WORKING WITH THE Web OBJECT

The Web object encapsulates most of the functionality that FrontPage exposes on a web site. The Web object contains properties and methods that enable manipulation of the web site and its contained files and folders programmatically. A Web object can encapsulate any type of web site that FrontPage can use.

Once a web site is opened into a Web object, there are a number of methods and properties that the programmer can use to manipulate its contents.

THE LocateFile, LocateFolder, AND LocateFile METHODS

These three methods give the programmer access to the individual elements of the web site: files in the web, folders in the web, and HTML content contained inside the files. Each of these methods take a URL as an argument and return an instance of the appropriate object, either a WebFile, WebFolder, or PageWindow object. Once the object is returned its methods and properties enable further access to the object's contents. See the "Working with Folders" and "Working with Files" sections later in this chapter for more information about the use of these methods.

THE Activate METHOD

Use the Activate method to make a particular Web in the Webs collection the active web. Making a web the "Active" web brings that window containing the web site to the foreground of all the other windows. For example, assuming that there are three webs opened into FrontPage and the window containing c:\my webs\webnumber1 is the foreground window, the following code activates the web at c:\my webs\webnumber3 and makes its window the active window.

```
Webs("c:\my webs\webnumber3").Activate
```

THE Close METHOD

Use the close method to close a web that is opened into FrontPage. For example, the following code closes a web named c:\my webs\mynewweb.

```
Webs("c:\my webs\mynewweb").Close
```

Executing the close method works exactly the same way as choosing the Close Web menu item from the File menu. Any pages that have been modified or are unsaved will prompt the user for action when the Close method for the web is executed.

THE ApplyTheme AND ApplyNavigationStructure METHODS

Both of these methods are used to apply changes made using the Themes and NavigationNode objects to the web. See the "Working with Themes and Borders" section later in this chapter for more information.

THE RecalcHyperlinks METHOD

One of the most important features of FrontPage is the ability to execute a recalculate hyperlinks command on the entire web. Recalculate hyperlinks does much more than simply regenerate the link information for a FrontPage-based web site. It also updates navigation structure and border information and synchronizes data for database components and category information. Use the RecalcHyperlinks method of the Web object to execute a recalculate hyperlinks command. The following example executes a recalculate hyperlinks command on the web at c:\my webs\mynewweb.

```
Webs("c:\my webs\mynewweb").RecalcHyperlinks
```

RecalcHyperlinks does not require any arguments.

THE Delete METHOD

Use the delete method to delete a website that is open in FrontPage. The Delete method takes one argument, WebDeleteFlags, which determines whether all of the web's content is deleted or just the FrontPage information. Use the fpDeleteEntireWeb const for the former and the fpDeleteFrontPageInfoFromWeb for the latter.

Executing the `Delete` method on the root web of the web site will remove all content files, regardless of what flag is specified.

In addition to the methods listed, the `Web` object exposes a number of properties used to get and set information about the web, as well as access the files and folders that are contained in the web.

THE URL PROPERTY

The `URL` property is a read-only value that corresponds to the location of the web on which it is exposed. The following example displays the URL of the current web in a message box.

```
MsgBox Webs("C:\my webs\mynewweb").URL
```

The `URL` property returns a fully qualified URL, absolute URL, so the above example returns the following string.

```
File:///c:/my webs/mynewweb
```

```
http://localhost/mynewweb
```

THE RevisionControlProject PROPERTY

FrontPage based web sites can use source control to manage changes made to the files and folders contained in the web. The `RevisionControlProject` property is a *read-write property (page 967)* that sets or gets the current source control project. If your web site is set up to use Visual SourceSafe (VSS) for source control, set this property to the project name of the VSS project to enable source control. If the web already has source control enabled for it, this property returns the project name. The following code sets the source control of the web `c:\my webs\mynewweb` to use the VSS project, `$/ournewweb`.

```
Webs("C:\my webs\mynewweb").RevisionControlProject = "$/ournewweb"
```

FrontPage 2000 can also use a lightweight version of source control called FrontPage Based Locking. To enable this type of source control, set `RevisionControlProject` to `<FrontPage-based Locking>`.

THE IsUnderRevisionControl PROPERTY

Use the `IsUnderRevisionControl` property to determine if a particular web has source control applied to it. The following example checks to see if the web at `c:\my webs\myneweb` has a source control project applied to it, and if it does it displays the project to the user.

```
If webs("c:\my webs\mynewweb").IsUnderRevisionControl Then
    MsgBox webs("c:\my webs\mynewweb").RevisionControlProject
End if
```

THE Theme PROPERTY

The Theme property gives access to the themes that are applied to the current web. Please see the section titled "Working with Themes and Borders," later in the chapter, for more information about the Themes collection.

THE Properties COLLECTION

The Properties collection gives the programmer access to the Meta Info for a particular web.

THE RootFolder OBJECT

Use the RootFolder property to get access to a WebFolder object the represents the *root folder (page 968)* or a FrontPage Web object. This WebFolder object contains all of the files and folders in a particular web site. The following example displays the URL of the root folder of the web site at c:\my webs\mynewweb. This is exactly the same value that is returned by the Web object.

```
MsgBox Webs("c:\my webs\mynewweb").RootFolder.Url
```

Please see the "Working with Folders" section for more information about the WebFolder object.

WORKING WITH FOLDERS

Folders in a FrontPage-based web site are exposed in the WOM as WebFolder objects. Each WebFolder object exposes a Folders collection that contains all the subfolders contained in the WebFolder. The Folders collection also exposes methods to add and remove folders from the collection, as well as properties to access the folders and determine their number. For example, the following example creates three news folders in the current web and then displays the number of folders in the web.

```
    Dim theWeb As Web
Dim theFolder As WebFolder

Set theWeb = Webs.Add("c:\my webs\mynewweb")

With theWeb.RootFolder
    .Folders.Add ("folder1")
    .Folders.Add ("folder2")
    .Folders.Add ("folder3")
End With

MsgBox theWeb.RootFolder.Folders.Count
```

Note

> The previous example adds three folders to the root folder of the web site. However, the last line of the program displays the number of folders contained in the root folder. You might expect the number to be three. However, the actual number is five. A default web in FrontPage contains two folders: Images and _Private.

The following code uses the Delete method of the Folders collection exposed on the RootFolder object to delete a folder contained in the web.

```
    Dim theWeb As Web
Dim theFolder As WebFolder

Set theWeb = Webs.Add("c:\my webs\mynewweb")
TheWeb.RootFolder.Folders.Delete("folder1")
```

The Delete method takes one argument, Index, which can be either a number or string specifying the index or URL of the folder.

Note

> The URL used as an index into the Folders collection (as well as the Files collection discussed in the next section) can be either absolute or relative. For example, the following two code segments are equivalent assuming that ActiveWeb is the web c:\my webs\mynewweb and it contains a folder named folder1.
>
> ```
> ActiveWeb.RootFolder.Folders("c:\my webs\mynewweb\folder1").URL
>         ActiveWeb.Rootfolder.Folders("folder1").URL
> ```

Both the Add method and the Item property of the Folders collection give access to the corresponding WebFolder objects. You can also use the LocateFolder method of the Web and WebFolder objects to get a WebFolder object for a particular folder in a web site. For example, the following code uses the LocateFolder method to retrieve the IsExecutable property of a folder named folder1 in the web at c:\my webs\mynewweb.

```
Dim theWeb As Web
Dim theFolder As WebFolder

Set theWeb = Webs.Add("c:\my webs\mynewweb")

Set theFolder = theWeb.LocateFolder("folder1")
MsgBox theFolder.IsExecutable
```

Note

> In the previous example, the IsExecutable property of the folder folder1 returns false. Because the web where the folder is contained is a disk-based web, it doesn't support setting the IsExecutable property. Attempting to set the property to true will result in an error message.

A `WebFolder` exposes methods and properties that encapsulate all of the functionality that FrontPage exposes to deal with folders contained in a web site.

THE `Delete` METHOD

Use the `Delete` method to remove a folder from a `Web` object. The web site must be opened in order to remove the `WebFolder` object. The following example deletes the folder `folder1` in the web site at `c:\my webs\mynewweb`.

```
Dim theWeb as Web
Dim theFolder as WebFolder
Set theWeb = Webs.Open("c:\my webs\mynewweb")
Set theFolder = theWeb.RootFolder.Folders("folder1").delete
```

> **Note**
>
> Executing the `Delete` method on the `RootFolder` object will delete the entire web site, so be careful!

THE `Copy` AND `Move` METHODS

Use the `Copy` and `Move` methods to make copies of folders and to move a particular folder to another area of the web. Both of these methods work on all of the subfolders and files of the `WebFolder`. Both methods take the following arguments: `DestinationURL`, `UpdateLinks`, and `ForceOverwrite`. `DestinationURL` can be an absolute or relative URL, but the destination URL must be within the current web site. Setting `UpdateLinks` to false keeps FrontPage from executing its default behavior of fixing up links to a folder that is moved to a new location. Setting `ForceOverwrite` to true forces FrontPage to replace the current folder without causing a runtime error, which is its default behavior. The following code uses the `Copy` and `Move` methods to rename a folder at `c:\my webs\mynewweb\folder1` to `c:\my webs\mynewweb\renamed_folder1` and then moves that folder to a new URL at `c:\my webs\mynewweb\mynewfolder1`.

```
Dim theWeb As Web
Dim theFolder As WebFolder, theRenamedFolder As WebFolder
Dim theNewFolder As WebFolder

Set theWeb = Webs.Add("c:\my webs\mynewweb")

Set theFolder = theWeb.LocateFolder("folder1")

Call theFolder.Copy("c:\my webs\mynewweb\renamed_folder1")
Set theRenamedFolder = theWeb.RootFolder.Folders("renamed_folder1")

Call theRenamedFolder.Move("c:\my webs\mynewweb\newfolder1")
Set theNewFolder = theWeb.RootFolder.Folders("newfolder1")
```

USING THE MakeWeb AND RemoveWeb METHODS AND THE IsWeb PROPERTY TO WORK WITH SUB-WEBS

One of the coolest and long awaited new features of FrontPage 2000 is the ability to create *sub-webs*. These webs exist inside another web and enable permissions, themes, and so on to be set differently from those of their parent.

There are two methods the FrontPage programmer can use to create sub-webs.

First, the Add method of the Webs collection can create sub-webs if a URL that points to a folder inside of an existing FrontPage based web site is passed to it.

Second, any folder that exists in a FrontPage based web site can be converted to a sub-web by using the MakeWeb method. MakeWeb adds the necessary FrontPage information to convert it to a sub-web. MakeWeb takes two optional arguments, UserName, and Password. These work the same as those exposed on the Web.Add method. If the currently logged-in user does not have the appropriate permission to create a web or sub-web, UserName and Password are required.

The following code creates a sub-web named mynewsubweb inside the existing website at c:\my webs\mynewweb by using the MakeWeb method.

```
Dim theWeb As Web
Dim theFolder As WebFolder

Set theWeb = Webs.Add("c:\my webs\mynewweb")
Set theFolder = theWeb.RootFolder.Folders.Add("mynewsubweb")
theFolder.MakeWeb
```

As far as the WOM is concerned, a sub-web is just a WebFolder with a special property, the IsWeb property, set to true. When iterating through the folders in a web, it is trivial to check the IsWeb property to determine whether a WebFolder is a sub-web. The following code iterates over the folders contained in the RootFolder of the currently opened web. When the code finds a WebFolder whose IsWeb property is true, it increments the variable iSubWebCount. Once the code is finished, iSubWebCount contains the number of sub-webs that exist inside of the RootFolder of the current web site.

```
Dim w As WebFolder
Dim iSubWebCount As Integer
iSubWebCount = 0

For Each w In ActiveWeb.RootFolder.Folders
    If w.IsWeb Then
        iSubWebCount = iSubWebCount + 1
    End If
Next w
MsgBox iSubWebCount
```

In addition to the methods mentioned previously, the WebFolder object also exposes a number of important properties.

THE URL PROPERTY

The URL property works the same way for the WebFolder object as it does for the Web object. URL always returns the absolute URL to the folder. It is read-only and cannot be set to a new value.

THE IsExecutable, IsReadable, AND IsWritable PROPERTIES

These three properties are very important in that they are used to set the permission levels for particular folders in a FrontPage-based web site. Requests from a web browser for files in a specific folder depend on certain permissions to be enabled or disabled for the folder. For example, many web servers have a folder called cgi-bin that exists in the root folder of the web site. This folder usually has its permission set such that any file placed in the folder is executable via browser request. Cgi scripts, programs, and so on are placed in the folder so they can be run. The following code example creates a new folder under the root folder of the web site http://www.bigcompany.com and marks it as executable by setting the IsExecutable property to true.

```
Dim theweb As Web
Dim thefolder As WebFolder
Set theweb = Webs.Open("http://www.bigcompany.com", "username", "password")
Set thefolder = theweb.RootFolder.Folders.Add("cgi-bin")
thefolder.IsExecutable = True
```

Caution

Marking a folder as executable for a web site means that *any* files in that folder are fair game. Make sure that if you set the IsExecutable property to true that you are sure no one will be able to place misbehaved executables into the folder.

The IsReadable and IsWritable properties work in much the same manner as the IsExecutable property. They are Boolean values that either enable of disable read-access and write-access for the specified folder. Again, make sure to be careful when setting these permission levels. Think about whether the folder you are setting the IsWritable property to true for really needs to have write access.

THE Files PROPERTY

The Files property is the most important property of the WebFolder object. This is the means by which files in the web are added, deleted, and modified. Accessing the Files collection returns an instance of a WebFiles collection. This collection represents all of the files located in a particular folder in a FrontPage-based web site. This includes all files, not just HTML or CSS files. The following example uses the Files property to obtain a WebFiles collection for the root folder of the web site at c:\my webs\mynewweb. Next, the code iterates over the collection, looking for GIF files, and displays the URL of any it finds in a message box.

```
Dim theweb As Web
Dim thefolder As WebFolder
Dim theFile As WebFile
```

```
Set theweb = Webs.Open("c:\my webs\mynewweb")
Set thefolder = theweb.RootFolder

For Each theFile In thefolder.Files
    If theFile.Extension = "gif" Then
        MsgBox theFile.Url
    End If
Next theFile
```

Now that you have had an introduction to the WebFiles collection, let's discuss how to use the collection to add, modify, and delete files in a FrontPage-based web site.

WORKING WITH FILES

Every file in a FrontPage-based web site can be represented using a WebFile object. There are two methods programmers can use to obtain WebFile objects for files in their web.

One method is to use the LocateFile method of the Application and Web objects. LocateFile takes one argument, FileURL, which is a string specifying an absolute or relative URL to a file in the FrontPage web. LocateFile returns a WebFile object that can then be used to modify the file it represents. The following code sample uses the LocateFile method to open the home page of the web site at c:\my webs\mynewweb.

```
Dim theweb As Web
Dim theFile As WebFile

Set theweb = Webs.Open("c:\my webs\mynewweb")
Set theFile = theweb.LocateFile("index.html")
If Not (theFile.IsOpen) Then
    theFile.Edit
End If
```

First the code in the previous sample gets a reference to the WebFile object for the home page. Next the code checks to see if the file is already open by checking the value of the IsOpen method of the WebFile object. If the file is not open, the code executes the Edit method of the WebFile object to open the file into Pages view of FrontPage.

A second method of accessing a WebFile object is via the WebFiles collection directly. Just as it did with the Webs and WebFolders collections, the Item property of the WebFiles collection enables the programmer to index into the collection and access a specific WebFile. Item takes one argument, Index, which can be either a number indicating the position or a string indicating the URL of the file. For example, the following code uses the Item property of the WebFiles collection to get a reference to the file catalog.htm and sets the title of the page to The Store Catalog.

```
Dim theweb As Web
Dim theFile As WebFile
Set theweb = Webs.Open("c:\my webs\mynewweb")
Set theFile = theweb.RootFolder.Files.Item("catalog.htm")
theFile.Title = "The Store Catalog"
```

THE WebFiles COLLECTION

The WebFiles collection exposes two important methods a programmer can use to create new files and remove existing files: Add and Delete. The Add method creates a new, blank HTML file in the specified folder. This file is exactly the same type of file generated by choosing the Normal Page template from the New File dialog box. Add takes one required argument, FileURL, which specifies the URL of the file to create. FileURL can be an *absolute* or *relative URL*. The following example uses the Add method to create a new file called prices.htm and adds it to the root folder of the web site at c:\my webs\mynewweb. The code then sets the title of the new file.

```
Dim theweb As Web
Dim theFile As WebFile
Set theweb = Webs.Open("c:\my webs\mynewweb")
Set theFile = theweb.RootFolder.Files.Add("prices.htm")
theFile.Title = "The Store Price List"
```

Now that you can add files to the collection, I guarantee you are going to want to know how to delete them. Use the Delete method of the WebFiles collection to remove existing files. For example, the following code deletes files created in the previous example and then adds a new file to take its place.

```
Dim theweb As Web
Dim theFile As WebFile
Set theweb = Webs.Open("c:\my webs\mynewweb")
Set theFile = theweb.RootFolder.Files.Add("prices2.htm")
theFile.Title = "The Real Store Price List"
theweb.RootFolder.Files.Delete ("prices.htm")
```

Caution

Be very careful with the Delete method of the WebFiles collection. For that matter, be careful with all Delete methods in the WOM. The whole point of using an object model to control an application is that no prompts appear during the automation. So, if you issue the Delete command on an object, it's gone. Poof! Do not pass go, do not collect your $200. Most actions in the DOM add to the undo stack, so you may be able to undo those changes. However, *none* of the actions exposed via the WOM are undoable.

THE WebFile OBJECT

As mentioned earlier, every file residing in a FrontPage-based web site has a WebFile object associated with it. Regardless of its type, the file's WebFile object exposes a number of important methods and properties that are used to manipulate the file.

THE Move AND Copy METHODS   Use the Move method to move an existing file to a new name or location. Move takes three arguments: DestinationURL, UpdateLinks, and ForceOverwrite. DestinationURL is a string value specifying the absolute or relative URL to which the file should be moved.

UpdateLinks is a Boolean value indicating whether FrontPage should update any links to this file in HTML pages located in the web site. The default value is false. If you don't care if links are broken (or you know that no pages link to this file) make sure to set it to false. This will increase the performance of the move.

ForceOverwrite is a Boolean value that indicates whether or not FrontPage should replace the file at DestinationURL, if one exists. If ForceOverWrite is false and a file does exist in the destination, a runtime error will occur, stopping your program.

The following example uses the Move method to rename the file prices2.htm in the web site c:\my webs\mynewweb to the URL, or prices.htm.

```
Dim theweb As Web
Dim theFile As WebFile
Set theweb = Webs.Open("c:\my webs\mynewweb")
Set theFile = theweb.RootFolder.Files.Item("prices2.htm")
Call theFile.Move("prices.htm", True, True)
```

The Copy method works the same way as the Move method, but leaves the original file intact. The following example copies the file c:\my webs\mynewweb\prices.htm to a new folder called archive in the same web.

```
Dim theweb As Web
Dim theFile As WebFile
Set theweb = Webs.Open("c:\my webs\mynewweb")
theweb.RootFolder.Folders.Add ("archive")
Set theFile = theweb.RootFolder.Files.Item("prices.htm")
Call theFile.Copy("archive/prices.htm", True, True)
```

Note

You cannot move or copy a file to a location outside the web. To export a file out of the web, use the SaveAs method of the PageWindow object described in the section "Working with PageWindows" later in this chapter.

THE Open AND Edit METHODS   Up to this point you may be wondering how to programmatically open pages into FrontPage. The Edit and Open methods of the WebFile object are the answer.

Use the Edit method to open HTML, ASP, and CSS pages into Pages view of FrontPage for editing. Edit works for any file type that has FrontPage as the default editor. The Edit method takes one optional argument, ViewMode. ViewMode can be any of the following:

```
FpPageViewNormal
FpPageViewDefault
FpPageViewHTML
FpPageViewNoFrames
FpPageViewNoWindow
FpPageViewPreview
```

Specifying one of these constant values for ViewMode determines what tab in Pages view is selected. Normally you will want to use the default value, FpPageViewNormal. However, if you want an HTML file to appear in HTML view instead of normal view, set the ViewMode argument to FpPageViewHTML.

The Edit method returns an instance of a PageWindow object, which can be used to modify the HTML content in the document itself. The PageWindow object is discussed later in the chapter and is discussed in Chapter 43.

The following example uses the Edit method to open every file in the root folder of the web site c:\my webs\mynewweb into a PageWindow object. Next, the code checks the length of the Images collection of the HTML document opened into the PageWindow to see if any images are embedded in the document.

```
Dim theweb As Web
Dim theFile As WebFile
Dim thePage As PageWindow
Set theweb = Webs.Open("c:\my webs\mynewweb")

For Each theFile In theweb.RootFolder.Files
    Set thePage = theFile.Edit(fpPageViewNormal)
    If thePage.document.images.Length > 0 Then
        MsgBox thePage.document.Url
    End If
Next theFile
```

Note

> The previous example uses the Images collection and its Length property. These are elements of the FrontPage Page Object Model (POM.) Please see Chapter 43 for more information about these and other POM objects.

Use the Open method to open files that are associated with applications other than FrontPage. When you use Open the result is the same as if you have double-clicking the specified file in the Windows Explorer. The application associated with the file is started and the file is opened into the application. For example, the following code opens the file proposal.doc that resides in the web site c:\my webs\mynewweb into Microsoft Word.

```
Dim theweb As Web
Dim theFile As WebFile

Set theweb = Webs.Open("c:\my webs\mynewweb")
theweb.Refresh
Set theFile = theweb.LocateFile("proposal.doc")
theFile.Open
```

The Open method does not return any object corresponding to the file's associated application. If you wish to modify the file, you must use the object model exposed on its associated application, if any exists. In the previous example, the object model of Microsoft Word must be used to modify the Word document proposal.doc.

THE URL PROPERTY   The URL property works the same as it did with the Web and WebFolder objects. It returns a string corresponding to the absolute URL of the file. For example, the following code displays the URL of the file c:\my webs\mynewweb\proposal.doc that you saw in the previous example.

```
Dim theweb As Web
Dim theFile As WebFile
Set theweb = Webs.Open("c:\my webs\mynewweb")
Set theFile = theweb.RootFolder.Files("proposal.doc")
MsgBox theFile.Url
```

PART

X

CH

44

THE Extension PROPERTY   Extension is a convenient property in that it exposes the three or four letter extension of a specific file for you, so you don't have to parse URLs in your code. The string returned from Extension corresponds exactly to all characters that occur after the period in the file's filename. Extension is a read-only property, meaning that you cannot set it to any value (unless you rename the file to a new extension).

THE IsOpen PROPERTY   Another convenient property, the IsOpen property returns a Boolean value indicating whether the specific file is currently opened into Pages view of FrontPage. If the file is open, IsOpen returns true. IsOpen is also a read-only property.

> **Note**
>
> IsOpen only checks to see if files are opened into FrontPage. Files opened via the Open method do not set IsOpen to true.

THE Name PROPERTY   Yet another convenience property, Name returns the actual filename of the file, without the rest of the URL information. Name is also a read-only property and can only be modified by renaming the file. The following code demonstrates the use of the Name property.

```
Dim theweb As Web
Dim theFile As WebFile
Set theweb = Webs.Open("c:\my webs\mynewweb")
For Each theFile In theweb.RootFolder.Files
    If theFile.Name = "index.htm" Or theFile.Name = "index.html" Then
        MsgBox "Found the Home Page!"
    End If
Next theFile
```

THE Title PROPERTY   The Title property is a shortcut use to get or set the title of a file. Setting the value of the Title property sets two values in FrontPage, a piece of MetaInfo for all files and the <TITLE> HTML tag if the file is an HTML document. The title of files is used throughout FrontPage to describe files.

WORKING WITH PageWindows

Now that you have the means to move, copy, and delete and edit files using the FrontPage WOM, you need to understand how to get at the content on those pages. The PageWindow object is the preferred method.

The PageWindow object encapsulates a page as it exists in the Pages view of FrontPage. The PageWindow exposes methods and properties to deal with saving content, access the HTML content directly, and the state of the page, and enables the closing of a page. The Web, WebFolder, and WebFile objects all had associated collections that were used to add and remove instances of the objects.

The PageWindow object is no exception. Its associated collection is the PageWindows collection. PageWindows is exposed on an object called a WebWindow. For the purposes of our discussion a WebWindow object is simply the main window of FrontPage to which all the pages and views are attached. To access the PageWindows collection, programmers must use the PageWindows property exposed on a WebWindow object. For example, the following code returns the number of pages currently opened into Pages view of the active FrontPage window.

```
MsgBox ActiveWebWindow.PageWindows.Count
```

The ActiveWebWindow property always returns an instance of a WebWindow object corresponding to the active FrontPage window. Each WebWindow object contains a PageWindows collection. For more information about WebWindows collection and the WebWindow object, see the section titled "Managing Web Publishing Using the WOM," later in this chapter, and Chapter 43.

There are two methods to open a file or create a new PageWindow object.

The first method uses the LocatePage method of the Application and Web objects. LocatePage only works with existing files—it doesn't create new files.

LocatePage takes two arguments, DocumentURL and ViewMode. DocumentURL can be any valid URL to a file. It can be a file on your local machine, a UNC path, another web site, and so on. Setting the value of ViewMode to any of the constant values contained in the enumerated type FpPageViewMode forces the page to open in a specific view.

For example, the following code opens the prices.htm file that resides in the web site C:\my webs\mynewweb into a Pages view and then displays the caption of the new PageWindow object in a message box.

```
Dim pw As PageWindow
Set pw = LocatePage("c:\my webs\mynewweb\prices.htm")
MsgBox pw.Caption
```

The second method used to open files into PageWindow objects is the Add method of the PageWindows collection. Add takes one argument, FileURL, which corresponds to the absolute or relative URL to the file to open. If FileURL is missing or is set to "", FrontPage creates a new page in Pages view and returns a reference to its PageWindow object. For example, the following code first opens the file c:\my webs\mynewweb\index.htm and then adds a new file to the web. The code displays the captions of both windows.

```
Dim theweb As Web
Dim pw1 As PageWindow, pw2 As PageWindow
Set theweb = Webs.Open("c:\my webs\mynewweb")
Set pw1 = theweb.ActiveWebWindow.PageWindows.Add("index.htm")
MsgBox pw1.Caption
Set pw2 = theweb.ActiveWebWindow.PageWindows.Add("")
MsgBox pw2.Caption
```

Now that we have the ability to open, access, and create `PageWindow` objects, we need more information on the objects themselves.

The `PageWindow` object corresponds to an HTML page opened into Pages view of FrontPage. The `PageWindow` exposes the functionality available for that page, like the caption of the page, whether the page has been modified, and so on.

It also exposes some very important links to the actual HTML content contained within the page. This content is exposed via a very extensive object model named the Page Object Model. Chapter 43 covers the POM and the associated methods exposed on the `PageWindow` in great detail. For brevity, the properties that access the POM, the `Document` and `FrameWindow` properties, have been left out of this discussion.

PART

X

CH

44

THE Caption PROPERTY

The `Caption` property corresponds exactly to the string that appears in the upper left-hand corner of a page in Pages view of FrontPage. `Caption` is a read-only property, meaning that its value cannot be modified directly. `Caption` returns the current URL of the page. If the page is unsaved, `Caption` returns a string of the form `"unsaved://"`. For example, the following code checks the `Caption` property of the `PageWindow` object for all pages currently open. If any of the pages are unsaved, the code displays their captions in a message box.

```
Dim pw As PageWindow

For Each pw In ActiveWebWindow.PageWindows
    If Left(pw.Caption, 11) = "unsaved:///" Then
        MsgBox pw.Caption
    End If
Next pw
```

THE File PROPERTY

The `File` property is important. `File` returns an instance of the `WebFile` object corresponding to the file opened into the `PageWindow`. If the `PageWindow` is unsaved, `File` returns `Null`. The following example uses the `File` property to get at the `WebFile` for each open `PageWindow`.

```
Dim pw As PageWindow
Dim theFile As WebFile
For Each pw In ActiveWebWindow.PageWindows
    If Not (pw.File Is Nothing) Then
        Set theFile = pw.File
            MsgBox theFile.Extension
    End If
Next pw
```

THE `ViewMode` PROPERTY   The `ViewMode` property enables the programmer to choose in the view to display the `PageWindow`. Setting the `ViewMode` property to the constant values contained in `FpPageViewMode` switches the page to the appropriate view. For example, the following code switched the current page to HTML view and back again to force a re-parse of the document.

```
ActivePageWindow.ViewMode = fpPageViewHtml
ActivePageWindow.ViewMode = fpPageViewNormal
```

THE `Activate` METHOD   Use the `Activate` method to make a specific `PageWindow` object become the active `PageWindow`. This gives the specified `PageWindow` the user focus in Pages view of FrontPage.

THE `Refresh` METHOD   Use the `Refresh` method to reload the current page from a saved state or to save and reload. This method corresponds to hitting F5 on a document or choosing `Refresh` from the View menu. Refresh takes one optional argument, `SaveChanges`, which indicates whether or not to save the current page before refreshing it.

THE `Close` METHOD   Use the `Close` method to dismiss a `PageWindow` object once you're finished using it. This is the equivalent of choosing Close from the File menu. `Close` takes one optional argument, `ForceSave`. `ForceSave` is a Boolean value indicating whether or not to save the contents of the page before dismissing it. `ForceSave` defaults to false, so changes will be lost if it is not specified. The following example uses the `Close` method to save and close all open page windows.

```
Dim pw as PageWindow
For Each pw In ActiveWebWindow.PageWindows
    pw.Close True
Next pw
```

THE `Save` AND `SaveAs` METHODS   Probably the most important methods on the `PageWindow` object, `Save` and `SaveAs` enable the programmer to save the current page or make a copy of the current page to a new location.

`Save` takes no arguments but only works for an already saved page. A runtime error will occur if `Save` is executed on an unsaved page. `Save` corresponds to hitting the Save button for an already saved page. The following example saves every page currently open if the `IsDirty` property of the specified `PageWindow` is true.

```
Dim pw As PageWindow
For Each pw In ActiveWebWindow.PageWindows
    If pw.IsDirty Then
        pw.Save
    End If
Next pw
```

Use SaveAs to save a specified page to a new location. SaveAs takes two arguments, DestinationURL, which is required, and ForceOverwrite, which is optional. DestinationURL can be any valid URL. You can use SaveAs to save a page to any location to which you have access, including HTTP-based webs, UNC paths, and so on. ForceOverwrite is a Boolean value indicating whether or not to replace any file that exists at DestinationURL. ForceOverwrite defaults to true, so be careful when using it. The following code saves the current page to a different filename using the SaveAs method.

```
ActivePageWindow.SaveAs "c:\my webs\mynewweb\inventory.htm", true
```

Note

The FrontPage 98 Export menu item has been replaced in FrontPage 2000 by the Save As menu item. The WOM works the same, there is no Export method, so programmers must use the SaveAs method to export files out of their web site.

WORKING WITH META INFO

Meta Info is information that the FrontPage client and FrontPage Server Extension maintain pertaining to webs and the files contained in them. Meta Info controls all manner of features in FrontPage, from keeping track of links between documents to determining what files should be published from a source web to its destination. Meta Info is a very powerful aspect of FrontPage.

Meta Info consists of a *key-value pair (page 981)* stored in a text file associated with the object it represents. For example, a FrontPage-based web site exposes a piece of Meta Info called vti_webservertype that corresponds to what type of web server a particular web resides on. For a disk-based web, this piece of Meta Info looks like this:

```
vti_webservertype:diskweb
```

The Properties collection of the WOM exposes methods and properties to deal with Meta Info.

Because Meta Info can come in any form—string, Boolean, numeric, lists of strings—the Properties collection works a bit differently than other collections exposed in the WOM. There is not a Property object per se, just basic VB types that correspond to each different type of Meta Info.

Two objects in the WOM expose the Properties collection: the Web object and the WebFile object. Each object uses different Meta Info key-value pairs to maintain information about the web.

Just as other collection in the WOM uses the Item property to access their objects, so does the Properties collection. However, the Item property for Properties only takes string values, not numerical indexed values. For example, the following code retrieves the value of the "vti_timecreated" meta key for the web at c:\my webs\mynewweb and outputs it into a message box.

```
MsgBox Webs.item("c:\my webs\mynewweb").Properties("vti_timecreated")
```

To modify a value for a Meta Info key, programmers can use the Item property directly. For example, the following code sets the "vti_navbuttonuplabel" meta info to a new string for the web site at c:\my webs\mynewweb. The "vti_navbuttonuplabel" Meta Info key controls the default label for the Up navigation bar.

```
Set theWeb = Webs.Item("c:\my webs\mynewweb")
TheWeb.Properties("vti_navbuttonuplabel") = "Up, Up and Away"
TheWeb. Properties.ApplyChanges()
```

THE Add METHOD

Use the Add method of the Properties collection to add a new key-value pair to the Meta Info for a specified object. The following code adds a new Meta Info key-value pair, "is_approved" to the Meta Info of the file c:\my webs\mynewweb\newlist.htm and sets its value to "true".

```
Dim theWeb As Web
Set theWeb = Webs.Item("c:\my webs\mynewweb")
Call theWeb.RootFolder.Files("newlist.htm").Properties.Add("is_approved", True)
Call theWeb.RootFolder.Files("newlist.htm").Properties.ApplyChanges
```

Attempting to add a Meta Info key-value pair that already exists simply replaces the value of the existing key.

THE Delete METHOD

Use the Delete method to remove a Meta Info key-value pair from the Meta Info associated with a specific Web or WebFile object. The following code deletes the "Is_Approved" meta key from the Meta Info for the file c:\my webs\mynewweb\newlist.htm.

```
Dim theWeb As Web
Set theWeb = Webs.Item("c:\my webs\mynewweb")
Call theWeb.RootFolder.Files("newlist.htm").Properties.Delete("is_approved")
Call theWeb.RootFolder.Files("newlist.htm").Properties.ApplyChanges
```

Attempting to delete a piece of Meta Info that does not exist generates a runtime error.

> **Note**
>
> Important! All changes made to Meta Info for a specified object are not committed until the ApplyChanges method for the object's Properties collection is executed.

Some Meta Info that is set by FrontPage is read-only, and some Meta Info must be accessed following specific rules. Please consult the VBA Online help in FrontPage VBE for more information about Meta Info key-values pairs.

MANAGING WEB PUBLISHING USING THE WOM

One of the most powerful features of FrontPage is its ability to publish a FrontPage-based web. The WOM exposes interfaces that can be used to control the publishing of a web site.

THE publish METHOD

The publish method is exposed on the Web object. Publish takes four arguments: DestinationURL, FpWebPublishFlags, UserName, and Password.

DestinationURL is a string indicating an absolute or relative URL where the current Web should be published.

FpWebPublishFlags is a combination of any of the following values: fpPublishAddToExistingWeb, fpPublishCopySubwebs, fpPublishIncremental, or fpPublishNone. These values can be added together to control the publishing method of the web.

UserName and PassWord are required if the currently logged-in user does not have permission to create or open web sites on the web server where DestinationURL is located.

Combine the different values of FpWebPublishFlags to control your publishing. For example, the following code publishes the current web to a non-existent web site.

```
Call ActiveWeb.Publish("c:\my webs\backup_web", fpPublishNone)
```

The preceding publish operation creates a new web site at c:\my webs\backup_web and copies each folder and file in the current web to the destination web.

The next code sample publishes just the changed pages in the current web to the web at c:\my webs\backup_web.

```
Call ActiveWeb.Publish("c:\my webs\backup_web",
fpPublishAddToExistingWeb+fpPublishIncremental)
```

This is the equivalent operation to clicking the Publish button on the standard toolbar *after* a web has already been published once.

For more information about controlling publishing using the Publish method, consult the FrontPage 2000 Online help for VBA.

WORKING WITH THEMES AND BORDERS

Themes and Borders are two very important features of FrontPage, and WOM exposes support for working with them.

THE Themes COLLECTION

The Themes collection exposes the list of themes currently available to be applied, but not the themes that are applied to an object. An instance of the Themes collection is exposed on the Application object as well as the Web object.

The Themes collection exposed on the Application object contains the collection of all theme files installed on the client machine. For example, FrontPage 2000 installs sixteen themes by default. These sixteen themes are automatically added to the Application object's Themes collection.

The Themes collection exposed on the Web object contains the themes currently applied to the web site. If a web-level theme is applied, there should be only one set of theme files in the web and therefore only one element in the Themes collection of the Web object. However, if several pages in the web have their own themes applied that are different from the web site's themes, the Themes collection will contain references to each of the themes.

THE Count PROPERTY Use the Count property to determine how many themes are located in the specified Themes collection. For example, the following code displays the number of themes currently applied to the web site corresponding to the ActiveWeb object.

```
MsgBox ActiveWeb.Themes.Count
```

THE Item PROPERTY Just as it does for other collections in the WOM, the Item property returns a Theme object. Item takes one argument, Index. This can be a string or index just like other collections. If a string is passed in, it must be the short name of the theme. For example, the following code checks the version of the Romanesque theme.

```
MsgBox ActiveWeb.Themes("rmnsque").Version
```

Using the numerical index to access themes is a more common scenario that using the string. For example, the following code iterates over the themes applied to the current web to determine if the "blends" theme is applied:

```
Dim theweb As Web
Dim x As Integer
Set theweb = Webs.Item("c:\my webs\mynewweb")
For x = 0 To theweb.Themes.Count - 1
    If theweb.Themes(x).Name = "blends" Then
        MsgBox "found the theme"
        Exit For
    End If
Next
```

THE Theme OBJECT

The Theme object represents an instance of a theme that can be applied. It does *not* represent the state of a theme as it is applied. To get this type of information, the programmer must use the ThemeProperties property of the specified object. The Theme object is simply for information. All of its properties are read-only.

THE Name PROPERTY The Name property of the Theme object returns the short name of the theme's install directory. For example, the following code displays the name of the first Theme object in the Application object's Themes collection.

```
MsgBox Application.Themes(0).Name
```

Note

The Name property is the most important property exposed on the Theme object. Its value is used to actually apply themes using the ApplyTheme method and to determine what theme is applied to specific objects.

THE Label PROPERTY   The Label property of the Theme object returns a string corresponding to the long name of the theme. This is the actual name of the theme that shows up in the Format Theme dialog box.

APPLYING THEMES

Themes are applied to specified object using the ApplyTheme method. The Web, WebFile, and PageWindow objects expose the ApplyTheme method. ApplyTheme takes two arguments: ThemeName and ThemeProperties. ThemeName corresponds to short names of the theme to be applied to the object. ThemeProperties can be any combination of the values shown in Table 44.2.

TABLE 44.2   THEME PROPERTIES

Theme Property Value	Effect
FpThemeActiveGraphics	Enables the Active Graphics option for the theme.
FpThemeBackgroundImage	Enables the Background Image option of the theme.
FpThemeCSS	Enables the Apply Theme Using CSS option for the theme.
FpThemeVividColors	Enables the Vivid Colors option of the theme.
FpThemeDefaultSettings	Applies the theme settings from the parent web's theme.
FpThemeName	The name of the theme that is currently applied to the object. (FpThemeName can only be used in a get of the ThemeProperties property.)
FpThemeNoBackgroundImage	Disables the background image of the specified theme.
FpThemeNoCSS	Disables the Apply Theme Using CSS option of the theme.
FpThemeNormalColors	Disables the Vivid Colors option of the theme.
FpThemeNormalGraphics	Disables the Active Graphics option for the theme.
FpThemePropertiesAll	Enables all the properties for the theme. This is equivalent to FpThemeActiveGraphics + FpThemeBackgroundImage + FpThemeCSS + FpThemeVividColors
FpThemePropertiesNone	Disables all the properties for the theme. This is equivalent to FpThemeNormalGraphics + FpThemeNoBackgroundImage + FpThemeNoCSS + FpThemeNormalColors

`ThemeProperties` corresponds to the four check boxes displayed on the Format Theme dialog box.

Combining these values when calling `ApplyTheme` determines which theme effects are enabled or disabled for the applied theme. For example, the following code applies the theme `"Blends"` to the entire web, enabling all of the theme options.

```
    Dim theweb As Web
Set theweb = Webs.Item("c:\my webs\mynewweb")
Call theweb.ApplyTheme("blends", fpThemePropertiesAll)
```

The next example uses the default settings from the web to apply the `"Blends"` theme to a newly added page.

```
Dim theweb As Web
Dim theFile As WebFile
Set theweb = Webs.Item("c:\my webs\mynewweb")
Set theFile = theweb.RootFolder.Files.Add("newpage.htm")
theFile.ApplyTheme "Default", fpThemeDefaultSettings
```

In the following example, a new page is added to the web. However, we don't want this page to have a theme, so we apply the `"None"` theme to it to avoid inheriting the web site's default theme.

```
Dim theweb As Web
Dim theFile As WebFile
Set theweb = Webs.Item("c:\my webs\mynewweb")
Set theFile = theweb.RootFolder.Files.Add("unthemed.htm")
theFile.ApplyTheme "None"
```

GETTING INFORMATION ABOUT AN APPLIED THEME

Now that you can programmatically apply themes and their associated options, you need a way to determine what theme is applied to what object and with what options. Each object that supports the `ApplyTheme` method also exposes the `ThemeProperties` property. This is an indexed property, which means that, although it is a property, it takes an argument in order to get or set its property. The `Web`, `WebFile`, and `PageWindow` objects all expose the `ThemeProperties` property.

All of the `FpThemeProperty` values shown in Table 44.2 can be used to index the `ThemeProperties` property. For example, the following code uses the `FpThemeName` constant to return the name of the theme applied to the active page in the Pages view of FrontPage.

```
msgbox activepagewindow.ThemeProperties(fpthemename)
```

The following example checks to see if the currently applied theme has its Background Image enabled. If not, the code then enables the Background Image option by replacing the current settings.

```
Dim theweb As Web
Dim theFile As WebFile
Dim currentprops As Integer

Set theweb = Webs.Item("c:\my webs\mynewweb")
```

```
If theweb.ThemeProperties(fpThemeBackgroundImage) = 0 Then
    currentprops = theweb.ThemeProperties(fpThemePropertiesAll)
    currentprops = currentprops + fpThemeBackgroundImage
    Call theweb.ApplyTheme(theweb.ThemeProperties(fpThemeName), currentprops)
End If
```

Getting the value of `ThemeProperties(FpThemePropertiesAll)` returns an integer that corresponds to the value of the currently enabled options added together. So, the previous code uses that fact to add one more option's value to the current property settings and then reapplies the current theme.

WORKING WITH SHARED BORDERS

Themes and shared borders go hand-in-hand in FrontPage. Shared borders are exposed in the WOM via the `SharedBorders` property exposed on the `Web` and `WebFile` object.

`SharedBorders` is an indexed property just like `ThemeProperties`. The property takes one of the five values listed in Table 44.3.

TABLE 44.3   SHARED BORDER PROPERTY VALUES

Property Value	Meaning
FpBorderTop	Enables the top border
FpBorderLeft	Enables the left border
FpBorderRight	Enables the right border
FpBorderBottom	Enables the bottom border
FpBorderAll	Enables all of the borders, equivalent to FpBorderTop + FpBorderLeft + FpBorderRight + FpBorderBottom

To enable or disable shared borders for specified objects, simply pass in the appropriate border property value and set the `SharedBorder` property to true or false. For example, the following code enables the top and left shared borders for the entire web.

```
Dim theweb As Web
Set theweb = Webs.Item("c:\my webs\mynewweb")
theweb.SharedBorders(fpBorderTop + fpBorderLeft) = True
```

Once a shared border is applied to an object, returning the value of `SharedBorder` with a specific border property value passed in returns a string that is the path to the border files. For example, assuming the previous code sample has been run, the following code displays `"_borders/top.htm"` in a message box.

```
Dim theweb As Web
Set theweb = Webs.Item("c:\my webs\mynewweb")
MsgBox theweb.SharedBorders(fpBorderTop)
```

Note

There is no direct support in the WOM for the Navigation Web-Bot that is added to shared borders by default. However, programmers can use the Page Object Model (POM) to access the navigation bot and make changes to its attributes. See Chapter 43 for more information.

WHERE TO GO FROM HERE

Now that you have a grasp of how the Web Object Model works, you will want to dive right in and start automating FrontPage. The thing to remember about the WOM, and any well-designed object model, is that its methods and properties should correspond to the UI of the feature. For example, for more information about what combinations to use when calling the `Publish` method of the `Web` object, consult the Publish Web dialog box. The option buttons at the bottom of the dialog box correspond to the `PublishFlags` argument that is passed in. The same holds for the `ThemeProperty` arguments, as well as for many more features exposed in the WOM.

For more detailed information about what meta-info is available to the programmer, see FrontPage 2000 VBA online help. A table of the key-value pairs and their descriptions is provided.

TROUBLESHOOTING

The FrontPage Visual Basic Editor will warn you automatically when you have generated a compiler error. The errors might not lead you directly to the problem at hand, but there are a few good places to start.

Make sure you didn't forget something: Most mistakes come when dealing with a long string of properties or collections such as `Web.RootFolder.Files.Count`. What would happen if you forgot the Files and entered `Web.RootFolder.Count`? You would receive an error. The Visual Basic Editor will offer a list of properties, methods, and events for each object as you type it. For example, when you type `Web.`, a list of properties comes up including the `RootFolder`. After you select the `RootFolder` and begin typing the period, the VB Editor will offer another list of choices. Selecting files from the list and typing the next period will offer any properties and methods available to the `Files` collection.

Check your parameters. Always make sure that you are passing the proper parameters to a function or property. If a function or property is expecting a string then you have to use quotes. Passing URL `http://www.microsoft.com` to the `Webs.Add` will give you a compiler error because the URL is not a string. If you pass `http://www.microsoft.com`, everything would work as planned. The VB Editor will list the parameters for an object or method so that you will usually know if you need a string or an integer.

The Visual Basic Editor has many time-saving features that can also reduce the number of errors that you might make. Try to look at any suggestions the VB Editor has to make because it can save you a lot of time.

PART

X

CH

44

CHAPTER 45

ACCESSING DOCUMENTS

In this chapter
by Bob Samer

Understanding the FrontPage 2000 Page Object Model

The Microsoft FrontPage 2000 Page Object Model (POM) is a superset of the Microsoft Internet Explorer 4.x Dynamic HTML object model.

Anyone who has used Dynamic HTML to create active HTML pages will find the FrontPage POM very familiar. The POM incorporates most of the design-time objects, methods, properties, and events of the DHTML object model.

Many of the runtime-type components of the DHTML object model do not make sense in the design time environment of FrontPage and are therefore not enabled in the POM.

In addition, a number of components that encapsulate specific FrontPage features are exposed in the POM. These include FrontPage components (formerly known as WebBots), Undo Transactions, and more.

Windows, Windows, and More Windows

The key to manipulating HTML pages using FrontPage Object Model is to understand the hierarchy of window objects that exist. There are three types of window objects in the FrontPage OM: the WebWindow object, the PageWindow object, which are both defined in the Web Object Model, and the FPHTMLWindow2 object, which is defined in the Page Object Model.

The WebWindow Object

The WebWindow object is actually part of the FrontPage Web Object Model (WOM). Please refer to Chapter 44, "Managing Webs with VBA," for a description of the rest of the WOM and a more detailed explanation of the WebWindow object.

The WebWindow corresponds directly to the window that appears when FrontPage is booted. It is the WebWindow that contains all of the different views that FrontPage supports and the open HTML pages. Each time the Window, New Window command is selected, a new WebWindow is created. When the last WebWindow is closed, FrontPage exits.

> **Note**
>
> The term WebWindow is a bit of a misnomer. It is not necessary to have a Web open in FrontPage to access a WebWindow.

The PageWindow Object

The PageWindow object is also a member of the WOM but is the only link from the WOM to the FrontPage POM. Each WebWindow object contains a number of PageWindow objects, corresponding to the number of pages opened into the current WebWindow.

These objects are arranged into a `PageWindows` collection and can be referenced by accessing the item property of the `PageWindows` collection. For example, the following code accesses the third HTML page opened into the Active `WebWindow`.

```
Set myPage1 = ActiveWebWindow.PageWindows(2)
```

Note

The collections in both the FrontPage WOM and POM are zero based. They are indexed beginning at zero. In this example, the code is actually returning the third `PageWindow`.

THE `FPHTMLWindow2` OBJECT

The `FPHTMLWindow2` object is another type of window object that the POM exposes. Each `PageWindow` object contains a reference to an `FPHTMLDocument` object.

This `FPHTMLDocument` object is the main means by which the HTML page is manipulated. Each `FPHTMLDocument` object exposes a `parentWindow` property. This property provides access to the `FPHTMLWindow2` object that "contains" the `FPHTMLDocument` object.

The `FPHTMLWindow2` object is important for two reasons:

1. It is the main method by which frames and framesets are manipulated in FrontPage (more on this later in the chapter).
2. The `IHTMLEventObj`, which is discussed in Chapter 46, "Using Events in FrontPage 2000," is exposed on the `FPHTMLWindow2` object. The `IHTMLEventObj` Object is used to respond to events generated by the FrontPage POM.

GETTING STARTED EDITING YOUR HTML PAGES USING THE FRONTPAGE OBJECT MODEL

There are three ways to open your HTML documents into Pages view and begin manipulating them by using the POM: the `Add` method of the `PageWindows` collection, the `LocatePage` method of the `Application` object, and the `Edit` method of the `WebFile` object. Each method has its advantages and disadvantages. Regardless of which method is chosen, each will return a `PageWindow` object that will enable the programmer to manipulate the HTML document.

Note

The `WebFile` object is discussed in Chapter 44.

THE `PageWindows` COLLECTION

As mentioned earlier, the `PageWindows` collection is the collection of all HTML or CSS documents open in Pages view of a FrontPage `WebWindow`.

USING THE Add METHOD

The Add method of the PageWindows collection takes one argument—the URL to the page the programmer wishes to open. This can be any type of URL: absolute, relative, file-based, UNC-based, and so on. However, if the URL is relative, the Web that it is relative to must be opened in FrontPage. The following code opens an HTML document named employees.htm, which resides in the current Web, in the Pages view of FrontPage.

```
Dim pw As PageWindow
Set pw = ActiveWebWindow.PageWindows.Add("employees.htm")
```

Note

You can create a new, blank HTML page by not passing in the URL argument. FrontPage will create a new HTML page as if the user had clicked the New Page button.

USING THE LocatePage METHOD

The LocatePage method of the Application object takes two arguments: documentURL and ViewMode. documentURL must be a valid absolute URL to an HTML page. ViewMode can be any of the following values: fpPageViewHTML, fpPageViewNormal, fpPageViewNoFrames, fpPageViewPreview, or fpPageViewNoWindow.

The ViewMode argument controls what view the PageWindow is opened into Pages view. If fpPageViewNoWindow is passed, the PageWindow is opened without UI.

The following example opens the HTML document at c:\temp\employess.htm into Pages view and switches to Preview mode.

```
Dim pw As PageWindow
Set pw = Application.LocatePage("c:\temp\employees.htm", fpPageViewPreview)
```

USING THE Edit METHOD OF THE WebFile OBJECT

The WebFile object is discussed earlier in the book; please refer to Chapter 44 for more information. The Edit method of the WebFile object is used to open HTML files that already exist inside of a FrontPage Web site. Edit takes one argument, ViewMode. The values for ViewMode are the same for the Edit method as for the LocatePage method. The following example opens a file called Employees.htm, which resides in a Web site at http://www.bigcompany.com, into a PageWindow object.

```
Dim pw As PageWindow
Dim wf As WebFile
Set wf = Webs("http://www.bigcompany.com").RootFolder.Files("Employees.htm")
Set pw = wf.Edit(fpPageViewHtml)
```

Note

> The `WebFile` object contains another method, `Open`, that can be used to open HTML files. While you can use `Open` to open HTML documents into FrontPage Pages view, you do so at your own risk. The `Open` method executes the application that is associated with the file's extension to open the file. Depending on how your system is setup, FrontPage may or may not be this application. To be safe, always use the `Edit` method to open HTML files from a Web into FrontPage.

MANIPULATING THE PageWindow

There are a few important methods and properties that need to be discussed before you get to hardcore document manipulation.

THE Save AND SaveAs METHODS

The `Save` and `SaveAs` methods are used for just what their names suggest, to save the contents of the HTML document open in Pages view. The `SaveAs` method takes two arguments: `DestinationURL` and `ForceOverwrite`.

`DestinationURL` is a string specifying any valid URL. If the URL is relative, the Web to which it is relative must be open.

`ForceOverwrite` is a Boolean value specifying whether the existing page should be overwritten. `ForceOverWrite` defaults to `false`; so make sure to pass `true` if you want to replace your changes. The following example opens an HTML file named `Employees.htm` into a `PageWindow` and then saves the file to another filename.

```
Dim pw As PageWindow
Set pw = ActiveWebWindow.PageWindows.Add("employees.htm")
pw.SaveAs "Employees_back.htm", True
```

Note

> The `Save` method will fail if called on a PageWindow that has not been saved once already. Make sure to call `SaveAs` for new pages before you call `Save`. The `IsDirty` property discussed mentioned shortly can help you decide which method to call.

THE Close METHOD

Just as the `Save` and `SaveAs` methods were self-explanatory, so is the `Close` method. `Close` is used to dismiss the PageWindow on which it is called. It takes one argument, `ForceSave`, which defaults to `false`. If `ForceSave` is set to `true`, invoking the `Close` method will save the HTML file before closing its `PageWindow`.

THE IsDirty PROPERTY

This very important property determines whether changes have been made to the PageWindow. If changes have been made to the PageWindow, IsDirty will return true; otherwise it will return false. IsDirty is a read-only property.

THE ViewMode PROPERTY

Another important property, ViewMode is a settable property that determines in what view the PageWindow is displayed.

ViewMode can be set to any of the following values: fpPageViewNormalView, fpPageViewHTMLView, fpPageViewPreview, or fpPageViewNoFrames.

Note

Once a PageWindow object is opened, its ViewMode property cannot be set to fpPageViewNoWindow.

THE Document PROPERTY

The Document property is very important. It provides the valuable link between the FrontPage Web Object Model and the Page Object Model. The Document property returns a reference to an FPHTMLDocument object. This object contains methods and properties that allow complete control over the structure and content of the document.

EXAMPLE—CREATING A NEW EMPLOYEE INFORMATION PAGE

The following example illustrates how an IS department could automate the creation of an employee contact page for new employees. The function works on the current Web and assumes that the Web has a folder called job_templates, where the adm.htm, engr.htm and sls.htm templates are stored. Depending on what values are passed to the functions, one of the templates is opened and saved to a new filename corresponding to the employee's name. The function uses a ByRef variable to return the PageWindow to its caller so the new employee page can be manipulated further.

```
Option Explicit
Public Enum JobCode
    Administrative
    Engineering
    Sales
End Enum


Function AddEmployeePageToWeb(sEmployeeName As String, Job As JobCode, _
oEmployeePage As PageWindow) As Boolean
```

```
With ActiveWeb.RootFolder.Folders("job_templates")
Select Case Job

Case JobCode.Administrative
Set oEmployeePage = .Files("adm.htm").Edit(fpPageViewNormal)
Case JobCode.Engineering
Set oEmployeePage = .Files("engr.htm").Edit(fpPageViewNormal)
Case JobCode.Sales
Set oEmployeePage = .Files("sls.htm").Edit(fpPageViewNormal)
Case Else
    Set oEmployeePage = Nothing
End Select
End With


If Not (oEmployeePage Is Nothing) Then
    Call oEmployeePage.SaveAs(sEmployeeName & ".htm", True)
    AddEmployeePageToWeb = True
Else
    AddEmployeePageToWeb = True
End If
End Function


Sub AddEmployee()
Dim pw As PageWindow
Dim sEmployeeName As String
sEmployeeName = "Jane Doe"
If AddEmployeePageToWeb(sEmployeeName, Engineering, pw) Then
    MsgBox "New Employee Page created for " _
    & sEmployeeName & " at " & pw.Document.Url
Else
    MsgBox "Could not create new employee page for " & sEmployeeName
End If
End Sub
```

MANIPULATION OF THE DOCUMENT

One of the dramatic and often useful ways to take control of your web is by manipulating the actual document.

FPHTMLDocument: NOT A WINDOW BUT IMPORTANT NONETHELESS

Now you come to the most important object in the entire FrontPage Page Object Model. The FPHTMLDocument object is the container for the rest of the HTML objects on the page.

This object exposes the methods and properties needed for high-level control of the document's contents. The FPHTMLDocument object can be accessed in one of two ways:

- The Application object's ActiveDocument property. The Application object is the top-level object in the FrontPage Object Model. See Chapter 44 for more information. This is the most direct method and doesn't require a reference to a PageWindow. The following code accesses the URL property of the FPHTMLDocument object for the active PageWindow object.

  ```
  myUrl = Application.ActiveDocument.url
  ```

- The Document property of a PageWindow object. The following code accesses the URL property of the FPHTMLDocument object for the second PageWindow object.

  ```
  myURL =ActiveWebWindow.PageWindows(1).Document.Url
  ```

UNDERSTANDING OBJECTS AND COLLECTIONS

The FrontPage 2000 POM exposes interfaces to access all elements on an HTML page. Depending on the context in which they are accessed, the elements are available via either an object element or a collection element.

FPPOM OBJECTS

Every HTML element in an HTML document corresponds to at least one object in the FrontPage POM. There are two different types of objects in the POM: the objects who use the IHTML naming convention and those that use the FPHTML naming convention. Objects whose names begin with the IHTML convention implement methods, properties, and events specific to the object type, but do not expose anything for general manipulation. On the other hand, objects whose names begin with the FPHTML convention expose all of the methods, properties, and events that their corresponding IHTML objects expose, as well as the more general methods, properties, and events.

A good example of this is the FPHTMLImage object. The src, border, and isMap properties are properties that the FrontPage POM exposes to work with the image objects. These properties are defined on the IHTMLImgElement object (along with a number of other properties.)

Now, the FrontPage POM also exposes a number of properties for dealing with generic HTML elements: the id property and the tagName property. These properties are defined on the IHTMLElement object.

So, as you may have guessed, the FrontPage POM takes the methods, properties, and events from both the `IHTMLImgElement` and `IHTMLElement` objects and exposes them in a conveniently named object: the `FPHTMLImg` object.

If you are still confused, an example should make the distinction clear. Assume that the following HTML is on a page opened into the Normal view of FrontPage.

```
<img id="myimage" border="0" src="Waves.gif" width="32" height="32">
```

The following code will get a reference to the `Waves.gif` image and retrieve information via its different object types.

```
Dim element As IHTMLElement
Dim image_element As IHTMLImgElement
Dim fp_image_element As FPHTMLImg

Set element = ActiveDocument.images(0)
Set image_element = element
Set fp_image_element = element

MsgBox element.tagName
MsgBox image_element.src
MsgBox fp_image_element.Id
```

The three objects all point to the `Waves.gif` image on the page, but each exposes different methods, properties, and events, depending on its type.

Note

> For the most part, it is not necessary to use IHTML-type objects. There are some exceptions, which you will deal with later. A programmer can always choose to use FPHTML-style objects.

See Table 45.1 for a list of HTML elements and their corresponding FrontPage POM object elements.

TABLE 45.1   HTML ELEMENTS AND THEIR CORRESPONDING FRONTPAGE PAGE OBJECT MODEL OBJECTS

HTML Element	POM Object Elements
\<A\>	FPHTMLAnchorELement
\<AREA\>	FPHTMLAreaElement
\<BASE\>	FPHTMLBaseElement
\<BASEFONT\>	FPHTMLBaseFontElement
\<BGSOUND\>	FPHTMLBGSound
\<BODY\>	FPHTMLBody
\<BR\>	FPHTMLBRElement

continues

TABLE 45.1   CONTINUED

HTML Element	POM Object Elements
<DD>	FPHTMLDDEElement
<DIV>	FPHTMLDivElement
<DL>	FPHTMLDListElement
<DT>	FPHTMLDTElement
<EMBED>	FPHTMLEmbed
<FIELDSET>	FPHTMLFieldSetElement
<FONT>	FPHTMLFontElement
<FORM>	FPHTMLFormElement
<FRAME>	FPHTMLFrameElement
<FRAMESET>	FPHTMLFrameSetSite
<WEBBOT>	FPHTMLFrontPageBotElement
<Hn>	FPHTMLHeaderElement
<HR>	FPHTMLHRElement
<IMG>	FPHTMLImg
<INPUT type="button">	FPHTMLInputButtonElement
<INPUT type="file">	FPHTMLInputFileElement
<INPUT type="hidden">	FPHTMLInputHiddenElement
<INPUT type="image">	FPHTMLInputImage
<INPUT type="text">	FPHTMLInputTextElement
<ISINDEX>	FPHTMLIsIndexElement
<LABEL>	FPHTMLLabelElement
<LEGEND>	FPHTMLLegendElement
<LI>	FPHTMLLIElement
<LINK>	FPHTMLLinkElement
<LIST>	FPHTMLListElement
<MAP>	FPHTMLMapElement
<MARQUEE>	FPHTMLMarqueeElement
<META>	FPHTMLMetaElement
<OBJECT>	FPHTMLObjectElement
<OL>	FPHTMLOListElement
<OPTION>	FPHTMLOptionElement
<input type="radio">	FPHTMLOptionButtoneElement

HTML Element	POM Object Elements
<P>	FPHTMLParaElement
<SCRIPT>	FPHTMLScriptEleement
<SELECT>	FPHTMLSelectElement
<SPAN>	FPHTMLSpanElement
<STYLE>	FPHTMLStyleElement
<TABLE>	FPHTMLTable
<CAPTION>	FPHTMLTableCaption
<TD>	FPHTMLTableCell
<COL> or <COLGROUP>	FPHTMLTableCol
<TR>	FPHTMLTableRow
<TEXTAREA>	FPHTMLTextArea
<TITLE>	FPHTMLTitleElement
<UL>	FPHTMLUListElement
<APPLET>	FPHTMLObjectElement

PART

X

CH

45

Table 45.1 lists the HTML Elements directly supported by Microsoft FrontPage and their corresponding FrontPage POM objects. Each of these elements has its own POM object with specific properties, methods, and events.

Where is the rest of the HTML set, you ask? Well, because the majority of the remaining HTML elements all have common properties, methods, and events, they can all be accessed via IHTMLElement objects. So, the <B> tag can be manipulated via an IHTMLElement object. A few special case elements require special elements in FrontPage. These are discussed in the next section.

There are a number of HTML elements for which the FrontPage POM does not provide support. The following is a list of those elements:

    <IFRAME>

    <BUTTON>

    <COMMENT>

    <!-->

    <!DOCTYPE>

Note

These objects are special in that FrontPage wraps them internally with FrontPage Web bots to better deal with them. Because of this, it is necessary to programmatically manipulate the WebBot element's events, properties, and methods to work with these objects. Accessing FrontPage Web bots via the POM is discussed in the next section.

FPHTMLFrontPageBotElement The `FPHTMLFrontPageBotElement` implements all of the methods, properties, and events of the `IHTMLElement` object as well as three extra methods: `GetBotAttribute`, `SetBotAttribute`, and `RemoveBotAttribute`. Because a FrontPage WebBot is essentially an HTML comment with attributes added to it, these methods are necessary to access the commented area and retrieve or set the WebBot's attributes. The following example demonstrates how to manipulate the FrontPage TimeStamp WebBot via the POM.

ACCESSING A FRONTPAGE WEBBOT The following HTML is a FrontPage TimeStamp WebBot. These elements can be inserted by choosing Insert, Time and Date from the FrontPage menu.

```
<!--WebBot bot="Timestamp" S-Type="EDITED" S-Format="%m/%d/%y" -->
```

that displays as

```
12/10/98
```

in the Normal view of FrontPage.

To access the WebBot object, you need to query into the document's `all` *collection (page 951)*. Collections are described in further detail in the next section. The following code gets a reference to the first `WebBot` object on the page and then changes its time stamp format by changing the `S-Format` attribute.

```
Dim wb As IHTMLFrontPageBotElement
Set wb = ActiveDocument.all.tags("WebBot").Item(0)
Call wb.setBotAttribute("S-Format", "%B %d, %Y %I:%M:%S %p")
```

After running the code, the TimeStamp WebBot displays as

```
December 10, 1998 01:13:56 AM
```

in the Normal view of FrontPage.

Finally, there are a number of POM objects that don't correspond directly to an HTML element, but are used for interaction with HTML elements. One example of these of objects is the `IHTMLTxtRange` object, used to work with ranges of text in the HTML document.

UNDERSTANDING COLLECTIONS IN THE FRONTPAGE POM

In addition to the object elements that were discussed in the previous section, the FrontPage POM also exposes a number of collections that programmers can use to work on groups of elements.

WHAT IS A COLLECTION?

A collection is defined as a series of like objects. Collections in the POM are just that: a series of objects that share a common property. This could be their type (all the `<B>` tags on a page) or their identifiers (all of the tags on a page whose `id` attribute is "me"). The POM has two types of collections: stock and user-defined.

The POM has a number of collections that are pre-defined for the programmer. These include those collections that correspond to the series of all the same HTML element in the documents. The Links collection of the FPHTMLDocument object is a good example of this kind of collection.

Whenever an <A> tag is added to the document, it is also added to the Links collection. At any given time, the programmer can query the Links collection to determine what hyperlinks are on the page. This is an example of a stock collection.

The following code checks the Forms collection of the ActiveDocument object to verify the number of forms on the page:

```
Dim iFormCount As Integer
iFormCount = ActiveDocument.forms.Length
```

When the code is executed, the number of <FORM> elements in the current HTML document is stored in the variable iFormCount.

Note

For most stock collections, the only way to change the number of items in a collection is to modify the document. For example, there is no add method on the FPHTMLDocument.Links collection, so to add a link to the collection, the programmer will have to add another <A> element to the document. The Areas collection of the FPHTMLMapElement is the exception to this rule because it allows additions and deletions via the add and remove methods. See Microsoft FrontPage 2000 VBA online help for more information.

In addition to the stock collections attached to many POM objects, the FrontPage POM allows the creation of user-defined collections. These collections are created by using the methods and properties of both the IHTMLElement object and the IHTMLElementCollection object.

All of the FrontPage POM objects that correspond to HTML elements (the objects in Table 45.1, for example) implement the properties, methods, and events exposed on the IHTMLElement object.

Two properties on the IHTMLElement object, all and children, allow the creation of the IHTMLElementCollection objects that allow user-defined collections.

THE all PROPERTY

The all property of the IHTMLElement object returns a collection of the remaining elements in the document below the current element. The collection is a non-hierarchical group, meaning that children and parents are listed on the same level. Accessing the all property of any FrontPage POM will return an IHTMLElementCollection that contains the remaining elements in the document.

The following HTML will create a form with two buttons on it in FrontPage.

```
<form method="POST" action="--WEBBOT-SELF--">
<p>
  <input type="submit" value="Submit" name="B1">
  <input type="reset" value="Reset" name="B2">
</p>
</form>
```

The following example uses the `all` property of an `FPHTMLFormElement` to return an `IHTMLElementCollection` object that will give access to the input button in the form that is created by the HTML just listed.

```
Dim form1 As FPHTMLFormElement
Dim submit_button As FPHTMLInputButtonElement

Set form1 = ActiveDocument.forms(0)
Set submit_button = form1.all(1)

sButtonCaption = submit_button.Value
```

Note

When inserting a Form element via the Insert, Form menu, FrontPage adds a wrapping `<P>` tag around any elements inside the form. For this reason, this example access uses the syntax `all(1)` to access the second element in the document after the Form element (skipping the `<P>` tag).

THE children COLLECTION

While the `all` property returned all of the remaining elements in the document below the current element, the `children` property will return just those elements that are both below the element in the document hierarchy and are immediate descendents of the element. The distinction may be a bit confusing, but an example should help. In the last section, you saw how to access a button element inside a Form element by using the `all` collection.

If the form created in the last section is on a page in Pages view of FrontPage, the following code will use the `children` collection to access the first button element on the form.

```
Dim form1 As FPHTMLFormElement
Dim para As FPHTMLParaElement
Dim submit_button As FPHTMLInputButtonElement
Dim sButtonCaption As String

Set form1 = ActiveDocument.forms(0)
Set para = form1.Children(0)
Set submit_button = para.Children(0)

sButtonCaption = submit_button.Value
```

PART

X

CH

45

Note

> You may be wondering why anyone would ever use the `children` property when all of the elements are accessible by using the `all` property. There is no reason a programmer cannot just use the `all` property, but the `children` property will come in handy in many situations. One use is to limit the search space when trying to locate a specific element in a specific part of the document. Searching just the immediate children elements is much simpler than doing a brute force search of every element on the page.

CREATING USER-DEFINED COLLECTIONS

The `all` and `children` properties both return instances of `IHTMLElementCollection` objects, which expose the `tags` and `item` methods. A programmer can create a collection in the FrontPage POM by these primary means.

THE `item` METHOD   The `item` method of the `IHTMLElementCollection` object enables the programmer to access either an individual element in the collection or create a new collection that is a subset of the original.

`item` takes two optional arguments, `name` and `index`. Both of these arguments are Variants. (Variants are a data type exposed by automation; see Chapter 43, "Introduction to Programming with Visual Basic for Applications," for more information.) Because they are Variants, the values can be either a number of a string.

If a string is passed in for `name` and nothing is passed for `index`, the FrontPage POM attempts to find the element or set of elements in the current collection (all, children or user-defined) that contains an `id` or `name` attribute equal to the `name` argument. If more than one instance is found, a new collection is created and returned. This new collection is of type `IHTMLElementCollection`. Using the item method in a situation where more than one element has the same `id` attribute is one way to create user-defined collections. The following example returns an `FPHTMLTable` object corresponding to the table on the page with an attribute `id` set to `mytable`.

```
Dim table As FPHTMLTable
Set table = ActiveDocument.all.Item("mytable")
sTableRows = table.rows.length
```

If more than one element on the page had the attribute `id="mytable"` (regardless of whether the other element was a table) this code listed would generate a runtime error. Because an object of type `IHTMLElementCollection` is returned, but the code is trying to assign it to a variable of type `FPHTMLTable`, Visual Basic will generate a "Type Mismatch" error.

If a number is passed in as `index` but no value is passed for `name`, the FrontPage POM returns the element at the ordinal position in the `all` collection. Using the `index` will always return only one object, but it does require that the programmer know the index number of the element. The following example demonstrates accessing the HTML element by passing in a numeric value to the `item` method of the `all` collection. The HTML is usually the first element on an HTML document, so it is accessed by using an index of zero.

```
Dim head As IHTMLElement
Set html = ActiveDocument.all(0)
iElementCount =html.all.Length
```

Note

Remember, there is no explicit object in the POM that represents the `<HEAD>` element, so a standard `IHTMLElement` is used instead.

If a string is passed in for `name` and a number is passed for `index`, the FrontPage POM assumes that a collection is being created of all the elements whose `name` and `id` attributes are `name` and returns the elements out of this new collection at the position specified in `index`. The following example demonstrates this use of the `name` and `index` properties.

```
Dim CorporateDivTag As FPHTMLDivElement
Set CorporateDivTag = ActiveDocument.all.Item("corporate_information", 1)
sDimension = CorporateDivTag.Style.Height & "," & CorporateDivTag.Style.Width
```

The example returns width and height of the second element on the page whose `id` attribute is set to `corporate_information`.

Tip #198

If you are unsure of how many elements exist in your document with the same `id` or `name` attribute, use the combination of the `name` and `index` properties with a value of zero for the `index`. For example

```
ActiveDocument.all.Item("corporate_information", 0)
```

will guarantee that the correct element will be returned (regardless of how many elements with the attribute exist on the document).

THE `tags` METHOD The `tags` method of the FrontPage POM is the second method by which programmers can create user-defined collections.

The `tags` method takes one argument, `tagName`, which is a string corresponding to the type of tag to add to the collection. The value of `tagName` should be the name of HTML element without the brackets. For example, to create a collection of all the `<TABLE>` elements in the documents, the programmer should set `tagName = "TABLE"`.

The `tags` method returns an instance of an `IHTMLElementCollection` that encompasses all of the elements in the page that were of the type specified in the `tagName` argument.

The following example returns a collection of all the tables on the document and then uses the collection to apply a style to all of the tables on the document by setting the `className` property of each table to a style named `CorporateStyle`.

```
Dim table As FPHTMLTable
Dim table_collection As IHTMLElementCollection
Set table_collection = ActiveDocument.all.tags("table")
```

```
For Each table In table_collection
    table.className = "CorporateStyle"
Next table
```

> **Note**
>
> For Each is a Visual Basic language construct that iterates over collections. For more information see Chapter 43.

USING PROPERTIES AND METHODS

FrontPage POM objects have properties and methods that are designed to allow the programmer to modify the content of the corresponding HTML elements and perform operations on an element or the entire document.

WORKING WITH PROPERTIES

POM object properties allow access to specific HTML attributes, such as the border attribute of a <TABLE> element, content values, such as the text inside a <B></B> tags construct, or to access other POM objects that allow further manipulation of the element or document.

USING THE getAttribute, setAttribute, AND removeAttribute METHODS The IHTMLElement object exposes the getAttribute, setAttribute, and removeAttribute methods. Because every POM object that corresponds to an HTML element implements the methods and properties of IHTMLElement, the programmer can always use these methods to directly manipulate the attributes for an element.

THE getAttribute METHOD Use the getAttribute to retrieve the value of an attribute for a specific HTML element. The getAttribute method takes two arguments: strAttributeName and lFlags.

strAttributeName is a string specifying the name of the attribute whose value the programmer wants to retrieve.

lFlags is an optional value that indicates whether to perform a case sensitive search. If lFlags is set to one, the attribute name specified in strAttributeName must match exactly with the attribute specified for the element. If more than one attribute of the same name is on the element, getAttribute returns the value of the last occurrence.

The following example uses the getAttribute method to get the border width of the first table located on the page.

```
Dim tag As IHTMLElement
Dim border_width As Integer
Set tag = ActiveDocument.all.tags("Table").Item(0)
border_width = tag.getAttribute("Border", 0)
```

THE setAttribute METHOD Use the setAttribute method to set an existing attribute to a new value or to create a new attribute. The setAttribute method takes three arguments: strAttributeName, AttributeValue, and lFlags.

strAttributeName is a string specifying the name of the attribute whose value the programmer wants to retrieve.

AttributeValue is a Variant specifying the value to give the attribute specified in strAttributeName.

lFlags is an optional value that indicates whether to perform a case sensitive search to find the attribute in the HTML element's list of attributes. If lFlags is set to one, the attribute name specified in strAttributeName must match exactly with the attribute specified for the element. If more than one attribute of the same name is on the element, setAttribute sets the value of the last occurrence.

The following example uses the setAttribute method to set the background color of the first table located on the current page.

```
Dim tag As IHTMLElement
Set tag = ActiveDocument.all.tags("Table").Item(0)
Call tag.setAttribute("bgColor", "Blue", 0)
```

Tip #199	Use the setAttribute method to add new attributes to an HTML element.

THE removeAttribute METHOD   Use the removeAttribute method to remove an attribute from an HTML element.

The removeAttribute method takes two arguments: strAttributeName and lFlags.

strAttributeName is a string specifying the name of the attribute to remove.

lFlags is an optional value that indicates whether to perform a case sensitive search. If lFlags is set to one, the attribute name specified in strAttributeName must match exactly with the attribute specified for the element.

If more than one attribute of the same name is on the element, removeAttribute removes the last occurrence of the attribute.

If the attribute was successfully removed, removeAttribute returns true, otherwise is returns false.

The following example uses the removeAttribute method to remove the id attribute from every element on the page.

```
Dim tag As IHTMLElement
For Each tag In ActiveDocument.all
    If Not (tag.removeAttribute("id")) Then
        Debug.Print "couldn't remove id attribute from: " & tag.tagName
    End If
Next tag
```

USING THE OBJECT'S EXPOSED PROPERTIES TO ACCESS ATTRIBUTES   In addition to the IHTMLElement methods mentioned in the last section, attributes can be modified via properties exposed on the corresponding POM object itself. For example, to modify the borderColor attribute of a <TABLE> element on the current page, the programmer could set the bordercolor attribute to red by using the following line of code:

```
ActiveDocument.all.tags("table").item(0).bordercolor = "red"
```

There are a number of properties exposed both on the IHTMLElement as well as the other POM objects that are used to affect the content of the element, but do not directly correspond to any specific attribute on the element. These cannot be set using the setAttribute method discussed in the last section. These must be set by using the properties for the specific object. The majority of these are exposed on the IHTMLElement. One example is the innerHTML.

This property doesn't correspond to any attribute, but does get and set the HTML content that appears within the opening and closing tags of an HTML element. For example, the following line of code would set the HTML inside the first <B> tag on the page to <I> Very Important Person </I>.

```
ActiveDocument.all.tags("b").Item(0).innerHTML _
= "<I> Very Important Person </I>"
```

For more information on properties exposed on specific objects, please consult the FrontPage 2000 VBA Help.

PART

X

CH

45

> **Note**
>
> The innerHTML property is a very important property used to add HTML content to an HTML Document by using the FrontPage POM.

USING THE expando METHOD TO ACCESS ATTRIBUTES   There is one more method used to access properties of objects in the FrontPage POM: the expando method. The expando method of setting and getting the values of properties enables the programmer to easily create or modify attributes without requiring the use of the setAttribute and getAttribute methods. The ability to use expando properties can be enabled or disabled on a per-document basis by changing the value of the expando property of the FPHTMLDocument object.

If expando is enabled for the document, the programmer can set and get arbitrary properties in the same manner as they would set and get the object's stock properties. The following example will demonstrate the use of the expando property to create a new attribute.

```
Dim table As FPHTMLTable
Set table = ActiveDocument.all.tags("table").Item(0)
ActiveDocument.expando = True
table.corporate_rating = 4.5
```

Note

Normally when using the Visual Basic Editor included with FrontPage 2000, typing an object's name followed by a . makes a list box appear next to the line of code. This list box contains the properties and methods that are available for the object. However, some properties on POM objects will not appear correctly. The expando property is one of these. When typing the third line of the previous example you will not see expando in the list of available properties for the ActiveDocument object. Please see Chapter 43 for more information.

This example creates a new attribute on the table object called corporate_rating and sets the value to 4.5.

Note

The expando property can be dangerous to programmers because it allows no control over case sensitivity. For example, a programmer might want to modify the value of an existing border attribute of a table object. The programmer might use the following code to accomplish the task:

```
ActiveDocument.all.tags("Table").item(0).Border = 10
```

However, if the attribute is border instead of Border, the programmer has just created a new attribute called border and the expected results will not appear.

To avoid these problems, you can disable the expando property for the current document by setting the expando property of the ActiveDocument object to false.

One added bonus of the expando functionality is that, when enabled, it allows programmers to call directly into any IHTMLElementCollection without using the item method of the collections. If expando is enabled, HTML elements are accessible via the their collections via their id or name property. For example, assuming a table with the id of table1 exists on the current page, the following code will set the table's background color to blue:

```
ActiveDocument.all.table1.bgColor = "blue"
```

PROPERTIES THAT RETURN OTHER POM OBJECTS   So far, you have learned about properties that directly correspond to HTML attributes and properties that affect the contents of and HTML element, like innerText. In addition to these, POM objects exposed properties that are used to access other POM objects that affect the particular object on which they are exposed. The all and children properties discussed in earlier sections are examples of these types of properties. They both return instances of IHTMLElementCollection objects that affect the content of the FPHTMLDocument object. Almost every object in the POM exposed other objects in some form. The following example demonstrates accessing the style property of a <P> element to set the inline style attribute by manipulating the instance of an FPHTMLStyle object that is returned from the style property.

```
Dim para As FPHTMLParaElement
Dim style As FPHTMLStyle
```

```
Set para = ActiveDocument.all.tags("p").Item(0)
Set style = para.style
With style
    .backgroundColor = "Gray"
    .fontSize = "7"
    .letterSpacing = "4px"
End With
```

WORKING WITH METHODS

You have already learned about a number of methods up to this point: the item and tags methods, setAttribute, getAttribute, removeAttribute, and so on. All objects in the POM expose some sort of method. These can range from the stock methods exposed on IHTMLElement to specialized methods that are only applicable to a specific element type. The following example uses the specialized method createTHead to create a header for an existing table and then uses the ScrollIntoView method (exposed for all HTML elements via the IHTMLElement object) to scroll the document so that the table is in view in the normal view of FrontPage:

```
Dim thead As FPHTMLTableSection
Dim table As FPHTMLTable
Set table = ActiveDocument.all.table1
Set thead = table.createTHead
thead.innerText = "Add new content here!"
table.scrollIntoView
```

There are far too many methods in the FrontPage POM to document here. For more information, please consult Microsoft FrontPage 2000 VBA Help.

MANIPULATING CONTENT IN THE DOCUMENT

The ability to add content to the document is what makes the FrontPage POM so great. An impressive array of methods and properties are exposed to give the programmer the freedom to access any and all parts of the HTML document.

> **Note**
>
> One of the big promises of FrontPage 2000 is 100 percent HTML preservation, which is an excellent feature that the FrontPage team worked long and hard to ensure. The FrontPage POM makes no such promises! Each of the methods and properties works with HTML text in a slightly different manner, and some methods do not allow the programmer to add invalid HTML to the document. Luckily, the POM is so rich and robust that there are ways to get any HTML (valid or invalid) into the document if the programmer works hard enough at it.

USING THE documentHTML PROPERTY TO REPLACE THE ENTIRE DOCUMENT

The documentHTML property exposed on the FPHTMLDocument object is a very useful property. This property exposes the entire text of the document as one contiguous string. This allows the complete replacement of the document content. Using the `documentHTML` property also allows the programmer to get at text that lies outside of the usual confines on an HTML document (outside of the `<HTML></HTML>` tags.) The following example replaces the text of one HTML document with the text of another, and then saves and closes both documents. The example uses the `PageWindow` and `WebWindow` objects, which are discussed in more detail in Chapter 44.

```
Dim OriginalDoc As PageWindow, TargetDoc As PageWindow
Set OriginalDoc = ActiveWebWindow.PageWindows.Add("myfav3.htm")
Set TargetDoc = ActiveWebWindow.PageWindows.Add("favorite.htm")
TargetDoc.Document.DocumentHTML = OriginalDoc.Document.DocumentHTML
TargetDoc.Save
TargetDoc.Close
OriginalDoc.Close
```

USING THE `outerHTML`, `innerHTML`, `outerTEXT`, AND `innerTEXT` PROPERTIES TO MANIPULATE CONTENT

These properties are exposed on the `IHTMLElement` object, so every POM object that corresponds to an HTML element has access to them. These properties allow more precision in HTML modification than what is available with the `documentHTML` property, but they still require the programmer access text as a string. Invalid HTML content will not be added when used with the `innerHTML` and `outerHTML` properties and will generate a runtime error.

THE `outerHTML` PROPERTY

The `outerHTML` property returns or sets the HTML content for an element up to an including the outer tags of the element. For example, `outerHTML` of the `<b>` tag listed next would return the string `<b> <u> Now on Sale! </u></b>`.

```
<b> <u> Now on Sale! </u></b>
```

One of the best uses of this property is to replace or delete elements. By setting an object's `outerHTML` property to new, valid HTML, the object will be replaced by the new element. The following example replaces the first `<TABLE>` element on the page with a `<p>` element.

```
Dim table As FPHTMLTable
Set table = ActiveDocument.all.tags("table").Item(0)
table.outerHTML = "<p> Tables are not allowed! </p>"
```

Tip #200	To delete an element from the document, set its `outerHTML` property to the empty string.

THE `outerText` PROPERTY

`outerTEXT` returns or sets the text of an element up to and including any text adjacent to the start and end tags of the element. For most POM elements, the `outerText` property works exactly like the `innerText` property. The following example stores the value of the text inside a table in the `sTableText` variable.

```
Dim table As FPHTMLTable
Dim sTableText As String
Set table = ActiveDocument.all.tags("table").Item(0)
sTableText = table.outerText
```

THE `innerHTML` PROPERTY The `innerHTML` property returns or sets the HTML content for an tag listed next would return the string `<u> Now on Sale! </u>`.

```
<b> <u> Now on Sale! </u> </b>
```

THE `innerText` PROPERTY The `innerTEXT` property returns or sets the text of an element up to but not including the start and end tags. The following example stores the value of the text inside a table in the `sTableText` variable.

```
Dim table As FPHTMLTable
Dim sTableText As String
Set table = ActiveDocument.all.tags("table").Item(0)
sTableText = table.innerText
```

USING THE `insertadjacentHTML` AND `insertadjacentText` METHODS

The `insertadjacentHTML` and `insertadjacentText` methods provide the most precise means to add content to the page. The methods take two arguments: `where` and `html`.

`where` is a string specifying a logical placement of the HTML with respect to the element that accessed. `where` can be any of the following string values: `BeforeBegin`, `AfterBegin`, `BeforeEnd`, `AfterEnd`.

`HTML` is a string that contains the HTML content to insert into the document. The string must be valid HTML or the method will fail.

Specifying `BeforeBegin` for `where` will insert the text immediately before the element.

Specifying `AfterBegin` for `where` will insert the text after the start of the element but before all other content in the element.

Specifying `BeforeEnd` for `where` will insert the text immediately before the end of the element but after all other content in the element.

Specifying `AfterEnd` for `where` will insert the text immediately after the end of the element.

The following example demonstrates the use of the `insertAdjacentHTML` method to add HTML content to an existing document. This example assumes that the following HTML appears on the current page in FrontPage.

```
<body>
        <h1>A New Home Computer </h1>
</body>
```

The following code adds a new HTML element in and around the `<h1>` tag to create new content for the page.

```
Dim elem As IHTMLElement
Dim sHTML As String

Set elem = ActiveDocument.all.tags("h1").Item(0)

sHTML = "<font size=""4"" color =""Blue"" > Don't you think you should</font>"
Call elem.insertAdjacentHTML("beforeBegin", sHTML)

sHTML = "<i> Buy Yourself a </i>"
Call elem.insertAdjacentHTML("AfterBegin", sHTML)

sHTML = "<p> They are the wave of the future </p>"
Call elem.insertAdjacentHTML("beforeEnd", sHTML)

sHTML = "and you don't want to miss the <font size=""7""
color=""#0000FF"">wave!</font>"
Call elem.insertAdjacentHTML("afterEnd", sHTML)
```

Running this code will add new content in and around the `<H1>` element.

The `insertadjacentText` method works exactly like the `insertadjacentHTML` method. It takes the same string values for `where` and takes a string as its second argument, `text`. The text specified in the `text` argument is added to the document as plain text. Any HTML constructs are encoded for display.

Using the `pasteHTML` Method

The `IHTMLTxtRange` object is mentioned earlier in this chapter as a means to work with text ranges in the document. One of its many uses is to add content to the page.

The `IHTMLTxtRange` object has a method called `pasteHTML` that will add content to the page for whatever range the `IHTMLTxtRange` encompasses.

The `pasteHTML` method adds content to the page using the same rules as the paste functionality of the FrontPage application.

`pasteHTML` takes one argument, `html`, which is a string that specifies the HTML to paste into the document. This string can contain invalid HTML. The `pasteHTML` method will attempt to paste the HTML into the document, removing any HTML constructs it cannot parse.

> **Note**
>
> The content in the `html` argument is not encoded, so any HTML constructs that appear within the string will be added to the page as HTML. For example, `pasteHTML("This is a <TABLE>")` will add `this is a <table> <tr> </tr></table>` to the document because FrontPage will add a valid table in place of the `<TABLE>` construct.

The following example creates an instance of the IHTMLTxtRange, moves the range to encompass the first table on the page, and then pastes new content over the table.

```
Dim r As IHTMLTxtRange
Dim table As FPHTMLTable
Dim sHTML As String

Set table = ActiveDocument.all.tags("table").Item(0)
Set r = ActiveDocument.body.createTextRange
Call r.moveToElementText(table)
r.Select
sHTML = "<b> This list is out-of-date. Please check back soon! </b>"
Call r.pasteHTML(sHTML)
```

OBJECT-SPECIFIC METHODS

There are a number of objects in the FrontPage POM that have special case methods and properties used to manipulate content related to the element.

TABLE INSERTION AND CREATION METHODS
The FPHTMLTable, FPHTMLTableRow, FPHTMLTableSection, and related objects expose a number of methods to create sections of the table, add new rows and cells, and so on. Two examples of these types of methods are the InsertRow and InsertCell methods. The following example uses these methods to dynamically add rows and cells to the first table on the current page.

```
Dim table As FPHTMLTable
Dim table_row As FPHTMLTableRow
Dim table_cell As FPHTMLTableCell
Dim x As Integer, y As Integer

Set table = ActiveDocument.all.tags("table").Item(0)

For x = 1 To 10
    Set table_row = table.insertRow
    For y = 1 To 10
        Set table_cell = table_row.insertCell
        table_cell.innerText = "Row =" & x & ", Column = " & y
    Next y
Next x
```

There are many other methods exposed on POM objects that allow specialized manipulation of the content related to the object. For more information on these methods and properties please see Microsoft FrontPage 2000 VBA online help.

WHAT ABOUT document.write(ln)?

Any reader familiar with HTML document scripting and/or Dynamic HTML is most likely asking themselves why the write and writeln methods have not been mentioned. These methods are exposed in the Internet Explorer Dynamic HTML object model as a means to create a new document at runtime. FrontPage is meant to be used in a design-time environment and, as such, does not support either of these methods.

WORKING WITH STYLES USING THE FRONTPAGE POM

Using both style sheets and inline styles are key to a professional looking and effective HTML document. The FrontPage POM exposes a wide array of objects, methods, and properties to manipulate this important area.

> **Note**
> The interfaces exposed by the FrontPage POM for manipulating styles in an HTML document contain a wide variety of objects, methods, and properties. This section deals with the most important of these, but does not come close to covering them all. For more information please see Microsoft FrontPage 2000 VBA online help.

FPHTMLStyleSheets COLLECTION

The FPHTMLStyleSheet exposes a collection of FPHTMLStyleSheet objects. It works similarly to the IHTMLElementCollection mentioned earlier in this chapter but does not support the tags method.

The FPHTMLStyleSheets collection is exposed for the FPHTMLDocument object via the StyleSheets property. This collection contains a series of FPHTMLStyleSheet objects representing all of the style sheets that are currently applied to the document. This includes embedded style sheets and style sheets that are linked or imported into the document.

The following example uses the stylesheets property to display the number of style sheets applied to the current document in a message box.

```
msgbox ActiveDocument.styleSheets.Length
```

FPHTMLStyleSheet OBJECT

This object represents a style sheet, either embedded or linked. It exposes a number of methods and properties to manipulate and get information about the style sheet.

> **Note**
> The FPHTMLStyleSheet object is used to provide an easy means to modify the contents of the style sheet it encompasses by exposing methods to add rules, remove rules, and so on. It is not the object that corresponds to the <STYLE> HTML element.

THE rules COLLECTION The FPHTMLStyleSheet object exposes a rules property that returns a collection of FPHTMLRuleStyle objects. Each of these objects encompasses a rule defined in the style sheet. FPHTMLRuleStyle objects are selected out of the rules collection by using either a numerical index or their selector text. For example, the following code places the text of the rule for <BODY> that is defined in the first stylesheet in the document into the variable sRuleCSS.

```
Dim ss As FPHTMLStyleSheet
Dim FirstRule As IHTMLStyleSheetRule
Dim sRuleCSS As String
```

```
Set ss = ActiveDocument.styleSheets(0)
Set FirstRule = ss.rules(0)
sRuleCSS = FirstRule.style.cssText
```

THE addRule METHOD   The FPHTMLStyleSheet object exposes a method to add new rules to the style sheet. This method accepts three arguments.

BstrSelector is a string specifying the selector text of element to which the rule should apply. This can be either one element or comma-separated list of elements.

BstrStyle is a string specifying the actual CSS rules to apply. The string should be valid CSS syntax specifying attribute value pairs of the form *attribute name: attribute value*. The string can also be a semi colon-delimited list of attribute name and attribute value pairs.

lIndex is an optional integer value that indicates where the rules should be placed in the style sheet.

The following code adds a new rule to the first style sheet in the document that sets the background-color CSS attribute to blue for the <TABLE>, <BODY>, and <P> elements.

```
Dim ss As FPHTMLStyleSheet
Set ss = ActiveDocument.styleSheets(0)
call ss.addRule("Body P Table", "background-color:blue;letter spacing:20px")
```

THE cssText PROPERTY   The cssText property of the FPHTMLStyleSheet object returns the entire text of all the rules defined in a style sheet as one contiguous string. This is a settable property that can be used to replace a style sheet's contents. The following code replaces adds a new rule to the first style sheet in the document by replacing the text of the style sheet.

```
Dim ss As FPHTMLStyleSheet
Dim sCSSText As String
Set ss = ActiveDocument.styleSheets(0)
sCSSText = ss.cssText
sCSSText = sCSSText & vbCrLf & "TABLE {position:absoslute};"
ss.cssText = sCSSText
```

THE FPHTMLStyle OBJECT

The FPHTMLStyle object is used to work with inline styles for HTML elements. The IHTMLElement exposes a property called style, which returns an instance of an FPHTMLStyle object. This object contains properties corresponding to all of the CSS attributes that can be defined in a style sheet's rules. When the style object is manipulated for an HTML element, a style attribute is added inline to the HTML elements tag. For example, the code below sets the letter-spacing CSS attribute to 20px for the <BODY> element by modifying the tag so is of the form <body style="letter-spacing:20px">.

```
Dim body_style As FPHTMLStyle
Set body_style = ActiveDocument.body.style
body_style.letterSpacing = "20px"
```

The FPHTMLStyle object exposes some methods and properties that are useful for dealing with inline styles.

THE getAttribute, setAttribute, AND removeAttribute METHODS   These methods work exactly like those defined on the IHTMLElement object that were discussed earlier in the chapter. They are primarily used to add, modify, or remove custom CSS attributes, but can also be used to work with regular CSS attributes as well. The following example code sets the background-color CSS attribute to the value green using the setAttribute method:

```
Dim table_style As FPHTMLStyle
Set table_style = ActiveDocument.all.tags("table").Item(0).style
Call table_style.setAttribute("background-color", "green")
```

THE cssText PROPERTY   This property of the FPHTMLStyle object returns the text of the style attribute defined for a particular object as one string. Like the cssText property of the FPHTMLStyleSheet object, this property is settable and can be used to replace the entire set of inline CSS attributes defined for the target object.

LINKING STYLE SHEETS USING THE FPHTMLLinkElement OBJECT

This POM object corresponds to a <LINK> HTML element and is the primary means of linking *style sheets (page 272)* into the current document. The FPHTMLLinkElement exposes three properties that are used to create a linked style sheet for an HTML document: rel, href, and type. Each of these properties is a string specifying the specifics of setting up the link. The following example code creates a new <LINK> object that links an existing style sheet named second.css to the current document.

```
Dim link As FPHTMLLinkElement
Dim head As IHTMLElement

Set head = ActiveDocument.all.tags("head").Item(0)
Call head.insertAdjacentHTML("BeforeEnd", "<link>")
Set link = ActiveDocument.all.tags("link").Item(0)
link.rel = "stylesheet"
link.href = "styles/second.css"
link.Type = "text/css"
```

WHAT ABOUT THE OTHER DHTML DYNAMIC STUFF?

As mentioned earlier with respect to the write and writeln methods of adding text to the document, the FrontPage 2000 POM is meant for use in a design-time environment. Features common to Dynamic HTML Web pages, like data binding, custom filters, and so on, do not make sense in a design-time environment, and so these types of features have not been implemented in the FrontPage 2000 POM.

PART

X

CH

45

> **Note**
>
> The FrontPage 2000 POM does not expose interfaces for these runtime types of features, but this does not mean that you cannot use the FrontPage POM to create pages in FrontPage that use these elements. For example, while FrontPage 2000 POM does not allow the programmer to create a page that reads from a database using DHTML *data binding* when the page is opened into FrontPage, the programmer is able to use the POM to create or modify the content of a page so that it supports data binding at browse time.

APPLYING THEMES AND SHARED BORDERS TO YOUR DOCUMENT

Two of the most important features of FrontPage are themes and shared borders. The FrontPage Object Model exposes objects, properties, and method to manipulate these exciting areas.

> **Note**
>
> The Theme and Shared Border interfaces defined in the FrontPage object model are not part of the POM. Because the POM is based on the Internet Explorer Dynamic HTML object model, no support for themes or shared borders is explicitly added to it, rather the interfaces are exposed on objects in the Web Object Model (WOM). The WOM is discussed in more detail in Chapter 44.

THE Themes COLLECTION

The FrontPage WOM exposes two themes collections, one corresponding to the current set of themes the client can apply to a Web and one that corresponds to the set of themes currently applied to a Web.

THE Application.Themes COLLECTION

This collection is the set of Theme objects that are available for application by the FrontPage OM. The available themes are exactly those that appear in the Apply Theme dialog box.

THE Web.Themes COLLECTION

This collection is the set of Theme objects that are currently applied to a Web. Normally, if a theme is applied at the Web level, this collection will only contain one Theme object. However, if pages in a Web have individually applied themes, this Themes collection will contain one Theme object for each of the applied themes.

THE Theme OBJECT

The Theme object encompasses a theme in FrontPage 2000. There are two important properties exposed on the Theme object: Name and Label.

Name is a property that returns the short name of a theme. This is important in that this string is used in the ApplyTheme method to apply a theme to a page. For example, if the theme is Bold Stripe, Label returns "boldstri".

Label is a property that returns the long name of a FrontPage theme. This string is exactly what shows up in the Themes dialog box in FrontPage. For example, if the theme is Bold Stripe, Label returns "Bold Stripe".

THE ApplyTheme METHOD

Use the ApplyTheme method to apply a specific theme to an HTML document. ApplyTheme is exposed on the PageWindow object and takes two arguments: ThemeName and ThemeProperties.

ThemeName is a string corresponding to the short name of the theme. For example, to apply the Bold Stripe theme, *ThemeName* should be set to "boldstri".

ThemeProperties is a combination of any of the following enumerated types used to specify what theme attributes are used when applying the theme.

The following example uses the ApplyTheme method to apply the blends theme to the current page, with all theme attributes enabled.

```
Call ActivePageWindow.ApplyTheme("blends", fpThemePropertiesAll)
```

The Themes collection, Theme objects, and the properties and method exposed to deal with Themes are discussed in more detail in Chapter 44.

ACCESSING SHARED BORDERS USING THE FRONTPAGE POM

FrontPage shared borders are applied by using the SharedBorders property exposed on the PageWindow and Web objects. Using the SharedBorders property to apply borders to a page or Web is covered in more detail in Chapter 44.

One very important aspect of working with shared borders using the FrontPage 2000 POM is understanding how the POM exposes pages with shared borders applied. The POM exposes the borders of a page as a series of <TABLE> elements. For example, if a page has the top, left, right, and bottom borders applied, the POM parses the page into three tables. Depending on which table is accessed, the content of the shared border can be read.

The first table, which corresponds to the top border, is a 1×1 table. Its content is included from the file _borders/top.htm.

The second table, which corresponds to the left and right borders and the content area, is a 1×3 table. The first cell contains the left border content included from _borders/left.htm, the middle cell contains the actual content of the document, and the third cell contains the right border content included from _borders/right.htm.

The third table, which corresponds to the bottom border, is a 1×1 table whose content is included from _borders/bottom.htm.

Note

Content should only be read from the border tables. Any modifications to content in the borders via the tables will temporarily update the border page, but will be lost when the entire page is saved. To make modifications to the border pages, open them directly into FrontPage from the _borders directory.

Also note, content for a page with shared borders on it *must* be added to the center cell of the center table. Adding content to a bordered document in any other way will result in the content being lost when the page is saved and closed.

The following example sets a number of FPHTMLTableCell objects equal to the shared border table cells and stores the content of each of the documents into variables, modifies the content of the bordered document, and then saves and closes the page.

```
Dim topborder As FPHTMLTableCell
Dim leftborder As FPHTMLTableCell
Dim rightborder As FPHTMLTableCell
Dim bottomborder As FPHTMLTableCell
Dim contentarea As FPHTMLTableCell

Dim sTopBorderContent As String
Dim sLeftBrderContent As String
Dim sRightBorderContent As String
Dim sBottomBorderContent As String
Dim sDocumentContent As String

Set topborder = ActiveDocument.all.tags("table").Item(0).rows(0).cells(0)
Set leftborder = ActiveDocument.all.tags("table").Item(1).rows(0).cells(0)
Set rightborder = ActiveDocument.all.tags("table").Item(1).rows(0).cells(2)
Set contentarea = ActiveDocument.all.tags("table").Item(1).rows(0).cells(1)
Set bottomborder = ActiveDocument.all.tags("table").Item(2).rows(0).cells(0)
Set topborder = ActiveDocument.all.tags("table").Item(0).rows(0).cells(0)

sTopBorderContent = topborder.innerHTML
sleftBorderContent = leftborder.innerHTML
srigthBorderContent = rightborder.innerHTML
sBottomBorderContent = bottomborder.innerHTML
sDocumentContent = contentarea.innerHTML

contentarea.innerHTML = sDocumentContent & "<B> modified on 12/11/98 </b>"

ActivePageWindow.Save
ActivePageWindow.Close
```

Note

There is no direct method exposed in the FrontPage OM to enable or disable the Navigation Bar features for shared border pages. However, these features are supplied by Navigation Bar WebBot, which is accessible using the FrontPage POM. Remember, changes made to a borders page are only saved if the actual border content page is opened in Pages view.

TROUBLESHOOTING

The FrontPage Page Object Model is based on the Internet Explorer 4.x Dynamic HTML Object Model. Because of this, its objects, methods, collections, and so on are not consistent with other Microsoft Office Objects Models. Because of this, programmers who are familiar with other Office Object Models might be confused because of this inconsistency.

For example, most Object Models expose a Count property that is used to return the number of elements contained in the collection. The FrontPage POM, to remain consistent with the IE4.x Object Model, exposes this property under the name Length.

There are many instances in the Page Object Model that are inconsistent with other Office applications but are exactly the same as those in the IE 4.x Object Model. For more information on these differences please consult the FrontPage 2000 Page Object Model online help. This help topic provides information on the differences between the POM and other Office applications.

DESIGNERS CORNER

Accessing and manipulating frames and framesets is one of the most frustrating things to do using the FrontPage 2000 Object Model. The following example shows how to access a frameset and its corresponding frames programmatically.

```
Option Explicit

Sub AccessFrames()
Dim fset As FPHTMLFrameSetSite
Dim frame As FPHTMLFrameElement
Dim i As Integer


Set fset = ActivePageWindow.FrameWindow.Document.all.tags("frameset").Item(0)

For i = 0 To fset.Document.all.tags("frame").Length - 1
    Set frame = fset.Document.all.tags("frame").Item(i)
    If frame.src = "main.htm" Then
        frame.src = "new_main.htm"
    End If
Next i

End Sub
```

CHAPTER 46

USING EVENTS IN FRONTPAGE 2000

In this chapter

by Bob Samer

INTRODUCTION TO EVENTS

Chapters 43, 44, and 45 covered the use of the Web Object Model (WOM), the Page Object Model (POM), and Visual Basic for Applications (VBA) to manipulate Webs and documents in FrontPage 2000. All of the examples given in those chapters have to be run manually. One of the most powerful aspects of using an Object Model is running code in response to an event.

An *event* is an occurrence in FrontPage that triggers a notification. VBA programs can run code in response to this notification to create programs that react to a user's operations in FrontPage.

WHAT EVENTS ARE AVAILABLE?

There are a number of *objects (page 548)* defined in the FrontPage object model that expose events. Events that provide notification about operations on the main FrontPage window are exposed on the Application object. For example, the OnBeforeWebPublish event is exposed on the Application object.

Page level events that correspond to user action on an HTML page are exposed on a per-object basis in the Page Object Model. For example, the POM's FPHTMLImg object exposes a number of events to deal with user actions on the image, including OnResize and OnClick.

Additionally, two more object models that are exposed for all Microsoft Office applications: the CommandBar OM and the COMAddIn OM. The CommandBar OM is discussed in some detail in this chapter, while the COMAddIn object model discussion will be deferred to Chapter 47, "Cross-Application Programming."

The CommandBar Object Model provides notification of user actions on the menu and toolbar system of FrontPage 2000. For example, the CommandBarButton object exposes an OnClick event. The CommandBar Object Model is common to all of the office applications. For more information on the CommandBar object model please see Chapter 47.

The COMAddIn Object Model exposes notification of application startup and COMAddIn connection events. For example, a COMAddIn exposes an OnStartupComplete event that is fired whenever the application that the COMAddIn is started up by has completed its startup procedures. This is the main method used to run a macro automatically when FrontPage 2000 is started.

For most Microsoft Office applications, there are two methods a programmer can use to catch events: choosing an event from a VBE project item and using the VBA withevents keyword to enable a procedure to catch and event.

Project items are a VBA feature that allows an application to define certain intrinsic objects. Doing so exposes the object's programming interfaces in the *VBE Project Explorer (page 933)*. A programmer can set properties directly on the objects as well as choose pre-defined event procedures for the objects.

Unfortunately, because of its architecture, the FrontPage 2000 Object Model does not expose any intrinsic objects as VBE project items, so the only method available to the FrontPage VBA programmer is the withevents keyword.

USING THE withevents KEYWORD TO CATCH EVENTS

To set up a program that can catch and respond to FrontPage 2000 generated events, a programmer must use the VBA withevents keyword. This keyword tells the Visual Basic Editor (or standalone Visual Basic) to setup event handlers for any events defined in the object.

> **Note**
>
> An *event handler* refers to a subprocedure defined in such a manner that the FrontPage Object Model makes a call into that procedure when its corresponding event is fired in the application.

PART

X

CH

46

Once an event handler is defined for a particular object, a programmer places the code that should run in response to the event inside the event handler procedure.

For example, Figure 46.1 shows the VBE Code Editor and an event handler for the OnPageOpen event defined for the FrontPage Application object.

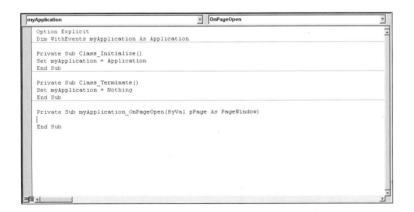

```
myApplication                          ▼  OnPageOpen                          ▼
    Option Explicit
    Dim WithEvents myApplication As Application

    Private Sub Class_Initialize()
    Set myApplication = Application
    End Sub

    Private Sub Class_Terminate()
    Set myApplication = Nothing
    End Sub

    Private Sub myApplication_OnPageOpen(ByVal pPage As PageWindow)
    |
    End Sub
```

Figure 46.1
An event handler for the Application object's OnPageOpen event.

To set up an event handler using the withevents keyword, choose an object in the object model that exposes events. Objects that expose or "source" events show up in the VBE Object Browser with a lightning bolt beside them. Figure 46.2 shows the events exposed for the Application object as seen in the *VBE Object Browser (page 950)*.

Figure 46.2
The Application object's events in the VBE Object Browser.

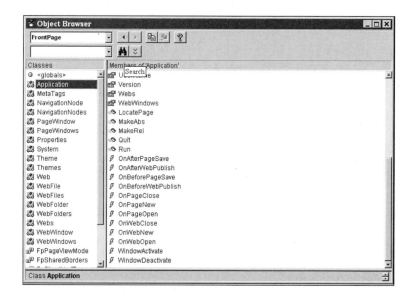

Once you have the appropriate object, define a declaration for it by using the withevents keyword. This will instruct VBE to generate handlers for the event that are available in the Procedure List Box of the VBE Code Editor. For example, the following code creates event handlers for the events exposed on the Page Object Model's FPHTMLDocument object.

```
Dim WithEvents myDoc As FPHTMLDocument
```

Once the line in this example is added to the Code Editor, the programmer can choose an event from the Procedure List Box. Doing so will create a stub subprocedure for the event that will be called in response to the event. For example, the following code shows an event handler for the OnClick event of the myDoc object from the previous example.

```
Private Function myDoc_onclick() As Boolean
End Function
```

Note

Variables (page 535) that use the withevents keyword can only be defined in a Class module or User Form module. Attempting to define them in a regular Code module will result in a compile time error from VBE.

For FrontPage to call into an event handler created via the withevents keyword, an instance of the variable that the keyword was applied to must be created. If the withevents variable is defined with public scope on a User Form module (it is defined outside of any procedure, for example), simply showing the User Form will create an instance of the withevents variable. Once the variable is created, FrontPage will call into its event handlers in response to all appropriate events. When the User Form is unloaded, all of its variables are destroyed. Once the withevents variables are destroyed, FrontPage calls none of its corresponding event handlers.

Using a *User Form* is an effective method to catch events, but it does force the programmer to show a form to the user. A better method is to create a class to contain your withevents variables. This will give you startup and shutdown procedures through which you can enable and disable events handling. For example, the following code defines a class that handles some of the key events defined for the FrontPage Application object.

```
Option Explicit

Dim WithEvents myApplication As Application

Private Sub Class_Initialize()
Set myApplication = Application
End Sub

Private Sub Class_Terminate()
Set myApplication = Nothing
End Sub

Private Sub myApplication_OnAfterPageSave(ByVal pPage As PageWindow, Success As
Boolean)
    MsgBox "OnAfterPageSave of the page " & pPage.document.Url
End Sub

Private Sub myApplication_OnAfterWebPublish(ByVal pWeb As Web, Success As Boolean)
    MsgBox "OnAfterWebPublish of the web " & pWeb.Url
End Sub

Private Sub myApplication_OnBeforePageSave(ByVal pPage As PageWindow, SaveAsUI As
Boolean, Cancel As Boolean)
    MsgBox "OnBeforePageSave of the page " & pPage.document.Url
End Sub

Private Sub myApplication_OnBeforeWebPublish(ByVal pWeb As Web, Destination As
String, Cancel As Boolean)
    MsgBox "OnBeforeWebPublish of the web " & pWeb.Url
End Sub
```

PART

X

CH

46

```
Private Sub myApplication_OnPageClose(ByVal pPage As PageWindow, Cancel As
Boolean)
    MsgBox "OnPageClose of the page " & pPage.document.Url
End Sub

Private Sub myApplication_OnPageNew(ByVal pPage As PageWindow)
    MsgBox "OnPageNew of the page " & pPage.document.Url
End Sub

Private Sub myApplication_OnPageOpen(ByVal pPage As PageWindow)
    MsgBox "OnPageOpen of the page " & pPage.document.Url
End Sub

Private Sub myApplication_OnWebClose(ByVal pWeb As Web, Cancel As Boolean)
    MsgBox "OnWebClose of the web " & pWeb.Url
End Sub

Private Sub myApplication_OnWebNew(ByVal pWeb As Web)
    MsgBox "OnWebNew of the web " & pWeb.Url
End Sub

Private Sub myApplication_OnWebOpen(ByVal pWeb As Web)
    MsgBox "OnWebOpen of the web " & pWeb.Url
End Sub
```

Don't let the amount of code scare you; the previous code sample sets up event handlers for every event defined for the FrontPage `Application` object. In practice, you will choose one or two events and define handlers for just those events.

Just as with User Form modules, `withevents` variables defined in *class modules* must be created to catch events. Use the VBA keyword `new` to create an instance of the class module. Calling `new` will in turn call the `Initialize` method of the newly created class. In the previous example, the `Initialize` method assigns the `withevents` variable `myDoc` to the `Application` object of the FrontPage Object Model. This instructs VBA to call into the events handlers defined in the class whenever an appropriate event is generated in FrontPage. The following example creates an instance of the class defined in the previous example. To run the example, insert a new class module into VBE and copy the class definition from the previous example onto it. Use the *VBE Properties window (page 937)* to name the class module `myclass`. Next, insert a new code module and add the following code.

```
Option Explicit
Public InstanceofMyClass As myClass

Sub EnableEvents()
Set InstanceofMyClass = New myClass
End Sub

Sub DisableEvents()
Set InstanceofMyClass = Nothing
End Sub
```

In the example, you define a public variable called InstanceofMyClass that is of type myClass. The variable is defined with public scope because you want it to hang around in memory trapping the events on the Application object until you instruct it to stop. Defining variables with public scope instructs VBE to keep the variable around until one of the following occurs: a runtime error, the variable is explicitly set to nothing, or the user chooses the Reset menu item from the Run menu. If the variable were defined inside of the EnableEvents procedure, it would have been created and destroyed within the scope of the procedure, which would not have allowed any events to be fired or caught.

To use the sample, run the EnableEvents procedure defined on your code module. Now try opening and closing pages and Webs, saving pages, and so on. You should get a message box prompt in response to each event. Once you are finished, run the DisableEvents method on your code module to stop catching events.

For the most part, you should declare your withevents variable with public scope and enable/disable events by instantiating and destroying the variable by using methods like the EnableEvents and DisableEvents methods in the example. However, there are a few instances where you will want to declare your withevents variable local to the procedure. For example, the following code publishes the active Web to a new site. The programmer wants to be notified when the publish operation is complete.

```
Sub VerifyPublish()
Dim LocalInstanceOfmyClass As myClass
Set LocalInstanceOfmyClass = New myClass

ActiveWeb.Publish "c:\my webs\mypublishedweb"

Set LocalInstanceOfmyClass = Nothing
End Sub
```

Because the withevents variable LocalInstanceOfMyClass is created and destroyed within the procedure, only events fired in because of code in the procedure will be caught. Once the procedure is has finished executing, no other event handlers will be called.

Using the withevents keyword to catch events is a standard method used across all Microsoft Office applications and Visual Basic.

USING THE FP WEB OBJECT MODEL TO RESPOND TO EVENTS

The Web Object Model (WOM) exposes twelve events on its Application object. These events provide notification of application-level operations. For example, the OnWebOpen event provides notification when any Web is opened into FrontPage. The event handler for each event defines a series of arguments that FrontPage passes in when the event is fired. For WOM events, this is usually a reference to the object that the event occurred on, like the Web object corresponding to the Web site that was opened, and potentially some informational arguments.

THE OnBeforePageSave EVENT

The OnBeforePageSave event is fired when a PageWindow is saved. The event is fired when any page opened into FrontPage is saved, whether the save is a manual operation by the user or is carried out programmatically. When the OnBeforePageSave event is fired, FrontPage passes in three arguments to the event handler: pPage, SaveAsUI, and Cancel.

THE SaveAsUI ARGUMENT

SaveAsUI is a Boolean value indicating whether the Save As dialog box is visible. The OnBeforePageSave event is fired before the actual save operation takes place. If the page that is being saved has not been saved at all (it is a new, unsaved page, for example), SaveAsUI is set to true. If the page has already been saved to some location, SaveAsUI is set to false. Using the SaveAsUI argument in conjunction with the Cancel property discussed in the next section will allow you to show your own Save As dialog box in response to the save operation.

THE Cancel ARGUMENT

Use the Cancel argument to cancel the Save operation. When FrontPage calls the OnBeforePageSave event handler, it passes the variable Cancel into the handler by reference. After the event handler code is executed, FrontPage checks the value of the Cancel argument. If Cancel has been set to true, FrontPage aborts the Save operation. By default, Cancel is set to false, indicating that FrontPage should carry out the save. If you wish to cancel the Save operation of the specified page, set Cancel to true inside your event handler.

THE pPage ARGUMENT

The pPage argument is a reference to the PageWindow object corresponding to the page that is being saved. Use the pPage object to get information about the page that is being saved.

The following example defines an event handler that uses the pPage argument and then the Cancel argument discussed in the previous section to cancel the Save operation if the page you are attempting to save contains any images. To run the example, insert a Class module and add the following code.

```
Option Explicit

Dim WithEvents myApplication As Application

Private Sub Class_Initialize()
Set myApplication = Application
End Sub

Private Sub Class_Terminate()
Set myApplication = Nothing
End Sub

Private Sub myApplication_OnBeforePageSave(ByVal pPage As PageWindow, SaveAsUI As
Boolean, Cancel As Boolean)
If pPage.document.images.Length > 0 Then
    Cancel = True
End If
End Sub
```

Next, use the *VBE Properties Window (page 937)* to name the class myClass. Finally insert a new code module and add the following code.

```
Option Explicit
Public InstanceofMyClass As myClass

Sub EnableEvents()
Set InstanceofMyClass = New myClass
End Sub

Sub DisableEvents()
Set InstanceofMyClass = Nothing
End Sub
```

Run the EnableEvents procedure, add a new blank page, and click the Save button on the toolbar. Notice that your page is saved. Now, close the page and add a new one. Add an image to the page using the Insert, Picture, Clip Art menu item. Choose a picture from the Clip Art gallery and insert it into the current page. Next, choose the Save button. Notice that your page is not saved. The event handler is working correctly.

THE OnAfterPageSave EVENT

The OnAfterPageSave event is fired after a Save operation is performed in FrontPage. The event is fired even if the Save operation is unsuccessful. When the OnAfterPageSave is fired, FrontPage passes the following arguments into the event handler: pPage and Success.

THE pPage ARGUMENT

Just as with the OnBeforePageSave event, the pPage argument is a reference to the PageWindow object of the page that was just saved. Use the pPage argument to get information from and manipulate the page.

THE Success ARGUMENT

The Success argument is a Boolean value indicating whether or not the save was successful. For example, if the path that the user saves to does not have enough space for the page, the OnAfterPageSave event is still fired, but the Success argument is set to false.

The following example uses the pPage and Success arguments to replace all replace all the Timestamp bots in the page with their resultant text. To run the code, replace all the code in the class module myclass from the previous example with the following code.

```
Option Explicit

Dim WithEvents myApplication As Application

Private Sub Class_Initialize()
Set myApplication = Application
End Sub

Private Sub Class_Terminate()
Set myApplication = Nothing
End Sub

Private Sub myApplication_OnAfterPageSave(ByVal pPage As PageWindow, Success As
Boolean)
Dim wb As FPHTMLFrontPageBotElement

If Success Then
    For Each wb In pPage.document.all.tags("Webbot")
        If wb.getBotAttribute("bot") = "Timestamp" Then
                wb.outerHTML = wb.innerHTML
        End If
    Next
End If
End Sub
```

Next, run the EnableEvents method on the code module inserted in the previous example. Add a new page and then insert a timestamp bot by choosing Date and Time from the Insert menu. Next click the Save button and specify a filename. Once the save is successful, click the area where you inserted the Timestamp bot. Notice that is has been replaced with just the date and time. The *WebBot (page 166)* should be gone entirely.

THE OnPageOpen EVENT

The OnPageOpen event if fired whenever a page is opened into FrontPage. The event is only called once for a frameset. Only one argument is passed into the event handler for OnPageOpen: pPage. Just as with the OnBeforePageSave and OnAfterPageSave events, pPage contains a reference to the PageWindow object corresponding to the page that is being opened into FrontPage. The following example checks to see if the page being opened is the admin_log.htm and verifies that the currently logged in user is the Administrator. If so, the page is opened. Otherwise the page is closed. To run the code, replace the code in the Class module myClass with the following code.

```
Option Explicit

Dim WithEvents myApplication As Application

Private Sub Class_Initialize()
Set myApplication = Application
End Sub

Private Sub Class_Terminate()
Set myApplication = Nothing
End Sub

Private Sub myApplication_OnPageOpen(ByVal pPage As PageWindow)
If pPage.document.nameProp = "admin_log" Then
    If UserName <> "Administrator" Then
        pPage.Close
    End If
End If

End Sub
```

Next, run the EnableEvents method on the code module inserted in the previous example. Create a new page called admin_log.htm and open it into Pages view. Notice that the page loads for a second and is then closed.

> **Note**
>
> Notice that the previous code will open the page if you are logged in as Administrator. If you are logged in as Administrator on the machine, you *will* be able to open the page.

The OnPageOpen event is called whenever a page is opened into Pages view of FrontPage, regardless of the method. For example, if the user is in Folders view and double clicks a page, the event is fired.

PART

X

CH

46

THE OnPageClose EVENT

The OnPageClose event is fired whenever a page is closed, regardless of the method used to close it. The event is only called once for a frameset. If any page is open when FrontPage is closed, the event is fired for each page. Also, if a page is open that resides in a Web, the event is fired when the Web is closed. When the event is fired, FrontPage passes two arguments into the event handler: pPage and Cancel.

THE pPage ARGUMENT

The pPage argument works just like all the other pPage arguments and allows access to the properties and methods of the PageWindow object corresponding to the page being closed.

THE Cancel ARGUMENT

Use the Cancel argument to cancel the close operation of the page.

The following example checks the page that is being closed to ensure that it has a title specified for it. If the title is not specified, a prompt is displayed to the user to determine whether he or she wants to close the page or not. To run the code, replace all the code in the class module myclass from the previous example with the following code.

```
Option Explicit

Dim WithEvents myApplication As Application

Private Sub Class_Initialize()
Set myApplication = Application
End Sub

Private Sub Class_Terminate()
Set myApplication = Nothing
End Sub


Private Sub myApplication_OnPageClose(ByVal pPage As PageWindow, Cancel As
Boolean)
If pPage.document.title = "" Then
    If MsgBox("No <TITLE> Element defined, Close?", vbYesNo, "No Title") = vbNo
Then
        Cancel = True
    End If
End If
End Sub
```

Next, run the `EnableEvents` method on the Code module inserted in the previous example. Add a new page and remove the `<TITLE>` element via HTML view. Now, close the page. Choose a filename for the page and click the Save button. Notice that you are prompted *after* the save event if you actually want to close the page.

THE OnPageNew EVENT

The `OnPageNew` event is fired when a new page is created in Pages view of FrontPage. The event is also fired when a new Web is created or an existing Web is opened. The event is not fired when a new page is created in a view other than Pages view. For example, creating a new page in Folders view doesn't fire the `OnPageNew` event. `OnPageNew` is only fired once for a new frameset.

THE pPage ARGUMENT

The `pPage` argument is a reference to a `PageWindow` object corresponding to the newly created page.

The following example checks to see if the new page is a style sheet by checking its file extension. If the new page is a style sheet, the page is closed. To run the code, replace all the code in the Class module `myclass` from the previous example with the following code.

```
Option Explicit

Dim WithEvents myApplication As Application

Private Sub Class_Initialize()
Set myApplication = Application
End Sub

Private Sub Class_Terminate()
Set myApplication = Nothing
End Sub

Private Sub myApplication_OnPageNew(ByVal pPage As PageWindow)
Dim sPageURL As String
sPageURL = pPage.Caption
If LCase(Right(sPageURL, Len(sPageURL) - (Len(sPageURL) - 3))) = "css" Then
    MsgBox "Cannot create new StyleSheets!", vbCritical, "Invalid New Page"
    pPage.Close
End If

End Sub
```

Next, run the `EnableEvents` method on the Code module inserted in the previous example. Now, create a new style sheet by choosing File, New Page. Choose a CSS template from the StyleSheets tab and choose OK. A message box will appear indicating that style sheet cannot be created. Once the user clicks the OK button on the message box, the new style sheet page is closed without being saved.

THE OnWebOpen EVENT

The `OnWebOpen` event is fired when a Web is opened into FrontPage. The event is fired regardless of the method used to open the Web. For example, opening a Web with the following code will fire the `OnWebOpen` event just as if the Web was manually opened.

```
Webs.Open("c:\my webs\mynewweb")
```

> **Note**
>
> The `OnWebOpen` event is fired when a new HTTP based Web site is created, but not fired when a new disk-based Web is created.

THE pWeb ARGUMENT

The `pWeb` argument is a reference to the `Web` object that corresponds to the FrontPage-based Web site that is being opened. Use `pPeb` to access methods and properties to get information from or manipulate the Web site.

For example, the following example restricts users from opening disk-based Webs by checking the `vti_webservertype` Meta information. If the Web is a disk-based Web, a message box is displayed and the Web is closed. To run the code, replace all the code in the class module `myclass` from the previous example with the following code.

```
Option Explicit

Dim WithEvents myApplication As Application

Private Sub Class_Initialize()
Set myApplication = Application
End Sub

Private Sub Class_Terminate()
Set myApplication = Nothing
End Sub

Private Sub myApplication_OnWebOpen(ByVal pWeb As Web)
If pWeb.Properties("vti_webservertype") = "diskweb" Then
    MsgBox "Disk Based Webs not allowed!", vbCritical, "Error"
    pWeb.Close
End If
End Sub
```

Next, run the EnableEvents method on the code module inserted in the previous example. Now, attempt to open a disk-based Web. Notice the message box that appears indicating that disk-based Webs are not allowed. Once the OK button is clicked, the Web is closed.

THE OnWebClose EVENT

The OnWebClose event is fired when any Web is closed in FrontPage. If a Web is open in FrontPage when the application is existed, the OnWebClose event is fired. FrontPage passes two arguments into the event handler in response the event: pWeb and Cancel.

THE pWeb ARGUMENT

The pWeb argument is a reference to the Web object that corresponds to the Web site that is being closed.

THE Cancel ARGUMENT

The Cancel argument is a Boolean value that FrontPage passes into the OnWebClose event handler to control whether the Web is actually closed. Setting the Cancel argument to true will force FrontPage to cancel the close operation for the Web and leave it open into FrontPage.

For example, the following code checks to see if the current Web has the Corporate theme applied to it. If not, the close operation is cancelled and the user is prompted to apply the correct theme.

> **Note**
>
> It is entirely possible for the code to apply the correct theme itself, but for the purposes of this example it notifies the user.

To run the code, replace all the code in the class module myclass from the previous example with the following code.

```
Option Explicit

Dim WithEvents myApplication As Application

Private Sub Class_Initialize()
Set myApplication = Application
End Sub

Private Sub Class_Terminate()
Set myApplication = Nothing
End Sub
```

PART

X

CH

46

```
Private Sub myApplication_OnWebClose(ByVal pWeb As Web, Cancel As Boolean)
If pWeb.ThemeProperties(fpThemeName) <> "Corporate" Then
    MsgBox "All webs need to have the Corporate Theme applied!", vbCritical,
"Wrong Theme!"
    Cancel = True
End If
End Sub
```

Next, run the EnableEvents method on the Code module inserted in the previous example. Now, create a new Web and then attempt to close it. Notice the message box that appears indicating that the incorrect theme has been applied. Once the OK button is clicked, the close operation is canceled.

> **Caution**
>
> You can easily get yourself into an endless loop if you are not careful with your events. For example, the previous example catches the OnWebClose event. If you indicate that a Web should be opened as a result of the OnWebClose event, and you have defined an OnWebOpen event handler like the ones you created earlier that call the Close method of the Web, an endless loop results.

THE OnWebNew EVENT

The OnWebNew event is fired whenever a new Web site is created using FrontPage. The one exception is creating a new sub-Web via the Convert To Web option from the context menu for a folder. In this case, the OnWebNew event is not called. FrontPage passes one argument into the event handler: pWeb.

THE pWeb ARGUMENT

The pWeb argument is a reference to the Web object corresponding to the Web site being created.

The following example traps the traps the OnWebNew event and applies the Top, Left, Right, and Bottom shared borders to the Web if not already applied. To run the code, replace all the code in the Class module myclass from the previous example with the following code.

```
Option Explicit

Dim WithEvents myApplication As Application

Private Sub Class_Initialize()
Set myApplication = Application
End Sub

Private Sub Class_Terminate()
Set myApplication = Nothing
End Sub
```

```
Private Sub myApplication_OnWebNew(ByVal pWeb As Web)
Dim AllBorders As Double
AllBorders = fpBorderLeft + fpBorderRight + fpBorderTop + fpBorderBottom

If pWeb.SharedBorders(fpBorderAll) <> AllBorders Then
    pWeb.SharedBorders(fpBorderAll) = True
End If
End Sub
```

Next, run the EnableEvents method on the code module inserted in the previous example. Now, create a new, one-page Web by choosing File, New Web, choose the One Page Web template and click OK. Notice that all four shared borders have been applied to the newly created Web site.

THE OnBeforeWebPublish EVENT

The OnBeforeWebPublish event is important in that a programmer can do some pre-processing of a Web site before it appears on the destination site. One example might be to strip out features added to Web that are not supported on a particular area. The OnBeforeWebPublish event is fired any time a Web is published in FrontPage. The application passes in three arguments to the event handler when the event is fired: pWeb, Destination, and Cancel.

THE pWeb ARGUMENT

The pWeb argument is a reference to the Web object corresponding to the Web that is being published. It is not a reference to the destination Web. Use the pWeb argument to get information from and manipulate the source Web site.

THE Destination ARGUMENT

The Destination argument is a string that is passed in by FrontPage specifying the URL of the target Web site of the publish. Because the destination Web site might not be a FrontPage-based Web site (it could be an FTP site, for example), a Web object cannot be passed back. Often the programmer will want to retain the value of the Destination argument so that the target Web can be opened later.

THE Cancel ARGUMENT

Just as you did with the other events, use the Cancel event to abort the Publish operation on the current Web. Setting Cancel to true will force FrontPage to stop the Publish operation when the event handler has finished execution.

The following example checks the current username. If it's not Administrator, the Publish operation is cancelled. If the user is the Administrator, the destination of the Publish operation is saved into the global variable sTargetWeb. This is important in that you will use it in the next example to open the target Web and do some post processing on the newly published Web.

To run the code, replace all the code in the Class module `myclass` from the previous example with the following code.

```
Option Explicit
Public sTargetWeb As String
Dim WithEvents myApplication As Application

Private Sub Class_Initialize()
Set myApplication = Application
End Sub

Private Sub Class_Terminate()
Set myApplication = Nothing
End Sub

Private Sub myApplication_OnBeforeWebPublish(ByVal pWeb As Web, Destination As
String, Cancel As Boolean)
    If UserName <> "Administrator" Then
        MsgBox "Only the Admin can publish this web", vbCritical, "Cannot
Publish!"
        Cancel = True
    Else
        sTargetWeb = Destination
    End If
End Sub
```

Next, run the `EnableEvents` method on the Code module inserted in the previous example. Now, create a new Web site and publish the Web to a new destination by selecting Publish from the File menu. If you are logged in to the machine under the account Administrator, the Web will be published correctly, otherwise you will get a prompt indicating that the Administrator can only publish the current Web.

> **Note**
>
> The `UserName` property of the `Application` object is a read-write property, meaning that you can set it to a new value. `UserName` is set to the current user initially, but you can easily set it to Administrator by using the following code
>
> `Username = "Administrator"`
>
> Because the property is not read-only, you may wish to use a different method to check the currently logged in user in the `OnBeforeWebPublish` event. For example, the Win32 API `GetUserName` can be used to get the "real" username of the currently logged in user, even if the `Application` object's `UserName` property has been set to a different value.

THE `OnAfterWebPublish` EVENT

The `OnAfterWebPublish` event is called after any Web is published in FrontPage. The event is fired regardless of the method used to publish. For example, the following code fires the `OnAfterWebPublish` event just as if the user had manually published the current Web.

```
ActiveWeb.Publish("c:\my webs\mynewweb")
```

FrontPage passes two arguments into the event handler for the OnAfterWebPublish event: pWeb and Success.

The pWeb Argument

Just as it does in the other event handlers, the pWeb argument is a reference to the Web object corresponding to the Web site that was published. It does not correspond to the destination Web site.

The Success Argument

The Success argument is a Boolean value indicating whether or not the Publish operation was successful. Because OnAfterWebPublish is fired even if the Publish operation fails, the Success argument can be checked to see if the operation succeeded. For example, if the disk space on the destination server runs out, the Publish operation will fail, but the OnAfterWebPublish event will still fire with the Success argument set to false.

The OnAfterPageSave event is an important means to do some post-publish processing on a Web site. For example, the following code replaces all webbot components on the home-page of the Web site with the generated HTML of the WebBot.

To run the code, replace all the code in the Class module myclass from the previous example with the following code.

```
Option Explicit
Public sTargetWeb As String
Dim WithEvents myApplication As Application

Private Sub Class_Initialize()
Set myApplication = Application
End Sub

Private Sub Class_Terminate()
Set myApplication = Nothing
End Sub

Private Sub myApplication_OnAfterWebPublish(ByVal pWeb As Web, Success As Boolean)
Dim oTargetWeb As Web
Dim pw As PageWindow
Stop
Dim wb As FPHTMLFrontPageBotElement
    If Success Then
        Set oTargetWeb = Webs.Open(sTargetWeb)
        Set pw = oTargetWeb.RootFolder.Files("index.htm").Edit
        For Each wb In pw.document.all.tags("webbot")
            wb.outerHTML = wb.innerHTML
        Next wb
        pw.Save
        pw.Close
    End If

End Sub
```

```
Private Sub myApplication_OnBeforeWebPublish(ByVal pWeb As Web, Destination As
String, Cancel As Boolean)
        sTargetWeb = Destination
End Sub
```

Next, run the EnableEvents method on the code module inserted in the previous example. Now, create a new *disk-based Web site* and add a Timestamp WebBot to the homepage of the Web site. Next, publish the Web site to a new Web. Notice that the OnBeforeWebPublish event is fired to set the global variable sTargetWeb to the URL of the destination Web. Next, the OnAfterWebPublish event is fired. The code in the OnAfterWebPublish event handler opens the destination Web's homepage, index.htm, and replaces the Timestamp webbot with its generated HTML.

USING THE FRONTPAGE POM TO RESPOND TO PAGE-LEVEL EVENTS

In addition to the events defined for Web-level events in the Web Object Model, the Page Object Model (POM) exposes a number of events for each of its objects. Each of the objects exposed in the *POM (page 992)* exposes events to provide notification of typical user interactions with the element.

The Page Object Model is based on the Internet Explorer DHTML object model and therefore inherits the event model. One item to note is the DHTML object model was created for a runtime environment. Because of this, some events make more sense than others when used in the design-time environment of Microsoft FrontPage.

For example, the DHTML object model exposes an OnClick event for most of its elements. This event makes sense in a design-time environment and is therefore exposed in the FrontPage Page Object Model. However, most elements in the DHTML object model also expose an OnAfterUpdate event. This event is a runtime-based event and has no function in a design-time environment and is therefore not exposed in the Page Object Model.

Event handlers for POM events are created in the same manner as those in the Web Object Model, through the use of withevents keyword. However, one important difference between the Page Object Model events and the WOM events is the lack of event handler arguments in the POM. Instead of passing in arguments to an event handler, FrontPage passes event information to the event's client by setting properties on a special event object. This object, the IHTMLEventObj, is accessible from anywhere on an HTML document via the parentWindow property of the document.

THE IHTMLEventObj ELEMENT

The IHTMLEventObj object is a public object that FrontPage uses to pass information about the generated event to an event handler. The object is always accessible in a program, but its properties are not initialized until an event occurs. To access the IHTMLEventObj, use the Event property of the FPHTMLWindow2 object. For example, the following code shows an event handler for the FPHTMLDocument object's OnMouseDown event.

```
Option Explicit
Dim WithEvents myDoc As FPHTMLDocument

Private Sub Class_Initialize()
Set myDoc = ActiveDocument
End Sub

Private Sub Class_Terminate()
Set myDoc = Nothing
End Sub

Private Sub myDoc_onmousedown()
Dim e As IHTMLEventObj
Set e = myDoc.parentWindow.event
MsgBox "The Event fired was the " & e.Type & " event!", vbOKOnly, "Event Fired"
End Sub
```

To run the event handler code, copy the code from the example into a new class module. Next, use the VBE Properties Window to rename the class module myPageClass. Now, insert a new code module and add the following code to it.

```
Option Explicit

Public myPageClassInstance As myPageClass

Sub EnableEvents()
Set myPageClassInstance = New myPageClass
End Sub

Sub DisableEvents()
Set myPageClassInstance = Nothing
End Sub
```

PART

X

CH

46

Now, run the EnableEvents procedure on the code module, switch to FrontPage and click the current document with the mouse. You should see the prompt shown in Figure 46.3, POM Event Handler.

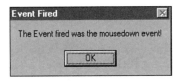

Figure 46.3
EnableEvents responds to a mouse click.

The previous example uses the type property of the IHTMLEventObj to display what event was fired. type is just one of the useful properties exposed on the event object. There are number of other properties that are exposed as well, each one important to the different types of events.

THE altKey PROPERTY

Use the altKey property to determine whether the user has the Alt key depressed when the event notification is triggered. The altKey property is a Boolean value, set to true if the Alt key was pressed during the event. For example, the following code fragment checks the value of the Alt key when the `OnClick` event is fired for the first `FPHTMLImg` object on the current document. To run the example, replace the code on the `myPageClass` class module with the following code.

```
Option Explicit
Dim WithEvents myImg As FPHTMLImg

Private Sub Class_Initialize()
Set myImg = ActiveDocument.images(0)
End Sub

Private Sub Class_Terminate()
Set myImg = Nothing
End Sub

Private Function myImg_onclick() As Boolean
Dim e As IHTMLEventObj
Set e = ActiveDocument.parentWindow.event

If e.altKey = True Then
    MsgBox "<ALT> key pressed while the image: " & myImg.href & " was clicked!"
End If
End Function
```

Next, make sure you have at least one image on the current page and run the `EnableEvents` procedure. Now, hold down the Alt key and click on the first image in your document with either mouse button. You should see the message box indicating that the `OnClick` event has fired and that the Alt key was depressed.

THE ctrlKey PROPERTY

The `IHTMLEventObj` object's `ctrlKey` property indicates the state of the Ctrl key during the event. If the Ctrl key is depressed, `ctrlKey` is set to `true`, otherwise it is `false`.

THE shiftKey PROPERTY

The `shiftKey` property works the same as the `altKey` and `ctrlKey` properties. If the Shift key is pressed when the event takes place, `shiftKey` is set to `true`, otherwise it is set to `false`.

THE keyCode PROPERTY

The `keyCode` property is set to the Unicode value of the key that caused the event to happen. If the event fired is `OnKeyDown`, `OnKeyPress`, or `OnKeyUp`, the `keyCode` property is set to the value of the key that generated the event. If the current event is not one of these three events, `keyCode` is set to 0. The `keyCode` property is read-write, meaning that it can be set to a new key value inside of the event handler. Doing so will replace the user's choice of keys with the new value for the `OnKeyDown` and `OnKeyPress` events.

THE button PROPERTY

Use the button property of the IHTMLEventObj to determine which button on the mouse was depressed when the event is fired. button is set to 0 if no mouse button was pressed, 1 if the left mouse button was depressed, 2 if the right mouse button was pressed, and 4 if the middle button was depressed.

THE cancelBubble PROPERTY

The cancelBubble property is a very important feature of the POM's event model. When a multiple event handlers are defined for nested objects, the value of the cancelBubble property determines whether or not the event of a child object is "bubbled" up to its parent's event handler. For example, if an OnClick event handler is defined for both an FPHTMLImg object and the FPHTMLDocument object that the image resides on, the OnClick event fired on the image will propagate to the document object by default. To avoid this, set the cancelBubble property to true. The following example sets the cancelBubble property to true in the image's OnClick event handler. Because cancelBubble is true, the document's OnClick event handler is not called, even though one is defined for it. Follow the instructions from the previous example to run the following code.

```
Option Explicit
Dim WithEvents myImg As FPHTMLImg
Dim WithEvents myDoc As FPHTMLDocument

Private Sub Class_Initialize()
Set myImg = ActiveDocument.images(0)
Set myDoc = ActiveDocument
End Sub

Private Sub Class_Terminate()
Set myImg = Nothing
Set myDoc = Nothing
End Sub

Private Function myDoc_onclick() As Boolean
Dim e As IHTMLEventObj
Set e = ActiveDocument.parentWindow.event
MsgBox "the OnClick event was fired for the Document"
End Function


Private Function myImg_onclick() As Boolean
Dim e As IHTMLEventObj
Set e = ActiveDocument.parentWindow.event
MsgBox "the OnClick event was fired for the Image"
e.cancelBubble = True
End Function
```

Once the EnableEvents procedure is executed, click the image inside of your document. Notice that the message box defined in the myImg_OnClick procedure is displayed, but the message box defined in the myDoc_OnClick procedure is not.

PART

X

CH

46

THE returnValue PROPERTY

This is the most important property exposed on IHTMLEventObj. By modifying this Boolean value, the programmer can enable or disable the default operation of the event. For example, setting returnValue to false for the OnMouseUp event will cancel the user's mouse click. The following code cancels the user's keystrokes in the first table in the current document by setting the returnValue property to false. To run the code, modify the myPageClass class module from the previous example, replacing its code with the following:

```
Option Explicit
Dim WithEvents myTable As FPHTMLTable

Private Sub Class_Initialize()
Set myTable = ActiveDocument.all.tags("table").Item(0)
End Sub

Private Sub Class_Terminate()
Set myTable = Nothing
End Sub


Private Function myTable_onkeypress() As Boolean
Dim e As IHTMLEventObj
Set e = ActiveDocument.parentWindow.event
e.returnvalue = False
End Function
```

Next, create a new page and add a 2×2 table to it. Now, run the EnableEvents procedure from the previous example and then attempt to type inside the table. Notice that your keystrokes are canceled. Now, type elsewhere in the document and notice that your keystrokes are not cancelled. This is a very powerful feature of the FrontPage POM event model. Having the ability to cancel the default operation of value will allow the programmer to substitute his or her own forms and code to respond to the users action.

THE srcElement PROPERTY

Another important property, the srcElement property, returns a reference to the IHTMLElement object corresponding to the object that fired the event. The object returned by this property is usually the object that had the action performed on it. For example, if an OnClick event handler is defined for the FPHTMLDocument object corresponding to the current document, the object returned by the srcElement will be the object that was under the mouse when the document was clicked. Only objects that are visible HTML elements are returned via the srcElement property. For example, if an OnResize event handler is defined for an FPHTMLWindow2 object corresponding to the current window and the window is resized, srcElement is set to Nothing because FPHTMLWindow2 is not a displayable HTML element.

THE x PROPERTY

The x property specifies the x coordinate on the screen corresponding to where an OnMouseDown, OnMouseUp, OnClick, OnDblClick, OnMouseOver, or OnMouseOut event occurred.

THE y PROPERTY

The y property works exactly like the x property except that is specifies the y coordinate on the screen for a mouse-generated event.

The x and y properties of the IHTMLEventObj are useful for a number of reasons, including providing information as a user moves the mouse over certain elements. For example, the following example displays a description of the element under the mouse in the status bar. By using the x and y properties of the IHTMLEventObj, in conjunction with the FPHTMLDocument object's ElementFromPoint method, the code gets the current element's title attribute and places this description into the FrontPage status bar. To run the example, replace the code in myPageClass from the previous example with the following code:

```
Option Explicit
Dim WithEvents myDoc As FPHTMLDocument

Private Sub Class_Initialize()
Set myDoc = ActiveDocument
End Sub

Private Sub Class_Terminate()
Set myDoc = Nothing
End Sub

Private Sub myDoc_onmouseover()
Dim e As IHTMLEventObj
Dim currentelement As IHTMLElement
Set e = ActiveDocument.parentWindow.event
Set currentelement = ActiveDocument.elementFromPoint(e.x, e.y)
ActiveDocument.parentWindow.status = currentelement.title
End Sub
```

Next create a new page and insert a number of elements. Make sure that each element has a title attribute set to some descriptive string value. For example, a title for a table element might use the following HTML:

```
<table title="January Cost Figures" border="1" width="100%">
```

Next, run the EnableEvents procedure from the previous example and move your mouse over the different elements you added. Notice that the status bar updates itself to show the title of the element that is currently under the mouse.

SOME COMMON PAGE OBJECT MODEL EVENTS

While there are many more events defined for the Page Object Model than those listed here, the following events cover the majority of the functionality most users will require for general use of events.

THE OnClick EVENT

The OnClick event is exposed for all HTML elements as well as the FPHTMLDocument object. OnClick is fired when the user presses and releases a mouse button over an element. OnClick is a combination of the OnMouseDown and OnMouseUp events. If both events are not fired, the

OnClick event is not fired. For example, assume that an OnClick event handler is defined for an FPHTMLTable element. If the user presses and holds the left mouse button inside the table, but then moves the mouse outside the table and releases it, the OnClick event is not called.

Note

> The OnClick event cannot be directly cancelled by setting the returnValue property to false, but the OnMouseUp event can be cancelled in this manner. Because both the OnClick and the OnDblClick events require the OnMouseUp event to fire before they fire themselves, canceling OnMouseUp effectively cancels OnClick and OnDblClick.

THE OnDblClick EVENT

The OnDblClick event fires when the user clicks twice in quick succession over an element. OnDblClick consists of the following chain of events: OnMouseDown, OnMouseUp, OnClick, OnMouseUp, and OnDblClick. Either mouse button can be used and as noted in the previous section the event can be cancelled by canceling the OnMouseUp event.

THE OnMouseDown EVENT

The event is fired when the user presses any mouse button. The event will be fired whether the user releases the button or not.

THE OnMouseUp EVENT

This event is fired when the user release either mouse button. This is the only cancelable event of the mouse type events, so setting the IHTMLEventObj object's returnValue property to false inside of the OnMouseUp event will cancel all other mouse-oriented events.

THE OnMouseMove EVENT

The OnMouseMove event is fired whenever the mouse is moved inside the confines of a page in Pages view of FrontPage. If the mouse moves outside the page, the event is not fired until the mouse moves back into the page. When this event is fired, the x and y properties are set for the IHTMLEventObj to the x and y coordinates of the mouse's current position with respect to the current page.

Using the OnMouseDown, OnMouseMove, and OnMouseUp events in conjunction allows the programmer to create custom drag-and-drop effects inside a FrontPage HTML page.

THE OnMouseOver EVENT

This is event is fired whenever the user moves the mouse over an element. The event is fired whenever the mouse first moves into the element's area and is only fired once unless the user moves out of the element's area and back in again. Once inside of the element, multiple OnMouseMove events are fired as the mouse pointer is moved around inside the element's area. The OnMouseOver event is fired for all HTML elements as well as the FPHTMLDocument object. The event is not defined for the FPHTMLWindow2 object.

THE OnKeyPress EVENT

The `OnKeyPress` event is fired whenever a key is pressed in the document. For the `OnKeyPress` event to fire, the `OnKeyDown` and `OnKeyUp` events must fire as well. When the `OnKeyPress` event is fired, the `keyCode` property of the `IHTMLEventObj` is set to the Unicode value of the key that was pressed. The `OnKeyPress` event is cancelable and is the means to cancel the `OnKeyDown` and `OnKeyUp` events as well. To cancel the `OnKeyPress` event, set the `returnValue` event of the `IHTMLEventObj` object to `false`. Also, a new keycode other than that the one corresponding to the key that generated the event can be substituted by setting the `keyCode` property of the `IHTMLEventObj` in the `OnKeyPress` event handler.

> **Note**
>
> The `keyCode` specified during the `OnKeyPress` event can be any key available on the keyboard, including the arrow keys, functions keys, and so on. However, the `keyCode` specified during the `OnKeyDown` and `OnKeyUp` events can only be an alphanumeric key.

THE OnKeyDown EVENT

This event is fired when the user presses a key down on the keyboard. `OnKeyDown` is not cancelable itself, but it will be canceled if the `OnKeyPress` is cancelled. Just as with the `OnKeyPress` event, the `keyCode` property of the `IHTMLEventObj` can be set to a new Unicode value to change the character that is added to the page.

THE OnKeyUp EVENT

This event is fired when the user releases a key on the keyboard. It is cancelable by canceling the `OnKeyPress` event associated with it.

THE OnResize EVENT

The `OnResize` event is fired whenever one of the applicable objects is resized. Most elements that can be resized in the application can create the `OnResize` event handler. For example, creating an `OnResize` event for a marquee or image is supported, as well as a handler for the `FPHTMLWindow2` object. `OnResize` is not cancelable and will not bubble up to the parent object.

There are many more events defined for each object in the FrontPage Page Object Model. For more information consult FrontPage online help under the `events` keyword.

USING THE COMMANDBAR OBJECT MODEL TO TRAP EVENTS

FrontPage 2000 includes the *Microsoft Office CommandBar object model*. This OM is common to all office application and allows the manipulation of the menu and toolbar system. Chapter 47 covers the use of the CommandBar object model in more detail. This section describes how to trap events for the menu and toolbar system by using CommandBar object model.

The CommandBar object model uses `withevents` variables to set up its events handlers, just like the POM and WOM objects.

There are two important events associated with the CommandBar object model: `Click` and `OnUpdate`.

THE `Click` EVENT OF THE `CommandBarButton` OBJECT

The `CommandBarButton` object represents a menu item in a FrontPage menu. When the menu item corresponding to a particular `CommandBarButton` object is selected, FrontPage passed two arguments into its event handler: `CTRL` and `CancelDefault`.

THE CTRL ARGUMENT

Use the `CTRL` element to get access to the menu item itself. `CTRL` is a reference to a `CommandBarControl` object corresponding to the menu item what was selected. Use the `CTRL` argument to get or set information about the menu item that caused the event. For example, the following example grays out the menu item once it has been selected. To run the example, insert a new class module, name it `myCBClass` and copy the following code onto the class module.

```
Option Explicit
Dim WithEvents cbutton As CommandBarButton

Private Sub Class_Initialize()
Set cbutton = CommandBars.ActiveMenuBar.Controls("Tools").Controls.Add(1, , , ,
True)
With cbutton
    .Caption = "My New Command"
    .Style = 1
    .Visible = True
End With
End Sub
```

```
Private Sub cbutton_Click(ByVal Ctrl As Office.CommandBarButton, CancelDefault As
Boolean)
    If Ctrl.Enabled Then
        Ctrl.Enabled = False
    End If
End Sub
```

Next, insert a new code module and add the following code to it.

```
Option Explicit
Public InstanceOfMyCBClass As myCBClass

Sub EnableEvents()
Set InstanceOfMyCBClass = New myCBClass
End Sub

Sub DisableEvents()
Set InstanceOfMyCBClass = New myCBClass
End Sub
```

Finally, run the EnableEvents procedure to execute the example. Now, choose the Tools menu and notice that a new menu item, My New Command, has appeared. Select the new menu item with your mouse and then drop the Tools menu again. Notice that the menu item is now grayed out. Setting the enabled property to false in the Click event handler defined in the previous code disabled the menu item.

THE CancelDefault ARGUMENT

The CancelDefault argument works for the CommandBarButton object in the same manner that the Cancel argument worked for the Web Object Model's OnBeforePageSave event. It is a read-write Boolean value that will cancel the default action for the CommandBarButton. If the CommandBarButton object for which the event handler is setup is a default FrontPage menu item, like the File, Exit menu item, setting CancelDefault to true will keep FrontPage from exiting when File, Exit is selected.

THE Update EVENT OF THE CommandBars OBJECT

One event of the CommandBar object model that is very important to understand to use the rest of the FrontPage OM is the Update event of the CommandBars object. This event is fired whenever a message is sent by Microsoft Windows or FrontPage instructing the CommandBars objects to update them. The Update event occurs when the user is typing, when the screen in minimized and maximized, when a menu or toolbar is selected, and many other times. When the Update event occurs, FrontPage does not pass in any arguments to the event handler.

> **Caution**
>
> The Update event is fired *often*, probably more often than you will anticipate, so don't place too much code in its event handler or FrontPage will slow to a crawl.

One important use of the Update event is to synchronize the target objects for the other object models in FrontPage. For example, a programmer can use the POM to set up an OnClick event handler for a specific image in a page. However, if the user drags and drops that image to a new area of the page or loads a new page with a new image, the event will not longer be enabled. So, programmers can use the Update event of the CommandBars object to re-assign the withevents variable for the image. The following example does just that, continually re-assigning the myImg variable to the new location of the image. To run the example, replace the code in myCBClass from the previous example with the following code:

```
Option Explicit
Dim WithEvents myImg As FPHTMLImg
Dim WithEvents cbars As CommandBars

Private Sub cbars_OnUpdate()
    Set myImg = Nothing
    Set myImg = ActiveDocument.images(0)
End Sub

Private Sub Class_Initialize()
```

```
    Set cbars = CommandBars
    Set myImg = ActiveDocument.images(0)
End Sub

Private Sub myImg_onmousedown()
MsgBox "MouseDown on image: " & myImg.href
End Sub
```

Next, add an image to your page and run the EnableEvents procedure from the previous example. Now, click the image and you should get the message box defined in the OnMouseDown event handler in the previous example. Next, drag and drop the image to a new area on the document and click again. Notice that the event is still enabled. Without the OnUpdate event handler constantly re-assigning your withevents variable, the event would have been disabled.

WRAPPING IT UP

Creating event handlers to respond to user actions is one of the most powerful features of any object model. In Chapter 47 you will see the object models and event models exposed in the other Microsoft Office products, in Visual Basic, and also in the COMAddIn object model. For more information on using events, please see the FrontPage 2000 VBA online help as well as the Microsoft Office Developer Network (MSDN).

TROUBLESHOOTING

There are over forty events exposed in the FrontPage 2000 Object Model, covering application-, web-, and page-level events. Adding these events increases the complexity of your programs.

You may encounter situations where your events are not firing or are firing in the incorrect order. Depending on what Object Model you are working with, the Web Object Model, the CommandBar Object Model, or the Page Object Model, there are different steps you should follow to troubleshoot your event code.

For events that are exposed on the Web and CommandBar level, like the OnWebOpen event, the majority of problems will be the same for all events. The best way to troubleshoot these events is to place a breakpoint in the Initialize event of your Class module. Using this method will allow you to "step" through the rest of your code to make sure that your event handler is actually being called.

For page level events there are a number of things to check. First, use the breakpoint method described in the previous paragraph to make sure that you event class is actually being created and the event handler is being called. Next, verify that the properties on the IHTMLEventObj are set to the correct value. In particular, check the cancelBubble property. If this property is set to true then no other events in the event chain will be called. For example, suppose your event class defines an event handler for both a table element as well as a table cell element contained inside the table. If the table cell event handler sets the

IHTMLEventObj's cancelBubble event to true then the table event handler will never receive notification that an event occurred on the table. This is a common problem when dealing with events for the POM.

For more information on what events are fired under what situations, please consult the Web Object Model and Page Object Model online help topics. To access this help, switch to VBE and hit F1.

DESIGNERS CORNER

Earlier in the chapter we talked about using Class modules to setup event handlers for FrontPage 2000 events. This is not the only method to catch events. UserForm modules can also be used to setup event handlers. The following example uses the withevents keyword discussed in this chapter to setup an OnClick event handler for the first image on the current page.

```
Option Explicit
Public WithEvents eimage As FrontPageEditor.FPHTMLImg

Private Function eimage_onclick() As Boolean
    MsgBox "OnClick for the Image"
End Function

Private Sub UserForm_Initialize()
Set eimage = ActivePageWindow.Document.images(0)
End Sub
```

The previous example is important because programmers will often not want to create a new Class module to work with events. One caveat of the above example is that the User Form module must be displayed in a modeless fashion, otherwise the user cannot click the image to generate the event.

PART

X

CH

46

CHAPTER **47**

CROSS-APPLICATION PROGRAMMING

In this chapter   *by Bob Samer*

WHAT IS CROSS-APPLICATION PROGRAMMING?

Cross-application programming refers to accessing one application's object model via another application's programming interface. For example, Microsoft FrontPage can access the object model of Microsoft Word to perform Word-specific manipulation of files in the FrontPage-based Web site. Likewise, the FrontPage 2000 OM can be accessed inside Microsoft Word.

All of the applications (as well as many other applications produced by Microsoft) contain the Visual Basic Editor (VBE). The VBE creates macros that automate each application's object model. The applications included in Microsoft Office 2000 premiere are Word, Excel, PowerPoint, Access, FrontPage, and Outlook. Each of these applications provides extensive object models in order to access their respective features.

HOW DO I GET ACCESS TO THE FRONTPAGE OBJECT MODEL?

All of the objects available in the FrontPage OM are available via the Application object. This is the standard method of accessing a Microsoft application's objects.

When users write macros in the Visual Basic Editor (VBE) included with FrontPage, the Application object is already created and ready to use. However, if an external application needs to use the object model, it must obtain a reference to the Application object via a different method. Applications that use Visual Basic as their automation language can use the CreateObject method to access the Application object.

> **Note**
>
> While Visual Basic is certainly the easiest automation language used to get access an Application's object model, any language that supports the correct interfaces can work with an object model. For example, Microsoft Visual C++ exposes a number of different methods to create and access object models.

The CreateObject method takes an identifier, or ProgID, that tells them what executable program to start in order to get access the Application object. In the case of FrontPage, the ProgID is FrontPage.Application. In a Visual Basic program that is run outside the FrontPage VBE, the following line of code creates an instance of the FrontPage Application object by passing its ProgID into the CreateObject method:

```
Set fp = CreateObject("FrontPage.Application")
```

The CreateObject method uses the ProgID to find the path in the Registry to the main FrontPage executable: frontpg.exe. Once the application is found, it is booted and a reference to its Application object is returned to the CreateObject method. This reference is then assigned to the variable fp in the previous example. The fp variable is then used in place of the `Application` object to access the rest of the FrontPage OM. For example, the following code uses the `fp` object from the last example to open a Web site into FrontPage:

```
Sub OpenWeb
Dim fp
Set fp = CreateObject("FrontPage.Application")
fp.Webs.Add ("c:\my webs\mynewweb2")
End Sub
```

Likewise, if you are working in the FrontPage VBE, the following code creates an instance of the `Application` object for Microsoft Word:

```
Set wrd = CreateObject("Word.Application")
```

Notice that you have not declared the `fp` object as any specific type. This means that type information specific to the FrontPage `Application` object is not available.

When a variable is used in a code editor that supports Visual Basic, the programmer normally sees a drop-down box when the `.` is typed after an object name. For example, typing `Application` followed by a `.` when in the FrontPage VBE forces a drop-down box to appear, displaying the names of all the *methods (page 535)* and *properties (page 612)* available on the object. The drop-down appears in this case because FrontPage VBE has a default reference to the library in which the `Application` object is defined. However, this reference is not created by default inside VBE in other applications or in standalone Visual Basic.

Use the References dialog box to create a reference to a library in a code editor that supports Visual Basic. In VBE, choose the References menu item from the Tools menu to display the dialog box. Figure 47.1 shows the References dialog box inside FrontPage.

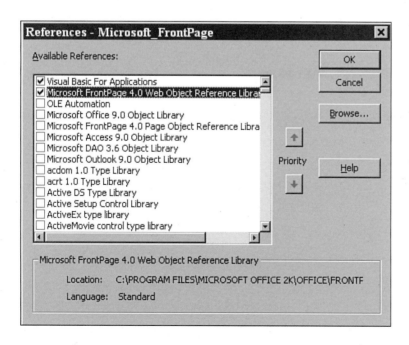

Figure 47.1
The References dialog enables you to quickly add references and begin using any COM library installed on your computer.

PART

X

CH

47

Note

In standalone Visual Basic, the References menu item is available from the Project menu. The References dialog box works exactly the same as it does in an Office application's VBE.

To add a reference to the FrontPage object models library, scroll down in the Available References list box until you see the Microsoft FrontPage Page Object Reference Library and the Microsoft FrontPage Web Object Reference Library. Place a check in both of the libraries and press the OK button. For example, if you are in the Microsoft Word VBE, your References dialog box should look like Figure 47.2: VBE References dialog box with FrontPage libraries referenced.

Figure 47.2
You can easily add references to all the Object Libraries in Office 2000 and develop an integrated application.

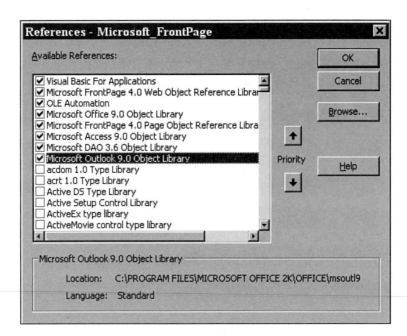

Adding references to both of these libraries allows VBE to look up type information for both the *Web Object Model (WOM)* and the *Page Object Model (POM) (page 992)* as long as variables are dimensioned with the correct keywords such as

```
Dim myweb As Web
```

Use the FrontPage keyword to preface variable types, such as the Application or Web objects, that are defined in the WOM. Likewise, use the FrontPageEditor keyword for objects defined in the POM, such as the FPHTMLDocument or FPHTMLBody objects.

For example, assuming that the correct reference has been created, the `fpapp` and `fpdoc` variables in the following example provide drop-down boxes that show the methods and properties available for the FrontPage `Application` object and the FrontPage `FPHTMLDocument` objects, respectively:

```
Sub ShowDropDown()
Dim fpapp As FrontPage.Application
Dim fpdoc As FrontPageEditor.FPHTMLDocument

Set fpapp = CreateObject("FrontPage.Application")
Set fpdoc = fpapp.ActiveDocument
End Sub
```

Note

When the `CreateObject` method is called, the Office application is booted up without any user interface visible. The application is created invisibly to allow the calling program to create a seamless user interface. The majority of the objects available in the application's object model should be available even when the no user interface is available. To make the application visible, set its `visible` property to `true`. The `visible` property is exposed on different object depending on what application's automation interface you are using. For example, setting the `visible` property of Word's `Application` object model to `true` makes the application visible. However, the FrontPage OM exposes the `visible` property on its `WebWindow` object. For example, the following code creates an instance of FrontPage and makes its main window visible.

```
Sub CreateFrontPageVisible()
Dim fp
Set fp = CreateObject("FrontPage.Application")
fp.ActiveWebWindow.Visible = True
End Sub
```

A WORD ABOUT THE OLD STUFF

You may be familiar with the legacy automation interfaces that were exposed in previous versions of FrontPage. While these interfaces were not an object model, they did expose a number of functions that programmers could call to manipulate the FrontPage Explorer and FrontPage Editor applications. These interfaces are still supported and available in FrontPage 2000 in exactly the same manner as the old FrontPage versions. The Explorer interfaces are available via the ProgID of `FrontPage.Explorer` and the Editor interfaces are available via the `FrontPage.Editor` ProgID.

For example, the following code creates two objects: `fpexplorer` and `fpeditor`. The former exposes the legacy calls for the FrontPage Explorer application and the latter exposed the FrontPage Editor application's functions:

```
    Sub CreateLegacyObject()
Dim fpeditor, fpexplorer
Set fpexplorer = CreateObject("FrontPage.Explorer")
Set fpeditor = CreateObject("FrontPage.Editor")
End Sub
```

While the legacy interfaces are available and should work correctly, Microsoft is downplaying them and is encouraging programmers to use the new object model. There are a number of features exposed in the legacy interfaces that made sense in a two-application model, but do not make sense in FrontPage 2000. For example, the FrontPage Editor interfaces exposed a function called vtiQuit. This made sense when the editor was in a separate application. However, now that the FrontPage Editor and Explorer are embedded in the same application, this method does not quit the application but instead returns an error.

THE REST OF THE FAMILY

Now that FrontPage is part of the Microsoft Office family of applications, it has the capability to access and manipulate each of the application object models in the suite. The other office applications—Word, Excel, Access, PowerPoint, and Outlook—all provide at least a minimal level of HTML content generation. One of Office 2000's big objectives is to provide the user many different ways to generate and manage his or her HTML content.

Excel, Word, Access, and PowerPoint all provide the capability to save files to and open files from a FrontPage-based Web site. In addition, because these Office applications are using the FrontPage server extensions under the hood, each provides some FrontPage-specific functionality in its user interface. For example, Word provides a Theme feature that allows you to apply FrontPage-based themes.

In addition to their interaction with the FrontPage server extensions, each of the Office applications can save its native document types to an HTML representation that can go from native document to HTML and back to native document again—a roundtrip. For example, a user can take a spreadsheet created in Excel 2000 (like the one in Figure 47.3) and save it to an HTML format.

The Excel 2000 spreadsheet's HTML format is a frames-based page that uses tab controls and the like to mimic the functionality of a normal Excel spreadsheet. The frames page is shown in Figure 47.4. The frame page can later be reopened into Excel and saved in the normal Excel document type. All of the information is roundtripped correctly.

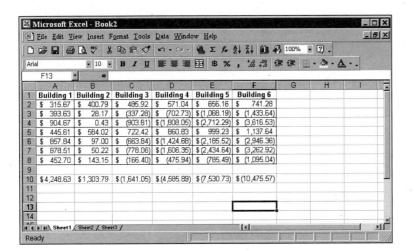

Figure 47.3
An average Excel spreadsheet before being saved as HTML.

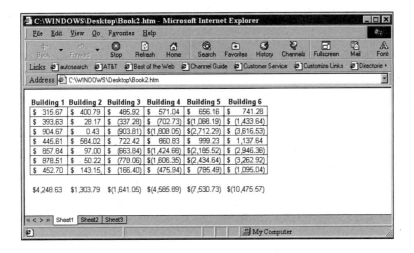

Figure 47.4
An average Excel spreadsheet saved as HTML. Notice that Excel no longer saves a GIF image of the spreadsheet but instead saves it as actual text and even allows for multiple sheets.

PART

X

CH

47

Is this sounding too good to be true? There are some drawbacks to using the Office applications to create your HTML content, the worst of which is that you get a mass of confusing HTML in your document. Office uses this content to preserve the Office document settings when saved to HTML and is then re-saved back to the Office document type. This extra content adds a great deal of complexity to the document as well as increases its size dramatically. For example, Figure 47.5 shows a Word document that is one sentence long, with a larger font and a red foreground color applied.

Figure 47.5
Even a simple page
such as this one will
generate a good deal
of HTML when it is
saved.

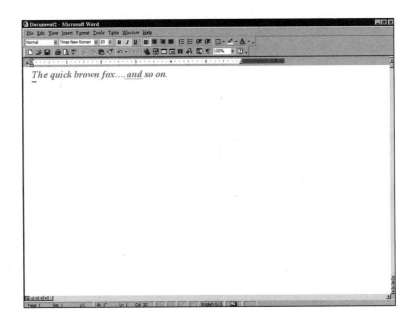

Saving this Word document as an HTML page generates the following HTML content:

```html
<html xmlns:o="urn:schemas-microsoft-com:office:office" xmlns:
w="urn:schemas-microsoft-com:office:word" xmlns="http://www.w3.org/TR/
REC-html40">

<head>
<meta http-equiv="Content-Type" content="text/html; charset=windows-1252">
<meta name="ProgId" content="FrontPage.Editor.Document">
<meta name="Generator" content="Microsoft FrontPage 4.0">
<meta name="Originator" content="Microsoft Word 9">
<link rel="File-List" href="The%20quick%20brown%20fox_files/filelist.xml">
<title>The quick brown fox…</title>
<!--[if gte mso 9]><xml>
 <o:DocumentProperties>
  <o:Author>Bob Samer</o:Author>
  <o:LastAuthor>Bob Samer</o:LastAuthor>
  <o:Revision>1</o:Revision>
  <o:TotalTime>2</o:TotalTime>
  <o:Created>1999-02-18T06:59:00Z</o:Created>
  <o:LastSaved>1999-02-18T07:01:00Z</o:LastSaved>
  <o:Pages>1</o:Pages>
  <o:Company>Dell Computer Corporation</o:Company>
  <o:Lines>1</o:Lines>
  <o:Paragraphs>1</o:Paragraphs>
  <o:Version>9.2601</o:Version>
 </o:DocumentProperties>
</xml><![endif]--><!--[if gte mso 9]><xml>
 <w:WordDocument>
```

```
 <w:DisplayHorizontalDrawingGridEvery>0</w:DisplayHorizontalDrawingGridEvery>
 <w:DisplayVerticalDrawingGridEvery>0</w:DisplayVerticalDrawingGridEvery>
 <w:UseMarginsForDrawingGridOrigin/>
 <w:Compatibility>
  <w:FootnoteLayoutLikeWW8/>
  <w:ShapeLayoutLikeWW8/>
  <w:AlignTablesRowByRow/>
  <w:ForgetLastTabAlignment/>
  <w:LayoutRawTableWidth/>
  <w:LayoutTableRowsApart/>
 </w:Compatibility>
 <w:BrowserLevel>MicrosoftInternetExplorer4</w:BrowserLevel>
 </w:WordDocument>
</xml><![endif]-->
<style>
<!--
 /* Style Definitions */
p.MsoNormal, li.MsoNormal, div.MsoNormal { mso-pagination: widow-orphan;
font-size: 10.0pt; font-family: Times New Roman;
                mso-fareast-font-family: Times New Roman; margin-left: 0in;
                margin-right: 0in; margin-top: 0in; margin-bottom: .0001pt }
@page Section1
    {size:8.5in 11.0in;
    margin:1.0in 1.25in 1.0in 1.25in;
    mso-header-margin:.5in;
    mso-footer-margin:.5in;
    mso-paper-source:0;}
div.Section1 { page: Section1 }
-->
</style>
</head>

<body lang="EN-US" style="tab-interval:.5in">

<div class="Section1">
  <p class="MsoNormal"><b><i><span style="font-size:20.0pt;mso-bidi-font-size:
10.0pt;
color:#FF6600">The quick brown fox….and so on.<o:p></o:p></span></i></b></p>
</div>

</body>

</html>
```

The moral of the story is that you should use FrontPage to generate the HTML if you want to have total control over the content.

USING MICROSOFT ACCESS

Because each of the other Office applications exposes an object model, FrontPage macros and programs can use their object models to apply their application's specific features to an HTML page. For example, the following code uses Microsoft Access object model to read records from a database and add those records to a table in an HTML page:

```
Sub AddRecordsTable()
Dim pw As PageWindow

Dim table As FPHTMLTable
Dim tr As FPHTMLTableRow
Dim td As FPHTMLTableCell

Dim access As access.Application
Dim db As DAO.Database
Dim tbl As DAO.TableDef
Dim rs As DAO.recordset
Dim fld As DAO.Field

Set access = CreateObject("Access.Application")
access.OpenCurrentDatabase ("c:\my documents\mydb.mdb")
Set db = access.CurrentDb

Set pw = ActiveWebWindow.PageWindows.Add
pw.Document.body.insertAdjacentHTML "BeforeEnd", "<table></table>"
Set table = pw.Document.body.all.tags("table").Item(0)
pw.SaveAs "c:\my documents\mydb_table.htm"

Set tbl = db.TableDefs("Contacts")
Set rs = tbl.OpenRecordset

Set tr = table.insertRow

For Each fld In rs.Fields
    Set td = tr.insertCell
    td.innerHTML = fld.Name
Next fld

While (Not (rs.EOF))
    Set tr = table.insertRow
    For Each fld In rs.Fields
        Set td = tr.insertCell
        td.innerHTML = fld.Value
    Next fld
    rs.MoveNext
Wend

pw.Save
pw.Close

db.Close
access.Quit
End Sub
```

To run the example, use Microsoft Access to create a database at c:\my document\mydb.mdb. Using Access, add a table named MyTable to the database you just created. Again, using Access, add a number of fields and value to the table. Boot FrontPage and switch to the *Visual Basic Editor (VBE) (page 932)*; insert a module and copy the code from the previous example onto the module. Run the AddRecordsTable macro to create a new HTML page and copy the rows of the database table into an HTML table on the page. Now examine what the code is doing in more detail.

The first three lines create and instance of the Microsoft Access application and open the database file c:\my documents\mydb.mdb into access.

```
Set access = CreateObject("Access.Application")
access.OpenCurrentDatabase ("c:\my documents\mydb.mdb")
Set db = access.CurrentDb
```

Just as it does with the FrontPage.Application ProgID, the CreateObject method uses the Access.Application ProgID to create an instance of Microsoft Access and return an instance of the Access main Application object. The code then calls the Access object model's method, OpenCurrentDatabase, with the path to the database. Once the database is opened, you use the currentDB property to store a reference to the DataBase object that represents the current database.

The next four lines of the previous example create a new page in HTML pages view and then insert a blank table onto the page. A reference to the newly inserted table is then stored in the variable table. Finally, the page is saved to c:\my documents\mydb_table.htm.

```
Set pw = ActiveWebWindow.PageWindows.Add
pw.Document.body.insertAdjacentHTML "BeforeEnd", "<table></table>"
Set table = pw.Document.body.all.tags("table").Item(0)
pw.SaveAs "c:\my documents\mydb_table.htm"
```

Next, a RecordSet object is opened for the first row of the mytable table. The header row for the table is built by iterating through this record's fields collection. As each field is found, a new cell is added to the first row of the HTML table on the current page:

```
Set tbl = db.TableDefs("myTable")
Set rs = tbl.OpenRecordset

Set tr = table.insertRow

For Each fld In rs.Fields
    Set td = tr.insertCell
    td.innerHTML = fld.Name
Next fld
```

The next set of statements builds the bulk of the new table:

```
While (Not (rs.EOF))
    Set tr = table.insertRow
    For Each fld In rs.Fields
        Set td = tr.insertCell
        td.innerHTML = fld.Value
    Next fld
    rs.MoveNext
Wend
```

Starting with the first record in the table, the code inserts a new row into the HTML for each row it finds in the database table. For each row inserted, a new cell is added to the current row of the HTML table corresponding to each field defined for the record. The value of the current record's current field is added to the cell by setting the cell's innerHTML property to equal the current field's value. Once each field in the current record has been

PART
X

CH
47

processed, the code moves on to the next record. This process repeats until the last record of the table is reached.

The final few lines of code save the new HTML page and then close the instance of Access that you created:

```
pw.Save
pw.Close

db.Close
access.Quit
```

Notice that you have to call the access object's Quit method to force it to exit. When Microsoft Access is created via the CreateObject method, it starts invisibly. If the Quit method is not called, a new instance of Access is started the next time createObject is called.

It may seem trivial to read out of a database and build an HTML page from the results, but the possibilities for extending the FrontPage design-time environment are limitless. For example, instead of building a static table from the database, a program could search out HTML elements with attributes set to query values, use these query values to look up a specific record and field value, and then fill in the value for the HTML element.

Note

If you have used the Internet Explorer *Dynamic HTML (page 506)* object model to do some HTML page scripting, the previous description may sound familiar. IE's DHTML exposes a feature called *databinding*, which is a runtime feature that binds HTML elements to database records and fields. Using the Access and FrontPage object models in conjunction, the design-time version of databinding is easy to accomplish.

USING MICROSOFT OUTLOOK

The previous example demonstrates how to use the Microsoft Access object model to create an HTML table from a database table. The next example uses the Microsoft Outlook application. Microsoft Outlook is an email and scheduling client that maintains a contacts list, containing email addresses, phone numbers, and so on. A user would ideally use the Save as Web Page feature when she wants to publish her contacts list on a Web page. This feature was not implemented in Outlook 2000.

Note

It is possible to export your contacts list to a database and then use that database to create a Web page; do so using either the previous example or Access' built-in HTML features.

Figure 47.6 shows Outlook's New Contact dialog box. As you can see, a contact entry form contains a great large number of fields, most of which can be left blank. In addition, a number of fields need to be *active* when they are placed into a Web page. For example, the

E-mail address field will need to have the `Mailto:` protocol added to it enabling you to click on an email address to open a New Mail Message window.

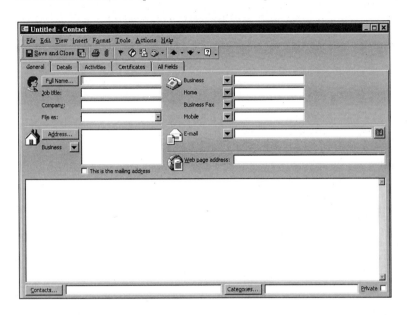

PART
X

CH
47

Figure 47.6
The New Contact dialog box is a swarm of fields to collect vital information.

```
Option Explicit

Sub BuildContactList()
Dim fpdoc As FrontPageEditor.FPHTMLDocument
Dim fppagewin As FrontPage.PageWindow
Dim myfolder As outlook.MAPIFolder
Dim ci As outlook.ContactItem
Dim outlook As outlook.Application

Dim contacttable As FPHTMLTable
Dim tr As FPHTMLTableRow
Dim td As FPHTMLTableCell

Set outlook = CreateObject("Outlook.Application")
Call outlook.Session.Logon(ShowDialog:=False)

Set fppagewin = LocatePage("c:\my webs\contacts.htm")
Set fpdoc = fppagewin.Document

        fpdoc.body.outerHTML = ""
        fpdoc.body.insertAdjacentHTML "BeforeEnd", "<table id=""contactlist"">
</table>"
        Set contacttable = fpdoc.all.contactlist
        Set myfolder = outlook.GetNamespace("MAPI").
    GetDefaultFolder(olFolderContacts)

        For Each ci In myfolder.Items
            Set tr = contacttable.insertRow
```

```
                    Set td = tr.insertCell
                    td.innerText = ci.FullName

                    Set td = tr.insertCell

                    td.innerHTML = "<a href=""" & ci.Email1Address & """>"
        & ci.Email1Address & "</a>"

                    Set td = tr.insertCell
                    td.innerText = ci.BusinessTelephoneNumber

                    Set td = tr.insertCell
                    td.innerHTML = "<a href=""" & ci.WebPage & """>"
        & ci.WebPage & "</a>"

            Next ci

            fppagewin.Save
            fppagewin.Close True

            outlook.Session.Logoff
            outlook.Quit
    End Sub
```

To run the example, make sure you have Microsoft Outlook installed on your local system. Then either ensure that you can log into your Outlook account without having specify a password or change the ShowDialog:=False to true in the second line of the example, which prompts you for your profile information.

Do you have some contacts added to your contact list? You should; select the Contacts item from the Outlook Bar at the left of the application. Add a contact by choosing the New Contact menu item from the File menu; the New Contact dialog box, shown in Figure 56.6, is displayed. Add the information you want to the fields and press OK.

Create a new HTML file using FrontPage at c:\my webs\contacts.htm. Alternatively, modify the path in the code to point to a file to which you want to add contact information.

Choose Tools, Macros, Visual Basic Editor. Insert a new Code module inside VBE in Outlook by choosing Insert, Module. Copy the code from the example into the module. To run the code and build an HTML table from your contacts list, run the BuildContactList procedure that you just added to your project. In addition, you need to add a reference to the Microsoft Outlook 9.0 Reference Library by using the References dialog box mentioned earlier in the chapter.

The first two lines of the macro create an instance of the Outlook application and attempt to log the current user in using the default *profile*:

```
Set outlook = CreateObject("Outlook.Application")
Call outlook.Session.Logon(ShowDialog:=False)
```

This will work fine for most users. If you have trouble and the macro seems to stop responding, try changing the second line to the following:

```
Call outlook.Session.Logon(ShowDialog:=False)
```

This forces outlook to display its Login dialog box, even if it was created without UI (as it was when you called CreateObject).

The next two statements open into FrontPage an existing file that will be used for the contact list. Also keep a reference to the FPHTMLDocument associated with the new page in the variable fpdoc:

```
Set fppagewin = LocatePage("c:\my webs\contacts.htm")
Set fpdoc = fppagewin.Document
```

The next three lines clear the contents of the contact list page and then add a new, blank table to the document with the ID contactlist. The code stores a reference to this table into the variable contactable:

```
fpdoc.body.outerHTML = ""
fpdoc.body.insertAdjacentHTML "BeforeEnd", "<table id=""contactlist"">
</table>"
Set contacttable = fpdoc.all.contactlist
```

The next line is pretty important. It tells Outlook to open the Contacts folder and to assign a reference for this folder into the myfolder variable:

```
Set myfolder = outlook.GetNamespace("MAPI").GetDefaultFolder
(olFolderContacts)
```

Note

> The GetNameSpace method may look a bit strange. Outlook uses this method to abstract what the real layout of an email data source looks like away from the code that wants to use it. The GetNameSpace() method returns a NameSpace object that provides methods for logging in, accessing its item, and so on. Currently, only the MAPI namespace is supported. This is the data source you want, so you can ask it for the Contacts folder once you get a reference to it.

PART

X

CH

47

Now that you have the folder you want to use, simply iterate through each item in the folder looking for the information that you want to put on the Web page. This example only collects the following data: full name, business telephone number, email address, and Web page.

The following statements from the previous example iterate through each contact item in the Contacts folder. A new row is added to the HTML table for each contact item found. Four cells are added to the row, corresponding to the four pieces of contact information you want to add to the page.

```
For Each ci In myfolder.Items
    Set tr = contacttable.insertRow

        Set td = tr.insertCell
        td.innerText = ci.FullName

        Set td = tr.insertCell
```

```
            td.innerHTML = "<a href=""" & ci.Email1Address & """>"
    & ci.Email1Address & "</a>"

            Set td = tr.insertCell
            td.innerText = ci.BusinessTelephoneNumber

            Set td = tr.insertCell
            td.innerHTML = "<a href=""" & ci.WebPage & """>"
    & ci.WebPage & "</a>"

        Next ci
```

Note that you want to add a hyperlink, not just the text for the email address and Web page. Add the anchor tag information to the beginning and end of the email address and Web page strings to do so.

Finally, the last four lines in the macro save and close the contacts page and log out of the current session by calling the session object's LogOff method. You also quit the Microsoft Outlook application.

```
    fppagewin.Save
    fppagewin.Close True

    outlook.Session.Logoff
    outlook.Quit
```

This is a simple example of using the Outlook object model inside FrontPage. There are many things that can be done between these two object models. For example, the code just discussed could be modified to run every time a new contact is added to the contact list. This is an easy way to keep a global contact list that is available to all users who have access to a Web browser.

Another cool idea is a macro that finds old files. (The user defines what constitutes an "old" file.) The macro could then send mail to the owner of that file informing them that their page has expired.

The possibilities available when using the FrontPage OM with other application's object models are truly limitless. Almost every Microsoft application, as well as many other companies' applications, exposes some sort of object model or programmable interface. Anything your heart desires can be added to extend Microsoft FrontPage when you use these interfaces in conjunction with the FrontPage.

WHERE TO GO FROM HERE

Depending on what type of feature or effect you are trying to create, you will have to choose the application that best suits your needs. The applications that are part of the Office suite—Microsoft Excel (spreadsheet), Microsoft Access (database), Microsoft Word (word processor), Microsoft PowerPoint (presentation package), and Microsoft Outlook (email and scheduling client)—provide a myriad of features that can be added to your code. For more information of these applications' object models, take a look at the online VBA help for the applications. In addition, the Microsoft Office 2000 Resource Kit will provide loads of useful information and examples.

TROUBLESHOOTING

One of the biggest problems that can occur is simply using the wrong method to do something. The `innerHTML` method is often confused with the `innerTEXT` method. If you accidentally used the `innerText` method to write HTML code, the HTML code would be converted by the `innerText` method so it could be displayed in the web page. When you see your HTML code being displayed in the browser, you might be led to believe you entered incorrect HTML code instead of having selected the wrong method.

The Visual Basic editor is very good at catching many formatting errors such as misplaced end quotes on a string or an extra parenthesis. When things do go wrong it is hard to determine where they might have occurred which makes debugging difficult. To make debugging easier you can insert your own simple breakpoints to alert you when you have reached a certain line of code. With VBA you can simply use message boxes saying "Made it here" to alert you to the fact that it reached the line of code where your breakpoint was with no errors. By moving your breakpoint around you can eventually prove that when you place your message box before line x your message box will appear, and if you place your message box immediately after line x it doesn't appear, which identifies line x as a problem.

DESIGNERS CORNER

So far, you've seen examples of how to write macros and programs using VBA and VB, but what else can you do with the programmability of Office 2000? Companies using Internet Information Server as a web server can leverage this programmability on the server itself. Since the server only requires one licensed copy of the product, this can leverage some of the programming power of Office 2000 for a fraction of the price.

Internet Information Servers uses a technology called Active Server Pages to allow both script and HTML to co-exist within the same document. ASP is quickly gaining momentum as one of the most popular forms of script writing because it uses VBScript, a subset of the Visual Basic language, as its default programming language. The other beauty of ASP is it is easily extensible through the use of COM objects, just like Word, Outlook, FrontPage and the rest of the Office 2000 suite of products.

The only real difference between a macro written in VBA and an ASP page written in VBScript is how you create objects. In VBA you would use `CreateObject` to create an instance of the `Word.Application` object. Since your VBScript is running on a web server, you need to ask the web server to create the object for you like so, `Server.CreateObject`. It's really that easy to go from one method to the other.

Have you ever tried sharing your Word documents and found that someone can't use it because they're running an earlier version of Word? What if you could place all your Word files in a central location on the web server and have the server create the needed document format and offer it for download?

Have you ever wished that a form could check your spelling? With the Word.Application object you could use the CheckSpelling method to check that each field has words that are properly spelled and list any words that are misspelled. You could even take this one step further and use the SuggestSpelling method to offer alternative spellings of the word just like you would see if you were using Word.

If you have ever tried keeping track of a phone list for a company then you know how easy it is for the list to become obsolete. Instead of trying to generate a new list every time there is a change and getting it out to the company, why not keep a list of employees in an Outlook Contact list. With a centralized list you can use the examples we covered in this chapter to create a server-side script that will generate a new contact page whenever you want.

APPENDIXES

FrontPage 2000 Resources on the Web

by Dennis Jones

In this chapter

WHAT'S ON THE MICROSOFT WEB SITE?

Before you go to all the trouble of searching magazines, Web sites, and even (perish the thought) other books, why not go straight to the horse's mouth? The horse, in this case, is Microsoft; the company offers two distinct places from which to get FrontPage information and resources.

> **Note** By the time you read this appendix, the FrontPage area of the Microsoft site (found at www.microsoft.com/frontpage) might well have changed.

MICROSOFT'S FRONTPAGE WEB SITE AND MICROSOFT'S OFFICE UPDATE SITE

- http://www.microsoft.com/frontpage
- http://officeupdate.microsoft.com/welcome/frontpage.htm

These two sites provide a variety of information and resources. They're dealt with together because they are relatively small.

The FrontPage section of the Office Update site is divided into four small sections:

- Welcome

    The Welcome area offers you links to official software updates for FrontPage, as well as recommendations to other information links.

- Updates

    This area contains links to information about each official FrontPage update.

- Downloads

    From here you can select each update you want to acquire and then proceed to the download for all those you have selected.

- Assistance

    As the name suggests, this area exists to provide further FrontPage assistance. Links connect you with the larger FrontPage information area of the SiteBuilder Network (see the following text for a description of this area), as well as to an online FrontPage tutorial. Other links take you to FrontPage user groups that exist on Microsoft's site, a Q&A area for FrontPage users, and a listing of popular topics and Microsoft Knowledge Base articles about the software. The page also provides links to other Microsoft information related to FrontPage, including a page devoted to helping you find a FrontPage host.

The FrontPage site itself (www.microsoft.com/frontpage) used to be the home for FrontPage information, but in recent months it has been largely stripped. By the time this book appears, all of it might well have been incorporated into the FrontPage area on the SiteBuilder Network (detailed in this section). For now, though, the site still offers the two strong areas:

■ **Find a Web Site Host**

This area of the MSFP site exists for FrontPage users who want to locate a host for their sites. Anyone can use it because Web site hosts who offer FrontPage support can host non-FrontPage Webs as well; the purpose here, however, is to let you find those who let you use FrontPage to create and manage your webs. To be sure, you can find many, many willing hosts from here.

Unfortunately, it's much less useful than it could be. It's categorized in only two ways: alphabetically or by state. Much more useful would be categories according to price, features, server type, and the like. Geographical location really doesn't matter much, so why bother with it? What you'll end up doing is simply going through the list as is, and that's a long, tedious process.

■ **Web Administrators**

If you're responsible for hosting Web sites in your organization, you'll want to visit the MSFP site's Web Administrators area. From here you can download the server extensions resource kit (SERK), get FAQs about the server extensions, and link to newsgroups about using the server extensions. You can also download the extensions themselves, as well as patches for Windows- and UNIX-based servers.

The entire area is especially useful for UNIX server administrators (UNIX is far and away the most common Web server platform) because it helps you decide whether to deploy them. If you'd like your UNIX administrators to install the extensions (many are reluctant), point them to this specific page to help them see what's available.

MICROSOFT'S SITEBUILDER NETWORK SITE

■ `http://www.microsoft.com/workshop/c-frame.htm#/workshop/languages/fp/default.asp`

Microsoft's SiteBuilder Network contains an absolute wealth of information for Web site developers, and part of it relates specifically to FrontPage. The URL given here will take you to the FrontPage information, and you'll find links in the frame along the left side; the links lead you to the following types of information.

FRONTPAGE TUTORIAL

If you want a hands-on guide when working with FrontPage, start with the tutorial. It is hardly extensive, but it provides enough to get you going. You can choose among the various lessons.

WEB SITE DESIGN

This lengthy area contains a wide range of hints, tips, and explanations for specific FrontPage features. New material is added frequently. This is an extremely useful area for page designers, with several of the topics leading to more extensive information on the FrontPage support site.

WEB SITE DEVELOPMENT AND FRONTPAGE SITE MANAGEMENT

If you're the developer or administrator of a public site, you'll find useful details in these two areas about several elements of FrontPage, ranging from creating and maintaining channels to detailed information about database connectivity.

PUBLISHING AND SERVER EXTENSIONS

In these two sections you can find information about FrontPage's publishing options, as well as the details and complexities of the FrontPage server extensions. You'll also find upgrades for existing server extensions and articles detailing installation and setup.

OTHER ACCESSIBLE AREAS

While you're on the FrontPage area of the SiteBuilder Network (SBN), check out the rest of SBN by clicking the collapsible menus at the top of the page. There you'll find an online magazine for site designers, workshops in a wide range of Web technologies, links to pages of tools, samples, and other downloadable resources, as well as information and downloads for trainers.

WEB SITES

While several Web sites devoted to FrontPage exist, no single resource is as extensive as the MSFP site. Still, all are worth keeping in a separate bookmarks or favorites folder, and indeed you might consider building your own local page consisting of links to the ones you find most useful. Many are definitely worth checking regularly to see if anything new has been added, or if something you didn't use before is suddenly of importance to you.

As with all Web sites of this kind, they tend to link to each other; you'll eventually find yourself in a kind of loop. Also with all Web sites of this kind, some are updated much more frequently than others, and some will undoubtedly be unavailable by the time you read this.

FRONTPAGE USER TIPS

- http://www.frontpage.to/support/fp98/home.html

This is a good supplement to the tips available at the MSFP site. You'll find tips for all versions of FrontPage, divided for earlier versions into Editor and Explorer tips. Also available are details on error messages and other problems, as well as special HTML coding such as RGB color codes and opening windows of specific sizes. A variety of Java scripts are included here, and the Miscellaneous section covers a number of useful topics (including tips on framesets).

FRONTPAGE REFUGEE CAMP

- `http://www.tntenterprises.com/frontpage/index.htm`

At the time of this writing, this site covers only FrontPage 98, but it's pretty obvious that such a complete site will have FrontPage 2000 information by the time you visit it. The site features tips for designers and administrators alike. The Infirmary section is especially useful if you're experiencing FrontPage frustration; you can talk to other FrontPage users via the discussion area to get even more advice.

LINKS TO MICROSOFT FRONTPAGE

- `http://www.cosy.sbg.ac.at/~ohaus/docs/frontpage.html`

This single-page Austrian site does exactly what it claims to do: offers links to other FrontPage resources on the Net (and not just those in English). The page is divided into forums, FAQs, discussion, software, tips, manuals, resources, and so on. The forums section takes you to a number of useful FrontPage-based sites, including one specifically designed for administrators using the Apache Web server. The most important section of this page, however, links you to FrontPage discussion areas on the Net, where you can ask questions of other FrontPage users.

THE COMPLETE WEBMASTER

- `http://abiglime.com/webmaster/articles/frontpage.htm`

The whole point of this useful site is to offer short tutorial-like articles about various FrontPage package elements. Articles include topics such as creating hover buttons and animated GIFs and designing your own templates, themes, and forms, database connectivity, frames, and so on. While none of the pieces give you all the features you can use, they work extremely well at helping you get started with specific tasks. There are similar (but less comprehensive) areas on this site for CGI, HTML, Java, and JavaScript, and there's also a well-populated bulletin board for questions and answers.

BUILDER.COM

- `http://www.builder.com/Authoring/FrontPage98/index.html`

Part of the huge CNET site (`http://www.cnet.com/`), the FrontPage section of the authoring area of Builder.com features a short introduction with links to several general web-building topics (not specifically a FrontPage topic), plus a list of very strong tutorials on a variety of topics. While "Using Keyboard Shortcuts" might not be your cup of tea, topics that cover turning data into tabular form and integrating FrontPage with Netscape Navigator might be precisely what you're looking for.

There are many more FrontPage sites available, but these five are among the best to get you started. The others are all available as links from several of these sites, so by all means click them all and see what you discover. The others don't offer much additional help, and some offered very little information at all.

NEWSGROUPS AND WEB DISCUSSIONS

Newsgroups and Web discussions devoted to FrontPage exist to let people discuss common issues, get answers to specific questions, and express opinions about features they find useful or useless. The Internet doesn't host a great number of either type of discussion group for FrontPage users, but those that do exist are well worth visiting. Ironically, those sites created by the FrontPage Discussion Wizard don't work as well in some ways than good old-fashioned newsgroups; newsgroup software offers far better ways to sort and filter the messages. Digging through a long list on a FrontPage-created Web site is always worth the time if it means you can get that one important answer, so be sure to take a look at all of these.

KEITH PARNELL'S USER TIPS FOR MICROSOFT FRONTPAGE

- http://www.frontpage.to/discussion/

This is part of the FrontPage User Tips site discussed earlier, but the discussion area merits a look all on its own. While you'll find that many of the dozens of messages have been written by a fairly consistent group of users, there's room to post anything you want here—and a reasonable chance you'll get the answers you need. The messages tend to be well written (hardly a guarantee with Internet discussion groups) and the range of topics is wide.

READY-TO-RUN SOFTWARE'S UNIX SUPPORT FOR THE FRONTPAGE SERVER EXTENSIONS

- http://www.rtr.com/fpsupport/discuss.htm

If you're a UNIX administrator using the FrontPage server extensions, or simply want to know more about the server extensions, this is a must-read. Given that UNIX servers, particularly the Apache, host the vast majority of Web sites (and that FrontPage is a package that many users of UNIX systems want to use), technical information about how the servers work with UNIX systems is crucial to the host administrator. This discussion forum features dozens of related messages, with several postings per day.

FRONTPAGE 98 FORUM

- http://www.austranet.com/disc1_toc.htm

While not as extensive as the two discussion groups examined above, this list features some good questions. Answers tend to be a bit long in coming, but it's certainly worth regular visits. Topics range from novice level through intermediate level.

FORUM FRONTPAGE

- `http://www.dwam.com/ForumFrontPage/`

This discussion forum is entirely in French. Not only are the topics wide ranging and well answered, but the site shows a very good use of the FrontPage Discussion Wizard. It's the most attractively designed discussion form of all those discussed here.

MIKE'S FRONTPAGE FAQ ARCHIVE

- `http://www.simplenet.com/frontpage/`

This is an extremely interesting idea. It combines a FrontPage discussion web with FrontPage FAQs. Users post answers to typical questions, and you can search a variety of FAQ sites accessible from the index page if you can't find the answer in the postings.

MICROSOFT NEWSGROUPS

Microsoft hosts a number of newsgroups dealing with FrontPage. These tend to be heavily populated, with questions about practically everything. That's good, but it's also easy to get lost. Get a good newsreader to access these (Outlook Express is okay, but several shareware readers offer more options) and keep track of what you've already read. Like all popular newsgroups, these are only as valuable as the time you put into them. The answers come from all over, including members of the FrontPage team at Microsoft.

The newsgroups are as follows:

`news://msnews.microsoft.com/microsoft.public.frontpage.client`: The main FrontPage newsgroup; this one features questions about any and all FrontPage topics. Visit unless you want answers about features dealt with in the following newsgroups.

`news://msnews.microsoft.com/microsoft.public.frontpage.extensions.windowsnt`: This group covers server extensions for Windows NT systems.

`news://msnews.microsoft.com/microsoft.public.frontpage.extensions.unix`: This group covers server extensions for UNIX boxes.

`news://msnews.microsoft.com/microsoft.public.frontpage.mac`: This group covers FrontPage for the Macintosh, still (inexplicably) in version 1.0.

Additional groups are in German, French, and Japanese.

ADD-ONS FOR FRONTPAGE USERS

There's no question that FrontPage 2000 is a full-featured package. There's also no question that no package, no matter how full featured, can do everything. In fact, one of the great traditions in the software industry has been the concept of the *add-on*, software that supplements existing software. Add-ons fill in gaps in the original software design, making the entire package more useful.

You can get add-ons for word processors (WordPerfect used to have hordes available), graphics programs, spreadsheet packages, database managers, personal information managers, and of course, Web browsers (that's what plug-ins are). You can get them for FrontPage as well. This appendix lists some of the available add-ons for your FrontPage package, along with some information about each.

> **Note**
>
> Visit this book's Web site at `http://www.nrandall.com/frontpage` for lists and reviews of FrontPage add-ons.

MICROSOFT ADD-ONS

Microsoft has posted several add-ons related to the FrontPage package on the FrontPage Web site.

MICROSOFT OFFICE 60 MINUTE INTRANET KIT

- `http://www.microsoft.com/office/intranet/solutions.htm`

This free kit, which you can get on CD-ROM or via download from the MS site, helps you use FrontPage to create an intranet. It comes with 12 predesigned intranets, which you open in FrontPage; from there you plug in the information you want. If you're considering setting up an intranet from scratch, start here.

The Foundation Intranet Template is related to this kit and is also on the MS site (`http://www.microsoft.com/office/intranet/modules.htm`). You can download this add-on, install it into FrontPage, and then download the modules available at the site (seven as of this writing). These include such useful things as a user training module, a document management module, and an advanced search module.

MICROSOFT SITE BUILDER NETWORK AND MICROSOFT GALLERY

- `http://www.microsoft.com/sitebuilder/`
- `http://www.microsoft.com/gallery/default.asp`

Don't argue, just join. It doesn't cost anything except a wee bit of HTML work (for level 1, at least) and you have access to huge amounts of information about—as the name suggests—building sites. New technologies, old and new methods—it's all here.

You can link to the tools and samples gallery from this site (`http://www.microsoft.com/gallery/default.asp`). Buttons link you from here to a wide selection of application tools, coding samples, images, sounds, fonts, and stylesheets, all available for download and use—highly useful stuff.

IMAGE COMPOSER

- `http://www.Microsoft.com/imagecomposer/default.asp`

Are you a heavy Image Composer user? You'll find some sample sprites, Web art, and animated GIFs to download from the IC site.

OTHER MICROSOFT RESOURCES

Several Microsoft offerings are useful for FrontPage users, especially since FrontPage is now expressly designed to work in conjunction with Office. What this means is that any Office add-on is also a FrontPage add-on, even if indirectly. Go to the Office site regularly (`http://www.Microsoft.com/office`) to see if anything new and useful has appeared; take advantage of trial downloads of products (such as Microsoft Liquid Motion) to determine if they will help you in your quest for the perfect site.

Of course, the most significant Microsoft resource is Office 2000 itself. Now that the package includes HTML as a native file type for all the suite components, and now that it includes direct online editing of Web pages, this is a seriously useful tool for FrontPage users.

THIRD-PARTY SOLUTIONS

If Microsoft were the only company offering FrontPage add-ons, this appendix wouldn't have much point in existing. Third-party offerings are springing up regularly, and Table A.1 takes a brief look at some of them:

TABLE A.1 THIRD-PARTY WEB SITES

Product Name and Publisher	Category	Free or Purchase	Description
First Themes Factory Auscomp `http://www.auscomp.com/ac_frames_ms.html`	Themes	Purchase; free sample	Themes in categories such as sports, entertainment, and the world
EB Themeshop `http://www.ebthemeshop.com/msindex.htm`	Themes	Purchase (subscription available) some free samples	Individual themes, theme packages, full year subscription
Theme Mart `http://www.thememart.com/default.asp?Ref=MFP`	Themes	Purchase	Large quantity of themes across a variety of categories
Theme Pak `http://www.themepak.com/index.asp?Ref=MFP`	Themes	Purchase	Large quantity of themes across a variety of categories

APP

A

continues

Table A.1   Continued

Product Name and Publisher	Category	Free or Purchase	Description
FrontLook Themes and Applet Package http://www.dpasoftware.com/fpoffer.htm	Themes, applets, clip art	Purchase; free sample	Application package for themes, Java applets, and clip art; includes wide range of samples
El Scripto JavaScript Components http://www.elscripto.com/info/fpuser.htm	Scripts	Purchase	Over a dozen JavaScript components; plugs into FrontPage menu bar
J-Bots Components http://www.websunlimited.com/jbotspromo2.htm	Components	Purchase; free sample	Several components for FrontPage, including image menus, image preloader, play music; plugs into FrontPage menu bar
RealMedia Plug-In http://www.real.com/products/tools/frontpage/	Streaming content	Purchase	Lets you provide links to RealAudio and RealVideo files; requires RealPublisher to create .ram files
SPG Web Tools http://www.spg-net.com/frontpageusers.html	Graphics	Purchase	Several plug-in tools for Image Composer
L&H Audio CafeLite http://www.lhs.com/speechtech/audiocafe/	Streaming content	Purchase, free version available	Tool for compressing and streaming audio files in your site
Storefront E-Commerce for FrontPage	E-commerce	Purchase	Package for creating a storefront for your site
JustAddCommerce http://www.richmediatech.com/index.html	E-commerce	Purchase	Lets you add a secure shopping cart to your site
Mercantec StoreBuilder http://www.mercantec.com/frontpage/	E-commerce	Purchase	Provides a built-in e-commerce design, or you can design your own
SalesCart Virtual Shopping Cart http://www.salescart.com/3rdparty.htm	E-commerce	Purchase	Lets you put a secure shopping cart on your site
ShopSite Express http://frontpage.shopsite.com/	E-commerce	Purchase	Lets you design and implement storefront sites

Product Name and Publisher	Category	Free or Purchase	Description
3D Impact http://www.crystalgraphics.com/ frontpage.download.html	Graphics	Free, but commercial version available	Produces 3D graphics; not specifically a FrontPage add-on
3D Space Publisher http://www.tgs.com/specials/ fp98/fp98.html	Graphics	Purchase	Produces 3D animations and Java, image editor
NetStudio http://www.netstudio.com/	Graphics	Purchase	Competitor to Image Composer, simplifies creation of Web graphics
Photos to Go http://www.photostogo.com/ premium/frontpage_promo.htm	Graphics	Purchase, free samples	Photographs for (legal) use on your site
WebSpice http://www.webspice.com/sampler/ fp98/webspice.html	Graphics	Purchase, free samples	Extensive collection of Web graphics

FRONTPAGE 2000 AND OFFICE 97

In this chapter   *by Dennis Jones*

USING WORD 97'S WEB TOOLS

If you're an experienced Microsoft Word 97 user, you might find it more convenient to construct Web pages by using that application than by way of an HTML editor. Word 97 does not give you the degree of control over the HTML formatting that you get with FrontPage 2000's page editor, but it can give you a head start.

Furthermore, if you have Word 97 documents that you would like to convert to HTML, doing so from Word is likely the most efficient approach.

The Web features in Word 97 are the Web toolbar, the insertion of hyperlinks, saving a Word document as an HTML file, the Web Page Wizard, and several tools specifically oriented toward editing Web pages.

Note

> For the following procedures to work, you must have installed the Web page authoring component when you installed Office 97. If you didn't do so, rerun the Office 97 Setup program and install the component before proceeding.

USING THE WEB TOOLBAR

The Web toolbar is available in Excel 97, Access 97, PowerPoint 97, and Access 97, but for convenience it's discussed in the context of Word.

If it is not already visible, you can turn on the toolbar by choosing View, Toolbars, and then clicking Web in the pop-up menu. The toolbar is actually a simple browser toolbar, with—from left to right—the following buttons (see Figure B.1):

- Back—Moves back one page.
- Forward—Moves forward one page.
- Stop—Stops the current network operation.
- Refresh Current Page—Reloads the page currently displayed.
- Start Page—Opens the default start page of the system's default browser.
- Search the Web—Opens the default search page of the system's default browser.
- Favorites—Opens the system's Favorites folder.
- Go—Allows navigation, plus user selection of start and search pages.
- Show Only Web Toolbar—Removes all toolbars but the Web toolbar.

Figure B.1
The Web toolbar in
Office 97 applications
offers the functions
of a simple browser.

INSERTING HYPERLINKS

Suppose that you have written a Word document, TRAPS.DOC, that discusses some problems with Excel worksheet functions and have saved it on the Windows Desktop. You are presently writing a guide, GUIDE.DOC, to using Office 97 as deployed at your firm. You would like to insert a hyperlink in GUIDE.DOC that points to TRAPS.DOC. To do so, take the following steps:

Tip #201

Before inserting hyperlinks into Office documents, save both the document with the hyperlink and the destination document.

1. Open GUIDE.DOC in Word. Just as you've done in FrontPage, select the text or image that you want to use as the link. (If you don't select something, Word inserts the full file name of the destination document as the hyperlink text.) The Insert Hyperlink dialog box appears when you choose Insert, Hyperlink (see Figure B.2).

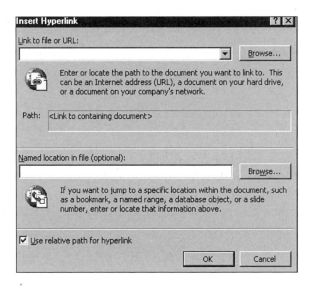

Figure B.2
Choose the destination for the Word hyperlink via the Insert Hyperlink dialog box.

APP

B

2. Choose the Browse button in the upper-right corner of the dialog box. The Link to File dialog box appears (see Figure B.3). Use this dialog box to locate and select the hyperlinks destination document, which in the example is TRAPS.DOC. When you've selected the destination file, choose OK.

Figure B.3
It's usually easier to browse to a destination file than to type its pathname or URL.

3. Choose OK when the Insert Hyperlink dialog box reappears. The dialog box closes. If you selected some text for the link, you'll see that it's now blue and underlined (see Figure B.4). Images serving as hyperlinks won't have changed in appearance.

Figure B.4
You can use a hyperlink for any file, as long as an application that displays that type of file is installed on the user's machine. Here, the hyperlink is to a Word document.

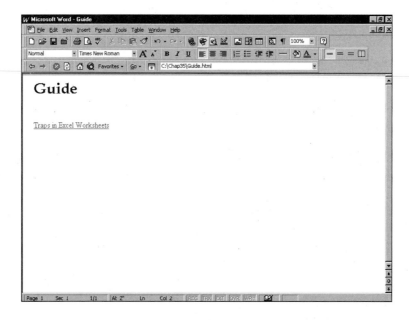

Note

If you're familiar with Office applications, you know about OLE links. These links behave differently than a hyperlink and you edit them by choosing Edit, Links. The Edit, Links command has nothing to do with hyperlinks, despite the confusing similarity of nomenclature.

You can now save both the hyperlinked document and the destination document as Word files or HTML files. To save them in Word 97 format, choose File, Save for each. To save them as HTML, choose File, Save As HTML for each. Now, if you prefer, you can import the HTML files into a FrontPage web.

In Word documents (documents in native Word format, not in HTML), hyperlinks are inserted as field codes. You can switch back and forth between viewing the hyperlink itself and viewing it as a field code. Right-click the hyperlink and choose Toggle Field Codes from the shortcut menu.

Caution

Saving a Word file as an HTML file doesn't change the destination filenames of the hyperlinks. If you create and link the files as Word documents and then save them as HTML files for import to a web, be sure you edit the hyperlinks in the newly created HTML files. This ensures that they point to the proper destinations. In other words, if a destination file that started life as a DOC file was then saved as an HTML file, the hyperlink pointing to it will have to be changed.

LINKING TO DESTINATIONS WITHIN DOCUMENTS

If the destination document is a long one and the point of interest in it isn't close to the beginning, you'll probably want to link to a *named location* in the file. This corresponds to HTML's *named anchor* tag. Follow these steps to insert such a link:

1. Open the destination document in Word. Locate the position you want to jump to and select some text as the named location.

2. Choose Insert, Bookmark. The Bookmark dialog box appears (see Figure B.5).

3. Type a name for the bookmark into the Bookmark Name text box and choose Add. Don't use spaces or reserved file characters (such as the asterisk) or the Add button will be grayed out. The dialog box vanishes and the bookmark is assigned the specified name.

4. Open the Word document that is to have the hyperlink in it. As you did earlier, select text or an image to be the link and choose Insert, Hyperlink. The Insert Hyperlink dialog box appears.

5. Use the upper-right Browse button in the dialog box to locate and select the destination file (the one where you just placed the bookmark). Make sure the file name appears correctly in the Link to File or URL text box.

6. Choose the lower-right Browse button. This opens the Bookmark dialog box, which now shows all the bookmarks located in the destination document (see Figure B.6).

Figure B.5
Use the Bookmark dialog box to insert named locations into documents.

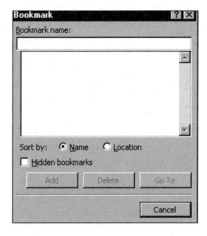

Figure B.6
The Bookmark dialog box shows all the bookmarks entered into a Word document.

7. Select the bookmark you want the hyperlink to jump to and choose OK to return to the Insert Hyperlink dialog box. Both text boxes in the dialog box now have entries (see Figure B.7). Choose OK again to close the dialog box and install the link. When you use the link, the bookmarked location appears in the document window.

You can, of course, work with either Word 97 documents or HTML documents to do this. However, remember this if you create and link the documents as Word 97 files: When you save them as HTML files, you need to edit the hyperlinks to point to the correct destinations. If you have a lot of links to set up, you might prefer to complete and save all the files as HTML documents before creating the hyperlinks.

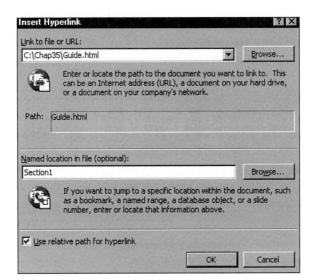

Figure B.7
Two text boxes need to be filled in order for a named location hyperlink to work properly.

Tip #202

When you create an Office document that will be the destination of a hyperlink in your web, do not save the destination document with an embedded blank in the filename—NEW CHART.XLS, for example. The resulting URL will not be evaluated properly because it is interpreted as ending with the W in NEW. If you ever encounter a broken hyperlink due to the inclusion of a space in the filename, insert a "%20" instead of the space itself.

USING THE PASTE AS HYPERLINK COMMAND WITH WORD DOCUMENTS

This is a very useful shortcut method and is by far the best way to create links between documents in different applications.

In the destination document, select some item (usually text) that will be the link target. This selected text actually functions as a named location, but you don't need to fuss with bookmarks because Word 97 creates its own special code for this named location.

When you've selected the text, choose Edit, Copy. Open the document where the link is to reside and place the insertion point where you want the link to appear. Choose Edit, Paste as Hyperlink. Any text selected as the named location in the destination page appears also as the hyperlink; you can edit it. If you chose an image as the named location, the image itself is placed in the origination page to serve as the hyperlink.

EDITING AND DELETING HYPERLINKS

To edit and delete hyperlinks, open the document with the hyperlink—it can be either a native Word 97 document or an HTML document—and right-click the hyperlink. Choose Hyperlink, Edit Hyperlink from the shortcut menu. This opens the Edit Hyperlink dialog

APP

B

box. This dialog box, except for its title and the presence of a Remove Link button, is identical to the Insert Hyperlink dialog box you saw in Figure B.2. Make the changes you want in the appropriate text boxes and choose OK. To remove the link entirely, choose Remove Link; the text or image loses its hyperlink properties.

If you want to change the wording of a textual link, right-click the link and choose Hyperlink, Select Hyperlink from the shortcut menu. With the link selected, type the new text. If you don't want to use the shortcut menu, drag across the link text to select it and type the new text.

MODIFYING LINK COLORS

The appearance of the hyperlink in Word 97 is governed by your choice of hyperlink style. The default appearance for a hyperlink uses the standard blue underlined font, and a followed hyperlink uses the standard violet underlined font. If consistency of appearance is not an issue, you can change the defaults by taking these steps:

1. Open a document that you have saved in HTML format.
2. Choose Format, Style and select Hyperlink from the Styles list box.
3. Choose Modify; choose Format from the Modify Style dialog box. Choose Font from the shortcut menu. In the Font dialog box, you can choose from different fonts, as well as from font styles, sizes, underline types, colors, and effects.
4. Repeat steps 2 and 3 for the followed hyperlink style.

After you have resaved the HTML document, your browser displays hyperlinks in the styles you selected.

VIEWING HTML SOURCE CODE

If you want to directly edit the page's HTML, you can do so by choosing View, HTML Source. This changes the Page view from a near-WYSIWYG appearance to straightforward HTML code. You can edit this code to get the effects you want on the page. When you've finished the edit, save the file and choose the Exit HTML Source button from the toolbar. The modified page appears in the Word workspace. Note that no syntax checking for errors is done. However, Word will alter manually entered HTML code if this code does not fit its internal validity checks. If you add HTML manually, verify that it remains as you want it by leaving HTML view and then re-entering that view.

USING THE WEB PAGE WIZARD

FrontPage 2000, as you already know, comes with a selection of page templates. If none of these quite suits your needs, you might try using Office 97's Web Page Wizard to create a more suitable specimen. Here's how to do it:

1. Choose File, New to open the New dialog box. From there, choose the Web Pages tab to open the Web Pages sheet.

2. Double-click the Web Page Wizard icon to open the Web Page Wizard's opening dialog box (see Figure B.8). Choose from several options—the example uses two-column layout—and then select Next. To assist you, the different templates appear behind the wizard dialog box as you make a choice.

Figure B.8
The Web Page Wizard assists you in creating a standard-layout Web page.

3. In the next dialog box, choose the overall appearance of the page from a list of eight possibilities. Click the flavor that best serves your needs and then choose Finish.

4. Edit the page to add your own information and images, as well as to modify the layout, if necessary. Save the page. (It defaults to saving as HTML unless you specify a different format.) Now you can import it into your FrontPage web.

Using Word 97's Other Web Tools

Word, even though it doesn't have FrontPage 2000's rich HTML editing capabilities, does have some other basic tools for Web page creation. If the page you're editing is an HTML file, you'll have some extra menu commands with which you can choose:

- Add Horizontal Lines—Choose Insert, Horizontal Line and select from a selection of weights and appearances.

- Add a Page Background Color—Choose Format, Background and select from a number of colors.

- Add Scrolling Text—Also known as a *marquee*. Choose Insert, Scrolling Text and use the resulting dialog box to create the text and set scroll direction and speed.

- Add Tables—Choose Table, Insert Table and select the number of columns and rows from the pop-up menu.

- Add a Video—Choose Insert, Video and use the resulting dialog box to set the video clip's source file and properties.

- Add Picture Bullets—Choose Format, Bullets and Numbering and select any of the bullet images.

App

B

- Add an Image—Choose Insert, Picture and select from clip art, image files, or charts.
- Add Background Sound—Choose Insert, Background Sound and select the sound file and its properties.

Note, however, that whenever the inserted items are files—video clips, images, sounds, and so on—these items should also be imported into the FrontPage web that hosts the page where they reside. The links to these various elements are broken if you import only the page's HTML file.

Note also that graphical elements that don't start out as files, such as bullets and lines, are saved as *GIF files (page 656)* in the current Word documents folder when you insert the element into the page; you'll find them in that folder when you get around to importing them into the web.

Note

A single Word document saved as HTML is actually saved as multiple files. It is a good idea to save Word-produced HTML documents to a separate folder so that your personal folder doesn't become cluttered with these multiple files.

USING EXCEL'S WEB TOOLS

The Web tools available to you in Excel are similar to those available in Word. You can save an Excel worksheet in HTML table format, as well as insert hyperlinks and view the Web toolbar.

There are also significant differences between Excel's Web capabilities and Word's. For example, Excel offers a method for building a web form and includes a new HYPERLINK() worksheet function.

SAVING EXCEL 97 WORKSHEET DATA TO AN EXISTING HTML PAGE

Note that in order to save Excel 97 worksheet data in HTML table format, you need to have included the Web page authoring component when you installed Office 97. Assuming this has been done, you have two possibilities—the existing page is already in a FrontPage web or the page has not yet been imported into a FrontPage web.

IF THE EXISTING HTML PAGE IS ALREADY IN A FRONTPAGE WEB

You must begin by hand-editing the HTML file that is to contain the Excel 97 table data. Open the file in FrontPage, click the HTML tab to go to HTML editing mode, and place the insertion point where you want the table's top margin to go. Type `<!--##Table##-->` into the page. This code is a signal to FrontPage to expect a table provided by Excel.

Save the page, close the page, and follow the next procedure:

1. Start FrontPage and open the web that contains the page you want.

2. Open the Excel 97 spreadsheet and select the range of cells you want to convert to HTML.

3. Choose File, Save as HTML. This opens the Internet Assistant Wizard (see Figure B.9). Edit the data ranges if necessary and then choose Next.

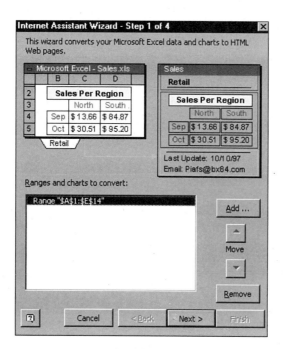

Figure B.9
The opening dialog box of the Internet Assistant Wizard lets you edit the ranges selected for the conversion.

4. Click the lower option button in the next wizard dialog box; this specifies that you want the data inserted as a table into an existing HTML page.

5. Choose Next. The third wizard dialog box allows you to open the page where the Excel data is to be inserted. Select the Open the File from My FrontPage Web option button and choose Browse. This opens a Pages Available dialog box, which displays the filenames of the pages in the open web (see Figure B.10). Select the file you want and choose OK to close the dialog box. Choose Next from the wizard dialog box.

Caution

The Pages Available dialog box displays only files that have an HTM extension. Those with an HTML extension won't appear. If you need a file with this extension, you have to type the page's URL into the URL Address text box of the wizard dialog box.

Figure B.10
You use the wizard's third dialog box to identify the Web page for the tabular Excel data.

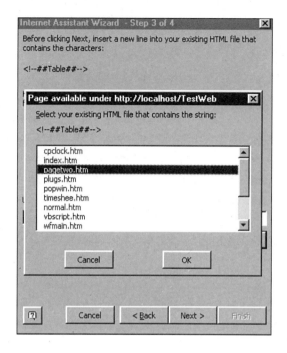

6. Select the Add the Result to My FrontPage Web option button in the wizard's final dialog box. The URL Address text box may not display the name of the file you selected in the previous dialog box. Assuming you still want this to be the save file for the Excel data, use Browse to open the Pages Available dialog box again and select that file. Choose OK, Finish. A dialog box appears and asks if you want to replace the existing file.

7. Choose Yes to insert the Excel tabular data into the page. (Despite the somewhat ambiguous dialog box, information already on the page will not be changed.)

8. Open the modified page in FrontPage Editor to see the results of your work. The table of Excel data will be there, along with several question mark HTML Markup icons above and below it. If you want to delete these icons, go ahead—they simply represent some commenting that you can see if you switch to HTML mode.

IF THE EXISTING HTML PAGE IS NOT IN A FRONTPAGE WEB

If you're adding Excel data to a page you haven't yet imported into a FrontPage web, begin by opening the page in an ASCII text editor, such as Windows Notepad. Place the insertion point where you want the table and then type `<!--##Table##-->`.

Save the page, close the page, and then follow these steps:

1. Open the Excel 97 spreadsheet and select the range of cells you want to convert to HTML.

2. Choose File, Save as HTML. This opens the Internet Assistant Wizard, as in the previous procedure (refer to Figure B.9). Edit the data ranges if necessary and choose Next.

3. Select the lower option button in the next wizard dialog box to specify that you want the data inserted as a table into an existing HTML page. Choose Next.

4. Select the Open the File Directly option button in the third wizard dialog box. Choose Browse to open the Select Your HTML File dialog box (see Figure B.11). In this dialog box, locate and select the file; choose Open to return to the wizard. You should now see the file's pathname in the Path of the Existing File text box.

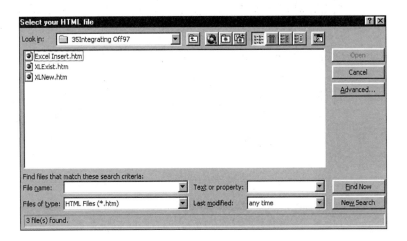

Figure B.11
Use this dialog box to locate the file in which the Excel tabular data will be inserted.

5. Choose Next. The final dialog box appears.

6. Select the Save the Result as an HTML File option button. Choose Browse to open the Save Your HTML Document As dialog box. Locate and select the file you want to receive the Excel data and choose Save to return to the wizard.

7. Choose Finish. When asked if you want to replace the existing file, choose Yes. Open the HTML file in a browser or in Word to see the results of your work.

APP

B

CREATING WEB PAGES FROM EXCEL 97 WORKSHEET DATA

In some cases, you don't want to place an Excel-derived table in an existing HTML page, but in one of its own. Excel 97's Internet Assistant Wizard provides an efficient way to do this.

1. Open the Excel 97 spreadsheet and select the range of cells you want to convert to HTML.

2. Choose File, Save as HTML. This opens the Internet Assistant Wizard, as in the previous procedures (refer to Figure B.9). Edit the data ranges if necessary and choose Next.

3. Mark the upper option button in the dialog box to specify that you want to create a new HTML document; choose Next.

4. Enter a title, to appear in the title bar of a browser window, a header as the first line on the page, a description, and horizontal lines in the dialog box (see Figure B.12). Add the items you want and choose Next.

Figure B.12
Customize your HTML table page's appearance by adding headers, descriptions, and lines.

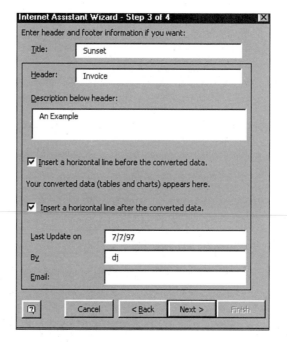

5. Select the Save the Result as an HTML File option button in the dialog box. Choose Browse to open the Save Your HTML Document As dialog box. In this dialog box, supply the path and filename for the new file and choose Save to return to the wizard dialog box.

6. Choose Finish. The new page is created and stored, ready for import into a FrontPage web.

INSERTING HYPERLINKS INTO EXCEL 97 WORKSHEETS

Putting a hyperlink into an Excel worksheet is simply a matter of selecting the cell where
you want the hyperlink and choosing Insert, Hyperlink. The Insert Hyperlink dialog box
appears; it has the same functionality as does Word's Insert Hyperlink dialog box (refer to
Figure B.2).

As you did earlier, fill in the Link to File or URL text box. If you want to link to a named
location, choose the lower Browse button (next to the Named Location in File text box).
This opens the Browse Excel Workbook dialog box, shown in Figure B.13.

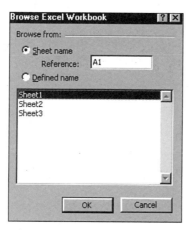

Figure B.13
Select either sheet
names and cell refer-
ences or Defined
Names as the named
location for a hyper-
link destination.

If you have already defined a name for the cell or the range, mark the Defined Name option
button, select the defined name from the list box, and choose OK to return to the Insert
Hyperlink dialog box. Choose OK to close the dialog box. When executed, the hyperlink
takes the user to that range and highlights it. Alternatively, you can simply specify a worksheet and cell reference.

You can also use the Copy/Paste as Hyperlink method (discussed in the earlier Word section) to insert hyperlinks within worksheets, across worksheets in the same workbook, or
across workbooks.

USING EXCEL 97'S HYPERLINK() FUNCTION

You can also create a hyperlink with Excel 97's new HYPERLINK() function. The syntax of this function is as follows:

```
=HYPERLINK(link location, friendly name)
```

link location is a reference to the destination file (including its path); friendly name is the text that's displayed in the cell containing the function. Entering the following code function in cell A1 would appear as Show Explanation in that cell:

```
=HYPERLINK("C:\My Documents\Background.doc","Show Explanation")
```

Clicking the cell would open the Word file BACKGROUND.DOC.

You can combine the HYPERLINK() function with other worksheet functions. Suppose that you want to display a hyperlink in cell C1, but only if the user has entered an invalid equation in cell A1—otherwise, you want nothing to appear in C1. Enter this formula in C1:

```
=IF(ISERROR(A1),HYPERLINK("C:\My Documents\HelpUser.doc","Click here for
➥help"),"")
```

If the user enters something such as =10/0 in cell A1—which returns the #DIV/0! error value—the IF() function calls the HYPERLINK() function that's nested within it. The HYPER-LINK() function then displays the Click here for help message in cell C1; if the user clicks it, the hyperlink opens the Word HELPUSER.DOC file.

If there's no error value in A1, the IF() function displays the empty text "".

USING POWERPOINT 97 WITH FRONTPAGE 2000

There's a wizard in PowerPoint 97 that helps you create a slideshow, which you can then import into a FrontPage 2000 web. Begin by opening (or creating and saving) the PowerPoint presentation you want in the web and then follow these steps:

1. Choose File, Save as HTML to start the Save as HTML Wizard in PowerPoint (see Figure B.14). You don't do anything in the first wizard dialog box, so choose Next.

2. Select the New Layout option button in the dialog box unless you have a saved layout you want to use. Choose Next.

3. Select the Standard option button in the dialog box unless you want a framed setup for the slideshow. Choose Next.

4. Decide if you want the graphics converted to GIF or JPEG or if you're using a PowerPoint animation. (You may never need to use the animation selection; FrontPage 98 lets you insert an animation file directly via the Insert, Active Elements, PowerPoint Animation command.) Choose Next.

5. Specify the monitor resolution your viewers are most likely to be using, as well as the width of screen the presentation is to occupy in the dialog box. Choose Next.

6. Create the information page options in the next dialog box. Choose Next.

7. Specify custom colors if you want them; otherwise select the Use Browser Colors option button in the dialog box. Choose Next.

8. Specify button style and layout styles, respectively, in the next two dialog boxes. Choose Next to move to the next dialog box. Here you specify the folder where the PowerPoint HTML file will be saved. Provide a folder name and choose Next. Choose Finish; PowerPoint readies the creation of the HTML slideshow.

9. Save the layout options you've developed in the preceding steps. If you want to do this, provide a name for the saved layout; otherwise choose Don't Save. The conversion process begins when that step is complete. When it completes successfully, you'll see a message stating as such.

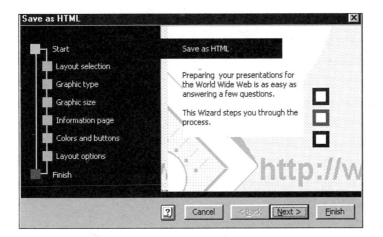

Figure B.14
Use the PowerPoint Save as HTML Wizard to create a set of files that FrontPage can use as a slideshow.

Now you must get the slideshow presentation into the FrontPage web. Switch to FrontPage, open the target web, and choose File, Import. Choose Add Folder to open the Browse for Folder dialog box. Locate the folder you named in step 8; select it and choose OK.

Now all the files in that folder are displayed in the list box of the FrontPage Web dialog box's Import File. Choosing OK creates a folder in the web with the name you gave in step 8, and the files are imported into it. If you inspect the folder, you'll see a file named INDEX.HTM. Open this in FrontPage Editor and preview it. You'll see something resembling what's shown in Figure B.15, which was made up in a plain-vanilla way with PowerPoint 97's Financial Performance template.

Caution

PowerPoint will not let you change the name of the TOC from index.htm to default.htm. Since IIS and PWS usually assume default.htm as the default page for each Web directory, take this into account when adding the presentation to a Web.

Figure B.15
The first page
(index.htm) of an
HTML-based
PowerPoint presenta-
tion provides a TOC.

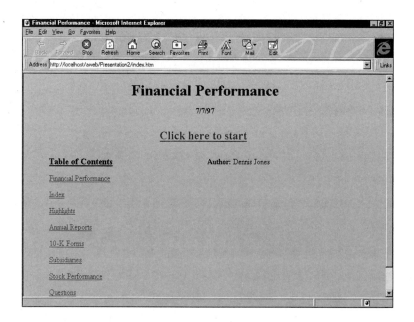

USING ACCESS 97'S WEB TOOLS WITH FRONTPAGE 2000

True database integration with FrontPage webs requires the use of FrontPage's database tools, as described in Part VIII, "Accessing Database Data with FrontPage." However, if you simply need to extract information from an existing database and put it into HTML form so a web can display it, Access 97 has a Save As HTML command that helps you do this.

In the following example you use the sample Northwind database that ships with Office 97. Begin by starting Access 97 and opening this database—which, if installed during setup, will be in C:\Program Files\Microsoft Office\Office\Samples (or in the directory where you installed Office, if you didn't use the default). If it's not there, you have to use Office 97 Setup to locate and install it.

Now follow these steps:

1. Choose File, Save as HTML. This opens the Publish to the Web Wizard. You don't need to provide any information in this dialog box, so choose Next.

2. Select which elements of the database you want to place in the Web page. To keep the example simple, click the Tables tab and select the Suppliers check box (see Figure B.16). Choose Next.

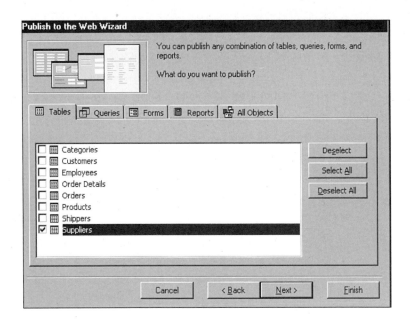

Figure B.16
You can select a wide range of information from the database.

3. If you have one, select a document template from the dialog box. Assume you have no template and choose Next.

4. Select the Static HTML option button if it isn't already. Choose Next.

5. Choose the destination folder for the HTML output in the dialog box. Because FrontPage is happier if it does its own file importing, select a suitable non–FrontPage folder by either typing it into the upper text box or using the Browse button. Choose Next.

6. Deselect the Yes I Want to Create a Home Page check box and choose Next.

7. Decide whether to save the selection and layout information you've provided so far, which makes a publication profile. If this profile is one you'll use often, select the check box to save the profile and choose Finish. Inspect the save folder when the wizard closes; you'll see the Web page file or files (as well as any required associated ones needed, such as graphics).

8. Close Access and import the file into the FrontPage web. You can see an example of the results in Figure B.17. The file has already been imported into a FrontPage web and is being viewed with the Preview in Browser command.

Figure B.17
Access 97's Save as HTML command makes it easy to prepare database information for use in a FrontPage web.

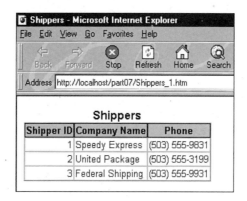

INDEX

Special Edition Using Microsoft FrontPage 2000

Thank you for purchasing *Special Edition Using Microsoft FrontPage 2000*, the most comprehensive book for advanced Microsoft FrontPage users. Please help us improve the next edition of *Special Edition Using Microsoft FrontPage 2000* to best fit your needs by taking a few minutes to answer these questions and then returning the survey to us.

Please tear out this form and mail it to the address on the back.

1. **Does your job involve training other users to use Microsoft FrontPage or Microsoft Office software or supporting other users in a help desk setting?**
   ❏ Yes   ❏ No

2. **Did you purchase FrontPage as part of Microsoft Office or as a standalone product?**
   ❏ Standalone (please skip to question 4)   ❏ Part of Office 2000 (please answer question 3)

3. **Which version of Microsoft Office 2000 do you own?**
   ❏ Standard   ❏ Professional   ❏ Developer Edition
   ❏ Small Business Edition ❏ Premium Edition   ❏ Not Sure

4. **Do you have Microsoft FrontPage for personal use or professional use?**
   ❏ Personal   ❏ Professional   ❏ Both

5. **Did you buy this book for personal use or professional use?**
   ❏ Personal   ❏ Professional   ❏ Both

6. **Where did you buy this book?**
   ❏ Bookstore   ❏ Direct from Publisher   ❏ Warehouse Club   oo Internet Site
   ❏ Computer Store   ❏ Office Club   ❏ Department Store   ❏ Consumer Electronics Store
   ❏ Mail Order   ❏ Other

7. **What operating system do you have on the computer(s) on which you use FrontPage 2000?**
   ❏ Windows 95   ❏ Windows 98   ❏ Windows NT 4   ❏ Windows 2000   ❏ Not Sure

8. **What other *Que Special Edition Using* books about Microsoft Office 2000 applications have you bought or do you plan to buy?**

   Special Edition Using Microsoft Office 2000
   ❏ Bought   ❏ Plan to buy

   Special Edition Using Microsoft Outlook 2000
   ❏ Bought   ❏ Plan to buy

   Special Edition Using Microsoft Access 2000
   ❏ Bought   ❏ Plan to buy

   Special Edition Using Microsoft Publisher 2000
   ❏ Bought   ❏ Plan to buy

   Special Edition Using Microsoft Word 2000
   ❏ Bought   ❏ Plan to buy

   Special Edition Using Microsoft PowerPoint 2000
   ❏ Bought   ❏ Plan to buy

   Special Edition Using Microsoft Excel 2000
   ❏ Bought   ❏ Plan to buy

9. **Please rate the following factors in making your decision to buy this book:**

   1 = Very Important   2 = Somewhat Important   3 = Not Important

Que brand name reputation	1 2 3	
Author reputation	1 2 3	
Length of book	1 2 3	
Thorough comparison of coverage versus other books	1 2 3	
Store clerk recommendation	1 2 3	
Other	1 2 3	

Special Edition Using brand name reputation	1 2 3
Price of book	1 2 3
Description of book on cover	1 2 3
Contents of CD-ROM with book	1 2 3
Recommendation of coworker, colleague, or friend	1 2 3

10. **Please rate the quality of the Tips in this book:**
    ❏ Excellent   ❏ Good   ❏ Fair   ❏ Poor

11. **Please check the appropriate box for each application to indicate how often you use the Office 2000 applications and what level of user you consider yourself with each:**

	I use this program...					*I consider my user level for this program...*		
	Over 4 hours daily	1-3 hours daily	A few minutes daily	Less than once a week	Never	Beginner	Intermediate	Expert
Word	❏	❏	❏	❏	❏	❏	❏	❏
Excel	❏	❏	❏	❏	❏	❏	❏	❏
PowerPoint	❏	❏	❏	❏	❏	❏	❏	❏
Publisher	❏	❏	❏	❏	❏	❏	❏	❏
Access	❏	❏	❏	❏	❏	❏	❏	❏
FrontPage	❏	❏	❏	❏	❏	❏	❏	❏
Outlook	❏	❏	❏	❏	❏	❏	❏	❏
PhotoDraw	❏	❏	❏	❏	❏	❏	❏	❏

12. **Please evaluate the amount and the level of coverage in this book for each FrontPage topic:**

	Amount of coverage			*Level of coverage*		
	Not enough	The right amount	Too much	Too low-level	The right level	Too advanced
Page Design	❏	❏	❏	❏	❏	❏
Web Management	❏	❏	❏	❏	❏	❏
Collaboration	❏	❏	❏	❏	❏	❏
Dynamic HTML	❏	❏	❏	❏	❏	❏
Databases Connectivity	❏	❏	❏	❏	❏	❏
FrontPage Server Extensions	❏	❏	❏	❏	❏	❏
Integration with Other Applications	❏	❏	❏	❏	❏	❏

13. **Please write any additional comments about this book, either positive or negative, here.**

14. **Please write today's date here.** _____

- **FOLD HERE AND TAPE TO MAIL**

Special Edition Using

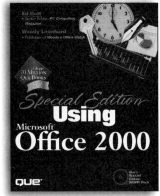

The One Source for Comprehensive Solutions™

The one stop shop for serious users, *Special Edition Using* offers readers a thorough understanding of software and technologies. Intermediate to advanced users get detailed coverage that is clearly presented and to the point.

Special Edition Using Microsoft Office 2000
Ed Bott
0-7897-1842-1
$39.99 US/
$59.95 CAN

Other Special Edition Using Titles

Special Edition Using Microsoft PowerPoint 2000
Patrice Rutledge
0-7897-1904-5
$39.99 US/$59.95 CAN

Special Edition Using Microsoft Access 2000
Roger Jennings
0-7897-1606-2
$39.99 US/$59.95 CAN

Special Edition Using Microsoft Outlook 2000
Gordon Padwick, Helen Feddema
0-7897-1909-6
$39.99 US/$59.95 CAN

Special Edition Using Microsoft Publisher 2000
Roger Parker
0-7897-1970-3
$39.99 US/$59.95 CAN

Special Edition Using Windows 98
Ed Bott
0-7897-1488-4
$39.99 US/$59.95 CAN

Special Edition Using HTML 4, Fifth Edition
Molly Holzschlag
0-7897-1851-0
$39.99 US/$59.95 CAN

Special Edition Using Java 1.2
Joe Weber
0-7897-1529-5
$39.99 US/$59.95 CAN

Special Edition Using Microsoft Word 2000
Bill Camarda
0-7897-1852-9
$39.99 US/
$59.95 CAN

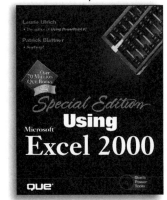

Special Edition Using Microsoft Excel 2000
Patrick Blattner
0-7897-1729-8
$39.99 US/
$59.95 CAN

que®

www.quecorp.com

All prices are subject to change.

By opening this package, you are agreeing to be bound by the following agreement:

Some of the software included with this product may be copyrighted, in which case all rights are reserved by the respective copyright holder. You are licensed to use software copyrighted by the Publisher and its licensors on a single computer. You may copy and/or modify the software as needed to facilitate your use of it on a single computer. Making copies of the software for any other purpose is a violation of the United States copyright laws.

This software is sold as is without warranty of any kind, either expressed or implied, including but not limited to the implied warranties of merchantability and fitness for a particular purpose. Neither the Publisher nor its dealers or distributors assumes any liability for any alleged or actual damages arising from the use of this program. (Some states do not allow for the exclusion of implied warranties, so the exclusion may not apply to you.)

This CD-ROM includes a full text electronic version of this book. This electronic version of this book is licensed to you for your individual use on one computer. You may make a single second copy of this electronic version for use by you on a second computer for which you are the primary user (for example, a laptop). You may not copy this to any network, intranet, the Internet, or any other form of distribution for use by anyone other than yourself. Any other use of this electronic version is a violation of U.S. and international copyright laws. If you would like to purchase a site license to use this material with more than one user, please contact Macmillan at license@mcp.com.

Windows 95 and Windows NT: If you have AutoPlay enabled, insert the CD-ROM and choose Installation Options from the displayed splash screen.

Note: If you have AutoPlay disabled on your computer, the CD-ROM will *not* automatically display the installation splash screen. To browse the CD-ROM manually, double-click on My Computer on the desktop, then right-click on your CD-ROM player icon and choose Explore from the shortcut menu. By doing this, you can immediately access the files for this CD-ROM.